MW00618622

ArtScroll Mesorah Series®

Rabbi Nosson Scherman / Rabbi Meir Zlotowitz
General Editors

קול התורה

THE
CALL
OF THE
TORAH

A PROJECT OF THE

Mesórah Heritage Foundation

OF
THE TORAH

An anthology of
interpretation and commentary
on the Five Books of Moses

by
Rabbi Elie Munk

Translated from the French by E. S. Mazer

THE CALL

Published by

Mesorah Publications, ltd

FIRST EDITION
First Impression ... September, 1994
Second Impression ... October 2000
Third Impression ... January 2001
Fourth Impression ... February 2003
Fifth Impression ... October 2008
Sixth Impression ... December 2011

Published and Distributed by
MESORAH PUBLICATIONS, Ltd.
4401 Second Avenue
Brooklyn, New York 11232

Distributed in Europe by
LEHMANNS
Unit E, Viking Business Park
Rolling Mill Road
Jarrow, Tyne & Wear NE32 3DP
England

Distributed in Australia & New Zealand by
GOLDS WORLD OF JUDAICA
3-13 William Street
Balaclava, Melbourne 3183
Victoria Australia

Distributed in Israel by
SIFRIATI / A. GITLER — BOOKS
6 Hayarkon Street
Bnei Brak 51127

Distributed in South Africa by
KOLLEL BOOKSHOP
Ivy Common 105 William Road
Norwood 2192, Johannesburg, South Africa

ARTSCROLL MESORAH SERIES®
THE CALL OF THE TORAH / Vol. 1 — Bereishis
© Copyright 1994, by MESORAH PUBLICATIONS, Ltd.
4401 Second Avenue / Brooklyn, N.Y. 11232 / (718) 921-9000 / www.artscroll.com

---

ISBN 10: 0-89906-040-4
ISBN 13: 978-0-89906-040-8

Typography by Compuscribe at ArtScroll Studios, Ltd.

Printed in the United States of America by Noble Book Press
Bound by Sefercraft, Quality Bookbinders, Ltd. Brooklyn, N.Y.

This volume is dedicated
to the memory of

Miriam Bronspigel ע״ה

מרים בת הרב אליהו הכהן ע״ה

נפטרה בדמי ימיה כ״ב סיון תשנ״ד
June 1, 1994

She was the daughter of the author of this work —
a true daughter in every way.
Wise and lively, sustained by indomitable faith and courage,
she endured much suffering for more than a decade
and never let it interfere with a life of heroic chessed,
love of Torah, dedication to her husband and children,
and remarkable service to people in need.

The wife of a rav and rosh yeshivah,
Rabbi Abba Bronspigel שליט״א,
she made Torah study the soul of her name,
and the paramount value of her children.

"Self" was not in her vocabulary.
She made many others grow and thrive,
as she brought love and health and caring
into countless other lives.
She was a testimony to the triumph of the spirit.

Her memory lives in the Torah
accomplishments of her family,
and in the hearts of the many whose
suffering she eased, while hiding her own.

ۋ Publishers' Preface

It has been our privilege to cooperate with the Munk family in publishing the English edition of their father's monumental commentary on the Torah.

Rav Elie Munk זצ״ל was outstanding in many ways, even uniquely so. He was the quintessential Rabbiner of the old school of German-Jewish greatness, the epitome of the path blazed by its founder, Rav Samson Raphael Hirsch. Rav Munk was an exceptional Torah scholar, *tzaddik*, inspirational and indefatigable leader of his communities in Ansbach, Germany and Paris, brave example of faith and ingenuity under the Nazis and in the flight to safety of his family and others, strong and imaginative builder of the new Jewish world in the aftermath of the War, battler for the bodies and souls of survivors of the Holocaust and refugees from North Africa who came to France when its empire crumbled.

Like his spiritual ancestor Rav Hirsch, and his teacher Rav Esriel Hildesheimer, head of the rabbinical seminary in Berlin, Rav Munk dealt with the needs of the people he was serving in the language they understood best. As a rabbi in Germany, he wrote in German. As a rabbi in France, he wrote in French. The wonder of it is that he was a consummate stylist in both languages. With the end of French control of Algeria and the massive influx of Jewish refugees to France, he saw the need to build religious institutions and create a Torah literature in their native tongue. Thus he began the massive undertaking that was the capstone of a great career: his commentary to the *Chumash*, קול התורה , *The Call of the Torah*. With this translation, it is now available to English-speaking Jews.

There are few commentaries in any language that so well combine classic commentary, Kabbalistic thought, and wise insights into human nature. It deserves to become a standard text, and we have every confidence that "The Munk Chumash" will be recognized as one of the classics of our time.

Rabbi Meir Zlotowitz / Rabbi Nosson Scherman

Elul 5754 / September 1994

◄§ Introduction

The aim of this commentary on the Five Books of Moses is to explain the Torah in accordance with the criteria of rational thinking, without losing sight of the overtones, associations, and intuitive aspects of meaning inherent in any work of spiritual truth.

This commentary does not claim to give new direction or to reveal new methods. Rather, it attempts to achieve its goal by basing itself on the authentic exegesis revealed in the Oral Law and on the teachings of our classic commentators, including those close to our own times such as Rabbis Isaac Arama, Judah ben Bezale (the *Maharal* of Prague), Isaiah Horowitz (the *Sheloh*), Chaim ben Attar and M.L. Malbim. It also draws from the enlightened commentaries of Rabbi S. R. Hirsch. But it keeps away from the homiletic genre and from philosophical speculation and clever constructions, brilliant but often artificial.

An objective appraisal of the content of the Bible and historical realities, however, shows that the criteria of the intellect are not always taken as the final word. They are transcended by another dimension, of a non-rational nature. Accordingly, this commentary on numerous occasions draws inspiration from the *Zohar* which goes back to the initial sources of the great truths, taking into account the totality of the natural and supernatural elements which form the fabric of our existence. In so doing, it is in line with the views of Rabbi Aryeh Leib of Gora, Kalwaria, Poland, the author of the ס׳ שפת אמת, who stated: "It is fitting and proper for everyone to learn at least the moral principles contained in the *Zohar* as well as its interpretations of the words of the Torah, insofar as they are accessible to us" (הסכמה לס׳ זהר תורה).

This method might seem tainted with eclecticism; it has nevertheless been chosen in order to avoid interpreting the Torah in the light of a ready-made, preconceived system or from a point of view that is fashioned from some subjective theory. The Torah can never be tied down to the discipline of a doctrine or a specific school of thought. Nevertheless, despite these efforts at objectivity, the interpretation of the word of God always remains an approximation. For the word emanating from the Divine has a universal character and its creative richness is infinite. Thus, man's interpretaion of Torah takes place in the confrontation between the Absolute and our earthly perspectives. "Is not My word as fire?" says the Lord, "and like a hammer that breaks the rock into pieces?" (*Jeremiah* 23:29). According to the explanation of the school of Hizkiyah, this simile employed by the prophet teaches us that "the divine word is split up into many sparks" (*Sanhedrin* 34a; quoted by *Rashi* on *Genesis* 33:20 and *Exodus* 6:9). What one may gather up of the truth is only "sparks" compared with the plenitude of the Divine light.

Our knowledge is thus reduced to only fragments and this is reflected in each page of this work. The reader will very often find hypothetical explanations, subjective thoughts, even divergent interpretations of the same phrase or subject. Indeed, there exists within tradition considerable latitude for free interpretation. But far from being an indication of inadequacies in the logic or composition of the sacred text, or proof of the uncertainty of our traditions, these differences of opinion go back to schools of thought or of doctrine which are independent of one another, or to distinct midrashic sources. Or more simply, they can also express different conjectures regarding the words and deeds of Biblical personages. And very often these explanations, far from excluding one another, are complementary and serve to complete each other. This was the reply which the prophet Elijah gave to a teacher of the law when the latter asked him to reveal the truth regarding a historical event for which a whole series of reasons had been give (*Megillah* 15b). Reality is, by its essence, of a complex nature. It does not always lend itself to the simplifications that theoreticians find so much to their liking.

This commentary does not tend to develop the laws and precepts of the Torah into the details of the *halachah*. For both the legislative sections and the historical passages, it endeavors to show the logical sequence in the arrangement of the subjects dealt with. And it attempts to bring out the harmonious unity which characterizes the Torah as a whole. But it favors drawing its inipiration from the exegetical principles adopted by *Ramban* (1193-1269) and stated in various parts of his writings. For this Sage, the change from the plural to the singular or vice versa in a passage referring to a group of people is part of the "way of Scripture, דרך הכתוב" and one need not seek out special reasons for it (*Genesis* 46:7). So too where the text repeats certain words or phrases simply in order to stress the importance of a subject or to return to a previous topic (*Exodus* 4:9). Repetitions are, moreover, characteristic of the prophetic style (*Job* 20). Furthermore, the Torah has a habit of making slight changes in the names of people and places when they are mentioned in different passages (*Deuteronomy* 10:10). These examples give evidence of an approach that relies on פשוטו של מקרא, *the plain meaning of the text, and* which takes into account "the way of Scripture." By so doing, *Ramban* stands in opposition to that tendency to seek out reasons of a moral, homiletic, or didactic sort that, when done by unqualified people, can be carried to excess. *Ramban's* commentary is also distinguished by the fact that it tends to explain the words of the Torah in terms of the context whereas some other commentators, for example *Rashi, Rashbam,* and *Ibn Ezra,* generally endeavor to explain the textual meaning. It is, though, fair to point out that in another connection *Ramban* protests against the "fanatics of the literal meaning, רודפי הפשט" (*Genesis* 11:2; 36:12) and that he never loses sight of the need to go beyond the plain sense of the Divine word and to seek out the hidden meaning (נסתר), even if it goes beyond the plain meaning of the text. And quite frequently, he undertakes to discern through historical events the transcendent and universal thought that presides over human destiny.

It is this path which has served as an example for us and for so many others — the Torah commentary of Rabbi Bachya ben Asher (who died in 1340), to name but one. This system is chosen with man himself in mind as the basis for consideration. It is focused on two vital points: the mind and the heart. And the mind takes precedence. These two centers are nourished both by rational commentaries and by those going into emotional and non-rational reasons.

Human psychology is nevertheless only the reflection of the universal soul. The microcosm is to be found in the macrocosm. Cosmology, then, describes for us the general laws which govern the universe. What these eternal laws are we learn from *Rashi* on the first verse in the Torah.

They are defined as the מדת הדין, which is the rigor, the severity of exact and unvarying logic, and then the מדת החסד, the principle of love which represents the source of the warmth of sentiment. The Torah is replete with this interplay between them. The Torah is replete with this and it is the Torah which gives us the dynamic and perpetually youthful picture of human existence. From this one can understand more clearly the juxtaposition, of the rationalist (*Rambam, Abarbanel, Hirsch,* etc.) and, on the other hand, the non-rationalist commentators (the *Zohar, Recanati, R' Bachya,* etc.). And in this lies the originality of this work.

⳽ Acknowledgments

We express our heartfelt gratitude to the wonderful staff of Mesorah Publications, and especially to Rabbis Meir Zlotowitz and Nosson Scherman for undertaking the immense task of publishing the English edition of our father's masterpiece. Through their devoted efforts they have made it possible for us to honor the memory of our beloved father, while at the same time giving the Jewish public access to his broad and deep understanding of the Torah.

We are also very grateful to Feldheim Publishers for originally publishing the commentary on *Genesis*, in 1980, and for their pioneering work in this project. We appreciate that they have given their consent for the entire series to be continued by Mesorah Publications.

We express our gratitude to Mr. E.S. Maser of Ottawa, Canada who translated the commentary from the original French. The translation of the *Chumash* text in this edition is taken from ArtScroll's Stone Edition of the *Chumash*.

We are also grateful to the entire staff of Mesorah Publications for presenting this work in such an attractive manner. In particular, we thank Eli Kroen for his striking design; Avrohom Biderman for coordinating the production; Mrs. Ethel Gottlieb, who proofread and made valuable suggestions; and Mrs. Mindy Breier, Mrs. Esty Dicker, Mrs. Esther Feierstein, Udi Herskovitz, and Leah Brocha Lasker who typed and corrected the manuscript.

The Munk Family

ספר בראשית
Sefer Bereishis

א　　　א בְּרֵאשִׁית בָּרָא אֱלֹהִים אֵת הַשָּׁמַיִם וְאֵת הָאָרֶץ:

1.

1. בְּרֵאשִׁית — *In the beginning*. Right with its first words, the Torah solemnly proclaims the great fundamental truth: God is the beginning and the origin of all things. The matter constituting the cosmos is not eternal, nor is it the primary source nor a regulator of all terrestrial life. It is God Who created matter out of nothing. It is He Who created the universe "at the beginning," that is to say, at a time depending solely on His own free will.

The Torah begins with an affirmation of creation *ex nihilo* יֵשׁ מֵאַיִן because on this affirmation is based the faith in a unique and omnipotent Creator Who is not Himself bound to matter, but Who has created the world with a definite purpose. If God had been confronted with pre-existing matter, then He would necessarily have been limited and the world of His making would not have been a free and perfect creation. With such matter God could only have made a world which would be relatively good but still nonetheless imperfect. All physical ills, all moral depravity, would then have had their origin in the imperfection of the primal matter, of the raw materials, and God Himself would have been incapable of delivering us from them. And under such circumstances man could no more be master of his body than God could be master of matter. Freedom would disappear from the world; a blind and disheartening necessity would rule over the earth together with its God and its humanity. This is the fallacious doctrine which is still fundamental to every heathen conception of life. This metaphysical lie deprives man of the truth, i.e. of consensus with reality, and, what is worse, it leads to the denial of freedom of will to both God and man, and thereby does away with every notion of morality.

The very first words of the Torah destroy this theory completely, proclaiming for all to hear that the substance and form of everything that exists have come from the omnipotent free will of the Creator. And in complete freedom, God continues to be Master of all beings, all forms, all substances, all forces which act on them and all the laws which govern their working and shape their forms. For it is His almighty absolutely free will which has created matter and which has imposed laws on it to give it form. Just as the Creator freely governs His universe, so too has He given man, into whom He has breathed a spark of His being, freedom over his own small world, freedom over his body and its forces. Thus man is a free-willed image of the free-willed Creator in a universe supremely governed by His omnipotence (R' *S.R. Hirsch*).

בָּרָא אֱלֹהִים — *Of God's creating*. The word "בָּרָא" is reserved for the Divine creation *ex nihilo*. For man's productive activity, the expression "make" or "form" is used. The concept of creation starting from nothing is given the force of a fundamental tenet of Judaism. For, as *Rambam* explains, denying this concept leads ultimately to the determinist philosophy of the eternity of the universe and this precludes all belief in prophecy and in miracles (*Guide for the*

1   ¹ *In the beginning of God's creating the heavens and the earth* —

Perplexed, Vol. 2, ch. 25). Creation out of nothing, on the other hand, is the fundamental principle which allows us to understand the freedom of the Divine will, and hence also the free will with which the Divine will has endowed mankind.

However, Jewish thinkers felt a need to analyze the concept of creation *ex nihilo* more closely. In their reflections on this concept they were confronted with the following problem: could the change from pure spirit to matter, accomplished by an act of the Divine will, have taken place directly, without an intermediate stage? In general, the answer was no. In fact, right from the start of his commentary on the Torah, one of our greatest sages, *Ramban*, points out that an intermediate factor exists between spirit and matter, a "dynamic force," as Plato had mentioned. The Greek philosophers called it *hylē* and it often appears in Jewish thought. *Hylē* is an amorphous indeterminate, indistinct force which the Torah designates as *tohu* (v. 2); its characteristics are not fixed (S. Munk edition, *Guide* 2:13) but its essential property is the power to confer form on potential being, thereby bringing it from potentiality to actuality.

This same factor appears in Lurianic Kabbalah in the form of Divine light emanating from the Infinite into space. It is composed of an infinity of isolated points and pours forth in an "atomized," corpuscular form. This world of punctiform lights, *olam ha'nekudos*, Luria also considers as *olam ha'tohu* "world of confusion, of disorder." The radiating force is equivalent to the *hylē* of the philosophers. In both cases, we are concerned with the same matter-building force whose characteristics seem not to be governed by the general continuity of natural laws. The fact remains that, in Jewish teaching, the concept of creation *ex nihilo* includes an intermediate factor between nothingness and matter, and this "dynamic force" spoken of by Jewish philosophers seems to be related to the concept of energy in nuclear physics. Both are taken as the factor involved in the organization of matter, both constitute the intermediate phase between the abstract and concrete.

Modern science has proved itself capable of discovering this concept, but will it be able to go even further? Will it someday discover the Creative Spirit which is at the origin of matter? It is well worth noting that science is progressing resolutely towards the abstract and the great Unity. Many physicists have described this evolution, which has been unfolding since the first days of scientific research. Did not the philosopher Hegel already have an inkling that "pure existence and nothingness are identical"? Science will advance "until we have arrived at a system having the greatest conceivable unity and the fewest number of concepts based on logic still compatible with observations made by our senses (i.e. an abstract system). We do not yet know if this will lead to a definite system .... However, as long as the struggle lasts, we will never give up the hope that this goal, the greatest of all goals, is truly attainable to a very high degree" (Einstein).

ב וְהָאָרֶץ הָיְתָה תֹהוּ וָבֹהוּ וְחֹשֶׁךְ עַל־פְּנֵי תְהוֹם וְרוּחַ
ג אֱלֹהִים מְרַחֶפֶת עַל־פְּנֵי הַמָּיִם: וַיֹּאמֶר אֱלֹהִים יְהִי־אוֹר

אֱלֹהִים — *God's.* The king of Egypt, Ptolemy (305-285 B.C.E.), summoned seventy-two elders and put them each in a separate room without telling them why. He went to each in turn and said, "Translate the Torah of Moses, your master, for me." God then prompted every one of them and they all had the same idea and without exception wrote, "God created in the beginning" (*Megillah* 9a).

The seventy-two elders who were the first to translate the Torah (into the version called the *Septuagint*) began by inverting the order of the first words of *Genesis*. This they did so as not to give the idea that "beginning" should be taken as subject of the sentence or that God had been preceded by another principle. However, as for the Torah itself, it does not take possible subjective errors into account. It mentions the ideas of time and creation before the name of God so that man will know, right from the beginning, that cognizance of the Creator can only be acquired through a knowledge of creation and an understanding of the varieties of earthly life. It is by observing and studying nature, by gaining an awareness of the Divine attributes, that one progressively approaches the cognizance of the name of God. "And you shall see My back, but My face shall not be seen" (*Exodus* 33:23). Man can come to know God only through His acts, His providence, or His word, but not in His very essence (*Akeidas Yitzchak*, R' Yitzchak Arama).

The Torah does not stipulate as an absolute act of faith that God exists. Indeed, the existence of God is presupposed throughout, but it is not the object of a proof, nor even of a doubt. But the word order in the initial verse of the Torah discreetly suggests that we seek out God in Creation and so progressively acquire with our intelligence that which faith puts forward to us at the beginning of our human experience. For faith is crowned by knowledge.

The Torah begins with a large ב, the second letter of the alphabet, as if to emphasize that the creation of the universe is only the second factor. From then on, it is up to man to go in quest of the first factor, which is the Creator Who precedes time.

2. וְהָאָרֶץ הָיְתָה תֹהוּ וָבֹהוּ — *When the earth was astonishingly empty.* It is the view of *Rashi, Ibn Ezra,* and other commentators that it is appropriate to consider the first two verses as one. "In the beginning of God's creating the heaven and the earth, when the earth was [still *tohu* and *vohu*] astonishingly empty. . . God said 'Let there be light.' " Hence, according to this interpretation, light was the creation of the first day whereas the original element had been created previously. This element included potentially both the substance (*tohu*) and the organizing principle (*vohu*) having the ability to give objects the form of a solid, a liquid, a gas, or a source of heat.

> ² *when the earth was astonishingly empty, with darkness upon the surface of the deep, and the Divine Presence hovered upon the surface of the waters —* ³ *God said, "Let there be light,"*

Given this conception, in which all future evolution was already potentially included in the first creative act, one can understand more clearly what the Sages meant when they taught (*Ethics of the Fathers* 5:1) "The world was created through ten divine utterances. Could it not have been created by a sole utterance? (Our explanation shows that in fact the first creative act did suffice for all creation). But it is for the punishment of the wicked, who mar a world created by ten utterances, and for giving merit to the righteous, who preserve a world created by ten utterances." This may be compared, it has been noted, to an architect who has a large window constructed not from one big sheet of glass but from ten smaller panes, reasoning that if someone throws a stone at the window, the damage will be limited to just one small pane. Similarly, the Creator constructed His universe with ten utterances rather than by just one creative act in order to limit the punishment of those who mar the world and to increase the merit of the righteous who keep alive each of the ten parts making up the edifice which is the universe (quoted in the name of *R' Chaim of Volozhin*).

וְחשֶׁךְ עַל־פְּנֵי תְהוֹם — *With darkness upon the surface of the deep.* Darkness is to be thought of not as an absence of light but as the effect of a creation *ad hoc*. This is the opinion of *Ramban* (and of the *Vilna Gaon* in ליקוטים לס׳ יצירה), who makes a specific reference to the wording of *Isaiah* (45:6-7) "I am God, there is none else . . . . I form the light and create darkness . . ." The creation of darkness seemingly precedes that of light and this order of creation reveals a characteristic of both nature and the physical realm. It is the principle of ascendancy in creation, going from negative to positive and from nothingness to being. And no matter what conditions confront us, this is the path which perfection must take.

וְרוּחַ אֱלֹהִים מְרַחֶפֶת עַל־פְּנֵי הַמָּיִם — *And the Divine Presence hovered upon the surface of the waters.* It is the mysterious, invisible and radiant presence of the Divine Being Which, hovering over inanimate matter, breathes into it the breath of life and makes it the substance of a living world. Water, the starting substance from which the universe was built, was "the first to extol the glory of God, as it is written (*Psalms* 93:4): '*Above the voices of many waters, above the mighty breakers of the sea (rises their hymn): God on high is mighty*' " (*Bereishis Rabbah*, ch. 5). *Rashi* explains accordingly, "The Throne of Glory was suspended in the air and hovered over the face of the waters . . ."

3. וַיֹּאמֶר אֱלֹהִים — *God said.* When applied to God, speaking signifies an act of will (*Rambam, Guide for the Perplexed* 1:65). However, Rabbi Judah Halevi amplifies this idea and, following the teachings of the *Sefer Yetzira*, demonstrates that thought, word, and deed are identical when referring to God.

ד וַיַּרְא אֱלֹהִים אֶת־הָאוֹר כִּי־טוֹב וַיַּבְדֵּל אֱלֹהִים

ה בֵּין הָאוֹר וּבֵין הַחֹשֶׁךְ: וַיִּקְרָא אֱלֹהִים ׀ לָאוֹר יוֹם וְלַחֹשֶׁךְ

קָרָא לָיְלָה וַיְהִי־עֶרֶב וַיְהִי־בֹקֶר יוֹם אֶחָד:

ו וַיֹּאמֶר אֱלֹהִים יְהִי רָקִיעַ בְּתוֹךְ הַמָּיִם וִיהִי מַבְדִּיל בֵּין מַיִם

ז לָמָיִם: וַיַּעַשׂ אֱלֹהִים אֶת־הָרָקִיעַ וַיַּבְדֵּל בֵּין הַמַּיִם אֲשֶׁר

In the terminology of this kabbalistic work, the three functions are called סְפָר, סִפּוּר, סֵפֶר. *Safar* (number) refers to intelligence; *sippur* (story) to speech; and *sefer* (book, letter) to the act. Because of the creative power inherent in their functional unity, these three are at the origin of the *sefiros* (סְפִירוֹת), spheres of emanation from the Divine (*Kuzari*, 4:25).

יְהִי־אוֹר — *Let there be light*. Since the time of creation, since man was first separated from the radiant celestial sphere by thick layers of matter, the most urgent task for us and for the future generations is to make light burst forth from the midst of the darkness (Rav Shneur Zalman of Liadi, *Tanya*, Chapter 36).

וַיְהִי־אוֹר — *And there was light*. This light, which is distinct from that subsequently radiated by the sun, is to dissipate the darkness which covers the abyss. The theory of cosmic nebulae provides an answer to the old problem of where light came from before the sun was created. The astronomer Halley wrote: "These nebulae completely resolve the problem which the biblical account of creation presents, namely, that light could have been produced without the sun."

4. וַיַּבְדֵּל אֱלֹהִים — *And God separated*. God did not have the light rule over the darkness, despite the fact that He called the light "good." Instead, He let the darkness subsist, separating it from the light. From the beginning of creation, God instituted the important principle of הַבְדָּלָה (separation) in the universe, (the prototype for which is the separation of genders into male and female). Thus He separated heaven and earth. In our prayers we praise "the One who separates the holy from the profane, light from darkness, Israel from the nations, the Sabbath from the six working days."

In the world plan separation, הַבְדָּלָה, is both stimulus and catalyst to life on earth. Indeed it is this universal polarization which gives man his earthly mission: to do everything in his power to overcome these dualisms and to bring about the Supreme Unity everywhere he possibly can. For everything springs from one unique source and everything instinctively tends to return to it. In the beginning, man and woman formed just one being but subsequently they were split into two distinct bodies. Hence the natural tendency to form "one flesh" is deeply rooted in their beings. It is the same for the other separations (*havdalos*) mentioned above. They should in no way be considered as naturally occurring and representing eternal, immutable, definitive states. The separation "between light and darkness" is destined to be overcome in the future when "a new light will shine over Zion." Likewise, through the spread and growth of the moral forces of mankind, the separation between Israel and the nations will disappear;

*and there was light. ⁴ God saw that the light was good, and God
separated between the light and the darkness. ⁵ God called to the
light: "Day," and to the darkness He called: "Night." And there
was evening and there was morning, one day.*

*⁶ God said, "Let there be a firmament in the midst of the
waters, and let it separate between water and water." ⁷ So God
made the firmament, and separated between the waters which*

all nations, all peoples, will at last be united in common worship of the One God.
All differences will dissolve to give honor to one supreme unity. Then the
distinction between the Sabbath and the other six days of the week will also
make way for "the time of continual Sabbath and continual rest in the World
to Come."

5. יוֹם אֶחָד — *One day. Rashi* notes that "The Torah does not use the phrase 'a
first day' whereas it does state 'a second day;' 'a third day,' etc. Why 'one'? It is
because God was One and alone in His universe." The dualism of light and
darkness, established in nature right from the first day of creation, is followed
in the Torah by a phrase which emphasizes the exclusive presence of God in the
universe. Despite the appearance of dualism within nature, God is One and One
alone. Among the most ancient aberrations of the human mind is the idea that
the oppositions, the antagonisms, observed in nature signified the presence of a
multiplicity of gods, and in particular of a dualism composed on one hand of a
divinity for day, life, and good, and on the other of a divinity for night, death,
and evil. In the final analysis, all ideological struggles and all the wars of religion
ever waged have hinged on the choice between the dualistic and the
monotheistic conceptions of the universe. It is striking how mankind in its
spiritual development is constantly evolving, albeit slowly and not without
reverses, toward a monistic theism which more and more approaches the Jewish
conception of monotheism. This verse concludes with the injunction "one," here
introduced for the first time just after the first dualistic phenomenon is instituted
in nature, in order to dispel any misunderstanding. And every morning, at
daybreak, the Jew who is preparing to proclaim the doctrine of pure monotheism
in the שְׁמַע יִשְׂרָאֵל emphatically reaffirms beforehand that both light and its
counterpart, darkness, have been created by the same God Who is One and
Unique יוֹצֵר אוֹר וּבוֹרֵא חֹשֶׁךְ, *Who forms light and creates darkness* and Who,
out of a world of apparent contradictions, brings forth perfect harmony (cf.
Berachos 11b).

6. וַיֹּאמֶר אֱלֹהִים יְהִי רָקִיעַ — *God said, "Let there be a firmament." Rashi*
comments: "This means, let the sky (firmament) become hardened. For although
the heavens were created on the first day, they were still in a fluid state,
solidifying only on the second day at God's thunderous command of 'Let the
firmament exist' — as a man become petrified with fright."

ח מִתַּחַת לָרָקִיעַ וּבֵין הַמַּיִם אֲשֶׁר מֵעַל לָרָקִיעַ וַיְהִי־כֵן: וַיִּקְרָא
אֱלֹהִים לָרָקִיעַ שָׁמָיִם וַיְהִי־עֶרֶב וַיְהִי־בֹקֶר יוֹם שֵׁנִי:
ט וַיֹּאמֶר אֱלֹהִים יִקָּווּ הַמַּיִם מִתַּחַת הַשָּׁמַיִם אֶל־מָקוֹם אֶחָד
י וְתֵרָאֶה הַיַּבָּשָׁה וַיְהִי־כֵן: וַיִּקְרָא אֱלֹהִים ׀ לַיַּבָּשָׁה אֶרֶץ
יא וּלְמִקְוֵה הַמַּיִם קָרָא יַמִּים וַיַּרְא אֱלֹהִים כִּי־טוֹב: וַיֹּאמֶר
אֱלֹהִים תַּדְשֵׁא הָאָרֶץ דֶּשֶׁא עֵשֶׂב מַזְרִיעַ זֶרַע עֵץ פְּרִי

The first day reveals to us the irresistible creative power of the Divine word. The second day shows that the Divine word alone suffices to arrest the violent surge of creation at its height and to transfix the elements of nature. The Master of the Universe has not surrendered Himself to His work. He remains in complete control, the absolute Master, and His word continues to be all-powerful. He does not merge with nature, but is freely enthroned above His creation, which He completely organizes and governs by His word. The work of transfixing the elements of creation is seen with the celestial bodies in outer space, where the earth's force of gravity no longer acts; these bodies are as if suspended in space. Do they not seem to be transfixed, as if petrified on hearing the thunderous Divine voice?

The meaning of "waters above the firmament" in the verse is difficult to state precisely. *Don Isaac Abarbanel* cites five different theories while *Ramban* emphasizes that this is one of the mysteries of creation and one should not expect an explanation of it from him, for even the Torah itself does not elaborate on it. However, modern science permits a better understanding of the Torah's reference to the separation of the waters below and the waters above. We now know that several atmospheric regions exist one above the other in the immensity of space, beyond what we call the heavens. Moreover, hydrogen is the basic element found in these zones, just as it is in all of creation.

In kabbalistic teaching, "the waters above" signify the male factor, active, fecundating, the source of dew and beneficial rains while "the waters beneath," forming oceans, rivers etc. (*Bereishis Rabbah*, ch. 4), represents the feminine, that is the passive, receptive, agent of form (*Midrash Hagadol*, *Genesis* 4). Life on earth is the fruit of the union of these two factors, and it is in this sense that the Sages of the Talmud speak of the distance between the two waters as being no greater than a "hairsbreadth." But, they elaborate, this distance can also be very great, for man has the power to disturb the harmonious union of the spheres of the universe and provoke great discord between the heavenly and earthly elements.

7. וַיְהִי כֵן — *And it was so.* Why is it that the Torah did not say of the second day: "God saw that it was good"? Because on that day there took place the separation of the waters, and since there was a separation, it was not good (*Midrash Hagadol*, ibid.). To be sure, there was a division on the first day as well,

were beneath the firmament and the waters which were above the firmament. And it was so. ⁸ God called to the firmament: "Heaven." And there was evening and there was morning, a second day.

⁹ God said, "Let the waters beneath the heaven be gathered into one area, and let the dry land appear." And it was so. ¹⁰ God called to the dry land: "Earth," and to the gathering of waters He called: "Seas." And God saw that it was good. ¹¹ God said, "Let the earth sprout vegetation: herbage yielding seed, fruit trees

but it was between elements of different kinds, light and darkness, whereas on the second day the separation involved just one category of substance, "the waters." And this separation, albeit indispensable to and a fundamental constituent of life, can never be termed "good."

10. וַיַּרְא אֱלֹהִים כִּי־טוֹב — *And God saw that it was good*. The third day of creation is the one in which the completed work is described as "good" not once but twice for it was on this day that the principle of love of the first day and that of law of the second day were brought into harmony. The first creative act is a gift of love offered to all created beings (חֶסֶד) and is expressed in the light which flooded the world. The second creative act introduces the organizing principle, the concept of law (דִין) which is intended to regulate, direct, and contain the expansive, bountiful outpouring of love. This organizing principle manifests itself on the second day in the distribution of the elements between the upper and lower spheres — the first organization of the created universe. But the third day sees the result of the harmonious collaboration between love and law (תִּפְאֶרֶת). The continents emerged from the ocean and nature was revealed in all its splendor, with "vegetation, plants, and fruit trees." As a creation of the third day, nature appears as the product of God's bountiful love and of the organizing action of natural law. And on this union is built the perfection and harmony of nature.

It is also, in another form, at the basis of the other aspects of creation, where the same elements of force and form, or to generalize, of spirit and matter, prevail. In every case, the fruit of this fertile union merits the words כִּי טוֹב, and *it was good.*

11. עֵץ פְּרִי עֹשֶׂה פְּרִי — *Fruit trees yielding fruit*. *Rashi* comments: "The tree also was to have the same taste as the fruit (the text says literally, 'tree of fruit'). But the earth disobeyed and brought forth trees producing fruit (verse 12) but not trees which were themselves fruit. This explains why, when man will later come to be punished for his sin, the earth will also be punished for this sin, and will be cursed." Some of our Sages think that if the earth was able to act contrary to God's orders it was because the creative freedom, which governed before the natural law was definitively established, gave a certain degree of liberty to the

יב עָשָׂה פְּרִי לְמִינוֹ אֲשֶׁר זַרְעוֹ־בוֹ עַל־הָאָרֶץ וַיְהִי־כֵן: וַתּוֹצֵא
הָאָרֶץ דֶּשֶׁא עֵשֶׂב מַזְרִיעַ זֶרַע לְמִינֵהוּ וְעֵץ עֹשֶׂה־פְּרִי אֲשֶׁר
יג זַרְעוֹ־בוֹ לְמִינֵהוּ וַיַּרְא אֱלֹהִים כִּי־טוֹב: וַיְהִי־עֶרֶב וַיְהִי־בֹקֶר
יוֹם שְׁלִישִׁי:
יד וַיֹּאמֶר אֱלֹהִים יְהִי מְאֹרֹת בִּרְקִיעַ הַשָּׁמַיִם לְהַבְדִּיל בֵּין
הַיּוֹם וּבֵין הַלָּיְלָה וְהָיוּ לְאֹתֹת וּלְמוֹעֲדִים וּלְיָמִים וְשָׁנִים:

elements (רע"ב). Moreover, note that the diverse parts of creation are considered to have a living soul and to be conscious of their existence (*Rambam, Hilchos Yesodei HaTorah* 3). They serve God fully of their own accord (*Chullin* 60b) and obey His laws "with joy and gladness" and "with respect and reverence" as we repeat often in our prayers.

The earth's sin mentioned here was committed before the advent of natural law, when the onrushing flow of successive creations was replaced by the all-powerful rhythm of the working of the universe. It stemmed from a feeling which, in itself, was just, but the consequent act was carried out overzealously. The earth was aware that God wanted to preserve the species and reasoned thus: When humankind will be created and become numerous, men will need large quantities of fruit for food. They will not want to wait patiently for years until the fruit grows but instead will fell the trees and use them for food, thereby killing them off rapidly. It is consequently better for the trees to have a taste which differs from that of the fruit (*Chizkuni*). Thus, the first sin committed within creation was one of "an excess of righteousness," which *Ecclesiastes* strongly criticizes in these words: "Be not righteous overmuch, neither make yourself over wise. Why should you destroy yourself?" (7:16). The fact remains that as a result of this misdeed, the ideal state in which the tree and its fruit have the same taste could not be realized. And since that time, creation suffers from a state of imperfection in which substance is not in harmony with form; there is opposition between them. Nevertheless, the Torah describes the work of this day as "good," consistent with the optimism which pervades the whole description of creation, where we find the word "good" so often repeated. Indeed, for the optimist a work which is intrinsically good remains so despite certain partial defects. (See also our commentary on 3:7.)

לְמִינוֹ — *After its kind*. The application of the law of organization within nature leads to the strict separation of species. This is characterized by the Divine command expressed in the word "לְמִינוֹ."

Rabbi S.R. Hirsch points out that our observation of nature confirms the rigorous application of this fundamental law which assigns to each created species its own sphere of existence and its own mission. "And you, son of man, respect this law when, in pursuing your calling, you attempt to intervene in the course of nature to exploit it for your benefit. Do not forget that God has only authorized you to tend creation and to keep it (2:15) but not to disturb its orderly

*yielding fruit each after its kind, containing its own seed on the
earth." And it was so.* [12] *And the earth brought forth vegetation:
herbage yielding seed after its kind, and trees yielding fruit, each
containing its seed after its kind. And God saw that it was good.*
[13] *And there was evening and there was morning, a third day.*
[14] *God said, "Let there be luminaries in the firmament of
the heaven to separate between the day and the night; and they
shall serve as signs, and for festivals, and for days and years;*

course of development through your own self-seeking. Do not forget this, and
do not try to interfere with this order by transferring forces inherent in one
species to another species distinct from it. That is why you have been forbidden
to breed animals of different species, to graft trees of diverse kinds, to mix
different kinds of material such as linen and wool (כִּלְאַיִם) and to cook together
foods of diverse kinds such as milk and meat" (*Horev*, Chapter 57).

14. וַיֹּאמֶר אֱלֹהִים יְהִי מְאֹרֹת — *God said, "Let there be luminaries."* The difference
between the creation of light on the first day and that of luminaries on the fourth
day has already been explained in verse 3. To be sure, many of the problems
posed by the Biblical description of the creation of light have not yet been solved
by the human mind — for example, the division into day and night. But at least
we are able to grasp very well the primary role ascribed by the Torah to the very
creation of light, which inaugurates the creation of the world and through
which, in the words of the *Zohar*, "were created all other creatures" (*Zohar
Chadash*, 8). "Light" is designated as the source of all energy in nature. Under
its influence, matter comes to life. Light is the *primum movens* of the elements,
the factor which gives all forces their dynamism. Not only does light promote
growth in the existing world, it also brings out the infinite variety of forms
which this world contains. Calling light the principle of all forms of matter and
of the atom, as we do here, is quite consistent with the assertion in physics that
light is at the foundation of all other physical phenomena. Note the relationship between light and heat, between light and magnetism. Physics teaches also
that "light potentially contains an infinitely varied energy which permits
immediate perception and through which the whole of the material world is
protected from every risk of annihilation. In contrast, the state of darkness is
always accompanied by a process tending toward destruction and death."

מְאֹרֹת — *Luminaries.* This word, notes *Rashi*, is written without the letter *vav*
(and can be read *m'eiros*, "curses"). The fourth day is a day of malediction, the
day when diphtheria menaces young children. Thus the Talmud teaches: on the
fourth day they used to fast to prevent diphtheria from smiting the young
(*Yerushalmi, Taanis* 4:3). The death of the young and innocent is a problem
which has often occupied our Sages. They strove to give non-rational solutions
by attributing such death to certain sins committed by the parents of these

טו וְהָיוּ לִמְאוֹרֹת בִּרְקִיעַ הַשָּׁמַיִם לְהָאִיר עַל־הָאָרֶץ וַיְהִי־
טז כֵן: וַיַּעַשׂ אֱלֹהִים אֶת־שְׁנֵי הַמְּאֹרֹת הַגְּדֹלִים אֶת־הַמָּאוֹר
הַגָּדֹל לְמֶמְשֶׁלֶת הַיּוֹם וְאֶת־הַמָּאוֹר הַקָּטֹן לְמֶמְשֶׁלֶת
יז הַלַּיְלָה וְאֵת הַכּוֹכָבִים: וַיִּתֵּן אֹתָם אֱלֹהִים בִּרְקִיעַ
יח הַשָּׁמָיִם לְהָאִיר עַל־הָאָרֶץ: וְלִמְשֹׁל בַּיּוֹם וּבַלַּיְלָה וּלֲהַבְדִּיל
יט בֵּין הָאוֹר וּבֵין הַחֹשֶׁךְ וַיַּרְא אֱלֹהִים כִּי־טוֹב: וַיְהִי־עֶרֶב
וַיְהִי־בֹקֶר יוֹם רְבִיעִי:
כ וַיֹּאמֶר אֱלֹהִים יִשְׁרְצוּ הַמַּיִם שֶׁרֶץ נֶפֶשׁ חַיָּה וְעוֹף יְעוֹפֵף
כא עַל־הָאָרֶץ עַל־פְּנֵי רְקִיעַ הַשָּׁמָיִם: וַיִּבְרָא אֱלֹהִים אֶת־

children (*Rashi* on *Deuteronomy* 24:16) or to hardship inflicted on the parents by Providence (*Tanchuma* on *Deuteronomy* 22:7) or to other causes depending on the very innocence of the children (*Rashi* on *Kesubos* 8b, beginning חשוב). Here in his commentary, *Rashi* notes that the death of the young and innocent may result from natural causes inherent in certain lacunae (discontinuities) within the workings of creation (מְאֹרַת חָסֵר כְּתִיב). Therefore, fasting and prayer appear to be the only recourse against this affliction.

וְהָיוּ לְאֹתֹת — *And they shall serve as signs.* Contrary to the usual conception, the Torah teaches that the sun and moon were created to serve as signs; for example, to set terrestrial time and the calendar. Only afterwards does the Torah add, "and they shall serve as luminaries." *Rashi* stresses that this latter role is subordinate: "And in addition to all of that they would serve to illuminate the world." Hence the stars were not indispensable as light sources, as is proved by the first three days of creation. Their primary function is to serve as signs to man, who sees in the phenomena of the starry heavens the prefiguration of earthly phenomena. In this way the interrelations between the sun and moon serve as "heavenly signs" for the relations between the nations of the world and Israel. Whereas the former follow their path on earth with splendor and brilliance just as the sun majestically traverses the heavens, Israel wanders in the somber kingdom of the night, even as the ever-shifting moon among the planets, unable to shine with its silver gleam until the sun has set.

The moon is also Israel's "sign" from another point of view. Its monthly regeneration after almost a complete disappearance is for Israel the heavenly pledge of its own perpetual renewal, despite the oft-repeated phases of its waning amidst the other nations. The monthly prayer of קִדּוּשׁ לְבָנָה, "Sanctification of the Moon," contains the most distinct expression of the more-than-symbolic meaning which is attached to the successive phases of the moon (see also our commentary on 3:8).

20. יִשְׁרְצוּ הַמַּיִם שֶׁרֶץ נֶפֶשׁ חַיָּה — *Let the waters teem with teeming living creatures.* The unfolding of creation takes two opposing paths. The emanating

¹⁵ *and they shall serve as luminaries in the firmament of the heaven to shine upon the earth." And it was so.* ¹⁶ *And God made the two great luminaries, the greater luminary to dominate the day and the lesser luminary to dominate the night; and the stars.* ¹⁷ *And God set them in the firmament of the heaven to give light upon the earth,* ¹⁸ *to dominate by day and by night, and to separate between the light and the darkness. And God saw that it was good.* ¹⁹ *And there was evening and there was morning, a fourth day.*

²⁰ *God said, "Let the waters teem with teeming living creatures, and fowl that fly about over the earth across the expanse of the heavens."* ²¹ *And God created the*

spheres go in successive stages from the transcendent world of pure spirit to the immanent spheres of life on earth in all its many manifestations. It is the initial unity which unfolds in the richness of its forms. As this evolution progresses, it is focused and goes from abstract to concrete. And so light from the first day is connected with the stars created on the fourth day; the waters and the atmosphere receive their living creatures on the fifth day; the earth, adorned with plant life on the third day, becomes inhabited on the sixth day. The farther the spheres are from their non-material Source, the more they appear in their "finished" incarnate form, relative to earthly dimensions. That is one path. But another evolution is occurring simultaneously in the opposite direction: matter is trying to attain the heights of the spirit. Indeed, creation follows a path along which spiritual forces come into play with ever-increasing importance. For creation is made to proceed from the inanimate (mineral) through the first elementary signs of a living soul (vegetable) to the world of animals endowed — as mentioned in this verse — with נֶפֶשׁ חַיָּה, *a living soul*, and finally to a world whose spiritual ascent reaches its summit with the creation of man who, in addition to his נֶפֶשׁ וְרוּחַ, a "vegetative" soul and a "feeling" soul is endowed with a נְשָׁמָה, *a spiritual soul*. The *n'shamah* which makes of man the creature which balances in himself the physical and spiritual forces places him in a central position between the celestial and the earthly spheres.

Thus, while God approaches man in successive stages, in successive degrees of emanation which go from the transcendent spheres of the spirit right to inanimate matter, the spiritual forces which are exiled on earth are tending to rise up again to God, going back by the same path. These forces create forms which come closer and closer to perfection and which culminate in man, who is constantly aspiring and striving to rejoin his Creator by elevating his soul, his mind and spirit. The reflected beam from man thus encounters the incident beam sent out by God (אוֹר יָשָׁר וְאוֹר חוֹזֵר). An excellent description of how all the creatures of the universe join together in a single choir to sing the glory of the Creator — in the two directions — is given in Psalm 148:1,7, הַלְלוּ אֶת ה' מִן

הַתַּנִּינִם הַגְּדֹלִים וְאֵת כָּל־נֶפֶשׁ הַחַיָּה ׀ הָרֹמֶשֶׂת אֲשֶׁר שָׁרְצוּ
הַמַּיִם לְמִינֵהֶם וְאֵת כָּל־עוֹף כָּנָף לְמִינֵהוּ וַיַּרְא אֱלֹהִים
כב כִּי־טוֹב: וַיְבָרֶךְ אֹתָם אֱלֹהִים לֵאמֹר פְּרוּ וּרְבוּ וּמִלְאוּ
כג אֶת־הַמַּיִם בַּיַּמִּים וְהָעוֹף יִרֶב בָּאָרֶץ: וַיְהִי־עֶרֶב וַיְהִי־בֹקֶר
יוֹם חֲמִישִׁי:
כד וַיֹּאמֶר אֱלֹהִים תּוֹצֵא הָאָרֶץ נֶפֶשׁ חַיָּה לְמִינָהּ בְּהֵמָה
כה וָרֶמֶשׂ וְחַיְתוֹ־אֶרֶץ לְמִינָהּ וַיְהִי־כֵן: וַיַּעַשׂ אֱלֹהִים אֶת־חַיַּת
הָאָרֶץ לְמִינָהּ וְאֶת־הַבְּהֵמָה לְמִינָהּ וְאֵת כָּל־רֶמֶשׂ הָאֲדָמָה

הַשָּׁמַיִם הַלְלוּהוּ בַּמְּרוֹמִים, *Praise Hashem from the Heavens; praise Him in the heights*, the sacred music first descends from the Heavens and the higher regions, and then it rises up from the earth to the heights of the celestial throne — הַלְלוּ אֶת ה' מִן הָאָרֶץ, *Praise Hashem from the earth* (see also *Rashi* on *Song of Songs* 7:2). Thus, the evolution of creation shows the way for mankind. For each human being there exists a path which takes him from the deepest recesses of earthly life, step by step, to the heights of existence. As he makes his way up the rungs of this universal ladder, he encounters God on the way.

21. הַתַּנִּינִם הַגְּדֹלִים — *The great sea-giants*. *Rashi* explains: *Taninim* are the large fish found in the sea. According to Rabbinic tradition, these were the Leviathan and its mate. God created them male and female and then slew the latter and stored her away to feed the righteous in the Hereafter. For had the leviathans multiplied, their offspring would have destroyed the world.

Rashi made a point of quoting this *aggadah* from the Talmud (*Bava Basra* 74b) as he felt that it contained an important lesson. One can therefore assume that he considered it important for man to be fully aware of how limited his spiritual horizons are. What man is allowed to see and observe gives him merely an extremely vague picture of the infinite grandeur and omnipotence of the Creator. Indeed, in every part of nature there exist creations which lie beyond man's range of perception; their size or their might is so overwhelming that he is incapable of having even the slightest idea of them. The light of the first day was of such brightness that it had to be replaced by sunlight, which is still too strong for man to look at without shielding his eyes. The firmament formed on the second day hides from us the immeasurable reaches of space. No imagination could have the vaguest conception of such enormity. Even the oceans and continents which appeared on the third day are so immense in size that after 5000 years of human investigation vast regions still remain unexplored. It is in this context that the Torah mentions the *taninim*, the sea serpents, members of the world of aquatic animals so powerful that "the world would have been destroyed" had the Creator allowed them to multiply.

How insignificant man feels in the presence of natural phenomena of such fantastic might and grandeur! Does he not seem like a worm compared with

*great sea-giants and every living being that creeps, with which
the waters teemed after their kinds; and all winged fowl of every
kind. And God saw that it was good.* [22] *God blessed them, saying, "Be fruitful and multiply, and fill the waters in the seas;
but the fowl shall increase on the earth."* [23] *And there was
evening and there was morning, a fifth day.*

[24] *God said, "Let the earth bring forth living creatures, each
according to its kind: animal, and creeping thing, and beast of
the land each according to its kind." And it was so.* [25] *God made
the beast of the earth according to its kind, and the animal
according to its kind, and every creeping being of the ground*

such gigantic creations! How then can man claim to want to know the
All-Powerful and to believe in Him only on condition that he understand His
eternal and absolute essence?

[Fish is the food especially favored on the Sabbath (מג״א 242:1) and has a
beneficial effect on the development of the intellect (*R' Bachya* 5:21).
Accordingly, the Leviathan will be the choice food offered to the righteous in
the Hereafter. On the other hand, eating the meat of animals is still considered
a concession, as is indicated in *Deuteronomy* 12:20.]

24. תּוֹצֵא הָאָרֶץ נֶפֶשׁ חַיָּה — *Let the earth bring forth living creatures.* Here too,
as with the days preceding, the new creation is completed on the following day.
The world of living creatures began to be formed on the fifth day and continues
on the sixth day to its completion. In general, we noted that there is no distinct
interruption between one day and the next. Rather, all creation unfolds in an
uninterrupted sequence and consequently there is a constant connection
between the seven stages of creation. The manifold elements of creation are thus
directly interconnected. And so in nature we find transitional forms between the
animal and vegetable kingdoms and between animal and man; for example:
algae, amphibious animals, and higher species of quadrupeds (cf. *Kuzari* 5:10):
"God has marvelously linked together all the beings of creation in a chain
wherein neighboring links differ almost imperceptibly, and this chain extends
all the way from the radiant angel to the smallest speck of dust."

It is pointed out by the philosopher R' Bachya ibn Pakuda that the principle
that creation is interwoven, interconnected, is borne out by many diverse
natural phenomena. For example, the seven colors of the rainbow are not
distinctly separated into a set of compartments but rather they form a spectrum
which is continuous, wherein the primary colors of the rainbow are bridged by
successions of hardly distinguishable intermediate shades. This principle
demonstrates that the different parts of creation cannot be due to the workings
of a number of divinities, each ruling separately, each in competition with the
rest. It shows us instead that there can only be One Creator, Who orders the
infinite richness of the varieties of creation into a coherent whole.

כו לְמִינֵהוּ וַיַּרְא אֱלֹהִים כִּי־טוֹב: וַיֹּאמֶר אֱלֹהִים נַעֲשֶׂה אָדָם
בְּצַלְמֵנוּ כִּדְמוּתֵנוּ וְיִרְדּוּ בִדְגַת הַיָּם וּבְעוֹף הַשָּׁמַיִם
וּבַבְּהֵמָה וּבְכָל־הָאָרֶץ וּבְכָל־הָרֶמֶשׂ הָרֹמֵשׂ עַל־הָאָרֶץ:

26. וַיֹּאמֶר אֱלֹהִים נַעֲשֶׂה אָדָם — *And God said, "Let us make Man."* Rashi
explains that although no one assisted God with creation and although heretics
may turn this plural form into an argument against monotheism, the Torah
did not wish to forego this opportunity to teach us the virtue of modesty: a
superior should consult with and seek the approval of his subordinates. On
the other hand, had the Torah stated: "I will make man," this would not
have taught us that God consulted with His "advisors" but rather that He
had formed this plan alone. Moreover, the counter-argument to the heretics is
found in the very next verse of the Torah: "God created the man," not "they
created."

Rashi's source for the above is the *Midrash Rabbah*. There it says even more
explicitly that when Moses came to this passage, which he was to write as God
dictated, he asked: "Why do You provide the heretics with a pretext (their
polytheistic theories seemingly being supported by the words 'Let us make
Man')?" God replied: "Write and let those who want to make the error make it.
Since man will be master of creation, it is appropriate for Me to ask the assent
of the higher and lower spheres before creating him. Men will thereby learn
from Me that the greatest must seek the approval of the smallest before
appointing a ruler over him."

Note that the Torah prefers to use an expression which might lead to
difficulties and be misinterpreted by polytheists rather than desist from
proclaiming an important moral lesson. The present example, appearing
right at the beginning of the Torah, is of prime importance. To be sure, there are
numerous passages in the Torah which can be misconstrued, which
are ambiguous or contain obscure terms or apparent contradictions. Schools
of biblical criticism pounce on such cases to cast doubt on the authenticity
and originality of the Scriptures, and they eagerly speculate on the presumed
authors of the Holy Writings, and go so far as to "resolve" these difficulties simply by changing and disfiguring the text or skipping parts of it. To
these aberrations of the human spirit, the Divine voice challenges: "Let those
who want to make the error make it." The moral, philosophical, historical,
and other teachings which the "incriminated" texts contain, and which
are generally clearly brought out by the Talmud, are infinitely more important that the fallacious conclusions which heretics might draw. For the Divine
Lawgiver, moral and doctrinal concerns take precedence over philological and
sometimes even historical questions. This idea of the Torah's universality, given
its place right at the beginning of *Genesis*, serves as notice; it is a signpost for
us as we encounter other textual difficulties in the Torah.

according to its kind. And God saw that it was good.

²⁶ *And God said, "Let us make Man in Our image, after Our likeness. They shall rule over the fish of the sea, the birds of the sky, and over the animal, the whole earth, and every creeping thing that creeps upon the earth."*

בְּצַלְמֵנוּ כִּדְמוּתֵנוּ — *In Our image, after Our likeness.* "The best of all explanations on this verse," writes *Ramban*, "is the one in which צֶלֶם refers to the facial features and expression and דְמוּת refers to the corporeal form which resembles those of the other earthly creatures. For man's body is like those of the other terrestrial beings but his soul is like the souls of heavenly beings."

It is the face of a holy and righteous person, alive with wisdom, goodness and love, which above all reflects the image of God. His magnanimity graces his features, his eyes shine with intelligence and understanding, the fire which burns within him bestows upon his whole being that radiance which made the Psalmist exclaim, "Yet You have made him but slightly less than the angels, and have crowned him with glory and honor" (*Psalms* 8:6).

In what sense is man created in the image of God? He bears within him a spark of the Divine spirit. Because of it he is "unique in the world just as God is unique above; he is the only earthly creature to be aware of good and evil" (*Rashi* on *Genesis* 3:22), for only he among all creatures has free will. Accordingly, his mind gives him the power to govern matter. To this spark he owes the immortality of his soul and the light of understanding which shines within him, permitting him to know God, to love Him and to cleave to Him.

God endowed each human being with this Divine spark by breathing into his nostrils the breath of life (*Genesis* 2:7). But the דְמוּת, the corporeal shape of man, albeit soil taken from the ground (ibid.), is also fashioned to resemble God. For *Rambam*, who is always careful to avoid the slightest hint of anthropomorphism, the words "image" and "likeness" are to be taken figuratively (*Guide for the Perplexed* 1:1). But in his interpretation of them, Rabbi Judah Halevi employs the concept of the microcosm: man is a miniature universe; in his physical and psychic makeup he is an exact reflection of the structure of the macrocosm, the world (*Kuzari* 4:25). This theory goes back to the very old סֵפֶר יְצִירָה attributed to the patriarch Avraham or, in the opinion of some historians, to the *Tanna*, Rabbi Akiva. It reveals the parallel which exists between man in his physical constitution and the universal soul in its functional structure. The head corresponds to the purely spiritual sphere of the metaphysical world; the chest, to the elements of will and action of the emanating spheres intermediate between spirit and matter. Lastly, the organs and parts of the lower body are the incarnation of physical functions of the material world (for more details, see *Kuzari*, ibid).

כז וַיִּבְרָא אֱלֹהִים ׀ אֶת־הָאָדָם בְּצַלְמוֹ בְּצֶלֶם אֱלֹהִים בָּרָא
כח אֹתוֹ זָכָר וּנְקֵבָה בָּרָא אֹתָם: וַיְבָרֶךְ אֹתָם אֱלֹהִים וַיֹּאמֶר
לָהֶם אֱלֹהִים פְּרוּ וּרְבוּ וּמִלְאוּ אֶת־הָאָרֶץ וְכִבְשֻׁהָ וּרְדוּ
בִּדְגַת הַיָּם וּבְעוֹף הַשָּׁמַיִם וּבְכָל־חַיָּה הָרֹמֶשֶׂת עַל־הָאָרֶץ:
כט וַיֹּאמֶר אֱלֹהִים הִנֵּה נָתַתִּי לָכֶם אֶת־כָּל־עֵשֶׂב ׀ זֹרֵעַ זֶרַע
אֲשֶׁר עַל־פְּנֵי כָל־הָאָרֶץ וְאֶת־כָּל־הָעֵץ אֲשֶׁר־בּוֹ פְרִי־עֵץ
ל זֹרֵעַ זָרַע לָכֶם יִהְיֶה לְאָכְלָה: וּלְכָל־חַיַּת הָאָרֶץ וּלְכָל־עוֹף
הַשָּׁמַיִם וּלְכֹל ׀ רוֹמֵשׂ עַל־הָאָרֶץ אֲשֶׁר־בּוֹ נֶפֶשׁ חַיָּה
לא אֶת־כָּל־יֶרֶק עֵשֶׂב לְאָכְלָה וַיְהִי־כֵן: וַיַּרְא אֱלֹהִים אֶת־כָּל־
אֲשֶׁר עָשָׂה וְהִנֵּה־טוֹב מְאֹד וַיְהִי־עֶרֶב וַיְהִי־בֹקֶר יוֹם הַשִּׁשִּׁי:

Thus, man represents, as it were, the "shadow" cast on the earth by the Divine Majesty (צֶלֶם being derived from צֵל, *shadow*, according to the interpretation of *R' Moshe Cordovero*).

27. וַיִּבְרָא אֱלֹהִים אֶת־הָאָדָם בְּצַלְמוֹ בְּצֶלֶם אֱלֹהִים — *So God created Man in His image, in the image of God*. From the way the Torah stresses that man was created "in God's image" we can presume the reasons for creation. Man appears as the highest stage in the hierarchy of creatures and if God wanted him to be created in His image, then the reason for this could only have been His wish to have His eternal bliss shared with these creatures who resembled Him.

The *Zohar* proclaims that God created the heavens and the earth through His love. The Almighty King, Who suffices unto Himself, voluntarily gave up a part of His Being in order to lavish His love on man, created in His form. He withdrew within Himself, giving to men the gift of His being, and from this act space was created. The relationship between God and life in the universe thus began in love, and in the same way, love is keeping its vigil beside the cradle of human life.

28. וַיְבָרֶךְ אֹתָם אֱלֹהִים וַיֹּאמֶר לָהֶם אֱלֹהִים פְּרוּ וּרְבוּ — *God blessed them and God said to them, "Be fruitful and multiply."* Right from the creation of the first couple, God brings them His blessing for the holiest and most basic task they have on earth, that of procreation. Rabbi Abahu said (allegorically), "God took the *kiddush*-cup and with it blessed the union of the first couple" (*Bereishis Rabbah*, ch. 8).

When husband and wife unite to procreate, they enter into a close partnership with God. How do those who claim to see in procreation nothing but a purely natural phenomenon, explain the presence of an immaterial soul in the newborn without referring to the Divine Creator's intervention? God's majesty hovers invisibly over the union of the procreating couple, ready to bless it by endowing the being which will develop with the breath of life that emanates from the celestial spheres.

²⁷ *So God created Man in His image, in the image of God He created him; male and female He created them.*

²⁸ *God blessed them and God said to them, "Be fruitful and multiply, fill the earth and subdue it; and rule over the fish of the sea, the bird of the sky, and every living thing that moves on the earth."*

²⁹ *God said, "Behold, I have given to you all herbage yielding seed that is on the surface of the entire earth, and every tree that has seed-yielding fruit; it shall be yours for food.* ³⁰ *And to every beast of the earth, to every bird of the sky, and to everything that moves on the earth, within which there is a living soul, every green herb is for food." And it was so.* ³¹ *And God saw all that He had made, and behold it was very good. And there was evening and there was morning, the sixth day.*

וּמִלְאוּ אֶת־הָאָרֶץ וְכִבְשֻׁהָ — *Fill the earth and subdue it.* The order given to the human race to subdue the earth implies the right to be master of and transform the earth's riches and resources and to appropriate them freely. This is a God-given right. Hence, man-made laws must protect the rights of ownership and condemn any damage done to another's property as a violation of a Divine right and as an affront to God. Founded on an inalienable God-given right, the norms of ownership offer absolute guarantees which no other reason advanced by men, be it occupation, accession, natural law, prescription, or social utility, can ever supplant. These Divine words coming on the first page of the Torah also serve as an example of the universal character of the law revealed in the Torah. This law proceeding from God is totally independent of the private interests of nations or social classes.

31. וְהִנֵּה־טוֹב מְאֹד — *And behold it was very good.* The work of the previous days of creation was called "good" but that of the last day is described as "very good" — טוֹב מְאֹד. To be sure, the excellence of a work only appears when it is finished and completed, whereas its parts, taken one by one, can appear to be just relatively good, being as they are but imperfect fragments of the whole. From this fact it follows that a sound knowledge of a subject presupposes a broad view of it, a view of its characteristics and properties in perspective. We often tend to prize specialization and to study beings and objects not as entities but "bit by bit." The compartmentalization of knowledge, the fragmenting of science into disciplines for "specialists," the excesses in the use of the analytical approach — these deprive us of perspective and cause us to lose sight of the whole. "Thus one grasps only bits of being, from which life has been banished; the sacred fire, the vital spirit, is taken away" (Goethe). Only insofar as scientists and philosophers have been able to go beyond the fragmenting conceptions which divide the universe into organic and inorganic worlds and a host of other disciplines, only when they have seen the world as a harmonious whole, have

ב א-ב וַיְכֻלּוּ הַשָּׁמַיִם וְהָאָרֶץ וְכָל־צְבָאָם: וַיְכַל אֱלֹהִים בַּיּוֹם הַשְּׁבִיעִי מְלַאכְתּוֹ אֲשֶׁר עָשָׂה וַיִּשְׁבֹּת בַּיּוֹם הַשְּׁבִיעִי

they been able to recognize the Living Spirit which quickens all parts of the universe.

Moreover, it is here, on the last day of creation, that our Sages in the Midrash first mention the presence of evil. Of course, considering the separate components of creation, one could think that they do not deserve the epithet "very good" because of the vices and imperfections which are included in them. But, seen as a whole, creation appears in all its excellence and the various kinds of evil assume their real significance when viewed in perspective. Indeed, as long as they are restrained, these diverse forms of evil contribute to the common good just as do human passions and the elemental forces of nature. Their presence is just as necessary for the harmony of creation as natural alloying with base metals is for the hardness of a substance. It is in this sense that Rabbi Meir said: "טוֹב מְאֹד זֶה הַמָּוֶת, very good includes even death"; and other sages added the evil inclination, Hell, etc. (*Bereishis Rabbah*, ch. 9; cf. *Ramban*; also *Guide for the Perplexed* 3:10).

Both morally and physically man is provided with matter which is not merely the best possible, but the only matter that is good. Despite its evident imperfections, this matter corresponds to the Divine plan, executed conscientiously and without restraint. And one can be sure that if God were not certain that His creation, fashioned by Him, was indeed the only one capable of fulfilling His goal, He would have made it otherwise. Thus, creation as it is must be able to reach full perfection and must contain in its intrinsic makeup all the necessary elements to do so. It is up to man to determine what these elements are, to isolate them and bring them into action in order to see the work of the six days of creations brought to complete perfection.

2.

1. וַיְכֻלּוּ הַשָּׁמַיִם וְהָאָרֶץ — *Thus the heaven and the earth were finished*. The word וַיְכֻלּוּ can mean "were ended," "were brought to perfection" (*Onkelos*), or "were completely finished." But it can also be linked with כְּלִי "object, instrument." In the latter case the sense would be that the potential world of *tohu* and *vohu* contained in the heavens and the earth needs to be bound up with a concrete object in order to become a living reality. Hence, it was only by connecting the heavens and the earth to their 'instruments" that "by the seventh day God completed His work which He had done" (*Recanati*).

However, the root כלה also signifies "to yearn" (as in *Psalms* 84:3). In his commentary *Ohr HaChaim*, Chaim ben Attar explains that when God finished Creation, He had to save His creatures from the inertia threatening every living being which lacks some higher aspiration, some higher goal. His creatures had to be given a deep longing for the Divine light. The term כָּלָה expresses this

2   ¹*Thus the heaven and the earth were finished, and all
their array. ²By the seventh day God completed His
work which He had done, and He abstained on the seventh day*

longing, which can attain the level of losing oneself completely in spiritual
contemplation. "The heavens, the earth, and all that is therein feel the yearning"
for their source of Divine emanation; it was a feeling of love that crowned
the work of creation. This gift, which is a vital principle of creation, was, as it
were, the gift of the Sabbath. By imparting the desire to strive for the ideal and
to come closer to their sources, the Sabbath gave a new soul to the works of
creation. This day continues as the day *par excellence* devoted to the soul's
aspirations for God. The Sabbath snatches the soul from the grip of worldly
cares and liberates it by providing a release for the metaphysical longings of
the soul; thus it offers the soul the means of fulfilling its supreme purpose on
earth (cf. *Beitzah* 16a). In this way the Sabbath has become the day of the נְשָׁמָה
יְתֵירָה, the new soul, and special Sabbath prayers appeal to this soul to sing
praises to God: נִשְׁמַת כָּל חַי תְּבָרֵךְ וגו׳, *the soul of every living being shall bless
Your Name.*

וְכָל־צְבָאָם — *And all their array*. Everything created in the heavens or on earth
forms a great צָבָא, a great army. The Creator and Master of the universe, Who
commands and draws up the host, is at its center. To each member He assigns
the place which befits him, where, with the powers he is granted, he is to fulfill
his particular mission. God draws up the master plan. Whether great or small,
no one is at his post by his own authority — we are all soldiers in God's army.
His is the power and the majesty, the wisdom, the will, and the command; our
duties are obedience and conscientiousness, loyalty, diligence, and industry.
There is no room for presumption here: man's greatest work is but a fragment,
and yet the slightest contribution is not lost in the complex whole so long as it
is carried out faithfully according to what the Supreme Commander of the host
expects. Nothing escapes God's notice, nothing is insignificant for the
realization of His plan. "Man is on earth in military service" (*Job* 7:1). And (ibid.
4:14) "One must stand fast until his relief comes, when God summons us to lead
us to another post" (*R' S.R. Hirsch*).

2. וַיְכַל אֱלֹהִים בַּיּוֹם הַשְּׁבִיעִי מְלַאכְתּוֹ אֲשֶׁר עָשָׂה — *By the seventh day God
completed His work which He had done*. The six days of creation are over.
Natural law, the all-powerful rhythm of the workings of the universe,
henceforth replaces the onrushing flow of successive creations. The Master
disappears behind His work. The omnipotence of the eternal law of nature thus
brings with it a serious danger, the danger that God will disappear from men's
minds. Hence the error of pantheism; hence the error of positivism. To combat
this danger, man needs to keep afresh the memory of the creation of the world,
of which Adam was the sole eyewitness — and at that he saw but a part of

ג מִכָּל־מְלַאכְתּוֹ אֲשֶׁר עָשָׂה: וַיְבָרֶךְ אֱלֹהִים אֶת־יוֹם הַשְּׁבִיעִי
וַיְקַדֵּשׁ אֹתוֹ כִּי בוֹ שָׁבַת מִכָּל־מְלַאכְתּוֹ אֲשֶׁר־בָּרָא אֱלֹהִים
לַעֲשׂוֹת:

creation (*R' S.R. Hirsch*). The Sabbath is thus זֵכֶר לְמַעֲשֵׂה בְרֵאשִׁית, a
remembrance of creation.

"The observance of the Sabbath is itself an acknowledgment of God, an
homage paid to the Creator of all. Indeed, he who rests on the Sabbath because
the work of Creation was finished on this day acknowledges that the world
had a beginning, and to recognize this beginning is to proclaim belief in
God, its Creator. However, he who ignores the Sabbath falls prey to doubts of
God's eternity; he loses his faith in the existence of the Creator of the world"
(*Kuzari* 2:4).

Furthermore, right from the beginning of life in the universe the Sabbath
makes its appearance as the day of liberation which triumphs over fate and
proclaims the complete freedom of the Creator. On the seventh day God ordered
the seething creative forces to stop. "These were in full swing and would have
continued to produce had not God revealing Himself as אֵל שַׁדַּי stopped them
with His supreme command: דַּי, enough" (שֶׁאָמַר לְעוֹלָם דַּי) — *Bereishis Rabbah*
10). For if one holds, as do the materialists, that the world owed its existence to
its own natural forces, how can one explain why these forces no longer act and
no longer create: Why do the same causes no longer have the same effects? Who
has placed a limit on their activity? The very fact that no new creation has come
about within living memory but that Sabbath does exist proves that this
Sabbath was preceded by a free creative force, conscious of itself and
all-powerful. The universe in its totality is not the purely physical result of
natural forces acting blindly and out of necessity. It is rather the work, of a moral
nature and order, emanating from a Creator Who acts in the infinite plenitude
of His wisdom, following a precise plan and by means of His free and
omnipotent will.

Thus, it is just this "stoppage of work" which gives the Sabbath all its
meaning. On the seventh day God raised up the creation of the world from the
constraints of material forces to the manifestation of Divine freedom which
finds expression in "rest." "What was the world still lacking?" asking *Rashi*.
"Rest — the Sabbath came and brought with it rest. Then the work of creation
was completed." And so the Torah records that God completed His work on the
seventh day and not on the sixth.

The fruit of the seventh day, rest, gives the work of the six preceding days
all its value and its dignity. Thus the Sabbath conquers the servitude to which
work inevitably leads. By giving mankind the gift of שַׁבָּת, God raised us to the
level of freedom, dignity, and equality for all. The Sabbath ennobles work and
crowns rest with glory. It establishes the realm of human dignity. To the slave,
denied a full portion in the human race, the Sabbath brings the right of accession

from all His work which He had done. ³ *God blessed the seventh day and sanctified it because on it He abstained from all His work which God created to make.*

to this freedom without which no earthly happiness is possible. The Sabbath, created just at the completion of creation, thus confers a moral character on all of creation. It is consequently a holiday not just for nature but also for humanity.

3. מִכָּל־מְלַאכְתּוֹ אֲשֶׁר־בָּרָא אֱלֹהִים לַעֲשׂוֹת — *From all His work which God created to make.* There are many interpretations for the word לַעֲשׂוֹת which concludes the chapter describing creation. Referring to chapter 11 of *Bereishis Rabbah*, *Rashi* explains that the work which was to have been accomplished on the seventh day, God did on the sixth, when twice as much was created. Each of the first five days included three creations whereas the sixth counted six creations on account of the "rest" expected on the seventh day. (Man as well will come to do twice as much on Friday in preparation for resting on the Sabbath).

The *Midrash Tanhuma* (and *Bereishis Rabbah* 7) interprets this verse as follows: God sanctified the seventh day when He ceased all His work which God was in the process of doing. This sudden cessation at the coming of the Sabbath gave rise to "the creation of demons." They remained as spirits devoid of corporeal form, the arrival of the Sabbath did not permit this work to be completely finished. The Midrash wants us to see that creation also includes maleficent, wandering, noxious spirits, all created during the dim twilight hours. They came into being just at the last minute of creation. Consequently they abhor broad daylight and seek their victims in the dimming twilight. Along similar lines the *Targum Yonasan* translates: the work which God had created and which He will create in future. According to *Recanati*, this way of translating the verse alludes to "the ten works of nature created on the eve of the Sabbath, at twilight," as enumerated in chapter 5 of *Ethics of the Fathers* (*Mishnah* 8). The activity of these ten creations and their effect will only become manifest some time after creation. *Rambam* gives the same interpretations in his commentary on the *Mishnah* (ibid.) and explains that the supernatural phenomena occurring in history have their origin here, in the work at twilight at the end of creation, when God put into nature the necessary conditions for their realization under particular circumstances.

Ibn Ezra and *Abarbanel* take לַעֲשׂוֹת to signify the permanence of the creative action. Creation, thanks to the Divine laws instilled in it, continues to act and to produce. "The Creator in His goodness renews each day the works of creation," as we say in our prayers. This opinion is based on the interpretation given by Rabbi Yitzhak in the *Zohar Chadash* (17a). For Rav Papa and Rav Oshaya, however, לַעֲשׂוֹת refers to the completion of creation which is entrusted to man (*Bereishis Rabbah* 11). The process of creation lasts as long as the conflict between good and evil remains unresolved. Ethically, the world is incomplete, unfinished, and mankind has the glorious privilege of being able to contribute

שני   ד אֵלֶּה תוֹלְדוֹת הַשָּׁמַיִם וְהָאָרֶץ בְּהִבָּרְאָם בְּיוֹם עֲשׂוֹת יהוה

to its perfection. Through moral conduct, men can bring about the victory of the forces of good. Thus as the story of creation draws to a close, the last word brings a new dimension to the history of humanity which is just beginning. It is now up to man to put the seal on God's work by his acts. The fate of creation is put in man's hands. The true completion of creation will come only when man has established the kingdom of God on earth. The Midrash expresses this idea when it describes the erection of the Temple in Jerusalem as crowning the creation of the world (*Pesikta Rabbasi* 6). "All the work for the house of God was completed וַתִּשְׁלַם כָּל הַמְּלָאכָה" (*I Kings* 7:51). This completion was the הַשְׁלָמָה, the perfection, which was brought to the "simple ending" of the works of the six days of creation וַיְכַל ... מְכָּל מְלַאכְתּוֹ אֲשֶׁר עָשָׂה. This is why the builder of the Temple is called שְׁלֹמֹה, King Shlomoh, for he brought the work of creation to perfection. Cf. our commentary on *Exodus* 25:31.

Developing this same historical view, *Ramban* and *R' Bachya* take the word לַעֲשׂוֹת to mean "to recur, to happen again" with respect to human history. The development of the seven days of creation faithfully recurs in the seven millennia of history, for "a thousand years in the eyes of the Lord are but as a day that passes" (*Psalms* 90:4). According to Jewish tradition, the history of humanity unfolds in a trilogy; each act covers 2000 years, the seventh millennium being the messianic era which is "complete Sabbath and everlasting peace" (*Avodah Zarah* 9a). Both sages demonstrate the parallel between the work of each of the seven days of creation and the historical features of each of the seven millennia in the history of the universe.

Consider the division of time into weeks. It owes its origin to the Torah's description of creation. Contrary to all other common times intervals (year, month, day, night), which are based on the motion of the stars and planets, the week has no other source than the Biblical narrative. Consequently, the fact that the civilized world has adopted a week of seven days ever since antiquity can be considered as an indirect proof of the veracity of the Torah (*Kuzari* 1:57; cf. *Ibn Ezra* on *Exodus* 16:1 and *Rambam, Guide* 3:43).

4. אֵלֶּה תוֹלְדוֹת — *These are the products.* R' Abahu observes that אֵלֶּה "these are" always denotes a contrast, a break with what preceded, while וְאֵלֶּה "*and* these are" introduces something continuous. In this verse, "These are the products of the heaven and the earth," what is the contrast? God had previously created worlds which had fallen short of the ideal. He destroyed them and returned them to a state of chaos. However, the world we live in does meet the standards for the ideal, and so God says: "These are the products..." This is a break with the previous worlds whose origins did not last, for they were returned to a state of chaos (*Shemos Rabbah* 30).

The Midrash quotes this saying of R' Abahu's several times (*Bereishis Rabbah* 3 and 9) and the cosmological idea on which it is founded has often been studied

> ⁴ *These are the products of the heaven and the earth*
> *when they were created in the day that HASHEM God made*

(cf. *Rambam*, *Guide* 2:30). Some Jewish scientists have utilized this idea, which admits there was life on earth before Genesis, to explain the geological formations, archaeological strata, prehistoric fossils, and other similar phenomena which give evidence that the world is millions of years old (*Tiferes Yisrael*, end of *Nezikim*; *Encyclopedia of Biblical Interpretation*, 1:86). The Jewish calendar refers to years counted in this present world; it does not deny the existence of previous worlds. As *Rabbi Judah Halevi* points out explicitly (*Kuzari* 1:67): "This idea is in no way opposed to religious faith." Moreover, from this notion we can now understand why no Divine orders announced the creation of heaven and earth as they did for the other creations. Indeed, heaven and earth endure "through the seven cycles of the world to the great Jubilee and the earthly creatures alone disappear and are recreated" (בחיי, בהר).

בְּהִבָּרְאָם — *When they were created.* The ה is written small according to the *Mesorah*. The word can thus be read בְּהֵ' בָּרְאָם; *with the ה He created them.* The Talmud does tell us that this world was created with a ה and the World to Come with the letter י (*Bavli*, *Menachos* 29b). *Rashi* gives an ethical interpretation and R' Bachya explains (consistent with the *Midrash* on *Psalms* 62) that the letter ה is the only one whose sound is a mere breath and demands no effort, in contrast to the other sounds which require movements of the lips, tongue, teeth, etc. This letter is therefore particularly well suited to illustrate the fact of creation *ex nihilo*. It is the best representation of what the Psalmist sang: "By the word of Hashem the heavens were made, and by the breath of His mouth, all their hosts" (*Psalms* 33:6). Cf. our commentary on 47:23.

בְּיוֹם עֲשׂוֹת ה' אֱלֹהִים — *In the day that HASHEM God made.* It is here, after the story of creation, that the Tetragrammaton, שֵׁם הֲוָיָה first appears as a name of God. The first chapter contained only the name אֱלֹהִים and *Rashi* notes in his commentary on the first verse of the Torah: "In the beginning, God intended to create the world according to the principle of Justice (*Elohim* is the name of God exercising justice). But He saw that the world could not endure so He brought mercy to the fore (הֲוָיָה reflects God's attribute of mercy) and joined it to justice. Hence it is written (at the beginning of Chapter 2): 'In the day that ה' אֱלֹהִים made earth and heaven.' "

In all of nature we see a perfect order, ruled by an immutable, unvarying and all-powerful Law. Consequently, throughout the first chapter, which is devoted to the creation of nature, God appears as אֱלֹהִים (having a numerical value of 86, the same as הַטֶּבַע, *nature*) which denotes God as the God of absolute power, of strict justice, and of eternal law — מִדַּת הַדִּין.

But as soon as the second chapter, and with it the history of mankind, commences, it is the מִדַּת הָרַחֲמִים, the name signifying God's love and mercy, which comes to the fore, to be united with the מִדַּת הַדִּין. If nature is governed

ה אֱלֹהִים אֶרֶץ וְשָׁמָיִם: וְכֹל ׀ שִׂיחַ הַשָּׂדֶה טֶרֶם יִהְיֶה
בָאָרֶץ וְכָל־עֵשֶׂב הַשָּׂדֶה טֶרֶם יִצְמָח כִּי לֹא הִמְטִיר
יְהוָה אֱלֹהִים עַל־הָאָרֶץ וְאָדָם אַיִן לַעֲבֹד אֶת־הָאֲדָמָה:
ו וְאֵד יַעֲלֶה מִן־הָאָרֶץ וְהִשְׁקָה אֶת־כָּל־פְּנֵי הָאֲדָמָה
ז וַיִּיצֶר יְהוָה אֱלֹהִים אֶת־הָאָדָם עָפָר מִן־הָאֲדָמָה וַיִּפַּח

by intangible laws, then the human sphere is governed by a law which is
tempered and softened with love. Note that at the end of this verse, the Torah
puts "earth" before "heaven" אֶרֶץ וְשָׁמָיִם as if to reinforce the change which has
just occurred with respect to the designation of God, with mercy not taking
precedence over justice. And the Biblical narrative from now on will be
concerned with the affairs of man.

That mercy takes priority over justice is illustrated by the episode
immediately following. The death sentence pronounced upon Adam for the first
sin will be commuted to banishment from paradise and exile (*Tanchuma
Masei*). Our Sages also followed this example of clemency and for all practical
purposes abolished the death penalty, meting out in its stead incarceration and
detention or other punishments. Hence the *Mishnah* states that if a *beis din*
(court of law) passes a death sentence once in seven years — according to R'
Elazar ben Azaryah, even once in seventy years — it is called a "pernicious
court" (*Makkos* 7a).

The problem of two Divine names being encountered in the first two chapters
of the Torah is a favorite subject of the pseudo-science of biblical criticism. Its
experts with their simplistic method "resolved" the problem by declaring that
these two chapters were written by two different people, one venerating the God
name E., the other, the one named J. This thesis ought to have been abandoned
for lack of proof. As for our Sages, they were quite well aware of exegetical
problems in the Torah, problems which biblical critics claimed to have
discovered, but the same typical contrast brought out right from the first page
of the Torah exists between all of this school's solutions and our Sages'
traditional method of interpretation.

5. וְכֹל שִׂיחַ הַשָּׂדֶה טֶרֶם יִהְיֶה בָאָרֶץ — *Now all the trees of the field were not yet on
the earth. Rashi* explains that God had not made it rain as there was no man to
work the land and to appreciate the benefits of the rain. When Adam came he
understood the need for rain and prayed for it. Rain fell and the trees and plants
grew. The Talmudical source for this *explanation* (*Chullin* 60b), quoted in the
name of R' Ashi, adds: "This teaches that God desires the prayers of the
righteous." *Recanati* concludes from the Torah's observation: it follows that the
benediction which comes from Heaven, to "water the ground everywhere" and
to make the earth fertile, depends on man, on his prayer, on his active will.

Just as the work of the six days of creation reaches completion, the Torah
makes us see that from now on, man is to play a key role in developing this

*earth and heaven — ⁵ now all the trees of the field were not yet
on the earth and all the herb of the field had not yet sprouted,
for HASHEM God had not sent rain upon the earth and there
was no man to work the soil. ⁶ A mist ascended from the
earth and watered the whole surface of the soil. ⁷ And HASHEM
God formed the man of dust from the ground, and He blew*

creation. He is to be God's collaborator; he is charged with keeping the harmony
of the universe. Everything will depend on his acts, on his conduct, and on his
efforts. Thus the Torah tells us at the beginning of human history that salvation
does not depend on the "mystery of grace" coming from God. It is instead up
to man to rouse Divine grace by his deeds and his prayers on this earth so that
this grace will grant him its providential benefits.

7. וַיִּיצֶר — *Formed*. The double *yud* in this word is an exceptional grammatical
construction (for the radical *yud* appears; it is usually omitted) and denotes a
double "forming" of man, according to our Sages. In man, the spiritual and the
temporal, "the good inclination and the evil inclination," are united. Man is
formed for this world and also for the next (*Rashi*); he contains in him both
heaven and earth. In וַיִּיצֶר only one *yud* is sounded; the other is quiescent,
indicating that of man's two-sided personality, one side is always dominant
while the other is only glimpsed. The noblest of men still belongs to the earth
and in the worst of men glimmerings of humanity still shine through.

We are deeply indebted to our Sages for having made us aware that man was
formed right from the start with both of these tendencies. Indeed, there exists
nothing which is evil in the absolute sense of the word, for the same Creator has
fashioned both the one side and the other, and each can serve the ideal of purity
and holiness. The sensual world and man's carnal nature are not the work of
Satan nor are they dedicated to him. To say otherwise is a lie, a fabrication which
has done the greatest harm to humanity! In Judaism, both tendencies in man are
the work of the Creator; heaven and earth, the immortal and the mortal, are both
intimately united within him.

[This dual nature consequently applies also to the sexual formation of man,
at least at his origins. *Rashi* comments (1:27) that initially man's physical being
was created with two sides, male and female, which afterwards were separated
(into two distinct sexes). According to our Sages, Adam was created
androgynous (*Berachos* 61a).

עָפָר מִן־הָאֲדָמָה — *Dust from the ground*. It is not written מֵאֲדָמָה but מִן הָאֲדָמָה
whereupon *Rashi* concludes: God collected soil from all parts of the world, from
the four corners of the earth; wherever man dies, the earth consents to be his
grave. Also expressed in this idea is that men of all continents and all climes are
brothers. Additionally, the formation of the superior human being is based on
constituents coming from the four corners of the world (הָאָדָם refers to the man
par excellence; cf. *Encyclopedia Talmudica*, article אָדָם — 1:76). Spiritually

ח בְּאַפָּיו נִשְׁמַת חַיִּים וַיְהִי הָאָדָם לְנֶפֶשׁ חַיָּה: וַיִּטַּע יהוה
אֱלֹהִים גַּן־בְּעֵדֶן מִקֶּדֶם וַיָּשֶׂם שָׁם אֶת־הָאָדָם אֲשֶׁר יָצָר:
ט וַיַּצְמַח יהוה אֱלֹהִים מִן־הָאֲדָמָה כָּל־עֵץ נֶחְמָד לְמַרְאֶה

speaking, human wisdom attains perfection only through the contributions of
the greatest minds the world over. As for the literal meaning, man *par excellence*
appears as the only one in all of creation to participate in all the elements of the
spiritual, sensory, and physical worlds, whereas the material, animal and
vegetable worlds on one hand and the metaphysical world on the other contain
only a specific part of all the universal forces. Man thus has things in common
with all parts of the universe.

Rashi continues: "Another interpretation is that the earth was collected from
the future site of the altar, whereof it is said 'An altar of earth you shall make
for Me' (*Exodus* 20:21). God said, 'Let this be the place of his atonement, and he
will be able to endure.' " *Rambam* elaborates: It is a generally accepted tradition
that at the very place where David and Solomon built the altar (of the Temple
in Jerusalem), Abraham had erected his altar to sacrifice Isaac, Noah had built
his altar on leaving the Ark, Cain and Abel had offered their sacrifices, and Adam
had offered a sacrifice after his creation. And it is at this place that he was created,
as our Sages said, "Man was created at the place of his atonement" (*Hilchos Bais
HaBechirah*, Ch.2). This means that sin is not an integral part of man's nature,
although he is formed of soil from the ground. He possesses the ability to rule
over sin and, by repentance, to be granted forgiveness by God. Hence the verse
mentions both names of God ה' אֱלֹהִים. Since man is a child of the earth, the
Creator is very close to him, like a father full of kindness מִדַּת הָרַחֲמִים = ה' (cf.
our commentary on 47:29).

וַיִּפַּח בְּאַפָּיו נִשְׁמַת חַיִּים — *And He blew into his nostrils the soul of life*. By receiving
the breath of life in his nostrils, in his countenance, man was elevated above the
other creatures both physically and spiritually. He thus stands in marked contrast
to plant life. The latter, rooted in the soil, draws up the life-giving sap it needs
from its roots, its lower extremities. As for the animal, its vital center is its heart,
a central part of the body. Man's life, however, is bonded to his spirit, to the
countenance which crowns his being. Man lifts his eyes upward and receives all
his strength "from above" when he hopes, desires, and thinks. The life breathed
into man's countenance upholds and sustains him, and so when he loses
consciousness he collapses.

נִשְׁמַת חַיִּים — *The soul of life*. The word נְשָׁמָה is reserved for the soul particular
to man. It distinguishes him from the other creatures, some of whom possess only
נֶפֶשׁ וְרוּחַ, a vegetative soul and a sensitive soul. The נְשָׁמָה is the emanation of the
Supreme Intelligence which constitutes man's resemblance to the Divine, as was
mentioned above. *Ibn Ezra* (7:22) notes that the assonance with שָׁמַיִם justifies
defining נְשָׁמָה as the emanation of the celestial spirit.

into his nostrils the soul of life; and man became a living being.
⁸ HASHEM God planted a garden in Eden, to the east, and placed
there the man whom He had formed. ⁹ And HASHEM God caused
to sprout from the ground every tree that was pleasing to the sight

Opinion is divided among our Sages as to the structure of the human soul. Some think of the soul as a simple principle with a triple function: vegetative, sensitive, and intellectual — as *Rambam* holds (*Shemoneh Perakim*, Ch. 1). Others consider the soul as being composed of three different parts. *Ramban* seems to share this opinion. He follows *Onkelos*, who translates the words נֶפֶשׁ חַיָּה in this verse as לְרוּחַ מְמַלְּלָא "speaking being." For him, then, once man receives the נִשְׁמַת חַיִּים, he becomes a personality endowed with the ability to think and to express his thoughts freely. He therefore possesses a soul which is particular to him.

Onkelos's translation has raised many comments among our Sages. According to this, what characterizes the human soul and what distinguishes it from the animal is the ability to speak. It implies that the formation of languages is to be attributed to a Divine miracle (*Kuzari* 4:25). However, the question remains: Was language given to man together with all its words and expressions, or did the vocabulary develop gradually as it was needed? *Malbim* studies this question in his commentary on the verse in which Adam names the animals (*Genesis* 2:20). The Torah does not exclude the opinion held by many psychologists that it is man's ability to express himself which forms and develops the intelligence, the latter being progressively refined by the use of language (*HaDe'ah VeHaDibur* 1:16). In any case, it is the רוּחַ מְמַלְּלָא, *the speaking spirit* which elevates man to resemble God. Indeed the word is the "divine seed" through which creation came into being. The word previously existed in the form of thought, for although speech is capable of expressing everything that is material, it is powerless to reveal what is not material. Now, it is this same property of the word which gives man a creative power here on earth, the repercussions of which can reach into the spheres of the cosmos (cf. verse 19; and *Sefer HaChinuch* §239, 350; Venice edition).

The *Zohar* however interprets וַיְהִי הָאָדָם לְנֶפֶשׁ חַיָּה in quite a different way: the Torah is expressing disdain of man. The Lord had crowned him with a soul imbued with holiness so that he could merit the future world. But man fell from his supreme nobility down to the level of the animal. R' Yehoshua adds that is why the Torah complains: And man became נֶפֶשׁ חַיָּה, a term designating (lit.) the soul of animals (1:24). The word וַיְהִי, let it be noted, occurs only twice in the description of creation — in this verse and in 1:3: וַיְהִי אוֹר. The word וַיְהִי always heralds the approach of trouble which in fact is an integral part of its meaning, as our Sages point out (*Megillah* 10b).

8. וַיִּטַּע ה׳ אֱלֹהִים גַּן בְּעֵדֶן מִקֶּדֶם — *HASHEM God planted a garden in Eden, to the east*. In the beginning was the ideal. The world which God created with His

וְטוֹב לְמַאֲכָל וְעֵץ הַחַיִּים בְּתוֹךְ הַגָּן וְעֵץ הַדַּעַת טוֹב וָרָע:
י וְנָהָר יֹצֵא מֵעֵדֶן לְהַשְׁקוֹת אֶת־הַגָּן וּמִשָּׁם יִפָּרֵד וְהָיָה
יא לְאַרְבָּעָה רָאשִׁים: שֵׁם הָאֶחָד פִּישׁוֹן הוּא הַסֹּבֵב אֵת כָּל־

boundless love was of a marvelous splendor and dazzling harmony. The whole universe was an Eden. But God "planted a garden in Eden to the east" and placed therein the man He had fashioned. He took him there, says R' Eliezer, as one takes a man to his palace, since Adam had come into the world on Mount Moriah whereas the garden was further to the east (*Pirkei D'Rabbi Eliezer* 12). Man's destiny was to live in pure joy, a sublime, divine joy, surrounded by all the beauty of nature, exulting in communion with God. God therefore placed man in the paradisical garden, setting no conditions on his happiness other than the cultivation and conservation of the garden.

The task of tending and keeping the garden of nature marks the beginning of human civilization. At the same time the Torah tells us that the garden was situated to the east. This first mention of direction underscores the importance of the cardinal points for all future development. The cradle of civilization is in the east. From here, the light of the spirit will take the same path on earth as the sun in the heavens, as the Psalmist says: "From the rising of the sun till its going down, the Lord's name will be praised" (113:3).

Onkelos and others however take מִקֶּדֶם to mean "from before," that is, before creation. The Talmud in *Pesachim* (54a) lists Paradise among the seven things which were created before the universe came into being. This means that Paradise was one of the seven essential elements for which the universe was created. Just as an architect draws up his blueprint before commencing his work, God established the plan of the principal consituents of the universe prior to creation.

9. וְעֵץ הַחַיִּים — *Also the Tree of Life*. The tree whose fruit brought longevity or eternal life was close to or had the same root as the Tree of Knowledge of Good and Bad, according to the Sages. The *Midrash Hagadol* relates that "the two trees were both in paradise. This is to teach you that man can find everything there. He who seeks the tree of life finds it there. He who seeks the tree of good and bad also finds it there. Man has two roads before him and can take the one he wants. If he wishes to follow the road of goodness, the door is open and he will find happiness. If he wants to follow the path of evil, the way is clear for him and he will come upon woes."

בְּתוֹךְ הַגָּן — *In the midst of the garden*. *Onkelos* translates "at the center" and *Rashi* also finds it necessary to stress "at the center" (rather than "within"). Why? A doctor once asked the *Chafetz Chaim*, Rabbi Yisrael Meir HaCohen, what merits doctors might have to be worthy of life in the World to Come. He answered by referring to this verse: "Our Sages stress that the Tree of Life was situated at the center of the garden. This was probably because the central point is equally accessible from all sides, so we do not think there is just one path to

and good for food; also the Tree of Life in the midst of the garden, and the Tree of Knowledge of Good and Bad.

10 A river issues forth from Eden to water the garden, and from there it is divided and becomes four headwaters. 11The name of the first is Pishon, the one that encircles the whole

arrive at the Tree of Life. It can be reached from all sides, that is, each man, whether he be Torah-scholar, scientist, or artisan, is capable of reaching it. 'In all your ways, acknowledge Him and He will direct your path' (*Proverbs* 3:6). And the Talmud tells us of the merits of the doctor, Abba, which earned him life in the World to Come" [*Taanis* 21b] (*Chafetz Chaim*). For the same reason the *ohel moed*, the tent of meeting wherein the Torah was contained, was situated at the center of the camp of the Israelites in the desert. Likewise, the *bimah* is the central point of each synagogue.

וְעֵץ הַדַּעַת טוב וָרָע — *And the Tree of Knowledge of Good and Bad*. The tree which wakens in man the knowledge of good and evil. Right from creation Adam possessed free will, but as long as he did not taste the forbidden fruit his soul was suffused with an eternal inner glow. It hovered majestically above good and evil, angelically pure, for Adam was above temptation. It had no effect on him.

Only after Adam had tasted the forbidden fruit was desire kindled within him. Then forces of evil were roused in him and, along with them, instincts and sexual passions. The first sin destroyed the marvelous harmony of the beginning. Hence the tree bears the name "the Tree of Knowledge of Good and Bad" עַל שֵׁם סוֹפוֹ because of what ultimately happened (*Rambam*, *Guide* 1:2, and *Ramban* 2:9).

10. וְנָהָר יֵצֵא מֵעֵדֶן לְהַשְׁקוֹת אֶת־הַגָּן — *A river issues forth from Eden to water the garden*. There is an Eden above and a garden below. The Eden above includes the supreme delights of the realms of the spirit and the garden below offers the marvels and joys of earthly life. The latter is watered by the river of overflowing richness which flows from the celestial Eden. The favorite day for this river to flow is the Sabbath: the first letters of the three words עֵדֶן — נָהָר — גַּן — form the word עֹנֶג which designates the sacred joy of the Sabbath, *oneg* Shabbat. Eden — river — garden are the three keywords for the Sabbath. On this day, the outpouring of blessings flows from the celestial Eden to water the terrestrial garden and this river is the counterpart of the one which rises from the earth to reach the heavenly Eden and to join with it. It rises from the earthly garden at the moment the *Kiddush* to sanctify the Sabbath is said on Friday night, it continues its ascent on the Sabbath morning with the prayers and Torah study, and on Sabbath afternoon at last its tastes the delights of the celestial Eden (*Recanati*). The Sabbath thus becomes the day on which material joys are united with the joys of the spirit.

11. שֵׁם הָאֶחָד פִּישׁוֹן — *The name of the first is Pishon*. According to *Rashi*, this is the Nile. After watering Eden, the river leaves it and flows underground to

יב אֶרֶץ הַחֲוִילָה אֲשֶׁר־שָׁם הַזָּהָב: וְזַהֲב הָאָרֶץ הַהִוא טוֹב שָׁם
יג הַבְּדֹלַח וְאֶבֶן הַשֹּׁהַם: וְשֵׁם־הַנָּהָר הַשֵּׁנִי גִּיחוֹן הוּא הַסּוֹבֵב
יד אֵת כָּל־אֶרֶץ כּוּשׁ: וְשֵׁם הַנָּהָר הַשְּׁלִישִׁי חִדֶּקֶל הוּא הַהֹלֵךְ
טו קִדְמַת אַשּׁוּר וְהַנָּהָר הָרְבִיעִי הוּא פְרָת: וַיִּקַּח יהוה אֱלֹהִים
טז אֶת־הָאָדָם וַיַּנִּחֵהוּ בְגַן־עֵדֶן לְעָבְדָהּ וּלְשָׁמְרָהּ: וַיְצַו יהוה

re-emerge in four different places as four new sources (for the word רָאשִׁים does not mean "branches"). Might this not give us the reason why it has never been possible to identify the sources of the Nile?

14. וְשֵׁם הַנָּהָר הַשְּׁלִישִׁי חִדֶּקֶל — *The name of the third river is Hiddekel.* This is usually considered to be the Tigris. The exact geographical location of Eden is not known for "it is not revealed to any mortal" (*Midrash Hagadol*). It is generally thought to be in the Middle Eastern region, near the equator. The Torah mentions four regions in this passage. All the abundance and all the richness of the choicest products of each of these regions could be found in Paradise.

Ramban quotes ancient Greek medical treatises and the famous doctor Assaf (9th century) to tell of the wise Asplagien of Macedonia. The latter, accompanied by forty expert healers, voyaged to India in search of therapeutic plants coming from the Tree of Life in Paradise. They arrived at the site but everyone of them was smitten by the "blade of the sword" which guarded the entrance. From that time onward medical science in these countries was lost until King Ataxerxes managed to re-establish it. These are authenticated facts, known to all in the Orient (שער הגמול).

15. וַיִּקַּח ה' אֱלֹהִים אֶת־הָאָדָם וַיַּנִּחֵהוּ בְגַן־עֵדֶן — *HASHEM God took the man and placed him in the Garden of Eden.* Our Sages are unanimous in the view that the story of Paradise is to be taken literally, but they also consider that at the same time it alludes, in all its details, to metaphysical facts in the upper worlds. For the earth with all it contains is only the reflection of the higher spheres. Thus, in the interpretations of philosophers such as *Rambam* (*Guide*, 2:30), we are not dealing merely with simple allegories or mythological fables but rather with applying the forms of incarnation in this world to the spheres of pure thought. Our Sages seek to discover the ideal world and its manifold aspects through the earthly phenomena known to us. And in this way, basing themselves on sayings in the Talmud, the *Zohar*, and the Midrash, our rabbis described the Garden of Eden, a paradise of delights of the spirit, a paradise promised to the souls of the righteous as a reward in the World to Come.

Here is how our Sages figuratively understood the story of paradise in its universal significance: One day, surrounded by his students, Rabbi Yochanan was speaking of the world, of God, and of the Torah. One disciple asked how they were interconnected. The master replied: "Consider a king who wished to plant a tree in his garden. He first passed through the garden to find a spring

land of Havilah, where the gold is. [12] *The gold of that land is good;
bedolach is there, and the shoham stone.* [13] *The name of the second
river is Gihon, the one that encircles the whole land of Cush.* [14] *The
name of the third river is Hiddekel, the one that flows toward the
east of Assyria; and the fourth river is the Euphrates.*

[15] *HASHEM God took the man and placed him in the Garden of
Eden, to work it and to guard it.* [16] *And HASHEM God commanded*

which would provide water for the tree. But unable to find one, he had a well
dug and then had the tree planted. And from then on the tree flourished, its roots
grew and strengthened, and it came into full blossom, for it was regularly being
provided with water from the well.

"The universe," concluded Rabbi Yochanan, "is like a tree planted by God.
It rises up in space, God's limitless garden. Its crown reaches the celestial throne
of the Divine Majesty, and its roots are buried in the depths of the earth, while
its trunk directly connects all parts of the tree, from roots to treetop. Its branches
and twigs spread out on all sides. This tree was planted to gladden man with its
fruits and blossoms and fragrance.

"But the sap, the life-blood rising in this tree which is the universe, comes
from the source which God created before the tree was planted. What is this
wellspring of universal life? It is the Torah. Its laws guarantee our existence just
as fresh, healthful water from the spring keeps the plant alive. Torah gives
creation its vitality and its vigor.

"Are you seeking life and its sovereign principle, Truth?" asked Rabbi
Yochanan of his students. "Heed, then, the exhortation of Isaiah which comes
down to you through the centuries: 'All of you who thirst, come and draw
water' " (*Zohar Chadash*, 116).

לְעָבְדָהּ וּלְשָׁמְרָהּ — *To work it and to guard it.* Even in a paradise where all the
earthly delights are offered to man, life is meaningless without duties and
unattractive unless its gifts are the result of deliberate effort. "And the Lord took
the man" as a father takes his son, and told him his duties "with pleasant words"
(*Rashi*). This was just as Adam was about to enter paradise as master and to be,
for the first time, "let free" (וַיַּנִּחֵהוּ) to use his own free will. Adam's duties
involved both the physical and spiritual realms. In the latter case, "to work it and
guard it" refers to cultivating spiritual values and keeping the Divine
commandments (*Targum Yonasan*). In the former case, these words apply to
tilling the soil. "See then the importance of work. Only after doing work was
the first man allowed to taste the produce of the earth. God puts Adam in the
Garden of Eden to cultivate and care for it — and only afterwards does He say,
'Of every tree of the garden you may freely eat.' " (*Avos D'Rabbi Nassan* 11).

16. וַיְצַו ה' אֱלֹהִים עַל־הָאָדָם — *And HASHEM God commanded the man.* With this
prohibition man's training for his high moral calling begins. This is the
commencement of human history and it illuminates the path for all future

יז אֱלֹהִים עַל־הָאָדָם לֵאמֹר מִכֹּל עֵץ־הַגָּן אָכֹל תֹּאכֵל: וּמֵעֵץ הַדַּעַת טוֹב וָרָע לֹא תֹאכַל מִמֶּנּוּ כִּי בְּיוֹם אֲכָלְךָ מִמֶּנּוּ

generations to follow. The fact that God first of all pronounces a prohibition instead of giving a command means implicitly that the one He addresses enjoys a new privilege: freedom. Moreover, it means that this freedom must play an active role and must become a dominant factor in the whole future history of mankind. But freedom is not just a privilege; it is also a test. God no longer imposes a formal materialized order in the form of instinct as He did for the animals; He leaves man free to choose between obedience and disobedience and this, for the first time, introduces conscience and will as the means by which man will progress. Man thus becomes master of his own fate. Because of this independence, from now on the individual alone is responsible for his actions. Even with respect to God man is independent, and this independence is therefore very real, for God Himself does not want to interfere with it. Spiritual progress no longer depends solely on God, Who gave up a part of His omnipotence for a created being in His creation, who can only advance by striving to do so, that is by an act of free will.

As creation begins, then, God begins His relationship with the universe with two successive acts of infinite loving-kindness. First He withdraws into Himself, making a gift of His Being to mankind — from this act of unselfishness comes the space for the universe. Then He once again renounces a part of His omnipotence to give mankind free will so that, by choosing good, man can be deserving of joy.

God's withdrawal into Himself accounts for His gift to man of freedom to choose. In no way does it contradict the fact that God knows in advance what man's choice will be and what will take place. To know in advance and to impose one's will are two different things; not only are they not equivalent but, from a logical point of view, they are not even related. Divine prescience is an inevitable logical consequence of the fact that for God neither time nor space exists. Hence the future is no less known to Him than the past or the present. Seen in this light, the question of the contradiction between free will and God's omniscience becomes meaningless (*Rambam*, *Hilchos Teshuvah*, 5:5).

However, examples from everyday life show even more strikingly than philosophical arguments that the question itself is not valid. A father who takes care to bring up his children lets them choose their future, their studies, and their livelihood once the children have reached a certain age. Very often the father knows in advance what this choice will be, despite each child's ongoing struggle to find out and discuss. Does the father's foreknowledge destroy the child's free will? When a teacher tells his pupils that they have the choice of continuing in the classroom for another hour or of being let out immediately, doesn't he know how each will decide? But does this prevent him from giving his pupils the possibility of making a free choice? (*Saadyah Gaon*, *Emunos VeDeos*, Chapter 4).

the man, saying, "Of every tree of the garden you may
freely eat; ¹⁷ *but of the Tree of Knowledge of Good and Bad,*
you must not eat thereof; for on the day you eat of it,

מִכֹּל עֵץ־הַגָּן אָכֹל תֹּאכֵל — *Of every tree of the garden you may freely eat*. The
Sages teach that the universal code of ethics is based on Divine revelation. Rabbi
Yochanan sees a suggestion of this here in the first precept addressed to man. He
teaches that seven commandments were imposed on the children of Noah —
that is, on the whole human race. They involve justice between man and man,
and prohibitions on idolatry, blasphemy, forbidden sexual relations, bloodshed,
theft, and eating the flesh of living animals (*Sanhedrin* 56b). *Rambam* describes
these laws in detail in his code, the *Mishneh Torah*. He considers that the seven
Noahide laws constitute as it were a common denominator of the ethical code
which the Divine lawgiver supplemented at the time of the patriarchs and
brought to completion at the time of Moses, with the giving of the Torah
(*Hilchos Melachim* 9:1).

These Noahide laws for the human race are considered to be the basis for
"natural law." No other single force has contributed as much to the makeup of
modern western law as the idea that there exists a discoverable natural law in
the universe. It represents a law which God placed at the very heart of human
nature at the moment of its creation. No matter how obscured it may be by sin,
this law subsists. It may be violated but it cannot be erased. Men can and must
encounter each other as men on this plane of natural law whose consequences
they have to face. From the beginning of modern history to the mid-eighteenth
century, every great jurist held this idea, which reached its zenith when Grotius
made it the basis of international law. The belief that a natural law does indeed
exist is so strongly rooted in men's hearts that, not surprisingly, the beginning
of this century witnessed the rebirth of these ancient theories.

The relationship between natural law and the seven Noahide laws was first
elucidated by John Selden, the greatest English scholar of the seventeenth
century, in his work *De Jure Naturali et Gentium juxta Disciplinam Ebraerum*
(1640) — (Natural Law and Civil Law According to the Hebrews). He speaks of
the "laws of Noah" of universal obligation and application, and of the laws
which are binding only on the Jews.

"Whoever among the gentiles fulfills the seven commandments to serve God
belongs to the righteous among the nations, and has his share in the World to
Come" (*Rambam*, ibid. 8:11).

17. וּמֵעֵץ. . .לֹא תֹאכַל מִמֶּנּוּ — *But of the Tree . . . you must not eat thereof*. The
first moral precept addressed to man is a prohibition, and not a rational one, not
a מִצְוָה שִׂכְלִית. All our perceptual faculties — taste, appeal to imagination, and
reason — rebel at this prohibition, which man would never have imagined on
his own. And what is more, even after man has been told of it, he is incapable
of finding any other reason for it than the absolute Divine will. It is a classic

יח מוֹת תָּמוּת: וַיֹּאמֶר יהוה אֱלֹהִים לֹא־טוֹב הֱיוֹת הָאָדָם לְבַדּוֹ

example of a חוק, a law without rational basis. Moreover it is a dietary law, and a law transmitted orally to man. It was to obeyed by Adam, Eve and their descendants. Hence this law included all the aspects of the future Law of Judaism which, in the words of our Sages, "the evil inclination and the non-Jewish world (יֵצֶר הָרָע וְאוּמוֹת הָעוֹלָם) have since earliest times resented and recoiled from" — specifically מִצְוַת לֹא תַעֲשֶׂה, חוק, תּוֹרָה שֶׁבְּעַל פֶּה, מַאֲכָלוֹת אֲסוּרוֹת. All of these were united in the prohibition which God set at the beginning of the history of the universe, לָדַעַת טוֹב וָרָע, so that one could know what man must consider as good and what must be rejected as evil. Hence, the condition for all moral life is the subordination of our physical nature to follow the will of God, and this condition is bound to the noble calling and the dignity of the human being. Man becomes worthy of the name by mastering the temptations of the senses. The exercise of self-discipline is always the first step in moral training. Still today, at every demand of the Law of God, each of us stands before the tree of knowledge and has to decide whether to follow the dictates of our senses, of our impure whims, of our animal instincts, or whether to obey the voice of God in the realization of our higher calling (R' S. R. Hirsch).

מוֹת תָּמוּת — *You shall surely die.* This means "you will become subject to death, you will become mortal." This interpretation resolves the problem that Adam and Eve did not die on the day of the sin but lived long afterward. It also assumes that man was originally destined for eternal life. In point of fact, the exact nature of death still remains an enigma in physiology. According to Isaiah (25:8), death is destined to disappear once mankind reunites with God, an era which would have already begun for Jewry with the giving of the Torah had the Divine Law been faithfully obeyed (*Avodah Zarah* 5a). *Ramban* observes: "Scientists claim that man was a mortal being right from the beginning since his body is composed of different elements and is therefore destined to disintegrate and die. But our Sages do not accept this. They teach that man would have been immortal if only he had not sinned. For the soul which emanates from the higher spheres confers eternal life and the Divine will in man since his creation constantly maintains him as a living being. Know that only skeptical materialists hold that man, being a compound, cannot escape destruction. But those who believe that the world is a product of the Divine free will profess that life endures as long as the Divine free will endures, and this is the simple truth."

Nevertheless, the *Zohar* and some teachers of the Midrash hold that both ideas are valid, that man was originally destined for eternal life and that death was built into man's creation. The latter view explains our verse as follows: "You will be liable to death, condemned to death." Why did Adam not die on the day of his sin? God granted him a reprieve as he repented in sincerity (*Zohar Chadash* 1:19). Or, as the Midrash answers, God in His mercy commuted the

you shall surely die."

    [18] *HASHEM God said, "It is not good that man be alone;*

death penalty to banishment from paradise and a life in exile (*Bamidbar Rabbah*, 23). This merciful act gave mankind the example of clemency to be followed for all time. Cf. *Tanchuma (Shemos* 13): Death was foreseen in the initial plan.

18. לֹא־טוֹב הֱיוֹת הָאָדָם לְבַדּוֹ — *It is not good that man be alone.* Do not think, says *R' Bachya,* that the Creator had been induced to change His plan after it had been carried out. This verse really applies to the beginning of creation. God had first created man to be both male and female, man and woman being bound back to back (this explains why man also has breasts). For absolute unity can exist only in God alone, never on earth (cf. *Rashi*). Accordingly, the unity of the Divine model was reflected on earth in the form of the union of the double principle, male and female. But "only when heaven and earth united for the first time to produce rain (verse 6) did the union of man and woman, patterned on nature, take place face to face. The desire of the female for the male resembles the mists which first rise from the earth heavenward; after having formed the clouds, the heavens water the earth. Man and wife are only truly united when they are face to face, and in this perfect union is born the reconciling principle, love" (*Zohar* 1:35a).

Of course man was able to reproduce in his androgynous form just as unicellular creatures can. He received the Divine blessing "Reproduce and multiply" when in this primitive form. But the reproductive act was then merely an instinctive reaction as it is for animals. What man lacked for his perfection was that this act should be the result of his free will, coming from a feeling of love. To give birth to this mediatory principle of love, God made a helper for him at his side, עֵזֶר כְּנֶגְדּוֹ, and thus created Eve (cf. *Ramban* and *Akeidas Yitzchak,* ch. 8).

God's boundless love was a factor at the origin of the world (*Psalms* 89:3). Likewise, it is love which must cause the seed of human life to develop and love must inspire the act of procreation. The deeper the love of the couple for each other, the more harmonious is their union. And it is in the intimate harmony forged by their love that the embrace of man and woman reaches its most perfect fruition.

אֶעֱשֶׂה־לוֹ עֵזֶר כְּנֶגְדּוֹ — *I will make him a helper corresponding to him.* This expression clearly indicates that woman is created to give man the physical, moral, and spiritual completion which he requires. Man's task on earth is too great for one to bear alone. He needs a helpmate at his side. Owing to woman, man's second self — through the close companionship of marriage — a man becomes truly a man. Without a wife, a man is more like half a man. And nothing in this definition refers to any sexual relationship. Consequently the role reserved for woman appears here as being invested with the highest

יט אֶעֱשֶׂה־לּוֹ עֵזֶר כְּנֶגְדּוֹ: וַיִּצֶר יהוֹה אֱלֹהִים מִן־הָאֲדָמָה
כָּל־חַיַּת הַשָּׂדֶה וְאֵת כָּל־עוֹף הַשָּׁמַיִם וַיָּבֵא אֶל־הָאָדָם
לִרְאוֹת מַה־יִּקְרָא־לּוֹ וְכֹל אֲשֶׁר יִקְרָא־לוֹ הָאָדָם נֶפֶשׁ חַיָּה
שלישי   כ הוּא שְׁמוֹ: וַיִּקְרָא הָאָדָם שֵׁמוֹת לְכָל־הַבְּהֵמָה וּלְעוֹף הַשָּׁמַיִם
כא וּלְכֹל חַיַּת הַשָּׂדֶה וּלְאָדָם לֹא־מָצָא עֵזֶר כְּנֶגְדּוֹ: וַיַּפֵּל יהוֹה
אֱלֹהִים | תַּרְדֵּמָה עַל־הָאָדָם וַיִּישָׁן וַיִּקַּח אַחַת מִצַּלְעֹתָיו
כב וַיִּסְגֹּר בָּשָׂר תַּחְתֶּנָּה: וַיִּבֶן יהוֹה אֱלֹהִים | אֶת־הַצֵּלָע

nobility. A helpmate means moreover that the wife is not the shadow or the slave of her husband, she is not the scorned object of a tyrannical husband as was witnessed in pagan antiquity. She is her husband's cherished and indispensable partner, a partner which no other creature in the world could have replaced.

From this verse our Rabbis concluded that marriage is a Divine institution and that only a married man is truly and fully alive. By proclaiming "It is not good that man be alone" the Torah condemns celibacy and implicitly declares it contrary to nature. Even when a man has fulfilled his obligation to procreate, he is forbidden to live without a wife. According to religious law, the wife has the right to fulfillment of conjugal duties by her husband, a right which is distinct from the duty of procreation (*Yevamos* 61b and *Even Ha'Ezer* 76).

19. וַיָּבֵא אֶל־הָאָדָם — *And brought them to the man.* God did not wish to "remove one of his sides" before Adam realized that no worthy companion was to be found among any of the other creatures; also Adam had to first feel the desire to have a companion suited to him (*Ramban*). God therefore brought all the animals and birds before Adam, male and female. Adam said, "Each one has his mate but I have no one" (*Rashi*). No species of the animal world can suit man for he seeks a deeper, fuller union with his partner than do the animals, who are destined merely to perpetuate their breed and who neither choose nor keep to just one mate (*Akeidas Yitzchak*, ch. 8).

לִרְאוֹת מַה־יִּקְרָא־לּוֹ — *To see what he would call each one. Recanati* explains מַה יִּקְרָא לוֹ as "what he would designate for himself." Adam characterized and classified the animals when he gave them their names. Thus he designated them according to their nature and in so doing he realized that none was like him, none resembled a human being. "For man" (verse 20 does not have "the man, הָאָדָם" with the definite article, as stated everywhere else), for God's vice-regent on earth, fashioned in God's image, there was no companion to share with him his noble calling. God had wanted Adam to designate his mate in order to endear her to him.

This name-giving required profound wisdom on Adam's part, for the name had to correspond to the nature, species, and sex of each creature. "Man's wisdom is superior to your wisdom," God replied to the angels, who were astonished at the privilege granted man. For man possesses the faculty of recognizing the nature of things and of giving them names. This is not possible for angels, who

*I will make him a helper corresponding to him." * [19] *Now,*
HASHEM *God had formed out of the ground every beast of*
the field and every bird of the sky, and brought them to the
man to see what he would call each one; and whatever the
man called each living creature, that remained its name.
[20] *And the man assigned names to all the cattle and to the*
birds of the sky and to every beast of the field; but as for
man, he did not find a helper corresponding to him.

[21] *So* HASHEM *God cast a deep sleep upon the man*
and he slept; and He took one of his sides and He filled
in flesh in its place. [22] *Then* HASHEM *God fashioned the side*

remain ignorant of the nature of things terrestrial. Consequently, the Torah
stresses that the name given to each animal by man — הוּא שְׁמוֹ — is a valid,
definitive name. This proves that the Hebrew language spoken by Adam
corresponds to the essential nature of things (*Ramban*; R' Judah Halevi, *Kuzari*
4:25; *et al.*). It is inspired by God or sanctioned by Him. On the other hand, with
respect to "and the man gave names ..." *Rambam* stresses the purely
conventional character of language (*Guide* 2:30) and R' S.R. Hirsch also
considers that language merely expresses the impression which man's mind
forms of things (cf. our commentary on verse 7; תורת העולה לרמ״א ג׳ ד׳).

21. וַיַּפֵּל ה׳ אֱלֹהִים תַּרְדֵּמָה עַל־הָאָדָם — *So* HASHEM *God cast a deep sleep upon the*
man. "For indeed He gives His beloved ones restful sleep"כֵּן יִתֵּן לִידִידוֹ שֵׁנָא
(*Psalms* 127:2). When man has tried his utmost to find what he desires, and all
in vain, Hashem still has unsuspected means of granting it to him. The Talmud
tells us that the greatest events happen בְּהֶסָּח הַדַּעַת (unexpectedly) when one
thinks of it the least — for example, the advent of the Messiah (who will come
unexpectedly). So too for important finds and discoveries. This also holds true
for great calamities and unhappy events such as the bite of a scorpion (*Sanhedrin*
97a). Now the Talmud states also that a wife is a man's greatest and most
marvelous find (*Berachos* 8a) and she was given to him just when he was
thinking of her least, during his sleep.

וַיִּקַּח אַחַת מִצַּלְעֹתָיו — *And He took one of his sides.* Because woman was originally
a part of man before she was separated, both man and woman instinctively have
the tendency to meet and to unite in order to "become one flesh." And when two
souls have found each other, they merge like two drops of quicksilver, proving
that originally they were one entity which appeared on earth in the form of two
different beings.

Rambam also emphasizes the general idea of this passage, namely that man
is made up of two factors, matter and form, which appear on earth as a duality
(masculine and feminine factors) but which in actual fact constitute one and the
same creation (*Guide* 2:30).

וַיִּסְגֹּר בָּשָׂר תַּחְתֶּנָּה — *And He filled in flesh in its place.* The difference in character

כג אֲשֶׁר־לָקַח מִן־הָאָדָם לְאִשָּׁה וַיְבִאֶהָ אֶל־הָאָדָם: וַיֹּאמֶר
הָאָדָם זֹאת הַפַּעַם עֶצֶם מֵעֲצָמַי וּבָשָׂר מִבְּשָׂרִי לְזֹאת
כד יִקָּרֵא אִשָּׁה כִּי מֵאִישׁ לֻקֳחָה־זֹּאת: עַל־כֵּן יַעֲזָב־
אִישׁ אֶת־אָבִיו וְאֶת־אִמּוֹ וְדָבַק בְּאִשְׁתּוֹ וְהָיוּ לְבָשָׂר אֶחָד:

and sound of voice between man and woman is related, our Sages tell us, to
their different origins, man coming from the soil of the earth (hence a deeper
"heavier" voice), and woman from the side of a human being already endowed
with all the attributes of existence. They also link the word וַיִּבֶן, which means
literally "He built" (v. 22), and which seems quite unusual here, with בִּינָה
meaning common sense, understanding, intuition. And our Sages conclude:
"This teaches us that God endowed woman with greater intuition than man."
Because she reaches maturity earlier, certain legal acts for a woman are
consequently valid from the twelfth year whereas those for a man are binding
only from his thirteenth year (Niddah 45b).

22. וַיִּבֶן ה' אֱלֹהִים אֶת־הַצֵּלָע ... לְאִשָּׁה וַיְבִאֶהָ אֶל־הָאָדָם — Then HASHEM God
fashioned the side ... into a woman, and He brought her to the man. He
entrusted woman to the angels who adorned her in finery and brought
her to the man, just as the bride's attendants lead the bride to the marriage
canopy to be united with her husband (Pesikta Zutrasa). The first wedding is recalled at every marriage ceremony, when God is thanked. We
bless Him "Who created man in His image, in the image of His likeness, and
formed for him (from his own body) a perpetual structure וְהִתְקִין לוֹ מִמֶּנּוּ בִּנְיַן
עֲדֵי עַד." This בִּנְיָן, this structure, recalls the term וַיִּבֶן in our verse; it means
that women builds for man the structure of generations which extends to
eternity.

23. זֹאת הַפַּעַם — This time. The word זֹאת, the feminine demonstrative
pronoun, occurs three times in this verse. It is considered as an "indicator"
of blessing, as Ramban notes in his commentary on the phrase וְזֹאת הַבְּרָכָה
(Deuteronomy 33:1). Designating the feminine gender, זֹאת indicates woman,
the source of the fertility and prosperity of the human race.

לְזֹאת יִקָּרֵא אִשָּׁה כִּי מֵאִישׁ לֻקֳחָה־זֹּאת — This shall be called Woman, for from
man was she taken. The Midrash Rabbah takes this as proof that Hebrew
was the original language. The form of almost all the proper nouns in Genesis
constitutes further proof. Rabbi Judah Halevi adds as examples the noun
אָדָם derived from the אֲדָמָה (Adam universally designating from the first
man); אִשָּׁה from אִישׁ; חַיָּה from חַי; קָנִיתִי from קַיִן; שֵׁת from שָׁת; נֹחַ from
(יְנַחֲמֵנּוּ). This fact is in no way contradicted by the statement in the
Talmud (Sanhedrin 38b) that Adam spoke Aramaic since, says Halevi,
Aramaic, Arabic, and Hebrew are interrelated and have analogous words,
expressions, and grammatical constructions, as encountered in all Semitic
languages. From a rational as much as a traditional viewpoint, Hebrew is the

that He had taken from the man into a woman, and He brought her to the man. [23] *And the man said, "This time it is bone of my bones and flesh of my flesh. This shall be called Woman, for from man was she taken."* [24] *Therefore a man shall leave his father and his mother and cling to his wife and they shall become one flesh.*

oldest of all languages. Its name comea from Ever (cf. *Ibn Ezra* on *Exodus* 1:16), the one who retained it after the confusion of tongues (*Kuzari* 2:68). In his work שָׂפָה בְּרוּרָה, *Ibn Ezra* demonstrates the correctness of these assertions.

For as long as he was alone, man was called אָדָם. But once he had a mate, he was called אִישׁ. This was because God wants to have His name associated with the marriage union. The letter י of אִישׁ and the letter ה of אִשָּׁה together form the divine Name (*Pirkei D'Rabbi Eliezer* 12). But this union becomes a "consuming fire" it if excludes the Divine presence — when these two letters are taken away only אֵשׁ (fire) remains (*Sotah* 17a).

The feminine form of אִישׁ is not really אִשָּׁה but אִישָׁה and *Ibn Ezra* points out that the strong *daggesh* in the letter *shin* of the word אִשָּׁה is to replace the consonantal *yud* which has disappeared. However, *Rabbi Yitzhak Arama* explains that the Torah wanted to avoid the true feminine form such as is used with animals: לָבִיא – לְבִיאָה; כֶּשֶׂב – כִּשְׂבָּה; פַּר – פָּרָה. In the animal kingdom, the difference between male and female is strictly sexual, whereas the role of a wife is to be a helpmate for her husband in all aspects of life. Consequently, the name of woman is not אִישָׁה (which would mean "she-man") but אִשָּׁה derived from the root אשש (to strengthen) as in *Isaiah* 46:8. Moreover it is to clearly bring out woman's very special role that she was made the object of a special creation, following that of man, in marked contrast to the animals where male and female were created simultaneously.

24. וְדָבַק בְּאִשְׁתּוֹ — *And cling to his wife.* This verse, spoken "by the Holy Spirit" (*Rashi*), contains the first commandment of the Torah and proclaims the law of marriage. This law is formulated in precise, definite terms and is irrespective of time, place, or race. It is of universal application and implicitly covers the sexual prohibitions binding on every human being, on every descendant of Adam and Noah (*Sanhedrin* 56b).

Marriage is a Divine institution. Its sacred character dates back to the beginnings of human society. It is part of the plan of creation. Monogamy is the prototype of marriage instituted by God — it is written "he shall cling to his wife" and not "to his wives." The word וְדָבַק, *to cling*, implies a permanent union permeated with fidelity. Although physically the stronger, it is man who must "cling" to his wife, whom he will respect as the greatest treasure he possesses on earth. In this way the bonds of love which unite the couple will remain indestructible.

ג   כה-א וַיִּהְיוּ שְׁנֵיהֶם עֲרוּמִּים הָאָדָם וְאִשְׁתּוֹ וְלֹא יִתְבֹּשָׁשׁוּ: וְהַנָּחָשׁ
הָיָה עָרוּם מִכֹּל חַיַּת הַשָּׂדֶה אֲשֶׁר עָשָׂה יהוה אֱלֹהִים
וַיֹּאמֶר אֶל־הָאִשָּׁה אַף כִּי־אָמַר אֱלֹהִים לֹא תֹאכְלוּ מִכֹּל

25. וְלֹא יִתְבֹּשָׁשׁוּ — *And they were not ashamed.* As long as they were in a state of complete purity, neither man nor his wife needed to be ashamed of their nakedness. The effect of sin created within them a sense of guilt and at the same time a sense of shame. Just like the human spirit, the human body is a Divine creation. It is not impure *per se*. All its functions, those which are called animal or sexual functions included, are made to serve God. The body is sanctified in its entirety inasmuch as God's service is faithfully carried out by it. But when man lets himself be conquered by sexual passions and lowers himself morally, he is filled with shame. Then he loses his stamp of the "Divine likeness" and, at the same time, his earthy paradise.

Hence of all creatures only man needs to cover his nakedness. He needs the "sign" of circumcision on his body to remind him of the duty to sanctify his sexual life. And he needs the other "sign" of *tzitzis*, fringes on his clothes, to remind him of the original reason for wearing them and to keep before him the warning following from this: not to be tempted by the desires "of the heart and of the eyes" which, as we will see, made man succumb to the temptation of the forbidden fruit.

3.

1. וְהַנָּחָשׁ הָיָה עָרוּם — *Now the serpent was cunning.* Today, no less than in the past, sin begins with a dialogue between animal instinct and human conscience. Which will win out? This is the crucial question. How one answers it decides not only his personal destiny but also the fate of future generations. In the final analysis, the history of mankind is nothing other than the history of man's attitude toward ethics and morality. At the beginning of this chapter interest is focused on this question; this is the question with which Adam is immediately confronted.

The story of the first sin is the story of all moral failings. In contradistinction to the animals, whose only law is obedience to their natural instincts, man has to willingly choose to do good. Yet he does not have within him the criteria for good and evil. Despite the collective efforts of the best minds over the centuries, man has not been able to discover the general rule for individual or group morality. Personal conscience, a celestial voice within us, only *encourages* us to be good and flee from evil. But what is good? What is evil? This, man can only learn from God. Now, since man lives only לְעָבְדָהּ וּלְשָׁמְרָהּ, *to work it and to guard it* (2:15), to serve God and the world, his own individual nature cannot constitute the ultimate criterion for his acts. This criterion must correspond to his higher calling; it is not to be identified merely with his sensual pleasures. Consider the paradisical tree, embellished with everything that can delight the senses; one's instincts would surely say

²⁵ *They were both naked, the man and his wife, and they were not ashamed.*

3   ¹**N**ow *the serpent was cunning beyond any beast of the field that* HASHEM *God had made. He said to the woman, "Did, perhaps, God say: 'You shall not eat of any*

"this tree is good," but the Divine word condemns it as evil. Hence the tree serves as the model and regulator of "the knowledge of good and bad" for man. The touchstone of human morality is the contrast between man and animal.

עָרוּם מִכֹּל חַיַּת הַשָּׂדֶה — *Cunning beyond any beast of the field.* The serpent represents, within creation, the incarnation of the principle of evil, whose presence has been explained in our commentary on 1:31. Our Sages tell us that the serpent, Satan, and the evil inclination all merge into one and the same force of evil (*Bava Basra* 16a).

Alas, there is no terrestrial paradise without its serpent. Temptation lies in wait for us within the delights of nature. The seductive voice of the serpent whispers in our ear. With his mortal venom he strives to poison man, and thenceforth the wonderful earthly paradise becomes a battleground. In the war between good and evil man finds the possibility of winning his greatest moral victories and thus comes to merit eternal happiness. The *Zohar* expresses it as follows: A king forbade his son to visit a harlot, but allowed her to come and rouse the passion of his son, for the purpose of increasing his son's merit. So it was with the serpent in Paradise (*Ohr HaChaim*, v.4).

The word עָרוּם appears in two successive verses, the first time meaning "naked" and the second "cunning," "crafty." *Rashi* explains the connection in his comments on verse 7: "naked" means "stripped of all morality, bereft of any Divine commandment." One who is naked in this sense becomes crafty and wicked. The serpent's nature as described here is reflected in his tortuous appearance and in his furtive, sinuous movements.

וַיֹּאמֶר אֶל־הָאִשָּׁה — *He said to the woman.* Several theories have been advanced to explain the fact that the serpent could talk. *Ibn Ezra* cites various opinions. In תּוֹרָה שְׁלֵמָה R' M. Kasher groups the different hypotheses including, among others, those which emphasize that the level of both mankind and animals before the first sin far surpassed our own. Moreover, all the creatures in Paradise lived in harmony and they were able to understand each other perfectly. It matters little, then by what means of communication this understanding was achieved (cf. also *Ramban* to *Leviticus* 26:6).

אַף כִּי־אָמַר אֱלֹהִים — *Did, perhaps, God say.* אַף means "although," "even if" and expresses revolt and opposition. The first words spoken by the eternal tempter express skepticism about God, and then a defiant challenge. Three other Biblical characters began their protestation or their call for rebellion by the word אַף: the chief baker (*Genesis* 40:16); Korah and his followers

ב עֵץ הַגָּן: וַתֹּאמֶר הָאִשָּׁה אֶל־הַנָּחָשׁ מִפְּרִי עֵץ־הַגָּן נֹאכֵל:
ג וּמִפְּרִי הָעֵץ אֲשֶׁר בְּתוֹךְ־הַגָּן אָמַר אֱלֹהִים לֹא תֹאכְלוּ
ד מִמֶּנּוּ וְלֹא תִגְּעוּ בּוֹ פֶּן תְּמֻתוּן: וַיֹּאמֶר הַנָּחָשׁ אֶל־הָאִשָּׁה
ה לֹא־מוֹת תְּמֻתוּן: כִּי יֹדֵעַ אֱלֹהִים כִּי בְּיוֹם אֲכָלְכֶם
מִמֶּנּוּ וְנִפְקְחוּ עֵינֵיכֶם וִהְיִיתֶם כֵּאלֹהִים יֹדְעֵי טוֹב וָרָע:

(*Numbers* 16:14) and Haman (*Esther* 5:12). And each was struck with אַף, which expresses Divine anger חֲרוֹן אַף (*Bereishis Rabbah* 19).

"And even if God said so." The dialogue between man and beast is here depicted. And even if God said so, do you have to obey? Isn't the inclination within you also a Divine voice? If it is wrong to enjoy these delights, why did God make then so attractive and why did He have you desire them? Hasn't He thus shown that desire and pleasure are to go together? God began by creating both desire and pleasure. Would He forbid them immediately afterwards? So speaks the animal, the serpent in each of us, sometimes guilelessly, sometimes clothed in the garb of philosophy, trying to dissuade us from obeying the Divine command which forbids us a sensual pleasure. And as before, it exaggerates and, in the little that is prohibited, it overlooks all that is morally permitted, and presents God's law of morality as the enemy of all sensual enjoyment (*R' S. R. Hirsch*).

Note that the serpent avoids the Divine name הַוָיָ, which is constantly used from the second chapter even up to the first half of this verse. The serpent accepts God only as אֱלֹהִים, only as Creator and Master of nature, but rejects the concept of הַוָיָ, of God's mercy over all His creatures. The snake does not use this name (either here or in verse 5), and even succeeds in making Eve adopt this heresy (v.3). The snake's venom thus begins its penetration into man's heart (*Akeidas Yitzhak* 3).

This verse seems abrupt, fragmentary: "Did perhaps, God say: 'You shall not eat of any tree of the garden'?" For *Ibn Ezra* this verse is the last of a series of implied sentences, previously spoken. *Rav Yitzhak Arama* takes an opposing view, namely that, as is woman's wont, Eve interrupted the serpent as he began to speak.

3. לֹא תֹאכְלוּ מִמֶּנּוּ וְלֹא תִגְּעוּ בּוֹ — *You shall neither eat of it nor touch it.* "The woman added something to the command she received. This is why she will later come to diminish it (by her disobedience). Thus it is written (*Proverbs* 30:6): 'Do not add to His words' " (*Rashi*). God forbade only eating the fruit of the tree; the woman added the prohibition of touching it. *Rashi* is referring here to the tractate *Sanhedrin* (29a) in the Talmud. In chapter 1 of *Avos D'Rabbi Nassan*, however, it is written that Adam added this prohibition, being moved by his conscience to provide a safeguard against sinning. This is, then, a typical example of putting up a סְיָיג, a "protective fence" around a law, and it shows that this protection follows naturally from the human conscience's caring about the

tree of the garden'?"

² *The woman said to the serpent, "Of the fruit of any tree of the garden we may eat.* ³ *Of the fruit of the tree which is in the center of the garden God has said: 'You shall neither eat of it nor touch it, lest you die.' "*

⁴ *The serpent said to the woman, "You will not surely die;* ⁵ *for God knows that on the day you eat of it your eyes will be opened and you will be like God, knowing good and bad."*

faithful fulfillment of a Divine commandment. Nevertheless our Sages warn us "Do not place the fence above the essential" so that it does not fall and destroy what it should protect. God had said: "On the day you eat of it you shall surely die," but Eve falsely reported it as "Do not touch it lest you die" and the serpent seized upon this allegation to trap her: "You touched the tree and you did not die. You will also not die after eating its fruit." This warning about protective measures should make us aware of their origin and of their importance. They should never be confused with a God-given commandment. The risk that a transgression of a rabbinical order will lead to transgressing a Divine commandment is greater when one forgets to designate the fences (סְיָגִים) or rabbinical decrees (גְּזֵירוֹת) as being rabbinical, מִצְוַת דְּרַבָּנָן, thus failing to distinguish them from מִצְוַת דְּאוֹרַיְיתָא, commandments recorded in the Torah. *Rambam* states that "one who declares a rabbinical prohibition to be a Torah prohibition is guilty of transgressing בַּל תּוֹסִיף, *you shall add nothing thereto* (הלכ׳ ממרים, פ״ב ה״ט). Adam had sinned by telling Eve that the prohibition of touching the tree, like that of eating the fruit, was of Divine origin.

4. וַיֹּאמֶר הַנָּחָשׁ אֶל־הָאִשָּׁה — *The serpent said to the woman.* The diabolical tempter wastes no time in taking advantage of Eve's exaggeration and shows her that she will not die from touching the tree. He "plays all the angles." He no longer hesitates to question the seriousness of the Divine prohibition; he arouses Eve's suspicion of the disinterestedness of the prohibition and even hints at God's jealousy as the true motive (*Rashi*). He excites her curiosity ("your eyes will be opened") and plays on her vanity ("you will be like God").

5. יֹדְעֵי טוֹב וָרָע — *Knowing good and bad. Rambam* explains that the knowledge of good and bad which would be obtained from eating the forbidden fruit cannot mean that man thereby has access to a higher degree of perfection, but rather that he falls from his original status. Indeed, before the sin, Adam possessed knowledge of the Truth. He was above earthy passions; they were powerless to undermine the clarity of his mind. So perfect was the objectivity of his view of things that he was able to distinguish true from false. But the sensual appetite, aroused in him as soon as he tasted the forbidden fruit, disturbed the original purity of his thought. From then on he was able to know only a part of the Truth, not the Truth in its entirety. He had fallen to the level of a man torn by his passions, only knowing what is good or bad for his sensual pleasures.

וַתֵּרֶא הָאִשָּׁה כִּי טוֹב הָעֵץ לְמַאֲכָל וְכִי תַאֲוָה־הוּא
לָעֵינַיִם וְנֶחְמָד הָעֵץ לְהַשְׂכִּיל וַתִּקַּח מִפִּרְיוֹ וַתֹּאכַל וַתִּתֵּן
גַּם־לְאִישָׁהּ עִמָּהּ וַיֹּאכַל: וַתִּפָּקַחְנָה עֵינֵי שְׁנֵיהֶם וַיֵּדְעוּ
כִּי עֵירֻמִּם הֵם וַיִּתְפְּרוּ עֲלֵה תְאֵנָה וַיַּעֲשׂוּ לָהֶם חֲגֹרֹת:

From the ideal region where reigns the celestial light of the spirit, Adam fell to
the level of physical sensuality where the idea of Truth and the Absolute is lost
(*Guide* 1:2). Accordingly, the expression וִהְיִיתֶם כֵּאלֹהִים is to be understood as
hyperbole, as *Rashi* explains: able to create worlds. The serpent uses this term to
impress Eve and to alienate her from God.

The Sages of the *Kabbalah* explain this differently. They begin by stressing
that the previous harmony of the universe rested on a perfect equilibrium
wherein each element, including the forces of good and evil, played a definite
role. But man, who holds a key position, destroyed the equilibrium when he
aroused the forces of evil. Once unleashed, they upset the Divine order of
creation. Goodness, which had originally appeared in unblemished sublime
majesty, succumbed in the general disorder that followed, as did all the elements
of creation. Good and evil, sacred and profane, ideas of beauty and ugliness, of
cleanliness and uncleanliness, were all jumbled together, floundering in utter
confusion. From the time that the first couple forsook the tree that gave eternal
life for the one that mixed together good and evil, men have been unable to
discern between good and evil, between justice and iniquity (*Zohar* 1:221; 3:107).
Since that day, humanity has had no other mission than to seek out and recover
the "holy sparks" that fell from the luminous heights and which are still
smoldering under the ashes of evil, in order to reunite them and reconstitute the
glowing light of moral and spiritual perfection.

As for Satan, he is still in his perfidious way trying to convince men that "they
will be like superior beings (cf. *Onkelos*), all enjoying good and evil together."

6. וַתֵּרֶא הָאִשָּׁה — *And the woman perceived*. All the senses, save the sense of
smell, played a part in the first sin and were sullied by it: sight ("the woman
perceived"); touch ("she took of its fruit"); taste ("and ate"); hearing ("they
heard"). The sense of smell, then, remains the purest sense. This is why the sweet
smell rising from the sacrifices pleases God (cf. *Rashi* to *Leviticus* 1:9). Of all the
senses, the olfactory sense is the most non-material (*Berachos* 43b). To have
ourselves permeated with the holiness of Sabbath, to keep its "fragrance" during
the weekdays, we turn to the sense of smell at the departure of the Sabbath (בִּרְכַּת
בְּשָׂמִים) with the spices for *Havdalah*. The prophet Isaiah tells us that the
Messiah will be recognized by his very acute sense of smell (11:3) for, of all of
the senses, only this one was not affected by the first sin (בני יששכר, אדר, מאמר
א'). For the same reason, we are advised to smell pleasant fragrances on the Day
of Atonement (מג״א, ס״ תרי״ב).

וַיֹּאכַל — *And he ate*. How could Adam, created by God's own hand, endowed
with unlimited perception of the universe and of humanity, called "thoroughly

⁶ *And the woman perceived that the tree was good for eating and that it was a delight to the eyes, and that the tree was desirable as a means to wisdom, and she took of its fruit and ate; and she gave also to her husband with her and he ate.* ⁷ *Then the eyes of both of them were opened and they realized that they were naked; and they sewed together a fig leaf and made themselves aprons.*

pious" by Rabbi Meir (*Eruvin* 18b) — how could he fall into sin? The answer is that "no one commits a transgression unless a spirit of folly has entered into him" (*Sotah* 3a). The father of humanity created in the image of God, also knew a moment of folly, and when the tempter came to seduce him Adam suddenly became a heretic and an apostate, or attempted to hide that he was circumcised (*Sanhedrin* 38b; cf. עֵין יעקב). Our Sages tell us, "the greater the person, the stronger his evil inclination" (*Sukkah* 52a). And later, his remorse and his repentance were immense (*Eruvin* ibid.).

7. וַתִּפָּקַחְנָה עֵינֵי שְׁנֵיהֶם — *Then the eyes of both of them were opened.* Rashi comments, "i.e., with wisdom. These words are not to be taken literally, as the end of the verse proves." Man was tempted with the promise of the knowledge of good and bad, but when he thought he had gained it, his eyes were opened. He perceived then that "he was naked" and that he knew nothing. Such was the conclusion that followed man's first acquired knowledge.

This, the beginning of knowledge, brought in its wake trials and tribulations, as King Solomon declared, "He who increases his knowledge, increases his pain" (*Ecclesiastes* 1:18).

When man's eyes are closed, as they are during much of his life, his insight and his mind are clear and penetrating. But once he opens his eyes, his visual horizon recedes and he sees no more than outward appearances. Thus, Adam, who had had within him the inner light of the prophets, lost this light once he tasted the forbidden fruit.

וַיֵּדְעוּ כִּי עֵירֻמִּם הֵם — *And they realized that they were naked.* Their sensual appetites and carnal desires were aroused once they had eaten of the forbidden fruit. The first couple felt shame in their nakedness for they realized that when the senses are allowed to dominate the spirit, human dignity is forfeited. They felt that this sin degraded them to the level of the animals and that they no longer represented the image of God on earth.

וַיִּתְפְּרוּ עֲלֵה תְאֵנָה — *And they sewed together a fig leaf.* This may be compared to a prince who sinned with a slave girl. The king, finding this out, expelled him from the palace. The prince went from door to door but no one would let him enter except for the slave girl who had sinned with him. So too with Adam. He was expelled from Paradise when he ate the forbidden fruit. He appealed to all the trees but none would receive him. They said to him: "Thief, you have deceived your Creator; do not touch me nor cut off my leaves." Only the fig tree whose fruit he had eaten (cf. *Rashi*) opened its branches to Adam and welcomed

ח וַיִּשְׁמְע֞וּ אֶת־ק֨וֹל יְהוָ֧ה אֱלֹהִ֛ים מִתְהַלֵּ֥ךְ בַּגָּ֖ן לְר֣וּחַ הַיּ֑וֹם
וַיִּתְחַבֵּ֨א הָֽאָדָ֜ם וְאִשְׁתּ֗וֹ מִפְּנֵי֙ יְהוָ֣ה אֱלֹהִ֔ים בְּת֖וֹךְ עֵ֣ץ
ט הַגָּֽן: וַיִּקְרָ֛א יְהוָ֥ה אֱלֹהִ֖ים אֶל־הָֽאָדָ֑ם וַיֹּ֥אמֶר ל֖וֹ אַיֶּֽכָּה:

him. Rabbi Yehoshua ben Levi answered: "Heaven forbid. God did not and will not reveal to man what that tree was. For see what is written: 'If a woman commits bestiality, both she and the animal shall die' (Leviticus 20:16). Did the animal sin? Yet it is killed lest, when it passes by, people say, because of this animal that woman was stoned.' The nature of this tree is not mentioned in the Torah for the same reason" (Bereishis Rabbah 15).

The text itself makes no reference to the apple tree as being the tree whose fruit was forbidden to Adam. However, the Tosafists connect the fruit with the esrog, the citron, which the Torah (Leviticus 23:40) calls the fruit of goodly trees (Shabbos 88a). Now the Midrash also names the esrog as the forbidden fruit (Rabbah, ibid.) since it is the only fruit which fits the description of the tree and its fruit having the same taste. This latter property recalls that the citron tree was the only tree which did not disobey the Divine command during creation (cf. Rashi to 1:12). Thus, it remained the favorite fruit because of its resemblance to the tree which bears it (See Sfas Emes on Succah, 35). Now, this same quality explains the double character of tree and plant exceptionally given to the esrog (Bikkurim 2:6 and Vilna Gaon comm. there). Ramban however considers the citron in a different light, namely with respect to its part in the festival of Succos (Leviticus ibid.). Let is also be noted that some consider grapes to be the forbidden fruit, for are they not frequently a source of unhappiness to men? Wheat, which once grew in the form of a shrub, is also mentioned; man's intelligence and knowledge awaken in him once he begins to eat bread.

8. וַיִּשְׁמְעוּ אֶת־קוֹל ה' אֱלֹהִים מִתְהַלֵּךְ — They heard the sound of HASHEM God manifesting Itself "The Shechinah (Divine Majesty) originally wanted to dwell on earth: עִיקַּר שְׁכִינָה בְּתַחְתּוֹנִים but withdrew to the first of the seven heavens when Adam sinned. It separated from the earth still more with each sin of mankind until Moses brought It back and the Shechinah dwelt then in the Tabernacle" (Bereishis Rabbah 19). It is generally thought that God associates closely with man only in exceptional, extraordinary, cases. The Sages point out the falsity of this assumption: עִיקַּר שְׁכִינָה בְּתַחְתּוֹנִים: Neither the missions of the prophets, nor the Divine revelation to the patriarchs, to Moses, and to Jewry are exceptional cases. On the contrary, it is this millennia-long separation between man and God, which is abnormal. We learn from the story of Paradise that the earth holds out to man the possibility of perfect harmonious co-existence with the elements of nature and with the animals, of standing upright among the creatures of creation, of serving as God's vice-regent on earth. In this condition man is accompanied by God, Who speaks to him, teaches him, and guides him. "But as for man — in glory he shall not repose, he is likened to the silenced." (Psalms 49:13). The supreme aim of the Torah will henceforth be to have the

⁸ *They heard the sound of* HASHEM *God manifesting Itself in the garden toward evening; and the man and his wife hid from* HASHEM *God among the trees of the garden.* ⁹ HASHEM *God called out to the man and said to him, "Where are you?"*

gates of Paradise re-open and to restore the harmony which reigned on earth between the animal kingdom and mankind. The ultimate objective of Torah is to cause the return to earth of the Divine Majesty. The Torah refers to this when it mentions the blessings in the era to come: וְהִתְהַלַּכְתִּי בְּתוֹכְכֶם "I will return in your midst" and *Rashi* explains, "I will walk with you in the Garden of Eden like one of you; you will have no need to tremble before Me" (*Leviticus* 26:12). Note the use of the reflexive verb form מִתְהַלֵּךְ בַּגָּן (rather than וְהָלַכְתִּי) in our verse; it brings to mind the reflexive form וְהִתְהַלַּכְתִּי of the blessings.

בַּגָּן לְרוּחַ הַיּוֹם — *In the garden toward evening.* I.e. to where the sun sets, the west. The fact that the first סְלוּק שְׁכִינָה, the first *withdrawal of the Shechinah*, took place to the west brings out the significance of the following: The Holy of the Holies קֹדֶשׁ הַקֳּדָשִׁים in the Temple was located in the west; the eternal light of the Sanctuary was the one turned to the west נֵר מַעֲרָבִי; and the last wall of the Temple where the *Shechinah* took refuge, never to leave, is the Western Wall הַכּוֹתֶל הַמַּעֲרָבִי (*Shemos Rabbah*, 2). Since the *Shechinah* gave Its farewell in the west, it is westward we look expectantly and hopefully. At the first sunset, man witnessed the first setting of the Divine light which illuminates his spirit. The Temple service, whose entire thrust is westward, is the powerful means by which we prepare the way for the *Shechinah's* return (*R' S.R. Hirsch*).

The *Shechinah's* withdrawal westward is also an indication of the course of history. Indeed, the evolution of universal history follows the movement of nature. Just as the stars traverse their route in the heavens from east to west, the light of the spirit arose with the dawn of humanity in the east and gradually progressed westward, winning over mankind, until it reached places and peoples poles apart. And the *Shechinah* waits in the west שְׁכִינָה לְעוֹלָם בְּמַעֲרָב (*Bava Basra* 25a). There It is paid homage by the stars for "The heaven's legions (arising from the east) bow down before You" (*Nehemiah* 9:6). There It waits for the tribute of mankind.

9. אַיֶּכָּה — *Where are you?* The word אַיֶּכָּה has the same letters as the word for "alas" (אֵיכָה) which expresses a painful sigh and sadness. The fact that God had to ask man "Where are you?" — "Why are you hiding? What have you done?" — is itself a cause of deep affliction, "you are no longer as you were before."

Although God surely knew where Adam was, this question is not purely rhetorical. It is the eternal question which God asks of man: "At what stage are you in your life? Where are you?" God has granted man a certain number of days and years in order that he fill them with good deeds toward his Creator and his fellowman. Hence He inquires of man, "Where are you in your life? In your

י וַיֹּאמֶר אֶת־קֹלְךָ שָׁמַעְתִּי בַּגָּן וָאִירָא כִּי־עֵירֹם אָנֹכִי
יא וָאֵחָבֵא: וַיֹּאמֶר מִי הִגִּיד לְךָ כִּי עֵירֹם אָתָּה הֲמִן־הָעֵץ
יב אֲשֶׁר צִוִּיתִיךָ לְבִלְתִּי אֲכָל־מִמֶּנּוּ אָכָלְתָּ: וַיֹּאמֶר הָאָדָם
הָאִשָּׁה אֲשֶׁר נָתַתָּה עִמָּדִי הִוא נָתְנָה־לִּי מִן־הָעֵץ
יג וָאֹכֵל: וַיֹּאמֶר יהוה אֱלֹהִים לָאִשָּׁה מַה־זֹּאת עָשִׂית
יד וַתֹּאמֶר הָאִשָּׁה הַנָּחָשׁ הִשִּׁיאַנִי וָאֹכֵל: וַיֹּאמֶר יהוה אֱלֹהִים
אֶל־הַנָּחָשׁ כִּי עָשִׂיתָ זֹּאת אָרוּר אַתָּה מִכָּל־הַבְּהֵמָה וּמִכֹּל

universe? How long have you lived and what have you done with your life during those years?" (אבני אזל).

10. וָאִירָא — *And I was afraid.* "Before man sins, his fellows treat him with deference and the animals respect him. But once he sins, fear grips him and makes him tremble before others. Prior to sinning, Adam heard the Divine voice while standing erect. Now, after the sin, he hides behind the trees, trembling with fright. Recall King Solomon the richest, wisest, most powerful of kings: after a moment of moral weakness and error, sixty armed warriors had to surround his bed with swords drawn, to protect him from his fear of the night" (*Midrash Rabbah* on *Song of Songs*, 3).

כִּי־עֵירֹם אָנֹכִי — *Because I am naked.* "A sin leads to another sin" say our Sages. Adam sins again by trying to use this excuse to cover up the truth. The personal pronoun אָנֹכִי stresses the personality and its characteristics more than does אֲנִי, the word commonly used for "I." "I am naked" thus means "stripped of my personality."

11. אָכָלְתָּ . . . הֲמִן־הָעֵץ — *Have you eaten of the tree?* Adam is offered the chance to confess and to repent — a sin unconfessed and not atoned for is a permanent sin. Right from the first of mankind's sins the doors of repentance are opened to him. It is God Himself who suggests to man that he can make amends and redeem himself from eternal damnation.

אֲשֶׁר צִוִּיתִיךָ לְבִלְתִּי אֲכָל־מִמֶּנּוּ — *From which I commanded you not to eat?* This phrase refers to what Rabbi Ya'akov the Maggid of Dubno explains by the following parable: A merchant who was spending the Sabbath at an inn kept his money in a small chest which he had brought with him. Not wanting to carry the key on the Sabbath, he decided to put it inside the chest, which locked automatically, and thought he would ask a locksmith to open it after the Sabbath. However, the dishonest innkeeper coveted his guest's money. He found a key of his own which opened the lock and he stole the contents of the chest in the merchant's absence. When the locksmith opened the chest after the Sabbath, the merchant was astonished to find it empty except for the key. Since the chest was locked, how could it have been opened?

God asked Adam: "I had created you such that you knew not passion. You were forbidden the fruit of that tree by My order. How then was your heart able

¹⁰ He said, "I heard the sound of You in the garden, and I was afraid because I am naked, so I hid."

¹¹ And He said, "Who told you that you are naked? Have you eaten of the tree from which I commanded you not to eat?"

¹² The man said, "The woman whom You gave to be with me — she gave me of the tree, and I ate."

¹³ And HASHEM God said to the woman, "What is this that you have done!"

The woman said, "The serpent deceived me, and I ate."

¹⁴ And HASHEM God said to the serpent, "Because you have done this, accursed are you beyond all the cattle and beyond all

to be opened to this desire?" Adam answered: "My heart was opened by another key ... the woman gave me the fruit of the tree and I ate."

12. הָאִשָּׁה — *The woman.* Adam now blames everyone except himself. First, "the woman." Next, with audacity and ungratefulness, he shifts part of the blame on God: "the woman whom You gave to be with me." The unusual form נָתַתָּה with the final ה (instead of נָתַתָּ) underscores this reproachful attitude towards God, as if to say: "It was Yourself Who gave her to me." The verbal form of another word also indicates Adam's defiant attitude. Instead of the usual form וְאָכַלְתִּי, our verse has וָאֹכֵל, a future tense with the conversive *vav*, which implies "I will eat," that is: "I will continue to eat."

14. אָרוּר אַתָּה — *Accursed are you.* Whoever sets his eyes on what is not his, is not granted what he seeks, and what he possesses is taken from him. So with the serpent. It coveted that which did not belong to him (Eve) and was deprived of what it had (the privilege of being a quadruped, and perhaps even a biped like man).

The Holy One, blessed is He, said: "I had destined the serpent to be king over every animal and beast. I had destined it to walk upright but now it will go upon its belly. I had declared: let its food be the same as man's; but now it will eat dust" (*Sotah* 9b).

If the desire to possess Eve was the serpent's motive for acting thus, as *Rashi* also points out at the beginning of this chapter, then its conduct constitutes persiflage toward God. The serpent slanders God by imputing motives of jealousy to Him (verse 5) — in this it hopes to alienate Eve from God, to have her more in its power. And so it was punished like the lepers who, because of their evil tongues, are banished from society and exiled outside of the three "camps" — the camp of the *Shechinah* within the holy enclosure, that of the Levites, and that of the Israelites (*Numbers* 5:1,2: cf. *Rashi*). In addition, the serpent had to undergo the threefold degradation just mentioned in the paragraph above, quoted from the Talmud. (The number of the punishments, with those mentioned in verse 15, totals six. The large letter *vav* in the word גָּחוֹן which refers to snakes הוֹלֵךְ עַל גָּחוֹן

חַיַּת הַשָּׂדֶה עַל־גְּחֹנְךָ תֵלֵךְ וְעָפָר תֹּאכַל כָּל־יְמֵי חַיֶּיךָ:
טו וְאֵיבָה I אָשִׁית בֵּינְךָ וּבֵין הָאִשָּׁה וּבֵין זַרְעֲךָ וּבֵין זַרְעָהּ
טז הוּא יְשׁוּפְךָ רֹאשׁ וְאַתָּה תְּשׁוּפֶנּוּ עָקֵב: אֶל־הָאִשָּׁה
אָמַר הַרְבָּה אַרְבֶּה עִצְּבוֹנֵךְ וְהֵרֹנֵךְ בְּעֶצֶב תֵּלְדִי בָנִים

(*Leviticus* 11:42) hints at these six punishments, the numerical value of *vav* being six.)

The serpent as a symbol still represents persiflage, scandalmongering, lying, envy and seduction. The serpent does evil solely out of spite, just like the slanderer. The animals one day will assemble near the serpent and say to him: "The lion attacks and devours his victim, the wolf tears and devours him, but as for you, what benefit do you derive?" The serpent will answer: "Go and ask the slanderer, for he too has no advantage, as it is said (*Ecclesiastes* 10:11) 'the charmer has no advantage' " (*Taanis* 8a).

Just as the serpent licks the dust of the earth, so the calumniator fills his mouth with dust and transforms his words into dirt (for example, עפרא בפומיה דאיוב, *Bava Basra* 15a). Both are unpardonable; their sin is forever irreparable כָּל יְמֵי חַיֶּיךָ, *all the days of your life.*

וּמִכֹּל חַיַּת הַשָּׂדֶה — *And beyond all beasts of the field.* "If it is cursed more than the domestic animals, is it not all the more so cursed above the wild animals? Hence our Sages learn (*Bechoros* 8b) that the serpent's gestation period lasts seven years." To this comment by *Rashi*, *Ramban* adds that this was confirmed as factual and that it is a typical example of the general truths which are contained in the words revealed in the Torah. J.L. Eilenburg in ס׳ מנחת יהודה comments: "If scientists nowadays observe a different gestation period for snakes, this is solely due to the fact that the natural conditions have changed over the centuries, as we observe in many fields נִשְׁתַּנָּה הַטֶּבַע."

וְעָפָר תֹּאכַל — *And dust shall you eat*, Conscious of the fact that the snake actually feeds on live animals, Rabbi Ami and Rabbi Assi interpret this verse as follows: Rabbi Ami teaches that to the serpent everything tastes like earth, even the tastiest food. According to Rabbi Assi, the serpent is sated only after having eaten earth (*Yoma* 75a).

Rabbi Yose said: See the difference between the Holy One, blessed is He, and man. When a man is very angry at his fellowman, he seeks to destroy him, whereas God cursed the snake but it still finds food everywhere. It climbs to rooftops and finds it. On the ground, it finds food. God cursed woman yet everyone runs after her; He cursed the earth, yet all get nourishment from it (ibid.).

However, our commentators ask: how was the snake really cursed, since it finds earth to eat everywhere? The author of ס׳ חפץ חיים answers that it is cursed because God said to it, as it were, "Find your food wherever you want, but have nothing more to do with Me." The snake is banished from the presence of God. It does not even have the consolation of being able to pray to God for its food.

*beasts of the field; upon your belly shall you go, and dust shall
you eat all the days of your life.* [15] *I will put enmity between
you and the woman, and between your offspring and her
offspring. He will pound your head, and you will bite his heel."*
[16] *To the woman He said, "I will greatly increase your suffering and your childbearing; in pain shall you bear children.*

כָּל־יְמֵי חַיֶּיךָ — *All the days of your life.* The principle of מִדָּה כְּנֶגֶד מִדָּה — the
nature of the punishment fits that of the crime — is applied right from the first
punishment. The sin concerns food, the penalty does likewise. The verdict "all
the days of your life" refers to this punishment, which will be everlasting, for
"although all ills will be cured in the World to Come, the snake will not be
healed; its suffering will last even in the Messianic Age כָּל יְמֵי חַיֶּיךָ" (*Bereishis
Rabbah*, 20). (From this Midrash, some rabbis conclude that the Sages, rather
than Ben Zoma, hold the correct view of the meaning of כָּל יְמֵי חַיֶּיךָ (*Berachos*
12b; also recorded in the Passover Haggadah.)

On the other hand these words do not apply to the malediction in the next
verse: "I will put enmity between you and the woman." The implacable hatred
existing between the descendants of Adam and Eve and those of the snake will
give way in the messianic era to the universal peace which will reign over
mankind and the animal kingdom alike. This time of tranquility and harmony
is depicted by the prophet Isaiah: "And the suckling will play near the viper's
nest, and on the asp's den the newborn will stretch out his hand" (11:8). Is it to
highlight this complete changeover to the ideal of goodness that the snake that
archetype of evil who formerly was the incarnation of horror and abasement,
became sometimes the emblem of the Messiah? It appears as such on the tribe
of Dan's banner (*Bamidbar Rabbah*, 2) and from this tribe comes the maternal
side of the Messiah (*Yalkut Bereishis* 49:15). For Bar Kochba, the snake was a
messianic insignia. The word "snake" נָחָשׁ is numerically equal to מָשִׁיחַ, which
signifies that these two ideas are interrelated — in the messianic era evil will cease
to exist. Why is the snake not included among the eight reptiles whose corpses
defile on contact (*Leviticus* 11:30)? Some of our Sages explain that it is because
the snake is set aside for purity in messianic times. (Others offer the more rational
explanation that after having put enmity between them, the Divine Lawgiver
did not want to prevent mankind from killing snakes, by declaring anyone
touching a snake's cadaver to be unclean.) *Rabbi Chaim ben Attar* holds that the
snake's uncleanness lies in its soul, that is, in its moral perversity, rather than in
its body. The snake is not included among the unclean reptiles mentioned in
Leviticus since it is condemned to eat the soil of the earth, and is therefore itself
likened to the earth which, by definition, can never take on this impurity. Hence,
the cadaver of a snake is not unclean (*Ohr HaChaim*; ibid.).

15. הוּא יְשׁוּפְךָ רֹאשׁ וְאַתָּה תְּשׁוּפֶנּוּ עָקֵב — *He will pound your head, and you will
bite his heel.* If we take the snake (or as in iconology, the crocodile) as a symbol

יז וּלְאָדָם אָמַר　　כִּי־שָׁמַעְתָּ תְּשׁוּקָתֵךְ וְהוּא יִמְשָׁל־בָּךְ:
כִּי־שָׁמַעְתָּ לְקוֹל אִשְׁתֶּךָ וַתֹּאכַל מִן־הָעֵץ אֲשֶׁר צִוִּיתִיךָ
לֵאמֹר לֹא תֹאכַל מִמֶּנּוּ אֲרוּרָה הָאֲדָמָה בַּעֲבוּרֶךָ
יח בְּעִצָּבוֹן תֹּאכֲלֶנָּה כֹּל יְמֵי חַיֶּיךָ: וְקוֹץ וְדַרְדַּר תַּצְמִיחַ
יט לָךְ וְאָכַלְתָּ אֶת־עֵשֶׂב הַשָּׂדֶה: בְּזֵעַת אַפֶּיךָ תֹּאכַל לֶחֶם

of concupiscence, this verse points out that man has more power over it than it does over him. Mankind can strike at the head of lust, but lust can reach only his heel, and that only when he is not on his guard. He can avoid the snake's bite just as he can avoid the sting of immoderate desire if only he remains constantly vigilant, always on his guard. But man can strike at the head of these desires only if they are dormant. Once he arouses them, excites them, and permits them to turn into lust, it is too late (R' S.R. Hirsch).

16. הַרְבָּה אַרְבֶּה עִצְּבוֹנֵךְ וְהֵרֹנֵךְ — I will greatly increase your suffering and your childbearing. Rashi explain that this refers to the woes of raising children, to the suffering of pregnancy, and, finally, "You will give birth to children painfully." The pains of childbirth are thus the punishment deserved by woman for the first sin. However, the Sages of the Talmud tell us that "pious women are not included in the decree against Eve this was so for Yocheved, the mother of Moses (Sotah 12a). Their labor is not necessarily painful. Moreover, the fact that the pains of childbirth are admittedly a Divine punishment does not forbid man from attempting to lessen the pain. Similarly, mankind has never considered it forbidden to soften the blow of the verdict "You will eat bread by the sweat of your brow" by technological or other means. It is reported by the Tosafists that in medieval times certain psychological means were in current use to alleviate labor pains, just as the midwives used them in Egypt (ibid. 11b).

17. כִּי־שָׁמַעְתָּ לְקוֹל אִשְׁתֶּךָ — Because you listened to the voice of your wife. Adam thought he could find an excuse for his sin by hiding behind the woman God had given him. Here he is being told that this argument is irrelevant. Man can never seek shelter behind another human being, even a prophet, if his purpose is to disobey the Divine commandments and to sin. This is evident, for when faced with דִּבְרֵי הָרַב וְדִבְרֵי הַתַּלְמִיד, דִּבְרֵי מִי שׁוֹמְעִין "words of the Master and words of the pupil, which does one obey?" Right from the beginning, the Torah stresses the idea of personal responsibility, an idea often scoffed at by mankind.

אֲרוּרָה הָאֲדָמָה בַּעֲבוּרֶךָ — Accursed is the ground because of you. The fall of Adam entails that of all of nature and that of all who come after him. This is the important lesson of the unity of creation which this verse teaches: everything is closely connected. Everything is interdependent. The bonds between generations and the interrelationships between the different domains of nature are so strong, absolutely rigorous, that man's responsibility for every one of his acts is as a consequence heightened immensely. For man is in the key position within creation. Each of his deeds, and often even his words, may have

Yet your craving shall be for your husband, and he shall rule over you."

[17] To Adam He said, "Because you listened to the voice of your wife and ate of the tree about which I commanded you saying, 'You shall not eat of it,' accursed is the ground because of you; through suffering shall you eat of it all the days of your life. [18] Thorns and thistles shall it sprout for you, and you shall eat the herb of the field. [19] By the sweat of your brow shall you eat bread

repercussions reaching to the most distant spheres. Because of natural heredity he can have a profound influence on his offspring, as much for good as for evil, and "traces" of his deeds continue to the heavenly spheres.

Thus his deeds have repercussions both in breadth and in depth, like the concentric circles formed by a stone dropped into a pool of water and carried far outward by the waves.

Man acts, as it were, as the conductor of the immense orchestra which is nature. All of nature forms a whole wherein each organism cooperates with and depends on every other, reacting to its slightest changes, just as within the microcosm of the human body. And so man, with nature's valuable assistance, is perfectly capable of establishing an era of peace and prosperity for all humanity just as well as he is able to upset and overthrow the natural order by unleashing harmful forces and having them shackle nature's resources and her richness. Is nature to become an earthly paradise or a hell of destruction? It all depends on man's will. When mankind respects the Divine plan of creation, nature lavishes all its benefits on him. But when he abuses his power and destroys the harmony of nature, it becomes his enemy.

This is what happened after the first sin, to which man succumbed by arousing the forces of evil. A sin is committed each time one disturbs the order of creation. The punishment that follows is not a simple repressive measure; it is rather the natural consequence of the disturbance which he caused to the pre-established order. (Cf. our commentary on *Leviticus* 26:11; *Ikkarim* 3:8 and של״ה, בית אחרון.) The first sin provoked man's fall and made him vulnerable to all base instincts, but this does not mean that he is in eternal disgrace. On the contrary, each individual fully possesses the ability to raise himself up by the effort of his will. He can thus reach the highest degree of purity. But the task has become more complex for it is much more difficult to restore an equilibrium that has been disturbed than to maintain one in its initial state. Henceforth, the whole problem of existence is to restore the harmony which originally existed.

19. בְּזֵעַת אַפֶּיךָ תֹּאכַל לֶחֶם — *By the sweat of your brow shall you eat bread*. Here, work, the ongoing condition of human existence, is represented as a curse with which God punishes man after the first sin. Were it not for his moral downfall, man would have enjoyed all of nature's pleasures freely and without any effort on his part. Nevertheless this early punishment designed as a torment to man has been considerably attenuated. God has turned it into a benefit, an asset. In

עַד שׁוּבְךָ אֶל־הָאֲדָמָה כִּי מִמֶּנָּה לֻקָּחְתָּ כִּי־עָפָר אַתָּה
כ וְאֶל־עָפָר תָּשׁוּב: וַיִּקְרָא הָאָדָם שֵׁם אִשְׁתּוֹ חַוָּה כִּי הִוא
כא הָיְתָה אֵם כָּל־חָי: וַיַּעַשׂ יהוה אֱלֹהִים לְאָדָם וּלְאִשְׁתּוֹ
כָּתְנוֹת עוֹר וַיַּלְבִּשֵׁם:

this regard the Sages of the Talmud bring out the contrast between the initial
verdict: "Thorns and thistles shall it sprout for you, and you shall eat the herb
of the field." and the final phrase: "By the sweat of your brow shall you eat
bread." They explain that tears fell from Adam when he heard that he would
have to eat thorns and thistles. "My donkey and I," he cried out, "will eat from
the same manger!" Then God answered: "By the sweat of your brow shall you
eat bread ." This sentence comforted and consoled Adam and he accepted the
work imposed on him cheerfully and with a sense of satisfaction. Jewish
teachings sums up his attitude thus: "Love work" (*Avos* 1). Far from considering
work as a necessary evil, the Psalmist exclaims: "When you eat of the labor of
your hands, happy will you be and it will be well with you" (127:2). The Sages
of the Talmud, echoing the Bible, praise the nobility and dignity of work in
many instances: through work human life acquires all its value. Thanks to it,
man's efforts acquire all their worth (*Avos D'Rabbi Nassan* 11). "A man who
lives from the labor of his hands is greater than the pious one who fears God"
(*Berachos* 8a).

20. כִּי הִוא הָיְתָה אֵם כָּל־חָי — *Because she had become the mother of all the living.*
Rashi comments that in this verse Adam resumes the interrupted naming of the
animals and living beings. Other Biblical commentators, however, hold that
Adam recognized that woman could no longer be the companion at his side who
would help him reach the ideal after the sin she had incited him to commit;
henceforth, her role would be limited to being "mother of all the living"
(*Malbim*). The Sages of the Midrash see Adam giving a hint of reproach towards
Eve in the assonance between the words חִוְיָא, *serpent* and the name חַוָּה, Eve.
It is as though Adam had said: "You who let yourself be seduced by the serpent,
for me you have become a serpent." R' Bachya associates the word חַוָּה with the
verb חַוָּה meaning to relate, to tell, to chatter (cf. *Job* 15:17); he notes that the name
of woman discreetly hides the vice by which she incites man to sin.

21. כָּתְנוֹת עוֹר — *Garments of skin.* Our Sages differ on what "garments of skin"
means. For some, they are garments made of the skin of animals. For others, they
are garments *for* the skin, covering the skin but not the soul of man. Rabbi
Yehudah teaches that before the sin, man was enveloped in a halo of light. He
appeared in a majestic splendor before all the creatures of heaven and earth. The
Psalmist is referring to this sublime appearance when he exclaims, "Yet You
have made him but slightly less than the angels, and crowned him with soul and
splendor" (8:6). But, after the sin, the halo of glory which illuminated man's spirit
disappeared; man was left only with "the garment which covers his skin." And

until you return to the ground, from which you were taken: For you are dust, and to dust shall you return.''

²⁰ *The man called his wife's name Eve, because she had become the mother of all the living.*

²¹ *And HASHEM God made for Adam and his wife garments of skin, and He clothed them.*

this is also how to understand the Midrash (*Bereishis Rabbah*, 20) which states: "The *sefer*-Torah of Rabbi Meir has כָּתְנוֹת אוֹר 'garments of light,' instead of כָּתְנוֹת עוֹר 'garments of skin,' " the two words אוֹר and עוֹר being homonyms. According to *Rambam* (quoted by מתנות כהונה ibid.) this version refers to the time before the sin, when man was bathed in light.

Rabbi Yitzchak adds that the covering of the human body before the sin was made of the matter which forms fingernails. Man's body then was radiant with the brilliant whiteness of the moon at the base of the nail; he was admired by all creatures. After the sin, he was deprived of this natural shield. Only a trace of its original brilliance remains at the moons of his nails (*Zohar* 2:208b). This trace of the enchanting ideal of a lost paradise is in our thoughts at the close of the Sabbath, as we say the *Havdalah* prayer. During this prayer, we gaze at the moons of our fingernails as though to express the longing to keep a trace of the radiant Sabbath during the week to come (ב״ח, או״ח, ס׳ רצ״ח).

The Midrash about Rabbi Meir's *sefer*-Torah contains an additional idea, according to Rav Yehudah Leib of Gora, Kalwaria, Poland, author of ס׳ שפת אמת. Not only the human body but, as it were, all of creation was clothed in "garments of skin" after the first sin. For man is just the reflection of the macrocosm. Before the sin, all of nature was inundated with the Divine light, which was of resplendent clarity to all creatures. But after the sin, God withdrew to higher spheres and nature became heavily veiled with "garments of skin." Man could only recognize God through this garment which hid God from his eyes. The word עוֹר "skin" has the same letters as the word עִוֵּר, *blind*. These "garments of skin" which envelop the whole universe make men blind. And yet they are also כָּתְנוֹת אוֹר, "garments of light," since, despite everything, they let the omnipotence of the Creator show through.

The human body, too, is not a hermetically sealed outer cover, for it allows the soul sheltered within to be glimpsed. But beware the one whose vices and moral degradation cause the skin of his body to be covered with "a tumor, a scab, or a bright spot" and thus obstruct the route leading to the soul. This man is declared unclean. אָדָם כִּי יִהְיֶה בְעוֹר בְּשָׂרוֹ שְׂאֵת אוֹ סַפַּחַת אוֹ בַהֶרֶת. . .וְטִמְּא אֹתוֹ, "If a person will have on the skin of his flesh, a *s'eis* or a *sapachas* or a *baheres*. . . and declare him contaminated" (*Leviticus* 13:2).

וַיַּלְבִּשֵׁם — *And He clothed them.* Their punishment is followed by Divine mercy. God Himself clothes the sinners despite their disobedient act and the Divine curse. From this example of goodness the Sages teach us that it is man's duty to

רביעי   כב וַיֹּאמֶר ו יהוה אֱלֹהִים הֵן הָאָדָם הָיָה כְּאַחַד מִמֶּנּוּ לָדַעַת טוֹב וָרָע וְעַתָּה ו פֶּן־יִשְׁלַח יָדוֹ וְלָקַח גַּם מֵעֵץ הַחַיִּים כג וְאָכַל וָחַי לְעֹלָם: וַיְשַׁלְּחֵהוּ יהוה אֱלֹהִים מִגַּן־עֵדֶן לַעֲבֹד כד אֶת־הָאֲדָמָה אֲשֶׁר לֻקַּח מִשָּׁם: וַיְגָרֶשׁ אֶת־הָאָדָם וַיַּשְׁכֵּן מִקֶּדֶם לְגַן־עֵדֶן אֶת־הַכְּרֻבִים וְאֵת לַהַט הַחֶרֶב הַמִּתְהַפֶּכֶת

imitate God by doing good deeds (*imitatio Dei*). It is highly characteristic that this manifestation of גְמִילוּת חֶסֶד, a charitable act, arises after the moral downfall of man. The downfall has indeed become the background against which man is best able to show this similarity to God. Every action which is selfish and degrading when done for ourselves becomes ennobled when dedicated to others. In the Jewish view, exerting oneself, בְּזֵעַת אַפּוֹ, to obtain bread and help for others is the way for man to truly resemble God. "Just as God clothed the naked, healed the sick, comforted the troubled, buried the dead, etc." is the basis of love for fellowman in Judaism, which has created the world's oldest humanitarian and benevolent society.

Thus, hardship and the need for assistance are the basis on which anyone who so wills can elevate himself to attain a likeness of God. Charity would have no basis were it not for the destitution which began here, at man's departure from Paradise. The fact that the practice of disinterested personal sacrifice for others has found so many souls willing and eager to give of themselves is the most powerful refutation of the lie which would have us believe that the first sin and the curse which it brought on man deprives him of the godliness of his being forevermore (R' S.R. Hirsch).

22. הָאָדָם הָיָה כְּאַחַד מִמֶּנּוּ — *Man has become like the Unique One among us.* Rabbi Wolf Heidenheim demonstrates that whenever the number אֶחָד is used in the construct state, as it appears here, it refers to a unit of inferior quality (עי' פ' קרח). The text would then mean: having tasted both good and evil, having participated in the original sin, man has become the last among the higher beings (cf. *Rashi*). Originally, he was intended to be the equal of the angels in moral and spiritual grandeur. But once he failed, tempted by evil, there was but one way left to make amends, that of death followed by a new existence made sublime by purity and holiness. It follows that man is not yet allowed to "reach out and take from the Tree of Life as well, and eat and live forever" (*Ohr HaChaim*). Considered in this way, death and resurrection appear as acts of Divine mercy. This is expressed in our prayers: מְחַיֶּה מֵתִים בְּרַחֲמִים רַבִּים, "He revives the dead with great mercy." The possibility of immortality is evident from this verse, independent of the meaning attached to "Tree of Life" which may be taken both literally and figuratively as *Ramban* implies (cf. *Recanati*, verse 24).

23. לַעֲבֹד אֶת־הָאֲדָמָה אֲשֶׁר לֻקַּח מִשָּׁם — *To work the soil from which he was taken.* If man can still be worthy of pity, only mother-earth from which he was taken

²² *And* HASHEM *God said, "Behold Man has become like the Unique One among us, knowing good and bad; and now, lest he put forth his hand and take also of the Tree of Life, and eat and live forever!"* ²³ *So* HASHEM *God banished him from the Garden of Eden, to work the soil from which he was taken.* ²⁴ *And having driven out the man, He stationed at the east of the Garden of Eden the Cherubim and the flame of the ever-turning sword,*

will provide consolation. He can no longer be the revered master of nature, but henceforth he will serve the earth, which will be his only comfort. The next verse contains a similar idea: man, expelled from Paradise, will settle in the east, outside of the garden. Rav teaches that it is always the east which receives criminals and offers them a place of refuge. So it was with Adam and Cain. Moses himself designated "three cities beyond the Jordan, to the east" for murderers (*Bereishis Rabbah*, 21). The east contains the cradle of civilization. It was "toward the east that man had been placed" originally (2:8, cf. *Tosafos* to *Bava Basra* 84a). It is thus eastward that the sinner seeks refuge and protection (cf. *Rashi* to 4:16).

24. וַיְגָרֶשׁ אֶת־הָאָדָם — *And having driven out the man.* Sin drives man away from the presence of God. If man banishes God from his universe he has to live in a wilderness instead of Eden. Humanity, once it has become impious, must henceforth recover its purity through ordeals of sorrow and death.

God has repudiated man. Although this act of repudiation is a punishment, at the same time it provides the way to salvation. For God has commuted the death penalty pronounced for the original sin to one of banishment. He has given man the chance to repent. "To guard the way to the Tree of Life" can indeed signify "to protect the tree so that man will not come back to it" but it can just as well mean "to protect and keep it so that man will not lose it and will one day be able to return to it." In fact, since that day when Paradise was lost to man, the whole story of humanity is nothing other than the search for the road back, the road leading to paradise on earth. Men have never given up this search; the millennia of history reflect the superhuman efforts and the tragic aberrations of mortals which are the stages to regaining this terrestrial paradise.

The Sages tell us that Adam and Eve discovered repentance immediately after banishment from Eden. They came closer to God outside Paradise than they had within. And so R' Nachman teaches that God has not repudiated man forever "like a כֹּהֵן, a priest, who is not permitted to take back the wife he repudiated." God has not banished man both from this world and from the World to Come, but He has repudiated man "like an Israelite, who can remarry the wife he has repudiated." He has banished him only from this world but not from the World to Come (*Bereishis Rabbah*, 21).

מִקֶּדֶם לְגַן־עֵדֶן — *At the east of the Garden of Eden.* In front of the garden. This is to be taken in a temporal rather than a spatial sense, following the *Midrash*

ד　א לִשְׁמֹר אֶת־דֶּרֶךְ עֵץ הַחַיִּים: וְהָאָדָם יָדַע אֶת־חַוָּה
אִשְׁתּוֹ וַתַּהַר וַתֵּלֶד אֶת־קַיִן וַתֹּאמֶר קָנִיתִי אִישׁ אֶת־

Rabbah, 21, and *Targum Yonasan*. "Before" (creation) the cherubim of Eden were already at their posts, that is, everything was in readiness before man's arrival into the world, to reward him if he deserved it. On the other hand, the punishment of Hell was also readied if man should fall. The cherubim, guardians of Paradise and upholders of the Divine glory (*Isaiah* 37:16), be it noted, carry "the flame of the ever-turning sword" and thus become "angels of destruction" (*Rashi*). Satan himself bears this "ever-turning sword." Depending on man's deeds, he too may become "an angel of mercy" as *Rashi* notes on *Numbers* 22:22).

The double-edged sword represents the insignia of the Garden of Eden since the fall of Adam, when good and evil began to merge. These forces no longer were rigorously separated as they had been at the beginning of creation. God had, right from the first day, separated light from darkness. But the fall of man brought confusion into moral ideas and man's earthly abode was placed under the sign of the angel who holds in store either the key to Paradise or the sword of Hell. It is written in the *Zohar*, "Man had become versatile. He assumed many guises, he turned sometimes to good, sometimes to evil; now toward prosecution and justice, now toward peace and love; now to life, now to death. He no longer remained constant. Hence, this place is named 'the blade of the revolving sword' which turns from one side to the other, from good to evil, from love to hate, from peace to war" (*Zohar* 3:107b).

Recanati adds that it is now clear why the terms of the Hebrew language are also often variable, and can be declined either in the masculine or in the feminine gender. God Himself can appear to man in the feminine gender, as is seen in *Leviticus* 9:4.

אֶת־דֶּרֶךְ עֵץ הַחַיִּים — *The way to the Tree of Life*. Rabbi Yishmael interprets this verse figuratively. The Tree of Life represents the Torah itself, in accordance with King Solomon's definition in *Proverbs* (3:18), and "way" symbolizes the way that leads to the Torah. This way is that of דֶּרֶךְ אֶרֶץ. R' Yishmael continues: There exists a set of general rules which are the "preliminaries" of the Torah and which serve as the introduction, so to speak, to it. These are a series of laws of moral conduct, gentility, common sense and propriety not recorded in the Torah though presupposed by it. The Sages have collected them in the Tractates דֶּרֶךְ אֶרֶץ רַבָּה וְזוּטָא. It is in this sense that these rules of דֶּרֶךְ אֶרֶץ antedate the Torah. "They precede it by twenty-six generations, as many generations as there were from creation to the birth of Moses" (*Vayikra Rabbah* 9; יומא, ישנים תוספ׳ ועי׳; פ״ה: ד״ה תשובה). In both the religious and the ethical domains the Torah makes the same assumption of a highly disciplined society at a very high level of morality. Hence the Torah has its prerequisites which man must satisfy before he has access to its riches.

to guard the way to the Tree of Life.

4   ¹*Now the man had known his wife Eve, and she conceived and bore Cain, saying, "I have acquired a man with*

4.

1. וְהָאָדָם יָדַע אֶת־חַנָּה אִשְׁתּוֹ — *Now the man had known his wife Eve.* This had taken place while they were still in Paradise, according to *Rashi's* explanation.

The expression יָדַע, *to know,* one's wife is a Biblical circumlocution for the conjugal act. Knowledge is the medium of love. The better a man knows his fellowman, his work, his studies, the better he loves him. Love deepens with knowledge, and this fact applies to love not only between husband and wife but also between man and God. As man increases his knowledge of the wonders of creation and of the revealed truths, love of God grows within him (*Rambam, Hilchos Yesodei HaTorah* 2:2 and *Rashi* to *Deuteronomy* 6:5). Since love is the fruit of knowledge, the word דַעַת may be used as a synonym for love. Hence love is based on a good measure of spirituality which endows it with more than a purely sensual character.

וַתַּהַר וַתֵּלֶד — *And she conceived and bore.* The Midrash and the *Zohar* give a more nuanced idea of the birth of Cain. They point out the fact (mentioned in 5:3) that "Adam had lived 130 years he begot in his likeness, and his image; and he named him Seth."

After their disobedience in Paradise, Adam and Eve practiced a long period of continence. The son Eve subsequently bore resembled them and was shaped as they were. However, the first two sons were conceived while the parents were morally corrupt and while the spirit of sin continued to be active. "Rabbi Abba said: When man seeks after the truth, when he assumes a spirit of holiness, and retains it, then the son he will have will also retain the spirit of holiness, as it is said (*Leviticus* 11:44; 20:7): *Sanctify yourselves and you shall become holy* (i.e. you will retain the holiness even through your children). But if man chooses evil, his spirit becomes defiled, his is the impure spirit which comes from evil, as it is written (*Leviticus* 11:43), *Do not make yourself impure lest you become impure.* Adam had become defiled, and Eve before him. Of this defilement she bore a son, a child of impurity. But the other son was fathered by Adam after he had repented. One came from the impure side, the other from the pure side. R' Eliezer taught: When the serpent sullied Eve with his defiling venom, she received this seed, and when Adam cohabited with her, she gave birth to two sons, one from the impure side, one from Adam. Thus Abel is of the likeness of the upper world and Cain of the lower, and hence they were later to go separate ways.

"Cain, the son of impure demons, of the evildoing and perverse serpent, became himself a murderer. He was the father of nests (קֵנִים) of impurity, of all evil spirits and demons" (*Zohar I:54a*).

קָנִיתִי אִישׁ — *I have acquired a man.* Eve's exclamation well describes the maternal feeling at the birth of her firstborn. The whole world was at her feet

ב יהוֹה: וַתֹּסֶף לָלֶדֶת אֶת־אָחִיו אֶת־הָבֶל וַיְהִי־הֶבֶל רֹעֵה
ג צֹאן וְקַיִן הָיָה עֹבֵד אֲדָמָה: וַיְהִי מִקֵּץ יָמִים וַיָּבֵא קַיִן
ד מִפְּרִי הָאֲדָמָה מִנְחָה לַיהוֹה: וְהֶבֶל הֵבִיא גַם־הוּא

but nothing was her own work until she gave birth. Then she experienced the feeling of having her very own treasure, the flesh of her flesh. While admiring this marvelous living being, while cognizant of the threefold miracle of conception, growth of the embryo, and birth, she was fully aware that this new life was not due solely to its parents — it was also due to the invisible assistance of God. Hence she exclaims, "I have produced a man with the help of God."

Right from this first birth of a human being, the Torah teaches us that the husband and wife cooperate closely with God when they unite to procreate. And those who want to see in procreation merely a purely natural phenomenon — can they explain the presence of a non-material soul in the being about to be born without referring to the intervention of the Divine Creator? His glory hovers invisibly above the union of husband and wife. He is ready to bless this union by giving to the body which will develop the breath of life emanating from the heavenly spheres (cf. *Rashi*).

אֶת־ה׳ — *With HASHEM.* Here, for the first time the Tetragrammaton (שֵׁם הֲוָיָ׳) stands alone, unaccompanied by the name אֱלֹהִים. This is because the Tetragrammaton signifies the מִדַּת הָרַחֲמִים, merciful God. Before this sin, man had considered God the God of justice, knowing only law and truth. Now, as man commences his life in exile, the Torah stresses the attribute of mercy (*Chizkuni*).

2. אֶת־אָחִיו אֶת־הָבֶל — *His brother Abel.* The author of *Sefer Chassidim* observes (§363) that הַשֵּׁם גּוֹרֵם, one's name may have a bearing on one's whole existence. The Torah shows this right from the birth of children to Adam and Eve. The children are characterized by their names.

Cain personifies possessiveness. His very name means "acquisition." As the firstborn, indeed he represents an acquisition for his parents. He is a farmer, attached to his land and highly interested in real estate. His son, a builder of cities, he will name Enoch, "foundation."

Abel appears as the complete antithesis of Cain. His name means "vanity." His fleeting existence without offspring justifies this name. According to *Ramban*, he was called הֶבֶל because his parents realized that הַכֹּל הֶבֶל, *all is vanity*, even the desire to possess as personified in Cain. This truth is expressed by the author of *Ecclesiastes* in the words: *But when I turned to all my works that my hands had wrought, and in the toil that I had toiled to accomplish: then, behold, all was vanity and a torture of the spirit, and there was no profit under the sun* (2:11).

וַיְהִי־הֶבֶל רֹעֵה צֹאן — *Abel became a shepherd.* The contrast in character between the two brothers is revealed in their choice of occupation. This contrast will reappear in the future development and interactions of agricultural and pastoral

*HASHEM." ² And additionally she bore his brother Abel. Abel
became a shepherd, and Cain became a tiller of the ground.
³ After a period of time, Cain brought an offering to HASHEM
of the fruit of the ground; ⁴ and as for Abel, he also brought*

peoples. Agriculture demands and absorbs all of man's physical strength. The
Divine words "by the sweat of your brow" are literally carried out in tilling the
earth. Agriculture gives rise to a pride in material possessions and in the value
they represent. On the one hand, agriculture is the basis of civilization; a great
part of the inventions and arts have been evoked by it. Cooperation, the very
cornerstone of life in society, in the state, is a basic demand of agriculture, which
thus sets the norms for social legislation. But, on the other hand, the agricultural
worker comes closer and closer to the level of the clod he serves. He begins
by bending his neck under the yoke of his desire for possessions; he ends by
bending his spirit. He gets caught by this effort. As a result, one man subjugates
and enslaves another. At the same time, the tiller of the soil comes to worship the forces of nature whose influence is seemingly critical for his
success. The agricultural peoples were the first to lose the pure consciousness of
God and humanity. They were the first to give themselves up to slavery and
polytheism.

In contrast, the pastoral life has many advantages. One is simply the fact that
shepherds are continually involved with living creatures; this demands humane
feelings and constant care from man. The instability of property in a shepherd's
life is a safeguard against placing too much value on both the property and its
owner. Less physical strength is called for than in agriculture; the mind is less
enslaved by the work and is freed for elevating thoughts of godliness and
goodness. Thus we find that our patriarchs were shepherds. Moses and David
tended their flocks. Note that the Egyptians hated shepherds and pastoral
people. Egyptian civilization was based on agricultural and it showed all the
symptoms described above, from slavery and polytheism to the total disregard
for human dignity. Only in that tribe of shepherds, our ancestors, were faith in
God, freedom, and man's likeness to his Creator to be found. The Egyptian
leaders knew very well why they were teaching their subjects to harbor an
overwhelming aversion to pastoral peoples. To be sure, man is, generally
speaking, destined more for an agricultural life than for a pastoral one. So is
Israel, as directed by the Torah itself. But by its commandments regarding the
Sabbath, the Sabbatical year, the laws of tithing, and similar laws, the Torah
protects Jewry against all excesses and anything leading to the worship of
property. As a consequence of these laws, the Torah resolves the problem of an
agricultural state which serves God, of a nation united in fraternity and freedom.
Without the Torah, the very existence of these ideals is threatened (*R' Hirsch;* cf.
our commentary to 46:32).

3. וַיָּבֵא קַיִן . . . מִנְחָה לַה' — *Cain brought an offering to HASHEM.* The word מִנְחָה
used here generally designates an offering of personal tribute to a superior.

מִבְּכֹרֹות צֹאנֹו וּמֵחֶלְבֵהֶן וַיִּשַׁע יהוֹה אֶל־הֶבֶל וְאֶל־
ה מִנְחָתֹו: וְאֶל־קַיִן וְאֶל־מִנְחָתֹו לֹא שָׁעָה וַיִּחַר לְקַיִן
ו מְאֹד וַיִּפְּלוּ פָּנָיו: וַיֹּאמֶר יהוֹה אֶל־קַיִן לָמָּה חָרָה לָךְ
ז וְלָמָּה נָפְלוּ פָנֶיךָ: הֲלֹוא אִם־תֵּיטִיב שְׂאֵת וְאִם לֹא תֵיטִיב

In this passage the idea of sacrifice appears for the first time. Note these two important points: First, idolatry had not yet come into existence, and so it is a mistake to believe that the sacrifices of *Leviticus* and *Numbers* are a concession to polytheism. The sacrifices came before polytheism; they are as old as humanity itself and hence can be nothing other than the expression of pure human thoughts and feelings. Second, there were already two kinds of offering in the very first sacrifice: one was rejected; the other accepted. It follows, then, that sacrifices never had an absolute value, and this contradicts the theory that only the prophets had the merit of proclaiming the doctrine of the wholly relative value of sacrifices. Of course idolaters offered sacrifices. But they offered prayers too, and one would have to abolish a lot if he wanted to avoid everything which degenerated in unworthy hands. It all depends on the meaning you attach to prayer and sacrifice. Two people can offer the same sacrifices or say the same prayers — and yet they can be quite different before God. This is the truth brought out by the first sacrifice (*R' Hirsch*).

מִפְּרִי הָאֲדָמָה — *Of the fruit of the ground.* In the sense of: some fruits or other. Hence, *Rashi* explains: poorer quality fruits. An *aggadah* states it was linseed. Why did Cain surprisingly take the initiative and offer the first sacrifice? And then, why did he make it of poor quality? This can only be explained as follows. We know of Cain's materialistic spirit from what was already said about his character and vocation. The Midrash reports that in discussion with his brother Abel, Cain affirmed: "There is no judge, no justice, no World to Come. There is neither reward for the righteous nor punishment for the wicked. And the world is not governed by love" (*Targum Yonasan*). The *Zohar* gives us further insight into Cain's inner thoughts by examining the first words of this verse: וַיְהִי מִקֵּץ יָמִים usually translated, *And it came to pass after a period of time.* Compare this expression which has the word יָמִים with that at the end of the book *Daniel:* לְקֵץ הַיָּמִין. The latter refers to the resurrection of the dead. It means, as *Rashi* explains, ". . . the end, when the right hand of God will triumph" (*Sanhedrin* 92a, ר״ה ואתה לך). But the expression מִקֵּץ יָמִים in our verse means literally "(starting from) the end of days." Cain is thinking of the end of days, of death, as he offers his sacrifice. Since he believes neither in life in the World to Come nor in the resurrection of the dead, he is terrified of the void which awaits him, terrified of the hidden forces which threaten his life and his belongings. He offers a sacrifice to gain favor from these; yet he feels no obligation to be generous in what is above all a "deal." Essentially, this is the kind of sacrifice offered by idolaters and it is because of this attitude that "He did not turn to Cain and to his offering." Here the Torah emphasizes that the

of the firstlings of his flock and from their choicest. HASHEM
turned to Abel and to his offering, [5] *but to Cain and to his offer-*
ing He did not turn. This annoyed Cain exceedingly, and
his countenance fell.

[6] *And HASHEM said to Cain, "Why are you annoyed, and*
why has your countenance fallen? [7] *Surely, if you improve*
yourself, you will be forgiven. But if you do not improve yourself,

offering was rejected much more because of Cain than because of the nature of
his sacrifice.

4. וְהֶבֶל הֵבִיא גַם־הוּא מִבְּכֹרוֹת צֹאנוֹ וּמֵחֶלְבֵהֶן — *And as for Abel, he also brought*
of the firstlings of his flock and from their choicest. Although Abel made
his offering "too," that is, only after his older brother did, it had a completely different meaning and was based on the purest and most humanly natural
motive for any sacrifice: thankfulness. It was to thank God for His infinite goodness and kindness that Abel chose the firstlings of his flock and
the choicest parts thereof. He put his heart into giving the offering. He
desired to make it of exceptional quality. *Rambam* points out that this
example should serve as a model for all who wish to offer a sacrifice to God
(הלכ' איסורי מזבח פ"ג י"א). Accordingly, God shows Himself favorable to Abel
and his sacrifice: a fire descends from Heaven and consumes his offering
(*Rashi*).

גַם־הוּא — *He also.* This expression implies that Abel shared some of his brother's
attitudes while disapproving of others. Both agreed to deny man's right over the
animals, but Abel allowed one exception: the sacrifice of an animal to honor
God, the absolute Ruler over all creatures. *R' Yosef Albo* presents the opinions
of the early Sages on this question in his *Sefer Halkkarim* (3:15).

5. וְאֶל־קַיִן וְאֶל־מִנְחָתוֹ לֹא שָׁעָה — *But to Cain and to his offering He did not turn.*
Cain did not find favor with Him. Here the younger is favored over the
firstborn, as if often the case in Biblical history. In fact, at the beginning of
human history no privilege of birth was envisioned. The firstborn son became
the trustee of the Divine message only in Abraham's time, and the Torah
confirms that the firstborn's privilege lasted only for a short time in Jewry. *R'*
Yitzchak Arama treats this question thoroughly in his book *Akeidas Yitzchak*
(cf. our commentary on 48:20).

6. לָמָּה חָרָה לָךְ וְלָמָּה נָפְלוּ פָנֶיךָ — *Why are you annoyed, and why has your*
countenance fallen? Man cannot raise himself up morally by anger or by
discouragement. Do not yield to anger, which deprives you of your lucidity
(*Pesachim* 66b) and your human dignity (נָפְלוּ פָנִים indicates that the face lost
the Divine radiance which illuminated it). Direct your thoughts exclusively to
accomplishing your one duty: to return to the right path. From history's
beginning the Torah shows us different cases of men confronted with this same

לַפֶּתַח חַטָּאת רֹבֵץ וְאֵלֶיךָ תְּשׁוּקָתוֹ וְאַתָּה תִּמְשָׁל־בּוֹ:
ח וַיֹּאמֶר קַיִן אֶל־הֶבֶל אָחִיו וַיְהִי בִּהְיוֹתָם בַּשָּׂדֶה וַיָּקָם קַיִן
ט אֶל־הֶבֶל אָחִיו וַיַּהַרְגֵהוּ: וַיֹּאמֶר יהוה אֶל־קַיִן אֵי הֶבֶל אָחִיךָ

quest. In so doing, the Torah points out that mankind's greatest problem is not economic, social, or political — it is essentially moral.

7. אִם־תֵּיטִיב — *If you improve yourself.* Then your sins will be remitted (*Onkelos* and *Rashi*); or, you will be able to lift it up, referring to Cain's fallen countenance (*Ibn Ezra*). This verse expresses the idea of moral regeneration consequent on improvement. This idea appears in the nine different interpretations, summarized in M.M. Kasher's *Encyclopedia of Biblical Interpretation.* Although God puts Cain in disgrace, He immediately gives him a chance for the moral rehabilitation which leads to forgiveness. In very few words our text formulates the prime, eternal, and universal ethical lesson: the salvation of man depends only on himself. If he does good, he will raise himself up; if he does evil, the temptation of sin will lie in wait for him but it will always remain within his power to triumph over it. This doctrine, so naturally humane, is in opposition not only to the idea of original sin but also to any theories of materialistic determinism and nihilistic fatalism. Here, no allusion to reward in a future life or to a punishment in Hell disturbs the purity of this moral imperative; no theological doctrine comes to restrict the universality of the ethical ideal.

לַפֶּתַח — *At the door. Rashi* renders: Your sin awaits you at the entrance of your grave, at the day of your death, at your day of judgment. Cain had experienced the sense of dependence which every human being feels — this had induced him to offer his sacrifice.

But he was unaware that reward awaits the righteous and punishment the wicked. Now God teaches this to him by revealing that the last judgment takes place "at the entrance of the grave." At that time, the slightest sin (חַטָּאת refers to involuntary sinning) comes forward to claim its atonement just as a creditor awaits the day of settlement to claim his due. All is paid back, either on earth or after death.

R' Yehudah HaNasi gives another meaning to this sentence in his answer to the Emperor Antoninus. The latter had asked: Does the evil inclination hold sway over man from conception or from birth? Rabbi answered: From conception. Antoninus objected that if this were so, the embryo, stirred by the evil inclination, would try to leave the mother's womb. Rabbi agreed and cited this verse as evidence, explaining that "at the entrance" refers to where the newborn emerges. In the same vein, R' Simlai taught that before birth the child is imbued with Divine knowledge; at his birth, "an angel strikes him on his mouth and causes him to forget the whole Torah" (*Niddah* 30b). This is why one sometimes has the vague feeling of having already known a fact one is just learning. To return to R' Yehudah, from interpretation of this text he concludes that the evil inclination attacks man from his birth whereas the good inclination

sin rests at the door. Its desire is toward you, yet you can conquer it."

⁸ *Cain spoke with his brother Abel. And it happened when they were in the field, that Cain rose up against his brother Abel and killed him.*

⁹ *HASHEM said to Cain, "Where is Abel your brother?"*

develops in him only when he becomes thirteen years of age (*Sanhedrin* 91b). And so, to protect the child from the evil inclination which assails him from birth, God sends His angels "to protect you in all your ways" (*Psalms* 91:11; cf. *Zohar* I:165b).

The Talmud teaches: R' Yehudah once asked Elijah the prophet why the Messiah was so long in coming. Elijah answered: "because sin crouches at the entrance." Sin intrudes at the last moment, just as the door of redemption is about to be opened (*Yoma* 19b).

חַטָּאת רֹבֵץ — *Sin rests.* The word חַטָּאת is feminine whereas the participle רֹבֵץ is in the masculine gender. The Sages of the Midrash explain: this is so because the word חַטָּאת (as distinct from חֵטְא) — derived from the *pi'el* conjugation — signifies that which causes one to sin, that is to say passion. Passion initially appears weak (like the feminine element), but if left by man to develop it finally becomes as powerful as the masculine element. The Talmud amplified this in the tractate *Sukkah* (52a).

8. וַיֹּאמֶר קַיִן אֶל־הֶבֶל אָחִיו — *Cain spoke with his brother Abel.* Cain scorns the hand generously offered to him and rushes headlong toward sin. Obstinately, he commits himself more and more to evil until he comes to murder.

Tradition teaches us that Cain, who was crazed with jealousy, began to argue with Abel concerning their respective rights and privileges or, in another version, their different points of view on the existence of God and on immortality. According to *Pirkei d'Rabbi Eliezer* (21), Cain desired Abel's twin-sister and wife, due to her exceptional beauty, and provoked him on this account. A violent dispute erupted. Cain struck Abel and, after vainly trying to find where he was vulnerable, stabbed him.

And so, the world's first brothers were implacable enemies. The older brother committed fratricide. The Torah shows us many examples of brothers, rivals, who fight and clash even to death. They bring about indescribable disasters with dire consequences felt for generations after. But the Torah also shows us brothers who cherish and respect each other and whose fraternal love is of such intensity that it brings out immortal values and inexhaustible sources of blessing for all generations. Such were the brothers Moses and Aaron. *How good and how pleasant it is for brothers to dwell together in unity!* (*Psalms* 133:1).

וַיַּהַרְגֵהוּ — *And killed him.* Just after God had shown favor to him, Abel suddenly dies a violent death. This proves to you that the soul is immortal and that its reward is reserved for it in the World to Come (*Baalei HaTosafos*).

י וַיֹּאמֶר לֹא יָדַ֒עְתִּי הֲשֹׁמֵר אָחִי אָנֹכִי: וַיֹּאמֶר מֶה עָשִׂיתָ קוֹל
יא דְּמֵי אָחִיךָ צֹעֲקִים אֵלַי מִן־הָאֲדָמָה: וְעַתָּה אָרוּר אָתָּה
מִן־הָאֲדָמָה אֲשֶׁר פָּצְתָה אֶת־פִּיהָ לָקַחַת אֶת־דְּמֵי אָחִיךָ
יב מִיָּדֶךָ: כִּי תַעֲבֹד אֶת־הָאֲדָמָה לֹא־תֹסֵף תֵּת־כֹּחָהּ לָךְ

But how can one explain this death from the viewpoint of Divine justice? Has it not been stated that no one dies unless he has sinned (except the four Biblical personages named in the Talmud, *Shabbos* 55b). The answer is that Abel sinned by growing arrogant once God had shown preference to him after his sacrifice. He desired then to fathom the mystery of God; he boldly sought to contemplate God in the majesty of His omnipotence. And so Abel deserved to die (cf. *Rashi* to *Exodus* 24:10). But his soul was to be reincarnated in Moses, a shepherd too, and then it was able to right this error, as it is said during the revelation at the burning bush (*Exodus* 3:6): *Moses hid his face for he was afraid to look upon God* (cf. *Ohr HaChaim*, verse 1). And this intellectual modesty was ultimately rewarded, for God later affirmed that "at the image of God does he (Moses) gaze" (*Numbers* 12:8) (תיקוני זוהר, מ״ב).

9. הֲשֹׁמֵר אָחִי אָנֹכִי — *Am I my brother's keeper?* Cain replied, "You, God, watch over all creatures and You ask me? This is like a thief who stole in the night and was not caught. The next morning a watchman catches him and asks accusingly, "Why have you stolen?" he replies, "I am a thief and I haven't given up my profession. But you, your duty was to guard the house. Why didn't you?" So Cain reasoned: "I killed him because You put an instinct for evil in me. It was You who killed him, had You not accepted his offering, I would never have been jealous of him." Then God answered Cain:

10. מֶה עָשִׂיתָ קוֹל דְּמֵי אָחִיךָ צֹעֲקִים אֵלַי — *What have you done? The blood of your brother cries out to Me.* But Cain replies: Master of the Universe! I never saw a death. How could I have known that he would die from my blows? And have You informants who come and tell You what men do? My parents are far away and do not know that I killed him. And You are in the heavens. How did You find out?

The Eternal then answers: Fool, the entire world is borne by Me! Cain exclaims: You bear the whole world and You cannot bear my sin?! (*Rabbah* 22 and *Tanchuma*). Sinners are never at a loss for excuses and pretexts. They are always ready to blame others for their faults.

קוֹל דְּמֵי אָחִיךָ — *The blood of your brother.* דְּמֵי, plural form, means: his blood and his descendants' blood (*Rashi*). Herein lies the basic difference between civil law and criminal law as the *Mishnah* (*Sanhedrin* 4:5) points out: "In civil suits man makes restitution for a wrong he did and is pardoned; in criminal cases, however, the culprit is held responsible not just for the blood of the victim but also of his descendants ever after."

And he said, "I do not know. Am I my brother's keeper?"
¹⁰ *Then He said, "What have you done? The voice of your brother's blood cries out to Me from the ground!* ¹¹ *Therefore, you are cursed more than the ground, which opened wide its mouth to receive your brother's blood from your hand.* ¹² *When you work the ground, it shall no longer yield its strength to you.*

מִן־הָאֲדָמָה — *From the ground.* The corpse of Abel lay on the ground and his blood flowed to the nearby trees and stones. The dog guarding Abel's flock now protected his body from the birds and animals. Cain (or, in another version, Adam and Eve) cried and did not know what to do with the corpse. He caught sight of a bird whose mate had died. Before them, it dug the earth and buried its mate. Cain said, "Let us do the same and bury Abel" (*Rabbah*, 22). This was how man learned that the dead are to be interred in the earth.

11. וְעַתָּה אָרוּר אָתָּה מִן־הָאֲדָמָה — *Therefore, you are cursed more than the ground.* Rashi explains: more than the ground, which had been cursed for its earlier sin (*Genesis* 1:11). But *Ibn Ezra* and *Ramban* translate: "By the earth which will no longer yield its richness as it did before. From now on you will have to work the earth harder and even then it will yield less than before."

אֲשֶׁר פָּצְתָה אֶת־פִּיהָ — *Which opened wide its mouth.* "The earth sinned once again when it opened its mouth to receive your brother's blood" (*Rashi*). The *Tosafists* explain that the earth somehow opened up and swallowed Abel's blood without leaving a trace. So, it became an accomplice to the murder (*Sanhedrin* 37b). Henceforth, the earth will no longer be able to protect murderers by concealing their innocent victims, "for the blood will bring guilt upon the Land; the Land will not have atonement for the blood that was spilled in it, except through the blood of the one who spilled it" (*Numbers* 35:33). Thus the earth, corrupted by blood, will yield only meager harvests as long as innocent blood is not atoned for (*Ramban*). This is why the earth, fearing further punishment, did not want to swallow up the Egyptians at the crossing of the Red Sea until God stretched out His right arm and swore to the earth that He would not condemn it (*Sifra Exodus* 15:12). Here again we see an example of the important principle of the unity of creation encompassing man together with nature.

12. נָע וָנָד תִּהְיֶה בָאָרֶץ — *You shall become a vagrant and a wanderer on earth.* נָע means roaming away from one's present home; נָד means shifting about constantly without finding peace. The Torah here foreshadows exile as the punishment for unintentional homicide (*Numbers* 35:11). Although this is a case of premeditated murder, Cain is shown clemency here either because his death would place the continuation of the human race in jeopardy (*Radak*); or because he knew neither the meaning of death nor the consequences of his blows (*Albo, Ikkarim* 3:15); or because he was not warned beforehand of the

יג נָ֥ע וָנָ֖ד תִּֽהְיֶ֣ה בָאָ֑רֶץ: וַיֹּ֥אמֶר קַ֖יִן אֶל־יהו֑ה גָּד֥וֹל עֲוֺנִ֖י מִנְּשֹֽׂא:
יד הֵן֩ גֵּרַ֨שְׁתָּ אֹתִ֜י הַיּ֗וֹם מֵעַל֙ פְּנֵ֣י הָֽאֲדָמָ֔ה וּמִפָּנֶ֖יךָ אֶסָּתֵ֑ר
טו וְהָיִ֜יתִי נָ֤ע וָנָד֙ בָּאָ֔רֶץ וְהָיָ֥ה כָל־מֹֽצְאִ֖י יַֽהַרְגֵ֑נִי: וַיֹּ֧אמֶר ל֣וֹ
יהו֗ה לָכֵן֙ כָּל־הֹרֵ֣ג קַ֔יִן שִׁבְעָתַ֖יִם יֻקָּ֑ם וַיָּ֨שֶׂם יהו֤ה לְקַ֨יִן֙ א֔וֹת
טז לְבִלְתִּ֥י הַכּוֹת־אֹת֖וֹ כָּל־מֹֽצְא֑וֹ: וַיֵּ֥צֵא קַ֖יִן מִלִּפְנֵ֣י יהו֑ה וַיֵּ֥שֶׁב
יז בְּאֶֽרֶץ־נ֖וֹד קִדְמַת־עֵֽדֶן: וַיֵּ֤דַע קַ֨יִן֙ אֶת־אִשְׁתּ֔וֹ וַתַּ֖הַר וַתֵּ֥לֶד

prohibition and penalty of murder (*Rabbah* 22). Nor could the death penalty be imposed for this crime without a court and witnesses (*R'Saadyah, Emun*os 3:9).

13. גָּדוֹל עֲוֺנִי מִנְּשֹׂא — *Is my iniquity too great to be borne?* In opposition to *Rashi,* most commentators hold that this verse is an expression of Cain's remorse after God had shown him the horror of his crime. In general, עָוֺן means sin, but it can also be used in the sense of punishment (*Radak*). Cain, then, is deploring the extreme harshness of his punishment and gives the reason for this in the next verse. But here again the character of the hardened sinner reappears. Here we have a קַיִן, conceived to be a possession (קָנִיתִי), himself obsessed with possessiveness (קִנְיָן), and incited to sin by jealousy (קִנְאָה). Thus קַיִן realizes he has lost everything, all because of his crime. Why is he sorry? It is not because he behaved improperly towards God and slew his brother. It is rather that he did irreparable harm to himself, as he himself admits in the next verse. Cain says: My sin is too great. Had I only killed my brother, I could bear it. But I didn't know that at the same time I condemned myself to death by this curse. The curse, the life of wandering, of fleeing, takes away my interest in life and in living.

14. וּמִפָּנֶיךָ אֶסָּתֵר — *Can I be hidden from Your presence?* When Cain was banished, the earth trembled under him wherever he went. The animals shuddered when he passed and exclaimed: "See the accursed murderer of his brother!" Cain broke into tears and cried out, "Where can I escape from Your Spirit? Where can I find refuge from Your presence? If I should ascend to heaven, You are there; and if I should make my bed in the nether world, You are there. If I should take the wings of the morning-dawn, if I should dwell in the uttermost parts of the sea, even there would Your hand lead me, and Your right hand would seize hold of me" (*Psalms* 139:7-12; *Rabbah* 22).

15. לָכֵן כָּל־הֹרֵג קַיִן — *Therefore, whoever slays Cain.* See *Rashi's* explanation of this incomplete sentence. But *Ramban* interprets it as follows: Whoever will dare to kill Cain will be avenged sevenfold, that is, to the limit.

וַיָּשֶׂם ה' לְקַיִן אוֹת — *And* HASHEM *placed a mark upon Cain.* On Cain's forehead He inscribed a letter of the Divine Name (*Rashi*). The Sages of the Midrash quote differing opinions on the nature of this sign, depending on whether they consider Cain to be a repentant sinner or not.

Some mention that God had Cain protected by a dog who guided him and fought off menacing beasts. Others explain that Cain himself became a warning

> *You shall become a vagrant and a wanderer on earth."*
>
> ¹³ *Cain said to HASHEM, "Is my iniquity too great to be borne?*
> ¹⁴ *Behold, You have banished me this day from the face of the earth*
> *— can I be hidden from Your presence? I must become a vagrant*
> *and a wanderer on earth; whoever meets me will kill me!"*
> ¹⁵ *HASHEM said to him, "Therefore, whoever slays Cain, before*
> *seven generations have passed he will be punished." And HASHEM*
> *placed a mark upon Cain, so that none that meet him might kill*
> *him.* ¹⁶ *Cain left the presence of HASHEM and settled in the land of*
> *Nod, east of Eden.*
>
> ¹⁷ *And Cain knew his wife, and she conceived and bore*

sign to murderers, or the herald of encouragement for the penitent (cf. next verse).

16. וַיֵּצֵא קַיִן מִלִּפְנֵי ה' — *Cain left the presence of HASHEM.* According to *Rashi* this means that he left with (a pretended) humility as if to (try to) fool God. Some of the Sages in the Midrash, however, explain that וַיֵּצֵא often implies "to leave, acquitted" as in *Exodus* 4:14. In fact, they add, Adam met Cain after the Divine sentence had been passed and asked him about it. He answered: "I repented and I admitted my wrongdoing." Thereupon Adam began beating his face and cried out: "The power of repentance is so great and I never realized it!" Then he began to sing: *A psalm, a song for the Sabbath day: it is a good thing to give thanks to God, and to sing praises to Your name, O Most High, tell in the morning of Your kindness, and of Your faithfulness in the nights . . . (Psalms 92:1-3).* Said R' Levi: This psalm was composed by Adam but later forgotten until Moses re-established it (cf. *Rashi, Psalms* 90:1). Adam, created (see *Pirkei D'Rabbi Eliezer*) and expelled from Paradise on the sixth day of creation, thought that the world would founder because of his sin when he witnessed the shadows of nightfall creep over the earth. The next morning, on the Sabbath day, he cried out in joy when the sun appeared on the horizon, *It is good to give thanks to God, to tell in the morning of Your kindness.* He welcomed the sunrise as a sign of grace from God and this encouraged him to confess his sin and repent. And for Adam the words טוֹב לְהֹדוֹת לַה', *it is good to give thanks to God,* mean: it is a good thing to confess to God (לְהֹדוֹת) relating to הִתְוַדָה; as in וְתֶן־לוֹ תוֹדָה — cf. *Joshua* 7:19). Thus the first Sabbath became the day of returning to God and so it remains to all eternity.

קַיִן . . . וַיֵּשֶׁב בְּאֶרֶץ־נוֹד — *Cain . . . and settled in the land of Nod.* That land to which all exiles flee (*Rashi*). (נָד means to be moving, to rove). Note that of the two words of punishment (נָע וְנָד ; a wanderer and an exile) applied to Cain, only the second appears here. Our Sages explain: this is because Cain repented after sentence was passed on him. And this teaches that repentance, like prayer, is able to halve the severity of punishment (*Rabbah* ibid.). The Talmud seems to suggest that Nod is a proper noun and interprets this verse as follows: Cain lived in (that

אֶת־חֲנֹוךְ וַיְהִי בֹּנֶה עִיר וַיִּקְרָא שֵׁם הָעִיר כְּשֵׁם בְּנֹו חֲנֹוךְ:
יח וַיִּוָּלֵד לַחֲנֹוךְ אֶת־עִירָד וְעִירָד יָלַד אֶת־מְחוּיָאֵל וּמְחִיָּיאֵל
יט יָלַד אֶת־מְתוּשָׁאֵל וּמְתוּשָׁאֵל יָלַד אֶת־לָמֶךְ: וַיִּקַּח־לֹו
כ לֶמֶךְ שְׁתֵּי נָשִׁים שֵׁם הָאַחַת עָדָה וְשֵׁם הַשֵּׁנִית צִלָּה: וַתֵּלֶד
כא עָדָה אֶת־יָבָל הוּא הָיָה אֲבִי יֹשֵׁב אֹהֶל וּמִקְנֶה: וְשֵׁם אָחִיו
כב יוּבָל הוּא הָיָה אֲבִי כָּל־תֹּפֵשׂ כִּנֹּור וְעוּגָב: וְצִלָּה גַם־הִוא
יָלְדָה אֶת־תּוּבַל קַיִן לֹטֵשׁ כָּל־חֹרֵשׁ נְחֹשֶׁת וּבַרְזֶל וַאֲחֹות
כג תּוּבַל־קַיִן נַעֲמָה: וַיֹּאמֶר לֶמֶךְ לְנָשָׁיו עָדָה וְצִלָּה שְׁמַעַן

is, *settled in*) the land of Nod. The Talmud concludes: This teaches that a fugitive's life in exile atones for half of his sins (since Cain was allowed to settle in Nod after his wandering; *Sanhedrin* 37b).

קִדְמַת־עֵדֶן — *East of Eden.* See our commentary on 3:23.

17. וַיְהִי בֹּנֶה עִיר — *He became a city-builder.* Cain thought he would die childless, so that when Enoch was born, he had to prepare for his future. He was now a nomad, an alien to the earth and to agriculture and had lost contact with God and with man. What,then, was left for him to do? Cain had only his own ability and intellectual resources to rely on and these led him quite naturally to build a city. As such, a city bears the mark of human intelligence and abilities. Crops from the land are transformed in the city to fill man's needs. Through art and industry the produce of the ground is given the imprint of man's intelligence.

Well aware of his destiny as wanderer and exile, Cain desired to perpetuate the memory of his offspring by naming the city he built after his son. But the Psalmist denounces the vanity of such ambitions of the wicked. *Their inward thought is that their houses shall continue forever and their dwelling-places to all generations; they call their lands after their own names. But man does not abide in his splendor ...* (Psalms 49:12-13).

R' Yehudah recalls the fate of this city: it was swallowed up in the Flood a few generations later (*Rabbah* 28). It is not through edifices of wood and stone that man should try to leave his mark for eternity but rather through accomplishments and creations of moral worth (cf. *Hirsch* to Numbers 32:42).

18. וַיִּוָּלֵד לַחֲנֹוךְ אֶת־עִירָד — *To Enoch was born Irad.* Cain and the five generations issuing from him perished in the Flood (*Shemos Rabbah* 31). Why then does the Torah give this genealogy? It is to show us God's forbearance. God granted Cain a long line of descendants so that, through *their* moral conduct, Cain might acquire the personal merit which could atone, at least partially, for his sin. But his offspring followed in their ancestor's footsteps and, as *Rashi* notes, they were depraved idolaters and forgers of instruments of death. Hence, the family did not survive, with one exception: Na'amah, the wife of Noah, was the only worthy descendant of Cain (cf. *Ramban*).

Enoch. He became a city-builder, and he named the city after
his son Enoch. ¹⁸ *To Enoch was born Irad, and Irad begot
Mehujael, and Mehujael begot Methushael, and Methushael
begot Lamech.*

*¹⁹ Lamech took to himself two wives: The name of one was
Adah, and the name of the second was Zillah. ²⁰ And Adah bore
Jabal; he was the first of those who dwell in tents and breed cattle.
²¹ The name of his brother was Jubal; he was the first of all who
handle the harp and flute. ²² And Zillah, too — she bore
Tubal-cain, who sharpened all cutting implements of copper and
iron. And the sister of Tubal-cain was Naamah.*

²³ And Lamech said to his wives, "Adah and Zillah, hear

Thus, from the beginning of history, the Torah illustrates that the downhill
path of sin, which began in the wake of the original sin, does not inexorably
lead to universal decadence. Quite the contrary, to each human being is left
complete freedom to uplift himself morally and to find personal salvation.

19. וַיִּקַּח־לוֹ לֶמֶךְ שְׁתֵּי נָשִׁים — *Lamech took to himself two wives.* It was Lamech
who instituted bigamy, for until then monogamy had been the rule. *Rashi*
explains: "This was the practice at the time of the Flood: there was one wife
for childbearing and one for pleasure, deliberately made sterile . . ."
The first wife was called Adah, the other Zillah. But Zillah had children as
well (גַּם הִוא; verse 22) either because the devices supposed to render her sterile
had no effect (*Baalei HaTosafos*) or because she had had children before marrying Lamech or before using these devices (*R' Wolf Heidenheim* on verse 4).

23. עָדָה וְצִלָּה שְׁמַעַן קוֹלִי — *Adah and Zillah, hear my voice.* The text of this
statement presents difficulties. Of the numerous explanations offered, we follow
Ramban's interpretation: It seems that Lamech was extremely knowledgeable
in all the arts. To his firstborn son he taught management of livestock; another
learned music from him; and the third was taught the art of forging instruments
of copper and iron to make lances and javelins for war. Lamech's wives thought
that he would follow his murderous ancestor when he began to invent such
instruments of death and destruction. They feared he would be punished.
Lamech reassured them: "Did I ever kill anyone, did I ever mortally wound a
child as Cain did? God will not punish me, but He will keep me from murdering
more than Cain. Dying from blows and wounds is more violent than murder
with a sword. The sword itself is not the cause of death and the swordmaker
commits no sin." Here *Ramban* touches on the ever-present problem of the
benefits of technological progress as weighed against the danger it poses to
mankind. Here for the very first time one begins to fear the blacksmith's art,
one feels terror at the possibly tragic consequences of technology which exist
alongside its peaceful uses, its contributions to advance our civilization. It is

קוֹלִי נְשֵׁי לֶמֶךְ הַאֲזֵנָּה אִמְרָתִי כִּי אִישׁ הָרַגְתִּי לְפִצְעִי
כד וְיֶלֶד לְחַבֻּרָתִי: כִּי שִׁבְעָתַיִם יֻקַּם־קָיִן וְלֶמֶךְ שִׁבְעִים
כה וְשִׁבְעָה: וַיֵּדַע אָדָם עוֹד אֶת־אִשְׁתּוֹ וַתֵּלֶד בֵּן וַתִּקְרָא
אֶת־שְׁמוֹ שֵׁת כִּי שָׁת־לִי אֱלֹהִים זֶרַע אַחֵר תַּחַת הֶבֶל
כו כִּי הֲרָגוֹ קָיִן: וּלְשֵׁת גַּם־הוּא יֻלַּד־בֵּן וַיִּקְרָא אֶת־שְׁמוֹ
ה שׁשׁי א אֱנוֹשׁ אָז הוּחַל לִקְרֹא בְּשֵׁם יהוה: זֶה סֵפֶר

highly significant that the Torah attributes the fear of these tragic outgrowths
to women, the guardians of the human race who are preoccupied with its
preservation. (The two parts of the song of Lamech are to be taken as
questions.)

24. כִּי שִׁבְעָתַיִם יֻקַּם־קָיִן — *If Cain suffered vengeance at seven generations* (i.e.
punished to the seventh generation). *Rashi* quotes the *Midrash Rabbah* to
explain: "Since God decreed that Cain's lineage would die out after seven
generations, Lamech's two wives separated from him after bearing children,
saying: 'What is the use of bringing children into the world just to have them
disappear? Tomorrow the Flood will carry all away ...' Lamech went to
complain about his wives to Adam. Replied he: 'You think you ought to
preoccupy yourself with the Divine decree? You do your duty; God will do
what He will.' "

Confidence in the omnipotent Creator, Who gives both life and the means
to sustain it, must win out over the forebodings and hesitations of husband and
wife, which, when the future threatens and fills them with doubt and fear,
might lead them to disobey the natural order, the Divine commandment:
Reproduce and multiply. To the couple who feel their courage falter, tradition
addresses this oft-quoted sentence: You do what you are commanded; God will
do that which He deems it best to do. This was also how Isaiah replied to a
king of Judah who wanted to remain unmarried because he had been told that
his children would not be virtuous, "What have you to do with the secrets of
the All-Merciful? It is not up to man to put himself in God's place" (*Berachos*
10a; cf. *Sotah* 12a and *Ohr HaChaim* on *Numbers* 3:39).

25. וַתִּקְרָא אֶת־שְׁמוֹ שֵׁת — *She ... named him Seth.* All the world's generations
descend from Seth (who is Noah's ancestor, whereas Cain's descendants
perished in the Flood) and so too all men of goodness and truth. R' Yose said:
This name is composed of the last two letters in the alphabet (ש-ת). After
having transgressed all the letters of the Torah, Adam repented. He began his
way back with the last two letters of the alphabet so that all the letters could
be put back in order. (After having turned the world order around, Adam
restored it by committing himself to return to the right path.) Hence he called
his son, born *in his likeness and his image* (5:3), שֵׁת. But only when Jewry
gathered at the foot of Mt. Sinai was there re-established the original order
which had reigned when heaven and earth were created. For it was then that

my voice; wives of Lemech, give ear to my speech: Have I slain a man by my wound and a child by my bruise? [24] *If Cain suffered vengeance at seven generations, then Lamech at seventy-seven!"*

[25] *Adam knew his wife again, and she bore a son and named him Seth, because: "God has provided me another child in place of Abel, for Cain had killed him."* [26] *And as for Seth, to him also a son was born, and he named him Enosh. Then to call in the Name of* HASHEM *became profaned.*

the covenant which God made with the world "by creating the foundation בָּרָא שִׁית —" (the verb שׁוּת means to place, to base on, to establish) was re-established. The first man broke this covenant but then repented and, when his son was born, Adam called him שֵׁת, the (new) foundation of the world. But conscious of his unworthiness, he omitted the letter י, *yud* from the word שִׁית. This letter is the sign of God Who made the covenant with the world. When Jewry accepted God's reign at Mount Sinai, this covenant was re-established with them. Then God placed the letter ב, first letter of the word בְּרִית (*covenant*), in the middle of the name שֵׁת (*foundation*) and made שַׁבָּת, the Sabbath, which thus became the basis and the foundation of the covenant between God and the Jewish people. וְשָׁמְרוּ בְנֵי יִשְׂרָאֵל אֶת הַשַּׁבָּת ... לְדֹרֹתָם בְּרִית עוֹלָם (*Zohar* 1:56a). The words שִׁית – שֵׁת – שַׁבָּת in their related structure designate the three fundamental stages of the cosmological, social and ethical evolution of life in the universe.

26. אָז הוּחַל. — *Then ... became profaned.* According to *Rashi* and most of our Sages, the verb הוּחַל is related to חוּלִין, *profanation.* "Men and lifeless objects were given Divine names by involving them in idolatrous cults and calling them gods," אָז הוּחַל לִקְרֹא בְּשֵׁם ה'.

The introduction to *Rambam's* treatise on laws concerning idolatry begins with this historical survey: "In the time of Enosh, men made a serious mistake. The sages of this era erred and Enosh himself among them. They considered that since God put stars and heavenly bodies in brilliant splendor above us to regulate life on earth and to be His first servants, then it is fitting to honor and glorify them. God, they reasoned, would want those which He made great and glorious to be venerated by man, just as a king wants others to honor those honored by him. Once they had this idea, men built temples to honor the stars, offered sacrifices, sang hymns, bowed down to them, all in order to receive Divine favor, in accord with this erroneous attitude. So idolatry began. The early pagans never denied God's existence nor held that all is attributable to the stars. The prophet Jeremiah confirms that in former times all men knew that God was the sole God, but they imagined that to worship stars was His will (10:7,8). Then, under the influence of false prophets who claimed to have received Divine messages and revelations, this worship degenerated into paganism and superstition. People next began to worship stars and heavenly

תּוֹלְדֹת אָדָם בְּיוֹם בְּרֹא אֱלֹהִים אָדָם בִּדְמוּת אֱלֹהִים עָשָׂה

bodies, and then forces of nature, simple objects and pictures, and finally statues of stone and wood to which they attributed magical powers. Except for some advanced thinkers such as Enoch, Methuselah, Noah, Shem and Eber, people gradually forgot the Name of God. This situation continued until the appearance of Abraham ...."

This account confirms the results of recent studies which lead to the increasingly widespread conviction that the worship of a single, supreme Deity dates from man's beginnings. Numerous arguments as well as old Babylonian and Greek traditions substantiate that monotheism existed in very early times and that it subsequently gradually degenerated. In convincing fashion, these corroborations refute the oft-encountered idea that monotheism evolved from polytheism, which is supposed to have its origins in fetishism or animism. This refutation is of particular importance since it is based on no less than the purest historical sources in the form of the earliest traditions. These tell us that polytheism was nothing other than a degenerate form of the original belief, which was monotheism.

5.

1. זֶה סֵפֶר תּוֹלְדֹת אָדָם — *This is the account of the descendants of Adam.* This is the enumeration (סְפִירָה) of the generations following Adam (*Rashi*). According to *Midrash Rabbah* (24) the emphasis is to be placed on זֶה סֵפֶר, these are the annals of the generations, in contrast to the generations previously mentioned which perished in the Flood. But now the family of Seth was perpetuated, thanks to one of them, Noah.

R' Yosef Albo considers this the real beginning of the Torah; the four preceding chapters served as its introduction. "Just as each science is preceded by a set of principles on which it is based, so too the Bible begins by setting out three fundamental principles: firstly, the existence of God (Chapter 1); secondly, Divine revelation — God reveals Himself to the first men, He teaches them, He guides them (Chapters 2-3:24); and thirdly, 'reward and punishment,' revealed to us throughout the fourth chapter in the story of Cain and Abel and the former's descendants." For *Albo* these three principles constitute the *ikkarim*, the basic articles of Jewish faith (1:11).

For *Albo*, then, this verse marks the beginning of the Torah and in this light one can understand all the better the exceptional importance ascribed to it. For example, Ben Azzai considers that it expresses the fundamental principle of the Torah to an even greater extent than the verse *Love your neighbor as yourself,* which in R' Akiva's view constitutes the Torah's basic teaching (*Sifra* to *Leviticus* 19). The latter verse bases universal brotherhood on the commandment of love for others whereas our verse teaches the unity of humankind in an infinitely greater and more elevated sense. Indeed, by beginning the account of human history with the words, *This is the account of the descendants of*

5 ¹*This is the account of the descendants of Adam — on the day that God created Man, He made him in the likeness of God.*

Adam, the Torah teaches us that each and every human being, whatever his race, color, or religion, is the child, created in God's image, of one and the same Father. Despite manifesting itself in varied and opposing ways, the whole of human history with its highs and lows is but a single entity. And just one single idea, despite striking contradictions and anomalies, lives and is being realized in humanity right from the unique being, Adam, formed in God's image. Man could not be "Adam" were the whole of this evolution not potentially in him. If, thanks to his free will, he is to be higher than the angels, then, because of this same freedom, he is also to have the chance to be lower than the animals. From the very beginning it was foreseen that Adam was capable of perversion. And, making no distinctions, our verse includes the depths of criminality and abject bestiality in the תוֹלְדֹת אָדָם, in that evolution which God inscribes in His annals of human history from the first Adam. The word תוֹלְדֹת is written defectively (missing a *vav*): it stresses that the defective specimens of humanity are nonetheless תוֹלְדֹת אָדָם, human beings formed in God's image, which can never be completely lost. This is the basic truth which stands at the head of universal history.

The second truth proclaims that "on the day God created Man, He made him in the likeness of God." Man's original state was not that of the primitive savage with a moral and spiritual crudeness almost bordering on the animal. Nor, on the other hand, is man's "resemblance to God" something supernatural which requires a renunciation of his natural character and needs a special training and culture. Quite the contrary, what we consider primitive man is really the opposite of natural man. The former, since he has forgotten the name of God, represents decadence and sinks to the level of an animal. In man's true natural state, he resembles God, his mind is radiant with intelligence, his soul pure and holy; his surroundings are to him like a paradise wherein he hears the Divine voice — all this is man's natural state, for *on the day that God created Man, He made him in the likeness of God.*

Thus, it is not without reason that the concept of man as a reflection of the Divine likeness is repeated here, after the fall occasioned by the first sin and followed by Cain's fratricide and Enosh's failing. The Creator Himself put the Divine likeness into man's nature. He formed man to meet this ideal just as He created the worm to play its role. It is He Who created man male and female, both formed equally in God's image, both sharing the same dignity, both receiving the same blessing, both together forming Adam. What is the final goal of the history of mankind? It is regaining this blessing, this humanity which is close to God, which resembles Him. It is coming ever nearer to this "natural condition" by constantly bettering ourselves and raising our level of existence (*R' S.R. Hirsch*).

זֶה סֵפֶר — *This is the account.* Basing themselves on the *Zohar*, some of our

ב אֹתוֹ: זָכָר וּנְקֵבָה בְּרָאָם וַיְבָרֶךְ אֹתָם וַיִּקְרָא אֶת־שְׁמָם
ג אָדָם בְּיוֹם הִבָּרְאָם: וַיְחִי אָדָם שְׁלֹשִׁים וּמְאַת שָׁנָה וַיּוֹלֶד
ד בִּדְמוּתוֹ כְּצַלְמוֹ וַיִּקְרָא אֶת־שְׁמוֹ שֵׁת: וַיִּהְיוּ יְמֵי־אָדָם
אַחֲרֵי הוֹלִידוֹ אֶת־שֵׁת שְׁמֹנֶה מֵאֹת שָׁנָה וַיּוֹלֶד בָּנִים וּבָנוֹת:

illustrious Sages such as the *Gaon R' Sherira, R' Yehudah HaLevi* (in *Kuzari* 3:65) and *Ramban* affirm the existence of a "book," revealed to Adam, which holds the key to the mysteries of the universe and of existence. This is the *Book of Raziel* (the name means "Divine secrets") and it deals with the physiognomic and theosophic sciences which were known to the High Priest Yishmael ben Elisha. This explains the fact that an important store of human knowledge came down to man in earliest times from suprarational sources and was transmitted from one generation to the next by oral tradition.

2. וַיִּקְרָא אֶת־שְׁמָם אָדָם . . . זָכָר וּנְקֵבָה בְּרָאָם — *He created them male and female . . . and called their name Man.* R' Elazar says: "A man without a wife is not a man (*adam*)." Only the bond uniting husband and wife can raise man to perfection. *Ramban*, however, commenting on *Exodus* 24:5, points out the purity of "the youths of the Children of Israel" who had yet to know women.

וַיְבָרֶךְ אֹתָם — *He blessed them.* Ben Azzai, who wanted to justify his bachelorhood but who nevertheless feared that his students would follow his example, quoted the verse זֶה סֵפֶר תּוֹלְדֹת אָדָם as the basic principle of the Torah. In so doing, he stressed the duty of procreation, which guarantees the preservation and continuity of humanity and, as he himself states, "the presence of God in society" (*Yevamos* 63b). But R' Akiva, whose disciples (at first numbering in the thousands) lacked a spirit of fraternity and cooperation and gradually dwindled away (*Yevamos* 62b), held another verse to be the basis of the Torah: *Love your fellowman like yourself* (*Sifra* to *Leviticus* 19; from R' C.E. Shapira, שער יששכר ח״א, מאמר חג הביכורים, ה׳).

3. וַיְחִי אָדָם שְׁלֹשִׁים וּמְאַת שָׁנָה — *When Adam had lived one hundred and thirty years. Rashi* adds, "Until now he had separated himself from his wife." Having yielded to temptation and suffered the terrible consequences — Cain's conduct and Abel's fate — Adam felt he must rid himself of even the slightest urge to do evil before reuniting with his wife. This he did to ensure that his future children would be pure in spirit and protected from sin. His self-imposed period of abstinence was filled with repentance and a striving for moral perfection. These difficult years of self-denial and self-discipline were rewarded as, for the first time, Adam fathered a being "in his likeness and his image," resembling his better self, itself formed in God's image. This is the first confirmation of the principle that: "The place of the repentants who have struggled with evil and triumphed over it is greater than that of the righteous who remain vulnerable to sin."

בִּדְמוּתוֹ כְּצַלְמוֹ — *In his likeness and his image.* "This teaches that Seth was born already circumcised (without a foreskin) just like his father Adam" (*Avos*

> ²He created them male and female. He blessed them and
> called their name Man on the day they were created —
> ³ when Adam had lived one hundred and thirty years,
> he begot in his likeness and his image, and he named him
> Seth. ⁴ And the days of Adam after begetting Seth were
> eight hundred years, and he begot sons and daughters.

D'Rabbi Nassan 2). R' Chaim ben Attar explains that man was originally created without a foreskin, as was the case with the thirteen righteous men (Avos D'Rabbi Nassan ibid.), including Moses and Jacob. Only after the first sin did the foreskin form — that is why it is now up to man to remove it by circumcision (cf. Ohr HaChaim to Leviticus 13:3).

From what has been said we see that the moral disposition of the parents has an influence on the future character of their children. This idea is studied thoroughly by the Kabbalist Moshe Cordovero in his book שיעור קומה (Chapter 34): "And if you say: since the child inherits the purity of soul of his parents, what merit will he then have for his own actions? We are talking here only of a predisposition to do good. But man's free will is unaffected; it still requires great and constant personal effort to reach perfection. What is important is that parents give birth to more than just the body of the child. They also transmit the natural predisposition which provides the 'springboard' for the soul."

Cordovero's view conflicts strikingly with that of Rambam. The latter, bypassing the law of spiritual heredity, holds that Adam referred to his son Seth as being formed in his likeness and his image only after he had raised and instructed him and had seen him reach perfection (Guide 1:7). Of Rambam's opinion, Cordovero comments: "He has erred in his interpretation because he lacked certain keys of wisdom."

4. וַיּוֹלֶד בָּנִים וּבָנוֹת — And he begot sons and daughters. R' Yehudah HaLevi (Kuzari 1:95) and other Sages are of the opinion that the first human beings each had but one son worthy of the Divine Inspiration and reflecting the ideal image of the first man. Humanity's nobility begins with Adam and continues through Seth and then Enosh, as the first verse of Chronicles solemnly proclaims. These represent segula (סְגוּלָה), the treasure of humanity. To honor them, the Torah calls them בְּנֵי אֱלֹהִים, sons of God. The number of years of their lives serves as the basis for reckoning the chronological table of universal history. For each of these representatives of the ten generations from Adam to Noah, the Torah repeats the lifespan in years, just after having given us enough information to deduce it ourselves. It then adds for each the word וַיָּמֹת, and he died, a word which does not appear in the genealogies of those coming after the Flood. What does this come to teach? The long lives of those mentioned here were full and active; when death came, it came as a redemption which crowned their lives. But the other "sons and daughters" also mentioned here are, in R' Yehudah HaLevi's view, just like chaff compared with wheat. The Torah only mentions them in passing.

ה וַיִּהְיוּ כָּל־יְמֵי אָדָם אֲשֶׁר־חַי תְּשַׁע מֵאוֹת שָׁנָה וּשְׁלֹשִׁים
ו שָׁנָה וַיָּמֹת: · · · · · · וַיְחִי־שֵׁת חָמֵשׁ שָׁנִים וּמְאַת
ז שָׁנָה וַיּוֹלֶד אֶת־אֱנוֹשׁ: וַיְחִי־שֵׁת אַחֲרֵי הוֹלִידוֹ אֶת־אֱנוֹשׁ
ח שְׁבַע שָׁנִים וּשְׁמֹנֶה מֵאוֹת שָׁנָה וַיּוֹלֶד בָּנִים וּבָנוֹת: וַיִּהְיוּ
כָּל־יְמֵי־שֵׁת שְׁתֵּים עֶשְׂרֵה שָׁנָה וּתְשַׁע מֵאוֹת שָׁנָה
ט וַיָּמֹת: · · · · · · וַיְחִי אֱנוֹשׁ תִּשְׁעִים שָׁנָה וַיּוֹלֶד אֶת־קֵינָן:
י וַיְחִי אֱנוֹשׁ אַחֲרֵי הוֹלִידוֹ אֶת־קֵינָן חֲמֵשׁ עֶשְׂרֵה שָׁנָה
יא וּשְׁמֹנֶה מֵאוֹת שָׁנָה וַיּוֹלֶד בָּנִים וּבָנוֹת: וַיִּהְיוּ כָּל־יְמֵי אֱנוֹשׁ

A tradition reported by R' Yirmiyahu ben Elazar attributes other progeny to
Adam. "In the years after the sin, when he was an anathema, Adam fathered
spirits, demons, and nocturnal phantoms, as it is written: *When Adam had lived
one hundred and thirty years, he begot in his likeness and his image.* Hence,
prior to this age he did not reproduce in his likeness. But an objection was raised
in the name of R' Meir: Adam was very pious. When he saw that he had caused
death to come (to the human race) he fasted for 130 years, took abstinence upon
himself, and girded himself only with fig leaves. How then did he father these
spirits? The answer: It was by the involuntary loss of semen" (*Eruvin* 18b).

Commenting on this verse, *Rav Sherira Gaon* (quoted by *Radak*) and
Rambam (*Guide* 1:7) explain that these beings engendered by Adam were
deformed and evil, half-man, half-animal. This anthropoid mammal is considered a degenerate creature brought into the world by perverted human beings
during the immoral and decadent generations of Enosh (*Bereishis Rabbah* 23)
and of the Tower of Babel (*Sanhedrin* 109a). According to the *Zohar* (1:54), the
ape was begotten by the acts of bestiality committed by Cain.

Hence the Sages of the Talmud and Midrash stand opposed to Darwinian
theories which have man descending from the ape. For the Rabbis, the ape is, on
the contrary, a malformation of man. [The traditional Jewish point of view on
the subject of the progressive evolution of species has been set down by Salomon
ibn Verga, a writer on mathematics and astronomy, in his book *Shevet Yehudah*
(ed. Wiener, p. 15).]

5. וַיִּהְיוּ כָּל־יְמֵי אָדָם אֲשֶׁר־חַי תְּשַׁע מֵאוֹת שָׁנָה וּשְׁלֹשִׁים שָׁנָה — *All the days that
Adam lived were nine hundred and thirty years.* This is the book of the
generations ... God showed Adam all future generations. He showed him
David, who was destined to live but three hours. Adam asked: "Can I not do
something for him? How many years have I to live?"

"A thousand years," was the reply (cf. *Bereishis Rabbah* 22; *Midrash Tehillim*
25).

"I wish to give him seventy years of my life. Let him reign and sing praises
to God!" Adam signed over these years to David, who alludes to this in *Psalms*
40:8): *I have come because of the scroll written about me* (*Yalkut Shimoni* 41).

⁵ *All the days that Adam lived were nine hundred and thirty years; and he died.*
⁶ *Seth lived one hundred and five years and begot Enosh.* ⁷ *And Seth lived eight hundred and seven years after begetting Enosh, and he begot sons and daughters.* ⁸ *All the days of Seth were nine hundred and twelve years; and he died.*
⁹ *Enosh lived ninety years, and begot Kenan.* ¹⁰ *And Enosh lived eight hundred and fifteen years after begetting Kenan, and he begot sons and daughters.* ¹¹ *All the days of Enosh were*

This Midrash brings out the close connection between the lives of Adam and David. The first is the father of mankind; the second, the father of the dynasty from which will come the Messiah. The whole history of the world is encompassed by these two giants of humanity. Their earthly missions are complementary and, taken together, are destined to form the historical cycle of man. Indeed, the second half of this cycle of six thousand years, leading to the messianic era, began with the advent of King David.

(Adam's example permits us to justify the practice of giving up some years of one's life in order to prolong the life of another stricken with a serious illness — *Sefer Chassidim*.)

6. שֵׁת... וַיּוֹלֶד אֶת־אֱנוֹשׁ — *Seth ... and begot Enosh*. Many exegetes consider that the fifth chapter of *Genesis* gives the Sethite genealogy. But it gives rather the genealogy of the descendants of Adam issuing through Seth (*Toldos Adam*).

The Torah lists ten generations from Adam to Noah. These were the bearers and trustees of man's great traditions. They transmitted them to Noah, who preserved them for the generations coming after the Flood. Hence we see how the original traditions were kept through the ages — note that Noah was a contemporary of Methuselah for six centuries, and that for 243 years Methuselah was a contemporary of Adam. Noah's father, Lamech, also knew Adam until he was 56 years of age (*R' Bachya*). These traditions concerned belief in God and the history of creation, and the Garden of Eden — the lost Paradise. This fund of knowledge was complemented by wisdom and by the discoveries which these generations made through their exceptional abilities and powers.

8. וַיִּהְיוּ כָּל־יְמֵי־שֵׁת שְׁתֵּים עֶשְׂרֵה שָׁנָה וּתְשַׁע מֵאוֹת שָׁנָה — *All the days of Seth were nine hundred and twelve years*. "Some think that here the word 'years' refers to a period shorter than the years we have now. This opinion is untenable from every point of view. In the episodes in *Genesis*, we note that the vitality of the people successively decreases. Even when it reaches the level we possess today, it is still designated by the same time unit, שָׁנָה. This word has always meant a period of revolution of a body about another: either of the earth around the sun or twelve revolutions of the moon around our planet" (*L. Wogue*).

11. וַיִּהְיוּ כָּל־יְמֵי אֱנוֹשׁ — *All the days of Enosh were*. The genealogy of the generations before the Flood finds a place in the traditions of almost all the

יב חָמֵשׁ שָׁנִים וּתְשַׁע מֵאוֹת שָׁנָה וַיָּמֹת: וַיְחִי קֵינָן
יג שִׁבְעִים שָׁנָה וַיּוֹלֶד אֶת־מַהֲלַלְאֵל: וַיְחִי קֵינָן אַחֲרֵי הוֹלִידוֹ
אֶת־מַהֲלַלְאֵל אַרְבָּעִים שָׁנָה וּשְׁמֹנֶה מֵאוֹת שָׁנָה וַיּוֹלֶד בָּנִים
יד וּבָנוֹת: וַיִּהְיוּ כָּל־יְמֵי קֵינָן עֶשֶׂר שָׁנִים וּתְשַׁע מֵאוֹת שָׁנָה
טו וַיָּמֹת: וַיְחִי מַהֲלַלְאֵל חָמֵשׁ שָׁנִים וְשִׁשִּׁים שָׁנָה
טז וַיּוֹלֶד אֶת־יָרֶד: וַיְחִי מַהֲלַלְאֵל אַחֲרֵי הוֹלִידוֹ אֶת־יֶרֶד
יז שְׁלֹשִׁים שָׁנָה וּשְׁמֹנֶה מֵאוֹת שָׁנָה וַיּוֹלֶד בָּנִים וּבָנוֹת: וַיִּהְיוּ
כָּל־יְמֵי מַהֲלַלְאֵל חָמֵשׁ וְתִשְׁעִים שָׁנָה וּשְׁמֹנֶה מֵאוֹת שָׁנָה
יח וַיָּמֹת: וַיְחִי־יֶרֶד שְׁתַּיִם וְשִׁשִּׁים שָׁנָה וּמְאַת שָׁנָה
יט וַיּוֹלֶד אֶת־חֲנוֹךְ: וַיְחִי־יֶרֶד אַחֲרֵי הוֹלִידוֹ אֶת־חֲנוֹךְ
כ שְׁמֹנֶה מֵאוֹת שָׁנָה וַיּוֹלֶד בָּנִים וּבָנוֹת: וַיִּהְיוּ כָּל־יְמֵי־יֶרֶד
כא שְׁתַּיִם וְשִׁשִּׁים שָׁנָה וּתְשַׁע מֵאוֹת שָׁנָה וַיָּמֹת: וַיְחִי
כב חֲנוֹךְ חָמֵשׁ וְשִׁשִּׁים שָׁנָה וַיּוֹלֶד אֶת־מְתוּשָׁלַח: וַיִּתְהַלֵּךְ
חֲנוֹךְ אֶת־הָאֱלֹהִים אַחֲרֵי הוֹלִידוֹ אֶת־מְתוּשֶׁלַח שְׁלֹשׁ
כג מֵאוֹת שָׁנָה וַיּוֹלֶד בָּנִים וּבָנוֹת: וַיְהִי כָּל־יְמֵי חֲנוֹךְ

peoples of antiquity — and parallels the Biblical account very closely. These peoples claim to descend from a race of "gods," usually ten in number, who lived and ruled for one thousand years. In particular, two "lists of kings" have been preserved, one Sumerian, the other Babylonian in origin. Both go back to the same source, which the Bible has maintained in its original purity and clarity. The chronological data for the first two millennia correspond quite closely with the historical traditions of the peoples of antiquity — and also, it should be added, with the results of archaeological findings. These results set the beginning of the Flood at 1656 years after the creation of the world (that is, 2104 years before the common era).

20. וַיִּהְיוּ כָּל־יְמֵי־יֶרֶד שְׁתַּיִם וְשִׁשִּׁים שָׁנָה וּתְשַׁע מֵאוֹת שָׁנָה — *All the days of Jared came to nine hundred and sixty-two years.* "The longevity of primitive races is taken for granted by scientists, independently of what tradition records, and surprises only the unschooled. In former times, man, plants, and animals not only grew to much larger size but were more vigorous and of stronger constitution than is the case nowadays. Virgil's *'Grandia mirabitur ossa'* is witness that the pagans of classical times also knew of this law of the gradual physical degeneration of the species" (*L. Wogue*).

Ramban, also, mentions this law in his commentary and explains that Adam's longevity was due to his physical perfection as a being created by God Himself. Even after being condemned to mortality, Adam was able to bequeath his extraordinary vigor to his descendants. However, atmospheric conditions after the Flood reduced the lifespan and only the righteous, such as the Patriarchs, were able to reach very old age, since "Fear of God increases man's days, but the

nine hundred and five years; and he died.

¹² *Kenan lived seventy years, and begot Mahalalel.* ¹³*And Kenan lived eight hundred and forty years after begetting Mahalalel, and he begot sons and daughters.* ¹⁴ *All the days of Kenan were nine hundred and ten years; and he died.*

¹⁵ *Mahalalel lived sixty-five years, and begot Jared.* ¹⁶ *And Mahalalel lived eight hundred and thirty years after begetting Jared, and he begot sons and daughters.* ¹⁷ *All the days of Mahalalel were eight hundred and ninety-five years; and he died.*

¹⁶*Jared lived one hundred and sixty-two years, and begot Enoch.* ¹⁹ *And Jared lived eight hundred years after begetting Enoch and he begot sons and daughters.* ²⁰ *All the days of Jared came to nine hundred and sixty-two years; and he died.*

²¹ *Enoch lived sixty-five years, and begot Methuselah.* ²² *Enoch walked with God for three hundred years after begetting Methuselah; and he begot sons and daughters.* ²³ *All the days of Enoch*

years of the wicked shall be shortened" (*Proverbs* 10:27).

Ramban strongly criticizes the view held by *Rambam* (*Guide* 2:47) that only those designated in the Torah enjoyed exceptional longevity, either because of their conduct or their nutrition or through a miracle, and that all the others had normal lifespans. This *Ramban* queries: Why did one group benefit from a miracle, while another did not? Why did their contemporaries and those coming after the Flood not adopt the same diet and style of living and so increase their longevity also?

R' Yomtov ben Avraham (*Ritva*) comes vigorously to *Rambam's* defense in his *Sefer HaZikaron*, Ch. 2. *Radak*, however, puts forward a different reason: "It is possible that God wanted the first generations of mankind to have long lives in order to give them time to acquire knowledge and to record this knowledge for posterity. Seventy years of life is not enough to acquire knowledge unless one has, as a basis, the knowledge gained by others in the past."

Flavius Josephus notes that astronomical observations at this period of ancient history required a lifetime of at least six hundred years (*Antiquities* I, 39). *Ibn Ezra* taught that the longevity enjoyed by the generations before the Flood will return in the messianic era, as Isaiah announces in 45:20 (ibid.).

22. וַיִּתְהַלֵּךְ חֲנוֹךְ אֶת־הָאֱלֹהִים — *Enoch walked with God.* He behaved as God wished. With this, the Bible arrives at the seventh generation from Adam, which, the Midrash (*Vayikra Rabbah* 29) tells us, is always outstanding. Enoch is also distinguished from his depraved era and he "trained himself" for holiness (חֲנוֹךְ is derived from חִנֵּךְ, *to educate*). He "walked with God," which, to avoid any anthropomorphism, *Onkelos* renders as "he walked in the fear of God." The *Targum Yerushalmi* translates: "he served God sincerely." A historical tradition reported in the *Book of Enoch* (סֵפֶר חֲנוֹךְ) states that Enoch was the king of

כד חָמֵשׁ וְשִׁשִּׁים שָׁנָה וּשְׁלֹשׁ מֵאוֹת שָׁנָה: וַיִּתְהַלֵּךְ חֲנוֹךְ

שביעי   כה אֶת־הָאֱלֹהִים וְאֵינֶנּוּ כִּי־לָקַח אֹתוֹ אֱלֹהִים: וַיְחִי

מְתוּשֶׁלַח שֶׁבַע וּשְׁמֹנִים שָׁנָה וּמְאַת שָׁנָה וַיּוֹלֶד אֶת־

כו לָמֶךְ: וַיְחִי מְתוּשֶׁלַח אַחֲרֵי הוֹלִידוֹ אֶת־לֶמֶךְ שְׁתַּיִם וּשְׁמוֹנִים

כז שָׁנָה וּשְׁבַע מֵאוֹת שָׁנָה וַיּוֹלֶד בָּנִים וּבָנוֹת: וַיִּהְיוּ

כָּל־יְמֵי מְתוּשֶׁלַח תֵּשַׁע וְשִׁשִּׁים שָׁנָה וּתְשַׁע מֵאוֹת שָׁנָה

כח וַיָּמֹת: וַיְחִי־לֶמֶךְ שְׁתַּיִם וּשְׁמֹנִים שָׁנָה וּמְאַת שָׁנָה

כט וַיּוֹלֶד בֵּן: וַיִּקְרָא אֶת־שְׁמוֹ נֹחַ לֵאמֹר זֶה יְנַחֲמֵנוּ מִמַּעֲשֵׂנוּ

ל וּמֵעִצְּבוֹן יָדֵינוּ מִן־הָאֲדָמָה אֲשֶׁר אֵרְרָהּ יהוה: וַיְחִי־לֶמֶךְ

Sippar, the city of the sun-god Shamash, and that he lived in close communion with God.

In Enoch's time a new spiritual decline was supposed to have taken place and only those with great moral strength were able to withstand the widespread immorality. "Ten generations lived from Adam to Noah. This shows you the mercifulness of God, for all those generations continued provoking Him until He finally brought the waters of the Flood upon them" (*Avos* 5:2). This is why Seth's descendants, beginning with Enoch, had Cainite names. At this time, these Cainites set out for Babylonia, which they succeeded in controlling thanks to their weapons of metal. Thus we find that Enoch, Methuselah and Lamech correspond to names of the sons of Cain: Enoch, Methushael, and Lamech. The name Methuselah, quite significantly, means a herald of arms (*Barsilai*, pp. 138, 165). Furthermore, there are indications that the descendants of Cain and of Seth began to intermarry at that time. This led to the total corruption of humanity before the deluge (*Genesis* 6:2; cf. *Ibn Ezra*). Thus we see Naamah, a sister of Tubal-cain, marry Noah (*Bereishis Rabbah* 23). But amidst this social and moral anarchy, Enoch served God, as the Torah stresses twice.

Many legends, both Jewish and pagan, deal with Enoch and with the mysterious circumstances of his death. According to rabbinical tradition, Enoch invented writing, arithmetic, and other branches of learning. He taught many laws which God had revealed to him, in particular those on the motions of heavenly bodies, which served as the basis for fixing the calendar (*Seder HaDoros*, ס' היובלים).

24. וְאֵינֶנּוּ כִּי־לָקַח אֹתוֹ אֱלֹהִים — *Then he was no more, for God had taken him.* The *Tosafists* (*Yevamos* 16b, ד"ה פסוק) point out that there are two different traditions regarding Enoch's death. The way it is described here attests to the fact that it was mysterious, perhaps supernatural. In any case, Enoch's demise at 365 was premature compared with the lifetimes of the other forefathers. R' Abahu (*Bereishis Rabbah* 25) says that Enoch died a natural death; according to the Sages of *Derech Eretz Zuta* 1 he "entered alive into Paradise" with the eight righteous men mentioned there. *Rashi* holds that Enoch died a natural but pre-

were three hundred and sixty-five years. ²⁴ *And Enoch walked with God; then he was no more, for God had taken him.*

²⁵ *Methuselah lived one hundred and eighty-seven years, and begot Lamech.* ²⁶ *And Methuselah lived seven hundred and eight-two years after begetting Lamech, and he begot sons and daughters.* ²⁷ *All the days of Methuselah were nine hundred and sixty-nine years; and he died.*

²⁸ *Lamech lived one hundred and eighty-two years, and begot a son.* ²⁹ *And he called his name Noah saying, "This one will bring us rest from our work and from the toil of our hands, from the ground which* HASHEM *had cursed."* ³⁰ *Lamech lived*

mature death and adds: Enoch was a just man but of weak conscience and easily swayed to evil. Hence God hurried to take him from this world before his time.

Such are the ways of God, concludes the *Zohar* (1:56b). When He knows that the fragrance emanating from one who is righteous begins to lose its quality, He hastens his end: He looks for the original fragrance and takes it back from the world. This is the meaning of the verse in the *Song of Songs: As long as the King* (God) *sits at his place* (man), *my nard sent forth its fragrance* (1:12). And if man ceases to possess this fragrance, then: *My beloved* (God) *is gone down to his garden* (the earth) *to the beds of spices ... to gather the lilies* (6:2). This is why righteous people are sometimes prematurely called away from this world.

Another explanation takes the words "he served God" as implying a reproach to Enoch, who withdrew from his fellowmen and, caring only for his own welfare, served God. The *Sefer HaYashar* confirms Enoch's pride in his הִתְבּוֹדְדוּת, his isolation. In this light, his premature death appears as a Divine punishment. Some Sages relate the version that "Enoch entered alive into Paradise" to the death of Adam, which occurred in the 298th year of Enoch's life. The disappearance of the first human being, even though he was created by God Himself, brought despair and skepticism to those who were left, unaware as they were of the existence of an afterworld and of the immortality of the soul. Hence, Enoch was carried to Heaven alive, in full view, in a fiery chariot drawn by fiery horses (ibid.). The people were shown that life does not come to an end with earthly death (*R' Bachya*).

28. וַיּוֹלֶד בֵּן ... לֶמֶךְ — *Lamech ... and begot a son.* Prior to this, the names of sons were mentioned immediately but here the name is withheld until the next verse in order to draw our attention to the special significance of this birth. Indeed, the birth of this son gave the people new hope for several reasons. Since Adam's death, he was the first descendant of the great Sethite dynasty (*Rashbam*). The curse upon Adam was supposed to disappear after his death, as it is said, *accursed is the ground because of you ... until you return to the ground from which you were taken ...* (3:17,19).

Moreover, the newborn was born circumcised and, according to an old

אַחֲרֵי הוֹלִידְוֹ אֶת־נֹחַ חָמֵשׁ וְתִשְׁעִים שָׁנָה וַחֲמֵשׁ מֵאֹת שָׁנָה
לא וַיּוֹלֶד בָּנִים וּבָנוֹת: וַיְהִי כָּל־יְמֵי־לֶמֶךְ שֶׁבַע וְשִׁבְעִים שָׁנָה
לב וּשְׁבַע מֵאֹת שָׁנָה וַיָּמֹת: וַיְהִי־נֹחַ
בֶּן־חֲמֵשׁ מֵאֹת שָׁנָה וַיּוֹלֶד נֹחַ אֶת־שֵׁם אֶת־חָם וְאֶת־
ו   א יָפֶת: וַיְהִי כִּי־הֵחֵל הָאָדָם לָרֹב עַל־פְּנֵי הָאֲדָמָה וּבָנוֹת
ב יֻלְּדוּ לָהֶם: וַיִּרְאוּ בְנֵי־הָאֱלֹהִים אֶת־בְּנוֹת הָאָדָם כִּי
ג טֹבֹת הֵנָּה וַיִּקְחוּ לָהֶם נָשִׁים מִכֹּל אֲשֶׁר בָּחָרוּ: וַיֹּאמֶר יהוה

tradition, the curse ceased at the birth of the first circumcised descendant
(*Tanchuma*). Other signs, too, foretold the special importance of Noah's birth:
"Because of the curse on the first man, the earth had produced only thorns and
nettles where grain had been sown. In Noah's time an end came to these
afflictions" (*Rashi*). Thus, with *Rashi*, we understand the prophetic tenor of the
emphatic: "*Lamech . . . begot a son (ben)* — one by whom the world would be
rebuilt (the word בֵּן being related to בָּנָה, *to construct*).

29. זֶה יְנַחֲמֵנוּ — *This one will bring us rest.* "The name does not correspond to
the interpretation, nor the interpretation to the name," R' Yochanan says, since
נֹחַ means "rest" whereas "comfort" is linked to a name like נַחְמָן or מְנַחֵם
(*Rabbah 25*). *Rashi* explains the name "Noah" in the sense of stoppage, relief. *R'
Bachya* states that נֹחַ is a diminutive of the word חֵן, which has the same letters.
This latter word means favor or grace and plays a key role in Noah's life. In fact,
the last verse in the *sidrah* of *Bereishis* proclaims, 'וְנֹחַ מָצָא חֵן בְּעֵינֵי ה, *But Noah
found grace in the eyes of Hashem.* It was taught in the school of R' Yishmael
that the fate of destruction was decreed against Noah, too, but he found grace
in God's eyes and benefited from an act of Divine mercy (*Sanhedrin 108a*).

The word זֶה (*this one*) bears two tonic accents ("notes") for the Torah reading
(תְּלִישָׁא וְגֵרְשַׁיִם) which *R' Bachya ibn Pakuda* explains in this way: Noah is the
tenth generation from Adam. The "tenth is consecrated to God" as in *Leviticus*
27:32, 'הָעֲשִׂירִי יִהְיֶה קֹּדֶשׁ לַה. Hence Noah's father hoped that he would bring
about a better world, a hope which he expressed as follows: "May the merit of
this one (Noah) cause This (God, Who is designated by זֶה, as in *Exodus* 15:2) to
console us in our travail and in our suffering, etc." The double tonic accent on
the word זֶה refers to this double meaning of the word. "Do not take these
niceties and discreet allusions lightly," *R' Bachya* concludes. "Even the notes for
the Torah reading come from Sinai. Even they contribute to a better understanding of the contents of the Torah."

6.

1. וַיְהִי כִּי־הֵחֵל הָאָדָם לָרֹב — *And it came to pass when Man began to increase.*
This chapter introduces the story of the Flood. In a few sentences the Torah
describes the underlying causes of the cataclysmic event: first, sexual depravity
which brought with it complete moral anarchy; later, social and moral corruption which put humanity's last hope for survival beyond reach (*Rashi*, verse 11).

five hundred and ninety-five years after begetting Noah, and he begot sons and daughters. ³¹ *All the days of Lamech were seven hundred and seventy-seven years; and he died.*

³² *When Noah was five hundred years old, Noah begot Shem, Ham, and Japheth.*

6   ¹*And it came to pass when Man began to increase upon the ground and daughters were born to them,* ² *the sons of the rulers saw that the daughters of man were good and they took themselves wives from whomever they chose.* ³ *And HASHEM said,*

וּבָנוֹת יֻלְּדוּ לָהֶם — *And daughters were born to them.* Scholars teach that in monogamous countries the number of male and female children are about equal, but where polygamy is the practice the number of females is double that of males. Now at the start of creation, people were monogamous and males were in the majority. But when Lamech, the descendant of Cain, married several wives, others followed his example and more daughters were born than sons. This natural phenomena is still in effect (*Malbim*).

Is the birth of a girl to be joyfully welcomed as a new source of fecundity and hence of blessings? So teaches R' Yochanan (*Bava Basra* 16a) and other Talmudic Sages (*Bereishis Rabbah* 26). On the other hand, in view of the harmful influence of women in the generations before the Flood, R' Shimon ben Lakish considers that the birth of a girl heralds quarrels. The first interpretation relates the infinitive לָרֹב of our verse to רְבִיָּה, *fertility,* and the second to מְרִיבָה, *quarrel* (cf. *Ramban* on *Genesis* 24:1).

2. וַיִּרְאוּ בְנֵי־הָאֱלֹהִים אֶת־בְּנוֹת הָאָדָם — *The sons of the rulers saw that the daughters of man. Rashi* gives two explanations for ''sons of the rulers'': children of princes, and judges — celestial beings carrying out a Divine mission. *Ibn Ezra* and others quote a third explanation: the sons of rulers were of the lineage of Seth and the daughters of man descended from Cain. The former are called בְּנֵי־הָאֱלֹהִים since the Sethites kept the Divine stamp, which reappeared with them (5:3). Nevertheless, as a consequence of not keeping their race pure, they were not able to save mankind. They intermarried with the Cainites, who developed an atheistic society which, despite being advanced in the arts and sciences, was to meet its doom in the Flood. Through intermarriage, the sons of Seth sank to the level of this impious generation and so they too deserved the death sentence which was passed on all humanity, save for one family. These verses are the Torah's first warning against intermarriage with idolaters.

כִּי טֹבֹת הֵנָּה — *That ... were good.* They considered only the outward appearance of the women, not caring about family background or the potential for raising children properly.

מִכֹּל אֲשֶׁר בָּחָרוּ — *From whomever they chose.* Clearly implying all excesses of an immoral generation. *Rashi* explains: even a married woman, even a male, even a beast. Adultery, pederasty, and bestiality lead to the destruction of humanity.

לֹא־יָד֨וֹן רוּחִ֤י בָֽאָדָם֙ לְעֹלָ֔ם בְּשַׁגַּ֖ם ה֣וּא בָשָׂ֑ר וְהָי֣וּ יָמָ֔יו

ד מֵאָ֥ה וְעֶשְׂרִ֖ים שָׁנָֽה: הַנְּפִלִ֞ים הָי֣וּ בָאָ֘רֶץ֮ בַּיָּמִ֣ים הָהֵם֒ וְגַ֣ם

אַֽחֲרֵי־כֵ֗ן אֲשֶׁ֨ר יָבֹ֜אוּ בְּנֵ֤י הָֽאֱלֹהִים֙ אֶל־בְּנ֣וֹת הָֽאָדָ֔ם וְיָֽלְד֖וּ

לָהֶ֑ם הֵ֧מָּה הַגִּבֹּרִ֛ים אֲשֶׁ֥ר מֵֽעוֹלָ֖ם אַנְשֵׁ֥י הַשֵּֽׁם:

מפטיר ה וַיַּ֣רְא יְהֹוָ֔ה כִּ֥י רַבָּ֛ה רָעַ֥ת הָֽאָדָ֖ם בָּאָ֑רֶץ וְכָל־יֵ֨צֶר֙ מַחְשְׁבֹ֣ת

3. לֹא־יָדוֹן רוּחִי בָאָדָם לְעֹלָם בְּשַׁגַּם הוּא בָשָׂר — *My spirit shall not contend evermore concerning Man since he is but flesh.* Seeing the sons of the Divine race marrying indiscriminately, God felt that His spirit, that is the Divine light, would soon no longer dominate the instincts of the flesh. Instead it risked "becoming flesh" itself. Man's spiritual force risked being submerged under the torrent of sensual passion. However, this verse can be taken in another way:

וְהָיוּ יָמָיו מֵאָה וְעֶשְׂרִים שָׁנָה — *His days shall be a hundred and twenty years.* This is the translation according to *Rashi.* Other commentators translate, "His lifespan will [eventually] become 120 years." R' M. C. Luzzatto explains: after Adam sinned, God wanted men to return to perfection solely by the attraction of the ideal of being holy, and not by imposing more laws upon them. Why did He grant them such long lives? It was in order to give them enough time to attain by themselves that degree of wisdom necessary for elevating themselves to holiness and to finding God. He offered them a respite of ten generations to realize this ideal. Noah could have been a veritable Messiah, a bearer of light and salvation for mankind. But he was too weak to stem the invading flood of immorality; he could not prevent the catastrophe. Then, since the "high road" to perfection by the ideal of holiness had met with failure, God decided to retrain humanity by using the "low road." This involves many laws and commandments destined to lead men to moral perfection. First, he promulgated laws for the "sons of Noah," and then those laws making up the Torah. At the same time, He shortened the human lifespan, since man no longer needed to seek the truth unaided, having now the Divine commandments as his guide. The example of Moses proves that a lifetime of 120 years is sufficient. (The Talmud teaches this lesson when it points out that the word בְּשַׁגַּם in our verse is "an allusion to Moses contained in the Torah" since its numerical value equals that of the word מֹשֶׁה; *Chullin* 139b.)

For God, a day lasts man's lifetime, 120 years. To be sure, this length of time can encompass a thousand years (*Psalms* 90:4) and the first generations had days of the latter sort. But just as days on earth can be shorter or longer depending on the season, so too the Divine day can be as short as 120 years, and even this figure is as approximate as considering daylight to last for exactly half of each day — often a part of these twelve hours is absorbed by the night. When man's life was shortened, his day became "short, and the task is great," as R' Tarfon taught (*Avos* 2:20). But even this reduced lifetime is enough for us to

"My spirit shall not contend evermore concerning Man since he is but flesh; his days shall be a hundred and twenty years."

⁴ The Nephilim were on the earth in those days — and also afterward when the sons of the rulers would consort with the daughters of man, who would bear to them. They were the mighty who, from old, were men of devastation.

⁵ HASHEM saw that the wickedness of Man was great upon the earth, and that every product of the thoughts of his

accomplish our task on earth, as *Rashi* points out in *Deuteronomy* (7:11) (אדיר במרום, י״א).

When the lifetime of 120 years of human existence reaches its own jubilee, after the cycle recurs fifty times, the world will enter its seventh millennium (*Avodah Zarah* 9a), the messianic era. Then, on a universal scale, the historical significance of the Jubilee Year will be realized. In the Torah's words: *And you shall sanctify the fiftieth year and proclaim freedom throughout the land for all its inhabitants* (*Leviticus* 25:10, cf. *R' Bachya* ibid.).

4. הַנְּפִלִים — *The Nephilim.* "From the verb נָפַל, *to fall.* They fell and caused humanity to fall" (*Rashi*). *Targum Yonasan* relates these giants to the "fallen angels" (שמחזאי ועוזיאל). *Yalkut Shimoni* (44) recounts that they descended from Heaven to prove to man that one could faithfully serve God even on earth. But then they themselves were corrupted by the "daughters of Adam" and from their cohabitation with them were born the mighty giants who were "of old the men of renown" such as Sihon and Og (*Niddah* 61a). וְגַם אַחֲרֵי כֵן, *and also afterward* — even after the Flood this race was perpetuated — since these two giants survived the Flood (ibid. נא תוספ׳ ד״ה נא). The school of R' Yishmael taught: On the Day of Atonement a scapegoat was offered to Azazel because evoking the angel of this name, who was unable to resist the temptation of sin, meant "expiation for the same sins committed by human beings" (*Yoma* 67b).

This verse is the source of numerous mythological stories about the fallen angels who corrupted the human race.

5. וַיַּרְא ה׳ — *HASHEM saw.* An anthropomorphism just as further on: *HASHEM reconsidered ... He had heartfelt sadness.* "People have for so long philosophized around these expressions in order to remove all thought of any corporeal form of God, that they have ultimately come to the danger of reducing even God's personality to an abstraction. Had this been the Torah's purpose, such expressions could easily have been avoided. But this latter danger is greater than the first. Indeed, these expressions safeguard two essential ideas: the free will of God and the free will of man. Not for nothing does it state *HASHEM saw,* etc. Man's depravity was not a matter of necessity. God had to see it before knowing it; hence this expression guarantees us that human liberty is a reality. And the fate that overtook mankind was not the result of a causality following from natural laws. Rather it was preceded by a Divine decision, a decision which

ו לִבּוֹ רַק רַע כָּל־הַיּוֹם: וַיִּנָּחֶם יהוה כִּי־עָשָׂה אֶת־הָאָדָם
ז בָּאָרֶץ וַיִּתְעַצֵּב אֶל־לִבּוֹ: וַיֹּאמֶר יהוה אֶמְחֶה אֶת־הָאָדָם
אֲשֶׁר־בָּרָאתִי מֵעַל פְּנֵי הָאֲדָמָה מֵאָדָם עַד־בְּהֵמָה עַד־
ח רֶמֶשׂ וְעַד־עוֹף הַשָּׁמָיִם כִּי נִחַמְתִּי כִּי עֲשִׂיתִם: וְנֹחַ מָצָא
חֵן בְּעֵינֵי יהוה:

pained the Decider. All this presupposes the personality of God as well as His
free will" (R' Hirsch). For Raavad, the awareness and consciousness of a
personal God is much more important than speculation on the Divine attributes
(הלכ' תשובה, פ"ג, ז'). R' Bachya and R' Yitzchak Arama also share this point of
view (עקידת יצחק, שער מ"ה).

וְכָל־יֵצֶר מַחְשְׁבֹת לִבּוֹ — Every product of the thoughts of his heart. In the Torah,
the heart is taken as the seat of thoughts. ("Lofty thoughts come from the heart,"
said Vauvenargues.) Hence, thoughts are often the "product" of an emotional
impulse, of a penchant or a passion (יֵצֶר) and not the outflow of a calm, pure
heart. "Every product of the thoughts" of the generation of the Flood was רַק רַע,
thoroughly bad. This word for bad is not the same as רָשָׁע (impious) and implies
sexual perversion, as in Genesis 38:7.

6. וַיִּתְעַצֵּב אֶל־לִבּוֹ — And He had heartfelt sadness. See Guide for the Perplexed
(1:29), where Rambam gives various interpretations. He also notes that God sent
no prophet to this unworthy generation but kept His affliction — and later His
mercy (8:21) — in His heart, until He revealed His inner thoughts to Moses.

R' Ami compares this with a king who conducts his affairs through a business
agent. If the king loses money, whom does he blame if not the agent? (Rabbah
26). So too, God ordered the earth to engender and sustain man. This mission
met with failure. Hence God felt resentment toward the earth. This is how to
understand our verse which does not have וַיִּתְעַצֵּב בְּלִבּוֹ (He was afflicted in His
heart) but אֶל־לִבּוֹ, toward his heart, concerning his heart. The words "His
heart" mean the earth, which holds the principal place in the works of creation.
The earth represents the treasure which God's love filled to the brim with
unheard-of richness and splendor. The earth is located at "the heart" of the
universe. This work is the object of God's joy (יִשְׂמַח ה' בְּמַעֲשָׂיו). He had given
it His heart; and in human terms He found He had to renounce the object of His
joy.

In this view, part of the responsibility for man's misdeeds is placed on the
earth, that is to say, on man's dependency on the earth. Thus, here the Torah
repeats the expression הָאָדָם בָּאָרֶץ, Man on earth (and not עַל הָאָרֶץ) on two
consecutive occasions. HASHEM saw that the wickedness of man was great upon
the earth ... And HASHEM reconsidered having made Man on earth. This sign
of indulgent clemency justifies the use of the Tetragrammaton (signifying pity)
in the verses announcing man's punishment, although subsequently, when

heart was but evil always. ⁶ And HASHEM *reconsidered having made Man on earth, and He had heartfelt sadness. ⁷ And* HASHEM *said, "I will blot out Man whom I created from the face of the ground — from man to animal, to creeping things, and to birds of the sky; for I have reconsidered My having made them." ⁸ But Noah found grace in the eyes of* HASHEM.

implacable justice will prevail, this name is replaced by אֱלֹהִים emphasizing the מִדַּת הַדִּין.

7. אֶמְחֶה אֶת־הָאָדָם — *I will blot out Man.* According to *Yalkut Shimoni,* this means total destruction, not only death and putrefaction but even the complete disappearance of the skeletons, including those parts of the body which our Sages tell us never rot. It is not surprising that so few vestiges of antediluvian human life have been discovered. In any case, passions influence the rate of decay, as our Sages have pointed out (*Shabbos* 152b), and this could have been a factor with a generation as perverse as the one at the time of the Flood.

מֵאָדָם עַד־בְּהֵמָה — *From man to animal.* Even at his destruction, man's greatness manifests itself in that his end brings along with it that of every living creature. The earth is exempt from the decree, but its surface, פְּנֵי הָאֲדָמָה, belongs to man's domain. Man is bound to objects not only physically but also in a moral, spiritual way. If man falls, the earth itself withers and is in mourning. The whole Bible is permeated with the idea of the organic unity of living creatures, encompassing men and animals.

8. וְנֹחַ מָצָא חֵן בְּעֵינֵי ה' — *But Noah found grace in the eyes of* HASHEM. This expression indicates the particular affection and esteem which God accords to an individual or to a people (as Israel: מָצָא חֵן בַּמִּדְבָּר). When God fulfilled Moses' dearest desire, He did so because Moses had found favor in His eyes (כִּי מָצָאתָ חֵן בְּעֵינַי; *Exodus* 33:17). This distinction is reserved for those who are the most deserving of God's friendship, even if there is not always a rational explanation for this, as R' Meir emphasizes (*Berachos* 7a).

Thus, with humanity on the verge of destruction, God concentrates His love on one man and on one family. On them He builds the future of the entire universe. One righteous being is capable, by himself, of saving all of humanity: וְצַדִּיק יְסוֹד עוֹלָם, *the righteous person is the foundation of the world* (*Proverbs* 10:25).

Ultimately, confidence in mankind wins out over bitter disappointment, indeed, over the failure of the creation of man. The *sidrah* of *Bereishis* began with the creation of the universe, an act inspired by infinite confidence in human nature, and it ends again on a note of confidence and optimism despite the most cruel failures. Even as the cataclysm is being prepared, we see hope reborn on the horizon. Once again, "the cure for the illness precedes the illness itself."

ט אֵלֶּה תּוֹלְדֹת נֹחַ נֹחַ אִישׁ צַדִּיק תָּמִים הָיָה בְּדֹרֹתָיו
י אֶת־הָאֱלֹהִים הִתְהַלֶּךְ־נֹחַ: וַיּוֹלֶד נֹחַ שְׁלֹשָׁה בָנִים אֶת־שֵׁם

9. אֵלֶּה תּוֹלְדֹת נֹחַ — *These are the offspring of Noah.* Just as the words אֵלֶּה
תוֹלְדוֹת הַשָּׁמַיִם וְהָאָרֶץ at the start of Chapter 2 announced a new development,
here, too, the words אֵלֶּה תּוֹלְדֹת נֹחַ open a new chapter in human history.
Mankind moves toward its destruction. Noah will be a second Adam. He will
become the ancestor of a new generation of human beings.

נֹחַ אִישׁ צַדִּיק — *Noah was a righteous man.* Later, he is called אִישׁ הָאֲדָמָה, *the*
man of the earth (9:20). Such a double characterization is also found for Joseph,
notes the *Zohar.* He too is called צַדִּיק (*Amos* 2:6) and also הוּא הַשַּׁלִּיט עַל הָאָרֶץ
— landlord and overseer for food (42:6). The word צַדִּיק refers to a righteous
person who retains his moral purity despite the many temptations which he
must face. Such was Noah amidst the depravity and perversion of his time. Such
was Joseph in the face of Potiphar's wife's attempts to seduce him. Now, as has
been noted on many occasions, the sphere of holiness attained by man through
his level of piety is the source of all material blessing. Thus קָדוֹשׁ וּבָרוּךְ are
correlatives wherever they appear. In this light one can understand that the
righteous, who have attained a high degree of holiness, are also the ones who
dispense the blessings of the earth to their fellowmen. So with Noah after the
Flood. He became an אִישׁ הָאֲדָמָה, that is, בַּעַל הָאֲדָמָה — the master of the earth
and dispenser of all its richness (*Zohar*). The righteous and holy Joseph fulfilled
the same function in Egypt. It was through their holiness that they became the
benefactors of their times.

צַדִּיק תָּמִים — *Righteous ... perfect.* For *Ramban* these words have a restrictive
meaning. The "perfectly righteous" is he who strictly obeys the imperatives of
complete justice (תָּמִים in his view modifies צַדִּיק, whereas for *Ibn Ezra* it modifies
אִישׁ). But Abraham surpassed Noah. To the ideal of justice, he added those of
charity and clemency (צְדָקָה וּמִשְׁפָּט), as the Torah indicates (*Genesis* 18:19).

בְּדֹרֹתָיו — *In his generations.* Those preceding and following the Flood. Is this
phrase meant to qualify and restrict the praise for Noah? Our Sages discuss this
and *Rashi* reports both sides, one favorable to Noah, in which he is righteous
even in an age of depravity, and one unfavorable: Noah is righteous but only
in the context of his immoral generation. Both of these views may be valid. The
battle Noah had to wage might leave some marks on one's strength of character.
But moral and irreproachable behavior in such an age carries more weight on the
Divine scales than even more perfect conduct in a better moral environment.
The words *Noah walked with God,* which complete the description of Noah in
this verse, can also be construed as being slightly critical. *Rashi* explains: "To
Abraham it is said: *Walk before Me* (17:1), whereas Noah had to walk *with* God,
needing His support. Abraham was strong enough in his righteousness to walk
alone, *before* God."

⁹ These are the offspring of Noah — Noah was a righteous
man, perfect in his generations; Noah walked with God. —
¹⁰ Noah had begotten three sons: Shem, Ham, and Japheth.

Why did Noah, so praised by the Torah and the inaugurator of a new world,
not become an Abraham? Why was he not able to be the great prophet for
monotheism at the time when humanity was reborn? This question is posed by
our Sages. What we have already observed supplies part of the answer to it. But
our Sages add that Noah was unable to fight vigorously enough against the
immorality of his age. He was unable to convince his fellowmen as Abraham
could. He did not intercede on their behalf before God, as Abraham did for the
people of Sodom. He accepted rescue from death for just himself and his family,
in contrast to Moses, who immediately cried out, when God threatened Israel
with destruction and offered to make him alone into a great nation: "Oh, forgive
their sin! And if not, blot me out of Your book which You have written"
(Exodus 32:32). Moses did not want to outlive his people under any
circumstances; he preferred to share their fate (Midrash and Zohar). In short,
then, Noah was the man who closed himself up inside in his "Ark," remaining
righteous for himself and his family, leaving the others to their fate.

To be sure, reply those of our Sages who judge Noah favorably, all
throughout the 120 years of building the Ark Noah did not relent from
reproving, warning, and explaining what was at stake to his contemporaries
(Rashi, verse 14) in order to bring about their repentance. He was unafraid of
their sarcasm, their ridicule, their threats and insults. Nevertheless, he kept a
certain distance from them, feeling that it would be better not to risk coming
under their influence over his own loyalty to God. He went so far as to abstain
from having a family until 500 years of age, whereas all his ancestors and
contemporaries had families much earlier. He was afraid to raise a family in so
corrupt a society. He feared that he would not be able to give them a wholesome
upbringing. Not until twenty years after the destruction was proclaimed, only
after 500 years of "walking with God," alone and solitary, did Noah have the
courage to become a father, after God had given him to understand that the
perpetuation of the human race would devolve upon him (Rashi ibid.).

Thus, whatever criticism Noah was subjected to, the Torah honors him with
the title צַדִּיק and approves of his conduct. It was Noah who, in the face of the
worst catastrophe which man has known, was found worthy to save the human
race. Noah has been criticized for not imploring God to save his generation as
Abraham did for Sodom's inhabitants, but Noah finds justification in that in his
time ten righteous people could not be found. Noah and his family, who
survived in the Ark, numbered only eight. Just like Abraham, Noah knew that
in such a case at least ten righteous people had to be found (cf. Ohr HaChaim,
who gives still other reasons to justify Noah).

10. אֶת־שֵׁם אֶת־חָם וְאֶת־יָפֶת — Shem, Ham, and Japheth. Three sons whose

יא אֶת־חָם וְאֶת־יָפֶת: וַתִּשָּׁחֵת הָאָרֶץ לִפְנֵי הָאֱלֹהִים וַתִּמָּלֵא
יב הָאָרֶץ חָמָס: וַיַּרְא אֱלֹהִים אֶת־הָאָרֶץ וְהִנֵּה נִשְׁחָתָה
יג כִּי־הִשְׁחִית כָּל־בָּשָׂר אֶת־דַּרְכּוֹ עַל־הָאָרֶץ: וַיֹּאמֶר
אֱלֹהִים לְנֹחַ קֵץ כָּל־בָּשָׂר בָּא לְפָנַי כִּי־מָלְאָה הָאָרֶץ
יד חָמָס מִפְּנֵיהֶם וְהִנְנִי מַשְׁחִיתָם אֶת־הָאָרֶץ: עֲשֵׂה לְךָ
תֵּבַת עֲצֵי־גֹפֶר קִנִּים תַּעֲשֶׂה אֶת־הַתֵּבָה וְכָפַרְתָּ אֹתָהּ
טו מִבַּיִת וּמִחוּץ בַּכֹּפֶר: וְזֶה אֲשֶׁר תַּעֲשֶׂה אֹתָהּ שְׁלֹשׁ

differences in character will show up throughout their lives and will leave a profound mark on their descendants. This fact can be a source of great comfort to us. Completely different though the various races of man appear, these differences existed even before the Flood and indeed were preserved by God for the future. This proves that they were part of the Divine plan, which is to realize the ultimate goal of history despite these differences in nationalities. Shem represents the spiritual man, Ham incarnates the races given to sensual passion, and Japheth is the father of peoples interested in the fine arts. All three were saved in the Ark and all three, together, then constituted the basis for populating the world once again (R' *S.R. Hirsch*).

Japheth was the eldest. "But Shem is mentioned first because he was righteous, born circumcised, and became the ancestor of Abraham" (*Rashi* to 5:32). "The third son," says R' Yehoshua, "is always cherished: Seth, son of Adam; Shem, son of Noah; Levi, son of Jacob; Moses, son of Amram ..." (*Tanchuma Yisro*).

11. וַתִּשָּׁחֵת הָאָרֶץ לִפְנֵי הָאֱלֹהִים וַתִּמָּלֵא הָאָרֶץ חָמָס — *Now the earth had become corrupt before God; and the earth had become filled with robbery.* At several points the Torah notes that moral corruption reigned. One might think that even if the youth were debauched, and marriages immoral, still, commerce and civic life in general would remain unaffected. However, when the corruption on earth is flaunted before God, no human institution can save the society from its ruin. Indeed, a society will never fall because of גֵּזֶל, open robbery, for it knows how to protect itself against such crimes, by prisons and penalties. But it is חָמָס which leads society to its destruction. This word means a crime committed through cunning or malice, a crime which human justice has not the means to pursue, a crime which only the voice of conscience could prevent. When this voice is smothered in a society wallowing in immorality, then nothing can avert the catastrophe.

13. קֵץ כָּל־בָּשָׂר — *The end of all flesh.* "Wherever you find debauchery and idolatry, a general destruction takes place which does not differentiate between the guilty and the innocent" (*Rashi*). Nonetheless, Noah was spared. A צַדִּיק גָּמוּר, a "perfectly righteous" person, remains invulnerable even at a time when "the angel of death receives the power to strike and no longer differentiates between the righteous and the sinful" (ע"ז ד' ע"א, מהרש"א ד"ה חלילה). But even

¹¹ *Now the earth had become corrupt before God; and the earth had become filled with robbery.* ¹² *And God saw the earth and behold it was corrupted, for all flesh had corrupted its way upon the earth.*

¹³ *God said to Noah, "The end of all flesh has come before Me, for the earth is filled with robbery through them; and behold, I am about to destroy them from the earth.* ¹⁴ *Make for yourself an Ark of gopher wood; make the Ark with compartments, and cover it inside and out with pitch.* ¹⁵ *This is how you should make — three*

he must not defy the angel of death. He should not expose himself to the danger but had best take refuge in his home, just as the Jews did in Egypt on the night when the firstborn of the Egyptians perished (*Exodus* 12:22). That is why God shut Noah in the Ark.

וְהִנְנִי מַשְׁחִיתָם אֶת־הָאָרֶץ — *And behold, I am about to destroy them from the earth.* *Rashi* comments: Even the three handsbreadth of the earth's surface which the plough turns were penetrated and washed away. The Midrash likens this to a prince who had a nurse. Whenever he behaved immorally, the nurse was punished. Likewise, the earth is punished when man is corrupt.

To a depth of three handsbreadth, the earth is called אֶרֶץ; deeper than this it is named אֲדָמָה. So says the *Sifsei Chachamim*, quoting *Maharshal*. Another definition is given by the author of the *Ohr HaChaim* (*Numbers* 16:31) and by *Malbim* (*Exodus* 20:21): אֲדָמָה applies to the surface and אֶרֶץ to the deeper layers of the earth. Be that as it may, the fact that the earth was itself affected and washed away by the Flood explains why its productivity lessened and has remained so to this day.

14. עֲשֵׂה לְךָ תֵּבַת עֲצֵי־גֹפֶר — *Make for yourself an Ark of gopher wood.* Only twice does the word תֵּבָה appear in the Torah: here and in *Exodus* 2:3, to designate the wicker basket which protected Moses and kept him from drowning in the Nile. In both cases, the תֵּבָה plays the same role; it saves a redeemer from death: the redeemer of humanity and the redeemer of the chosen people. In both cases it serves as a prefiguration of "the Ark of the Covenant" (אֲרוֹן הַבְּרִית), which contained the treasure of humanity. In one case it was Moses, the future prophet of the covenant with Jewry, who was protected; in the other Noah, to whom God promised the covenant with mankind just as he entered the Ark, as it is written: *But I will establish My covenant with you, and you shall enter the Ark* (verse 18). Thus, the sacred Ark has remained for Jewry the symbol of their salvation and the salvation of all mankind.

15. וְזֶה אֲשֶׁר תַּעֲשֶׂה אֹתָהּ — *This is how you should make it.* These words are found in just one other context: regarding the sacrifices for the Altar of the Tabernacle (*Exodus* 29:38). The *Baal HaTurim* says this is a hint to Noah to build an altar on leaving the Ark. That God prescribed the exact measurements to which the Ark was to be built, as He did also only for the Altar of the

מֵאוֹת אַמָּה אֹרֶךְ הַתֵּבָה חֲמִשִּׁים אַמָּה רָחְבָּהּ וּשְׁלֹשִׁים
אַמָּה קוֹמָתָהּ: צֹהַר l תַּעֲשֶׂה לַתֵּבָה וְאֶל־אַמָּה תְּכַלֶּנָּה
מִלְמַעְלָה וּפֶתַח הַתֵּבָה בְּצִדָּהּ תָּשִׂים תַּחְתִּיִּם שְׁנִיִּם
וּשְׁלִשִׁים תַּעֲשֶׂהָ: וַאֲנִי הִנְנִי מֵבִיא אֶת־הַמַּבּוּל מַיִם
עַל־הָאָרֶץ לְשַׁחֵת כָּל־בָּשָׂר אֲשֶׁר־בּוֹ רוּחַ חַיִּים מִתַּחַת
הַשָּׁמָיִם כֹּל אֲשֶׁר־בָּאָרֶץ יִגְוָע: וַהֲקִמֹתִי אֶת־בְּרִיתִי
אִתָּךְ וּבָאתָ אֶל־הַתֵּבָה אַתָּה וּבָנֶיךָ וְאִשְׁתְּךָ וּנְשֵׁי־בָנֶיךָ

Tabernacle, suggests an analogy between Ark and Altar. Just as the latter confers holiness on sacrifices offered to God and consumed on its brazier, so, too, the Ark will rise in sanctity above the waves and, symbolizing humanity's altar, will offer the homage of innumerable sacrifices to God (cf. verse 18).

שְׁלֹשׁ מֵאוֹת אַמָּה אֹרֶךְ הַתֵּבָה — *Three hundred cubits the length of the Ark.* "The Torah teaches that the width of a boat should be one-sixth its length, and its height one-tenth its length" (Midrash). The Ark measured about 500 feet long, over 80 feet wide, and about 50 feet high. How could an ark of this size contain thousands of animals? And among them, species of gigantic size such as the monster Re'em which surely could not have been confined on one of the three decks? (*Zevachim* 11b). *Ramban* replies that only a miracle can explain this, but although God could well have chosen other ways to save Noah's family and the animals, He wanted to reduce His supernatural intervention to a minimum and, to this end, He ordered the construction of an ark of impressive size. Because, for "every miracle which the Torah and the Prophets recount, man must do what is in his power to do, while the rest remains in God's hands."

16. צֹהַר תַּעֲשֶׂה לַתֵּבָה — *A window shall you make for the Ark.* צֹהַר is related to זֹהַר (brightness, splendor) and סֹהַר (prison), as in *Genesis* 39:20. The believer can find himself enclosed in an ark in the midst of a catastrophe; yet brightness still shines within him thanks to his faith and unwavering confidence in God. Such was Joseph, who was "put into the prison in which the king's prisoners were imprisoned: וַיְהִי שָׁם בְּבֵית הַסֹּהַר, and he was there in a luminous place."

Rashi reports two meanings for צֹהַר: for some it means a window; for others, a precious stone, radiating light. The fact that *Rashi* quotes both opinions implies that he recognized both as valid and complementary. Indeed, when large-scale disaster is imminent, a righteous person such as Noah does not stop at enjoying the light which glows in his home with his family. Instead, he makes a window to look out at the world, to realize what is going on around him so as to be ready to help as much as he can when the time comes.

תַּחְתִּיִּם שְׁנִיִּם וּשְׁלִשִׁים — *Bottom, second, and third decks.* The *Zohar* applies this verse from *Proverbs* to the Ark: "The name of God [protects like] a strong tower, to which the righteous runs and is placed in safety" (18:10).

hundred cubits the length of the Ark; fifty cubits its width; and thirty cubits its height. [16] *A window shall you make for the Ark, and to a cubit finish it from above. Put the entrance of the Ark in its side; make it with bottom, second, and third decks.*

[17] *"And as for Me — Behold, I am about to bring the Flood-waters upon the earth to destroy all flesh in which there is a breath of life from under the heavens; everything that is in the earth shall expire.* [18] *But I will establish My covenant with you, and you shall enter the Ark — you, your sons, your wife, and your sons' wives*

Indeed, the Ark harboring its inhabitants under God's sign resembled a strong tower. It was composed of three stories: the top one, where people dwelt; the middle one for the animals; and the lowest one for refuse (*Rashi*). In his book ח״ב, שׁל״ה, ס׳, R' Isaiah Horowitz describes the rich lessons which Noah was to draw from this gradual ascent from the earthly spheres in order to merit Divine protection.

17. וַאֲנִי הִנְנִי מֵבִיא — *And as for Me — Behold, I am about to bring.* וַאֲנִי הִנְנִי is an emphatic expression meaning "with joy" (*Rashi* to Numbers 18:8). Also implied is a certain eagerness: "I am now ready to agree with those who have long urged Me with the words: 'What is man, that You are mindful of him?'" (*Rashi*). After the affliction which made Him sorrowfully change His initial plans (6:6), God decided to have done with this world in order to build a better one on its ruins. This is the reason for His readiness and haste.

18. אֶת־בְּרִיתִי — *My covenant.* בְּרִית does not mean a pact based on mutual agreement, but frequently refers to a solemn promise whose validity is confirmed. Hence here, just after announcing the Flood, God reaffirms the permanent validity of the covenant made with man when the world began, which is included in the blessing: *Be fruitful and multiply and fill the land, etc.* Henceforth, this covenant will be carried on by Noah and his family. "Never has a covenant, a *bris*, been more necessary than this one with Noah. The boards of the Ark surely were not the actual means of salvation, otherwise others could also have saved themselves in this way. The Ark was only Noah's indispensable contribution to his own rescue, but the real salvation and survival required the quite special protection of Divine Providence" (*R' S.R. Hirsch*).

אַתָּה וּבָנֶיךָ וְאִשְׁתְּךָ וּנְשֵׁי־בָנֶיךָ אִתָּךְ — *You, your sons, your wife, and your sons' wives with you.* "Men and women separated. We learn from this that sexual relations were forbidden" (*Rashi*) until the Flood was over, out of respect for the dead, out of solidarity with mankind's suffering and grief, out of a desire to preserve the holy atmosphere within the Ark, a symbol of the sanctuary and the Altar (cf. our commentary to verse 15). The three creatures who trespassed this interdiction were severely punished: Noah's son Ham, the raven, and the dog (*Sanhedrin* 108b). The law is still that one should abstain from sexual relations

יט אִתָּךְ: וּמִכָּל־הָחַי מִכָּל־בָּשָׂר שְׁנַיִם מִכָּל תָּבִיא אֶל־הַתֵּבָה

כ לְהַחֲיֹת אִתָּךְ זָכָר וּנְקֵבָה יִהְיוּ: מֵהָעוֹף לְמִינֵהוּ וּמִן־

הַבְּהֵמָה לְמִינָהּ מִכֹּל רֶמֶשׂ הָאֲדָמָה לְמִינֵהוּ שְׁנַיִם מִכֹּל

כא יָבֹאוּ אֵלֶיךָ לְהַחֲיוֹת: וְאַתָּה קַח־לְךָ מִכָּל־מַאֲכָל אֲשֶׁר

כב יֵאָכֵל וְאָסַפְתָּ אֵלֶיךָ וְהָיָה לְךָ וְלָהֶם לְאָכְלָה: וַיַּעַשׂ נֹחַ

ז א כְּכֹל אֲשֶׁר צִוָּה אֹתוֹ אֱלֹהִים כֵּן עָשָׂה: וַיֹּאמֶר יהוה לְנֹחַ

בֹּא־אַתָּה וְכָל־בֵּיתְךָ אֶל־הַתֵּבָה כִּי־אֹתְךָ רָאִיתִי צַדִּיק לְפָנַי

ב בַּדּוֹר הַזֶּה: מִכֹּל | הַבְּהֵמָה הַטְּהוֹרָה תִּקַּח־לְךָ שִׁבְעָה

שִׁבְעָה אִישׁ וְאִשְׁתּוֹ וּמִן־הַבְּהֵמָה אֲשֶׁר לֹא טְהֹרָה הִוא

in times of famine or widespread calamity, as is stated in the *Shulchan Aruch, Orach Chaim* §240:12. Cf. our commentary to 4:24.

19. וּמִכָּל־הָחַי — *And from all that lives.* "Even demons" (*Rashi*). The Midrash (*Rabbah* 32) adds: The demon of falsehood came to Noah to enter the Ark. Noah told him, "Find yourself a companion. Only pairs can enter here." He left to do so and found the demon of thievery and said, "I want to enter the Ark but I need a companion; will you come with me?" Thievery replied: "What will you give me if I do?" Falsehood then promised to give up anything he would acquire and, side by side, they entered the Ark. Since then, as the proverb has it, "Whatever is sown by falsehood is reaped by thievery."

20. מֵהָעוֹף לְמִינֵהוּ — *From each bird according to its kind.* The three categories (fowl, quadrupeds, reptiles) are listed in order of greatest number of pure animals in each species. Fowl, first in the list, includes the greatest number of pure specimens (*Chullin* 63b).

22. וַיַּעַשׂ נֹחַ כְּכֹל אֲשֶׁר צִוָּה אֹתוֹ אֱלֹהִים — *Noah did according to everything God commanded him.* This, notes *Rashi*, refers to building the Ark. Similar words occur in 7:5, but there the reference is to entering the Ark. Despite death-threats from his fellowmen during the 120 years needed to build the Ark, despite the apparently insoluble problems of lodging and feeding the thousands of animals — and our Sages stress the innumerable difficulties involved (*Rabbah* 31; cf. *Ibn Ezra*) — Noah carried out his orders in every detail.

7.

1. וַיֹּאמֶר ה' לְנֹחַ — *Then HASHEM said to Noah.* The Divine name אֱלֹהִים had been used since the beginning of this *sidrah.* Now it is replaced throughout chapter 7 by the Tetragrammaton שֵׁם הֲוָיָ'. Previously God acted primarily through His aspect of justice; now He appears as the God of love who readies a new world for the future. Moreover, *Ramban* observes that this is also the chapter which contains the first preparations for the sacrifice which Noah will offer to God on leaving the Ark, as brought out by *Rashi* on verse 2. It is after this offering that God will pledge: "Never again shall there be a flood to destroy the earth." The

with you. ¹⁹ *And from all that lives, of all flesh, two of each shall you bring into the Ark to keep alive with you; they shall be male and female.* ²⁰ *From each bird according to its kind, and from each animal according to its kind, and from each thing that creeps on the ground according to its kind, two of each shall come to you to keep alive.*

²¹ *And as for you, take yourself of every food that is eaten and gather it in to yourself, that it shall be as food for you and for them.''* ²² *Noah did according to everything God commanded him, so he did.*

7 ¹ *Then HASHEM said to Noah, ''Come to the Ark, you and all your household, for it is you that I have seen to be righteous before Me in this generation.* ² *Of every clean animal take unto you seven pairs, a male with its mate, and of the animal that is not clean,*

Tetragrammaton is always used with respect to sacrifices since it always refers exclusively to God. The name אֱלֹהִים, on the other hand, can refer on occasion to judges, strange gods, etc. (*Kuzari* 4:1). Thus, whenever sacrifices are referred to, the Torah uses the name הֲוָיָ' for God in order to unequivocally consecrate the sacrifices not to any intermediary but to God alone (cf. *Ramban, Leviticus* 1:9).

2. מִכֹּל הַבְּהֵמָה הַטְּהוֹרָה — *Of every clean animal.* It was said about the animals in general: *They shall come to you,* but here, for the pure animals, it is written: *take unto you.* Pure animals are mentioned here for the first time. Despite the fact that animals were not yet permitted as food for man and although the difference between pure and impure animals was to come later with the promulgation of the Torah at Sinai, nevertheless Noah selected the animals meeting the criteria for purity. This was necessary, even so long ago, because of the coming sacrifices — Noahides had and have the right to offer animals for sacrifice, but only pure ones (*Zevachim* 115a). It follows that Jews must eat only that which may be offered in sacrifice by any human being. The table of the Jew is at the same level as the altar of the Noahides (*R' Hirsch*). The criteria for pure and impure animals will be given in *Leviticus* 11.

שִׁבְעָה שִׁבְעָה אִישׁ וְאִשְׁתּוֹ — *Seven pairs, a male with its mate.* The Torah attaches great importance to the number seven, but there are differing opinions as to why it does so. For *Ibn Ezra* (*Numbers* 23:1) seven represents perfection since it is the only number completely independent of the decimal system. Indeed, it is the only number which is neither a product nor a factor of the other numbers up to ten. *Rambam* notes that the number seven specifies the weekly cycle, instituted by God at creation, and placed between the daily (solar) cycle of twenty-four hours and the monthly (lunar) cycle of twenty-eight days (quoted by *R' Bachya*). In the *Zohar,* the number seven is made up of all the emanating spheres of the earthly world. These spheres encompass the elements of the

ג שְׁנַיִם אִישׁ וְאִשְׁתּוֹ: גַּם מֵעוֹף הַשָּׁמַיִם שִׁבְעָה שִׁבְעָה זָכָר
ד וּנְקֵבָה לְחַיּוֹת זֶרַע עַל־פְּנֵי כָל־הָאָרֶץ: כִּי לְיָמִים עוֹד שִׁבְעָה
אָנֹכִי מַמְטִיר עַל־הָאָרֶץ אַרְבָּעִים יוֹם וְאַרְבָּעִים לָיְלָה
וּמָחִיתִי אֶת־כָּל־הַיְקוּם אֲשֶׁר עָשִׂיתִי מֵעַל פְּנֵי הָאֲדָמָה:

moral, physical and historical domains, going from love (חֶסֶד) to kingship (מַלְכוּת), and through their interaction they guarantee universal harmony. The number seven has a holy character because in it resides the mystery of the Divine order of nature. *R' S.R. Hirsch* demonstrates that the number six is the sign of the visible world, created in six days, whereas seven is that of its completion by the covenant with God (*Collected Works* III:305). Developing ideas from the old סֵפֶר הַיְצִירָה, which is traditionally ascribed to the patriarch Abraham or to *R' Akiva, R' Yehudah HaLevi* teaches that the basic factors in both cosmological and psychological orders constitute a hexagon. The seventh factor is the universal spirit which crowns it (*Kuzari* 4:25). *R' Isaiah Horowitz* develops the same idea (של"ה, מסכת חולין). This factor is, then, the source of blessings, the radiating center which sends out the vital forces to reach the elements around it. Although the seventh to be created, this factor is nonetheless the "first in thought," that is to say, in the initial plan it was the starting point (cf. *Maharal, Tiferes Yisrael* 40).

3. מֵעוֹף הַשָּׁמַיִם — *Of the birds of the heavens. Rashi* explains that this refers only to the pure birds (which will also later serve as a sacrifice) although the Torah does not specifically use the word "pure" here as it did for the animals. According to *Chizkuni*, when the Talmud reports (*Zevachim* 116a) that Noah recognized the pure species by whether the Ark accepted them or rejected them (cf. *Rashi* 6:20), it is referring only to species of birds, not to the quadrupeds. Noah was able to tell which quadrupeds were pure because "he had studied Torah," that is, he had knowledge of its laws. In his commentary חִידּוּשֵׁי אַגָּדוֹת (ibid.), *R' S. Edels* contests this distinction between fowl and animals but *R' Moshe Sofer* upholds and justifies it (*Toras Moshe*). Be that as it may, the seven pairs of pure species were necessary not to perpetuate the race but "so that Noah could offer some of them as sacrifices when he came out of the Ark" (*Rashi*). And if the Torah uses the expression לְחַיּוֹת זֶרַע here, it is meant to be taken figuratively: it is thanks to the sacrifices offered on leaving the Ark that God promised to restore life on earth (*Ramban* to 8:1).

4. כִּי לְיָמִים עוֹד שִׁבְעָה — *For in seven more days time. Rashi* explains: These were the seven days of mourning for Methuselah the righteous. For his sake, God delayed the punishment for the world. If you count Methuselah's years, you will find that he died when Noah was 600 years old. The seven-day postponement was to bring people to repent when they realized the loss of the righteous person who had just died. The significance of his death was brought home to them in eulogies. This explanation is amplified by the Talmud when

two, a male with its mate; ³ *of the birds of the heavens also, seven pairs, male and female, to keep seed alive upon the face of all the earth.* ⁴ *For in seven more days time I will send rain upon the earth, forty days and forty nights, and I will blot out all existence that I have made from upon the face of the ground."*

it states that "the seven days were a last stay of execution granted to this perverted generation after the reprieve of 120 years in order to give them yet another, but this time final, chance to repent (*Sanhedrin* 108a). From a psychological point of view, one can understand that the repeated warnings over a span of 120 years finally lost their influence, and what was needed was a last appeal for repentance. During those seven days, the memory of Methuselah's exemplary life should have made the people reflect; furthermore, the sight of the animals thronging into the Ark was a supreme warning to them of the imminent catastrophe.

R' Zeira explains the week of mourning preceding the Flood in a more general way (*Yerushalmi, Moed Katan* 3:5). After expressing deep hurt (6:6), God Himself set aside a week of mourning, just before the cataclysm began. Similarly, He commanded Aaron and his sons to observe the "seven days" (שִׁבְעָה) before death came to his other two sons Nadab and Abihu. But the sense of what is prescribed here comes clearly from the text itself: *And at the door of the tent of meeting shall you abide day and night seven days, and keep the charge of God that you not die (Leviticus 8:35).*

From these thoughts, it seems that the week of mourning was originally meant to be a week of reflection, of meditation. It was meant to give people who had long before deserved to die (as was the case with the generation of the Flood and with Aaron's two sons — cf. *Rashi* on *Exodus* 24:11) a last chance to receive God's pardon through prayer and repentance. This was also King David's attitude: when his son was ill, he fasted and besought God; but when, on the seventh day, his son died, he *arose, washed and anointed himself, and changed his garments and asked that they should set food before him.* And he answered his astonished servants: *While the child was yet alive, I fasted and wept; because I thought: Who knows, but that God will be gracious to me, that the child may live? But now that he is dead, why should I fast? Can I restore him?* (*II Samuel* 12:22). Cf. *Midrash Tanchuma* פ׳ שמיני, beginning, and our commentary to 50:10.

אַרְבָּעִים יוֹם וְאַרְבָּעִים לָיְלָה — *Forty days and forty nights.* Rashi observes that this is "corresponding to the forty days of formation of the fetus, because their misbehavior obliged their Creator to create children from illegitimate unions." The forty-day period means that the catastrophe was destined to lead to a rebirth of mankind — a completely new generation had to be formed. Because of the forty days needed to "form the fetus," the ethical formation, the moral coming-of-age for man, is also connected with the number forty. The

ה־י וַיַּעַשׂ נֹחַ כְּכֹל אֲשֶׁר־צִוָּהוּ יהוה: וְנֹחַ בֶּן־שֵׁשׁ מֵאוֹת שָׁנָה
ז וְהַמַּבּוּל הָיָה מַיִם עַל־הָאָרֶץ: וַיָּבֹא נֹחַ וּבָנָיו וְאִשְׁתּוֹ
ח וּנְשֵׁי־בָנָיו אִתּוֹ אֶל־הַתֵּבָה מִפְּנֵי מֵי הַמַּבּוּל: מִן־
הַבְּהֵמָה הַטְּהוֹרָה וּמִן־הַבְּהֵמָה אֲשֶׁר אֵינֶנָּה טְהֹרָה וּמִן־
ט הָעוֹף וְכֹל אֲשֶׁר־רֹמֵשׂ עַל־הָאֲדָמָה: שְׁנַיִם שְׁנַיִם בָּאוּ
אֶל־נֹחַ אֶל־הַתֵּבָה זָכָר וּנְקֵבָה כַּאֲשֶׁר צִוָּה אֱלֹהִים אֶת־
י נֹחַ: וַיְהִי לְשִׁבְעַת הַיָּמִים וּמֵי הַמַּבּוּל הָיוּ עַל־הָאָרֶץ:

punishment inflicted in order to expiate a sin and to put a fallen man back on his feet consists of forty lashes. Ritual purification is attained through immersion in a *mikveh* containing forty measures of natural water. Jewry's "upbringing" in the desert lasted forty years. Moses was raised into the ideal of the Torah during the forty days he stayed on Mount Sinai (*Recanati*).

וּמָחִיתִי אֶת־כָּל־הַיְקוּם — *And I will blot out all existence.* R' Shimon notes the exceptional use of the word אָנֹכִי here. It refers to God in His omnipotence and brings to mind the great, solemn אָנֹכִי heard at Sinai — אָנֹכִי ה' אֱלֹהֶיךָ.

The destruction of the world by the blotting out of every being is but the consequence of the defiance shown by men to the universal moral law proclaimed on Mount Sinai. It is just because of this אָנֹכִי, the first word of the moral law, that the world cannot survive (מכילתא דרשב"י, יתרו כ' ב').

5. וַיַּעַשׂ נֹחַ כְּכֹל אֲשֶׁר־צִוָּהוּ ה' — *And Noah did according to everything that HASHEM had commanded him.* The frequent repetition of this phrase draws our attention to the fact that Noah did not follow his own plans nor his own impulses in order to save himself and his family. He did only what God commanded; but this he did completely, placing his confidence in God. Often in recounting the obedience of the righteous, the Torah says: he did what God commanded him. It does so to remind us of an important principle: גָּדוֹל הַמְצֻוֶּה וְעוֹשֶׂה מִמִּי שֶׁאֵינוֹ מְצֻוֶּה וְעוֹשֶׂה — greater is he who is commanded and acts accordingly than he who acts on his own initiative." Contrary to widely-held opinion, the greatest value is placed on an act carried out to accomplish God's will, whereas a deed done from personal motives has only a subjective value. Accordingly, each time we carry out a moral or religious act we stress that we are accomplishing God's will: אֲשֶׁר קִדְּשָׁנוּ בְּמִצְוֹתָיו וְצִוָּנוּ.

6. וְנֹחַ בֶּן־שֵׁשׁ מֵאוֹת שָׁנָה — *Noah was six hundred years old.* Just as the sixtieth year marks the "age of wisdom" (שנא' בישישים חכמה, cf. *Avos* 5:21; *Tosafos*) for the generations following the Flood, so did the 600th year have the same significance for antediluvian generations. Noah had to acquire the crown of wisdom, כֶּתֶר חָכְמָה, which took 600 years, before God could call him a צַדִּיק תָּמִים, worthy of carrying on the unbroken chain of humanity. Toward the 600th year of the sixth millennium, adds the *Zohar*, "the Floodgates of heaven will open," unleashing a Flood of new knowledge which will permit man to

⁵ *And Noah did according to everything that HASHEM had commanded him.*

⁶ *Noah was six hundred years old when the Flood was water upon the earth.* ⁷ *Noah, with his sons, his wife, and his sons' wives with him, went into the Ark because of the waters of the Flood.* ⁸ *Of the clean animal, of the animal that is not clean, of the birds, and of each thing that creeps upon the ground,* ⁹ *two by two they came to Noah into the Ark, male and female, as God had commanded Noah.* ¹⁰ *And it came to pass after the seven-day period that the waters of the Flood were upon the earth.*

make astonishing discoveries and to uncover eternal truths. (This time corresponds to the middle of the nineteenth century.)

7. וַיָּבֹא נֹחַ וּבָנָיו — *Noah, with his sons ... went.* Verses 6 to 11 refer to verse 5; they specify how Noah carried out God's commands (*Ramban*). *Rashi's* explanation, that Noah was of little faith and did not enter the Ark until the rising waters compelled him to do so, is contradicted by *Radak, Ibn Ezra,* and *Ramban,* who take the expression מִפְּנֵי מֵי הַמַּבּוּל to mean: in fear of the waters of the Flood (and not: in the face of the threat of the Floodwaters).

8. וּמִן־הַבְּהֵמָה אֲשֶׁר אֵינֶנָּה טְהֹרָה — *Of the animal that is not clean.* One should never let a vulgar word pass from his lips. Here the Torah uses eight extra letters in order not to write "impure animals" (*Pesachim* 3a). And so it has remained the practice to use a circumlocution when describing a vile, unseemly or odious object. However, an exception is made in the chapters of *Leviticus* where the specifications of the Law require that categorical and straightforward language be used.

9. כַּאֲשֶׁר צִוָּה אֱלֹהִים אֶת־נֹחַ — *As God had commanded Noah.* In the similar phrase in verse 1, God is called ה׳ whereas here He is called אֱלֹהִים. Above, the Divine command concerned the entry of Noah and his family into the Ark, whereas verses 8 and 9 deal with the entry of the quadrupeds, the birds, and the creeping animals. God gives orders not only to men but also to nature's animals, in other words, ה׳ is also אֱלֹהִים. The Divine words rule over both the kingdom of man and the natural laws of the universe. God gives orders to Noah so that he may carry them out unhindered. He also leads the animals to Noah in such a way that he can accomplish the Divine mission.

10. וַיְהִי לְשִׁבְעַת הַיָּמִים — *And it came to pass after the seven-day period.* The verses which follow, with their exact dates, tell how everything occurred just as had been announced in advance. Hence, far from being in the realm of the blind forces of nature, the catastrophe appears as being the effect of Divine Providence, just like the miracles in Egypt, also generally announced beforehand. We see here a sort of journal, a historical record of Noah which, in contrast to the scientific opinion attributing the Flood to a natural phenomenon,

יא בִּשְׁנַת שֵׁשׁ־מֵאוֹת שָׁנָה לְחַיֵּי־נֹחַ בַּחֹדֶשׁ הַשֵּׁנִי בְּשִׁבְעָה־
עָשָׂר יוֹם לַחֹדֶשׁ בַּיּוֹם הַזֶּה נִבְקְעוּ כָּל־מַעְיְנֹת תְּהוֹם
יב רַבָּה וַאֲרֻבֹּת הַשָּׁמַיִם נִפְתָּחוּ: וַיְהִי הַגֶּשֶׁם עַל־הָאָרֶץ
יג אַרְבָּעִים יוֹם וְאַרְבָּעִים לָיְלָה: בְּעֶצֶם הַיּוֹם הַזֶּה בָּא נֹחַ
וְשֵׁם־וְחָם וָיֶפֶת בְּנֵי־נֹחַ וְאֵשֶׁת נֹחַ וּשְׁלֹשֶׁת נְשֵׁי־בָנָיו אִתָּם
יד אֶל־הַתֵּבָה: הֵמָּה וְכָל־הַחַיָּה לְמִינָהּ וְכָל־הַבְּהֵמָה לְמִינָהּ
וְכָל־הָרֶמֶשׂ הָרֹמֵשׂ עַל־הָאָרֶץ לְמִינֵהוּ וְכָל־הָעוֹף לְמִינֵהוּ
טו כֹּל צִפּוֹר כָּל־כָּנָף: וַיָּבֹאוּ אֶל־נֹחַ אֶל־הַתֵּבָה שְׁנַיִם שְׁנַיִם
טז מִכָּל־הַבָּשָׂר אֲשֶׁר־בּוֹ רוּחַ חַיִּים: וְהַבָּאִים זָכָר וּנְקֵבָה
מִכָּל־בָּשָׂר בָּאוּ כַּאֲשֶׁר צִוָּה אֹתוֹ אֱלֹהִים וַיִּסְגֹּר יהוה בַּעֲדוֹ:

shows us two powers faithfully obeying God's will: Noah on the one hand and unreasoning nature on the other. The birds in the air, the crawling worms, all knew the way to Noah "at God's command." All came to Noah "two by two, male and female" (hence, not at all in a natural manner) and likewise, the torrential Flood swept over the earth only on the day decreed by God (R' Hirsch). The following verse gives an even better glimpse of this supernatural quality.

11. בַּחֹדֶשׁ הַשֵּׁנִי — *In the second month.* R' Eliezer says *Cheshvan,* whereas R' Yehoshua holds that it is *Iyar* (*Rashi*). For R' Yehoshua the Flood began in spring, and on the seventeenth of the month when "the constellation of Pleiades is in its descendancy and the fountains are drying up." Hence an act of Providence was needed for unleashing the massive flow of water. For R' Eliezer, the Flood began in autumn, yet here too supernatural intervention was needed, in this case to raise the temperature of the water to intense heat. "For they had sinned with ardent passion, and so were punished with boiling waters" (*Rosh Hashanah* 11b).

From this, both R' Yitzchak Arama (*Akeidas Yitzchak* 13) and *Maharal* (גבורות ה', הקדמה) conclude that those like R' Levi ben Gershon (*Ralbag*) who attempt to deny at all costs that acts of Providence play a role in manifest miracles (e.g. *Joshua* 10:13 and *II Kings* 20:9) and prefer to attribute such acts of Divine Providence to the occurrence of simply natural phenomena, are much in error. The simultaneous outflow from "all the fountains of the great deep and the windows of the heavens" is another indication of the supernatural character of the Flood (*Malbim*).

12. וַיְהִי הַגֶּשֶׁם עַל־הָאָרֶץ — *And the rain was upon the earth.* הַגֶּשֶׁם, with the definite article. This implies that it was a rain referred to previously. Indeed, it was the same rain found at the beginning of creation, as R' Levi explains: "When the world was created, God was glorified only by the waters, as it is said: *From the noise of great waters, from the mighty billows of the sea* (the words of praise ring out): *HASHEM excels on high* (Psalms 93:4). This is like a king who

¹¹ *In the six hundredth year of Noah's life, in the second month, on the seventeenth day of the month, on that day all the fountains of the great deep burst forth; and the windows of the heavens were opened.* ¹² *And the rain was upon the earth forty days and forty nights.*

¹³ *On that very day Noah came, with Shem, Ham, and Japheth, Noah's sons, with Noah's wife, and the three wives of his sons with them, into the Ark —* ¹⁴ *they and every beast after its kind, every animal after its kind, every creeping thing that creeps on the earth after its kind, and every bird after its kind, and every bird of any kind of wing.* ¹⁵ *They came to Noah into the Ark; two by two of all flesh in which there was a breath of life.* ¹⁶ *Thus they that came, came male and female of all flesh, as God had commanded him. And* HASHEM *shut it on his behalf.*

built a palace and kept mute servants therein. The servants paid homage to him by signs and gestures. 'How much greater glory will I have with servants who can speak,' thought the king. But when this came about, the servants proclaimed, 'This palace is not the king's, it belongs to us.' The king decided to bring back the mute servants he had had before. So too with the world. When God was paid homage by the waters of the deep, He said: 'If these waters with no mouth and no words do glorify Me, then how much greater homage will I receive from men, when I create them.' But generations of mankind continually revolted against God . . . hence God declared: 'Let them disappear and make way for the waters which had filled the earth previously' " (*Rabbah* 5).

Moreover, it is understandable why the fountains of the great deep gushed forth first: at the beginning of creation, these "waters below" had covered the earth's surface but were then forced back to the oceans. On the other hand, the "waters above" did not hurry to leave their privileged position around the celestial throne (*Shemos Rabbah* 15).

13. בְּעֶצֶם הַיּוֹם הַזֶּה — *On that very day.* Cf. *Rashi to Deuteronomy* 32:48.

בְּנֵי־נֹחַ וְאֵשֶׁת נֹחַ — *Noah's sons, with Noah's wife.* Noah's name is repeated three times in this verse. When you cherish someone, you like to repeat his name often. But when you detest someone, you avoid speaking his name: so with Saul, enemy of David (*I Samuel* 20:27) and with the enemies of Mordechai (*Esther* 6:3).

15. וַיָּבֹאוּ אֶל־נֹחַ — *They came to Noah.* Man appears here in his supreme dignity. All the animals come to him. It is he who saves them and protects them.

16. וַיִּסְגֹּר ה' בַּעֲדוֹ — *And* HASHEM *shut it on his behalf.* It was up to man to welcome the living creatures into his Ark. But it was God, and God alone, who "closed the door." Indeed, which man would dare affirm that a creature is no longer worthy of joining those in the Ark of salvation?

שלישי

יז וַיְהִי הַמַּבּוּל אַרְבָּעִים יוֹם עַל־הָאָרֶץ וַיִּרְבּוּ הַמַּיִם וַיִּשְׂאוּ
אֶת־הַתֵּבָה וַתָּרָם מֵעַל הָאָרֶץ: יח וַיִּגְבְּרוּ הַמַּיִם וַיִּרְבּוּ
מְאֹד עַל־הָאָרֶץ וַתֵּלֶךְ הַתֵּבָה עַל־פְּנֵי הַמָּיִם: יט וְהַמַּיִם
גָּבְרוּ מְאֹד מְאֹד עַל־הָאָרֶץ וַיְכֻסּוּ כָּל־הֶהָרִים הַגְּבֹהִים
כ אֲשֶׁר־תַּחַת כָּל־הַשָּׁמָיִם: חֲמֵשׁ עֶשְׂרֵה אַמָּה מִלְמַעְלָה
כא גָּבְרוּ הַמָּיִם וַיְכֻסּוּ הֶהָרִים: וַיִּגְוַע כָּל־בָּשָׂר | הָרֹמֵשׂ
עַל־הָאָרֶץ בָּעוֹף וּבַבְּהֵמָה וּבַחַיָּה וּבְכָל־הַשֶּׁרֶץ הַשֹּׁרֵץ
כב עַל־הָאָרֶץ וְכֹל הָאָדָם: כֹּל אֲשֶׁר נִשְׁמַת־רוּחַ חַיִּים בְּאַפָּיו
כג מִכֹּל אֲשֶׁר בֶּחָרָבָה מֵתוּ: וַיִּמַח אֶת־כָּל־הַיְקוּם | אֲשֶׁר |
עַל־פְּנֵי הָאֲדָמָה מֵאָדָם עַד־בְּהֵמָה עַד־רֶמֶשׂ וְעַד־עוֹף
הַשָּׁמַיִם וַיִּמָּחוּ מִן־הָאָרֶץ וַיִּשָּׁאֶר אַךְ־נֹחַ וַאֲשֶׁר אִתּוֹ בַּתֵּבָה:

17. וַיְהִי הַמַּבּוּל אַרְבָּעִים יוֹם — *When the Flood ... forty days.* "The waters continued to swell after the forty days and they then raised up the Ark" (*Ibn Ezra*). But according to *Rashi* the waters swelled up "by themselves" during the forty days. Some relate this to the natural turbulence of the water, others to an increase in volume due to the intense heat (verse 11). However, *R' Chaim ben Attar* stresses that the water increased by itself in its irresistible desire to carry out the Divine command to perfection.

21. וַיִּגְוַע כָּל־בָּשָׂר ... וְכֹל הָאָדָם — *And all flesh ... expired ... and all mankind.* Birds, cattle, beasts and insects perished whereas man lived on. As though acting with reluctance, God held off His destruction to the last moment in the hope that mankind would repent. (The different order given in verse 23 just summarizes what the Torah had specified previously.)

22. נִשְׁמַת־רוּחַ חַיִּים — *The breath of the spirit of life.* Since the word applies only to the soul of man, and since this verse concerns all creatures, *Rashi* interprets it here in the sense of "breath" and explains: all those with the breath of life.

However, the *Masorah* mentions four instances where this word is found in the Bible. The first, at man's creation (*Genesis* 2:7), states וַיִּפַּח בְּאַפָּיו נִשְׁמַת חַיִּים. The second is this verse. The third is in *Proverbs* (20:27), where it is written: נֵר ה' נִשְׁמַת אָדָם חֹפֵשׂ כָּל חַדְרֵי בָטֶן. The fourth is found in *Isaiah* (30:33) concerning the king of Assyria: נִשְׁמַת ה' כְּנַחַל גָּפְרִית בֹּעֲרָה בָּהּ, *the Divine soul was [for him]* like a stream of sulfur in which he was consumed.

The four passages trace the soul's destinies on earth. At the beginning of creation God breathed a soul into man's nostrils. But the soul's calling is given in the verse of *Proverbs: A Divine light is the soul of man, penetrating all the inner chambers of the body.* The soul must not remain bound up *in man's face* (בְּאַפָּיו, his nostrils or face) but should sanctify his whole being (כָּל חַדְרֵי בָטֶן), to the farthest corners of his physical personality. The king of Assyria had besmirched his soul, so for him, it became *like a stream of sulfur in which he was consumed.*

> ¹⁷ When the Flood was on the earth forty days, the waters increased and raised the Ark so that it was lifted above the earth. ¹⁸ The waters strengthened and increased greatly upon the earth, and the Ark drifted upon the surface of the waters. ¹⁹ The waters strengthened very much upon the earth, all the high mountains which are under the entire heavens were covered. ²⁰ Fifteen cubits upward did the waters strengthen, and the mountains were covered. ²¹ And all flesh that moves upon the earth expired — among the birds, the animals, the beasts, and all the creeping things that creep upon the earth, and all mankind. ²² All in whose nostrils was the breath of the spirit of life, of everything that was on dry land, died. ²³ And He blotted out all existence that was on the face of the ground — from man to animals to creeping things and to the bird of the heavens; and they were blotted out from the earth. Only Noah survived, and those with him in the Ark.

Now, at the generation of the Flood, man failed to make the soul rule over his entire being. Hence this generation had to disappear — and this is suggested by our verse: "Each one who has a living soul [only] in his face, must perish."

מִכֹּל אֲשֶׁר בֶּחָרָבָה — Of everything that was on dry land. Rashi notes: "But not the fish of the sea." Some hold that the fish were also to be destroyed but they fled to the ocean (Rabbah 32). R' Bachya states that the fish were especially blessed when they were created; this blessing protected them at all times (Genesis 1:22). Another tradition has it that the fish "did not corrupt their ways by crossbreeding, as other creatures did (Pesikta Zutrasa). Kabbalists teach that the laws governing social and sexual behavior were decreed only for men and animals, but not for aquatic animals (ס' הקנה). Rashi alludes to this when he explains why Psalms 82 is called the Psalm of the Third day: on the third day of creation, dry land appeared — and it is on it that justice and law will reign (Tamid 33). Hence the fish of the sea were not punished as men and the animals were.

These various opinions all lead to the same conclusion (also given by the Talmud, Zevachim 113a) that fish were not harmed in the world-wide cataclysm.

23. וַיִּשָּׁאֶר אַךְ־נֹחַ — Only Noah survived. Before the Flood, Noah was called "perfectly righteous" compared with his generation. Now that they had disappeared, there was "only Noah" left, just Noah before God. Having failed to save his fellowmen, Noah is now stripped of his attributes.

Ibn Ezra sees this phrase in another way. For him it is proof that the Land of Israel was also submerged by the Flood, since nothing was left but Noah and the Ark. A discussion, based on the interpretation of a passage in Ezekiel (22:24), takes place on this topic between R' Shimon ben Lakish and R' Yochanan (Zevachim ibid.). The latter teaches that the Floodwaters did not sweep over the

ח כד-א וַיִּגְבְּרוּ הַמַּיִם עַל־הָאָרֶץ חֲמִשִּׁים וּמְאַת יוֹם: וַיִּזְכֹּר
אֱלֹהִים אֶת־נֹחַ וְאֵת כָּל־הַחַיָּה וְאֶת־כָּל־הַבְּהֵמָה אֲשֶׁר
אִתּוֹ בַּתֵּבָה וַיַּעֲבֵר אֱלֹהִים רוּחַ עַל־הָאָרֶץ וַיָּשֹׁכּוּ הַמָּיִם:

Land of Israel but its inhabitants died in the intense heat generated by the
boiling waters. Noah and his family could have taken refuge on the Land of
Israel's high mountains but instead the arduous construction of the Ark was
imposed on them in order to serve as a warning to the others (*Maharsha*).

Another opinion (also adopted by *Ramban*) suggests that although the Land
of Israel was spared from the torrential rains and the outflows from the deep, it
was nevertheless inundated by Floodwaters from neighboring countries, since
"no barrier" could stop the onrushing waters. Accordingly, not all vegetation
was washed away, as it was in other countries, and the trees remained (עי' תוספ'
ד"ה לא, זבחים שם).

Why was the Land of Israel spared? Not because of the virtue of its
inhabitants, but because it was an earthly extension (הֲדוֹם רַגְלָיו) of the Throne
of the Divine Majesty (*R' Bachya*). Over the Land of Israel, *HASHEM will remain
enthroned as King, even amidst the waters of the Flood* (*Psalms* 29:10).

24. וַיִּגְבְּרוּ הַמַּיִם ... חֲמִשִּׁים וּמְאַת יוֹם — *And the waters strengthened ... a
hundred and fifty days.* Stories from almost every nation, excepting Nordic and
tropical races, deal with the Flood. The terrible catastrophe began in Babylonia
in the year 1656 after creation (that is, 2104 B.C.E.), which date coincides
approximately with those reported in the myths. Many of the details in the
numerous old legends remind us of the Torah's description, which incidentally
has been completely confirmed by recent archaeological research. Closest in
detail to the Biblical account is the description in an Assyro-Babylonian text
known as the "Epic of Gilgamesh." Gilgamesh, a hero of Uruk in Babylonia,
learns the story of the Flood from his ancestor, Ut-Napishtim (Day of life), who
is the Babylonian Noah. There have been many contradictory views on the
quasi-universality of the Flood theme. Despite their interest, however, the
scientific or comparative approaches (influenced by the philosophical systems in
vogue when they were offered, and discarded as quickly as they have been built
up) are hardly destined to enrich our knowledge of the Biblical text.

The ideological differences existing between mythological accounts and the
Torah text are basic: on the one hand, polytheism, terror of the gods before the
disaster, an arbitrary decision, etc.; on the other hand, the One God associates the
Flood with the notion of sin, and crowns it with an everlasting covenant. The
Divine words translate the great principles of universal life "into the language
of man," that is, into facts really having their place in the unfolding of history.
In contrast to the polytheistic peoples who deformed historical truth and
invented a mythology which is "the perversion of history," only the Torah kept
record of the authentic facts and their real significance. "The Biblical account of
the Flood is still even today capable of awakening the world's conscience. It was

²⁴ *And the waters strengthened on the earth a hundred and fifty days.*

8   ¹*God remembered Noah and all the beasts and all the animals that were with him in the Ark, and God caused a spirit to pass over the earth, and the waters subsided.*

written with this moral and pedagogical intent. The non-biblical accounts ignore this aspect completely" (*A. Jeremias*).

8.

1. וַיִּזְכֹּר אֱלֹהִים אֶת־נֹחַ — *God remembered Noah.* This chapter's first words proclaim the basic principle of Divine Providence. Amidst the devastation, God recalls Noah's family and the innocent animals, specks on the rushing Floodwaters. He unleashes unrelenting justice on a guilty humanity in a paroxysm of fury, while He lets the inhabitants of the Ark sink into oblivion for five months in order to shelter them from inexorable justice. In this way God spares them during the "final judgment." When justice has been done and the punishment carried out, He remembers those who had thought themselves forgotten and who were giving up hope of Divine salvation (*Zohar* 1:69b).

"God remembers" — in these words the idea of Divine Providence often finds expression in the Torah. This concept is amplified by our Sages in the second part of the Rosh Hashanah *Musaf* prayer, called זִכְרוֹנוֹת, as R' *Yosef Albo* notes (*Ikkarim* 1:4). "You remember all works, there is nothing hidden from Your eyes ... the remembrance of all creatures rises before You and You examine all their deeds ... Thus in Your love did You remember Noah, granting him merciful aid when You sent the Flood to destroy all creatures because of their evil doings. Then You remembered him to make his descendants as numerous as the soil of the earth, as the sand of the sea ...".

Although this verse highlights God's clemency, the Divine name אֱלֹהִים, designating the attribute of justice, reappears here. This is to stress that God remembered Noah by virtue of the principle of justice. That spirit of justice which condemned humanity to death is the same which saved the only man worthy of God's love on his own merits.

וְאֵת כָּל־הַחַיָּה וְאֶת־כָּל־הַבְּהֵמָה — *And all the beasts and all the animals.* Does Providence then also extend to the animals? Were they too, because of their merit (for not having been corrupt previously and for remaining chaste within the Ark), in receipt of God's solicitude, as *Rashi* affirms? Or was it Noah's merit that protected them, as is recounted in the Midrash (*Rabbah* 33)? The Midrash bases itself on a verse in *Psalms*, אָדָם וּבְהֵמָה תּוֹשִׁיעַ ה׳, *You save both man and beast, Hashem* (36:7), signifying that the animals benefit from man's merit. Or did the animals' salvation come from the Divine will to perpetuate the races and species formed at the Creation, as *Ramban* maintains, since "animals have neither merit nor sin"?

ב וַיִּסָּכְרוּ מַעְיְנֹת תְּהוֹם וַאֲרֻבֹּת הַשָּׁמָיִם וַיִּכָּלֵא הַגֶּשֶׁם

ג מִן־הַשָּׁמָיִם: וַיָּשֻׁבוּ הַמַּיִם מֵעַל הָאָרֶץ הָלוֹךְ וָשׁוֹב וַיַּחְסְרוּ

ד הַמַּיִם מִקְצֵה חֲמִשִּׁים וּמְאַת יוֹם: וַתָּנַח הַתֵּבָה בַּחֹדֶשׁ

ה הַשְּׁבִיעִי בְּשִׁבְעָה־עָשָׂר יוֹם לַחֹדֶשׁ עַל הָרֵי אֲרָרָט: וְהַמַּיִם

הָיוּ הָלוֹךְ וְחָסוֹר עַד הַחֹדֶשׁ הָעֲשִׂירִי בָּעֲשִׂירִי בְּאֶחָד

ו לַחֹדֶשׁ נִרְאוּ רָאשֵׁי הֶהָרִים: וַיְהִי מִקֵּץ אַרְבָּעִים יוֹם

ז וַיִּפְתַּח נֹחַ אֶת־חַלּוֹן הַתֵּבָה אֲשֶׁר עָשָׂה: וַיְשַׁלַּח אֶת־הָעֹרֵב

Three opinions on this problem (not counting that of the materialists who deny any kind of Divine intervention and who attribute everything to chance) are quoted in *Sefer HaChinuch* (The Book of Education) סימן קס״ח ascribed to R' Aharon HaLevi. Some hold that Divine Providence for the individual (הַשְׁגָּחָה פְּרָטִית) extends to animals as well as to human beings. Others claim that this providence extends even to material objects, no movement occurring on earth without the express will of God. But the author of *Sefer HaChinuch* finds this opinion far from logical. The third opinion is that "transmitted to us by our great Sages and by minds who continually sought the truth." It states that the animals enjoy a הַשְׁגָּחָה כְּלָלִית, *collective Providence*, which is destined to conserve and perpetuate the species in their diversity, whereas human beings benefit from an individual Providence. This is also the view of *Rambam* (*Guide* 3:17), *Ramban* (quoted above) and *Recanati*.

וַיַּעֲבֵר אֱלֹהִים רוּחַ — *And God caused a spirit to pass*. Rashi explains: It was a spirit of consolation and appeasement which passed before Him concerning the earth. This is the same Divine spirit which "hovered over the water" at the start of creation. For "a covenant is made with the waters, that they become calm whenever the Divine spirit passes over them" (*Rabbah* 2). We often observe the peaceful calm after a storm which only a few minutes before was breaking in all its fury. Then one feels a breath of love from God (ibid.) passing over the earth, like a breath from the World to Come.

2. וַיִּסָּכְרוּ מַעְיְנֹת — *The fountains ... were closed*. Rashi notes that those fountains beneficial to the world continued to flow, such as the hot springs of Tiberias. Thus, when God punishes the world, He can turn the punishment into a source of blessing and benefit. Such was the Dead Sea which issued from the destruction of Sodom. Pious Jews often hold hot springs in particular esteem and have faith in their therapeutic effects — basing themselves on what is alluded to here when the Torah states מַעְיְנֹת, but not כָּל מַעְיְנֹת, not *all fountains*.

4. עַל הָרֵי אֲרָרָט — *Upon the mountains of Ararat*. A mountain range in Armenia, north of Mesopotamia, 5156 meters (about 17,000 feet) in altitude. According to the היובלים ס', the Ark rested on the mountain named Lubbar. The region is that of Kurdistan (*Targumim*).

5. בָּעֲשִׂירִי בְּאֶחָד לַחֹדֶשׁ — *In the tenth month, on the first of the month*. How long did each of the various stages of the Flood last? This is a topic of discussion by

² *The fountains of the deep and the windows of the heavens were closed, and the rain from heaven was restrained.* ³ *The waters then receded from upon the earth, receding continuously, and the waters diminished at the end of a hundred and fifty days.* ⁴ *And the Ark came to rest in the seventh month, on the seventeenth day of the month, upon the mountains of Ararat.* ⁵ *The waters were continuously diminishing until the tenth month. In the tenth month, on the first of the month, the tops of the mountains became visible.*

⁶ *And it came to pass at the end of forty days, that Noah opened the window of the Ark which he had made.* ⁷ *He sent out the raven,*

Rashi and Ramban and continues with later scholars. It is a question of the exact significance of the 150 days (rising or falling of water level, stationary waters, or impossibility of the Ark settling) on the one hand, and, on the other, of understanding the ordinal number of the month involved, as some ordinal numbers seem to refer to the beginning of the year and others to the beginning of the Flood. Rashi, following R' Yehoshua (Rosh Hashanah 27a) holds that the world was created in the month of Nissan. Ramban follows R' Eliezer, stating that creation occurred in Tishrei (Ibn Ezra shares Rashi's opinion here but follows that of R' Eliezer in the ס׳ העבור).

Be that as it may, both Sages conclude that the disaster ended on the first of Tishrei. On this day Noah sent forth the "dove of peace" which did not return again, for the waters were dried up from the earth (verse 13). Thus, from earliest times, the day of Rosh Hashanah has been the herald of the reconciliation between God and His creatures.

6. וַיְהִי מִקֵּץ אַרְבָּעִים יוֹם — *And it came to pass at the end of forty days.* "There is a time for everything, and everything has its time under the sun." The Midrash applies these words of *Ecclesiastes* (3:1) to Adam when he entered and was expelled from Paradise, and to Noah when he entered and left the Ark. *Maharal* explains that the events in our lives do not happen fortuitously but come at the proper time, when they are meant to happen. Thus, Adam's entry into Paradise was part of a providential plan; so was his expulsion, since sin potentially exists in every human being. For the same reason, Noah's entry into the Ark came at the appointed time but his departure did not occur just because the ground had dried. It had to take place, since it was provided for in God's plan that the world would be restored. A host of other historical events are to be considered in the same light. Man does not escape his destiny; for better or for worse, everything happens when its time comes (*Tiferes Yisrael*, ch.25).

7. וַיְשַׁלַּח אֶת־הָעֹרֵב — *He sent out the raven.* The raven refused to leave, arguing that since he was of an impure species, only two of his kind had been taken into the Ark and if he "were not to return to the Ark, how would the species be perpetuated?" Irritated at this, Noah replied: "What does it matter, for of what

ח וַיֵּצֵא יָצוֹא וָשׁוֹב עַד־יְבֹשֶׁת הַמַּיִם מֵעַל הָאָרֶץ: וַיְשַׁלַּח
אֶת־הַיּוֹנָה מֵאִתּוֹ לִרְאוֹת הֲקַלּוּ הַמַּיִם מֵעַל פְּנֵי הָאֲדָמָה:
ט וְלֹא־מָצְאָה הַיּוֹנָה מָנוֹחַ לְכַף־רַגְלָהּ וַתָּשָׁב אֵלָיו אֶל־
הַתֵּבָה כִּי־מַיִם עַל־פְּנֵי כָל־הָאָרֶץ וַיִּשְׁלַח יָדוֹ וַיִּקָּחֶהָ וַיָּבֵא
אֹתָהּ אֵלָיו אֶל־הַתֵּבָה: וַיָּחֶל עוֹד שִׁבְעַת יָמִים אֲחֵרִים וַיֹּסֶף
יא שַׁלַּח אֶת־הַיּוֹנָה מִן־הַתֵּבָה: וַתָּבֹא אֵלָיו הַיּוֹנָה לְעֵת עֶרֶב
וְהִנֵּה עֲלֵה־זַיִת טָרָף בְּפִיהָ וַיֵּדַע נֹחַ כִּי־קַלּוּ הַמַּיִם מֵעַל
יב הָאָרֶץ: וַיִּיָּחֶל עוֹד שִׁבְעַת יָמִים אֲחֵרִים וַיְשַׁלַּח אֶת־הַיּוֹנָה
יג וְלֹא־יָסְפָה שׁוּב־אֵלָיו עוֹד: וַיְהִי בְּאַחַת וְשֵׁשׁ־מֵאוֹת שָׁנָה

use are you to the world? You are fit neither for food nor for sacrifice in the Temple!" But God reprimanded Noah, saying: "The day will come when the raven's usefulness will become evident. A righteous man, the prophet Elijah, will come and punish the world with drought. Night and day, the raven will bring him bread and meat to feed him." Then the raven left but did not return, and sustained itself by feeding on carrion (*Rabbah* 33).

וַיֵּצֵא יָצוֹא וָשׁוֹב — *And it kept going and returning.* "The raven did not do what it was told, in contrast to the dove which carried out its mission. The raven was an abject creature who had violated the Divine command to remain chaste during the Flood, whereas the dove was pure and remained pure" (cf. our commentary to 7:18). We learn from this that one should entrust only a worthy and deserving person with carrying out a mission for good and useful ends (*Pirkei D' Rabbi Eliezer* פכ"ג).

8. וַיְשַׁלַּח אֶת־הַיּוֹנָה מֵאִתּוֹ — *Then he sent out the dove from him.* The dove, which brought back the olive leaf, has become the universal symbol for peace whereas the Torah shows us the raven, hovering before the window of the Ark, as a bad omen. *Radak* reminds us that the dove has a natural gift for carrying or bringing back messages, as carrier pigeons prove. The dove is distinguished by the fact that "it does not feed on carrion and is modest while mating" (*Eruvin* 100b).

9. וְלֹא־מָצְאָה הַיּוֹנָה מָנוֹחַ לְכַף־רַגְלָהּ . . . וַיָּבֵא אֹתָהּ אֵלָיו אֶל־הַתֵּבָה — *But the dove could not find a resting place for the sole of its foot . . . and brought it to him to the Ark.* Our Sages find much in common between the nature and behavior of the dove and of the "community of Israel." The *Song of Songs* exalts Jewry in these words: *Lo, you are beautiful, my beloved; lo, you are beautiful: your eyes are those of a dove* (1:15). Further on, Jewry is often called "My dove, my perfect one, etc." Just as the dove brought light to the world in Noah's time (by its presence and its new message), so too does Jewry's message bring light to the world. In the relations between Jewry and the other nations, the *Zohar* sees parallels with the vicissitudes of the dove and the raven in their flight to the world outside (*Zohar Chadash*, 33). And R' Shimon states: Had it found a

*and it kept going and returning until the waters dried from upon
the earth.* [8] *Then he sent out the dove from him to see whether
the waters had subsided from the face of the ground.* [9] *But the
dove could not find a resting place for the sole of its foot, and
it returned to him to the Ark, for water was upon the surface
of all the earth. So he put forth his hand, and took it, and brought
it to him to the Ark.* [10] *He waited again another seven days, and
again sent out the dove from the Ark.* [11] *The dove came back to
him in the evening — and behold! an olive leaf it had plucked
with its bill! And Noah knew that the waters had subsided from
upon the earth.* [12] *Then he waited again another seven days and
sent the dove forth; and it did not return to him anymore.*

[13] *And it came to pass in the six hundred and first year,*

resting-place, the dove would not have flown back to the Ark; had Jewry found
a resting-place among the nations, she would not have returned to her nest . . .
(*Rabbah* 33).

10. וַיֹּסֶף שַׁלַּח אֶת־הַיּוֹנָה מִן־הַתֵּבָה — *And again sent out the dove from the Ark.*
Thrice in a row was the dove sent from the Ark. It returned the first time, just
as Jewry returned to Him from the first exile in Babylonia. The second time, the
dove returned to Noah at evening with an olive leaf in its beak. So was Jewry
again exiled with the Greeks. But their spiritual horizon was darkened by the
influence of Greek culture and Jewry then returned to God only at nightfall
"holding in her bill an olive leaf," symbol of the olive oil which the
Hasmoneans lit (at Chanukah) to revive Jewry's spiritual light. Then, when sent
away for the third time, the dove did not return. Jewry, too, has not come back
from its present exile amid the Edomite nations, but note that it says, "it did not
return to him anymore" and not "he no longer returned to her." This teaches
you that the dove is free to return when she wishes. God is ready to welcome
her; He is awaiting her return (*Zohar* ibid.).

11. טָרָף בְּפִיהָ — *It had plucked with its bill.* טָרָף means "it had torn it" (*Rashi*).
The leaf was plucked from a tree rather than found floating on the water. Hence
Noah concluded that "the waters were abated from the earth" (*Radak*).
Rashi explains: "I claim that the bird was male, and therefore sometimes
the masculine is used and sometimes the feminine. The word יוֹנָה itself is
feminine. For example: 'Like doves by streamlets of water (כְּיוֹנִים רְחֲצוֹת),' in
Song of Songs (5:12)."
However, in his commentary on *Song of Songs*, *Rashi* contradicts this last
statement, for there he claims the word רְחֲצוֹת modifies עֵינָיו which is feminine.
Some sages take this contradiction as confirmation of the assertion made by
Chida (in *Shem HaGedolim*) that the commentary attributed to *Rashi* on *Song
of Songs* was not really written by him.

בָּרִאשׁוֹן בְּאֶחָד לַחֹדֶשׁ חָרְבוּ הַמַּיִם מֵעַל הָאָרֶץ וַיָּסַר
נֹחַ אֶת־מִכְסֵה הַתֵּבָה וַיַּרְא וְהִנֵּה חָרְבוּ פְּנֵי הָאֲדָמָה:
יד וּבַחֹדֶשׁ הַשֵּׁנִי בְּשִׁבְעָה וְעֶשְׂרִים יוֹם לַחֹדֶשׁ יָבְשָׁה
רביעי טו-טז הָאָרֶץ: 　　וַיְדַבֵּר אֱלֹהִים אֶל־נֹחַ לֵאמֹר: צֵא מִן־הַתֵּבָה
יז אַתָּה וְאִשְׁתְּךָ וּבָנֶיךָ וּנְשֵׁי־בָנֶיךָ אִתָּךְ: כָּל־הַחַיָּה אֲשֶׁר־
אִתְּךָ מִכָּל־בָּשָׂר בָּעוֹף וּבַבְּהֵמָה וּבְכָל־הָרֶמֶשׂ הָרֹמֵשׂ
הַיַּצֵא ק' עַל־הָאָרֶץ °הוֹצֵא אִתָּךְ וְשָׁרְצוּ בָאָרֶץ וּפָרוּ וְרָבוּ עַל־
יח-יט הָאָרֶץ: וַיֵּצֵא־נֹחַ וּבָנָיו וְאִשְׁתּוֹ וּנְשֵׁי־בָנָיו אִתּוֹ: כָּל־הַחַיָּה

---

13. בָּרִאשׁוֹן — *In the first month.* "*Tishrei*, according to R' Eliezer; *Nissan* in the opinion of R' Yehoshua," reports *Rashi.* See *Maharal's* polemic against R' Eliyahu Mizrachi concerning the relationships between this Tannaitic controversy and the corresponding one which the *Tannaim* had about the month of creation (*Gur Aryeh*).

14. בְּשִׁבְעָה וְעֶשְׂרִים יוֹם לַחֹדֶשׁ — *On the twenty-seventh day of the month.* "The judgment of the generation of the deluge lasted a whole year" (*Rashi*). Also that of the Egyptians and of Iyov continued for a year. So too will the judgment of Gog and Magog take an entire year. The conclusion is that "judgment of sinners in Hell lasts for a year." This conclusion has a certain bearing on the nature of the year of mourning for the immediate family, as is seen in *Shulchan Aruch, Yoreh Deah* §376:4.

16. צֵא מִן־הַתֵּבָה — *Go forth from the Ark.* Despite the fact that living there was extremely trying, Noah waited for explicit Divine instructions before leaving the Ark. "Noah slept not a wink in the Ark since he and his sons were preoccupied with bringing each animal its food at the proper time. So much so, in fact, that the phoenix had pity on their tiredness and refused to eat in order to save the human inhabitants of the Ark from extra work. Noah then blessed this bird: 'May God spare you from ever dying' .... The 360 rooms and halls of the Ark were filled with noise from all the animals. The males were placed on one side, the females on the other, for they were forbidden to mate while God's wrath was kindled on the earth .... Once Noah was late in giving the lion its food and was bitten on the heel, causing him to limp for the rest of his days. Because of this, he could no longer serve as a priest. The waters rose incessantly and buffeted the Ark. Noah and his sons cried out to God: 'O God! hear our prayer, we can no longer bear what is happening. Let us see Your Countenance, O God. Have pity on us, deliver us and save us' " (ס' הישר פ' נח and *Sanhedrin* 108b).

Despite everything, Noah patiently awaited authorization to leave the Ark. He had been disappointed in not being able to leave the Ark after the first "seven days" (verse 10) and patiently waited another seven days. In verse 12, the word וַיָּחֶל is not in the usual *piel* or *hiphil* form of the verb (יחל) but in the *niphal* form. This implies the idea of waiting in disappointment. Nonetheless,

in the first month, on the first of the month, the waters dried
from upon the earth; Noah removed the covering of the Ark, and
looked — and behold! the surface of the ground had dried. [14] And
in the second month, on the twenty-seventh day of the month,
the earth was fully dried.
  [15] God spoke to Noah, saying, [16] "Go forth from the Ark:
you and your wife, your sons, and your sons' wives with you.
[17] Every living being that is with you of all flesh, of birds,
of animals, and moving things that move on the earth — order
them out with you, and let them teem on the earth and be fruitful and multiply on the earth." [18] So Noah went forth, and his
sons, his wife, and his sons' wives with him. [19] Every living being,

whenever his sons urged him to leave, Noah spoke out in unequivocal
opposition: "God forbid! We entered at God's command, we shall leave only at
God's command! (*Tanchuma*). In addition, because of the curse which the world
had suffered, Noah was in dread of his duty to procreate anew. Then God swore
never to devastate the world again by Flood, as it is said, *I have sworn that the
waters of Noah should no more pass over the earth* (*Isaiah* 54:9). God
commanded Noah to leave the Ark and immediately blessed him, and the
animals, with prosperity and fruitfulness (verse 17; *Rabbah* 34).
  Noah's conduct served as an example to three young men. When Chananiah,
Mishael, and Azariah were cast into the fiery furnace by King Nebuchadnezzar
of Babylonia, they refused to leave it until they received the order from the king
himself (*Daniel* 3:26; cf. *Tanchuma*).

18. וַיֵּצֵא־נֹחַ וּבָנָיו וְאִשְׁתּוֹ וּנְשֵׁי־בָנָיו אִתּוֹ — *So Noah went forth, and his sons, his
wife, and his sons' wives with him.* But God had specified a different order:
"You and your wife, and your sons and your sons' wives" (verse 16). This slight
change indicates that even on leaving the Ark Noah continued to keep the sexes
separated and hence from mating although God had just now authorized the
inhabitants of the Ark to procreate. R' Yehudah says that this excess of piety led
Noah to debauchery for he then became drunk and violated a sexual
prohibition. R' Nechemiah answers back, "Just the contrary. Noah's spirit of
holiness made him and his children deserving of a distinction reserved only for
the righteous, that is, to hear the Divine words and blessing addressed to them
directly (*Genesis* 9:8; *Rabbah* 35).

19. לְמִשְׁפְּחֹתֵיהֶם — *By their families. Rashi:* They undertook to unite henceforth
only with their own species. This explanation refers at the same time to what R'
Yochanan says (and which is commented on in several ways) in *Sanhedrin*
108b: לְמִשְׁפְּחֹתֵיהֶם וְלֹא הֵם (cf. *Maharsha* ibid.). The word stressed here is
לְמִשְׁפְּחֹתֵיהֶם; when the animals leave the Ark, on the threshold of a new world,
this word comes to remind us of the supreme importance of the law concerning
the respecting of the species (לְמִינֵיהֶם) contained in the first chapter of the Torah.

כָּל־הָרֶ֫מֶשׂ וְכָל־הָע֗וֹף כֹּ֤ל רוֹמֵ֣שׂ עַל־הָאָ֔רֶץ לְמִשְׁפְּחֹ֣תֵיהֶ֔ם
כ יָצְא֖וּ מִן־הַתֵּבָֽה: וַיִּ֧בֶן נֹ֛חַ מִזְבֵּ֖חַ לַֽיהֹוָ֑ה וַיִּקַּ֣ח מִכֹּ֣ל |

20. וַיִּבֶן נֹחַ מִזְבֵּחַ לַה' — *Then Noah built an altar to HASHEM.* Nothing could better show the deep significance of the sacrifices and the falsity of all theories disparaging them than this passage which first introduces us to the altar and the burnt offering.

For a complete year Noah had devoted himself to keeping the animals alive and now, just after saving them, he sacrifices them! And this sacrifice is of such far-reaching importance for world history that the whole future development of the world and mankind appears (in verses 21 and 22) as the consequence of, or in some way the reply to, Noah's offering. What was the meaning of the building of the altar and the sacrifice that they could result in so basic a covenant? It is evident from many passages in the Bible that the altar signifies an elevation of the earth towards the heavens, built by man's own hands. Ezekiel calls the altar הַראֵל, the Mount of the Almighty. The altar had to be built of stones but was an elevation of the earth by human activity in order to dedicate it to God. Taking a single stone and offering sacrifices on it would mean remaining on nature's terms. But building an altar expresses the desire to rise up above the level of nature in order to seek the level of the God-like free-willed human being who dedicates himself to God from this base. In building an altar to God on the restored earth, Noah, the ancestor of the humanity to come, wanted to dedicate this earth to be a place where men would add stone upon stone, until the entire earth becomes a holy mountain!

When other nations sought their gods, they left the human sphere, believing they could find them more easily in nature. Certainly, God can be discovered in nature too. But He is even closer to us, and in all His splendor, in the sphere of human life when it is pure and healthy. Here His love is revealed; in nature is revealed His omnipotence. Thus, the מִזְבֵּחַ, *altar*, is a dedicated, consecrated place, whereas מַצֵבָה is but a stone set up in nature. This thought is of such importance for Jewish law that around the altar no tree was allowed to be found; not even a board reminding one of a tree was allowed to be seen in the building enclosing the altar (*R' S.R. Hirsch*).

וַיַּעַל עלֹת בַּמִּזְבֵּחַ — *And offered burnt-offerings on the altar.* What motivated Noah to offer a sacrifice to God? It was his desire to consecrate the earth and its inhabitants henceforth to serve God. Noah also felt infinite gratitude for the Divine grace which he and his family had just received, as the Midrash points out (*Pirkei D'Rabbi Eliezer* פכ"ג).

The *Zohar*, however, notes that Noah's sacrifices are described as עלֹת, holocausts, burnt-offerings. Now, this class of sacrifice is meant for expiating sins committed not in deed but in thought (הִרְהוּרֵי עֲבֵרָה). Cain and Abel offered מְנָחוֹת, *offerings of homage,* and the Talmud notes that the Noahides in general do not offer שְׁלָמִים, *offerings in gratitude. Maharsha* explains that this is

every creeping thing, and every bird, everything that moves
on earth came out of the Ark by their families.
²⁰ Then Noah built an altar to HASHEM and took of every

because these sacrifices are partly consumed by their owners, but the Noahides
do not keep the laws of purity required for this (*Zevachim* 116a).

The *Zohar* asks: What was the sin mentally committed by Noah? He doubted
the permanency of his covenant with God, thinking that the benefits which
Providence had heaped upon him had deprived him of that merit which would
have justified keeping this covenant. Furthermore, looking over the world
ravaged by the deluge, Noah could not help wondering: How could God, called
merciful and compassionate, do such a thing, showing no pity for His creatures?
God replied, "Now you think of this? Why didn't you pray to Me when I
announced the Flood and commanded you to build your Ark? I waited long
years for your prayer on behalf of your fellowmen. But when you learned that
you would be saved in the Ark, you never thought of praying for the others (ט"ס
ובהשמטות). And now, when the world is destroyed, the devastation bothers
you!"

These thoughts gave Noah a feeling of guilt and this was, in part, why he
offered a sacrifice.

Rashi gives us an explanation with a much different insight: Noah said to
himself, "If God had me bring seven pairs of some animals into the Ark, it must
be to sacrifice some of them." Considered in this light, Noah was answering a
discreet invitation from God when he offered the sacrifices. All future legislation
about sacrifices gives us to understand that the offering of sacrifices is wanted
by God. Is it not defined as לֶחֶם אִשֶּׁה לַה׳, nourishing the Divine flame on earth?
Hence, of all forms of worship, sacrifice is the preferred. When the Altar
transforms the offering of flesh into an ethereal flame springing heavenward,
this sacrifice of love becomes "a pleasant odor to God." More detailed
explanations on the significance of the sacrifices will follow in the commentary
on פ׳ הקרבנות.

Let it suffice here to point out the full import of *Rashi's* words. Many exegetes
and rationalist historians have indeed wanted to show that right from the
beginning man had attributed senses to God and felt that he was obliged to offer
Him gifts to gain His favor. And so he offered sacrifices of what he himself
preferred to consume. Confirmation of this theory lies in the fact that the first
sacrifices offered by men were not done so at God's command, but rather spontaneously, on their own. It was only much later that God prescribed sacrifices,
at a time when sacrifices were the rule with pagan peoples. In restricting and
considerably limiting this cult, God's intention was to draw Jews progressively
away from it, and to erase from their heart any vestige of paganism.

This theory is called the anthropopathic theory. It is partly based on the
spontaneity of the first sacrifices. Interpreting *Rambam's* teaching, which has
points in common with this theory, and defending it against *Ramban (Guide*

הַבְּהֵמָה הַטְּהֹרָה וּמִכּל הָעוֹף הַטָּהוֹר וַיַּעַל עֹלֹת בַּמִּזְבֵּחַ:
כא וַיָּרַח יהוה אֶת־רֵיחַ הַנִּיחֹחַ וַיֹּאמֶר יהוה אֶל־לִבּוֹ לֹא אֹסִף
לְקַלֵּל עוֹד אֶת־הָאֲדָמָה בַּעֲבוּר הָאָדָם כִּי יֵצֶר לֵב הָאָדָם רַע

3:32), *Don Isaac Abarbanel* states that Adam, Cain, Abel and Noah all offered sacrifices with this in mind. Their sacrifices led them to humility, to a belief in the existence of God and of Divine Providence. Hence God let this cult be practiced, although totally erroneous ideas became introduced into it.

But the untenability of this rationalist theory has often been demonstrated. *Rashi's* remark, which stresses that Noah's sacrifice was not completely spontaneous but at least suggested by God, takes on its full significance when confronting these speculations. As for the reasons which could have prompted such a "suggestion," they will become evident in what follows.

21. וַיָּרַח ה' אֶת־רֵיחַ הַנִּיחֹחַ — *HASHEM smelled the pleasing aroma.* R' Chanina said: Whoever becomes pacified thanks to the atmosphere created by wine has something of the spirit of his Creator. He follows God's good example. God needed only to smell the pleasant odor of Noah's sacrifice to swear never to curse the world again (*Eruvin* 65b according to *Rashi*). Our Sages say: the pious are hard to anger, but easy to appease (*Avos* 5:14). From Adam to Noah, God had waited ten generations under continual provocation before He brought down the Flood. This is to show how great is His long-suffering (ibid. 5:2). And then, here, Noah's sacrifice suffices to appease the Divine anger instantly. "The sweet savor" denotes a spiritual joy. Indeed, of all the senses, the sense of smell gives the purest and most abstract sensation. Our Sages ask: What is the joy which the soul delights in but not the body? It is a sweet smell (*Berachos* 43b; cf. our commentary on 3:6). The word נִיחֹחַ is considered by some to be derived from the *piel* form of נוחה and by others from the noun נוֹחַ. It means satisfaction (*Targumim*) or appeasement (*Ibn Ezra*) or acquiescence (*R' Hirsch*).

The spiritual satisfaction which Noah's sacrifice brought to God is based on the very idea of "sacrifice." Noah concretizes this ideal of serving God with his sacrifice. The true servant of God is not a visionary, not a sage plunged into mystical contemplation, not a subtle philosopher, not a fanatic or exalted prophet. His religion, far from being limited to prayers, beliefs, ritual practices, or mortification, is first and foremost made up of absolute devotion to God. This devotion knows no bounds, it is never-failing, ready to sacrifice fortune, life itself, one's dearest affections, everything, for the love of God. The sacrifices are but the concretization of this ecstasy of devotion. Hence our Sages say: When God smelled the pleasant odor emanating from Noah's sacrifice, it reminded Him (for the past and the future merge in God) of the pleasant odor (רֵיחַ נִיחֹחַ) which rose from the sacrifice when Abraham entered the fiery furnace out of love for God, and of the same pleasant odor which came from the sacrifice of Chananyah, Mishael and Azaryah, who also entered the furnace at Nebuchadnezzar's command, and then, of the voluntary sacrifice of innumerable victims

*clean animal and of every clean bird, and offered burnt-offerings
on the altar.* [21] *HASHEM smelled the pleasing aroma, and HASHEM
said in His heart: "I will not continue to curse again the
ground because of man, since the imagery of man's heart is evil*

of persecution, massacred for קִידוּשׁ הַשֵּׁם (*Rabbah* 34). It was the pleasant odor
rising up from the earth throughout the centuries of history which made God
henceforth bestow His blessings on mankind despite the fact that "the
inclination of man's heart is evil from his youth."

Another Midrash teaches that when he left the Ark and saw the immensity
of the disaster, Noah broke down in tears. This righteous man's sincere
supplication to spare the world from such catastrophes in the future was heard
by God because it was accompanied by a threefold pleasant odor: from the burnt
offering, from the prayer, and from the merits of a righteous person. Hence God
commanded later: רֵיחַ נִיחֹחִי תִּשְׁמְרוּ לְהַקְרִיב לִי (*Numbers* 28:2), which means:
You shall observe to offer Me the pleasant odor of Noah, the רֵיחַ of Noah נֹחַ
(נִיחוֹחִי), made up of the odor of the burnt-offering, prayer, and good deeds
(*Zohar Chadash, Noach*).

וַיֹּאמֶר ה' אֶל־לִבּוֹ — *And HASHEM said to his heart.* In our commentary on 6:5, we
have drawn attention to the importance of the anthropomorphic expressions
which abound in the Torah. The danger of thinking of God in too corporeal a
way is much less serious than that of reducing Him by philosophical speculation
to an abstract, transcendent, and metaphysical idea. It is much more important
to be convinced of the personal existence of God and of His close ties with men
than to speculate on the irrational attributes of unity and incorporeality which
have scarcely more connection with the morality of our lives than algebraic
symbols. Our expression parallels the phrase וַיִּתְעַצֵּב אֶל־לִבּוֹ used previously (6:6)
before justice was meted out on the earth. But now that the past has been washed
away, it is the richness of God's love and mercy which speaks out for the future
preservation of the world. Our Sages note that the text has אֶל־לִבּוֹ and not בְּלִבּוֹ.
This form serves as an example for man, possessing free will, not to be בִּרְשׁוּת
לִבּוֹ, a slave of his feelings and sentiments. Whenever it is a question of men who
can serve as examples for us, the words אֶל לִבּוֹ are used literally: "he speaks *to*
his heart," whereas with the impious the word used is בְּלִבּוֹ, *in* his heart. Hence,
it is written here וַיֹּאמֶר ה' אֶל־לִבּוֹ. All the מִדּוֹת הָרַחֲמִים stood before God and
pleaded for the future salvation of humanity. And although the world was still
far from its ultimate goal, God saw in Noah's sacrifice an impassioned desire to
reach this goal and He proclaimed לֹא אֹסִף לְקַלֵּל עוֹד אֶת הָאֲדָמָה, *I will not
continue to curse again the ground* (*R' Hirsch*).

כִּי יֵצֶר לֵב הָאָדָם רַע מִנְּעֻרָיו — *Since the imagery of man's heart is evil from his
youth.* Referring to discussions in the Talmud (*Nedarim* 32b), *Rambam* explains
that uncontrolled instincts are active in children before they can be held in check
by the reasoning faculties which are developed at adolescence (*Guide* 3:22). This

מִנְּעֻרָיו וְלֹא־אֹסֵף עוֹד לְהַכּוֹת אֶת־כָּל־חַי כַּאֲשֶׁר עָשִׂיתִי:
כב עֹד כָּל־יְמֵי הָאָרֶץ זֶרַע וְקָצִיר וְקֹר וָחֹם וְקַיִץ וָחֹרֶף וְיוֹם וָלַיְלָה
ט א לֹא יִשְׁבֹּתוּ: וַיְבָרֶךְ אֱלֹהִים אֶת־נֹחַ וְאֶת־בָּנָיו וַיֹּאמֶר לָהֶם

constitutes, as it were, extenuating circumstances for human weakness and
henceforth the Creator takes this into account. Moreover, it follows that the legal
responsibility of the child is to be strictly limited, as is discussed in the Talmud in
the tractate *Bava Metzia* 10b (cf. שי״ד אלפים ב׳ ,ח״ה ,הרדב״ז תש׳).

R' *Hirsch* interprets this same verse as follows: Even if the inclination of the
human heart [again] be evil from its youth, I will not again smite living beings as
I have done before, but I will bring them up — in the manner described in the
next verse. R' *Yitzchak Arama* stresses the contrast between *Genesis* 6:5, where
the impulse of the heart is described as "solely evil, all the time" (that is, over
one's lifetime) and this passage where only childhood is emphasized.

Indeed, the Flood taught men a terrible lesson and had a sobering effect on
their hearts. Moreover, the forces of evil aroused by the first sin began to weaken
in the human soul. Then, too, as with the earth, the vital force in the new
generations diminished and life became more arduous; giving oneself up to the
pleasures of life became more precarious. Man was therefore capable of reaching
higher moral perfection after the Flood than before it, following the fall of
Adam. In the future, instincts were to rule unbridled only in childhood, as
originally foreseen, and in view of this improvement in moral conditions for life
on earth, God was able to swear that mankind would survive.

22. יִשְׁבֹּתוּ לֹא ... הָאָרֶץ כָּל־יְמֵי עֹד — *Continuously, all the days of the earth ...
shall not cease.* This verse is generally taken as announcing that the regular
cycle of the seasons and days, which had been disturbed during the deluge, will
never again be disturbed.

This view takes for granted that the same seasons we have today existed
before the Flood. But this does not seem to correspond with the early traditions.
Indeed, R' Yitzchak holds that before the Flood the land had to be cultivated
only once every forty years, it was eternally spring, and the seasons and
temperatures were the same on all continents. Communication from one end of
the earth to the other was not difficult, for men had enormous physical strength
and the continents were not yet separated from one another (*Rabbah* 35). They
did separate after the Flood and since then men has only very gradually
succeeded in conquering the earth's vastness by artificial means.

Consequently, the changes of season indicated here are to be taken as a
postdiluvian innovation. This is why R' Shmuel ben Nachman would later cry
out when the weather would cause him to have headaches: "Do you see what we
owe to the Generation of the Flood!" (ibid.). Stability in climatic conditions and
the extraordinary longevity enjoyed before the Flood are considered as essential
causes of the general depravity of the times. The changes which took place in the
shape of the continents and in atmospheric conditions are confirmed by research

from his youth; nor will I again continue to smite every living being, as I have done. [22] *Continuously, all the days of the earth, seedtime and harvest, cold and heat, summer and winter, day and night, shall not cease.'*

9   [1]*God blessed Noah and his sons, and He said to them,*

in the fields of geology and physical geography. Archaeological remains, fossils and traces of the primitive age show that the distribution of seasons and temperatures differed from those we have now and that the shaping of the continents by oceans, rivers, mountains, and deserts are of a period more recent than Creation. A saying of our Sages seems to indicate that the Flood was caused by altering the positions of certain constellations, which, in turn, brought about a disturbance in the telluric equilibrium (*Berachos* 59a). Our Sages consider in any case that the change of seasons came about only after the Flood.

To be sure, the earth had previously undergone certain periods of change. But they had followed one another at long intervals. Hence, men had enjoyed long periods of stability in nature and in the physical realm. This led them to an easy and frivolous existence, scarcely requiring any effort or struggle on their part. When these long carefree ages encouraged increasing evil and were witness to "old רְשָׁעִים, rich, opulent, and immoral," massive destruction became inevitable.

But henceforth, the plan for mankind's upbringing which was to assure the permanency of life on earth without further recourse to such catastrophes would be based on the principle that different seasons and climatic conditions will always exist on earth simultaneously. And the break-up of the continents and territories was included in the fundamental change solemnly proclaimed here.

Because of these new conditions, man became dependent on his physical environment. It no longer sufficed to "sow once every forty years." Continual changes in nature and its loss of vigor compared with antediluvian conditions now exacted ceaseless effort from humanity. Moreover, the new conditions served to create more complex individuals, different in goodness but also in the degree of evil. Another consequence of the more frequent and more rapid change in natural phenomena was that the human lifespan was shortened. It has remained approximately at its present level since the end of the Flood.

Now evil instincts have a barrier which prevents them from permanent victory. Even the most powerful tyrant can scarcely maintain his rule for over fifty years. For as long as each generation lived 700 or 800 years, the young, who were moved with purer and nobler feelings than their already corrupted elders, were not given the chance to bring their idealism into play and to advance civilization. Now, with the new social order, human genius can look forward and can open to youth the road to hope and to a better future.

Thus this new phase in the education of mankind is inaugurated by the principle of diversity among individuals and thence among peoples, encouraged by the separation of the continents. The quicker change of generations means

ב פְּרוּ וּרְבוּ וּמִלְאוּ אֶת־הָאָרֶץ: וּמוֹרַאֲכֶם וְחִתְּכֶם יִהְיֶה עַל
כָּל־חַיַּת הָאָרֶץ וְעַל כָּל־עוֹף הַשָּׁמָיִם בְּכֹל אֲשֶׁר תִּרְמֹשׂ
ג הָאֲדָמָה וּבְכָל־דְּגֵי הַיָּם בְּיֶדְכֶם נִתָּנוּ: כָּל־רֶמֶשׂ אֲשֶׁר
הוּא־חַי לָכֶם יִהְיֶה לְאָכְלָה כְּיֶרֶק עֵשֶׂב נָתַתִּי לָכֶם אֶת־כֹּל:

that young and vigorous peoples will replace degenerate nations so that, as history
unfolds, decadence can never again spread over the whole earth (*R' Hirsch*).

9.

1. פְּרוּ וּרְבוּ — *Be fruitful and multiply.* This blessing gives implicit reassurance to
Noah and his sons about the fate of their descendants. It is reiterated in verse 7,
in order to "emphasize that men must henceforth fulfill the duty of procreation,
or to summon them to fill the earth, that is, to spread over it and not to
concentrate in a single area as did those who built the Tower of Babel"
(*Ramban*).

2. וּמוֹרַאֲכֶם וְחִתְּכֶם יִהְיֶה עַל כָּל־חַיַּת הָאָרֶץ — *The fear of you and the dread of you
shall be upon every beast of the earth.* This marks a new stage in the
relationship between man and the animals. At Creation, man was granted
dominion over the animals (1:28); here this power is restricted. From now on the
animals will fear and respect only the man who is pure, innocent and without
reproach, the one whose face still reflects God's image. No longer does man
enjoy as absolute a supremacy over beast as he did before his moral downfall.
His right to domesticate animals is no longer unlimited. How can man, who has
fallen to the level of the beasts, still rule as master over them? But the animals
also were warned about man (verse 5). *Rashi* explains why: Because the
generation of the Flood sinned, they were given over to the dominion of the wild
animals, who now had mastery over them as it is said: *They are like the beasts
that perish* (*Psalms* 49:21). Hence it was now necessary to warn the animals
about them.

3. לָכֶם יִהְיֶה לְאָכְלָה — *Shall be food for you.* "I had not allowed Adam to eat flesh,
only the herbage of the fields. Now for you, just as Adam was free to eat the
vegetation, I give you everything to eat" (*Rashi*).

The change in food solemnly proclaimed here is the first instruction which
man received after the Flood. It was to inaugurate the new order instituted
within humanity. The fact that the moral reformation of man begins with a
"dietary law" proves the fundamental importance attached to it. Most of the
reasons advanced to explain this change in diet do not seem to encompass this
historical evolution (a concession to Noah for having rescued and nourished the
animals during the deluge; a reward to Noah for having obtained the Divine
covenant with humanity through his sacrifice; the need for a more substantial
diet because of a weakening of the human body and a reduction in man's
life-span; a special permission granted to man who now, after the Flood, has
access to a higher degree of morality).

"Be fruitful and multiply and fill the land. ² *The fear of you and the dread of you shall be upon every beast of the earth and upon every bird of the heavens, in everything that moves on earth and in all the fish of the sea; in your hand they are given.* ³ *Every moving thing that lives shall be food for you; like the green herbage I have given you everything.*

The new era spelled the end of the vegetarian diet which had been in force from creation for 1656 years. Far from calming man's behavior, this diet had been powerless to prevent him from becoming cruel, egoistic, and perverse. Accordingly, a new orientation was now called for. It was part of a new method of moral training, which was to permit all of creation to raise itself up, progressively, to holiness.

R' M. Cordovero writes: "The whole universe is like a temple where all sing the glory of God (*Psalms* 29:9). At every rung of the ladder extending from the depths of life on earth to the sublimest regions of the spirit, all the elements reach upwards and strive to come ever closer to the holy, Divine source of life and blessing. Indeed, in nature there exists a hierarchical order which extends right down to inorganic elements, differentiated by the measure of the vitality which they receive from the supreme source of the Divine light. This sequential connection of the spheres of creation encompasses the mineral, vegetable, animal, and human realms. The continual rise of each constituent occurs step by step. Thus, rain falls on the earth, it waters the earth, it helps the seed to germinate. The seed assimilates and transforms elements in the earth to grow into a plant. The plant is eaten by animals, and the vegetable element, thanks to this transmigration, reaches a level of existence where the soul begins to shine forth on the purely physical world. Ultimately, man consumes the flesh of the animals, which becomes part of the man himself. The animal comes ever closer to the source of light contained in the spiritual soul. In this way, the different elements of nature ascend to the threshold of the metaphysical world, where the unfettered human soul will rejoin the heavenly sphere of absolute holiness" (פרדס רמונים, שער כ"ד, פ"י).

Seen in this perspective, the authorization for eating meat is a part of the universal uplifting of the spheres of creation to the heights of holiness.

However, adds R' Yitzchak Luria, this authorization was not in effect before the Flood. At creation's beginnings, the Divine plan foresaw that holiness would spread from heaven on its route earthward. Radiating from the supreme source, it was to penetrate to the lowest levels of the emanating spheres. Thus the sacrifice offered by Adam consecrated the entire animal species and gave it its stamp of holiness. But as soon as the animals "corrupted their ways" a new access to holiness had to be found. It was the one which characterized the postdiluvian era and it concerned all creatures which had given themselves to debauchery. This new approach to holiness was an infinitely more arduous path, climbing from the depths upward, step by step, past all levels of creation.

ד-ה אַךְ־בָּשָׂר בְּנַפְשׁוֹ דָמוֹ לֹא תֹאכֵלוּ: וְאַ֤ךְ אֶת־דִּמְכֶם
לְנַפְשֹׁתֵיכֶם֙ אֶדְרֹשׁ מִיַּ֤ד כָּל־חַיָּה אֶדְרְשֶׁ֔נּוּ וּמִיַּ֣ד הָֽאָדָ֔ם
ו מִיַּד֙ אִ֣ישׁ אָחִ֔יו אֶדְרֹשׁ אֶת־נֶ֥פֶשׁ הָֽאָדָם: שֹׁפֵךְ֙ דַּ֣ם הָֽאָדָ֔ם
בָּֽאָדָ֖ם דָּמ֣וֹ יִשָּׁפֵ֑ךְ כִּ֚י בְּצֶ֣לֶם אֱלֹהִ֔ים עָשָׂ֖ה אֶת־הָֽאָדָֽם:

Thus the change in diet, coming at the beginning of a new epoch in human history, is characteristic of profound changes in the physical and moral development of the human race from that time onward.

4. אַךְ־בָּשָׂר בְּנַפְשׁוֹ דָמוֹ לֹא תֹאכֵלוּ — *But flesh; with its soul its blood you shall not eat. Rashi* explains: this first forbids taking flesh from an animal which is still alive; then follows the interdiction of eating the blood of a living animal (cf.*Rambam Hilchos Melachim* 9:10).

Although the Torah authorizes eating meat for the reasons given above, it does so only on certain conditions, thus limiting and restricting the allowed practice. Here is a typical example of the Torah's method of instruction. Judaism does not require an austere life nor does it demand a vegetarian diet. What it does want is to sanctify human life in all its manifestations. Together with complete moral freedom for the individual, the Torah wanted to give him the means of making the best use of it, of experiencing life and its joys without losing one's soul or compromising one's greatness among the creatures of creation. Hence, around what it permitted, Judaism placed certain precepts which serve to control man's instincts. They prevent him from becoming a slave to his sensual appetites and descending to a bestial level. These precepts help him maintain his dignity as a human being. The constant self-discipline and self-denial which they demand puts the stamp of holiness on our sensual pleasures.

The prohibitions of this verse act in this direction. Forbidding cruelty to animals, prohibiting the consumption of blood — these are the bases for most of the laws relating to the Jewish method of slaughtering animals (*shechitah*) and of preparing meat for food (making meat kosher), laws which Jews have observed from time immemorial. But here they are addressed to the sons of Noah, that is, to all of humanity, which brings out the universal value of the Biblical laws, at least in their basic principles. Indeed, there can be but one truth, valid for Jew and non-Jew alike. The difference is that for the Jews, who are the "advance party" of the nations, the duties are more numerous and stricter than for the others.

5. אֶת־דִּמְכֶם . . . אֶדְרֹשׁ — *Your blood . . . I will demand.* "I have allowed you to take the lives of animals; but I will require those who (in committing suicide) shed their own blood to answer for it" (*Rashi*).

I might think, continues the Midrash, that the prohibition of suicide would apply even to a case like that of Chananyah, Mishael and Azaryah, who threw themselves into the fiery furnace to sanctify God's name before King

⁴ *But flesh; with its soul its blood you shall not eat.* ⁵ *However, your blood which belongs to your souls I will demand, of every beast will I demand it; but of man, of every man for that of his brother I will demand the soul of man.* ⁶ *Whoever sheds the blood of man, by man shall his blood be shed; for in the image of God He made man.*

Nebuchadnezzar (*Daniel* 3:17). This is not so, because our verse begins with an adverb which has a case like the following: when Saul was wounded by the Philistines during battle, he said to his armor-bearer, *Draw your sword and thrust me through, lest these uncircumcised come and thrust me through and wantonly ill-use me* (*I Samuel* 31:4; see also *Ralbag* on *II Samuel* 1:16). In Saul's case it was a question of avoiding the "profanation of God's name" and the shame upon Israel which would have occurred had the king of Israel been slaughtered at the hand of the enemy. But aside from these cases and the ones mentioned by *Rambam* (*Hilchos Yesodei HaTorah* 5:4), suicide (as well as euthanasia) remains forbidden because "man is not the complete master of his body" (שו״ע הרב, חלק ה', סע ד').

מִיַּד אִישׁ אָחִיו — *Of every man for that of his brother.* Cf. *Rashi* to *Exodus* 21:13.

6. שֹׁפֵךְ דַּם הָאָדָם — *Whoever sheds the blood of man.* On what is based the inviolability and sanctity of human life? Man was made in God's image. This is the only justification which is valid in the absolute. It permits no distinction to be made between men of different races, religions, or colors, nor between masters and slaves, nor between friends and enemies. It confers on each individual a natural dignity which keeps from shame even the wrongdoer who is being punished (*Deuteronomy* 25:3) and even the corpse of a man condemned to death (*Deuteronomy* 21:23). It is the offense to the dignity of human beings created in God's image which provides the basic reason underlying the juridical sanctions within Biblical legislation — and not at all the *jus talionis* (right of retaliation) nor the idea of deterrence, as has often been claimed in reference to *Deuteronomy* 13:11 etc. (cf. *R' Hirsch*).

בָּאָדָם דָּמוֹ יִשָּׁפֵךְ — *By man shall his blood be shed.* R' Yitzchak Luria explained that the murderer's blood must be shed because he shed human blood in man (שפך דם הָאָדָם בָּאָדָם), that is, the blood of the descendants contained in that of the victim. His disciple *R' Chaim Vital* raised an objection, quoting *Onkelos'* interpretation which renders בָּאָדָם as "with witnesses." If there are witnesses to the murder, you are to put the murderer to death. But the master replied: Both interpretations are complementary. If the one murdered would have had descendants, Providence would ensure that witnesses were present when the murder was committed so that human justice could punish the murderer.

In the other case, the murderer only smote a man virtually dead and no witnesses are required. It is in this way that *Rashi's* comment on *Exodus* 2:12 should be taken.

חמישי   ז-ח   וְאַתֶּם פְּרוּ וּרְבוּ שִׁרְצוּ בָאָרֶץ וּרְבוּ־בָהּ:   וַיֹּאמֶר

ט   אֱלֹהִים אֶל־נֹחַ וְאֶל־בָּנָיו אִתּוֹ לֵאמֹר: וַאֲנִי הִנְנִי מֵקִים

י   אֶת־בְּרִיתִי אִתְּכֶם וְאֶת־זַרְעֲכֶם אַחֲרֵיכֶם: וְאֵת כָּל־נֶפֶשׁ

הַחַיָּה אֲשֶׁר אִתְּכֶם בָּעוֹף בַּבְּהֵמָה וּבְכָל־חַיַּת הָאָרֶץ אִתְּכֶם

יא   מִכֹּל יֹצְאֵי הַתֵּבָה לְכֹל חַיַּת הָאָרֶץ: וַהֲקִמֹתִי אֶת־בְּרִיתִי

אִתְּכֶם וְלֹא־יִכָּרֵת כָּל־בָּשָׂר עוֹד מִמֵּי הַמַּבּוּל וְלֹא־יִהְיֶה

יב   עוֹד מַבּוּל לְשַׁחֵת הָאָרֶץ: וַיֹּאמֶר אֱלֹהִים זֹאת אוֹת־הַבְּרִית

אֲשֶׁר־אֲנִי נֹתֵן בֵּינִי וּבֵינֵיכֶם וּבֵין כָּל־נֶפֶשׁ חַיָּה אֲשֶׁר אִתְּכֶם

7. וְאַתֶּם פְּרוּ וּרְבוּ — *And you, be fruitful and multiply.* The same words had been cited previously (*Genesis* 1:28), where *Rashi* and *Ramban* take them to be a blessing. Here, however, they are a command. (Cf. א׳ שיק, המצות למהר"ם ס׳).

8. וַיֹּאמֶר אֱלֹהִים אֶל־נֹחַ וְאֶל־בָּנָיו — *And God said to Noah and to his sons.* Cf. our commentary on 8:18. The expression וַיֹּאמֶר אֱלֹהִים is given here, a change from the וַיְדַבֵּר א׳ of 8:15. The former signifies a specification of the more general discourse implied in the verb דבר (שב"ט) ס׳, אילת השחר, מלבים).

9. וַאֲנִי הִנְנִי מֵקִים אֶת־בְּרִיתִי — *And as for Me, behold, I establish My covenant.* An emphatic expression, a counterpart to that used when the Flood was unleashed (6:17; cf. our commentary ibid.). Now that man has suffered his punishment and made atonement, God is ready and eager to make a covenant with him — it is the same readiness with which He wiped corruption off the face of the earth. Hence *Rashi* explains this verse in terms corresponding to those used above for the destruction: I am ready to confirm My promise, to give you a covenant to ratify it, and I give you this sign.

11. וְלֹא־יִכָּרֵת כָּל־בָּשָׂר עוֹד מִמֵּי הַמַּבּוּל — *Never again shall all flesh be cut off by the waters of the flood.* Note the Talmud in *Sotah* 11a: The Egyptians said, "Come, let us deal wisely with him" (*Exodus* 1:10). They should have said "with them." But, explains R' Chama ben Chanina, the Egyptians meant: Let us go and outsmart Him (the Redeemer of the Jews). Shall we attack them with fire? Their God has proclaimed that He will punish by fire (*Isaiah* 66:15). By sword? Their God punishes "with his sword drawn in his hand" (*Numbers* 22:23). The Egyptians knew that God punishes according to the principle of מִדָּה כְּנֶגֶד מִדָּה, *measure for measure,* and so they sought a way of destroying the Jews which could never come back on them "measure for measure." They decided to smite the Jews with water (every newborn male was to be thrown into the river) since God had already promised never to devastate the earth again by flood. But they did not know that He had promised this only with respect to the earth as a whole, but not for individual nations. Or again, He promised never to bring devastation on the earth again by flood, but He did not give assurance that men would not of their own accord rush into water and drown. And this is just what happened to the Egyptians, who "were fleeing towards it" (*Exodus* 14:27).

> ⁷ *And you, be fruitful and multiply; teem on the earth and multiply on it."*
>
> ⁸ *And God said to Noah and to his sons with him saying:* ⁹ *"And as for Me, behold, I establish My covenant with you and with your offspring after you,* ¹⁰ *and with every living being that is with you — with the birds, with the animals, and with every beast of the land with you — of all that departed the Ark, to every beast of the earth.* ¹¹ *And I will confirm My covenant with you: Never again shall all flesh be cut off by the waters of the flood, and never again shall there be a flood to destroy the earth."*
>
> ¹²*And God said, "This is the sign of the covenant that I give between Me and you, and every living being that is with you,*

Thus, Jewish tradition considerably limits the scope of the Divine promise; it does not refer to smaller-scale floods, nor to the destruction of an entire nation by shipwreck, nor to destruction by a means other than water. This gives rise to certain questions. What is the reason for this "relative," restricted promise? And then, what is the nature of Divine justice? No one was bothered by these problems more than Abraham. When God told him of the imminent destruction of Sodom, he cried out (*Genesis* 18:25): חָלִלָה לְּךָ הֲשֹׁפֵט כָּל־הָאָרֶץ לֹא יַעֲשֶׂה מִשְׁפָּט, *It would* be *sacrilege to You! Shall the Judge of all the earth not do justice?* And the Sages explain the sense of this outcry by having Abraham say: "Did You not swear never again to bring a flood upon the world? Why then do You use this ploy of making a distinction between a flood of water and a flood of fire? You will not be absolved of Your oath!" R' Shimon ben Lakish has Abraham object in these words: "If you want justice, You cannot have the world. You cannot have it both ways. If You do not want to temper somewhat (the principle of strict justice) the world cannot exist." Then God paid homage to the "love of righteousness and hatred of wickedness" which Abraham showed (*Psalms* 45:8; *Bereishis Rabbah* 39). And Abraham immediately took the opportunity to have God "temper somewhat the principle of strict justice" and implored God to save the whole city for the sake of its few righteous inhabitants. Unfortunately there were no righteous people to be found. Then the deluge of flame raged over Sodom, for such a punishment was not excluded by the covenant which God had contracted with Noah.

12. זֹאת אוֹת־הַבְּרִית — *This is the sign of the covenant. Ramban* recalls this phrase in connection with the sacred service of the High Priest on the Day of Atonement (*Leviticus* 16:3). There we find the words: בְּזֹאת יָבֹא אַהֲרֹן אֶל הַקֹּדֶשׁ, *With this shall Aaron enter the Sanctuary.* Now, the word בְּזֹאת (*with this*) alludes to the word זֹאת in our verse concerning the covenant between God and man. With "this," the Divine promise of mercy and clemency for mankind, valid for all generations (לְדֹרֹת עוֹלָם), the High Priest will enter the Sanctuary on Yom Kippur to ask God for atonement. The Torah repeats

יג לְדֹרֹת עוֹלָם: אֶת־קַשְׁתִּי נָתַתִּי בֶּעָנָן וְהָיְתָה לְאוֹת בְּרִית

יד בֵּינִי וּבֵין הָאָרֶץ: וְהָיָה בְּעַנְנִי עָנָן עַל־הָאָרֶץ וְנִרְאֲתָה הַקֶּשֶׁת

טו בֶּעָנָן: וְזָכַרְתִּי אֶת־בְּרִיתִי אֲשֶׁר בֵּינִי וּבֵינֵיכֶם וּבֵין כָּל־נֶפֶשׁ
חַיָּה בְּכָל־בָּשָׂר וְלֹא־יִהְיֶה עוֹד הַמַּיִם לְמַבּוּל לְשַׁחֵת כָּל־

טז בָּשָׂר: וְהָיְתָה הַקֶּשֶׁת בֶּעָנָן וּרְאִיתִיהָ לִזְכֹּר בְּרִית עוֹלָם בֵּין
אֱלֹהִים וּבֵין כָּל־נֶפֶשׁ חַיָּה בְּכָל־בָּשָׂר אֲשֶׁר עַל־הָאָרֶץ:

this same expression twice, here and in verse 17, to bring out the full significance
of this covenant.

13. אֶת־קַשְׁתִּי נָתַתִּי בֶּעָנָן — *I have set My rainbow in the cloud.* The stars and
celestial phenomena, from the time they were created, were destined to serve as
"signs" for man (וְהָיוּ לְאֹתֹת; *Genesis* 1:14). The moon became Jewry's emblem,
the sun symbolized the other nations, the stars were designated as a pledge to
Abraham regarding his descendants. Here the rainbow appears as a sign of the
covenant established with Noah for the salvation of mankind.

As a natural phenomenon resulting from the refraction of the sun's rays
through cloud, the rainbow was in existence from creation. But only after the
Flood did it assume the particular significance of a sign of the covenant. So holds
Ramban (and others) who points to the past tense of the verb נָתַתִּי in this verse
as proof that the rainbow was previously in existence. *Ibn Ezra* disagrees, despite
the statement in Mishnah *Avos* (5:8) which counts the rainbow among the "ten
objects created on the sixth day at twilight," that is, just at the end of the work
of creation. *Abarbanel* considers that, because of the changes in cosmic
conditions following the Flood, people were then able to see the rainbow, which
previously they had not perceived. For *Maharal*, the rainbow is, to be sure, a
natural phenomenon, but here the Torah gives the primary cause for its
formation (the cause of the cause), which is metaphysical. Nature was created
with man in mind, in such a way that his moral conduct can have repercussions
on natural phenomena. A case in point was the first sin, after which nature
produced thorns and thistles (באר הגולה ד׳; ו׳). This interdependence, this
interaction, also explains the tradition which *Rashi* quotes: "Some generations
had no need of this sign, because they were perfectly righteous. Such were the
generations of Chizkiyah, king of Judah, and of R' Shimon bar Yochai.

What is the specific relationship between the rainbow and the covenant with
mankind? Some of our Sages believe it to be symbolized in the shape of the
rainbow. Its position of rest heralds peace, for a bow turned toward the earth
would have signified God's intention to smite the earth, just as the hunter turns
his bow and arrow towards his target. Since the bow is turned heavenwards, this
is not the case.

The Kabbalists consider that the continuous spectrum of colors in the rainbow
reflects the Divine attributes in their nuanced variety. Indeed the prophet Ezekiel
says: *Like the appearance of the bow that is in the cloud on the day of rain, so*

to generations forever: [13] *I have set My rainbow in the cloud,
and it shall be a sign of the covenant between Me and the
earth.* [14] *And it shall happen, when I place a cloud over the
earth, and the bow will be seen in the cloud,* [15] *I will remember
My covenant between Me and you and every living being
among all flesh, and the water shall never again become a flood
to destroy all flesh.* [16] *And the bow shall be in the cloud, and I
will look upon it to remember the everlasting covenant between
God and every living being, among all flesh that is on earth.''*

*was the appearance of the brightness round about; this was the appearance of
the likeness of the Glory of HASHEM. And when I saw it, I fell upon my face, and
I heard the voice of One that spoke* (1:28). And just as the rainbow is a
binding-together of a sevenfold radiation, so too is the light emanating from
God's presence to be considered the radiance of a sevenfold goodness. Our daily
prayers allude to these seven attributes of the Divine light in שִׂים שָׁלוֹם: *Bless us
all alike, our Father, with the light of Your countenance, for by the light of Your
countenance have You given us, HASHEM our God, a Torah of life,
lovingkindness, charity, blessing, mercy, life and peace.* Consequently, the
seven colors are in some way the projections of the attributes of Divine love.
Because of this, God proclaimed: "When I wish to bring darkness and desolation
upon the earth (cf. *Rashi* on verse 14) the bow will be seen in the clouds . . . and
I shall see it to recall a permanent covenant, etc."

Thus the rainbow was recognized as a reflection of the *Shechinah.* It follows
that one should not stare at it, nor should one point it out to those with him. He
should rather do as Moses did before the burning bush and hide his face from
it, for *he was afraid to look upon God* (*Exodus* 3:6) (*Racanati*). The enjoyment
of the Divine light in its bright splendor is reserved for the righteous in the
messianic era (*Zohar*).

16. וּרְאִיתִיהָ לִזְכֹּר בְּרִית עוֹלָם — *And I will look upon it to remember the
everlasting covenant.* Does God need to look upon it in order to remember?
There is no forgetting with God! Or was the rainbow needed to remind Jewry
of the punishment of the Flood? But that was recorded in the Torah — how
could it be forgotten? And the rainbow was not needed by the other nations
because they were non-believers and "disbelievers" and the Flood meant
nothing to them. In reality, "the sign through which God recalls His miracles"
זֵכֶר עָשָׂה לְנִפְלְאוֹתָיו is meant for mankind. Thus it is not written, *And I will look
upon it that I may remember,* but *to remember,* (וּרְאִיתִיהָ לִזְכֹּר) that is, so that
the righteous remember and bless the One Who "remembers the covenant (בָּרוּךְ
זוֹכֵר הַבְּרִית), Who is faithful to His covenant and makes good His word." (These
are the words of the blessing said on seeing a rainbow.) When the rainbow
appears in the clouds, let everyone be aware that "I recall." Let men not lose
heart, let them not have doubts about Divine justice, even when the world is

יז וַיֹּאמֶר אֱלֹהִים אֶל־נֹחַ זֹאת אוֹת־הַבְּרִית אֲשֶׁר הֲקִמֹתִי בֵּינִי
וּבֵין כָּל־בָּשָׂר אֲשֶׁר עַל־הָאָרֶץ:

ששי יח וַיִּהְיוּ בְנֵי־נֹחַ הַיֹּצְאִים מִן־הַתֵּבָה שֵׁם וְחָם וָיָפֶת וְחָם הוּא

יט אֲבִי כְנָעַן: שְׁלֹשָׁה אֵלֶּה בְּנֵי־נֹחַ וּמֵאֵלֶּה נָפְצָה כָל־הָאָרֶץ:

כ־כא וַיָּחֶל נֹחַ אִישׁ הָאֲדָמָה וַיִּטַּע כָּרֶם: וַיֵּשְׁתְּ מִן־הַיַּיִן וַיִּשְׁכָּר

plunged into darkness and desolation. But let them see in the rainbow the pledge
of the eternal pact between Creator and created, and in it the assurance that the
Eternal is leading the world to its destiny, even though times be hard. As for the
Eternal, He does not know forgetfulness; He needs no sign to remember ('ס
(חסידים, כ"י סי' תתתשל"ד, פארמא).

18. בְּנֵי־נֹחַ הַיֹּצְאִים מִן־הַתֵּבָה — *The sons of Noah who came out of the Ark*. One
might have hoped that their stay in the Ark would have had a decisive influence
on the character and spirit of Noah's sons. Indeed, in several places and right up
to the first days following the Flood, the Torah does not name them but speaks
simply of Noah and his sons. During that period they were the sons of a righteous
person and had come closer to God, Whose words they all heard. But scarcely
out of the Ark, they reverted to their pre-Flood behavior: three brothers, each
going his own way, coming closer to or straying from God. Japheth, the eldest,
learned nothing from the events which befell him and was relegated to be
mentioned last.

וְחָם הוּא אֲבִי כְנָעַן — *Ham being the father of Canaan*. This detail, which the Torah
repeats further on, is highly significant. It is important to keep in mind that when
the Jewish people received the Torah, they were well acquainted with the
Canaanite tribe and were making ready to conquer its territory. Accordingly, the
text puts great emphasis here on the origin of this people, which explains its moral
perversion, an ancestral heritage and inescapable cause of its imminent downfall.
The phrase "Ham is the father of Canaan" therefore serves as a stern warning
to Jewry. The text seems to say to the future conquerors of the land of Canaan:
"Never forget that the idolatrous population of this land is doomed to be wiped
out because of the moral debauchery rooted in it from its earliest ancestor. Beware
of following its example, lest the promised land disgorge you also. Above all,
watch over and preserve the moral purity of your people for your own salvation."

The word חָם is found in three other places in the Bible; each time it refers to
a state of heat (See *Baal HaTurim*, quoting the *Rosh* on *Exodus* 16:21). So too here,
applying to Noah's son, it designates a hot-blooded character, one of feverish
temperament given to sensuality.

19. שְׁלֹשָׁה אֵלֶּה בְּנֵי־נֹחַ — *These three were the sons of Noah*. All three had the
same father, a perfectly righteous man, and yet they were so different from each
other! All mankind was divided and separated into individual types, branching
out from these three. All future differentiation in human types goes back to these
three "archetypes."

¹⁷ And God said to Noah, "This is the sign of the covenant that I have confirmed between Me and all flesh that is upon the earth."

¹⁸ The sons of Noah who came out of the Ark were Shem, Ham, and Japheth — Ham being the father of Canaan. ¹⁹ These three were the sons of Noah, and from these the whole world was spread out.

²⁰ Noah, the man of the earth, debased himself and planted a vineyard. ²¹ He drank of the wine and became drunk,

20. וַיָּחֶל נֹחַ — Noah ... debased himself. Rashi remarks that: "וַיָּחֶל is related to חוּלִין, something profane. Noah profaned himself. He should have begun by planting something else."

Noah's first preoccupation after the Flood was not to devote all his efforts to the moral and spiritual rebuilding of the world. It was to plant a vineyard. This is judged a "profanation" a debasement of himself. God said to him: "Noah, shouldn't you have learned your lesson from Adam's sin and its consequences?" (According to R' Meir, the forbidden fruit was the fruit of the vine; Sanhedrin 70b.)

Noah escapes the terrible calamity, he comes out safe and sound from a nightmarish existence in the Ark lasting an interminable year, and yet his first thought is to taste life's pleasures once more. Noah, formerly called אִישׁ צַדִּיק, after his ordeal becomes אִישׁ הָאֲדָמָה, the man of the earth. R' Berachya observes: See the difference between Noah's tragic fall and Moses' uninterrupted rise. For at the beginning of his career Moses was called אִישׁ מִצְרִי, an Egyptian man (Exodus 2:19), and at the end, אִישׁ הָאֱלֹהִים, the man of God (Deuteronomy 33:1; Bereishis Rabbah 36).

וַיִּטַּע כָּרֶם — And planted a vineyard. "Satan came toward him and offered to help him in the planting. Noah accepted. What did Satan do then? He took a sheep and slaughtered it over the vine. Then he did likewise with a lion, and then a pig. The earth of the vineyard was watered with the blood of these animals. On the very day it was planted, the vine bloomed and bore fruit. On that same day, Noah gathered the grapes, pressed them and drank. Why did Satan do this? When a man drinks one glass of wine, he stays meek as a lamb; with two glasses, he becomes strong as a lion, believing no one is his equal. But when three or four are imbibed, he resembles a pig — he dirties his clothes and wallows in filth."

The drinker who is incapable of controlling his vice stumbles along the downhill path which leads to shame. This idea also finds expression in the Talmud. It notes that the coordinating conjunction ו (meaning and) is repeated thirteen times in the five verses recounting Noah's drunkenness. If he cannot control himself, the drunkard is dragged by his passion from degradation to degradation; his thirteen steps downward lead him to defy, God, characterized by His thirteen attributes of mercy (Sanhedrin 70a; ועי' של"ה).

כב וַיִּתְגַּל בְּתוֹךְ אָהֳלֹה: וַיַּרְא חָם אֲבִי כְנַעַן אֵת עֶרְוַת אָבִיו
כג וַיַּגֵּד לִשְׁנֵי־אֶחָיו בַּחוּץ: וַיִּקַּח שֵׁם וָיֶפֶת אֶת־הַשִּׂמְלָה
וַיָּשִׂימוּ עַל־שְׁכֶם שְׁנֵיהֶם וַיֵּלְכוּ אֲחֹרַנִּית וַיְכַסּוּ אֵת עֶרְוַת
כד אֲבִיהֶם וּפְנֵיהֶם אֲחֹרַנִּית וְעֶרְוַת אֲבִיהֶם לֹא רָאוּ: וַיִּיקֶץ נֹחַ
כה מִיֵּינוֹ וַיֵּדַע אֵת אֲשֶׁר־עָשָׂה לוֹ בְּנוֹ הַקָּטָן: וַיֹּאמֶר אָרוּר כְּנָעַן

Just before קִדּוּשׁ is said over wine to sanctify the Sabbath or a festival, one says סַבְרִי מָרָנָן which is addressed to those listening. It means תְּנוּ דַעְתְּכֶם, *pay attention*, since wine can lead to drunkenness and since it brought a curse on the world (*Tanchuma, Pekudei*).

21. וַיִּתְגַּל — *And he uncovered himself.* The word וַיִּתְגַּל contains the same letters as גָּלִיּוֹת, *exiles* (*Baal HaTurim*). The Midrash makes a similar observation based on the verbal form of וַיִּתְגַּל, which could mean *he was exiled*. It draws the lesson that just as drink caused Noah to flee in shame, it will force those of his descendants who take to it to become fugitives. Such was the case with the ten tribes of Israel who were exiled "because of wine" (*Amos* 6:6); so too with the tribes of Judah and Benjamin (*Isaiah* 28:7).

אָהֳלֹה — *His tent.* אָהֳלֹה is written with the feminine pronoun suffix. Our sages say it was his wife's tent. When he felt the wine going to his head, Noah took refuge where he hoped no one would see him. He did not want his children to see him in a drunken state.

22. וַיַּרְא חָם אֲבִי כְנַעַן אֵת עֶרְוַת אָבִיו — *Ham, the father of Canaan, saw his father's nakedness.* The other children remained outside out of respect and decency. But Ham boldly entered the tent. What is worse, he was a father himself and his experience with his own children should have made him feel quite differently toward his father. But not only did he see the shame of his father, he took pleasure in telling his brothers, with sneers and derision (*Pirkei D'Rabbi Eliezer* 23).

We have already pointed out that by emphasizing the words אֲבִי כְנַעַן, the fact that Ham is the father of Canaan, the Torah has in its sights the degenerate population of Canaan. It wants to impress on the Jewish people the origins of this degeneration. Israel was flanked by two Hamitic peoples: Egypt, where it was exposed to social decadence, and Canaan, whose moral decay it was well aware of. Here, then, the Torah gives us the origin of this depravity — the relationship between Ham and his father!

Man's universe is built entirely on the relationship between child and parent. As long as children see their parents entrusted with the Divine mission, as long as children respect the spiritual being within their parents, humanity will develop in a healthy way. But without this, when the child is only given the physical aspect of his father to honor, and no longer feels a sense of decency in respecting his parents, then the branch is severed. The past will no longer be

and he uncovered himself within his tent. ²² Ham, the father of Canaan, saw his father's nakedness and told his two brothers outside. ²³ And Shem and Japheth took a garment, laid it upon both their shoulders, and they walked backwards, and covered their father's nakedness; their faces were turned away, and they saw not their father's nakedness.
    ²⁴ Noah awoke from his wine and realized what his small son had done to him. ²⁵ And he said, "Cursed is Canaan;

capable of leading to an ever-improving future. And so, when the Jewish nation was led to the borders of the Promised Land, which was to be evacuated to make room for them, they were shown this moral decadence and its consequences. Then they were told: see, this decadence began with the first act of disrespect which the ancestor of this populace showed toward his father (*R' Hirsch*).

וַיַּגֵּד לִשְׁנֵי־אֶחָיו — *And told his two brothers.* This explains why a Caananite slave was freed if his master caused permanent damage to his eye or made him lose a tooth (*Exodus* 21:26-27). The curse of slavery on the sons of Canaan goes back to the sin of their ancestor, a sin committed with the organs of sight and speech (וַיַּרְא, וַיַּגֵּד). Now if the slave loses the use of one of these organs, punishment has been exacted and the curse loses its *raison d'etre* (*Rabbah* ibid. and *Rashi*).

23. וַיִּקַּח שֵׁם וָיֶפֶת אֶת־הַשִּׂמְלָה — *And Shem and Japheth took a garment.* Rashi interprets as follows: since Shem was more eager than Japheth to carry out the *mitzvah*, his sons will deserve to wear the *tallis*, with its fringes, *tzitzis*. As for Japheth's sons, they will merit having a proper burial. And as for Ham, who did not respect his father, the prophet Isaiah will describe how his descendants will be punished (20:4). Very often our Sages show us how a simple good deed of the ancestors is of benefit to their children to the latest generations (or how the virtue of the forefathers continues to bear fruit and to develop progressively) and how, conversely, sins of the ancestors have grave repercussions down the chain of the generations. It is as the Divine word proclaimed in the Decalogue: "For I, Hᴀꜱʜᴇᴍ, your God, am the jealous Almighty, Who visits the iniquity of the fathers upon the children unto the third and fourth generation of those who hate Me; and shows mercy unto the thousandth generation of those who love Me and keep My commandments."

24. נֹחַ . . . וַיֵּדַע אֵת אֲשֶׁר־עָשָׂה לוֹ בְּנוֹ הַקָּטָן — *Noah . . . and realized what his small son had done to him.* The general opinion is that this refers to Ham. But for *Ibn Ezra* (based on *Pirkei D'Rabbi Eliezer* 23) it refers to Canaan, fourth and youngest son of Ham, who was a bad influence on his father. The expression "he realized what he had done to him" implies some material act. To be sure, verse 22 speaks of sight and speech, but would these require a punishment as severe and full of consequence as the curse? This is the argument which *Maharal* (באר הגולה, ה׳) advances against those critical of the affirmation of Rav and

כו עֶבֶד עֲבָדִים יִהְיֶה לְאֶחָיו: וַיֹּאמֶר בָּרוּךְ יהוה אֱלֹהֵי שֵׁם
כז וִיהִי כְנַעַן עֶבֶד לָמוֹ: יַפְתְּ אֱלֹהִים לְיֶפֶת וְיִשְׁכֹּן בְּאָהֳלֵי־

Shmuel: one holds that the son castrated the father; the other, that he committed an act of pederasty with him (*Sanhedrin* 70a).

"Why did Ham make his father a eunuch? He said to his brothers: Adam had two sons and one killed the other to inherit the world. And our father has three sons — and he wants a fourth?" (*Rashi*).

25. עֶבֶד עֲבָדִים יִהְיֶה לְאֶחָיו — *A slave of slaves shall he be to his brothers.* What led Noah to condemn his unworthy son to slavery as punishment for his misdeeds? *Rashi* answers: "Because of you I will not have a fourth son to serve me. (Noah and his sons had had to work extremely hard, to their utmost, in the Ark. Noah had then hoped that his sons would be able to rest and be waited upon by slaves after the deluge, and that he himself would be served by a fourth son — *Midrash Rabbah*). Then cursed be your own fourth son; he will be enslaved by the descendants of your older brothers who now will have to look after me." Here we find the first mention of the division between masters and slaves in society. Moral decay was its prime cause.

Ibn Ezra explains that at first Canaan was to be a slave to both God and the descendants of Shem. This is taken from the plural לָמוֹ in verse 26: *And let Canaan be a slave to them.* Bondage under the descendants of Shem constitutes the surest means of bringing the Canaanite slaves closer to the ideal of moral purity, of leading them "under the wings of the *Shechinah*." It is in this spirit that the author of *Sefer HaChinuch* (§331) interprets the Mosaic law concerning Canaanite slaves (*Leviticus* 25:46). The real source of this law is found here in this verse.

R' S.R. Hirsch sees slavery as the fatal consequence of man's inability to control his instincts. Whoever lacks the will to control his passions becomes first the slave of his own senses and then the slave of other people. But he who knows how to remain in control of his nature and how to forego the enslavement of his sensual appetites will never let himself be led about and enticed, not even by chains of gold. He may go under, perish — but he can never be enslaved. So it is with individuals and so it is with nations.

For *Sforno*, slavery means a degradation to the lowest level of the social hierarchy, whose goal is to preserve the other social strata from the baneful influence of moral depravity.

Quite different is the point of view of *Ramban*. Right from the first verse of the Torah (keeping in mind the words of R' Yitzchak quoted by *Rashi*) he points out that *Genesis* opens with a description of history in order to explain to the world the origin of the Jewish people's legitimate rights to the Promised Land. The story of Noah's sons fits into this thesis. It teaches us that Canaan, whose offspring inhabited the land after the Flood (indeed, its name then was אֶרֶץ כְּנַעַן), was condemned to slavery and this was his own fault. Accordingly, the land of Canaan was promised to Abraham. For the original inhabitants continued in

a slave of slaves shall he be to his brothers."
    26 And he said, "Blessed is HASHEM, the God of Shem; and let Canaan be a slave to them.
    27 "May God extend Japheth, but he will dwell in the tents of

their depraved ways and were not worthy of possessing the jewel of lands. They were expelled, just as Adam was made to leave Paradise, just as the generation of the Flood was wiped off the earth, just as the generation of the Tower of Babel was dispersed throughout the world. Since the dawn of humanity, this has been the principle of Divine justice: when a nation reaches the lowest level of corruption, it must disappear and make way for a younger and purer nation. Thus God gave to the Jews *lands occupied by other peoples . . . so that they might observe His statutes and respect His laws* (*Psalms* 105:44-45). But even before occupying the land, they were warned: *Do not defile yourselves in any of these things* (sexual immorality); *for in all these the nations are defiled, which I cast out from before you . . . Beware that the land not disgorge you also, when you defile it, as it disgorged the nation that was before you* (*Leviticus* 18:28).

Indeed, *Ramban* adds, in the Divine plan which covers all eternity, the Holy Land was destined for Jewry right from the beginning. This idea is seen in Moses' final speech (*Deuteronomy* 32:8). But God first gave it to Canaan who, as slaves, kept it for the Jews. This is why Noah repeats twice here that Canaan is to be the slave of Shem. This is like a man who entrusts the possessions of the son of his master to his slave. The latter will keep them until the son grows up and takes possession of them himself (10:15). It is also in this spirit that Geviha ben Pesisa, in the presence of Alexander of Macedonia, refuted the territorial claims of the descendants of Canaan to the Promised Land (*Sanhedrin* 91a).

26. בָּרוּךְ ה' אֱלֹהֵי שֵׁם — *Blessed is HASHEM, the God of Shem.* Through this concise phrase is glimpsed the thankful joy which Noah felt from thoughts of his son Shem, who remained a faithful servant of God, Whom Noah himself had always loved. To Shem and his descendants falls the task of bringing about the victory of moral, spiritual, and religious values based on belief in God. It is their responsibility to spread the great religious ideas throughout the world.

וִיהִי כְנַעַן עֶבֶד לָמוֹ — *And let Canaan be a slave to them.* "The Jewish people were created to teach others to know God and also to devote themselves to serving Him. If these people turned part of themselves into slaves, the latter could not accomplish their supreme *raison d'etre.* Hence the Jewish people will be served by those among the nations of the world who, by their own fault, were condemned to servitude" (*Sefer HaChinuch*, ed. Venice, §331).

27. יַפְתְּ אֱלֹהִים לְיֶפֶת — *May God extend Japheth.* Onkelos translates: "give much room." Japheth's blessing refers to the expansion of his domain, that is, to worldly prosperity and widespread dominion. But he is to "dwell in the tents of Shem." Friendly relations should exist between the Semitic and Japhetic races. This is the first of the universal forecasts in the Bible. It envisages the day when

כח שֵׁם וַיְהִי כְנַעַן עֶבֶד לָמוֹ: וַיְחִי־נֹחַ אַחַר הַמַּבּוּל שְׁלֹשׁ מֵאוֹת
כט שָׁנָה וַחֲמִשִּׁים שָׁנָה: וַיִּהְיוּ כָּל־יְמֵי־נֹחַ תְּשַׁע מֵאוֹת שָׁנָה
וַחֲמִשִּׁים שָׁנָה וַיָּמֹת:

י א וְאֵלֶּה תּוֹלְדֹת בְּנֵי־נֹחַ שֵׁם חָם וָיָפֶת וַיִּוָּלְדוּ לָהֶם בָּנִים אַחַר

hostility between nations will be forgotten, when they will unite in common worship of the One God.

The word Japheth also means "beauty." The Rabbis thus interpret this verse: Let Japhetic beauty dwell in Semitic tents (*Megillah* 9b). They applied this recommendation more particularly to the use of Greek to translate the Torah since it was "the most beautiful language of the descendants of Japheth" (*Rashi* ibid.). In Chapter 10, verse 2, יָוָן (Greece) is named as a son of Japheth; it is he who most perfectly incarnates the essential character of Japheth, just as עֵבֶר, the Hebrew, is the most faithful representative of the spirit of Shem.

Noah's words to his children had universal impact on human history, as his three sons became the fathers of humanity after the Flood. Shem was the progenitor of the Semitic races, Ham essentially of the African peoples, and Japheth was the ancestor of the Indo-European nations. If today, after millennia of history, we try to sum up in a few words the contribution of each group to humanity, we could do no better than use the words of Noah's blessing: "Let God give Japheth the sense of beauty, but may He dwell in the tents of Shem, and let Canaan be their slave." Retrospectively, we see that Japheth, the ancestor of the Greeks, developed the cult of beauty and oriented man toward an esthetic culture. On the other hand, thanks to the tents of Shem, the great religious ideas were spread throughout the world. And it is true that until our own day the African peoples descending from Ham were the slaves of the white races.

These ideas permit us to conclude that, all in all, culture contains three essential elements: spiritual forces, emotional forces, and physical forces which quicken man's sensual life. Ham and his descendants represent the last, whereas the Semites incarnate the spiritual sphere (שֵׁם means *name*, that is, the abstract idea of an object, a purely spiritual factor). But between spirit and sensuality is the intermediate force of sensibility, of the sensitive life belonging to Japheth and his descendants. Here the substance comes from the physical domain, but the attributes, the essential characteristics, are taken from the spiritual. Hence this force is a link between the other two opposing spheres and is, as it were, the springboard by which the brutal, sensual force is to raise itself to gain access to the spiritual sphere. The Greek cult of beauty, attributed to Japheth, serves to calm one's disposition, to raise one's heart toward an esthetic ideal, and to bring out a love of perfect form. Only by passing through this intermediate Japhetic stage can Ham redeem himself and reach the heights where "dwells the God of Shem." This is why the "beauty of Japheth is to dwell in the tents of Shem." For Shem to carry out its mission of raising up by its ideal the hearts of all its brethren toward God, it must grant the Hellenic aspirations a place in its tent.

Shem; may Canaan be a slave to them."
²⁸ Noah lived after the Flood three hundred fifty years.
²⁹ And all the days of Noah were nine hundred fifty years; and
he died.

10 ¹These are the descendants of the sons of Noah: Shem, Ham,
and Japheth; sons were born to them after the Flood.

With this view of history, the famous Rabbi of Frankfurt, R' Samson Raphael
Hirsch, developed his doctrine known as תּוֹרָה עִם דֶּרֶךְ אֶרֶץ, Torah im Derech
Eretz. To a clearly defined extent, it supports a connection between Torah and
general culture. It declares as legitimate, from our Sages' point of view, the
integration of secular studies — "the culture of Japheth" as expressed in the arts,
literature, and the sciences — into the Jewish education program as long as the
secular studies do not contradict Judaism. On the contrary, they may make
valuable contributions to it (Works, II, "Der Hellenismus und das Judentum").

28. וַיְחִי־נֹחַ אַחַר הַמַּבּוּל שְׁלֹשׁ מֵאוֹת שָׁנָה וַחֲמִשִּׁים שָׁנָה — Noah lived after the Flood
three hundred fifty years. Noah lived long enough to see his family increase to
a large size — in fulfillment of the Divine benediction given them to multiply
rapidly after the Flood. To his descendants Noah was able to transmit the great
traditions about the creation of the world, Paradise, the first sin, etc., which he
himself had received from his ancestors. He also told of his first-hand experience
of Divine omnipotence as manifested in the Flood. Thus was formed the stock
of historical traditions which would become so widespread among men (cf. our
commentary on the next verse).

10.

1. וְאֵלֶּה תּוֹלְדֹת בְּנֵי־נֹחַ — These are the descendants of the sons of Noah. This
chapter traces the nations of the earth from Noah's sons. The principal races and
peoples known on earth are arranged as different branches of one great family.
Thus, all the nations have sprung from the same ancestry. All men are therefore
brothers. This sublime conception of the unity of the human race logically
follows from the belief in the unity of God and, like it, forms one of the
cornerstones of the edifice of Judaism. Polytheism could never rise to the idea of
humanity. "Heathen society was vitiated by failure to recognize the moral
obligation involved in our common humanity" (Elmslie). There is, therefore, no
parallel to this chapter in the literature of other peoples. Hence it has been called
a "Messianic document."

While the surpassing importance of this chapter is based on the philosophy
of history which it develops for us, the "table of the nations" drawn up here
remains, according to all results of archaeological exploration, an ethnographic
original document of the first rank which nothing can replace (Kautzsch). In all
its essential details, its trustworthiness has been vindicated by the ancient
monuments and inscriptions (Hertz).

ב הַמַּבּוּל: בְּנֵי יֶפֶת גֹּמֶר וּמָגוֹג וּמָדַי וְיָוָן וְתֻבָל וּמֶשֶׁךְ וְתִירָס:

ג-ד וּבְנֵי גֹמֶר אַשְׁכְּנַז וְרִיפַת וְתֹגַרְמָה: וּבְנֵי יָוָן אֱלִישָׁה וְתַרְשִׁישׁ

ה כִּתִּים וְדֹדָנִים: מֵאֵלֶּה נִפְרְדוּ אִיֵּי הַגּוֹיִם בְּאַרְצֹתָם אִישׁ

ו לִלְשֹׁנוֹ לְמִשְׁפְּחֹתָם בְּגוֹיֵהֶם: וּבְנֵי חָם כּוּשׁ וּמִצְרַיִם וּפוּט

ז וּכְנָעַן: וּבְנֵי כוּשׁ סְבָא וַחֲוִילָה וְסַבְתָּה וְרַעְמָה וְסַבְתְּכָא וּבְנֵי

ח רַעְמָה שְׁבָא וּדְדָן: וְכוּשׁ יָלַד אֶת־נִמְרֹד הוּא הֵחֵל לִהְיוֹת גִּבֹּר

ט בָּאָרֶץ: הוּא־הָיָה גִבֹּר־צַיִד לִפְנֵי יהוה עַל־כֵּן יֵאָמַר כְּנִמְרֹד

י גִּבּוֹר צַיִד לִפְנֵי יהוה: וַתְּהִי רֵאשִׁית מַמְלַכְתּוֹ בָּבֶל וְאֶרֶךְ

Other ideas, on a different plane, add still more to these words. They reveal the fact that Divine Providence reigns over nations and their history just as it does over nature. *When the Most High gave to the nations their inheritance, when He separated the sons of Adam, He set the borders of the peoples according to the number of the Children of Israel* (Deuteronomy 32:8). The distribution of peoples over the face of the earth takes into account the fact that, when the time comes, the Jewish people will take possession of the area situated *at the center of the earth* (Ezekiel 38:12), which is the central point at the crossroads of three continents. From here the rays of the light of truth will emanate to all parts of the world (see also *Rashi* ibid.). In addition, this chapter shows that the patriarch Abraham is a direct descendant of Shem, and this is historically necessary in order to justify his right to the Promised Land (*Ramban*).

For *Rambam*, this genealogical table is further proof of the creation of the world. He demonstrates that Abraham knew Noah (he was fifty-eight years old when Noah died; *Ibn Ezra* on 6:9) and Noah's father Lemech was fifty-six years of age at Adam's death (*Guide* 3:50). Thus there was a rather short "chain of tradition" from creation to the time of the patriarchs. And when they proclaimed the truth about creation by God they could count on earwitnesses to confirm their words. Abraham was the fourth link in the unbroken chain of tradition beginning from Adam. Moreover, Isaac and Jacob both knew Shem, Noah's son. He taught them the Divine laws; Jacob was fifty years old when Shem died. It was Jacob who transmitted all the great truths learned from this witness of the Flood to his generation which went down to Egypt, and to Pharaoh and his servants. "And so, those who received these truths could easily verify them, because one cannot lie about facts that go back only four or five generations." This was one of the arguments which *Ramban* used in Barcelona in 1263, during his debates with the apostate Dominican friar Pablo before James I, king of Spain and Aragon (דרשת הרמב"ן).

וַיִּוָּלְדוּ לָהֶם בָּנִים אַחַר הַמַּבּוּל — *Sons were born to them after the Flood.* Cf. *Rashi* on 5:32.

2. בְּנֵי יֶפֶת — *The sons of Japheth.* Some of the following are names of nations or countries as well as persons whose signification cannot always be firmly

² *The sons of Japheth: Gomer, Magog, Madai, Javan, Tubal, Meshech, and Tiras.* ³ *The sons of Gomer: Ashkenaz, Riphath, and Togarmah.* ⁴ *The sons of Javan: Elishah and Tarshish, the Kittim and the Dodanim.* ⁵ *From these the islands of the nations were separated in their lands — each according to its language, by their families, in their nations.*

⁶ *The sons of Ham: Cush, Mizraim, Put, and Canaan.* ⁷ *The sons of Cush: Seba, Havilah, Sabtah, Raamah, and Sabteca. The sons of Raamah: Sheba and Dedan.*

⁸ *And Cush begot Nimrod. He was the first to be a mighty man on earth.* ⁹ *He was a mighty hunter before* HASHEM; *therefore it is said: "Like Nimrod a mighty hunter before* HASHEM." ¹⁰ *The beginning of his kingdom was Babel, Erech,*

established. Hence we merely point out that, in general, Japheth's offspring are the Indo-European peoples. However, the Mongols are a Japhetic people through their ancestor Magog. Javan was the founding father of Greece, or more exactly of Ionia (יָוָן = יוֹן = Ion) and his eldest son, Elishah, is considered as being the Greek "Hellas." The descendants of Japheth generally inhabited the countries north of the Middle East, Ham's descendants dwelt in the south, and the Semites occupied the central region. However, the offspring of Kush, from Ham's family remained in Babylonia.

The principal peoples formed by Japheth's offspring are Germanic, Mongol, Medean, Hellenic, and Slavic.

6. וּבְנֵי חָם — *The sons of Ham.* They made up the peoples of Egypt, Ethiopia, Somalia, and Canaan. They spread to several parts of Africa, Phoenicia, and Palestine. The black color of this race is considered a Divine punishment inflicted upon Ham as a consequence of his moral corruption and the grave sin he committed against his father (*Rabbah* 36).

8. וְכוּשׁ יָלַד אֶת־נִמְרֹד — *And Cush begot Nimrod.* Nimrod — the first conqueror, the first despot, a powerful hunter before God. *Rashi* explains that Nimrod "captured men's thoughts and incited them to rebel against God. Hence it is said of a man who sins by bravado, who knows his Master and yet is bent on rebelling against Him, that he is 'like Nimrod, a mighty hunter, defiant before God.' "

In later times Nimrod became the archenemy of Abraham. Long before Abraham was born, Providence had prepared the arrival of his antagonist and then had put him in Abraham's path. Many a time he had to defend himself against Nimrod, stand up to him, and even attack him outright. Only by relentlessly struggling against the opposition which he encounters can man be led to affirm his personality and to reach true greatness. It was inevitable that before he could become the advocate of truth Abraham needed a cruel and brutal antagonist. *For God has made one to oppose the other* (*Ecclesiastes* 7:14).

יא וְאַבֵּד וְכַלְנֶה בְּאֶרֶץ שִׁנְעָר: מִן־הָאָרֶץ הַהִוא יָצָא אַשּׁוּר
יב וַיִּבֶן אֶת־נִינְוֵה וְאֶת־רְחֹבֹת עִיר וְאֶת־כָּלַח: וְאֶת־רֶסֶן בֵּין־
יג נִינְוֵה וּבֵין כֶּלַח הִוא הָעִיר הַגְּדֹלָה: וּמִצְרַיִם יָלַד אֶת־
יד לוּדִים וְאֶת־עֲנָמִים וְאֶת־לְהָבִים וְאֶת־נַפְתֻּחִים: וְאֶת־
פַּתְרֻסִים וְאֶת־כַּסְלֻחִים אֲשֶׁר יָצְאוּ מִשָּׁם פְּלִשְׁתִּים וְאֶת־
טו כַּפְתֹּרִים: וּכְנַעַן יָלַד אֶת־צִידֹן בְּכֹרוֹ וְאֶת־חֵת:
טז-יז וְאֶת־הַיְבוּסִי וְאֶת־הָאֱמֹרִי וְאֵת הַגִּרְגָּשִׁי: וְאֶת־הַחִוִּי וְאֶת־
יח הָעַרְקִי וְאֶת־הַסִּינִי: וְאֶת־הָאַרְוָדִי וְאֶת־הַצְּמָרִי וְאֶת־
יט הַחֲמָתִי וְאַחַר נָפֹצוּ מִשְׁפְּחוֹת הַכְּנַעֲנִי: וַיְהִי גְּבוּל הַכְּנַעֲנִי
מִצִּידֹן בֹּאֲכָה גְרָרָה עַד־עַזָּה בֹּאֲכָה סְדֹמָה וַעֲמֹרָה וְאַדְמָה
כ וּצְבֹיִם עַד־לָשַׁע: אֵלֶּה בְנֵי־חָם לְמִשְׁפְּחֹתָם לִלְשֹׁנֹתָם
כא בְּאַרְצֹתָם בְּגוֹיֵהֶם: וּלְשֵׁם יֻלַּד גַּם־הוּא אֲבִי כָּל־
כב בְּנֵי־עֵבֶר אֲחִי יֶפֶת הַגָּדוֹל: בְּנֵי שֵׁם עֵילָם וְאַשּׁוּר וְאַרְפַּכְשַׁד
כג-כד וְלוּד וַאֲרָם: וּבְנֵי אֲרָם עוּץ וְחוּל וְגֶתֶר וָמַשׁ: וְאַרְפַּכְשַׁד
כה יָלַד אֶת־שָׁלַח וְשֶׁלַח יָלַד אֶת־עֵבֶר: וּלְעֵבֶר יֻלַּד שְׁנֵי בָנִים
שֵׁם הָאֶחָד פֶּלֶג כִּי בְיָמָיו נִפְלְגָה הָאָרֶץ וְשֵׁם אָחִיו יָקְטָן:

After reigning over the several provinces named here, Nimrod as absolute monarch provoked the people into building the Tower of Babel. The failure of this enterprise caused the defection of his subjects to such an extent that he had to confine himself to his Babylonian kingdom. There, the young Abraham revolted against his idolatrous cult. He was cast into the fiery furnace at Nimrod's command, and exited victoriously. Much later, during the war of the kings, Nimrod participated under the name of Amraphel (*Rashi* on 14:1) and was again defeated by Abraham. He died from Esau's blows on the day that Esau sold his birthright. Esau stripped him of his cloak, which came from Paradise and which had magical power over the animals. It was on this same day that Abraham died (see our commentary on 25:27 and 29).

11. מִן־הָאָרֶץ הַהִוא יָצָא אַשּׁוּר — *From that land Ashur went forth. Rashi* explains: When Ashur saw his sons following Nimrod and rebelling against God by building the tower, he withdrew from them and built Nineveh and other cities. Ashur, who was of Semitic stock, was the only man besides Abraham with courage enough to escape from Nimrod's clutches. But unlike Abraham, he did not want to fight back, preferring instead to leave his land. He built large cities, and Nineveh, the famous city of antiquity, remained alive with the spirit of its founder for many generations after. Indeed, it was saved from the destruction which threatened it thanks to the piety of its king, as is reported in the Book of *Jonah*.

Accad, and Calneh in the land of Shinar. [11] *From that land Ashur went forth and built Nineveh, Rehovoth-ir, Calah,* [12] *and Resen between Nineveh and Calah, that is the great city.*

[13] *And Mizraim begot Ludim, Anamim, Lehabim, Naphtuhim,* [14] *Pathrusim, and Casluhim, whence the Philistines came forth, and Caphtorim.*

[15] *Canaan begot Zidon his firstborn, and Heth;* [16] *and the Jebusite, the Amorite, the Girgashite,* [17] *the Hivite, the Arkite, the Sinite,* [18] *the Arvadite, the Zemarite, and the Hamathite. Afterward, the families of the Canaanites branched out.* [19] *And the Canaanite boundary extended from Zidon going toward Gerar, as far as Gaza; going toward Sodom, Gomorrah, Admah, and Zeboiim, as far as Lasha.* [20] *These are the descendants of Ham, by their families, by their languages, in their lands, in their nations.*

[21] *And to Shem, also to him were born; he was the ancestor of all those who lived on the other side; the brother of Japheth the elder.* [22] *The sons of Shem: Elam, Asshur, Arpachshad, Lud, and Aram.* [23] *The sons of Aram: Uz, Hul, Gether, and Mash.* [24] *Arpachshad begot Shelah, and Shelah begot Eber.* [25] *And to Eber were born two sons: The name of the first was Peleg, for in his days the earth was divided; and the name of his brother was Joktan.*

15. וּכְנַעַן יָלַד — *Canaan begot.* Ten descendants of Canaan are mentioned here. They founded the ten Canaanite peoples whose inheritance was promised to Abraham's descendants. The latter, however, took over the land of seven of these peoples. The territories of the three remaining peoples are reserved for the kingdom of Israel in messianic times (*R' Bachya*).

21. וּלְשֵׁם יֻלַּד גַּם־הוּא — *And to Shem, also to him were born.* Shem was the father of the whole race of עֵבֶר, whence the word Hebrew is derived as *Ibn Ezra* notes. Those peoples mentioned here were mainly inhabitants of Persia, Assyria, the Arabian Gulf, Syria, and other countries in Asia Minor.

The names enumerated in this chapter total seventy (not including Nimrod, who appears not as founder of a people but important in his own right for the role he is to play). Thus we see the first appearance of the number seventy, which in Jewish tradition usually represents the total number of nations in the world and which moreover has remained approximately the case even to our day. The seventy nations parallel the seventy souls of Jacob's family (*Genesis* 46:27), who constitute the nucleus of the Jewish people. This people is in some ways a reflection of the various peoples of the world, just as on another level the Land of Israel represents the focus from which rays emanate to the countries of the world. Jewry and the Holy Land are to the nations and to the countries of the world as microcosm is to macrocosm. *R' Yehudah*

כו וְיָקְטָן יָלַד אֶת־אַלְמוֹדָד וְאֶת־שָׁלֶף וְאֶת־חֲצַרְמָוֶת וְאֶת־
כז-כח יָרַח: וְאֶת־הֲדוֹרָם וְאֶת־אוּזָל וְאֶת־דִּקְלָה: וְאֶת־עוֹבָל וְאֶת־
כט אֲבִימָאֵל וְאֶת־שְׁבָא: וְאֶת־אוֹפִר וְאֶת־חֲוִילָה וְאֶת־יוֹבָב
ל כָּל־אֵלֶּה בְּנֵי יָקְטָן: וַיְהִי מוֹשָׁבָם מִמֵּשָׁא בֹּאֲכָה סְפָרָה הַר
לא הַקֶּדֶם: אֵלֶּה בְנֵי־שֵׁם לְמִשְׁפְּחֹתָם לִלְשֹׁנֹתָם בְּאַרְצֹתָם
לב לְגוֹיֵהֶם: אֵלֶּה מִשְׁפְּחֹת בְּנֵי־נֹחַ לְתוֹלְדֹתָם בְּגוֹיֵהֶם וּמֵאֵלֶּה
נִפְרְדוּ הַגּוֹיִם בָּאָרֶץ אַחַר הַמַּבּוּל:
יא שביעי א-ב וַיְהִי כָל־הָאָרֶץ שָׂפָה אֶחָת וּדְבָרִים אֲחָדִים: וַיְהִי בְּנָסְעָם
ג מִקֶּדֶם וַיִּמְצְאוּ בִקְעָה בְּאֶרֶץ שִׁנְעָר וַיֵּשְׁבוּ שָׁם: וַיֹּאמְרוּ
אִישׁ אֶל־רֵעֵהוּ הָבָה נִלְבְּנָה לְבֵנִים וְנִשְׂרְפָה לִשְׂרֵפָה וַתְּהִי
ד לָהֶם הַלְּבֵנָה לְאָבֶן וְהַחֵמָר הָיָה לָהֶם לַחֹמֶר: וַיֹּאמְרוּ
הָבָה ׀ נִבְנֶה־לָּנוּ עִיר וּמִגְדָּל וְרֹאשׁוֹ בַשָּׁמַיִם וְנַעֲשֶׂה־

HaLevi expressed this idea by comparing Jewry to the heart of the nations; it is the organ which constitutes the *force vitale* of the whole organism and it feels the pains and sufferings of each of its parts before the others (*Kuzari* 2:36).

11.

1. כָל־הָאָרֶץ — *The whole earth*. "Though you pound a fool in a mortar, in the midst of grains of wheat with a pestle, still would his folly not depart from him" (*Proverbs* 27:22). The Midrash applies this verse to "the generation of the Tower of Babel." Having learned nothing from the Flood, they began again 340 years later (cf. *Rashi* and our commentary on 10:25) to rebel against God. This, despite the presence among them of Noah and his sons, and of Abraham, who was then forty-eight years old and was already proclaiming the omnipotence of God (*Radak*).

2. וַיְהִי בְּנָסְעָם מִקֶּדֶם — *And it came to pass, when they migrated from the east*. See our commentary on *Genesis* 4:16. They left their homeland: their hearts forsook the One Who preceded the world קַדְמוֹנוֹ שֶׁל עוֹלָם (*Rabbah* 35).

3. וַיֹּאמְרוּ אִישׁ אֶל־רֵעֵהוּ — *They said to one another*. What exactly was the sin committed by this generation? So ask our Sages, since the punishment indicated in the text does not seem to fit the seriousness of the crime. Some answers refer to the words of the text, for example those given by *Rashi* at the beginning of the chapter. However, *Ramban* objects to "those who stick to just the literal meaning." He limits himself to pointing out the significant fact that the account of the Tower of Babel contains only the Tetragrammaton, whereas the story of the Flood regularly has the word אֱלֹהִים. As for the Kabbalists, they restrict themselves to affirming that the generation of the Tower of Babel wanted to separate the last *sefira*, מַלְכוּת, from the nine preceding ones. All in all, the real motives of the tower builders are not at all clear from the text.

²⁶ *Joktan begot Almodad, Sheleph, Hazarmaveth, Jerah,*
²⁷ *Hadoram, Uzal, Diklah,* ²⁸ *Obal, Abimael, Sheba,* ²⁹ *Ophir,*
Havilah, and Jobab; all these were the sons of Joktan. ³⁰ *Their*
dwelling place extended from Mesha going toward Sephar,
the mountain to the east. ³¹ *These are the descendants of*
Shem according to their families, by their languages, in their
lands, by their nations.

³² *These are the families of Noah's descendants, according*
to their generations, by their nations; and from these the nations
were separated on the earth after the Flood.

11
¹*The whole earth was of one language and of common purpose.*
² *And it came to pass, when they migrated from the east*
they found a plain in the land of Shinar and settled there.
³ *They said to one another, "Come, let us make bricks and burn*
them in fire." And the brick served them as stone, and the lime
served them as mortar. ⁴ *And they said, "Come, let us build us*
a city, and a tower with its top in the heavens, and let us make

These various points of view are united in a single perspective by *R' Yehudah L. Bloch* of Telshe in his book שעורי דעת ח"ג. He emphasizes that the Sages of the Midrash give the apparent or more obvious reasons while the Kabbalists reveal the secret or subconscious motives. Hence it seems that the initial intention of Nimrod and his generation was to group the people in one area in order to concentrate more effectively on discovering the hidden forces of nature. Harnessing them would afford protection against all natural disasters and evil forces. This collectivity would also serve as a shield against war and social hardship. Accordingly, they assembled in the valley of Shinar, which subsequently became Babylonian territory, and built the "holy city" of Babel. There, as a rallying point, as a sign of their might, and as a mark of defiance to God above, they built a gigantic three-storied tower which rose up more than 200 meters (650 feet) into the sky.

There was nothing wrong with this in itself, although the exploitation of newly-discovered forces in nature could lead to the result that "nothing they are planning to do will be withheld from them." What was heretical, though, was the afterthought they had of turning against God. These men thought that by knowing the secrets of nature they would no longer have to depend on Divine Providence. The union of all races and all classes of society would free them from God's omnipotence. That was their ultimate goal, their ulterior motive.

The Torah records only the obvious, expressed motive: *Let us build us a city, and a tower with its top in the heavens, and let us make a name for ourselves, lest we be dispersed across the whole earth.* But tradition records the various deeper, underlying reasons which nevertheless all lead to the same result. Thus some said, "From the tower top we will wage war with God." These words are

ה לָּנוּ שֵׁם פֶּן־נָפוּץ עַל־פְּנֵי כָל־הָאָרֶץ: וַיֵּרֶד יהוה לִרְאֹת
ו אֶת־הָעִיר וְאֶת־הַמִּגְדָּל אֲשֶׁר בָּנוּ בְּנֵי הָאָדָם: וַיֹּאמֶר יהוה
הֵן עַם אֶחָד וְשָׂפָה אַחַת לְכֻלָּם וְזֶה הַחִלָּם לַעֲשׂוֹת וְעַתָּה
ז לֹא־יִבָּצֵר מֵהֶם כֹּל אֲשֶׁר יָזְמוּ לַעֲשׂוֹת: הָבָה נֵרְדָה וְנָבְלָה
ח שָׁם שְׂפָתָם אֲשֶׁר לֹא יִשְׁמְעוּ אִישׁ שְׂפַת רֵעֵהוּ: וַיָּפֶץ יהוה
ט אֹתָם מִשָּׁם עַל־פְּנֵי כָל־הָאָרֶץ וַיַּחְדְּלוּ לִבְנֹת הָעִיר: עַל־כֵּן

attributed to descendants of Ham, unscrupulous and depraved. Shem's offspring
wanted to erect a memorial to those whose corpses covered the plain of Shinar
after the deluge. The descendants of Japheth, given to culture and rationaliza-
tions, thought of buttressing the heaven by means of powerful substructures.
They claimed that the sky would break open over the earth every 1656 years,
as it just had during the deluge.

Ramban adds that they rebelled against God as the שֵׁם הֲוָיָ, which is the
designation that this passage always uses. As is seen in *Exodus* 6:3, this
name refers to God as absolute Master of human destiny Who exercises His
Providence supremely over mankind. (In contrast, the chapter describing the
Flood contains only the name אֱלֹהִים. The generation of the Flood lived violent,
debauched lives but still did not deny the concept of Providence.) The same
idea is expressed by the Kabbalists. They say that the men who built the
tower wanted to separate the tenth *sefira*, מַלְכוּת, from the others. The first
nine represent Divine attributes whereas מַלְכוּת signifies the realization of the
Divine Presence in history, which has as its final outcome the establishment of
the kingdom of God on earth. Now it was just this messianic fulfillment which
the tower-builders wished to compromise when they proclaimed their
independence from Providence and their wish to build history on their own
terms.

4. וְנַעֲשֶׂה־לָּנוּ שֵׁם — *And let us make a name for ourselves.* "These words reveal
the true attitude of the tower-builders. Becoming conscious of one's ego can lead
to two possible reactions: humility or pride. Being obsessed with our paltriness
and smallness can serve to stimulate our efforts to do something for humanity
or it can lead us to rebel against an inexorable destiny, to try to break out of our
human limitations by revolting against God. The men of Babel deliberately chose
pride. They refused to admit that the worth of the individual is based only on
his contribution to society. Their tower was utterly useless. It was merely the
grotesque concretization of an overweening pride which believed it could wipe
out the eternal boundaries between man and God. And God destroyed their
egoistical plans. He scattered them over the earth. He erected the impassable
barriers of language and way of speech and made it forever impossible for any
permanent coalition to arise against Him. Men were separated and realized how
vain their dream of greatness was. Now weakened, obliged to depend on their
individual resources and deprived of close cooperation with neighboring nations,

a name for ourselves, lest we be dispersed across the whole earth."

⁵ *HASHEM descended to look at the city and tower which the sons of man built,⁶ and HASHEM said, "Behold, they are one people with one language for all, and this they begin to do! And now, should it not be withheld from them all they propose to do?⁷ Come, let us descend and there confuse their language, that they should not understand one another's language."*

⁸ *And HASHEM dispersed them from there over the face of the whole earth; and they stopped building the city.⁹ That is why it*

people will again have to find how to utilize human genius patiently and efficiently for the greatest good for all humanity.

"With Babel, men lost their unity. All their efforts will now be directed to cling to their place in the sun and to defend it against jealous neighbors. The world will be preoccupied now with material matters. Without reaching the degree of perversion of the old world, it vegetates in drudgery and is blind to the light which is to brighten the future. The pure flame of the name of God will not spring forth until Abraham, born in a pagan land from modest parents, will call on all men not 'to make a name for themselves,' but to glorify the name of God (לִקְרֹא בְּשֵׁם ה'). He will teach them charity and love. He will become forever the symbol of the peace which will be re-established between God and man" (*R' S.R. Hirsch*).

5. וַיֵּרֶד ה' — *HASHEM descended.* Ramban explains that the term "descended" when applied to God refers to a descent on the scale of the Divine attributes. It was as though God left His pedestal of love and descended to the lower level of complete justice (*Genesis* 18:21). He came down to exact justice and to punish, as *Onkelos* translates. But it is still ה', the מִדַּת הָרַחֲמִים, which comes down, still a God full of gentleness. Despite the sin of apostasy committed by the rebellious generation, God brings neither death nor destruction for He takes into account the spirit of brotherhood which united them (cf. *Rashi*).

8. וַיָּפֶץ ה' אֹתָם — *And HASHEM dispersed them.* Tradition tells us that the tower-builders suffered three punishments. The Semites, who wished to perpetuate the memory of the Flood's victims with a memorial (see above, verse 3), were scattered over the earth — the lesson of the Flood should have been taught to the living and not commemorated in stone. The Hamites, who intended to wage war with God, were banished and "were transformed into monkeys and demons" (*Sanhedrin* 109a), the image of their degeneration and decadence. As for the offspring of Japheth, who had wanted to erect a gigantic temple to their idols — their common language, the mainstay of their collective strength, was taken from them. They were forced to abandon their ominous plan (דברי ירמיהו).

עַל־פְּנֵי כָל־הָאָרֶץ — *Over the face of the whole earth.* It should be borne in mind that the scattering of mankind over the earth was called for, in the Divine plan,

קָרָא שְׁמָהּ בָּבֶל כִּי־שָׁם בָּלַל יהוה שְׂפַת כָּל־הָאָרֶץ וּמִשָּׁם
הֱפִיצָם יהוה עַל־פְּנֵי כָּל־הָאָרֶץ:

right from the beginning. Just after the Flood, God had blessed mankind with these words: *Be fruitful and multiply and fill the land* (9:1). And, referring to a verse in *Isaiah, Rashi* mentions a tradition which has it that one-third of the world is inhabited by man, one-third is desert, and one-third is oceans and rivers (*Isaiah* 40:12). Hence, from this point of view, the question of relating cause and effect for the tower-builders still remains unanswered, as Rabbi Chaim ben Attar suggests in his commentary.

9. כִּי־שָׁם בָּלַל ה׳ שְׂפַת כָּל־הָאָרֶץ — *Because it was there that HASHEM confused the language of the whole earth.* Again here, the principle of מִדָּה כְּנֶגֶד מִדָּה comes into play. Man's attempt to establish a universal hegemony in order to rebel against God is punished by the confusion of languages which inevitably leads to widespread scattering of peoples.

There is another lesson in this chastisement: organized society should have as its goal not the excessive conformity of its elements but rather a harmonious unity, with each component participating according to its own calling.

Jewish tradition considers Hebrew the original language. After the Tower of Babel, the other languages sprang from it. Many have suggested that languages have a common origin, although this has not been generally recognized.

Idioms in Hamitic and Semitic languages are certainly linguistically related. Moreover, it is possible, albeit sometimes difficult, to establish common origins between Semitic and Indo-European languages. Similarities and indeed identical elements of vocabulary serve as a basis for these comparative studies. For these languages, a close relationship can be established between words expressing concepts used since earliest man: names of planets and stars; minerals, plants, animals; description of human beings — age, sex, parts of body, family and kinship terms; description of space, time, number, and measures; designation of occupations or other primary activities, and of war and weapons.

Compared with other languages, Hebrew best fits the Bible's description of דְּבָרִים אֲחָדִים, "few words." Words in Hebrew are generally made up of two letters which contain the basic meaning. This meaning can then be adapted to numerous nuances of thought by the addition of a third letter. Structured in this way, a language really needs just a few words. For example, take the two letters ח and ר; they can be combined with almost all the letters of the alphabet to produce a considerable number of words. With these combinations they can take on sixty-five different meanings. The ability to make the appropriate combinations was based on a highly developed uniformity of thought as well as on a very thorough knowledge of the initial meaning of each letter. It was precisely this aptitude which disappeared with the tower and as a result a multitude of idioms derived directly or indirectly from Hebrew came into existence.

Hebrew alone kept its original purity, a purity characterized by simplicity, coupled with its highly intellectual structure.

> *was called Babel, because it was there that HASHEM confused the language of the whole earth, and from there HASHEM scattered them over the face of the whole earth.*

Apart from these philological aspects, the "holy language" stands out because of its reflection of objective truth, as *R' S.R. Hirsch* points out in several of his works. When words are used to designate persons or objects in other languages, they mark a subjective relationship between man and his surroundings, based on sense perception. In the "holy language" words express objective concepts, independent of any personal contingencies. This gives them a more absolute value in comparison with the relative approximations afforded in existing languages.

Let us imagine a language in which every expression gives only the real nature of the objects it describes and not merely our subjective relation with them. In this language, words dealing with law and morality, physics and metaphysics, would have no other object than to tell us what their elements are and what they should represent for us. Such a language would create a uniform doctrine, a uniform view, of the world and existence. It would embrace universal wisdom; its breakdown would have the gravest consequences. For example, let us attempt to do without using the English word "have." Hebrew does not possess this word. "Have" involves a physical idea, *habere, avere*, to languish after something, and when you possess it, you "have" it. Imagine that this word did not exist and that one only considers his that which is allotted to him, לו, as Hebrew expresses it. Then even the very idea of "mine" and "yours" as distinct property does not exist, for it is inconceivable except in terms of the relationship of object to personality. Now, introducing the notion of "have" into this conception would have no less than a revolutionary effect. It would transform a legal term into a notion of the law of the strongest (*R' S.R. Hirsch* develops analogous examples for Hebrew words concerning justice, virtue, religion, life, people, family, etc.)

The change which came at the time of the "dispersed generation" saw the subjective, arbitrary point of view gain the upper hand over the principle of objective truth. The collectivist policy underlying the building of the tower had gone down to a resounding defeat. It turned into individualistic doctrines which absolutely refused to recognize any authority, even God. This "new wave" led to the establishment of an egocentric civilization. But, in God's hands, such excesses become the means of salvation in man's moral development.

10. אֵלֶּה תּוֹלְדֹת שֵׁם — *These are the descendants of Shem.* The Torah obviously attaches considerable interest to the genealogies of the earliest generations. It of course wants to inform us of the historical circumstances and changes which resulted in the worldwide distribution of the families of nations. But there is another purpose. When the Torah traces the Semitic lineage in particular, it wants to show us that the patriarchs were not superhuman beings but were born

י אֵ֣לֶּה תּֽוֹלְדֹ֣ת שֵׁ֔ם שֵׁ֚ם בֶּן־מְאַ֣ת שָׁנָ֔ה וַיּ֖וֹלֶד אֶת־אַרְפַּכְשָׁ֑ד

יא שְׁנָתַ֖יִם אַחַ֣ר הַמַּבּֽוּל: וַֽיְחִי־שֵׁ֗ם אַֽחֲרֵי֙ הֽוֹלִיד֣וֹ אֶת־אַרְפַּכְשָׁ֔ד

יב חֲמֵ֥שׁ מֵא֖וֹת שָׁנָ֑ה וַיּ֥וֹלֶד בָּנִ֖ים וּבָנֽוֹת: וְאַרְפַּכְשַׁ֣ד חַ֔י

יג חָמֵ֥שׁ וּשְׁלֹשִׁ֖ים שָׁנָ֑ה וַיּ֖וֹלֶד אֶת־שָֽׁלַח: וַֽיְחִ֣י אַרְפַּכְשַׁ֗ד אַֽחֲרֵי֙

הֽוֹלִיד֣וֹ אֶת־שֶׁ֔לַח שָׁלֹ֣שׁ שָׁנִ֔ים וְאַרְבַּ֥ע מֵא֖וֹת שָׁנָ֑ה וַיּ֥וֹלֶד בָּנִ֖ים

יד וּבָנֽוֹת: וְשֶׁ֥לַח חַ֖י שְׁלֹשִׁ֣ים שָׁנָ֑ה וַיּ֖וֹלֶד אֶת־עֵֽבֶר:

טו וַֽיְחִי־שֶׁ֗לַח אַֽחֲרֵי֙ הֽוֹלִיד֣וֹ אֶת־עֵ֔בֶר שָׁלֹ֥שׁ שָׁנִ֖ים וְאַרְבַּ֣ע

טז מֵא֣וֹת שָׁנָ֑ה וַיּ֥וֹלֶד בָּנִ֖ים וּבָנֽוֹת: וַֽיְחִי־עֵ֕בֶר

יז אַרְבַּ֥ע וּשְׁלֹשִׁ֖ים שָׁנָ֑ה וַיּ֖וֹלֶד אֶת־פָּֽלֶג: וַֽיְחִי־עֵ֗בֶר אַֽחֲרֵי֙

הֽוֹלִיד֣וֹ אֶת־פֶּ֔לֶג שְׁלֹשִׁ֣ים שָׁנָ֔ה וְאַרְבַּ֥ע מֵא֖וֹת שָׁנָ֑ה וַיּ֥וֹלֶד

יח בָּנִ֖ים וּבָנֽוֹת: וַֽיְחִי־פֶ֕לֶג שְׁלֹשִׁ֥ים שָׁנָ֖ה וַיּ֥וֹלֶד אֶת־

יט רְעֽוּ: וַֽיְחִי־פֶ֗לֶג אַֽחֲרֵי֙ הֽוֹלִיד֣וֹ אֶת־רְע֔וּ תֵּ֥שַׁע שָׁנִ֖ים וּמָאתַ֣יִם

כ שָׁנָ֑ה וַיּ֥וֹלֶד בָּנִ֖ים וּבָנֽוֹת: וַֽיְחִ֣י רְע֔וּ שְׁתַּ֥יִם

כא וּשְׁלֹשִׁ֖ים שָׁנָ֑ה וַיּ֖וֹלֶד אֶת־שְׂרֽוּג: וַֽיְחִ֣י רְע֗וּ אַֽחֲרֵי֙ הֽוֹלִיד֣וֹ

אֶת־שְׂר֔וּג שֶׁ֥בַע שָׁנִ֖ים וּמָאתַ֣יִם שָׁנָ֑ה וַיּ֥וֹלֶד בָּנִ֖ים

כב וּבָנֽוֹת: וַֽיְחִ֣י שְׂר֔וּג שְׁלֹשִׁ֖ים שָׁנָ֑ה וַיּ֖וֹלֶד אֶת־

כג נָחֽוֹר: וַֽיְחִ֣י שְׂר֗וּג אַֽחֲרֵי֙ הֽוֹלִיד֣וֹ אֶת־נָח֔וֹר מָאתַ֣יִם שָׁנָ֑ה וַיּ֥וֹלֶד

כד בָּנִ֖ים וּבָנֽוֹת: וַֽיְחִ֣י נָח֔וֹר תֵּ֥שַׁע וְעֶשְׂרִ֖ים שָׁנָ֑ה וַיּ֖וֹלֶד

כה אֶת־תָּֽרַח: וַֽיְחִ֣י נָח֗וֹר אַֽחֲרֵי֙ הֽוֹלִיד֣וֹ אֶת־תֶּ֔רַח תְּשַֽׁע־עֶשְׂרֵ֥ה

כו שָׁנָ֖ה וּמְאַ֣ת שָׁנָ֑ה וַיּ֥וֹלֶד בָּנִ֖ים וּבָנֽוֹת: וַֽיְחִי־

תֶ֖רַח שִׁבְעִ֣ים שָׁנָ֑ה וַיּ֗וֹלֶד אֶת־אַבְרָ֔ם אֶת־נָח֖וֹר וְאֶת־הָרָֽן:

---

of a father and mother whose ancestors are known. They were simply human beings who had no other merit than that of seeking the truth on their own initiative and through their own moral and spiritual efforts. In enumerating the families of Shem, the word וַיָּמׇת, *and he died*, never appears, although it did in preceding genealogies. *R' Bachya* explains that this is because the Messiah, the redeemer of mankind, will be of Semitic ancestry. This lineage is immortal, just as the messianic idea itself is, because דָּוִד מֶלֶךְ יִשְׂרָאֵל חַי וְקַיָם, *David king of Israel lives and remains always in our midst.*

וַיּוֹלֶד אֶת־אַרְפַּכְשָׁד — *When he begot Arpachshad.* Arpachshad, Shem's third son, was born two years after the Flood (2102 B.C.E.). Horite documents found at Nuzu (and dating from the fifteenth century B.C.E.) show that the area near Nineveh was called Arrapka, probably identical to the biblical Arpachshad. The most famous descendant of Shem was Ever (b. 2037 B.C.E.) who was close to his ancestor Shem and became the repository of the old traditions. He lived into Jacob's time; Jacob studied his spiritual heritage in "the tents of Shem and

¹⁰ *These are the descendants of Shem: Shem was one hundred years old when he begot Arpachshad, two years after the Flood.* ¹¹ *And Shem lived five hundred years after begetting Arpachshad, and he begot sons and daughters.*

¹² *Arpachshad had lived thirty-five years when he begot Shelah.* ¹³ *And Arpachshad lived four hundred three years after begetting Shelah; and he begot sons and daughters.*

¹⁴ *Shelah had lived thirty years when he begot Eber.* ¹⁵ *And Shelah lived four hundred and three years after begetting Eber, and begot sons and daughters.*

¹⁶ *When Eber had lived thirty-four years, he begot Peleg.* ¹⁷ *And Eber lived four hundred and thirty years after begetting Peleg, and he begot sons and daughters.*

¹⁸ *When Peleg had lived thirty years, he begot Reu.* ¹⁹ *And Peleg lived two hundred and nine years after begetting Reu, and he begot sons and daughters.*

²⁰ *When Reu had lived thirty-two years, he begot Serug.* ²¹ *And Reu lived two hundred and seven years after begetting Serug, and he begot sons and daughters.*

²² *When Serug had lived thirty years, he begot Nahor.* ²³ *And Serug lived two hundred years after begetting Nahor, and he begot sons and daughters.*

²⁴ *When Nahor had lived twenty-nine years, he begot Terah.* ²⁵ *And Nahor lived one hundred nineteen years after begetting Terah, and he begot sons and daughters.*

²⁶ *When Terah had lived seventy years, he begot Abram, Nahor, and Haran.*

Eber" (*Rashi, Genesis* 25:27). The word "Hebrew" probably comes from Eber, as *Ibn Ezra* notes (*Genesis* 10:21).

According to the Torah, and the ancient steles as well, the Hebrews were originally a nomadic people occupying the steppes of Mesopotamia from the end of the third to the beginning of the second millennium before the common era. A survey of the patriarchs and the localities named after them shows that their first primitive settlement was located in the valleys of the Euphrates and its surroundings, and in particular at Khabur, west and northwest of Mesopotamia. Here the population was predominantly Hebrew. Hence, Joshua's words are confirmed: *On the other side of the river* (Euphrates) *did your ancestors dwell from the beginning* (24:2).

26. וַיְחִי־תֶרַח שִׁבְעִים שָׁנָה — *When Terah had lived seventy years.* The two elder sons, Abram and Nahor, were born in Mesopotamia, but Haran was born in Haran and died there (cf. *Ramban,* and *Maharal's* discussion in גבורות ה', פ״ה).

כז וְאֵ֣לֶּה תּוֹלְדֹ֣ת תֶּ֔רַח תֶּ֖רַח הוֹלִ֣יד אֶת־אַבְרָ֔ם אֶת־נָח֖וֹר

כח וְאֶת־הָרָ֑ן וְהָרָ֖ן הוֹלִ֣יד אֶת־ל֑וֹט: וַיָּ֣מׇת הָרָ֗ן עַל־פְּנֵ֛י תֶּ֥רַח אָבִ֖יו

מפטיר כט בְּאֶ֣רֶץ מוֹלַדְתּ֔וֹ בְּא֖וּר כַּשְׂדִּֽים: וַיִּקַּ֨ח אַבְרָ֧ם וְנָח֛וֹר לָהֶ֖ם נָשִׁ֑ים

Tradition ascribes to Terah the position of an army officer serving the king of Ur (*Sefer HaYashar*).

Recent excavations at the site of the old Ur in Chaldea give a fairly complete picture of conditions in Abram's time. Ur, one of the oldest cities, had a quarter of a million inhabitants. It was consecrated to the moon-god called Nannar. Innumerable idols were worshiped but the moon-god reigned supreme. A three-story pyramidal tower was dedicated to him. This tower still existed in Abram's time. Nearly every house had chapels and altars for household gods. Religion in Ur was blatant polytheism. In fact, ancient texts give the names of 5,000 Sumeria gods or of 5,000 different names for an infinite number of gods, all under the moon-god, who was not, however, involved in the daily needs of the people.

The description of Terah given by our Sages (and first cited in the apocryphal *Book of Jubilees*) has him as an idolmaker (which does not necessarily contradict what was just quoted from the *Sefer HaYashar*) and this agrees very well with these historical facts. Trafficking in idols was certainly a lucrative profession at a time when each person worshiped his own idol in his house. Some historians think that Terah left Ur after Hammurabi of Babylonia conquered it, when military forays were directed against it to block trade routes and ruin its economic life. Terah intended to go to Canaan, but stopped on the way, at Haran. This city is situated on the road leading westward from Mesopotamia. There converged the highways, the major trade routes, from Babylonia lying to the south, Nineveh to the east, and Damascus to the west. Haran answered Terah's commercial needs; it was, moreover, the second most important city in Mesopotamia. And it was dedicated to the moon-god which Terah had already worshiped in Ur.

28. בְּא֖וּר כַּשְׂדִּֽים — *In Ur Kasdim*. It is of utmost interest to determine how Abram came upon the ideal which was subsequently to become the spiritual heritage of universal scope. The Torah is extremely discreet on this point. It seems to want to modestly spread a veil over the birth of the holy on earth, just as it does for the birth of life itself. Nonetheless, the Torah lets us read between the lines and we can therefore try to find how Abram became the founder of the universal monotheistic religions.

The first verses of Abram's story contain only vague indications. The first is alluded to in the name of the city, אוּר כַּשְׂדִּים, so called because of the fiery furnace (אוּר) into which Abram was thrown by King Nimrod for having broken his father's idols. God miraculously saved Abram from the flames, as *Rashi* relates. This implies that Abram had long before recognized God, and had worshiped Him openly, and, as a "faithful servant," he had no fear of

> ²⁷ Now these are the chronicles of Terah: Terah begot
> Abram, Nahor, and Haran; and Haran begot Lot. ²⁸ Haran
> died in the lifetime of Terah his father, in his native land,
> in Ur Kasdim. ²⁹ And Abram and Nahor took themselves wives;

risking a certain conflict with his father, with Nimrod, the despotic absolute
monarch of that time, or with the whole idolatrous population around him. In
fact, tradition tells us that Abram began to believe in God as Creator and then
as a personal God when he was three years old. Another version puts his age at
forty years when this occurred (cf. Rambam הלכי עכוי"ם ה'"ג וכסף משנה שם).

It was his own reflections coupled with the gift of intuition (to which our
Sages refer when they speak of the two "kidneys" which inspired the patriarch
— Bereshis Rabbah 95) which led Abram to conclude that there must be
Supreme Ruler of the universe Who governs the world, Who establishes the
laws of nature and the paths of the constellations. This concurred with what
Abram had heard from Noah, who knew the tradition of the creation of the
world from his father, Lemech, a contemporary of Adam himself. Abram's own
reasoning had led to ideas which this evidence corroborated. He set down these
precious teachings in a book called סֵפֶר הַיְצִירָה (Kuzari 4:25) and added the
result of his own observations and conclusions. But what made him a giant in
the history of mankind was the eloquence and forcefulness with which he
preached the truth and converted others to his faith. It was the indomitable
courage he showed in fiercely opposing the idolatrous cult, and it was above all
his boundless love of God. This love manifested itself, on the one hand, in an
unceasing love of others and, on the other, in continuous, unlimited, unhesitant,
and unwavering devotion to God. Abram was not a visionary, not a sage
immersed in mystical contemplation, not an erudite philosopher, not a fanatic
or exalted prophet. He was, quite simply, a man, a seeker after truth with a
generous heart and a fervent soul. Abram's religion was not limited to prayers,
beliefs, rituals, or mortifications. It was first and foremost made up of devotion,
ceaseless devotion despite all obstacles. Abram's religion demands the complete
self. It admits of no duplicity. For man must be whole, integral. There must be
a unity in his life, just as God is One in the universe.

The first of the ten trials inflicted on Abram, and over which he triumphed,
was the "fiery furnace." Nimrod had ordered Abram to be thrown into it
because of his revolutionary agitation in favor of belief in God. Abram was
saved from the flames through a miracle (Avos 5:4). Another version recounts
that Nimrod freed Abram from imprisonment as he did not want to make a
martyr of him and it considers this turn of events a נֵס נִסְתָּר, hidden miracle. Be
that as it may, after realizing the mortal dangers they faced at Ur, Terah and his
son Abram decided to leave and head westward. They journeyed from Ur and
settled first in Haran (Ramban). (The historians' explanation cited in the
commentary on verse 26 seems to fall short of doing justice to the exceptional
historical importance attached to the events surrounding the life of Abram.)

שֵׁם אֵשֶׁת־אַבְרָם שָׂרָי וְשֵׁם אֵשֶׁת־נָחוֹר מִלְכָּה בַּת־הָרָן
ל-לא אֲבִי־מִלְכָּה וַאֲבִי יִסְכָּה: וַתְּהִי שָׂרַי עֲקָרָה אֵין לָהּ וָלָד: וַיִּקַּח
תֶּרַח אֶת־אַבְרָם בְּנוֹ וְאֶת־לוֹט בֶּן־הָרָן בֶּן־בְּנוֹ וְאֵת שָׂרַי
כַּלָּתוֹ אֵשֶׁת אַבְרָם בְּנוֹ וַיֵּצְאוּ אִתָּם מֵאוּר כַּשְׂדִּים לָלֶכֶת
לב אַרְצָה כְּנַעַן וַיָּבֹאוּ עַד־חָרָן וַיֵּשְׁבוּ שָׁם: וַיִּהְיוּ יְמֵי־תֶרַח
חָמֵשׁ שָׁנִים וּמָאתַיִם שָׁנָה וַיָּמָת תֶּרַח בְּחָרָן:

But the *Zohar* gives a deeper, psychological reason for this trip. The Torah begins the story of Abram's life by recounting his many journeys (from Mesopotamia to Ur, thence to Haran and then Canaan). The *Zohar* takes this as an indication of inner anguish reflected in an outward instability. What Abram so ardently sought he could not succeed in finding where he was. Paganism colored everything, poisoned the atmosphere, and rose up like a barrier between God and himself. It prevented him from living a life of perfect holiness. The seeker of truth moved constantly here and there in quest of the absolute, until, at last, God revealed Himself to the seventy-five-year-old Abram, for the first time, to say to him: *Go . . . to the land that I will show you.*

(Referring to Abram's story, R' *Yitzchak Arama*, in *Akeidas Yitzchak*, 16, compares the two roads to truth: Torah and tradition on the one hand, and logical reflection and experience on the other. See also *Kuzari* 4:17 and 27.)

And so, Abram was never "touched by grace." It was entirely his own effort, his own perseverance and enthusiasm in the search for truth and in absolute faithfulness to God, which earned him the opportunity of receiving the Divine word, and this after long years filled with trials and sacrifice. This word was but a response to the burning love which filled Abram's heart to overflowing. "The spark from below ignited the flame from above" (cf. R' *Bachya ibn Pakuda*, *Duties of the Heart* 14).

30. וַתְּהִי שָׂרַי עֲקָרָה — *And Sarai was barren.* Just like Rebecca and Rachel, the wives of Isaac and Jacob, Sarah gives birth only through an act of Providence. Some explain that the wives of the patriarchs were barren in order to evoke prayers from their husbands, for "God desires the prayers of the righteous" (*Yevamos* 64a). Then the child who would be born would be much more than a gift of nature. He would be born at the price of tears from his mother and supplications from his righteous father. He would be designated from birth as being the child of Providence.

the name of Abram's wife was Sarai, and the name of Nahor's wife was Milcah, the daughter of Haran, the father of Milcah and the father of Iscah. ³⁰ And Sarai was barren, she had no child.

³¹ Terah took his son Abram, and Lot the son of Haran, his grandson, and his daughter-in-law Sarai, the wife of Abram his son, and they departed with them from Ur Kasdim to go to the land of Canaan; they arrived at Haran and they settled there.

³² The days of Terah were two hundred and five years, and Terah died in Haran.

But other Sages hold that these matriarchs were barren in order to complete the sharp break with the past and its harmful influences. The birth of the people of God needed a new creation, starting from nothing (יֵשׁ מֵאַיִן). The old sources must go dry. Only a completely fresh source can create a new family which is healthy and pure.

(The fact of Sarai's barrenness is immediately followed in the Torah by the departure for Canaan. This suggests that the hope of conceiving children in the Holy Land might have been one of the reasons for this move — *Ohr HaChaim*.)

32. וַיָּמָת תֶּרַח בְּחָרָן — *And Terah died in Haran.* The Torah leaves us in doubt as to whether Terah recognized God before he died, as *Ramban* thinks. Did he stop midway in his search for truth just as he did on his way to the Holy Land? Be that as it may, Terah has his "part in the World to Come," for if God punishes children for the sins of their fathers, He also rewards parents for the merits of their children. "The tree is judged by its fruit." All kinds of wood can be used on the altar, except wood from the olive tree and the vine. This is because their fruit (oil and wine) serve as holy offerings (cf. *Ramban; Rabbah* 38).

The final letter of the final word of the chapter, בְּחָרָן, is written upside down in the masoretic text. According to *Rashi*, this signifies that until Abram, God's anger (חָרָן) lay over the world (cf. *Bereshis Rabbah* 70 on *Genesis* 29:4, מֵחָרָן אֲנַחְנוּ).

The Talmud states in more general terms that the first two millennia, from the genesis of humanity to Abram's time, witnessed the age of *tohu-vohu*, of confusion, of a world plunged into chaos. It was a time of great catastrophes because of the first sin, which had upset the Divine order and destroyed universal harmony. Now here, as it were, the Torah puts a finishing touch, a final bold stroke, to end this period. It now turns its attention to the next two millennia, which are dominated by the Divine revelation on Mount Sinai and by the Torah's reign within the Jewish nation (*Avodah Zarah* 9a).

יב א וַיֹּאמֶר יהוה אֶל־אַבְרָם לֶךְ־לְךָ מֵאַרְצְךָ וּמִמּוֹלַדְתְּךָ וּמִבֵּית
ב אָבִיךָ אֶל־הָאָרֶץ אֲשֶׁר אַרְאֶךָּ: וְאֶעֶשְׂךָ לְגוֹי גָּדוֹל וַאֲבָרֶכְךָ
ג וַאֲגַדְּלָה שְׁמֶךָ וֶהְיֵה בְּרָכָה: וַאֲבָרֲכָה מְבָרְכֶיךָ וּמְקַלֶּלְךָ אָאֹר

12.

1. וַיֹּאמֶר ה' אֶל־אַבְרָם — *HASHEM said to Abram.* The Divine word addressed to a human being, spontaneously and without prior justification of his personal merit! But this has been explained at the end of the previous chapter. The Divine call was really only the long-awaited answer to a life filled with devotion, sacrifice and incessant struggle, seventy-five years dedicated to glorifying God. The Midrash begins its comments on this chapter with a quote from *Psalms* 45 (much of this psalm has been applied to Abraham): *Hearken, O daughter, and see, and incline your ear, forget your own people and your father's house* (v.11). *R' Chaim ben Attar* notes that outside the Holy Land Abram could only hear the Divine voice, but later, when he entered it, HASHEM *appeared to Abram and said* (verse 7). And so the Psalmist's words should be taken in this way: *Hearken, O daughter* (in Babylonia) *and see* (in the Holy Land). So too, the Babylonian Talmud always uses the phrase תָּא שְׁמַע, *come and hear*, whereas the Jerusalem Talmud has תָּא חֲזִי, *come and see.* The revelation of the Divine is only offered to man in the Holy Land. Elsewhere, the vision of the Absolute remains fragmentary (*Kuzari*, ibid.).

לֶךְ־לְךָ — *Go for yourself.* The call to separate oneself from homeland, birthplace and father's house constituted the first step toward the realization of Judaism. To be a Jew means to break with "the crowd" out of love for God and to accept the sacrifice of isolation.

The ethical value of the principle of isolation has been brought out by *R' Bachya ibn Pakuda*, author of *Chovos Halevavos* (*Duties of the Heart*), in Part III, 5 (dialogue between reason and the heart).

The Divine command לֶךְ לְךָ, *go for yourself*, is put at the head of Judaism. It implies the will to go it alone with God if need be. The idea of "majority rule" is indeed legitimate. But when the majority's values do not meet the criterion of Divine truth, man has the duty to separate himself and to remain "alone for himself" and with his God.

How could we have existed and how could we continue to exist if Abram had not given us the courage to be a minority?

Should Judaism be of the times. "Up-to-date Judaism!" The loudest protest against it is Judaism's first words, לֶךְ לְךָ. As soon as Abram appears, he stands in opposition to the spirit of the times. Amidst a perverted, idolatrous, immoral society, idolizing power, almost completely wiping out the name of God, Abram willingly gives up all the family and social closeness so dear to people. He becomes a bearer of God's message and throws a protest in the face of the gods worshiped by all the nations. This demands courage and the deep conviction of the truth of the message itself. This demands an enduring consciousness of a

12   ¹Hᴀsʜᴇᴍ *said to Abram, "Go for yourself from your land, from your relatives, and from your father's house to the land that I will show you. ²And I will make of you a great nation; I will bless you, and make your name great, and you shall be a blessing. ³I will bless those who bless you, and him who curses you I will curse;*

messianic mission. This demands the Jewish conception of God, and Jewish confidence and boldness — in short, that obstinacy and persistence which characterizes the Jew (R' Hirsch).

מֵאַרְצְךָ — *From your land.* Although the land of Canaan was full of idols and paganism, as tradition stresses (*Avodah Zarah* 45a), it was still more suitable than Ur and Haran for receiving Abram's message. In Canaan he proclaimed the Name of God, built altars, and converted idolaters without being molested and cursed, as had been the case in his country of birth. Thus his strategy was different in Canaan. He did not go about smashing idols and scorning his own safety, but, seeing that people were listening to him, he preached the acknowledged truth and sought only to gain converts (*Chasam Sofer*). In this sense *Rashi* explains that his departure was "for his own good and for his happiness."

אֶל־הָאָרֶץ אֲשֶׁר אַרְאֶךָּ — *To the land that I will show you.* Abram received a similar command just as he was about to sacrifice Isaac. There too, the destination was not immediately revealed: *Go to . . . one of the mountains which I shall tell you* (22:2). When, in times of great trial, the Jew has to leave his father's home or is called on to sacrifice his child in his love for God, he must know but one sole duty: that of following God blindly wherever He will lead him.

2. וְאֶעֶשְׂךָ לְגוֹי גָּדוֹל וַאֲבָרֶכְךָ וַאֲגַדְּלָה שְׁמֶךָ — *And I will make of you a great nation; I will bless you, and make your name great.* *Rashi* explains: "God promised him children, prosperity and fame. Another explanation: *I will make of you a great nation* — hence we say (in the *Amidah*), "God of Abraham"; *I will bless You* — thus we say, "God of Isaac"; *and make Your name great* — "God of Jacob." These two interpretations are complementary. They reflect the struggle of good and evil in Abram's heart. The evil inclination urged Abram to obey the Divine commandment in order to have children, wealth and fame. But the good inclination retorted: the intention should be solely for the grandeur and glory of the Name of God which, thanks to this journey and its future consequences, will be manifested as the God of Abraham, of Isaac, and of Jacob. It was with this thought that Abram set out, not with the desire to be gratified with material blessing (*Ohev Yisrael*).

וֶהְיֵה בְּרָכָה — *And you shall be a blessing.* Consequently, the first benediction of the *Amidah* will end with your name alone (*Magen Avraham*). In his book *HaKesav VeHaKabbalah*, *R' Yaakov Tzvi Meklenburg* explains this remark of *Rashi's* as follows: Abram alone recognized God through his own intellectual investigation, whereas Isaac and Jacob already had it as a family tradition. At

ד וְנִבְרְכוּ בְךָ כֹּל מִשְׁפְּחֹת הָאֲדָמָה: וַיֵּלֶךְ אַבְרָם כַּאֲשֶׁר דִּבֶּר
אֵלָיו יהוה וַיֵּלֶךְ אִתּוֹ לוֹט וְאַבְרָם בֶּן־חָמֵשׁ שָׁנִים וְשִׁבְעִים
ה שָׁנָה בְּצֵאתוֹ מֵחָרָן: וַיִּקַּח אַבְרָם אֶת־שָׂרַי אִשְׁתּוֹ וְאֶת־לוֹט
בֶּן־אָחִיו וְאֶת־כָּל־רְכוּשָׁם אֲשֶׁר רָכָשׁוּ וְאֶת־הַנֶּפֶשׁ אֲשֶׁר־
עָשׂוּ בְחָרָן וַיֵּצְאוּ לָלֶכֶת אַרְצָה כְּנַעַן וַיָּבֹאוּ אַרְצָה כְּנַעַן:

the end of time, the light of the spirit will shine forth so brightly that knowledge of the truth will be based on reason itself and not on tradition, as the prophet Isaiah exclaims: *The earth shall be full of the knowledge of God as the waters cover the sea* (11:9).

Now, our text refers to this. The benediction (of the generations) will end on the name of Abraham, the one who is the symbol of the pure knowledge of God.

3. וַאֲבָרֲכָה מְבָרְכֶיךָ — *I will bless those who bless you.* As Abram leaves his home to begin a new life, God blesses him with seven different benedictions. So too, at the threshold of their new lives, as they leave their parents' homes, newlyweds receive a sevenfold benediction, the *sheva berachos.*

"The souls of the righteous are fashioned at the foot of the heavenly throne to go and inspire the human bodies and to guide them along the right path. When God sends these souls from the holy spheres down to the lower regions, He blesses them with a sevenfold benediction just as He blessed Abram when he went into the impurity of Canaan. The soul has the same function that the body of Abram had in a pagan land. It is also אַב־רָם, the "supreme father" of the body. Thus God says to the soul, 'Go away from your land, from the neighborhood of your birth, and from your Father's home, to the body I shall show you ...' Abram went as God had told him. But Lot, his nephew, doggedly stayed with him. So too, the evil inclination slips into the body just as the soul arrives. The argument which will take place between Abram and Lot reflects that inner conflict in the human body between the good and the evil inclinations until they come to a parting of the ways, Lot choosing places of pleasure and debauchery, Abram choosing that difficult land where one seeks and finds God" (זהר חדש).

וְנִבְרְכוּ בְךָ כֹּל מִשְׁפְּחֹת הָאֲדָמָה — *And all the families of the earth shall bless themselves by you.* Regarding this, *Rambam (Guide* 3:29) notes: "We see today most of the world glorifying the same forefather of believers and blessing each other through recalling his deeds. Even some who do not descend from him claim to do so. His enemies have all disappeared. Today all are aware of his greatness, except for the last sectarians of an almost extinct religion with vestiges at the farthest corners of the earth, such as the miscreant Turks in the far north, and the Hindus at the extreme south ..."

5. וַיִּקַּח אַבְרָם ... וְאֶת־לוֹט בֶּן־אָחִיו — *Abram took ... and Lot, his brother's son.* "With his prophetic vision, he saw that the Messiah, the son of David, would descend from Lot" (*Zohar*). Indeed, Lot's daughter became the mother of the

and all the families of the earth shall bless themselves by you."
⁴ *So Abram went as HASHEM had spoken to him, and Lot
went with him; Abram was seventy-five years old when
he left Haran.* ⁵ *Abram took his wife Sarai and Lot, his
brother's son, and all their wealth that they had amassed,
and the souls they made in Haran; and they left to go to
the land of Canaan, and they came to the land of Canaan.*

Moabites, from whom descended Ruth, the ancestress of David. Consequently
Abram wished to instruct Lot to become a faithful servant to God, for Lot was
of as indecisive a character as his father Haran, who was always wavering
between Nimrod and Abram (*Rashi* on 11:28).

וְאֶת־הַנֶּפֶשׁ אֲשֶׁר־עָשׂוּ בְחָרָן — *And the souls they made in Haran.* "Whom they
had bought in under the wings of the *Shechinah.* Abram brought the men to
God, and Sarai, the women" (*Rashi*). What became of these proselytes? No
further mention in made of them for they dispersed when they saw that Abram's
children no longer showed them hospitality and charity to the same
extraordinary degree that the "father of peoples and believers" had (ר״ח
מאלבכסנדר).

וַיֵּצְאוּ לָלֶכֶת אַרְצָה כְּנַעַן — *And they left to go to the land of Canaan.* Terah had
already set the land of Canaan as his destination, but he stopped halfway (11:31).
After receiving the command to put still more distance between himself and his
birthplace, Abram (as if instinctively) continues on the route to Canaan. He
wants to get there on his own and the Divine word encourages him, for "Heaven
helps those whose intentions are pure" (*Shabbos* 104a). But man must take the
first step himself (*Zohar*).

Although Canaan was occupied by the most degenerate Hamitic tribes,
Abram felt drawn toward it. This was so because Shem, Noah's son who had
kept all his faith in God, was ruler over Jerusalem, which had not yet fallen to
the Canaanites. According to another tradition, Moriah, where the sacrifice of
Isaac occurred (and subsequently the site of the altar and of the Temple) was
where Noah and even Abel had offered their sacrifices. This spot was predestined
for the moral and spiritual rebirth of mankind. Also, according to an ancient
tradition, the land of Canaan was spared from the devastation of the Flood. One
can see why Abram, forced to flee Chaldea where he was alone in his beliefs,
felt a yearning for the country which men had inhabited when they were still
nearer to God (*Sforno*).

וַיָּבֹאוּ אַרְצָה כְּנַעַן — *And they came to the land of Canaan.* Abram was not born
in the Holy Land but in Mesopotamia. At seventy-five he arrived in Canaan
after long journeys and much hardship. Adam also did not enter the world in
Paradise but outside of it, and *God took the man and placed him in the Garden
of Eden* (2:15).

וֹ וַיַּעֲבֹר אַבְרָם בָּאָרֶץ עַד מְקוֹם שְׁכֶם עַד אֵלוֹן מוֹרֶה
ז וְהַכְּנַעֲנִי אָז בָּאָרֶץ: וַיֵּרָא יהוה אֶל־אַבְרָם וַיֹּאמֶר לְזַרְעֲךָ
אֶתֵּן אֶת־הָאָרֶץ הַזֹּאת וַיִּבֶן שָׁם מִזְבֵּחַ לַיהוה הַנִּרְאֶה

The most sacred object, the one which constitutes the ideal of perfection, never comes simply as a gift from heaven. It is never given to man right at his birth. He has to go and get it, and to earn it through his own personal efforts.

Abram's journey to Canaan still symbolizes Jewry's relationship to its land. The bonds between nations and their homelands are generally the result of a long evolution. Once a nation has its territory, over the generations it forms a sentimental attachment to it, founded on reminiscences of past history, on cultural affinities from the particular conditions of the country, and on the common destiny. Not so with Jewry.

The Jewish nation was created long before it came into possession of its land. But the land was promised to the Jewish people from its beginnings. The land was designated as the indispensable means of carrying out Jewry's messianic mission. The land was never to be taken for granted or as a permanent possession. It still remains an objective to be reached an ideal to be realized, a supreme good to be gained. Without the land, Jewry cannot attain its national unity, cannot realize its cultural message, its messianic calling. Hence the deep yearning which Jews unceasingly feel for the Promised Land. The Jewish people's connection with its country is not based on history but on metaphysics. Thus, the land is the object of Jewry's eternal desire, a desire which cannot be satisfied until the Jewish nation lives on it and in harmony with it (*A. Y. Kook, Commentary on Prayers*, Introduction).

6. וַיַּעֲבֹר אַבְרָם בָּאָרֶץ עַד מְקוֹם שְׁכֶם — *Abram passed into the land as far as the site of Shechem.* Aside from *Rashi's* explanation for mentioning Shechem in this verse, let us consider two others. *Ramban* stresses that "whatever happened to the patriarchs serves as a sign for their descendants." Thus, Abram's travels in Canaan mark the route taken in Joshua's time during the conquest of the Promised Land. But before receiving the Divine promise giving him the land, Abram dwelt in Shechem. Shechem was also conquered, by Simeon and Levi, before Canaan was taken. Furthermore, Shechem was situated on the plain of Moreh, which was the first place reached by the Jews after they crossed the Jordan to conquer Canaan, as is seen in *Deuteronomy* 11:30. And here, after crossing the Jordan, the Jewish nation was blessed (ibid. 27:12).

Thus, it turned out that Abram was to plant the flag of Judaism and bring his ideal of holiness and moral purity to triumph amidst the most decadent and vicious people of his time. If this ideal reflects the absolute truth, it must be capable of transforming beasts into angels. The earth which gave rise to perversion must also be able to produce perfection, for man's moral development, his moral ascent, is bound neither to time nor to space. A country may well influence its inhabitants, but the Divine in us, our rising up to God, remains

⁶ *Abram passed into the land as far as the site of Shechem, until the Plain of Moreh. The Canaanite was then in the land.*

⁷ *HASHEM appeared to Abram and said, "To your offspring I will give this land." So he built an altar there to HASHEM Who appeared*

within reach for the Laplander in Lapland just as it does for the Greek in his country. An Abram can live amidst murderers. A land can bear both criminal and prophet. This country, so sensitive that it had to "disgorge its inhabitants" because of their depravity, is the very land which God chooses as a place for His people. If this people, although קְשֵׁה עוֹרֶף, *stiff-necked* and far from cooperative, will be won over by the sacred flame (אֵשׁ דָּת) of the Divine law on this land, then no people, no race could be insensitive to this flame. The victory of the Divine over the earthly begins with the most hardened of peoples (עַז שֶׁבָּאוּמוֹת) and on the most refractory of lands (*Bereishis Rabbah* 64).

Maharal shows the similarity between the immoral Hamitic populations among which Abram was born and raised and the "crucible" of polytheistic Egypt where Jewry's national character was forged. Both Abram and the Jewish people had to be exposed to the depths of an abject existence in order to reach the heights of holiness. *Who can make a clean thing out of an unclean? Is it not [solely] the One God?* (*Job* 14:4). So with Abram, born of Terah the idolater. So with the Jewish nation, created amidst pagan peoples (גבורות ה' פ"ה)! Cf. our commentary on 49:28.

וְהַכְּנַעֲנִי אָז בָּאָרֶץ — *The Canaanite was then in the land.* See our commentary on 9:25. Later the Torah (13:7) will speak of the Canaanites who *were then dwelling in the land* (אָז יֹשֵׁב בָּאָרֶץ); the more general phrase used in our verse means: the Canaanite spirit, which implies a subversive, perverse, immoral state of mind (*R' Bachya*).

7. וַיֵּרָא ה' אֶל־אַבְרָם — *HASHEM appeared to Abram.* On the threshold of the Holy Land, God reveals Himself to the patriarch and gives this land to his offspring. Men had previously heard the Divine voice, but now for the first time a man perceives the Divine Majesty in a prophetic vision. For the one who has elevated his senses and instincts to holiness, the wall existing between created and Creator since the first sin crumbles. There is no longer any obstacle to a clear vision of the Divinity (*Meshech Chochmah*). Abram understood that the presence of idolaters, which has just been mentioned, could not obscure the intensity of the radiant holiness in the Holy Land. The *"Shechinah* remains there amidst the impure"* (*Rashi, Leviticus* 16:16).

וַיִּבֶן שָׁם מִזְבֵּחַ לַה' הַנִּרְאֶה אֵלָיו — *So he built an altar there to HASHEM Who appeared to him.* Abram worshiped God with his whole being. After desiring for so long to "contemplate" the Almighty, Abram is carried away with thankfulness and humility before God "Who appeared to him." He builds his first altar with these feelings, although thoughts of "his descendants and the possession of this land which had just been announced" (*Rashi*) remain on his mind.

ח אֵלָיו: וַיַּעְתֵּק מִשָּׁם הָהָרָה מִקֶּדֶם לְבֵית־אֵל וַיֵּט אָהֳלֹה
בֵּית־אֵל מִיָּם וְהָעַי מִקֶּדֶם וַיִּבֶן־שָׁם מִזְבֵּחַ לַיהוֹה וַיִּקְרָא
ט בְּשֵׁם יהוֹה: וַיִּסַּע אַבְרָם הָלוֹךְ וְנָסוֹעַ הַנֶּגְבָּה:
י וַיְהִי רָעָב בָּאָרֶץ וַיֵּרֶד אַבְרָם מִצְרַיְמָה לָגוּר שָׁם כִּי־כָבֵד
יא הָרָעָב בָּאָרֶץ: וַיְהִי כַּאֲשֶׁר הִקְרִיב לָבוֹא מִצְרָיְמָה וַיֹּאמֶר

(On the nature and degree of Abram's gift of prophecy, see *Rambam, Guide* 2:45).

8. וַיַּעְתֵּק מִשָּׁם הָהָרָה — *From there he relocated to the mountain.* (הָהָרָה = הַר ה'). This is the mountain of God, Mount Moriah, where the Temple of Jerusalem would later be erected. There Abram set up a second altar, representing the second stage of his service to God. The first altar was dedicated to "Hashem Who appeared to him," whereas this one was consecrated simply to God, without qualification, i.e., to God the invisible Who sits enthroned in the Heavens (*Zohar*).

וַיִּקְרָא בְּשֵׁם ה' — *And invoked HASHEM by Name.* It was here, at the site where Jerusalem would stand, at the universal starting point for the Divine word, that Abram began to proclaim, to preach, to teach belief in God. He began a large-scale missionary effort. This marked a turning-point in history, for at that moment the second two-thousand-year cycle of human history began, which was characterized by the revelation at Mount Sinai and by the Torah's reign (*Avodah Zarah* 9a).

The patriarch Isaac also built an altar and there proclaimed the name of God to people who still did not believe in Him (*Genesis* 26:25). But the Torah mentions nothing of this kind about Jacob. Indeed, in his time, God's Name was already known in Canaan, and Jacob's many sons spread the knowledge of God to the pagans. From then on, the whole family of Israel became the herald of the King of the Universe (*Ramban*).

9. וַיִּסַּע אַבְרָם הָלוֹךְ וְנָסוֹעַ הַנֶּגְבָּה — *Then Abram journeyed on, journeying steadily toward the south.* The south is where light has its reign. Hence the great golden candelabrum in the Temple, symbolizing the light of Torah, was located in the south part of the Temple court. "Whoever wishes to acquire wisdom, let him face southward" when praying (*Bava Basra* 25b). "But whoever wishes material wealth, let him face northward," where the table with the showbread was situated in the Temple (ibid.). In all his journeys, Abram went from north to south. He forsook temporal wealth for spiritual riches (cf. 20:1 and *Rashi* 21:34).

But נֶגֶב also refers to the southern, most arid part of Canaan, which is covered by the Negev desert. There Abram settled. For twenty-six years he dwelt in Beer-sheba (*Rashi*). This desert was to be inhabited by the Amalekites, the archenemies of the Jewish people (*Numbers* 13:29) and it was here the twelve spies first visited (ibid. 13:17). Abram constantly makes his way toward the

to him. ⁸ From there he relocated to the mountain east of Beth-el and pitched his tent, with Beth-el on the west and Ai on the east; and he built there an altar to HASHEM and invoked HASHEM by Name. ⁹ Then Abram journeyed on, journeying steadily toward the south.

¹⁰ There was a famine in the land, and Abram descended to Egypt to sojourn there, for the famine was severe in the land. ¹¹ And it occurred, as he was about to enter Egypt, he said

Negev. This desert is the ultimate objective of his travels through Canaan. Thus he "shows the way" for his descendants, for whom the Negev will ultimately be transformed into a fertile, flowering land, and represents the high point of their route to the land of their ancestors. And in their songs, the Negev evokes the messianic era, when HASHEM *will bring back our captives, as [He brings back] the streams in the Negev (Psalms* 126:4).

In three trips, from the northern tip of Canaan to Shechem, thence to Beth-El and finally to the Negev, Abram crosses the whole land from north to south. During his journey, Abram built two altars, one near Shechem, the other near Beth-El. In this way the patriarch symbolically took possession of the land and left his mark on it. His sacred calling would henceforth be permanent, for eternity.

10. וַיְהִי רָעָב בָּאָרֶץ — *There was a famine in the land.* Why does the Torah often dwell on the description of unimportant events in the lives of Biblical personages? The Torah wants to show us what their moral and religious attitudes were when they were confronted with the problems and conflicts which everyone must face. The Torah prefers living examples of the behavior of holy people to moral treatises or discussion of religious principles. The general concept of the Bible demonstrates that more value is placed on education through example than through lessons in ethics.

The story of the famine in Canaan is to be considered in this light. Abram had just received the Divine command to leave Chaldea and to enter Canaan. Then, soon after his arrival, there is a famine, "worse than any other," as tradition tells us. How will Abram react to it? Will he be mistrustful of God? Will he recriminate? But Abram does not hesitate even for a moment. He accepts this new trial with the absolute faith of the righteous (אֱמוּנָה שְׁלֵמָה). He accepts the famine and acts in a sensible way, which the Talmud makes explicit: "When famine breaks out, leave for another place ... even if it has its dangers" (*Bava Kamma* 60b). Abram does not find it opportune to remain in Canaan waiting for a new miracle to save him and his family. The one who was miraculously saved from the fiery furnace, into which he was thrown for his love of God, does not want to depend on a miracle when it is a case of the salvation of his own being. "One should not depend on miracles" (*Pesachim* 64b). Hence he takes all the rational steps to escape the calamity. Later on, when danger threatens Sarai,

אֶל־שָׂרַי אִשְׁתּוֹ הִנֵּה־נָא יָדַעְתִּי כִּי אִשָּׁה יְפַת־מַרְאֶה אָתְּ:
יב וְהָיָה כִּי־יִרְאוּ אֹתָךְ הַמִּצְרִים וְאָמְרוּ אִשְׁתּוֹ זֹאת וְהָרְגוּ אֹתִי
יג וְאֹתָךְ יְחַיּוּ: אִמְרִי־נָא אֲחֹתִי אָתְּ לְמַעַן יִיטַב־לִי בַעֲבוּרֵךְ
יד וְחָיְתָה נַפְשִׁי בִּגְלָלֵךְ: וַיְהִי כְּבוֹא אַבְרָם מִצְרָיְמָה וַיִּרְאוּ
טו הַמִּצְרִים אֶת־הָאִשָּׁה כִּי־יָפָה הִוא מְאֹד: וַיִּרְאוּ אֹתָהּ שָׂרֵי
פַרְעֹה וַיְהַלְלוּ אֹתָהּ אֶל־פַּרְעֹה וַתֻּקַּח הָאִשָּׁה בֵּית פַּרְעֹה:
טז וּלְאַבְרָם הֵיטִיב בַּעֲבוּרָהּ וַיְהִי־לוֹ צֹאן־וּבָקָר וַחֲמֹרִים
יז וַעֲבָדִים וּשְׁפָחֹת וַאֲתֹנֹת וּגְמַלִּים: וַיְנַגַּע יהוה ׀ אֶת־פַּרְעֹה
נְגָעִים גְּדֹלִים וְאֶת־בֵּיתוֹ עַל־דְּבַר שָׂרַי אֵשֶׁת אַבְרָם:

שני

he will even prefer to tell a half-truth than to rest passively in the expectation
of a providential miracle.

(This interpretation of Abram's behavior is consistent with that of *Radak, R'
Moshe Sofer*, and *R' Chaim ben Attar*; but *Ramban* considers that the departure
into Egypt and the stratagem used to protect Sarai constitute a bad lack of
confidence on Abram's part; his view is contradicted by *Maharal* (דברי בס' – וע'
שאול גבורות ה' פ"ט).

11. הִנֵּה־נָא יָדַעְתִּי כִּי אִשָּׁה יְפַת־מַרְאֶה אָתְּ — *See now, I have known that you are
a woman of beautiful appearance.* Abram's reaction on approaching the "dark
continent" seems quite natural. *Rashi* expresses it in these terms: "We now come
into a land whose people are dark-skinned and ugly. They are brothers of the
Ethiopians and are not accustomed to seeing a beautiful woman."

12. וְאָמְרוּ אִשְׁתּוֹ זֹאת וְהָרְגוּ אֹתִי — *They will say, 'This is his wife!'; then they will
kill me.* In the immoral civilization of the Egyptians and the Philistines,
an unmarried woman had more protection than a married one! The
latter, especially a foreigner, faced certain danger. The husband was killed
and the wife abducted. But an unmarried woman accompanied by her
brother was a different situation. They hoped to win her by gaining her
brother's favor.

13. אִמְרִי־נָא אֲחֹתִי אָתְּ — *Please say that you are my sister.* Later, Abram will
explain concerning Sarai: *She is indeed my sister, my father's daughter, though
not my mother's daughter* (20:12). Thus it was a half-truth, which Abram
thought he could tell when they were doubly threatened with murder and rape.

By passing Sarai off as his sister, Abram hoped to gain time through making
excessive demands for her hand. In this spirit *Rashi* interprets the words, "so
that I will receive benefit for you" as follows: "so that they will give me
presents." Abram who later will say, "I swear . . . I will take nothing of yours,
from a thread to a shoelace" to the king of Sodom was surely not eager to amass
wealth. But he wanted to show his wife that the gifts which the Egyptians
would offer in return for her hand in marriage would permit him to prolong
negotiations until providential help would come or until the famine would end.

to his wife Sarai, "See now, I have known that you are a woman of beautiful appearance. ¹² And it shall occur, when the Egyptians will see you, they will say, 'This is his wife!'; then they will kill me, but you they will let live. ¹³ Please say that you are my sister, that it may go well with me for your sake, and that I may live on account of you."

¹⁴ But it occurred, with Abram's coming to Egypt, the Egyptians saw that the woman was very beautiful. ¹⁵ When the officials of Pharaoh saw her, they lauded her for Pharaoh, and the woman was taken to Pharaoh's house. ¹⁶ And he treated Abram well for her sake, and he acquired sheep, cattle, donkeys, slaves and maidservants, female donkeys, and camels.

¹⁷ But HASHEM afflicted Pharaoh along with his household with severe plagues because of the matter of Sarai, the wife of Abram.

As a result he would live because of her. Nevertheless, Abram never wanted to profit materially from these gifts. He did not touch them but gave every one of them to the children of his concubines, as Rashi tells us (25:6). Cf. our commentary on 14:22.

15. וַתֻּקַּח הָאִשָּׁה בֵּית פַּרְעֹה — And the woman was taken to Pharaoh's house. The only case which Abram did not foresee was that the king would want Sarai for himself. The king was the only one who could offer whatever amount of money was asked. Hence Abram was obliged to accept sheep, cattle, donkeys, slaves and maidservants, female donkeys, and camels. Now there was no escape. Abram and Sarai took refuge in the last resort of the Jew in times of distress: prayer. Each prayed fervently to God for help. And He, the "shield of Abraham," answered their prayers, as it is said, לֹא־יְאֻנֶּה לַצַּדִּיק כָּל־אָוֶן, No wrong can come to the righteous (Proverbs 12:21; cf. Tanchuma).

17. וַיְנַגַּע ה' אֶת־פַּרְעֹה נְגָעִים גְּדֹלִים — But HASHEM afflicted Pharaoh ... with severe plagues. "He punished kings for their (the Jews') sake, saying 'Touch not My anointed, and do My prophets no harm!' " (Psalms 105:14-15; I Chronicles 16:21; Midrash Psalms 105).

עַל־דְּבַר שָׂרַי אֵשֶׁת אַבְרָם — Because of the matter of Sarai, the wife of Abram. עַל־דְּבַר שָׂרַי means literally "because of Sarai's word." She had never accepted the request of her husband; she had never claimed to be his sister. She had kept quiet even when abducted to Pharaoh's palace. But when he was afflicted with terrible plagues, he urged her to tell the truth. Then she admitted that she was Abram's wife and this was the "word of Sarai" which explained to him why he was being punished (Ramban). Nonetheless, the king does not retract his gifts to Abram, even after learning of his stratagem; and the Torah deems this worthy of mention. It expressly makes a point of noting this at the beginning of the next chapter (ibid.).

יח וַיִּקְרָא פַרְעֹה לְאַבְרָם וַיֹּאמֶר מַה־זֹּאת עָשִׂיתָ לִּי לָמָּה
יט לֹא־הִגַּדְתָּ לִּי כִּי אִשְׁתְּךָ הִוא: לָמָה אָמַרְתָּ אֲחֹתִי הִוא וָאֶקַּח
כ אֹתָהּ לִי לְאִשָּׁה וְעַתָּה הִנֵּה אִשְׁתְּךָ קַח וָלֵךְ: וַיְצַו עָלָיו
פַרְעֹה אֲנָשִׁים וַיְשַׁלְּחוּ אֹתוֹ וְאֶת־אִשְׁתּוֹ וְאֶת־כָּל־אֲשֶׁר־לוֹ:
יג א וַיַּעַל אַבְרָם מִמִּצְרַיִם הוּא וְאִשְׁתּוֹ וְכָל־אֲשֶׁר־
ב לוֹ וְלוֹט עִמּוֹ הַנֶּגְבָּה: וְאַבְרָם כָּבֵד מְאֹד בַּמִּקְנֶה בַּכֶּסֶף
ג וּבַזָּהָב: וַיֵּלֶךְ לְמַסָּעָיו מִנֶּגֶב וְעַד־בֵּית־אֵל עַד־הַמָּקוֹם
אֲשֶׁר־הָיָה שָׁם אָהֳלֹה בַּתְּחִלָּה בֵּין בֵּית־אֵל וּבֵין הָעָי:

18. מַה־זֹּאת עָשִׂיתָ לִּי — *What is this you have done to me?* "Pharaoh is indignant, and rightly so. He severely reprimands Abram and sends him away forthwith." This is the usual non-Jewish interpretation. In reality, in a country where the husband of a beautiful woman ran the risk of death in order that his wife could be carried off to the king's harem, Pharaoh was scarcely justified in showing such indignation towards Abram. A large part of the reproach meant for Abram goes back to Pharaoh. But the ever-precarious situation of the Jew amid the nations is such that he prefers not to answer back, no matter how unjustified the reproach, as long as they let him go in peace. The gentiles would understand neither his actions nor the position he is in. And so Abram does not answer back. It is true that under quite similar circumstances he does explain his behavior to King Abimelech of Gerar. But Abimelech showed himself much kinder toward Abram than the Pharaoh of Egypt (20:15).

20. וַיְצַו עָלָיו פַרְעֹה אֲנָשִׁים — *So Pharaoh gave men orders concerning him.* "To accompany him and to protect him" (*Rashi*). Our Sages tell us that the travels and events in Abram's life re-echo on an infinitely larger stage, that of the history of the Jewish people. The journey into Egypt, the famine in Canaan which preceded it, taking possession of Canaan, the discord with Ishmael the father of Islam, etc. — all was to come about again in the history of the Jewish nation. "God said unto our father Abraham, 'Go and show the way before them' " (*Bereishis Rabbah* 40). And so the first patriarch showed his children the way not only to their spiritual calling but also to their historical destiny. The latter is a function of the former. Seen in this light, the present narrative is situated in a general historical perspective. By "going down to Egypt" Abram anticipates the opening of the road to the future; and the last phrase, *Pharaoh gave men orders concerning him and they escorted him,* is re-echoed in the last act of the exodus from Egypt, *Pharaoh sent the people out* (*Exodus* 13:17). On both occasions the people came out with lavish gifts (cf. our commentary on 14:22), which permitted them to build the Tabernacle in the desert.

13.

1. וַיַּעַל אַבְרָם מִמִּצְרַיִם — *So Abram went up from Egypt.* R' Shimon said: "Abraham went up from Egypt uninfluenced by its immorality. For Adam and

¹⁸ *Pharaoh summoned Abram and said, "What is this you have done to me? Why did you not tell me that she is your wife?* ¹⁹ *Why did you say, 'She is my sister,' so that I would take her as my wife? Now, here is your wife; take her and go!"* ²⁰ *So Pharaoh gave men orders concerning him, and they escorted him and his wife and all that was his.*

13 ¹ So *Abram went up from Egypt, he with his wife and all that was his — and Lot with him — to the south.* ² *Now Abram was very laden with livestock, silver, and gold.* ³ *He proceeded on his journeys from the south to Beth-el to the place where his tent had been at first, between Beth-el and Ai,*

Noah contact with the outside world, fraught with temptation, was harmful. But far from being seduced by Egyptian civilization, Abraham returned to exactly the same 'level of wisdom' which he had left. Thus his exile into Egypt was not a moral downfall. On the contrary, Abraham triumphed over this test and his return to the Holy Land was an עֲלִיָּה, a step upward. What is more, after building altars, proclaiming the Name of God, and receiving the Divine revelation at Beth-El, Abraham felt that in order to reach the highest degree of holiness he still had to be exposed to corruption and to purify his soul in the 'crucible' of Egypt. And so he 'went down' into this land of perdition, but it was a descent in order to rise up (יְרִידָה צֹרֶךְ עֲלִיָּה). So too with Jewry, who could become the people of God only after they had faced and withstood the Egyptian influence. And then they 'went up' to the Holy Land" (*Zohar*).

2. וְאַבְרָם כָּבֵד מְאֹד — *Now Abram was very laden.* He amassed material wealth during his three months in Egypt (see *Rashi* on 21:34) but this was matched by the spiritual riches he acquired from Egyptian sages and astrologers. Later, Abram introduced Zoroaster to the knowledge of astronomy. In the constellations of the planets, he had observed certain changes which had occurred since the Flood in the order of creation (*Sefer HaYashar* 32b).

3. וַיֵּלֶךְ לְמַסָּעָיו — *He proceeded on his journeys.* On his return, he paid back his debts (*Rashi*). But had he left Canaan in such dire straits that he needed to go into debt? And whom could he count on to give credit to a fugitive in his condition?

But *Rashi's* remark contains another idea. Wherever he went, Abram was proclaiming the power of God, Creator of heaven and earth, and calling men to His service. Many though did not believe him and asked: if Abram is telling the truth, why does this God let His faithful servant wander about endlessly? Why doesn't He reward him with happiness, calm, rest? Abram could not answer these questions, all the more so as the wanderings were inflicted upon him as tests of his love of God. And so he remained "in the debt" of his fellows. But when he returned rich and famous thanks to a miracle with Pharaoh which

ד אֶל־מְקוֹם הַמִּזְבֵּחַ אֲשֶׁר־עָשָׂה שָׁם בָּרִאשֹׁנָה וַיִּקְרָא שָׁם

שלישי ה אַבְרָם בְּשֵׁם יהוה: וְגַם־לְלוֹט הַהֹלֵךְ אֶת־אַבְרָם הָיָה צֹאן־

ו וּבָקָר וְאֹהָלִים: וְלֹא־נָשָׂא אֹתָם הָאָרֶץ לָשֶׁבֶת יַחְדָּו כִּי־הָיָה

ז רְכוּשָׁם רָב וְלֹא יָכְלוּ לָשֶׁבֶת יַחְדָּו: וַיְהִי־רִיב בֵּין רֹעֵי מִקְנֵה־

אַבְרָם וּבֵין רֹעֵי מִקְנֵה־לוֹט וְהַכְּנַעֲנִי וְהַפְּרִזִּי אָז יֹשֵׁב בָּאָרֶץ:

ח וַיֹּאמֶר אַבְרָם אֶל־לוֹט אַל־נָא תְהִי מְרִיבָה בֵּינִי וּבֵינֶךָ וּבֵין

ט רֹעַי וּבֵין רֹעֶיךָ כִּי־אֲנָשִׁים אַחִים אֲנָחְנוּ: הֲלֹא כָל־הָאָרֶץ

לְפָנֶיךָ הִפָּרֶד נָא מֵעָלָי אִם־הַשְּׂמֹאל וְאֵימִנָה וְאִם־הַיָּמִין

everyone knew about, he was able to "pay back his debts" by answering his detractors (הרב מקאזמיר).

4. אֶל־מְקוֹם הַמִּזְבֵּחַ — *To the site of the altar.* The text seems to want to say that Abram returned to the place where he had previously built an altar. "Thinking that pagans had sullied the altar with offerings to idols during his absence, Abram did not want to sacrifice on it. He did away with it and sacrificed instead on the *site* of the altar, i.e., on the site where the altar had been, which had retained its sanctity" (*Meshech Chochmah*).

The words אֶל־מְקוֹם הַמִּזְבֵּחַ can also imply that Abram spiritually regained "the level of the altar' which he had previously built. All the riches and knowledge which he gained, all the honor given him by the king of Egypt, were not able to cause his absolute fidelity to waver even for an instant. Abram returned straightaway to the place where he belonged: the place of the altar. As has been mentioned (12:8) this site was on Mount Moriah, from where later the Torah was to spread out to all parts of the world. Here Abram, the father of all believers, wants to reside; this is his "headquarters." He has but one goal in life — לִקְרֹא בְּשֵׁם ה׳, to proclaim the name of God. And, scarcely back from the exile which has bestowed on him fame and fortune, he immediately takes up his missionary work once again.

7. וַיְהִי־רִיב — *And there was quarreling.* Rashi explains what it was about: Abram's herdsmen accused Lot's of theft for using fields which did not belong to them. Lot's men retorted that it was their land because it had been given to Abram and, since Abram was childless, Lot would be his heir. Abram's men replied that "The Canaanite and the Perizzite were then dwelling in the land." Consequently, at that time Abram did not yet have a right to it.

But this gives only the apparent reason for the quarrel. The underlying cause which led to the separation is brought out by the *Zohar.* Lot wanted to return to the idolatry practiced by the inhabitants of the land. The text alludes to this when it stresses in the same verse, *The Canaanite and the Perizzite were then dwelling in the land.* Mixing with these pagans was at the root of the quarrel between Abram and his nephew. Lot persisted in his desire to serve idols, even after Abram's invitation to separate from him: וַיִּסַּע לוֹט מִקֶּדֶם, *And Lot journeyed from the east.* Rashi explains that allegorically this means that "he separated

⁴ to the site of the altar which he had erected there at first; and there Abram invoked HASHEM by Name.

⁵ Also Lot who went with Abram had flocks, cattle, and tents. ⁶ And the land could not support them dwelling together for their possessions were abundant and they were unable to dwell together. ⁷ And there was quarreling between the herdsmen of Abram's livestock and the herdsmen of Lot's livestock — and the Canaanite and the Perizzite were then dwelling in the land.

⁸ So Abram said to Lot: "Please let there be no strife between me and you, and between my herdsmen and your herdsmen, for we are kinsmen. ⁹ Is not all the land before you? Please separate from me: If you go left then I will go right, and if you go right

himself from the One Who existed before the world came into being (קַדְמוֹן; cf. our commentary on 11:2). Lot said: 'I want neither Abram nor his God.' " Like his father Haran, Lot was unstable and changeable (cf. *Rashi* on 11:28). When he left Chaldea, he chose to follow Abram and his God, but on his return from polytheistic Egypt, he favored the pagans and their idols. He had become rich in his association with Abram and now he wanted to be on his own.

8. כִּי־אֲנָשִׁים אַחִים אֲנָחְנוּ — *For we are kinsmen. Rashi* explains: they were just close relatives. But the Midrash says that Abram and Lot resembled each other, they had the same look. Abram probably wanted to tell Lot: "Let us go separate ways for we have nothing in common but outward appearance."

9. הִפָּרֶד נָא מֵעָלָי — *Please separate from me.* The word הִפָּרֶד expresses a more complete separation than its synonym הִבָּדֵל. It is an emphatic expression. Abram is accommodating, indulgent, and hospitable to all strangers. But with his own nephew he is strict and uncompromising when he realizes that Lot is forsaking his faith and seeking the company of the Sodomites.

But more, the verb פרד means a definitive separation. Indeed, Abram foresaw that this parting of the ways would extend to all future generations; it would forbid marriages between his descendants and Lot's. The latter, who formed the Amonite and Moabite nations, are referred to explicitly when the Torah states: *An Amonite or a Moabite shall not enter into the assembly of God . . . none of them shall enter there forever (Deuteronomy 23:1,4).* Nevertheless, from these peoples two women of exceptional valor, Ruth the Moabitess and Na'amah the Amonitess, became illustrious mothers in Israel: in association with our word הִפָּרֶד, tradition calls the two פְּרֵדוֹת טוֹבוֹת (*Bava Kamma* 38b; Amonite and Moabite women were not included in the prohibition mentioned above). Some commentators also admit that when Abram used the word הִפָּרֶד he wanted to reply to the insult of Lot's men toward him: פְּרֵדָה עֲקָרָה, *sterile mule* (cf. *Bereishis Rabbah* 41).

אִם־הַשְּׂמֹאל וְאֵימִנָה — *If you go left then I will go right.* R' Yochanan interprets Abram's words in this way: if you go to the left, that is to the north, then I will

יְ וְאַשְׂמְאִילָה: וַיִּשָּׂא־לוֹט אֶת־עֵינָיו וַיַּרְא אֶת־כָּל־כִּכַּר הַיַּרְדֵּן כִּי כֻלָּהּ מַשְׁקֶה לִפְנֵי | שַׁחֵת יהוה אֶת־סְדֹם וְאֶת־עֲמֹרָה יא כְּגַן־יהוה כְּאֶרֶץ מִצְרַיִם בֹּאֲכָה צֹעַר: וַיִּבְחַר־לוֹ לוֹט אֵת כָּל־כִּכַּר הַיַּרְדֵּן וַיִּסַּע לוֹט מִקֶּדֶם וַיִּפָּרְדוּ אִישׁ מֵעַל אָחִיו: יב אַבְרָם יָשַׁב בְּאֶרֶץ־כְּנָעַן וְלוֹט יָשַׁב בְּעָרֵי הַכִּכָּר וַיֶּאֱהַל עַד־ יג-יד סְדֹם: וְאַנְשֵׁי סְדֹם רָעִים וְחַטָּאִים לַיהוה מְאֹד: וַיהוה אָמַר אֶל־אַבְרָם אַחֲרֵי הִפָּרֶד־לוֹט מֵעִמּוֹ שָׂא־נָא עֵינֶיךָ וּרְאֵה טו מִן־הַמָּקוֹם אֲשֶׁר־אַתָּה שָׁם צָפֹנָה וָנֶגְבָּה וָקֵדְמָה וָיָמָּה: כִּי אֶת־כָּל־הָאָרֶץ אֲשֶׁר־אַתָּה רֹאֶה לְךָ אֶתְּנֶנָּה וּלְזַרְעֲךָ עַד־ טז עוֹלָם: וְשַׂמְתִּי אֶת־זַרְעֲךָ כַּעֲפַר הָאָרֶץ אֲשֶׁר | אִם־יוּכַל אִישׁ

go to the right, southwards. If not, I will go to the right and I will make you go to the left, to the north. The form וְאַשְׂמְאִילָה (rather than וְאַשְׂמָאלָה) is a הִפְעִיל, a causative verb. Indeed, Abram wanted at all costs to go southward, for the reasons given in our commentary on 12:9 (*Bereishis Rabbah* 41).

10. וַיִּשָּׂא־לוֹט אֶת־עֵינָיו — *So Lot raised his eyes.* The same expression is used when Potiphar's wife looks lasciviously at Joseph (*Genesis* 39:7). R' Yose notes that all the terms of this verse contain a nuance of sensual desire (in detail, *Bereishis Rabbah* ibid.). "Whoever burns with insatiable hunger will end by eating his own flesh. So with Lot: his lust ultimately led him to commit incest" (ibid.).

כְּגַן־ה' כְּאֶרֶץ מִצְרַיִם — *Like the garden of HASHEM, like the land of Egypt.* "Just as the Garden of Eden did not need to be watered, so it was in Egypt and in the land of Sodom. All the world's delights were to be found there. And the inhabitants permitted no one to share them" (*Zohar*). Before the salt sea was formed, following the destruction of Sodom, the Jordan watered the vast basin of the whole region and made it extremely fertile "both for trees and for plants."

14. וַה' אָמַר אֶל־אַבְרָם — *HASHEM said to Abram.* From the time that his traveling companion began to deny God in his heart, the *Shechinah* had moved away from Abram. Just after Lot separated from Abram, the *Shechinah* revealed Itself to him once more. God does not tolerate the righteous and the impious living side by side. *For the scepter of wickedness will not rest upon the lot of the righteous* (*Psalms* 125:3).

אַחֲרֵי הִפָּרֶד־לוֹט מֵעִמּוֹ — *After Lot had parted from him.* R' Yehudah and R' Nechemiah disagree on the exact meaning of this phrase. Does it mean that God had waited for Lot to leave because He was displeased with Abram, displeased that he had brought Lot with him despite the command to leave all his family? Or, on the contrary, does it mean that God was displeased that Abram sent Lot away although he was infinitely hospitable to all the others? The form וַה', *And HASHEM* (with the coordinating conjunction) designates God surrounded by the heavenly tribunal and sitting in judgment over His creatures

then I will go left.''

¹⁰ *So Lot raised his eyes and saw the entire plain of the Jordan that it was well watered everywhere — before HASHEM destroyed Sodom and Gomorrah —like the garden of HASHEM, like the land of Egypt, going toward Zoar.* ¹¹ *So Lot chose for himself the whole plain of the Jordan, and Lot journeyed from the east; thus they parted, one from his brother.*

¹² *Abram dwelled in the land of Canaan while Lot dwelled in the cities of the plain and pitched his tents as far as Sodom.* ¹³ *Now the people of Sodom were wicked and sinful toward HASHEM, exceedingly.*

¹⁴ *HASHEM said to Abram after Lot had parted from him, ''Raise now your eyes and look out from where you are: northward, southward, eastward and westward.* ¹⁵ *For all the land that you see, to you will I give it, and to your descendants forever.* ¹⁶ *I will make your offspring as the dust of the earth so that if one can*

(ירוש׳ ברכות, פ״ט ה״ז); quoted by *Rashi*, 19:24). The question remains unanswered.

שָׂא־נָא עֵינֶיךָ — *Raise now your eyes.* Do not gaze at this land in the ordinary way. Do not see merely outward appearances, such as the presence of the Canaanites and their depraved ways. But lift up your eyes and look at the land, heighten your awareness and see the land in perspective. Realize that *all the land that you see, to you will I give it,* for it is stamped from now on with a holiness which befits your calling (*Meshech Chochmah*).

15. לְךָ אֶתְּנֶנָּה וּלְזַרְעֲךָ עַד־עוֹלָם — *To you will I give it, and to your descendants forever.* When Abram's nephew leaves, God renews the promise made previously (12:7). This is because, for want of a son, Abram had considered his nephew as his probable heir through whom the Divine promise would be fulfilled.

Again the patriarch hears that the land will be given to his descendants. But considering Sarai's sterility, this is seemingly impossible. The first Jew is already trained to place himself entirely in God's hands, to have complete confidence in God. He is already trained to look at nature and the empirical as not being made up of absolute and irreversible factors.

עַד־עוֹלָם — *Forever.* This does not imply that they will always be in possession of the land. But it will belong to them, even as it was given to Abram here, without his ever being in actual possession of it (*R' S. R. Hirsch*).

16. וְשַׂמְתִּי . . . כַּעֲפַר הָאָרֶץ — *I will make . . . as the dust of the earth.* As the dust covers the earth from one end to the other, so too will your descendants be dispersed the world over; as metals disintegrate in the dust, which endures after them, so too will your descendants cause the breakdown of pagan peoples, yet will permanently endure, even though, like dust, they will be trampled by their enemies (*Midrash*).

יז לִמְנוֹת אֶת־עֲפַר הָאָרֶץ גַּם זַרְעֲךָ יִמָּנֶה: קוּם הִתְהַלֵּךְ בָּאָרֶץ
יח לְאָרְכָּהּ וּלְרָחְבָּהּ כִּי לְךָ אֶתְּנֶנָּה: וַיֶּאֱהַל אַבְרָם וַיָּבֹא וַיֵּשֶׁב
בְּאֵלֹנֵי מַמְרֵא אֲשֶׁר בְּחֶבְרוֹן וַיִּבֶן־שָׁם מִזְבֵּחַ לַיהוָה:

יד רביעי א וַיְהִי בִּימֵי אַמְרָפֶל מֶלֶךְ־שִׁנְעָר אַרְיוֹךְ מֶלֶךְ אֶלָּסָר כְּדָרְלָעֹמֶר

17. קוּם הִתְהַלֵּךְ בָּאָרֶץ לְאָרְכָּהּ וּלְרָחְבָּהּ — *Arise, walk about the land through its length and breadth!* From these words the Talmud concludes that the act of walking over the length and breadth of a property to which one has rights constitutes a means of acquisition (*Bava Basra* 100a). In this way Abram gains the rights of acquisition to the land he was promised for his descendants; he walks through the land from one end to the other (חֲזָקָה) so that, our Sages tell us, "it will be easy for his children to conquer." *Rashi* explains that they will have the status of heirs to the land. They will not be like thieves, nor will Satan (i.e. the enemy) be able to accuse them, nor will justice find a pretext to fault them (ibid.).

Ramban makes the following point: know that every Divine decree reaches definitive realization when it leaves the potential and is concretized and actualized through an action, be it even a formality or a fiction. This is why the prophets carried out certain prophetic acts, as with Jeremiah (51:63) and Elisha (*II Kings* 13:18-19). Along the same lines, Abram had to carry out the formality of acquisition (חֲזָקָה) over the land and a series of other concrete acts which opened the way to the future history of his descendants.

This ideas has wide application. It helps us also to understand certain external acts, often qualified as pure formality, both in the historical and legislative domains of Judaism. *R' S. R. Hirsch* interprets them as symbolic acts whose purpose is to awaken in the Jewish conscience those thoughts and feelings which give rise to strong, definite commitment (*Collected Works*, III, 213-254). For *Ramban*, however, these same acts serve to inscribe certain eternal values in the reality of historical, moral, or social events by initiating the concretization of these values. Seen in this way, prophetic acts or laws qualified as "signs" have a much deeper function than merely to represent symbolic signs. They direct our outlook, they turn our whole personality in the desired direction, they orient us in our historical destiny (ועי' דרשות הר"ן, דרוש ב').

18. בְּחֶבְרוֹן — *In Hebron.* Flavius Josephus speaks of this city as being more ancient than Memphis in Egypt.

14.

1. וַיְהִי בִּימֵי אַמְרָפֶל — *And it happened in the days of Amraphel.* Here we have the oldest case of war and conflict between kings in all history. What is the Torah's purpose in recounting these events?

Various answers are given by our Sages. Some hold that the chapter makes an important point regarding the special character of the Holy Land. King Amraphel of Babylonia (Shinar), identified with the "powerful hunter" Nimrod

count the dust of the earth, then your offspring, too, can be counted. ¹⁷ Arise, walk about the land through its length and breadth! For to you will I give it." ¹⁸ And Abram moved his tent and came and dwelled in the plains of Mamre which are in Hebron; and he built there an altar to HASHEM.

14 ¹*And it happened in the days of Amraphel, king of Shinar; Arioch, king of Ellasar; Chedorlaomer, king of*

(10:9), had given himself absolute powers as king (See *Maharsha, Eruvin* 53a). His despotism enabled him to misuse the collective forces of the nation for his own purposes, under the cloak of patriotism and at the cost of the welfare of the individual. This policy spread rapidly, so that history then was just the history of kings, not of people. An area as small as the Jordan valley had no fewer than five kings, a king to every town. Later on, in Joshua's time, a small area had thirty-one kings. Still other nobles were even more powerful kings; they ruled over provinces or large territories such as Babylonia and Media. Through their conquests, they became rulers even over other kings.

The large number of tiny kingdoms in this region is generally attributed to the superabundance, the fertility of the soil. Opulence and riches lead a people to an easy, carefree, luxurious life, the breeding-ground for personal ambition and desire for power. The small kingdoms were in turn made subordinate to a powerful foreign king, such as Chedorlaomer, king of Elam. The kings of these small kingdoms willingly paid an annual tribute to him if it meant that they could have peace and security to rule and enjoy royal status in their lands.

Here, the ancestor of the future Jewish people observed that opulence reduces a people to enslavement, both literally and figuratively. There is no internal or external freedom for any nation except by submission to moral law. But for Abram this experience was to have still more specific significance. The land on which he stood was promised to his children and yet his first experience on it was famine — his second — war. Thus he realized that neither material abundance nor political independence was inherent in the land itself. In both respects the land of Israel stood in complete contrast to Egypt. Just as its fertility was entirely dependent on rain from Heaven, so too its political position was such that it could offer no natural resistance to invaders. Left to itself, the land of Israel lay open to famine and political dependence. It is situated in the "navel" of the world, where Asia, Africa, and Europe meet, and hardly any world war has occurred without its being drawn into it. And this is precisely why it was chosen. If, despite everything, this land could produce a national life which no conqueror would dare attack even though its borders were left undefended, as was the case three times a year, and if all the kingdoms of the world fought and killed each other while "no sword would dare pass through this land," this flowering yet defenseless land, then the nations of the world would see that God dwells in this land! "God resides in her palaces, He is become known as their true fortress" (*Psalms* 48:4).

ב מֶלֶךְ עֵילָם וְתִדְעָל מֶלֶךְ גּוֹיִם: עָשׂוּ מִלְחָמָה אֶת־בֶּרַע מֶלֶךְ
סְדֹם וְאֶת־בִּרְשַׁע מֶלֶךְ עֲמֹרָה שִׁנְאָב ׀ מֶלֶךְ אַדְמָה וְשֶׁמְאֵבֶר
ג מֶלֶךְ °צְבֹיִים וּמֶלֶךְ בֶּלַע הִיא־צֹעַר: כָּל־אֵלֶּה חָבְרוּ
ד אֶל־עֵמֶק הַשִּׂדִּים הוּא יָם הַמֶּלַח: שְׁתֵּים עֶשְׂרֵה שָׁנָה עָבְדוּ
ה אֶת־כְּדָרְלָעֹמֶר וּשְׁלֹשׁ־עֶשְׂרֵה שָׁנָה מָרָדוּ: וּבְאַרְבַּע עֶשְׂרֵה
שָׁנָה בָּא כְדָרְלָעֹמֶר וְהַמְּלָכִים אֲשֶׁר אִתּוֹ וַיַּכּוּ אֶת־רְפָאִים

צְבוֹיִם ק'

For Abram, this event was one of the most important in his life. The wealthy lords of the land had been conquered, had become subjects of Chedorlaomer, had finally rebelled against him — and they must have been powerful since Chedorlaomer the great king called for his allies to help subdue them — and had been beaten. And now Abram, with only his household — but with God as his ally — succeeds in overcoming this most powerful of earthly kings. Abram literally reconquers the land. He chases Chedorlaomer from one end of the land to the other, from Hebron to Damascus, drives him out, and frees the land. He lives to see the promise of לְךָ אֶתְּנֶנָּה, *to you will I give it*, literally carried out (*R' S. R. Hirsch*).

Another important aspect of this chapter is stressed by our Sages. An analogy can be drawn between the four victorious kingdoms and the ד' מַלְכִיּוֹת, the four world-empires which dominate human history. At least two can be clearly recognized: Shinar is Babylonia; Elam is Media-Persia. From earliest times they had raided and made military expeditions to the Holy land and surrounding countries, which at first were conquered. Thus the prophets had a vision of the "four kingdoms" everywhere victorious, conquerors of lands and peoples including the Land of Israel until finally, with God's help, the Jewish nation wins and becomes the redeemer of humanity (cf. *Ramban*).

אַמְרָפֶל מֶלֶךְ־שִׁנְעָר — *Amraphel, king of Shinar*. This king is generally identified with Hammurabi, the illustrious, enlightened king of Babylonia. He reigned from 1945-1902 B.C.E. and united the city-states of the north and south into a centralized empire. He conquered Soubartou and Assyria and enlarged his territory on the Euphrates and the Tigris to the Persian Gulf. He promulgated new laws, the Code of Hammurabi, which was engraved on stone. In fact the Louvre contains one of these, discovered in Susa in 1901. According to *Onkelos*, the Shinar ruled by Amraphel is none other than Babylonia. Shinar is just one of its Egyptian names (cf. 10:10). Certain scholars hypothesize that Shinar is the same as Sumer, a region of lower Mesopotamia inhabited by the Sumerians. Their civilization greatly influenced the development of the whole Near East.

Rashi quotes the opinion of the *Amoraim*, Rav and Shmuel, that Amraphel is identified with Nimrod. He was called Amraphel because he had said (אָמַר) to Abram: cast yourself (פּוֹל) into the fiery furnace. He was also called Nimrod because he made the world rebel (הִמְרִיד) against God. One is his proper name,

Elam, and Tidal, king of Goiim, ² that these made war on Bera,
king of Sodom; Birsha, king of Gomorrah; Shinab, king of
Admah; Shemeber, king of Zeboiim; and the king of Bela, which
is Zoar. ³ All these had joined at the Valley of Siddim, now the
Salt Sea. ⁴ Twelve years they served Chedorlaomer, and they
rebelled thirteen years. ⁵ In the fourteenth year, Chedorlaomer
and the kings who were with him came and struck the Rephaim

the other is an epithet (*R' Eliyahu Mizrachi*). The *Sefer HaYashar* tells us that
after the Tower of Babel, which he instigated, had failed and was followed
by the confusion of languages, large numbers of Nimrod's followers left him.
The only ones to remain loyal were the people of Shinar. Confronted with this
new situation, he took on a new name. However, in his book *Mevo HaTalmud*
(*A Student's Guide to the Talmud*, chapter 21), *R' Zvi Hirsh Chajes* maintains
that our Sages "had the habit of identifying two different people of equal
stature with respect to their virtues or vices in order to increase our esteem of
the righteous and to make the wicked even more detestable." According to him,
then, this would also be the sense of the tradition identifying Amraphel with
Nimrod.

2. אֶת־בֶּרַע מֶלֶךְ סְדֹם — *Bera, king of Sodom. Rashi* explains his name: evil (רַע)
toward God, evil toward men. The names which follow are also explained in
an allegorical manner. The author just quoted, *R' Chajes*, states that the Sages
had a tradition which said the names used in the Torah contain indications
of the character or future destiny of their bearers. As a consequence, they looked
a priori for the deep meaning just as the old saying has it: "*Nomen est omen.*"
The Talmud also states the rule שְׁמָא גְּרִים — the name is an omen (*Berachos*
7b). *R' Yehudah HaLevi* says that the essence of one's character is reflected
in the name which one bears (*Kuzari* 4:1). But there are exceptions: some have
excellent names but do evil and vice versa (*Bamidbar Rabbah* 16). Thus the
name of a righteous person is not always a good omen, and the opposite case
can also occur (ס' חסידים סעי' רמ"ד). *R' Yose* and *R' Shimon ben Gamliel* declare
that in early times those who foresaw the destinies of their children, either
through the gift of prophecy or through knowledge of their family
background, gave them names which corresponded to their future destiny,
whereas we give them the names of our ancestors (*Bereishis Rabbah* 37).

4. שְׁתֵּים עֶשְׂרֵה שָׁנָה עָבְדוּ — *Twelve years they served.* In his responsa, *R' Shlomo*
ben Aderes (תשובות הרשב"א) takes issue with those such as Philo of Alexandria
who explain the text allegorically. For them the war of the four kings against
five would signify the battle of the four natural elements (earth, air, water, fire)
against the five senses with which man is endowed, i.e. the battle for control
between man and nature.

But *R' Ephraim of Luntshitz*, author of the book עוֹלְלֹת אפרים, recognizes
the legitimacy of such דְרָשׁוֹת as long as they claim only to interpret the "hidden

בְּעַשְׁתְּרֹת קַרְנַ֫יִם וְאֶת־הַזּוּזִים בְּהֶם וְאֵת הָאֵימִים בְּשָׁוֵ֫ה
ו קִרְיָתָ֫יִם: וְאֶת־הַחֹרִ֫י בְּהַרְרָם שֵׂעִיר עַ֫ד אֵיל פָּארָ֫ן אֲשֶׁר
ז עַל־הַמִּדְבָּ֫ר: וַיָּשֻׁ֫בוּ וַיָּבֹ֫אוּ אֶל־עֵ֫ין מִשְׁפָּט הִוא קָדֵ֫שׁ וַיַּכּ֫וּ
אֶת־כָּל־שְׂדֵ֫ה הָעֲמָלֵקִ֫י וְגַ֫ם אֶת־הָאֱמֹרִ֫י הַיֹּשֵׁ֫ב בְּחַצְצֹ֫ן
ח תָּמָ֫ר: וַיֵּצֵ֫א מֶֽלֶךְ־סְדֹם וּמֶ֫לֶךְ עֲמֹרָ֫ה וּמֶ֫לֶךְ אַדְמָה וּמֶ֫לֶךְ
צבוֹיֵם ק' צְבוֹיִ֫ים וּמֶ֫לֶךְ בֶּ֫לַע הִוא־צֹ֫עַר וַיַּֽעַרְכ֫וּ אִתָּם מִלְחָמָ֫ה בְּעֵ֫מֶק
ט הַשִּׂדִּ֫ים: אֵ֫ת כְּדָרְלָעֹ֫מֶר מֶ֫לֶךְ עֵילָ֫ם וְתִדְעָל מֶ֫לֶךְ גּוֹיִ֫ם
וְאַמְרָפֶל֙ מֶ֫לֶךְ שִׁנְעָ֫ר וְאַרְי֫וֹךְ מֶ֫לֶךְ אֶלָּסָ֫ר אַרְבָּעָ֫ה מְלָכִ֫ים
י אֶת־הַחֲמִשָּׁ֫ה: וְעֵ֫מֶק הַשִּׂדִּ֫ים בֶּ֫אֱרֹת בֶּ֫אֱרֹת חֵמָ֫ר וַיָּנֻ֫סוּ
מֶֽלֶךְ־סְדֹ֫ם וַעֲמֹרָ֫ה וַיִּפְּלוּ־שָׁ֫מָּה וְהַנִּשְׁאָרִ֫ים הֶ֫רָה נָּ֫סוּ:
יא וַיִּקְח֫וּ אֶת־כָּל־רְכֻ֫שׁ סְדֹ֫ם וַעֲמֹרָ֫ה וְאֶת־כָּל־אָכְלָ֫ם וַיֵּלֵֽכוּ:

meaning" of the text without being intended as a substitute for the literal
meaning. He explains the verse in relation to the first twelve years in the life
of man, when the five senses (of the soul) are enslaved by the four elements
of nature. Indeed, tradition states that man's natural instincts rule unopposed
by his reason until he is thirteen (*Nedarim* 32b; *Avos D'Rabbi Nosson* 16:2).
But in the thirteenth year, they rebel. At this age the spiritual forces of the
soul begin to oppose the elemental forces of physical nature. Accordingly,
"full-scale war" breaks out in the fourteenth year when the latter try to regain
lost ground. After a fierce battle raging back and forth, it is Abram, the
incarnation of Divine law, who finally comes to liberate the five kings
(representing the factors of the soul) for good from the subjugation of the four
kings, who personify the four basic elements of nature (cf. *M. M. Kasher*, לך
מכאן manuscript: מדרש הבאור quoting ,section 24 ,page 497 ,לך, תורה שלמה
.(סמכו חכמים שבן י"ג יצא מרשות אביו)

10. בֶּאֱרֹת בֶּאֱרֹת חֵמָר — *Was full of bitumen wells. Rashi:* The Midrash tells
us that they sank into the clay, but a miracle occurred and the king of Sodom
was able to reach safety. There were some people who had refused to believe
that Abram miraculously emerged unharmed from the fiery furnace of Ur
Kasdim. But now that the king of Sodom had come safely out of the clay pits,
they began to believe retrospectively in Abram's miracle, too.

Ramban asks: How was the miracle for the king of Sodom more convincing
than that which saved Abram? Would it not, on the contrary, give the pagans
reason to believe even more in their own religion, since the miracle happened
to a pagan king? Might they not simply be led to conclude that all miracles
are witchcraft? He answers that the miracle occurred just as the victorious
Abram passed in front of the pit, intending to save the king of Sodom. Thus
everyone recognized that the miracle happened only because of Abram. *R'
Eliyahu Mizrachi* explains that the miraculous rescue of the king of Sodom
convinced the pagans of the existence of supernatural intervention; this they

at Ashteroth-karnaim, the Zuzim in Ham, the Emim at Shaveh-kiriathaim; ⁶ *and the Horites in their mountains of Seir, as far as the Plain of Paran which is by the desert.* ⁷ *Then they turned back and came to En-mishpat, which is Kadesh; they struck all the territory of the Amalakites; and also the Amorites who dwell in Hazazon-tamar.*

⁸ *And the king of Sodom went forth with the king of Gomorrah, the king of Admah, the king of Zeboiim and the king of Bela, which is Zoar, and engaged them in battle in the Valley of Siddim:* ⁹ *With Chedorlaomer, king of Elam; Tidal, king of Goiim; Amraphel, king of Shinar; and Arioch, king of Ellasar — four kings against five.*

¹⁰ *The Valley of Siddim was full of bitumen wells. The kings of Sodom and Gomorrah fled and fell into them while the rest fled to a mountain.* ¹¹ *The seized all the wealth of Sodom and Gomorrah and all their food and they departed.*

had not previously believed possible. The fact that such intervention had happened for Abram because he opposed idol worship made them realize the truth of his message. *Maharal* explains: the Divine assistance which Abram received in his amazing victory over the four mighty kings was so striking to the pagans that they now understood what had occurred at the clay pits. They realized that the miraculous rescue of the king of Sodom could only have been wrought by the God of Abram. This revelation won them over to his cause.

11. וַיֵּלֵכוּ ... אֶת־כָּל־רְכֻשׁ וַיִּקְחוּ — *They seized all the wealth ... and they departed.* The following verse repeats that the victors departed after capturing Lot and his wealth. This repetition shows that their objective was to capture Sodom, and more particularly Lot himself. And so the Midrash teaches that the war of the kings was the sixth of the ten trials which Abram had to undergo. For the kings had Abram in mind and only "began with his nephew Lot" (*Pirkei D'Rabbi Eliezer* 27). And the *Zohar* makes it even more explicit: this war was, in the final analysis, Abram's war. The mighty kings wanted to kill him because he turned the population away from idolatry and led them to a love of God. But as soon as they had taken Lot prisoner they went their way, for he looked like Abram (cf. *Rashi*, 13:8) to such an extent that at first they thought he was Abram. Abram rushed to the rescue of his nephew. He decided forthwith and, although his temperament inclined toward pity for all creatures, he showed himself a courageous, intrepid fighter. The Divine Presence, which began again to spread over the earth thanks to Abram, accompanied him into battle, for Abram had implored his Helper: *O God, take no rest for Yourself, be not silent and keep not still, O Almighty. For Your enemies make a tumult and they that hate You have lifted up their head* (Psalms 83:2-3).

יב וַיִּקְחוּ אֶת־לוֹט וְאֶת־רְכֻשׁוֹ בֶּן־אֲחִי אַבְרָם וַיֵּלֵכוּ וְהוּא
יג יֹשֵׁב בִּסְדֹם: וַיָּבֹא הַפָּלִיט וַיַּגֵּד לְאַבְרָם הָעִבְרִי וְהוּא שֹׁכֵן
בְּאֵלֹנֵי מַמְרֵא הָאֱמֹרִי אֲחִי אֶשְׁכֹּל וַאֲחִי עָנֵר וְהֵם בַּעֲלֵי
יד בְרִית־אַבְרָם: וַיִּשְׁמַע אַבְרָם כִּי נִשְׁבָּה אָחִיו וַיָּרֶק אֶת־

12. וְהוּא יֹשֵׁב בִּסְדֹם — *For he was residing in Sodom.* We were already told that Lot was Abram's nephew and that he lived in Sodom. But the Torah surely has a reason for mentioning it here again. Lot was not born a Sodomite, since he was Abram's nephew. Had he remained as he was, he would not have been in danger and he could have hoped that, although he was close to the fighting, as a stranger he would have been spared and sheltered from Chedorlaomer's revenge. But he had become an inhabitant of Sodom, a citizen, and as such he had to pay the price. This is a warning to the members of the family of Abram which has been borne out through the centuries of Jewish history. Remaining faithful to the Jewish calling and destiny means that one has to do without a good deal, to be sure, but one also saves oneself from a good deal; one seems to be borne upon כַּנְפֵי שְׁכִינָה, *the wings of the Shechinah.* Jewish ghettos existed not only against the Jews but also for them. Within them Jews remained protected from the many evils which in the Middle Ages befell the people outside. But the vulgar, the sensual, never learn. Lot should have learned from his experiences to avoid Sodom. Nevertheless we find him at the final catastrophe still living in Sodom (*R' S. R. Hirsch*).

13. וַיָּבֹא הַפָּלִיט — *Then there came the fugitive. Rashi* quotes the Midrash: "This is Og (the king of Bashan), the giant who survived the Flood. He was hoping that Abram would be killed in battle so that he could marry Sarai." But another Midrash designates the Archangel Michael (called 'the fugitive" or "the rejected") as announcing the news to Abram (*Pirkei D'Rabbi Eliezer* ibid.). These interpretations are evidently contradictory; they remind us that man sees merely outward appearances. The event itself is clear: a fugitive came to tell Abram that his nephew had been captured. But why did this happen? It is quite impossible to ascertain the motives, the reasons for this announcement. Was it an angel from heaven who came to bring good news? Or was it a coarse, unrefined mortal with evil intentions? Lacking evidence to the contrary, Abram took it for good. Indeed Og, the Talmud tells us, was rewarded "for bringing joy to the righteous" (*Niddah* 61a) and for indirectly contributing to an act of קִדּוּשׁ הַשֵּׁם, *sanctification of the Holy Name* through Abram's victory and his noble attitude after the defeat of the kings. His reward was exceptional longevity (*Bereishis Rabbah* 42). And Moses himself feared to enter into battle against Og because of the merit which he had acquired by giving the news to Abram, notwithstanding the fact that he had come with evil intentions (*Rashi on Numbers* 21:34).

Maharal adds: Do not be surprised at Og's longevity, which extended over approximately nine centuries — from the time of the Flood to the wars preceding

¹² *And they captured Lot and his possessions — Abram's nephew — and they left; for he was residing in Sodom.*
¹³ *Then there came the fugitive and told Abram, the Ivri, who dwelt in the plains of Mamre, the Amorite, the brother of Eshcol and the brother of Aner, these being Abram's allies.* ¹⁴ *And when Abram heard that his kinsman was taken captive, he armed his*

the death of Moses. Human vitality was much greater at creation and in the centuries following. Its effects were felt right up to King David's reign, at the end of the first half of the cycle of human history. But since then, exceptional cases of this kind are no longer encountered. (However, *Maharal* does not exclude the possibility that Og is the name of a whole dynasty and that this name could refer to various members of the same royal lineage.)

וְהֵם בַּעֲלֵי בְרִית־אַבְרָם — *These being Abram's allies.* Not אַנְשֵׁי בְּרִיתוֹ, which would mean allies on an equal footing, but בַּעֲלֵי בְרִית, that is, masters of the covenant of Abram. It was not Abram who took them into his circle of friends but Aner, Eshcol and Mamre who welcomed him into theirs; they were the "masters of the covenant" whereas he was the stranger. Yet he was such an imposing personality that they did not hesitate to accept him as their ally and friend. Hence Abram had no fear of preserving his individuality among the Amorites and of appearing as a stranger who was merely tolerated. He remained Abram the Hebrew (הָעִבְרִי), that is, the stranger who came from the other side (עֵבֶר) of the river, or, as R' Yehoshua explains, the one who stands on the other side, the one "beyond," standing in opposition to all humanity, and known as such, וְהוּא שֹׁכֵן, he is just a temporary resident with the Amorites. But he is not a יֹשֵׁב, not a real inhabitant, as Lot wants to be in Sodom. Abram's attitude can serve as an example to his descendants whenever they dwell in a land not their own. The Jew must remain a Jew, must remain a moderate, not troubling the public order of his society. He must develop and organize the conditions of his Jewish life in such a way that others seek his friendship and not vice versa. Every good man recognizes that in authentic, complete Judaism there is the realization of humanism *par excellence.* For to be a Jew means to be a man, but on a higher plane. Let the children of Abram remain solely Jews, but Jews in the full sense of the word, and although only "residents" they will be partners in the "covenant of nations." Abram does not seek to ensure this alliance by forsaking or compromising his mission (*R' S. R. Hirsch*).

14. וַיִּשְׁמַע אַבְרָם כִּי נִשְׁבָּה אָחִיו — *And when Abram heard that his kinsman* [lit. *brother*] *was taken captive.* Prior to this Abram had called Lot his nephew or his relative. But as soon as he learns of his misfortune, Abram calls Lot his brother, even though, because of Lot's apostasy, Abram just previously had cause to leave him. Now Abram was not entirely uninvolved in the death of Haran, who was his brother and the father of Lot, and he surely felt an increased

חֲנִיכָיו יְלִידֵי בֵיתֹו שְׁמֹנָה עָשָׂר וּשְׁלֹשׁ מֵאֹות וַיִּרְדֹּף עַד־דָּן:
טו וַיֵּחָלֵק עֲלֵיהֶם ׀ לַיְלָה הוּא וַעֲבָדָיו וַיַּכֵּם וַיִּרְדְּפֵם עַד־חֹובָה
טז אֲשֶׁר מִשְּׂמֹאל לְדַמָּשֶׂק: וַיָּשֶׁב אֵת כָּל־הָרְכֻשׁ וְגַם אֶת־לֹוט
יז אָחִיו וּרְכֻשֹׁו הֵשִׁיב וְגַם אֶת־הַנָּשִׁים וְאֶת־הָעָם: וַיֵּצֵא מֶלֶךְ־
סְדֹם לִקְרָאתֹו אַחֲרֵי שׁוּבֹו מֵהַכֹּות אֶת־כְּדָרְלָעֹמֶר וְאֶת־
הַמְּלָכִים אֲשֶׁר אִתֹּו אֶל־עֵמֶק שָׁוֵה הוּא עֵמֶק הַמֶּלֶךְ:

responsibility toward his nephew. Haran had died in the fiery furnace; he went to his death in an act of קִדּוּשׁ הַשֵּׁם although his faith was unsteady (Rashi on 11:28). Nevertheless, he died a martyr and his son deserved to be helped wholeheartedly. In addition Lot had willingly left his homeland and followed Abram. Had it not been for Abram, Lot would have remained at home. Thus Abram felt morally obligated to come to Lot's rescue at Sodom (Ramban on 19:29). But this obligation did not concern the servants raised in his house. And Abram was punished "for having imposed military duty on these disciples of the Sages" (Nedarim 32a). Abram's eagerness to save his nephew gives us the first example of Jewish solidarity.

וַיָּרֶק אֶת־חֲנִיכָיו — He armed his disciples. Rashi notes that the word חֲנִיכָיו is to be read חֲנִיכֹו, in the singular, i.e. the one who had been trained, schooled. It refers primarily to Eliezer, who was taught by Abram to observe the Divine commandments.

שְׁמֹנָה עָשָׂר וּשְׁלֹשׁ מֵאֹות — Three hundred and eighteen. Our Sages say this refers solely to Eliezer, for the numerical value of his name totals 318. The Targum Yonasan recounts: He had armed the children of his house, ready for war, but they did not want to accompany him. Then he chose from among them Eliezer, the son of Nimrod, whose strength was equal to that of 318 youths.

עַד־דָּן — As far as Dan. At Dan, Abram's strength faltered because he prophetically foresaw that his sons would one day build the idol of a calf there (Rashi). The shadow of sin — that was the obstacle which stopped Abram as well as his descendants in the pursuit of their enemies.

15. וַיֵּחָלֵק עֲלֵיהֶם לַיְלָה הוּא וַעֲבָדָיו — And he with his servants deployed against them at night. While pursuing them, they split up to catch those who were fleeing in different directions (Rashi). R' Yitzchak Arama describes the care with which Abram worked out his strategy, considering that help from heaven comes only to those who have first done everything humanly possible to succeed (chapter 16). And so God helped the patriarch with miracles. Indeed, this night was the night of miracles for Israel, as Rashi cites in the name of the Midrash.

The Midrash keeps the original word-order intact: "the night was divided in two." Abram's miracle occurred in the first half of the night. The second half was kept for the night of Exodus from Egypt. This night, which saw so many miracles for Jewry throughout its history, was the night predestined by HASHEM ... for all the descendants of Israel throughout their generations (Exodus 12:42).

disciples who had been born in his house — three hundred and eighteen — and he pursued them as far as Dan. ¹⁵ *And he with his servants deployed against them at night and struck them; he pursued them as far as Hobah which is to the north of Damascus.* ¹⁶ *He brought back all the possessions; he also brought back his kinsman, Lot, with his possessions, as well as the women and the people.*

¹⁷ *The king of Sodom went out to meet him after his return from defeating Chedorlaomer and the kings that were with him, to the Valley of Shaveh which is the king's valley.*

For Abram, providential help came in his battle with the mighty kings and *his sword rendered things into dust, his bow made all as driven stubble; he pursued them, passed along in safety by a path which his feet had not gone over before.* These verses from *Isaiah* (41:2-3) are applied to Abram, who triumphed over his adversaries through these miracles" (*Taanis* 21b).

Since that night of the fourteenth of *Nissan* when Abram unhesitatingly rushed to help his nephew — even though Lot had openly forsaken his faith in God — God has rewarded the generosity of the patriarch. On this same night He has often come to the help of Abram's descendants, bestowing on them His miraculous salvation, even though they were not always worthy of it.

וַיִּרְדְּפֵם עַד־חוֹבָה אֲשֶׁר מִשְּׂמֹאל לְדַמָּשֶׂק — *He pursued them as far as Hobah which is to the north of Damascus.* R' Abahu said: when the righteous sees the forsaken who is the prisoner of his own faults, he goes to him; perhaps he will bring him back to do good. He draws the sinner to him and instructs him in what is right, as it is said, *He pursued them as far as Dan,* that is, he followed him right to the place of justice (דִּין = דָּן) to save him from Hell. But he goes still further, sparing no effort day and night — *And he with his servants deployed against them at night and struck them; he pursued them as far as Hobah.* This means that he went so far as to discipline sinners physically and to uncover for them their חוֹבָה, *fault,* which they committed by going to the left, instead of taking the "right" road. But the righteous person finally succeeds in bringing all earthly goods back (וַיָּשֶׁב אֵת כָּל הָרְכֻשׁ) to their true destination, and "he also brought back his kinsman, Lot, with his posessions, as well as the women and the people" to God. They were helpless to resist the strong influence of Abram's purity and his faith. See how great is the reward of the one who brings his fellowman back to God! The "king of justice," מַלְכִּי־צֶדֶק, reigning in the heavenly Jerusalem, meaning the Archangel Michael, the priest of God Most High, goes out to meet him and to offer him friendship and hospitality (*Zohar Chadash*).

17. אֶל־עֵמֶק שָׁוֵה — *To the Valley of Shaveh.* This means the "united valley," the valley where all nations were united, where all unanimously agreed to have Abram as their king, their leader, their guide (*Rashi*). It was not the great miracle at Ur Kasdim nor those regarding the friendship with the Egyptian Pharaoh; it

יח וּמַלְכִּי־צֶדֶק מֶלֶךְ שָׁלֵם הוֹצִיא לֶחֶם וָיָיִן וְהוּא כֹהֵן לְאֵל
יט עֶלְיוֹן: וַיְבָרְכֵהוּ וַיֹּאמַר בָּרוּךְ אַבְרָם לְאֵל עֶלְיוֹן קֹנֵה שָׁמַיִם

was not Abram's life shining with holiness and kindness nor his mission to proclaim the God of Heaven and Earth — it was not these which made the nations extend the royal scepter to Abram. Only his courage and military victories earned him their homage and gratitude. But Abram declined their honors, replying, "Has not the world its supreme Ruler and its all-powerful God?" (*Midrash Rabbah*).

The king of Sodom went to meet Abram not to ask him for something, but to honor him. He accompanied him to Salem. When he saw how magnanimous Abram was, offering a tithe of the spoil to Malchizedek, the king of Sodom also asked for a share, although he had no right to it. This explains why the Torah interrupts the story of the latter's going out to meet Abram with an account of the welcome extended to Abram by the king of Salem (*Ramban* verse 20).

18. מֶלֶךְ שָׁלֵם — *King of Salem*. Salem was the original name for Jerusalem, as *Onkelos* mentions. The name Jerusalem never expressly appears in the Torah, for the reasons which *Rambam* gives (*Guide* 3:45): to avoid causing jealousy among the other nations, to avert attempts at conquest by them, and to prevent jealousy among the tribes of Israel, each of which would want to have the future holy city located in its territory.

The first designation, given by Malchizedek, the "king of justice" (who is Shem, son of Noah), is "Salem," an allusion to peace. Later, Abraham will call this same place ה׳ יִרְאֶה, *HASHEM manifests Himself there* (22:14). But God did not want to vex Shem the righteous nor Abram the righteous, so He combined the two names and called the city יְרוּשָׁלַיִם (*Bereishis Rabbah* 56). So constituted, "Jerusalem" means, according to the Kabbalists, the place of "the perfect fear of God," since יִרְאֶה (will appear) and יִרְאָה (fear) are homonyms. But the author of the ס' של"ה, *R' Isaiah Horowitz*, points out that if the early name given by Abram precedes that given by Shem, although Shem came first, it is because Jerusalem must designate the city where the Divine Majesty "will manifest Itself to the full" in the messianic era. Note that יְרוּ has a numerical value of 216 (just like יִרְאָה, from which it is derived) which corresponds to the great Divine Name of 72 letters repeated three times (cf. *Bereishis Rabbah* on 15:14). This plenitude of the Divine Omnipotence will be manifested in its universal scope starting from Jerusalem. The letter *yud*, the first letter of the Tetragrammaton, was introduced into the word שָׁלֵם to form יְרוּשָׁלַיִם, in order to stress that Jerusalem means the city of the "Divine revelation *par excellence*" (של"ה, בית דוד). For *R' S. R. Hirsch*, Shalem was the city where the king, Shem son of Noah, wanted צֶדֶק, *justice*, to rule as an instrument of שָׁלֵם, *peace*. The nations already had an old tradition that the future redemption of mankind would come through justice, and this tradition crystallized from earliest times in the city of Jerusalem "which is at the center of the inhabited world and which faces the temple of

¹⁸ *But Malchi-zedek, king of Salem, brought out bread and wine; he was a priest of God, the Most High.* ¹⁹ *He blessed him saying: "Blessed is Abram of God, the Most High, Maker of heaven*

celestial spheres" (*Ramban*). *Radak* adds: This is the city of peace which does not tolerate the reign of injustice and violence for long but disgorges its iniquitous inhabitants.

וְהוּא כֹהֵן לְאֵל עֶלְיוֹן — *He was a priest of God, the Most High.* Being one of Noah's sons, the king of Salem had survived the Flood in the Ark. He could have no doubts about the existence and omnipotence of the absolute Master of nature. Thus he became His earthly advocate; he became the priest of God supreme. The bitter memory of the sinfulness before the Flood and the horrendous disaster which it brought about led him to build a society, at least in his own kingdom, based on the strict application of צֶדֶק, *justice.*

However, Abram's belief and attitude to God differed from Malchizedek's. R' Shimon bar Yochai notes that Abram was the first man to call God אָדוֹן, which implies the idea of a personal God (*Berachos* 7b). Abram was the first to recognize that God is not only the Creator of heaven and earth but that each one of us personally depends upon Him to survive. He is therefore for every individual: אֲדֹנָי, *my Master.* Now, in blessing Abram, Malchizedek first refers to *the Most High, Maker of heaven and earth.* Then he blesses *the Most High, Who had delivered your foes into your hand.* In so doing, he also admits the providential action of the Creator of nature. But Abram reverses this order. He puts the glorification of the personal God first by invoking God with the Name הֲוָיָ׳ אֵל עֶלְיוֹן וגו׳ (verse 22). To the Divine appellation mentioned by Malchizedek, Abram prefixes the Divine Name הֲוָיָ which designates the personal care of Divine Providence, rewarding or punishing each person according to his deeds (*Rashi, Exodus* 6:2). For Abram, experiencing this God very close to us takes precedence over the abstract knowledge of God, Creator of heaven and earth. This Abrahamic conception has remained the view of Judaism. It is seen for example in the form of our blessings: בָּרוּךְ אַתָּה ה׳ אֱלֹהֵינוּ מֶלֶךְ הָעוֹלָם, *Blessed are You, HASHEM our God, King of the universe.* Here the Name הֲוָיָ precedes the designation of Master of the universe. (So too, when we say אָבִינוּ מַלְכֵּנוּ, *Our Father, our King.*)

Why was the dignity of כְּהוּנָה, *priesthood,* taken from the descendants of Malchizedek and given to the children of Abram? It was because Malchizedek reversed the order of the essential ideas; he relegated the principle of Divine Providence to second place (*Nedarim* 32b).

20. וּבָרוּךְ אֵל עֶלְיוֹן — *And blessed be God, the Most High.* The *Zohar* emphasizes that the structure of Malchizedek's blessings serves as a model for the formulation of *berachos* in our prayers. He begins with the benediction going "from lower to higher" (in verse 19) and ends with that going in the opposite direction (verse 20). To be sure, the word בָּרוּךְ is a homonym, as *R' Yosef Albo*

כ וָאָרֶץ: וּבָרוּךְ אֵל עֶלְיוֹן אֲשֶׁר־מִגֵּן צָרֶיךָ בְּיָדֶךָ וַיִּתֶּן־לוֹ מַעֲשֵׂר
חמישי   כא מִכֹּל: וַיֹּאמֶר מֶלֶךְ־סְדֹם אֶל־אַבְרָם תֶּן־לִי הַנֶּפֶשׁ וְהָרְכֻשׁ
כב קַח־לָךְ: וַיֹּאמֶר אַבְרָם אֶל־מֶלֶךְ סְדֹם הֲרִמֹתִי יָדִי אֶל־יהוה
כג אֵל עֶלְיוֹן קֹנֵה שָׁמַיִם וָאָרֶץ: אִם־מִחוּט וְעַד שְׂרוֹךְ־נַעַל
וְאִם־אֶקַּח מִכָּל־אֲשֶׁר־לָךְ וְלֹא תֹאמַר אֲנִי הֶעֱשַׁרְתִּי אֶת־

demonstrates (*Ikkarim* 2:26). It refers both to the one who receives the blessing and to the one who dispenses it. Thus, just like Malchizedek's words, וּבָרוּךְ אֵל עֶלְיוֹן, the words of our *berachos*, בָּרוּךְ אַתָּה ה', express the wish that the Supreme Divine Source of all blesings be blessed, that is to say, increase, flourish, never run dry. But the outflow of heavenly blessing pours forth only insofar as the "love from below," expressed in man's good deeds, devotion to God, and fervor in religious practice, stimulates that from above (עי' עין יעקב, ברכות ז). This is the blessing going from "lower to higher" and this is the one Malchizedek first speaks of. He wants to say: "Abram is blessing the Supreme Almighty One because His universal kingdom manifests itself to mortals' eyes, thanks to him, his example, and his words. Thus the blessing coming from Abram's good works becomes the stimulant for the blessings which Heaven bestows on him when his enemies are delivered into his hands."

It is in this sense that the Midrash interprets the words of King Malchizedek: "Abram blesses the Supreme Almighty One by making Him known to all as Maker of heaven and earth." Thus he becomes in a sense the partner of the Creator, an idea which the Torah hints at by not explicitly giving the subject of the verb קנה. It then can also refer to Abram (chapter 43).

וַיִּתֶּן־לוֹ מַעֲשֵׂר מִכֹּל — *And he gave him a tenth of everything. Rambam* states that Isaac was the first to give a tithe, as is seen from *Genesis* 26:12 (cf. *Rashi* ibid.). But *R' Avraham ben David* says it was Abram and bases his argument on this verse. It seems, explain the commentaries, that *Rambam* considers the tithe taken by Abram on all the spoils as a friendly gesture toward Malchizedek but not as the legal tithing which is primarily due on the produce of the field, as is seen in *Deuteronomy* 14:22 (*Hilchos Melachim* 9). Be that as it may, the first patriarch "showed the way for his children" once more here, as has been the case so many times. He offered the tithe to the *Kohen*, and did so in Jerusalem itself, as the Torah later commands expressly (*Deuteronomy* ibid.).

21. תֶּן־לִי הַנֶּפֶשׁ וְהָרְכֻשׁ קַח־לָךְ — *Give me the people and take the possessions for yourself.* When the king of Sodom saw Abram considering the spoils as rightfully his own (for he had tithed it), and since he wanted to appear grateful to his liberator, he made an offer to Abram to keep the wealth, gently hinting that the material profit from it might interest him. The king asked only for the prisoners of war. But the rights of war legitimized the victor's prerogative of keeping the prisoners in his own country or of demanding a ransom for them. Abram, though, did not want to use his prerogative. He meant to do a public act

and earth; [20] *and blessed be God, the Most High, Who has delivered your foes into your hand"; and he gave him a tenth of everything.*

[21] *The king of Sodom said to Abram: "Give me the people and take the possessions for yourself."*

[22] *Abram said to the king of Sodom: "I lift up my hand to* HASHEM, *God, the Most High, Maker of heaven and earth,* [23] *if so much as a thread to a shoestrap; or if I shall take from anything of yours! So you shall not say, 'It is I who made Abram rich.'*

of קִדּוּשׁ הַשֵּׁם by showing that he was totally disinterested. He even went so far as to desist from holding them captive. In so doing, however, he deprived himself of an exceptional opportunity to lead sinners to the knowledge of God. And this decision of his is criticized by some of our Sages (see our commentary to verse 23).

22. הֲרִמֹתִי יָדִי אֶל־ה' — *I lift up my hand to* HASHEM. "The righteous adjure their inclination, in order to keep themselves from the evil influence coming from them" (*Sifre, Va'eschanan* 33). So also did Joseph, Boaz and David (*Midrash Ruth*).

Why did Abram accept the lavish gifts of Pharaoh in Egypt without hesitation, while he indignantly refused the offer of the king of Sodom? We have answered this in our commentary on 12:15. Here it is a question of an exercise in futility which would oblige Abram to make concessions repugnant to him. But another explanation is put forward by the author of ס' תכלת מרדכי. Abram accepted gifts on leaving Egypt because he wished at all costs to "open the way to the future" for his descendants. The latter also were to receive gifts on leaving Egypt, *jewels of silver and jewels of gold,* and had to accept them to be able to build the Tabernacle, with its rich ornaments of gold and silver, in the desert. But this reason is not valid with respect to the king of Sodom's offer. Hence Abram rejects it in no uncertain terms (cf. our commentary to *Exodus* 3:22).

23. אִם־מִחוּט וְעַד שְׂרוֹךְ־נַעַל — *If so much as a thread to a shoestrap.* "This stylistic image takes in all that covers a person from head to toe. The thread alludes to the fine ribbons which girls wear on their heads as adornment (*Tur* on the Torah).

Rabbah said: As a reward for these words said by Abram, God gave two commandments to his children, the azure thread of the *tzitzis* and the thong of the *tefillin* (*Sotah* 17a). The sense of these words might be: the ideal of Abram's existence was to win men over to the Divine truth and to bring them "under the wings of the *Shechinah.*" His solemn oath to the king of Sodom was made in this spirit. Abram wanted to do a public act of קִדּוּשׁ הַשֵּׁם. In speaking of these commandments, which crown the head of the Jew, the Torah states: *And all the peoples of the earth shall see that the name of* HASHEM *is called upon you; and they shall respect you* (*Deuteronomy* 28:10). But R' Yochanan is of a different opinion regarding the patriarch's behavior, as we saw above.

כד אַבְרָם: בִּלְעָדַי רַק אֲשֶׁר אָכְלוּ הַנְּעָרִים וְחֵלֶק הָאֲנָשִׁים
אֲשֶׁר הָלְכוּ אִתִּי עָנֵר אֶשְׁכֹּל וּמַמְרֵא הֵם יִקְחוּ
חֶלְקָם: אַחַר ׀ הַדְּבָרִים הָאֵלֶּה הָיָה דְבַר־יהוה אֶל־ טו א
אַבְרָם בַּמַּחֲזֶה לֵאמֹר אַל־תִּירָא אַבְרָם אָנֹכִי מָגֵן לָךְ שְׂכָרְךָ

מִכָּל־אֲשֶׁר־לָךְ — *From anything of yours.* "R' Yochanan says: 'Because Abram missed a chance to bring some people to God (when he gave the prisoners to the king of Sodom) he was punished and his children were enslaved in Egypt" (*Nedarim* 32b). "At least, this was one of the several reasons for the exile along with sins committed earlier," adds the *Rosh* (ibid.). In any case, R' Yochanan condemns the patriarch's decision when he had to choose between his missionary duty and that of קִדּוּשׁ הַשֵּׁם (see verse 21).

A similar reproach is directed once again at Abram, who was nonetheless the "father of proselytes." He should not have repulsed the pagan princess Timna when she came to convert. He was not convinced of her sincerity and wanted to accept neither her nor her sons. But then, after being rejected by Isaac and Jacob as well, she became the concubine of Eliphaz, the son of Esau. She bore him Amalek, the future unrelenting enemy of Jewry (*Genesis* 36:12; cf. *Sanhedrin* 99b; also see our commentary on 36:12).

24. רַק אֲשֶׁר אָכְלוּ הַנְּעָרִים — *Only what the young men have eaten. Rashi* explains: the servants who accompanied me; and also Aner, Eshcol and Mamre. Although my servants went into battle and Aner and his companions just stayed to guard the camp, they are also entitled to their portion. King David learned this rule of distribution from Abram (*I Samuel* 30:24-25). Hence it is written, *and it happened from that day and forward that he made it a statute, etc.* In reality David just reinstituted an old statute promulgated by Abram and applied in the Torah itself in *Numbers* 31:27. Nevertheless, the text attributes it to David: *he made it a statute.* From this we learn that whoever reinstates a law which had fallen into disuse is considered as having promulgated it (*Midrash Lekach Tov*).

15.

1. אַחַר הַדְּבָרִים הָאֵלֶּה — *After these events.* Abram had just reached the height of his career. After his glorious military victory, the peoples of Canaan had offered him the royal crown. He had greatly impressed others both by his courage and by his sublime ideal. He was good, rich and powerful. It was evident that "God was with him in all he did" as Abimelech later said to him. He was now seventy-three years old (*Tosafos* on *Berachos* 7b).

But anguish dwelt in this righteous heart. *Targum Yonasan* advances several reasons: "Perhaps the miraculous defeat of the four kings and the nine armies was already the reward for my virtues — and I am to receive no share in the World to Come... Perhaps the friends and allies of the victims will take up arms against me and, with none of my good deeds now left to protect me, I will be

²⁴ *Far from me! Only what the young men have eaten, and the share of the men who accompanied me: Aner, Eshcol, and Mamre — they will take their portion.''*

15 ¹*After these events, the word of HASHEM came to Abram in a vision saying, "Fear not, Abram, I am a shield for you;*

the cause of a חִלּוּל הַשֵּׁם, *a profanation of the name of God* ... perhaps I have caused the death of innocent people ...''

But *happy is the man who always dreads* (*Proverbs* 28:14). For *a wise man is fearful, and departs from evil; but the fool excites himself and is confident* (ibid. 14:16). Abram had little confidence in himself, despite the rich blessings lavished on him by God when he came to the Holy Land. Was he still worthy of them? "Trust not in yourself until the day of your death" (*Avos* 2:5).

It was then that the Divine word came to him, saying: "Fear not, Abram, I am a shield for you, to protect you from the mightiest armies, from every punishment. You will not be punished for those whom you killed in battle. And as for the torment you feel in thinking that your fund of good deeds has been depleted, know that these deeds still remain in profusion" (*Rashi* and *Targum*).

הָיָה דְבַר־ה' אֶל־אַבְרָם בַּמַּחֲזֶה — *The word of HASHEM came to Abram in a vision.* Our Sages count ten forms of prophecy which differ depending on the prophet and on the time of the revelation. Moses attained the highest degree of prophecy, as the Torah indicates. As for Abram, "his power was great, for to Abram God revealed Himself by דִּבּוּר (stern words) and by מַחֲזֶה (vision), two forms of prophecy denoting an ominous message (see *Isaiah* 21:2: חָזוּת קָשָׁה הֻגַּד לִי). These two terms מַחֲזֶה and דִּבּוּר are used here to designate the new revelation to Abram" (*Rabbah* 44).

Until now Abram's life had been in continuous ascent. Beginning as an unknown, he had become the leader of his era and especially its leading spiritual figure. Every new advance can come only from the vicissitudes of destiny or from the "school of hard knocks." Now Abram receives a Divine revelation which is somber, full of anguish, and which makes him tremble (as *Rambam* points out in (*Hilchos Yesodei HaTorah* 7:2). In this way too, God appeared to the prophet Balaam אֲשֶׁר מַחֲזֵה שַׁדַּי יֶחֱזֶה נֹפֵל וּגְלוּי עֵינָיִם, *sees the vision of the Almighty, fallen down, yet with open eyes* (*Numbers* 24:4). Thus Abram braces himself to receive a grave message. But the Divine word then reassures him: "Fear not, Abram, I am a shield for you." The ordeal of exile for his descendants, soon to be announced to him, is indispensable if they are to fulfill their historical calling. And Abram must know that the sacrifices, ordeals, and acts of abnegation will constitute the training which Jewry needs in order to carry out its universal mission. But he must also know that under all circumstances, under all conditions, God will remain "the shield" of the people of Abram and that their "reward is very great."

ב הַרְבֵּה מְאֹד: וַיֹּאמֶר אַבְרָם אֲדֹנָי יֱהֹוִה מַה־תִּתֶּן־לִי וְאָנֹכִי

ג הוֹלֵךְ עֲרִירִי וּבֶן־מֶשֶׁק בֵּיתִי הוּא דַּמֶּשֶׂק אֱלִיעֶזֶר: וַיֹּאמֶר

אַבְרָם הֵן לִי לֹא נָתַתָּה זָרַע וְהִנֵּה בֶן־בֵּיתִי יוֹרֵשׁ אֹתִי:

Of course, Abram never asked for a reward. The idea had never crossed his mind. Had he not just turned down an offer of reward from the king of Sodom with indignation? But if man ought not to serve God out of self-interest, nevertheless Providence intends to reward the righteous and to inflict punishment on evildoers. That is a law built into the plan of creation. But the reward is not in this world. *Oh, how great is Your goodness, which You have stored up for those who fear You, which You have wrought for those who trust in You (Psalms 31:20)*. R' Tarfon said: "Know that the grant of reward unto the righteous will be in the World to Come" (*Avos* 2:21). The promise of the great reward refers to the World to Come (*Rabbah* ibid.).

אָנֹכִי מָגֵן לָךְ — *I am a shield for you*. Just as the one guarding himself with his shield fears neither lance nor javelin, so too I will protect you, you and your children, if they guard themselves (with the shield formed) with the words of the Torah, as it is said (*Proverbs* 30:5), *Every saying of God is perfect, a shield unto those who seek shelter in it* (*Tanchuma*).

The nations of the world cry out: "Why does God cherish Abram so? Why did He save him from the fiery furnace? From the quarrel of kings? From the war of the armies? From every one of his ordeals?" God answers them: "I will show you why. If I command him to sacrifice his son to Me, Abram obeys Me in perfect trust. Therefore I take him under My protection, and say to him: אָנֹכִי מָגֵן לָךְ. And in their daily prayers (מָגֵן אַבְרָהָם) his children will bless this Divine help, which is always ready to manifest Itself. They will remember that מָגֵן הוּא לְכֹל הַחוֹסִים בּו *He is a shield to all who trust in Him* (*Psalms* 18:31; *Midrash* ibid.).

Rambam notes that "Divine protection is proportionate to the degree of perfection attained by the individual. Thus God promises to protect Abraham like a shield. To Isaac He promises: *I will be with you and bless you* (*Genesis* 26:3); to Jacob: *I am with you; I will guard you wherever you go* (ibid. 28:15); to Moses: *For I shall be with you — and this is your sign that I have sent you* (*Exodus* 3:12); to Joshua: *As I was with Moses, so shall I be with you; I shall not let you fail, nor forsake you* (*Joshua* 1:5). This concept of Divine Providence is one of the basic foundations of Judaism" (*Guide* 3:18).

2. ה' אֱלֹהִים מַה־תִּתֶּן־לִי — *My Lord, HASHEM/ELOHIM: What can You give me*. This cry of despair lets us see into Abram's soul. What good were earthly possessions to Abram if a worthy child who would continue his work after him was denied to him? The attitude of the ancestor of the Jewish people toward children is that they are the most cherished of treasures. This has also remained the attitude of his descendants to this day. Within other societies of antiquity children had no rights, no protection, no human dignity; this was true even in

your reward is very great."

² *And Abram said, "My Lord, HASHEM/ELOHIM: What can You give me seeing that I go childless, and the steward of my house is the Damascene Eliezer?"*

³ *Then Abram said, "See, to me You have given no offspring; and see, my steward inherits me . . ."*

the most enlightened of those societies. In Greece, weak children were left to die on lonely mountains. The Roman historian Tacitus deemed it a contemptible prejudice of the Jews that "it is a crime among them to kill any child." The Rabbis, on the other hand, spoke of little children as "the Messiah's of mankind." For them, the child represents the perpetual regenerative force in mankind, because in the child God continually gives humanity a chance to make good its mistakes, to improve its ways.

Abram introduces his prayer for a child with the double Name, אד' א. In *Deuteronomy* (3:24) Moses begins a prayer in the same way. There *Rashi* explains the meaning of these two terms: merciful in His justice. And *Maharal* interprets Abram's thinking in this way: O God, You Who reign in absolute justice, grant me nevertheless Your mercy. Abram knew very well that because of sterility — both his and his wife's — he could never have children according to the ordinary laws of nature, but only through an act of Divine kindness. Thus, further on, he will consider the promise of offspring as an act of "charity" (וַיַּחְשְׁבֶהָ לּוֹ צְדָקָה; verse 6, see *Ramban* ad loc.). For *Maharal*, the attribute of justice is implicit in the first Name and that of mercy in the second. This resolves the question which *Radak* asks here on the order of the two names (*Gur Aryeh*, שם). *Ramban* writes: It is true that Abram had already heard the Divine promise of *to your offspring I will give this land* (12:7). But the righteous are never sure of irrevocable promises in this world. They always are afraid that a sin, even one committed involuntarily, might come and compromise the effect of the promise (cf. *Berachos* 4a). This possibility was always on Abram's mind, especially since he was still childless though on in years and also since he was afraid of being no longer worthy for having caused innocent people to go to their deaths in the war of the kings.

וְאָנֹכִי הוֹלֵךְ עֲרִירִי — *Seeing that I go childless.* R' Yochanan said: Abram and David said the same thing: If I have children who are going to arouse Your anger, I would rather go childless. This helps us to understand Abram's words: What will You give me? (implying: If You will give me unworthy children,) I prefer to go childless. So, too, with David (see *Psalms* 139:23).

3. וַיֹּאמֶר אַבְרָם — *Then Abram said.* These two words are a repetition of the beginning of the previous sentence. (Moreover, these two verses have just about the same content.) This means that the first sentence was Abram's thought (he said it to himself) whereas the second was what he spoke out (אבן שועיב, בשם ר' חנניא). But according to R' Shimon, Abram wanted to express his conviction

ד וְהִנֵּה דְבַר־יהוה אֵלָיו לֵאמֹר לֹא יִירָשְׁךָ זֶה כִּי־אִם אֲשֶׁר
ה יֵצֵא מִמֵּעֶיךָ הוּא יִירָשֶׁךָ: וַיּוֹצֵא אֹתוֹ הַחוּצָה וַיֹּאמֶר
הַבֶּט־נָא הַשָּׁמַיְמָה וּסְפֹר הַכּוֹכָבִים אִם־תּוּכַל לִסְפֹּר
ו אֹתָם וַיֹּאמֶר לוֹ כֹּה יִהְיֶה זַרְעֶךָ: וְהֶאֱמִן בַּיהוה וַיַּחְשְׁבֶהָ

— seemingly confirmed by his knowledge of astrology — that he would never have children. And thus, although his life was not yet half over, and although stating the obvious, as he did, seemed very bold, he cried out: "You have not given me children" (*Rabbah* 44).

4. וְהִנֵּה דְבַר־ה׳ אֵלָיו לֵאמֹר — *Suddenly, the word of HASHEM came to him, saying.* The term וְהִנֵּה is emphatic; it implies a feeling of joy (cf. our commentary on 6:17). According to *Ramban*, this word indicates that God suddenly interrupted Abram's tale of woe and cut short his arguments to confirm the joyful news.

5. וַיּוֹצֵא אֹתוֹ הַחוּצָה — *And He took him outside.* Literally, He took him outside his tent to see the stars. *Rashi* quotes first the literal meaning and thus seems to hold that these events really took place and are not just part of a vision which Abram had, as is held by *Rambam* (*Guide* 2:46) and *Ramban* (verse 12). Several commentators take up the discussion on this point. *Maharsha* notes that the midrashic interpretation arises from the difficulty of the literal meaning (*Shabbos* 156a). The Midrash, which *Rashi* also quotes, interprets the verse in this way: Go out from your destiny such as it is written in the stars. You have seen in the stars that you are not to have children. Indeed, Abram is not to have a child but *Abraham* will. Sarai will not have a child but *Sarah* will. I am going to give you a different name; your destiny will now be different.

The Talmudic source for this Midrash (*Shabbos* ibid.) concludes that אֵין מַזָּל לְיִשְׂרָאֵל. Jewry does not come under the sway of the stars (מַזָּל includes more particularly the signs of the zodiac). Judaism teaches that the determinism of a destiny "written in the stars" is not irrevocable. It can be appealed. There are ways of influencing the course of human destiny which are "the ultimate." These are first and foremost the return to God (תְּשׁוּבָה), prayer (תְּפִלָּה), and charitable acts (צְדָקָה). A change of name (שִׁנּוּי הַשֵּׁם) and a change of place (שִׁנּוּי הַמָּקוֹם) are the outward signs of a much deeper change occurring in one's existence (*Rosh Hashanah* 16b, cf. *Maharsha*). Idolaters blindly believe in predestination. For them, events will happen or not happen just as is noted down in their horoscopes, and they resignedly take "destiny" as absolutely irrevocable. But Abram, as a microcosm of the Jewish nation, is told that he has the power to "transcend his astrological destiny" and to dominate it by the means which we have just mentioned.

However, these factors of personal merit only come into play in the fortunes of the individual but not in those of Jewry as a nation. Referring to the explanations of our Sages, *Maharsha* (*Shabbos* ibid.) shows that national

> ⁴ *Suddenly, the word of* HASHEM *came to him, saying: "That one will not inherit you. Only him that shall come forth from within you shall inherit you."* ⁵ *And He took him outside, and said, "Gaze, now, toward the Heavens, and count the stars if you are able to count them!" And He said to him, "So shall your offspring be!"* ⁶ *And he trusted in* HASHEM, *and He reckoned it*

destinies depend on different criteria. *Rashi* alludes to this in the third explanation he gives to this verse: God brought Abram away from the earth to a place above the stars. Thus the text uses the word הַבֶּט which means (usually) "to look at from above; to look downward." Taking the verse figuratively in this way lets us assume that Abram's offspring will be on a higher level than the earthly and the material. While the fortunes of other nations are governed by natural, physical, socio-economic contingencies, Jewry's history is a history of the spirit. Jewry's grandeur and its decadence follow the rise and fall of its moral and spiritual strength. In contrast to the other nations, Jewry can reach a degree of holiness in which the spirit can conquer matter; where the spirit is so strong that by itself it can animate the nation as a whole, where with a minimum of natural means it can assure the nation of eternal life. Jewry's existence can endure for millennia without a country, without a government, without a common language, solely on the strength of its spirit. Its national destiny is the striking manifestation of the reality of the supernatural and the Divine, and of the existence of miracles in life on earth.

וּסְפֹר הַכּוֹכָבִים — *And count the stars.* The stars of the heavens and the sand of the sea are the two metaphors used by God when He announced to Abram that "so shall your offspring be." But these two images are at opposite extremes. The innumerable stars shine in the immensity of space whereas the sand is trampled on by everyone. This double image reflects a characteristic of the Jewish people, the stiff-necked people, obstinate and willful, for good and also for evil, as will be evidenced throughout its history. Jewry will almost never know a bourgeois, peaceful, or stable existence. Its rise will be meteoric just as its descent will be to the very depths. Conquered, subjugated, the Jewish nation will undergo sufferings no other nation will ever know. But victorious, triumphant, once again coming to the fore, Jewry will attain unthought-of heights. "When Jewry rises, it does so up to the stars; when it falls, it falls right down to the sand of the sea" (*Rashi to Esther* 6:13).

כֹּה יִהְיֶה זַרְעֶךָ — *So shall your offspring be.* The text uses the adverb כֹּה. This same adverb is used in description of the sacrifice of Isaac, נֵלְכָה עַד כֹּה, *will go yonder* (*Genesis* 22:5) and in the priestly blessing כֹּה תְבָרְכוּ, *so shall you bless* (*Numbers* 6:23). This relationship permits us to interpret the verse as follows: May your offspring follow the example of Abram and his son, going forward in perfect single-heartedness and devotion, עַד כֹּה, even to the point of supreme

ששי   ז לָּוֹ צְדָקָה: וַיֹּאמֶר אֵלָיו אֲנִי יהוֹה אֲשֶׁר הוֹצֵאתִיךָ מֵאוּר כַּשְׂדִּים
ח לָתֶת לְךָ אֶת־הָאָרֶץ הַזֹּאת לְרִשְׁתָּהּ: וַיֹּאמַר אֲדֹנָי יהוֹה
ט בַּמָּה אֵדַע כִּי אִירָשֶׁנָּה: וַיֹּאמֶר אֵלָיו קְחָה לִי עֶגְלָה מְשֻׁלֶּשֶׁת

sacrifice in honor of God, and then they will merit the Divine benediction transmitted by the *Kohanim*.

6. וְהֶאֱמִן בַּה׳ — *And he trusted in HASHEM.* Abram had no children but he had faith in God's word promising him offspring as innumerable as the stars in heaven. He was ready to wait until God chose, never doubting His word. Indeed, he had to wait twenty-five years to have a child (the numerical value of the word כֹּה is twenty-five — *Baal HaTurim*). The sign of true belief in God is an unwavering confidence which steadfastly asserts itself despite disappointments, despite all the circumstances which seem to oppose the object of the belief. Hence God considers this act as a proof of piety (עי׳ גבורות ה׳ למהר״ל, פרק ז׳).

"It is written וְהֶאֱמִן rather than וַיַּאֲמֵן, no doubt because it is not so much a casual belief as a permanent, complete trust, at least from this moment on. Now, it is known that habitual action is most often expressed in Hebrew by the future, which is given here by the past tense with the conversive *vav*" (*Wogue*).

וַיַּחְשְׁבֶהָ לּוֹ צְדָקָה — *And He reckoned it to him as righteousness.* Cf. our commentary on verse 2. The author of *Sefer Chofetz Chaim* notes that Abram had recognized the Creator through his own powers of reasoning. But here the Torah's praise for him refers to his אֱמוּנָה, *faith*. Faith remains the essential foundation, the bedrock: *The righteous man lives by his faith* (Habakkuk 2:4). Consider one who is shipwrecked, who runs the risk of drowning, and sees a tree lying in the water, close to shore. He will try to catch hold of the trunk, not the branches. Now the Torah, which contains the object of our faith, is also עֵץ חַיִּים, *the tree of life*, which we must seize by its "trunk," by its very essence.

7. וַיֹּאמֶר אֵלָיו — *He said to him.* These new Divine words which announce the possession of the land of Israel to Abram were said three years before the words which directly precede them in the Torah. This is demonstrated by *Tosafos* on *Berachos* 7b. Events in the Torah are not always arranged in strict chronological order. Sometimes other connections cause events far apart in time to be mentioned together in one chapter (אֵין מוּקְדָּם וּמְאוּחָר בַּתּוֹרָה). Furthermore, the first revelation happened at night ("gaze now toward the Heavens and count the stars") and the second in the daytime (as the sun was setting). *Rambam* and other sages are however of the opinion that Abram had just one prophetic vision, during the day, but it was made up of two successive phases (*Guide* 2:41; ibid. 45, degree 8; cf. *Abarbanel*; cf. also our commentary on verse 18).

אֲשֶׁר הוֹצֵאתִיךָ מֵאוּר כַּשְׂדִּים לָתֶת לְךָ אֶת־הָאָרֶץ הַזֹּאת לְרִשְׁתָּהּ — *Who brought you out of Ur Kasdim to give you this land to inherit it.* Abram had to go through the fiery furnace (brought to mind by the name Ur Kasdim) to be worthy of possessing the Holy Land. Here, once more, the patriarch "shows the way" for

to him as righteousness.

⁷ *He said to him, "I am* HASHEM *Who brought you out of Ur Kasdim to give you this land to inherit it."*

⁸ *He said, "My Lord,* HASHEM/ELOHIM: *Whereby shall I know that I am to inherit it?"*

⁹ *And He said to him, "Take to Me three heifers, three goats,*

his children: the crematorium prepared the way for taking possession of Israel. And when Abram asks the question: How can I know? — that is, "Tell me by what merit will my children continue to dwell in it" — he is answered, "by the merit of sacrifices" (*Rashi*). From the beginning of our history "sacrifices" were the price we had to pay to acquire the Promised Land. *I passed by you, and I saw you wallowing in your own blood and I said to you, 'In your blood you will live'; and I said to you, 'in your blood you will live' (Ezekiel 16:6).*

8. וַיֹּאמַר . . . בַּמָּה אֵדַע כִּי אִירָשֶׁנָּה — *He said . . . Whereby shall I know that I am to inherit it?* What is Abram really asking? Two points of view exist on how his question is to be taken. One is given by R' Chiya ben Chanina, who said: Abram did not aggressively demand to know. He simply wondered by what merit he was deserving of the Promised Land. God answered him: By the merit of the sacrifices which your children will bring. And He said to him: "Take to Me three heifers, etc." as a symbol of the future sacrifices. This opinion is quoted by *Rashi*. *Ramban* states that, far from doubting God's word, Abram wished to ascertain whether the promise was unconditional, definite, and independent of sins which he or his offspring might commit in the future. "Would the promise be revoked if the Canaanites repented?" Abram wondered. "How can I know that I will possess the land come what may?" The answer came to him through the unconditional covenant which God then made with him.

A different point of view is given by the *Amora* Shmuel: "Our father Abraham was punished and his children enslaved in Egypt for 210 years because he went too far in asking about the Divine promises: How can I know?" (*Nedarim* 32a). This question opens the way to doubt in the Divine words and is considered a grave failing on the part of the patriarch (*Tanchuma, Vayigash* 2). Thus one can understand what *R' M. C. Luzzatto* writes in *The Path of the Righteous* (Chapter 4): "God is extremely demanding with the most pious of the faithful. Consider Abraham, whom God called 'My friend' (*Isaiah* 41:8) but who nonetheless did not escape punishment for a few words spoken negligently, *Whereby shall I know?* You can see from this how careful one must be with every word spoken before God." Several authors, in particular *Abarbanel* and *Maharal*, list the various presumed reasons for the slavery in Egypt and attempt to interrelate them. Our Sages held that this exile was a Divine punishment which had its relevant causes and our verse is surely at the root of their investigation of those causes, even though they go back to much earlier generations. Their investigations seemed to them all the more imperative since

י וְעֵז מְשֻׁלֶּשֶׁת וְאַיִל מְשֻׁלָּשׁ וְתֹר וְגוֹזָל: וַיִּקַּח־לוֹ אֶת־
כָּל־אֵלֶּה וַיְבַתֵּר אֹתָם בַּתָּוֶךְ וַיִּתֵּן אִישׁ־בִּתְרוֹ לִקְרַאת
יא רֵעֵהוּ וְאֶת־הַצִּפֹּר לֹא בָתָר: וַיֵּרֶד הָעַיִט עַל־הַפְּגָרִים
יב וַיַּשֵּׁב אֹתָם אַבְרָם: וַיְהִי הַשֶּׁמֶשׁ לָבוֹא וְתַרְדֵּמָה נָפְלָה
עַל־אַבְרָם וְהִנֵּה אֵימָה חֲשֵׁכָה גְדֹלָה נֹפֶלֶת עָלָיו:

the Torah itself gives us no moral reason for the Egyptian exile as it does for the Babylonian exile (גבורות ה׳ פ״ט).

Seen in this light, there appears a cause and effect relationship between the patriarch's skepticism and the exile in Egypt. Indeed, in a fleeting moment of weakness, even the strongest believers may feel in themselves a flicker of doubt, doubt which may itself be justified in several ways. In this case, the questions of the merit of the offspring, of sufficient personal merit, of the possible repentance of the idol-worshipers, all came up at the same time. But on the other hand, the messianic mission reserved for the children of Abram, and the national discipline which it demands, does not have room for even the slightest doubt of the absolute truth of the Divine words. Hence it was obligatory to root out even the smallest trace of doubt from the soul of the Jewish people in order to prepare them properly for all time for their twofold role of a holy people and martyr of humanity. Thanks to the hardship, severe but chastening, of the exile, the children of Abram cleave to their God in unalterable, eternal union.

9. קְחָה לִי עֶגְלָה מְשֻׁלֶּשֶׁת — *Take to Me three heifers*. As *Rashi* makes clear, this Divine command carried out by Abram is a prefiguration of the sacrifices. Our Sages tell us: "Abram said to God: How can I know that I will take possession of the land? Perhaps one day the Jewish people will sin. You would then deal with them as you dealt with the generation of the Flood and the generation of the Tower of Babel. God answered: No! And Abram replied: Let me know how I will take possession of the land (referring to his offspring). And God said: 'Take to Me three heifers, etc'. Abram answered: This (i.e. the sacrifices) is useful only as long as the Temple is in existence, but what will happen to them when it exists no longer? Then God said to him: My son, I have provided chapters relating to the sacrifices for them. As long as they read these chapters, I will consider it as if they had actually offered the sacrifices and I will pardon all their sins" (*Taanis* 27b).

In numerous places in Jewish literature we find this same idea, that the study of those parts of the Torah related to the sacrifices serves to replace them in absolving us from our sins. We find further that the study of these Torah prescriptions about sacrifice replaces not only sin and guilt offerings but also free-will and thank-offerings. Referring to *Sotah* 21a, *Maharsha* considers that the Torah serves to replace sacrifices because it keeps man from sin and has therefore a preventative effect. *R' Bachya* (on *Leviticus* 7:33) holds that a given sacrifice could be replaced only by the Torah portions related specifically to it

three rams, a turtledove, and a young dove." [10] He took all these to Him: he cut them in the center, and placed each piece opposite its counterpart. The birds, however, he did not cut up.

[11] *Birds of prey descended upon the carcasses, and Abram drove them away.*

[12] *And it happened, as the sun was about to set, a deep sleep fell upon Abram; and behold — a dread! great darkness fell upon him.*

because the daily repetition and deep study of these prescriptions allow us to see more and more clearly the basic concept involved. As a result, this deepens our commitment and feelings of devotion and it heightens the sensitivity of our moral conscience.

10. וַיְבַתֵּר אֹתָם — *He cut them.* ". . . The practice in making a covenant was to cut up an animal and to pass between the pieces (as in *Jeremiah* 34:19). Here, the column of smoke and the flame which passed between the pieces are the messengers of the *Shechinah*, Who is fire" (*Rashi*). The *Shechinah* passes between the animals which represent the other nations swooping down on Jewry to devour it (cf. verse 11), and this passage "between the halves" breaks the destructive force of the enemies of Abram (*Maharal*). R' Yosef Albo explains the symbolism of this action with reference to the covenant: "Just as the two parts of the animal formed its whole body when it was alive, with each part feeling the hurt and the pain of the other as well as its own, so too with people entering a covenant. They will have to form a single entity until death comes to separate them. They will have to help one another, rescue each other in times of danger, warn the other when danger threatens" (*Ikkarim* 4:45).

וְאֶת־הַצִּפֹּר לֹא בָתָר — *The birds, however, he did not cut up.* This parallels the instructions in *Leviticus* (1:17) for the sacrificial service.

11. וַיֵּרֶד הָעַיִט עַל־הַפְּגָרִים — *Birds of prey descended upon the carcasses.* R' Assi says: This alludes to the nations of the world which come to attack Israel. Abram tires to disperse them by force, but to no avail. Then he uses the only weapon which will work: bringing them to fear God, תְּשׁוּבָה. This is the hidden meaning in the words וַיַּשֵּׁב אֹתָם אַבְרָם (*Rabbah* 44).

12. אֵימָה חֲשֵׁכָה גְדֹלָה — *A dread! great darkness.* "This refers to the anguish and darkness of the exile" (*Rashi*). The verse itself alludes to the four nations which enslaved Jewry. "Dread" refers to Babylonia, which only oppressed the Jewish people physically; "darkness" describes Persia and Media, who wanted to tear out Jewry's soul; "great" recalls the persecution by the Greeks, who tried hard to extinguish Jewry's spiritual light completely. And "fell upon him" alludes to the Edomite or Roman nations which sought to break the Jewish people not only physically but also by moral and spiritual persecution (גבורות ה', פ' ח').

יג וַיֹּאמֶר לְאַבְרָם יָדֹעַ תֵּדַע כִּי־גֵר ׀ יִהְיֶה זַרְעֲךָ בְּאֶרֶץ לֹא
יד לָהֶם וַעֲבָדוּם וְעִנּוּ אֹתָם אַרְבַּע מֵאוֹת שָׁנָה: וְגַם אֶת־
הַגּוֹי אֲשֶׁר יַעֲבֹדוּ דָּן אָנֹכִי וְאַחֲרֵי־כֵן יֵצְאוּ בִּרְכֻשׁ גָּדוֹל:
טו וְאַתָּה תָּבוֹא אֶל־אֲבֹתֶיךָ בְּשָׁלוֹם תִּקָּבֵר בְּשֵׂיבָה טוֹבָה:
טז וְדוֹר רְבִיעִי יָשׁוּבוּ הֵנָּה כִּי לֹא־שָׁלֵם עֲוֺן הָאֱמֹרִי עַד־הֵנָּה:

13. יָדֹעַ תֵּדַע — *Know with certainty.* The verb is repeated in order to give this proclamation, which is of fundamental importance for the history of the Jewish people, still greater impact. Announcing the calamity long in advance of its occurrence will make the people realize that it is a part of the Divine overall plan. Its effect on the morale of the people will then be less serious than if it had come as a sudden surprise.

אַרְבַּע מֵאוֹת שָׁנָה — *Four hundred years.* Rashi (and others) show in what sense the number 400 is to be taken, for elsewhere the Torah mentions 430 years as the length of the stay in Egypt (*Exodus* 12:40). But how long the exiles will last, the date of the end of our hardships, these are still shrouded in mystery. They remain unrevealed: *Indeed, this is laid up in store with Me. It is sealed up in My treasuries,* says God (*Deuteronomy* 32:34). He reveals them to no human being, all the more so as the time involved can vary depending on the degree of perfection which Jewry attains (*Shemos Rabbah* ibid.). The date of a happy event is given exactly. It is much heralded and well-publicized. On the other hand, the dates of tragic events remain as deep in mystery "as the deep abysses" (*Tanchuma* to *Numbers* 1:1). However, aware of the inability of the non-Jewish world to understand such subtleties in the Torah, the seventy translators were led to modify the text of their Greek translation on this point, as the Talmud recounts (*Megillah* 9a).

On the significance of the number 400, see our commentary on 7:4.

14. וְגַם אֶת־הַגּוֹי אֲשֶׁר יַעֲבֹדוּ דָּן אָנֹכִי — *But also the nation that they shall serve, I shall judge.* Rambam asks: "Since God had decreed that the Jews would be enslaved in Egypt, why did He punish the Egyptians? It was because He had only proclaimed in general terms that the children of Abram would become slaves in a foreign land; thus each individual Egyptian was still free not to oppress them if he so desired." *Ravad* takes issue with this explanation. He makes the point that the Egyptians deserved punishment even before this because of their perversions. But their blasphemous insolence toward God and His envoy served to hasten their downfall (*Hilchos Teshuvah,* ch 6). *Ramban* also considers *Rambam's* explanation to be insufficient. In his view, the punishment of the Egyptians was justified by the fact that they went beyond the degree of hardship foreseen in the announcement to Abram. They drowned newborn Jewish boys in the Nile, they oppressed the slaves in inhumane fashion, and they tried to exterminate them. Many texts are quoted in support of this view, as well as for other examples of Jewish martyrdom. The debate

¹³ And He said to Abram, "Know with certainty that your offspring shall be aliens in a land not their own, they will serve them, and they will oppress them four hundred years. ¹⁴But also the nation that they shall serve, I shall judge, and afterwards they shall leave with great wealth. ¹⁵ As for you: you shall come to your ancestors in peace; you shall be buried in a good old age. ¹⁶ And the fourth generation shall return here, for the iniquity of the Amorite shall not yet be full until then."

between *Rambam* and *Ramban* is continued down through the centuries, with proponents of each viewpoint bringing in new arguments. But *R' Chaim ben Attar* considers the whole discussion groundless. All those, he writes, who persecute and make martyrs of the descendants of Abram are guilty; for they act not to carry out a Divine command but to unleash their hatred of the Jewish religion which differs from all the rest, and which at the same time makes its adherents stand out from all other people. And through the religion, it is really God Himself Who is the target of their burning hatred and wild fanaticism. This is alluded to in our verse, which can be translated in this way: "And in addition to the nation which they will enslave, they accuse Me (אָנֹכִי, the same personal pronoun used by God at the beginning of the Decalogue) . . . ."

And so the verse ends with the words: *and afterwards they shall leave with great wealth*. The oppression of the slaves was motivated solely by base instincts and not at all by the desire to carry out a Divine decree. Hence the oppressors as a nation cannot be exempt from reparations for the material wrongs done to victims of theft and plunder. Using this argument, Geviha ben Pesisa claimed reparations from the Egyptians for the Jews whom they stripped of their rights and possessions (*Sanhedrin* 91a; ע״פ אור החיים). Cf. our commentary on 45:18.

15. וְאַתָּה תָּבוֹא אֶל־אֲבֹתֶיךָ בְּשָׁלוֹם — *As for you: you shall come to your ancestors in peace*. Abram's death is foretold in one of these remarkable phrases attesting that the doctrine of immortality was not unknown to the ancient Hebrews. Indeed, here the return of the soul to the souls of the fathers is kept quite separate from the burial of the body. It is evident that there is no connection between the two, since Abram was buried in Canaan whereas all his ancestors had died and were buried in Mesopotamia (*M. M. Kalisch*).

תִּקָּבֵר בְּשֵׂיבָה טוֹבָה — *You shall be buried in a good old age*. See *Rashi* on *Genesis* 25:9 — Yishmael repented.

16. וְדוֹר רְבִיעִי יָשׁוּבוּ הֵנָּה — *And the fourth generation shall return here*. Does this mean the fourth generation of Jews starting from the descent into Egypt? Such is the view of *Rashi, Rambam* (פיה״מ עדיות פ״ב, ט) and others. Or does, it refer, as *Ramban, Ravad* and others hold, to the fourth generation of Amorites? R' Akiva himself, commenting on this verse in the Mishnah (*Eduyos* 2:9), scarcely helps to clarify this question. Also *Ibn Ezra* demonstrates that we cannot

יז וַיְהִי הַשֶּׁמֶשׁ בָּאָה וַעֲלָטָה הָיָה וְהִנֵּה תַנּוּר עָשָׁן וְלַפִּיד אֵשׁ
יח אֲשֶׁר עָבַר בֵּין הַגְּזָרִים הָאֵלֶּה: בַּיּוֹם הַהוּא כָּרַת יהוה אֶת־

ascertain the number of years to be counted as a generation. Thus, here once again it appears that the end of the exile and its sufferings remain shrouded in mystery, as was stressed in our commentary to verse 13. And R' Yehudah explains: How long the exile will last is expressed in one place in years (400) and in another in generations (four). This is to tell you: If Jewry repents, they will be delivered after four generations: and if not, after 400 years (*Tanchuma, Exodus* 12; *Ibn Ezra,* commentary at the end of *Job; Ramban* to *Genesis* 46:15).

But it should also be remembered that through Jewry's history there have always been intervals of some generations between the end of the exile and the possession of the Promised Land. *When Pharaoh had let the people go, God led them not by the way of the land of the Philistines, although that was near ... but led them about, by way of the wilderness* (*Exodus* 13:17-18). R' Shimon bar Yochai explains that this was done because the people were too imbued with the spirit of materialism from their contact with the other nations. They needed a period of transition in order to raise themselves up toward the ideal of the Torah before the land could be restored to them (*Yalkut Shemos* ibid.). Thus, the "four generations" may also take into account the forty years of wandering in the desert before entry into the Holy Land (cf. *Ramban* on *Exodus* 12:40).

כִּי לֹא־שָׁלֵם עֲוֹן הָאֱמֹרִי — *For the iniquity of the Amorite shall not yet be full.* This nation is mentioned here because it was the most powerful and the most perverted of Canaanite peoples. Accordingly, its name always serves as a general designation for the debauched inhabitants of Canaan, as is seen in *Rashi* on *Leviticus* 18:3.

Only when their iniquity is full will they deserve to be expelled from their land, for God punishes a people only when "its measure of sin is full" (*Rashi*). R' Meir Simcha of Denaburg (Dvinsk) adds: Of course, with His prescience, God knew that the measure of iniquity of the Amorites would be full one day, but as for Abram, he must have wondered about the possibility of their repentance. Now this alternative is actually implied in the Divine words, as follows: Either the Amorites' iniquity will be full and your descendants will then be justified in conquering their land or else they will return to God and willingly obey the Divine wish of giving up the land to the children of the patriarch, in accordance with the ancestral tradition known from the days of Noah (as *Rashi* points out on 9:26; *Meshech Chochmah*).

17. וַיְהִי הַשֶּׁמֶשׁ בָּאָה — *So it happened: The sun set.* Said R' Yochanan: God showed four things to Abram — Hell and the (tyranny of the) foreign powers; the giving of the Torah and the Temple. He said to him: "As long as your children are preoccupied with the latter two, they will be safe from the first two. But if they forsake one of the latter two, they will have to face one of the first two. Which do you prefer, Hell or the rule of foreign kings?" Rav Huna said:

> [17] *So it happened: The sun set, and it was very dark. Behold —*
> *there was a smoky furnace and a torch of fire which passed*
> *between these pieces.* [18]*On that day HASHEM made a covenant with*

Abram was perplexed for a whole day, he did not know which to choose. God
said to him: "Abram, make your choice." And He advised him to choose living
under foreign rule. This is what the word לֵאמֹר, *saying* to him, refers to in the
next verse: That day, God made a covenant with Abram, saying . . . (*Rabbah* 44).

The smoking furnace and the flaming torch which appeared to Abram
parallel "Mount Sinai altogether on smoke because God had descended upon it
in the midst of flame, and its smoke ascended like the smoke of a furnace"
(*Exodus* 19:18). So too here the Divine Majesty descended in a torch of flame and
amid a furnace of smoke and "passed between the pieces" to ratify the covenant
with Abram.

In this revelation the patriarch sees the promulgation of the Torah on Mount
Sinai and the sacrifices to be offered in the Temple in Jerusalem. But, at the
opposite extreme, this same vision can symbolize Hell's purgatory or the flames
rising from the stakes which foreign kings erected to torture the descendants of
Abram. Abram understood. Either the Torah and the Temple — or Hell and the
horrors of exile under the tyranny of hostile powers. Such were the conditions
implied in the solemn covenant which was to be binding through the millennia
of Jewry's history. Forsaking the Torah or the Temple by Jewry will have to
bring with it a heavenly punishment, either in עוֹלָם הַבָּא, the World to Come,
with the afflictions of Hell, or in עוֹלָם הַזֶּה, this world, through hardship and
suffering at the hands of the nations of the world. Abram remained in a
quandary. He could not bring himself to choose the exile with its suffering,
fearing that his children would not be able to withstand the hardship, fearing
that they would be lost among the other nations. But God reassured him. *Their
rock* (Abram) *would have given them over* (to the sufferings of Hell) *but
HASHEM delivered them up* (to be subjects of foreign powers) (*Deuteronomy*
32:30). Thus did Abram accept the exile and its afflictions for his children.

18. בַּיּוֹם הַהוּא — *On that day.* It was the fifteenth of *Nissan*, the day of the
exodus from Egypt, a day of glory for Jewry, when the patriarch heard the
historical promise concerning the Holy Land. Later, when the Jewish people is
about to leave Egypt, the Torah will say, *At the end of 430 years, on that
selfsame day* (*Exodus* 12:41). And *Rashi* notes there: "This teaches us that when
the time came God did not delay their freedom even for an instant. Now, on the
fifteenth of *Nissan* the angels had come to Abraham to bring him the good
news. On the fifteenth of *Nissan* Isaac was born, and on the fifteenth of *Nissan*
the בְּרִית בֵּין הַבְּתָרִים, *Covenant Between the Parts*, was made."

כָּרַת ה׳ — *HASHEM made a covenant.* The official, formal giving-over of the
Holy Land to Abram and his offspring now ratifies the acquisition that had
symbolically taken place earlier (13:14-18). God, King of the Universe, gives His

אַבְרָם בְּרִית לֵאמֹר לְזַרְעֲךָ נָתַתִּי אֶת־הָאָרֶץ הַזֹּאת מִנְּהַר
יט מִצְרַיִם עַד־הַנָּהָר הַגָּדֹל נְהַר־פְּרָת: אֶת־הַקֵּינִי וְאֶת־הַקְּנִזִּי
כ-כא וְאֵת הַקַּדְמֹנִי: וְאֶת־הַחִתִּי וְאֶת־הַפְּרִזִּי וְאֶת־הָרְפָאִים: וְאֶת־
א הָאֱמֹרִי וְאֶת־הַכְּנַעֲנִי וְאֶת־הַגִּרְגָּשִׁי וְאֶת־הַיְבוּסִי: וְשָׂרַי   **טז**
אֵשֶׁת אַבְרָם לֹא יָלְדָה לוֹ וְלָהּ שִׁפְחָה מִצְרִית וּשְׁמָהּ הָגָר:

guarantee to Abram, whose offspring obtain inalienable right to the land which extends "from the river of Egypt till the Euphrates River."

According to *Ramban*, the various promises God makes to Abram reflect his degree of merit. Hence they increase progressively in value and importance, from the first (12:7) to the last, made at the time of the circumcision (17:8). But R' Isaiah Horowitz, basing himself on the *Tosafos* on *Berachos* 7b, stresses that the promise in our verse precedes the others by several years. Chronologically, it came first. And so it contains the revelation of torments, hardships, calamities for the future. The first phase of the spiritual world built by Abram suffers the same setbacks as the primitive ages of the physical world erected by God. The second stage sees a consolidation under the reign of Torah. And so the second promise follows the report of people converting to Abram's religion (12:5 and 7). The last promise took place under the sign of the circumcision (17:8), which symbolizes the close covenant between Jewry and God, for it envisages an era of messianic peace when the Holy Land will be "the everlasting possession of Jewry and God will be their God, their guardian" (*Shelah*).

נָתַתִּי — *Have I given.* The past tense used here indicates that this land has long been destined for Jewry, as we can also see from *Deuteronomy* 32:8 (cf. *Ibn Ezra* ibid.: "since the generation of the Tower of Babel").

מִנְּהַר מִצְרַיִם — *From the river of Egypt.* According to the *Targumim* and the *Aruch*, this is the Nile, identical to שיחור which *Ibn Ezra* names explicitly. Or, according to an ancient tradition, it is the Wadi El Arish, which formed the border between Egypt and Palestine (see *Encyclopedia Talmudis*, art. ארץ ישראל).

נְהַר־פְּרָת — *The Euphrates River.* This river constituted the ideal boundary for the territory of the Jewish nation, which was attained in the days of King Solomon (*I Kings* 5:1). The area delimited here takes in the whole sweep of the Middle East.

19. אֶת־הַקֵּינִי וְאֶת־הַקְּנִזִּי וְאֵת הַקַּדְמֹנִי — *The Kennite, the Kenizzite, and the Kadmonite.* Ten nations are mentioned here. But Jewry will only take over from seven. Three are reserved for the future (*Rashi*). *Rambam* adds that this refers to the messianic era, when Jewry will have the merit of observing all the Divine commandments and of loving God fully and ever-faithfully, as it is said: *When* HASHEM, *your God, enlarges your border, as He has sworn unto your fathers, and gives you all the land which He promised to give unto your fathers, on condition that you keep all this law to do it, which I command you this day, to*

*Abram, saying, "To your descendants have I given this land, from
the river of Egypt to the great river, the Euphrates River: ¹⁹ the
Kennite, the Kenizzite, and the Kadmonite; ²⁰ the Hittite, the
Perizzite, and the Rephaim; ²¹ the Amorite, the Canaanite, the
Girgashite, and the Jebusite."*

16   ¹Now Sarai, Abram's wife, had borne him no children. She
had an Egyptian maidservant whose name was Hagar.

love HASHEM your God, and to walk ever in His ways (*Deuteronomy* 19:8-9;
Ramban ibid.). When this will come about, three new Cities of Refuge will be
added to the six existing ones; they will be situated within the borders of these
three nations.

21. וְאֶת־הָאֱמֹרִי וְאֶת־הַכְּנַעֲנִי וגו׳ — *The Amorite, the Canaanite.* From a review of
the territories conquered by Abram during his raid against the four kings
(Chapter 14), it is seen that the same localities are mentioned once again, but in
reverse order, when the Jewish nation takes possession of the land in the time
of Moses and Joshua (*Numbers* 34; *Deuteronomy* 3). Thus the territories
conquered by the Jews are the very same as those over which Abram had
already acquired rights through conquest, a conquest whose legitimacy had
officially been recognized when Malchizedek, king of Jerusalem, paid homage
to him. The covenant "between the halves" now serves as confirmation, by
Divine right, of the historical right acquired through the symbolic act of the
conquest.

16.

1. וְשָׂרַי אֵשֶׁת אַבְרָם לֹא יָלְדָה לוֹ — *Now Sarai, Abram's wife, had borne him no
children.* Fifteen years had passed since the solemn announcement that Abram
would have many descendants. Sarai must have thought that her sterility would
explain why this promise had still not been fulfilled so many years later. What
she now proposes to her husband reflects a Babylonian custom which had
acquired the force of a law: the husband of a childless woman could marry a
concubine but the latter was not to have the same status as the wife.

R' Yehudah said: "The sow has produced ten little ones and the ewe has not
a single lamb. Abram had just been presented with ten Canaanite peoples and
Sarai had not a single child!" (*Rabbah* 44). This illustrates the contrast between
the end of the preceding chapter and the beginning of this one.

וְלָהּ שִׁפְחָה מִצְרִית — *She had an Egyptian maidservant.* A noteworthy fact. The
Mechilta tells us: No slave, male or female, ever came out of Egypt as a free
person, save Hagar (*Mechilta Shemos* 1). *Rashi* reveals the reason: She was
Pharaoh's daughter. When he saw the miracles wrought for Sarai, he said,
"Better my daughter a servant in this house than mistress of another house." In
Chapter 12, verse 16, the word "maidservant" is written defectively. This alludes
to the fact that Pharaoh's gift consisted of just this single maidservant. Sarai had

ב וַתֹּאמֶר שָׂרַי אֶל־אַבְרָם הִנֵּה־נָא עֲצָרַנִי יהוה מִלֶּדֶת בֹּא־
נָא אֶל־שִׁפְחָתִי אוּלַי אִבָּנֶה מִמֶּנָּה וַיִּשְׁמַע אַבְרָם לְקוֹל
ג שָׂרָי: וַתִּקַּח שָׂרַי אֵשֶׁת־אַבְרָם אֶת־הָגָר הַמִּצְרִית שִׁפְחָתָהּ
מִקֵּץ עֶשֶׂר שָׁנִים לְשֶׁבֶת אַבְרָם בְּאֶרֶץ כְּנָעַן וַתִּתֵּן אֹתָהּ
ד לְאַבְרָם אִישָׁהּ לוֹ לְאִשָּׁה: וַיָּבֹא אֶל־הָגָר וַתַּהַר וַתֵּרֶא

accepted Hagar as a personal tribute; so too, had Abram received Eliezer, the
son of Nimrod, to be his servant after the miracle in Ur Kasdim (*Midrash
Aggadah*).

If Sarai's maidservant had been a Canaanite, Abram would not have married
her, just as he later forbade his son to marry a Canaanite (24:3) (cf. *Ramban*
on 25:6).

2. הִנֵּה־נָא עֲצָרַנִי ה׳ מִלֶּדֶת — *See now*, HASHEM *has restrained me from bearing*.
Just after her marriage the text had said, *And Sarai was barren, she had no child*
(11:30). Why is this idea repeated? R' Nachman explains: it implies that Sarai did
not even have a womb (*Yevamos* 64a). Our verse alludes to this. However, it has
been noted that when the Torah repeats *she had no child* it wants to limit the
scope of the words. Sarah was barren, but only physically, not spiritually. By her
spirit, she inspired multitudes of pagans to embrace her faith and to become,
spiritually speaking, her children.

אוּלַי אִבָּנֶה מִמֶּנָּה — *Perhaps I will be built up through her*. It is not unusual for
a woman to give birth after having adopted a child. Thus *Rashi* explains: With
the merit for bringing a rival into my own house (and adopting her child).
Rebecca and Rachel also went childless for a time. They implored God in the
hope that their wish would be answered. But Sarai does not pray. She gives her
maidservant over to her husband. Probably she could not see how giving birth
was possible for her, since her physiological nature removed any hopes she
might have had. It thus seemed useless to her to pray for something materially
impossible. But Rebecca and Rachel were aware of the miracle which had
happened to Sarah. They knew that the course of nature can be changed by the
Almighty and they prayed for Divine mercy.

וַיִּשְׁמַע אַבְרָם לְקוֹל שָׂרָי — *And Abram heeded the voice of Sarai*. "The Holy Spirit
which spoke through her voice" (*Rashi*). The form שָׁמַע לְ . . . used here (instead
of the prefix בְּ or the word אֶת) implies to listen carefully in order to pick out the
inflections of the voice which reveal its true character. Hence, by listening
carefully not only to Sarai's words but to the tone of her voice, Abram perceived
the *voice*, the קוֹל, which came from the רוּחַ הַקּוֹדֶשׁ. (We find another example
of this in *Deuteronomy* 4:12.) Then, when Abram understood that Sarai's
request reflected the Divine will, he did it at once, as if it had been a command.
The proposal "Consort, now, with my maidservant" was for Abram truly an
ordeal. He could not fathom how his spiritual heir, who would carry on the

> ² *And Sarai said to Abram, "See, now, HASHEM has restrained me from bearing; consort, now, with my maidservant, perhaps I will be built up through her." And Abram heeded the voice of Sarai.*
> ³ *So Sarai, Abram's wife, took Hagar the Egyptian, her maidservant — after ten years of Abram's dwelling in the Land of Canaan — and gave her to Abram her husband, to him as a wife.*
> ⁴*He consorted with Hagar and she conceived; and when she saw*

knowledge of all his great truths, could be the child of a slave and not of his wife Sarai. But once again, he faithfully obeyed the voice of the Holy Spirit which he had recognized. This was the fifth of the ten ordeals inflicted on Abram (Midrash to *Psalms* 18:31).

Why did the Divine will subject Abram to this ordeal? *R' Chaim ben Attar* and *Malbim* reply that it was because of the general law of natural selection. Abram himself was affected by an atavism formed by ancestral generations of idolaters. For his offspring, there was need to extract, to eliminate, in order to separate the wheat from the chaff. The precious elements of the patriarchs' offspring could only be obtained through a very gradual process of elimination. Hence Ishmael had to come before Isaac; Esau had to precede Jacob. The extraction of raw materials precedes the recovery of pure elements. Several authors develop this theory (called the theory of בֵּרוּר) in slightly different ways. In particular, it is discussed by *R' Saadyah Gaon* (*Emunos VeDeos*, Chapter 8), *R' Yehudah HaLevi* (*Kuzari* 1:95), and *R' M. C. Luzzatto* (*Klach Pischei Chochmah*, 47).

3. וַתִּקַּח שָׂרַי — *So Sarai ... took.* She persuaded her with words. "Fortunate are you to have the privilege of being united with this pure and holy man" (*Rashi*). Sarai's spirit of sacrifice goes so far as to make use of all her powers of persuasion in order to convince her reticent husband and her maidservant, the latter unwilling because of Abram's advanced age (*Midrash Aggadah*). But Sarai in no way abdicates any of her rights, in no way lets her love diminish in intensity ... as the Torah discreetly tells us when it adds right here אֵשֶׁת אַבְרָם, she remained fully the wife of Abram. (The expression וַתִּקַּח, *she took*, cannot in this context be taken literally; it means rather, "she persuaded her" with her words. *Rashi* often explains it in this way, e.g. *Leviticus* 8:2.)

מִקֵּץ עֶשֶׂר שָׁנִים — *After ten years.* "The time limit for a wife who has no children. After this time the husband has to marry another ... but the years spent outside of *Eretz Yisrael* are not counted" (*Rashi*). See *Even HaEzer* 154:10 on the legal dispositions regarding this rule.

וַתִּתֵּן אֹתָהּ ... לוֹ לְאִשָּׁה — *And gave her ... to him as a wife.* Out of respect for her husband's dignity, Sarai wanted her maidservant to be elevated to the status of wife, although legally she could only have had a concubine's status (*Ramban* ibid. and 25:6).

ה כִּי הָרָתָה וַתֵּקַל גְּבִרְתָּהּ בְּעֵינֶיהָ: וַתֹּאמֶר שָׂרַי אֶל־אַבְרָם
חֲמָסִי עָלֶיךָ אָנֹכִי נָתַתִּי שִׁפְחָתִי בְּחֵיקֶךָ וַתֵּרֶא כִּי הָרָתָה
ו וָאֵקַל בְּעֵינֶיהָ יִשְׁפֹּט יהוה בֵּינִי וּבֵינֶיךָ: וַיֹּאמֶר אַבְרָם
אֶל־שָׂרַי הִנֵּה שִׁפְחָתֵךְ בְּיָדֵךְ עֲשִׂי־לָהּ הַטּוֹב בְּעֵינָיִךְ
ז וַתְּעַנֶּהָ שָׂרַי וַתִּבְרַח מִפָּנֶיהָ: וַיִּמְצָאָהּ מַלְאַךְ יהוה עַל־עֵין
ח הַמַּיִם בַּמִּדְבָּר עַל־הָעַיִן בְּדֶרֶךְ שׁוּר: וַיֹּאמַר הָגָר שִׁפְחַת
שָׂרַי אֵי־מִזֶּה בָאת וְאָנָה תֵלֵכִי וַתֹּאמֶר מִפְּנֵי שָׂרַי גְּבִרְתִּי
ט אָנֹכִי בֹּרַחַת: וַיֹּאמֶר לָהּ מַלְאַךְ יהוה שׁוּבִי אֶל־גְּבִרְתֵּךְ

5. חֲמָסִי עָלֶיךָ — *The outrage against me is due to you!* In addition to the grievances cited by *Rashi, Targum Yerushalmi* has her say the following to her husband: "I left my land, my home, my father's house, and followed you for the sake of belief in God ... Then, as I was childless, I gave you my Egyptian maidservant to have a child that I could raise. But as soon as she saw that she had conceived, I became despised in her eyes. Let Hashem judge between us, in mercy (יִשְׁפֹּט ה' = מִדַּת הָרַחֲמִים; the name HASHEM refers to the attribute of mercy), let Him cause peace to reign between us, let it be that the world be restored by the two of us, without need of the son of Hagar the Egyptian, the descendant of those who cast you into the fiery furnace at Ur Kasdim.

6. הִנֵּה שִׁפְחָתֵךְ בְּיָדֵךְ — *Behold! — your maidservant is in your hand.* Although Sarai wanted Hagar to become Abram's wife, she nonetheless intended Hagar to still remain her servant. For she wanted to raise the child by herself. That was the condition underlying her actions. When she saw Hagar's arrogance on becoming pregnant, Sarai understood that all her hopes would be dashed. Hence her very great disappointment.

עֲשִׂי־לָהּ הַטּוֹב בְּעֵינָיִךְ — *Do to her as you see fit.* A typical example of the humility of Abram's soul (נֶפֶשׁ שְׁפֵלָה), one of his three greatest virtues (*Rambam, Avos* 5:19).

וַתְּעַנֶּהָ שָׂרַי — *And Sarai dealt harshly with her.* "Our matriarch Sarai was wrong to have acted in this way; so was Abram for allowing her to do so. And so God saw Hagar's misery and gave her a son who became the ancestor of an unruly people, a race which was to treat the descendants of Abraham and Sarah very harshly." This opinion of *Ramban* does not pass unchallenged. But it seems to be based on the *Zohar*, which considers that although, when she fled a second time, Hagar was guilty of returning to idolatry (as *Rashi* indicates on *Genesis* 21:14), nevertheless during her first flight it was Sarai who was in the wrong. Once again we see the words of the Decalogue being applied: God visits the iniquity of the fathers upon the children ...

7. וַיִּמְצָאָהּ מַלְאַךְ ה' — *An angel of HASHEM found her.* She fled into the desert, hoping not to be found by any of her acquaintances. An angel found her עַל עֵין

that she had conceived, her mistress was lowered in her esteem.
⁵ So Sarai said to Abram, "The outrage against me is due to you!
It was I who gave my maidservant into your bosom, and now that
she sees that she has conceived, I became lowered in her esteem.
Let HASHEM judge between me and you!"

⁶ Abram said to Sarai, "Behold! — your maidservant is in your
hand; do to her as you see fit." And Sarai dealt harshly with her,
so she fled from her.

⁷ An angel of HASHEM found her by the spring of water in the
desert, at the spring on the road to Shur. ⁸ And he said, "Hagar,
maidservant of Sarai, where have you come from and where are
you going?" And she said, "I am running away from Sarai my
mistress."

⁹ And an angel of HASHEM said to her, "Return to your mistress,

הַמַּיִם, *by the spring of water.* She had hidden there because it was a well in the midst of the desert which led to Egypt, her birthplace. This spring became famous because of Hagar, but it had already been known, as it was located "on the road to Shur," which is the most desolate, arid, and hostile desert (cf. *Exodus* 15:22) of all. Hence it was a most welcome stopover for all the caravans crossing this desert (*R' Hirsch*).

8. הָגָר שִׁפְחַת שָׂרַי — *Hagar, maidservant of Sarai.* Although Hagar had fled because she no longer wanted to be a slave, when the angel calls her "maidservant of Sarai" she answers: "I am running away from Sarai my mistress." this is just what the proverb means, says Rabbah, when it says, "If others call you a donkey, put on a saddle" (*Bava Kamma* 92b) — do not blind yourself from realizing it (*Rashi* ibid.).

וַתֹּאמֶר מִפְּנֵי שָׂרַי גְּבִרְתִּי אָנֹכִי בֹּרַחַת — *And she said, "I am running away from Sarai my mistress."* Of the angel's two questions, Hagar answers only the first: "Where have you come from?" But the question, "Where are you going?" she leaves unanswered. To be sure, the fugitive knows where he came from but rarely where he is going.

9. שׁוּבִי אֶל־גְּבִרְתֵּךְ — *Return to your mistress.* Verses 9, 10 and 11 comprise three separate speeches. The first is the condition, the second the promise, the third the task and its result. Verse 9 says: "Go back of your own free will to your mistress and submit yourself to her." This sacrifice constitutes the condition. The son is to develop and be born under the influence of the free-willed recognition of Sarai's authority. He is to grow up under Sarai's guidance. But Hagar does not move.

Verse 10: "On these terms you will become the ancestress of countless descendants." Hagar still remains impassive.

Verses 11 and 12: "Your descendants will become the freest of all men." That was sufficient. For that price she is ready to submit (*R' S.R. Hirsch*).

וְהִתְעַנִּי תַּחַת יָדֶיהָ: וַיֹּאמֶר לָהּ מַלְאַךְ יהוה הַרְבָּה אַרְבֶּה
אֶת־זַרְעֵךְ וְלֹא יִסָּפֵר מֵרֹב: וַיֹּאמֶר לָהּ מַלְאַךְ יהוה הִנָּךְ
הָרָה וְיֹלַדְתְּ בֵּן וְקָרָאת שְׁמוֹ יִשְׁמָעֵאל כִּי־שָׁמַע יהוה
אֶל־עָנְיֵךְ: וְהוּא יִהְיֶה פֶּרֶא אָדָם יָדוֹ בַכֹּל וְיַד כֹּל בּוֹ

10. וַיֹּאמֶר לָהּ מַלְאַךְ ה' — *And an angel of HASHEM said to her.* When R' Shimon
bar Yochai was in Rome to intercede on behalf of the Jews during persecutions, he exclaimed, "Thrice has an angel appeared to the slave of our ancestors'
house, but not once to me! Let the miracle which I await happen somehow!"
(*Meilah* 17a).

The fact that an angel speaks several times to Hagar is considered a great
distinction by our Sages. "Frequent visitors to Abram's house were accustomed
to encounter angels" (*Rabbah* 45). Some hold that each sentence was spoken by
a different angel and that there were four or five in all (ibid.).

But others consider that a single message transmitted by an angel specially
sent for this purpose is a greater mark of esteem than three messages delivered
separately by several messengers; Hagar was not worthy of a special envoy.

Rambam goes even further. Following his general theory about prophecy, he
considers that the angels spoken of in these verses were not real beings. Hagar
was not a prophetess. She could not have Divine revelations, only visions or
apparitions during which she heard celestial voices, similar to a בַּת קוֹל, speaking
to her. *Rambam* points out that the expression וַיִּמְצָאָהּ in verse 7 indicates a
fortuitous meeting; it is again used when the angel meets Joseph (37:15; cf. *Rashi*
ibid.) to inform him where his brothers had gone. Now Joseph was only
seventeen years old at the time and surely did not yet have gifts of prophecy.
Thus it may be a question of a "very opportune meeting" not related to a
prophetic revelation.

11. וְקָרָאת שְׁמוֹ יִשְׁמָעֵאל — *You shall name him Ishmael.* The Midrash notes that
despite what this name was to signify (God has heard your affliction), the word
יִשְׁמָעֵאל is in the future tense, and is to be translated, "the Almighty will hear
your affliction," that is, all your future afflictions (*Pirkei D' Rabbi Eliezer* פל״ב).
This name brings out the principal idea that Hagar is to represent: The
consciousness of Providence which watches over man, his misery, and his
affliction; Providence which not only sees but listens, that is, which hears the
moans of this affliction and judges them. But, subsequently, the children of
Ishmael have enlarged this concept. They have built it into a doctrine which
teaches man's dependence on God "Who hears all," not only with respect to
man's will but also to his deeds and destiny. This concept leads ultimately to a
rigid system wherein man is subjugated and powerless before absolute decrees
from God. It leads to predestination of good and evil. It leads to fatalism.

יִשְׁמָעֵאל — *Ishmael.* "Balaam said: Of all the seventy nations which God has
created, He gave His name (אֵל) only to Israel and, for the same reason, to

and submit yourself to her domination."
    ¹⁰ *And an angel of HASHEM said to her, "I will greatly increase
your offspring, and they will not be counted for abundance."*
    ¹¹ *And an angel of HASHEM said to her, "Behold, you will
conceive, and give birth to a son; you shall name him Ishmael, for
HASHEM has heard your prayer. ¹² And he shall be a wild-ass of a
man: his hand against everyone, and everyone's hand against*

Ishmael. Hence both have powers sanctioned by God. This is what Balaam
implies when he says (*Numbers* 24:23): אוֹי מִי יִחְיֶה מִשֻּׂמוֹ אֵל, Alas, who will be
able to outlive the one in whom (i.e. in whose name) 'El' has a place (that is,
Ishmael = יִשְׁמָעֵאל מִשֻּׂמוֹ אֵל). For in the end of days it will be the sons of Ishmael
who will wage wars in the Holy Land and they carry in their name the name
of God!" (*Pirkei D' Rabbi Eliezer* פ״ל).

12. פֶּרֶא אָדָם — *A wild-ass of a man.* A vivid description of the sons of the desert,
owning no authority, save that of their own chief, reckless of life, treacherous
toward strangers, a nomadic people ever ready for war or pillage (Driver). The
history of the Arabs, the Bedouins, and the Tartars, reputedly the descendants
of Ishmael, confirms this prophecy, at least as we believe we understand it
(Wogue).

    According to *Sforno*, the two words of the expression פֶּרֶא אָדָם indicate
that Ishmael is the possessor of a double heritage: from his mother's side פֶּרֶא —
a wild ass, a passion for independence, a thirst for freedom; from his father's side
אָדָם, an aspiration to human perfection. If it is true that a spark of Abram's spirit
will be found in Ishmael, that the savants of the Arab nations have derived
many of their ideas from the treasures of Abram, that in spirit we really feel a
brotherhood with the sons of Ishmael, then it is nonetheless true that Ishmael did
not have Sarai for a mother. This means that moral purity, the consecration of
the body and the senses which is the exclusive work of the Jewish mother, is
wanting. Between Hagar and Sarai there will always be the difference that exists
between a well-organized, well-disciplined life and a wild, unruly, violent
existence. It can be said that the Arab peoples have developed their Jewish side,
the spirit, to such a point that at one time their philosophers served as mentors
to the Jews. But one must be born of a Jewish mother to know the real meaning
of "to serve God with all your heart, with all your soul, and with all your might."

יָדוֹ בַכּל — *His hand against everyone.* Robbery. *Rashi* explains: "When God
gave the Torah on Mount Sinai, *He appeared coming from the mountains of
Paran* (*Deuteronomy* 33:2), inhabited by the sons of Ishmael (*Genesis* 21:21). He
had asked them, 'Would you accept the Torah?' They asked, 'What does it say?'
He answered, 'You shall not steal.' Then they replied, 'But our ancestor was
blessed with the words: *His hand against everyone!*' And they refused to accept
the Torah, as did all the other nations to whom God had offered it before He
gave it to the Jewish people" (*Sifre, Deuteronomy* ibid.).

יג וְעַל־פְּנֵי כָל־אֶחָיו יִשְׁכֹּן: וַתִּקְרָא שֵׁם־יהוה הַדֹּבֵר אֵלֶיהָ
יד אַתָּה אֵל רֳאִי כִּי אָמְרָה הֲגַם הֲלֹם רָאִיתִי אַחֲרֵי רֹאִי: עַל־
כֵּן קָרָא לַבְּאֵר בְּאֵר לַחַי רֹאִי הִנֵּה בֵין־קָדֵשׁ וּבֵין
טו בָּרֶד: וַתֵּלֶד הָגָר לְאַבְרָם בֵּן וַיִּקְרָא אַבְרָם שֶׁם־בְּנוֹ
טז אֲשֶׁר־יָלְדָה הָגָר יִשְׁמָעֵאל: וְאַבְרָם בֶּן־שְׁמֹנִים שָׁנָה וְשֵׁשׁ
יז א שָׁנִים בְּלֶדֶת־הָגָר אֶת־יִשְׁמָעֵאל לְאַבְרָם: וַיְהִי
אַבְרָם בֶּן־תִּשְׁעִים שָׁנָה וְתֵשַׁע שָׁנִים וַיֵּרָא יהוה אֶל־

וְעַל־פְּנֵי כָל־אֶחָיו יִשְׁכֹּן — *And over all his brothers shall he dwell.* Ishmael and his descendants took upon themselves to carry out the *mitzvah* of circumcision. Thus they entered into the Covenant of Abraham, but only partly so, since they did not accept the other Torah *mitzvos.* They went halfway and do not deserve to be called אָדָם, *man,* as Jewry is called (*Ezekiel* 34:31), but rather are qualified as פֶּרֶא אָדָם, half man, half savage. Circumcision, which they carry out only in part, confers a certain degree of integrity on them, as is said regarding this commandment addressed to Abram: By carrying out the commandment of circumcision you will be תָּמִים, *whole* (*Rashi* on 17:1). The Torah alludes to this when it says וַה' בֵּרַךְ אֶת אַבְרָהָם בַּכֹּל, *And Hashem had blessed Abraham with everything* (24:1), i.e., in the fact of being complete, whole. Because of circumcision, Ishmael participated in this blessing also — הִנֵּה בֵּרַכְתִּי אֹתוֹ (17:20), which the Torah implies with the words יָדוֹ בַכֹּל, he has a share in the blessing granted to Abraham. Hence, he cannot be compared to an ordinary convert; he is Abram's son, an offspring of the very source of holiness. He holds a privileged position among the other peoples. He shall dwell over (עַל פְּנֵי) all his brothers (*Zohar*).

13. וַתִּקְרָא שֵׁם־ה' הַדֹּבֵר אֵלֶיהָ — *And she called the Name of HASHEM Who spoke to her.* Hagar had left Abram's house in hot anger and in spitefulness. She thought that this constituted at the same time a break with God. The apparition which she had just seen astonished her and she cried out in joy: "Could I ever have thought that even here, in the desert, I would see God's messengers again just as I used to see them in Abram's house . . ." (*Rashi*).

אַתָּה אֵל רֳאִי — *You are the God of Vision.* This, according to *Onkelos,* is the meaning of אַתָּה אֵל רֳאִי. He takes the first רֳאִי as verbal and the second as a noun (נְתִינָה לָגֵר). Hagar recognizes God as He Who sees all, and especially the humiliation of the humiliated (*Rashi*). But God's angel had previously said: God has heard your affliction . . . Now in the Torah שָׁמַע, *to hear,* often implies *to understand,* whereas *to see* refers to external appearances. It follows that the words "God hears" express, to human perception, a deeper, more encompassing, Divine power than does the expression "God sees." Hagar did not grasp this important shade of meaning, but these two attributes taken together constitute the basis for the belief in הַשְׁגָּחָה פְּרָטִית, *individual Providence.* "God hears and

him; and over all his brothers shall he dwell."

¹³ *And she called the Name of HASHEM Who spoke to her "You are the God of Vision," for she said, "Could I have seen even here after having seen?"* ¹⁴ *Therefore the well was called "The Well of the Living One." It is between Kadesh and Bered.*

¹⁵ *Hagar bore Abram a son and Abram called the name of his son that Hagar bore him Ishmael.* ¹⁶*And Abram was eighty-six years old when Hagar bore Ishmael to Abram.*

17   ¹*When Abram was ninety-nine years old, HASHEM appeared to*

sees all" — this credo of the sons of Ishmael subsequently became the supreme principle for them. The idea of personal responsibility, the doctrine of free will — these were relegated to positions of much lesser importance. The consequences which this had on Islam were mentioned in our commentary on verse 11.

14. עַל־כֵּן קָרָא לַבְּאֵר — *Therefore the well was called.* The angel ordered that the Divine revelation be perpetuated in the name of the child about to be born. But Jewish tradition would have it that the site of the revelation should also serve as a reminder of it through its name, as we see again in *Genesis* 28:19.

16. וְאַבְרָם בֶּן־שְׁמֹנִים שָׁנָה וְשֵׁשׁ שָׁנִים — *And Abram was eighty-six years old.* *Rashi* adds: "This was written in praise of Ishmael. Ishmael will thus be thirteen years old and still will not resist being circumcised." But in the next chapter (17:25) the text says explicitly that Ishmael was thirteen years of age at the time of his circumcision. Why then this repetition? The answer is that the Torah wants to bring out the full impact of this fact in order to have us better understand the underlying causes that motivated the extreme ordeal of the binding of Isaac, as *Rashi* explains them in 22:1.

17.

1. וַיְהִי אַבְרָם בֶּן־תִּשְׁעִים שָׁנָה וְתֵשַׁע שָׁנִים — *When Abram was ninety-nine years old.* "This verse is to be studied carefully, for it contains several difficulties." With these words the *Zohar* begins its reflections on our text. It continues, "Did Abram not have visions before he reached ninety-nine? Why then does the Torah stress his age? The reason is that now, with this revelation, he begins a new life. The text emphasizes this break with his past life in the special way it expresses 'ninety-nine years.' " In Hebrew syntax, in counting years the smaller number (i.e., the units digit) precedes the larger. But here we have an exception to this rule. First comes the ninety, then the nine. The *Zohar* explains: This is to teach you that the first ninety years formed a whole, a complete stage in Abram's life, as distinct from the years which followed. The "ninety" is followed by the word "year" in the singular as if to emphasize that this whole existence counted for just one year, whereas the nine years which followed,

leading up to Abram's higher, "heightened" existence, are given the plural form. From now on, each year counts for itself, each year is a step which one must climb to reach the summit of existence.

By beginning the chapter with mention of the patriarch's age, the Torah draws our attention also to the direct relationship existing between his advanced age and the revelation which follows.

Abram already had a long life behind him. He might have considered himself to have reached the height of perfection. Now he learns that he is just starting out.

This fact is important from two points of view. Some consider that "if one just does one's moral and humanitarian duty in life, God is satisfied. And Judaism asks only that." Others profess that to be a Jew is different from being simply a man; it is a sort of variation in the human condition. If the Torah did not tell us here that Abram was ninety-nine when the founding covenant of Judaism, based on the commandment of circumcision, was concluded with him, we could have thought that all of Abram's great virtues, as recorded until now, resulted from a covenant entered into from his youth, and that these virtues represented the highest of attainments. Now, this life of perfect morality preceded the *milah*, the sign of membership in Judaism. The appeal now addressed to Abram: וֶהְיֵה תָמִים, *be perfect*, presupposes that the ideal of humanity, of purely humane virtues, has already been realized. The covenant with Abram thus constitutes a higher perfection of the human virtues: be a man before being a Jew. And you will be far from it if you only accomplish the virtues of Abram recounted so far. Being as generous, as human, as conciliating, as disinterested, and without a personal agenda, etc. as Abram was up to this point leads only to the ideal of what every Noachian should be. First God led the patriarch successively through all the levels of moral training and had made him resolve all that which God demands from every human being. Then He appeared to him a second time and said, "I am אֵל שַׁדַּי, walk before Me and be perfect!"

Now Abram must reach a higher level still, that of the Torah. Its prototype is the commandment of circumcision, which is at the threshold of existence for the Jew. Abram had to learn that, to be a Jew, serving God through being moral and practicing the moral virtues is not enough. The covenant established with God for the greatest good of all humanity demands more from Abram and his offspring. It demands absolute free-willed obedience to the Law proclaimed by God. For He alone knows the secret of universal harmony, that harmony which is the basis for the salvation of the world and of its individuals and peoples. And He alone is able to promulgate those laws capable of restoring this harmony which has been disturbed from the day of the first sin.

The covenant with Abram is devoted to the realization of this task for humanity. With it begins a new phase of history. This chapter shows us the very first aspects of this covenant: God promises Abraham that he will become the father of a multitude of nations and will possess the land of Canaan — and Abraham undertakes to give unreserved obedience to the Divine law. Thus, the first step toward the accomplishment of the universal mission is now taken (R' S.R. Hirsch).

Another theme is brought out by *Midrash Rabbah* to explain why Abram's age is given at the beginning of this chapter: Abram was not circumcised at the age of forty-eight, when he recognized God, but when he was ninety-nine, in order "not to close the door to the proselytes" who, even if advanced in years, can follow the example of the first Jew. Nor was Abram circumcised at eighty-six, when Ishmael was born, for God wanted to wait until he attained the age when passion and impulse had lost their vigor, so that Isaac would be an offspring imbued with holiness.

אֲנִי־אֵל שַׁדַּי — *I am El Shaddai.* Regarding the meaning of the name שַׁדַּי our Sages are of various opinions. *Rashi* says that this name is derived from דַּי which means "enough" and its meaning depends on the context. Here it is taken to mean: I have enough Divine power for all creatures. Thus, serve Me and I will be your God and your Protector. And so, just when God gives Abraham the commandment of *milah* which will serve to isolate him from the others, God calls Himself by this name. It reminds us that God will suffice completely for Abraham; He will take him under His invincible protection and He will belong to him and be his all the more intimately: I will be your God and your Protector. The Midrash gives a different perspective: "God said to the world: It is enough for Me (שֶׁאָמַר לְעוֹלָמוֹ דַּי) if I have just one human being who walks loyally before Me and just one people ready to follow Me!"

Ibn Ezra and *Ramban* consider that this name is derived from שָׁדַד, designating God as מְשַׁדֵּד מַעֲרָכוֹת, He Who dominates and controls the natural order. Hence the usual English translation for שַׁדַּי, *Almighty*, which in its Latin form is used by the Vulgate. This Divine name designates then "God as Master of nature Who works invisible miracles," that is, those not requiring changes in the laws of nature. Often the patriarchs and their children enjoyed such miracles; this justifies the use of the name שַׁדַּי revealed to Abram. But we never see this name in the story of Moses. There, only the Tetragrammaton is used, for it refers to the absolute Master of the universe Who does supernatural miracles, as Moses and his contemporaries witnessed: the Ten Plagues, splitting the Red Sea, manna, the miraculous well, etc. With this conception of the two Divine names, we can understand the words addressed to Moses: "I revealed myself to Abraham, to Isaac and to Jacob as אֵל שַׁדַּי; but by My name ה׳ I did not make Myself known to them" (*Exodus* 6:3).

Rambam explains שַׁדַּי as characterizing God, sufficient unto Himself (*Guide* 1:63). *R' Bachya ibn Pakuda*, however, writes that this name is mentioned at the beginning of the chapter devoted to the commandment of circumcision because it brings out its profound moral significance. It is indeed because God "said to His universe: Enough!" (שֶׁאָמַר לְעוֹלָמוֹ דַּי;) and so arrested the expansive outflow of creative substance that man, created in His image, is also capable of "circumscribing" his elemental forces and can contain them within fixed limits.

אַבְרָם וַיֹּאמֶר אֵלָיו אֲנִי־אֵל שַׁדַּי הִתְהַלֵּךְ לְפָנַי וֶהְיֵה תָמִים:
ב וְאֶתְּנָה בְרִיתִי בֵּינִי וּבֵינֶךָ וְאַרְבֶּה אוֹתְךָ בִּמְאֹד מְאֹד:

The commandment of *milah* is called upon to give him the means to do so. Accordingly, it is placed under the sign of the Divine name: שַׁדַּי.

הִתְהַלֵּךְ לְפָנַי — *Walk before Me.* Proclaim My majesty to others, just like a herald who walks before his king, announcing his glory and grandeur. "See the difference between Noah and Abram. Of Noah, the Torah says he *walked with God*, that is at his side (6:9). But of the second it is said, *Walk before Me.*" R' Yochanan said: "This is like a king who had two sons. He took the younger by the hand, afraid he would fall, while the elder walked ahead by himself. So too, God made Noah walk by His side, lest he fall into the evil ways of his generation. But Abram walked all alone before God" (*Rabbah* 30). Since then Abram and his descendants have remained in the forefront of belief in One God.

וֶהְיֵה תָמִים — *And be perfect. Rashi* gives several interpretations of this "second commandment." First he links this verse with another in *Deuteronomy* (18:13) which also commands being תָמִים although in a different context: תָמִים תִּהְיֶה עִם ה' אֱלֹהֶיךָ, *you shall be wholehearted with Hashem, your God.* In both cases *Rashi* takes this word to mean "having complete confidence in God, accepting all trials unquestioningly, whole-heartedly." This notion of confident acceptance, never demanding explanations, ties in with the interpretation which *Ibn Ezra* gives here to the word תָמִים: Do not ask why the *milah* exists.

These ideas regarding the command וֶהְיֵה תָמִים, given at the head of the chapter whose main object is the commandment of circumcision, imply that the underlying reasons for it are beyond our comprehension, Indeed, the covenant is called a סוֹד ה', *a Divine secret* (*Rabbah* 49); the numerous reasons suggested for it are at best approximations. No one saw this more clearly than *Onkelos* (Aquila) the proselyte. In answer to the reproaches of his uncle, the emperor Hadrian, he affirmed that comprehending the Torah is subordinate to the act of circumcision. The relationship of cause and effect existing between them can only be of a mystical nature (*Tanchuma* to *Exodus* 21).

Another explanation: By carrying out the commandment of circumcision, you will become whole (תָמִים), whereas if you remain uncircumcised you bear a defect. Here *Rashi's* view is shared by the author of the *Sefer HaChinuch* (presumably R' Aharon HaLevi) and also by R' Z. E. Shapira, author of the ס' דֶרֶךְ פִּקוּדֶיךָ. They hold that God wanted His work to be brought to completion by man himself. He created him with a physical defect in order to make man understand that, just as his physical completion depends on himself, so too man's attainment of moral perfection is under his control (§2).

R' M. C. Luzzatto adds that the Torah itself, by its last sentence in the story of creation, אֲשֶׁר בָּרָא אֱלֹהִים לַעֲשׂוֹת (2:3) indicates that man must associate himself with the work of creation by participating personally in bringing it to perfection. Now, to reach this goal, circumcision represents what is to be man's

Abram and said to him, "I am El Shaddai; walk before Me and be perfect. ² I will set My covenant between Me and you, and I will increase you most exceedingly."

first step in this participation (אדיר במרום, ג׳ ס״ב). This also seems to be the idea behind R' Akiva's answer to Turnus Rufus as recorded in *Midrash Tanchuma* on *Leviticus* 12:3. But *Rambam* takes strong exception to "those who thought that circumcision made up for what was lacking in creation (and this opinion was not without its legitimate critics). How could nature be deficient so as to require external completion?" (*Guide* 3:49).

Rashi quotes the Midrash: "Be whole (in the name you, Abram, now bear). It lacks the letter ה, having a numerical value of 5. I will add this letter to your name which will then total 248, the number of parts of the human body." Our Sages tell us that up to this time Abram was master of his 243 parts but that afterwards he also ruled over his two eyes, his two ears, and his reproductive organ (*Nedarim* 32b). Before being circumcised Abram had mastery over all his body except for the senses which most people succeed only rarely in controlling. From then on, a new task awaited him: the new covenant implies that the senses and the instincts which one generally blindly obeys are to be subordinated and freely dominated by the human will. All instincts, even the most powerful, must be mastered in the name of God Almighty (שַׁדַּי) Who sets limits on the free reign of the elements. The Jew must be alive with the Divine spirit, not only where it is a question of being human but in all aspects of his life. On the decision to submit *all* one's acts (and not just one's thoughts and feelings) to God's direction of one's own free will has God built up the whole edifice of Abraham and of the Jewish nation (*R' S. R. Hirsch*).

2. וְאֶתְּנָה בְרִיתִי — *I will set My covenant.* Jewish destiny is not based on natural events. One cannot consider that the Jews have a "pragmatic" history in the usual sense of the word. Isaac, the first Jewish son, would never have come into the world according to the laws of nature. Jews would long since have disappeared if the natural order had determined their existence as a nation. Jewry's historical existence is founded not on a contract but on a covenant, a Divine covenant, absolute in character, completely independent of all external conditions and contingencies.

The perpetual, unchangeable sign of this covenant is circumcision. The fundamental importance of *milah* can be seen from the fact that the word בְּרִית is repeated thirteen times in this chapter (*Nedarim* 32b), whereas *Rambam* tells us that the other *mitzvos* in the Torah were sealed only by a threefold covenant (סוף הלכ׳ מילה). The number thirteen alludes to the World to Come, which is also characterized by this number; circumcision is the first "landmark" on the way to the World to Come (ילקות סופר; cf. *Yerushalmi, Avodah Zarah* 3:1).

Here the expression *I will set* (lit. "give") *My covenant* is used in contrast to the usual phrase employed previously: "I will establish" or "conclude." By having the sign of the circumcision engraved on the flesh of Abraham and his

ג־ד וַיִּפֹּל אַבְרָם עַל־פָּנָיו וַיְדַבֵּר אִתּוֹ אֱלֹהִים לֵאמֹר: אֲנִי הִנֵּה
ה בְרִיתִי אִתָּךְ וְהָיִיתָ לְאַב הֲמוֹן גּוֹיִם: וְלֹא־יִקָּרֵא עוֹד אֶת־שִׁמְךָ

offspring, He in a way takes back the covenant and then "bequeaths it" to the patriarch.

3. וַיִּפֹּל אַבְרָם עַל־פָּנָיו — *Abram threw himself upon his face.* In this spontaneous reaction, filled with humility, Abram expressed his acceptance and his profound thankfulness for the covenant which God offered him (*Sforno*).

But *Rashi* explains that Abram fell down out of fear of the presence of God. Before being circumcised, he did not have the strength to bear the presence of the Holy Spirit over him. So too with Balaam (*Numbers* 24:4). Abram reacted in this same way during the earlier revelations, although the Torah does not expressly say so. But mention of it is just made here to have us connect it with the circumcision (*Yafeh To'ar*).

וַיְדַבֵּר אִתּוֹ אֱלֹהִים — *And God spoke with him.* For the first time in the story of Abram the name אֱלֹהִים is used. As soon as Abram accepts the covenant, the Eternal enters into a personal relationship with him, as it were. For the Divine Name יהוה designates God as the transcendent, infinite, absolute Being whereas the name אֱלֹהִים calls to mind God in His relationships with creation and its creatures. Hence, of the names of God, only אֱלֹהִים takes the pronominal suffixes. Just as the covenant between Abram and "his God" is about to be sealed, there appears the Divine name which will later be spoken of as אֱלֹהֵי אַבְרָהָם, the God to Whom Abraham completely devoted himself, He Who was Abraham's protecting "shield." This intimacy is further highlighted by the use of the preposition אֶת in the phrase וַיְדַבֵּר אִתּוֹ. This preposition expresses a much closer relationship than does the more usual עִם, as *Malbim* demonstrates with numerous examples (*Leviticus* 1:3).

Furthermore, the word לֵאמֹר is also used here for the first time, in the Divine words addressed to Abram. It indicates that what is about to be said is to be retold and repeated. Until now Divine revelations had occurred in a "vision" which remained secret, for God speaks to the uncircumcised only under exceptional circumstances. But here the speech is direct, without artifice; it is public, because the mission with which it invests Abram is of universal consequence and concerns the whole of mankind.

4. וְהָיִיתָ לְאַב הֲמוֹן גּוֹיִם — *You shall be a father of a multitude of nations.* Abram feared the isolation which circumcision would bring upon him. He thought that it would create a barrier between him and the uncircumcised. This barrier would prevent him from having his spirit radiate out to them and bring them to God. His whole life's work was thus threatened with failure. Converted pagans would not consent to submit to the commandment of circumcision.

Accordingly, God gives His solemn assurance that Abraham will become the spiritual father of a multitude of nations. It is often the case that the word אַב

³ *Abram threw himself upon his face, and God spoke with him saying,* ⁴*"As for Me, this is My covenant with you: You shall be a father of a multitude of nations;* ⁵ *your name shall no longer be*

designates spiritual paternity. This meaning is confirmed through the letter ה which is added to the name אַבְרָם as this promise is made. Of all the letters, this one is the most "immaterial": just a breath, scarcely audible, not an articulated sound. Hence the letter ה represents a material void. Integrated into the name of the patriarch, it indicates that it is not a question of physical paternity, but paternity in the spiritual sense. This extends over "a multitude of nations" of both Jewish and non-Jewish stock, as *Rashi* points out (in contrast to the view of *Onkelos* and *Ramban*, who consider it a question of physical paternity).

Right here, on the threshold of the creation of the Jewish people, the particularistic and, at the same time, universalistic character of the people of Israel is first proclaimed. And, typically, this occurs with the commandment which marks Jewry's distinctiveness more than any other. Circumcision, to be sure, serves to segregate the children of Abram from other peoples. But the separation brought about by this commandment allows Jewry to shelter its national genius from all external sources which threaten it. Now, for Jewry, spiritual conquests are based solely on the persuasive force which comes from the truth, and not on personal mission work nor on inhumane methods such as are practiced by the fanatics of other religions. Therefore, in order to let its ideal shine forth, the Jewish people is not at all compelled to intermix with the other nations and thus be exposed to outside influences which could sully its special character. Quite the contrary, it is by remaining true to itself, to its truths, to its principles, that the Jewish nation is better able to carry out its mission. The suggestive power of its truths is such that Jewry can remain itself, without sacrificing anything of its existence. In this sense, circumcision is its best protection. But Jewry's particularism will always remain in the service of its universal mission.

5. וְלֹא־יִקָּרֵא עוֹד אֶת־שִׁמְךָ אַבְרָם — *Your name shall no longer be called Abram.* Whoever calls Abraham, "Abram" transgresses either a positive commandment or a prohibition, the Talmud tells us (*Berachos* 13a). However, one may call Jacob equally well by his other name Israel, the name which God gave him. Abraham's case is different because he became a new person with circumcision, when he received his new name. The *milah* means a new physical condition which signifies a distinct break with the past, socially as well as morally and physically. Return is no longer possible. The old Abram is gone forever. Abraham belongs to another world. He lives in another sphere.

But this was not so with Jacob. His change of name did not bring with it a definite change of personality. Both names, Jacob and Israel, are valid; the prophets often call the Children of Israel by the name Jacob. Indeed, Jewry remains a people with a double identity: "Israel" when conscious of its calling

שביעי   אַבְרָם וְהָיָה שִׁמְךָ אַבְרָהָם כִּי אַב־הֲמוֹן גּוֹיִם נְתַתִּיךָ:
ו וְהִפְרֵתִי אֹתְךָ בִּמְאֹד מְאֹד וּנְתַתִּיךָ לְגוֹיִם וּמְלָכִים מִמְּךָ
ז יֵצֵאוּ: וַהֲקִמֹתִי אֶת־בְּרִיתִי בֵּינִי וּבֵינֶךָ וּבֵין זַרְעֲךָ אַחֲרֶיךָ
לְדֹרֹתָם לִבְרִית עוֹלָם לִהְיוֹת לְךָ לֵאלֹהִים וּלְזַרְעֲךָ
ח אַחֲרֶיךָ: וְנָתַתִּי לְךָ וּלְזַרְעֲךָ אַחֲרֶיךָ אֵת ׀ אֶרֶץ מְגֻרֶיךָ אֵת
כָּל־אֶרֶץ כְּנַעַן לַאֲחֻזַּת עוֹלָם וְהָיִיתִי לָהֶם לֵאלֹהִים:

to be "a fighter for God," proud, courageous; "Jacob" when weak, indecisive, and vulnerable to sin.

כִּי אַב־הֲמוֹן גּוֹיִם נְתַתִּיךָ — *For I have made you the father of a multitude of nations.* In his prayers, the proselyte has the right to say the words אֱלֹהֵינוּ וֵאלֹהֵי אֲבוֹתֵינוּ, *our God and the God of our forefathers,* and עַל הָאָרֶץ שֶׁהִנְחַלְתָּ לַאֲבוֹתֵינוּ, *the land You have given to our forefathers as a heritage* because Abraham is the father of all who "come under the wings of the *Shechinah*" (*Tosafos* on *Bava Basra* 81a). For the same reason he has the right to offer the first fruits with the accompanying prayer, as stated in *Deuteronomy* 26:3, in which we thank God for having given us the land "which He swore to our ancestors to give to us" (*Rambam, Hilchos Bikkurim* 4:3).

6. וְהִפְרֵתִי אֹתְךָ בִּמְאֹד מְאֹד — *I will make you most exceedingly fruitful.* The adverb מְאֹד is repeated twice just as it is in *Avos* (4:4), מְאֹד מְאֹד הֱוֵי שְׁפַל רוּחַ, *be exceedingly humble.* Modesty, says *Rambam,* is the only virtue where an excess is not an evil, but is, on the contrary, desirable. *Rashi* points out the connection between modesty and having many offspring in his comments on the genealogy of יָקְטָן (*Genesis* 10:26): "He was humble and small in his own eyes (קָטָן), hence he merited establishing so many families." It was because the moon consented to make itself small before the sun during creation that it had the merit of being perpetually surrounded by a host of stars (*Chullin* 60b). In Egypt, the Jewish people lived in exceedingly humble fashion, and so they were blessed with exceeding fruitfulness, פָּרוּ וַיִּשְׁרְצוּ וַיִּרְבּוּ בִּמְאֹד מְאֹד (*Exodus* 1:7). Our verse hints at this relationship with its words בִּמְאֹד מְאֹד (*Sfas Emes*).

7. אֶת־בְּרִיתִי בֵּינִי וּבֵינֶךָ — *My covenant between Me and you.* Circumcision was commanded only for Abraham and his descendants, as it is said, *between Me and you and between your offspring after you.* Now the descendants of Ishmael are not included (as it is said, "Isaac's descendants will be called yours"). Esau's offspring are also excluded because Jacob is the one who is heir to Abraham and to his blessing. He, then, is the only one to keep the covenant and only his descendants are bound by circumcision (*Rambam, Hilchos Melachim* 4:7). History has borne out these Divine words. No other people shares in the covenant of circumcision in its authentic form (which includes ablation of the foreskin מִילָה and uncovering the glans, פְּרִיעָה). Circumcision remains the Divine seal engraved on the flesh of Abraham's descendants. It is reserved for Jewry just like

*called Abram, but your name shall be Abraham, for I have made you the father of a multitude of nations; * *⁶ I will make you most exceedingly fruitful, and make nations of you; and kings shall descend from you. ⁷ I will ratify My covenant between Me and you and between your offspring after you, throughout their generations, as an everlasting covenant, to be a God to you and to your offspring after you; ⁸ and I will give to you and to your offspring after you the land of your sojourns — the whole of the land of Canaan — as an everlasting possession; and I shall be a God to them."*

the Sabbath, which is also an eternal convenant and sign between "Me and the Children of Israel" (בְּרִית עוֹלָם בֵּינִי וּבֵין בְּנֵי יִשְׂרָאֵל אוֹת הִיא לְעֹלָם).

לִהְיוֹת לְךָ לֵאלֹהִים — *To be a God to you.* This is the ultimate, supreme goal of the covenant. אֲנִי לְדוֹדִי וְדוֹדִי לִי, *I am my beloved's and my beloved is mine.* This image borrowed from the loving couple will serve King Solomon to describe the covenant between Jewry and God. The covenant is first and foremost a covenant of love; so *Rashi* defines it in verse 2. But the text gives a finer shade of meaning. When it speaks of the covenant, it states its ultimate objective: לִהְיוֹת לְךָ לֵאלֹהִים, and these words imply: to *become* your God. But in the next verse, mentioning possession of the promised land, it is written: "I shall *be* a God to them." This latter expression implies a more immediate, more direct relationship than the former. This prompts *Rashi* to interpret: There I will be your God, but a Jew who dwells outside the Holy Land is as though he had no God (hyperbole alluding to the frequent soul-conflicts which the Jew suffers when he lives amid the other nations, far from the land of his forefathers).

וּלְזַרְעֲךָ אַחֲרֶיךָ — *And to your offspring after you.* The word אַחֲרֶיךָ is repeated several times in this chapter, although it seems superfluous. The *Gaon* Rav Natrunai explains in a different context: An apostate has no right to the inheritance of his Jewish father. That was shown to me in a dream in which heaven told me the words "your descendants after you," that is, resembling you, worthy of you. An apostate is one who forsakes the holy camp of Jewry and its heritage (תש׳ הגאונים סי׳ כג׳).

8. לַאֲחֻזַּת עוֹלָם — *As an everlasting possession.* The first act of the covenant concerns the constitution of the people; the second refers to possession of the land. This order of priorities is very revealing. It shows us that the existence of the people is independent of the land. What is more, the land given over to Abraham as a gift appears as a land which his descendants are to conquer. The two words מַתָּנָה, *gift,* and אֲחֻזָה or יְרוּשָׁה (taking possession in the sense of conquering; as עֲלֵה רֵשׁ in *Deuteronomy* 1:21 and elsewhere) are often used together in reference to the Promised Land. The Torah gives us to understand that if the land was magnanimously given to Abraham, it will nonetheless have to be deserved,

ט וַיֹּאמֶר אֱלֹהִים אֶל־אַבְרָהָם וְאַתָּה אֶת־בְּרִיתִי תִשְׁמֹר אַתָּה
י וְזַרְעֲךָ אַחֲרֶיךָ לְדֹרֹתָם: זֹאת בְּרִיתִי אֲשֶׁר תִּשְׁמְרוּ בֵּינִי
יא וּבֵינֵיכֶם וּבֵין זַרְעֲךָ אַחֲרֶיךָ הִמּוֹל לָכֶם כָּל־זָכָר: וּנְמַלְתֶּם אֶת

earned by the unceasing efforts of his offspring. Each generation has to begin
again for itself the "conquest" of the Holy Land.

[But, starting from a legal point of view, other scholars stress that the land of
Canaan which was given as a gift to Abraham in perpetuity acquires the status
of a legitimate inheritance for his children. The prophet Michah alludes to this in
the words: תִּתֵּן אֱמֶת לְיַעֲקֹב, חֶסֶד לְאַבְרָהָם, וגו׳, *You give to Jacob as an inalienable
right what was an act of kindness to Abraham and what You have sworn to our
fathers from the earliest times (Micah 7:20).*]

9. וְאַתָּה אֶת־בְּרִיתִי תִשְׁמֹר — *And as for you, you shall keep My covenant.*
According to *Rashi*, this is an imperative. Grammatically, it can also be taken as
being in the future tense. This would then mean that Abraham is assured that his
posterity, as well as himself, would keep the covenant in their generations, לְדֹרֹתָם
(this word is written defectively, without the *vav*, to show that the covenant will
be kept even by those generations which are morally wanting).

Taken in this sense, Abraham is put at ease after the anguish he felt at God's
words, *Walk before Me and be perfect!* (*Nedarim* 32b). How would he ever
manage to reach such a high ideal? How could he impose it on his offspring?
Wasn't it above and beyond the moral capabilities of man and especially of a
group? Then God reassured him that future generations would remain loyal to
the covenant. [If the expression וֶהְיֵה תָמִים likewise contains a promise for the
future, based on the moral effect of circumcision, rather than being construed as
a command, as *Rashi* would have it, then this would resolve *Ramban's* objection
to *Rambam* who omitted this commandment in his enumeration of the 613
commandments (השגות הרמב"ן לס׳ המצות, מצוה ח׳).]

10. הִמּוֹל לָכֶם כָּל־זָכָר — *Every male among you shall be circumcised.* The
commandment of circumcision is one of those called a חֹק, that is, a Divine law
whose reasons are unknown to us. So concludes the Midrash (*Tanchuma* 17)
referring to the words of the Psalmist: וַיַּעֲמִידֶהָ לְיַעֲקֹב לְחֹק, *He established it unto
Jacob as a statute* (חֹק), *unto Israel as an everlasting covenant* (105:10).
Accordingly, the prayers which accompany the circumcision contain the
paraphrase חֹק בִּשְׁאֵרוֹ שָׂם, *and placed the mark of the decree in his flesh.*

Nevertheless, we are advised to seek out possible reasons for this
commandment in order to understand and appreciate its educational and moral
value. The following interpretations result from such a search.

Rambam, Ramban, and others consider that one of the purposes of this
commandment is to diminish sexual passion (*Guide* 3:49). (The attenuation of the
libido is attributed to a dulling of the nervous sensitivity of the uncovered glans
due to the incessant rubbing against clothing which causes the skin to harden.

⁹ God said to Abraham, "And as for you, you shall keep
My covenant — you and your offspring after you throughout
their generations. ¹⁰ This is My covenant which you shall keep
between Me and you and your descendants after you: Every
male among you shall be circumcised. ¹¹ You shall circumcise the

But it also follows from a weakening of the erectile organ and from a limitation
of turgescence.)

Thus, scarcely having entered the world, the Jew is put on the road to
self-control. Circumcision is but the first stage in the progressive education of the
Jew. It is succeeded by a long series of steps, religious and moral, all permeated
with a moral purity which envelops him in an atmosphere of chastity and human
dignity and prevents him from falling to the level of an animal.

Some, including Philo of Alexandria, see circumcision as a hygienic measure
conditioned by the climate and living conditions of the Orient. Moreover, it is
recognized that circumcision always has various effects on hygiene. It has
prophylactic powers against a large number of ailments and is a highly efficient
preventative against cancer of the genitals. But these are the natural consequences
of circumcision, and not the reasons we are after!

Some would see in circumcision a trace of primitive rites which made their way
into Jewish tradition. To be sure, many other peoples are also acquainted with it.
But as is often the case, pagans have borrowed religious ideas or acts which
originally were pure and noble, and have deformed and degraded them into
superstitious practices, magic ceremonies, or mythological symbols. In this way
our holidays were reduced to popular celebrations at the solstices, our Sabbath
was given the character of the first social victory of the proletariat over the
exploiting class, the solemnity of Yom Kippur was transformed in pagan cults to
a time of flagellation and mortification.

But if the pagans have "profaned and sullied our sanctuary," circumcision still
remains for us the Divine seal cut into our flesh to sanctify the most powerful
instinct, the one most stamped with sensuality. None of the natural faculties in us
is of itself good or bad. It all depends on how we use it. Hence intellectual
curiosity, inventive genius, the procreative urge, familial love, these are all urges
in man which, taken one by one, could lead to instability, even to debauchery in
many cases. But when they are coordinated under a single higher will, they
engender a continual harmony and development. The law given to Abraham is
an admirable demonstration of this. It condemns neither the desire nor the joys of
life. It encourages neither abstinence nor continence. It does not seek that violent
repression of the senses which cuts man off from society, changes his nature, and
renders him useless to his fellowman. Satisfying one's sensual appetites produces
effects which are even more disastrous. They turn man into a beast, degrade him
deeply. They impede the upward flight of his soul, they stifle the most noble
beats of his heart and snuff out the Divine spark within him.

יב בְּשַׂר עָרְלַתְכֶם וְהָיָה לְאוֹת בְּרִית בֵּינִי וּבֵינֵיכֶם: וּבֶן־שְׁמֹנַת
יָמִים יִמּוֹל לָכֶם כָּל־זָכָר לְדֹרֹתֵיכֶם יְלִיד בָּיִת וּמִקְנַת־כֶּסֶף

In addition to complete free will in moral matters, God wanted to give Jewry's adherents the means of making the best use of this freedom by living their lives, with their joys, to the full, but without compromising their souls and their greatness among the other creatures. The first law on the road of human life leading to this result is circumcision. By placing the Divine seal on man's body, it sanctifies the most violent and most animal of instincts and the genital area, which hitherto had been considered as the seat of impure, unmentionable activities. Through circumcision man becomes conscious of the Divine to the depths of his being. The *milah* now invites him to enter into the select group of "servants of God" so that the complete man may become the perfect artisan of the Divine plan.

11. וְהָיָה לְאוֹת בְּרִית בֵּינִי וּבֵינֵיכֶם — *And that shall be the sign of the covenant between Me and you.* As it were, the master's seal on his servant (*Sforno* and others). No matter what reasons have been or will be advanced for circumcision, Abraham and his descendants feel far removed from such ideas. For them circumcision is simply the symbol of the dedication of Abraham and his offspring to God. It is the rite of the covenant. And the faithfulness and devotion which have characterized this fundamental institution of Judaism for all time have known no bounds. Jewish men and women have always been ready to die in its defense. The Maccabean martyrs died for it. Jewish mothers were slain by King Antiochus's officers because they had dared to "bring their children into the covenant of Abraham" (*I Maccabees* 1:61). During the terrible Hadrianic persecutions, during the Inquisition — whenever tyrants tried to uproot the Jewish faith — Jews were ready to give up their possessions and their lives to safeguard this tradition. Even Baruch Spinoza, who was anathematized as an apostate, declared: "I consider the sign of the covenant so important that in my view it alone is sufficient to maintain the separate existence of the Jewish people forever."

In his book *The Kuzari, R' Yehudah HaLevi* brings out another aspect of the sign of the covenant: The Divine practices are neither commanded nor rejected by our intellect. They are observed just as a sick person obeys the orders of his physician. Consider circumcision. It has nothing to do with analogic thought or with the constitution of social life. Yet Abraham subjected his person and his children to it, although this must have caused him much pain — he was nearly 100 years old! On Abraham's person this became a sign that the spirit of God will hover over him and his descendants, as it is written: *I will ratify My covenant between Me and you and between your offspring after you* (verse 7).

The Khazar replied: Indeed, you have duly accepted this law and you perform it with great zeal, with a public ceremony to praise it and to bring out its basic concept. Hence it brings blessings. Other peoples desired to imitate you, but they

flesh of your foreskin, and that shall be the sign of the covenant between Me and you. [12] *At the age of eight days every male among you shall be circumcised, throughout your generations — he that is born in the household or purchased with money*

only had the pain, without the joy which can only be felt by him who remembers the cause for which he bears the pain (3:7-8).

12. וּבֶן־שְׁמֹנַת יָמִים יִמּוֹל לָכֶם כָּל־זָכָר — *At the age of eight days every male among you shall be circumcised.* This very early age is considered a fringe benefit of circumcision. It has been observed that cancer of the penis does not occur when the child is circumcised at the age of eight days but it does occur, for example, in Muslims who are circumcised at 3 to 14 years of age. This disease is very commonly encountered in some parts of Asia where circumcision is not practiced at all.

But in Jewish thought there is a connection between the eighth day prescribed for circumcision and the offering of sacrifices. The idea of sacrifice has an important place similar to the performance of the *milah*. The *milah* is to be carried out on the eighth day after birth just as an animal cannot be sacrificed until the eighth day (*Leviticus* 22:27). R' Levi said: This is like a king who is visiting one of his provinces. He has proclaimed, "All who wish to pay homage to me must do so to the Queen first." So too, God proclaims: "Whoever wishes to offer his sacrifice to Me must first acknowledge the Queen Sabbath." Thus a sacrifice could not be accepted before the eighth day; and the covenant of circumcision cannot be celebrated before the eighth day, so that the newborn could first pay homage to the Sabbath (*Sefer HaBahir*).

The *Zohar* and Kabbalists put much stress on the symbols of sacrifice included in the circumcision ceremony. The blood brings atonement to the one offering the sacrifice or to the father who has his son circumcised. But the value of circumcision is greater, for it is corporeal, not just material, as is the case when an animal is offered. After the circumcision, the foreskin is put into a cup containing some earth. This is reminiscent of the altar filled with earth on which sacrifices were offered (*Exodus* 20:21). For one who has his son circumcised is like one who builds an altar for his sacrifices.

Circumcision is only the first sacrifice which the Jew is to make in order to carry out his earthly mission. The Torah which established the ideal of "sanctification through sacrifice" has made the concept of sacrifice one of prime importance. It places the act of sacrifice in the midst of its legislation.

In no matter which domain of existence, there can be no harmonious union without each of its spheres coming to present its sacrifice, with its full consent, on the altar of humanity! There can never be union, peace and harmony without the sacrificing of a bit of sovereignty both by the individual and the community.

And so the Jew is invited to participate in this requirement right from the start of his life. The sacrifice of "flesh and blood" which begins with circumcision and

יג מִכֹּל בֶּן־נֵכָר אֲשֶׁר לֹא מִזַּרְעֲךָ הוּא: הִמּוֹל ׀ יִמּוֹל יְלִיד
בֵּיתְךָ וּמִקְנַת כַּסְפֶּךָ וְהָיְתָה בְרִיתִי בִּבְשַׂרְכֶם לִבְרִית
יד עוֹלָם: וְעָרֵל ׀ זָכָר אֲשֶׁר לֹא־יִמּוֹל אֶת־בְּשַׂר עָרְלָתוֹ

continues later with other forms of abnegation, constitutes the means of permitting a close, intimate bond between the physical side of human nature and the spiritual sphere. Removing the flesh of the foreskin therefore symbolizes the tribute which man has to pay to the Divine order of creation as long as he participates in life on this earth.

וּמִקְנַת־כֶּסֶף מִכֹּל בֶּן־נֵכָר אֲשֶׁר לֹא מִזַּרְעֲךָ הוּא — Or *purchased with money from any stranger who is not of your offspring. Rambam* states the law concerning the slave explicitly in this fashion: He who buys a pagan slave unwilling to be circumcised or to observe the commandments which slaves must observe, should look after him personally (in order to convince him) for twelve months; if the slave still refuses, his master is to sell him back to a pagan or to someone outside the Holy Land (*Hilchos Avadim* 8:12). Jewish legislation concerning the Canaanite slave was directed at attracting him toward the knowledge and love of God and hence raising him to a moral and social level which would have been inaccessible to him in his previous condition. Now, here, circumcision is seen to be the fundamental requirement for "entry into the covenant of Abraham." No one can be welcomed into this covenant without bearing its sign on himself. It is a prerequisite. So answered R' Eliezer when King Agrippas asked him: "Since God attaches so much importance to circumcision, why isn't it one of the Ten Commandments?" R' Eliezer replied: "It comes before them. Did not Jeremiah say, *Thus says HASHEM: If not for My covenant* (of circumcision) *day and night, then I cease to appoint the laws of heaven and earth!*" (33:25). This prophet wants us to see that the covenant of circumcision is the basis for moral life just as the laws of nature serve as a base for physical life (cf. *Tanchuma*). Circumcision predisposes man to physical and spiritual perfection whereas the other 612 commandments provide him the means of reaching this perfection.

R' M. C. Luzzatto expresses this same idea in referring us to the words of *Deuteronomy* (30:12): מִי יַעֲלֶה־לָּנוּ הַשָּׁמַיְמָה, *who shall go up for us to heaven?* The initial letters of these four words form the word מִילָה. From this we infer that circumcision can raise us to higher spheres by making us fit to welcome the Divine spirit. And the last letters of these words form the ineffable name of God, הֲוָיֳ, to tell us that the sanctifying power of the *milah* emanates directly from God, and that it remains an impenetrable mystery for us. All in all, circumcision makes us receptive to Divine revelation and predisposes us to a pure, moral life. He whose flesh is marked with the "seal of the holy covenant" will never be capable of complete moral degradation. "God swore to Abraham that no one who is circumcised will enter Hell" (*Tanchuma*). And Abraham "sits before the gates of Hell to watch that no one who is circumcised enters therein" (*Bereishis Rabbah* 48). Whereas the gates of Hell are open for the uncircumcised (*Ezekiel* 32:24), just

from any stranger who is not of your offspring. ¹³ *He that is born in your household or purchased with your money shall surely be circumcised. Thus, My covenant shall be in your flesh for an everlasting covenant.* ¹⁴ *An uncircumcised male the flesh of whose foreskin shall not be circumcised*

as they are for the apostate (*Psalms* 55:21), circumcision opens the way that leads to the World to Come (as was mentioned in our commentary to verse 2).

13. הִמּוֹל יִמּוֹל יְלִיד בֵּיתְךָ וּמִקְנַת כַּסְפֶּךָ — *He that is born in your household or purchased with your money shall surely be circumcised.* "A repetition of the last part of the previous verse, but without the words, *eight days old.* Hence there will be some who will be circumcised after the eighth day, as the Talmud explains in the tractate *Shabbos* (137b)." With these words *Rashi* points out that the Torah reiterates the law of circumcision with respect to gentiles "not descended from you" and grants them, in certain cases, the option of not making the eighth day a compulsory condition for the circumcision. This shows that although it was concluded between God and Abraham and his descendants, the covenant does not exclude all others. The door is open to those who are "not descended from you" and who wish to enter into the covenant. Moreover, when they enter, they do so with the same rights and the same obligations. This important clause is loudly proclaimed at the very moment the covenant is concluded.

בְּרִיתִי בִּבְשַׂרְכֶם — *My covenant shall be in your flesh.* The term בָּשָׂר designates more specifically the reproductive organ, as several of our Sages point out. However, *Rashi* quotes the saying of R' Nassan (*Shabbos* 108a) to this effect: the expression וְעָרֵל זָכָר in the next verse serves as an indication to Abraham that circumcision is to be performed "at the place where male and female are distinguishable." The *Midrash Tanchuma* adds: Abraham was still perplexed and did not know how to proceed. Then God Himself helped him, as it is said, וְכָרוֹת עִמּוֹ הַבְּרִית, *He made* [lit. *cut*] *the covenant of circumcision with him* (*Nehemiah* 9:8), instead of the more usual phrase וְכָרוֹת לוֹ.

14. עָרְלָתוֹ — וְעָרֵל זָכָר אֲשֶׁר לֹא־יִמּוֹל אֶת־בְּשַׂר עָרְלָתוֹ — *An uncircumcised male the flesh of whose foreskin shall not be circumcised.* According to the Talmud, the various formulations of the commandment in this chapter refer to various cases (*Kiddushin* 29a). First it is the father's duty to have his son circumcised (Abraham circumcised his son Isaac, 21:4). If the father has not done so, the obligation falls on the *beis din,* that is, on the local religious authorities — the text alludes to them when it uses the impersonal expression in verse 10: הִמּוֹל לָכֶם כָּל־זָכָר, to have every male among you circumcised. If the *beis din* has not done so, then the person himself is obliged to circumcise himself, as the words of our verse tell us: וְעָרֵל זָכָר אֲשֶׁר לֹא־יִמּוֹל אֶת־בְּשַׂר עָרְלָתוֹ, *an uncircumcised male the flesh of whose foreskin shall not be circumcised.*

טו וְנִכְרְתָה הַנֶּפֶשׁ הַהִוא מֵעַמֶּיהָ אֶת־בְּרִיתִי הֵפַר: וַיֹּאמֶר
אֱלֹהִים אֶל־אַבְרָהָם שָׂרַי אִשְׁתְּךָ לֹא־תִקְרָא אֶת־שְׁמָהּ
טז שָׂרָי כִּי שָׂרָה שְׁמָהּ: וּבֵרַכְתִּי אֹתָהּ וְגַם נָתַתִּי מִמֶּנָּה לְךָ בֵּן

וְנִכְרְתָה הַנֶּפֶשׁ הַהִוא מֵעַמֶּיהָ — *That soul shall be cut off from its people.* This is the
second punishment announced in the Torah, the first being the death penalty
proclaimed after the first sin, for murder. כָּרֵת indicates a punishment from
Heaven which can take different forms but which always signifies a rupture, a
cutting-off. Whoever is punished with כָּרֵת no longer has ties with his people, he
lives cut off from them, i.e., excluded from the community of the righteous.
When the Torah speaks of the punishment כָּרֵת, it regularly uses the expression
וְנִכְרְתָה מֵיִשְׂרָאֵל or מִקֶּרֶב עַמּוֹ, thus implying that the guilty one will be cut off,
extirpated, from his people. Just once does the Torah express this as a severance
with respect to God: וְנִכְרְתָה הַנֶּפֶשׁ הַהִיא מִלְּפָנַי, אֲנִי ה׳ — *that person shall be cut off
from before Me* (*Leviticus* 22:3). Our Sages explain: You might have thought
that the sinner is cut off from Jewry but that he might still go to another people.
Hence the Torah tells us: *that person shall be cut off from before Me.* Now, God
is everywhere. Where could the guilty one go to escape His presence? (*Mechilta
Bo,* 70).

According to *Rambam,* a person who consciously remains uncircumcised
until he dies is then liable to this penalty. *R' Abraham ben David,* however,
considers that one is guilty of the punishment of כָּרֵת each day he remains
uncircumcised (פ״א, ה״ב, וכ״מ שם).

Cutting off a soul is like the breaking-off of a branch cut from the trunk, the
core which gave it life. It cannot be re-attached to its life-source. This punishment follows the principle of מִדָּה כְּנֶגֶד מִדָּה, *measure for measure.* The guilty one
has violated My covenant (אֶת בְּרִיתִי הֵפַר), and so he will be punished by breaking the bonds which attach his soul to the source. Know that the penalty of כָּרֵת
is not the same for all who deserve it. The perfectly righteous person who "slips
up" and follows his desire to eat a piece of lard (the size of an olive) must undergo
כָּרֵת (*Leviticus* 7:25) but this does not mean he will thereby lose his share in the
World to Come. This share is reserved for every Jew, as our Sages tell us, except
for apostates and rebels. But כָּרֵת sometimes refer to the body and sometimes to
the soul. He whose merits surpass his sins, even if the latter include sins punishable by כָּרֵת, will undergo the physical punishment and will die a premature
death. But he will keep his share in the World to Come (he is cut off only מֵעַמָּיו,
only *from his people,* that is, from the living). But the one who commits many
sins suffers the other kind of כָּרֵת: the soul of the sinner is deprived of life in the
World to Come. It is to this sinful soul that the verses in *Leviticus* refer: *That
person shall be cut off from before Me* (22:3), and again, *That soul I shall
destroy* (23:30). These sinners do not undergo physical punishment. They may
even reach old age in this world, as it is said (*Ecclesiastes* 7:15): "There is many a
wicked man who lives long in his wickedness" (*Recanati*).

— that soul shall be cut off from its people; he has invalidated My covenant."

¹⁵ *And God said to Abraham, "As for Sarai your wife — do not call her name Sarai, for Sarah is her name. ¹⁶ I will bless her; indeed, I will give you a son through her;*

15. שָׂרַי אִשְׁתְּךָ — *As for Sarai your wife.* Nothing could better illustrate the importance which the Torah attaches to the wife's role in the development of the nation than this passage devoted to Sarai. Everything had already been said about Abraham's future offspring, and the fact that Ishmael had been born before the latest promises proves that this offspring was to come from Sarai, not from Hagar. But again the Divine word comes to Abraham, this time to honor Sarai with a new name, conferred by God Himself to bless her and announce her motherhood. In this way God pays homage to her and emphasizes the importance of her maternal mission. Her influence on the upbringing of her son will be decisive. By stressing the leading role which the first Jewish mother is to play alongside her husband, the Torah makes us conscious of the enormous responsibility which rests on the Jewish wife and mother.

Our Sages describe Sarah as a model Jewish wife. To her they apply Solomon's words: *A virtuous woman is a crown to her husband (Proverbs 12:4).* R' Acha interprets: "It is he who finds his crown in her, not she in him." Moreover, add the Rabbis, she is superior to her husband in her intuition, as it is said, *Whatever Sarah tells you, heed her voice (Genesis 21:12).* Indeed, R' Yehoshua ben Korcha holds that Sarai did better still. She took the letter *yud* from her name and split it into two halves; one *hey* (which has half the numerical value of *yud*) she kept for herself (שָׂרָה) and the other was for her husband (אַבְרָהָם). When one considers that *yud* is the initial letter of the Divine name, this sharing signifies that Sarah was able to associate her husband with the Divine spirit which manifested itself in her through her gifts of prophecy. Another of our Sages teaches that the *yud* withdrawn from Sarai's name was given to Joshua when Moses changed his name from הוֹשֵׁעַ to יְהוֹשֻׁעַ (*Numbers* 13:16). Sarai wanted to communicate a part of her spirit to the one who would be destined to lead the Jewish people into Canaan in order to conquer it. She had (symbolically) been the first to conquer this land and prayed that the future conquest would be made with the same spirit of devotion and sacrifice which had always inspired her (*Bereishis Rabbah*). This spirit was to remain imprinted in Joshua's name.

כִּי שָׂרָה שְׁמָהּ — *For Sarah is her name.* The letter *yud*, a sign of the masculine (in verbal prefixes in the future tense and in pronominal suffixes) is replaced by the letter *hey*, indicating the feminine and symbolizing fertility. Henceforth both Sarah and Abraham will bear this letter in them. In addition to new names, it will confer upon them new personalities characterized by fertility and by fruitfulness, both in the physical sense, with respect to paternity, and, in a spiritual sense, as the patrons of nations (*Kli Yakar*).

16. וּבֵרַכְתִּי אֹתָהּ — *I will bless her.* The double blessing in this verse refers to the

יז וּבֵרַכְתִּיהָ וְהָיְתָה לְגוֹיִם מַלְכֵי עַמִּים מִמֶּנָּה יִהְיוּ: וַיִּפֹּל
אַבְרָהָם עַל־פָּנָיו וַיִּצְחָק וַיֹּאמֶר בְּלִבּוֹ הַלְּבֶן מֵאָה־שָׁנָה
יח יִוָּלֵד וְאִם־שָׂרָה הֲבַת־תִּשְׁעִים שָׁנָה תֵּלֵד: וַיֹּאמֶר אַבְרָהָם
יט אֶל־הָאֱלֹהִים לוּ יִשְׁמָעֵאל יִחְיֶה לְפָנֶיךָ: וַיֹּאמֶר אֱלֹהִים
אֲבָל שָׂרָה אִשְׁתְּךָ יֹלֶדֶת לְךָ בֵּן וְקָרָאתָ אֶת־שְׁמוֹ יִצְחָק

birth of a son and to raising him. The first blessing comes to annul the curse of
Eve — *in pain shall you bear children* (3:16). Sarah gave birth without pain, as
tradition teaches (*Daas Zekeinim* on *Genesis* 21:2). The second blessing brings
the gift of raising a child without sorrow, without vexation. Abraham and his
wife had the joy of raising their son with this blessing, as R' Yehudah mentions
in *Sanhedrin* 19a (*Sforno*).

17. וַיִּפֹּל אַבְרָהָם עַל־פָּנָיו — *And Abraham threw himself upon his face.* We have
already been told in verse 3 that Abraham did so. There, R' Bachya says, it was
a sign of humility as the prophet prepared to welcome the Divine revelation. But
here, the second time Abraham prostrates himself, it is the spontaneous reaction
of a father beseeching Divine mercy for his son: הַכֹּל בִּזְכוּת הִשְׁתַּחֲוָיָה our Sages
tell us (*Bereishis Rabbah* 56). The greatest blessings granted to man were but
responses to the fervent adoration and deep emotion which motivated him to
prostrate himself before God.

וַיֹּאמֶר בְּלִבּוֹ — *And he thought.* Is this double objection which comes to
Abraham's mind, causing him to smile, evidence of a hint of doubt regarding
God's word? The words וַיֹּאמֶר בְּלִבּוֹ seems to suggest that it is. Our Sages tell us
that with the righteous the words וַיֹּאמֶר אֶל לִבּוֹ are used, for the righteous person
controls the thoughts and feelings of his heart. On the other hand, וַיֹּאמֶר בְּלִבּוֹ
is used with reference to a wicked person, who speaks "*in* his heart," for he is
prisoner of his thoughts and inclinations. But here we come across the sole
exception to this rule: Abraham said to himself (in his heart). In a moment of
weakness the patriarch let himself be carried away in a manner unworthy of
him. His reactions were valid for ordinary people but not for one who had
experienced a century of Providence's exceptional care. For a brief moment, he
was the prisoner of his own heart.

18. לוּ יִשְׁמָעֵאל יִחְיֶה לְפָנֶיךָ — *O that Ishmael might live before You!* R' Chiya
sighed and wept when he began to explain the verse, *And Sarai was barren, she
had no child* (11:30). He interpreted the words וַתְּהִי שָׂרַי as וַי עַל זֶה, *woe for this*,
woe for the moment when Hagar gave birth to Ishmael. R' Yose asked him to
explain, for "had Sarah too not had a son born from this source of holiness?" He
answered, "This is what I heard from R' Shimon bar Yochai: Alas for Sarah who
waited so long to have a child. She offered Hagar to Abraham and because of
Sarai's proposal the time was propitious for the bondwoman: She was able to
acquire some of her rights and she bore a son to Abraham. When Abraham

I will bless her and she shall give rise to nations; kings of peoples will rise from her."

¹⁷ And Abraham threw himself upon his face and laughed; and he thought, "Shall a child be born to a hundred-year-old man? And shall Sarah — a ninety-year-old woman — give birth?" ¹⁸ And Abraham said to God, "O that Ishmael might live before You!" ¹⁹ God said, "Nonetheless, your wife Sarah will bear you a son and you shall call his name Isaac;

received word from God about Isaac, he cried out, 'If only Ishmael would live in awe of You.' Abraham was so attached to Ishmael that God promised him, *Regarding Ishmael I have heard you: I have blessed him, etc.* Then Ishmael grew up, was circumcised and entered into the holy covenant before Isaac was born. For 400 years, the patron-angel of the sons of Ishmael came before God to claim their part of the Divine inheritance, for they too were circumcised, just like the sons of Isaac. But they received this reply: 'The sons of Isaac are circumcised correctly; not so with you [Ishmael who was circumcised at thirteen years of age had the foreskin cut but he did not want to bear having the skin folded back; his descendants kept the same incomplete kind of circumcision (מִילָה בְּלִי פְּרִיעָה)]. Moreover, the sons of Isaac carry the sign of the circumcision from the age of eight days; for you, this comes only much later.' Nevertheless, God granted them a part of the Holy Land and let the children of Ishmael reign over it while it was deserted for a long time. This reign, which enabled them to keep the children of Isaac in the background, has lasted as long as the reward for the incomplete circumcision. But at the end of the evolution of history, the children of Ishmael will wage brutal wars on land and on sea, and in the vicinity of Jerusalem. The world conflagration which they will provoke will ultimately lead to the coming of the messianic era" (*Zohar*).

19. וְקָרָאתָ אֶת־שְׁמוֹ יִצְחָק — *And you shall call his name Isaac.* יִצְחָק does not mean "he who laughs" nor "he who rejoices." It means he who "causes laughter," who brings a smile to the lips of his parents, both to Abraham (verse 17) and to Sarah (18:12). The word צָחַק generally indicates an ironic or mocking laugh, brought about by something ridiculous, something inconceivable.

The fact that the announcement of the coming birth of their son provoked laughter is of exceptional significance; so important is it that God left that mark for eternity in the name of this son. Why is this so? The following considerations will help bring out the reasons.

It is surely paradoxical to expect that a 100-year-old man, and his 90-year-old wife who had never before had children, should now give birth. And then to expect a great nation to arise, to place the hopes of the whole future of mankind on this late-born only child — that is surely an absurdity, if one takes only the natural course of events into account. Placing the very greatest expectations on the very smallest, almost non-existent, beginnings seems grotesque. This

וַהֲקִמֹתִ֨י אֶת־בְּרִיתִ֤י אִתּוֹ֙ לִבְרִ֣ית עוֹלָ֔ם לְזַרְע֖וֹ אַחֲרָֽיו:

כ וּֽלְיִשְׁמָעֵאל֮ שְׁמַעְתִּיךָ֒ הִנֵּ֣ה ׀ בֵּרַ֣כְתִּי אֹת֗וֹ וְהִפְרֵיתִ֥י אֹת֛וֹ וְהִרְבֵּיתִ֥י אֹת֖וֹ בִּמְאֹ֣ד מְאֹ֑ד שְׁנֵים־עָשָׂ֤ר נְשִׂיאִם֙ יוֹלִ֔יד

כא וּנְתַתִּ֖יו לְג֥וֹי גָּדֽוֹל: וְאֶת־בְּרִיתִ֖י אָקִ֣ים אֶת־יִצְחָ֑ק אֲשֶׁר֩ תֵּלֵ֨ד

כב לְךָ֤ שָׂרָה֙ לַמּוֹעֵ֣ד הַזֶּ֔ה בַּשָּׁנָ֖ה הָאַחֶֽרֶת: וַיְכַ֖ל לְדַבֵּ֣ר אִתּ֑וֹ וַיַּ֣עַל

כג אֱלֹהִ֔ים מֵעַ֖ל אַבְרָהָֽם: וַיִּקַּ֨ח אַבְרָהָ֜ם אֶת־יִשְׁמָעֵ֣אל בְּנ֗וֹ וְאֵ֨ת כָּל־יְלִידֵ֤י בֵיתוֹ֙ וְאֵת֙ כָּל־מִקְנַ֣ת כַּסְפּ֔וֹ כָּל־זָכָ֕ר בְּאַנְשֵׁ֖י בֵּ֣ית אַבְרָהָ֑ם וַיָּ֗מָל אֶת־בְּשַׂ֤ר עָרְלָתָם֙ בְּעֶ֨צֶם֙ הַיּ֣וֹם הַזֶּ֔ה

contrast was so great that Abraham, with all his confidence in God, could not help laughing. And this burst of laughter is considered as being so characteristic that it is to be perpetuated for all future generations in the name of the child about to be born.

The beginnings of the Jewish people are completely "ridiculous." To the one who considers only natural causality, ordinary cause and effect, the Jewish people and its history and messianic hopes — indeed its whole existence as a nation — must appear as the most unwarranted, laughable pretention. It only makes sense — and then becomes perfectly realistic — when one bases one's understanding on the first and supreme causality which gives rise to all the other causalities in existence, when one reckons on the all-pervasive, completely free, almighty will as one's starting point. The patriarchs were to realize this truth right from the beginning and their descendants were all to keep it uppermost in their minds. That was why God waited for this "absurd" age of the first patriarch before producing the first seed of this nation. He waited to fulfill His promise until all human hopes of its realization had ended. For it was a question of creating a people who, in opposition to all the ordinary laws of world history, were to be from their beginnings and ever onward an אֱלֹהִים צְבָא, a Divine sign, and who therefore must appear to be a most impossible, absolutely inexplicable phenomenon to all narrow-minded people who deny the existence of God. The burst of laughter which follows the Jew as he makes his way through history confirms that God leads him on his way. It does not bother him in the least, for he has been prepared from the beginning for this (R' S. R. Hirsch).

20. שְׁנֵים־עָשָׂר נְשִׂיאִם יוֹלִיד — He will beget twelve princes. "Also this has God made in equal measure against the other" (Ecclesiastes 7:14). "For example," says R' Akiva, "Paradise versus Hell; the kingdom of the righteous against that of the wicked" (Chagigah 15a). Implicit in the structure of creation is that to every positive element there is a corresponding negative element. The law of polarity on which the universe is based results in the division of the cosmos into a masculine and feminine factor, just as it results in the separation of the principle of day from that of night. This same dualism, which bears within it the seed of future evolution, appears in the sphere of history in the form of the twelve tribes of Israel confronting the twelve princes of Ishmael (Recanati).

and I will fulfill My covenant with him as an everlasting covenant for his offspring after him. ²⁰ *But regarding Ishmael I have heard you: I have blessed him, will make him fruitful, and will increase him most exceedingly; he will beget twelve princes and I will make him into a great nation.* ²¹ *But I will maintain My covenant through Isaac whom Sarah will bear to you by this time next year."* ²² *And when He had finished speaking with him, God ascended from upon Abraham.*

²³ *Then Abraham took his son Ishmael and all those servants born in his household and all those he had purchased for money — all the male members of Abraham's house — and he circumcised the flesh of their surplusage on that very day*

וּנְתַתִּיו לְגוֹי גָּדוֹל — *And I will make him into a great nation.* In his *Letter to Yemen, Rambam* vigorously attacks those who see in the words בִּמְאֹד מְאֹד a reference to the prophet of Islam. The numerical value of the latter's name (מְחַמַּד) equals that of these two words.

21. וְאֶת־בְּרִיתִי אָקִים אֶת־יִצְחָק — *But I will maintain My covenant through Isaac.* R' Abba said: "We have here an *a fortiori* argument: What is true for the son of the bondwoman is all the more so valid for the son of the wife. Verse 20 says concerning Ishmael: *I have blessed him, will make him fruitful. . . and I will make him into a great nation.* All the more so then will I establish My covenant with Isaac." But on this explanation quoted by *Rashi*, one could ask: If this is indeed an *a fortiori* argument, why did the Torah need to state the conclusion explicitly? An answer is given by the author of the בני ישׁשכר — the Torah wanted to affirm what Abraham had hoped for but what he could conclude only through a subjective argument: God had indeed already promised to establish His eternal covenant with Isaac and his descendants after him (לְזַרְעוֹ אַחֲרָיו). The term אַחֲרָיו implies that the offspring will walk in the ancestor's footsteps and will follow his example (verse 19). Abraham might well have taken this implication as a condition *sine qua non* for maintaining the covenant. But when he heard the Divine promise granting an unconditional blessing to Ishmael and his seed, then he assumed that the covenant with Isaac would, *a fortiori*, be unconditional too (verse 20). And so, God confirms his assumption: "I will maintain My covenant through Isaac" (verse 21) — this time without adding the clause לְזַרְעוֹ אַחֲרָיו with its tacit implication (חי' תשרי, מאמר י"ב).

22. וַיַּעַל אֱלֹהִים מֵעַל אַבְרָהָם — *God ascended from upon Abraham. Rashi:* This is a refined expression with reference to the *Shechinah.* From this we learn that the righteous are the "vehicle" (lit. "chariot") for God. The highest perfection which man can reach on earth is when he is seen in the eyes of his fellowmen as "God's agent on earth." The righteous person whose inspired countenance radiates the Divine spirit, whose entire personality reflects heavenly light, is the

מפטיר כד כַּאֲשֶׁר דִּבֶּר אִתּוֹ אֱלֹהִים: וְאַבְרָהָם בֶּן־תִּשְׁעִים וָתֵשַׁע שָׁנָה
כה בְּהִמֹּלוֹ בְּשַׂר עָרְלָתוֹ: וְיִשְׁמָעֵאל בְּנוֹ בֶּן־שְׁלֹשׁ עֶשְׂרֵה שָׁנָה
כו בְּהִמֹּלוֹ אֵת בְּשַׂר עָרְלָתוֹ: בְּעֶצֶם הַיּוֹם הַזֶּה נִמּוֹל אַבְרָהָם
כז וְיִשְׁמָעֵאל בְּנוֹ: וְכָל־אַנְשֵׁי בֵיתוֹ יְלִיד בָּיִת וּמִקְנַת־כֶּסֶף מֵאֵת
בֶּן־נֵכָר נִמֹּלוּ אִתּוֹ:

one who becomes the custodian of the "chariot of triumph" which spreads
God's glory and has His majesty acclaimed wherever he goes.

Quoting the Midrash (*Bereishis Rabbah* 47) *Ramban* stresses that the three
patriarchs in particular are described as representing the "Divine chariot" on
which the *Shechinah* is majestically borne. But the righteous in general also
deserve the honorable title מֶרְכָּבָה לַשְּׁכִינָה (as *Rashi* points out) to the extent that
each of them brings to his fellowmen the revelation of one of the aspects of the
greatness of the supreme being (*Maharal*). The righteous are the supports and
heralds of the Divine Majesty on earth, just as the angels in the prophet
Ezekiel's vision (ch. 1) are the bearers of the Divine Chariot (מֶרְכָּבָה) in celestial
realms.

23. כַּאֲשֶׁר דִּבֶּר אִתּוֹ אֱלֹהִים — *As God had spoken with him.* Tradition tells us that
"Abraham fulfilled all the Torah before it was given" (*Kiddushin* 82a).
However, before carrying out the circumcision, he waited for a Divine order
stipulating this explicitly. For Abraham knew that "he who acts on a command
is more worthy than he who acts spontaneously, on his own" (*Kiddushin* 31a).
Therefore, Abraham was able to fulfill all the other *mitzvos* on his own
initiative, and still carry them out again, a second time, when God would
command it. All, except for circumcision.

Another view is offered by our Sages: Abraham did not want to perform the
circumcision before he was commanded to do so because he felt that, unbidden,
it would constitute mutilation of the body, a forbidden act (*R' Eliyahu
Mizrachi*).

24. בְּהִמֹּלוֹ בְּשַׂר עָרְלָתוֹ — *When he was circumcised on the flesh of his
surplusage.* In the next verse, referring to Ishmael, this phrase is repeated
exactly, save for the preposition אֵת, which is missing here. *Rashi* (quoting the
Midrash) explains that this is an indication that פְּרִיעָה was not required of
Abraham or, as Rav in the Talmud (*Yevamos* 71b) interprets, it was not
commanded of him. However, *Tosafos* add that in any case Abraham did the
פְּרִיעָה on his own (ibid. ד״ה לא). This initiative can be simply explained in the
light of our commentary on the previous verse. Abraham awaited the Divine
commandment before carrying out the circumcision. But once he had received
it, he hurried to carry it out in its entirety and he did the last part (the פְּרִיעָה) of

as God had spoken with him. [24] *Abraham was ninety-nine when he was circumcised on the flesh of his surplusage;* [25] *And his son Ishmael was thirteen years old when he was circumcised on the flesh of his surplusage.* [26] *On that very day was Abraham circumcised with Ishmael his son,* [27] *and all the people of his household, born in his household and purchased for money from a stranger, were circumcised with him.*

his own accord, just as he had already fulfilled the other *mitzvos* of the Torah since he knew all their details.

The benediction for the circumcision, לְהַכְנִיסוֹ בִּבְרִיתוֹ שֶׁל אַבְרָהָם אָבִינוּ, is said by the father between the מִילָה and the פְּרִיעָה. Hence it is an exception to the rule of עוֹבֵר לַעֲשִׂיָּתָן which stipulates that the *berachah* must precede the fulfillment of the *mitzvah*. This problem is considered by R' *Moshe Sofer* in his Addenda to *Yoreh Deah* No. 249. It may be, a more general interpretation, that the "covenant with Abraham" is only open to the child after מִילָה which is considered then as a preparation for the *mitzvah*. The existence of the בַּעַל בְּרִית begins only from that moment. Consequently, the *berachah* is directed at his future (cf. *Tosafos* on *Shabbos* 137b, ד״ה אבי) and this is stressed by the guests who reply to the father's benediction: "May the child enter to Torah, *mitzvos*, *chuppah*, and good deeds just as he has now been introduced into the covenant of Abraham." The true fulfillment of the covenant has only just commenced and so the *berachah* is to be taken as preceding the *mitzvah* (עוֹבֵר לַעֲשִׂיָּתָן).

25. וְיִשְׁמָעֵאל בְּנוֹ בֶּן־שְׁלֹשׁ עֶשְׂרֵה שָׁנָה — *And Ishmael, his son, was thirteen years old.* Cf. our commentary to 16:16.

26. בְּעֶצֶם הַיּוֹם הַזֶּה נִמּוֹל אַבְרָהָם — *On that very day was Abraham circumcised.* The phrase בְּעֶצֶם הַיּוֹם הַזֶּה will be repeated in the context of Yom Kippur (*Leviticus* 23:28). Accordingly, these two identical phrases are connected and the Midrash concludes: Abraham was circumcised on Yom Kippur. Each year, on this day, God recalls the blood of Abraham's circumcision and absolves us of our sins. The phrase כִּי־בַיּוֹם הַזֶּה יְכַפֵּר עֲלֵיכֶם, *for on this day He will absolve you* (*Leviticus* 16:30) re-echoes the expression בְּעֶצֶם הַיּוֹם הַזֶּה (*Pirkei D'Rabbi Eliezer* 29; cf. *Tosafos* on *Rosh Hashanah* 11b, ד״ה אלא).

27. וְכָל־אַנְשֵׁי בֵיתוֹ . . . וּמִקְנַת־כֶּסֶף — *And all the people of his household . . . and purchased for money.* The pagan who comes to convert willingly submits to being circumcised but remains attached to his origins until the seventh generation (cf. *Rashi* on *Exodus* 18:9). As for slaves who have been circumcised, one cannot count on them before the sixteenth generation (*Yerushalmi, Horayos* 3). Hence, the slaves who were circumcised with Abraham did not remain faithful to the Jewish people, neither they nor their descendants (*Pirkei D'Rabbi Eliezer* 29).

יח   א וַיֵּרָא אֵלָיו יהוה בְּאֵלֹנֵי מַמְרֵא וְהוּא יֹשֵׁב פֶּתַח־הָאֹהֶל
ב כְּחֹם הַיּוֹם: וַיִּשָּׂא עֵינָיו וַיַּרְא וְהִנֵּה שְׁלֹשָׁה אֲנָשִׁים נִצָּבִים
עָלָיו וַיַּרְא וַיָּרָץ לִקְרָאתָם מִפֶּתַח הָאֹהֶל וַיִּשְׁתַּחוּ אָרְצָה:

18.

1. וַיֵּרָא אֵלָיו ה' — *HASHEM appeared to him.* Abraham had just carried out the act of circumcision. He feared lest this sign of the covenant prove to be a barrier between him and others, condemning him to isolation. And so God appeared to him to make him understand that even if circumcision alienated him from men, it brought Abraham still closer to Him and made him worthy of "receiving a visit from God, Who came to inquire about his health" (*Rashi* and *Rabbah* 47).

But this new dignity meant increased responsibilities. By entering into the covenant, Abraham became "father of a multitude of nations," that is, invested with a moral responsibility like that of a father toward his children. As בְּנֵי בְּרִית, *children of the covenant,* the patriarch's descendants also have a moral responsibility toward the nations, as an older brother does toward his younger brothers. This is why the Torah calls them בְּנִי בְכוֹרִי, the *firstborn son* among the children of God.

No sooner has Abraham entered into the covenant than he is made aware of his "paternal" role. Indeed, the revelation, whose main object was to "visit the sick," solemnly announces the fate in store for the city of Sodom and its inhabitants (verse 20). Although circumcision now distinguishes him from his contemporaries, Abraham has to remain aware of the solidarity which continues to unite him with those of his generation. Their fate directly concerns him. He can no more remain indifferent to their destiny than a father can ignore the fate of his children. Later, the Sages will declare: "If you see a greatly troubled generation, go forth and examine (the acts of) the judges of the Jewish people, for all retribution that comes to the world comes only on account of the judges of the Jewish people" (*Shabbos* 139a).

וְהוּא יֹשֵׁב פֶּתַח־הָאֹהֶל — *While he was sitting at the entrance of the tent.* This is typical of Abraham: he was seated at the feet of his Master to receive the Divine teaching (likewise, the Jewish people remain seated while reciting שְׁמַע יִשְׂרָאֵל in prayer, to receive the Divine message addressed to them); seated at the entrance of Jewry's tent to welcome all those who wish to enter into the covenant; seated at the entrance of his home to offer hospitality to all strangers, whatever their religion; seated at the entry to Hell to bar the way to anyone bearing the sign of the covenant (*Rabbah* ibid.). At the exodus from Egypt, the blood of the covenant likewise appeared as a sign of protection on the lintels and doorposts of the Jewish homes (*Exodus* 12:23).

כְּחֹם הַיּוֹם — *In the heat of the day.* The charitable sun carries healing in its rays (*Malachi* 3:20). The text, adds *Ramban,* emphasizes these details in order to draw our attention to the fact that at that moment Abraham had no thought of readying himself for an act of prophecy. He was in no condition to devote

18   ¹Hashem appeared to him in the plains of Mamre while he
was sitting at the entrance of the tent in the heat of the
day. ² He lifted his eyes and saw: And behold! three men
were standing over him. He perceived, so he ran toward them
from the entrance of the tent, and bowed toward the ground.

himself to prayer or deep mystical contemplation. He was just recovering from
the effects of the circumcision and was looking for an opportunity to be hospitable. Yet, it was at this very moment that he received the Divine revelation.

This fact is of considerable significance for understanding the Jewish
concept of prophecy, and how it has been misconstrued! Some have wanted to
identify it with a state of exaltation or ecstasy or of trance and clairvoyance.
And even some Jewish philosophical doctrines, are they not imbued with the
idea that הִתְבּוֹדְדוּת as a method — physical and spiritual abstraction, isolation
of man and thought — leads to prophecy? But what a gulf there is between
such theories and true prophecy! It is not abstract contemplation but life itself,
suffused with devotion to God, which draws the Holy Spirit to itself. The Sages
have emphasized that prophecy is not the product of a morbid imagination, nor
of a state of excitement or supersensitiveness; the Divine spirit, they tell us,
dwells neither with a man in a depressed or sorrowful state nor with one in a
state of levity or frivolity, but only with the man who is experiencing the joy
of performing a *mitzvah* (*Shabbos* 30b). And whenever the Torah speaks of a
revelation to someone in a dream, the dream itself is then only the medium of
Divine communication and not the expression of a visionary or ecstatic state.
Here we see Abraham becoming a נָבִיא at a time of complete clarity of mind
(*R' S. R. Hirsch*).

2. וַיַּרְא וְהִנֵּה שְׁלֹשָׁה אֲנָשִׁים — *And saw and behold! three men. Rashi* explains:
"One to announce the good news concerning Sarah (Michael), the second to
overthrow Sodom (Gabriel) and the third to heal Abraham (Rafael)." But if
"one messenger does not carry out two missions," as *Rashi* tells us, then why
did the angel Michael also go to save Lot? *R' Bachya* answers that it was
because the same principle of love was involved in both missions and so one
angel was authorized to carry out both. But he cannot do so when the missions
involve two opposite principles, such as strict punishment and mercy. For the
"peace which reigns in the celestial heights" (*Job* 25:2) is built on a hierarchical
order governing the assignment of the functions of each factor of creation.

נִצָּבִים עָלָיו וַיַּרְא וַיָּרָץ לִקְרָאתָם — *Standing over him. He perceived, so he ran
toward them.* If they were standing near him, then how can one explain that
"he ran toward them"? And why is the word וַיַּרְא, *he perceived*, stated twice in
this verse?

These peculiarities, replies the author of the ס' שלַ"ה, reveal the doubt
prevailing in Abraham's heart. Were these three Arab travelers or were they
angels in human guise, as their bearing led him to believe? Abraham saw three

ג וַיֹּאמַר אֲדֹנָי אִם־נָא מָצָאתִי חֵן בְּעֵינֶיךָ אַל־נָא תַעֲבֹר
ד מֵעַל עַבְדֶּךָ: יֻקַּח־נָא מְעַט־מַיִם וְרַחֲצוּ רַגְלֵיכֶם וְהִשָּׁעֲנוּ
ה תַּחַת הָעֵץ: וְאֶקְחָה פַת־לֶחֶם וְסַעֲדוּ לִבְּכֶם אַחַר
תַּעֲבֹרוּ כִּי־עַל־כֵּן עֲבַרְתֶּם עַל־עַבְדְּכֶם וַיֹּאמְרוּ כֵּן
ו תַּעֲשֶׂה כַּאֲשֶׁר דִּבַּרְתָּ: וַיְמַהֵר אַבְרָהָם הָאֹהֱלָה אֶל־שָׂרָה
וַיֹּאמֶר מַהֲרִי שְׁלֹשׁ סְאִים קֶמַח סֹלֶת לוּשִׁי וַעֲשִׂי עֻגוֹת:
ז וְאֶל־הַבָּקָר רָץ אַבְרָהָם וַיִּקַּח בֶּן־בָּקָר רַךְ וָטוֹב וַיִּתֵּן

strangers and wanted to run to meet them, but he glimpsed in them superior beings, עָלָיו, superior to his human level. He let this uncertainty determine his conduct toward the three men. On the one hand he made them wash their feet, thinking they were Arabs who worship the dust of their feet, for he took care not to allow anything connected with idolatry to enter his house. He had a fine meal prepared for them in order to refresh themselves. But, on the other hand, he "prostrated himself on the ground" before them, thus giving them the honor due Divine messengers. And in addressing them, or the greatest of the three, he ambiguously used the name אד׳, having either the secular meaning of "sirs" or the religious meaning of "God." The meal which he offered had, then, the significance of a sacrifice offered in homage to God. (In the choice of cattle, etc., it foreshadows the future sacrificial worship; cf. *Rashi* on *Numbers* 7:21.)

3. וַיֹּאמַר אֲדֹנָי — *And he said, "My Lord."* Rashi cites the two opinions given in the Talmud (*Shevuos* 35b) concerning the real meaning of the word אד׳, for this word can be taken either in a sacred or a profane sense. The fact that the Masoretes punctuated this name with a *kamatz* seems to prove, adds R' Bachya ibn Pakuda, that they understood it to refer to God. For nouns formed with the *kamatz* indicate the absolute state whereas those with the *patach* are in the construct. Consequently, the word אד׳ written with a *kamatz* designates God, but when formed with a *patach* it refers to men. R' Bachya concludes: it is therefore of the utmost importance not to confuse these two vowels, not only in writing but also in pronunciation, where the difference must also be distinctly noticeable. (This remark is an argument in favor of the pronunciation of the Ashkenazim.)

אַל־נָא תַעֲבֹר מֵעַל עַבְדֶּךָ — *Please pass not away from Your servant.* This is addressed to God, Whom Abraham asks to wait so that he can go and attend to the strangers (*Rashi*). R' Yehudah teaches: from this we conclude that hospitality to wayfarers is greater than welcoming the presence of the *Shechinah* (*Shabbos* 127a). Here, immediately following the covenant with Abraham, the Torah shows us that the first duty of the Jew is that of being hospitable to every person, whatever his origin. And the purely humane duty to be good, charitable, and gracious comes before the religious duty to welcome the *Shechinah* and carry out the Divine service.

³ *And he said, "My Lord, if I find favor in Your eyes, please pass not away from Your servant."*

⁴ *"Let some water be brought and wash your feet, and recline beneath the tree.* ⁵ *I will fetch a morsel of bread that you may sustain yourselves, then go on — inasmuch as you have passed your servant's way." They said, "Do so, just as you have said."*

⁶ *So Abraham hastened to the tent to Sarah and said, "Hurry! Three se'ahs of meal, fine flour! Knead and make cakes!"* ⁷ *Then Abraham ran to the cattle, took a calf, tender and good, and gave*

5. וְאֶקְחָה פַת-לֶחֶם — *I will fetch a morsel of bread.* The feast prepared by Abraham has a three-fold significance. First, it is the expression of love for others — a trait characteristic of the patriarch. However, as *Rashi* points out further on, Abraham thought of this charitable act as a chance to bring the men to love God: "After his guests had eaten and drunk, Abraham would say to them: 'Bless Him of Whose food you have partaken. You think that you have eaten my food. Not so; it belongs to the One Who, by His word, created the world'" (21:33). Furthermore, the feast took the place of a sacrifice offering in thanksgiving to God. Abraham had not yet shown his gratefulness for the gift of the covenant and the Divine promises of such worth. He considered the arrival of the heavenly messengers to be the providential opportunity to present his offering in the form of a sacrifice. This is what he means by his statement here, "since (to give me the opportunity of a holy offering) you have come by your servant." And the banquet which the patriarch offers to the angels is a prefiguration of the "feast of the righteous" to be held in the messianic era. It is a preview of the ideal repast with the righteous seated at the table, surrounded by archangels, in an atmosphere of serene holiness in honor of God.

This three-fold significance brings out the value of the סְעוּדַת מִצְוָה, the feast dedicated to a *mitzvah.* At such a meal, the food itself is elevated to sanctity, because of the *mitzvah* which attends the feast and also because of the words of Torah which accompany it. (The text alludes to these Torah discussions when it says, וְהִשָּׁעֲנוּ תַּחַת הָעֵץ, *recline beneath the tree;* here the tree recalls to mind the tree of life, designated as the Torah in *Proverbs* 3:18; *Mechilta* on *Exodus* 15:25.)

אַחַר תַּעֲבֹרוּ — *Then go on.* אַחַר תַּעֲבֹרוּ instead of וְתַעֲבֹרוּ, a simpler form which would have sufficed to express the thought. This is an example of the importance the Torah gives to stylistic perfection, as the Talmud points out in *Nedarim* 37b (עִטוּר סוֹפְרִים, Scriptural embellishments, according to *Rabbeinu Nissim*).

7. וְאֶל-הַבָּקָר רָץ אַבְרָהָם — *Then Abraham ran to the cattle.* The interpretation of the whole of this narrative gives rise to a vigorous controversy between *Rambam* and *Ramban.* The former maintains that Abraham had a prophetic vision, as indicated in the first verse of the chapter. The description of the angels' visit, the patriarch's welcome, his eagerness and hospitality, as well as the

ח אֶל־הַנַּעַר וַיְמַהֵר לַעֲשׂוֹת אֹתוֹ: וַיִּקַּח חֶמְאָה וְחָלָב
וּבֶן־הַבָּקָר אֲשֶׁר עָשָׂה וַיִּתֵּן לִפְנֵיהֶם וְהוּא עֹמֵד עֲלֵיהֶם
ט תַּחַת הָעֵץ וַיֹּאכֵלוּ: וַיֹּאמְרוּ אֵלָיו אַיֵּה שָׂרָה אִשְׁתֶּךָ וַיֹּאמֶר
י הִנֵּה בָאֹהֶל: וַיֹּאמֶר שׁוֹב אָשׁוּב אֵלֶיךָ כָּעֵת חַיָּה וְהִנֵּה־
בֵן לְשָׂרָה אִשְׁתֶּךָ וְשָׂרָה שֹׁמַעַת פֶּתַח הָאֹהֶל וְהוּא
יא אַחֲרָיו: וְאַבְרָהָם וְשָׂרָה זְקֵנִים בָּאִים בַּיָּמִים חָדַל לִהְיוֹת
יב לְשָׂרָה אֹרַח כַּנָּשִׁים: וַתִּצְחַק שָׂרָה בְּקִרְבָּהּ לֵאמֹר אַחֲרֵי
יג בְלֹתִי הָיְתָה־לִּי עֶדְנָה וַאדֹנִי זָקֵן: וַיֹּאמֶר יהוה אֶל־אַבְרָהָם
לָמָּה זֶּה צָחֲקָה שָׂרָה לֵאמֹר הַאַף אֻמְנָם אֵלֵד וַאֲנִי זָקַנְתִּי:
יד הֲיִפָּלֵא מֵיהוה דָּבָר לַמּוֹעֵד אָשׁוּב אֵלֶיךָ כָּעֵת חַיָּה וּלְשָׂרָה

announcement to Sarah, did not really occur but represent the details of this vision (*Guide* 2:42). But *Ramban* holds that this is a case of personified angels, visible only to pure, pious, and inspired men. And so, the facts related here are to be taken literally. When the Torah in other contexts mentions that angels appear or speak to a human being, this is not ascribable to a prophetic state but to an *ad hoc* revelation or a dream. Although *Ramban* gives numerous arguments and examples in defense of his thesis, *Rambam's* view is upheld by such thinkers as *Abarbanel* and *R' Yomtov ben Avraham* (*Ritva*).

אֶל־הַבָּקָר — *To the cattle.* The calf had fled and had stopped at the mouth of the cave of Machpelah. Abraham ran in pursuit and caught up with it. He marveled at the cave where the first human couple, Adam and Eve, lay buried. He then felt a desire to be buried one day at their side (*Pirkei D'Rabbi Eliezer* 36). But the owners of the field were completely unaware of this cave (*Ramban on* 23:9). Several hours after discovering his future burial place, Abraham received the news of the son to be born to him through his wife Sarah. To Abraham this must have seemed a new sign of favor from Providence. (The Midrash dwells upon the similarity of the words בָּקָר and קֶבֶר.)

10. וַיֹּאמֶר שׁוֹב אָשׁוּב אֵלֶיךָ — *And he said, ''I will surely return to you.''* Up to this point Abraham did not know whether his guests were wayfarers or angels. It was the announcement of the birth of Isaac that revealed the Divine Presence to him. Indeed, the *Zohar* observes that none other than God could guarantee Sarah a son ''since the key of birth, especially in the case of a barren woman, rests in the hands of God' (*Taanis* 2a). And so it was the Divine voice which announced שׁוֹב אָשׁוּב, *I will surely return* (as the use of the first person singular indicates). The word וַיֹּאמֶר, without any indication of the subject, also generally refers to God. Similarly, He is the implied subject of the sentences וְהוּא עֹמֵד עֲלֵיהֶם תַּחַת הָעֵץ and וְהוּא אַחֲרָיו. The Divine Presence hovered invisibly over the entire scene announcing the miraculous birth of the son of Abraham and Sarah.

שׁוֹב אָשׁוּב — *I will surely return.* The term שׁוֹב אָשׁוּב means, I will return ''to remember Sarah'' (as will be recorded in 21:1) and I will return to give life a

it to the youth who hurried to prepare it. ⁸ *He took cream and milk and the calf which he had prepared, and placed these before them; he stood over them beneath the tree and they ate.*

⁹ *They said to him, "Where is Sarah your wife?" And he said, "Behold! — in the tent!"*

¹⁰ *And he said, "I will surely return to you at this time next year, and behold Sarah your wife will have a son." Now Sarah was listening at the entrance of the tent which was behind him.*

¹¹ *Now Abraham and Sarah were old, well on in years; the manner of women had ceased to be with Sarah —*

¹² *And Sarah laughed at herself, saying, "After I have withered shall I again have delicate skin? And my husband is old!"*

¹³ *Then HASHEM said to Abraham, "Why is it that Sarah laughed, saying: 'Shall I in truth bear a child, though I have aged?'* ¹⁴ *— Is anything beyond HASHEM?! At the appointed time I will return to you at this time next year, and Sarah will have*

second time to Isaac at the time of his sacrifice, when his soul will be on the point of leaving him (*Pirkei D'Rabbi Eliezer* 31).

12. וַתִּצְחַק שָׂרָה בְּקִרְבָּהּ — *And Sarah laughed at herself.* "There is nothing astonishing in Sarah's behavior. She cannot bring herself to believe something so improbable and smiles skeptically when her husband confirms that she will be a mother at a very advanced age. She does not suspect that this smile will accompany her descendants throughout their history, nor that the world will shrug its shoulders when the Jewish nation has pretensions of living contrary to all human experience. People will always have the same interest in the Jewish people that they have in a curiosity of nature. Our existence will disturb men, we will have the courage and insolence to survive persecutions without number, to sustain ourselves, although weakened, long after our formidable enemies have disappeared. Since Isaac we live contrary to historic and natural 'laws,' for ever since our beginning we have been sustained and supported by the task to which the Divine will has called us" (*R' S. R. Hirsch*).

13. לָמָּה זֶּה צָחֲקָה שָׂרָה — *Why is it that Sarah laughed?* According to the usual translation of 17:17 (since the root צחק appears there too), Abraham also laughed when he heard the news of the birth of a son to Sarah and yet he did not suffer Divine reproach for doing so. The present translation, following *Onkelos* and *Ramban*, explains this difference by taking Abraham's laughter as a laughter of gladness and Sarah's as one of ridicule. But the *Midrash HaGadol* explains: "When two people, one a great personage, the other insignificant, have acted wrongly, the lesser is blamed and the greater understands by himself."

14. לְמוֹעֵד אָשׁוּב — *At the appointed time I will return.* Cf. *Rashi* on 21:2: He made a mark on the wall and said to him: "When the sun comes around to

שני   טו בֶּן: וַתְּכַחֵשׁ שָׂרָה ׀ לֵאמֹר לֹא צָחַקְתִּי כִּי ׀ יָרֵאָה וַיֹּאמֶר ׀ לֹא
טז כִּי צָחָקְתְּ: וַיָּקֻמוּ מִשָּׁם הָאֲנָשִׁים וַיַּשְׁקִפוּ עַל־פְּנֵי סְדֹם
יז וְאַבְרָהָם הֹלֵךְ עִמָּם לְשַׁלְּחָם: וַיהֹוָה אָמָר הַמֲכַסֶּה אֲנִי
יח מֵאַבְרָהָם אֲשֶׁר אֲנִי עֹשֶׂה: וְאַבְרָהָם הָיוֹ יִהְיֶה לְגוֹי גָּדוֹל
יט וְעָצוּם וְנִבְרְכוּ־בוֹ כֹּל גּוֹיֵי הָאָרֶץ: כִּי יְדַעְתִּיו לְמַעַן אֲשֶׁר יְצַוֶּה

this mark next year, Sarah will give birth." As *Rashi* points out on verse 10, the
announcement took place on Passover and Isaac was born the following
Passover. Sarah conceived on Rosh Hashanah [as we are reminded by the
reading of the episode וה' פָּקַד אֶת־שָׂרָה (*Genesis* 21) on this festival] and some
of our Sages hold that the year had an extra month, so that Isaac came into the
world after Sarah's seventh month of pregnancy. The discussion is reported in
the Talmud (*Rosh Hashanah* 11a).

וּלְשָׂרָה בֵן — *And Sarah will have a son.* The promise of a son was given
following an act of hospitality performed with love and generosity. Let all
childless couples who want to see their wish fulfilled do as Abraham and Sarah
did, and pay particular attention to the *mitzvah* of hospitality (של"ה).

15. וַתְּכַחֵשׁ שָׂרָה . . . כִּי יָרֵאָה — *Sarah denied it . . . for she was frightened.* But
later, at Isaac's birth, she explained what she meant: "What God has done to me
will make people laugh. Whoever hears it will laugh for me" (see 21:6).

16. וַיָּקֻמוּ מִשָּׁם הָאֲנָשִׁים — *So the men got up from there.* They rose up and with
the hospitality "from there" still fresh in their minds they headed for Sodom to
save the nephew of so virtuous and charitable a man. For *And so it was when
God destroyed the cities of the plain that God remembered Abraham; so He
sent Lot from amidst the upheaval when He overturned . . .* (19:29).

וַיַּשְׁקִפוּ — *And gazed down.* The verb הִשְׁקִיף, says *Rashi*, always indicates an evil
intention. There is just one exception: *Look out from your holy habitation*
(*Deuteronomy* 26:15). However, the *Zohar* considers the expression וַיַּשְׁקִפוּ in
our verse to be comparable to the exception. Here it means a look of pity,
motivated by the kindnesses which they had just received from Lot's uncle
Abraham. When God is about to punish a population, He first provides an
opportunity for those He loves to acquire merit, to do an act of kindness. Thus,
the plague on Sodom was preceded by the visit of the poor strangers to
Abraham's house, and subsequently to Lot's. Both the uncle and his nephew
offered them hospitality, and when the angel of destruction swooped down on
Sodom he saw the sign of the *mitzvah* in Lot. He gave him a "benevolent look"
and saved him from misfortune.

לְשַׁלְּחָם — *To escort them.* "He thought they were ordinary travelers." In
contrast to this explanation of *Rashi's*, the *Zohar* notes in the name of R' Elazar:
He knew they were angels, but he acted toward them as he did with all his
guests. Accompanying guests is indeed an important part of the duty of

a son."

¹⁵ *Sarah denied it, saying, "I did not laugh," for she was frightened. But he said, "No, you laughed indeed."*

¹⁶ *So the men got up from there, and gazed down toward Sodom, while Abraham walked with them to escort them.*

¹⁷ *And HASHEM said, "Shall I conceal from Abraham what I do,* ¹⁸ *now that Abraham is surely to become a great and mighty nation, and all the nations of the earth shall bless themselves by him?* ¹⁹ *For I have loved him, because he commands*

hospitality. When Abraham accompanied his guests, God, surrounded by the celestial tribunal, lingered with this righteous person, revealed His plans to him and granted him His protection en route. This *mitzvah* is such that the one who performs it retains the *Shechinah* with him on his way.

17. הַמְכַסֶּה אֲנִי מֵאַבְרָהָם אֲשֶׁר אֲנִי עֹשֶׂה — *Shall I conceal from Abraham what I do. Rashi* cites R' Yehudah's explanation: "It is not proper that I should do what I am about to do to Sodom without his knowledge. Can I destroy the children without telling the father, My beloved, to whom I have given all this land and the five cities concerned?" However, R' Levi mentions a different reason. Abraham was deeply perplexed about the generation of the Flood. He thought it impossible that there were not ten or twenty righteous people whose merit could have saved them. Accordingly, God intended to inform him that the region of Sodom did not have ten righteous people. Job had the same preoccupation as Abraham with the problem of theodicy, but he made a hasty judgment when he declared, *It is all the same; therefore I say He will cause the innocent and the wicked to perish* (9:22). As for Abraham, he weighed his words more carefully: *Will You also stamp out the righteous along with the wicked?*

Moreover, God wants Abraham to know and to teach his descendants that great catastrophes are due to acts of providential justice, which is always vigilant and cannot be defied with impunity. For fifty-two years Providence had vainly waited for the inhabitants of Sodom to return to their moral duty (*Tanchuma*).

18. וְאַבְרָהָם הָיוֹ יִהְיֶה — *Now that Abraham is surely to become. Rashi:* The Midrash here applies its principle: the memory of a righteous person is a blessing (זֵכֶר צַדִּיק לִבְרָכָה; *Proverbs* 10:7). The moment He mentions him, He blesses him." However, one might object: given that Abraham's intervention was fruitless, why does the Torah mention it so prominently and what is the point of saying, particularly at this point in the text, that the memory of a righteous man is to be blessed? It is because Abraham showed for all generations how a man must intercede on behalf of his proscribed brothers: by proclaiming the principle that a minority of righteous people can redeem the sins of the majority. Thus, what endures of the "memory of the righteous" is the blessing

אֶת־בָּנָיו וְאֶת־בֵּיתוֹ אַחֲרָיו וְשָׁמְרוּ דֶּרֶךְ יהוה לַעֲשׂוֹת צְדָקָה
וּמִשְׁפָּט לְמַעַן הָבִיא יהוה עַל־אַבְרָהָם אֵת אֲשֶׁר־דִּבֶּר עָלָיו:
כ וַיֹּאמֶר יהוה זַעֲקַת סְדֹם וַעֲמֹרָה כִּי־רָבָּה וְחַטָּאתָם כִּי כָבְדָה

that his plea brings to future generations, when Abraham will have become "a great and powerful nation."

19. כִּי יְדַעְתִּיו — *For I have loved him* [lit. *I know him*]. "One who loves another brings him near in order to know him better. And why is God fond of him? Because *he commands his children . . . that they keep the way of* HASHEM" (*Rashi*).

The knowledge of God and His Law was kept in Abraham's time by certain people such as Shem, the son of Noah, and his great-grandson Eber, who had the gift of prophecy (cf. *Rashi* on 10:25). They taught their knowledge and traditions in the *beis hamidrash* which bore their names. But they did not have the persuasive power to convince their contemporaries and to cause the Divine light to shine upon humanity. Only Abraham attained the role of an apostle of truth whose influence on the minds of others was strong enough to leave a definite imprint on their lives. Hence the Torah emphasizes the patriarch's accomplishments in his mission as teacher, starting with his own children and family, to be deserving of the love which God lavished upon him. This mission, which begins in the family home and thenceforth spreads in ever-widening circles to men of all extractions, appears here as being, *sub specie aeternitatis*, the foundation of Judaism.

This verse is the source of the duty of the father to educate his children in "the ways of God." This duty includes educating the daughters as well as the sons (אֶת־בָּנָיו וְאֶת־בֵּיתוֹ). On the other hand the duty of teaching Torah stipulated in *Deuteronomy* 11:19 applies only to teaching the sons (*Meshech Chochmah*).

לַעֲשׂוֹת צְדָקָה וּמִשְׁפָּט — *Doing charity and justice.* The children are to "Keep the way of HASHEM," consistent with the order Abraham previously received: *Walk before Me and be perfect* (17:1). To accomplish this goal God gave His people the *milah*, the eternal symbol of the duty to live a life of moral purity. This *mitzvah* is one of the חֻקִּים, the laws which tend to purify and sanctify our physical life: מִצְוֹת שֶׁבֵּין אָדָם לַמָּקוֹם. The first Divine commandment to Abraham was followed by a second which, this time, includes practicing love and justice. It is in the domain of מִצְוֹת שֶׁבֵּין אָדָם לַחֲבֵרוֹ. This order of succession has remained characteristic of Judaic legislation.

Every human being has the right to מִשְׁפָּט, that is, to just treatment from his fellowman. צְדָקָה, which signifies love of others and charity, is not included among legal rights, but it can be solicited in the name of God, as it is God Who teaches us this virtue. Thus, the Jewish concept differs from the practice of haughtily giving alms as a gesture of charity to the poor who receive in humility. *Tzedakah* is rather an obligation whose benefits go back to the poor

his children and his household after him that they keep the way
of HASHEM, doing charity and justice, in order that HASHEM might
then bring upon Abraham that which He had spoken of him."
²⁰ *So HASHEM said, "Because the outcry of Sodom and Gomorrah*
has become great, and because their sin has been very grave,

in the name of God and whose acceptance by them in no way carries with it any humiliation.

(Contrary to the rule, here the term צְדָקָה precedes מִשְׁפָּט. The latter usually comes first, for the practice of justice must be assured in all circumstances, independent of the religious duty of charity. To be charitable and yet dishonest would be in fact a hypocritical and reprehensible attitude. But the Torah probably wishes to bring out the contrast between the moral Jewish concept, which raises צְדָקָה to the level of a religious duty, and the depraved morality of Sodom, where the practice of love and charity was branded a criminal act.)

The great testament which Abraham leaves to his descendants is summed up in these words: וְשָׁמְרוּ דֶּרֶךְ ה' לַעֲשׂוֹת צְדָקָה וּמִשְׁפָּט. The text does not say וַיַּעֲשׂוּ but לַעֲשׂוֹת. This means that these imperatives cannot be separated, but are interdependent. Love and justice can only be accomplished by following "God's way." For He is not only the Master of our destinies, but also the exclusive source of our knowledge of law and ethics (*R' S. R. Hirsch*).

20. וַיֹּאמֶר ה' — *So HASHEM said*. Whenever the Torah mentions Divine speech in this chapter, the name הֲוָיָ', which refers to the attribute of love (מִדַּת הָרַחֲמִים) is used. But each time Abraham speaks to God, he invokes the name אד', referring to מִדַּת הַדִּין, the principle of justice. Abraham considers that God is judging the inhabitants of Sodom according to the rigorous criteria of justice — but he is answered that the judgment is passed taking into account the imperatives of love.

זַעֲקַת סְדֹם וַעֲמֹרָה כִּי־רָבָּה — *Because the outcry of Sodom and Gomorrah has become great*. The word רַבָּה is an allusion to רִיבָה, *a young woman*; the cry of a young woman tortured to death for having given food to a poor man (*Sanhedrin* 109b). It is said that she was a daughter of Lot (*Pirkei D'Rabbi Eliezer* 25).

It is characteristic that the crimes blamed on Sodom are above all in the social and moral realms (*R' Bachya*). "This was the crime of Sodom," proclaims the prophet Ezekiel: "The pride of having an abundance of food and comfort and security was hers and her daughters', and she did not strengthen the hand of the poor and the needy. They were haughty, they committed abominations before Me, and I suppressed them when I saw it" (16:49-50). Tradition tells us that the inhabitants of Sodom practiced xenophobia to such an extent that even people of that time, who themselves were little aware of humanitarian principles, were frightened of them. Their moral perversion is seen in their words to the two strangers [the phrase "so that we may know (can become intimate with) them,"

כא מְאֹד: אֵרֲדָה־נָּא וְאֶרְאֶ֔ה הַכְּצַעֲקָתָ֛הּ הַבָּ֥אָה אֵלַ֖י עָשׂ֣וּ ׀ כָּלָ֑ה
כב וְאִם־לֹ֖א אֵדָֽעָה: וַיִּפְנ֤וּ מִשָּׁם֙ הָֽאֲנָשִׁ֔ים וַיֵּלְכ֖וּ סְדֹ֑מָה וְאַ֨בְרָהָ֔ם
כג עוֹדֶ֥נּוּ עֹמֵ֖ד לִפְנֵ֥י יְהוָֽה: וַיִּגַּ֥שׁ אַבְרָהָ֖ם וַיֹּאמַ֑ר הַאַ֣ף תִּסְפֶּ֔ה

19:5, is a euphemism with a very precise meaning]. Moreover, all classes of the
population of Sodom had become corrupt, young and old, everyone everywhere.
It is probably this seemingly unfathomable extension of the crime, the
participation of all the inhabitants in the outrage against morals, which
condemned them to so terrifying a fate.

The Midrash relates the two words רַבָּה, one used here, the other concerning
the deluge (6:5), and concludes that the inhabitants of Sodom relapsed into crime
and committed the same sins as those of the generation of the Flood. The latter
were punished by a flood of water, the former by a deluge of fire. The people
at the time of the Flood used to follow the merchants' wagons filled with lupines
and each would take less than a *pruta's* worth, so that by the time the wagon
left the city it was empty. But the people could not be prosecuted, for the *pruta*
was the smallest coin in use and when less than a *pruta's* worth was stolen the
victim had no redress (*Rabbah* 31). This jealous greed, devoid of all feelings of
generosity, is branded with infamy in the *Ethics of the Fathers:* "What is mine
is mine, what is yours is yours — this is the characteristic of Sodom" (5:13).

21. אֵרֲדָה־נָּא וְאֶרְאֶה — *I will descend and see.* See our commentary to 11:5. R'
Shimon bar Yochai used to say, "This is one of ten Divine descents mentioned
in the Torah." R' Abba adds, "This proves that God gave them the opportunity
of repenting" (*Rabbah* 49). When men become prisoners of their passions to the
extent that they no longer find the strength or the will to uplift themselves
morally, God offers them His help, He "goes down to them" and thus opens the
gate of repentance to them. Some remain indifferent but others then feel in the
depths of their souls that they are drawn toward good, as did Lot and his
daughters, and the spark of love for God is once again kindled in their hearts.
This experience is renewed each year during the "ten days of repentance" when
God draws near to man and "lets Himself be found by all who search for Him."

וְאִם־לֹא אֵדָעָה — *And if not, I will know.* This phrase leaves the final decision open
and gives Abraham the opportunity to intercede on behalf of the condemned
population. Similarly, God addresses Moses after the sin of the Golden Calf in
a way which, as *Rashi* explains it, "opens a door and makes him see that the
outcome depends upon him. If he will pray for them, He will not destroy them"
(*Exodus* 23:10). It appears once again that the moral responsibility for the whole
generation devolves upon the righteous one who inspires his era.

22. וְאַבְרָהָם עוֹדֶנּוּ עֹמֵד לִפְנֵי ה' — *While Abraham was still standing before
HASHEM.* Although the men had advanced toward Sodom to destroy it, Abraham
remained standing before God to beg for mercy. "Even when the sharp sword
rests upon a man's neck, he should not despair of Divine mercy" (*Berachos* 10a).

²¹ *I will descend and see: If they act in accordance with its outcry*
— then destruction! And if not, I will know."
²² *The men had turned from there and went to Sodom, while*
Abraham was still standing before HASHEM.
²³ *Abraham came forward and said, "Will You also stamp out*

Rashi observes that the text should have said, "HASHEM stood yet before
Abraham," for it was God Who had come toward him to say, 'The outcry of
Sodom has become great." This is indeed "a correction of the Scribes." This
passage which Rashi quoted from the Midrash is explained by Rashba (R'
Shlomo ben Adereth) who says that this is not really a correction, but a
paraphrase of the text aimed at avoiding the disrespectful form, "HASHEM stood
yet before Abraham" (quoted by Halichos Olam and R' Eliyahu Mizrachi).

23. וַיִּגַּשׁ אַבְרָהָם וַיֹּאמַר — *Abraham came forward and said.* What thought
prompted Abraham's course of action? He was aware that Noah had remained
silent and asked nothing of God when it was announced to him that, "The end
of all flesh has come before Me." And so, when God announced His intention
of destroying the sinful cities, Abraham interceded at once. R' Elazar adds,
"Abraham's intervention was also imperfect, for he prayed only that the
righteous not perish with the guilty. But Moses' supplication reached perfection,
for when God made known His will to destroy the Jewish people following the
sin of the Golden Calf, Moses prayed for forgiveness on behalf of everyone,
including the guilty, and desisted only when he had obtained a general pardon;
and he did so at the risk of destroying himself: *If not, blot me out of Your book*
which You have written (Exodus 32:32; Zohar).

Rashi adds: "We find the term הַגָּשָׁה used for battle, appeasement, and prayer.
Abraham drew near for all three purposes. He spoke harshly, he sought conciliation, and later on he will resort to prayer." This example of harsh discussion
with God in the attempt to save human life was subsequently followed by all
truly righteous men — Isaac, Moses, David and, more recently, by the great
tzaddikim, the spiritual leaders of the Chassidim. The entire scene which unfolds
in this passage shows us that God, Whose judgments are judgments of absolute
justice, wishes to rally men to help and care for their fellowmen.

הַאַף תִּסְפֶּה צַדִּיק עִם־רָשָׁע — *Will You also stamp out the righteous along with the*
wicked? The presence of the perverted and debauched Sodomites, who
nevertheless lived in luxury in a rich paradisical setting, was a standing challenge
directed at the patriarch, who was preaching obedience to God, goodness,
morality and virtue in a spirit of absolute disinterestedness. However, when the
catastrophe hovering over Sodom becomes imminent, Abraham pleads for the
safety of her inhabitants. For his ultimate moral objective is not the suppression
of sinners but the abolition of sin. *Let sins disappear from the earth and the*
wicked be no more (Psalms 104:35): יִתַּמּוּ חַטָּאִים וְלֹא חוֹטְאִים — let the sins
disappear, not those who commit them (Berachos 10a).

כד צַדִּיק עִם־רָשָׁע: אוּלַי יֵשׁ חֲמִשִּׁים צַדִּיקִם בְּתוֹךְ הָעִיר הַאַף
רִשֶׁא מִקִּידְצַה מִשְׁמֵחַ וְעָמֵל סוּקְמָל אַשְׁתְּ־אֹלֵן הִפֶּסְתְּ
כה ־סֵע קִידְצַ תִּימֵהָל הִזֶה רִבְדֵבּ ׀ תִּשְׁעָמֶ וְרֹל הַלָּלֵח :הִבְּרְקֹבּ
אֵל יֹרְאֶהָ־לֵבּ טִפֶּשֵׁה וְרֹל הַלָּלֵח עַשְׁרְבֵּ קִידְצַבּ הִיֵהֹן עֲשָׁר

24. אוּלַי יֵשׁ חֲמִשִּׁים צַדִּיקִם — *What if there should be fifty righteous people?*
Rashi explains, "Ten righteous in each city, as there were five cities." But, in the
face of God's negative reply, Abraham continues to implore for the salvation
of four cities which could be saved by forty righteous, three cities by thirty, two
by twenty, and one by ten. But once the principle that a city could be saved by
the presence of ten righteous men was admitted, why did Abraham have to
recommence his plea each time? *Ramban* replies, "Because he thought that the
presence of a greater number of righteous had more weight than a lesser
number" (cf. *Rashi* on *Leviticus* 26:8). And so, God assured him that the
presence of ten righteous had the same effect as that of fifty. (According to
Ramban, the patriarch always asks pardon for all five cities, contrary to *Rashi's*
opinion.)

25. חָלִלָה לְּךְ — *It would be a sacrilege to You. Rashi* explains, "If You say the
righteous will not save the wicked, why then would You kill the righteous?"
Abraham's exclamation in this verse, "Will the Judge of all the world not do
justice?" shows us his perplexity in the face of Divine justice. The sentence has
a rather rhetorical nature, for Abraham does not doubt, but wishes to
understand why the righteous must share the fate of the wicked. Abraham does
not know that the city has no righteous people, but God confirms to him what
he seems to admit as being obvious — namely, that the city would be saved if
any righteous lived there. This criterion of justice is so important that Scripture
reproduces the entire dialogue, in the course of which it is proclaimed in several
places. It represents, in effect, the counterpart of the fundamental law of
collective responsibility (cf. *Rashi* on 21:6).

Every organized society is governed by this absolute rule, whose primary
source goes back to the Bible and the Talmud (*Deuteronomy* 29:28; *Sanhedrin*
43b). Men are interdependent as much for good as for evil, as much in good
fortune as in misfortune. Just as each individual must subordinate his personal
welfare to the common good, so is he responsible, to the extent of his influence,
for the moral state of the society. This burden grows in proportion to the degree
of his personal power and, as a consequence, it renders the nation responsible
for the moral and social level of the citizens, as well as for unprosecuted offenses
and crimes perpetrated on its territory.

But, conversely, the individual is also supported by the society with respect
to its material and moral benefits. Indeed, he profits from its material
advantages, not because of a charitable action, but as a result of the legitimate right of social welfare, based on the law of joint responsibility. As for
the moral benefit due to the society, the principle is openly proclaimed for

the righteous along with the wicked? ²⁴ *What if there should
be fifty righteous people in the midst of the city? Would You
still stamp it out rather than spare the place for the sake of
the fifty righteous people within it?* ²⁵ *It would be sacrilege
to You to do such a thing, to bring death upon the righteous
along with the wicked; so the righteous will be like the wicked.
It would be sacrilege to You! Shall the Judge of all the earth not*

the first time in the course of our passage relating to the destruction of the
city of Sodom.

Who can say how many collective punishments have been earned but never
took place in the course of history, owing to the presence of men of
righteousness and integrity living within the society?

The idea that "God pardons the entire country because of the just" will be
developed to its ultimate limit. It will show all of society as "a group of over-
lapping joint responsibilities" which extends its circle ever wider to the nations
and, similarly, to succeeding generations. Thus it will create the notion of the
responsibility of parents in its twofold aspect: the "transgression of fathers" and
the "merit of fathers." This brief outline shows us that the law of collective
responsibility raises the community to a very high level of moral discipline.

חָלִלָה לָּךְ — *It would be sacrilege to You.* The repetition of this exclamation in
the same sentence shows us how worried Abraham was by חִלּוּל הַשֵּׁם,
profanation of the Divine name which the judgment of Sodom might provoke.
The second time, the words חָלִלָה לָּךְ refer to the World to Come, according to
Rashi. Maharal explains: this indicates that in Abraham's eyes the compensat-
ing justice of the World to Come could not justify an iniquitous decree in the
present world. The חִלּוּל הַשֵּׁם remains, even though there is compensation in the
World to Come.

But the Sages of the Midrash see, in the repetition of the exclamation, the
expression of Abraham's anguish and disapproval. R' Eliezer puts the following
words into the mouth of the patriarch: "Have You not sworn not to devastate
the world again by a Flood? I am astonished that You wish to misuse the good
faith of men and to punish them by a deluge of fire in place of a flood. How
will You free yourself of Your oath?" R' Shimon ben Lakish interprets
Abraham's thought thus: "If You wish to maintain the world, there cannot be
absolute justice; if You desire absolute justice, the world cannot exist. Why do
You take such advantage of the situation? You want the world and yet You
want absolute justice! If You do not forgo ever so little (of the realization of
absolute justice), the world will be unable to exist." God cried out, "Abraham,
*you love justice, you hate iniquity; that is why God has consecrated you
through gladness, in preference over your companions (Psalms* 45:8).
Accordingly, you are the first to whom I have addressed My speech in ten
generations" (*Rabbah* 39).

כו יַעֲשֶׂה מִשְׁפָּט: וַיֹּאמֶר יהוֹה אִם־אֶמְצָא בִסְדֹם חֲמִשִּׁים
כז צַדִּיקִם בְּתוֹךְ הָעִיר וְנָשָׂאתִי לְכָל־הַמָּקוֹם בַּעֲבוּרָם: וַיַּעַן
אַבְרָהָם וַיֹּאמַר הִנֵּה־נָא הוֹאַלְתִּי לְדַבֵּר אֶל־אֲדֹנָי וְאָנֹכִי
כח עָפָר וָאֵפֶר: אוּלַי יַחְסְרוּן חֲמִשִּׁים הַצַּדִּיקִם חֲמִשָּׁה
הֲתַשְׁחִית בַּחֲמִשָּׁה אֶת־כָּל־הָעִיר וַיֹּאמֶר לֹא אַשְׁחִית
כט אִם־אֶמְצָא שָׁם אַרְבָּעִים וַחֲמִשָּׁה: וַיֹּסֶף עוֹד לְדַבֵּר אֵלָיו
וַיֹּאמַר אוּלַי יִמָּצְאוּן שָׁם אַרְבָּעִים וַיֹּאמֶר לֹא אֶעֱשֶׂה
ל בַּעֲבוּר הָאַרְבָּעִים: וַיֹּאמֶר אַל־נָא יִחַר לַאדֹנָי וַאֲדַבֵּרָה
אוּלַי יִמָּצְאוּן שָׁם שְׁלֹשִׁים וַיֹּאמֶר לֹא אֶעֱשֶׂה אִם־אֶמְצָא
לא שָׁם שְׁלֹשִׁים: וַיֹּאמֶר הִנֵּה־נָא הוֹאַלְתִּי לְדַבֵּר אֶל־אֲדֹנָי אוּלַי
יִמָּצְאוּן שָׁם עֶשְׂרִים וַיֹּאמֶר לֹא אַשְׁחִית בַּעֲבוּר הָעֶשְׂרִים:
לב וַיֹּאמֶר אַל־נָא יִחַר לַאדֹנָי וַאֲדַבְּרָה אַךְ־הַפַּעַם אוּלַי
יִמָּצְאוּן שָׁם עֲשָׂרָה וַיֹּאמֶר לֹא אַשְׁחִית בַּעֲבוּר הָעֲשָׂרָה:
לג וַיֵּלֶךְ יהוֹה כַּאֲשֶׁר כִּלָּה לְדַבֵּר אֶל־אַבְרָהָם וְאַבְרָהָם
יט שלישי א שָׁב לִמְקֹמוֹ: וַיָּבֹאוּ שְׁנֵי הַמַּלְאָכִים סְדֹמָה בָּעֶרֶב וְלוֹט

26. חֲמִשִּׁים צַדִּיקִם בְּתוֹךְ הָעִיר — *Fifty righteous people in the midst of the city*. Throughout this chapter, the word צַדִּיקִם is written "defectively," that is, without the consonant *yud* (*Rabbah* 49). This indicates that the "righteous" supposedly living in Sodom could not have been so in the absolute sense, but only in comparison with the impious of the city; they could only be righteous "in the midst of the city." In fact, had they been perfectly righteous they would not have died with the wicked, for, says, R' Yosef, "From the moment the angel of destruction receives permission to destroy, he does not distinguish righteous from wicked" (*Bava Kamma* 60a), but he stops nevertheless before the perfectly righteous (צַדִּיק גָּמוּר; see *Ein Yaakov* ibid.). However, in stressing the words בְּתוֹךְ הָעִיר, *in the midst of the city*, Abraham hoped to obtain pardon even for those who were righteous only in comparison with the other citizens (*Malbim*).

32. וַיֹּאמֶר לֹא אַשְׁחִית בַּעֲבוּר הָעֲשָׂרָה — *And He said, "I will not destroy on account of the ten."* R' Shimon bar Yochai used to say that the world could be saved on the merit of one single righteous person, as it is written, וְצַדִּיק יְסוֹד עוֹלָם, *the righteous one is the foundation of the world* (*Proverbs* 10:25). But this can only refer to a righteous person of exceptional perfection and saintliness. In other cases, ten is the minimum number of the righteous required to communicate the sacred faith to the community (*Berachos* 50a; cf. *Ohr HaChaim*). If the proscribed cities had contained ten righteous people, Divine justice would not have despaired of the possibility of a better future and a more moral life for the entire population. It would have preserved the population for this future. And man must also persevere himself where God has not despaired. He must

do justice?"

²⁶ *And HASHEM said, "If I find in Sodom fifty righteous people in the midst of the city, then I would spare the entire place on their account."*

²⁷ *Abraham responded and said, "Behold, now, I desired to speak to my Lord although I am but dust and ash.* ²⁸ *What if the fifty righteous people should lack five? Would You destroy the entire city because of the five?" And He said, "I will not destroy if I find there forty-five."*

²⁹ *He further continued to speak to Him and he said, "What if forty would be found there?" And He said, "I will not act on account of the forty."*

³⁰ *And he said, "Let not my Lord be annoyed and I will speak: What if thirty would be found there?" And He said, "I will not act if I find there thirty."*

³¹ *So he said, "Behold, now, I desired to speak to my Lord: What if twenty would be found there?" And He said, "I will not destroy on account of the twenty."*

³² *So he said, "Let not my Lord be annoyed and I will speak but this once: What if ten would be found there?" And He said, "I will not destroy on account of the ten."*

³³ *HASHEM departed when He had finished speaking to Abraham, and Abraham returned to his place.*

19   ¹*The two angels came to Sodom in the evening and Lot*

undertake to do good, with confidence, even when faced with a completely lost society, and when the final victory could appear only as the result of a remote future (*R' S. R. Hirsch*).

33. וְאַבְרָהָם שָׁב לִמְקֹמוֹ — *And Abraham returned to his place.* This means that he returned to his former principle in spite of the disappointment he had just had. Without allowing himself to be disconcerted, he continued immediately to dedicate himself to the exercising of charity and hospitality (*R' Bachya*). He "did not budge," and we see him recommence later on (19:27), although this time not to call for justice but to ask for mercy.

19.

1. וַיָּבֹאוּ שְׁנֵי הַמַּלְאָכִים — *The two angels came.* This is the first time these strangers are called angels. The exemplary hospitality of Lot could then be explained by the fact that he recognized them as such, which would certainly diminish his merit in comparison with Abraham, who saw before him only ordinary men. But some commentators think that contact with superior beings

יֹשֵׁב בְּשַׁעַר־סְדֹם וַיַּרְא־לוֹט וַיָּקָם לִקְרָאתָם וַיִּשְׁתַּחוּ אַפַּיִם
ב אָרְצָה: וַיֹּאמֶר הִנֶּה נָּא־אֲדֹנַי סוּרוּ נָא אֶל־בֵּית עַבְדְּכֶם
וְלִינוּ וְרַחֲצוּ רַגְלֵיכֶם וְהִשְׁכַּמְתֶּם וַהֲלַכְתֶּם לְדַרְכְּכֶם וַיֹּאמְרוּ
ג לֹא כִּי בָרְחוֹב נָלִין: וַיִּפְצַר־בָּם מְאֹד וַיָּסֻרוּ אֵלָיו וַיָּבֹאוּ
ד אֶל־בֵּיתוֹ וַיַּעַשׂ לָהֶם מִשְׁתֶּה וּמַצּוֹת אָפָה וַיֹּאכֵלוּ: טֶרֶם
יִשְׁכָּבוּ וְאַנְשֵׁי הָעִיר אַנְשֵׁי סְדֹם נָסַבּוּ עַל־הַבַּיִת מִנַּעַר
ה וְעַד־זָקֵן כָּל־הָעָם מִקָּצֶה: וַיִּקְרְאוּ אֶל־לוֹט וַיֹּאמְרוּ לוֹ אַיֵּה
הָאֲנָשִׁים אֲשֶׁר־בָּאוּ אֵלֶיךָ הַלָּיְלָה הוֹצִיאֵם אֵלֵינוּ וְנֵדְעָה
ו־ז אֹתָם: וַיֵּצֵא אֲלֵהֶם לוֹט הַפֶּתְחָה וְהַדֶּלֶת סָגַר אַחֲרָיו: וַיֹּאמַר

gave rise, in Lot, to an outburst of love and kindness. The exercise of these
virtues which he had acquired during his long association with Abraham had
been repressed since his sojourn with the Sodomites and a spark was sufficient
to rekindle the flame. And so Lot showed himself extremely zealous and defied
the formal prohibition against welcoming strangers. But what a contrast with
the well-wishing spirit of Abraham's house! Here, neither wife nor child shared
in the *mitzvah*. Lot was alone with what he had learned in his uncle's house. It
is he who prepared the meal and baked the cakes.

2. וְלִינוּ וְרַחֲצוּ רַגְלֵיכֶם — *Spend the night and wash your feet.* Abraham had said
first "wash" (18:4), then "rest." But Lot thought, according to *Rashi's*
interpretation, "If the Sodomites come to my house and see that these two men
have already washed, they will accuse me, saying, 'They have already spent
two or three nights with you and you did not inform us.' Therefore, it is better
for them to remain with dust on their feet in order to appear as though they had
just arrived." Thus, he first said "spend the night," then "wash."

However, *Rashi* previously gave an entirely different explanation: "Abraham thought the strangers were Arabs who prostrate themselves before the
dust of their feet, and he took care not to admit the object of an idolatrous cult
to his house. But Lot, who was not so particular, invited them first to enter and
then to wash" (18:4).

Thus, Lot's conduct can be interpreted in two ways. It could have resulted
from favorable sentiment toward the strangers or from culpable complicity in
a pagan cult. What human being can ever reveal the obscure motives within the
soul of a personality as inconsistent as that of Lot?

3. וַיַּעַשׂ לָהֶם מִשְׁתֶּה — *He made a feast for them.* מִשְׁתֶּה implies a feast at which
wine is served. The term is not used for the meal offered by Abraham to the
strangers. In fact, remarks *Sforno*, Lot liked wine, as his end proves when he
allowed himself to be inebriated by his daughters and committed incest.

4. אַנְשֵׁי סְדֹם נָסַבּוּ עַל־הַבַּיִת — *Sodomites converged upon the house.* The text
presents the striking contrast between two diametrically opposed mentalities:
the morals of Israel and the morals of Sodom. On one hand, savage and cruel

was sitting at the gate of Sodom; now Lot saw and stood up to meet them and he bowed, face to the ground. ² *And he said, "Behold now, my lords; turn about, please, to your servant's house; spend the night and wash your feet, then wake up early and go your way!" And they said, "No, rather we will spend the night in the square."*

³ *And he urged them very much, so they turned toward him and came to his house; he made a feast for them and baked matzos, and they ate.*

⁴ *They had not yet lain down when the townspeople, Sodomites, converged upon the house, from young to old, all the people from every quarter.* ⁵ *And they called to Lot and said to him, "Where are the men who came to you tonight? Bring them out to us that we may know them."* ⁶ *Lot went out to them to the entrance, and shut the door behind him.* ⁷ *And he said,*

hatred brought the men of Sodom to refuse to welcome the men who came that evening within the walls of the city. On the other, a house was open to all in distress, a hand always prepared to welcome and assist. The quality of generous hospitality is the most prominent feature of the heritage of Abraham. Greed and egoism will always be the obvious signs of a detachment from the great principles of Judaism. It is by his goodness of heart and his practice of charity that you will recognize the worthy descendant of the patriarchs (*Yerushalmi, Kiddushin* 4:1).

5. וְנֵדְעָה אֹתָם — *That we may know them.* A known euphemism for pederasty. It is from the unspeakable penchant of the inhabitants of Sodom that the word "sodomy" is metaphorically derived. Scripture lingers over the description of the events of that night to show that fundamental depravity and immorality extended to all classes of the population without exception, beginning with the very youngest, as *Rashi* emphasizes in verse 11. God had granted the inhabitants one last respite (18:21), but their abject and criminal behavior during that night furnished irrefutable proof of their guilt, both individual and collective. They had surrounded Lot's house in order to set an example which would serve as a lesson to anyone who might henceforth be tempted to commit the crime of hospitality. They had decided to treat the strangers with ferocious cruelty. The Talmud (*Sanhedrin* 109a) reports numerous examples of the abominable habits of the Sodomite population which justify the punishment pronounced by Jewish tradition "The men of Sodom do not have a share in the World to Come, although they will be revived for the final judgment," according to the Sages (cf. ibid.). R' Abba adds, "All the creatures will be present, for God is merciful; when they have undergone their chastisement, they are no longer pursued with the ultimate severity" (*Zohar*).

ח אַל־נָא אַחַי תָּרֵעוּ: הִנֵּה־נָא לִי שְׁתֵּי בָנוֹת אֲשֶׁר לֹא־יָדְעוּ
אִישׁ אוֹצִיאָה־נָּא אֶתְהֶן אֲלֵיכֶם וַעֲשׂוּ לָהֶן כַּטּוֹב בְּעֵינֵיכֶם
רַק לָאֲנָשִׁים הָאֵל אַל־תַּעֲשׂוּ דָבָר כִּי־עַל־כֵּן בָּאוּ בְּצֵל
ט קֹרָתִי: וַיֹּאמְרוּ ׀ גֶּשׁ־הָלְאָה וַיֹּאמְרוּ הָאֶחָד בָּא־לָגוּר
וַיִּשְׁפֹּט שָׁפוֹט עַתָּה נָרַע לְךָ מֵהֶם וַיִּפְצְרוּ בָאִישׁ בְּלוֹט
י מְאֹד וַיִּגְּשׁוּ לִשְׁבֹּר הַדָּלֶת: וַיִּשְׁלְחוּ הָאֲנָשִׁים אֶת־יָדָם
יא וַיָּבִיאוּ אֶת־לוֹט אֲלֵיהֶם הַבָּיְתָה וְאֶת־הַדֶּלֶת סָגָרוּ: וְאֶת־
הָאֲנָשִׁים אֲשֶׁר־פֶּתַח הַבַּיִת הִכּוּ בַּסַּנְוֵרִים מִקָּטֹן וְעַד־גָּדוֹל
יב וַיִּלְאוּ לִמְצֹא הַפָּתַח: וַיֹּאמְרוּ הָאֲנָשִׁים אֶל־לוֹט עֹד מִי־לְךָ
פֹה חָתָן וּבָנֶיךָ וּבְנֹתֶיךָ וְכֹל אֲשֶׁר־לְךָ בָּעִיר הוֹצֵא
יג מִן־הַמָּקוֹם: כִּי־מַשְׁחִתִים אֲנַחְנוּ אֶת־הַמָּקוֹם הַזֶּה כִּי־גָדְלָה
יד צַעֲקָתָם אֶת־פְּנֵי יהוה וַיְשַׁלְּחֵנוּ יהוה לְשַׁחֲתָהּ: וַיֵּצֵא לוֹט
וַיְדַבֵּר ׀ אֶל־חֲתָנָיו ׀ לֹקְחֵי בְנֹתָיו וַיֹּאמֶר קוּמוּ צְּאוּ
מִן־הַמָּקוֹם הַזֶּה כִּי־מַשְׁחִית יהוה אֶת־הָעִיר וַיְהִי כִמְצַחֵק
טו בְּעֵינֵי חֲתָנָיו: וּכְמוֹ הַשַּׁחַר עָלָה וַיָּאִיצוּ הַמַּלְאָכִים בְּלוֹט

8. לִי שְׁתֵּי בָנוֹת — *I have two daughters.* The ransom which Lot is prepared to pay for the protection of the lives of the guests who have passed through his door is immoral and inhumane, but it does not seem abnormal in relation to the oriental habits of the time. "You deliver your daughter to debauchery," cried a voice from heaven, "instead of defending their honor to the death! Your sin will finally return to you and through them you will succumb to incest." R' Nachman cites the following aphorism in this regard: "he who is affected by a voracious hunger finally eats his own flesh" (*Tanchuma*). [*Ramban* establishes the comparison between the sin of Lot and that of "the concubine of Gibah" (*Judges* 19), which was, however, less serious than this one.]

11. וְאֶת־הָאֲנָשִׁים . . . הִכּוּ בַּסַּנְוֵרִים — *And the men . . . they struck with blindness.* According to ערוך, from cataracts. For *Ibn Ezra* and *Rashbam*, it is a "blindness of the eyes and the spirit." *Rashi* (on *II Kings* 6:18) explains that the term signifies a dizziness which causes sight to dim.

12. הוֹצֵא מִן־הַמָּקוֹם — *Remove from the place.* The Midrash elaborates: "One should save from fire (on the Sabbath day) the case of the holy book along with the holy book; the case holding *tefillin* along with the *tefillin*" (*Shabbos* 116b). "This teaches you: Happy are the righteous and happy are those who cling to them. God had in fact remembered Abraham and had caused Lot to escape from the midst of destruction (verse 29), by 'saving also from fire' Abraham's relatives found with him" (*Tanchuma*).

13. כִּי־מַשְׁחִתִים אֲנַחְנוּ אֶת־הַמָּקוֹם הַזֶּה — *For we are about to destroy this place.*

"I beg you, my brothers, do not act wickedly. [8] *See, now, I have two daughters who have never known a man. I shall bring them out to you and do to them as you please; but to these men do nothing inasmuch as they have come under the shelter of my roof."*

[9] *And they said, "Stand back!" Then they said, "This fellow came to sojourn and would act as a judge? Now we will treat you worse than them!" They pressed exceedingly upon the man, upon Lot, and they approached to break the door.*

[10] *The men stretched out their hand and brought Lot into the house with them, and closed the door.* [11] *And the men who were at the entrance of the house they struck with blindness, from small to great; and they tried vainly to find the entrance.* [12] *Then the men said to Lot, "Whom else do you have here — a son-in-law, your sons, or your daughters? All that you have in the city remove from the place,* [13] *for we are about to destroy this place; for their outcry has become great before HASHEM, so HASHEM has sent us to destroy it."*

[14] *So Lot went out and spoke to his sons-in-law, [and] the betrothed of his daughters, and he said, "Get up and leave this place, for HASHEM is about to destroy the city!" But he seemed like a jester in the eyes of his sons-in-law.*

[15] *And just as dawn was breaking, the angels urged Lot on*

The angels were punished, says R' Shimon, for having announced the Divine plan in these terms (*Rabbah* 50). In fact, a Divine decree can always be revoked through men's repentance. Now, the definite form of the angels' announcement of the end of Sodom must have removed all hope of pardon from Lot and discouraged him and his fellow-citizens from all moral efforts. The angels had thus been guilty of an inexact or incomplete revelation whose consequences could have been serious. However, upon hearing the end of the sentence of the angels, *so* HASHEM *has sent us to destroy it*, Lot understood that ultimate recourse was still possible. The last words left a glimmer of hope. Accordingly, he then went to warn his sons-in-law. He said to them, "Get up and leave this place," hoping that this gesture would rouse the inhabitants to repent (*Meshech Chochmah*).

14. וַיְהִי כִמְצַחֵק בְּעֵינֵי חֲתָנָיו — *But he seemed like a jester in the eyes of his sons-in-law.* The sons-in-law said to him, "Fool! The city is full of joy and liveliness, the inhabitants live in happiness, and you maintain that it will be destroyed?" (*Rabbah* 50).

15. וּכְמוֹ הַשַּׁחַר עָלָה — *And just as dawn was breaking.* The Talmud determines the length of the interval between dawn and sunrise from this verse and verse 23 (*Pesachim* 94a).

לֵאמֹ֔ר ק֣וּם קַ֠ח אֶֽת־אִשְׁתְּךָ֜ וְאֶת־שְׁתֵּ֤י בְנֹתֶ֙יךָ֙ הַנִּמְצָאֹ֔ת פֶּן־
טז תִּסָּפֶ֖ה בַּעֲוֺ֥ן הָעִֽיר׃ וַיִּתְמַהְמָ֓הּ ׀ וַיַּחֲזִ֨יקוּ הָאֲנָשִׁ֜ים בְּיָד֣וֹ וּבְיַד־
אִשְׁתּ֗וֹ וּבְיַד֙ שְׁתֵּ֣י בְנֹתָ֔יו בְּחֶמְלַ֥ת יְהוָ֖ה עָלָ֑יו וַיֹּצִאֻ֥הוּ וַיַּנִּחֻ֖הוּ
יז מִח֥וּץ לָעִֽיר׃ וַיְהִי֩ כְהוֹצִיאָ֨ם אֹתָ֜ם הַח֗וּצָה וַיֹּ֙אמֶר֙ הִמָּלֵ֣ט
עַל־נַפְשֶׁ֔ךָ אַל־תַּבִּ֣יט אַחֲרֶ֔יךָ וְאַל־תַּעֲמֹ֖ד בְּכָל־הַכִּכָּ֑ר הָהָ֥רָה
יח-יט הִמָּלֵ֖ט פֶּן־תִּסָּפֶֽה׃ וַיֹּ֥אמֶר ל֖וֹט אֲלֵהֶ֑ם אַל־נָ֖א אֲדֹנָֽי׃ הִנֵּה־נָ֠א
מָצָ֨א עַבְדְּךָ֜ חֵ֘ן בְּעֵינֶ֒יךָ֒ וַתַּגְדֵּ֣ל חַסְדְּךָ֗ אֲשֶׁ֤ר עָשִׂ֙יתָ֙ עִמָּדִ֔י
לְהַחֲי֖וֹת אֶת־נַפְשִׁ֑י וְאָנֹכִ֗י לֹ֤א אוּכַל֙ לְהִמָּלֵ֣ט הָהָ֔רָה פֶּן־
כ תִּדְבָּקַ֥נִי הָרָעָ֖ה וָמַֽתִּי׃ הִנֵּה־נָ֠א הָעִ֨יר הַזֹּ֧את קְרֹבָ֛ה לָנ֥וּס שָׁ֖מָּה
וְהִ֣וא מִצְעָ֑ר אִמָּלְטָ֨ה נָּ֜א שָׁ֗מָּה הֲלֹ֥א מִצְעָ֛ר הִ֖וא וּתְחִ֥י נַפְשִֽׁי׃
רביעי כא וַיֹּ֣אמֶר אֵלָ֔יו הִנֵּה֙ נָשָׂ֣אתִי פָנֶ֔יךָ גַּ֖ם לַדָּבָ֣ר הַזֶּ֑ה לְבִלְתִּ֛י הָפְכִּ֥י
כב אֶת־הָעִ֖יר אֲשֶׁ֥ר דִּבַּֽרְתָּ׃ מַהֵר֙ הִמָּלֵ֣ט שָׁ֔מָּה כִּ֚י לֹ֣א אוּכַל֙
לַעֲשׂ֣וֹת דָּבָ֔ר עַד־בֹּאֲךָ֖ שָׁ֑מָּה עַל־כֵּ֛ן קָרָ֥א שֵׁם־הָעִ֖יר צֽוֹעַר׃

הַנִּמְצָאֹת — *Who are present. Rashi* explains the literal meaning ("your daughters who are present in your house, ready to be saved"), but he draws our attention indirectly to "another interpretation of the Midrash." The latter relates the term הַנִּמְצָאֹת to the phrase מָצָאתִי דָּוִד עַבְדִּי, *I have found* (discovered) *David, My servant* (*Psalms* 89:21), and concludes that this discovery refers back to Sodom where the two daughters of Lot "were discovered." Indeed, they became the founders of the peoples of Moab and Amon, as the end of the present chapter will make clear, and these peoples were at the origin of the Davidic dynasty.

16. וַיִּתְמַהְמָהּ — *Still he lingered*. In order to bring all his belongings (*Rashi*). The syntax of the word וַיִּתְמַהְמָהּ is explained more precisely by the Midrash, "תְּמָהוֹן אַחַר תְּמָהוֹן, *hesitation after hesitation.*" The term thus illustrates clearly the character of Lot, as Scripture constantly presents it: hesitant, indecisive, and irresolute. In addition, the importance of the word is stressed by the very rare Torah-reading "note" which accompanies it — שַׁלְשֶׁלֶת. Something imitative can be found in the form as well as the traditional singing of this note, as in that of וַיְמָאֵן, *adamantly refused* (*Genesis* 39:8). See *S. Parchon, Machberes He'Aruch* I, f. 5b (*Wogue*).

17. אַל־תַּבִּיט אַחֲרֶיךָ — *Do not look behind you.* "You have done evil just as they have. It is by Abraham's merit that you are saved! You do not deserve to see the punishment that will strike them while you are spared" (*Rashi*). Whoever is saved from calamity by his own merit has the right to contemplate the victims of Divine chastisement, like the Jews at the shore of the Red Sea who "saw the Egyptians dead" (*Exodus* 14:30). *When God is for me, among those who help me,* said the Psalmist, *I shall indeed look upon the punishment of my foes* (118:7). (See the account of the ס׳ שער בת רבים, *Genesis* 6:16, on this principle applied to several Biblical passages.) But *Ramban*, among others,

saying: "Get up — take your wife and your two daughters who are present, lest you be swept away because of the sin of the city!"

¹⁶ *Still he lingered — so the men grasped him by his hand, his wife's hand, and the hand of his two daughters in HASHEM's mercy on him; and they took him out and left him outside the city.* ¹⁷ *And it was as they took them out that one said: "Flee for your life! Do not look behind you nor stop anywhere in all the plain; flee to the mountain lest you be swept away."* ¹⁸ *Lot said to them: "Please, no! My Lord —* ¹⁹ *See, now, Your servant has found grace in Your eyes and Your kindness was great which You did with me to save my life; but I cannot escape to the mountain lest the evil attach itself to me and I die.* ²⁰ *Behold, please, this city is near enough to escape there and it is small; I shall flee there. Is it not small? — and I will live."* ²¹ *And He replied to him: "Behold, I have granted you consideration even regarding this, that I not overturn the city about which you have spoken.* ²² *Hurry, flee there, for I cannot do a thing until you arrive there." He therefore called the name of the city Zoar.*

admits that the contemplation of the misfortune or the suffering of others can bring with it physical and moral ills. R' Eliezer adds that at the moment that the Omnipresent descends to earth to show His anger with men, no one has the right to harden his heart and stare at it with impunity (*Pirkei D'Rabbi Eliezer* 25).

הָהָרָה הִמָּלֵט — *Flee to the mountain.* The sentence includes a metaphorical meaning: "Search for safety near Abraham, who represents the summit of the moral world." But Lot replies, "I cannot escape toward the mountain, for Abraham has said to me (13:9): 'Separate from me.' "

20. הִנֵּה־נָא הָעִיר הַזֹּאת קְרֹבָה — *Behold, please, this city is near enough.* It is said in the name of Rav, "Man must always seek to live in a city populated just recently, for its sins are thus fewer, as our sentence shows" (*Shabbos* 10b). *Rashi* calculates that the city of Sodom, founded after the dispersion of the Tower of Babel, had been in existence for fifty-two years, whereas Zoar was founded one year after Sodom and its neighboring cities. The two letters of the word נָא, in the sentence spoken by Lot, add up to the number fifty-one. Apparently, the difference of a single year is hardly tangible. It is only justified in the light of Divine justice, which condemns solely "when the measure is full," as the example in *Genesis* 15:16 shows us; the sins of one year can suffice to upset the equilibrium of the scales of justice and cause them to turn to the side of the prosecution.

כג־כד הַשֶּׁמֶשׁ יָצָא עַל־הָאָרֶץ וְלוֹט בָּא צֹעֲרָה: וַיהוָה הִמְטִיר עַל־
כה סְדֹם וְעַל־עֲמֹרָה גָּפְרִית וָאֵשׁ מֵאֵת יהוה מִן־הַשָּׁמָיִם: וַיַּהֲפֹךְ
אֶת־הֶעָרִים הָאֵל וְאֵת כָּל־הַכִּכָּר וְאֵת כָּל־יֹשְׁבֵי הֶעָרִים
כו וְצֶמַח הָאֲדָמָה: וַתַּבֵּט אִשְׁתּוֹ מֵאַחֲרָיו וַתְּהִי נְצִיב מֶלַח:

23. הַשֶּׁמֶשׁ יָצָא עַל־הָאָרֶץ — *The sun rose upon the earth.* When Lot arrived in Zoar at sunrise, the destruction had already taken place. This follows from the beginning of the next sentence, in which the form of the verb הִמְטִיר is to be interpreted, according to *Malbim,* in the pluperfect: "HASHEM had made it rain." *Malbim* establishes the rule of syntax according to which the past tense of a verb following its subject indicates the pluperfect, whereas it indicates the imperfect when it precedes the subject. The *Midrash Rabbah* (and *Tosafos* to *Chullin* 91b) also makes it clear that the destruction had taken place by the end of the night.

When a punishment rages on earth, remarks *Recanati,* it generally begins during the nocturnal hours: *The weavers of dark plots shall labor in darkness* (*Isaiah* 29:15). The "three messengers of misfortune (מַשְׁחִית אַף וְחֵמָה) then have free reign" (*Midrash Ruth*). Therefore, we begin our evening prayer with the sentence from *Psalms* (78:38), וְהוּא רַחוּם, which implores God "not to destroy (מַשְׁחִית) but instead to turn away His anger (אַף), and not to stir up all His wrath (חֵמָה)." This verse was chosen because it contains thirteen words, which allude to the thirteen attributes of Divine mercy and to their absolute power over the three messengers of misfortune. But its recitation is omitted on the eve of the Sabbath, which brings the reign of peace to the living as well as to the dead.

24. וַה' הִמְטִיר — *Now HASHEM had caused . . . to rain.* "Wherever it is written, *And HASHEM,* this refers to Him and His heavenly tribunal" (*Rashi*). Thus the punishment appeared as the result of the postulates of justice, as well as those of love, given that the Divine name used here, הֲוָי, normally indicates the God of love and mercy. Indeed, as ruthless as the punishment was, it nevertheless spared one family, which was able to escape. And this family contained the seed of the future redeemer of humanity. Moreover, declares *Ramban,* the extreme severity of the sanction served the higher interest of the land of Israel. To be sure, other populations committed the same crimes and abominations without being punished with extermination. But, since the Promised land is "the sanctuary of HASHEM" (*Jeremiah* 7:4), where the state of holiness must attain a higher level than in other countries, God wanted to preserve the Jewish people from moral decadence and He presented them, right within the land itself, with the dreadful example of the cities of Sodom, Gomorrah, etc., destroyed forever because of their corruption and perversion. It is the Torah itself which points this out in connection with the psychological effect caused by the indelible spectacle of desolation (*Deuteronomy* 29). Considered in this light, the terrifying punishment also had a beneficial side, emanating from Divine clemency.

23 *The sun rose upon the earth and Lot arrived at Zoar.* 24 *Now HASHEM had caused sulfur and fire to rain upon Sodom and Gomorrah, from HASHEM, out of heaven.* 25 *He overturned these cities and the entire plain, with all the inhabitants of the cities and the vegetation of the soil.* 26 *His wife peered behind him and she became a pillar of salt.*

גָּפְרִית וָאֵשׁ — *Sulfur and fire.* First rain, which then turned to sulfur and fire (*Rashi*). R' Yehoshua ben Levi said, "God is long-suffering with everything except depraved morals." R' Shimon bar Yochai maintains that the death penalty by fire is the most severe of the four methods of execution, for it is reserved for the crime of debauchery. Thus it is said, *If the daughter of a Kohen is dishonored by adultery . . . she shall perish by fire* (*Leviticus* 21:9). This was the penalty to which Judah condemned Tamar for a similar crime (*Genesis* 38:24). Accordingly, it was fire which fell upon the inhabitants of Sodom because of their dissolute morals (*Tanchuma*).

מֵאֵת ה' מִן־הַשָּׁמָיִם — *From HASHEM, out of heaven.* Contemplating the desolate region of the Dead Sea and the high salt content of its waters, where these cities once flourished, the observer notes the volcanic nature of its soil. He might be led to attribute the destruction of the five proscribed cities to an ordinary natural phenomenon. And so the Divine words are repeated in our verse, as if to exclude this theory. God made it rain — God Himself from the heavenly heights. The observer confuses the cause and the effect: the present condition of the soil is not the cause of the catastrophe, but the result. Its origin is due not to a volcanic eruption but to a providential element, "out of heaven."

26. וַתַּבֵּט אִשְׁתּוֹ מֵאַחֲרָיו — *His wife peered behind him.* The *Targum Yerushalmi* explains, "She was a native of Sodom and wanted to see what had become of her father's house. She then became a statue of salt until the resurrection of the dead." R' Eliezer relates that her first name was Edith (*Pirkei D'Rabbi Eliezer* 25). She stopped en route and became, at the same time as the soil and the inhabitants of Sodom, a victim of the sulfur-salt petrification brought upon the entire region (פי' הטור בשם הרא"ש). But contrary to this natural explanation, the Talmud and certain *midrashim* admit that Lot's wife became a statue after arriving at Zoar, and in a miraculous way. Whoever sees this statue should pronounce the benediction reserved for Divine punishment: בָּרוּךְ דַּיַּן הָאֱמֶת. This obligation is nevertheless not codified by *Rambam* (*Berachos* 54a). This, writes רד"ל, is because the statue was swallowed up by the Dead Sea following an earthquake. But it "was still standing" at the time of R' Eliezer (ibid.), and Flavius Josephus reports having seen it.

The Torah makes a point of relating this event because it renders the behavior of Lot's daughters more comprehensible to us. If their mother had been alive, the daughters would not have been able to act as they did (פי' הטור).

כז וַיַּשְׁכֵּם אַבְרָהָם בַּבֹּקֶר אֶל־הַמָּקוֹם אֲשֶׁר־עָמַד שָׁם אֶת־
פְּנֵי יהוה: כח וַיַּשְׁקֵף עַל־פְּנֵי סְדֹם וַעֲמֹרָה וְעַל כָּל־פְּנֵי אֶרֶץ
הַכִּכָּר וַיַּרְא וְהִנֵּה עָלָה קִיטֹר הָאָרֶץ כְּקִיטֹר הַכִּבְשָׁן: כט וַיְהִי
בְּשַׁחֵת אֱלֹהִים אֶת־עָרֵי הַכִּכָּר וַיִּזְכֹּר אֱלֹהִים אֶת־אַבְרָהָם
וַיְשַׁלַּח אֶת־לוֹט מִתּוֹךְ הַהֲפֵכָה בַּהֲפֹךְ אֶת־הֶעָרִים אֲשֶׁר־
יָשַׁב בָּהֵן לוֹט: ל וַיַּעַל לוֹט מִצּוֹעַר וַיֵּשֶׁב בָּהָר וּשְׁתֵּי בְנֹתָיו
עִמּוֹ כִּי יָרֵא לָשֶׁבֶת בְּצוֹעַר וַיֵּשֶׁב בַּמְּעָרָה הוּא וּשְׁתֵּי בְנֹתָיו:
לא וַתֹּאמֶר הַבְּכִירָה אֶל־הַצְּעִירָה אָבִינוּ זָקֵן וְאִישׁ אֵין בָּאָרֶץ
לב לָבוֹא עָלֵינוּ כְּדֶרֶךְ כָּל־הָאָרֶץ: לְכָה נַשְׁקֶה אֶת־אָבִינוּ

---

27. וַיַּשְׁכֵּם אַבְרָהָם בַּבֹּקֶר אֶל־הַמָּקוֹם — *Abraham arose early in the morning to the place.* The place where he had accompanied the angels and where he had interceded on behalf of the Sodomites (18:22). After this intervention, based on the principles of justice, proved ineffective, Abraham attempted to beg for Divine mercy. Early rising is characteristic of Abraham's personality, always eager to perform a *mitzvah* as soon as possible. We find this same phrase in the section about the sacrifice of Isaac (22:3) and, referring to this verse, the Sages conclude that Abraham gave the first example of "the morning prayer" (*Berachos* 26a; cf. commentary to 24:63). He also showed the importance of a fixed place for prayers, by returning "to the place where he had stood before God" (*Berachos* 6b). Prayer confers a certain holiness upon the place where it is recited regularly, and the call which constantly rises from the same place toward God builds up such an attraction that "God Himself inquires after the one who is accustomed to attend synagogue daily and one day does not attend" (ibid.).

28. וַיַּשְׁקֵף עַל־פְּנֵי סְדֹם — *And he gazed down upon Sodom.* The thought of the imminent fate of the five cities had profoundly affected Abraham. After spending a sleepless night, he rose early in the morning and glanced, with an impassioned look, at the place of Divine justice.

29. וַיְהִי בְּשַׁחֵת אֱלֹהִים — *And so it was when God destroyed.* Whereas the Divine name appearing in this chapter is always שֵׁם הֲוָיָ, denoting מִדַּת הָרַחֲמִים, the principle of love, our verse twice cites the name אֱלֹהִים, expressing the attribute of justice. Lot saw that his salvation was an act of mercy, but for Abraham the salvation of his nephew, the only relatively righteous man of Sodom, was the manifestation of the Divine justice he had begged for in his dialogue with God.

וַיִּזְכֹּר אֱלֹהִים אֶת־אַבְרָהָם — *That God remembered Abraham.* "What did He recall concerning Abraham? Regarding Lot. He had remembered that Lot knew that Sarah was Abraham's wife. When he heard Abraham say to the Egyptians, 'She is my sister,' Lot did not disclose the fact but had pity on him. Therefore, the Holy One, Blessed is He, pitied Lot." This explanation of *Rashi's* emphasizes that the bonds of kinship are not in themselves sufficient to benefit a member

²⁷ *Abraham arose early in the morning to the place where he had stood before HASHEM.* ²⁸ *And he gazed down upon Sodom and Gomorrah and the entire surface of the land of the plain; and saw — and behold! the smoke of the earth rose like the smoke of a kiln.* ²⁹ *And so it was when God destroyed the cities of the plain that God remembered Abraham; so He sent Lot from amidst the upheaval when He overturned the cities in which Lot had lived.* ³⁰ *Now Lot went up from Zoar and settled on the mountain, his two daughters with him, for he was afraid to remain in Zoar; he dwelt in a cave, he with his two daughters.* ³¹ *The older one said to the younger, "Our father is old and there is no man in the land to marry us in the usual manner.* ³² *Come, let us ply our father*

of the family of a righteous man on the latter's merit if he cannot claim a minimum of personal merit himself. *Maharal* goes more thoroughly into this. He considers that there existed a certain closeness of character between the two men in spite of the antagonism of their doctrines and mentality. Lot, to a certain extent, understood his uncle. And so he respected his secret about Sarah. Similarly, he exercised his ingenuity to imitate his uncle's marvelous virtue of hospitality. These qualities developed in him the virtue which engendered a lineage worthy of the greatest destinies. *Ramban* mentions the merit of Lot for having of his own accord accompanied his uncle in his peregrinations through a foreign country. "Without Abraham, he would still have been in Haran and not in Sodom. Accordingly, it was not fitting that he should die there." "Be that as it may," remarks *Recanati*, "it seems to me from this passage that the merit of the righteous protects his own family, even if they do not follow in his footsteps, on condition, however, that they are not fundamentally evil, as our Sages have observed with respect to David and his son Absalom" (cf. *Ezekiel* 14:16).

32. לְכָה נַשְׁקֶה אֶת־אָבִינוּ יַיִן — *Come, let us ply our father with wine.* The prime motives of the daughters of Lot in committing their ignoble act are the subject of a discussion between Rav Huna and Rav Shimon (*Rabbah* 51). The former affirms that their intention was pure, לְשֵׁם שָׁמַיִם. They believed that the world has just been devastated and that their mother had just died, leaving them the only women on earth. They thought they had been saved with their father in order to assure the continuation of the human species and they accomplished their imagined duty by cohabiting with him. Other traditions report that they feared they would never marry, for men would avoid them in the future inasmuch as they were natives of the accursed city. And so the Talmud ordains that the reading and public explanation of this passage do not constitute a dishonor for Abraham (*Megillah* 25b). R' Shimon, on the other hand, deems that the daughters of Lot committed an act of perversion, led astray by their spirit of debauchery. It appears, however, that the Talmud (*Nazir* 23a) and our classic authors (such as *Ramban, R' Bachya,* and many others) tend more to

לג יַיִן וְנִשְׁכְּבָה עִמּוֹ וּנְחַיֶּה מֵאָבִינוּ זָרַע: וַתַּשְׁקֶיןָ אֶת־אֲבִיהֶן
יַיִן בַּלַּיְלָה הוּא וַתָּבֹא הַבְּכִירָה וַתִּשְׁכַּב אֶת־אָבִיהָ וְלֹא־
לד יָדַע בְּשִׁכְבָהּ וּבְקוּמָהּ: וַיְהִי מִמָּחֳרָת וַתֹּאמֶר הַבְּכִירָה
אֶל־הַצְּעִירָה הֵן־שָׁכַבְתִּי אֶמֶשׁ אֶת־אָבִי נַשְׁקֶנּוּ יַיִן גַּם־
לה הַלַּיְלָה וּבֹאִי שִׁכְבִי עִמּוֹ וּנְחַיֶּה מֵאָבִינוּ זָרַע: וַתַּשְׁקֶיןָ גַּם
בַּלַּיְלָה הַהוּא אֶת־אֲבִיהֶן יָיִן וַתָּקָם הַצְּעִירָה וַתִּשְׁכַּב עִמּוֹ
לו וְלֹא־יָדַע בְּשִׁכְבָהּ וּבְקֻמָהּ: וַתַּהֲרֶיןָ שְׁתֵּי בְנוֹת־לוֹט מֵאֲבִיהֶן:

accuse the father than his daughters. Knowing that cohabitation of a father with his daughter was tolerated by the sons of Noah, they nevertheless inebriated their father because their sense of decency forbade their inviting him to cohabit; or because this union, although permissible, was nevertheless considered odious (*Tosafos* to *Nazir* ibid.); or because they dreaded that future generations would consider it so. As for the father, the text alludes to his total lack of scruples in verse 33 by putting a dot over the letter *vav* in the word וּבְקוּמָהּ, *and of her getting up* (whereas the letter does not appear in verse 35, in reference to the younger sister). *Rashi* explains, "Lot knew when she arose and, despite this, on the following night he did not guard against excessive drink."

It seems, according to the opinions of our Sages, that different motives moved the daughters of Lot, that even their pure intentions were not devoid of voluptuous instincts. From a psychological point of view, this form of interpretation corresponds much better, no doubt, to the complexity of the human soul than an overly simplistic one. The fact remains that both elements of their character reappear in the lineage of the two peoples they founded. The spirit of debauchery manifested itself anew in the conduct of the daughters of Moab, who tried to seduce the Jews and to separate them from their faith (*Numbers* 25:2); on the other hand, their self-sacrifice for the salvation of humanity reaffirmed itself in the historic Divine call of David and his dynasty which issued, through their ancestress Ruth, from the descendants of Moab.

The Davidic dynasty, destined to give birth at the end of time to the Messiah son of David, was indeed "discovered in Sodom" according to the Midrash. The fact that the future redeemer of humanity had his origin in an incestuous union seems to be surrounded by mystery. It is all the more disturbing as it is repeated in the paternal ancestry of David. Ruth the Moabitess, the ancestress of David, married Boaz, born of the tribe of Judah. Now, the origin of this tribe similarly goes back to an apparently incestuous relationship — that of Judah with Tamar, his daughter-in-law (*Genesis* 38:16; cf. *Leviticus* 18:15). These historical events are assuredly not fortuitous. They have deep meaning. Accordingly, it is permissible to presume that the future redeemer of humanity must carry in his veins an impure, non-Jewish

with wine and lay with him that we may give life to offspring through our father."

³³ *So they plied their father with wine on that night; and the older one came and lay with her father, and he was not aware of her lying down and of her getting up.*

³⁴ *And it was on the next day that the older one said to the younger, "Behold, I lay with my father last night; let us ply him with wine tonight as well, and you come lay with him that we may give life to offspring through our father."*

³⁵ *So they plied their father with wine that night also; and the younger one got up and lay with him, and he was not aware of her lying down and of her getting up.*

³⁶ *Thus, Lot's two daughters conceived from their father.*

drop of blood, in order to understand in some measure the feelings of all human beings and to share their weaknesses, and so, through the twin influences of his personality and his language, to be able to find the path to their heart and to lead them back to God (cf. *Ohr HaChaim* of *R' Chaim ben Attar, Genesis* 49:9).

וְנִשְׁכְּבָה עִמּוֹ — *And lay with him.* If God had judged Lot's daughters according to their acts, they would have been condemned to death. But in judging them He took into account their intentions, which were good, and He punished them only by excluding their male descendants from joining the Jewish people (*Deuteronomy* 23:4). The Talmud (*Nazir* 23a) studies the problem of the relationship between an evil act and a good intention. It concludes that Lot and his daughters were judged differently for the same sin and it applies to Lot the prophet Hosea's condemnation (14:10): *Straight are the ways of God . . . but sinners will stumble in them,* whereas the rest of this same verse applies to his daughters: *and the just do walk in them.*

33. וְלֹא־יָדַע בְּשִׁכְבָה — *And he was not aware of her lying down.* It has already been pointed out that in the diacritical point over the *vav* in the word וּבְקוּמָה the Sages see an allusion to the guilt of Lot, persisting in his state of drunkenness (*Horayos* 10b). This fact gives the reason for the law which excludes only the men (but not the women) of Moab and Amon from entry into the community of Jewry (*Midrash Rabbah;* cf. *Even HaEzer* 4:2).

וּבְקוּמָה — *And of her getting up.* An allusion to Ruth, a descendant of the Moabites, who "remained prostrate at the feet of Boaz until morning and arose before the hour at which one can discern another" (*Ruth* 3:14). It was much too soon in history for Lot and Boaz to be able to discern the immense importance of the acts they had just effected (*Zohar*).

36. וַתַּהֲרֶיןָ שְׁתֵּי בְנוֹת־לוֹט — *Thus, Lot's two daughters conceived.* See our commentary on 13:9.

לז וַתֵּ֤לֶד הַבְּכִירָה֙ בֵּ֔ן וַתִּקְרָ֥א שְׁמ֖וֹ מוֹאָ֑ב ה֥וּא אֲבִי־מוֹאָ֖ב
לח עַד־הַיּֽוֹם: וְהַצְּעִירָ֤ה גַם־הִוא֙ יֶ֣לְדָה בֵּ֔ן וַתִּקְרָ֥א שְׁמ֖וֹ בֶּן־
כ א עַמִּ֑י ה֛וּא אֲבִ֥י בְנֵֽי־עַמּ֖וֹן עַד־הַיּֽוֹם: וַיִּסַּ֨ע
מִשָּׁ֤ם אַבְרָהָם֙ אַ֣רְצָה הַנֶּ֔גֶב וַיֵּ֥שֶׁב בֵּין־קָדֵ֖שׁ וּבֵ֣ין שׁ֑וּר
ב וַיָּ֖גָר בִּגְרָֽר: וַיֹּ֧אמֶר אַבְרָהָ֛ם אֶל־שָׂרָ֥ה אִשְׁתּ֖וֹ אֲחֹ֣תִי הִ֑וא
ג וַיִּשְׁלַ֗ח אֲבִימֶ֨לֶךְ֙ מֶ֣לֶךְ גְּרָ֔ר וַיִּקַּ֖ח אֶת־שָׂרָֽה: וַיָּבֹ֧א אֱלֹהִ֛ים

38. וַתִּקְרָא שְׁמוֹ בֶּן־עַמִּי — *And she called his name Ben-Ammi* [lit. *son of my people*]. R' Chiya bar Abba weighs the qualities of the two daughters of Lot. The elder showed herself more eager than the younger in accomplishing the duty of procreation. Accordingly, her posterity acceded to royalty sooner, through David and Solomon, than the younger's, whose descendant, Naamah the Amonitess, was the mother of King Rehoboam, grandson of David (*I Kings* 14:21). The younger daughter, on the other hand, showed more discretion in naming her son than the elder. The latter named him "son of the father," the former "son of my people." The younger was rewarded: her descendants never became the tributary of an enemy, which was not the case with the descendants of the elder (*Deuteronomy* 14:9; cf. *Bava Kamma* 38b).

20.

1. וַיִּסַּע מִשָּׁם אַבְרָהָם — *Abraham journeyed from there*. Scripture does not give specific motives for this departure, as it did in 12:10, where Abraham's move was justified by the famine in Canaan. *Rashi* gives two different reasons which may well be complementary. First, the desire to move away from Lot, who had a bad name for having cohabited with his daughters, and, second, "Abraham went away when he saw that the cities had been destroyed and that there were no more passersby."

This latter reason seems more in accord with the character of Abraham as the Torah describes him. His kindness and his need for action impelled him to help others and to be hospitable. But, before all else, he was "the father of the believers," and his *raison d'etre* was but to proclaim monotheism to all. His legendary hospitality enabled him to introduce his guests to God and convert them to serve Him. And so, when he saw that the cities of the Dead Sea basin were lost, and "that there were no more passersby," he left that region, where he had worked for God for twenty-five years (*Rashi* to 21:34), and at once went to another part of the country to continue his mission there, without allowing himself even a moment of discouragement. Such a sentiment would have been quite understandable after the failure of so many dogged efforts, but the unshakeable faith of Abraham won out over despair.

Faithful to his principle of spiritual conquest of the southern areas of the country, the most arid and the most hostile to all human culture (12:9), Abraham was going to establish himself in the Negev, close by the formidable desert of Shur. But he settled at Gerar, the residence of the kings of the

³⁷ *The older bore a son and she called his name Moab; he is the ancestor of Moab until this day.* ³⁸ *And the younger one also bore a son and she called his name Ben-Ammi; he is the ancestor of the children of Ammon until this day.*

20

¹ *A*braham *journeyed from there to the region of the south and settled between Kadesh and Shur, and he sojourned in Gerar.* ² *Abraham said of Sarah his wife, "She is my sister";* *so Abimelech, king of Gerar, sent, and took Sarah.* ³ *And God came*

Philistines, a city situated at the crossroads of Kadesh and Shur, where he was certain to be able to offer hospitality to numerous passersby.

2. וַיֹּאמֶר אַבְרָהָם אֶל־שָׂרָה אִשְׁתּוֹ — *Abraham said of Sarah his wife.* The patriarch was so imbued with his Divine mission that he did not hesitate to risk his own life and that of his wife. However, he did not wish to trust in a miracle for their safety and he had recourse to the subterfuge he had already used previously. "He who has once benefited from a miracle must not expect a second, for his merits have diminished" (*Zohar*). It is the presentation of these examples of the conduct of the patriarchs in difficult circumstances which obliges the Torah to relate in detail the events of their lives, including those which seem to us to have no historical importance, as is the case with this passage. As a whole, these numerous examples constitute the line of conduct for every Jew to adopt in the face of the great and small problems of existence. The story of the patriarchs represents the framework of the Jewish ethic.

אֲחֹתִי הִוא — *"She is my sister."* According to the *Zohar*, there is an additional meaning implied by these words. Seeing that the *Shechinah* did not cease hovering over the saintly Sarah's abode, Abraham did not count on his own merits but sought to cling even more to his wife. And so he said in speaking of her, "She is my sister," for one cannot renounce his sister as he can his wife. (The comparison with a sister implies the notion of inseparability, as in *Proverbs 7:4: Say to wisdom, "You are my sister."*) Now, it was just at the time when he made his way to Egypt, and to the country of the Philistines as well, that Abraham felt the need to express his indissoluble attachment to God, Whose holy presence was drawn to Sarah. This is like a man who wishes to descend into a deep pit, but for fear of being unable to rise back out of it, he attaches a rope ladder to the edge of the pit and then descends in complete calm. Thus, before going down into a land full of idolatry, Abraham fixed "the rope of faith" for himself by clinging to the *Shechinah*. Then he went down, certain of his ability to rise again, unharmed, whenever he wanted.

וַיִּשְׁלַח אֲבִימֶלֶךְ ... וַיִּקַּח אֶת־שָׂרָה — *Abimelech ... sent, and took Sarah.* When she had been abducted by the Pharaoh of Egypt, she was sixty-five years old and could still have been very beautiful. Now, she was ninety-years-old. How could she have preserved her beauty? *Ramban* responds that she had found

אֶל־אֲבִימֶ֫לֶךְ בַּחֲל֣וֹם הַלַּ֑יְלָה וַיֹּ֣אמֶר ל֗וֹ הִנְּךָ֥ מֵת֙ עַל־
ד הָאִשָּׁ֣ה אֲשֶׁר־לָקַ֔חְתָּ וְהִ֖וא בְּעֻ֣לַת בָּֽעַל: וַאֲבִימֶ֕לֶךְ לֹ֥א
ה קָרַ֖ב אֵלֶ֑יהָ וַיֹּאמַ֕ר אֲדֹנָ֕י הֲג֥וֹי גַּם־צַדִּ֖יק תַּֽהֲרֹֽג: הֲלֹ֨א
ה֤וּא אָֽמַר־לִי֙ אֲחֹ֣תִי הִ֔וא וְהִֽיא־גַם־הִ֖וא אָֽמְרָ֣ה אָחִ֣י ה֑וּא
ו בְּתָם־לְבָבִ֛י וּבְנִקְיֹ֥ן כַּפַּ֖י עָשִׂ֥יתִי זֹֽאת: וַיֹּ֩אמֶר֩ אֵלָ֨יו הָֽאֱלֹהִ֜ים
בַּֽחֲלֹ֗ם גַּ֣ם אָֽנֹכִ֣י יָדַ֘עְתִּי֘ כִּ֤י בְתָם־לְבָֽבְךָ֙ עָשִׂ֣יתָ זֹּ֔את
וָֽאֶחְשֹׂ֧ךְ גַּם־אָֽנֹכִ֛י אֽוֹתְךָ֖ מֵֽחֲטוֹ־לִ֑י עַל־כֵּ֥ן לֹֽא־נְתַתִּ֖יךָ

her beauty and her femininity once more when the angels announced her impending pregnancy, as the Talmud indicates (*Bava Metziah* 87a). This explanation fits better with the passage about the consequences of her being carried off than that given by *Abarbanel* in the name of *Rabbeinu Nissim*, who states that Abimelech simply wanted to honor the illustrious patriarch who was his guest.

3. וַיָּבֹא אֱלֹהִים אֶל־אֲבִימֶלֶךְ — *And God came to Abimelech.* "Long after Sarah was led to the unwitting king" (*Ramban*). *Rambam* elaborates, "When it is said, 'God came to such a person in a dream of the night,' it is not a question of prophecy, and this person is not a prophet. In fact, it means merely that a warning came to this person from God, and we are then told that this warning was made in a dream. Certainly we do not doubt that Laban the Aramean was a complete scoundrel as well as an idolater; and as for Abimelech, although among his people he was a pious man, our father Abraham said of his city and his realm, 'There is no fear of God in this place.' Nevertheless, it is said of Laban and of Abimelech that God appeared to them in a dream of the night — quite different from a nocturnal vision, like that mentioned regarding the patriarch Jacob (46:2). This is why *Onkelos* translates, 'There came a speech from God' (וַאֲתָא מֵימַר מִן קֳדָם ה׳) and not 'God revealed Himself' (וְאִתְגְּלִי ה׳)" (*Guide* 2:41).

עַל־הָאִשָּׁה אֲשֶׁר־לָקַחְתָּ — *Because of the woman you have taken.* Theft and adultery, the two crimes charged here, are both mortal sins for the sons of Noah, as is pointed out in the Talmud in *Sanhedrin* 57a. (Nevertheless, the moral level of Abimelech was still superior to that of the Egyptian Pharaoh, and so he was spared from the "terrible plagues" which were inflicted upon the latter.) According to *Rambam*, the moral responsibility of every human being is derivable from this important statement: "For God, justice is something absolutely necessary; that is He rewards the pious man for all his pure and upright actions, even though he is not ordered to do them through a prophet, and He punishes each evil act, even though it has not been forbidden by a prophet; for it is still forbidden to him by the natural sentiment which prohibits injustice and iniquity" (*Guide* 3:17).

5. וְהִיא־גַם־הוּא אָמְרָה — *And she, too, herself said.* "Eleven times the word הִיא is written in the Torah in the masculine (הוּא) but pronounced in the feminine,

*to Abimelech in a dream by night and said to him, "Behold you
are to die because of the woman you have taken; moreover she is
a married woman."*

⁴ *Now Abimelech had not approached her; so he said, "O my
Lord, will You slay a nation even though it is righteous?* ⁵ *Did not
he himself tell me: 'She is my sister'? And she, too, herself said:
'He is my brother!' In the innocence of my heart and integrity of
my hands have I done this."*

⁶ *And God said to him in the dream, "I, too, knew that it was in
the innocence of your heart that you did this, and I, too, prevented
you from sinning against Me; that is why I did not permit you*

הִיא. In our verse, this occurs twice" (*Avos D'Rabbi Nosson* 34). It was really
Abraham who affirmed that she was his sister while Sarah remained silent, just
as she had in Egypt, for the reasons pointed out in our commentary to 12:17. But
Abimelech interpreted her silence as acquiescence.

בְּתָם־לְבָבִי — *In the innocence of my heart.* This means, according to *Rashi*, "I
had no intention of sinning." The following term, "integrity," literally
"cleanness of hand," means "I am innocent of all transgression for I have not
touched her." But God answers him, "It is certainly true that you did not intend
to sin (for you did not know that Sarah was Abraham's wife). But do not speak
of the purity of your hands." God had him understand that even if he really had
acted "with integrity," he was nevertheless far from being in a state of
innocence. For even if Sarah had only been Abraham's unmarried sister, is it
right that every female foreigner entering the country should be at the disposal
of the prince for his pleasure? And even if the customs of Gerar sanctioned such
action, they were nonetheless still sins before God, and it was up to the prince
to sanction only those customs that complied with ethical conduct.

6. מֵחֲטוֹ — *From sinning.* This word is written defectively (without the letter א)
in the Masoretic text, so that it can be related to the word מַחַט, *needle.* Every sin,
explains the *Zohar* metaphorically, is like a needle sticking into the living flesh
of the Divinity (ibid.). The Talmud deduces from the expression מֵחֲטוֹ־לִי, *from
sinning against Me,* that the punishment regarding the sin which Abimelech
committed in ignorance of the fact that Sarah was Abraham's wife is left solely
to the celestial tribunal, although the guilt is also evident to human judges
(*Tosafos* to *Makkos* 9a). This is based on the fact "that Abimelech should have
learned how to act, but did not," as is mentioned in the same Talmudic passage,
in its analysis of the following verse.

עַל־כֵּן לֹא־נְתַתִּיךְ לִנְגֹּעַ אֵלֶיהָ — *That is why I did not permit you to touch her.* "It
was not by your own restraint that you did not touch her. It is I who prevented
you from doing evil; I did not give you the strength" (*Rashi*). Referring to the
words עָצֹר עָצַר, *completely restrained,* twice repeated in verse 18, the *Midrash*

ז לִנְגֹּעַ אֵלֶיהָ: וְעַתָּה הָשֵׁב אֵשֶׁת־הָאִישׁ כִּי־נָבִיא הוּא
וְיִתְפַּלֵּל בַּעַדְךָ וֶחְיֵה וְאִם־אֵינְךָ מֵשִׁיב דַּע כִּי־מוֹת תָּמוּת
ח אַתָּה וְכָל־אֲשֶׁר־לָךְ: וַיַּשְׁכֵּם אֲבִימֶלֶךְ בַּבֹּקֶר וַיִּקְרָא לְכָל־
עֲבָדָיו וַיְדַבֵּר אֶת־כָּל־הַדְּבָרִים הָאֵלֶּה בְּאָזְנֵיהֶם וַיִּירְאוּ
ט הָאֲנָשִׁים מְאֹד: וַיִּקְרָא אֲבִימֶלֶךְ לְאַבְרָהָם וַיֹּאמֶר לוֹ
מֶה־עָשִׂיתָ לָּנוּ וּמֶה־חָטָאתִי לָךְ כִּי־הֵבֵאתָ עָלַי וְעַל־
מַמְלַכְתִּי חֲטָאָה גְדֹלָה מַעֲשִׂים אֲשֶׁר לֹא־יֵעָשׂוּ עָשִׂיתָ
י עִמָּדִי: וַיֹּאמֶר אֲבִימֶלֶךְ אֶל־אַבְרָהָם מָה רָאִיתָ כִּי עָשִׂיתָ
יא אֶת־הַדָּבָר הַזֶּה: וַיֹּאמֶר אַבְרָהָם כִּי אָמַרְתִּי רַק אֵין־יִרְאַת
יב אֱלֹהִים בַּמָּקוֹם הַזֶּה וַהֲרָגוּנִי עַל־דְּבַר אִשְׁתִּי: וְגַם־אָמְנָה
אֲחֹתִי בַת־אָבִי הִוא אַךְ לֹא בַת־אִמִּי וַתְּהִי־לִי לְאִשָּׁה:

Rabbah tells us that Abimelech was stricken with an occlusion of the genital organs from the time Sarah entered his palace. But, although she had already been in his house for a long time, the king did not realize the cause of this ailment until he heard the Divine warning in the dream of the night (*Ramban*).

7. כִּי־נָבִיא הוּא — *For he is a prophet.* And had he not been a prophet, would he not have had to return the wife to her husband? But the text means: "In any case, restore the wife to her husband, whoever he may be. And as for your objection, 'Do You kill nations even when they are righteous? Didn't he tell me, "She is my sister"?' know, Abimelech, that this man Abraham is a prophet and he knew in advance how you would behave. When a stranger arrives in a city, he is asked whether he would like to eat or drink, but he is not asked first whether this woman is his wife or his sister" (*Makkos* 9b). Abimelech should have understood that Abraham's statement about Sarah was just the subterfuge which he was forced to use because of the immoral way of welcoming strangers to the royal palace. Abimelech was guilty of not having learned how to behave properly.

וְיִתְפַּלֵּל בַּעַדְךָ וֶחְיֵה — *And he will pray for you and you will live.* The Sages point out: When one has humiliated his neighbor, he must pay him compensation. But he will only be absolved of the offense when he asks pardon, even if he should bring all the world's "rams of Nevayos," for it is written: "Now return the man's wife — for he is a prophet — so that he will pray for you." This implies, notes *Meiri,* that you should ask him to pardon you so willingly that he will even pray for you (*Bava Kamma* 92a; *Rambam* פ״ה ט׳ חובל ומזיק).

8. וַיִּירְאוּ הָאֲנָשִׁים מְאֹד — *And the people were very frightened.* They could see the smoke of Sodom rising like a blazing furnace and they said to each other, "The messengers who were sent there are now coming to visit us" (*Rabbah* 52). Moreover, it was a "bad dream," like the one Abimelech had just had, which provoked the first manifestation of the fear of God (*Berachos* 55a).

to touch her. ⁷ But now, return the man's wife for he is a prophet, and he will pray for you and you will live, but if you do not return her, be aware that you shall surely die: you and all that is yours."

⁸ Abimelech arose early next morning; he summoned all his servants and told them all of these things in their ears, and the people were very frightened. ⁹ Then Abimelech summoned Abraham and said to him, "What have you done to us? How have I sinned against you that you brought upon me and my kingdom such great sin? Deeds that ought not to be done have you done to me!" ¹⁰ And Abimelech said to Abraham, "What did you see that you did such a thing?'

¹¹ And Abraham said, "Because I said, 'There is but no fear of God in this place and they will slay me because of my wife.' ¹² Moreover, she is indeed my sister, my father's daughter, though not my mother's daughter; and she became my wife.

9. מֶה־עָשִׂיתָ לָּנוּ — What have you done to us? Abimelech's reaction resembled that of Pharaoh of Egypt and prompts the same observations. Cf. our commentary on 12:18, where the reason for Abraham's different attitude toward Abimelech is given.

11. רַק אֵין־יִרְאַת אֱלֹהִים בַּמָּקוֹם הַזֶּה — There is but no fear of God in this place. Abraham seems to want to reply, "Neither civilization nor the ethics of your nation, of which you boast, is a sufficient guarantee of morality, since the fear of God is lacking in your realm."

The adverb רַק at the beginning of this phrase has a restrictive meaning, as usual. R' Eliezer interprets it thus: "The fear of God was not entirely lacking among the Philistines, since the text has just said, the people were very frightened. But it was limited. It only manifested itself when the news of a Divine rebuke was announced (ילק״ש, רמז נ״ז). Accordingly it was purely external. That is why the Torah here used the term יִרְאַת אֱלֹהִים, fear of the God of justice, and not the usual יִרְאַת ה', fear permeated with a veneration of the God of love (של״ה, עשרה מאמרות).

For Abraham, the fear of God meant, if not the ultimate goal, then the fundamental basis for all moral life, as will be seen in 22:12. Here Abraham shows that for him this moral criterion has an absolute value. "God has no other treasure in His world more precious than the fear of Heaven" (Shabbos 31b).

12. בַּת־אָבִי הוּא — My father's daughter. The Torah sometimes uses the terms "son" and "daughter" to mean grandson or granddaughter. Sarah, whom tradition identifies with Iscah, daughter of Haran (Rashi on 11:29), was in fact the granddaughter of Terah and Abraham's niece. Ramban severely criticizes the patriarch's conduct in again placing his wife's life in danger. He says it is of little importance whether Abraham said truthfully or not that Sarah was his sister, since he concealed the essential fact that she was also his wife.

יג וַיְהִי כַּאֲשֶׁר הִתְעוּ אֹתִי אֱלֹהִים מִבֵּית אָבִי וָאֹמַר לָהּ
זֶה חַסְדֵּךְ אֲשֶׁר תַּעֲשִׂי עִמָּדִי אֶל כָּל־הַמָּקוֹם אֲשֶׁר נָבוֹא
יד שָׁמָּה אִמְרִי־לִי אָחִי הוּא: וַיִּקַּח אֲבִימֶלֶךְ צֹאן וּבָקָר
וַעֲבָדִים וּשְׁפָחֹת וַיִּתֵּן לְאַבְרָהָם וַיָּשֶׁב לוֹ אֵת שָׂרָה אִשְׁתּוֹ:
טו וַיֹּאמֶר אֲבִימֶלֶךְ הִנֵּה אַרְצִי לְפָנֶיךָ בַּטּוֹב בְּעֵינֶיךָ שֵׁב:
טז וּלְשָׂרָה אָמַר הִנֵּה נָתַתִּי אֶלֶף כֶּסֶף לְאָחִיךְ הִנֵּה הוּא־לָךְ
יז כְּסוּת עֵינַיִם לְכֹל אֲשֶׁר אִתָּךְ וְאֵת כֹּל וְנֹכָחַת: וַיִּתְפַּלֵּל
אַבְרָהָם אֶל־הָאֱלֹהִים וַיִּרְפָּא אֱלֹהִים אֶת־אֲבִימֶלֶךְ
יח וְאֶת־אִשְׁתּוֹ וְאַמְהֹתָיו וַיֵּלֵדוּ: כִּי־עָצֹר עָצַר יהוה בְּעַד
כָּל־רֶחֶם לְבֵית אֲבִימֶלֶךְ עַל־דְּבַר שָׂרָה אֵשֶׁת אַבְרָהָם:

The Bible frequently reports the faults and the virtues of its heroes in a perfectly objective way. It never considers passing over their weaknesses or strayings in silence. But the moral character of our great Biblical personages is not thereby diminished; on the contrary, they gain by the full significance of the message which they address to us. If they shone in our eyes with a flawless brilliance, we would consider them as being endowed with a nature different from our own. Their virtues would appear to us as the result of a superior organization of character, devoid of passions and internal struggles, so that these virtues could not be attributed to their merit and they could not serve as examples for us. Thus, it is the errors of Moses, his outbursts of anger, which confer upon his modesty its inestimable value. It appears to us as the result of a very great attempt at willpower and self-discipline which we must imitate because it is in our power to do so (R' S. R' Hirsch).

13. וַיְהִי כַּאֲשֶׁר הִתְעוּ אֹתִי אֱלֹהִים — And so it was, when God caused me to wander. "Each time the name of God is used in the story of Abraham it is sacred, except in our verse, where it is profane (and designates idols). But some say it is sacred here as well" (Yerushalmi, Megillah 1:9). Rashi draws from this latter idea and explains, "When God had me leave my paternal home and I found myself wandering and buffeted about from place to place . . . I said to her, etc. . . ." But Onkelos translates: "When the nations strayed after their idols God brought me from my paternal home to worship and serve Him."

Rashi generally reports Onkelos' words, but here, exceptionally, he just says: "Onkelos has translated as he has translated." R' Meir Shapiro of Lublin interprets the inner thought that Rashi wanted to express by this phrase in the following manner: "It is known that Onkelos (Aquila of Pontus) was a pagan who converted and who renounced a high position in an idolatrous cult to become a loyal follower of God. He came upon his own destiny in the words of our sentence and he translated it accordingly. This is what Rashi wanted to bring out in a few concise words: He translated the verse as he interpreted his own life."

אֶל כָּל־הַמָּקוֹם אֲשֶׁר נָבוֹא שָׁמָּה — To whatever place we come. Abraham had

¹³ *And so it was, when God caused me to wander from my father's house, I said to her, 'Let this be your kindness which you shall do for me — to whatever place we come, say of me: He is my brother.'*"

¹⁴ *So Abimelech took flocks and cattle and servants and maidservants and gave them to Abraham; and he returned his wife Sarah to him.*

¹⁵ *And Abimelech said, "Behold, my land is before you: settle wherever you see fit." *¹⁶* And to Sarah he said, "Behold, I have given your brother a thousand pieces of silver. Behold! Let it be for you an eye-covering for all who are with you; and to all you will be vindicated."*

¹⁷ *Abraham prayed to God, and God healed Abimelech, his wife, and his maids, and they were relieved; *¹⁸* for HASHEM had completely restrained every orifice of the household of Abimelech, because of Sarah, the wife of Abraham.*

addressed this request to Sarah from their first voyage to Egypt. She was always to say, "He is my brother," and this agreement was not repeated when they went to Gerar (*Ramban*).

16. וּלְשָׂרָה אָמַר — *And to Sarah he said.* According to *Radak, Ibn Ezra,* and others, the sense of this difficult verse would be as follows: The fact that, even as king, I tried to redeem myself in such spectacular fashion from the single time I had approached you will assure you in the future of such protection (a covering of the eyes, which guards against improper glances) among your entourage. Consequently you will be able to introduce yourself candidly to anyone without having to disguise your identity.

However, in the tone of this sentence R' Yitzchak perceives a reproach to Sarah: "You have blindfolded me" (by declaring a false identity) — הִנֵּה הוּא־לָךְ, "Let the covering of the eyes fall back on you!"

"Do not take any curse lightly, not even that of a common man. For Abimelech's curse was realized with Sarah's son, Isaac, whose vision was dimmed" (27:1; *Bava Kamma* 93a: א״ת כסות אלא כסיית עינים).

17. וַיִּתְפַּלֵּל אַבְרָהָם . . . וַיִּרְפָּא אֱלֹהִים אֶת־אֲבִימֶלֶךְ — *Abraham prayed . . . and God healed Abimelech.* From where do we learn that an offended party to whom the offender has apologized must not show himself unwilling to forgive? From the verse, *Abraham prayed to God, etc.* (*Bava Kamma* ibid.). This is the first time in the Torah, adds the *Midrash Rabbah,* that mention is made of a man's prayer to God. And this prayer is that of a husband who has just been mocked, and it is spoken in favor of the health of his "rival" stricken with a physical disability!

18. כִּי־עָצֹר עָצַר ה׳ — *For HASHEM had completely restrained.* Cf. our commentary on verse 6.

עַל־דְּבַר שָׂרָה — *Because of Sarah.* The occlusion of the genital organs with which

כא

א וַיהוָה פָּקַד אֶת־שָׂרָה כַּאֲשֶׁר אָמָר וַיַּעַשׂ יהוָה לְשָׂרָה כַּאֲשֶׁר
ב דִּבֵּר: וַתַּהַר וַתֵּלֶד שָׂרָה לְאַבְרָהָם בֵּן לִזְקֻנָיו לַמּוֹעֵד
ג אֲשֶׁר־דִּבֶּר אֹתוֹ אֱלֹהִים: וַיִּקְרָא אַבְרָהָם אֶת־שֶׁם־בְּנוֹ
ד הַנּוֹלַד־לוֹ אֲשֶׁר־יָלְדָה־לּוֹ שָׂרָה יִצְחָק: וַיָּמָל אַבְרָהָם
אֶת־יִצְחָק בְּנוֹ בֶּן־שְׁמֹנַת יָמִים כַּאֲשֶׁר צִוָּה אֹתוֹ אֱלֹהִים:
חמישי   ה וְאַבְרָהָם בֶּן־מְאַת שָׁנָה בְּהִוָּלֶד לוֹ אֵת יִצְחָק בְּנוֹ:

Abimelech was stricken, as *Rashi* reports (verse 9), was produced "because of Sarah" so that no one could say, "It is by Abimelech that she is pregnant" (*R' Chaim ben Attar*).

21.

1. נַה׳ פָּקַד אֶת־שָׂרָה — *HASHEM had remembered Sarah.* This expression implies an act of Providence going beyond the laws of nature, according to the *Zohar.* Sarah's giving birth indeed appeared to be a supernatural phenomenon. Generally the term זְכִירָה transmits the idea of a providential intervention, as was explained in 8:1, when Noah was miraculously saved in the midst of the flood's waves. Similarly here, פְּקִידָה precedes עֲשִׂיָה just as the decision precedes the action.

The Talmud emphasizes in several passages that Sarah's prayer was granted on the day of Rosh Hashanah (*Berachos* 29b). On that day, explains *Rashi,* God remembers sterile wives, and fulfilling their prayers, renders them fertile, as was the case also with Rachel and with Hannah, the mother of the prophet Samuel (and, according to certain of our authorities, Rebecca). Rosh Hashanah is the time when זְכְרוֹנוֹת, *the remembrances* of our merits, rise up before God and when great providential decisions are made concerning individual and national destinies, as the *Mussaf* prayer of Rosh Hashanah describes. Consequently, this chapter was chosen for the Torah reading on the first day of that festival.

כַּאֲשֶׁר דִּבֵּר — *As He had spoken.* The repetition in this verse occurs because Scripture wants to emphasize that the miracle occurred exactly as it had been foretold (*Radak*). But Rava explains that the words כַּאֲשֶׁר אָמָר in the first half of the verse refer to Abraham's speech about Abimelech, discussed at the end of the preceding chapter. "From where do we learn that he who prays for something for his neighbor, while he himself requires the same, will be answered first? From Abraham, who interceded so that the wife and slaves of Abimelech could give birth; but it was his wife Sarah, who gave birth first; that is why the two passages are close together in the text" (*Bava Kamma* 92a). The *Tosafists* add, "This is not a question of the gift of the birth itself, for that had already been announced earlier by the angels, but rather of an easy delivery." The fact that Sarah, like other righteous women, gave birth without pain has already been pointed out in 3:16.

2. בֵּן לִזְקֻנָיו — *A son . . . in his old age.* The Midrash interprets the word לִזְקֻנָיו as a compound from זִיו אִיקוֹנִין שֶׁלּוֹ, his face resembled that of his father. The same

21   ¹H*ASHEM had remembered Sarah as He had said; and* H*ASHEM did for Sarah as He had spoken.* ² *Sarah conceived and bore a son unto Abraham in his old age, at the appointed time of which God had spoken with him.* ³ *Abraham called the name of his son who was born to him — whom Sarah had borne him — Isaac.*

    ⁴ *Abraham circumcised his son Isaac at the age of eight days as God had commanded him.* ⁵ *And Abraham was a hundred years old when his son Isaac was born to him.*

---

observation is made for Joseph, the son of the patriarch Jacob. זְקֻנִים are the years when a man thinks about the end of his life and again feels the desire for a lineage fit to succeed him in the moral sense and to perpetuate his spiritual heritage. Thus, the son who promises to be a worthy descendant of his aged father is called בֶּן לִזְקֻנָיו. Now, Isaac was destined from birth to fulfill this mission, and his parents recognized the promising future of their child in his countenance, which already reflected the image of his father.

3. וַיִּקְרָא אַבְרָהָם אֶת־שֶׁם־בְּנוֹ הַנּוֹלַד־לוֹ . . . יִצְחָק — *Abraham called the name of his son who was born to him . . . Isaac.* The significance of this name has already been commented upon in 17:19. The first Jewish child was called יִצְחָק because he brought a skeptical smile to all those who did not believe in Divine Providence and in miracles. The derisive laugh heard at the cradle of the Jewish people is the same as that which accompanies them along with their "pretensions" to a universal messianism throughout the centuries of history. It will accompany them until the realization of the Biblical prophecies and the epoch of which it is said, אָז יִמָּלֵא שְׂחוֹק פִּינוּ, *then shall our mouth be filled with laughter* (*Psalms* 126:2). This laugh of the future will no longer be צְחוֹק, a mocking, derisive laugh, but שְׂחוֹק, a laughter of gladness, full of love (*R' S. R. Hirsch*).

4. בֶּן־שְׁמֹנַת יָמִים — *At the age of eight days.* Accordingly, one customarily greets the newborn, when he is led to the *milah*, with the words בָּרוּךְ הַבָּא, for the word הַבָּא corresponds in numerical value to eight (*Baalei HaTosafos*).

כַּאֲשֶׁר צִוָּה אֹתוֹ אֱלֹהִים — *As God had commanded him.* With the same eagerness and joy as when he had performed his own *milah*, which God Himself had commanded. He offered a great feast on the day of his son's circumcision, as the *Tosafists* read between the lines of verse 8: (בְּיוֹם הִגָּמֵל, הג־מָל), on the eighth day, according to the numerical value of הג (8); cf. *Shabbos* 130a). Rabban Shimon ben Gamliel concluded: "Every *mitzvah* which Jewry accepted with joy, such as *milah*, it still performs in gladness" (*Shabbos* ibid.).

5. וְאַבְרָהָם בֶּן־מְאַת שָׁנָה — *And Abraham was a hundred years old.* *Ramban*, in several passages, dwells upon the fact that the advanced age at which the patriarch became the father of a child does not constitute a real miracle. He recalls that forty years later Abraham had six sons by Keturah, as the Torah points out

וַתֹּאמֶר שָׂרָה צְחֹק עָשָׂה לִי אֱלֹהִים כָּל־הַשֹּׁמֵעַ יִצְחַק־לִי: ו
וַתֹּאמֶר מִי מִלֵּל לְאַבְרָהָם הֵינִיקָה בָנִים שָׂרָה כִּי־יָלַדְתִּי בֵן ז
לִזְקֻנָיו: וַיִּגְדַּל הַיֶּלֶד וַיִּגָּמַל וַיַּעַשׂ אַבְרָהָם מִשְׁתֶּה גָדוֹל בְּיוֹם ח
הִגָּמֵל אֶת־יִצְחָק: וַתֵּרֶא שָׂרָה אֶת־בֶּן־הָגָר הַמִּצְרִית אֲשֶׁר־ ט

at the beginning of Chapter 25. Besides, at the age of 100, Abraham had just entered the second half of his life. The miracle was rather that he had a child from Sarah, at age 90, whose menstrual cycle had stopped. Thus it can be understood that the Torah does not draw attention to the pregnancy of Jochebed, mother of Moses, at the age of 130 as a miracle (cf. *Sotah* 12a), for advanced age does not at all preclude the retention of all physiological functions (*Ramban* on 46:15).

6. יִצְחַק־לִי — *Will laugh for me.* Rashi explains, "will rejoice with me. Along with Sarah, God remembered many other barren women. Many sick people were cured on that day. Many prayers were answered. There was great joy in the world." This is a typical example of a "collective blessing" emanating from the righteous. It is the counterpart of the principle of collective responsibility, described in our commentary to 18:25. זֵכֶר צַדִּיק לִבְרָכָה, when the memory of the righteous rises before God it brings about a general blessing.

7. מִי מִלֵּל לְאַבְרָהָם — *Who is the One Who said to Abraham.* "Instead of the usual verb דִּבֵּר, Sarah uses the verb מִלֵּל. The three letters of the root מלל give the numerical value of 100: when Abraham will be 100 years old" (*Rashi*). In analogous fashion, Hannah, mother of the prophet Samuel, cries out in her song of gladness: עָלַץ לִבִּי בַּה', *My heart exults in God.* The *Yalkut Shimoni* (*I Samuel* 2:1) points out that the three letters of the word עָלַץ (to exult) indicate in their numerical values the three great dates in the lives of Abraham and Sarah as they awaited their child. ע (70) recalls the seventy years of age at which time Abraham was promised a posterity at the covenant בֵּין הַבְּתָרִים; ל (30) are the thirty years Abraham had to wait before seeing the realization of the promise; צ (90) corresponds to Sarah's age when she became a mother.

הֵינִיקָה בָנִים שָׂרָה — *Sarah would nurse children.* "Though they be numerous who laugh on account of me, who among them could describe to Abraham just one word of what the weaning of this child represents for me! In him I nourish the entire future of a nation; I am, thanks to him, the mother of all his lineage, for he will carry the torch lit by his father." Sarah did not nourish just one child; in educating and raising her son, she nourished the multitude of her children (הֵינִיקָה בָנִים שָׂרָה, *Sarah would nurse children*, in the plural).

8. וַיִּגְדַּל הַיֶּלֶד וַיִּגָּמַל — *The child grew and was weaned.* Rashi: "at the end of twenty-four months." We find in the apocryphal book of *2 Maccabees* that mothers weaned their children when they were three years old (7:27). Indeed, *R' Bachya ibn Pakuda* explains, it is usual to make a celebration on the day of the birth or the circumcision of a son. But Abraham postponed the feast until the

⁶ *Sarah said, "God has made laughter for me; whoever hears will laugh for me."* ⁷ *And she said, "Who is the One Who said to Abraham, 'Sarah would nurse children'? For I have borne a son in his old age!"*

⁸ *The child grew and was weaned. Abraham made a great feast on the day Isaac was weaned.*

⁹ *Sarah saw the son of Hagar, the Egyptian, whom she had*

day of weaning, for this day marked the beginning of his son's spiritual life. Do not be astonished at this precocious age, for had not Abraham himself "recognized the Creator from the age of three"? Accordingly he wanted to introduce his son to reflect on things Divine from his tenderest infancy, as the prophet Isaiah similarly recommends: *To whom shall he teach knowledge? And whom shall he give to understand doctrine? Those that are weaned from the milk, those that are taken from the breasts* (28:9). Jewish education begins with the first awakening of the spirit in the child scarcely come into the world. *You have founded Your might*, will say the Psalmist, *out of the mouths of babes and sucklings* (8:3).

מִשְׁתֶּה גָדוֹל — *A great feast.* "Because the great men of the epoch, Shem, Eber, and Abimelech, were there" (*Rashi*). According to *Midrash Rabbah*, the thirty-one kings of Canaan were also there, as well as the giant Og, the eternal skeptic, who had come to see the miracle predicted by God. "The children of this baby will one day punish you for your mocking of the God of Abraham," cried out a celestial voice, alluding to the death of the giant, related in *Numbers* 21:34.

R' Shimon said: Whoever enjoys himself on his festive days without giving joy to the poor is accused by Satan, who causes him the worst torments. Who exerted himself more than Abraham in acts of charity for all creatures? Nevertheless, when he made his feast, he invited only the great men of his time. Consequently, Satan descended and stayed at his door, disguised as a beggar. But no one paid any attention to him. Abraham served the kings and princes. Sarah was busy suckling the children of the princesses. For people had said, "Isaac is not the child of Sarah, he is a foundling" (cf. *Rashi* on verse 7). Immediately, Satan went to carry his accusation before God: "Master of the world! You call Abraham 'My friend.' Now, he is offering a feast but gives nothing to the poor. He has not even offered a dove as a sacrifice in Your honor." The feast was thus disturbed by Satan. And God decreed that Abraham would be put on trial by the binding of Isaac, which ultimately resulted in the death of Sarah (noted by *Rashi* on 22:1 and 23:2; *Zohar* 1:118).

9. וַתֵּרֶא שָׂרָה אֶת־בֶּן־הָגָר ... אֲשֶׁר־יָלָדָה — *Sarah saw the son of Hagar ... whom she had born.* At the beginning of *Exodus*, the Sages of the Midrash note the perfect harmony which prevailed among the patriarch Jacob and his twelve sons as they went down of a common accord to sojourn in Egyptian exile. The Sages also emphasize that such exemplary harmony was lacking in the homes

י יָלְדָה לְאַבְרָהָם מְצַחֵק: וַתֹּאמֶר לְאַבְרָהָם גָּרֵשׁ הָאָמָה הַזֹּאת
וְאֶת־בְּנָהּ כִּי לֹא יִירַשׁ בֶּן־הָאָמָה הַזֹּאת עִם־בְּנִי עִם־יִצְחָק:
יא-יב וַיֵּרַע הַדָּבָר מְאֹד בְּעֵינֵי אַבְרָהָם עַל אוֹדֹת בְּנוֹ: וַיֹּאמֶר
אֱלֹהִים אֶל־אַבְרָהָם אַל־יֵרַע בְּעֵינֶיךָ עַל־הַנַּעַר וְעַל־אֲמָתֶךָ
כֹּל אֲשֶׁר תֹּאמַר אֵלֶיךָ שָׂרָה שְׁמַע בְּקֹלָהּ כִּי בְיִצְחָק יִקָּרֵא
יג לְךָ זָרַע: וְגַם אֶת־בֶּן־הָאָמָה לְגוֹי אֲשִׂימֶנּוּ כִּי זַרְעֲךָ הוּא:

of Abraham and Isaac. The Sages do not hesitate to blame the patriarchs themselves, and in this connection they quote the verse from *Proverbs:* "To spare the rod is to hate the child; but to take care to correct him is to love him" (13:24). Abraham and Isaac were both too indulgent with their sons, whereas Jacob educated his children with greater authority, although he had a weakness (with heavy consequences) for Joseph.

Abraham was not insensitive to the manifestations of love which he received from Ishmael, just as Isaac, in the following generation, allowed himself to fall into "the snare of the fine words" of Esau (*Rabbah* ibid.). In both cases, it was the mother who was more clear-sighted than the father. Sarah realized that Ishmael, who she so much hoped would become his father's spiritual heir, resembled his mother Hagar more and more as he grew up. She called him "the son of Hagar the Egyptian," which characterized his entire personality, but Abraham always saw in him "his son" (verse 11).

מְצַחֵק — *Mocking. Rashi* explains that Ishmael was guilty of idolatry, debauchery, and murder. This opinion is attributed to R' Akiva, according to the Talmudic texts (*Rosh Hashanah* 18b and *Tosefta, Sotah* 6). But R' Shimon professes a second opinion, also quoted by *Rashi*, according to which Ishmael argued with Isaac about the inheritance, as is seen from Sarah's declaration in the following verse. R' Shimon, then, finds his interpretation "more probable than that of R' Akiva," but *Rashi* seems to want to consider the two opinions complementary. As for *Ramban*, he considers that Ishmael's jeering, derisive laughter was heard on the very day of Isaac's feast and not several years later, as the preceding explanations suggest. It was about the legitimacy of the birth of Isaac, a subject which concerned Ishmael because of his rights of inheritance. Thus, instead of espousing the faith of Abraham, Ishmael adopted a derisive, cynical sneer, characteristic of the world of the pagans.

10. גָּרֵשׁ הָאָמָה הַזֹּאת — *Drive out this slavewoman.* "Because she dismissed Hagar the Egyptian from her house, the descendants of Sarah were punished and driven out of Egypt" (*Baal HaTurim*). The relationship between Sarah and Hagar surely underwent numerous vicissitudes and saw profound changes. But, given that the decision to dismiss Hagar was approved by God, why was it liable to punishment? The answer is that although the decision seemed justified with respect to Ishmael's conduct, it was nevertheless blameworthy, for Sarah ought

born to Abraham, mocking. ¹⁰ *So she said to Abraham, "Drive out this slavewoman with her son, for the son of that slavewoman shall not inherit with my son, with Isaac!"*

¹¹ *The matter greatly distressed Abraham regarding his son.* ¹² *So God said to Abraham, "Be not distressed over the youth or your slavewoman: Whatever Sarah tells you, heed her voice, since through Isaac will offspring be considered yours.* ¹³ *But the son of the slavewoman as well will I make into a nation for he is your offspring."*

to have exerted her influence on Ishmael's upbringing at the opportune time so that the conflict would never have broken out.

כִּי לֹא יִירַשׁ בֶּן־הָאָמָה הַזֹּאת עִם־בְּנִי עִם־יִצְחָק — *For the son of that slavewoman shall not inherit with my son, with Isaac.* "I know that he will not share the faith with him and he will not have a common share with him either in this world or in the World to Come. And God approved of Sarah's words, for the sacred lineage had to live its own life in order to preserve its special character" (*Zohar*). *The scepter of wickedness shall not rest upon the lot of the righteous* said the Psalmist (125:3).

11. וַיֵּרַע הַדָּבָר מְאֹד בְּעֵינֵי אַבְרָהָם — *The matter greatly distressed Abraham.* "Of all the trials which afflicted Abraham, this dismissal was particularly painful to him" (*Pirkei D'Rabbi Eliezer* 31). Throughout his life he had led innumerable pagans to love God, and now he found himself forced to expel his own son because he had turned away from the right path. Up to now, Abraham had not realized the evil tendencies in the character of his oldest son. "Depravity in a man's house is worse than the war of Gog and Magog" (*Berachos* 7b). But he accepted this new test (the eighth or, according to some, the ninth of his ten tests) with his usual confidence in God; and as soon as he had recognized the Divine will, he rose "early in he morning," always eager to accomplish this will and to carry it out without complaint.

עַל אוֹדֹת בְּנוֹ — *Regarding his son.* Abraham hoped that association with Isaac would influence Ishmael for the better and, to this end, he wanted to keep him at home. But Sarah, whose prophetic power was superior to Abraham's (*Rashi* on verse 12) foresaw, on the contrary, the ill-omened influence of Ishmael on his younger brother. God then ordered Abraham to listen to the voice of his wife. "When hot water is poured into cold water, the hot water is cooled" (*Chofetz Chaim*).

12. שְׁמַע בְּקֹלָה — *Heed her voice.* Obedience is expressed in Hebrew not by שָׁמַע הַדָּבָר, but by שָׁמַע בְּקוֹל, to listen to a person's voice, not only to his speech. One obeys because this voice has spoken, and not because of the words and their content. Listen to Sarah's voice, obey it, even if you are displeased by her words. Trust her, for she has a better feel for the truth than you. Women generally have a more accurate view of nuances of character (cf. our commentary to 16:2).

יד וַיַּשְׁכֵּם אַבְרָהָם ׀ בַּבֹּקֶר וַיִּקַּח־לֶחֶם וְחֵמַת מַיִם וַיִּתֵּן אֶל־הָגָר
שָׂם עַל־שִׁכְמָהּ וְאֶת־הַיֶּלֶד וַיְשַׁלְּחֶהָ וַתֵּלֶךְ וַתֵּתַע בְּמִדְבַּר
טו בְּאֵר שָׁבַע: וַיִּכְלוּ הַמַּיִם מִן־הַחֵמֶת וַתַּשְׁלֵךְ אֶת־הַיֶּלֶד תַּחַת
טז אַחַד הַשִּׂיחִם: וַתֵּלֶךְ וַתֵּשֶׁב לָהּ מִנֶּגֶד הַרְחֵק כִּמְטַחֲוֵי קֶשֶׁת
כִּי אָמְרָה אַל־אֶרְאֶה בְּמוֹת הַיָּלֶד וַתֵּשֶׁב מִנֶּגֶד וַתִּשָּׂא
יז אֶת־קֹלָהּ וַתֵּבְךְּ: וַיִּשְׁמַע אֱלֹהִים אֶת־קוֹל הַנַּעַר וַיִּקְרָא
מַלְאַךְ אֱלֹהִים ׀ אֶל־הָגָר מִן־הַשָּׁמַיִם וַיֹּאמֶר לָהּ מַה־לָּךְ הָגָר
אַל־תִּירְאִי כִּי־שָׁמַע אֱלֹהִים אֶל־קוֹל הַנַּעַר בַּאֲשֶׁר הוּא־

כִּי בְיִצְחָק יִקָּרֵא לְךָ זָרַע — *Since through Isaac will offspring be considered yours.*
The Talmud interprets the word בְּיִצְחָק in a restrictive sense: your posterity,
bearing your name, will not be the entire race of Isaac, but only a part of this
race: בְּיִצְחָק וְלֹא כָּל יִצְחָק, which excludes Esau and his descendants (*Nedarim*
31a; see our commentary on 16:2).

14. וַיְשַׁלְּחֶהָ — *And sent her off.* This implies a legal act of repudiation. In order to
remove Isaac and his descendants from the harmful influence of Ishmael and his
Egyptian mother, Sarah in her great foresight knew that a complete rupture was
now needed. Though a radical measure, it was called for by the circumstances.
The divorce had to be effected in such a way that mother and son would appear
to the house of Abraham (according to the "letter of the law") strictly as a
bondwoman and her son. Later, Abraham would be free to grant Hagar a status
more in keeping with his spirit of generosity and his personal sentiments. This
he did after the marriage of Isaac (*Rashi* on 25:1).

וַתֵּלֶךְ וַתֵּתַע — *She departed, and strayed.* To be taken figuratively. As soon as
she was dismissed from Abraham's family, she strayed and returned to the
pagan cult of her father's house. And so God heard not her plea but her son's,
just as in their first flight into the desert (16:11).

15. וַתַּשְׁלֵךְ אֶת־הַיֶּלֶד — *She cast off the boy.* Hagar's behavior is extremely
characteristic and denotes the brutality of the Hamitic nature. A Jewish mother
would not have abandoned her child; she would have stayed by him even if all
she could do was to calm him or ease his suffering, even if only to soothe him for
a fraction of a second. To withdraw and remain passive because one does not
wish to see misery is no proof of pity but rather a sign of cruel, primitive egotism.
In every being moved by human sentiments, a sense of duty wins out over the
most violent emotions. It can make one forget his own pain to care for and help
another, even when the only good he can do is to give the other the comfort and
consolation of knowing another person is near (*R' S. R. Hirsch*).

16. וַתֵּלֶךְ וַתֵּשֶׁב לָהּ מִנֶּגֶד — *She went and sat herself down at a distance.* Hagar
had proceeded to "the desert of Beer-sheba," a name given in anticipation (verse
31). It is believed that the city of Beer-sheba was on the southern Philistine
border and it was there that Abraham prayed and proclaimed the name of God

¹⁴ *So Abraham awoke early in the morning, took bread and a skin of water, and gave them to Hagar. He placed them on her shoulder along with the boy, and sent her off. She departed, and strayed in the desert of Beer-sheba.*

¹⁵ *When the water of the skin was consumed, she cast off the boy beneath one of the trees.* ¹⁶ *She went and sat herself down at a distance, some bowshots away, for she said, "Let me not see the death of the child." And she sat at a distance, lifted her voice, and wept.*

¹⁷ *God heard the cry of the youth, and an angel of God called to Hagar from heaven and said to her, "What troubles you, Hagar? Fear not, for God has heeded the cry of the youth in his*

(verse 33). The "gate of the heavens" is also situated in this region (*Rashi* to 28:10-17). Aware of these facts, Hagar sat down here, "facing the gate of the heavens" where "the ladder set up on the earth" rises to carry prayers to the celestial spheres. Consequently, the prayer of Ishmael was fulfilled בַּאֲשֶׁר הוּא שָׁם, because he was there, because of his location (*Meshech Chochmah*).

17. וַיִּשְׁמַע אֱלֹהִים אֶת־קוֹל הַנַּעַר — *God heard the cry of the youth.* Ishmael was overcome with thirst. He collapsed amid the thornbushes of the desert and cried out, "Master of the world! If you would quench my thirst, let me drink. But do not leave me to die the most horrible of all deaths — from thirst!" And God granted this prayer (*Pirkei D'Rabbi Eliezer* 30). This passage is always read in the synagogue on the first day of Rosh Hashanah. It reminds us that on this day of repentance "though all the gates of prayer are closed, that of tears is not closed" (*Berachos* 32b).

וַיִּקְרָא מַלְאַךְ אֱלֹהִים אֶל־הָגָר מִן־הַשָּׁמַיִם — *And an angel of God called to Hagar from heaven.* When Hagar first fled the angels had spoken directly to her. In fact, she was used to seeing angels in Abraham's house and later returned to it. But here, he divorced himself from her. And so the angel called to her only from the heavens (cf. *Rashi* on 16:13). Abraham was also called by an angel from heaven during the binding of Isaac, but there the reason is different. His sacrifice resembled that offered by the High Priest in the Holy of Holies on the Day of Atonement. No one could enter here, not even an angel. Similarly, access to Mount Moriah was forbidden to the angels when Isaac was bound and the angel could call Abraham only from heaven (*Meshech Chochmah*).

בַּאֲשֶׁר הוּא־שָׁם — *In his present state.* Rashi quotes the Talmud (*Rosh Hashanah* 16a) which explains that man is judged by his present behavior and not by his future conduct. God answers the angels who plead against Ishmael's descendants: "At this moment what is he? Righteous or wicked? Righteous, I judge him 'as he is now,' according to what he is doing at present." This is the meaning of "in his present state."

יח שָׁם: קוּמִי שְׂאִי אֶת־הַנַּעַר וְהַחֲזִיקִי אֶת־יָדֵךְ בּוֹ כִּי־לְגוֹי גָּדוֹל
יט אֲשִׂימֶנּוּ: וַיִּפְקַח אֱלֹהִים אֶת־עֵינֶיהָ וַתֵּרֶא בְּאֵר מָיִם וַתֵּלֶךְ
כ וַתְּמַלֵּא אֶת־הַחֵמֶת מַיִם וַתַּשְׁקְ אֶת־הַנָּעַר: וַיְהִי אֱלֹהִים
כא אֶת־הַנַּעַר וַיִּגְדָּל וַיֵּשֶׁב בַּמִּדְבָּר וַיְהִי רֹבֶה קַשָּׁת: וַיֵּשֶׁב
בְּמִדְבַּר פָּארָן וַתִּקַּח־לוֹ אִמּוֹ אִשָּׁה מֵאֶרֶץ מִצְרָיִם:
ששי כב וַיְהִי בָּעֵת הַהִוא וַיֹּאמֶר אֲבִימֶלֶךְ וּפִיכֹל שַׂר־צְבָאוֹ אֶל־
כג אַבְרָהָם לֵאמֹר אֱלֹהִים עִמְּךָ בְּכֹל אֲשֶׁר־אַתָּה עֹשֶׂה: וְעַתָּה

The commentators of the Talmud ask about the difference between Ishmael's case and that of the "stubborn and rebellious son" who is given the death penalty (*Deuteronomy* 21:21) because he is judged, right from that moment, according to his end. He is considered irrevocably lost (*Sanhedrin* 71b). The difference, answer some of our Sages, is that for a son of Abraham, as Ishmael was, hope of a return to the ideal is never abandoned. But this is a vain hope for a stubborn and rebellious son, born, as tradition explains, from a union with a woman (יְפַת תּוֹאַר) taken captive in war (*Deuteronomy* 21:10-14). Note that there the Torah portion dealing with her immediately precedes that of the rebellious son. Purity of origin remains the criterion.

But other exegetes pose the question: How can Ishmael be called righteous, judging from his present behavior, when he was accused of idolatry and immorality, as *Rashi* points out on verse 9? The *Zohar* replies that "as he then was" (that is, not yet twenty years of age) Ishmael was still not responsible for his actions from the point of view of the heavenly tribunal. Others hold that Ishmael was judged on criteria applying to nations and peoples, since he was destined to become the ancestor of "a great nation." In fact, in numerous passages in the Torah we find that the consequences, for Israel, of grave sins such as idolatry and debauchery are less severe for the צִבּוּר, which can point to its other distinguished qualities as a group, than for the individual. Accordingly, the *Shechinah* "dwells with them, even in the midst of their impurity" (*Leviticus* 16:16). But on the other hand, the moral shortcomings of a nation which affect its social life carry heavy sanctions; these can have far-reaching consequences as to cause the withdrawal of the *Shechinah* (cf. *Meshech Chochmah*, *Exodus* 14:29).

18. קוּמִי שְׂאִי אֶת־הַנַּעַר — *Arise, lift up the youth.* After having let him drink (*Ramban*). Ishmael is between two stages of life, childhood and adolescence and is called either נַעַר or יֶלֶד. According to tradition he was sixteen or seventeen. (At seventeen Joseph is also designated as יֶלֶד in *Genesis* 37:30 and as נַעַר in 37:2.)

Nevertheless, his mother carried him on her shoulders (verse 14), which is not surprising in an age when the average lifetime was from 120 to 170 years, and a boy of seventeen years corresponded to a ten- or eleven-year-old boy in our day.

וְהַחֲזִיקִי אֶת־יָדֵךְ בּוֹ — *And grasp your hand upon him.* The mother who supports her son in order to lead him to safety feels her own strength increase

present state. ¹⁸ *Arise, lift up the youth and grasp your hand upon him, for I will make a great nation of him."*

¹⁹ *Then God opened her eyes and she perceived a well of water; she went and filled the skin with water and gave the youth to drink.*

²⁰ *God was with the youth and he grew up; he dwelt in the desert and became an accomplished archer.* ²¹ *He lived in the desert of Paran, and his mother took a wife for him from the land of Egypt.*

²² *At that time, Abimelech and Phicol his general said to Abraham, "God is with you in all that you do.* ²³ *Now*

tenfold, the literal translation of וְהַחֲזִיקִי אֶת־יָדֵךְ בּוֹ is "strengthen your hand by him."

19. וַיִּפְקַח אֱלֹהִים אֶת־עֵינֶיהָ — *Then God opened her eyes.* The word פָּקַח is only used in the figurative sense of expanding intellectual vision. It does not refer to the recovery of the sense of sight; e.g. "God opened her eyes": Not that there was a veil over the eyes, which was removed; but one experienced another state in which new sources of knowledge were received (*Guide* 1:2).

21. מֵאֶרֶץ מִצְרָיִם — *From the land of Egypt. Rashi* notes, "From the place where she had been raised. As the proverb has it: Throw a stick into the air and it falls back where it came from." R' Eliezer adds, "Abraham went to visit his son Ishamel three years after his departure. He had promised Sarah not to dismount from his camel at Ishmael's place. Abraham arrived at midday and met his son's wife. He asked her where Ishmael could be found, and she replied that he had gone to the desert with his mother to pick dates. He said to her, 'Give me a little water and some bread, for I am tired from my trip through the desert.' She answered: 'I have neither bread nor water.' He said to her: 'When Ishmael returns, tell him that an old man from Canaan came and said that the threshold to the house needs repairing.' When his wife had carried out this request, Ishmael sent her away and his mother had him marry a wife from her own family, named Petuma. Three years later Abraham went back to see his son. Ishmael was absent as before, but his wife gave Abraham drink and food. Then Abraham prayed and blessed his house. When Ishmael learned of this on his return, he understood that his father still loved him" (*Pirkei D'Rabbi Eliezer* 30). Later on, he went back to his father's house at Beer-sheba and was with Abraham at the time of the binding of Isaac (*Rashi* on 22:3).

22. בָּעֵת הַהִוא — *At that time.* The many miracles from which Abraham had benefited, and especially that of the birth of Isaac, which had just occurred and which pointed to a close-at-hand realization of the Divine words, "I shall give this land to your descendants," prompted Abimelech to ask Abraham for a friendship treaty which would last for three generations. Far from considering Abraham an ordinary individual, the Philistine king saw in him the progenitor

הִשָּׁבְעָה לִּי בֵאלֹהִים הֵנָּה אִם־תִּשְׁקֹר לִי וּלְנִינִי וּלְנֶכְדִּי
כַּחֶסֶד אֲשֶׁר־עָשִׂיתִי עִמְּךָ תַּעֲשֶׂה עִמָּדִי וְעִם־הָאָרֶץ אֲשֶׁר־
כד־כה גַּרְתָּה בָּהּ: וַיֹּאמֶר אַבְרָהָם אָנֹכִי אִשָּׁבֵעַ: וְהוֹכִחַ אַבְרָהָם
אֶת־אֲבִימֶלֶךְ עַל־אֹדוֹת בְּאֵר הַמַּיִם אֲשֶׁר גָּזְלוּ עַבְדֵי
כו אֲבִימֶלֶךְ: וַיֹּאמֶר אֲבִימֶלֶךְ לֹא יָדַעְתִּי מִי עָשָׂה אֶת־הַדָּבָר
הַזֶּה וְגַם־אַתָּה לֹא־הִגַּדְתָּ לִי וְגַם אָנֹכִי לֹא שָׁמַעְתִּי בִּלְתִּי
כז הַיּוֹם: וַיִּקַּח אַבְרָהָם צֹאן וּבָקָר וַיִּתֵּן לַאֲבִימֶלֶךְ וַיִּכְרְתוּ
כח שְׁנֵיהֶם בְּרִית: וַיַּצֵּב אַבְרָהָם אֶת־שֶׁבַע כִּבְשֹׂת הַצֹּאן לְבַדְּהֶן:
כט וַיֹּאמֶר אֲבִימֶלֶךְ אֶל־אַבְרָהָם מָה הֵנָּה שֶׁבַע כְּבָשֹׂת הָאֵלֶּה
ל אֲשֶׁר הִצַּבְתָּ לְבַדָּנָה: וַיֹּאמֶר כִּי אֶת־שֶׁבַע כְּבָשֹׂת תִּקַּח

of a nation whose friendship and favor were important. Abraham was therefore qualified to sign a political treaty. The king shows complete confidence in Abraham's influence on his descendants. He has no doubt that they will consider themselves bound by their ancestor's word.

In keeping with the profound meaning of the story of the patriarchs, this passage about the pact of friendship between Abraham and the Philistine king is a forerunner of the fraternal alliance which the nations will offer to Jewry after they recognize that "God is with you in all that you do."

23. הֵנָּה הַשָּׁבְעָה לִּי בֵאלֹהִים — *Swear to me here by God.* הֵנָּה is an allusion to the two words הֵנָּה in 15:16: "the fourth generation will return *here* (to Canaan) for the iniquity of the Amorite shall not yet be full until *then.*" As a result Abimelech proposes an alliance to last for three generations, until Abraham's descendants return.

24. אָנֹכִי אִשָּׁבֵעַ — *I will swear.* Instead of using the usual personal pronoun אֲנִי, Abraham says אָנֹכִי, a term which adds weight to the first person singular pronoun. By thus stressing his own person, Abraham wishes to emphasize, "It is I, myself alone, who will swear." For "association with an idolater is prohibited so that the latter will not be led to swear by his idol" (*Sanhedrin* 63a). Unable to refuse this treaty with the king who had rendered him some service, Abraham wanted at least to avoid making him swear by his idol.

25. וְהוֹכִחַ אַבְרָהָם אֶת־אֲבִימֶלֶךְ — *Then Abraham disputed with Abimelech.* What is at stake in the discussion immediately following the conclusion of the treaty is of highly symbolic value. The well of water so often mentioned in the Bible represents the source of purity and fecundity. The prophet Jeremiah goes so far as to use it as the image of the Divinity itself: "They have forsaken Me, the source of living waters, to hew out for themselves cisterns, broken cisterns that cannot hold water" (2:13).

This symbolic aspect also underlies the dialogue in our text. By demanding the return of the wells he had dug, Abraham makes his new ally understand that

swear to me here by God that you will not deal falsely with me nor with my son nor with my grandson; according to the kindness that I have done with you, do with me, and with the land in which you have sojourned." [24] *And Abraham said, "I will swear."* [25] *Then Abraham disputed with Abimelech regarding the well of water that Abimelech's servants had seized.* [26] *But Abimelech said, "I do not know who did this thing; furthermore, you have never told me, and moreover I myself have heard nothing of it except for today."*

[27] *So Abraham took flocks and cattle and gave them to Abimelech; and the two of them entered into a covenant.* [28] *Abraham set seven ewes of the flock by themselves.* [29] *And Abimelech said to Abraham, "What are these seven ewes which you have set by them-selves?"*

[30] *And he replied, "Because you are to take these seven ewes*

he intends to remain the master of his "source of living waters," that is, the source of his inspiration. Even if he did consent to make a treaty with a pagan king, the latter must know that it is a political treaty but it includes no sort of communion on the spiritual plane. Abraham considered this right of cultural autonomy so important that he was intent on solemnly confirming it with Abimelech. For this he set aside seven ewe-lambs and offered to give them to him. By accepting them out of his hand, Abimelech attested to Abraham's formal right to "dig his own well." Hence "that place was called Beer-sheba: because there the two of them took an oath." This name brings out the great importance which Abraham attached to the incident of the well, at first sight so commonplace. The place was not called "the treaty of the oath" but Beer-sheba, "the source of the oath," in order to emphasize that to Abraham the safeguarding of his "source of inspiration" remained the essential factor in his treaty with Abimelech. The place name בְּאֵר שֶׁבַע is an eternal reminder of this important detail.

26. לֹא יָדַעְתִּי מִי עָשָׂה אֶת־הַדָּבָר הַזֶּה — *I do not know who did this thing.* This was Abimelech's reply to Abraham's reproach. He then turned to Pichol, his chief of staff, and said: "You also did not tell me of it." And Pichol replied, "I did not know of it before today." Hence the apparent repetitions in this verse (*Sfas Emes*).

27. וַיִּכְרְתוּ שְׁנֵיהֶם בְּרִית — *And the two of them entered into a covenant.* In spite of the pact, they remained "the two of them." Abraham refused to be closely united with his ally.

30. כִּי אֶת־שֶׁבַע כְּבָשֹׂת תִּקַּח מִיָּדִי — *Because you are to take these seven ewes from me.* The Sages of the Midrash disapprove of these gifts from Abraham to the Philistine king, which are in addition to the smaller livestock and the oxen already given as a symbol of the alliance. In their view, despite his precautions

מִיָּדִי בַּעֲבוּר תִּהְיֶה־לִּי לְעֵדָה כִּי חָפַרְתִּי אֶת־הַבְּאֵר הַזְּאת:
לא עַל־כֵּן קָרָא לַמָּקוֹם הַהוּא בְּאֵר שָׁבַע כִּי שָׁם נִשְׁבְּעוּ שְׁנֵיהֶם:
לב וַיִּכְרְתוּ בְרִית בִּבְאֵר שָׁבַע וַיָּקָם אֲבִימֶלֶךְ וּפִיכֹל שַׂר־צְבָאוֹ
לג וַיָּשֻׁבוּ אֶל־אֶרֶץ פְּלִשְׁתִּים: וַיִּטַּע אֶשֶׁל בִּבְאֵר שָׁבַע וַיִּקְרָא־
לד שָׁם בְּשֵׁם יהוה אֵל עוֹלָם: וַיָּגָר אַבְרָהָם בְּאֶרֶץ פְּלִשְׁתִּים יָמִים
רַבִּים:

and reservations, the patriarch went too far in his pact of friendship with a pagan king. And did not this treaty determine the future of the land which was promised to him and his descendants? True, it was only for a time, but did Abraham have the right, was he free to limit it, even for three generations? Accordingly, his confident and amiable attitude was not at all rewarded. The Philistines waged war more often with the Jews, right from their arrival in Canaan, than all the other peoples of these lands. And the consequences were serious in many respects for the future of the Jewish people during the period of the judges and the kings (cf. *Rabbah* 56). Finally the covenant foundered in bloody battles right in the heart of Jerusalem, which in David's time was occupied by the Jebusites, descendants of Abimelech! "King David and his men marched on Jerusalem against the Jebusites who occupied the land; but they said to David, 'You will not enter until you have removed the blind and the lame,' meaning that David could not enter. Nevertheless David captured the stronghold of Zion, the city of David, and David said on that day, 'Whoever will smite the Jebusites must reach to the summit and the lame and the blind that are hateful to David's soul'" (*II Samuel* 5:6-8). *Rashi* and *Radak* report that the Jebusites had put together two banners, one with an image of a blind man, the other showing a lame one. These represented the patriarch Isaac, who became blind, and the patriarch Jacob, who became lame after his battle with the angel. They kept citing the oath of the covenant which Abraham had sworn to their ancestor Abimelech. And so, the Jews could not conquer Jerusalem when they arrived in Canaan, for the standards reminded them of the covenant, which was still in force (*Joshua* 15:63 and *Rashi*). But in David's time the Jebusites were no longer of the third generation after Abimelech. The covenant was no longer valid. Joab, son of Tzeruyah (David's sister), was the first to go up, defeat the Jebusites, and become leader. David took over the fortress, which was therefore named "City of David" [*I Chronicles* 11:7; Jerusalem was formerly called Jebus (ibid.].

Such are the mysterious ways of Providence. Undoubtedly, Abraham's friendly gesture to the pagan king was made to avoid objections and grievances. But it was nevertheless owing to this alliance that Jerusalem was conquered only at the very last, well after the rest of the territory of Canaan. This is another case of the well-established rule that the most sacred possessions are granted to man only after he has made his supreme effort to obtain them אַחֲרוֹן אַחֲרוֹן חָבִיב; (*Bereishis Rabbah* 76). What is dearest to us is saved for the last.

from me, that it may serve me as testimony that I dug this well."
³¹ *Therefore that place was called Beer-sheba because there the two of them took an oath.* ³² *Thus, they entered into a covenant at Beer-sheba; Abimelech then arose, with Phicol, his general, and they returned to the land of the Philistines.*
³³ *He planted an 'eshel' in Beer-sheba, and there he proclaimed the Name of HASHEM, God of the Universe.* ³⁴ *And Abraham sojourned in the land of the Philistines many years.*

כִּי חָפַרְתִּי אֶת־הַבְּאֵר הַזֹּאת — *That I dug this well. Rashi:* The shepherds of Abimelech were looking for an argument and said, "We dug it." Then they all agreed that the one at whose approach the water would come up was the rightful owner. The water came up as Abraham approached. Abraham, notes *R' E. Mizrachi,* wanted water for his flock; he set aside seven ewes, certain that the water would come up when they approached. He decided beforehand to make a gift of them to Abimelech, for they would help to prove him right. But *Maharal* questions how Abraham could be so certain of the impending miracle. He had no doubt that the blessing which would make the well productive and the water come forth would only be bestowed on the rightful owner of the well and not upon those who had stolen it.

31. כִּי שָׁם נִשְׁבְּעוּ שְׁנֵיהֶם — *Because there the two of them took an oath.* R' Chama ben Chanina says, "Abimelech's oath was broken in the time of Shimshon the judge. It is said of him, 'He shall begin to deliver the Jewish people out of the hand of the Philistines' " (*Judges* 13:5). The word יָחֵל in this verse is taken as a derivate of חָלַל, *to profane, to violate.* Shimshon had the right to break the oath, for the Philistines had violated it long before (*Rashi* to *Sotah* 10a). When one party violates an oath sworn to another, the other is exempt from it also (*Yoreh Deah* 236:6). Nevertheless, David respected the oath until its legal expiration, until the advent of the fourth generation, as mentioned above.

33. וַיִּטַּע אֶשֶׁל בִּבְאֵר שָׁבַע — *He planted an 'eshel' in Beer-sheba.* "On the meaning of the word אֶשֶׁל Rav and Shmuel disagree. One says it is a garden in which he gathered fruits to serve at the table to his guests. The other says, an inn where passersby could be welcomed and where all sorts of fruit were served. It was there that Abraham called upon the name of God. After his guests had eaten and drunk Abraham would say to them, "Bless Him to Whom belongs the food which you have eaten. You think that you have eaten my food? Not so; it belongs to the One Who created the world.' "

Be that as it may, whether אֶשֶׁל denotes a garden or an inn, for Abraham, generous hospitality represented the very best means of bringing pagans to the love and knowledge of God. His missionary activity was based on a love of others and was intimately linked with material aid. That seemed to him all the more natural since, for Abraham, material nourishment was only a pretext for dispensing spiritual nourishment. Every meal in his home was sanctified by

כב *שביעי* א וַיְהִי אַחַר הַדְּבָרִים הָאֵלֶּה וְהָאֱלֹהִים נִסָּה אֶת־אַבְרָהָם

discussions on sacred matters and because of this it was enhanced to the level of a Divine service. For a righteous man like Abraham, a meal, like every activity in a person's life, is not an end in itself but is focused on serving God.

הי׳ אֵל עוֹלָם — *HASHEM, God of the Universe.* According to *Ramban*, the term עוֹלָם refers to space, to the universe. This expression specifies that Abraham proclaimed God as Master of the universe and its elements. But *Rambam* takes עוֹלָם in a temporal sense. He interprets it as meaning "the everlasting God." "Time," he says, "is something created by God . . . . Consequently, the creation of the world by God could not have a temporal beginning, could not have been preceded by the existence of time, as time itself was among the things created . . . . Abraham our father was the first to teach this view, after he had established it by philosophical research. That is why he proclaimed the name of the everlasting God, אֵל עוֹלָם, that is, preceding time" (*Guide* 2:13).

22.

1. וַיְהִי אַחַר הַדְּבָרִים הָאֵלֶּה וְהָאֱלֹהִים נִסָּה אֶת־אַבְרָהָם — *And it happened after these things that God tested Abraham.* There are many views on the motive and the meaning of the binding of Isaac, which represented so severe a test for Abraham. Let us say at the outset that if these opinions appear contradictory, they are nevertheless not mutually exclusive on the plane of the Divine spirit, universal in essence. Infinite thought embraces all the elements which escape human perception.

Rambam is the first who strongly emphasizes that the idea of a test is not that God wants to test and try man in order to discover what He had not known previously. It should be realized that every time the Torah speaks of a test, this test has no other object or goal than to have men learn what they must do or believe. The story of Abraham regarding the binding of Isaac thus comprises two great fundamental ideas in Judaism. The first is to teach us how far we must go in our love and fear of God. Abraham was ordered to do something which could not be compared with any sacrifice, whether of money or even of life; it was the most extraordinary thing that could have happened in the world, one of those things which one would think human nature not capable of accepting. Imagine a childless man, driven by an extreme desire to have children, possessing great fortune and highly esteemed, longing that his race become a nation; if he has a son, after despairing so long of ever having one, what love, what passion he will have for this son!

Nevertheless, fearing God and wishing to obey His command, Abraham puts this cherished son in the background. He renounces all he has hoped for from his son and consents to sacrifice him after a few days' voyage. If our father Abraham hurried to sacrifice Isaac, it was not out of fear that God would kill him, but solely because it is the duty of mortals to love and fear God without the slightest hope for reward, without the slightest chastisement. If the angel

22   ¹*And it happened after these things that God tested Abraham*

then says to him, "... for now I know that you are a God-fearing man," it means, "this act which earns you without reservation the epithet יְרֵא אֱלֹהִים, a God-fearing person, will make known to all mortals how far their fear of God must reach. You are to know that this idea has been confirmed in the Torah, for in it we are told that its contents as a whole have just one aim, which is the fear of God" (cf. *Deuteronomy* 28:58). This is one of the two ideas expressed in the *Akeidah* passage.

The second idea is that the prophets must take whatever is revealed to them by God as reality, for just because this revelation occurs, as we have pointed out, in a dream or vision, and through the imagination, it does not follow that what they hear or see in a parable cannot be counted on, or even that it is open to doubt. We are therefore told that everything the prophet sees in his prophetic vision is real and true and certain for him, that he doubts none of it and that he considers it as real as anything perceived by his senses or intellect. The proof is that Abraham hurried to sacrifice the son he loved even though the command to do so came to him in a dream or vision. But had the prophetic dream been obscure for the prophets, had there remained any doubt or uncertainty regarding what they had perceived in a prophetic vision, they would not have been so eager to carry out what was repugnant to human nature, and if Abraham had had doubts he would not have consented to perform an act of such gravity (*Guide* 3:24).

Ramban, along with *R' Bachya* and *R' Yehudah HaLevi* (*Kuzari* 5:20) stresses that temptation always comes to bring out the best in man. One's acts depend only on his free will. Accordingly, God tests him so that he can concretize through action that which only existed in his mind and then be rewarded for good deeds as well as for good intentions. We can now understand why "God tries (only) the righteous" (*Psalms* 11:5), for He knows that they will triumph and increase their merits still further (*Bereishis Rabbah* 34). An ordeal gives the righteous person a chance to elevate himself to a new level of perfection, as will be shown further on (see our commentary on verse 12).

According to the Midrash and the *Zohar*, the test of the *Akeidah* is to serve as an example of absolute devotion to Divine will. The word נִסָּה meaning *he tested* is related to נֵס, *flag* and calls to mind Isaiah's words: הָרִימוּ נֵס עַל הָעַמִּים (62:10): *Lift up a flag over the peoples*. In the eyes of the nations, Abraham's superhuman conduct during his ordeal made him the standard-bearer for the love of God. It also brought to them the justification for the miracles and exceptional kindness which God had lavished on him (*Rabbah* 55).

Other scholars, however, consider the *Akeidah* a Divine chastisement inflicted on the patriarch, as will be seen later on.

אַחַר הַדְּבָרִים הָאֵלֶּה — *After these things.* This introduction — which can also be taken as "after these words" — implies that the *Akeidah* came in the wake of certain deeds or certain words.

ג וַיֹּאמֶר אֵלָיו אַבְרָהָם וַיֹּאמֶר הִנֵּנִי: וַיֹּאמֶר קַח־נָא אֶת־
בִּנְךָ אֶת־יְחִידְךָ אֲשֶׁר־אָהַבְתָּ אֶת־יִצְחָק וְלֶךְ־לְךָ אֶל־
אֶרֶץ הַמֹּרִיָּה וְהַעֲלֵהוּ שָׁם לְעֹלָה עַל אַחַד הֶהָרִים אֲשֶׁר

Rashi cites here Satan's accusations already mentioned in our commentary on 21:8. According to this account, the sacrifice of Isaac seems due to a diabolical plot. But *Rashi* quotes a second version: "Following Ishmael's boast against Isaac (that Ishmael had consented to be circumcised at thirteen), Isaac said to him: "You wish to make trouble for me because of one limb? Should God say to me, 'Offer your entire self to Me as a sacrifice,' I would not run away." Seen in this light, the test arose out of a contest of ideals. Abraham himself was tormented with doubt and wondered about the reasons for the test. Was it imposed to allow him to acquit himself from a spiteful accusation (thus coming as a corrective process), or, on the contrary, was it to afford him a new opportunity to manifest his boundless devotion to God (in which case from start to finish it would be a new opportunity for growth in holiness)? This inner torment persisted until Abraham heard the angel forbid him to lay a hand on his son. Then he knew that the real purpose of the test was the manifestation of his absolute obedience to God, and not the sacrifice of his son that Satan had demanded.

Yet who would dare to claim knowledge of the designs of God, to be able to determine His intentions? Surely Abraham did not dare to assert that his test was only aimed at moral perfection to the exclusion of any notion of punishment. And so, our Sages record certain ideas which bring out Abraham's sin and his guilt. The introductory words themselves, "and it happened after these things," allude to the link between the test and the events immediately preceding. This refers to the pact of friendship between Abraham and Abimelech, the Philistine king. "The ministering angels assembled and cried out before God: 'Master of the Universe! the only one whom you chose among the seventy nations of the world has gone and made an alliance with pagans!' God replied, 'He has but one son, born to him when he was 100 years old. I shall order him to sacrifice this son to Me as an offering. If he accepts — good; if not, you are right' " (*Tanna D'Bei Eliyahu* 7). In this light, the term נִסָּה אֶת־אַבְרָהָם means "God disturbed and saddened Abraham," the word נִסָּה being related to the expression נְסִיסִין, the *Targum* translation of זָעֲפִים, *aggrieved*, in *Genesis* 40:6 (R' *Bachya*).

Rashbam adds in his commentary: "Divine anger was kindled against Abraham. For God had given the land of the Philistines (along with the rest of the Promised Land) to the patriarch, but he made a pact of friendship with Abimelech for three generations (whereas its inhabitants were to have been completely exterminated). Accordingly, God commanded Abraham to offer up his son as a sacrifice in order to show him just what could happen from making an alliance on his own, an alliance which put a commitment on the future destiny of the Promised Land (cf. our commentary on 21:30).

From this we see that the motive of retribution must not be discounted from among the various underlying causes of Abraham's ordeal.

and said to him, "Abraham," and he replied, "Here I am."
*² And He said, "Please take your son, your only one, whom
you love — Isaac — and go to the land of Moriah; bring him
up there as an offering upon one of the mountains which*

וְהָאֱלֹהִים — *That God.* Literally, "and God." In confirmation of the opinion just stated, the Divine name used here presents God as Judge demanding strict justice amid the celestial tribunal. R' Eliezer says, "Just as the expression וַה', *and HASHEM,* denotes the God of love with His tribunal, so too the form וְהָאֱלֹהִים with the conjunction *vav* denotes the God of justice with His tribunal" (*Yalkut*).

נִסָּה אֶת־אַבְרָהָם — *Tested Abraham.* Was the test only for Abraham and not for Isaac? The *Zohar* points out that if Isaac had refused to go, Abraham would not have been responsible, since Isaac was thirty-seven years old at this time and was thus held accountable for his actions. But the text says נִסָּה אֶת־אַבְרָהָם (not נִסָּה לְאַבְרָהָם) and the use of the preposition אֶת here implies that Isaac too was being tested — "with Abraham." (Note that the preposition אֶת can also mean "with.") The test was first for Abraham, then for Isaac, and it was meant, according to the *Zohar's* terminology, to seal the union of water with fire and fire with water. This imagery means that, through the *Akeidah,* Abraham's personality was to achieve that harmonious unity which he still lacked. His heart was full of goodness and love. But to reach a perfect unity in himself, he had to unite these "calm waters" with the "raging fire" of a relentless discipline, ready even for supreme sacrifice. Isaac, on the other hand, had a soul which was attached to justice and legality. Hence, he could only bring complete harmony to his being through an act of supreme devotion to God, an act which only an infinite love can inspire. R' Shimon bar Yochai said: The greatest blessing is to have contrasting elements brought into harmony on earth just as God brings the elements of fire and water into harmony in the celestial regions (*Yalkut* to *Job* 25:2).

וַיֹּאמֶר אֵלָיו אַבְרָהָם — *And said to him, "Abraham."* The Torah teaches us the rule of proper conduct that one calls a person by name before speaking to him (*Yoma* 4b). The disjunctive Torah-reading "note" (tonic accent) טִפְּחָא on the word אַבְרָהָם is very characteristic; it indicates that Abraham's affirmative reply instantly followed the Divine call (*R' Hirsch*). Abraham commits himself fully; he is ready for anything, for any new duty, for any sacrifice, even for death (*Tanchuma*). הִנֵּנִי, *here I am,* is the word most characteristic of Abraham's piety, which remains a living example for every Jew. His religion is as far removed from mystical contemplation as it is from naive faith or theological philosophy. Above all else, it is absolute devotion to the Divine will. It was this same eager response, "Here I am," which sprang from the lips of Samuel, of Elisha, of innumerable servants of God who consecrated their lives to the glory of God without the slightest hesitation.

2. אֶת־בִּנְךָ אֶת־יְחִידְךָ — *Your son, your only one.* The word יְחִידְךָ refers to the word יְחִידָה, *unique,* which is one of the five names for the human soul (*Rabbah*

ג אָמַ֣ר אֵלָ֑יו: וַיַּשְׁכֵּ֨ם אַבְרָהָ֜ם בַּבֹּ֗קֶר וַֽיַּחֲבֹשׁ֙ אֶת־חֲמֹר֔ו
וַיִּקַּ֞ח אֶת־שְׁנֵ֤י נְעָרָיו֙ אִתּ֔וֹ וְאֵ֖ת יִצְחָ֣ק בְּנ֑וֹ וַיְבַקַּע֙ עֲצֵ֣י
עֹלָ֔ה וַיָּ֣קָם וַיֵּ֔לֶךְ אֶל־הַמָּק֖וֹם אֲשֶׁר־אָֽמַר־ל֥וֹ הָאֱלֹהִֽים:
ד בַּיּ֣וֹם הַשְּׁלִישִׁ֗י וַיִּשָּׂ֨א אַבְרָהָ֧ם אֶת־עֵינָ֛יו וַיַּ֖רְא אֶת־

14). It is mentioned in *Psalms* (22:21) and elsewhere. For Abraham, offering his
son Isaac as a sacrifice meant sacrificing his own life since this son embodied his
only hope for the future of his mission (*Sifre to Deuteronomy* 313). When
Abraham gave his son, he gave his soul.

וְלֶךְ־לְךָ אֶל־אֶרֶץ הַמֹּרִיָּה — *And go to the land of Moriah.* The same Divine
command לֶךְ־לְךָ appeared at the beginning of Abraham's story (12:1). It occurs
here a second time, at the zenith of his life. "We do not know," the Sages tell us,
"which of the two commands is of greater importance. But the fact that the
Moriah region is explicitly named here (whereas the first time the text had said,
to the land that I will show you) demonstrates that the second לֶךְ־לְךָ has a greater
value than the first" (*Rabbah* 55). This phrase stresses that the command to go
to Moriah, the future site of the Sanctuary, in order to serve God, has priority
over that to leave one's birthplace to go to the Promised Land. Going up to the
Temple Mount is an even more ideal objective than *aliyah* to the Land of Israel.

הַמֹּרִיָּה — *Moriah. Rashi:* This is Jerusalem. As in *II Chronicles* 3:1, "To build the
house of God at Jerusalem, on Mount Moriah." This place, say our Sages, was
originally a plain. But when it was chosen as the site of the *Akeidah*, the
surrounding hills came together to form a mountain where the plain had been.
Hence it is called הַר הַמֹּרִיָּה, the mountain formed from the fear of God (מֵירְאָתוֹ
שֶׁל הקב"ה נַעֲשָׂה הַר). And when Abraham approached it he "perceived the place
from afar" (*Tanchuma*). The Midrash expresses the idea that an insignificant
and hitherto unknown place can suddenly be elevated to dizzying heights by
becoming the setting for an act of *Kiddush Hashem* (sanctification of the Divine
name) of sublime grandeur. But *Rashi* also quotes *Onkelos'* explanation: "Land
of the service." This refers to the service of the incense (עֲבוֹדַת הַקְּטֹרֶת), which
contained myrrh (in Hebrew מֹר, related to מוֹרִיָּה), nard, and other aromatic
plants. Thus, the name of the mountain reminds us of the place where the
sweetest perfume (רֵיחַ נִיחֹחַ) ever given off by a sacrifice rose toward God.

וְהַעֲלֵהוּ שָׁם לְעֹלָה — *Bring him up there as an offering.* Abraham's merit was all
the greater since human sacrifice was among the most abominable forms of
idolatry which he had relentlessly subjected to public condemnation in the name
of God, and now he himself suddenly receives the Divine command to proceed
with the sacrifice of his own son. Although this command upset all his teachings
and all his efforts, he did not hesitate. The faithful servant, Abraham, blindly
obeyed the Divine will.

Certainly he could not suspect that God wanted nothing from him but proof
of his obedience. In fact, the "sacrifice" of Isaac became the most striking

I shall tell you."

³ *So Abraham woke up early in the morning and he saddled his donkey; he took his two young men with him and Isaac, his son; he split the wood for the offering, and stood up and went to the place of which God had spoken to him.*

⁴ *On the third day, Abraham raised his eyes and perceived the*

demonstration in all of history *against* human sacrifice. The Divine intervention to prevent the sacrifice appeared, at the time, much more astonishing than the order to carry it out.

The first effect of this ordeal was to show Abraham and his descendants after him how much God abhors human sacrifice. In contrast to the cruel pagan divinities, God requires of man only his moral devotion. Moses warned his people not to serve God in the ways of the neighboring nations: *For every abomination to God, which He hates, have they done unto their gods; for even their sons and their daughters do they burn in the fire to their gods! (Deuteronomy 12:31).* So too did all the prophets brand this hideous aberration with infamy; they ceased doing so only when they had made all Jewry share their horror. Through their teachings, *Gehinnom*, the name of the valley where perverted kings performed this hideous rite, became synonymous with Hell.

3. בַּבֹּקֶר . . . וַיַּשְׁכֵּם — *Early in the morning.* From this we learn that the zealous carry out a *mitzvah* as soon as they can (*Pesachim* 4a; cf. *Tosafos*). Twice before, the text uses the same words, וַיַּשְׁכֵּם אַבְרָהָם בַּבֹּקֶר, to denote Abraham's eagerness and zeal at the break of day (19:27 and 21:14). However, the earlier cases are not as convincing; for the first relates to Abraham's plea on behalf of the doomed city of Sodom and the second to the dismissal of Ishmael, with God's explicit approval. Consequently, the lesson of eagerness and zeal is learned only from the ordeal of the *Akeidah*. Although everything — logic, sentiment, nature, instinct — rebels against this *mitzvah*, the patriarch's enthusiasm made him rise "early in the morning" to carry out the Divine command to the letter (cf. *Rashi* on *Numbers* 22:21).

וַיַּחֲבֹשׁ אֶת־חֲמֹרוֹ — *And he saddled his donkey.* חֲמוֹר, donkey, and חֹמֶר, matter, are homonyms. And so the text can be taken, "he harnessed his nature and the material part of his being in order to dominate his natural sentiments (the source of paternal love, as in *Sefer HaChinuch, Mitzvah* 263) and to remove from his idealism all constraints" (תכלת מרדכי).

4. בַּיּוֹם הַשְּׁלִישִׁי — *On the third day.* The *Midrash Tanchuma* gives a dramatic account of the three days of the journey, filled with the Machiavellian stratagems of the tempter to deter father and son from the straight path. Satan joins them on the way and uses every seductive argument, every perfidious ruse, to draw them into his trap. He puts so many obstacles in their path that it becomes intolerable. Then Abraham implores God to save him from the clutches of the

ה הַמָּקוֹם מֵרָחֹק: וַיֹּאמֶר אַבְרָהָם אֶל־נְעָרָיו שְׁבוּ־לָכֶם
פֹּה עִם־הַחֲמוֹר וַאֲנִי וְהַנַּעַר נֵלְכָה עַד־כֹּה וְנִשְׁתַּחֲוֶה
ו וְנָשׁוּבָה אֲלֵיכֶם: וַיִּקַּח אַבְרָהָם אֶת־עֲצֵי הָעֹלָה וַיָּשֶׂם
עַל־יִצְחָק בְּנוֹ וַיִּקַּח בְּיָדוֹ אֶת־הָאֵשׁ וְאֶת־הַמַּאֲכֶלֶת

demon and to let him perform his *mitzvah*. And so, finally, on the third day, Abraham lifts up his eyes and perceives the place where a cloud hovers over the mountain.

For the righteous, the Midrash tells us, the obstacles which pile up on the path of duty are the work of Satan. But the many difficulties must not discourage them, but rather should spur them on. Their fierce tenacity and determination will ultimately be rewarded and they will see, rising before them, bright summits where Divine blessing awaits them.

וַיַּרְא אֶת־הַמָּקוֹם מֵרָחֹק — *And perceived the place from afar*. The "place" is a reference to the place mentioned regarding Jacob: *He took from the stones of the place* (28:11) — the same place where the *Akeidah* occurred. Fully aware of the Divine promise regarding the posterity of Isaac that would bear his name (21:12), Abraham foresaw that this promise would be fulfilled with the third generation. Although incapable of comprehending the sequence of events unfolding just as he was about to sacrifice Isaac, Abraham nevertheless believed the Divine words and "lifted up his eyes (to the third generation) and saw Jacob from afar" (*Zohar*).

שְׁבוּ־לָכֶם פֹּה עִם הַחֲמוֹר — *Stay here by yourselves with the donkey*. 5. The righteous have a presentiment of the sacred place when they draw near to it, but the wicked, whose senses are dull, feel nothing. Abraham said to Isaac: "My son, do you see, as I do, a cloud close to the mountain?" He replied, "Yes." Then Abraham asked the two servants what they saw. They answered, "Nothing." He said to them: "Since the donkey sees nothing and you see nothing, stay with the donkey at the foot of the mountain" (*Rabbah* 56).

From this it is concluded that the Canaanite slave is on the same level as the beast. This has certain legal consequences regarding his personal status (*Kiddushin* 68a) but does not however affect his worth as a human being (*Kesubos* 111a).

וְהַנַּעַר — *And the lad*. Rabbinical tradition calculates his age then at thirty-seven years. However, *Ibn Ezra* points out that with Isaac at this age, the test should have been directed as much to him as to Abraham. But from the text, the ordeal seems to have been just for Abraham. Hence, logically, Isaac must have been about thirteen years old when he obediently followed his father, unsuspicious of the significance of his journey.

נֵלְכָה עַד־כֹּה — *Will go yonder*. R' Nachman said: The priestly blessing יְבָרֶכְךָ וְיִשְׁמְרֶךָ is due to Isaac's merit. The word כֹּה which introduces this blessing (*Numbers* 6:23) is also used at Isaac's sacrifice: נֵלְכָה עַד־כֹּה — "I and the lad will go yonder" (*Bamidbar Rabbah* 43). Love and filial respect as admirably displayed

place from afar. ⁵ And Abraham said to his young men, "Stay
here by yourselves with the donkey, while I and the lad will go
yonder; we will worship and we will return to you."

⁶ And Abraham took the wood for the offering, and placed
it on Isaac, his son. He took in his hand the fire and the knife,

in the words, *I and the lad will go yonder; we will worship (God)* are at the
foundations of the Divine blessing accorded to succeeding generations.

Only Abraham and his son went to the top of the mountain. No one else was
to be present at the solemn moment of the sacrifice to God. The Divine service
requires man to be completely alone before God. Just as on the Day of Atonement
the High Priest will enter the Holy of Holies alone in order to perform the sacred
service, so too Abraham was alone before God as he ascended the highest
pinnacle of sanctity to offer his homage to God on a solitary summit (cf. our
commentary on 21:17; *Pirkei D'Rabbi Eliezer* 31).

וְנִשְׁתַּחֲוֶה — *We will worship.* (lit. *prostrate ourselves*). The servants knew that
Abraham was going to offer a sacrifice when he took the wood for the offering.
But he said to them simply, "We will worship." Indeed the gesture of prostration
perfectly expresses the sense of sacrifice. To prostrate oneself before God, to
surrender one's complete soul to His will, that is what sacrifice symbolically
expresses. For Abraham, the sacrifice signifies nothing other than הִשְׁתַּחֲוָיָה.

וְנָשׁוּבָה אֲלֵיכֶם — *And we will return to you.* He prophesied that they would both
return (*Rashi*). "Conclude from this," said R' Yochanan, "that a covenant is
sealed with the lips in the sense that words once spoken — unknowingly
referring to the future — come true" (*Moed Katan* 18a).

6. וַיָּשֶׂם עַל־יִצְחָק בְּנוֹ — *And placed it on Isaac his son.* When they arrived at the
foot of the holy mountain, Abraham decorated his son just as the offerings of
the first fruits were adorned upon approaching Jerusalem (*Bikkurim* 3; from the
סְלִיחָה: אִם אָפֵס רוֹבַע הַקֵּן).

הַמַּאֲכֶלֶת — *The knife. Rashi* points out that the noun מַאֲכֶלֶת is related to the word
אֲכִילָה, *eating:* "The knife prepares the flesh for eating." And on the same theme
the Sages of the Midrash add: "Everything which Israel eats in this world is due
to the merit of this knife" (*Rabbah* 56). Here the Sages wanted to put into words
our age-old experience which teaches us that the blessings enjoyed by Jewry in
this world are the fruit of the martyrs and blood of countless sacrifices. And at
their origins, how often one finds the butcher-knife! In our day, has not the blood
of millions of victims of Nazi persecution given birth to the State of Israel? The
prophet Ezekiel expresses this same idea in these words: I passed by you (said
God) and I saw you wallowing in your own blood and I said to you, "In your
blood you will live" (בְּדָמַיִךְ חֲיִי) (16:6).

וַיֵּלְכוּ שְׁנֵיהֶם יַחְדָּו — *And the two of them went together.* Abraham knew that he
was about to sacrifice his son, yet he went with the same willingness and joy as

ז וַיֵּלְכוּ שְׁנֵיהֶם יַחְדָּו: וַיֹּאמֶר יִצְחָק אֶל־אַבְרָהָם אָבִיו וַיֹּאמֶר
אָבִי וַיֹּאמֶר הִנֶּנִּי בְנִי וַיֹּאמֶר הִנֵּה הָאֵשׁ וְהָעֵצִים וְאַיֵּה הַשֶּׂה
ח לְעֹלָה: וַיֹּאמֶר אַבְרָהָם אֱלֹהִים יִרְאֶה־לּוֹ הַשֶּׂה לְעֹלָה בְּנִי
ט וַיֵּלְכוּ שְׁנֵיהֶם יַחְדָּו: וַיָּבֹאוּ אֶל־הַמָּקוֹם אֲשֶׁר אָמַר־לוֹ
הָאֱלֹהִים וַיִּבֶן שָׁם אַבְרָהָם אֶת־הַמִּזְבֵּחַ וַיַּעֲרֹךְ אֶת־הָעֵצִים
וַיַּעֲקֹד אֶת־יִצְחָק בְּנוֹ וַיָּשֶׂם אֹתוֹ עַל־הַמִּזְבֵּחַ מִמַּעַל
י לָעֵצִים: וַיִּשְׁלַח אַבְרָהָם אֶת־יָדוֹ וַיִּקַּח אֶת־הַמַּאֲכֶלֶת
יא לִשְׁחֹט אֶת־בְּנוֹ: וַיִּקְרָא אֵלָיו מַלְאַךְ יהוה מִן־הַשָּׁמַיִם

Isaac, who suspected nothing (*Rashi*). But on the other hand our Sages record that "tears flowed from Abraham's eyes" when he went to sacrifice his son (*Yalkut*) and that he prayed to God for his well-being as is seen in the *selichos* prayer מִי שֶׁעָנָה לְאַבְרָהָם בְּהַר הַמּוֹרִיָּה; (cf. *Mishnah Taanis* 2:4 and *Tosafos Yom Tov*). R' Yisrael Salanter resolves this contradiction with his psychological doctrine based on the two elements of lucid consciousness and the subconscious (אור ישראל, מכתב ו'). The former urged Abraham to "willingness and joy"; the latter, harboring the shadows of paternal instinct, provoked a reaction of sadness and affliction.

7. וַיֹּאמֶר יִצְחָק אֶל־אַבְרָהָם אָבִיו — *Then Isaac spoke to Abraham his father.* The father and son had not yet spoken to each other. The silent, serious attitude of the father was enough for his son to guess the gravity of the task. Finally, according to the Midrash, they spoke — after Satan, disguised as a human being, approached Isaac and attempted to lead him astray. "Wretched one, son of a wretched woman! How many times she fasted, how many supplications to Heaven until you were born! And now this old man at your side has gone insane and is about to sacrifice you!" At once, Isaac turned to his father and said: "Father, this is what this man said to me. But then, where is the lamb for an offering?" (פסיקתא, פרק מ').

And Abraham replied, "As for us, we are to bring the wood, the fire, and the knife, and to be prepared for any sacrifice. Whatever God chooses and whatever happens will be solely by His will. Let us leave the decision to God." With these words Abraham told his son all he had to know. "We have only to build the altar and leave to God the problem of providing the sacrifice which He in His wisdom will choose" — and the two of them went off together.

8. אֱלֹהִים יִרְאֶה־לּוֹ הַשֶּׂה — *God will seek out for Himself the lamb.* Rashi: "He will see it and choose it for Himself. And if there is no lamb for the sacrifice, it will be you, my son. And even though Isaac understood that he was going to be sacrificed, they went off together in the same spirit." The grandeur of Isaac's soul, which "understood that he was going to be sacrificed," was equal to that of Abraham's. Isaac had received no Divine command; he had only learned of his duty from the words of his father, as a תּוֹרָה שֶׁבְּעַל פֶּה, an *oral tradition*. At no time, however — as extraordinary as it may seem — did Isaac doubt his father's

and the two of them went together. ⁷ *Then Isaac spoke to Abraham his father and said, "Father — "*

And he said, "Here I am, my son."

And he said, "Here are the fire and the wood, but where is the lamb for the offering?"

⁸ *And Abraham said, "God will seek out for Himself the lamb for the offering, my son." And the two of them went together.*

⁹ *They arrived at the place of which God had spoken to him; Abraham built the altar there, and arranged the wood; he bound Isaac, his son, and he placed him on the altar atop the wood.* ¹⁰ *Abraham stretched out his hand, and took the knife to slaughter his son.*

¹¹ *And an angel of HASHEM called to him from heaven, and said,*

word. The incomparable force which has maintained the vigor of our people throughout its history, the living tradition passing from father to son, was already active within him. Our Sages ask how Isaac could believe in such a הוֹרָאַת שָׁעָה (*ad hoc* ruling) of Abraham's. The reply is היכא דמוחזק שאני (*Sanhedrin* 89b); it was not because of a special legality but because Isaac knew well that his father was a confirmed prophet; he could not lie. He needed no other confirmation.

9. מִמַּעַל לָעֵצִים — *Atop the wood.* Why above it? While building the altar, Abraham had thought of the celestial throne of the Divine Majesty surrounded by *seraphim,* who were standing above it (*Isaiah* 6:2): עֹמְדִים מִמַּעַל לוֹ. Spellbound by this vision, he placed his son in the same position as the *seraphim* around the heavenly throne (*Rabbah* 56).

10. וַיִּשְׁלַח אַבְרָהָם אֶת־יָדוֹ — *Abraham stretched out his hand.* From this moment, Isaac was consecrated as an offering according to the general law of sacrifice. And so, throughout his life, he retained the sacred character of עוֹלָה תְּמִימָה, *a perfect offering.* This imposed certain restrictions on him, as *Rashi* points out on 26:2: "*Do not descend to Egypt* (says God to Isaac), for you are an offering dedicated completely to God, and the lands outside the Holy Land are not worthy of you." Similarly, see *Rashi* on 25:26.

לִשְׁחֹט אֶת־בְּנוֹ — *To slaughter his son.* Isaac said to his son, "Bind me well, for if you don't, I may thrash out from the pain and disturb you, and your sacrifice might then turn out to be invalid! You might lose your reward in the World to Come." Abraham's eyes were fixed on Isaac's, but Isaac was contemplating the angels of the celestial world. At this instant, the angels sprang up and cried out to one another: "Have you seen these two righteous men on earth, one sacrificing, the other offering himself up? The one who sacrifices does not hesitate and the other holds out his throat to be slaughtered!" (*Targum Yerushalmi*).

11. וַיִּקְרָא אֵלָיו מַלְאַךְ ה׳ — *And an angel of HASHEM called to him.* God said to the angels, "Since it is your accusations which have put Abraham to the test (see our

יב וַיֹּאמֶר אַבְרָהָם ׀ אַבְרָהָם וַיֹּאמֶר הִנֵּנִי: וַיֹּאמֶר אַל־תִּשְׁלַח
יָדְךָ אֶל־הַנַּעַר וְאַל־תַּעַשׂ לוֹ מְאוּמָה כִּי ׀ עַתָּה יָדַעְתִּי כִּי־
יְרֵא אֱלֹהִים אַתָּה וְלֹא חָשַׂכְתָּ אֶת־בִּנְךָ אֶת־יְחִידְךָ מִמֶּנִּי:

commentary on verse 1), let one of you go to save Isaac, now that you have seen the futility of such accusations" (*Midrash HaGadol*). From the start, the test from the Divine point of view was unnecessary, as shown at the beginning of this chapter. But it allowed God to "reply to Satan and the pagan nations who asked in wonderment why Abraham was the beloved of God" (*Rashi* on verse 12). Accordingly, it was not God but one of the accusers who intervened at the critical moment.

מִן־הַשָּׁמַיִם — *From heaven.* Cf. our commentary on 21:17.

אַבְרָהָם אַבְרָהָם — *Abraham! Abraham!* Jacob, Samuel, and Moses were also addressed in this way, with their names repeated. In all cases a *p'sik* (vertical stroke) separates the two names, except for Moses (*Exodus* 3:4). The reason for this exception is that Moses was summoned by God to rescue the Jews enslaved in Egypt. For this, there was not a single moment to spare, not even time for a pause in the call to Moses.

Another explanation: all the prophets met with some pauses in the manifestation which reached them from God, except for Moses, who was a prophet throughout his life with no interruption (*Shemos Rabbah* 2).

12. אַל־תִּשְׁלַח יָדְךָ אֶל־הַנַּעַר — *Do not stretch out your hand against the lad.* *Rashi*: To slay him. Then Abraham said: "If so, I have come here for nothing. I will at least cause him a slight wound to draw a few drops of blood." God answered him: "Nor harm him — do not create any defect in him." The patriarch felt that to transmit to his heirs the spiritual strength needed for unconditional devotion to God it was essential to seal this manifestation of devotion through some concrete act. He wanted to cause at least one drop of blood to flow, for without it the will for the devotion would exist only potentially, but not actually. However, God put Abraham's mind at ease by assuring him that his unequaled example was already sufficient to implant the virtue of מְסִירַת נֶפֶשׁ, *self-sacrifice* in the souls of his descendants.

כִּי עַתָּה יָדַעְתִּי — *For now I know.* If the Torah uses this expression here, even though no new knowledge can be brought to God, it is because the knowledge of a deed after it is performed is necessarily different from that before, as is seen for example in *Genesis* 12:11, "Now I have known that you are a woman of beautiful appearance," a fact which Abraham already knew. In these examples, "to know" signifies confirmation of earlier knowledge. With respect to God, this knowledge does not imply any change from a previous state. The Torah employs the term solely because it must use expressions which man can comprehend. "Now I know that you are a God-fearing man" thus means "you have now proven by your actions that it is not fear of punishment which motivates you, but genuine reverence permeated with love." Hence, the prophet

"Abraham! Abraham!"
And he said, "Here I am."
¹² *And he said, "Do not stretch out your hand against the lad*
nor do anything to him for now I know that you are a God-fearing
man, since you have not withheld your son, your only one, from
Me."

Isaiah (41:8) describes Abraham with the words: *Abraham who loves me* (*R'*
Yosef Albo, Ikkarim 4:13).

This harmonious union of fear and love of God characterizes Abraham's
piety (and Job's). It is brought out by R' Meir in *Sotah* 35a. Numerous
Midrashim also develop the same theme. In this light the words יְרֵא אֱלֹהִים used
here are to be taken as they are explained in the *Zohar*, which distinguishes
between יִרְאַת הָעוֹנֶשׁ *fear of punishment,* and יִרְאַת הָרוֹמְמוּת, *veneration of*
Divine grandeur. In the latter the factor of love ennobles the primitive dread of
punishment. After Abraham's extraordinary devotion, God proclaims that he
now has the supreme degree of reverence of God יִרְאַת הָרוֹמְמוּת. (On the
relationship between fear and love see also, תניא, פמ״א; של״ה, י׳ מאמרות; עיקרים
(לר״י אלבו, ג:לה; ר׳ בחיי חובות הלבבות, ש׳ הפרישות.

Two conflicting views shed light on Abraham's rise to perfection through
the *Akeidah.* The first involves *Rashi's* definition of love and fear: "One who
acts out of love is not like one who acts out of fear. He who serves his master
in fear, when importuned will leave him and go away" (*Deuteronomy* 6:5).
From this it appears that the fear of God which was able to inspire Abraham
many times in previous acts of devotion could still not be considered the
driving force behind an act which demanded superhuman self-abnegation. The
willingness to sacrifice Isaac can only be explained by an infinite love of God.

The *Vilna Gaon,* however, considers that the earlier merits of the patriarch
arose from his intrinsic goodness and profound natural love of others. On the
other hand, the test of the *Akeidah* made him rise to the point where he
triumphed over his own nature and where, in fear of God, he could arrive at a
unity in his own personality. It is in this sense that *Rashi's* remark on verse 2
should be taken: God said to Abraham, "I beseech you to succeed in this test for
Me, so that none can say 'the first tests proved nothing.' "

13. וַיִּשָּׂא אַבְרָהָם אֶת־עֵינָיו וַיַּרְא — *And Abraham raised his eyes and saw.* This
phrase indicates that the patriarch did not just chance to look at the ram.
Instead, he raised his eyes and looked about intending to find something which
would serve as an offering to God. "Abraham said to God, 'I cannot go back
down from here without offering a sacrifice' " (*Tanchuma, Shelach* 14).

If we try to understand the thoughts which prompted Abraham to seek
another sacrifice in place of his son, it seems we could presume that they both
considered themselves guilty of a sin committed unconsciously or inadver-
tently, since sins of this type are also punishable according to Divine law.
Abraham felt that if God had renounced the offering which He had demanded

יג וַיִּשָּׂא אַבְרָהָם אֶת־עֵינָיו וַיַּרְא וְהִנֵּה־אַיִל אַחַר נֶאֱחַז בַּסְּבַךְ
בְּקַרְנָיו וַיֵּלֶךְ אַבְרָהָם וַיִּקַּח אֶת־הָאַיִל וַיַּעֲלֵהוּ לְעֹלָה תַּחַת

earlier, then his sin had still not been atoned for. The one who receives the gift of life, he concluded, must "redeem himself" with an offering, a gift, or a sacrifice in his place. This same concept is expressed in *Job: The soul (of a man) who draws near to the grave — his life seems delivered to the agents of death. If there is, then, an angel who intercedes for him, one among a thousand to vouch for his merit, who accords him grace and says, "Deliver him from going down to the pit, I have found his ransom" — then his flesh again finds the vigor of a child's, he is restored to the days of his youth . . .* (33:22-25).

The idea of "personal redemption" plays an important role in the sources of our tradition. It is found again in the Torah in the form of a material gift כֹּפֶר נֶפֶשׁ (*Exodus* 21:12), or as an animal sacrifice called simply כַּפָּרָה, which signifies both atonement and redemption. The Sages of the Talmud refer to this doctrine (*Berachos* 62b), as do our eminent thinkers (*Ramban* on *Leviticus* 16:8). But the principle of redemption is made clear by the Torah itself in the last chapter of *Leviticus*. As it concludes the book in which the laws of sacrifices are promulgated, the Torah develops the idea of redemption of the individual through an offering of his own estimated worth. It describes in detail the legal standards for the redemption of objects or animals consecrated to God and the laws governing replacement of sacrificial animals. Comparing the beginning and end of the book of *Leviticus*, the Sages of the Midrash (end of *Tanchuma*) bring out the importance of the principle of redemption (תְּמוּרָה וּגְאוּלָה) within the general concept of sacrifice. As a consequence, *Rashi* explains why Abraham sacrificed the ram by referring to this principle: "For each rite which he performed, he said this prayer: May it be the will of God to accept this sacrifice as though I had performed it on my son, as though my son had been slaughtered, as though his blood had been spilled, as though his skin had been removed, as though my son had been consumed and had turned to ashes."

The fact that an animal can become the victim of a man's sin fits into the general concept of the collective responsibility of creation. Animals can be called upon to suffer because of man, but they can also benefit from his merits, as was the case when the animals were saved in Noah's ark during the Flood. Other examples are given in *Vayikra Rabbah* 27.

The possibility which man has of legally redeeming himself through a gift or sacrifice was granted to him by the grace of God right from the beginning of creation. In some manner, because it is of prime importance, it was integrated into the works of creation just before the start of human history. This is what our Sages wanted to express when they taught that the ram which Abraham sacrificed had been created at twilight on the last day of creation (*Avos* 5:8)

¹³ *And Abraham raised his eyes and saw — behold, a ram! — afterwards, caught in the thicket by its horns; so Abraham went and took the ram and offered it up as an offering instead of his son.*

and then became entangled at the very site of the future sanctuary, the materialization *par excellence* of the idea of atonement (cf. *Pirkei D'Rabbi Eliezer* 31). Moreover the word אַחַר in our verse has the disjunctive "note" (*zakef gadol*) which makes it stand out and emphasizes that the function of the ram was "to replace," "to substitute for." It was "another" Isaac to be offered; אַחַר, "another," will henceforth be the motto of sacrifice, whose guiding principle is that of redemption.

אַחַר נֶאֱחַז בַּסְּבַךְ בְּקַרְנָיו — *Afterwards, caught in the thicket by its horns.* R' Yehudah declares: אַחַר, *later,* when Israel will be completely ensnared in her sins, this horn will come to her rescue and save her from her predicament (*Bereishis Rabbah* 56). This rescuing ram's horn is the *shofar.* Each year on Rosh Hashanah its blasts recall the *Akeidah* which, tradition, tells us, took place on that same date. (Some Sages, however, hold that the *Akeidah* took place on the Day of Atonement.) The exceptional importance attached to the blowing of the *shofar* can be explained in the light of what was stated above. The *shofar* reminds us that in His kindness God accepts the offering of the guilty one condemned to death as "the redemption of his person." "Sound the shofar before Me," says God, "and I will remember the sacrifice of Isaac in your favor" (*Rosh Hashanah* 16a).

On the other hand, the *shofar* recalls that Israel's greatest virtues stem from the act of the *Akeidah.* Limitless devotion to Divine service, messianic faith, spiritual strength to obey the law, the unrelenting struggle for the glory of God, the holy enthusiasm of the love of God which composes immortal hymns — these are the qualities which Israel has inherited from its ancestors by virtue of the superhuman trials which they were able to overcome. According to R' Eliezer's allegory, from the five organs and parts of the sacrificed ram of which "no part was lost," five virtues were derived: the ram's ashes formed the base of the altar in the Temple; its right horn will herald the messianic redemption; its left horn was the one which was heard at the revelation on Mount Sinai; its skin was used for the sash of Elijah the prophet, the valiant defender of the glory of God; and its tendons were used to make the ten strings for the Psalmist David's harp (*Pirkei D'Rabbi Eliezer*, ibid.). The prodigious and constant influence which Abraham's test has had on the spiritual, moral, and religious level of his descendants is thus seen in its historical perspective. And so, numerous times on Rosh Hashanah we evoke the memory of the *Akeidah* as an inexhaustible source of our moral strength while praying that we may continue to benefit from the immense merit of the patriarchs and that we ourselves may, through our own devotion, deserve the rich blessings which rewarded Abraham.

יד בְּנוֹ: וַיִּקְרָא אַבְרָהָם שֵׁם־הַמָּקוֹם הַהוּא יהוה | יִרְאֶה אֲשֶׁר

טו יֵאָמֵר הַיּוֹם בְּהַר יהוה יֵרָאֶה: וַיִּקְרָא מַלְאַךְ יהוה אֶל־

טז אַבְרָהָם שֵׁנִית מִן־הַשָּׁמָיִם: וַיֹּאמֶר בִּי נִשְׁבַּעְתִּי נְאֻם־יהוה כִּי

14. וַיִּקְרָא אַבְרָהָם שֵׁם־הַמָּקוֹם הַהוּא ה' יִרְאֶה — *And Abraham called the name of that site "HASHEM Yireh."* The patriarch sums up the significance of Mount Moriah in these words: ה' יִרְאֶה, *HASHEM sees!* This name is clearly connected with Abraham's earlier reply to his son: אֱלֹהִים יִרְאֶה־לּוֹ הַשֶּׂה, *God will seek out for Himself the lamb.* To Abraham, the scene which has just unfolded includes a most important lesson: God sees, knows, and chooses even where man sees nothing and understands nothing of the reasons of His will. It is for God to see and to choose, and for us to obey. When God revealed the Torah to His people, He significantly added here the words, *as it is said to this day, one is seen on the Mount of HASHEM.* Each of us is seen by God, Whose gaze contemplates and judges us. Three times a year the Jew is to go up to Mount Moriah, to the place of the Sanctuary, there to "be seen by HASHEM" (*Exodus* 23:17) and to renew, through sacrifice, the pledge of the *Akeidah.*

בְּהַר ה' יֵרָאֶה — *On the mountain HASHEM will be seen.* Onkelos translates: Abraham worshiped and prayed here and said before God, "Let future generations worship in this very place and say (on this day): 'On this mountain Abraham worshiped Hashem.'" Referring to this interpretation *Rambam* writes, "It is known that idolaters sought to build their temples and erect their idols in the highest place they could find (see *Deuteronomy* 12:2). That is why our father Abraham chose Mount Moriah, the highest mountain in this region (see *Ezekiel* 20:40) and there proclaimed God's unity, marked out the Sanctuary, and set it exactly to the west. The Holy of Holies was indeed in the west, as the Sages tell us in tractate *Bava Basra* 25a, and it was our father Abraham who determined its position (cf. *Rambam, Guide des Egarés,* trans. by S. Munk, III. p. 469). He did so, it seems to me for this reason. At that time it was very widely held that one should worship the sun, which was taken for a divinity. Undoubtedly everyone turned eastward to pray. And so our father Abraham set the western side of Mount Moriah as the site of the Sanctuary in order to have the people turn their backs on the sun. Do you not see what the Jews did when their disloyalty and infidelity made them revert to these old, perverse ways? *They turned their backs toward the Temple of Hashem, and their faces toward the east; and they were prostrating themselves eastward toward the sun (Ezekiel 8:16).* Understand this important point well. Moreover, I do not doubt that this place chosen by Abraham in prophetic vision was also known to Moses our teacher and to many others . . ." (*Guide* 3:45). However, see our commentary on *Genesis* 3:8, which gives a different idea for the significance of the western side.

יֵרָאֶה — *Will be seen.* Cf. our commentary on 14:18 for the etymology and significance of the name יְרוּשָׁלַיִם.

15. וַיִּקְרָא מַלְאַךְ ה' . . . שֵׁנִית — *The angel of HASHEM called . . . a second time.* Why

¹⁴ *And Abraham called the name of that site "HASHEM Yireh," as it is said this day, on the mountain HASHEM will be seen.*
¹⁵ *The angel of HASHEM called to Abraham a second time from heaven.* ¹⁶ *And he said, "By Myself I swear — the word of HASHEM*

a second time? When the angel said the first time, "Do not stretch our your hand against the lad," Abraham had replied, "Who are you?" He said, "An angel." He replied, "The order to sacrifice my son was given to me by God Himself; if He wants me to desist, He will tell me Himself." And so the angel called a second time and this time reported the "words of God," Who "swore by Himself." Abraham replied, "You have sworn; I will also swear that I will not leave the altar before saying what I have to say. I want You to hear my grievances. Yesterday You said to me, '(Only) through Isaac will (your) descendants be called yours.' Then You tell me, 'Take your son . . . and bring him up there as an offering.' Now You say to me, 'Do not stretch out your hand against the lad.' And yet, I restrained myself and did not answer back. Thus when the children of Isaac will be guilty and will find themselves in distress, consider his sacrifice, pardon them, and deliver them from their anguish" (*Tanchuma*; see יפ״ת on the correct sequence of these phrases).

Following this intervention, notes another Midrash, God prescribed the daily sacrifice of two lambs, one to be offered in the morning, the other in the evening. He remembers the sacrifice of Isaac each time Israel recites the verse (*Leviticus* 1:11): וְשָׁחַט אֹתוֹ וגו׳, *He shall kill it on the side of the altar northward before God.* "I call Heaven and earth to witness," adds the Midrash, "every person, Jew or non-Jew, man or woman, manservant or maidservant, whoever shall read this verse, for him God will remember the binding of Isaac" (*Vayikra Rabbah* 2). The adoption of this verse in our daily prayers stems from this source, as R' Yosef Karo points out (*Orach Chaim* 1).

The daily morning and evening sacrifices are the expression of the will to devote oneself totally to God, not only at the high points of the festivals but also right within the normal course of everyday life. To be Jewish means to be constantly ready for sacrifice, which above all calls for self-control, for submission of our will to God's will. These acts of will constitute the prerequisite for all moral development. The exceptional character of Abraham's sacrifice lies in the fact that he was able to dominate his nature to such a degree that he without hesitation subordinated his paternal love to his love for God. Now, this profound meaning of sacrifice is explained by the verse וְשָׁחַט אֹתוֹ, *and he shall kill it*, for the victory over our own ego is also considered as an act of "killing" the instinct (cf. *Sukkah* 52b). Whoever achieves this act of piety of Abraham's within himself, Jew or non-Jew, man or woman, manservant or maidservant, earns the blessing of the sacrifice of Isaac which was announced to the patriarch long ago.

16. בִּי נִשְׁבַּעְתִּי — *By Myself I swear.* Cf. *Rashi* on *Exodus* 32:13: אֲשֶׁר נִשְׁבַּעְתָּ לָהֶם בָּךְ, *You have sworn* (to the patriarchs) *by Yourself:* "You did not swear to them

יַעַן אֲשֶׁר עָשִׂיתָ אֶת־הַדָּבָר הַזֶּה וְלֹא חָשַׂכְתָּ אֶת־
יז בִּנְךָ אֶת־יְחִידֶךָ: כִּי־בָרֵךְ אֲבָרֶכְךָ וְהַרְבָּה אַרְבֶּה אֶת־
זַרְעֲךָ כְּכוֹכְבֵי הַשָּׁמַיִם וְכַחוֹל אֲשֶׁר עַל־שְׂפַת הַיָּם וְיִרַשׁ
יח זַרְעֲךָ אֵת שַׁעַר אֹיְבָיו: וְהִתְבָּרְכוּ בְזַרְעֲךָ כֹּל גּוֹיֵי הָאָרֶץ
יט עֵקֶב אֲשֶׁר שָׁמַעְתָּ בְּקֹלִי: וַיָּשָׁב אַבְרָהָם אֶל־נְעָרָיו
וַיָּקֻמוּ וַיֵּלְכוּ יַחְדָּו אֶל־בְּאֵר שָׁבַע וַיֵּשֶׁב אַבְרָהָם בִּבְאֵר
שָׁבַע:

by something destined to disappear, not by heaven nor by earth, not by mountains nor by hills, but by Your everlasting Self, Whose oath will remain forever . . . ."

וְלֹא חָשַׂכְתָּ אֶת־בִּנְךָ אֶת־יְחִידֶךָ — *And have not withheld your son, your only one.* Through the revolt of the Maccabees, down to the present, how many times has the act of Abraham served as a stirring example to Jews called on to die for their faith or to "not withhold their child, their only one!" Compelled to make the terrible choice of renouncing their faith or of suffering martyrdom, the binding of Isaac again came alive in the spirit of our ancestors, men and women, and they chose martyrdom. The *Akeidah* became the ideal of the martyrdom which the Jew may be called upon to undergo for the sanctification of God's name. From earliest times the liturgy has included numerous references to the *Akeidah* and a long series of synagogue hymns deal with this theme (*piyutim*). In the Middle Ages, the *Akeidah* gave fathers and mothers the superhuman courage to sacrifice themselves and their children rather than to submit to idolatry or conversion. But in our day many have lost their understanding of martyrdom. They do not realize that the greatest moral triumph of humanity is the steadfastness of unshakable principles defended to the death. There exists no noble idea in human history which has not demanded the sacrifice of human life. But no nation on earth has offered as many sacrifices as Israel for the ideals of truth, justice, human dignity, and freedom. Israel has become "the classic people of martyrdom" (M. Schreiner). Few chapters of the Bible have had a more profound and more lasting influence on the spirit and lives of men than the chapter of the *Akeidah.*

17. כִּי־בָרֵךְ אֲבָרֶכְךָ — *That I shall surely bless you.* I.e., I will indeed unconditionally bless you. What has hitherto been only an alliance and hence dependent on the mutual fulfillment of certain conditions now becomes an unconditional oath. For through the *Akeidah* Abraham not only fulfilled the supreme goal of his life but at the same time he ensured its faithful fulfillment on the part of his offspring. Herein lies the merit of the *Akeidah.* It caused the ideal of mortal perfection to enter the spirit of the patriarch's lineage, and shines forth so brightly as an eternal example that because of this double factor — the glorious example plus the natural moral and spiritual disposition which they

*— that because you have done this thing, and have not withheld
your son, your only one, [17] that I shall surely bless you and greatly
increase your offering like the stars of the heavens and like the
sand on the seashore; and your offspring shall inherit the gate
of its enemy. [18] And all the nations of the earth shall bless
themselves by your offspring, because you have listened to My
voice.''*

[19] *Abraham returned to his young men, and they stood up and
went together to Beer-sheba, and Abraham stayed at Beer-sheba.*

inherit — the people of Israel can never be entirely lost. They will finally once
more rise to their saintly calling even though almost succumbing to the deepest
aberrations along the way. Thus, at this solemn hour God could promise His
eternal blessing to the descendants of Abraham (*R' S. R. Hirsch*).

וְיִרַשׁ זַרְעֲךָ אֵת שַׁעַר אֹיְבָיו — *And your offspring shall inherit the gate of its enemy.*
As *Ramban* notes, this is the new blessing to be added to the promises already
made before. Your descendants will never perish but will on the contrary
continue their triumphal march through the nations. For the future belongs to
the spirit of the *Akeidah*. They will conquer a hostile and stubborn world. (The
word שַׁעַר is close in meaning to "forum," and the conquest implied in the
expression וְיִרַשׁ זַרְעֲךָ is of essentially spiritual and moral, or social, character.)
   The promise of the spiritual conquest of humanity by the Jewish people
represents the supreme reward granted to Abraham after he had triumphed over
the most formidable of his ten trials, the *Akeidah*.

18. וְהִתְבָּרֲכוּ בְזַרְעֲךָ כֹּל גּוֹיֵי הָאָרֶץ — *And all the nations of the earth shall bless
themselves by your offspring.* To perpetuate the spirit of the *Akeidah*
throughout humanity in order to have humankind share in the promises of the
Divine blessings — this is the legacy of Abraham, this is the mission of his
children, the Jewish people.

19. וַיָּשָׁב אַבְרָהָם אֶל־נְעָרָיו — *Abraham returned to his young men.* Before, at the
outset of the great test, only Abraham and Isaac "went together" וַיֵּלְכוּ שְׁנֵיהֶם
יַחְדָּו. Now, after reaching the summit of human ethics, they start back and as
they do so they "go together" (וַיֵּלְכוּ יַחְדָּו) with their servants. They do not behave
haughtily, they do not consider themselves superior. They come back as though
nothing had happened. The modesty which they show us here is the mark of
true greatness.

20. וַיְהִי אַחֲרֵי הַדְּבָרִים הָאֵלֶּה — *It came to pass after these things.* Literally "those
words." What Abraham said to himself after the sacrifice of Isaac (*Rashi*). The
word אַחֲרֵי used here is not the same as אַחַר. One means "immediately
afterwards"; the other, "long after." But opinions differ as to which meaning
each word actually has (cf. *Maharal*; according to פי' הטור, the word אַחַר means
"immediately after" whereas אַחֲרֵי can have either meaning).

מפטיר כ וַיְהִ֗י אַחֲרֵי֙ הַדְּבָרִ֣ים הָאֵ֔לֶּה וַיֻּגַּ֥ד לְאַבְרָהָ֖ם לֵאמֹ֑ר הִנֵּ֠ה יָֽלְדָ֨ה
כא מִלְכָּ֥ה גַם־הִ֛וא בָּנִ֖ים לְנָח֥וֹר אָחִֽיךָ: אֶת־ע֥וּץ בְּכֹר֖וֹ וְאֶת־בּ֣וּז
כב אָחִ֑יו וְאֶת־קְמוּאֵ֖ל אֲבִ֥י אֲרָֽם: וְאֶת־כֶּ֣שֶׂד וְאֶת־חֲז֔וֹ וְאֶת־
כג פִּלְדָּ֖שׁ וְאֶת־יִדְלָ֑ף וְאֵ֖ת בְּתוּאֵֽל: וּבְתוּאֵ֖ל יָלַ֣ד אֶת־רִבְקָ֑ה
כד שְׁמֹנָ֥ה אֵ֙לֶּה֙ יָֽלְדָ֣ה מִלְכָּ֔ה לְנָח֖וֹר אֲחִ֣י אַבְרָהָֽם: וּפִֽילַגְשׁ֖וֹ
וּשְׁמָ֣הּ רְאוּמָ֑ה וַתֵּ֤לֶד גַּם־הִוא֙ אֶת־טֶ֣בַח וְאֶת־גַּ֔חַם וְאֶת־
תַּ֖חַשׁ וְאֶת־מַֽעֲכָֽה:

Be that as it may, upon returning from Mount Moriah Abraham said to himself, "Had my son been sacrificed, he would have died without children. I should have him marry one of the daughters of Aner, Eshkol, and Mamre." Then the Holy One, Blessed is He, told him of the birth of Rebecca, destined for Isaac. (The term וַיֻּגַּד implies a revelation by the רוּחַ הַקֹּדֶשׁ, as is noted by the מד' אור האפלה; cf. *Rashi* to *Genesis* 27:42.)

Besides this explanation, quoted by *Rashi*, the Midrash gives another: On his return from Mount Moriah, Abraham said to himself that even though Satan's slanderous accusations against Isaac had been proven false, there still remained the fear that harmful traces would mark Isaac's offspring. Then God said to him: "Do not fear any further troubles. The one who will be afflicted with them in your stead has just come into the world. He is Utz, the firstborn of your brother Nahor, whom the Torah names here אֶת עוּץ בְּכֹרוֹ." This name alludes to Job, the man from the land of Utz (*Job* 1:1) who was subjected to a series of harsh ordeals. [According to a tradition cited in the Jerusalem Talmud (*Sotah* 5:6), Job lived at the time of the patriarch.]

Even though it is shown to be false, the slander spread by a sinister enemy can still leave traces and have a harmful effect on the life of an innocent victim. But Providence can safeguard the righteous by diverting the aftermath toward a third party. The latter may himself be guilty and deserving of punishment, as with the examples cited by *Isaiah* (43:4) in history. Or he may be innocent, and then the tribulations come upon him as יִסּוּרִים שֶׁל אַהֲבָה, hardships that will, after he triumphs over them, bring him heavenly blessings, as we see with Job (42:10).

Here for the first time we find the idea of a man being offered as fodder to the forces of evil in order to have him bear the sufferings of others. This is the most sublime form of the idea of sacrificing oneself for the salvation of one's fellowman (של"ה, פ' וירא).

21. וְאֶת־קְמוּאֵ֖ל אֲבִ֥י אֲרָֽם — *Kemuel, the father of Aram.* Tradition identifies Kemuel with Balaam, the future Midianite prophet, "the father of Aramaic

²⁰ *It came to pass after these things, that Abraham was told,*
saying: Behold, Milcah too has borne children to Nahor, your
brother: ²¹ *Uz, his firstborn; Buz, his brother; Kemuel, the father*
of Aram; ²² *and Chesed, Hazo, Pildash, Jidlaph, and Bethuel;*
²³ *And Bethuel begot Rebecca. These eight Milcah bore to Nahor,*
Abraham's brother. ²⁴ *And his concubine, whose name was*
Reumah, also bore children: Tebah, Gaham, Tahash, and
Maacah.

sorcery" (*Targum Yerushalmi*). His name alludes to the one who "rose up
against God (קָם אֵל) and against His people" by trying to destroy them with his
power to curse (*Tanchuma*). His mother Milcah, Abraham's niece, had given
birth at the same time as Sarah and through her merit, as the expression גַּם הוא
(which refers to Sarah's blessing mentioned in 21:6; cf. our commentary) brings
out. Nevertheless, Balaam became a traitor and a relentless enemy of Jewry. How
many times has Jewish history borne out Isaiah's assertion that *your destroyers*
and they who laid you waste have come out of you (49:17). Cf. our commentary
on *Exodus* 1:10.

23. וּבְתוּאֵל יָלַד אֶת־רִבְקָה — *And Bethuel begot Rebecca.* R' Yochanan said,
"No righteous person leaves this world without another righteous one having
been born, as it is said (*Ecclesiastes* 1:4-5): *One generation passes away and*
another generation comes ... the sun also rises and the sun goes down,
and striving to reach its place it rises again there (*Yoma* 38b). Thus, here, the
Torah relates the birth of Rebecca before it reports the death of Sarah (*Rabbah*
58).

24. וּפִילַגְשׁוֹ ... וַתֵּלֶד גַּם־הִוא — *And his concubine ... also bore children.* Rashi
explains that this whole genealogy is given only in order to come to the
verse concerning Rebecca. The Sages of the Midrash, however, note that
the four names in this verse indicate four names of rebellion (contrary to
Ramban's opinion). According to R' *Chaim ben Attar*, the genealogy is a
reminder to us that the birth of the righteous is accompanied by that of
unworthy and heretical elements. Along with the good wheat grows the
chaff. Such are the consequences of the jumble of good and evil which has
permeated creation since the first sin. The birth of the righteous occurs in a world
waiting to take advantage of them. Rebecca came into the world as "a rose
among thorns" (*Midrash Rabbah* to *Song of Songs* 2:2) and despite iniquitous
parents, brothers, and surroundings, she maintained her angelic purity (*Rashi* on
25:20).

כג   א וַיִּהְיוּ חַיֵּי שָׂרָה מֵאָה שָׁנָה וְעֶשְׂרִים שָׁנָה וְשֶׁבַע שָׁנִים שְׁנֵי חַיֵּי
ב שָׂרָה: וַתָּמָת שָׂרָה בְּקִרְיַת אַרְבַּע הִוא חֶבְרוֹן בְּאֶרֶץ כְּנָעַן

23.

1. וַיִּהְיוּ חַיֵּי שָׂרָה מֵאָה שָׁנָה וְעֶשְׂרִים שָׁנָה וְשֶׁבַע שָׁנִים — *Sarah's lifetime was one hundred years, twenty years, and seven years.* The passage about Sarah's death immediately follows that of the sacrifice of Isaac for, *Rashi* explains, upon learning that her child had been bound upon the altar, that he was ready to be sacrificed, and that he very nearly was, her soul left her and she died. Such is the lot of the righteous on earth. Abraham returns from Mount Moriah with his heart full of joy that he was able to save his son and that he received new Divine blessings, even greater than before. Surely he rejoices at the thought of being able to share his good fortune with his wife, at the very moment he reaches the apotheosis of his life. Yet it is just at this moment that a new ordeal cruelly confronts him: he learns the terrible news of his wife's death.

Rashi will explain on a similar occasion in the life of the patriarch Jacob: The righteous aspire to live in happiness. But God says: Are they not satisfied with what the World to Come has in store for them? They also want happiness in this world! (37:2). Accordingly, it should not be at all surprising to see the righteous going from one trial to another.

Rashi's account of the circumstances surrounding Sarah's death is based on the words of R' Eliezer (*Pirkei D'Rabbi Eliezer* 32) which tell that Satan, who was vexed by his failure to dissuade Abraham and his son from obeying God, deliberately went to provoke Sarah's death. He brutally told her of her son's imminent death. Does this therefore mean that Sarah was innocent when she died? Or was her premature death, caused by diabolical intervention, to be taken as a providential chastisement for a transgression which she had committed earlier? Such is the opinion of R' Chanan, who teaches: Whoever accuses his fellowman before God (instead of bringing his case before an earthly court) will be punished first. For example, Sarah accused her husband, saying: "The outrage against me is due to you (you did not defend me before Hagar); let God judge between me and you!" (16:5). Called upon to render justice, God gave His verdict. It was against Sarah. She died prematurely, thirty-eight years before her husband (*Bava Kamma* 93a and *Bereishis Rabbah* 45). (Justice demands atonement for a previous error, as was shown in our commentary to 21:8.)

וַיִּהְיוּ חַיֵּי שָׂרָה — *Sarah's lifetime.* But for this occasion, the Torah never records a woman's age. The *Zohar* calls attention to this exception in order to stress the unequaled value of Sarah's life. It is not written וַתְּחִי שָׂרָה, the usual form, but וַיִּהְיוּ חַיֵּי שָׂרָה, which further emphasizes the notion of a life lived on a higher level. Moreover, the verse reiterates שְׁנֵי חַיֵּי שָׂרָה, *the years of Sarah's life*, and this suggests that the Torah wants to allude to a double life — that of this world and that of the World to Come. Sarah, the *Zohar* writes, was pure and righteous.

23 ¹**S**arah's lifetime was one hundred years, twenty years, and seven years; the years of Sarah's life. ² Sarah died in Kiriath-arba which is Hebron in the land of Canaan;

During her stay on earth she never allowed herself to be sullied by sin, as Eve had. Her saintly life continues in the hereafter; this continuation is implied in the word וַיִּהְיוּ (rather than וַתְּחִי), which also means to remain, to abide, as in Ecclesiastes 11:2. [וַיִּהְיוּ has a numerical value of thirty-seven, a reference to the thirty-seven years from Isaac's birth, which represented the true life of Sarah (Zohar).]

מֵאָה שָׁנָה וְעֶשְׂרִים שָׁנָה וְשֶׁבַע שָׁנִים — One hundred years, twenty years, and seven years. Why is Sarah's age divided into three separate segments? In order to teach you that for the righteous each day and each segment of life counts as much as the entire life taken as a whole (Midrash HaGadol). Rashi explains further: "The word 'year' is repeated with each number to tell you that it requires interpretation. At one hundred Sarah was as she was at twenty, without sin . . . at twenty she was just as beautiful as she had been at seven." But several exegetes bring out the original, seemingly more logical version of this quotation as it appears in Yalkut to Psalms 37: At one hundred she was as beautiful as at twenty; at twenty she was as much without sin as at seven (Rashi, ed. Berliner).

שְׁנֵי חַיֵּי שָׂרָה — The years of Sarah's life. R' Chaim ben Attar explains that this last part of the verse refers to the remainder of the years which Sarah was destined to live had she not died prematurely. The end of the sentence teaches us that God does not deprive the righteous person who dies prematurely of the merit of the years initially destined for him (cf. Tanchuma to Exodus 30:12, where this idea is treated at length).

2. בְּקִרְיַת אַרְבַּע — Kiriath-arba. The old name for Hebron, mentioned in the book of Judges (1:10). Here the Israelites conquered three giants, tribal chieftains, the sons of a man named Arba (Joshua 15:13). "There is no area in the land of Israel more rocky than Hebron; that is why it had been destined as a burial ground. Despite this, Hebron was still seven times better than Zoan, royal residence and privileged region of Egypt" (Rashi on Numbers 13:22).

Why does the Torah give the original name Kiriath Arba, since it immediately adds the name normally used? Rashi explains that the word אַרְבַּע refers either to the four giants living there or to the four couples buried there. The Zohar, however, sees in the name קִרְיַת אַרְבַּע a reference to the four letters of the Divine name (i.e., the Tetragrammaton, שֵׁם הַוָיָ'). Just as Aaron, Miriam, and Moses all expired by the Divine kiss, Sarah too died innocent and pure, in "the enclosure (קִרְיַת = city, surrounding wall) of the four" letters of the Ineffable Name.

חֶבְרוֹן בְּאֶרֶץ כְּנָעַן — Hebron in the land of Canaan. The Torah stresses here and in verse 19 that Sarah died in the land of Canaan and was buried there. This

ג וַיָּבֹא אַבְרָהָם לִסְפֹּד לְשָׂרָה וְלִבְכֹּתָהּ: וַיָּקָם אַבְרָהָם מֵעַל
ד פְּנֵי מֵתוֹ וַיְדַבֵּר אֶל־בְּנֵי־חֵת לֵאמֹר: גֵּר־וְתוֹשָׁב אָנֹכִי
עִמָּכֶם תְּנוּ לִי אֲחֻזַּת־קֶבֶר עִמָּכֶם וְאֶקְבְּרָה מֵתִי מִלְּפָנָי:

detail can give us the explanation of why she died in Hebron. She had lived in Beer-sheba and no explanation is given for her moving from there. However, one can see why her death and burial should have taken place in Canaan and not in Beer-sheba, which was located in Philistine territory. Indeed, it was essential for the future of the Jewish people that the tombs of the patriarchs be situated in the Promised Land. Throughout the centuries of history, in all the lands of the dispersion, they represented the eternal symbol of the homeland and the rallying point for the whole nation, And so, Sarah's move to Hebron, where she died, was an act of Providence. Abraham would have had no valid reason for wanting to buy the cave of Machpelah from the sons of Heth had Sarah died in Beer-sheba and not in Hebron.

וַיָּבֹא אַבְרָהָם וְגוֹ' — *And Abraham came, etc.* The question was raised: "Is the funeral oration in honor of the living or the dead?" This is important in the case where the dead person had asked not to have a eulogy or where the surviving family does not want one. Come and hear: Abraham came to eulogize Sarah and to bewail her. Now if you say that this is in honor of the living, how could Sarah's body have been left unburied in order to honor Abraham? [The Talmud considers that Abraham was separated from Sarah at the moment of her death. Right after the *Akeidah* on Mount Moriah, Abraham returned to Beer-sheba, as stated at the end of the previous chapter. According to certain traditions, Isaac too was far away, his father having taken him from Mount Moriah to the school of Shem and Eber (*Rabbah* 56). Hence, Abraham came back alone from Beer-sheba to Hebron, where Sarah had gone for reasons unknown. Now if you admit that a eulogy is made to honor the surviving family, then there was no reason for delaying Sarah's burial, since they were absent.] But the Talmud does not accept this as a conclusive argument and replies: Sarah herself wanted Abraham to be honored through her (*Sanhedrin* 46b).

וְלִבְכֹּתָהּ — *And to bewail her.* According to the *Masorah*, the letter כ in the word וְלִבְכֹּתָהּ is written smaller than the other letters. This seems to point to a certain constraint in the expression of grief. Indeed, for the righteous person convinced of the immortality of the soul, death means only a temporary separation and he does not give way to excessive sadness.

3. וַיָּקָם אַבְרָהָם מֵעַל פְּנֵי מֵתוֹ — *Abraham rose up from the presence of his dead.* Although the sacrifice of Isaac had indirectly caused Sarah's death, Abraham did not regret in the least having faithfully obeyed the command of the *Akeidah*. Not only did the painful test not diminish in the slightest his faith in God but, on the contrary, through it Abraham was able to attain a new level of moral perfection. He "rose up higher in the presence of his dead one."

and Abraham came to eulogize Sarah and to bewail her.
³ *Abraham rose up from the presence of his dead, and spoke to*
the children of Heth, saying: ⁴ *"I am an alien and a resident*
among you; grant me an estate for a burial site with you, that
I may bury my dead from before me."

וַיְדַבֵּר אֶל־בְּנֵי־חֵת — *And spoke to the children of Heth.* These were the Hittites, descendants of Canaan (10:15). R' Eliezer said: "How much ink has flowed, how many pens have been worn out to write the words בְּנֵי חֵת ten times in the Torah (eight times in this passage, once in 25:10, and once again in 49:32)! Ten times, as many as the Ten Commandments. This is to teach you that if one assists (lit. clarifies) a righteous man in his business dealings, it is as important as observing the Ten Commandments" (*Rabbah* chap. 58). The same master also teaches that the righteous are scrupulously careful in financial transactions "because they never stretch out their hands to robbery" (*Chullin* 91a). Hence they are extremely strict in these matter. For Abraham, a business transaction requires the same moral consciousness as that which is to inspire the observance of the Ten Commandments.

4. גֵּר־וְתוֹשָׁב אָנֹכִי עִמָּכֶם — *I am an alien* (sojourner) *and a resident* (dweller) *among you.* By prefacing his negotiations with these words, Abraham wanted to inform the others of his position: "Give me willingly what I ask, as a sojourner. If not, I shall claim it as a dweller among you and shall take a burial-place by rights, for God has said to me, 'I shall give this land to your descendants' " (*Rashi*). Abraham's state of mind is clearly seen from these opening words. He has to acquire the land rapidly and does not for the moment wish to enter into any discussion about his true rights: "give me possession of the burial-place either as a sojourner or as a dweller."

וְאֶקְבְּרָה מֵתִי מִלְּפָנָי — *That I may bury my dead from before me.* This is the first reference in the Bible to burial of the dead. Abraham places very great importance on assuring "his dead" of an honorable burial-place and his descendants have inherited this same preoccupation from him. Many of the rules concerning forms of burial and the mourning period are derived from the details of this passage.

As a wrapping for the soul which comes from the celestial spheres, the human body is lavished with the greatest care during its earthly life and the most profound respect at the moment the soul leaves it. *The body returns to the earth whence it came and the spirit ascends again to God Who gave it* (*Ecclesiastes* 12:7). The body is returned to the earth to blend again with it, while the soul remains and "ascends again to God." For Judaism, burial of the mortal remains signifies that the material part of man finally disintegrates, while the spiritual soul survives in its individuality. The pagans who believed in the transmigration of souls considered the body as the only perpetual part of the human being. Consequently they practiced necromancy, embalmed their corpses, mummified

ה-ו וַיַּעֲנוּ בְנֵי־חֵת אֶת־אַבְרָהָם לֵאמֹר לוֹ: שְׁמָעֵנוּ | אֲדֹנִי נְשִׂיא
אֱלֹהִים אַתָּה בְּתוֹכֵנוּ בְּמִבְחַר קְבָרֵינוּ קְבֹר אֶת־מֵתֶךָ אִישׁ
ז מִמֶּנּוּ אֶת־קִבְרוֹ לֹא־יִכְלֶה מִמְּךָ מִקְּבֹר מֵתֶךָ: וַיָּקָם אַבְרָהָם
ח וַיִּשְׁתַּחוּ לְעַם־הָאָרֶץ לִבְנֵי־חֵת: וַיְדַבֵּר אִתָּם לֵאמֹר אִם־יֵשׁ
אֶת־נַפְשְׁכֶם לִקְבֹּר אֶת־מֵתִי מִלְּפָנַי שְׁמָעוּנִי וּפִגְעוּ־לִי
ט בְּעֶפְרוֹן בֶּן־צֹחַר: וְיִתֶּן־לִי אֶת־מְעָרַת הַמַּכְפֵּלָה אֲשֶׁר־לוֹ

them, and erected mausoleums and pyramids in their honor. Opposed to this materialist concept is the nihilist doctrine of freethinkers. They show their belief in nothingness after death by having their dead cremated. But Judaism affirms its faith in the immortality of the soul by returning the body to its original source without deifying or annihilating it, while the immaterial and imperishable soul rejoins its sphere of emanation in the metaphysical regions.

The exceptional importance which Abraham attached to the acquisition of a burial place for Sarah was certainly in keeping with his desire to reveal these fundamental principles of monotheistic religion to the pagan people of Canaan.

6. נְשִׂיא אֱלֹהִים אַתָּה בְּתוֹכֵנוּ — *You are a prince of God in our midst.* R' Yose the Galilean said, "Since the abominable practices of the Egyptians are considered on a par with those of the Canaanites, why did the latter live in peace longer than the Egyptians? It is because they behaved in a worthy fashion toward Abraham. They honored him, even though they did not share his views" (ת"כ, *Leviticus* 18:3).

אִישׁ מִמֶּנּוּ אֶת־קִבְרוֹ לֹא־יִכְלֶה מִמְּךָ — *Any of us will not withhold his burial place from you.* Such has always been the fate of the righteous person. People scarcely worry about his needs during his lifetime. But they are ready to offer him a grave the moment he dies. The Jewish scholar, תַּלְמִיד חָכָם, also knows the same fate: When he dies, everyone becomes his relative (*Moed Kattan* 25a).

7. וַיִּשְׁתַּחוּ לְעַם־הָאָרֶץ — *And bowed down to the members of the council.* Although he bowed down before the members of the council, it was meant for God, Whom Abraham wanted to thank for the affirmative reply of the Hittites. However, the patriarch did not at all want to bury his dead in those family plots which the Hittites wanted to offer him. He intended to have permanent ownership of the cave which he longed for, the one which belonged to Ephron.

לְעַם־הָאָרֶץ — *To the members of the council.* The expression עַם הָאָרֶץ was used in later Hebrew to denote an ignorant man. But, of the forty-nine times it occurs in Scripture, in forty-two it refers neither to people, nor to an ignorant individual, but to the common assembly which forms the political or administrative council of the land.

8. וּפִגְעוּ־לִי בְּעֶפְרוֹן — *And intercede for me with Ephron.* Abraham had long been aware of the cave of Machpelah, situated at the end of Ephron the Hittite's field in Hebron. He had discovered the cave while chasing the fleeing "young calf"

⁵ And the children of Heth answered Abraham, saying to him: ⁶ "Hear us, my lord: You are a prince of God in our midst; in the choicest of our burial places bury your dead, any of us will not withhold his burial place from you, from burying your dead."
⁷ Then Abraham rose up and bowed down to the members of the council, to the children of Heth. ⁸ He spoke to them saying: "If it is truly your will to bury my dead from before me, heed me, and intercede for me with Ephron son of Zohar. ⁹ Let him grant me the Cave of Machpelah which is his,

which he intended to give to the three strangers who came to visit him after the circumcision (see our commentary on 18:7). He had caught the calf in front of the cave, where it had stopped. Abraham had smelt the sweet fragrance of Paradise wafting from the cave, and had had a vision of dazzling light. He recognized then that the cave contained the graves of Adam and Eve. From that time onward he was obsessed with obtaining this cave as the burial place for himself and his family. With all his soul he wanted to own it, and waited for the right moment to make it his (Zohar).

But after Sarah died, Abraham could not negotiate directly with Ephron for the cave. With the esteem the people of Hebron had for him, Abraham would have offended them had he spoken to just one individual without consulting the city council. And so he proceeded with tact and diplomacy. First he gave a preamble which in general terms revealed his request to bury his wife (ibid.). Then, having won over the council, he begged them to intercede with Ephron on his behalf.

Why was Abraham so anxious to acquire the burial place of Adam and Eve as a family possession in perpetuity? To be sure, every nation has its pantheon, which usually contains the remains of its national heroes and represents a high point of patriotic sentiment. But Abraham, in contrast, wanted to make the Jewish pantheon a symbol of the spirit of universalism. For him, Judaism was the realization of the mission of Adam, that is, of man *par excellence.* After the ideal plan conceived for all humanity had failed, following the original sin, Abraham was the first to attempt to repair this flaw and to fulfill this calling for humanity. Basically his religion was that of every human being. "You are Adam" (man *par excellence*) said the prophet Ezekiel to the Jews (34:31). And the Divine commandments addressed to the Jewish people were given in order that *man do them and live by them* (Leviticus 18:5). They are offered to all men regardless of race, regardless of origin.

This universal character was of the utmost importance for the patriarch. It determined the choice of the burial place for Abraham and his family. Abraham considered himself the successor and repository of Adam's mission, and he did not hesitate to pay any price, including the renunciation of the city of Jerusalem

אֲשֶׁ֣ר בְּקָצֵ֣ה שָׂדֵ֗הוּ בְּכֶ֨סֶף מָלֵ֤א יִתְּנֶ֨נָּה֙ לִּ֔י בְּתוֹכְכֶ֖ם
י לַאֲחֻזַּת־קָֽבֶר: וְעֶפְר֥וֹן יֹשֵׁ֖ב בְּת֣וֹךְ בְּנֵי־חֵ֑ת וַיַּ֩עַן֩ עֶפְר֨וֹן הַֽחִתִּ֤י
אֶת־אַבְרָהָם֙ בְּאָזְנֵ֣י בְנֵי־חֵ֔ת לְכֹ֛ל בָּאֵ֥י שַֽׁעַר־עִיר֖וֹ לֵאמֹֽר:
יא לֹֽא־אֲדֹנִ֣י שְׁמָעֵ֔נִי הַשָּׂדֶה֙ נָתַ֣תִּי לָ֔ךְ וְהַמְּעָרָ֥ה אֲשֶׁר־בּ֖וֹ לְךָ֣
יב נְתַתִּ֑יהָ לְעֵינֵ֧י בְנֵֽי־עַמִּ֛י נְתַתִּ֥יהָ לָּ֖ךְ קְבֹ֥ר מֵתֶֽךָ: וַיִּשְׁתַּ֨חוּ֙
יג אַבְרָהָ֔ם לִפְנֵ֖י עַם־הָאָֽרֶץ: וַיְדַבֵּ֨ר אֶל־עֶפְר֜וֹן בְּאָזְנֵ֣י עַם־
הָאָ֘רֶץ֮ לֵאמֹר֒ אַ֛ךְ אִם־אַתָּ֥ה ל֖וּ שְׁמָעֵ֑נִי נָתַ֜תִּי כֶּ֤סֶף הַשָּׂדֶה֙

(see our commentary to verse 16), in order to assure himself of ownership of the cave wherein the first couple lay buried.

9. וְיִתֶּן־לִי — *Let him grant me.* Abraham anticipated all possible arguments which his possession of the cave would entail, both then and in the future. At the moment of acquisition he took all the precautions imaginable. He called attention to the legal form of donation as well as of sale in order to prevent any restrictive clause or mental reservation which might subsequently be connected with one of these two procedures. Moreover, he was anxious to conclude the acquisition publicly in order to ensure that the transaction would not be invalidated by mortgages or prior charges on the property or by claims regarding priority in option rights brought forward by neighbors or by any other interested parties.

אֶת־מְעָרַת הַמַּכְפֵּלָה — *The Cave of Machpelah.* *Rashi* gives two explanations for the name מַכְפֵּלָה, which is derived from כֶּפֶל, *double*: Because the ground itself had a second story above it, or because of its couples. *Ramban* objects to looking for a special interpretation of the proper name by which this cave was always known. Nevertheless, for the *Zohar* the name מַכְפֵּלָה has the meaning of "double." The cave where the righteous find eternal rest is but the double, the counterpart, of the celestial residence where their souls soar and enjoy the bliss of the hereafter.

11. לֹֽא־אֲדֹנִי — *No, my lord.* "You will not purchase it with money" (*Rashi*). Is this generous offer of a donation, thrice repeated in this verse, just part of the typical oriental setting replete with grandiloquent declamations which are hardly taken seriously by the speaker? Is the offer insincere or is it genuine? Opinions are divided. R' Elazar chooses the first hypothesis (*Bava Metziah* 87a). But the *Zohar* elaborates that Ephron placed little value on the cave and was totally unaware of its contents. Only Abraham through prophetic intuition was able to perceive the ethereal radiance from the cave. Only he could realize the saintly treasures which it harbored. But Ephron had seen nothing and suspected nothing. We have already observed this difference between Abraham's hypersensitivity and the dulled sensitivity of simple mortals during the *Akeidah* (in our commentary to 22:5). And so Ephron did not know why Abraham showed excessive interest in the cave. He took the whole affair lightly,

on the edge of his field; let him grant it to me for its full
price, in your midst, as an estate for a burial site."

¹⁰ Now, Ephron was sitting in the midst of the children of
Heth; and Ephron the Hittite responded to Abraham in the
hearing of the children of Heth, for all who come to the gate
of his city, saying: ¹¹ "No, my lord; heed me! I have given
you the field, and as for the cave that is in it, I have given
it to you; In the view of the children of my people have I
given it to you; bury your dead." ¹² So Abraham bowed down
before the members of the council. ¹³ He spoke to Ephron in
the hearing of the members of the council, saying: "Rather,
if only you would heed me! I give you the price of the field,

detachedly. Ephron willingly offered to make Abraham a gift of the cave at the
end of his field and even added the field itself (which Abraham had not asked
for). He did so either with an ulterior motive or because he thought it
inconceivable that Abraham should possess the cave without having the field
giving access to it (Ramban). [The Rama on Choshen Mishpat 232:18 deals with
the legal value of a sale effected in ignorance of the real value of the
merchandise. See on this R' Chaim ben Attar's commentary on our verse.]

12. וַיִּשְׁתַּחוּ אַבְרָהָם לִפְנֵי עַם־הָאָרֶץ — So Abraham bowed down before the
members of the council. For the second time Abraham makes this gesture of
humility which is also an expression of his deep gratitude. The full impact of this
state of mind is brought out by the words of the Talmud quoted by Rashi on
Exodus 6:9: God said to Moses (after he had criticized His conduct at the start
of his mission), "Alas for those who have disappeared never to be found again!
Well can I mourn the death of the patriarchs! Often I revealed Myself to them
as Almighty God and they did not criticize My conduct nor ask Me (as you do),
'What is Your name?' I had said to Abraham: 'Arise, walk through the length
and breadth of this land, for I shall give it to you.' Yet, when he wanted to bury
Sarah, he had to purchase the burial-place which he found for her, at
considerable expense. And despite all this he did not criticize My actions"
(Sanhedrin 111a). Our verse now lets us add: Not only did he not criticize them,
but he even showed profound gratitude when he managed to acquire the burial
place for Sarah. From this one can see why a statement in the היובלים ס' tells us
that the death and burial of Sarah were among the ten trials which Abraham
had to overcome.

13. קַח מִמֶּנִּי — Accept it from me. The legal form of Jewish marriage makes
reference to the act of selling Ephron's field. The Talmud compares the term
employed in acquiring this field — קַח מִמֶּנִּי — with the analogous expression
used in Deuteronomy 24:1 for the act of marriage, כִּי יִקַּח אִישׁ אִשָּׁה. It concludes
that acquisition via a sum of money is one of the legal forms of marriage
(Kiddushin 4b).

יד קַח מִמֶּנִּי וְאֶקְבְּרָה אֶת־מֵתִי שָׁמָּה: וַיַּעַן עֶפְרוֹן אֶת־אַבְרָהָם

טו לֵאמֹר לוֹ: אֲדֹנִי שְׁמָעֵנִי אֶרֶץ אַרְבַּע מֵאֹת שֶׁקֶל־כֶּסֶף בֵּינִי

טז וּבֵינְךָ מַה־הִוא וְאֶת־מֵתְךָ קְבֹר: וַיִּשְׁמַע אַבְרָהָם אֶל־עֶפְרוֹן

וַיִּשְׁקֹל אַבְרָהָם לְעֶפְרֹן אֶת־הַכֶּסֶף אֲשֶׁר דִּבֶּר בְּאָזְנֵי

שני   יז בְנֵי־חֵת אַרְבַּע מֵאוֹת שֶׁקֶל כֶּסֶף עֹבֵר לַסֹּחֵר: וַיָּקָם ׀ שְׂדֵה

עֶפְרוֹן אֲשֶׁר בַּמַּכְפֵּלָה אֲשֶׁר לִפְנֵי מַמְרֵא הַשָּׂדֶה וְהַמְּעָרָה

אֲשֶׁר־בּוֹ וְכָל־הָעֵץ אֲשֶׁר בַּשָּׂדֶה אֲשֶׁר בְּכָל־גְּבֻלוֹ סָבִיב:

יח לְאַבְרָהָם לְמִקְנָה לְעֵינֵי בְנֵי־חֵת בְּכֹל בָּאֵי שַׁעַר־עִירוֹ:

Some modernists have found this judicial form displeasing and have reproachfully derided Mosaic religion. "The Jew buys his wife!" they say. Indeed he does! He does acquire her. But then she will accordingly be his, his alone and his forever. Unlike the modernists, in his eyes his wife will be the most treasured possession he has on earth. For him, the marriage contract is definitive and inviolable. And the bonds of love uniting the couple will remain indissoluble, even beyond the "field of death" (קיחה קיחה משדה עפרון).

15. אֶרֶץ אַרְבַּע מֵאֹת שֶׁקֶל־כֶּסֶף — *Land worth four hundred silver shekels*. Ephron was aware of the Divine announcement which promised possession of the land of Canaan to Abraham's descendants after 400 years. This period corresponds to eight jubilee cycles. Now the price of redemption of inherited land was set at fifty shekels of silver per jubilee period (*Leviticus* 27:16; cf. *Rashi*). Hence Ephron asked Abraham for 400 shekels in payment of his field. He is even more specific: בֵּינִי וּבֵינְךָ, this price is calculated for the period between me (i.e. when the field belongs to me) and you (when it will become yours through the Divine promise). Hence if you do not buy it, מַה־הִוא, what does it matter? It will ultimately be yours in any case (ישמח משה).

16. וַיִּשְׁמַע אַבְרָהָם אֶל־עֶפְרוֹן — *Abraham heeded Ephron*. When Abraham implored the Hittites to let him have the cave of Machpelah for a good price and with no strings attached, they at first refused. And so, Abraham had to prostrate himself on two occasions before the common people of the region in order to secure their agreement. They said to him: "We know that God will give your descendants all these territories. Swear to us first that your descendants will never take possession of Jebus without the consent of the Jebusites, and in return you will have the cave of Machpelah." Hence it is written here *Abraham heeded Ephron* (שָׁמַע אֶל always indicates acquiescence), and then *Abraham weighed out to Ephron the price etc.* (*Pirkei D'Rabbi Eliezer* 36).

Jebus is the former name of Jerusalem (*I Chronicles* 11:6), inhabited of old by the Hittites, who are of Canaanite descent. It has already been noted that Abraham's friendship treaty with Abimelech the Philistine king had grave repercussions when David prepared to conquer Jerusalem (see our commentary to 21:30). In another *aggadic* version, these same events are depicted as the tragic

accept it from me, that I may bury my dead there."

¹⁴ And Ephron replied to Abraham, saying to him: ¹⁵ "My lord, heed me! Land worth four hundred silver shekels; between me and you — what is it? Bury your dead."

¹⁶ Abraham heeded Ephron, and Abraham weighed out to Ephron the price which he had mentioned in the hearing of the children of Heth, four hundred silver shekels in negotiable currency. ¹⁷ And Ephron's field, which was in Machpelah, facing Mamre, the field and the cave within it and all the trees in the field, within all its surrounding boundaries, was confirmed ¹⁸ as Abraham's as a purchase in the view of the children of Heth, among all who came to the gate of his city.

result of the oath which Abraham made to the Hittites while transacting the purchase of the cave of Machpelah. It seems that a double fate hovered over the Holy City, as though the many tribulations which accompanied its capture were to be a stern warning to the Jewish people never to let themselves be induced to make treaties or promises of friendship with pagan nations (see also our commentary to 23:8).

שֶׁקֶל כֶּסֶף עֹבֵר לַסֹּחֵר — Silver shekels in negotiable currency. Acceptable everywhere (Onkelos). Wherever the Torah speaks of shekels it means selas; in the prophets the litra is meant; in the Writings (Hagiographa), the centenarium (100 selas). But an exception to this is the money given Ephron, which, although recorded in the Torah, involves shekels equivalent to centenaria. "There are places where centenaria are referred to as shekels" (Bechoros 50a). This detail indicates that Abraham gave Ephron shekels which were acceptable the world over.

17-18. וַיָּקָם שְׂדֵה עֶפְרוֹן . . . לְאַבְרָהָם לְמִקְנָה — And Ephron's field . . . was confirmed as Abraham's as a purchase. The last verses of the chapter contain nothing other than an exact description of the location of the cave of Machpelah and a reminder that Abraham and his offspring would have perpetual title to it. The same insistence and the same wealth of detail recur at the end of Genesis when Jacob gives his children final instructions for his burial in the Holy Land (49:29-32).

There are three places, say our Sages, where the peoples of the world cannot contest our title to property. These are the cave of Machpelah, the Temple site, and Joseph's tomb — the first in view of the precise particulars given and repeated here, the second by virtue of the purchase contract made by David and mentioned explicitly in I Chronicles 21:24-25, and the third because of the legal acquisition reported by the Torah: "He bought the parcel of land upon which he pitched his tent from the children of Hamor, Shechem's father, for one hundred kesitahs (Genesis 33:19; Rabbah ibid.). This place was called Shechem, and here Joseph was buried, as Rashi points out on Genesis 48:22.

יט וְאַחֲרֵי־כֵן קָבַר אַבְרָהָם אֶת־שָׂרָה אִשְׁתּוֹ אֶל־מְעָרַת שְׂדֵה
כ הַמַּכְפֵּלָה עַל־פְּנֵי מַמְרֵא הִוא חֶבְרוֹן בְּאֶרֶץ כְּנָעַן: וַיָּקָם
הַשָּׂדֶה וְהַמְּעָרָה אֲשֶׁר־בּוֹ לְאַבְרָהָם לַאֲחֻזַּת־קָבֶר מֵאֵת
בְּנֵי־חֵת: וְאַבְרָהָם זָקֵן בָּא
כד א
ב בַּיָּמִים וַיהוָה בֵּרַךְ אֶת־אַבְרָהָם בַּכֹּל: וַיֹּאמֶר אַבְרָהָם

However, no matter what precautions the most eminent Biblical figures took in anticipation of the future vicissitudes of history, no other holy places gave rise to as many conflicts, disputes, and court cases as these three places. Jewry's destiny would have it that for long centuries these sites would be in foreign and enemy hands. Even now (1977) the three sites are under Arab authority, though nominally in Jewish hands.

Did Providence wish to use these three examples to show just how artificial business deals turn out to be when it is a matter of establishing the permanence of Jewry's most sacred possessions in the world? Or must one rather conclude that the *Shechinah* and Its protecting care are themselves absent from the Holy Land when Jewry is banished in distant exile, or faltering in its observance of God's Torah even while in the Holy Land?

19. וְאַחֲרֵי־כֵן קָבַר אַבְרָהָם אֶת־שָׂרָה אִשְׁתּוֹ — *And afterwards Abraham buried Sarah his wife.* The *Zohar* explains: "that is, after having appeased the fears of the first couple who were lying in the cave, Adam and Eve. When the mortal remains of the righteous and saintly Sarah were brought in, Adam and Eve began to fear that the memory of their sin would again be brought before the celestial tribunal and they would have to face unfavorable comparisons. They did not want to allow Sarah to enter. But Abraham promised to pray for them. After this he buried Sarah, his wife. The text does not state קָבַר שָׂרָה but קָבַר אֶת־שָׂרָה, which implies that he buried someone 'with Sarah,' namely Eve herself." Abraham and Sarah were the first human beings who undertook to repair the tragic consequences of the first sin. Owing to them, the souls of the first couple were able to find their repose in the hereafter. Abraham and Sarah's lives on earth were the best prayers for the salvation of these souls. And when the body of Sarah entered the cave of Machpelah, for Eve it was like a "second burial" which allowed her soul at last to be truly at peace.

24.

1. וְאַבְרָהָם זָקֵן — *Now Abraham was old.* He was 137 years old at that time and he lived another 38 years. But suddenly he felt old after his wife died.

On the other hand, Abraham's aging is considered one of the seven phenomena brought about after creation. "Before him, old age did not exist" (*Sanhedrin* 103b). Age remained invisible; it did not show up in the crown of white hair which gives the elderly their venerable appearance. "God heeded Abraham's prayer to look old so that no one would take Isaac for Abraham or vice versa" (ibid.). *The hair of his head, white as pure wool (Daniel 7:9)*

¹⁹ *And afterwards Abraham buried Sarah his wife in the cave of the field of Machpelah facing Mamre, which is Hebron, in the land of Canaan. ²⁰ Thus, the field with its cave confirmed as Abraham's as an estate for a burial site, from the children of Heth.*

24   ¹*Now Abraham was old, well on in years, and HASHEM had blessed Abraham with everything. ² And Abraham said*

symbolically represents "splendor and majesty" (*Tanchuma*). God graced man with this sign "which He bears Himself, so that one will know who deserves to be honored" (ibid.). On this verse, the Sages of the Midrash depict mature age as a title of honor which is to bring respect and veneration. Old age has a positive value *per se*. It is a guarantee of tradition whose continuity is assured by the chain of generations. Hence the authority of a teacher among the Jewish people must be legitimized by age or signs of age; witness the example of R' Elazar ben Azaryah (*Bereishis Rabbah* 28). In this concept, Judaism, which teaches respect for old age as a positive commandment, stands diametrically opposed to Greek polytheism which puts adolescence at the center of life. One values the cult of beauty and physical strength; the other, respect for family and for tradition.

בָּא בַּיָּמִים — *Well on in years*. Literally, "in *the* days" (with the definite article). In this supplementary detail the Sages of the Midrash see a reference to the fact that Abraham "advanced toward the days *par excellence*" — those of the next world. They tell us that the days of his earthly life were, for him, just a "passage leading to the next world." His life was made up of "double days," those of existence here on earth and, potentially, those of the World to Come. For the Jew, life on earth is not an end in itself. Even in old age he continues to "advance toward the days to come."

וַה' בֵּרַךְ אֶת־אַבְרָהָם — *And HASHEM had blessed Abraham*. He blessed him after Sarah's death so that no one would say "Abraham merely benefited from the merit of his saintly wife" (*Tanchuma*).

בַּכֹּל — *With everything*. Rashi explains: the word בַּכֹּל, *with everything*, has a numerical value (52) equal to בֵּן, *son*. And since he had a son, he now had to find a wife for him. This explanation derives from the opinion of R' Meir, for whom the blessing was that Abraham had just a son but no daughter. But R' Yehudah considers that the blessing "with everything" also includes a daughter. Others are of the opinion that Abraham had a daughter whose name was בַּכֹּל (*Bava Basra* 16b).

Maharal interprets the words of these *Tannaim* as follows: R' Meir holds that the blessing would not have been complete if Abraham had had a daughter; since if the patriarch had no Jewish (male) descendants, she would have been obliged to marry a Canaanite or an Aramean and might eventually have been lost to the spirit and house of Abraham. R' Yehudah is of the opinion that a perfect blessing most certainly includes the gift of a daughter — the value of this blessing does

אֶל־עַבְדּוֹ זְקַן בֵּיתוֹ הַמּשֵׁל בְּכָל־אֲשֶׁר־לוֹ שִׂים־נָא יָדְךָ
ג תַּחַת יְרֵכִי: וְאַשְׁבִּיעֲךָ בַּיהוה אֱלֹהֵי הַשָּׁמַיִם וֵאלֹהֵי הָאָרֶץ
אֲשֶׁר לֹא־תִקַּח אִשָּׁה לִבְנִי מִבְּנוֹת הַכְּנַעֲנִי אֲשֶׁר אָנֹכִי יוֹשֵׁב
ד בְּקִרְבּוֹ: כִּי אֶל־אַרְצִי וְאֶל־מוֹלַדְתִּי תֵּלֵךְ וְלָקַחְתָּ אִשָּׁה לִבְנִי
ה לְיִצְחָק: וַיֹּאמֶר אֵלָיו הָעֶבֶד אוּלַי לֹא־תֹאבֶה הָאִשָּׁה לָלֶכֶת
אַחֲרַי אֶל־הָאָרֶץ הַזֹּאת הֶהָשֵׁב אָשִׁיב אֶת־בִּנְךָ אֶל־הָאָרֶץ
ו אֲשֶׁר־יָצָאתָ מִשָּׁם: וַיֹּאמֶר אֵלָיו אַבְרָהָם הִשָּׁמֶר לְךָ פֶּן־
ז תָּשִׁיב אֶת־בְּנִי שָׁמָּה: יהוה ׀ אֱלֹהֵי הַשָּׁמַיִם אֲשֶׁר לְקָחַנִי

not depend on what future consequences she might have to bear. She is a benefit
per se. But others think that because of the immense prestige which the Divine
benediction in all things conferred upon him, even without a daughter Abraham
still had the same spiritual influence over the pagan world as he would have had
with a daughter's help — with her ties through marriage and her influence as
a mother. It is in this sense that the words "his daughter was named 'blessed with
everything' " are to be taken.

2. וַיֹּאמֶר אַבְרָהָם אֶל־עַבְדּוֹ — *And Abraham said to his servant.* The ample space
and profuse detail which the Torah devotes to Isaac's marriage are an indication
of the importance it attaches to this event. Indeed there is no event in the life of
a Jewish father more important than the marriage of his child. No details are left
to chance; nothing is overlooked. Isaac's mother has just passed away, her earthly
task finished. From now on her soul will watch over her son's destiny from on
high, for "the merit of the parents protects the children." And so Abraham does
not wait until the year of mourning is over before busying himself with the
preparations for his son's marriage. He now makes all the arrangements,
counting on the help of Providence and the aid of זְכוּת אָבוֹת, Sarah's merit.

The Torah dwells at length on the fact that this first Jewish marriage was
arranged through an intermediary, a "matchmaker" (שַׁדְכָן). It even seems to
want to emphasize the virtues of this method. One wonders: how could Isaac
trust the choice of a third party even if it was Eliezer, the faithful and longtime
servant of his father?

The Jewish approach, however, recommends this as the way to conjugal
happiness. For the man who looks for a wife on his own leaves himself open to
influence by purely external impressions or transient feelings and passions
which may very well vanish soon after the marriage. And the consequences of
this are tragic situations. But a third party with the advantage of experience, age,
and wisdom would be more objective, freer of prejudice, free from emotional
factors. Hence his choice would present a better guarantee of mutual
understanding for the couple's future (*R' Dessler, Michtav Me'Eliyahu*, p. 73).

שִׂים־נָא יָדְךָ תַּחַת יְרֵכִי — *Place now your hand under my thigh.* Cf. *Tosafos* on
Shavuos 38b. Also see our commentary to 47:29.

to his servant, the elder of his household who controlled all that
was his: "Place now your hand under my thigh. ³ And I will have
you swear by HASHEM, God of heaven and God of earth, that you
not take a wife for my son from the daughters of the Canaanites,
among whom I dwell. ⁴ Rather, to my land and to my kindred shall
you go and take a wife for my son for Isaac."

⁵ The servant said to him: "Perhaps the woman shall not wish
to follow me to this land; shall I take your son back to the land from
which you departed?" ⁶ Abraham answered him, 'Beware not to
return my son to there. ⁷ HASHEM, God of heaven, Who took me

3. אֲשֶׁר לֹא־תִקַּח אִשָּׁה לִבְנִי — *That you not take a wife for my son.* Between a son
of Abraham and a daughter of Canaan there is a spiritual and moral abyss so
profound that any understanding between them remains forever illusory. The
son of Abraham must not under any circumstances come under the influence of
a Canaanite woman. However, the patriarch does accept marriage with an
Aramean woman, of his land and his birthplace. To be sure, the inhabitants of
Aram were idolaters too. But Abraham knew their basic character. He knew that
it was healthy and pure and that among them idolatry was just an intellectual
deviation which could be corrected. But the Canaanites were morally corrupt;
they were perverted to the very depth of their souls and Abraham could not hold
out any hope of finding a pure, chaste, and innocent woman among them, one
who could offer his son the treasure of nobility of sentiments and conduct
(*Drashos HaRan* ch.5).

6. הִשָּׁמֶר לְךָ פֶּן־תָּשִׁיב אֶת־בְּנִי — *Beware not to return my son.* On no pretext
whatsoever is Isaac to leave his father's house. Abraham forbids his son even so
natural and spontaneous a gesture as visiting the home of his chosen one and
introducing himself to her family. It seems that Abraham's motives can be found
in his constant concern for sheltering his son from all influences able to
jeopardize the purity of his religious ideas. Abraham does not close his eyes to
the attractions of the east, with its exuberance and sensuality, which stand in
marked contrast to life on the plains of Canaan. Even at the risk of being
considered a boor scornful of the most established customs, Abraham is going
to ask Isaac's future wife to follow his own example and deliberately leave
parents, brothers, and sisters. He will ask her to break away from a confused past
in an idolatrous environment just as he himself has done to devote her life to a
new future. And it is through this decision facing Rebecca that Abraham awaits
confirmation of his choice of bride for his son.

7. ה' אֱלֹהֵי הַשָּׁמַיִם — *HASHEM, God of heaven.* Here Abraham does not add *God
of earth* as above, where he said: *I will have you swear by HASHEM, God of
heaven and God of earth.* Abraham meant: "Now, He is the God of the heavens
and the earth, for I have accustomed His creatures to proclaim His name. But
when He took me out of my father's house, He was God of the heavens but not

מִבֵּית אָבִי֙ וּמֵאֶ֣רֶץ מֽוֹלַדְתִּ֔י וַֽאֲשֶׁ֨ר דִּבֶּר־לִ֜י וַֽאֲשֶׁ֥ר נִשְׁבַּֽע־
לִ֣י לֵאמֹ֔ר לְזַ֨רְעֲךָ֔ אֶתֵּ֖ן אֶת־הָאָ֣רֶץ הַזֹּ֑את ה֚וּא יִשְׁלַ֣ח
ח מַלְאָכוֹ֙ לְפָנֶ֔יךָ וְלָֽקַחְתָּ֥ אִשָּׁ֛ה לִבְנִ֖י מִשָּֽׁם: וְאִם־לֹ֨א תֹאבֶ֜ה
הָֽאִשָּׁה֙ לָלֶ֣כֶת אַֽחֲרֶ֔יךָ וְנִקִּ֕יתָ מִשְּׁבֻֽעָתִ֖י זֹ֑את רַ֣ק אֶת־בְּנִ֔י
ט לֹ֥א תָשֵׁ֖ב שָֽׁמָּה: וַיָּ֤שֶׂם הָעֶ֨בֶד֙ אֶת־יָד֔וֹ תַּ֛חַת יֶ֥רֶךְ אַבְרָהָ֖ם
י אֲדֹנָ֑יו וַיִּשָּׁ֣בַֽע ל֔וֹ עַל־הַדָּבָ֖ר הַזֶּֽה: וַיִּקַּ֣ח הָ֠עֶ֠בֶד עֲשָׂרָ֨ה
גְמַלִּ֜ים מִגְּמַלֵּ֤י אֲדֹנָיו֙ וַיֵּ֔לֶךְ וְכָל־ט֥וּב אֲדֹנָ֖יו בְּיָד֑וֹ וַיָּ֗קָם וַיֵּ֛לֶךְ
יא אֶל־אֲרַ֥ם נַֽהֲרַ֖יִם אֶל־עִ֥יר נָחֽוֹר: וַיַּבְרֵ֧ךְ הַגְּמַלִּ֛ים מִח֥וּץ
לָעִ֖יר אֶל־בְּאֵ֣ר הַמָּ֑יִם לְעֵ֣ת עֶ֔רֶב לְעֵ֖ת צֵ֥את הַשֹּֽׁאֲבֹֽת:

God of the earth, for men were not aware of Him and His name was not widely
known on earth" (*Rashi*). This is why the words (מַלְכוּת) מֶלֶךְ הָעוֹלָם do not
appear in the opening *berachah* of the first of the eighteen benedictions, the
benediction which makes reference to Abraham in the daily *Amidah*. When the
Patriarch first began to proclaim the name of God, He was still not yet known
as the King of the universe (דעת זקנים מבעלי תוספות).

הוּא יִשְׁלַח מַלְאָכוֹ לְפָנֶיךָ — *He will send His angel before you.* An optative
expression, a wish, explains the *Zohar*. Although Abraham had already made
Eliezer swear, he had no confidence in the success of his mission until he had
implored Divine aid. "May God send you His angel" — the angel who watches
over the covenant with Abraham, whose sacred insignia is circumcision.
Accordingly, the word מִילָה may be formed from the initial letters of the four
words הוּא יִשְׁלַח מַלְאָכוֹ לְפָנֶיךָ.

8. וְאִם־לֹא תֹאבֶה הָאִשָּׁה לָלֶכֶת אַחֲרֶיךָ — *But if the woman will not wish to follow
you.* Although Abraham has complete confidence that Providence will aid him
to realize his desire, he is still prepared to admit the possibility of
disappointment. This attitude reflects one of the great principles of trust in God
(R' Bachya ibn Pakuda, *Duties of the Heart* 4:1).

וְנִקִּיתָ מִשְּׁבֻעָתִי זֹאת — *You shall then be absolved of this oath of mine.* This is
the categorical reply which Abraham gives to his distraught slave's question:
"If the woman will be unwilling to follow me, am I to take your son somewhere else?" The patriarch answers: "Be especially careful not to take my
son back to the land which I have left. And as for you, you will be free of
any further commitment, your mission will be over. What will then become
of my son? I rely entirely on Divine Providence to look after him when
every last human effort has met with failure." This is the meaning *Ramban*
gives to Abraham's reply. But *Rashi* interprets differently: "You will be clear
of my oath as far as any foreign women are concerned. You are then to take
one of the daughters of Aner, Eshkol or Mamre as a wife for Isaac." These
were Abraham's allies. Despite their Canaanite origin, they had often given

from the house of my father and from the land of my birth; Who spoke concerning me, and Who swore to me saying, 'To your offspring will I give this land,' He will send His angel before you, and you will take a wife for my son from there. [8] *But if the woman will not wish to follow you, you shall then be absolved of this oath of mine. However, do not return my son to there.''*

[9] *So the servant placed his hand under the thigh of Abraham his master and swore to him regarding this matter.* [10] *Then the servant took ten camels of his master's camels and set out with all the bounty of his master in his hand and made his way to Aram Naharaim to the city of Nahor.* [11] *He made the camels kneel down outside the city towards a well of water at evening time, the time when women come out to draw.*

proof of their sincere friendship and of their attachment to the ideals of the patriarch.

10. אֲרַם נַהֲרַיִם — *Aram Naharaim* (lit. *Syria of the double river*). This refers to the Syria of the two rivers (the Euphrates and the Tigris), i.e. Mesopotamia.

עִיר נָחוֹר — *The city of Nahor.* The city in which Nahor and his family dwelt, Haran.

11. אֶל־בְּאֵר — *Towards a well.* In several instances the Bible paints a poetic picture of a meeting by a well leading to marriage. In addition to the example of Isaac and Rebecca, there are the marriages of Jacob and Rachel, and of Moses and Zipporah. The Torah in this way wants to show us water from the ground as the symbol of purity and the sign of fertility. *And the Divine Presence hovered upon the surface of the the waters* (*Genesis* 1:2). The Jewish woman feels herself drawn towards natural water, which constitutes the source of purity in her conjugal life. Conversely, the pure waters which gush forth from the soil rise to meet the woman who personifies the ideals of purity and chastity (cf. *Bereishis Rabbah* 60: "the waters of the well rose toward Rebecca"). These marriages "by the well" thus symbolize the ideal of purity which should form the basis for all conjugal life.

לְעֵת עֶרֶב — *At evening time.* The same time as that mentioned later (verse 63) when, after reciting his prayer, Isaac looks up and discovers his future wife. This is the time which best fits Isaac's personality and destiny. His father Abraham rose like a star in the firmament of humanity. He made the world resplendent with his love of God and love of others. He was like the radiance of dawn. It was he who instituted the morning prayer (*Berachos* 26b). But Isaac sees his fortunes waning in comparison with the glorious rise of his father. Isaac's life no longer resembles the rising sun with its dazzling brightness; rather it is like the close of day as the shadows of night are approaching. And so Isaac's time is twilight, designated as the time of דִּינָא קַשְׁיָא, of harshness in nature and in existence. At

יב וַיֹּאמַר ׀ יהוֹה אֱלֹהֵי אֲדֹנִי אַבְרָהָם הַקְרֵה־נָא לְפָנַי הַיּוֹם
יג וַעֲשֵׂה־חֶסֶד עִם אֲדֹנִי אַבְרָהָם: הִנֵּה אָנֹכִי נִצָּב עַל־עֵין
יד הַמָּיִם וּבְנוֹת אַנְשֵׁי הָעִיר יֹצְאֹת לִשְׁאֹב מָיִם: וְהָיָה הַנַּעֲרָ
אֲשֶׁר אֹמַר אֵלֶיהָ הַטִּי־נָא כַדֵּךְ וְאֶשְׁתֶּה וְאָמְרָה שְׁתֵה וְגַם־
גְּמַלֶּיךָ אַשְׁקֶה אֹתָהּ הֹכַחְתָּ לְעַבְדְּךָ לְיִצְחָק וּבָהּ אֵדַע כִּי־
טו עָשִׂיתָ חֶסֶד עִם־אֲדֹנִי: וַיְהִי־הוּא טֶרֶם כִּלָּה לְדַבֵּר וְהִנֵּה
רִבְקָה יֹצֵאת אֲשֶׁר יֻלְּדָה לִבְתוּאֵל בֶּן־מִלְכָּה אֵשֶׁת נָחוֹר אֲחִי

day's end, Isaac chooses to address God in prayer (מִנְחָה) and give account of his actions.

Isaac's character also differs from his father's. Feelings of love overflowed in Abraham's spirit. In Isaac these were subordinated to the rigorous discipline of obedience to God. The bonds that bind Isaac to the sacred altar, ready for sacrifice, are the symbol of this submission with absolute devotion. The early-morning eagerness so enthusiastically manifested by the father gives way in Isaac to harsh discipline, which asserts itself at the trying hours of the day, just before the day ends.

And so Isaac's destiny is bound up with the time of evening. It was then that Eliezer made his way to the well to meet Isaac's future wife. Water is the element of tenderness (חֶסֶד), the symbol of peaceful elements having the power to appease and temper the harsh forces of nature. It is through the intimate blending of this gentleness, representative of femininity, and the severe rigor which is the essential trait of Isaac's character that Eliezer wants to see perfect harmony created in the union of the future couple (from the *Zohar*). Accordingly, it is by the well of water that events take place which lead to the finding of a wife for Isaac.

12. וַיֹּאמַר — *And he said*. The importance of the word וַיֹּאמַר is brought out by the Torah-reading "note" שַׁלְשֶׁלֶת which appears only four times in the Pentateuch. This note gives emphasis to Eliezer's exclamation: God of my master Abraham, You began today with a miracle for me by shortening my journey (see *Rashi* on verse 42). Please, manifest Yourself to me once more and end my mission this very day (*Rabbah* 60).

14. הַנַּעֲרָ — *The maiden*. Here and further on the word הַנַּעֲרָ is written defectively — the final letter ה is missing. "This is because Rebecca was then only three years old. But do not be astonished that she was already able to go out to draw water. In those times girls of three were like ten-year-olds nowadays. They were already nubile at that age" (*Sechel Tov*).

וְגַם־גְּמַלֶּיךָ אַשְׁקֶה — *And I will even water your camels*. Eliezer just wanted a mouthful of water for himself. But the maiden who voluntarily offered to water his camels also would, in so doing, give proof of her goodness. Kindness to animals is a virtue which Judaism holds in particular esteem. The Talmud

¹² *And he said, "HASHEM, God of my master Abraham, may You so arrange it for me this day that You do kindness with my master Abraham. ¹³ See, I stand here by the spring of water and the daughters of the townsmen come out to draw. ¹⁴ Let it be that the maiden to whom I shall say, 'Please tip over your jug so I may drink,' and who replies, 'Drink, and I will even water your camels,' her will You have designated for Your servant, for Isaac; and may I know through her that You have done kindness with my master."*

¹⁵ *And it was when he had not yet finished speaking that suddenly Rebecca was coming out — she who had been born to Bethuel the son of Milcah the wife of Nahor, brother*

stipulates that a meal must not be served until the animals have been fed. Eliezer wanted nobleness of sentiment to be the only criterion in the choice of a wife for Isac. In this he anticipates the author of *Proverbs*, who declares: *Charm is deceptive and beauty is vain; only a God-fearing woman will be praised* (31:30).

אֹתָהּ הֹכַחְתָּ לְעַבְדְּךָ לְיִצְחָק — *Her will You have designated for Your servant for Isaac.* Some of our Sages disapprove of asking for a sign to point out the maiden designated by God. In this approach they see a certain similarity to pagan customs which put faith in omens to guide man along his way. However, Eliezer's words could be taken in the sense of determining the character of Isaac's wife-to-be who, above all else, would have to behave charitably to others, even to a foreign slave. This trait has henceforth become the chief virtue of the Jewish woman. (See the controversy on this subject between *Rambam* and *Ravad* in הלכ׳ עכו״ם פי״א ה״ד).

Be that as it may, God answered Eliezer immediately. Eliezer was one of the three Biblical personages, along with Saul and and Yiftah, whose requests were improper. For could not the maiden with the qualities he specified be lame or blind? But out of love for Abraham, God generously fulfilled his wish and sent Rebecca (*Taanis* 4a; cf. *Tosafos* there).

15. וַיְהִי־הוּא טֶרֶם כִּלָּה לְדַבֵּר — *And it was when he had not yet finished speaking.* The personal pronoun הוא is not necessary for the comprehension of the phrase — it could have been stated more simply: וַיְהִי כְּכַלּוֹתוּ לְדַבֵּר. But this pronoun refers to Him, God Himself (as in *Psalms* 100:3). He helped Eliezer in his mission by having the angel Abraham had called for, accompany him. This angel was "sent before him" (verse 7). Indeed, he preceded him so well that Eliezer witnessed his mission accomplished even before he had finished speaking. When the narrative reaches this point, Eliezer is no longer called an עֶבֶד, *servant*, for he is now surrounded by the invisible presence of the angel. Now he is called אִישׁ, which frequently designates a title of honor for a human being (*R' Bachya*).

טז אַבְרָהָם וְכַדָּהּ עַל־שִׁכְמָהּ: וְהַנַּעֲרָ טֹבַת מַרְאֶה מְאֹד בְּתוּלָה

יז וְאִישׁ לֹא יְדָעָהּ וַתֵּרֶד הָעַיְנָה וַתְּמַלֵּא כַדָּהּ וַתָּעַל: וַיָּרָץ הָעֶבֶד

יח לִקְרָאתָהּ וַיֹּאמֶר הַגְמִיאִינִי נָא מְעַט־מַיִם מִכַּדֵּךְ: וַתֹּאמֶר

יט שְׁתֵה אֲדֹנִי וַתְּמַהֵר וַתֹּרֶד כַּדָּהּ עַל־יָדָהּ וַתַּשְׁקֵהוּ: וַתְּכַל

לְהַשְׁקֹתוֹ וַתֹּאמֶר גַּם לִגְמַלֶּיךָ אֶשְׁאָב עַד אִם־כִּלּוּ לִשְׁתֹּת:

כ וַתְּמַהֵר וַתְּעַר כַּדָּהּ אֶל־הַשֹּׁקֶת וַתָּרָץ עוֹד אֶל־הַבְּאֵר לִשְׁאֹב

כא וַתִּשְׁאַב לְכָל־גְּמַלָּיו: וְהָאִישׁ מִשְׁתָּאֵה לָהּ מַחֲרִישׁ לָדַעַת

כב הַהִצְלִיחַ יהוה דַּרְכּוֹ אִם־לֹא: וַיְהִי כַּאֲשֶׁר כִּלּוּ הַגְּמַלִּים

לִשְׁתּוֹת וַיִּקַּח הָאִישׁ נֶזֶם זָהָב בֶּקַע מִשְׁקָלוֹ וּשְׁנֵי צְמִידִים

כג עַל־יָדֶיהָ עֲשָׂרָה זָהָב מִשְׁקָלָם: וַיֹּאמֶר בַּת־מִי אַתְּ הַגִּידִי

כד נָא לִי הֲיֵשׁ בֵּית־אָבִיךְ מָקוֹם לָנוּ לָלִין: וַתֹּאמֶר אֵלָיו בַּת־

כה בְּתוּאֵל אָנֹכִי בֶּן־מִלְכָּה אֲשֶׁר יָלְדָה לְנָחוֹר: וַתֹּאמֶר אֵלָיו

כו גַּם־תֶּבֶן גַּם־מִסְפּוֹא רַב עִמָּנוּ גַּם־מָקוֹם לָלוּן: וַיִּקֹּד הָאִישׁ

כז וַיִּשְׁתַּחוּ לַיהוה: וַיֹּאמֶר בָּרוּךְ יהוה אֱלֹהֵי אֲדֹנִי אַבְרָהָם אֲשֶׁר

לֹא־עָזַב חַסְדּוֹ וַאֲמִתּוֹ מֵעִם אֲדֹנִי אָנֹכִי בַּדֶּרֶךְ נָחַנִי יהוה

כח בֵּית אֲחֵי אֲדֹנִי: וַתָּרָץ הַנַּעֲרָ וַתַּגֵּד לְבֵית אִמָּהּ כַּדְּבָרִים

כט הָאֵלֶּה: וּלְרִבְקָה אָח וּשְׁמוֹ לָבָן וַיָּרָץ לָבָן אֶל־הָאִישׁ הַחוּצָה

ל אֶל־הָעָיִן: וַיְהִי | כִּרְאֹת אֶת־הַנֶּזֶם וְאֶת־הַצְּמִדִים עַל־יְדֵי

אֲחֹתוֹ וּכְשָׁמְעוֹ אֶת־דִּבְרֵי רִבְקָה אֲחֹתוֹ לֵאמֹר כֹּה־דִבֶּר אֵלַי

הָאִישׁ וַיָּבֹא אֶל־הָאִישׁ וְהִנֵּה עֹמֵד עַל־הַגְּמַלִּים עַל־הָעָיִן:

לא וַיֹּאמֶר בּוֹא בְּרוּךְ יהוה לָמָּה תַעֲמֹד בַּחוּץ וְאָנֹכִי פִּנִּיתִי

לב הַבַּיִת וּמָקוֹם לַגְּמַלִּים: וַיָּבֹא הָאִישׁ הַבַּיְתָה וַיְפַתַּח הַגְּמַלִּים

רביעי

---

16. וְאִישׁ לֹא יְדָעָהּ — *Whom no man had known.* Bethuel, king of the city of Nahor, had instituted the *jus primae noctis*. His subjects consented to this outrage as long as the king's own daughter was not exempted. It was just as Eliezer arrived in Haran that she was to be taken by her father (she had just reached the age of three years and one day — see *Niddah* 44b). And so God brought about the death of Bethuel (*Rashi* on verse 55) in order to save Rebecca from disgrace (*Yalkut*).

Other sources indicate that Rebecca was fourteen years old at that time (*Yevamos* 61b and *Tosafos* there; cf. our commentary to verse 14 above).

29. וּלְרִבְקָה אָח וּשְׁמוֹ לָבָן — *Rebecca had a brother whose name was Laban.* When impious people are referred to, their proper name is usually put before the word "name," i.e. נָבָל שְׁמוֹ. But for the righteous, the order is reversed. What merit did Laban have to be designated here in the form reserved for the righteous? The merit of having wanted to defend the honor of his sister. When he saw the rings and bracelets on her, he had the impression that the stranger

of Abraham — with her jug upon her shoulder. [16] *Now the maiden was very fair to look upon; a virgin whom no man had known. She descended to the spring, filled her jug and ascended.* [17] *The servant ran towards her and said, "Let me sip, if you please, a little water from your jug."* [18] *She said, "Drink, my lord," and quickly she lowered her jug to her hand and gave him drink.*

[19] *When she finished giving him drink, she said, "I will draw water even for your camels until they have finished drinking."* [20] *So she hurried and emptied her jug into the trough and kept running to the well to draw water; and she drew for all his camels.* [21] *The man was astonished at her, reflecting silently to know whether HASHEM had made his journey successful or not.* [22] *And it was, when the camels had finished drinking, the man took a golden nose ring, its weight was a beka, and two bracelets on her arms, ten gold shekels was their weight.* [23] *And he said, "Whose daughter are you? Pray tell me. Is there room in your father's house for us to spend the night?"*

[24] *She said to him, "I am the daughter of Bethuel the son of Milcah whom she bore to Nahor."* [25] *And she said to him, "Even straw and feed is plentiful with us as well as place to lodge."*

[26] *So the man bowed low and prostrated himself to HASHEM.* [27] *He said, "Blessed is HASHEM, God of my master Abraham, Who has not withheld His kindness and truth from my master. As for me, HASHEM has guided me on the way to the house of my master's brothers."*

[28] *The maiden ran and told her mother's household according to these events.* [29] *Rebecca had a brother whose name was Laban: Laban ran to the man, outside to the spring.* [30] *For upon seeing the nose ring, and the bracelets on his sister's hands, and upon his hearing his sister Rebecca's words, saying, "Thus has the man spoken to me," he approached the man, who was still standing by the camels by the spring.* [31] *He said, "Come, O blessed of HASHEM! Why should you stand outside when I have cleared the house, and place for the camels?"*

[32] *So the man entered the house, and unmuzzled the camels.*

wanted to seduce her. He angrily rushed toward Eliezer to give him what he thought he deserved. But when Laban saw Eliezer as he stood by the camels at the spring surrounded by his men and with the speech and bearing of a great lord, he realized that he had misjudged him. Then Laban greeted him and welcomed him, saying: "Come, O blessed of HASHEM" (*Bamidbar Rabbah* 6).

וַיִּתֶּן תֶּבֶן וּמִסְפּוֹא לַגְּמַלִּים וּמַיִם לִרְחֹץ רַגְלָיו וְרַגְלֵי
הָאֲנָשִׁים אֲשֶׁר אִתּוֹ: °וַיּישֶׂם לְפָנָיו לֶאֱכֹל וַיֹּאמֶר לֹא אֹכַל ‎לג‎ °וַיּוּשַׂם ק'
עַד אִם־דִּבַּרְתִּי דְּבָרָי וַיֹּאמֶר דַּבֵּר: וַיֹּאמַר עֶבֶד אַבְרָהָם ‎לד‎
אָנֹכִי: וַיהוָֹה בֵּרַךְ אֶת־אֲדֹנִי מְאֹד וַיִּגְדָּל וַיִּתֶּן־לוֹ צֹאן וּבָקָר ‎לה‎
וְכֶסֶף וְזָהָב וַעֲבָדִם וּשְׁפָחֹת וּגְמַלִּים וַחֲמֹרִים: וַתֵּלֶד שָׂרָה ‎לו‎
אֵשֶׁת אֲדֹנִי בֵן לַאדֹנִי אַחֲרֵי זִקְנָתָהּ וַיִּתֶּן־לוֹ אֶת־כָּל־אֲשֶׁר־
לוֹ: וַיַּשְׁבִּעֵנִי אֲדֹנִי לֵאמֹר לֹא־תִקַּח אִשָּׁה לִבְנִי מִבְּנוֹת ‎לז‎
הַכְּנַעֲנִי אֲשֶׁר אָנֹכִי יֹשֵׁב בְּאַרְצוֹ: אִם־לֹא אֶל־בֵּית־אָבִי ‎לח‎
תֵּלֵךְ וְאֶל־מִשְׁפַּחְתִּי וְלָקַחְתָּ אִשָּׁה לִבְנִי: וָאֹמַר אֶל־אֲדֹנִי ‎לט‎
אֻלַי לֹא־תֵלֵךְ הָאִשָּׁה אַחֲרָי: וַיֹּאמֶר אֵלַי יהוָֹה אֲשֶׁר־ ‎מ‎
הִתְהַלַּכְתִּי לְפָנָיו יִשְׁלַח מַלְאָכוֹ אִתָּךְ וְהִצְלִיחַ דַּרְכֶּךָ
וְלָקַחְתָּ אִשָּׁה לִבְנִי מִמִּשְׁפַּחְתִּי וּמִבֵּית אָבִי: אָז תִּנָּקֶה ‎מא‎
מֵאָלָתִי כִּי תָבוֹא אֶל־מִשְׁפַּחְתִּי וְאִם־לֹא יִתְּנוּ לָךְ וְהָיִיתָ
נָקִי מֵאָלָתִי: וָאָבֹא הַיּוֹם אֶל־הָעָיִן וָאֹמַר יהוָֹה אֱלֹהֵי ‎מב‎
אֲדֹנִי אַבְרָהָם אִם־יֶשְׁךָ־נָּא מַצְלִיחַ דַּרְכִּי אֲשֶׁר אָנֹכִי הֹלֵךְ
עָלֶיהָ: הִנֵּה אָנֹכִי נִצָּב עַל־עֵין הַמָּיִם וְהָיָה הָעַלְמָה הַיֹּצֵאת ‎מג‎
לִשְׁאֹב וְאָמַרְתִּי אֵלֶיהָ הַשְׁקִינִי־נָא מְעַט־מַיִם מִכַּדֵּךְ:

34. עֶבֶד אַבְרָהָם אָנֹכִי — *A servant of Abraham am I.* These words are characteristic of Eliezer in more than one respect. He conducted himself by the rule. "Do not wait for your inferiorities to be discovered by others but declare them yourself." At the same time he was so devoted to his master that he considered being his servant more of an honor than being a free citizen. The idea of declaring that he was a friend or a relative of Abraham did not even enter his mind. Eliezer's whole personality together with his manner of speaking had such a profound effect on Abraham's relatives that they renounced their intention to harm him (*Bava Kamma* 92b and *Bereishis Rabbah* 60).

39. אֻלַי לֹא־תֵלֵךְ הָאִשָּׁה — *Perhaps the woman will not follow.* The word אֻלַי, *perhaps,* is written without a *vav,* and the Midrash reads it אֵלַי, *toward me.* Eliezer himself had a daughter and tried to induce Abraham to tell him that his daughter should marry Isaac. Abraham responded, "My son is blessed and you are cursed (being a descendant of Canaan, whom Noah cursed in *Genesis* 9:25): The cursed cannot be united with the blessed" (*Rashi*). Why, one may ask, does *Rashi* not make this comment earlier, when Eliezer questions Abraham (in verse 5) as he receives details of his mission? Rav Avraham Mordechai of Ger (Gora Kalwaria, Poland) replies: Frequently a man does not admit to himself his own ulterior motives

*He gave straw and feed for the camels, and water to bathe his feet
and the feet of the men who were with him.* [33] *Food was set before
him, but he said, "I will not eat until I have spoken my piece."*
And he said, "Speak."

[34] *Then he said, "A servant of Abraham am I.* [35] *HASHEM has
greatly blessed my master, and he prospered; He has given him
flocks, cattle, silver and gold, servants and maidservants, camels
and donkeys.* [36] *Sarah, my master's wife, bore my master a son
after she had grown old, and he gave him all that he possesses.*
[37] *And my master had me take an oath saying, 'Do not take a wife
for my son from the daughters of the Canaanites in whose land I
dwell.* [38] *Unless you go to my father's house and to my family and
take a wife for my son.'* [39] *And I said to my master, 'Perhaps the
woman will not follow me?'* [40] *He replied to me, 'HASHEM, before
Whom I have walked, will send His angel with you and make your
journey successful, and you will take a wife for my son from my
family and my father's house.* [41] *Then will you be absolved from
my oath when you have come to my family; and if they will not
give her to you, then, you shall be absolved from my oath.'*
[42] *"I came today to the spring and said, 'HASHEM, God of my
master Abraham, if You would graciously make successful the
way on which I go.* [43] *Behold, I am standing by the spring of water;
let it be that the young woman who comes out to draw and to whom
I shall say, "Please give me some water to drink from your jug,"*

or his secret interests. He only realizes them when he finds out that he has
been disappointed. Such was the case with Eliezer at the home of Abraham's
relatives when he saw that Rebecca fulfilled the conditions for being Isaac's
wife.

42. וָאָבֹא הַיּוֹם — *I came today.* R' Acha said: "The conversation of the servants
of the patriarchs is more precious to God than the Torah of their children. For
the whole episode of Eliezer is repeated here twice whereas many essential
points of the Torah are merely hinted at" (*Rashi*). The method of deducing
important laws from certain allusions in the text is destined to add to Jewry's
merit. The Jewish people delve into the slightest details of the sacred text in
order to discover the Divine will. But the Torah does not lack for words when
it comes to clearly bringing out the moral principles such as those which are
to direct the preparations for a marriage. It develops them thoroughly and
connects them with the original thought of the patriarchs as faithfully reflected
even in the words and deeds of their servants. No detail is superfluous, no
repetition is extraneous, where uniting the lives of two human beings in
matrimony is at stake.

מד וְאָמְרָה אֵלַי גַּם־אַתָּה שְׁתֵה וְגַם לִגְמַלֶּיךָ אֶשְׁאָב הִוא
הָאִשָּׁה אֲשֶׁר־הֹכִיחַ יהוה לְבֶן־אֲדֹנִי: אֲנִי טֶרֶם אֲכַלֶּה לְדַבֵּר מה
אֶל־לִבִּי וְהִנֵּה רִבְקָה יֹצֵאת וְכַדָּהּ עַל־שִׁכְמָהּ וַתֵּרֶד הָעַיְנָה
וַתִּשְׁאָב וָאֹמַר אֵלֶיהָ הַשְׁקִינִי נָא: וַתְּמַהֵר וַתּוֹרֶד כַּדָּהּ מו
מֵעָלֶיהָ וַתֹּאמֶר שְׁתֵה וְגַם־גְּמַלֶּיךָ אַשְׁקֶה וָאֵשְׁתְּ וְגַם
הַגְּמַלִּים הִשְׁקָתָה: וָאֶשְׁאַל אֹתָהּ וָאֹמַר בַּת־מִי אַתְּ וַתֹּאמֶר מז
בַּת־בְּתוּאֵל בֶּן־נָחוֹר אֲשֶׁר יָלְדָה־לּוֹ מִלְכָּה וָאָשִׂם הַנֶּזֶם
עַל־אַפָּהּ וְהַצְּמִידִים עַל־יָדֶיהָ: וָאֶקֹּד וָאֶשְׁתַּחֲוֶה לַיהוה מח
וָאֲבָרֵךְ אֶת־יהוה אֱלֹהֵי אֲדֹנִי אַבְרָהָם אֲשֶׁר הִנְחַנִי בְּדֶרֶךְ
אֱמֶת לָקַחַת אֶת־בַּת־אֲחִי אֲדֹנִי לִבְנוֹ: וְעַתָּה אִם־יֶשְׁכֶם מט
עֹשִׂים חֶסֶד וֶאֱמֶת אֶת־אֲדֹנִי הַגִּידוּ לִי וְאִם־לֹא הַגִּידוּ לִי
וְאֶפְנֶה עַל־יָמִין אוֹ עַל־שְׂמֹאל: וַיַּעַן לָבָן וּבְתוּאֵל וַיֹּאמְרוּ נ
מֵיהוה יָצָא הַדָּבָר לֹא נוּכַל דַּבֵּר אֵלֶיךָ רַע אוֹ־טוֹב:
הִנֵּה־רִבְקָה לְפָנֶיךָ קַח וָלֵךְ וּתְהִי אִשָּׁה לְבֶן־אֲדֹנֶיךָ כַּאֲשֶׁר נא
דִּבֶּר יהוה: וַיְהִי כַּאֲשֶׁר שָׁמַע עֶבֶד אַבְרָהָם אֶת־דִּבְרֵיהֶם נב
חמישי   וַיִּשְׁתַּחוּ אַרְצָה לַיהוה: וַיּוֹצֵא הָעֶבֶד כְּלֵי־כֶסֶף וּכְלֵי זָהָב נג
וּבְגָדִים וַיִּתֵּן לְרִבְקָה וּמִגְדָּנֹת נָתַן לְאָחִיהָ וּלְאִמָּהּ: וַיֹּאכְלוּ נד
וַיִּשְׁתּוּ הוּא וְהָאֲנָשִׁים אֲשֶׁר־עִמּוֹ וַיָּלִינוּ וַיָּקוּמוּ בַבֹּקֶר
וַיֹּאמֶר שַׁלְּחֻנִי לַאדֹנִי: וַיֹּאמֶר אָחִיהָ וְאִמָּהּ תֵּשֵׁב הַנַּעֲרָ נה
אִתָּנוּ יָמִים אוֹ עָשׂוֹר אַחַר תֵּלֵךְ: וַיֹּאמֶר אֲלֵהֶם אַל־ נו
תְּאַחֲרוּ אֹתִי וַיהוה הִצְלִיחַ דַּרְכִּי שַׁלְּחוּנִי וְאֵלְכָה לַאדֹנִי:
נז-נח וַיֹּאמְרוּ נִקְרָא לַנַּעֲרָ וְנִשְׁאֲלָה אֶת־פִּיהָ: וַיִּקְרְאוּ לְרִבְקָה
וַיֹּאמְרוּ אֵלֶיהָ הֲתֵלְכִי עִם־הָאִישׁ הַזֶּה וַתֹּאמֶר אֵלֵךְ:

49. וְאֶפְנֶה עַל־יָמִין אוֹ עַל־שְׂמֹאל — *And I will turn to the right or to the left.*
The *Targum Yonasan* translates: southwards or northwards. The Arabic
language also identifies south with the right and north with the left on the
assumption that the observer is facing east (cf. *Rashi* to *Genesis* 35:18 and
Tosafos Yom Tov ‫רמאי פ״ה, א׳‬). This geographic positioning explains *Rashi's*
interpretation: to the right hand means to the daughters of Ishmael, who
inhabited the south of the land; to the left means to the daughters of Lot, who
lived in the north.

50. מֵי׳ יָצָא הַדָּבָר — *The matter stemmed from HASHEM.* The idea that
marriages are made in heaven stems from these words. It is reaffirmed in the
Prophets (*Judges* 14:4) and in the Writings (*Proverbs* 19:14). But the Sages of
the Midrash wonder יָצָא מֵהֵיכָן — "from when did it come? Some reply מֵהַר
הַמֹּרִיָּה, from what occurred on Mount Moriah as recorded just before (ch. 22),

⁴⁴ *and who will answer, "You may also drink and I will draw water for your camels, too," she shall be the woman whom HASHEM has designated for my master's son.'* ⁴⁵ *I had not yet finished meditating when suddenly Rebecca came out with a jug on her shoulder, and descended to the spring and drew water. Then I said to her, 'Please give me a drink.'* ⁴⁶ *She hurried and lowered her jug from upon herself and said, 'Drink, and I will even water your camels.' So I drank and she watered the camels also.*

⁴⁷ *"Then I questioned her and said, 'Whose daughter are you?' And she said, 'The daughter of Bethuel, son of Nahor, whom Milcah bore to him.' And I placed the ring on her nose and the bracelets on her hands.* ⁴⁸ *Then I bowed and prostrated myself to HASHEM and blessed HASHEM, God of my master Abraham, Who led me on a true path to take the daughter of my master's brother for his son.* ⁴⁹ *And now, if you intend to do kindness and truth with my master, tell me; and if not, tell me, and I will turn to the right or to the left."*

⁵⁰ *Then Laban and Bethuel answered and said, "The matter stemmed from HASHEM! We can say to you neither bad nor good.* ⁵¹ *Here, Rebecca is before you; take her and go, and let her be a wife to your master's son as HASHEM has spoken."* ⁵² *And it was, when Abraham's servant heard their words, he prostrated himself to the ground unto HASHEM.* ⁵³ *The servant brought out objects of silver and gold, and garments, and gave them to Rebecca; and delicious fruits he gave to her brother and her mother.* ⁵⁴ *They ate and drank, he and the men who were with him, and they spent the night; when they arose next morning, he said, "Send me to my master."*

⁵⁵ *Her brother and mother said, "Let the maiden remain with us a year or ten [months]; then she will go."* ⁵⁶ *He said to them, "Do not delay me now that HASHEM had made my journey successful. Send me, and I will go to my master."* ⁵⁷ *And they said, "Let us call the maiden and ask her decision."*

⁵⁸ *They called Rebecca and said to her, "Will you go with this man?"*

And she said, "I will go."

when the young husband-to-be gave proof of extraordinary devotion which earned him the Divine blessing. Others in their reply refer to the words: *Let her be a wife to your master's son* (verse 51). Hence, for some, the main factor in the choice of a mate is his personal merit (יִחוּס עַצְמִי); others see the ethical integrity of the family (*a wife to your master's son*) and the "merit of the fathers" as the best guarantee for the virtue of his progeny (יִחוּס מִשְׁפַּחְתִּי).

נט וַיְשַׁלְּחוּ אֶת־רִבְקָה אֲחֹתָם וְאֶת־מֵנִקְתָּהּ וְאֶת־עֶבֶד אַבְרָהָם
ס וְאֶת־אֲנָשָׁיו: וַיְבָרְכוּ אֶת־רִבְקָה וַיֹּאמְרוּ לָהּ אֲחֹתֵנוּ אַתְּ הֲיִי
סא לְאַלְפֵי רְבָבָה וְיִירַשׁ זַרְעֵךְ אֵת שַׁעַר שֹׂנְאָיו: וַתָּקׇם רִבְקָה
וְנַעֲרֹתֶיהָ וַתִּרְכַּבְנָה עַל־הַגְּמַלִּים וַתֵּלַכְנָה אַחֲרֵי הָאִישׁ
סב וַיִּקַּח הָעֶבֶד אֶת־רִבְקָה וַיֵּלַךְ: וְיִצְחָק בָּא מִבּוֹא בְּאֵר לַחַי
סג רֹאִי וְהוּא יוֹשֵׁב בְּאֶרֶץ הַנֶּגֶב: וַיֵּצֵא יִצְחָק לָשׂוּחַ בַּשָּׂדֶה
סד לִפְנוֹת עָרֶב וַיִּשָּׂא עֵינָיו וַיַּרְא וְהִנֵּה גְמַלִּים בָּאִים: וַתִּשָּׂא
רִבְקָה אֶת־עֵינֶיהָ וַתֵּרֶא אֶת־יִצְחָק וַתִּפֹּל מֵעַל הַגָּמָל:
סה וַתֹּאמֶר אֶל־הָעֶבֶד מִי־הָאִישׁ הַלָּזֶה הַהֹלֵךְ בַּשָּׂדֶה לִקְרָאתֵנוּ
סו וַיֹּאמֶר הָעֶבֶד הוּא אֲדֹנִי וַתִּקַּח הַצָּעִיף וַתִּתְכָּס: וַיְסַפֵּר
הָעֶבֶד לְיִצְחָק אֵת כָּל־הַדְּבָרִים אֲשֶׁר עָשָׂה: וַיְבִאֶהָ יִצְחָק
סז הָאֹהֱלָה שָׂרָה אִמּוֹ וַיִּקַּח אֶת־רִבְקָה וַתְּהִי־לוֹ לְאִשָּׁה
וַיֶּאֱהָבֶהָ וַיִּנָּחֵם יִצְחָק אַחֲרֵי אִמּוֹ:

These moral and ethical factors are the basic elements whence comes the Divine blessing.

58. וַתֹּאמֶר אֵלֵךְ — *And she said, "I will go."* Rebecca's reply is given in such a peremptory manner that *Rashi* concludes: "I will go on my own — even if you do not wish it." One must conclude that Rebecca felt herself instinctively attracted by the noble manners and goodness of Abraham's servant and by his marvelous belief in God which shone forth in every word. This feeling awakened a deep echo in her and she understood that in Isaac she would find a spirit akin to her own.

The next verse reinforces the intensity of her determination.

60. אַתְּ הֲיִי לְאַלְפֵי רְבָבָה — *May you come to be thousands of myriads.* Abraham's family, and many others as well, were aware of the Divine promises regarding the historical destiny of the patriarch's descendants, as was pointed out in our commentary to 21:22. This explains why Rebecca received that particular blessing from Laban and from her mother, as *Rashi* notes in his commentary.

62. וְיִצְחָק בָּא מִבּוֹא בְּאֵר לַחַי רֹאִי — *Now Isaac came from having gone to Beer-lahai-roi.* It was at this well that Hagar had sought refuge (16:14). Accordingly *Rashi* explains: "Isaac had gone there to bring Hagar back as a wife for his father Abraham." While the father sends his servant to find a wife for his son, the son thinks only of restoring the conjugal home of his recently-widowed father. Only after Isaac brings Abraham's former wife back to him does he go to pray to Providence regarding his own impending marriage. What a contrast between the spirit of our forefathers — so natural and so human — on the one hand and, on the other, the mentality of our own age, so often affected by unwholesome sentimentality!

⁵⁹ *So they escorted Rebecca their sister, and her nurse, as well as Abraham's servant and his men.* ⁶⁰ *They blessed Rebecca and said to her, "Our sister, may you come to be thousands of myriads, and may your offspring inherit the gate of its foes."*

⁶¹ *Then Rebecca arose with her maidens; they rode upon the camels and proceeded after the man; the servant took Rebecca and went.*

⁶² *Now Isaac came from having gone to Beer-lahai-roi, for he dwelt in the south country.* ⁶³ *Isaac went out to supplicate in the field towards evening and he raised his eyes and saw, and behold! camels were coming.* ⁶⁴ *And Rebecca raised her eyes and saw Isaac; she inclined while upon the camel.* ⁶⁵ *And she said to the servant, "Who is that man walking in the field toward us?"*

And the servant said, "He is my master." She then took the veil and covered herself. ⁶⁶ *The servant told Isaac all the things he had done.* ⁶⁷ *And Isaac brought her into the tent of Sarah his mother; he married Rebecca, she became his wife, and he loved her; and thus was Isaac consoled after his mother.*

63. וַיֵּצֵא יִצְחָק לָשׂוּחַ בַּשָּׂדֶה — *Isaac went out to supplicate in the field. Rashi:* "The word שׂוּחַ means prayer. (Similarly in *Psalms* 102:1.) R' Shimon said, "Did he not have a house or another place to pray? Yet he prayed in the field which Abraham had acquired, near the cave of Machpelah. There Isaac perceived what seemed to him a perfume from Paradise and there he felt the closeness of the *Shechinah*" (*Zohar*). Thus it was to his mother's grave that Isaac went in order to collect his thoughts before making the most important decision of his life.

לִפְנוֹת עָרֶב — *Towards evening.* Cf. our commentary to verse 11 and to 28:11.

64. וַתִּפֹּל מֵעַל הַגָּמָל — *She inclined while upon the camel. Onkelos* explains that Rebecca bowed toward the ground as soon as she heard from Eliezer that the "very lordly man" (*Rashi*) who was coming across the field to meet them was Isaac. Here the Torah teaches a rule of modesty: the young woman must bow and cover herself with a veil (v. 65) before the man who is to be her husband (*Radak and Chizkuni*).

67. וַיְבִאֶהָ יִצְחָק הָאֹהֱלָה שָׂרָה אִמּוֹ — *And Isaac brought her into the tent of Sarah his mother.* Here again is a principle which is still maintained among Abraham's progeny: The longer she was his wife, the more he loved her. Just like this marriage of the first son of the Jewish people, the majority of Jewish marriages are not contracted on the basis of momentary passion. The parents and relatives consult with each other to find out whether the young people are well matched; and then their love for one another deepens as they come to know each other better. In contrast to most non-Jewish marriages, where usually only feelings of "love" precede the marriage — and these risk giving way to grave deceptions

כה ששי א-ב וַיֹּסֶף אַבְרָהָם וַיִּקַּח אִשָּׁה וּשְׁמָהּ קְטוּרָה: וַתֵּלֶד לוֹ אֶת־
זִמְרָן וְאֶת־יָקְשָׁן וְאֶת־מְדָן וְאֶת־מִדְיָן וְאֶת־יִשְׁבָּק וְאֶת־
ג שׁוּחַ: וְיָקְשָׁן יָלַד אֶת־שְׁבָא וְאֶת־דְּדָן וּבְנֵי דְדָן הָיוּ אַשּׁוּרִם
ד וּלְטוּשִׁם וּלְאֻמִּים: וּבְנֵי מִדְיָן עֵיפָה וָעֵפֶר וַחֲנֹךְ וַאֲבִידָע

with time — the union of Rebecca and Isaac was not initially motivated by love.
They were united with a common will and joined for the same sake: the
continuation of the house of Abraham. It was only after Isaac had taken her as
his wife that "he loved her." Thus love represents the outcome of shared
experiences. Far from being the supreme goal, marriage is only the beginning of
a life together which gives love an ever more profound and more authentic
meaning (R' S. R. Hirsch).

As long as Sarah was alive, notes Rashi, a lamp was lit from one Sabbath eve
to the next; the benediction was made over the dough (which she kneaded); and
a cloud hovered over the tent. When she died this all ceased, but when Rebecca
came everything began once again.

These three hallmarks of Sarah's tent correspond to the three main duties of
the Jewish wife: to light Sabbath lights (הַדְלָקָה), to separate challah from the
dough, which assures a blessing from above (חַלָּה), and to observe the laws of
purity of conjugal life (טָהֳרַת הַמִּשְׁפָּחָה). They draw the presence and protection
of the Divine Majesty which hovers invisibly over the home as in a column of
"cloud over the tent."

25.

1. וַיֹּסֶף אַבְרָהָם וַיִּקַּח אִשָּׁה — Abraham proceeded and took a wife. From this we
learn that a husband bereaved of his wife will marry off his children and
afterwards remarry (Midrash). For "even if a widower has fulfilled the
commandment to procreate, rabbinic law stipulates that he is not to remain
without a wife lest he come to have impure thoughts. Moreover, it is fitting to
continue the duty of procreation, just as Abraham 'continued' — וַיֹּסֶף — despite
his advanced age, and so bring more children into the world than before"
(רמב"ם, הל' אישות, ט"ו, ט"ז). In this connection our Sages advise us to heed the
counsel of Ecclesiastes: In the morning [of your life] sow your seeds and in the
evening withhold not your hand for you know not which will prosper, whether
this or that, and perhaps they will both be equally good (11:6).

וּשְׁמָהּ קְטוּרָה — Whose name was Keturah. Another name for Hagar, as Rashi
explains. But Ramban holds that this woman was a former Canaanite slave,
called a concubine in the first chapter of Chronicles. "Do not be surprised," adds
R' Bachya, "that Abraham married a Canaanite woman while making his
servant swear not to take one as a wife for his son. This precaution was essential
for Isaac, as he was the repository of his father's faith. But when Isaac married
a woman from his father's family, there was no longer any obstacle preventing
Abraham from marrying a Canaanite woman."

25   ¹*Abraham proceeded and took a wife whose name was Keturah.*
²*She bore him Zimran, Jokshan, Medan, Midian, Ishbak and*
Shuah. ³*Jokshan begot Sheba and Dedan, and the children*
of Dedan were Asshurim, Letushim, and Leummim. ⁴*And*
the children of Midian: Ephah [and] Epher, Hanoch, Abida,

Abraham's remarriage in the latter days of his life was but the continuation
(וַיֹּסֶף), in a new form, of the task to which he had devoted his entire existence:
the propagation of the belief in God. By virtue of his missionary spirit, reinforced
by extraordinary intelligence and eloquence, and through his love of others, his
kindness and his hospitality, Abraham had succeeded in converting entire
nations to his ideal (cf. 'רמב״ם, הל' עבודת כוכבים א). Now, with Isaac's marriage
ensuring that the whole of his spiritual heritage would continue in perpetuity,
Abraham undertook to form new generations — to be sure, less imbued with his
spirit and his ideal than Isaac, the son of his wife Sarah, but nevertheless capable
of carrying his Divine message to still other pagan peoples. And so, as soon as
they grew up, Abraham sent these children to the far-off lands of Asia. He was
aware that these children, born of foreign mothers, could not be messengers of
his doctrine in all its purity. But still he understood that the first rays of light
which they would carry to these regions, still spiritually in darkness, would
gradually disperse the shadows of night to make way for the radiant brightness
of truth. The one who had known so many disappointments in his missionary
activity, even with those very close to him, never let himself be overcome by
feelings of discouragement. וַיֹּסֶף אַבְרָהָם, *Abraham continued*, thus becomes the
motto of his life and these two words serve to introduce the chapter which
relates Abraham's death. They contain the message which he addresses to all his
descendants from beyond the grave. Abraham's perseverance triumphed over
all obstacles and ultimately won over humanity to the truth of monotheism (cf.
Rambam, Melachim 12, ed. Rome; Mosad Harav Kook, and Alumim).

2. . . . וַתֵּלֶד לוֹ אֶת־זִמְרָן. — *She bore him Zimran, etc.* Of Abraham's children, Isaac
was the one who most perfectly embodied the saintly ideal which was the
inheritance of his father. But the patriarch wanted this core of saintliness to be
surrounded by a sacred zone, just as Shabbos, a day of holiness, overflows its
own bounds and forms a zone around itself. Its heralding rays envelop both the
hours which precede it and those which serve to prolong it at nightfall (מוֹסִיף מִן
הַחוֹל עַל הַקֹּדֶשׁ). So too, the nucleus of holiness that Isaac represented availed
itself of his brother Ishmael, born fourteen years before him, to send out the
heralding rays which began to illuminate the horizon of humanity. And it
continued past its own limits through the children of Keturah, the younger
brothers and sisters of Isaac (*Sfas Emes*).

4. וָעֵפֶר — *[and] Epher.* Quoting the historian Alexander, Flavius Josephus
(*Antiquities* I:, 15) reports that Epher led an army into Libya and took possession

ה וְאֶלְדָּעָה כָּל־אֵלֶּה בְּנֵי קְטוּרָה: וַיִּתֵּן אַבְרָהָם אֶת־כָּל־אֲשֶׁר־
ו לוֹ לְיִצְחָק: וְלִבְנֵי הַפִּילַגְשִׁים אֲשֶׁר לְאַבְרָהָם נָתַן אַבְרָהָם
מַתָּנֹת וַיְשַׁלְּחֵם מֵעַל יִצְחָק בְּנוֹ בְּעוֹדֶנּוּ חַי קֵדְמָה אֶל־אֶרֶץ
ז קֶדֶם: וְאֵלֶּה יְמֵי שְׁנֵי־חַיֵּי אַבְרָהָם אֲשֶׁר־חָי מְאַת שָׁנָה
ח וְשִׁבְעִים שָׁנָה וְחָמֵשׁ שָׁנִים: וַיִּגְוַע וַיָּמָת אַבְרָהָם בְּשֵׂיבָה
ט טוֹבָה זָקֵן וְשָׂבֵעַ וַיֵּאָסֶף אֶל־עַמָּיו: וַיִּקְבְּרוּ אֹתוֹ יִצְחָק
וְיִשְׁמָעֵאל בָּנָיו אֶל־מְעָרַת הַמַּכְפֵּלָה אֶל־שְׂדֵה עֶפְרֹן

of it. The African continent derives its name from this grandson of Abraham. Many other countries of Asia minor and the Arabian peninsula, such as Chaldea, Aram-Tzovah, and Aram-Naharaim (Mesopotamia) likewise seem to have been founded by descendants or members of the family of Abraham.

כָּל־אֵלֶּה בְּנֵי קְטוּרָה — *All these were the descendants of Keturah.* Although both they and their descendants were subject to the obligation of circumcision (רמב״ם, הל׳ מלכים, פ״י, י׳) spiritually they still remained the children of Keturah and they practiced idolatry (*Rabbah* 61). Why then did God Himself command Abraham to marry her, as our Sages point out (ע״פ הַדִּבּוּר, *Bereishis Rabbah* 61)? It was because He knew that some of the offspring would bring the light of the Torah to idolatrous peoples (*Sefer Chassidim* §1171). Such was the case with Jethro, a descendant of Keturah who became the father-in-law of Moses (*Seder Olam*).

5. וַיִּתֵּן אַבְרָהָם אֶת־כָּל־אֲשֶׁר־לוֹ לְיִצְחָק — *Abraham gave all that he had to Isaac.* Isaac had brought Rebecca into the tent of his mother Sarah, and Abraham, when he remarried, never again set foot in this tent with his new wife. No other woman save Rebecca dwelt in the tent where Sarah had lived and where her spirit still reigned. Thus it was that Abraham handed over to his son "everything he owned," that is, the home of the woman who had been his greatest treasure on earth (*Zohar*).

The *Zohar* explains also that the word כֹּל in the phrase וַה׳ בֵּרַךְ אֶת־אַבְרָהָם בַּכֹּל (24:1) refers to the "complete blessing" bestowed on Abraham. This blessing is expressed by the permanent closeness of the *Shechinah* (cf. *Isaiah* 43:7). It was this blessing which the patriarch bequeathed to his son Isaac (אֶת־כָּל־אֲשֶׁר־לוֹ).

6. נָתַן אַבְרָהָם מַתָּנֹת — *Abraham gave gifts.* Our Sages explain: he handed over to them the "name of impurity" (*Rashi*). This is in regard to the knowledge of magic which teaches how to combat evil spirits and demons. Abraham himself had acquired this knowledge during his sojourn in Egypt (see our commentary to 13:2). He subsequently sent the sons of his concubines to the Far East, to the land of Kedem, where they practiced these tainted arts. This knowledge was later passed on by magicians such as Laban, Balaam and his father Beor (cf. *Numbers* 23:7). In praise of King Solomon's great wisdom, the book of *I Kings* records that *his wisdom was greater than that of all the inhabitants of Kedem* (5:10).

and Eldaah; all these were the descendants of Keturah. [5] *Abraham gave all that he had to Isaac.* [6] *But to the concubine-children who were Abraham's, Abraham gave gifts; then he sent them away from Isaac his son, while he was still alive, eastward to the land of the east.*

[7] *Now these are the days of the years of Abraham's life which he lived: a hundred years, seventy years, and five years.* [8] *And Abraham expired and died at a good old age, mature and content, and he was gathered to his people.* [9] *His sons Isaac and Ishmael buried him in the cave of Machpelah, in the field of Ephron the son*

Rashi adds another explanation: "He gave them those gifts which he had received because of Sarah, for he did not wish to derive any benefit from them." (See our commentary to 12:16).

וַיְשַׁלְּחֵם מֵעַל יִצְחָק בְּנוֹ — *He sent them away from Isaac his son.* The children of Ishmael and of Keturah came with a lawsuit against the Jewish people before Alexander of Macedonia. They pleaded: "The land of Canaan belongs as much to us as to you, for the descendants of Ishmael and Keturah are just as much children of Abraham as Isaac." . . . Geviha ben Pesisa replied to them, "You bring your proof from the Torah. Then I too shall do the same. The Torah states: *Abraham gave all that he had to Isaac. But to the concubine-children who were Abraham's, Abraham gave gifts.* Now if a father made a bequest to his children during his lifetime and then sent them far away from the other, do they still have the right to assert a claim?" (*Sanhedrin* 91a).

בְּעוֹדֶנּוּ חַי — *While he was still alive.* While Abraham yet lived, so that a dispute would not erupt among the children after their father's death (*Zohar*).

7. וְאֵלֶּה יְמֵי שְׁנֵי־חַיֵּי אַבְרָהָם אֲשֶׁר־חָי — *Now these are the days of the years of Abraham's life which he lived.* The purpose of the duplication in the text, writing both *life* and *he lived,* is to emphasize that he was able to enjoy life during all of his 175 years. But "he died five years before his time had come, so that he would not see his grandson Esau behave wickedly while he was alive. On the very day of his death, Esau rebelled against God" (*Rashi* to 15:15).

8. בְּשֵׂיבָה טוֹבָה — *At a good old age.* This means that Ishmael repented while Abraham was still alive (*Rashi,* ibid.).

זָקֵן וְשָׂבֵעַ — *Mature and content.* It is a virtue of the righteous not to covet unnecessary material objects but to be content with what they have. The statement affirming that "no one dies possessing even one half-of his desires" (*Koheles Rabbah* 1:34) refers to the rest of humanity. But out text also means that God "shows the righteous, while they are still living, the reward which awaits them in the World to Come" (*Rabbah* 62). The righteous person is satiated by this vision, while he falls peacefully asleep for his eternal slumber (*Ramban*).

י בֶּן־צֹחַר הַחִתִּי אֲשֶׁר עַל־פְּנֵי מַמְרֵא: הַשָּׂדֶה אֲשֶׁר־
קָנָה אַבְרָהָם מֵאֵת בְּנֵי־חֵת שָׁמָּה קֻבַּר אַבְרָהָם וְשָׂרָה
יא אִשְׁתּוֹ: וַיְהִי אַחֲרֵי מוֹת אַבְרָהָם וַיְבָרֶךְ אֱלֹהִים אֶת־
יִצְחָק בְּנוֹ וַיֵּשֶׁב יִצְחָק עִם־בְּאֵר לַחַי רֹאִי:

שביעי   יב וְאֵלֶּה תֹּלְדֹת יִשְׁמָעֵאל בֶּן־אַבְרָהָם אֲשֶׁר יָלְדָה הָגָר
יג הַמִּצְרִית שִׁפְחַת שָׂרָה לְאַבְרָהָם: וְאֵלֶּה שְׁמוֹת בְּנֵי
יִשְׁמָעֵאל בִּשְׁמֹתָם לְתוֹלְדֹתָם בְּכֹר יִשְׁמָעֵאל נְבָיֹת וְקֵדָר
יד-טו וְאַדְבְּאֵל וּמִבְשָׂם: וּמִשְׁמָע וְדוּמָה וּמַשָּׂא: חֲדַד וְתֵימָא
מפטיר   טז יְטוּר נָפִישׁ וָקֵדְמָה: אֵלֶּה הֵם בְּנֵי יִשְׁמָעֵאל וְאֵלֶּה
שְׁמֹתָם בְּחַצְרֵיהֶם וּבְטִירֹתָם שְׁנֵים־עָשָׂר נְשִׂיאִם לְאֻמֹּתָם:

וַיֵּאָסֶף אֶל־עַמָּיו — *And he was gathered to his people.* This is not to be taken literally, since his relatives had been buried in Mesopotamia. But in these words there is a reference to immortality, just as in the corresponding verse, 15:15. Indeed, from this passage the burial of human remains is clearly distinct from the souls' return to the sheaf of souls of other human beings. The Torah does not explicitly teach the immortality of the soul. For a people which recognizes the Torah it is self-evident. The soul is immortal for it is nothing other than the Divine breath placed by God into the human body (2:7). It constitutes the element of metaphysical origin which enables man to serve the Divine will in complete freedom. Judaism without this concept is inconceivable. Yet it does not teach this concept any more than it does the concept that God exists, a concept which indeed is presupposed by the very first words of the Torah — בְּרֵאשִׁית בָּרָא אֱלֹהִים. And when *Ecclesiastes* declares: *the spirit returns to God* (12:7), it is not at all preaching immortality but merely undertaking to describe life and death, citing the return of the spirit to God as one stage in this process. It was not until recent times, when freethinking sects attempted to deny the principle of immortality, that it appeared necessary to teach it formally as a basic tenet of Judaism (R' S. R. Hirsch).

10. הַשָּׂדֶה אֲשֶׁר־קָנָה אַבְרָהָם — *The field that Abraham had bought.* For the details regarding the cave of Machpelah see our commentary to 23:17.

11. וַיְהִי אַחֲרֵי מוֹת אַבְרָהָם וַיְבָרֶךְ אֱלֹהִים אֶת־יִצְחָק בְּנוֹ — *And it was after the death of Abraham that God blessed Isaac his son.* The Midrah (quoted in brief by *Rashi*) develops the conflict facing Abraham with the following comparison. "The owner of a garden places it under the care of a gardener, who is also to water it and look after its upkeep. The gardener notices two trees intertwined, one bearing poisonous fruit, the other succulent fruit. He wonders to himself, 'If I water the good tree, the bad one will benefit and will develop as well. And if I do not water at all, how will the good tree ever develop?' So he reflects on this and decides, 'I am just the owner's gardener. I will water the rest of the garden and when the owner returns he will do what he thinks best.' "

of Zohar the Hittite, facing Mamre. [10] The field that Abraham had bought from the children of Heth, there Abraham was buried, and Sarah his wife. [11] And it was after the death of Abraham that God blessed Isaac his son, and Isaac settled near Beer-lahai-roi.

[12] These are the descendants of Ishmael, Abraham's son, whom Hagar the Egyptian, Sarah's maidservant, bore to Abraham. [13] These are the names of the sons of Ishmael by their names, in order of their birth: Ishmael's firstborn Nebaioth, Kedar, Adbeel, and Mibsam, [14] Mishma, Dumah, and Massa, [15] Hadad and Tema, Jetur, Naphish, and Kedem. [16] These are the sons of Ishmael, and these are their names by their open cities and by their strongholds, twelve chieftains for their nations.

Hence Abraham, whom God entrusted with the power to bless whomever he wanted (as *Rashi* states on *Genesis* 12:2), was afraid to bless his own son Isaac, for he saw that Isaac had given birth to the wicked Esau in addition to the righteous Jacob. So Abraham said, "Let the Master of blessings Himself come and bless whomever He sees fit to bless." And so, God came after the death of Abraham and blessed Isaac.

The whole story of the patriarchs demonstrates how difficult it is for a man to give his blessing to others. Abraham was perplexed by the problem arising from his power to bless others; he preferred to abstain from using it. He bequeathed the hereditary gift of blessing to his son Isaac (*Rashi* on 25:5). Isaac gave it to his sons, Jacob and Esau; this resulted in a dramatic conflict within the family with repercussions for long centuries afterwards. As for Jacob, inspiration failed him just as he was preparing to bless his children before his death. The words he addressed to his oldest son Reuben gave rise to quarrels among the sons, and Moses had to re-establish the fraternal peace within the family of Israel in his last blessing (*Bereishis Rabbah* 100).

Later, the power of blessing was entrusted to the *Kohanim*, but the form was set in general terms, and refers equally to all individuals. It is this form which parents use to bless their children. As for the blessings given by saintly men to those whom they deem worthy, these depend on a supplication addressed to Providence in the knowledge that *God fulfills the will of those who fear Him* (*Psalms* 145:19).

14. וּמִשְׁמָע וְדוּמָה וּמַשָּׂא — *Mishma, Dumah, and Massa.* At the end of his *Epistle to Yemen* (אִגֶּרֶת תֵּימָן), *Rambam* speaks of the Moslem oppression of the Jews. He quotes this verse containing the names of Ishmael's children and explains, "Our Sages enjoin us to bear the treachery of the Ishmaelites and their lies with indifference. This they derived from the verse which names the children of Ishmael. The names mean שְׁמַע דוֹם וְשָׂא, *listen, be quiet, and bear it.*

16. שְׁנֵים־עָשָׂר נְשִׂיאָם לְאֻמֹּתָם — *Twelve chieftains for their nations.* Cf. our commentary to 17:20.

יז וְאֵ֗לֶּה שְׁנֵי֙ חַיֵּ֣י יִשְׁמָעֵ֔אל מְאַ֥ת שָׁנָ֛ה וּשְׁלֹשִׁ֥ים שָׁנָ֖ה וְשֶׁ֣בַע
יח שָׁנִ֑ים וַיִּגְוַ֣ע וַיָּ֔מָת וַיֵּאָ֖סֶף אֶל־עַמָּֽיו: וַיִּשְׁכְּנ֞וּ מֵֽחֲוִילָ֣ה עַד־
שׁ֗וּר אֲשֶׁר֙ עַל־פְּנֵ֣י מִצְרַ֔יִם בֹּאֲכָ֖ה אַשּׁ֑וּרָה עַל־פְּנֵ֥י כָל־אֶחָ֖יו
נָפָֽל:

---

17. וְאֵלֶּה שְׁנֵי חַיֵּי יִשְׁמָעֵאל — *These were the years of Ishmael's life.* According to *Rashi*, Ishmael's lifespan is given in order to make a connection with the years which Jacob lived. *Ramban* adds that our Sages gave other reasons as well (*Rabbah* 62), but that the essential motive is the fact that Ishmael had repented and became righteous. Consequently the Torah gives his lifespan just as it does for other righteous persons.

וַיִּגְוַע — *When he expired.* The term וַיִּגְוַע is used only in reference to the

¹⁷ *These were the years of Ishmael's life: a hundred and thirty-seven years, when he expired and died, and was gathered to his people.* ¹⁸ *They dwelt from Havilah to Shur — which is near Egypt — toward Assyria; over all his brothers he dwelt.*

righteous (*Rashi*). Indeed, the latter do not die a sudden death, but expire slowly, in order to be able to repent and "set their houses in order" (*II Kings* 20:1) before they die, as the Talmud emphasizes (*Moed Katan* 28a). Cf. *Ramban.*

18. עַל־פְּנֵי כָל־אֶחָיו נָפָל — *Over all his brothers he dwelt.* Literally, "he fell." The next verse begins, *And these are the offspring of Isaac.* This teaches you that when Ishmael falls at the end of days, only then will the history of Isaac commence, under the reign of the Messiah (*Baal HaTurim*).

יט וְאֵלֶּה תּוֹלְדֹת יִצְחָק בֶּן־אַבְרָהָם אַבְרָהָם הוֹלִיד אֶת־יִצְחָק:
כ וַיְהִי יִצְחָק בֶּן־אַרְבָּעִים שָׁנָה בְּקַחְתּוֹ אֶת־רִבְקָה בַּת־בְּתוּאֵל
הָאֲרַמִּי מִפַּדַּן אֲרָם אֲחוֹת לָבָן הָאֲרַמִּי לוֹ לְאִשָּׁה: וַיֶּעְתַּר כא
יִצְחָק לַיהוה לְנֹכַח אִשְׁתּוֹ כִּי עֲקָרָה הִוא וַיֵּעָתֶר לוֹ יהוה
כב וַתַּהַר רִבְקָה אִשְׁתּוֹ: וַיִּתְרֹצְצוּ הַבָּנִים בְּקִרְבָּהּ וַתֹּאמֶר אִם־כֵּן

19. אַבְרָהָם הוֹלִיד אֶת־יִצְחָק — *Abraham begot Isaac*. Despite the multitude of proselytes converted to Abraham's faith and all the children of his wife Keturah and of his son Ishmael previously mentioned, Isaac was the only worthy successor of the patriarch. Solely in Isaac was his spirit most perfectly embodied. In the spiritual sense Isaac was truly the "only son" of Abraham according to the words of God Himself (22:2). The spiritual and physical resemblances between father and son became still more striking after the father's death; so much so that all those who beheld Isaac exclaimed: "Surely this is the son of Abraham" (*Zohar*).

20. וַיְהִי יִצְחָק בֶּן־אַרְבָּעִים שָׁנָה — *Isaac was forty years old*. The Torah states Isaac's age explicitly. Probably it wants to give us the reason he waited so long before marrying: Rebecca was born just when he returned from Mount Moriah and Isaac had to wait a long time to marry her. He was older than she and this allowed him to train her entirely as he felt best and to make an ideal wife and mother of her, despite the natural tendencies toward evil she had probably inherited from her parents. The Torah shows us here that it is permissible to pass the marriageable age rather than to marry an unworthy woman. Isaac's son Jacob followed this example and waited much longer before marrying (cf. our commentary on 26:34).

Isaac was sixty when his sons were born. He had to reach this "age of intelligence" (*Avos* 5:24) in order to be able to endow his spiritual heir, Jacob, with the maximum of moral perfection (*Zohar*).

בַּת־בְּתוּאֵל — *Daughter of Bethuel*. She was the daughter of an evil person, the sister of an evil person, and she dwelt in a wicked land (*Rashi*). In contrast, Isaac came from a family which lived by justice, virtue, and charity. Providence therefore united violence with kindness so that the fruit of this union would be perfect, permeated with a harmony of strength and gentleness.

אֲחוֹת לָבָן — *Sister of Laban*. Most boys take after their mother's brothers (cf. *Rashi* to *Exodus* 6:23). Hence, it should not be surprising that a woman as saintly as Rebecca was able to bear a son like Esau.

21. וַיֶּעְתַּר — *Entreated*. "To repeat and insist in prayer ... The verb עתר denotes insistence and repetition of the same act" (*Rashi*). However, it is not good to be too insistent in one's prayers, even when it involves praying for the blessing of having an offspring. Take Isaac, for example. Although God granted his wish, his son Esau became corrupt and was a source of heartbreak to his parents (*Sefer Sheivet Musar*).

¹⁹**A**nd these are the offspring of Isaac son of Abraham — Abraham begot Isaac. ²⁰ Isaac was forty years old when he took Rebecca, daughter of Bethuel the Aramean from Paddan Aram, sister of Laban the Aramean, as a wife for himself. ²¹ Isaac entreated HASHEM opposite his wife, because she was barren. HASHEM allowed Himself to be entreated by him, and his wife Rebecca conceived.

²² The children agitated within her, and she said, "If so,

כִּי עֲקָרָה הוא — *Because she was barren.* Unlike Abraham, his father, Isaac did not want to marry a bondwoman, for the binding on Mount Moriah had made of him an offering consecrated wholly to God (*Rashi* on verse 26). And so he had no recourse but prayer for having children. Isaac went to Mount Moriah to pray, for it was there, during the sacrifice, that God had promised his father: "I shall multiply your descendants" (*Targum Yonasan*).

וַיֵּעָתֶר לוֹ ה' — *HASHEM allowed Himself to be entreated by him.* R. Yitzchak said, "Why were the Patriarchs barren? It was because God desires the prayer of the righteous" (*Yevamos* 64a). A wild tree, says a proverb, grows by itself, but a fruit tree needs to be cultivated. Even before birth, the righteous one needs special care for his future development. His parents' prayer to God for his arrival into the world is the first step in assisting the child to be born with the Divine blessing.

Rashi emphasizes that it was Isaac's own prayer that God granted, not that of his wife. The prayer of a righteous son of a wicked man does not have the same value as the prayer of the righteous son of a righteous man (*Rashi*). However, for leading the prayers there is a controversy regarding the preference to be accorded the son of a righteous man over one born into a wicked family but who returns to God of his own accord (ט״ז א״ח נ״ג ס״ק ג').

22. וַיִּתְרֹצֲצוּ הַבָּנִים בְּקִרְבָּה — *The children agitated within her.* "The wicked are estranged from the womb." From this verse (*Psalms* 58:4) R' Levi brings out that Esau's implacable hatred for Jacob did not begin just from their birth, but went back still earlier. It manifested itself even in the womb of the mother, as *Rashi* relates: "When their mother passed before the school of Torah conducted by Shem and Ever, Jacob ran and struggled to come out; when she passed in front of gates of idolatry, Esau struggled to come out ... Another explanation: They struggled against one another and quarreled over the inheritance of the two worlds."

Hence, the path of the two rival brothers seems to have been set out *a priori*, even before birth. Their future personalities are already represented in their embryonic stage. Would this not confirm the teachings of some scholars who contend that the first gestures of a human being indicate the tendencies and desires which will be manifested throughout his life? From the tenderest age, the child conceals the man. The art of the educator will be precisely to have perfect knowledge of the mental makeup of the youngster and, far from harming it, he

כג לָמָּה זֶּה אָנֹכִי וַתֵּלֶךְ לִדְרֹשׁ אֶת־יהוה: וַיֹּאמֶר יהוה לָהּ
גוים ק׳ שְׁנֵי °גיים בְּבִטְנֵךְ וּשְׁנֵי לְאֻמִּים מִמֵּעַיִךְ יִפָּרֵדוּ וּלְאֹם
כד מִלְאֹם יֶאֱמָץ וְרַב יַעֲבֹד צָעִיר: וַיִּמְלְאוּ יָמֶיהָ לָלֶדֶת וְהִנֵּה

will try to use it for the best to make him a useful member of society. It does no
good to try to suppress an attitude or to impose any other upon him. The future
man appears potentially in the embryo. Accordingly, it is only through infinite
patience and perfect understanding that one may become able to guide the
young person, advise him, and help him. The story of these twins will be a living
example of good and bad approaches to education. The former will consist in
observing the child and חֲנוֹךְ לַנַּעַר עַל פִּי דַרְכּוֹ "bringing him up in accordance
with his own way, his presumed life's path" (*Proverbs* 22:6); the latter lies
in seeing the child not as he is, but as he should be. The former will not submit to any deceit; the latter will, sooner or later, be driven to total defeat
(*R' S.R. Hirsch*).

אִם־כֵּן לָמָּה זֶּה אָנֹכִי — "*If so, why am I thus?*" Rebecca cried out to God, "If it
is thus, if Esau wants to destroy Jacob and his children, then לָמָּה זֶּה אָנֹכִי — what
good will it be to proclaim at Sinai, אָנֹכִי, *I am Hashem your God* — to whom
will You say these words?" (*Midrash HaGadol*).

וַתֵּלֶךְ לִדְרֹשׁ אֶת־ה׳ — *And she went to inquire of* HASHEM. At the school of Shem
and Ever (*Rashi*). Going up to this school, situated at sacred Mount Moriah, was
"going to inquire of HASHEM." The object of this inquiry was to learn the
reasons for her violent pains.

23. שְׁנֵי גוֹיִם בְּבִטְנֵךְ — *Two nations are in your womb.* Shem, the son of Noah,
replied to her, "I shall entrust you with a secret which you must keep to yourself.
Two future peoples are forming in your womb. But how will it contain them
when the whole world will not be large enough for them to live together in
peace? These two peoples (גוֹיִם) are destined to form two independent nations
(לְאֻמִּים), which will be distinct, if not opposite, in their characters, ideals, and
objectives. The two children are the symbol of the eternal conflict between
Divine law and brute force. The struggle recommences in each generation and
it determines the course of history. Its result remains uncertain for centuries and
centuries, but it will turn out that one day the stronger will pay tribute to the
weaker. They will never be equal in greatness. When one rises, the other will fall.
From one will come a Solomon who will build the Temple; from the other, a
Vespasian who will destroy it. From Jacob will come prophets; from Esau, lords"
(cf. Midrash on *Psalms* 9:5).

וּשְׁנֵי לְאֻמִּים מִמֵּעַיִךְ יִפָּרֵדוּ — *Two regimes from your insides shall be separated.*
One going toward his wickedness, the other toward his integrity (*Rashi*). But,
asks *Maharal*, are we not taught that the evil inclination begins to exert its
influence on the soul only from birth (*Sanhedrin 91a*)? Yet here we see Esau
trying to "run to the gates of idolatry" while still an embryo in his mother's

why am I thus?" And she went to inquire of HASHEM.

²³ *And HASHEM said to her: "Two nations are in your womb;
two regimes from your insides shall be separated; the might
shall pass from one regime to the other, and the elder shall
serve the younger."*

²⁴ *When her term to bear grew full, then behold!*

womb! Here, for Esau, it is not a question of the effect of his evil inclination.
Rather, Esau was under the influence of the law of nature involving
quasi-magnetic attraction of similar elements. Idolatry "polarized" and attracted
the kindred soul of Esau.

Whatever the case, the Torah is anxious to make us see that the relentless
hostility separating Jacob and Esau for as long as they live does not stem from
jealousy or from political or economic rivalry, but that it goes back to congenital
differences in character which manifested themselves even while the brothers
were still in the womb. The fierce hatred between them thus appears to be a
basic condition, an *a priori* fact, a providential factor of history which
escapes the control of the will. Hence we can understand Rabbi Shimon bar
Yochai's categorical statement: "It is an axiom that Esau hates Jacob" (cf. *Rashi*
to *Genesis* 33:4).

In Talmudic sources and in Midrashic literature the names Esau-Edom are
often identified with Rome. *Rashi* echoes these traditions when he connects the
"fatness of the earth," mentioned in Isaac's blessing to Esau, with Italy (27:39;
cf. *Rashi* to *Numbers* 24:19). Later, when Rome adopted Christianity, the same
appellation was conferred upon the whole of the Christian world. Flavius
Josephus records that Tz'fo, a grandson of Esau (*Genesis* 36:11), was the founder
of Rome, which eventually became the center of Christianity (*Ramban* on
49:31). Since then, it has become traditional to consider the Christians as
representative of Esau's offspring and the Jews as descendants of Jacob. The
antagonism between Jacob and Esau is thus symbolic of that between Rome and
Jerusalem; and the reasons underlying this antagonism are also applicable to the
Jewish and Christian worlds. One can therefore conclude that the hostility of
Christian anti-Semites is not based on religious, political, or economic grounds;
nor is it based on any other definite motive. It is of an irrational nature, for it goes
back to the prenatal stage. It was already manifest in the womb, where an
unrelenting struggle was carried on between two brothers representing two
worlds with a deep gulf separating them. Note that it has never been possible
to discover and identify the true motives of anti-Semitism through logical
analysis, despite the countless studies devoted to it.

24. וְהִנֵּה תוֹמִם בְּבִטְנָהּ — *Then behold! there were twins in her womb.* Rebecca
already knew that she would give birth to twins. But nevertheless she was
surprised, as is indicated by the word וְהִנֵּה which frequently denotes surprise.
Here the mother's reaction is related to the fact that the twins were physically

כה תוֹמִם בְּבִטְנָהּ: וַיֵּצֵא הָרִאשׁוֹן אַדְמוֹנִי כֻּלּוֹ כְּאַדֶּרֶת
כו שֵׂעָר וַיִּקְרְאוּ שְׁמוֹ עֵשָׂו: וְאַחֲרֵי־כֵן יָצָא אָחִיו וְיָדוֹ
אֹחֶזֶת בַּעֲקֵב עֵשָׂו וַיִּקְרָא שְׁמוֹ יַעֲקֹב וְיִצְחָק בֶּן־שִׁשִּׁים
כז שָׁנָה בְּלֶדֶת אֹתָם: וַיִּגְדְּלוּ הַנְּעָרִים וַיְהִי עֵשָׂו אִישׁ יֹדֵעַ

completely different, whereas they usually resemble each other. One was ruddy and hirsute, the other fair and smooth. Moreover, Jacob was born circumcised, as indicated in this verse by the abridged form of the word תָּמִים which can mean perfect [i.e. without a foreskin, as referred to in *Genesis* 17:1] (*Chizkuni*). Hence it is Jacob, the beloved of God (*Malachi* 1:2), the one consecrated to God right from his mother's womb, who is referred to in the prayer recited at each circumcision ceremony — אֲשֶׁר קִדֵּשׁ יְדִיד מִבֶּטֶן — *Who sanctified the beloved one from the womb* , ערוך ע׳ ידיד; see, however, *Rashi* and *Tosafos* on *Shabbos* 137b).

וְהִנֵּה תוֹמִם — *Then behold! there were twins.* The month of *Sivan*, the third month of the calendar, is placed under the zodiacal sign of Gemini (twins). It was in this month that God gave the Torah in order to offer to Esau, born under the sign of the twins, and his posterity a direct approach to the Divine law (*Pesikta D'Rav Kahana* פ׳ בחודש השלישי).

25. וַיֵּצֵא הָרִאשׁוֹן אַדְמוֹנִי — *The first one emerged red.* Said R' Yehudah: If you see a red-haired man, know that he may be wicked like Esau or righteous like David, King of Israel, who was also ruddy at birth [*I Samuel* 16:12] (*Midrash HaGadol*). *Rashi* takes ruddiness "as a sign that he will shed blood." But David spilled the blood of the enemies of God and his wars were carried out to honor the name of God (*Rabbah*, 63). The choice to do good or evil remains in man's power, no matter what his nature.

Esau remained uncircumcised because of his ruddy appearance. His father attributed this to poor blood circulation and hesitated to put the sign of the covenant on his son. Isaac decided to wait until Esau was thirteen, the age when his brother Ishmael had been circumcised. But when the time came, Esau refused to comply with his father's wish and he remained uncircumcised (cf. *Rambam, Hilchos Melachim* 10:7). In contrast to his brother, Jacob had the rare distinction of coming into the world already adorned with the sign of the covenant.

Why was Esau first to see the light of day? So that all the impurities inside the womb could go out with him. It is like the keeper of a bathhouse who first rinses out the bath and then goes to bathe the royal prince (*Midrash*).

We have already drawn attention (on the occasion of Ishmael's birth) to the importance of this concept, which considers not only physical impurities but also the moral impurities from generations back which had accumulated in the maternal soul.

26. וְיָדוֹ אֹחֶזֶת בַּעֲקֵב עֵשָׂו — *His hand grasping on to the heel of Esau.* The *Zohar* asks: Can you imagine that the baby's hand really held on to his brother's foot? Certainly not, but it seized the person that forced Jacob back — עֲקֵב עֵשָׂו. Esau is to be compared to the serpent in Paradise who was cursed by God in these

there were twins in her womb. [25] *The first one emerged red, entirely
like a hairy mantle; so they named him Esau.* [26] *After that his
brother emerged with his hand grasping on to the heel of Esau; so
he called his name Jacob; Isaac was sixty years old when she bore
them.*

[27] *The lads grew up and Esau became one who knows*

terms: וְאַתָּה תְּשׁוּפֶנּוּ עָקֵב, *"[He will pound your head] and you will bite his heel"*
(3:15). Hence the designation עֵקֶב עֵשָׂו refers to the serpent; just like the serpent,
Esau acts maliciously, craftily, in underhanded ways. This characteristic of
Esau's will govern Jacob's attitude toward him throughout his lifetime. In
confrontations with his brother, Jacob will seize his heel, that is, he will "fight
fire with fire," as the Psalmist declares: *With the crooked, You act perversely*
(18:27). He will be ingenious, cunning, crafty and will try to forestall his brother's
evil designs and foil his ruses in order to prevent him from sullying the
Sanctuary of Jewry. The whole future conduct of Jacob towards Esau can be
explained in this perspective.

Geographically, the location of the Holy Land, which seems to reach out its
hand from the confines of the Mediterranean toward the heel of the Italian
"boot," Esau's domain (*Rashi* on 27:39), presents us with the best illustration of
the Torah's words. The historical rivalry between Rome and Jerusalem thus
shows up right from the birth of the twins. "The kingdom of one will scarcely
have come to an end before the other will rise up at once to take over from him"
(*Rashi*).

וַיִּקְרָא שְׁמוֹ יַעֲקֹב — *So he called his name Jacob.* The Holy One, Blessed is He, gave
him that name (*Rashi*). According to the *Zohar*, the name יַעֲקֹב given by God
means "he will be [the master of] the heel of Esau" (see above), that is, with his
intelligence he will foil the attacks which Esau will plan against him by forcing
Esau back by the heel. Hence *Onkelos* translates the word וַיַּעְקְבֵנִי as וְחַכְּמַנִי *he
has outsmarted me* (27:36).

27. וַיִּגְדְּלוּ הַנְּעָרִים — *The lads grew up.* Abraham personally took charge of
raising his grandchildren, as the Torah may be implying (18:19). But he died
when they reached the age of fifteen. Immediately, Esau broke away and turned
openly to idolatry.

אִישׁ יֹדֵעַ צַיִד — *One who knows hunting.* Cf. our commentary to *Genesis* 10:9.
Rashi explains that Esau was "an idler, hunting animals and birds with his bow."
This term recalls to mind the one describing Nimrod (ibid.). Indeed, Esau had
managed to defeat Nimrod and strip him of his tunic adorned with figures
representing animals and birds. It had the power of attracting animals so that
whoever wore it became a great hunter. This tunic came from the כָּתְנוֹת עוֹר —
garments of skin — which God had made for the first couple and which Noah
had kept in the Ark during the deluge. Subsequently, Shem and Ever watched
over these garments, but Nimrod managed to snatch them away. According to

כח צֵיד אִישׁ שָׂדֶה וְיַעֲקֹב אִישׁ תָּם יֹשֵׁב אֹהָלִים: וַיֶּאֱהַב
יִצְחָק אֶת־עֵשָׂו כִּי־צַיִד בְּפִיו וְרִבְקָה אֹהֶבֶת אֶת־יַעֲקֹב:
כט-ל וַיָּזֶד יַעֲקֹב נָזִיד וַיָּבֹא עֵשָׂו מִן־הַשָּׂדֶה וְהוּא עָיֵף: וַיֹּאמֶר
עֵשָׂו אֶל־יַעֲקֹב הַלְעִיטֵנִי נָא מִן־הָאָדֹם הָאָדֹם הַזֶּה כִּי

some traditions, they were made of the skin of the serpent of Paradise. This is
what *Onkelos* alludes to when he translates גְּבַר נַחְשִׁירְכָן — the man with (the
skin of) the serpent on his hips (נָחָשׁ יָרֵךְ) (*Pirkei D'Rabbi Eliezer*, 24). This
passage bears out the description of Esau's personality given in our commentary
on the preceding verse.

אִישׁ תָּם — *A wholesome man.* Knowing nothing of all this, (Jacob knew nothing
about Esau's actions, mentioned above) his heart and lips spoke the same
language. He who is not skillful at cheating is called *tam* (*Rashi*). But *Onkelos*
translates גְּבַר שְׁלִים — *a perfect man.* The *Zohar* points out that Jacob's stage of
perfection exceeds Abraham's for Abraham is called תָּמִים (17:1) but Jacob is
called תָּם, which expresses the absolute form of perfection. Indeed, in his own
being Jacob achieved the harmonious union of those virtues which his forebears
possessed only singly: the infinite love of God and man which was Abraham's
great attribute, and the spirit of obedience and harsh discipline, Isaac's hallmark.
(Abraham embodies the ideal of חֶסֶד, *love and kindness,* Isaac that of דִּין, *justice
and stringency,* and Jacob רַחֲמִים, *compassion* = תִּפְאֶרֶת, *splendor and honor,* the
Zohar explains.)

יֹשֵׁב אֹהָלִים — *Abiding in tents.* This refers to the tent of Shem and the tent of
Ever (*Rashi*), where Jacob studied the Divine law. His grandfather had had the
soul of a missionary, of a preacher, and continuously proclaimed the majesty of
God to his contemporaries — וַיִּקְרָא בְּשֵׁם ה' אֵל עוֹלָם. His missionary work was
his *raison d'etre;* his life's goal was to convince men and lead them to God. But
the grandson was no longer possessed of this missionizing flame. His nature led
him to concentrate on the study and knowledge of God. Thus the patriarchs
show us two fundamental concepts, both equally legitimate: expansion and
concentration (הקדמה, קצר חובת הלבבות; cf. our commentary on 35:27).

28. וַיֶּאֱהַב יִצְחָק אֶת־עֵשָׂו — *Isaac loved Esau.* Although he is described as an evil
person who, like the hunters "wandering in the fields," was inclined to shed
blood and treat animals harshly, Esau is nevertheless praised for his filial love,
and in particular for his great devotion to his father. Rabban Shimon ben
Gamliel said: "I have served my father all my life but I have not accomplished
even one-hundredth of what Esau did for his father" (*Rabbah* 65). Jacob was
aware of his brother's moral superiority in this domain. He dreaded any
comparison concerning the fulfillment of this particular *mitzvah,* for it might
have proved disastrous for himself (ibid. 76). Hence Isaac loved Esau for "he
brought him venison to eat." But Esau's love for his father was purely emotional,
not based on obedience to a Divine command, and was consequently unstable.

> *hunting, a man of the field; but Jacob was a whole-*
> *some man, abiding in tents.* [28] *Isaac loved Esau for game*
> *was in his mouth; but Rebecca loved Jacob.*
>   [29] *Jacob simmered a stew, and Esau came in from*
> *the field, and he was exhausted.* [30] *Esau said to Jacob,*
> *"Pour into me, now, some of that very red stuff for I am*

It was so unstable in fact that Esau ultimately came to desire his father's immediate death: "May the days of mourning for my father draw near, then I will kill my brother Jacob" (27:41).

R' Yehudah, quoted in the *Zohar*, gives quite a different view. In response to a question posed by his son he explains that Isaac loved Esau just as one element feels itself attracted to another of the same species. Isaac recognized that his son Esau had the same basic personality as he did. The dominant trait in their characters was מִדַּת הַדִּין — a spirit of harshness — although it manifested itself differently in each. Isaac's strictness became the source of his obedience and unconditional discipline with respect to God. But Esau's severity brought him to use brute strength and to treat men and animals ruthlessly.

29. וַיָּבֹא עֵשָׂו מִן־הַשָּׂדֶה וְהוּא עָיֵף — *Esau came in from the field, and he was exhausted. Rashi* elaborates: "tired from killing." That day he had killed his old hunting rival, King Nimrod. That day too saw the death of his grandfather Abraham. For a long time Esau had striven to suppress his immoral passions and his instinct to violence. He had done this out of respect for the patriarch. But as soon as Abraham died, Esau gave these feelings free rein. With his moralizing grandfather dead at last and the dangerous rival slain, Esau felt liberated. He saw opening before him the grand life of the fields, a life of freedom. Under such circumstances, of what importance to him were the rights of the firstborn which, in his eyes, meant only more obligations to be met in the service of God?

30. הַלְעִיטֵנִי — *Pour into me.* Abraham's slave Eliezer had said הַגְמִיאִינִי, *Let me sip* (24:17), whereas the gluttonous and voracious Esau says הַלְעִיטֵנִי, *pour into me.* Indeed, *the righteous eats to appease his hunger, but the stomach of the wicked is never satisfied* (*Proverbs* 13:25).

הָאָדֹם הָאָדֹם הַזֶּה — *That very red stuff.* I.e. red lentils meant for his father. His father was to have them for the first mourner's meal after Abraham's death. Cf. *Rashi*, who also explains the connection between a plate of lentils and mourning. Adam and Eve ate lentils after Abel was murdered, as did Haran's parents after Haran died in the fiery furnace (*Midrash*).

The mourner's meal which Jacob prepared occasioned a lively ideological discussion between the brothers, during which Esau categorically denied belief in the immortality of the soul, in the resurrection of the dead and, ultimately, in the existence of God. Jacob then asked him, "Since you claim that there is neither a future world nor reward in the hereafter, why do you value the birthright which calls for serving God?" So began the bargaining over the birthright. Jacob

לא עָיֵף אָנֹכִי עַל־כֵּן קָרָא־שְׁמוֹ אֱדוֹם: וַיֹּאמֶר יַעֲקֹב מִכְרָה כַיּוֹם
לב אֶת־בְּכֹרָתְךָ לִי: וַיֹּאמֶר עֵשָׂו הִנֵּה אָנֹכִי הוֹלֵךְ לָמוּת
לג וְלָמָּה־זֶּה לִי בְּכֹרָה: וַיֹּאמֶר יַעֲקֹב הִשָּׁבְעָה לִּי כַּיּוֹם וַיִּשָּׁבַע
לד לוֹ וַיִּמְכֹּר אֶת־בְּכֹרָתוֹ לְיַעֲקֹב: וְיַעֲקֹב נָתַן לְעֵשָׂו לֶחֶם וּנְזִיד
עֲדָשִׁים וַיֹּאכַל וַיֵּשְׁתְּ וַיָּקָם וַיֵּלַךְ וַיִּבֶז עֵשָׂו אֶת־הַבְּכֹרָה:

had long suspected his brother of not caring about it and he was waiting for an opportunity to put him to the test. This opportunity came spontaneously on the day that their grandfather died (ibid.).

עַל־כֵּן קָרָא־שְׁמוֹ אֱדוֹם — *He therefore called his name Edom.* Red or red-haired. Esau had an affinity for the color red, the color of blood. It was the food's red color which attracted him much more than its quality. The red complexion he was born with did not give him the nickname "Edom"; it was rather his particular affinity for red which earned him the name.

31. מִכְרָה כַיּוֹם — *Sell, as this day. Rashi* explains, "Just as this day is clear, so make a real and clear sale of it to me." But according to *Ramban* and *Rashbam,* the term כַיּוֹם signifies "immediately."

אֶת־בְּכֹרָתְךָ — *Your birthright.* As the sacrificial service is the responsibility of the firstborn, Jacob said: "It is not fitting that this wicked person should bring offerings to the Holy One, Blessed is He" (*Rashi*).

Much has been said about this pact between the two boys. Some critics see it as a children's game, having at most a certain psychological interest. Others think they see in it the first manifestation of the "mercantile" spirit of the Jew, who knows how to profit from every opportunity and particularly from the ignorance of others. But both these views miss the point. The point here is that two concepts, two theses, two ideals confronted one another. The objective is the continuation of the spiritual heritage of Abraham and its application on a vast scale. In Jacob's thinking, the firstborn's main task will be to ensure the permanence of family traditions and thus to carry on with complete continuity what the founder of the family had begun. For Esau this responsibility is unacceptable. It involves considerable sacrifice and a devotion which would constantly curb his freedom to follow his innate tendencies. What is important to Esau is not a long and exacting labor which would bear fruit only after his death, but immediate enjoyment and momentary physical satisfaction. What would he do with the birthright, which was more of a duty than a right? A mouthful of bread, a succulent plate of lentils, are of infinitely greater value to him than all these ideas. In Jacob's mind, the sale of the birthright was but a proof of supreme scorn, which he had long suspected. And it was hardly any question of Esau's renouncing his rights to a material inheritance — in what follows we see that Esau goes on to acquire a considerable fortune and become rich and powerful. But as for Jacob, the possessions which he will manage to acquire in Laban's house will be the

exhausted." (He therefore called his name Edom.)

³¹ *Jacob said, "Sell, as this day, your birthright to me."*

³² *And Esau said, "Look, I am going to die, so of what use to me is a birthright?"*

³³ *Jacob said, "Swear to me as this day"; he swore to him and sold his birthright to Jacob.* ³⁴ *Jacob gave Esau bread and lentil stew, and he ate and drank, got up and left; thus, Esau spurned the birthright.*

fruit of dogged labor and not a fortune obtained through inheritance (*R' S.R. Hirsch*).

32. אָנֹכִי הוֹלֵךְ לָמוּת — *I am going to die. Rashi* gives two interpretations of Esau's reply: The birthright is unstable and will disappear. The sacrificial service will not always remain the responsibility of the firstborn, for later it will pass to the tribe of Levi. Besides, what does this service consist of? There are so many precautions to take, so many sanctions, transgression of which is penalized by death . . . I am going to die on account of it, so why should I want it?

Other commentators consider that Esau knew he was in danger of losing his life any day because of the risks of being a hunter. And so he did not count on personally inheriting anything from his father, and thus lost interest in his birthright. *Ibn Ezra* quotes commentators who hold that this lack of interest in the birthright stemmed from Isaac's poverty, a fact which seems to be borne out by several remarks in the Biblical text. But *Ramban* demonstrates at length the error of this view. He maintains that before the Torah was given, the birthright carried with it only the privilege of worship, but not judicial or material advantages.

33. הִשָּׁבְעָה לִי — *Swear to me.* Jacob knew his brother very well. He knew that he was not a believer but that he still feared the curse which would follow the violation of an oath, just as he believed in the value of a blessing. Accordingly, Jacob made him swear by the life of his father because he knew that Esau was very close to him. Esau could not be made to swear by the sign of the covenant for he did not have this sign, nor by the name of God for he was not a believer (*Midrash*).

וַיִּמְכֹּר אֶת־בְּכֹרָתוֹ לְיַעֲקֹב — *And sold his birthright to Jacob.* Jacob realized the corrupt character of his brother. Hence he considered it justifiable to give up something to him with the sole purpose of being able to devote himself to Divine service in total quietude. This example of the ancestor was of value to the descendants and they adopted it in their confrontations with Esau's descendants, as *Ramban* notes on *Leviticus* 16:8. And *R' Yehudah HaChassid* justifies Jacob's conduct when he concludes: "Learn from this that a righteous person is permitted to use artifice to obtain a *sefer Torah* or a sacred object in the possession of a wicked person" (*Daas Zekeinim* from *Baalei Tosafos*).

34. וְיַעֲקֹב נָתַן לְעֵשָׂו לֶחֶם וּנְזִיד עֲדָשִׁים — *Jacob gave Esau bread and lentil stew.* In addition to a substantial amount of money (*Lekach Tov*) and the superb sword of

כו   א וַיְהִי רָעָב בָּאָרֶץ מִלְּבַד הָרָעָב הָרִאשׁוֹן אֲשֶׁר הָיָה בִּימֵי
אַבְרָהָם וַיֵּלֶךְ יִצְחָק אֶל־אֲבִימֶלֶךְ מֶלֶךְ־פְּלִשְׁתִּים גְּרָרָה:
ב וַיֵּרָא אֵלָיו יהוה וַיֹּאמֶר אַל־תֵּרֵד מִצְרָיְמָה שְׁכֹן בָּאָרֶץ
ג אֲשֶׁר אֹמַר אֵלֶיךָ: גּוּר בָּאָרֶץ הַזֹּאת וְאֶהְיֶה עִמְּךָ וַאֲבָרֲכֶךָּ
כִּי־לְךָ וּלְזַרְעֲךָ אֶתֵּן אֶת־כָּל־הָאֲרָצֹת הָאֵל וַהֲקִמֹתִי
ד אֶת־הַשְּׁבֻעָה אֲשֶׁר נִשְׁבַּעְתִּי לְאַבְרָהָם אָבִיךָ: וְהִרְבֵּיתִי
אֶת־זַרְעֲךָ כְּכוֹכְבֵי הַשָּׁמַיִם וְנָתַתִּי לְזַרְעֲךָ אֵת כָּל־הָאֲרָצֹת
ה הָאֵל וְהִתְבָּרֲכוּ בְזַרְעֲךָ כֹּל גּוֹיֵי הָאָרֶץ: עֵקֶב אֲשֶׁר־שָׁמַע
אַבְרָהָם בְּקֹלִי וַיִּשְׁמֹר מִשְׁמַרְתִּי מִצְוֺתַי חֻקּוֹתַי וְתוֹרֹתָי:

Methuselah, which Isaac inherited from Abraham and presented to Jacob (*Sechel Tov*).

וַיִּבֶז עֵשָׂו אֶת־הַבְּכֹרָה — *Thus, Esau spurned the birthright*. Noting the consonance of the words בְּכֹרָה (*birthright*) and בְּרָכָה (*blessing*), R' Shmuel teaches: Esau exclaims, "What good is the birthright to me?" And the Holy Spirit replies: "What good will the blessing [which you will try to get for yourself at any cost] be to you? (*Midrash HaGadol*).

26.

1. וַיְהִי רָעָב בָּאָרֶץ — *There was a famine in the land*. The *Zohar* considers this calamity as a test meant especially for Isaac, for *God tests the righteous* (*Psalms* 11:5). He tested Adam and Noah and both succumbed, whereas the patriarchs triumphed in their tests of faith. God surely knows the hearts of men without needing to test them, but the purpose of such tests is to give the servants of God the opportunity to increase in moral stature and to raise themselves to the supreme degree of perfection (נִסָּה, *to test*, being related to נָשָׂא, *to raise*; cf. *Rashi* to *Exodus* 20:17).

וַיֵּלֶךְ יִצְחָק אֶל־אֲבִימֶלֶךְ מֶלֶךְ־פְּלִשְׁתִּים — *And Isaac went to Abimelech king of the Philistines*. The land of the Philistines constitutes the shortest route from Canaan to Egypt, as the Torah later points out (*Exodus* 13:17). Isaac wanted to go to Egypt, the land of plenty, just as his father had on a similar occasion. Presumably Abimelech is the son of the king of the same name who reigned in Abraham's time (*Onkelos*).

2. אַל־תֵּרֵד מִצְרָיְמָה — *Do not descend to Egypt*. *Rashi* gives the reason: "You are an offering totally consecrated to God (עוֹלָה תְּמִימָה; cf. our commentary to 22:12); the lands outside the Holy Land are not worthy of you (just as the burnt offering is not to go out חוּץ מִן הַקְּלָעִים, *beyond the sacred enclosure of the Temple*)." To *Ramban*, the prohibition of going to Egypt comprises yet another historically important reference. Abraham's travels in this country traced the route for his descendants who were to dwell there during their first exile. But Isaac's stay in the land of the Philistines, where his father had formerly dwelt,

26 ¹*There was a famine in the land, aside from the first famine that was in the days of Abraham; and Isaac went to Abimelech king of the Philistines, to Gerar. ² HASHEM appeared to him and said, "Do not descend to Egypt; dwell in the land that I shall indicate to you. ³ Sojourn in this land and I will be with you and bless you; for to you and your offspring will I give all these lands, and establish the oath that I swore to Abraham your father: ⁴ 'I will increase your offspring like the stars of the heavens; and will give to your offspring all these lands;' and all the nations of the earth shall bless themselves by your offspring. ⁵ Because Abraham obeyed My voice, and observed My safeguards, My commandments, My decrees, and My Torahs."*

corresponded to the second exile in Babylonia, the land of Abraham's birth. King Abimelech's changing attitude toward him was later mirrored in the fickle behavior of the Babylonian kings toward the exiles.

3. גּוּר בָּאָרֶץ הַזֹּאת — *Sojourn in this land.* In the previous verse it was said *dwell in the land . . .* The Torah now repeats this injunction but makes it more specific: גּוּר — be a גֵּר — a stranger in this land. Indeed, no matter in which land a man finds himself, he may only consider himself a guest of God, Who remains its absolute Master. "This verse teaches you that the righteous feel themselves strangers wherever they are in this world" (*Midrash HaGadol*).

אֶת־כָּל־הָאֲרָצֹת הָאֵל — *All these lands.* The demonstrative pronoun הָאֵל is a short form of הָאֵלֶּה, *these* (*Rashi*). The Midrash interprets הָאֵל as being related to אֵילֵי הָאָרֶץ, *the mighty of the land* (*Ezekiel* 17:13). It emphasizes the notion of strength and toughness: these hard, refractory lands I give to you and your descendants. The same form is found repeated in the next verse.

Just as the Jewish people, right from their origins, have been characterized as עַם קְשֵׁה עוֹרֶף, *a stiff-necked people,* so too the Land of Israel is designated as an arid and barren territory, on occasion afflicted with famine. It is precisely this land which God promises to the patriarchs so that, by their carrying out the Divine laws, it may bloom and be transformed into a land flowing with milk and honey. This example will show the peoples of the world the path every man must take in order to be the creator of his own blessings, even under the worst of natural conditions. It is in this sense that Isaac's seed will be a blessing for all the nations of the earth (*R' S.R. Hirsch*).

5. עֵקֶב אֲשֶׁר־שָׁמַע אַבְרָהָם בְּקֹלִי — *Because Abraham obeyed My voice.* The celestial blessings are bestowed on Isaac because of the merits of his father Abraham. Cf. our commentary to verse 24.

וַיִּשְׁמֹר מִשְׁמַרְתִּי — *And observed My safeguards.* In the words of this verse *Rashi* sees confirmation of the rabbinical tradition (*Rabbah* 95) that Abraham observed all the regulations of the Torah, including the rabbinical prohibitions

שני

ו־ז וַיֵּשֶׁב יִצְחָק בִּגְרָר: וַיִּשְׁאֲלוּ אַנְשֵׁי הַמָּקוֹם לְאִשְׁתּוֹ וַיֹּאמֶר
אֲחֹתִי הִוא כִּי יָרֵא לֵאמֹר אִשְׁתִּי פֶּן־יַהַרְגֻנִי אַנְשֵׁי הַמָּקוֹם
ח עַל־רִבְקָה כִּי־טוֹבַת מַרְאֶה הִוא: וַיְהִי כִּי אָרְכוּ־לוֹ שָׁם
הַיָּמִים וַיַּשְׁקֵף אֲבִימֶלֶךְ מֶלֶךְ פְּלִשְׁתִּים בְּעַד הַחַלּוֹן וַיַּרְא
ט וְהִנֵּה יִצְחָק מְצַחֵק אֵת רִבְקָה אִשְׁתּוֹ: וַיִּקְרָא אֲבִימֶלֶךְ
לְיִצְחָק וַיֹּאמֶר אַךְ הִנֵּה אִשְׁתְּךָ הִוא וְאֵיךְ אָמַרְתָּ אֲחֹתִי הִוא
י וַיֹּאמֶר אֵלָיו יִצְחָק כִּי אָמַרְתִּי פֶּן־אָמוּת עָלֶיהָ: וַיֹּאמֶר
אֲבִימֶלֶךְ מַה־זֹּאת עָשִׂיתָ לָּנוּ כִּמְעַט שָׁכַב אַחַד הָעָם
יא אֶת־אִשְׁתֶּךָ וְהֵבֵאתָ עָלֵינוּ אָשָׁם: וַיְצַו אֲבִימֶלֶךְ אֶת־כָּל־

and the teachings of the Oral Law, even before the Torah was given on Mount Sinai. He knew them through his gift of prophecy (רוּחַ הַקֹּדֶשׁ) and transmitted them to his descendants.

However, *Ramban* objects that there were a certain number of Mosaic laws which the patriarchs did not observe, in particular that prohibiting the marrying of two sisters. Accordingly he thinks that in the case of the patriarchs' observance of the Torah was limited to the time when they were living in the Promised Land. This opinion is contradicted by *R' Chaim ben Attar* (*Genesis* 49:3) who holds that first and foremost the patriarchs observed the Noachian precepts and the Mosaic laws while allowing rare exceptions for reasons he explains, including also prophecy. *Sforno, Ibn Ezra* and *Radak* share his opinion, while *Maharal* considers that the patriarchs observed only the positive commandments (מִצְווֹת עֲשֵׂה) but not the prohibitions. The latter are intended only for those to whom God has formally made known His will whereas the other commandments can be carried out by anyone whose love of God brings him to manifest his feelings of adoration. Abraham was the only patriarch to observe the Divine laws, both positive and negative, in their entirety (*Gur Aryeh* 46:6; cf. our commentary to 29:28).

6. וַיֵּשֶׁב יִצְחָק בִּגְרָר — *So Isaac settled in Gerar.* This, notes the *Masorah,* is one of the fourteen Torah verses composed of just three words. Indeed, it could serve as a chapter heading. Isaac established himself in Gerar — just where his father had lived through the tragic experience of seeing his wife Sarah abducted by King Abimelech (20:1). Of this city Abraham had declared: *There is but no fear of God in this place* (ibid. v. 11). It follows, then, that Isaac's decision to dwell in Gerar was a mistake fraught with consequences. He failed to learn from his father's experiences, and this error was at the root of the troubles which he brought upon himself in this city. [God had commanded him only to stay in Canaan, but Isaac chose the city of Gerar on his own initiative.] These moral considerations can explain why the Torah relates the events which followed, although seemingly they are of secondary importance. Twice before, the same incident occurred in the lives of his parents. But the son still neglects to learn from these events and becomes the victim of his carelessness.

⁶ *So Isaac settled in Gerar.* ⁷ *When the men of the place asked about his wife, he said, "She is my sister" — for he was afraid to say "my wife" — "lest the men of the place kill me because of Rebecca for she is fair to look upon!"*

⁸ *And it came to pass, as his days there lengthened, that Abimelech king of the Philistines gazed down through the window and saw — behold! Isaac was jesting with his wife Rebecca.* ⁹ *Abimelech summoned Isaac and said, "But look! She is your wife! How could you say, 'She is my sister?'"*

Isaac said to him, "Because I said that I would be killed because of her."

¹⁰ *Abimelech said, "What is this that you have done to us? One of the people has nearly lain with your wife, and you would have brought guilt upon us!"* ¹¹ *Abimelech then warned all the*

---

8. וַיְהִי כִּי אָרְכוּ־לוֹ שָׁם הַיָּמִים — *And it came to pass, as his days there lengthened.* *Rashi* explains: Isaac said to himself: "From now on I need not worry," for until that time no one had done anything to him. And he was no longer on his guard.

But another interpretation from the Midrash mentions a verse from the prophet Ezekiel: *The days are lasting long, and lost is every vision* (12:22). This quotation alludes to Abimelech's dream of the night in which God had warned him regarding Sarah: *"Behold you are to die because of the woman you have taken; moreover she is a married woman"* (20:3). The warning was forgotten in time and Abimelech again succumbed to temptation, this time for Rebecca. In this interpretation the beginning of our verse is to be translated, "When the days had lasted long for him there, Abimelech ..." Thus the entire verse refers to the king of the Philistines, with the implication that he was the same Abimelech who lived in Abraham's time. But according to *Rashi* the first part of the verse refers to Isaac.

וַיַּשְׁקֵף אֲבִימֶלֶךְ ... בְּעַד הַחַלּוֹן — *Abimelech ... gazed down through the window.* The *Zohar* negates *Rashi's* explanation, "He saw them making love," saying that the righteous respect the prohibition against cohabitation during the daytime. Accordingly, the *Zohar* points out that the expression, "gazed down through the window," is also used in the sense of contemplating the stars for soothsaying (e.g. *Judges* 5:28). Through his astrology Abimelech saw that Rebecca was really Isaac's wife.

9. אַךְ הִנֵּה אִשְׁתְּךָ הִוא — *But look! She is your wife.* The word אַךְ always indicates a restriction. Abimelech said to Isaac, "At first, you were great and esteemed in our eyes. Now that you have lied to us, you are nothing" (*Midrash HaGadol*).

כִּי אָמַרְתִּי פֶּן־אָמוּת עָלֶיהָ — *Because I said that I would be killed because of her.* This teaches you that it is permissible to resort to a falsehood in a case of extreme danger (cf. *Yevamos* 65b).

יב הָעָם לֵאמֹר הַנֹּגֵעַ בָּאִישׁ הַזֶּה וּבְאִשְׁתּוֹ מוֹת יוּמָת: וַיִּזְרַע
יִצְחָק בָּאָרֶץ הַהִוא וַיִּמְצָא בַּשָּׁנָה הַהִוא מֵאָה שְׁעָרִים
יג וַיְבָרֲכֵהוּ יהוה: וַיִּגְדַּל הָאִישׁ וַיֵּלֶךְ הָלוֹךְ וְגָדֵל עַד כִּי־
יד גָדַל מְאֹד: וַיְהִי־לוֹ מִקְנֵה־צֹאן וּמִקְנֵה בָקָר וַעֲבֻדָּה רַבָּה
טו וַיְקַנְאוּ אֹתוֹ פְּלִשְׁתִּים: וְכָל־הַבְּאֵרֹת אֲשֶׁר חָפְרוּ עַבְדֵי
אָבִיו בִּימֵי אַבְרָהָם אָבִיו סִתְּמוּם פְּלִשְׁתִּים וַיְמַלְאוּם
טז עָפָר: וַיֹּאמֶר אֲבִימֶלֶךְ אֶל־יִצְחָק לֵךְ מֵעִמָּנוּ כִּי־עָצַמְתָּ
יז מִמֶּנּוּ מְאֹד: וַיֵּלֶךְ מִשָּׁם יִצְחָק וַיִּחַן בְּנַחַל־גְּרָר וַיֵּשֶׁב שָׁם:

שלישי

11. הַנֹּגֵעַ בָּאִישׁ הַזֶּה — *Whoever molests this man.* Abimelech remembers the
solemn warning which God had given him previously: *"But if you do not return
her, be aware that you shall surely die: you and all that is yours."* (20:7). This
warning was of utmost importance for all future times. It was the first time that
God had informed the people on Abraham's route how important the patriarch
was. Now, the same incident recurs in the life of Abraham's son and in the midst
of the Philistines. It was here that Isaac had come into the world and it was the
Philistines who were to be in constant proximity to the Jewish people. And so
the event related here takes on the significance of a warning: אַל תִּגְּעוּ בִמְשִׁיחָי
וְלִנְבִיאַי אַל תָּרֵעוּ, *do not touch My anointed, do no harm to My prophets* (*Psalms*
105:15).

12. וַיִּזְרַע יִצְחָק בָּאָרֶץ הַהִוא — *Isaac sowed in that land.* Isaac was supposedly the
first Jew to live in exile while still within Canaanite territory, as *Rashi* points out
on *Genesis* 15:13. גּוּר בָּאָרֶץ הַזֹּאת, *Sojourn in this land,* he was told by God (verse
3). And so, in contrast to his father, Isaac decided to provide for his family by
working the soil. He felt that this means of subsistence would attract less
hostility towards the "foreign Jew" from those around than commerce or
exploitation of the riches of the land. He was the first to show the moral and
practical value of personal labor and agrarian economy.

וַיִּמְצָא ... מֵאָה שְׁעָרִים — *He reaped a hundredfold.* *Rashi* explains, "They
estimated what he should have harvested and he harvested a hundred times this
estimate." The Midrash raises an objection: but we know that blessing does not
extend over what is weighed, measured, or counted (*Bava Metziah* 42a).
However, this estimate was necessary for setting aside the tithes. As a
consequence *Rambam* notes that the institution of tithing for the poor of the
land was first practiced by Isaac (*Hilchos Melachim* 9:3; cf. our commentary to
14:20). He distributed the tithe to the poor of the land and God recompensed him
with a new blessing. [This is why the words וַיְבָרֲכֵהוּ ה', *thus had* HASHEM
blessed him, come at the end of the sentence and not at the beginning.]

14. וַיְקַנְאוּ אֹתוֹ פְּלִשְׁתִּים — *And the Philistines envied him.* This jealousy initiated
a whole chain of events and a new period of exile, which began with Isaac (and
which was referred to in the announcement to Abraham — גֵּר יִהְיֶה זַרְעֲךָ בְּאֶרֶץ

people saying, "Whoever molests this man or his wife shall surely die."

¹² Isaac sowed in that land, and in that year he reaped a hundredfold; thus had HASHEM blessed him. ¹³ The man became great and kept becoming greater until he was very great. ¹⁴ He had acquired flocks and herds and many enterprises; and the Philistines envied him.

¹⁵ All the wells that his father's servants had dug in the days of Abraham his father, the Philistines stopped up, and filled them with earth. ¹⁶ And Abimelech said to Isaac, "Go away from us for you have become much mightier than we!" ¹⁷ So Isaac departed from there and encamped in the valley of Gerar, and dwelled there.

לֹא לָהֶם, *your offspring shall be aliens in a land not their own* (15:13). To be sure, Abraham was also a stranger in the land, but he had achieved such respect and admiration that everyone considered him נְשִׂיא אֱלֹהִים, *a prince of God.* Isaac, though, became an object of jealousy, indeed, of unconcealed hatred in the eyes of the populace. As for Jacob, a large part of his life was lived in a state of servitude. These three phases correspond to the three aspects of the lives of the Jews among the nations. In each of these aspects — servitude, envied power, and respected greatness — Jewry's task is to manifest its fidelity to the Divine covenant. In return, this covenant remains its constant protective shield and guarantee of its salvation. Jewry experiences these three stages historically, but in reverse order. Not so long ago, it suffered trials of misery and servitude and triumphed over them. Its current phase consists in living free and independent among the nations, without having to fear braving opposition and jealousy. This is the new exile-test we still have to pass. Then we can look forward to the last stage of exile: to win the respect and admiration of the nations, as did Abraham, because of our specific mission. Then, history will have accomplished what the Torah describes as our program for exile and redemption — וְזָכַרְתִּי אֶת בְּרִיתִי יַעֲקוֹב וְאַף אֶת בְּרִיתִי יִצְחָק וגו׳, *I will remember My covenant with Jacob . . . with Isaac . . . with Avraham* (*Leviticus* 26:42). Note that the Torah names the three phases of the covenants with the patriarchs in reverse order, conforming with the actual development of Jewish history (*R' S.R. Hirsch*).

15. וְכָל־הַבְּאֵרֹת אֲשֶׁר חָפְרוּ — *All the wells . . . had dug.* On the evident importance Scripture attaches to the episodes involving the wells, the patriarchs dug, see our commentary to 21:25 and 29:1.

R' Bachya explains that this passage refers to the pagans whom Abraham had converted. "To dig a well" is a metaphor for "to open the heart," hitherto closed. The wells dug in Abraham's time were filled in by the Philistines; that is, impelled by feelings of jealousy, they made the proselytes return to idolatry. They again closed their hearts and filled them with dust, i.e., with contemptible and worthless theories. (Perhaps *Rashi* wants to allude to the double meaning

יח וַיָּשָׁב יִצְחָק וַיַּחְפֹּר ׀ אֶת־בְּאֵרֹת הַמַּיִם אֲשֶׁר חָפְרוּ בִּימֵי
אַבְרָהָם אָבִיו וַיְסַתְּמוּם פְּלִשְׁתִּים אַחֲרֵי מוֹת אַבְרָהָם וַיִּקְרָא
יט לָהֶן שֵׁמוֹת כַּשֵּׁמֹת אֲשֶׁר־קָרָא לָהֶן אָבִיו: וַיַּחְפְּרוּ עַבְדֵי־
כ יִצְחָק בַּנָּחַל וַיִּמְצְאוּ־שָׁם בְּאֵר מַיִם חַיִּים: וַיָּרִיבוּ רֹעֵי גְרָר
עִם־רֹעֵי יִצְחָק לֵאמֹר לָנוּ הַמָּיִם וַיִּקְרָא שֵׁם־הַבְּאֵר עֵשֶׂק
כא כִּי הִתְעַשְּׂקוּ עִמּוֹ: וַיַּחְפְּרוּ בְּאֵר אַחֶרֶת וַיָּרִיבוּ גַּם־עָלֶיהָ
כב וַיִּקְרָא שְׁמָהּ שִׂטְנָה: וַיַּעְתֵּק מִשָּׁם וַיַּחְפֹּר בְּאֵר אַחֶרֶת וְלֹא
רָבוּ עָלֶיהָ וַיִּקְרָא שְׁמָהּ רְחֹבוֹת וַיֹּאמֶר כִּי־עַתָּה הִרְחִיב
רביעי כג-כד יהוה לָנוּ וּפָרִינוּ בָאָרֶץ: וַיַּעַל מִשָּׁם בְּאֵר שָׁבַע: וַיֵּרָא אֵלָיו

of this verse when he mentions that the Talmud uses a word identical to סְתָמוּם in the expression "a plugged-up heart.") But ultimately, Isaac redug the water wells that they had dug in his father Abraham's lifetime, and which the Philistines had sealed off after Abraham's death; and he named them as his father had named them" (verse 18). Proselytes receive new names after their conversion.

18. וַיִּקְרָא לָהֶן שֵׁמוֹת כַּשֵּׁמֹת אֲשֶׁר־קָרָא לָהֶן אָבִיו — *And he called them by the same names that his father had called them.* Moved by a feeling of filial piety, Isaac kept the names that his father had given the wells. This teaches us the extent to which our ancestral teachings must be maintained. Undoubtedly, it was to reward his respect for the original names that Isaac's own name was never changed, although the names of Abraham and Jacob were (*R' Saadyah Gaon,* quoted by *R' Bachya*).

20. לָנוּ הַמָּיִם — *The water is ours.* All the facts related here and in Chapter 21 demonstrate that it was legitimate to dig a well and that the well belonged to whoever dug it. Moreover, here it was a question of "living" fresh water, מַיִם חַיִּים, springing up from the depths of the earth. Consequently, it could not have been prejudicial to the interests of any person whatsoever. Despite this, Isaac was subjected to severe quarrels and wranglings, just as the Jew in exile has been through the centuries, "You dug the well? The hole is yours, but the water is ours!"

וַיִּקְרָא שֵׁם־הַבְּאֵר עֵשֶׂק — *So he called the name of that well Esek (contention).* Consistent with the idea he developed previously, *Ramban* explains that the episode of the wells which Isaac dug, of secondary importance in itself, alludes to Jewry's future history. The "well of living water" allegorically designates the sacred Temple, as in the expression used by the prophet Jeremiah (17:13). The First Temple was the object of numerous quarrels and disputes which ultimately led to its ruin. The Second Temple also foundered amid the violent opposition and enmity of the nations. The names עֵשֶׂק and שִׂטְנָה — *contention* and *harassment* — thus evoke the destinies of the first two Temples, which figuratively represent the "wellspring" of the Jewish nation. But Isaac dug a

18 *And Isaac dug anew the wells of water which they had dug in the days of Abraham his father and the Philistines had stopped up after Abraham's death; and he called them by the same names that his father had called them.*

19 *Isaac's servants dug in the valley and found there a well of fresh water.* 20 *The herdsmen of Gerar quarreled with Isaac's herdsmen saying, "The water is ours," so he called the name of that well Esek because they involved themselves with him.* 21 *Then they dug another well, and they quarreled over that also; so he called its name Sitnah.* 22 *He relocated from there and dug another well; they did not quarrel over it, so he called its name Rehoboth, and said, "For now HASHEM has granted us ample space, and we can be fruitful in the land."*

23 *He went up from there to Beer-sheba.* 24 *HASHEM appeared*

third well, over which no one quarreled. He called this one רְחֹבוֹת — *expansion* — saying, "For now God has given us room, so that we can reproduce in the land." The Temple in messianic times will be like this well. It will be erected in the time of our "expanded borders" (*Deuteronomy* 19:8) and will stand out because of the splendor of its vast spaces (*Ezekiel* 41:7). It will witness neither contention nor harassment.

22. וַיַּעְתֵּק מִשָּׁם — *He relocated from there.* For the second time, Isaac leaves his place of residence in search of a less hostile populace. The Sages of the Midrash quote the prophet Isaiah, *Go my people, enter into your chambers and shut your door behind you; hide yourself for but a little moment until the fury has passed away* (26:20). Why defy the adversity which pursues you? Hide yourself for a short while just as Isaac did from the hostility of the Philistines. Their rage quickly passed and Abimelech and his generals went to see Isaac to solicit his friendship (*Tanchuma Vayeitzei* 5). The Sages want to present Isaac's conduct as an example for us to follow when calamity dogs men's footsteps.

23. וַיַּעַל מִשָּׁם בְּאֵר שָׁבַע — *He went up from there to Beer-sheba.* Until now it was the hostility of the Philistines which had forced Isaac to keep to himself. And God did not appear to Isaac as long as he was compelled to live in isolation by external circumstances. He left Isaac alone, exposed to the jealousy and hatred of his environment with no promise of rescue. This test showed the way for the life that Isaac's descendants endured during the centuries of their existence in ghettos. But it was just when Isaac deliberately chose to dwell in isolation — even though in so doing he was finally assured of living in peace — that God appeared to him, blessed him, and promised to protect him. Isaac returned voluntarily to Beer-sheba. Here he had spent his youth alone with his father, here his father had devoted himself to his great spiritual calling, and here Abraham had received the Divine command to sacrifice him on Mount Moriah (21:33).

יהוה֙ בַּלַּ֣יְלָה הַה֔וּא וַיֹּ֗אמֶר אָנֹכִ֕י אֱלֹהֵ֖י אַבְרָהָ֣ם אָבִ֑יךָ
אַל־תִּירָא֙ כִּֽי־אִתְּךָ֣ אָנֹ֔כִי וּבֵֽרַכְתִּ֙יךָ֙ וְהִרְבֵּיתִ֣י אֶת־זַרְעֲךָ֔
כה בַּֽעֲב֖וּר אַבְרָהָ֣ם עַבְדִּֽי: וַיִּ֧בֶן שָׁ֣ם מִזְבֵּ֗חַ וַיִּקְרָא֙ בְּשֵׁ֣ם יהוה֔
כו וַיֶּט־שָׁ֖ם אָֽהֳל֑וֹ וַיִּכְרוּ־שָׁ֥ם עַבְדֵֽי־יִצְחָ֖ק בְּאֵֽר: וַֽאֲבִימֶ֕לֶךְ הָלַ֥ךְ
כז אֵלָ֖יו מִגְּרָ֑ר וַֽאֲחֻזַּת֙ מֵֽרֵעֵ֔הוּ וּפִיכֹ֖ל שַׂר־צְבָאֽוֹ: וַיֹּ֤אמֶר אֲלֵהֶ֙ם
יִצְחָ֔ק מַדּ֖וּעַ בָּאתֶ֣ם אֵלָ֑י וְאַתֶּם֙ שְׂנֵאתֶ֣ם אֹתִ֔י וַתְּשַׁלְּח֖וּנִי
כח מֵֽאִתְּכֶֽם: וַיֹּֽאמְר֗וּ רָא֣וֹ רָאִ֘ינוּ֮ כִּֽי־הָיָ֣ה יהוה֣ | עִמָּךְ֒ וַנֹּ֗אמֶר תְּהִ֣י
כט נָ֥א אָלָ֛ה בֵּֽינוֹתֵ֖ינוּ בֵּינֵ֣ינוּ וּבֵינֶ֑ךָ וְנִכְרְתָ֥ה בְרִ֖ית עִמָּֽךְ: אִם־
תַּֽעֲשֵׂ֨ה עִמָּ֜נוּ רָעָ֗ה כַּֽאֲשֶׁר֙ לֹ֣א נְגַֽעֲנ֔וּךָ וְכַֽאֲשֶׁ֨ר עָשִׂ֤ינוּ עִמְּךָ֙
חמישי   ל רַק־ט֗וֹב וַנְּשַׁלֵּֽחֲךָ֙ בְּשָׁל֔וֹם אַתָּ֥ה עַתָּ֖ה בְּר֣וּךְ יהוֽה: וַיַּ֤עַשׂ לָהֶם֙
לא מִשְׁתֶּ֔ה וַיֹּֽאכְל֖וּ וַיִּשְׁתּֽוּ: וַיַּשְׁכִּ֣ימוּ בַבֹּ֔קֶר וַיִּשָּֽׁבְע֖וּ אִ֣ישׁ לְאָחִ֑יו

---

24. וַיֵּרָא אֵלָיו ה' בַּלַּיְלָה הַהוּא — *HASHEM appeared to him that night.* Joseph said to Potiphar's wife, "When the Holy One, Blessed is He, revealed Himself to my ancestors it was usually at night. We see this with Abraham (15:1), Isaac (our verse) and Jacob (28:12). If I listen to you, God will find me impure when He wants to reveal Himself to me" (*Bereishis Rabbah* 87).

אָנֹכִי אֱלֹהֵי אַבְרָהָם אָבִיךָ — *I am the God of your father Abraham.* In emphasizing the fact that the blessing conferred upon him derives from the merit of his father Abraham, whom He called עַבְדִּי, *My servant* (an epithet used only here), God makes clear to Isaac all that He expects from him.

בַּעֲבוּר אַבְרָהָם עַבְדִּי — *Because of Abraham My servant.* R' Eliezer said: "All the kindnesses accorded Isaac were due to the merit of his father. His own merits will be recompensed only in the distant future (*Midrash HaGadol*). This opinion is borne out by a passage in the Talmud which describes Isaac as the true redeemer of the Jewish people on the day of the final judgment (*Shabbos* 89b). There he is called the "father of the people" in accordance with *Isaiah 63:16*.

25. וַיִּבֶן שָׁם מִזְבֵּחַ — *He built an altar there.* Isaac immediately builds an altar at Beer-sheba and proclaims the name of God, just as his father did at this very place (21:33). He does not wait to examine the soil or to see whether water is to be found. Yet here everything comes to him even before he desires it. His servants find water just as soon as they start to dig, and the prince who had expelled him now visits him in his refuge and shows him great honor. How much anxiety had Isaac previously suffered just to attain all this, and without success!

28. תְּהִי נָא אָלָה בֵּינוֹתֵינוּ בֵּינֵינוּ וּבֵינֶךָ — *Let the oath between ourselves now be between us and you.* *Rashi* explains: "Let the oath that is between us since your father's time continue now between ourselves and you." The renewal of the treaty drawn up with Abraham for a number of generations (21:23) had become necessary, adds *Ramban*, because the Philistines realized that they had violated

to him that night and said, "I am the God of your father
Abraham: Fear not, for I am with you; I will bless you and
increase your offspring because of Abraham My servant."
²⁵ He built an altar there, invoked HASHEM by Name, and there
he pitched his tent; there Isaac's servants dug a well.

²⁶ Abimelech went to him from Gerar with a group of his
friends and Phicol, general of his legion. ²⁷ Isaac said to him,
"Why have you come to me? You hate me and drove me away
from you!"

²⁸ And they said, "We have indeed seen that HASHEM has been
with you, so we said, 'Let the oath between ourselves now be
between us and you, and let us make a covenant with you:
²⁹ If you do evil with us...! Just as we have not molested
you, and just as we have done with you only good, and sent
you away in peace — Now, you, O blessed of HASHEM!' "

³⁰ He made them a feast and they ate and drank. ³¹ They
awoke early in the morning and swore to one another;

it when they expelled Isaac from their territory. They now feared that Isaac's
descendants would take revenge on their own descendants. They still
remembered Abraham's spectacular victory over the supposedly invincible
Canaanite kings and they had good reason to dread the aggressiveness of
his descendants. But Isaac remained loyal to the oath which his father swore
just as, throughout the centuries of history, the Jewish people has always
remained faithful to its legal commitments and treaties, regardless of
circumstances.

29. וַנְּשַׁלֵּחֲךָ בְּשָׁלוֹם — And sent you away in peace. The Philistines felt it was a
great kindness to let Isaac go without stripping him of his possessions. In their
eyes this justified a new pact of friendship. This is like the lion who has a bone
stuck in his throat. No animal can dislodge it until a long-necked bird says to
him, "Give me a reward and I'll take it out of your throat." The lion replies, "I'll
give you whatever you wish." The bird puts her head into the lion's throat and
draws out the bone. Then she says to him, "Give me my reward." The lion
replies, "Is it not enough that you have been in my mouth and have come out
unharmed?" Likewise Abimelech says to Isaac, "We have done you a great favor
by allowing you to leave in peace, for our practice is to mistreat all strangers"
(Daas Zekeinim from Baalei Tosafos).

30. וַיַּעַשׂ לָהֶם מִשְׁתֶּה — He made then a feast. When a Jew has the privilege
of being seated at the table of a righteous man and sharing his meal, he
feels deeply impressed by the example of holiness which he observes. But
Abimelech feels nothing. He eats and drinks and the next morning goes on
his way (R' Bunam).

לב וַיְשַׁלְּחֵם יִצְחָק וַיֵּלְכוּ מֵאִתּוֹ בְּשָׁלוֹם: וַיְהִי ׀ בַּיּוֹם הַהוּא
וַיָּבֹאוּ עַבְדֵי יִצְחָק וַיַּגִּדוּ לוֹ עַל־אֹדוֹת הַבְּאֵר אֲשֶׁר חָפָרוּ
לג וַיֹּאמְרוּ לוֹ מָצָאנוּ מָיִם: וַיִּקְרָא אֹתָהּ שִׁבְעָה עַל־כֵּן שֵׁם־
הָעִיר בְּאֵר שֶׁבַע עַד הַיּוֹם הַזֶּה:
לד וַיְהִי
עֵשָׂו בֶּן־אַרְבָּעִים שָׁנָה וַיִּקַּח אִשָּׁה אֶת־יְהוּדִית בַּת־בְּאֵרִי
לה הַחִתִּי וְאֶת־בָּשְׂמַת בַּת־אֵילֹן הַחִתִּי: וַתִּהְיֶיןָ מֹרַת רוּחַ
כז א לְיִצְחָק וּלְרִבְקָה: וַיְהִי כִּי־זָקֵן יִצְחָק וַתִּכְהֶיןָ עֵינָיו

33. וַיִּקְרָא אֹתָהּ שִׁבְעָה — *And he named it Shibah.* It means "oath," because of the treaty (which contained an oath). So interprets *Rashi, Ramban,* and *Rashbam.* This name goes back to Abraham (21:3). But it was given a second time following the new oath which became necessary when the Philistines violated the treaty. Henceforth, the city will permanently bear this name — "until this very day."

It is important, however, to note that twice (here and with Abraham, 21:28-31) the Torah connects digging wells and making a treaty with a foreign power. The significance of this has been discussed in the previous chapter. Digging a well just after signing a treaty takes on a symbolic importance corresponding to a "mental reservation." The well of living water on the material plane is equivalent to the source of inspiration on the spiritual plane; the patriarchs are determined to make it clear to their partners, right from the moment the friendship treaty was signed, that they will never share their cultural life. They will draw spiritual nourishment only from their own sources, from their own wellsprings. A treaty with a pagan king will not "rub off" on their spiritual life — the latter is "private property," untouchable. And so the well dug at the time of a pact will be "seven times" sacred and consequently will be named Beer-sheba. (*Sforno* notes that the word שֶׁבַע, with a *segol* as one of the vowels, designates the number seven, whereas the same name as given by Abraham has a *kamatz* and is related to the word "oath.")

34. וַיְהִי עֵשָׂו בֶּן־אַרְבָּעִים שָׁנָה — *When Esau was forty years old. Rashi* points out the hypocrisy of Esau. He is compared to a pig who lies down and proudly shows off his hooves as if to say, "You see, I am a kosher animal." For at least twenty-five years Esau had been taking wives away from their husbands and doing violence to them. Now that he is forty, he hypocritically exclaims, "My father took a wife at forty; I shall follow his example." Moreover, *Rashi* points out that the name Judith, which Esau gave to his wife, was intended to mislead Isaac. She was originally called Aholibamah. Esau had renamed her Judith to give the impression that she had renounced idolatry and to deceive his father into believing it (36:2). Moreover, she died childless (*Rashbam* ibid.), for Esau had reverted to the "antediluvian custom of having two wives, one to bring children into the world, the other for pleasure, deliberately sterilized, bedecked like a bride and fed delicacies" (*Rashi* on 4:19).

then Isaac saw them off and they departed from him in peace.
³² *And it was on that very day that Isaac's servants came and told him about the well they had dug, and they said to him, "We have found water!"* ³³ *And he named it Shibah; therefore, the name of the city is Beer-sheba until this very day.*

³⁴ *When Esau was forty years old, he took as a wife Judith daughter of Beeri the Hittite, and Basemath daughter of Elon the Hittite;* ³⁵ *and they were a source of spiritual rebellion to Isaac and to Rebecca.*

27 ¹ A*nd it came to pass, when Isaac had become old, and his eyes*

וַיִּקַּח אִשָּׁה — *He took as a wife.* After the years of famine had ended, Isaac sent his younger son Jacob to the school of Shem to study Divine Law. There Jacob remained thirty-two years. As for Esau, he refused to go to study and remained in his father's house. His only occupation was hunting, but he pursued peaceful passers-by in order to rob them, just as he stalked game.

On one of his hunting expeditions, Esau found his way to Mount Seir, where he met Judith, a Canaanite woman. He married her and brought her to his father's house. When Shem died ten years later, Jacob returned to his father's home. He was then fifty years old. Six years later Rebecca heard the good news of the birth of twin daughters, Leah and Rachel, to her sister-in-law Adina, Laban's wife. She urged Jacob never to marry any of the daughters of Canaan but instead to take a wife from the house of Abraham. Jacob replied that Abraham's prohibition against marrying a Canaanite had remained engraved in his mind — because of it he had preferred to remain a bachelor even into his sixties, although for twenty-three years he was exposed to his brother's reproaches for not following his example in this regard. But Jacob intended to wait until he could marry a woman of the family of Abraham (*Sefer HaYovlim* 25).

וַתִּהְיֶיןָ מֹרַת רוּחַ לְיִצְחָק וּלְרִבְקָה .35 — *And they were a source of spiritual rebellion to Isaac and to Rebecca.* Esau's marriages demonstrated how totally incapable he was of being the representative of the mission of Abraham. The Abrahamic principle is lost in a household ruled by two women of Hittite origin. The Midrash calls attention to the fact that Isaac is named in this verse before Rebecca despite his unconcealed sympathy for his son Esau, as the text has testified (25:28). But here it was a question of formal opposition to the sacred principles of Isaac as well as of Rebecca.

Accordingly, these two verses represent a real introduction to the passage which follows.

27.

וַיְהִי כִּי־זָקֵן יִצְחָק .1 — *And it came to pass, when Isaac had become old.* When the word וַיְהִי introduces a passage, it indicates that there is cause for sorrow connected with the passage (*Megillah* 11a). Here, there is a double reason: First,

מֵרְאֹת וַיִּקְרָא אֶת־עֵשָׂו ׀ בְּנוֹ הַגָּדֹל וַיֹּאמֶר אֵלָיו בְּנִי

ב וַיֹּאמֶר אֵלָיו הִנֵּנִי: וַיֹּאמֶר הִנֵּה־נָא זָקַנְתִּי לֹא יָדַעְתִּי יוֹם

ג מוֹתִי: וְעַתָּה שָׂא־נָא כֵלֶיךָ תֶּלְיְךָ וְקַשְׁתֶּךָ וְצֵא הַשָּׂדֶה

ד   וְצוּדָה לִּי °צֵידָה: וַעֲשֵׂה־לִי מַטְעַמִּים כַּאֲשֶׁר אָהַבְתִּי

צַיִד ק׳   וְהָבִיאָה לִּי וְאֹכֵלָה בַּעֲבוּר תְּבָרֶכְךָ נַפְשִׁי בְּטֶרֶם אָמוּת:

for Isaac who had successfully surmounted a series of tests. He also had seen the offer of friendship extended to him by his former enemies. He was now at the high point of his life. But the happiness which he now begins to enjoy is to be short-lived. His horizons abruptly cloud over and Isaac sees gulfs of hatred opening up right in his own family. Another cause for sorrow was that the blessings for Jacob and his descendants could be obtained only by devious means and at the price of much hardship.

וַתִּכְהֶיןָ עֵינָיו מֵרְאֹת — *And his eyes dimmed from seeing.* Isaac had begged God for physical suffering. His argument was: "If a man dies without suffering, his sentence in the hereafter will be brought upon him with full force. It is much better that he atone on earth, through his suffering." God replied, "Your request is justified. I shall begin with you" (*Rabbah* 65).

On the day of final judgment, adds the author of the *Sefer Chofetz Chaim*, the faults of man can outweigh his merits and the verdict may condemn him. But physical suffering while he is living, which has the effect of atonement, can then tip the scales of justice in the man's favor.

However, *Rashi* quotes different explanations which the Midrash gives for Isaac's blindness: His vision was dimmed from the smoke (of the idolatrous offerings) of Esau's wives (as alluded to in the previous verse). Another explanation: When Isaac was bound to the altar, just as his father was about to sacrifice him, the heavens opened, the angels serving God saw him, they cried, and their tears flowed and fell into Isaac's eyes. Since that event his vision remained dimmed. This allegorical interpretation reminds us that Isaac's infirmity goes back to the time of his voluntary sacrifice on Mount Moriah. God had refused to accept the gift of his whole person; but by giving him this infirmity, God showed Isaac that He had accepted the sacrifice, made in love, which Isaac was determined to offer.

Rabbi Yitzchak gives another reason for Isaac's blindness, which makes it seem to be his own fault. He points to the prohibition: *And you shall take no gifts for corruption, for a gift of corruption blinds those who can see* ... (*Exodus* 23:8). Isaac did accept gifts from his impious son — the venison and savory food which he loved (verse 4). These corrupted him, with the result that "his eyes dimmed." This explanation contains the idea that Isaac had become blind toward his son Esau, blind to his faults. Hence this verse, set right at the start of the whole episode, clearly indicates the underlying cause of the patriarch's unjustified preference for

dimmed from seeing, that he summoned Esau, his older son, and said to him, "My son." And he said to him, "Here I am." [2] *And he said, "See, now, I have aged; I know not the day of my death.* [3] *Now sharpen, if you please, your gear — your sword and your bow — and go out to the field and hunt game for me.* [4] *Then make me delicacies such as I love and bring it to me and I will eat, so that my soul may bless you before I die."*

Esau. It sheds light on the Torah's appraisal of Isaac's conduct toward his children.

Be that as it may, Isaac's disability turned out to be of benefit to Jacob. Without it he would not have enjoyed the blessings of his father. Under the circumstances, God treated Isaac as a doctor treats a patient who is forbidden to drink wine despite a strong craving for it. In order to appease him, the doctor orders him to be given hot water in the dark, which he will be told is wine (*Rabbah* 65). Because of his blindness, Isaac mistook Jacob for Esau.

וַיֹּאמֶר אֵלָיו הִנֵּנִי — *And he said to him, "Here I am."* Like silver dross laid over an earthen vessel, so are burning lips with a bad heart (*Proverbs* 26:23). This is the image of Esau, who eagerly replies, "Here I am," and yet says in his heart, "When will he die?" as is stated a little further on (verse 41): *"May the days of mourning for my father draw near, then I will kill my brother Jacob"* (*Tanchuma*).

2. הִנֵּה־נָא זָקַנְתִּי — *See, now, I have aged.* Isaac was then 123 years old, and he lived another 57 years. This teaches you that, in our times, with our shorter life expectancy, it is advisable to think of one's ultimate end right from the age of 50, and to be prepared with the "provisions" for the final journey (*Chofetz Chaim*).

3. וְצוּדָה לִי צָיִד — *And hunt game for me.* The letter ה at the end of the word צָיִד as it is written (כְּתִיב) — צידה, indicates that Isaac taught Esau the five criteria for clean animals (cf. *Baal HaTurim, Yoreh De'ah* §79).

4. וַעֲשֵׂה־לִי מַטְעַמִּים — *Then make me delicacies.* Neither Jacob nor Moses had need of a plate of food or any other means of elation in order to give their blessings. If Isaac found this necessary it was for the following reason: although he did not suspect the extent of his son's perversity, he still did not consider Esau worthy of the paternal blessing without his performing some formal act of filial devotion. And so Isaac sent Esau to prepare a plate of tasty food which would give him enjoyment (*Sforno*).

Ramban considers that the sumptuous fare which he liked affected Isaac as music did the prophet Elisha. In his desire to draw the prophetic spirit to himself Elisha exclaimed, "But now bring me a musician." When the musician played, the inspiration of God came upon him (*II Kings* 3:15). To be inspired with רוּחַ הַקֹּדֶשׁ, Divine Inspiration, Isaac had to have recourse to a means of

ה וְרִבְקָה שֹׁמַעַת בְּדַבֵּר יִצְחָק אֶל־עֵשָׂו בְּנוֹ וַיֵּלֶךְ עֵשָׂו הַשָּׂדֶה
ו לָצוּד צַיִד לְהָבִיא: וְרִבְקָה אָמְרָה אֶל־יַעֲקֹב בְּנָהּ לֵאמֹר
הִנֵּה שָׁמַעְתִּי אֶת־אָבִיךָ מְדַבֵּר אֶל־עֵשָׂו אָחִיךָ לֵאמֹר:
ז הָבִיאָה לִּי צַיִד וַעֲשֵׂה־לִי מַטְעַמִּים וְאֹכֵלָה וַאֲבָרֶכְכָה
ח לִפְנֵי יהוה לִפְנֵי מוֹתִי: וְעַתָּה בְנִי שְׁמַע בְּקֹלִי לַאֲשֶׁר

exaltation such as the excellent dish prepared by his firstborn son. This was because the gift of prophecy had forsaken him ever since the pagan women living under his roof filled the house with the smoke of incense which they offered to idols (*Ramban* on 25:34). The first verse of this chapter, which announces Isaac's loss of vision, also means that he had lost his gifts of prophetic vision (*Midrash Rabbah* 65). The feast which he commanded Esau to provide was meant to transport Isaac's soul to a state of exaltation and enable him to draw Divine Inspiration to himself. This was indispensable to Isaac, for the blessing he was just about to give would entrust his son with the Abrahamic mission of universal significance (cf. שעורי דעת by Rabbi Y.L. Bloch of Telshe, Vol. 1, Chapter 15).

בַּעֲבוּר תְּבָרֶכְךָ נַפְשִׁי בְּטֶרֶם אָמוּת — *So that my soul may bless you before I die.* Here *Abarbanel* analyzes the various forms of blessing: those which God addresses to man and those which one man gives to another. But *Ibn Ezra* (on verse 40) explains that our text concerns a blessing of a righteous man, which is essentially a prayer to Providence for the welfare of the one being blessed. This prayer was fulfilled — the blessings were realized — not right away, but as the history of Isaac's descendants unfolded. For the realization of a blessing is not bound just to the one being blessed at the time; it can be fulfilled in the destinies of his off-spring, as *Rashbam* emphasizes (*Deuteronomy* 7:9). Cf. our commentary to 28:4.

בְּטֶרֶם אָמוּת — *Before I die.* A blessing is more effective when given before death, for the soul is more detached from all that is material. For this reason Jacob and Moses gave their blessings before dying (*Sforno*).

5. וְרִבְקָה שֹׁמַעַת — *Now Rebecca was listening.* The verbal form שֹׁמַעַת is equivalent to the present indicative. It means here that she 'kept hearing" Isaac's words through her prophetic spirit, as the *Targum Yonasan* notes. Seen in this light, Rebecca acted under Divine Inspiration and from here on all her words and actions take on still more profound significance. As for Isaac, he also calls upon the prophetic spirit, so that Rebecca will later say to her son that his father wishes to give his blessing to Esau לִפְנֵי ה', *before God,* the only time this phrase is used in this passage. Nevertheless, the true character of his favorite son was not revealed to him; Isaac, even as a prophet, remained mistaken about his children, as noted in our commentary on verse 1.

6. וְרִבְקָה אָמְרָה אֶל־יַעֲקֹב בְּנָהּ — *But Rebecca had said to Jacob her son.* This verse marks the beginning of the conflict which comes to the surface between the

⁵ *Now Rebecca was listening as Isaac spoke to Esau his son; and Esau went to the field to hunt game to bring.* ⁶ *But Rebecca had said to Jacob her son, saying, "Behold I heard your father speaking to your brother Esau saying,* ⁷ *'Bring me some game and make me delicacies to eat, and I will bless you in the presence of HASHEM before my death.'* ⁸ *So now, my son, heed my voice to that which*

husband and wife, after smoldering for a long time right within the home itself. Most of our early commentators refrain from trying to somehow justify Isaac's behavior; it is generally admitted that he made an error in judgment in his blind preference for Esau. As the patriarch prepares to transmit the solemn blessing of his father to Esau, as he is about to invest him with all the dignity of the head of the household and the future head of the messianic nation, Isaac considers his firstborn son worthy of his sacred mission even though he is not unaware of some of his evil deeds. But he believes in Esau. He places his paternal confidence in his firstborn son. Isaac is convinced that Esau will succeed in improving himself and vanquishing his adolescent penchants. He blesses him with the hope that "God will agree" (*Rashi*) with his words and that Esau would have Heaven's help to overcome his weaknesses (*R' Chaim ben Attar*).

"Never will anyone be able to equal Esau in fulfilling the duty of filial devotion," report the Sages of the Midrash (*Rabbah*, 65). Accordingly, we might suppose that with the realization of this eminent virtue in his son, Isaac felt that Esau was fit to become the repository of the high family traditions and the herald of the sacred message of Abraham.

But Rebecca was not taken in. Often, a mother understands the nature and character of her children better than the father. She had long known that Esau's wicked instinct outweighed his good qualities. She knew of his duplicity, his hypocrisy, his appetite for the sensual, his brutality to animals, and his desire for monetary gain. In her eyes, Esau was a materialist to the depths of his soul, while Jacob embodies the idealistic spirit of Abraham and Isaac with his whole being.

Furthermore, Rebecca had not forgotten the revelation she received during her pregnancy with the twins — *the elder shall serve the younger* (25:33). However, she had never told her husband about this revelation, either because it had been given to her as a secret for herself alone (cf. our commentary, ibid.) — which she did not intend to divulge and thus risk opposing the plans of Providence (*Ramban*) — or else because she was extremely reserved in her relationship with Isaac. Right from the moment she first met her future husband she *took her veil and covered herself* (24:65); she was always humble and modest in his presence. This reserve kept her from speaking frankly about her problems or worries as Sarah had done with Abraham and Rachel with Jacob (נצי"ב). Hence, Rebecca never told him that she disagreed with the blind confidence he placed in their son Esau.

ט אֲנִי מְצַוֶּה אֹתָךְ: לֶךְ־נָא אֶל־הַצֹּאן וְקַח־לִי מִשָּׁם שְׁנֵי גְּדָיֵי
עִזִּים טֹבִים וְאֶעֱשֶׂה אֹתָם מַטְעַמִּים לְאָבִיךָ כַּאֲשֶׁר אָהֵב:
יא וְהֵבֵאתָ לְאָבִיךָ וְאָכָל בַּעֲבֻר אֲשֶׁר יְבָרֶכְךָ לִפְנֵי מוֹתוֹ: וַיֹּאמֶר
יַעֲקֹב אֶל־רִבְקָה אִמּוֹ הֵן עֵשָׂו אָחִי אִישׁ שָׂעִר וְאָנֹכִי אִישׁ
יב חָלָק: אוּלַי יְמֻשֵּׁנִי אָבִי וְהָיִיתִי בְעֵינָיו כִּמְתַעְתֵּעַ וְהֵבֵאתִי
יג עָלַי קְלָלָה וְלֹא בְרָכָה: וַתֹּאמֶר לוֹ אִמּוֹ עָלַי קִלְלָתְךָ בְּנִי
יד אַךְ שְׁמַע בְּקֹלִי וְלֵךְ קַח־לִי: וַיֵּלֶךְ וַיִּקַּח וַיָּבֵא לְאִמּוֹ וַתַּעַשׂ
טו אִמּוֹ מַטְעַמִּים כַּאֲשֶׁר אָהֵב אָבִיו: וַתִּקַּח רִבְקָה אֶת־בִּגְדֵי
עֵשָׂו בְּנָהּ הַגָּדֹל הַחֲמֻדֹת אֲשֶׁר אִתָּהּ בַּבָּיִת וַתַּלְבֵּשׁ
טז אֶת־יַעֲקֹב בְּנָהּ הַקָּטָן: וְאֵת עֹרֹת גְּדָיֵי הָעִזִּים הִלְבִּישָׁה
יז עַל־יָדָיו וְעַל חֶלְקַת צַוָּארָיו: וַתִּתֵּן אֶת־הַמַּטְעַמִּים וְאֶת־
יח הַלֶּחֶם אֲשֶׁר עָשָׂתָה בְּיַד יַעֲקֹב בְּנָהּ: וַיָּבֹא אֶל־אָבִיו
יט וַיֹּאמֶר אָבִי וַיֹּאמֶר הִנֶּנִּי מִי אַתָּה בְּנִי: וַיֹּאמֶר יַעֲקֹב אֶל־
אָבִיו אָנֹכִי עֵשָׂו בְּכֹרֶךָ עָשִׂיתִי כַּאֲשֶׁר דִּבַּרְתָּ אֵלָי קוּם־נָא
כ שְׁבָה וְאָכְלָה מִצֵּידִי בַּעֲבוּר תְּבָרֲכַנִּי נַפְשֶׁךָ: וַיֹּאמֶר יִצְחָק
אֶל־בְּנוֹ מַה־זֶּה מִהַרְתָּ לִמְצֹא בְּנִי וַיֹּאמֶר כִּי הִקְרָה יהוה
כא אֱלֹהֶיךָ לְפָנָי: וַיֹּאמֶר יִצְחָק אֶל־יַעֲקֹב גְּשָׁה־נָּא וַאֲמֻשְׁךָ
כב בְּנִי הַאַתָּה זֶה בְּנִי עֵשָׂו אִם־לֹא: וַיִּגַּשׁ יַעֲקֹב אֶל־יִצְחָק
אָבִיו וַיְמֻשֵּׁהוּ וַיֹּאמֶר הַקֹּל קוֹל יַעֲקֹב וְהַיָּדַיִם יְדֵי עֵשָׂו:

9. שְׁנֵי גְּדָיֵי עִזִּים טֹבִים — *Two choice young kids of the goats.* Was Isaac's meal, then, made up of both kids? One was destined to be the paschal sacrifice and the other she made into a good meal. This explanation, given by *Rashi*, refers to the tradition that Isaac blessed his son on the day on which Pesach would take place in the future. But the *Zohar* adds in the name of R' Yehudah that the two kids are the counterparts of the two goats which the children of Jacob would one day be called upon to sacrifice in the Yom Kippur service. One of these two goats will be offered in homage to God; the other will be the atoning sacrifice laden with Jewry's sins. Thus they bring atonement for the acts, carried out using the two kids, which caused strife between the two brothers (cf. *Ramban* on *Leviticus* 16:8; cf. also *Tanchuma*, in the name of R' Helbo).

13. עָלַי קִלְלָתְךָ בְּנִי — *Your curse be on me, my son.* Rebecca allayed his fears, saying: "When Adam was cursed, it was upon his mother, symbolized by the earth that the curse fell. I too am prepared to take your curse upon myself. Besides, if the worst comes about, I would go to your father and say to him, 'Esau is wicked and Jacob is righteous.'" She was absolutely sure of herself, for she had received the prophetic assurance that "the elder shall serve the younger" (*Midrash HaGadol* and *Targum*).

I command you. ⁹ *Go now to the flock and fetch me from there two choice young kids of the goats, and I will make of them delicacies for your father, as he loves.* ¹⁰ *Then bring it to your father and he shall eat, so that he may bless you before his death."*

¹¹ *Jacob replied to Rebecca, his mother, "But my brother Esau is a hairy man and I am a smooth-skinned man.* ¹² *Perhaps my father will feel me and I shall be as a mocker in his eyes; I will thus bring upon myself a curse rather than a blessing."* ¹³ *But his mother said to him, "Your curse be on me, my son; only heed my voice and go fetch them for me."* ¹⁴ *So he went, fetched, and brought to his mother, and his mother made delicacies as his father loved.* ¹⁵ *Rebecca then took her older son Esau's clean garments which were with her in the house, and clothed Jacob her young son.* ¹⁶ *With the skins of the goat-kids she covered his arms and the his smooth-skinned neck.* ¹⁷ *She placed the delicacies and the bread which she had made into the hand of her son Jacob.*

¹⁸ *And he came to his father and said, "Father," and he said, "Here I am; who are you, my son?"* ¹⁹ *Jacob said to his father, "It is I, Esau your firstborn; I have done as you told me; rise up, please, sit and eat of my game that your soul may bless me."*

²⁰ *Isaac said to his son, "How is it that you were so quick to find, my son?" And he said, "Because HASHEM your God arranged it for me."* ²¹ *And Isaac said to Jacob, "Come close, if you please, so I can feel you, my son; are you, indeed, my son Esau or not?"*

²² *So Jacob drew close to Isaac his father who felt him and said, "The voice is Jacob's voice, but the hands are Esau's hands."*

14. וַיֵּלֶךְ וַיִּקַּח וַיָּבֵא לְאִמּוֹ — *So he went, fetched, and brought to his mother.* Each of these actions is mentioned separately. This indicates that each required a conscious effort on Jacob's part. It pained him to do them. He did them reluctantly and solely out of obedience to his mother (*Midrash*). Accordingly, observes R' E. Dessler, Jacob cannot be considered a common liar; it is rather Esau, the hypocrite, the one who knew how to brag about his integrity, who deserves this epithet (*Michtav Me'Eliyah*).

20. הִקְרָה ה' אֱלֹהֶיךָ לְפָנָי — *HASHEM, your God, arranged it for me.* This term designates a fortuitous meeting, due to good luck. Such meetings had already occurred on two occasions in Isaac's life — at the sacrifice on Mount Moriah (22:13) and on the occasion of his marriage (24:12) — and the son did not miss pointing this out to his father (*Midrash*).

22. הַקֹּל קוֹל יַעֲקֹב — *The voice is Jacob's voice.* Our Sages interpret: Jacob's only power lay in his voice, the voice of prayer and the study of Torah. But Esau's weapons are none other than his hands, i.e. brute strength. "The nations of the

כג וְלֹא הִכִּירוֹ כִּי־הָיוּ יָדָיו כִּידֵי עֵשָׂו אָחִיו שְׂעִרֹת וַיְבָרְכֵהוּ:

כד-כה וַיֹּאמֶר אַתָּה זֶה בְּנִי עֵשָׂו וַיֹּאמֶר אָנִי: וַיֹּאמֶר הַגִּשָׁה לִּי
וְאֹכְלָה מִצֵּיד בְּנִי לְמַעַן תְּבָרֶכְךָ נַפְשִׁי וַיַּגֶּשׁ־לוֹ וַיֹּאכַל וַיָּבֵא

כו לוֹ יַיִן וַיֵּשְׁתְּ: וַיֹּאמֶר אֵלָיו יִצְחָק אָבִיו גְּשָׁה־נָּא וּשְׁקָה־

כז לִּי בְּנִי: וַיִּגַּשׁ וַיִּשַּׁק־לוֹ וַיָּרַח אֶת־רֵיחַ בְּגָדָיו וַיְבָרְכֵהוּ

ששי   כח וַיֹּאמֶר רְאֵה רֵיחַ בְּנִי כְּרֵיחַ שָׂדֶה אֲשֶׁר בֵּרְכוֹ יהוה: וְיִתֶּן־
לְךָ הָאֱלֹהִים מִטַּל הַשָּׁמַיִם וּמִשְׁמַנֵּי הָאָרֶץ וְרֹב דָּגָן

world have had no greater philosopher than Balaam the son of Beor. They came to him and asked, 'Do you think that we will be able to defeat this nation (the Jews)?' He replied, 'Go and see their synagogues and houses of study. If you find children there who make their voices heard, you will have no power over them. For their ancestor promised them, 'As long as the voice of Jacob is heard, the hands of Esau are powerless against him' " (*Midrash*).

25. וַיָּבֵא לוֹ יַיִן וַיֵּשְׁתְּ — *He brought him wine and he drank.* The prosodists, determined to stress this phrase, marked the word לוֹ with the very rare tonic accent ("note") מֵרְכָא־כְּפוּלָה. In this way they draw our attention to what remains unexpressed in this verse, namely, the miracle which must have occurred for Jacob to offer his father wine even though he had received none from his mother. The *Targum Yonasan* explains that an angel came to bring Jacob tasty wine which had been kept in its grapes since the creation of the world. This wine brought out blessings, and not the opposite as is frequently the case with ordinary wine. It spurred Isaac on to give his blessing, just as this same wine had previously done with King Malki-Zedek of Shalem (14:18) (*Tanchuma*).

27. וַיָּרַח אֶת רֵיחַ בְּגָדָיו — *He smelled the fragrance of his garments.* But there is no odor more disagreeable than that of the hide of the goat! This teaches us that it had been permeated with a fragrance of the Garden of Eden. To this explanation given by *Rashi*, the *Zohar* adds, "The clothes worn by Jacob belonged to Esau, who through covetousness had taken them from King Nimrod, the great hunter. They had originally belonged to the first couple when they lived in Paradise (as was mentioned above in our commentary to 25:27). Noah kept them in the Ark during the Flood, Nimrod subsequently appropriated them for himself, and then Esau took possession of them; but by that time they had lost the celestial fragrance of the Garden of Eden. Nevertheless, as soon as Jacob clothed himself in them they regained their original fragrance. For Jacob had the same physiognomy as Adam; he was a pure and righteous being, formed in the image of the first man." (Before his death, Jacob bequeathed these clothes to Joseph. Cf. our commentary to 48:22.)

How did Isaac recognize the fragrance of "a field which Hashem had blessed," i.e. of Paradise? He sensed the same sublime fragrance which had enveloped him while he was bound as a sacrifice on the altar on Mount Moriah

²³ *But he did not recognize him because his hands were hairy like those of Esau his brother; so he blessed him.* ²⁴ *He said, "You are, indeed, my son Esau!" And he said, "I am."* ²⁵ *He said, "Serve me and let me eat of my son's game that my soul may bless you." So he served him and he ate, and he brought him wine and he drank.*

²⁶ *Then his father Isaac said to him, "Come close, if you please, and kiss me, my son."* ²⁷ *So he drew close and kissed him; he smelled the fragrance of his garments and blessed him; he said, "See, the fragrance of my son is like the fragrance of a field which HASHEM had blessed —* ²⁸ *And may God give you of the dew of the heavens and of the fatness of the earth, and abundant grain*

(מוֹרִיָּה derived from מוֹר, *myrrh*); it was the same fragrance which he had known when he used to pray in the field beside the cave of Machpelah, his mother's burial place (cf. our commentary to 24:63). Isaac recognized this wondrous perfume of Paradise which he had not encountered for so many years and at once he understood that the son now before him was a holy person, an angel, worthy of his blessing. He blessed him without hesitation. Moreover, it is with these exceptional circumstances still in his thoughts that Isaac later will insist to Esau: גַּם־בָּרוּךְ יִהְיֶה, *Indeed, he shall remain blessed!* (verse 33).

28. וְיִתֶּן־לְךָ הָאֱלֹהִים מִטַּל הַשָּׁמַיִם — *And may God give you of the dew of the heavens.* The *Zohar* gives these blessings, and the exceptional circumstances surrounded them, a deeper meaning. It sees them as the first step in repairing the harm caused to humanity by the ruses and lies of the serpent of Paradise at the beginning of *Genesis*. The treacherous serpent provoked the first sin, which brought a curse on mankind and on the earth itself. And that is how the forces of evil deprive man of the kindnesses and bliss which God has reserved for humanity. Now, Jacob was the first man capable of restoring to the earth the initial blessings which the Creator had wanted to lavish upon it. Physically and morally, he resembled Adam. He was the beloved of God (*Malachi* 1:2), destined to inaugurate a new cycle of blessings upon terrestrial life. But this honest and loyal man was obliged to resort to trickery in order to recapture the prize of the blessings, blessings which the forces of evil had snatched away from men by similar means. To the words earlier in *Genesis* וְהַנָּחָשׁ הָיָה עָרוּם (3:1), *the serpent was cunning*, the phrase in our passage answers back: בָּא אָחִיךָ בְּמִרְמָה (v. 35), *your brother came with cleverness.*

Thus Jacob regained the blessings, initially destined for the righteous and pious, but which fell into the hands of the wicked only through guile and trickery. Until now, the blessing received by the patriarchs Abraham and Isaac referred to their offspring, to the Promised Land, or to the future of the family of Abraham. But the blessing addressed to Jacob concerns material wealth, the fertility of the soil, and the prosperity of the earth. At last the curse pronounced on the earth, and on man who must work it since the time of the first sin, seems to have been lifted. The righteous can once again hope to live in peace with God

וְיִשְׁתַּחֲוּ ק' כט וְתִירֹֽשׁ: יַֽעַבְדוּךָ עַמִּים °וְיִשְׁתַּחֲוּ לְךָ לְאֻמִּים הֱוֵה גְבִיר
לְאַחֶיךָ וְיִשְׁתַּחֲוּ לְךָ בְּנֵי אִמֶּךָ אֹרְרֶיךָ אָרוּר וּֽמְבָרְכֶיךָ
בָּרֽוּךְ: ל וַיְהִי כַּֽאֲשֶׁר כִּלָּה יִצְחָק לְבָרֵךְ אֶֽת־יַֽעֲקֹב וַיְהִי אַךְ
יָצֹא יָצָא יַֽעֲקֹב מֵאֵת פְּנֵי יִצְחָק אָבִיו וְעֵשָׂו אָחִיו בָּא מִצֵּידֽוֹ:
לא וַיַּעַשׂ גַּם־הוּא מַטְעַמִּים וַיָּבֵא לְאָבִיו וַיֹּאמֶר לְאָבִיו יָקֻם אָבִי
וְיֹאכַל מִצֵּיד בְּנוֹ בַּֽעֲבֻר תְּבָֽרְכַנִּי נַפְשֶׁךָ: לב וַיֹּאמֶר לוֹ יִצְחָק
אָבִיו מִי־אָתָּה וַיֹּאמֶר אֲנִי בִּנְךָ בְכֹֽרְךָ עֵשָׂו: לג וַיֶּֽחֱרַד יִצְחָק
חֲרָדָה גְּדֹלָה עַד־מְאֹד וַיֹּאמֶר מִֽי־אֵפוֹא הוּא הַצָּֽד־

and nature in a Garden of Eden, as had been the design of the Divine plan right
from Creation.

Seen in this perspective, the first phrase וְיִתֶּן־לְךָ הָֽאֱלֹהִים מִטַּל הַשָּׁמַיִם, *and
may God give you of the dew of the heavens*, is the reply to the curse on
Adam: בְּעִצָּבוֹן תֹּאכֲלֶנָּה, *through suffering shall you eat of it* (3:17). The next
phrase, וּמִשְׁמַנֵּי הָאָרֶץ, *and of the fatness of the earth*, supplants the words
אֲרוּרָה הָֽאֲדָמָה בַּֽעֲבוּרֶךָ, *accursed is the ground because of you* (ibid.). The
words וְרֹב דָּגָן וְתִירשׁ, *and abundant grain and wine*, come to annul the curse,
וְקוֹץ וְדַרְדַּר תַּצְמִיחַ *thorns and thistles shall it sprout for you* (ibid. v. 18).
Lastly, the blessing יַֽעַבְדוּךָ עַמִּים, *peoples will serve you*, abolishes the
verdict, בְּזֵעַת אַפֶּיךָ תֹּאכַל לֶחֶם, *by the sweat of your brow shall you eat bread*
(ibid. v. 19).

But these blessings were not given unconditionally. The Divine name אֱלֹהִים,
invoked at the beginning of the first sentence, designates God as Supreme
Judge (מִדַּת הַדִּין) and emphasizes that the blessings are given subject to the
criterion of justice based on personal merit. "If it is due to you, He will give it
to you; and if not, He will not give it to you," says *Rashi*. And further on, when
Esau was blessed after Jacob had been made his master, *Rashi* says: "When
Jewry will transgress against the Torah and you will have reason to moan and
to complain about the blessings accorded him, then you will throw off his
yoke" (verse 40).

In fact, notes the *Zohar*, Jacob and his descendants have never enjoyed the
rich material blessings given by Isaac. They are still being kept for the future.
Cf. our commentary to 28:4.

30. כַּֽאֲשֶׁר כִּלָּה יִצְחָק לְבָרֵךְ אֶֽת־יַֽעֲקֹב — *When Isaac had finished blessing Jacob.*
The letter ל in the word כִּלָּה is one of the 44 in the Torah whose vertical stroke
is to be curved back (ס' התגין). This form must allude to the fact that the
blessing just pronounced departs from the celestial heights and comes down to
this world. Indeed, in it God Himself is invoked as the dispenser of the blessing
(וְיִתֶּן לְךָ הָֽאֱלֹהִים), whereas the parallel blessing addressed to Esau makes no
mention of the name of God, so that it can be interpreted as being simply the
fortuitous result of natural circumstances.

and wine. ²⁹ *Peoples will serve you, and regimes will prostrate themselves to you; be a lord to your kinsmen, and your mother's sons will prostrate themselves to you; cursed be they who curse you, and blessed be they who bless you."*

³⁰ *And it was, when Isaac had finished blessing Jacob, and Jacob had scarcely left from the presence of Isaac his father, that Esau his brother came back from his hunt.* ³¹ *He, too, made delicacies, and brought them to his father; he said to his father, "Let my father rise and eat of his son's game, so that your soul will bless me."*

³² *Isaac his father said to him, "Who are you?" And he said, "I am your firstborn son Esau."* ³³ *Then Isaac trembled in very great perplexity, and said, "Who — where — is the one who hunted*

וַיְהִי אַךְ יָצֹא יָצָא יַעֲקֹב מֵאֵת פְּנֵי יִצְחָק אָבִיו — *And Jacob had scarcely left from the presence of Isaac his father.* In the figurative sense: Jacob/Israel no sooner leaves the path of his fathers than Esau, his rival brother, comes to threaten him with his weapons (*Midrash*).

33. וַיֶּחֱרַד יִצְחָק חֲרָדָה גְדֹלָה עַד־מְאֹד — *Then Isaac trembled in very great perplexity.* Rashi explains, quoting the Midrash, "He saw Hell opened before him." It was at this moment that Isaac realized, in a flash, just how completely he had misjudged the character of his son Esau. With Jacob in his presence he had sensed the fragrance of Paradise and, as it were, a mysterious presence which made him want to give the richest and most perfect blessing. And so, when Esau entered, Isaac wondered, "Who, — where — is the one?" מִי אֵפוֹא = אֵיפֹה. But this invisible force now abandoned Isaac and when Esau arrived the vision of Hell replaced the sublime fragrance of Paradise. He understood that Jacob had been surrounded by the holy presence of the *Shechinah.* It was not so with Esau. And Isaac then became terrified. "What do the words עַד מְאֹד mean? They indicate that Isaac had never known such fear in his whole life. Even when bound to the altar to be sacrificed, even when the knife was at his throat, he had not been gripped with a fear such as he experienced when Esau entered and he saw the abyss begin to open before him" (*Zohar*).

גַּם־בָּרוּךְ יִהְיֶה — *Indeed, he shall remain blessed.* It was like a heavenly voice which spoke these words when Isaac had said, "I partook of all when you had not yet come and I blessed him." Come and see how all approved of the blessing given to Jacob, the higher beings as well as the lower ones. Even the guardian spirit of Esau finally consented to the blessings received by Jacob although they were meant for Esau (*Genesis* 32:27). When they met that night, Jacob declared to Esau's guardian spirit, *I will not let you go unless you bless me* (32:27) [read not *unless you bless me* — for the verb is in the past tense — but *unless you approve of my previous blessings*]. And he blessed him there (וַיְבָרֶךְ אֹתוֹ שָׁם; 32:30), that is, he acknowledged all the blessings which Jacob had received from his father (*Zohar*).

צַיִד וָאֹבַל מִכֹּל בְּטֶרֶם תָּבוֹא וָאֲבָרֲכֵהוּ גַּם־
לד בָּרוּךְ יִהְיֶה: כִּשְׁמֹעַ עֵשָׂו אֶת־דִּבְרֵי אָבִיו וַיִּצְעַק צְעָקָה
גְדֹלָה וּמָרָה עַד־מְאֹד וַיֹּאמֶר לְאָבִיו בָּרֲכֵנִי גַם־אָנִי
לה-לו אָבִי: וַיֹּאמֶר בָּא אָחִיךָ בְּמִרְמָה וַיִּקַּח בִּרְכָתֶךָ: וַיֹּאמֶר הֲכִי
קָרָא שְׁמוֹ יַעֲקֹב וַיַּעְקְבֵנִי זֶה פַעֲמַיִם אֶת־בְּכֹרָתִי לָקָח
וְהִנֵּה עַתָּה לָקַח בִּרְכָתִי וַיֹּאמַר הֲלֹא־אָצַלְתָּ לִּי בְּרָכָה:

34. עֵשָׂו ... וַיִּצְעַק צְעָקָה גְדֹלָה וּמָרָה — *Esau ... he cried out an exceedingly great
and bitter cry.* R' Chanina (*Rabbah*, 67) severely criticizes those who profess
that God is magnanimous and absolves the righteous of wrongs which they
commit. God only "extends time to debtors." He is long-suffering but
ultimately exacts His payment. Consider the patriarch Jacob, who caused Esau
to cry bitterly. These cries were repaid in Shushan, where Jacob's offspring also
cried out bitterly on account of Esau's descendants, as recorded in *Esther* (4:1).
Esau shed three tears, says the *Midrash Tanchuma*: One fell from his right eye,
one from the left eye and the third, the bitterest, he held back and never let fall.
It is this third tear which has us eat "a bread of tears" and drink "tears in great
measure" (*Psalms* 80:6) during our exile.

The *Zohar* quotes several other examples of punishments inflicted upon
Jacob or his posterity which correspond in their nature to wrongs done to Esau
(following the principle of מִדָּה כְּנֶגֶד מִדָּה). Concludes the *Zohar*, "He was
punished despite the fact that God approved of the blessings. This shows us
that everything is repaid, even wrongs committed against others but which
come from an action which in itself is good and just."

35. בְּמִרְמָה — *With cleverness.* On having to resort to guile in order to obtain
the blessing, see our commentary to verse 28 and to 25:26.

Rashi explains, after Onkelos בְּחָכְמְתָא, "with intelligence," probably
alluding to the verse in *Proverbs*, אֲנִי חָכְמָה שָׁכַנְתִּי עָרְמָה, *I, intelligence, dwell
with guile* (8:12). This expression means that guile is the daughter of
intelligence. To *Ibn Ezra*, Jacob is beguiled by lying, but the author of *Sefer
Chassidim* attempts to show that he was not guilty of any real falsehood
(§946). *Rambam* defines the term עָרְמָה as a permissible ruse and the term מִרְמָה
as a prohibited ruse (פיה"מ ריש פ"ד תמורה). But this definition refers to terms
used in the Mishnah, terms whose meanings differ from the Biblical terms (תוס'
ט"י ibid.). Nevertheless, right from the moment he blessed Jacob, Isaac had had
the revelation that Jacob deserved this blessing and was to remain its
beneficiary. Accordingly, he replied to Esau: "He has acquired your blessing
even though he came with guile!" (cf. *Ramban*).

36. הֲכִי קָרָא שְׁמוֹ יַעֲקֹב — *Is it because his name was called Jacob.* Esau does not
say נִקְרָא שְׁמוֹ יַעֲקֹב — *he is named Jacob* — but uses a form which could mean
"He called him Jacob," alluding to God, Who had given him this name, as
Rashi mentions on 25:26. Esau spluttered in rage as he spoke these words and

game, brought it to me, and I partook of all when you had not yet come, and I blessed him? Indeed, he shall remain blessed!"

³⁴ *When Esau heard his father's words, he cried out an exceedingly great and bitter cry, and said to his father, "Bless me too, Father!"*

³⁵ *But he said, "Your brother came with cleverness and took your blessing."*

³⁶ *He said, "Is it because his name was called Jacob that he outwitted me these two times? — He took away my birthright and see, now he took away my blessing!" Then he said, "Have you not reserved a blessing for me?"*

cried out, "He has ambushed me twice: he took my birthright and he just now took my blessing!" The demonstrative pronoun זֶה in the phrase זֶה פַעֲמַיִם (*these two times*), indicates that the trickery concerned "this same word" twice, namely, the word בְּכֹרָתִי, which is reversible to give בִּרְכָתִי. Until now, Esau had attached no value to the birthright. He had totally despised it. But now he discovered that the rich ancestral blessings depended on this right! Too late he realized that בְּרָכָה and בְּכֹרָה form only one word (*Zohar*).

וַיַּעְקְבֵנִי זֶה פַעֲמַיִם — *He outwitted me these two times.* Cf. our commentary to 25:26, concerning *Onkelos'* translation of the word וַיַּעְקְבֵנִי — *he has outsmarted me.* But, *Ibn Ezra* relates this term to עָקֹב and, as in the phrase עָקֹב הַלֵּב (*Jeremiah* 17:9), it means "to take a crooked, cunning route." According to *Rashi*, "to set a trap." Be that as it may, the name יַעֲקֹב includes the idea of a devious path pursued with malice or guile to reach one's ends.

This definition of Jacob's name is confirmed by the fact that he was led to trick his brother on two occasions. But still it stands in strange contrast to that characteristic of Jacob — *God has bestowed truth unto Jacob* — mentioned by the prophet Michah (7:20) and repeated by philosophers and Kabbalists as the predominant quality of his personality and the ideal to be achieved in his life. This patriarch, by nature honest and full of integrity, dwelling peacefully in his tent (25:27) and enamored of truth, was to struggle his whole life through with adversaries such as Esau and Laban, individuals full of deceit, hypocrisy, and guile. He later saw hatred and lies even among his own children (with Joseph and his brothers) and witnessed the trickery of Simeon and Levi regarding Shechem. This tragic personage was obliged to settle the moral conflicts which Providence seemed to reserve for him more than for anyone else. But the painful trials thrust upon him gave Jacob the opportunity of raising the virtue of truth to its highest perfection, through unrelenting confrontation with the elements opposing it. In this life-struggle, Jacob remained pure and honest. Truth always wins out in the end and Jacob emerged from his ordeals with greater stature and nobility.

But with its wealth of detail describing the episode of the blessing taken from Esau, the Torah also wants to make us see that guile and cleverness are the

לז וַיַּעַן יִצְחָק וַיֹּאמֶר לְעֵשָׂו הֵן גְּבִיר שַׂמְתִּיו לָךְ וְאֶת־כָּל־
אֶחָיו נָתַתִּי לוֹ לַעֲבָדִים וְדָגָן וְתִירֹשׁ סְמַכְתִּיו וּלְכָה אֵפוֹא
לח מָה אֶעֱשֶׂה בְּנִי: וַיֹּאמֶר עֵשָׂו אֶל־אָבִיו הַבְרָכָה אַחַת
הִוא־לְךָ אָבִי בָּרֲכֵנִי גַם־אָנִי אָבִי וַיִּשָּׂא עֵשָׂו קֹלוֹ וַיֵּבְךְּ:
לט וַיַּעַן יִצְחָק אָבִיו וַיֹּאמֶר אֵלָיו הִנֵּה מִשְׁמַנֵּי הָאָרֶץ יִהְיֶה
מ מוֹשָׁבֶךָ וּמִטַּל הַשָּׁמַיִם מֵעָל: וְעַל־חַרְבְּךָ תִחְיֶה וְאֶת־

defenses which Jacob — the symbol of the entire Jewish nation — is at times
compelled to use in the struggle against his rival Esau. The latter has no scruples
when it comes to pursuing his goals; he does not hesitate to resort to hypocritical
lies and deceit. In its millennial combat against the enemies which threaten
its very existence, the Jewish people has been confronted with impossible
situations and was within its rights to act as the patriarch did. When the
struggle is perilous and unequal, Jacob's descendants are able to use devious
means to escape from the dangerous, ruthless enemy. The theme of their right
to do so in case of moral or physical danger is developed both in the Talmud
(*Megillah* 13b) and the *Zohar*: the conclusions have been mentioned in our
commentary to 25:26.

However, this recourse to "crooked paths" can only be of a temporary nature.
Jacob, whose name alludes to these paths, did not keep this name for long. God
Who had given him this name soon changed it, saying, *Your name shall not
always be called Jacob, but Israel* (35:10). And *Rashi* explains: "The name
'Jacob' designates one who lies in wait to take someone by surprise (עָקְבָה), but
you will bear the name 'Israel,' which means princely (שַׂר) and noble." This
change thus indicates Jacob's accession to a higher level of achievement with
respect to his holy mission of "fighting for God — יִשְׂרָאֵל" (following 32:29).
Nevertheless, the name Jacob does not permanently disappear; it frequently
appears beside the name Israel. The ways and means indicated by the name
Jacob continue to operate over the long centuries of the epic struggle between
Israel and his brothers, i.e., between the Jewish and non-Jewish worlds. Only at
the end of time will the third name, Jeshurun, completely replace that of Jacob.
For the name Jeshurun signifies uprightness (derived from יָשָׁר). It only appears
in the last chapters of the Torah which open up the perspective on the end of
time, and it emphasizes that Jewry will then at last follow a straight and
unswerving path, without detours and without straying. It is of this epoch that
the prophet Isaiah speaks when he proclaims (40:4): וְהָיָה הֶעָקֹב לְמִישׁוֹר, *the
crooked shall be made straight* (עָקֹב and מִישׁוֹר reflect the two names יַעֲקֹב,
Jacob, and יְשׁוּרוּן, Jeshurun).

37. וּלְכָה אֵפוֹא מָה אֶעֱשֶׂה בְּנִי — *And for you, where — what can I do, my son?* The
unusual spelling of וּלְךָ, written here וּלְכָה, prompts the *Targum Yonasan* to give
it the sense of הֲלִיכָה and to translate, "Go away, do not bother me." Similarly,
R' Shimon ben Lakish adds his interpretation of the word אֵפוֹא as related to אַף,

³⁷ *Isaac answered, and said to Esau, "Behold, a lord have I made him over you, and all his kin have I given him as servants; with grain and wine have I supported him, and for you, where — what can I do, my son?"*

³⁸ *And Esau said to his father, "Have you but one blessing, Father? Bless me too, Father!" And Esau raised his voice and wept.*

³⁹ *So Isaac his father answered, and said to him: "Behold, of the fatness of the earth shall be your dwelling and of the dew of the heavens from above. ⁴⁰ By your sword you shall live, but your*

anger. Anger was one of Esau's bad qualities; his mother was in dread of its effects (verse 45; *Rabbah* 67). The expression וּלְכָה אֵפוֹא thus assumes the meaning, "Go away, quick-tempered one!"

After seeing how he misjudged Esau, Isaac considers him unworthy of any blessing. But Esau answers his father cleverly — he, with Cain and Menasheh son of Chizkiyah, was one of the people who made objections which on the surface seemed quite relevant (*Sanhedrin* 101b) — saying, "Have you but one blessing, my father? Had Jacob and I both been righteous, would not your God have had two blessings for us?" (Likewise, Jacob will bless his twelve sons with a different blessing for each.) And when Isaac saw his son burst into tears he pitied him and blessed him. For, despite everything, Esau remained his beloved son (cf. *Rashi* on *Psalms* 80:16) because of the close similarly in their characters, as was quoted from the *Zohar* in our commentary to 25:28. Isaac still affectionately calls Esau בְּנִי, *my son.*

39. הִנֵּה מִשְׁמַנֵּי הָאָרֶץ יִהְיֶה מוֹשָׁבֶךָ — *Behold, of the fatness of the earth shall be your dwelling.* *Rashi,* quoting the Midrash, explains: "This is the Italy of the Greeks." (See our commentary to 25:26.) The same words — מִשְׁמַנֵּי הָאָרֶץ — are employed in the blessing addressed to Jacob and refer there to the soil of the Promised Land, which the patriarch bequeaths to him (28:4). The Midrash concludes from this that "of the fatness of the earth shall be your dwelling" promised to Esau also refer to a land just as fertile, none other than Italy.

וּמִטַּל הַשָּׁמַיִם מֵעַל — *And of the dew of the heavens from above.* R' Shimon bar Yochai said: Although the blessings for Jacob are given in almost the same terms, do not think that they are identical. They are in fact quite divergent. For his son Jacob, the patriarch asks for blessings granted by God Himself — וְיִתֶּן לְךָ הָאֱלֹהִים. But the blessings for Esau, although similar in content, do not evoke the Divine name; this indicates that they might result solely from the interplay of the laws of nature and not from any special act of Providence.

Moreover, in Esau's blessing, but not in Jacob's, *the fatness of the earth* precedes *the dew of the heavens.* This matches the spiritual outlook of the two brothers. In Esau's eyes the good things of the earth take precedence over the benefits coming from heaven. Jacob's outlook, on the other hand, is directed more to heaven and the blessings coming down from the celestial spheres are

אָחִיךָ תַּעֲבֹד וְהָיָה כַּאֲשֶׁר תָּרִיד וּפָרַקְתָּ עֻלּוֹ מֵעַל צַוָּארֶךָ:

מא וַיִּשְׂטֹם עֵשָׂו אֶת־יַעֲקֹב עַל־הַבְּרָכָה אֲשֶׁר בֵּרְכוֹ אָבִיו וַיֹּאמֶר
עֵשָׂו בְּלִבּוֹ יִקְרְבוּ יְמֵי אֵבֶל אָבִי וְאַהַרְגָה אֶת־יַעֲקֹב אָחִי:

מב וַיֻּגַּד לְרִבְקָה אֶת־דִּבְרֵי עֵשָׂו בְּנָהּ הַגָּדֹל וַתִּשְׁלַח וַתִּקְרָא
לְיַעֲקֹב בְּנָהּ הַקָּטָן וַתֹּאמֶר אֵלָיו הִנֵּה עֵשָׂו אָחִיךָ מִתְנַחֵם
לְךָ לְהָרְגֶךָ: מג וְעַתָּה בְנִי שְׁמַע בְּקֹלִי וְקוּם בְּרַח־לְךָ אֶל־

dearer to him than those which depend on the fertility of the soil. And each
material blessing he sees only as the earthly reflection of a spiritual blessing; and
these spiritual blessings are infinitely more precious to him than mere material
blessings (*Zohar*).

40. וְעַל־חַרְבְּךָ תִחְיֶה — *By your sword you shall live.* When Jacob came before
him, Isaac sensed at once the presence of the *Shechinah* and prophetic
inspiration. But these had completely forsaken him when Esau arrived. He knew
then that Esau would not be the spiritual heir of the patriarchs and he implored
God to grant him at least the blessings of this world, befitting his character and
his tastes. And so, he gave him the blessing for his exploits in battle in view of
his love of hunting and war (ibid.).

וְאֶת־אָחִיךָ תַּעֲבֹד — *But your brother you shall serve.* This prediction has not yet
come to pass: Esau has never served Jacob. For Jacob did not wish to make use
of the privilege accorded him in the words: *be a lord to your kinsmen* (verse 29).
Accordingly, several times he called his brother אֲדֹנִי, *my lord.* Indeed, Jacob
moved far away and left his blessings for the end of days, while those of Esau
— as far as material riches were concerned — came about in his lifetime.

This point made by the *Zohar* constitutes the reply to the Roman reaction
mentioned in the Talmud (*Avodah Zarah* 11b). The Talmud relates that every
seventy years the Romans celebrated a festival, a masquerade on the theme: "An
imposter was the brother of our ancestor (Esau). What good is swindling to the
swindler and cheating to the deceiver? Jacob wanted to steal the blessing of our
ancestor, his brother, but what good did it do him to be blessed with the words
הֱוֵה גְבִיר לְאַחֶיךָ, *be a lord to your kinsmen* — it never came true!" (Cf. our
commentary to 28:4.)

וְהָיָה כַּאֲשֶׁר תָּרִיד — *Yet it shall be that when you are aggrieved.* Cf. *Rashi* on the
meaning of the word תָּרִיד: "When Israel transgresses against the Torah and you
have reason to moan and complain about the blessings granted to him, then you
will cast off his yoke." The domination which Esau will then be authorized to
exert over Israel will be limited to "casting off his yoke," but no more. It has
never included the right to persecute, or make pogroms, or compel martyrdom,
or annihilate.

41. יִקְרְבוּ יְמֵי אֵבֶל אָבִי — *May the days of mourning for my father draw near.*
Esau said to himself, "I shall not do as Cain did. He slew his brother Abel while
his father yet lived, and his father then begot Seth. As for me, I shall await the

brother you shall serve; yet it shall be that when you are aggrieved, you may cast off his yoke from upon your neck."

⁴¹ *Now Esau harbored hatred toward Jacob because of the blessing with which his father had blessed him; and Esau thought, "May the days of mourning for my father draw near, then I will kill my brother Jacob."*

⁴² *When Rebecca was told of the words of her older son Esau, she sent and summoned Jacob her younger son and said to him, "Behold, your brother Esau is consoling himself regarding you to kill you.* ⁴³ *So now, my son, heed my voice and arise; flee to*

days of mourning for my father and then I will kill my brother Jacob and be left as the sole heir" (*Targum Yonasan*).

On the other hand, realizing that he could not under any circumstances kill his father himself, Esau thought of joining forces with his uncle Ishmael. He assumed that Ishmael would share his reasons for hating his father; Isaac had thwarted Ishmael regarding his privileges as firstborn and had made him leave his father's house empty-handed. Ishmael would naturally be his nephew's ally. So Esau went to him with the intention of marrying his daughter and hinting that he should kill Isaac, after which Esau would kill Jacob and then Ishmael himself (*Midrash Shocher Tov*). This would leave Esau as sole heir to Abraham and Isaac. But all of these diabolical schemes collapsed when Ishmael died just after his daughter was betrothed to Esau (*Rashi* to 29:8).

וְאַהַרְגָה אֶת־יַעֲקֹב אָחִי — *Then I will kill my brother Jacob.* Speaking of Esau, the prophet Ovadiah exclaims: *Because of your violence against your brother Jacob, shame will cover you and you will be cut off forever* (1:10). The *Tosafists* comment: We find that Esau only had evil intentions toward Jacob, but he never carried them out. This teaches you that with idolaters wicked intentions are likened to the deed itself (cf. *Kiddushin* 39b; on the relationship between intentions and actions cf. chapter 9 of ס' משנת ר' אליעזר).

42. וַיֻּגַּד לְרִבְקָה אֶת־דִּבְרֵי עֵשָׂו בְּנָהּ הַגָּדֹל — *When Rebecca was told of the words of her older son Esau.* What Esau thought in his heart was revealed to her by the Holy Spirit. This explanation of *Rashi's* is contradicted by *Ramban*, who mentions that the expression אֲמִירָה בַּלֵּב — *to say to oneself* — is often used when one makes a mental decision or commits oneself, even when this decision is verbalized. But what mother does not guess the most intimate thoughts of her children?

43. בְּרַח־לְךָ אֶל־לָבָן אָחִי — *Flee to my brother Laban.* The righteous, as a rule of conduct, bow to the necessities of the hour and go to seek temporary refuge elsewhere. So it was with Jacob, Moses and David. For "whoever tries to force circumstances (by facing them) is himself forced by circumstances" (*Berachos* 64a; cf. our commentary to 26:22).

מד לָבָן אָחִי חָרָנָה: וְיָשַׁבְתָּ עִמּוֹ יָמִים אֲחָדִים עַד אֲשֶׁר־תָּשׁוּב
מה חֲמַת אָחִיךְ: עַד־שׁוּב אַף־אָחִיךְ מִמְּךָ וְשָׁכַח אֵת אֲשֶׁר־
עָשִׂיתָ לּוֹ וְשָׁלַחְתִּי וּלְקַחְתִּיךָ מִשָּׁם לָמָה אֶשְׁכַּל גַּם־שְׁנֵיכֶם
מו יוֹם אֶחָד: וַתֹּאמֶר רִבְקָה אֶל־יִצְחָק קַצְתִּי בְחַיַּי מִפְּנֵי בְּנוֹת
חֵת אִם־לֹקֵחַ יַעֲקֹב אִשָּׁה מִבְּנוֹת־חֵת כָּאֵלֶּה מִבְּנוֹת הָאָרֶץ
כח א לָמָּה לִי חַיִּים: וַיִּקְרָא יִצְחָק אֶל־יַעֲקֹב וַיְבָרֶךְ אֹתוֹ וַיְצַוֵּהוּ
ב וַיֹּאמֶר לוֹ לֹא־תִקַּח אִשָּׁה מִבְּנוֹת כְּנָעַן: קוּם לֵךְ פַּדֶּנָה אֲרָם
בֵּיתָה בְתוּאֵל אֲבִי אִמֶּךָ וְקַח־לְךָ מִשָּׁם אִשָּׁה מִבְּנוֹת לָבָן

44. עַד אֲשֶׁר־תָּשׁוּב חֲמַת אָחִיךְ — *Until your brother's wrath subsides.* Twice in a row the saintly Rebecca expresses hope that Esau's fury will subside. But the wicked react in a contrary manner, as the prophet Amos emphasizes: *His anger tore in pieces continually and he kept his wrath forever* (1:11).

45. וְשָׁלַחְתִּי וּלְקַחְתִּיךָ מִשָּׁם — *Then I will send and bring you from there.* From the remainder of the passage it seems that Rebecca never again saw her son Jacob. Her intervention in Isaac's blessing took a turn which, certainly, she had not expected. She was forced to send her son away and never had the good fortune of seeing him again, for his absence lasted thirty-six years. In these tragic developments is one to see a punishment tantamount to disapproval of Rebecca's mode of conduct? She meant well in applying the principle that the end justifies the means, but it seems that possibly Providence did not sanction every detail in her decision. Should one perhaps interpret these events as trials inflicted on the righteous or as reparations for the wrongs done to Esau (in the sense given in our commentary to verse 34)?

לָמָה אֶשְׁכַּל גַּם־שְׁנֵיכֶם יוֹם אֶחָד — *Why should I be bereaved of both of you on the same day? Rashi* explains: Inspired by the Holy Spirit, she prophesied that they would both die on the same day, as the Talmud tells us (*Sotah* 13a). For every curse uttered by a sage will come to pass, even if it is conditional (*Makkos* 11a).

The conjunction גַּם in the expression גַּם שְׁנֵיכֶם includes Rebecca herself. If she lost her two sons on the same day, she too would die, of grief. Jacob did not want to flee from danger, for he deemed it his duty to remain in his father's home in order to carry out the *mitzvah* of honoring father and mother and to perfect himself still more in the knowledge of God.

To be sure, he was already quite old and still unmarried, but the prospect of seeking a wife in a pagan milieu disturbed him. For the second time, he found himself in disagreement with his mother's wishes. Accordingly, she had to use all her maternal authority, make the most of sentimental arguments, and even call upon Isaac to formally command his son Jacob in order to finally convince him (*Sefer Chassidim*, §1902).

46. קַצְתִּי בְחַיַּי — *I am disgusted with my life.* To save Jacob's life Rebecca was obliged to inform Jacob of Esau's criminal designs, but she still did not wish to

my brother Laban, to Charan. ⁴⁴ *And remain with him a short while*
until your brother's wrath subsides. ⁴⁵ *Until your brother's anger*
against you subsides and he forgets what you have done to him;
then I will send and bring you from there; why should I be
bereaved of both of you on the same day?'

⁴⁶ *Rebecca said to Isaac, "I am disgusted with my life on account*
of the daughters of Heth; if Jacob takes a wife of the daughters of
Heth like these, of the daughters of the land, what is life to me?'

28   ¹*So Isaac summoned Jacob and blessed him; he instructed him,*
and said to him, "Do not take a wife from the Canaanite women.
² *Arise, go to Paddan-aram, to the house of Bethuel your mother's*
father, and take a wife from there from the daughters of Laban

speak of them to her husband. She did not want to disturb him still more
with reports of his son's wickedness. And so she gave a different reason for
Jacob's departure (*R' Chaim ben Attar*). The ק, first letter of the word קַצְתִּי,
is written smaller than the others and may be explained as the Masoretic indication that the reason given here in this verse was not the principal one.

28.

1. וַיִּקְרָא יִצְחָק אֶל־יַעֲקֹב וַיְבָרֶךְ אֹתוֹ — *So Isaac summoned Jacob and blessed him.*
R' Abahu said: Jacob's hold on the earlier blessings was weak. One might have
said that had he not deceived his father he would not have received them. So
Isaac now confirmed them of his own accord and on his own initiative. This
is like a young prince who furtively takes a piece of gold belonging to his
father. His father says to him, "Why this secrecy? Come, take it openly!"
(*Midrash*).

לֹא־תִקַּח אִשָּׁה מִבְּנוֹת כְּנָעַן — *Do not take a wife from the Canaanite women.* So
great was Isaac's confidence in his son that he blessed him without making it
conditional on any promise of obedience from Jacob. Only after blessing him
did Isaac tell Jacob what he wanted him to do with respect to taking a wife,
remembering that Abraham had previously expressed the same wish for him.
This wish remained absolutely essential for the historic mission of the family
of Abraham (cf. our commentary to 24:3).

2. בֵּיתָה בְתוּאֵל אֲבִי אִמֶּךְ — *To the house of Bethuel your mother's father.* The
same verse contains a second reference to "your mother" ("from the daughters
of Laban, your mother's brother"). Although Jacob dreaded going to look for
a wife among the idolatrous family of Bethuel, Isaac wanted him to understand
that in a place where someone as pure as his mother had been born and
perfectly raised, Jacob could very well find a life-companion, despite the
presence of a Laban.

ג אֲחִי אִמֶּךָ: וְאֵל שַׁדַּי יְבָרֵךְ אֹתְךָ וְיַפְרְךָ וְיַרְבֶּךָ וְהָיִיתָ
ד לִקְהַל עַמִּים: וְיִתֶּן־לְךָ אֶת־בִּרְכַּת אַבְרָהָם לְךָ וּלְזַרְעֲךָ
אִתָּךְ לְרִשְׁתְּךָ אֶת־אֶרֶץ מְגֻרֶיךָ אֲשֶׁר־נָתַן אֱלֹהִים
ה לְאַבְרָהָם: וַיִּשְׁלַח יִצְחָק אֶת־יַעֲקֹב וַיֵּלֶךְ פַּדֶּנָה אֲרָם
אֶל־לָבָן בֶּן־בְּתוּאֵל הָאֲרַמִּי אֲחִי רִבְקָה אֵם יַעֲקֹב
ו וְעֵשָׂו: וַיַּרְא עֵשָׂו כִּי־בֵרַךְ יִצְחָק אֶת־יַעֲקֹב וְשִׁלַּח אֹתוֹ

    שביעי

3. וְאֵל שַׁדַּי ... וְיַפְרְךָ וְיַרְבֶּךָ — *Almighty God ... make you fruitful and make you numerous.* The name שַׁדַּי is usually invoked when the blessing of "being fruitful and multiplying" is asked for (e.g. 35:11 and 48:3; cf. בעה"ט ibid.). *Rashi* explains this name in the following way: "I have enough (דַּי) Divine power for all the creatures ..." This word has the same meaning throughout the Torah and it must be understood according to the context (17:1). To this idea the other commentators add that of omnipotence (מְשַׁדֵּד מַעֲרָכוֹת), so that שַׁדַּי may be defined, "God Who, through His omnipotence over the elements of nature, dispenses blessings even where physical conditions would preclude childbearing" (cf. our commentary to 17:1). The *Zohar* also gives this definition.

Thus far, Isaac had not wanted to make mention of having children in his blessings, for Esau's wives were a cause of sorrow to him. He waited until Jacob had agreed to go to Aram and marry a woman of his family before giving him this blessing.

4. וְיִתֶּן־לְךָ אֶת־בִּרְכַּת אַבְרָהָם — *May He grant you the blessing of Abraham.* Here Jacob is formally invested with carrying on the mission of Abraham and, because of this very fact, becomes the heir to the Divine blessings granted to the ancestor: *I will make of you a great nation* (12:2), *and all the nations of the earth shall bless themselves by your offspring* (22:18), *and I will give to you ... the land of your sojourns ... the whole of the land of Canaan* (17:8).

R' Yose said, "Come and see how many blessings were bestowed upon Jacob! The first he obtained from his father through guile; the second, God gave him on his return from Laban (35:9); the third he received from Esau's guardian angel (32:30); and again he was blessed by his father before he set out for Paddan-aram. Seeing himself surrounded with so many blessings, Jacob wondered, "Which one should I first make use of?' He decided to retain the least rich of all, namely, the one which his father had given him before he went to Aram. Certainly it too was important, but it comprised fewer blessings concerning earthly riches than did the others. Jacob said to himself, 'I want to derive benefit right now from this blessing; the others I will leave for the future, for the needs of my children. Someday they will have to fight for their lives against powerful and imposing armies and then the blessings kept in store for them will come to their rescue from all directions. But for me, one blessing is all I need to deal with Esau.' This is like a king who sends his guards after the common thieves and pirates, but keeps his armies, cannons, and generals for

your mother's brother. [3] *And may Almighty God bless you, make you fruitful and make you numerous, and may you be a congregation of peoples.* [4] *May He grant you the blessing of Abraham to you and to your offspring with you, that you may possess the land of your sojourns which God gave to Abraham.''* [5] *So Isaac sent away Jacob and he went toward Paddan-aram, to Laban the son of Bethuel the Aramean, brother of Rebecca, mother of Jacob and Esau. —* [6] *When Esau saw that Isaac had blessed Jacob and sent him off*

battle against his enemies. The prophet Michah is alluding to these arrangements made by the patriarch when he proclaims (5:6): וְהָיָה שְׁאֵרִית יַעֲקֹב — *the remnant [of the blessings] of Jacob — shall be in the midst of many peoples* (enemies) *as dew from God, as showers upon the grass, that hopes not for man and waits not for the sons of man''* (Zohar).

5. וַיִּשְׁלַח יִצְחָק אֶת־יַעֲקֹב — *So Isaac sent away Jacob.* The Midrash puts the words of *Psalms* 121 into the mouth of Jacob as he sets out alone for a foreign land in search of his life-companion: *A song to the ascents. I raise my eyes upon the mountains* (אֶשָּׂא עֵינַי אֶל הֶהָרִים). The word הֶהָרִים could be read as הַהוֹרִים — *the parents.* The sentence then comes to mean, ''I raise my eyes to my parents [as I wonder], מֵאַיִן יָבוֹא עֶזְרִי — *whence will come my help —* to be beside me?'' (a wife being called עֵזֶר כְּנֶגְדּוֹ in *Genesis* 2:20). As the son travels far from home in search of a wife, he raises his eyes to his parents and reflects on their example and their merits. Jacob reflected: ''When Eliezer went to seek a wife for his master's son, he had with him *ten camels and all his master's goods*; I have neither necklaces nor bracelets! Then he decided to place all his confidence in God: עֶזְרִי מֵעִם ה׳ עֹשֵׂה שָׁמַיִם וָאָרֶץ — *My 'help' is from Hashem, Maker of heaven and earth.''* From then on Jacob went his way in confidence, unafraid of the fierce hatred of his brother whom he had left behind in his father's house. The psalm expresses these feelings: *He will not allow your foot to falter; your Guardian will not slumber . . . Hashem will protect you from every evil; He will guard your soul. Hashem will guard your departure and your arrival, from this time and forever* (Rabbah 68).

אֵם יַעֲקֹב וְעֵשָׂו — *Mother of Jacob and Esau.* Rashi remarks, ''I do not know what this phrase wants to teach us.'' According to R' S.R. Hirsch, it emphasizes that despite her previous actions toward Esau, Rebecca always felt that she was the mother of *both* sons. She acted solely from objective considerations and with pure motives, and did not yield to her personal preference for Jacob. If Jacob is named here before Esau, the latter is nevertheless designated earlier as the elder son while Jacob is called the younger son of Rebecca (27:15). Whatever her disappointments, her sorrows and her trials, she remained the mother of both her children.

פַּדֶּנָה אֲרָם לָקַחַת־לוֹ מִשָּׁם אִשָּׁה בְּבָרֲכוֹ אֹתוֹ וַיְצַו עָלָיו

מפטיר   ז לֵאמֹר לֹא־תִקַּח אִשָּׁה מִבְּנוֹת כְּנָעַן: וַיִּשְׁמַע יַעֲקֹב אֶל־אָבִיו

ח וְאֶל־אִמּוֹ וַיֵּלֶךְ פַּדֶּנָה אֲרָם: וַיַּרְא עֵשָׂו כִּי רָעוֹת בְּנוֹת כְּנָעַן

ט בְּעֵינֵי יִצְחָק אָבִיו: וַיֵּלֶךְ עֵשָׂו אֶל־יִשְׁמָעֵאל וַיִּקַּח אֶת־

מָחֲלַת | בַּת־יִשְׁמָעֵאל בֶּן־אַבְרָהָם אֲחוֹת נְבָיוֹת עַל־נָשָׁיו לוֹ

לְאִשָּׁה:

6. וַיְצַו עָלָיו לֵאמֹר — *He commanded him saying.* Here לֵאמֹר means, "saying for all future generations" (*Sechel Tov*). The command remains valid for posterity and for all time. The word לֵאמֹר occasionally is taken to mean לְדוֹרוֹת — for future generations, as in *Genesis* 28:20 according to *Bereishis Rabbah* 70.

7. וַיִּשְׁמַע יַעֲקֹב אֶל־אָבִיו וְאֶל־אִמּוֹ וַיֵּלֶךְ פַּדֶּנָה אֲרָם — *And that Jacob obeyed his father and mother and went to Paddan-aram.* Some must travel great distances to find their spouse, others see their spouse coming toward them. Isaac saw Rebecca come to him, but on the other hand his son had to travel a long distance to meet his future wife (*Midrash*).

9. וַיֵּלֶךְ עֵשָׂו אֶל־יִשְׁמָעֵאל — *So Esau went to Ishmael.* Rabba asked Rabbi ben Mari, "From where comes the proverb, 'A bad date-palm will usually make its way to a grove of barren trees'?" He replied, "It is written in the Torah, *So Esau went to Ishmael*" (*Bava Kamma* 92b). Indeed, the children of Hagar were not at all fit to be united with the descendants of Abraham, as the *Tosafists*

to Paddan-aram to take himself a wife from there, as he blessed him he commanded him, saying, "You shall not take a wife from among the daughters of Canaan"; [7] *and that Jacob obeyed his father and mother and went to Paddan-aram;* [8] *then Esau perceived that the daughters of Canaan were evil in the eyes of Isaac, his father.* [9] *So Esau went to Ishmael and took Mahalath, the daughter of Ishmael son of Abraham, sister of Nebaioth, in addition to his wives, as a wife for himself.*

point out in connection with Abraham's daughter (*Bava Basra* 141a, ד״ה בת).
Cf. our commentary to 17:41.

וַיִּקַּח אֶת־מָחֲלַת — *And took Mahalath.* Was she really named "Mahalath?" More likely she was called "Basmath," as she is specifically designated in 36:3. But here, on the occasion of her marriage, she is called מָחֲלַת. This is to tell you that her husband's sins were forgiven that day (מָחֲלַת — she *caused pardon*, derived from מָחַל). The newly-married man is one of those whose transgressions are pardoned on their day of honor (*Yerushalmi, Bikkurim* 3:3). But the question arises: Why is this lesson taught just on the occasion of the marriage of Esau who is usually considered an immoral being and a heretic? Because it applies even to this type of individual. It should also be noted that Esau felt a desire to repent at this time (*Rabbah* 67). The groom begins a new existence. Accordingly, the sins of his past are forgiven so that he may build his future on new foundations, sound and solid. But Esau did not know how to take advantage of this opportunity and his good intentions were soon forgotten.

יא וַיֵּצֵא יַעֲקֹב מִבְּאֵר שָׁבַע וַיֵּלֶךְ חָרָנָה: וַיִּפְגַּע בַּמָּקוֹם וַיָּלֶן שָׁם
כִּי־בָא הַשֶּׁמֶשׁ וַיִּקַּח מֵאַבְנֵי הַמָּקוֹם וַיָּשֶׂם מְרַאֲשֹׁתָיו וַיִּשְׁכַּב
יב בַּמָּקוֹם הַהוּא: וַיַּחֲלֹם וְהִנֵּה סֻלָּם מֻצָּב אַרְצָה וְרֹאשׁוֹ מַגִּיעַ

10. וַיֵּצֵא יַעֲקֹב מִבְּאֵר שָׁבַע — *Jacob departed from Beer-sheba. Rashi* devotes his long explanation of the last verse of the preceding section to demonstrating that "Jacob went to study with his ancestor Eber, the great-grandson of Noah. There he remained hidden for fourteen years and only afterwards did he go to Haran." Thus Jacob stayed for a long time in the house of study before going to his uncle Laban's. He considered it essential to be deeply imbued with the spirit of sacred studies, as well as with the fear and love of God, before facing an idolatrous environment in a strange land full of temptation and with the gravest of moral and spiritual dangers awaiting him. Next, he went to Beer-sheba, for he thought, "My father and mother told me to go to Aram, outside the Promised Land. I shall go first to Beer-sheba. There, where my father was refused permission by God to leave this land, I may learn whether God approves of my departure" (*Rabbah*, 68). The city where Jacob had received his father's blessings was not Beer-sheba but Hebron, as *Ramban* demonstrates with reference to *Genesis* 35:27, whereas the city of Beer-sheba mentioned in 26:33 in connection with Isaac is not the same as Abraham's Beer-sheba (*Rashbam* ibid.). The prime importance of this latter city for carrying out the historical mission of Abraham and Isaac has been emphasized in our commentary to 26:23. We can thus see why Jacob went there to collect his thoughts before going to make his home and begin a new existence in a strange land.

11. וַיִּפְגַּע בַּמָּקוֹם — *He encountered the place. Rashi* explains: The Torah does not give the name of the place. But it is "the place" (already known) which is named elsewhere; it is Mount Moriah, as is written, *Abraham . . . perceived the place from afar* (22:4). Our Sages have explained the word וַיִּפְגַּע in the sense of praying. Jeremiah uses it in this sense (7:16): *Neither lift up cry nor prayer for them nor make intercession to Me.* From these words וַיִּפְגַּע and וַיָּלֶן we conclude that it was Jacob who instituted the evening prayer — עַרְבִית.

According to the tradition reported in *Berachos* 26b, the morning service was instituted by Abraham, the afternoon service by Isaac, and the evening service by Jacob. These different times of day call to mind the place that each patriarch's destiny occupies in the temporal world. Abraham's destiny appears in light as it rises and radiates outward. Not only is the patriarch not the object of envy or enmity, but he is even revered as the "prince of God." Isaac's place in the world already appears to be smaller; the sun, which had shone brightly on his father, has passed its peak. Around him Isaac sees only jealousy; he is spurned and forced to withdraw into himself and his family. Right from Isaac's birth the prediction, *Your offspring shall be aliens* (15:13), begins to come true. Then for Jacob, destiny becomes overcast with the night shadows; his life is but a series of painful trials and the outward joys of life are his only for a short time, and only very rarely.

> [10] *Jacob departed from Beer-sheba and went toward Haran.* [11] *He encountered the place and spent the night there because the sun had set; he took from the stones of the place which he arranged around his head, and lay down in that place.* [12] *And he dreamt, and behold! A ladder was set earthward and its top reached*

Nevertheless, despite their very different destinies, the three patriarchs came to find the path to God through their prayers; they bequeathed to us these prayers which teach us how to come closer to God in the different circumstances of our lives: in the morning rays, the expression of radiant plenitude which calls us to life and gratitude (שַׁחֲרִית); in the setting sun, the symbol of the decline of our own personal destinies, inviting us to a spiritual meditation (מִנְחָה); and at night in the hours of anguish and uncertainty which urge us to take refuge in God (עַרְבִית).

12. וַיַּחֲלֹם — *And he dreamt.* Many interpretations are given to this dream. Consistent with the concept mentioned in the preceding verse, that Jacob prayed in the place of the future Sanctuary where his forefathers had also prayed and where "prayer rises to Heaven," the ladder Jacob saw in his dream represents the ascent of prayer toward the celestial spheres. The angels rose up from the earth, carrying the supplications of men to the celestial throne and then came back to them again, laden with heavenly blessings.

Rambam quotes a passage from the *Midrash Tanchuma* (which does not appear in our present editions) indicating that the ladder had four rungs. These correspond to the four stages which thought must pass through in order to reach God (*Guide* 2:10; cf. אגרת לר׳ חסדאי).

A ladder was set earthward — here the ladder designates the place and relationships of the different beings in the universe. *A ladder set earthward* designates the terrestrial world, the world of perception and experience from which emanates all worldly knowledge. *Its top reached heavenward* teaches us that knowledge progresses from the world of the senses toward the world of saintly beings and higher spheres. *And angels of God were ascending and descending on it* alludes to the super-sensible world of the angels, where knowledge penetrates still deeper; and finally, the fourth and last stage of spiritual evolution represents the goal of knowledge and, at the same time, of prayer: *And behold! Hashem was standing over him* (following the commentary of *Ibn Tibbon,* ibid.).

In his work של"ה, R' Isaiah Halevi Horowitz attempts a synthesis of the rationalist method with that of Kabbalah. He explains that the four worlds of the philosophers are identical to the four worlds of Kabbalah, namely: the world of material phenomena — עוֹלָם הָעֲשִׂיָּה; the world of formation — עוֹלָם הַיְצִירָה; the world of creation or of forces — עוֹלָם הַבְּרִיאָה; and the world of ideas — עוֹלָם הָאֲצִילוּת.

But while the worlds of Kabbalah represent the stages of development of the Divine emanation, the four worlds of the philosophers designate only the

יג הַשָּׁמַ֔יְמָה וְהִנֵּה֙ מַלְאֲכֵ֣י אֱלֹהִ֔ים עֹלִ֥ים וְיֹרְדִ֖ים בּֽוֹ: וְהִנֵּ֨ה יהו֜ה
נִצָּ֣ב עָלָיו֮ וַיֹּאמַר֒ אֲנִ֣י יהו֗ה אֱלֹהֵי֙ אַבְרָהָ֣ם אָבִ֔יךָ וֵאלֹהֵ֖י
יִצְחָ֑ק הָאָ֗רֶץ אֲשֶׁ֤ר אַתָּה֙ שֹׁכֵ֣ב עָלֶ֔יהָ לְךָ֥ אֶתְּנֶ֖נָּה וּלְזַרְעֶֽךָ:
יד וְהָיָ֤ה זַרְעֲךָ֙ כַּעֲפַ֣ר הָאָ֔רֶץ וּפָרַצְתָּ֛ יָ֥מָּה וָקֵ֖דְמָה וְצָפֹ֣נָה וָנֶ֑גְבָּה
טו וְנִבְרֲכ֥וּ בְךָ֛ כָּל־מִשְׁפְּחֹ֥ת הָאֲדָמָ֖ה וּבְזַרְעֶֽךָ: וְהִנֵּ֨ה אָנֹכִ֜י עִמָּ֗ךְ

different phases through which human knowledge must evolve, starting from the perception of the phenomena and culminating in the vision of the absolute. The four successive stages correspond point by point to the process by which nature teaches us. Thus, the thinking mind must raise itself up the ladder of knowledge until it gains access to the Creator of the universe; so too, man when he prays must first pass through these four worlds, in order to be able to find, as Jacob did, at the top of the ladder, the God Whom he seeks with his intelligence and his heart.

These four worlds correspond to the four major parts of our daily prayers. the first part takes us to בָּרוּךְ שֶׁאָמַר and refers to the world of action and natural phenomena (עוֹלָם הָעֲשִׂיָּה); the second part extends from בָּרוּךְ שֶׁאָמַר to בָּרְכוּ — it rises toward the world of nature and forms (עוֹלָם הַיְצִירָה); the next part includes the קְרִיאַת שְׁמַע and its blessings and it leads us to the world in which all the forces acting in the universe are related to the One God, Creator of heaven and earth (עוֹלָם הַבְּרִיאָה); the last part consists of the שְׁמוֹנֶה עֶשְׂרֵה where we find God, Master of all personal and universal destinies, and we pour out our hearts to Him (עוֹלָם הָאֲצִילוּת).

מַלְאֲכֵי אֱלֹהִים עֹלִים וְיֹרְדִים בּוֹ — *Angels of God were ascending and descending on it.* R' Eliezer explains that Jacob's dream was a prophetic one and in it God revealed the reign and rise and fall of the four kingdoms which would enslave his descendants (the kingdoms of Babylon, Media, Greece, and Edom-Rome). The angels are the "guardians" of these kingdoms in the celestial spheres. But God appeared at the top of the ladder and promised to give Jacob, the embodiment of the Jewish people, His protection: *I will guard you wherever you go, and I will return you to this soil.* Abraham had also had a similar vision in the "Covenant Between the Parts" (בְּרִית בֵּין הַבְּתָרִים) and had heard the Divine words promising final redemption after the exile (15:18) (*Pirkei D'Rabbi Eliezer* 31; quoted by *Rambam*; cf. *Hilchos Yesodei HaTorah* 7:3 on the various forms of prophecy).

13. וְהִנֵּה ה' נִצָּב עָלָיו — *And behold! HASHEM was standing over him. Rashi:* "to protect him." *Ramban,* who also takes the preposition עָלָיו as referring to Jacob and not to the ladder, interprets this thought more explicitly. The prophetic dream revealed to Jacob that all terrestrial life is governed by intermediate forces (the angels of God) which, after drawing their substance from the Supreme Being, "descend" to enrich this lower world. Jacob and his offspring are the only

heavenward; and behold! angels of God were ascending and descending on it.

¹³ *And behold! HASHEM was standing over him, and He said, "I am HASHEM, God of Abraham your father and God of Isaac; the ground upon which you are lying, to you will I give it and to your descendants.* ¹⁴ *Your offspring shall be as the dust of the earth, and you shall spread out powerfully westward, eastward, northward and southward; and all the families of the earth shall bless themselves by you and by your offspring.* ¹⁵ *Behold, I am with you;*

ones not entrusted to the hands of these agents of the Creator; they depend on Him alone. It is God Himself Who stands over Jacob to protect him at all times and to save him from evil forces. For the Jewish people is "Hashem's portion; Jacob is the measure of His inheritance" (*Deuteronomy* 32:9). This concept mirrors the Talmudic statement (*Shabbos* 156a) that Jewry is not subject to the blind laws of natural destinies — אֵין מַזָּל לְיִשְׂרָאֵל — Jewry is under the immediate protection of the Master of the universe.

וַיֹּאמֶר — *And He said.* For the first time in his life Jacob is personally addressed by Divine speech. Just as with Abraham, this first revelation takes place just as he gives up a peaceful existence at home to emigrate to a strange land. This is characteristic of the destiny of the Jews. God invests the family of Abraham with a mission which is destined to be accomplished, above all, in exile. To be Jewish means to remain faithful to God while in the midst of the other nations.

אֲנִי ה׳ אֱלֹהֵי אַבְרָהָם אָבִיךָ — *I am HASHEM, God of Abraham your father.* This case is exceptional in the Torah: the grandfather is called "father" whereas the father is mentioned simply by his first name. Obviously, it cannot be a question of physical derivation. But this form of address makes it clear to Jacob that Abraham is his spiritual father, Isaac being only an intermediary link. You are the son of him to whom I said, הִתְהַלֵּךְ לְפָנַי וֶהְיֵה תָמִים, *Walk before Me and be perfect (Genesis* 17:1) — you be his son and heir! In Jacob, the first one to build a completely Jewish household, the Abrahamic future was to begin its realization (*R' S.R. Hirsch*).

14. וְהָיָה זַרְעֲךָ כַּעֲפַר הָאָרֶץ — *Your offspring shall be as the dust of the earth.* After being subjected to the scorn of others and treated like dirt, your posterity will spread to the east, west, north and south and all the families of the earth will be blessed through you. Jacob is the beloved of God (*Malachi* 1:2) and receives the promise of an "inheritance without limits" in future times — נַחֲלָה בְּלִי מְצָרִים. This stands in contrast to the promises made to Abraham and Isaac wherein the heritage of their descendants was limited, reduced to borders. The verse in *Isaiah* in which God says: "I will make you ride upon the high places of the earth and make you rejoice in the heritage of Jacob your father..." is a reference to Jacob's privileged position (58:14; cf. *Shabbos* 118a).

וּשְׁמַרְתִּ֙יךָ֙ בְּכֹ֣ל אֲשֶׁר־תֵּלֵ֔ךְ וַהֲשִׁ֣בֹתִ֔יךָ אֶל־הָאֲדָמָ֖ה הַזֹּ֑את
כִּ֚י לֹ֣א אֶֽעֱזָבְךָ֔ עַ֚ד אֲשֶׁ֣ר אִם־עָשִׂ֔יתִי אֵ֥ת אֲשֶׁר־דִּבַּ֖רְתִּי
לָֽךְ: טז וַיִּיקַ֣ץ יַעֲקֹב֮ מִשְּׁנָתוֹ֒ וַיֹּ֗אמֶר אָכֵן֙ יֵ֣שׁ יהו֔ה בַּמָּק֖וֹם
הַזֶּ֑ה וְאָנֹכִ֖י לֹ֥א יָדָֽעְתִּי: יז וַיִּירָא֙ וַיֹּאמַ֔ר מַה־נּוֹרָ֖א הַמָּק֣וֹם
הַזֶּ֑ה אֵ֣ין זֶ֗ה כִּ֚י אִם־בֵּ֣ית אֱלֹהִ֔ים וְזֶ֖ה שַׁ֥עַר הַשָּׁמָֽיִם:

15. וּשְׁמַרְתִּיךָ בְּכֹל אֲשֶׁר־תֵּלֵךְ — *I will guard you wherever you go.* In the same vein, *Rambam* points out that the promise of protection granted to Jacob is more important than those given to the first two patriarchs. To Abraham, it was said, *I am a shield for you* (15:1); to Isaac, *I will be with you and bless you* (26:3). Consistent with the thesis which he develops in his *Guide to the Perplexed* (3:18), when he comes to our present verse, *Rambam* shows that the degree to which Providence watches over men varies as to their degree of perfection. See our commentary on 25:27 regarding the stage of perfection attained by Jacob as compared with the other patriarchs.

עַד אֲשֶׁר אִם־עָשִׂיתִי — *Until I will have done.* This does not mean that God will abandon Jacob as soon as He has fulfilled His promise. For the preposition עַד, *until*, means here, as it often does elsewhere, *forever* (e.g. *Isaiah* 26:4, 64:8, etc.; cf. *Deuteronomy* 34:6). On the other hand, the repetition of the word אֲשֶׁר in this verse has the sense of absolute confirmation (אִישּׁוּר), having the same force as an oath. In fact, the realization of the promise of Divine protection will never reach the point where it definitely ceases (פ' הריב"א).

16. וַיִּיקַץ יַעֲקֹב מִשְּׁנָתוֹ — *Jacob awoke from his sleep.* R' Yochanan explained the word מִשְּׁנָתוֹ, *from his sleep,* as though it had been written מִמִּשְׁנָתוֹ, *from his Mishnah;* that is, when he awoke he was already involved with studying the meaning of his dream. "Since he studied the law continuously, day and night, he kept right on searching for the meaning of his dream" (cf. *Baal HaTurim*).

וְאָנֹכִי לֹא יָדָעְתִּי — *And I did not know.* "Is it indeed so astonishing that he had not known the significance of the place? Certainly not, but Kabbalistically, this is perplexing that he had not been judged worthy of 'knowing the name אָנֹכִי' of God. For the first time he had had a Divine revelation, but in it God had made Himself known to him by אֲנִי ה', whereas to Abraham and Isaac He had revealed Himself by the title אָנֹכִי (15:1; 26:24). This אָנֹכִי, *I,* is the title of Majesty. It designates God at the time of the creation of the world (*Jeremiah* 26:5) and at the proclamation of the Decalogue (*Exodus* 20:2). Accordingly, Jacob 'became frightened' (verse 17), afraid that he was unworthy of his forefathers. He felt that his imperfection was due to his unmarried state, because of which he could not aspire to a more perfect Divine revelation. Then he cried out, 'how awesome is this place! (מַה נּוֹרָא וכו'). *This is none other than the abode of God* (which I have not yet founded) — אֵין זֶה כִּי אִם־בֵּית אֱלֹהִים — *and this is the gate of the heavens* וְזֶה שַׁעַר הַשָּׁמָיִם' "(*Zohar*).

*I will guard you wherever you go, and I will return you to this soil;
for I will not forsake you until I will have done what I have spoken
about you."*

¹⁶ *Jacob awoke from his sleep and said, "Surely HASHEM is present
in this place and I did not know!"* ¹⁷ *And he became frightened and
said, "How awesome is this place! This is none other than the abode
of God and this is the gate of the heavens!"*

Later, when Jacob was married and the father of a family, God did reveal
Himself to him as אָנֹכִי (31:13). And when he spoke to his children from his
deathbed, Jacob reminded them that God had revealed Himself to all the
patriarchs with this Name and that God had proclaimed it at the time of the
descent into Egypt (46:4). Jacob concluded, "And when you hear God coming
to you with the name אָנֹכִי to save you, you will know that He is with you."
Therefore, it was as אָנֹכִי that God revealed himself to Moses at the burning bush
(*Exodus* 3:6; *Pesikta* 21).

17. אֵין זֶה כִּי אִם־בֵּית אֱלֹהִים — *This is none other than the abode of God.* Jacob leaves
his parents' house to found a Jewish home and brings with him nothing more
than what makes up his own personality. This is what this section proclaims
from the outset, and all that follows revolves around founding this home. Jacob
was the first to affirm that God is to be sought out first of all in the family and
the home. He was the one who conceived the idea of the "House of God" (בֵּית
אֱלֹהִים), meaning that the most important and closest place of Divine
manifestation is the place where human souls blossom and flourish, where man
contributes what he himself is, in order to build his life and forge his activity out
of it (יעקב קראו בית; *Midrash Psalms* 81).

God is not only the Creator of nature and God of history; He is God within
the home which men build in order to carry out His will. The vision of the ladder
means that the family home must raise itself to ideal spheres and so constitute
the "chariot," the support for the Divine Majesty on earth (מֶרְכָּבָה לַשְּׁכִינָה).
And just as the ladder reaching up into the heavens was inclined so that its
middle rung was above the location of the future Sanctuary (*Rashi*), so must the
home be built as a מִקְדָּשׁ מְעַט — *a miniature Sanctuary* — and elevate itself up
to the heights where the King of kings sits enthroned, ever ready to bless and
to protect.

Jacob's first reaction to his dream was spontaneous: "It is right here, not in the
celestial heights, that God is to be found. He is to be found wherever a guiltless
man finds repose and peace. Divine glory is not to be sought in the heavens; its
place is in the lives of human beings." Jacob experienced concern (וַיִּירָא) at the
idea that mortal man is called upon to be the bearer of the Divine Majesty; he
realized the extent and gravity of the task awaiting whoever prepares to build
a home where "God is to dwell," a home which is to become a "gate to heaven,"
by bringing the earthly and the heavenly spheres ever closer together (*R' S.R.
Hirsch*).

יח וַיַּשְׁכֵּם יַעֲקֹב בַּבֹּקֶר וַיִּקַּח אֶת־הָאֶבֶן אֲשֶׁר־שָׂם מְרַאֲשֹׁתָיו
יט וַיָּשֶׂם אֹתָהּ מַצֵּבָה וַיִּצֹק שֶׁמֶן עַל־רֹאשָׁהּ: וַיִּקְרָא אֶת־שֵׁם־
כ הַמָּקוֹם הַהוּא בֵּית־אֵל וְאוּלָם לוּז שֵׁם־הָעִיר לָרִאשֹׁנָה: וַיִּדַּר
    יַעֲקֹב נֶדֶר לֵאמֹר אִם־יִהְיֶה אֱלֹהִים עִמָּדִי וּשְׁמָרַנִי בַּדֶּרֶךְ הַזֶּה
כא אֲשֶׁר אָנֹכִי הוֹלֵךְ וְנָתַן־לִי לֶחֶם לֶאֱכֹל וּבֶגֶד לִלְבֹּשׁ: וְשַׁבְתִּי
כב בְשָׁלוֹם אֶל־בֵּית אָבִי וְהָיָה יהוה לִי לֵאלֹהִים: וְהָאֶבֶן הַזֹּאת

וְזֶה שַׁעַר הַשָּׁמָיִם — *And this is the gate of the heavens.* R' Shimon bar Yochai said that the earthly Sanctuary is situated just opposite the celestial Sanctuary. The distance separating them, he adds figuratively, is only eighteen miles (corresponding to the word זֶה in our sentence). This statement expresses the idea that the distance one must go through to raise himself from the temporal to the spiritual and from the profane to the sacred is not at all that great. The two spheres are side by side; and if reality often shows them to us as separated by a deep gulf, then it is the fault of man, not of the Creator (*Rabbah* 69).

18. וַיָּשֶׂם אֹתָהּ מַצֵּבָה — *He . . . set it up as a pillar.* Cf. *Rashi* on *Deuteronomy* 16:22.

19. וְאוּלָם לוּז שֵׁם־הָעִיר לָרִאשֹׁנָה — *However, Luz was the city's name originally.* Following the opinion of R' Yose (*Rabbah*, 69), *Ramban* holds that the city originally called Luz is none other than Jerusalem, called by Jacob בֵּית אֵל, *House of God.* (The Gaon of Vilna demonstrates that Jacob gave the name Beth-el to three different cities; *Joshua* 16:2.)

The fact that the Torah gives the original place name here and again in 35:6 shows that it attaches a certain importance to this name. The word לוּז also denotes the לוּז הַשִּׁדְרָה, the bone in the spine which is absolutely indestructible, which resists all elements, even fire. Its name also indicates that it is shaped like a hazelnut (cf. *Genesis* 30:37). The resurrection of the dead will start with this bone (*Leviticus Rabbah* 18). It does not draw its nourishment from ordinary food, it never changes in form, nor does it decompose after death like the bones of the human skeleton. Accordingly, the name לוּז was given to a city where the angel of death has no influence (*Sotah* 46a). One can hold, then, that Jerusalem bore the name לוּז originally because it is the "eternal city" which resists all destruction and always renews itself out of its ashes (cf. *Siddur Yaavetz*, commentary on the prayers of מוֹצָשׁ"ק). And it is starting from Zion that the moral and spiritual resurrection of humanity will come about (cf. *R' Bachya*).

20. וַיִּדַּר יַעֲקֹב נֶדֶר לֵאמֹר — *Then Jacob took a vow, saying.* Here the term לֵאמֹר implies saying to the future generations — that they too should vow in times of distress (see the Talmudic discussion in *Nedarim* 9a and *Yoreh De'ah* 203:5). Thus King David cried out, *I will fulfill my vows to You . . . which my mouth spoke when I was in distress* (*Psalms* 66:13-14).

אִם־יִהְיֶה אֱלֹהִים עִמָּדִי — *If God will be with me. Rashi* explains: "If God will keep His promises to be with me, even as He said to me, *I am with you . . .*" But the

¹⁸ *Jacob arose early in the morning and took the stone that he placed around his head and set it up as a pillar; and he poured oil on its top.* ¹⁹ *And he named that place Beth-el; however, Luz was the city's name originally.*

²⁰ *Then Jacob took a vow, saying, "If God will be with me, will guard me on this way that I am going; will give me bread to eat and clothes to wear;* ²¹ *and I return in peace to my father's house, and HASHEM will be a God to me —* ²² *then this stone*

Zohar asks, "Did Jacob really doubt the fulfillment of the Divine promises? Certainly not, but he thought, 'I was dreaming. Now, some dreams reveal the truth, others do not. If the promises I heard in my dream come true, I will know that it was a revelation.' " The Sages of the Midrash emphasize here the fact that in this world there are no irrevocable promises for the righteous person — he is always afraid that a sin he might commit will bring about cancellation of the Divine promises. Here, because of this fear, Jacob resorts to terms of doubt. But with a series of analogous examples *Ramban* demonstrates that the form אִם וגו׳ does not always express doubt; quite frequently it introduces an idea referring to the future — "When such a condition will come about."

וּשְׁמָרַנִי בַּדֶּרֶךְ הַזֶּה אֲשֶׁר אָנֹכִי הוֹלֵךְ — *Will guard me on this way that I am going.* Jacob was to emigrate and go into exile. Accordingly, the wish he expresses, as he sets out on his peregrinations toward an uncertain future full of danger, puts into words the desires or hopes which every Jew has when he leaves his home to go into exile. Before praying for subsistence, he implores God to be with him and protect him. He does not wish to succumb morally, like so many others, in the struggle for one's daily bread which awaits him. In this struggle, countless human beings lose their faith and morality and become nonbelievers or delinquents. Therefore, Jacob prays that God should "protect him"; that, as the Sages of the Midrash understand it, keep him from serious error, from injustice, from infringing upon the rights of others, from abandoning his faith, from debauchery and slander. His supreme request thus concerns safeguarding his moral personality. He next prays that God accord him modest living conditions (food to eat and clothing to wear) and, finally, that He permit him to return to his family and his father's house "in peace." This peace refers firstly to external peace, which the wandering Jew needs more than anyone but, as *Rashi* emphasizes, it also includes the idea of "integrity," i.e. of preservation from all sin. And last, what is important to Jacob is to remain himself incorruptible and complete, "without learning anything from Laban's example" — in short, to return to his parents a perfect Jew, having triumphed over the dangers of assimilation with the other nations.

21. וְהָיָה ה׳ לִי לֵאלֹהִים — *And HASHEM will be a God to me. Rashi* interprets the verse in this sense: His name will rest upon me from beginning to end; there will be no blemish in my descendants, as God has said to me — *to be a God to you*

אֲשֶׁר־שַׂמְתִּי מַצֵּבָה יִהְיֶה בֵּית אֱלֹהִים וְכֹל אֲשֶׁר תִּתֶּן־
כט שני א לִי עַשֵּׂר אֲעַשְּׂרֶנּוּ לָךְ: וַיִּשָּׂא יַעֲקֹב רַגְלָיו וַיֵּלֶךְ אַרְצָה

and to your offspring after you (17:7). But *Ramban, Ibn Ezra, R' Chaim ben
Attar* and the other commentators all have different explanations for this verse.
According to *Sforno*, Jacob is pledging not only to recognize God as the heavenly
Father Who bestows blessings, protects His creatures, and envelops them with
His infinite love (מִדַּת הָרַחֲמִים), but also to serve him as אֱלֹהִים — the supreme
Judge Who made the Law and Who demands rectitude and morality under all
the circumstances which man encounters. And God will one day say to Jacob's
descendants, "I have made you a free nation, לִהְיוֹת לָכֶם לֵאלֹהִים, in order to be
for you God Who demands that the ideal of morality and justice be realized."

R' Levi said: God took the words of the patriarchs and made of them the key
of the liberation of their children. Said God to Jacob, "You said וְהָיָה ה' וגו'. So
too, I will announce to your children all the kindnesses, blessings and promises
for the future with the same word — וְהָיָה; as in *Zechariah* 14:8; *Isaiah* 7:21; ibid.
11:11; *Joel* 4:18; and *Isaiah* 27:13. The term וְהָיָה has a very specific meaning. The
conversive *vav* placed before the verb in the past tense הָיָה (*it was*) transforms
it into the future tense (*it will be*). The converse also applies: the future form יְהִי
becomes a past form when the conversive *vav* precedes it. This grammatical
peculiarity hints that whenever our glorious past serves as a foundation for
building the future, the result is joy and great promise for that future: וְהָיָה בַּיּוֹם
הַהוּא..., *and it shall come to pass on that day — the great trumpet of liberation
will resound, etc.* (*Isaiah* 27:13). But whenever a Jew wants to reject our future
by forgetting the past, by pretending to consider it without substance, then
sadness and despair take over: אֵין וַיְהִי אֶלָּא לְשׁוֹן צָרָה. Although he was on the
threshold of a new life of wandering, full of bleak prospects, Jacob nevertheless
believed in the future and placed all his confidence in Providence. And God
promised to give his children fulfillment with the same term which Jacob had
used to express his serene confidence in the future (*Rabbah*, 70).

22. וְהָאֶבֶן הַזֹּאת אֲשֶׁר־שַׂמְתִּי מַצֵּבָה — *Then this stone which I have set up as a
pillar.* R' Eliezer taught: And what did God do? This stone, which had served
to protect the patriarch, He buried in the depths of the abyss and used it to
stabilize the world, just as one lays the cornerstone of a building. That is why
this stone is called אֶבֶן שְׁתִיָּה (from the verb שׁוּת, *to place*). It is situated at the
center of the world, where the world began to form. There the Holy of Holies
was built in the Temple of Jerusalem (*Pirkei D'Rabbi Eliezer* 35).

However, sources in the Talmud (*Yoma* 53b) and *Zohar* indicate that
the formation of the world began with the אֶבֶן שְׁתִיָּה. According to tradition,
the history of this stone goes back to the epoch of creation, then to the time
of Abraham, Jacob and the prophets. The term הַמָּקוֹם, meaning simply *the
place* and recurring so often in Scripture, designates the location of this
foundation stone. This stone now marks the beginning of the founding of

which I have set up as a pillar shall become a house of God, and
whatever You will give me, I shall repeatedly tithe to You."

29   ¹*So Jacob lifted his feet, and went toward the land of*

the בֵּית יִשְׂרָאֵל, *family of Israel*, which is to be identified with the house of
God (בֵּית אֱלֹהִים) serving as the very fountainhead of the בֵּית הַמִּקְדָּשׁ, *Sanctu-*
ary. This foundation constitutes the definitive consolidation of the world, whose
"foundation stone" is thus established a second time. And when, at
the end of his life, Jacob recalls the stages of his past, he exclaims, "מִשָּׁם רֹעֶה
אֶבֶן יִשְׂרָאֵל, thanks to God, Who from there (Beth-el) tended (watched over
and guarded) the stone which Israel (had erected there)" (*Genesis* 49:24). For
him this stone remains the triple symbol of Creation, the Sanctuary and
the Jewish home.

וְכֹל אֲשֶׁר תִּתֶּן־לִי עַשֵּׂר אֲעַשְּׂרֶנּוּ לָךְ — *And whatever You will give me I shall*
repeatedly tithe to You. Besides his pledge to remain always a faithful servant
of God and to found a home which would be a "house of God," Jacob does not
forget to include in his vow a commitment to do good to others, by consecrating
a tenth of all he will possess for sacred use. To be sure, this commitment referred
to possessions which did not as yet exist, and the promise depended entirely on
future circumstances; nevertheless, it was still valid, as *Rambam* explains in his
Mishneh Torah (הל׳ ערכין, פ״ו, ל״א).

Jacob gave us the first example of making a vow in a time of distress, and at
that time he instituted the offering of a tithe (*Tanchuma Re'eh*; see, however,
our commentary on *Genesis* 14:20 and 26:12). Essentially, this *mitzvah* applied
only in the Holy Land, and Jacob's vow as he left this land could refer only to
the time when he would come back to it. But right from his departure, he thought
of fulfilling it on his return. This attitude shows us the contrast between Jacob
and his brother Esau. The latter, on the very soil of the Holy Land, hypocritically
asked his father insidious questions on how to perform this *mitzvah* (cf. *Rashi*
on 25:28).

A heretic one day asked R' Meir, "You maintain that your ancestor Jacob was
an honest man. Then since he had vowed to tithe all that God had granted him,
why did he not tithe his children?" He replied, "He did so by consecrating his
son Levi to Divine service. This son was the most suitable for this sacred mission"
(*Radak*). [Not counting Reuben and Joseph, the firstborn sons of Leah and
Rachel, who were consecrated to God by birth, Jacob tithed his remaining ten
sons (*Rabbah*, 70).] Jacob had already been personally reproached for negligence
in fulfilling his vow by the angel who had attacked him at night and prevented
him from crossing the ford of Yabok (32:23). This negligence was a fault which
rendered him vulnerable to his brother's rivalry. And so, he immediately decided
to dedicate Levi to the Divine service (*Pirkei D'Rabbi Eliezer* 37). However, *Ibn*
Ezra remarks that it is fitting to interpret this Midrash symbolically, as the
setting aside of a tithe is required only for the harvest and livestock.

ב בְנֵי־קֶדֶם: וַיַּרְא וְהִנֵּה בְאֵר בַּשָּׂדֶה וְהִנֵּה־שָׁם שְׁלֹשָׁה עֶדְרֵי־
צֹאן רֹבְצִים עָלֶיהָ כִּי מִן־הַבְּאֵר הַהִוא יַשְׁקוּ הָעֲדָרִים וְהָאֶבֶן
ג גְּדֹלָה עַל־פִּי הַבְּאֵר: וְנֶאֶסְפוּ־שָׁמָּה כָל־הָעֲדָרִים וְגָלֲלוּ
אֶת־הָאֶבֶן מֵעַל פִּי הַבְּאֵר וְהִשְׁקוּ אֶת־הַצֹּאן וְהֵשִׁיבוּ אֶת־
ד הָאֶבֶן עַל־פִּי הַבְּאֵר לִמְקֹמָהּ: וַיֹּאמֶר לָהֶם יַעֲקֹב אַחַי מֵאַיִן
ה אַתֶּם וַיֹּאמְרוּ מֵחָרָן אֲנָחְנוּ: וַיֹּאמֶר לָהֶם הַיְדַעְתֶּם אֶת־
ו לָבָן בֶּן־נָחוֹר וַיֹּאמְרוּ יָדָעְנוּ: וַיֹּאמֶר לָהֶם הֲשָׁלוֹם לוֹ וַיֹּאמְרוּ
ז שָׁלוֹם וְהִנֵּה רָחֵל בִּתּוֹ בָּאָה עִם־הַצֹּאן: וַיֹּאמֶר הֵן עוֹד
הַיּוֹם גָּדוֹל לֹא־עֵת הֵאָסֵף הַמִּקְנֶה הַשְׁקוּ הַצֹּאן וּלְכוּ רְעוּ:
ח וַיֹּאמְרוּ לֹא נוּכַל עַד אֲשֶׁר יֵאָסְפוּ כָּל־הָעֲדָרִים וְגָלֲלוּ אֶת־
ט הָאֶבֶן מֵעַל פִּי הַבְּאֵר וְהִשְׁקִינוּ הַצֹּאן: עוֹדֶנּוּ מְדַבֵּר עִמָּם
י וְרָחֵל ׀ בָּאָה עִם־הַצֹּאן אֲשֶׁר לְאָבִיהָ כִּי רֹעָה הִוא: וַיְהִי

29.

1. יַעֲקֹב ... וַיֵּלֶךְ אַרְצָה בְנֵי־קֶדֶם — *Jacob ... went toward the land of the easterners.* Since Laban lived in Haran, why did Jacob head toward the land of בְּנֵי קֶדֶם? He had said to himself, "When my father wanted to marry, Abraham sent his servant, who came upon a well of water and there found the woman who became my mother. Now, in Haran I have not found a well, a fountain, or a stream." So he headed eastward in the direction of the land of the בְּנֵי קֶדֶם. Soon he discovered a well, not far from Haran (*Zohar*).

The Torah gives several instances of marriages "by a well." The significance of such marriages has been brought out in our commentary to 21:25. Like his father, Jacob wanted to arrange for his marriage near sources of purity and holiness.

2. וַיַּרְא וְהִנֵּה בְאֵר בַּשָּׂדֶה — *He looked, and behold — a well in the field!* The Torah makes a point of giving minute details about watering the sheep. This prompts our Sages to consider that the passage hints at a message of a general nature which refers to the future destinies of the family of Abraham. As was shown in commentary to chapter 26, the well symbolizes the source of inspiration emanating from the Divine Spirit. The concrete manifestation on earth of this source of inspiration is represented by the Sanctuary, by the *Sanhedrin*, or in a more limited way by the synagogue. So in the Midrash our Sages tell us how the details recorded here apply symbolically to these manifestations.

The *Zohar* compares the story of Jacob's marriage to that of Moses, related in *Exodus* 2:15. It was Moses who achieved the highest degree of holiness accessible to mortal man. He "ascended to God" (*Exodus* 19:3) and abstained from conjugal relations (*Deuteronomy* 5:27 and 28). He was "the man of God" (ibid.

the easterners. ² *He looked, and behold — a well in the field! And behold! three flocks of sheep lay there beside it, for from that well they would water the flocks, and the stone over the mouth of the well was large.* ³ *When all the flocks would be assembled there they would roll the stone from the mouth of the well and water the sheep; then they would put back the stone over the mouth of the well, in its place.*

⁴ *Jacob said to them, "My brothers, where are you from?" And they said, "We are from Charan."* ⁵ *He said to them, "Do you know Laban the son of Nahor?" And they said, "We know."* ⁶ *Then he said to them, "Is it well with him?" They answered, "It is well; and see — his daughter Rachel is coming with the flock!"*

⁷ *He said, "Look, the day is still long; it is not yet time to bring the livestock in; water the flock and go on grazing."* ⁸ *But they said, "We will be unable to, until all the flocks will have been gathered and they will roll the stone off the mouth of the well; we will then water the flock."*

⁹ *While he was still speaking with them, Rachel had arrived with her father's flock, for she was a shepherdess.* ¹⁰ *And it was,*

33:1). And so, the text says of the well where Moses met his future wife, וַיֵּשֶׁב עַל הַבְּאֵר, *he sat by a well* (*Exodus* 2:15) [where the word "well" allegorically assumes the meaning of the place of marriage]. Moreover, the word בְּאֵר occurs just once in the story of Moses while it is mentioned seven times in the account of Jacob's marriage. This insistence brings out the fact that the patriarch did not attain the same degree of holiness as Moses. Jacob lingered by the well and stopped to contemplate it (וַיַּרְא וְהִנֵּה בְאֵר), whereas Moses lived unconcerned with earthly contingencies and ultimately "apart from his wife" (*Rashi* on *Numbers* 12:1; cf. our commentary to verse 27).

7. הֵן עוֹד הַיּוֹם גָּדוֹל — *Look, the day is still long. Rashi* comments, "This means if you are hired by the day, you have not yet finished your day's work; and even if the animals are your own, it is still not yet time to bring in the cattle." And the Midrash adds, "You may conclude from this example that if a righteous man passes by a place where he sees a misdeed taking place, his duty is to protest it and not to say, 'This is none of my business' " (*Midrash Lekach Tov*). In the passage which follows, the Torah bears witness to the fact that Jacob demanded the same absolute rectitude and conscientiousness of himself as he did of others (31:6 and 40).

9. וְרָחֵל בָּאָה עִם־הַצֹּאן אֲשֶׁר לְאָבִיהָ — *Rachel had arrived with her father's flock.* But Leah was not a shepherdess. She stayed at home for she was the elder of the twin sisters and she was to marry (Midrash ibid.). Cf. our commentary to verse 26 and to 35:18.

כַּאֲשֶׁר֩ רָאָ֨ה יַעֲקֹ֜ב אֶת־רָחֵ֗ל בַּת־לָבָן֙ אֲחִ֣י אִמּ֔וֹ וְאֶת־צֹ֥אן
לָבָ֖ן אֲחִ֣י אִמּ֑וֹ וַיִּגַּ֣שׁ יַעֲקֹ֗ב וַיָּ֤גֶל אֶת־הָאֶ֨בֶן֙ מֵעַל֙ פִּ֣י הַבְּאֵ֔ר

יא וַיַּ֕שְׁקְ אֶת־צֹ֥אן לָבָ֖ן אֲחִ֥י אִמּֽוֹ: וַיִּשַּׁ֥ק יַעֲקֹ֖ב לְרָחֵ֑ל וַיִּשָּׂ֥א
יב אֶת־קֹל֖וֹ וַיֵּֽבְךְּ: וַיַּגֵּ֨ד יַעֲקֹ֜ב לְרָחֵ֗ל כִּ֣י אֲחִ֤י אָבִ֨יהָ֙ ה֔וּא וְכִ֥י
יג בֶן־רִבְקָ֖ה ה֑וּא וַתָּ֖רָץ וַתַּגֵּ֥ד לְאָבִֽיהָ: וַיְהִי֩ כִשְׁמֹ֨עַ לָבָ֜ן אֶת־
שֵׁ֣מַע ׀ יַעֲקֹ֣ב בֶּן־אֲחֹת֗וֹ וַיָּ֤רָץ לִקְרָאתוֹ֙ וַיְחַבֶּק־לוֹ֙ וַיְנַשֶּׁק־ל֔וֹ
וַיְבִיאֵ֖הוּ אֶל־בֵּית֑וֹ וַיְסַפֵּ֣ר לְלָבָ֔ן אֵ֥ת כָּל־הַדְּבָרִ֖ים הָאֵֽלֶּה:
יד וַיֹּ֤אמֶר לוֹ֙ לָבָ֔ן אַ֛ךְ עַצְמִ֥י וּבְשָׂרִ֖י אָ֑תָּה וַיֵּ֥שֶׁב עִמּ֖וֹ חֹ֥דֶשׁ יָמִֽים:
טו וַיֹּ֤אמֶר לָבָן֙ לְיַעֲקֹ֔ב הֲכִֽי־אָחִ֣י אַ֔תָּה וַעֲבַדְתַּ֖נִי חִנָּ֑ם הַגִּ֥ידָה לִּ֖י
טז מַה־מַּשְׂכֻּרְתֶּֽךָ: וּלְלָבָ֖ן שְׁתֵּ֣י בָנ֑וֹת שֵׁ֤ם הַגְּדֹלָה֙ לֵאָ֔ה וְשֵׁ֥ם
יז הַקְּטַנָּ֖ה רָחֵֽל: וְעֵינֵ֥י לֵאָ֖ה רַכּ֑וֹת וְרָחֵל֙ הָֽיְתָ֔ה יְפַת־תֹּ֖אַר

10. אֶת־רָחֵ֗ל בַּת־לָבָן֙ אֲחִ֣י אִמּ֔וֹ — *Rachel, daughter of Laban his mother's brother.*
Three times in this verse the Torah repeats that Laban was the brother of Jacob's
mother — for the memory of his mother was ever-present in Jacob's mind in all
that he did here. In Rachel he recognized the living image of his mother, whose
niece Rachel was. He kissed her at once and, were it not for the repeated
references to the memory of his mother, one might have thought that this was
an act of gallantry toward a pretty shepherdess. But in her Jacob saw only his
close kin. This also explains why he cried when he embraced her. For a long time
Jacob had wandered without encountering a kindred spirit. But now, suddenly
he found himself face to face with a cousin and in a flash saw his mother's face
once again. Overcome by emotion, he burst into tears. These tears prove that the
kiss was altogether chaste (*R' S.R. Hirsch*).

Ibn Ezra remarks that when the verb נָשַׁק, *to embrace*, is followed by the
preposition ל of the dative case, as in this verse (11), it means to kiss the head or
the shoulder, but when it takes the preposition אֶת, it means to kiss on the mouth
(*Genesis 27:26*).

יַעֲקֹב וַיָּגֶל אֶת־הָאֶבֶן — *Jacob . . . and rolled the stone.* As one would remove the
cork from the mouth of a bottle — to inform you that he had great strength
(*Rashi*). Jacob came to Haran empty-handed, as *Rashi* points out in his
commentary on this verse. The only treasure which he had taken from his
father's house was his own robust health and physical strength — but it was a
treasure of inestimable worth. His strength was immense and the Midrash states
that he often used it. Just how strong he was can be seen from the results of his
struggle with the angel (32:25) from which he emerged in glory. His children
inherited his physical qualities, as we see from the exploits of Judah and his
brothers (in their epic confrontation with Joseph, as recounted in the Midrash);
so too with Simeon and Levi (34:25). Even his grandson Manasseh, Joseph's son,
demonstrated similar prowess. When Joseph wanted to have his brother Simeon
imprisoned, he left it to his valiant warriors to arrest him but they could not

when Jacob saw Rachel, daughter of Laban his mother's brother, and the flock of Laban his mother's brother, Jacob came forward and rolled the stone off the mouth of the well and watered the sheep of Laban his mother's brother. [11] *Then Jacob kissed Rachel; and he raised his voice and wept.* [12] *Jacob told Rachel that he was her father's relative, and that he was Rebecca's son; then she ran and told her father.*

[13] *And it was, when Laban heard the news of Jacob his sister's son, he ran toward him, embraced him, kissed him, and took him to his house; he recounted to Laban all these events.* [14] *Then Laban said to him, "Nevertheless, you are my flesh and blood!" And he stayed with him a month's time.*

[15] *Then Laban said to Jacob, "Just because you are my relative, should you serve me for nothing? Tell me: What are your wages?"*

[16] *(Laban had two daughters. The name of the older one was Leah and the name of the younger one was Rachel* [17] *Leah's eyes were tender, while Rachel was beautiful of form*

subdue him. Then he entrusted his son Manasseh with taking him to prison. Manasseh struck him on the shoulder and Simeon collapsed. He turned to his brothers and called out to them, "The blow I just received is not from an Egyptian; it could only have come from one of our own blood" (*Tanchuma Vayigash* 4).

12. וַיַּגֵּד יַעֲקֹב לְרָחֵל כִּי אֲחִי אָבִיהָ הוּא — *Jacob told Rachel that he was her father's relative* (lit. *brother*). But was he not her father's nephew? Indeed he was. But he told her that he had come to marry one of his uncle's daughters and asked her whether she wanted to be his wife. She had replied in the affirmative, immediately adding, "My father is crafty and you are no match for him." Jacob asked what to watch for in the way of trickery. She replied, "I have an older sister and he does not want me to marry before she does." Jacob replied, "If it is cunning he wants, I am his brother (i.e. his equal) but if it is fairness that he seeks, then I am the son of Rebecca" (*Rabbah*). Is it then permissible for the righteous to resort to deception? Yes, from this verse (*II Samuel* 22:27): *With the pure be sincere and with the deceiver, cunning.* Jacob then gave her signs in order to recognize her on the marriage night, but Rachel revealed them to her sister in order to spare her shame. This is why Jacob was tricked (*Bava Basra* 123a). Ultimately, however, the innate honesty of the patriarch certainly got the better of his uncle's trickery.

15. וַעֲבַדְתַּנִי חִנָּם — *Should you serve me for nothing?* As soon as he took up residence in Laban's house, Jacob no longer allowed Rachel to tend the flocks. he took over this task himself.

שלישי   יח וַיֶּאֱהַב יַעֲקֹב אֶת־רָחֵל וַיֹּאמֶר אֶעֱבָדְךָ שֶׁבַע
יט שָׁנִים בְּרָחֵל בִּתְּךָ הַקְּטַנָּה: וַיֹּאמֶר לָבָן טוֹב תִּתִּי אֹתָהּ לָךְ
כ מִתִּתִּי אֹתָהּ לְאִישׁ אַחֵר שְׁבָה עִמָּדִי: וַיַּעֲבֹד יַעֲקֹב בְּרָחֵל
שֶׁבַע שָׁנִים וַיִּהְיוּ בְעֵינָיו כְּיָמִים אֲחָדִים בְּאַהֲבָתוֹ אֹתָהּ:
כא וַיֹּאמֶר יַעֲקֹב אֶל־לָבָן הָבָה אֶת־אִשְׁתִּי כִּי מָלְאוּ יָמָי וְאָבוֹאָה

17. וְרָחֵל הָיְתָה יְפַת־תֹּאַר וִיפַת מַרְאֶה — *Rachel('s face) was beautiful of form and beautiful of appearance.* The terms תֹּאַר and מַרְאֶה are interpreted in this way by *Rashi. Midrash Lekach Tov* refers them to the form of her body and the beauty of the face while *R' Chaim ben Attar* holds that one of the terms signifies beauty, the other the charm of the personality.

The Torah praises feminine beauty in several instances, especially in connection with the patriarchs' wives. It certainly does not consider beauty a virtue in itself, and King Solomon describes it as "deceitful and vain" alongside the virtue of piety (*Proverbs* 31:30). Nevertheless, the Torah does esteem true beauty as the physical reflection of a beautiful soul. A bride with beautiful eyes needs no proof of her other qualities (*Taanis* 24a). What is more, physical beauty, like the splendors of nature, can be considered one of the forms in which the Divinity and the sublime love of the Creator are revealed. This theme recurs in many of the psalms.

In his psychological treatise entitled "Eight Chapters" (*Shemoneh Perakim*, ch. 5), *Rambam* stipulates that the purely spiritual pleasure which the perfection of esthetic forms gives is one of the means by which a person who aspires to the knowledge of truth can elevate himself to spheres of abstract thought. Beauty has an exalting effect on the human soul; ugliness, on the other hand, has a depressing effect. It is in this connection, continues *Rambam*, that one is to understand the Talmudic statement describing it as "good fortune" for a scholar to have a wife with a pleasant face (*Shabbos* 25a).

18. אֶעֱבָדְךָ שֶׁבַע שָׁנִים בְּרָחֵל — *I will work for you seven years, for Rachel.* Why did he not propose ten or twelve years? Several answers are given to this question posed by the *Zohar. R' Bachya* holds that Jacob wanted to wait until Rachel reached twelve years of age for she was then only five. But the book *Seder HaDoros* has it that she was was 15 or even 21 years of age at the time. *Rashi* cites a different explanation. The seven years are the "short while" which Jacob's mother had told him to stay with Laban: *Remain with him a short while until your brother's wrath subsides.* Later, when Jacob saw Esau again for the first time in 34 years, he *bowed earthward seven times until he reached his brother* (33:3). Jacob thought of the truth which Solomon expressed in these terms: *A righteous man falls seven times and rises up again (Proverbs* 24:16).

The *Zohar* states that the waiting period was necessary for Jacob to educate Rachel to his own way of thinking before marrying her and making her the future mother of his children, since she had been raised in an idolatrous

> *and beautiful of appearance.)*
> ¹⁸ *Jacob loved Rachel, so he said, "I will work for you seven years, for Rachel your younger daughter."*
> ¹⁹ *Laban said, "It is better that I give her to you than that I give her to another man; remain with me." * ²⁰ *So Jacob worked seven years for Rachel and they seemed to him a few days because of his love for her.*
> ²¹ *Jacob said to Laban, "Deliver my wife for my term is fulfilled, and I will consort with her."*

environment. Thus he acted just as his father had regarding his own marriage, as was shown in our commentary 25:20. (Certain *Midrashim* consider the seven years as the normal period of servitude foreseen for a Jewish servant, foreshadowing *Exodus* 21:2.)

19. טוֹב תִּתִּי אֹתָהּ לָךְ — *It is better that I give her to you.* Both here and further on (30:34) we see that Laban accepts Jacob's proposals without discussion: "Agreed! If only it will be as you say." All the same, he ultimately tricked him in both cases (cf. ibid., verse 36, *Rashi*). One can only conclude that Laban's acceptance of Jacob's offers was not sincere and concealed dishonest, ulterior motives. A man of integrity discusses the conditions of a proposed transaction because he intends to respect them rigorously; but the hypocrite discusses nothing for his mind is already made up to cheat in some way or other, sooner or later, and he wants to leave his partner with the illusion of his good faith.

20. וַיַּעֲבֹד יַעֲקֹב בְּרָחֵל שֶׁבַע שָׁנִים — *So Jacob worked seven years for Rachel.* The prophet Hosea exclaims, *Jacob fled into the fields of Aram and Israel served for a wife, and was a shepherd for a wife* (12:13). The prophet wants his contemporaries, who feign to have forgotten God and pride themselves on their own strength, to remember their past. He shows them the extremely humble beginnings of the Jewish people. Jacob came to Aram as a refugee and he who was one day to be Israel, the herald of monotheism, was obliged to serve as a slave before establishing a home. He had to "serve for a wife and be a shepherd for a wife." And only Divine intervention protected him when he came back from Aram (31:24). He had fled his own land and again he had to flee a foreign land to come back. When at last the hour of liberation arrived for his children, who meanwhile had become a nation, they again found themselves enslaved. And the one who came to free them was neither king nor general, but a prophet. "By a prophet did God bring Israel up out of Egypt, and by a prophet was he guarded (ibid. 14). Whatever Jewry represents for humanity, as well as for itself, it owes solely to Divine Providence. This is the lesson which the prophet Hosea means to draw from the modest beginnings of the patriarch Jacob.

21. וְאָבוֹאָה אֵלֶיהָ — *And I will consort with her. Rashi* points out, "The most dissolute of people would not dare to speak in this way. But Jacob was 84 years old and had to start his family." *R' Bachya*, though, explains that the patriarchs

כב אֵלֶיהָ: וַיֶּאֱסֹף לָבָן אֶת־כָּל־אַנְשֵׁי הַמָּקוֹם וַיַּעַשׂ מִשְׁתֶּה:
כג וַיְהִי בָעֶרֶב וַיִּקַּח אֶת־לֵאָה בִתּוֹ וַיָּבֵא אֹתָהּ אֵלָיו וַיָּבֹא
כד אֵלֶיהָ: וַיִּתֵּן לָבָן לָהּ אֶת־זִלְפָּה שִׁפְחָתוֹ לְלֵאָה בִתּוֹ
כה שִׁפְחָה: וַיְהִי בַבֹּקֶר וְהִנֵּה־הִוא לֵאָה וַיֹּאמֶר אֶל־לָבָן
מַה־זֹּאת עָשִׂיתָ לִּי הֲלֹא בְרָחֵל עָבַדְתִּי עִמָּךְ וְלָמָּה
כו רִמִּיתָנִי: וַיֹּאמֶר לָבָן לֹא־יֵעָשֶׂה כֵן בִּמְקוֹמֵנוּ לָתֵת הַצְּעִירָה

and their wives lived on a very high spiritual plane and for them cohabitation was a natural function, free of sensuality. It was a pure act carried out for the duty of procreation. Thus Jacob's words are free from any frivolous thought. (The *Maharal* develops this thesis at length in *Be'er HaGolah,* 5.)

22. וַיֶּאֱסֹף לָבָן אֶת־כָּל־אַנְשֵׁי הַמָּקוֹם — *So Laban gathered all the people of the place.* This gathering preceded the feast which he offered to all the inhabitants. For Laban had devised a new scheme to take advantage of his nephew. He gathered all the men and said to them, "You know we are short of water in our city. Now, since this righteous man who is my nephew arrived here, the water is blessed and it gushes forth in abundance. Do you not want him to remain with us another seven years?" They replied, "Surely, do as you see fit." Then he said to them, "If you agree, I will deceive him and give him Leah for a wife. Since he loves Rachel very much, he will work here another seven years." They replied, "Do as you please." Then Laban demanded pledges from them as guarantees that they would not divulge the secret. Everyone brought him his pledge and Laban made the men a feast, during which they handed them over to him. That is why Laban is called לָבָן הָאֲרַמִּי, for he tricked even the men of his own city, Aram. He never gave them back their pledges (*Midrash*).

23. וַיְהִי בָעֶרֶב וַיִּקַּח אֶת־לֵאָה בִתּוֹ — *And it was in the evening, that he took Leah his daughter.* One cannot get the best of a cunning scoundrel whether through words or force. It does no good even to lock him up in a dungeon. Didn't Jacob take all the necessary precautions? He had said, "I will work for you seven years for Rachel." You might say then, he meant another Rachel nearby. So he specified, "your daughter." You might say, "I will change Leah's name them to Rachel." And so he again specified, "the younger." But all these precautions were to no avail (cf. *Rashi* on verse 18).

24. וַיִּתֵּן לָבָן לָהּ אֶת־זִלְפָּה שִׁפְחָתוֹ — *And Laban gave her Zilpah his maidservant.* The text then repeats, *a maidservant to Leah his daughter.* So too later on (verse 29) in connection with Bilhah, given as a bondwoman to Rachel. The Torah seems to want to emphasize that Laban showered kindness upon his daughters but offered his son-in-law nothing. Bilhah and Zilpah were also daughters of Laban, as *Rashi* notes in 31:50, but he gave them as bondwomen because their mother was only his concubine.

25. וַיְהִי בַבֹּקֶר וְהִנֵּה־הִוא לֵאָה — *And it was, in the morning, that behold it was Leah!* "In the morning" — hence at night it was not Leah. Indeed, Jacob had

²² *So Laban gathered all the people of the place and made a feast.*
²³ *And it was in the evening, that he took Leah his daughter and brought her to him; and he consorted with her.*
²⁴ *— And Laban gave her Zilpah his maidservant — a maidservant to Leah his daughter.*
²⁵ *And it was, in the morning, that behold it was Leah! So he said to Laban, "What is this you have done to me? Was it not for Rachel that I worked for you? Why have you deceived me?"*
²⁶ *Laban said, "Such is not done in our place, to give the younger*

prearranged signs with Rachel for the wedding night. But when Rachel saw that Leah was being given to Jacob, she said to herself, "My sister will be humiliated." And she told her these signs (*Rashi*).

Rachel's act of supreme abnegation for the sake of her sister is considered of a moral value great enough to assure her eternal merit. When the First Temple fell into enemy hands and the Jews were taken into captivity in Babylonia, the patriarchs and Moses intervened from beyond the grave. They begged for God's kindness and asked Him to put an end to the people's suffering. The Midrash allegorically describes their arguments and their means of persuasion to obtain Divine clemency. Each of them referred, in moving terms, to his own merits. But God did not heed any of their supplications. Then Rachel's voice was heard: "Master of the Universe! You know that Jacob loved me with boundless love and that he served my father for seven years so that he could marry me. And when our wedding day came, my father decided to put my sister in my place; but I was not jealous of her. If I, who am nothing but ashes and dust, was not jealous of my rival, how could You, Master of the Universe, be jealous of idols worshiped by the Jews but which are as nought?" God's pity was at once roused and He proclaimed, "I will grant your prayer, Rachel, and I will bring Jewry back to its homeland." The prophet Jeremiah extols this promise of God in these words (31:14-16): *A voice is heard in Ramah, groaning, lamenting and bitterly weeping. Rachel is weeping for her children. She refuses to be comforted for her lost children. Thus says God: "Keep your voice from weeping, and your eyes from tears. For there is a reward for your work," says God, "and they will return from the land of the enemy. Yes, there is hope for your future," says God, "and children will return to their border"* (*Lamentations Rabbah* 1).

וְלָמָּה רִמִּיתָנִי — *Why have you deceived me?* See our commentary to 27:36.

26. לֹא־יֵעָשֶׂה כֵן בִּמְקוֹמֵנוּ — *Such is not done in our place.* The two sisters were twins, with Leah coming into the world before Rachel. However, discussing the birth of the twins Esau and Jacob, *Rashi* explains that the first twin born is really the last to be conceived and, conversely, the first to be conceived is the last born. Hence Jacob, who came into the world after Esau, considered the birthright legally his (cf. 25:26). He drew the same conclusion regarding Rachel and

כז לִפְנֵי הַבְּכִירָה: מַלֵּא שְׁבֻעַ זֹאת וְנִתְּנָה לְךָ גַּם־אֶת־
זֹאת בַּעֲבֹדָה אֲשֶׁר תַּעֲבֹד עִמָּדִי עוֹד שֶׁבַע־שָׁנִים אֲחֵרוֹת:
כח וַיַּעַשׂ יַעֲקֹב כֵּן וַיְמַלֵּא שְׁבֻעַ זֹאת וַיִּתֶּן־לוֹ אֶת־
כט רָחֵל בִּתּוֹ לוֹ לְאִשָּׁה: וַיִּתֵּן לָבָן לְרָחֵל בִּתּוֹ אֶת־בִּלְהָה
ל שִׁפְחָתוֹ לָהּ לְשִׁפְחָה: וַיָּבֹא גַּם אֶל־רָחֵל וַיֶּאֱהַב גַּם־
אֶת־רָחֵל מִלֵּאָה וַיַּעֲבֹד עִמּוֹ עוֹד שֶׁבַע־שָׁנִים אֲחֵרוֹת:

considered her the elder. But Laban answered him, "In our place, with twins, it
is the one who first comes into the world who is considered the elder" (*Chida*).

27. מַלֵּא שְׁבֻעַ זֹאת — *Complete the week of this one.* Rambam refers to this
sentence when he codifies the prohibition of mixing two different rejoicings [for
example, the celebration of marriage on a festival] (הל' אישות, פ"י, י"ד). In his
responsa, R' Y.S. Nathanson discusses *Ramban's* objections to this conclusion
and establishes the following principle: No *mitzvah* can be based on what
preceded the revelation on Sinai, but a moral principle can indeed be inferred
from such a happening (שו"ת שואל ומשיב מהד' ד' ח"א).

וְנִתְּנָה לְךָ גַּם־אֶת־זֹאת — *And we will give you the other one, too.* When Jacob
arrived at Laban's house, Laban felt embarrassed for he did not know how to
ensure that Jacob would go to work for him. He went to consult his household
gods who revealed to him that: "Jacob wants nothing but a wife. He is attracted
to women and if he ever threatens to leave you, offer him another wife and he
will not go" (*Yalkut Reuveni*). The *Zohar* also notes the allusion which comes
from the relationship between the word נָקְבָה, *to set a salary*, in chapter 30:28
and נְקֵבָה, *woman*. (Cf. our commentary to 29:2.)

28. וַיִּתֶּן־לוֹ אֶת־רָחֵל בִּתּוֹ לוֹ לְאִשָּׁה — *And he gave him Rachel his daughter to him
as a wife.* The fact that Jacob married two sisters, thus violating a prohibition
of the Torah (*Leviticus* 18:18), is considered a flaw in his piety (*Pesachim* 119b).
Moreover, this seems to be in contradiction with what the Midrash affirms, that
the patriarchs performed all the precepts of the Torah (*Genesis Rabbah*, chapter
95). *Ramban* and *R' Bachya* attempt to resolve this contradiction by suggesting
that the patriarchs fulfilled the Torah only within the Promised Land. Jacob was
outside the borders of this land when he married the two sisters (cf. *Genesis* 26:5).
But this opinion is contested and *Maharal* (תפא' ישר' פ"ב), along with R' *Chaim
ben Attar* (on *Genesis* 49:3) hold that the patriarchs only observed the Noachian
precepts which are the universal foundation for ethics, and also the positive
commandments of the Torah since they reflect loving God, whereas the
prohibitions of the Torah are directed more especially toward those who
formally received them at the Revelation on Sinai (cf. our commentary to 26:5).
But, whatever the case, the union with two sisters barred the way for the
patriarch to attain the ultimate degree of perfection, a fact which does not
prevent the Torah, out of respect for Jacob, from omitting its sanction against

before the elder. ²⁷ *Complete the week of this one and we will give you the other one too, for the work which you will perform for me yet another seven years.''*

²⁸ *So Jacob did so and he completed the week for her; and he gave him Rachel his daughter to him as a wife.* ²⁹ *And Laban gave Rachel his daughter Bilhah his maidservant — to her as a maidservant.* ³⁰ *He consorted also with Rachel and loved Rachel even more than Leah; and he worked for him yet another seven years.*

union with two sisters in the chapter which deals with sanctions against illicit marriages (cf. *R' Bachya* on *Leviticus* 20:21). The Kabbalistic explanation of Jacob's marriage is given by *Recanati* on *Leviticus* 18:6 (עי׳ נמוקי שמואל, פסחים קי״ט; וע׳ע מהרש״א יומא כ״ח; וש״ת הרדב״ז, ח״ב סי׳ תרצ״ו).

30. וַיֶּאֱהַב גַּם־אֶת־רָחֵל מִלֵּאָה — *And loved Rachel even more than Leah.* But the following verse tells us that Jacob hated Leah. This leads the *Midrashim* to describe how Jacob's feelings toward her changed. Although she was not the one his heart chose, he loved her at first, as one loves the first woman of his life (*Sanhedrin* 22a, following *Proverbs* 5:18: *Rejoice with the wife of your youth*) and he did so even in addition to Rachel, גַּם־אֶת־רָחֵל, whom he loved with the deepest affection. But his feelings for Leah quickly turned to hatred. For when he realized how he had been tricked on the wedding night he said to her, "Deceiver, daughter of a deceiver! You have become your father's accomplice and are just as treacherous as he." She answered him, "And you! Did you not trick your father when he asked, 'Is it you, my son Esau?' And you replied, 'I am Esau, your firstborn.' Did your father not tell Esau about you, saying, 'Your brother came with cleverness' (27:35)? And you think you have the right to reproach me for my deception?"

Jacob made no reply to these cutting words. Did he feel that the way he was tricked had to be accepted as reflecting Divine will, just as his father had without hesitation accepted his own ruse when he exclaimed, (ibid. v. 33) "Indeed, he shall remain blessed"? Or did Jacob consider that he had just received due punishment for having deceived his brother, even though he had only acted on his mother's formal command and did not feel that he was at all guilty?

In any case, Leah's reaction created an atmosphere full of bitterness which lasted between them for a very long time. At first Jacob even thought of divorce. He doubted Leah's sincerity and her morality, fearing the effects of what she might have inherited from her father. He remembered his father's insistence that Esau repudiate his wives because of their evil character. He lived in fear that marriage to Leah might compromise his noble destiny by giving him unworthy children. But very soon she became pregnant and from this Jacob concluded that Providence wanted her to remain his wife. (These circumstances might explain the fact that Leah conceived right from the first union, as noted in *Tosafos* to

לא וַיַּרְא יהוה כִּי־שְׂנוּאָה לֵאָה וַיִּפְתַּח אֶת־רַחְמָהּ וְרָחֵל
עֲקָרָה: לב וַתַּהַר לֵאָה וַתֵּלֶד בֵּן וַתִּקְרָא שְׁמוֹ רְאוּבֵן כִּי
אָמְרָה כִּי־רָאָה יהוה בְּעָנְיִי כִּי עַתָּה יֶאֱהָבַנִי אִישִׁי:

Yevamos 76a, in contrast to the general rule mentioned in the Talmud in
Yevamos 34a. Besides, Leah's children were born prematurely, in the seventh
month of her pregnancy. As a result, she managed to bring her first four sons
into the world in three years. Cf. *Sforno* on 30:8.)

Despite this, Jacob kept on harboring resentment toward Leah for a long time,
even after Rachel died. And it was only on his deathbed, when he realized the
profound piety which ennobled each of his sons without exception, that he paid
homage to Leah's great and sincere devotion. *Then Israel prostrated himself* עַל
רֹאשׁ הַמִּטָּה, *towards the head of his bed* (47:31), i.e. to Leah, the one who had
borne him more than half of all his children (*Rabbah* and *Tanchuma*).

31. וַיַּרְא ה' — *HASHEM saw.* The verb "to see" when referring to God has the
sense of an intellectual perception, as *Rambam* explains in his *Guide* (1:4).
Hence, in this sense, we are to take it that God alone "saw" what no one else
could see, namely the hatred which Jacob had deep in his heart for Leah. Jacob
was able to conceal his feeling and perhaps even Leah herself did not suspect just
how deep his hostility went! But God also knew that she did not deserve it, for
she was a righteous and virtuous woman. Accordingly, He decided to assist this
unfortunate woman who was suffering unjustly, just as He "saw" the plight of
the unfortunate descendants of Israel who were being oppressed in Egypt; and
this "seeing" was a means of "directing His heart toward them and not keeping
from them any longer" (*Rashi* on *Exodus* 2:25).

כִּי־שְׂנוּאָה לֵאָה — *That Leah was unloved.* We see, however, that of all the
children born to Jacob, Leah's children were the best, despite the fact that
the children of a hated wife are, generally speaking, a bad lot (cf. *Nedarim* 20b).
The *Zohar* explains that the hatred which this sincerely pious wife had to bear
had the effect of relegating her to the background. Indeed, her whole life
was spent in the shadow of her sister Rachel's life. For Rachel, from the
beginning, everything occurred in the open. With Leah it was different. Events
in her life followed one another in the mystery of the unknown. Jacob did not
know that the one for whom he had served Laban seven years was Leah. He did
not know that Leah was the one with whom he had spent the first night of his
marriage; and finally, the Torah shrouds the date and circumstances of her death
in mystery whereas Rachel's tomb stands as a monument on a main
thoroughfare. The veil which was spread over the whole of Leah's life had a
beneficial effect, for "blessing abounds solely in what is hidden from sight"
(*Taanis* 8b). And so she was blessed with numerous and magnificent children
(*Zohar*). Judah and Levi became the heads of the dynasties of the Jewish nation
— the kingdom and priesthood — while Rachel's children played relatively
secondary roles.

---

³¹ *HASHEM saw that Leah was unloved, so He opened her womb; but Rachel remained barren.*

³² *Leah conceived and bore a son, and she called his name Reuben, as she had declared, "Because HASHEM has discerned my humiliation, for now my husband will love me."*

וַיִּפְתַּח אֶת־רַחְמָהּ — *So He opened her womb.* The Sages of the Midrash explain the verse, *For Hashem regards the way of the righteous (Psalms 1:6).* Leah, a righteous, pious woman, deserved Divine solicitude all the more since the torment which she had to endure from Jacob was not justified. Just the thought that she might have one day been Esau's had so terrified her that it ravaged her features. Her eyes became weak "because she feared she was destined for Esau and cried over it. Everyone was saying, Rebecca has two sons, Laban has two daughters; the elder will marry the elder and the younger the younger" (*Rashi* on verse 17). With all her soul Leah was hoping instead to give children to righteous Jacob. "God heard her prayer, for she wanted very much to found numerous tribes" (30:17, *Rashi*). He made her fertile although by nature she was barren (*Pesikta D'Rav Kahana,* 20). God thus redeemed Leah in her husband's eyes and rewarded her for her suffering, being lenient toward her although she had consented to obey Laban's order to take Rachel's place in the bridal chamber (cf. *Ramban*). The Divine name ה׳ brings out this merciful aspect, whereas in the parallel wording of *Exodus 2:25,* וַיַּרְא אֱלֹהִים אֶת־בְּנֵי יִשְׂרָאֵל וַיֵּדַע אֱלֹהִים, *God saw the Children of Israel; and God knew,* the name אֱלֹהִים is used.

32. וַתִּקְרָא שְׁמוֹ רְאוּבֵן — *And she called his name Reuben.* The names Leah gave to her children express the purity of her intentions. They bring out the happiness which she felt at being the wife of the patriarch. At the same time they reflect the immense gratitude of a fulfilled mother toward Providence. Blessing her in this way, Providence did justice to her with respect to her husband and permitted her to win his affection. Hence she calls her first son רְאוּבֵן, for "Hashem has discerned my humiliation, (a reference to וַיַּרְא ה׳ in the previous verse); for now my husband will love me."

Rashi, however, cites the explanation of R' Elazar (*Berachos* 7b): Leah said: "See (רְאוּ) the difference between my son (בֵּן) and the son of my father-in-law. The latter sold his birthright to Jacob but my son will not sell his to Joseph. Nor will he protest the preference for Joseph. Not only that, he will even want to rescue Joseph from the pit."

Some have wondered what could have prompted R' Elazar to look for a different interpretation from that given explicitly by the Torah itself. It has been thought that Leah's expression רְאוּ, *see,* hints at a deeper meaning since the singular form רְאֵה would have been sufficient. Also, the syllable בֵּן seems superfluous in the light of the reason for the name as given in the Torah — it would seem that a more appropriate name for Leah's son would have been רְאָה עֲנִי (*Maharsha,* ibid.). The Gaon of Vilna holds that the verse itself implies still another reason — which is not expressed — for in all the following names the

לג וַתַּהַר עוֹד וַתֵּלֶד בֵּן וַתֹּאמֶר כִּי־שָׁמַע יהוה כִּי־שְׂנוּאָה אָנֹכִי
וַיִּתֶּן־לִי גַּם־אֶת־זֶה וַתִּקְרָא שְׁמוֹ שִׁמְעוֹן: לד וַתַּהַר עוֹד וַתֵּלֶד בֵּן
וַתֹּאמֶר עַתָּה הַפַּעַם יִלָּוֶה אִישִׁי אֵלַי כִּי־יָלַדְתִּי לוֹ שְׁלֹשָׁה

reason for the name precedes the name itself, whereas here the name is given *a priori*. This implies, then, that this name is not derived solely from the reason mentioned explicitly in the verse.

Be that as it may, R' Elazar's explanation refers to certain events which had not yet come to pass at the time the name was given. Accordingly, it is held that Leah gave this name to the child through prophetic inspiration (רוּחַ הַקֹּדֶשׁ), but was not completely aware of its true import (שֶׁלֹּא מִדַּעַת) [cf. commentaries on *Berachos* ibid.]. The name as it is, then, expresses a twofold sentiment: gratitude to Providence and profound joy at having been spared the dreaded union with Esau (cf. our commentary on verse 31: "See the difference between my son and Esau!").

The influence of one's name on his future destiny is brought out by R' Elazar (*Berachos* ibid.) in reference to the naming of Reuben. *R' Chaim ben Attar* considers one's name as characteristic of his personality (*Genesis* 35:10; so too *Radak* on *Psalms* 24:4); in his Talmudic commentary חפץ ה' (on *Berachos* 13a) he holds that the name which a father gives his son corresponds to that which the Creator gives to his soul in the higher spheres. However, R' Jacob ibn Habib, author of ס' עין יעקב, stresses that R' Elazar's declaration שמא גרים implies only that the name serves as an indicator of what may possibly take place, but it does not unconditionally prejudge; in no way does it jeopardize the principle of indeterminism (consistent with R' Akiva's teaching in *Avos* 3:19).

The *Zohar* finds something else discreetly hinted at in the name רְאוּבֵן. While with Leah on his wedding night Jacob had thought of another woman, namely her sister Rachel. Now, children conceived in such a frame of mind are afflicted with a defect (cf. *Nedarim* 20b). So, when Leah gave birth to a boy who was "perfectly formed and with an intelligent look" (*Pirkei D'Rabbi Eliezer* , 36) she was overjoyed. She cried out: "See, a son (well-formed and without a blemish!)" and at once named him רְאוּבֵן. The *Zohar* concludes that God took into account that Jacob had acted in perfect innocence. And, the *Zohar* adds, everything depends ultimately on moral integrity and on the purity of the intention.

33. כִּי־שָׁמַע ה' כִּי־שְׂנוּאָה אָנֹכִי — *Because HASHEM has heard that I am unloved.* Leah realized that her husband still bore some resentment toward her even after the birth of their first child. She "was still hated" and God had heard her prayer by "giving her this one too." The name שִׁמְעוֹן thus means *Hashem heard*.

At the birth of Leah's first son, she had referred to the sense of vision — "Hashem saw"; at the birth of the second, she spoke of the sense of hearing — "Hashem heard." The latter expression implies Divine intervention following a more direct and less impersonal investigation than that which is the consequence of vision. According to R' Moshe Cordovero, when these two terms are applied

³³ *And she conceived again and bore a son and declared,*
"Because HASHEM *has heard that I am unloved, He has given me*
this one also," and she called his name Simeon.

³⁴ *Again she conceived, and bore a son and declared, "This time*
my husband will become attached to me for I have borne him three

to God they refer to acts of Providence. God judges and acts in accordance with
what He has seen or heard regarding men's conduct. But the slight difference in
meaning between these two terms concerns the quality of Divine judgment. The
field of vision takes in much more than that of hearing. Hence the expression
"Hashem saw" implies a view from above and from a distance where
conclusions are reached objectively, without consideration for the reasons and
motives put forward by those involved. In this case, the judgment is based on
strict law — מִדַּת הַדִּין. On the other hand, the words "Hashem heard" mean that
Providence lends an ear to the complaints and sighs of distress which rise up
from the earth, and God hears them. Hence these words refer to a judgment
based on mercy — מִדַּת הָרַחֲמִים.

So when one says, "God has heard my prayer or my grievance, etc." it means
that after having listened, judged, and appraised it, He has answered it (שׁעור
קומה, ס"ו).

And here, with these words, Leah wanted to express that the second child
proved to her, even more than the first, that God had heard and judged her case,
had found her worthy of His mercy, and had rewarded her with kindness even
beyond what she was entitled to.

34. עַתָּה הַפַּעַם יִלָּוֶה אִישִׁי אֵלַי — *This time my husband will become attached to*
me. The birth of a third son gives Leah the feeling that she has finally become
her sister's equal for the affections of her husband. She hopes that from now on
she will have the permanent closeness with her husband that she has longed for,
and she means to express this ardent desire in the name which her son will bear.

However, the name of the son who was destined to found the tribe of the
priests and prime servants of God must contain far more than an expression of
his mother's feelings. It must reflect his religious and national calling.
Accordingly, the name "Levi" has a second meaning. *Rashi* notes this other
meaning while pointing out that, in marked contrast with the other cases, it is
not written here "She called his name," but rather "He called his name Levi."
God Himself put this name on Leah's lips: "He sent the angel Gabriel, who
brought the child before Him. He bestowed this name upon him along with the
twenty-four gifts that are the tribute due to the priests. Because He had
accompanied him with these gifts, He called him לֵוִי (which means, *to*
accompany)." Hence, the name Levi emphasizes the future priestly calling of
Leah's third son. "He accompanied God, by serving Him" (*Targum Yonasan* on
Numbers 18:2). Levi was chosen by his father to preside over the school
(yeshivah) which he had set up for his children, and Levi's descendants

לה בָנִים עַל־כֵּן קָרָא־שְׁמוֹ לֵוִי: וַתַּהַר עוֹד וַתֵּלֶד בֵּן וַתֹּאמֶר
הַפַּעַם אוֹדֶה אֶת־יהוה עַל־כֵּן קָרְאָה שְׁמוֹ יְהוּדָה וַתַּעֲמֹד
א מִלֶּדֶת: וַתֵּרֶא רָחֵל כִּי לֹא יָלְדָה לְיַעֲקֹב וַתְּקַנֵּא רָחֵל בַּאֲחֹתָהּ
וַתֹּאמֶר אֶל־יַעֲקֹב הָבָה־לִּי בָנִים וְאִם־אַיִן מֵתָה אָנֹכִי:

ל

remained the masters and faithful guardians of the ancestral traditions. Never
did the tribe of Levi practice idolatry, as the other tribes temporarily did (רמב״ם,
הל׳ עכו״ם, פ״א).

עַל־כֵּן — *Therefore.* Whenever the expression עַל כֵּן is used for one of the sons,
it heralds a large number of descendants (*Rashi*). [According to M.M. Kasher in
Torah Sheleimah, this is not necessarily to be taken as a cause and effect
relationship; it is rather a statement of fact in reference to the tribes of Judah and
Dan.] An exception is made for the tribe of Levi, as its members were responsible
for guarding the Holy Ark, and sins committed in this context resulted in death
(ibid.). See in this regard the comments of *Ramban* and *R' Chaim ben Attar* on
Numbers 3:14. The latter demonstrates that the tribe of Levi became very
numerous in the period after Moses' death.

קָרָא־שְׁמוֹ לֵוִי — *He called his name Levi.* This name is composed of three letters:
לָ־וִ־י; so too is the name of his most illustrious descendant מֹשֶׁה. Each was the
third child of his parents and Jacob himself was the third of the patriarchs. The
Midrash extols the third element of a group in various areas of our lives and
considers it to be the element reaching the highest perfection. Such is also the
case with the tribe of Levi, of whom the Torah will say, *At that time Hashem
set apart* (i.e. chose) *the tribe of Levi, etc.''* (*Deuteronomy* 10:8; *Tanchuma* on
Exodus 19:1).

35. הַפַּעַם אוֹדֶה אֶת־ה׳ — *This time let me gratefully praise HASHEM.* Said R' Levi,
Leah had a grateful nature. She took charge of the scepter of gratitude and
bequeathed it to her offspring. The name יְהוּדָה encompasses both meanings of
its root — הדה, *gratitude* and אדה, *admission* as when he says צָדְקָה מִמֶּנִּי (38:26).
So did David and Daniel, both of the tribe of Judah (*Psalms* 107:1 and *Daniel*
2:23). Thus, through the virtue of its ancestor, the royal tribe was kept free from
arrogance. The feeling of profound gratitude to God never left it for an instant.
Rachel, on the other hand, excelled in the virtue of silence. She observed the most
complete silence on the night of Leah's marriage. Later, her children inherited
this quality from her. Benjamin kept secret the sale of his brother. Saul and
Esther, both from the tribe of Benjamin, also kept their secrets (*I Samuel* 10:16
and *Esther* 2:20). And this virtue became the key to their deliverance.

קָרְאָה שְׁמוֹ יְהוּדָה — *She called his name Judah.* Later on, the name of his tribe
will serve to designate all of Jacob's descendants, who will be called ''Yehudim,''
or ''Jews.'' In the name יְהוּדָה the Ineffable Name of God (שֵׁם הֲוָיָ׳) is glimpsed
as it shines forth on the Jews. Their destiny is forever linked to the Divine Name
and this destiny will be fulfilled when the Messiah, from the tribe of Judah,

sons"; therefore He called his name Levi.

³⁵ She conceived again, and bore a son and declared, "This time let me gratefully praise HASHEM"; therefore she called his name Judah; then she stopped giving birth.

30   ¹Rachel saw that she had not borne children to Jacob, so Rachel became envious of her sister; she said to Jacob, "Give me children — otherwise I am dead."

causes the Name which is engraved in their own to be worshiped by all men and by all nations (cf. our commentary to 32:29).

וַתַּעֲמֹד מִלֶּדֶת — *Then she stopped giving birth.* The triangle is the representation of the three dimensions making up the non-material world of the spirit חָכְמָה־בִּינָה־דַעַת (wisdom-insight-knowledge) and likewise that of moral forces חֶסֶד־דִּין־רַחֲמִים (kindness-justice-compassion). But the political and social domain, conditioned by history, rests on a broader foundation. It is represented by the rectangle (or the parallelogram of forces). History is added to the first three to form a fourth dimension. Its final outcome is the establishment of the kingdom of God on earth (מַלְכוּת). This is the meaning of the saying שְׁלֹשָׁה אָבוֹת — three are the patriarchs, i.e. the sources of spiritual inspiration; אַרְבַּע אִמָּהוֹת — four are the matriarchs, that is, the agents of terrestrial life. The letter ד, with a numerical value of four and calling to mind the four dimensions, is introduced in the midst of the Ineffable Name הֲוָיָ — the name of Divine royalty — to form the name יְהוּדָה, the artisan of the future kingdom of God (*Zohar*).

Levi, Leah's third son and founder of the priestly tribe, is the keeper of the spiritual and moral ideal. Judah, her fourth son, is the founder of the Messianic rule, whose supreme objective is the kingdom of God. Hence his very being brings to mind the final evolution of history. And so the Torah notes that after the birth of Judah, the mother of Israel's tribes *stopped giving birth*.

30.

1. וַתְּקַנֵּא רָחֵל בַּאֲחֹתָהּ — *So Rachel became envious of her sister.* "Jealousy is cruel as the grave" (*Song of Songs* 8:6) and spares neither the greatest nor the saintliest of men. Rachel succumbed to it. So did the patriarch Isaac. When Isaac arrived at Mount Moriah for the supreme sacrifice, Satan came and whispered in his ear, "All the finery your mother made for you will go to Ishmael, who is rejected in your house." Isaac, hitherto unshakable, became jealous and cried out, "My father, my father have pity on me!" (*Midrash Rabbah*, ibid.). Even Moses, who desired so much to be allowed to enter Canaan as his life drew to a close, nevertheless cried out when he saw Joshua taking his place and instructing the people, "Better death a hundred times than the pangs of jealousy!" (*Devarim Rabbah*, chapter 8).

הָבָה־לִּי בָנִים — *Give me children.* The two sisters differ as much in character as in appearance. Leah calmly accepts the vicissitudes of her fate. But Rachel

ב וַיִּחַר־אַף יַעֲקֹב בְּרָחֵל וַיֹּאמֶר הֲתַחַת אֱלֹהִים אָנֹכִי
ג אֲשֶׁר־מָנַע מִמֵּךְ פְּרִי־בָטֶן: וַתֹּאמֶר הִנֵּה אֲמָתִי בִלְהָה
בֹּא אֵלֶיהָ וְתֵלֵד עַל־בִּרְכַּי וְאִבָּנֶה גַם־אָנֹכִי מִמֶּנָּה:
ד וַתִּתֶּן־לוֹ אֶת־בִּלְהָה שִׁפְחָתָהּ לְאִשָּׁה וַיָּבֹא אֵלֶיהָ יַעֲקֹב:
ה-ו וַתַּהַר בִּלְהָה וַתֵּלֶד לְיַעֲקֹב בֵּן: וַתֹּאמֶר רָחֵל דָּנַנִּי
אֱלֹהִים וְגַם שָׁמַע בְּקֹלִי וַיִּתֶּן־לִי בֵּן עַל־כֵּן קָרְאָה שְׁמוֹ דָּן:

---

appears irritable and quick-tempered. She seems destined to have a life like a flame which blazes up and burns intensely before going out. Her brief existence will be rich, even violent. Her love for Jacob will be her whole life. And yet Leah, the wife in the background, will have more happiness in her married life and her family than Rachel, the favored wife, who will come to know the seriousness and anxiety of being a wife and mother. Together the two women will form that unique source which will nourish an entire people, and Jewish tradition has justly seen them as equals with an equal right to our respect (R' S.R. Hirsch; cf. סדר עולם רבה פ"ב).

וְאִם־אַיִן מֵתָה אָנֹכִי — *Otherwise I am dead.* "Because," explains *Rashi*, "one who has no children is considered dead." But *Ramban* interprets: "or else I will die of grief."

2. וַיִּחַר־אַף יַעֲקֹב בְּרָחֵל — *Jacob's anger flared up at Rachel.* He said, "Am I instead of God?" That is, "It is not to me that you must address your request, but to God" (*Onkelos*). But God held Jacob accountable for his refusal to intercede on Rachel's behalf and in this connection the Midrash quotes the Biblical verse, *Should a wise man advance futile reasons . . . should he reason with unprofitable talk, or with speeches wherewith he can do no good?* (Job 15:2). Replied God: Is this the way to reply to the distressed? The day will come when your sons will hear Rachel's son answer back to them: הֲתַחַת אֱלֹהִים אָנִי, *Am I instead of God?* Joseph will one day answer in the same words that Jacob has just spoken but he will do so with love, not spite. For Joseph's answer will mean a refusal to punish, while Jacob's meant that he did not want to help (*Rabbah* 71; *Genesis* 50:19).

אֲשֶׁר־מָנַע מִמֵּךְ פְּרִי־בָטֶן — *Who has withheld from you fruit of the womb?* The Midrash reports the dialogue which took place between the husband and wife.

Rachel: Did your father treat your mother this way? No. He prayed on her behalf.

Jacob: I am not like my father. He had no children at the time; I already have.

Rachel: Remember your grandfather Abraham. He already had a son (Ishmael) when he prayed to God on behalf of your grandmother.

Jacob: Would you be capable of what my grandmother did?

Rachel: What did she do?

Jacob: She had her rival brought into the house.

² *Jacob's anger flared up at Rachel, and he said, "Am I instead of God Who has withheld from you fruit of the womb?"*
³ *She said, "Here is my maid Bilhah, consort with her, that she may bear upon my knees and I too may be built up through her."*
⁴ *So she gave him Bilhah her maidservant as a wife, and Jacob consorted with her.* ⁵ *Bilhah conceived and bore Jacob a son.*
⁶ *Then Rachel said, "God has judged me, He has also heard my voice and has given me a son." She therefore called his name Dan.*

Rachel: If that is the obstacle, here is my maidservant Bilhah; go to her. *I too,* גַּם־אָנֹכִי, will become a mother through her, just as Sarah became a mother through her maidservant" (*Rabbah,* ibid.).

Ramban adds that Jacob's anger might have been provoked by Rachel's threat that she would die of grief — he considered it a ploy to intimidate him — or by her insistence that he guarantee children through prayers which could not possibly be rejected. This pretentiousness made Jacob refuse and Rachel then resolved to pray to God herself that He "make her fertile," as is recorded in verse 22.

3. וְאִבָּנֶה גַם־אָנֹכִי מִמֶּנָּה — *I too may be built up through her.* Cf. our commentary on 16:2.

4. לְאִשָּׁה. וַתִּתֶּן־לוֹ אֶת־בִּלְהָה שִׁפְחָתָהּ — *So she gave him Bilhah her maidservant as a wife.* In the previous verse Bilhah was called אָמָה, a Jewish maidservant, and not שִׁפְחָה, which generally means a Canaanite maidservant. In reality, she was one of Laban's daughters, as *Rashi* notes on 31:50. But Rachel gave her to Jacob as a legitimate wife (לְאִשָּׁה) and not as a concubine. Bilhah, however, even when she became pregnant, behaved modestly toward Rachel, her mistress. She remained a שִׁפְחָה, *servant*, in contrast to Hagar, who acted insolently toward Sarah as soon as she became pregnant.

5. בִּלְהָה וַתֵּלֶד לְיַעֲקֹב בֵּן — *Bilhah . . . and bore Jacob a son.* וַתֵּלֶד לְיַעֲקֹב בֵּן — these words are repeated at the birth of every son of the handmaids. This form of expression emphasizes that these children were acknowledged by the patriarch to have the same status as the children of Leah and Rachel in every respect.

6. דָּנַנִּי אֱלֹהִים — *God has judged me. Rashi:* "He had judged me and had condemned me (by refusing to grant me children); then He again judged me and recognized my merit — and He gave me a son." And so, she named him דָּן (*adjudged*). It is a good thing to be prudent with words. When Rachel's first child was born to her "in her arms," she called on the Attribute of Justice and referred to the Divine Name אֱלֹהִים which designates God in His quality of supreme Judge (מִדַּת הַדִּין). Thus the principle of justice got hold of and ultimately turned against Rachel, who had appealed to it with too much insistence. And she died prematurely at the birth of her son Benjamin (*R' Bachya*). Cf. our commentary to 35:18.

זַתַּהַר עוֹד וַתֵּלֶד בִּלְהָה שִׁפְחַת רָחֵל בֵּן שֵׁנִי לְיַעֲקֹב:
ח וַתֹּאמֶר רָחֵל נַפְתּוּלֵי אֱלֹהִים ׀ נִפְתַּלְתִּי עִם־אֲחֹתִי גַּם־
ט יָכֹלְתִּי וַתִּקְרָא שְׁמוֹ נַפְתָּלִי: וַתֵּרֶא לֵאָה כִּי עָמְדָה מִלֶּדֶת
וַתִּקַּח אֶת־זִלְפָּה שִׁפְחָתָהּ וַתִּתֵּן אֹתָהּ לְיַעֲקֹב לְאִשָּׁה:
יא וַתֵּלֶד זִלְפָּה שִׁפְחַת לֵאָה לְיַעֲקֹב בֵּן: וַתֹּאמֶר לֵאָה
בָּא גָד ק׳ יב בְּגָד וַתִּקְרָא אֶת־שְׁמוֹ גָּד: וַתֵּלֶד זִלְפָּה שִׁפְחַת לֵאָה בֵּן
יג שֵׁנִי לְיַעֲקֹב: וַתֹּאמֶר לֵאָה בְּאָשְׁרִי כִּי אִשְּׁרוּנִי בָּנוֹת
רביעי יד וַתִּקְרָא אֶת־שְׁמוֹ אָשֵׁר: וַיֵּלֶךְ רְאוּבֵן בִּימֵי קְצִיר־חִטִּים
וַיִּמְצָא דוּדָאִים בַּשָּׂדֶה וַיָּבֵא אֹתָם אֶל־לֵאָה אִמּוֹ

7. וַתֵּלֶד בִּלְהָה ... בֵּן שֵׁנִי לְיַעֲקֹב — *Bilhah ... bore Jacob a second son.* Sforno demonstrates that Jacob's marriage to Zilpah took place before the birth of this second son. So too *Ibn Ezra* on verse 23.

8. נַפְתּוּלֵי אֱלֹהִים נִפְתַּלְתִּי — *Sacred schemes have I maneuvered.* Several explanations have been given to interpret the name נַפְתָּלִי. *Rashi* quotes that of the grammarian *Menachem ben Saruk*, "I have become closer with my sister, as desired by God, in order to deserve children"; his own, "I have turned every which way, I have insisted and struggled many a time before God, to be my sister's equal"; and that of *Onkelos*, "I have offered prayers acceptable to God and have been answered." *Radak* explains, "I have waged a Divine struggle against my sister and have defeated her" similarly, *Ibn Ezra. Sforno* (on verse 16) says, "We have struggled in honor of God, my sister and I (to create the family of Israel) by giving our maidservants as wives to the patriarch (cf. preceding verse) and by our ardent prayers to God." What these different interpretations all have in common is the emphasis placed on the virtue of personal effort (הִשְׁתַּדְּלוּת). One does not count on a miracle but tries everything within his power in order to achieve his goal (*Sforno* ibid.; cf. also *Ramban* on 49:21).

9. וַתִּקַּח אֶת־זִלְפָּה שִׁפְחָתָהּ — *She took Zilpah her maidservant. Ramban* wonders what reasons Leah could have had for giving her handmaid to Jacob for a wife. That her sister did this we understand, for she had no children. However, Leah already had four children. Moreover, is it normal for a wife to want to add to the number of her husband's wives? But Leah knew by the prophetic spirit that Jacob was to have twelve children and she was motivated by a profound desire to give him the greatest number of these children, even if this meant giving him her handmaid as a wife. On the other hand, she understood that the long-foreseen time (15:16) for taking possession of the Promised Land was drawing near and it was now becoming necessary to ensure that the family of Abraham had numerous offspring. Since the first two patriarchs had had but few children there was now a need to create the nucleus of the future nation and in order to do so Jacob had to have several wives.

⁷ *Bilhah, Rachel's maidservant, conceived again and bore Jacob a second son.* ⁸ *And Rachel said, "Sacred schemes have I maneuvered to equal my sister, and I have also prevailed!" And she called his name Naphtali.*

⁹ *When Leah saw that she had stopped giving birth, she took Zilpah her maidservant and gave her to Jacob as a wife.* ¹⁰ *Zilpah, Leah's maidservant, bore Jacob a son.* ¹¹ *And Leah declared, "Good luck has come!" So she called his name Gad.*

¹² *Zilpah, Leah's maidservant, bore a second son to Jacob.* ¹³ *Leah declared, "In my good fortune! For women have deemed me fortunate!" So she called his name Asher.*

¹⁴ *Reuben went out in the days of the wheat harvest; he found dudaim in the field and brought them to Leah his mother;*

11. נַתִּקְרָא אֶת־שְׁמוֹ גָּד — *So she called his name Gad.* According to *Rashi* and *Onkelos*, the word בְּגָד means, "Good luck has come — בָּא בְּמַזָּל טוֹב." "But," adds *Rashi*, "I do not know why the two words בָּא גָד are written here as one word, בְּגָד." The *Zohar* (on *Genesis* 49:19) explains why this word is written defectively: Gad was a child of good fortune. He was to be the most perfect of the twelve sons. But his descendants abruptly swerved from the right path and went astray, like a river which suddenly deviates from a straight line and makes a crooked turn. The children of Gad made the choice of settling in Transjordan and voluntarily alienated themselves from the source of sanctity which the Holy Land represents. The word בְּגָד, written incompletely, alludes to the fact that part of their good fortune was missing.

Written this way, the word בְּגָד can also mean treachery. The tribe of Gad was guilty of treachery (or infidelity) toward the Holy Land.

13. נַתִּקְרָא אֶת־שְׁמוֹ אָשֵׁר — *So she called his name Asher.* When Zilpah's second son was born, Leah cried out, "Happy am I! בְּאָשְׁרִי, for the daughters will call me happy" (cf. our commentary to 49:20). The names Leah gave to her bondwoman's two children confirm her grateful nature, which has already been mentioned in our commentary to 29:35. Leah is filled with happiness and wants to keep her feelings alive in the names of her children. גָּד and אָשֵׁר are, in a way, synonymous; the *Zohar* (ibid.) points out that the tribe of Asher made amends for the sin committed by the tribe of Gad. While the former wanted to settle on the other side of the Jordan, the tribe of Asher took up residence right in the midst of the Promised Land: *From Asher — his bread will have richness, and he will provide kingly delicacies* (49:20). The good fortune experienced by Leah, which she expressed in Asher's name, smiled similarly upon him throughout his history. As the Midrash notes here, Asher has both אוֹשֶׁר, *happiness*, and עוֹשֶׁר, *wealth*; and he redeems his brother Gad.

14. וַיֵּלֶךְ רְאוּבֵן — *Reuben went.* He was about seven years old at the time (*Midrashim*).

טו וַתֹּאמֶר רָחֵל אֶל־לֵאָה תְּנִי־נָא לִי מִדּוּדָאֵי בְּנֵךְ: וַתֹּאמֶר
לָהּ הַמְעַט קַחְתֵּךְ אֶת־אִישִׁי וְלָקַחַת גַּם אֶת־דּוּדָאֵי בְּנִי
וַתֹּאמֶר רָחֵל לָכֵן יִשְׁכַּב עִמָּךְ הַלַּיְלָה תַּחַת דּוּדָאֵי בְנֵךְ:
טז וַיָּבֹא יַעֲקֹב מִן־הַשָּׂדֶה בָּעֶרֶב וַתֵּצֵא לֵאָה לִקְרָאתוֹ
וַתֹּאמֶר אֵלַי תָּבוֹא כִּי שָׂכֹר שְׂכַרְתִּיךָ בְּדוּדָאֵי בְּנִי וַיִּשְׁכַּב
עִמָּהּ בַּלַּיְלָה הוּא: וַיִּשְׁמַע אֱלֹהִים אֶל־לֵאָה וַתַּהַר וַתֵּלֶד
יח לְיַעֲקֹב בֵּן חֲמִישִׁי: וַתֹּאמֶר לֵאָה נָתַן אֱלֹהִים שְׂכָרִי

בִּימֵי קְצִיר־חִטִּים — *In the days of the wheat harvest.* Menasseh, the son of King Chizkiyah, sat at the rostrum interpreting the Law in a scoffing tone. He was saying (among other things), "Did Moses have nothing to do but relate how Reuben went in the days of the wheat harvest and found some *dudaim* in the field?" (He considered these details superfluous.) However, it was explained in the name of Rav, "Here, the Torah wants to praise the fathers of the Jewish tribes. This was the harvest time and, nevertheless, Reuben did not touch anyone else's property to bring back wheat or barley. Instead he gathered something free, something which no one cared about" (*Sanhedrin* 99b).

דּוּדָאִים — *Dudaim.* While R' Levi considers that the דּוּדָאִים are cypresses (Latin: *cyperus rotundus*), Rav (and probably R' Yonasan) holds that they are mandrakes (*Sanhedrin* ibid.); this latter opinion is also shared by *Onkelos* and *Ibn Ezra*. The mandrake is a "herb with a fleshy root, generally bifurcated, reminiscent of a human body with two legs. It is said to have aphrodisiac properties. But Reuben only brought the flowers or the fruits. These have the form of an apple and are sweet smelling" (*Ramban*).

תְּנִי־נָא לִי מִדּוּדָאֵי בְּנֵךְ — *Please give me some of your son's dudaim.* Nothing exists on earth which does not have a purpose on a higher plane. Take the *dudaim.* These plants of little value nevertheless served as the indirect means by which Providence brought about the birth of two children. These children grew into two future tribes of Israel. The first child, Issachar, distinguished himself by the same quality as the jasmines have, although on a higher level. הַדּוּדָאִים נָתְנוּ רֵיחַ, *The jasmines give forth fragrance* (*Song of Songs* 7:14). So too, Issachar gives forth "the perfume of the Torah" more than all the other tribes (*Zohar*). This passage consequently draws our attention to the fact that no creation exists in the world "which has not its place" (cf. *Avos* 4:3; and our commentary to verse 20).

15. הַמְעַט קַחְתֵּךְ אֶת־אִישִׁי — *Was your taking my husband insignificant?* For Rachel did not allow him to go to Leah (*Zohar*).

לָכֵן יִשְׁכַּב עִמָּךְ הַלַּיְלָה — *Therefore, he shall lie with you tonight. Rashi:* "This night was mine and I give it to you in exchange for your son's flowers. And because she disdained the company of this righteous man, she did not merit being buried with him." "She prophesied the future without knowing it when she declared, יִשְׁכַּב עִמָּךְ הַלַּיְלָה — he will rest with you in eternal night" (*Midrashim*).

> Rachel said to Leah, "Please give me some of your son's dudaim."
> [15] But she said to her, "Was your taking my husband insignifi-
> cant? — And now to take even my son's dudaim!" Rachel said,
> "Therefore, he shall lie with you tonight in return for your son's
> dudaim."
>
> [16] When Jacob came from the field in the evening, Leah went
> out to meet him and said, "It is to me that you must come for I
> have clearly hired you with my son's dudaim." So he lay with
> her that night.
>
> [17] God hearkened to Leah; and she conceived and bore Jacob a
> fifth son. [18] And Leah declared, "God has granted me my reward

16. וַתֵּצֵא לֵאָה לִקְרָאתוֹ — *Leah went out to meet him.* Such a gesture might appear immodest; however, this is not the case here. Leah went out to meet her husband so that she should not have to seek him in her sister's tent where he was headed. Wanting to avoid humiliating her sister, she had watched for Jacob's return at nightfall, for during the day he was away pasturing Laban's flocks. She had heard the braying of the ass carrying Jacob and ran out to meet him. This is what is alluded to in 49:14: *Issachar is a strong-boned donkey* (חֲמֹר גָּרֶם), which can also be taken to mean: "Issachar — an ass was the cause for him." As for Jacob, he immediately acceded to Leah's request when she hurried to inform him of Rachel's consent. She let him know that Rachel was in possession of some *dudaim;* this would not displease him in view of the reputation which these plants had for increasing fertility. Indeed, Jacob wished that Rachel would have children and he certainly did not despise the use of stimulants, even though he put all his trust in providential action (*Zohar*).

כִּי שָׂכֹר שְׂכַרְתִּיךָ — *For I have clearly hired you.* This expression does not signify that the sisters merely made a deal for the right to spend a night with Jacob, but it is to be taken in the sense which *Rashi* gives it: "I have given Rachel her due for this." However, it is also possible that Leah wanted to give expression to her ardent desire to "give birth to numerous tribes," and she did so by not overlooking any means of attaining this goal. And this included "paying the price" in order to have the right to be with her husband.

בַּלַּיְלָה הוּא — *That night.* Instead of the pronoun הַהוּא, the text employs the word הוּא which contains an indirect reference to Him, the Holy One, Blessed is He. "He Himself was present that night and He helped in the conception of the child" (*Rashi*). This comment is better understood when we recall the words in 29:35, that Leah *stopped giving birth.* It was only through Divine intervention that she subsequently had two more children for God alone knew the purity of her intentions and God alone knew that she deserved to be blessed anew.

18. נָתַן אֱלֹהִים שְׂכָרִי אֲשֶׁר־נָתַתִּי שִׁפְחָתִי לְאִישִׁי — *God has granted me my reward because I gave my maidservant to my husband.* The name יִשָּׂשכָר refers both to this reward (שְׂכָרִי) and to the hiring (שָׂכָר) with the *dudaim* mentioned in

יט אֲשֶׁר־נָתַתִּי שִׁפְחָתִי לְאִישִׁי וַתִּקְרָא שְׁמוֹ יִשָּׂשכָר: וַתַּהַר עוֹד

כ לֵאָה וַתֵּלֶד בֵּן־שִׁשִּׁי לְיַעֲקֹב: וַתֹּאמֶר לֵאָה זְבָדַנִי אֱלֹהִים ׀

אֹתִי זֶבֶד טוֹב הַפַּעַם יִזְבְּלֵנִי אִישִׁי כִּי־יָלַדְתִּי לוֹ שִׁשָּׁה בָנִים

כא וַתִּקְרָא אֶת־שְׁמוֹ זְבֻלוּן: וְאַחַר יָלְדָה בַּת וַתִּקְרָא אֶת־

כב שְׁמָהּ דִּינָה: וַיִּזְכֹּר אֱלֹהִים אֶת־רָחֵל וַיִּשְׁמַע אֵלֶיהָ אֱלֹהִים

verse 16. This double meaning may explain why the name יִשָּׂשכָר contains the letter ש twice. When we read it, however, only one ש is pronounced, as though the name was written יִשָׂכָר. This is because Leah considered the birth of her son a reward for having given her maidservant to her husband; she did not value the seemingly much less important act of giving up the *dudaim* (רבעה"ת). According to this interpretation, the word יִשָּׂשכָר is normally read with just one ש, except here, where the name is first mentioned in the Torah. *Ibn Ezra* and *Radak* (I *Chronicles* 15:24) give a grammatical explanation: When two identical letters come together in the same word, often only the first is pronounced. (According to this, one would always pronounce the word יִשָׂכָר). A third explanation points out that Issachar's son, named יוֹב in *Genesis* 46:13, is referred to as יָשׁוּב in *Numbers* 26:24. This son complained to his father of being named יוֹב, the name of an idol in those times. Issachar then took one of the letters ש from his own name and added it to his son's name and henceforth his son was called יָשׁוּב. Based on this, in the Torah readings some pronounce all the letters of the name יִשָּׂשכָר until they come to the name יָשׁוּב in *Parashas Pinchas* and from then on they read it as יִשָׂכָר (רבעה"ת). Still others pronounce both letters ש of יִשָּׂשכָר only in the book of *Genesis*.

וַתִּקְרָא שְׁמוֹ יִשָּׂשכָר — *So she called his name Issachar*. This name means יֵשׁ שָׂכָר, *there is a reward*. The tribe of Issachar was the one which devoted itself entirely to the study of Torah, as is seen in the book of I *Chronicles* (12:33). Now, study of Torah is promised a greater reward than all other *mitzvos* — תַּלְמוּד תּוֹרָה כְּנֶגֶד כֻּלָּם (Peah 1:1). In this sense the book of *Proverbs* (8:21) says, לְהַנְחִיל אֹהֲבַי יֵשׁ, *I have those who love Me to receive reward* — where יֵשׁ is an allusion to יֵשׁ שָׂכָר (*Zohar*). The Torah must be studied לִשְׁמָהּ, for its own sake, not with one's own interests (שָׂכָר) in mind. But according to the Talmudic dictum in *Pesachim* 50b, it is permissible to begin its study שֶׁלֹּא לִשְׁמָהּ, in the hope that complete disinterestedness will take over in the future. This can explain the custom of pronouncing the name Issachar the first time as יִשָּׂשכָר = יֵשׁ שָׂכָר and from then on always as יִשָׂכָר.

19. וַתַּהַר עוֹד לֵאָה — *Then Leah conceived again*. In order to dedicate itself to the study of Torah with full peace of mind, the tribe of Issachar had to be free of all material worries. Accordingly, the tribe of Zebulun took upon itself to guarantee its subsistence, and the two tribes loyally shared the merit and the reward for the *mitzvah* of תַּלְמוּד תּוֹרָה (*Bereishis Rabbah* 72). But such an ideal partnership presupposes a never-failing spirit of brotherhood, free of all jealousy. Only true

because I gave my maidservant to my husband." So she called his name Issachar.

¹⁹ Then Leah conceived again and bore Jacob a sixth son. ²⁰ Leah said, "God has endowed me with a good endowment; now my husband will make his permanent home with me for I have borne him six sons." So she called his name Zebulun. ²¹ Afterwards, she bore a daughter and she called her name Dinah.

²² God remembered Rachel; God hearkened to her and He

brothers are capable of collaborating in a sacred venture on such a high level, and that is why Providence blessed Leah one more time after the birth of Issachar. She gave birth to Zebulun and the two brothers, born of the same father and mother, began their partnership in a spirit of unselfishness and total loyalty to each other.

20. זְבָדַנִי אֱלֹהִים אֹתִי זֵבֶד טוֹב — *God has endowed me with a good endowment.* As with the preceding names, the name זְבָלוּן, *Zebulun,* also has a double meaning. it expresses Leah's gratitude for receiving a double portion, i.e. half of all the children who will form the future family of Israel, and also it puts into words Leah's hope that now יִזְבְּלֵנִי אִישִׁי, *my husband will make his permanent home with me (Rashi).* However, the word זֵבֶד in our verse, which *Onkelos* translates as חֵלֶק "a portion," occurs nowhere else in the Torah. *Ramban* explains it as the Aramaic term for the Hebrew צֵדָה meaning provision or portion (cf. *Onkelos* to *Genesis* 42:25, where צֵדָה is translated זְוָדִין; the interchanging of the letters ו and ב is common). In this meaning, the word זֵבֶד has remained the motto of the tribe of Zebulun's calling; to furnish provisions for its brother-tribe Issachar, absorbed in the study of Torah. (In this light, one can understand the midrashic statement that the *dudaim* brought on the birth of not just one tribe but two.)

21. דִּינָה — *Dinah. Rashi:* Our teachers explain, "Leah pronounced judgment (דִּין) against herself: If this too is a male, then my sister Rachel will not even be the equal of one of the handmaids. She then prayed regarding the child and it was a girl."

But, asks R' Yosef, does it not say in the Mishnah (*Berachos* 54), "If one's wife is already pregnant, it is useless for him to pray for the birth of a male child" (for the sex is determined right at the time of conception)? Leah's case, it is answered, was different, either because it was an instance of supernatural intervention or because she had prayed within the first forty days after conception [when a change is still possible] (*Berachos* 60a). Other sources, however, referring to *Jeremiah* 18:4, grant that changes may occur until just before birth.

The name דִּינָה, *Dinah,* is derived from דִּין, *judgment,* according to R' Yehoshua. But R' Chanina explains, "Leah and the two bondwomen assembled and prayed: We have enough boys! דַּיֵּנוּ זְכָרִים (hence the name דִּינָה). Let Rachel also be remembered!" (*Rabbah* 72).

22. וַיִּזְכֹּר אֱלֹהִים אֶת־רָחֵל — *God remembered Rachel.* God remembered her on the day of Rosh Hashanah. Such was the case also for Sarah and for Hannah, mother

כג וַיִּפְתַּח אֶת־רַחְמָהּ: וַתַּהַר וַתֵּלֶד בֵּן וַתֹּאמֶר אָסַף אֱלֹהִים
כד אֶת־חֶרְפָּתִי: וַתִּקְרָא אֶת־שְׁמוֹ יוֹסֵף לֵאמֹר יֹסֵף יהוה לִי בֵּן
כה אַחֵר: וַיְהִי כַּאֲשֶׁר יָלְדָה רָחֵל אֶת־יוֹסֵף וַיֹּאמֶר יַעֲקֹב אֶל־לָבָן
כו שַׁלְּחֵנִי וְאֵלְכָה אֶל־מְקוֹמִי וּלְאַרְצִי: תְּנָה אֶת־נָשַׁי וְאֶת־יְלָדַי

of the prophet Samuel (*Rosh Hashanah* 11b). On this day of judgment, He had listened to Leah's דִּין, as noted on the previous verse, as well as to the combined prayers of Leah, Bilhah and Zilpah on behalf of Rachel and also to the "multiple prayers" of Rachel herself (*Midrash*). He had taken into account Rachel's great merit and the mental anguish she suffered when she thought she might ultimately have to marry Esau (*Rashi*). Hence, answering Rachel's prayers was really an act of justice. The Torah emphasizes this by repeating the Divine name אֱלֹהִים (signifying God as supreme judge, מִדַּת הַדִּין) twice in our verse. But as for her future happiness, Rachel expects it to come only through Divine grace and when she prays for another son she invokes the Divine name ה' — מִדַּת הָרַחֲמִים.

When the Torah tells us that God remembered Sarah, it uses the term וַה' פָּקַד, whereas here it uses the verb זָכַר. For Sarah, the remembering of her maternal desire and her prayers preceded God's visit (=פְּקִידָה, an allusion to the conception), as is seen from 17:21: *But I will maintain My covenant through Isaac, whom Sarah will bear to you by this time next year.* But for Rachel Divine intervention was more immediate, hence more miraculous. Moreover, the term פָּקַד, which relates more particularly to conception, refers to the female, whereas the verb זָכַר calls to mind the word זָכָר, the male. Now the act of remembering, of which our verse speaks, was at the origin of the birth of Joseph, the very one who is considered, in relation to his brothers, representative of the masculine element of the patriarchal family. Indeed, he was the active and productive element who, through his deeds, brought the history of Jacob's children to fruition, while the brothers submitted to his law. The words וַיִּזְכֹּר וְגו' can thus be understood in this way: "God gave Rachel the [future] great man" of the family of Jacob (*Zohar*).

וַיִּשְׁמַע אֵלֶיהָ אֱלֹהִים — *God hearkened to her.* Cf. our commentary to verse 2.

וַיִּפְתַּח אֶת־רַחְמָהּ — *And He opened her womb.* The sentence implies that she was by nature barren. Rachel was the only one of the mothers (including the handmaids Bilhah and Zilpah) whose name did not contain the letter ה. This letter is the sign of fertility; it is "with it that God formed this world" (cf. *Rashi* on *Genesis* 2:4). It was added to the names of Abram and Sarai to give them the ability to procreate. But for Rachel, who had neither the natural ability nor even the letter ה, the sign of procreation, Providence worked a miracle by making her fertile. For, adds R' Yochanan, God holds in His own hands three keys which He never entrusts to messengers: the keys of procreation, of rain and good weather, and of resurrection (*Taanis* 2b). The miracle of Rachel's pregnancy was certainly more evident than that wrought for Leah (cf. our commentary on

opened her womb. ²³ *She conceived and bore a son, and said, "God has taken away my disgrace."* ²⁴ *So she called his name Joseph, saying, "May HASHEM add on for me another son."*

²⁵ *And it was, when Rachel had given birth to Joseph, Jacob said to Laban, "Grant me leave that I may go to my place and to my land.* ²⁶ *Give me my wives and my children*

29:31) for the Torah explicitly mentions Rachel's barrenness (ibid.) whereas for Leah it is left unsaid.

23. אָסַף אֱלֹהִים — *God has taken away.* The verb אָסַף is one of those words with two opposing meanings. It signifies to hide (the shame of being childless) and to add (another child). Hence the name יוֹסֵף on one hand includes homage to Providence for the kindness of removing past shame and, on the other, a prayer for a future blessing. The *Zohar* calls attention to the connection between יוֹסֵף and the prayer of מוּסָף, *Mussaf.* Rachel felt that the joyous special day on which God had remembered her and she had brought a child into the world was a propitious time to pray for a new blessing and she cried out, "May God give me another son!" Indeed, when *God has been mindful of us, He will bless: He will bless the house of Israel; He will bless the house of Aaron.* יֹסֵף ה' עֲלֵיכֶם, *God increase to you more and more [His blessings], to you and your children (Psalms* 115:14). In this same spirit, the supplementary prayer of *Mussaf* also enables us to pray for additional blessings and specifically only on joyous, special days. While the three patriarchs are the initiators of the three prayers of *Shacharis, Minchah* and *Maariv,* Joseph embodies in his name the very idea of the prayers of *Mussaf (Recanati, Parashas Mikeitz).*

24. בֶּן אַחֵר — *Another son.* אַחֵר also means "different." Let him be *different* from his brothers. They who formed the ten tribes ultimately sank into oblivion but Benjamin, with the tribe of Judah, constituted the imperishable nucleus of the Jewish nation (*Rabbah* 73).

25. וַיְהִי כַּאֲשֶׁר יָלְדָה רָחֵל אֶת-יוֹסֵף — *And it was, when Rachel had given birth to Joseph.* "Why did he wait for Joseph's birth before deciding to go back to his parents' home? Because it had been revealed to him that the house of Esau would fall at the hands of Joseph's children, as the prophet Ovadiah confirmed (1:18, *Bava Basra* 123b). "Now," Jacob exclaimed, "I no longer have anything to fear from Esau and his legions" (*Targum Yonasan*). Joseph's children, explains *Maharal* (ibid.), distinguished themselves from others by their extremely modest conduct. They do not mix with the outside world, as *Rashi* notes on *Genesis* 48:16. Such virtues ultimately triumph over the brute force of an Esau with his legions.

שַׁלְּחֵנִי וְאֵלְכָה אֶל-מְקוֹמִי — *Grant me leave that I may go to my place.* About this time, Rebecca sent her nurse Deborah and two of Isaac's servants to Jacob with a message for him to return to his father's house since the fourteen-year period

אֲשֶׁר עֲבַדְתִּי אֹתְךָ בָּהֶן וְאֵלֵכָה כִּי אַתָּה יָדַעְתָּ אֶת־עֲבֹדָתִי

כז אֲשֶׁר עֲבַדְתִּיךָ: וַיֹּאמֶר אֵלָיו לָבָן אִם־נָא מָצָאתִי חֵן

חמישי כח בְּעֵינֶיךָ נִחַשְׁתִּי וַיְבָרֲכֵנִי יהוה בִּגְלָלֶךָ: וַיֹּאמַר נָקְבָה

כט שְׂכָרְךָ עָלַי וְאֶתֵּנָה: וַיֹּאמֶר אֵלָיו אַתָּה יָדַעְתָּ אֵת אֲשֶׁר

ל עֲבַדְתִּיךָ וְאֵת אֲשֶׁר־הָיָה מִקְנְךָ אִתִּי: כִּי מְעַט אֲשֶׁר־הָיָה

לְךָ לְפָנַי וַיִּפְרֹץ לָרֹב וַיְבָרֶךְ יהוה אֹתְךָ לְרַגְלִי וְעַתָּה מָתַי

לא אֶעֱשֶׂה גַם־אָנֹכִי לְבֵיתִי: וַיֹּאמֶר מָה אֶתֶּן־לָךְ וַיֹּאמֶר יַעֲקֹב

לֹא־תִתֶּן־לִי מְאוּמָה אִם־תַּעֲשֶׂה־לִּי הַדָּבָר הַזֶּה אָשׁוּבָה

of his servitude had come to an end. Jacob informed Laban of this message from his mother and then asked Laban's permission to go back to his land (*Yashar* 57b).

26. תְּנָה אֶת־נָשַׁי — *Give me my wives.* "I do not wish to leave without your permission" (*Rashi*). Moses also asked his father-in-law's permission to leave for Egypt (*Rashi* on *Exodus* 4:18). Both had historically important missions to carry out in their land. Nevertheless, their moral conscience prevented them from undertaking these missions without first obtaining permission to leave from their host, no matter if it was a Laban who unscrupulously tricked even his own son-in-law.

However, Jacob consented to stay with Laban six more years (cf. 31:41); and then finally he left without Laban's permission — in fact, he fled. This was just when Rachel became pregnant again. No matter what, Jacob did not want his twelfth son, the one who was to complete the family of Israel, to come into the world outside the Promised Land. He knew also that the *Shechinah* (Divine Presence) would hover closely over the family only within the confines of the Holy Land (cf. *Rashi* on 31:3). It was then that he resolved to forgo his irascible father-in-law's permission, unlike Moses, whose father-in-law was fair to him (*Zohar*).

כִּי אַתָּה יָדַעְתָּ אֶת־עֲבֹדָתִי — *For you are aware of my service.* Very few human beings have gone through fourteen years of labor as Jacob did. And he had not done all this work for his wives and children, but solely for the right to marry two wives who, into the bargain, brought him no dowry. Nevertheless, these fourteen years laid the foundation for the family and national life of the house of Jacob. They were suffused with nobility of spirit, moral devotion, and the ideal inspiration and motivation of a sacred challenge for creating the family of Israel. They also show the key position occupied by the Jewish wife in her home, thus categorically shattering the myth of the inferiority of women within the framework of the Jewish religion, a myth based on ideas of the oriental way of life. At the end of the fourteen years, Jacob was no better off financially than when he had started working for Laban. His only new "acquisitions" were the worries caused by his large family and his only riches were what he had brought

for whom I have served you, and I will go; for you are aware of my service that I labored for you."
²⁷ *But Laban said to him, "If I have found favor in your eyes! — I have learned by divination that HASHEM has blessed me on account of you."* ²⁸ *And he said, "Specify your wage to me and I will give it."* ²⁹ *But he said to him, "You know how I served you and what your livestock were with me.* ³⁰ *For the little that you had before I came has expanded substantially as HASHEM has blessed you with my coming; and now, when will I also do something for my own house?'*
³¹ *He said, "What shall I give you?' And Jacob said, "Do not give me anything; if you will do this thing for me, I will resume*

with him when he left his parents, namely his intelligence and his physical strength.

27. נִחַשְׁתִּי — *I have learned by divination.* Laban still was very eager to have Jacob work for him for wages amounting to nothing more than his meals. He hypocritically speaks in self-righteous tones, not admitting that he would like to keep Jacob because of his great ability, which would have led him to make some concrete proposal, but letting Jacob know that he is moved only by a נִיחוּש — a sort of superstitious belief. Laban believes that the God of Jacob has blessed him on account of this pious servant.

28. וַיֹּאמַר נָקְבָה שְׂכָרְךָ — *And he said, "Specify your wage."* Laban had hoped that his pious nephew would be flattered (by his offer) and would consent to stay on with him under the same conditions as before. But as Jacob remained silent, he was obliged to ask what his conditions for remaining were. The break in the middle of the episode marks this pause in Laban's proposal (R' S.R. Hirsch).

וְאֶתֵּנָה — *And I will give it.* The letter ה at the end of this word may denote either the optative mood or the feminine gender. "I give her to you" — referring to the daughters Laban had given Jacob in exchange for his labor (as was quoted from the Zohar in our commentary to 29:27). The same reference is contained in the word נָקְבָה in our verse, for this word can also mean *wife*, meaning to give Jacob yet more wives.

30. לְרַגְלִי — *With my coming.* "That is to say," explains Rambam, "because of me," or, "as a kindness to me" (Guide 1:28). Rashi's explanation on Yoma (38b) is similar (ד"ה רגלי).

31. לֹא-תִתֶּן-לִי מְאוּמָה — *Do not give me anything.* Jacob was extremely mistrustful of Laban, having experienced too much of his bad faith. Time had not yet healed the old wounds and Jacob made up his mind to rely solely on his own exceptional knowledge and his skill as a shepherd.

אִם-תַּעֲשֶׂה-לִי הַדָּבָר הַזֶּה — *If you will do this thing for me.* Cf. Rashi on Bava Metzia 94a (ועי' קצה"ת, סי' של"ב, אות ו'; ד"ה כל).

לב אֶעֱבֹר בְּכָל־צֹאנְךָ הַיּוֹם הָסֵר מִשָּׁם כָּל־שֶׂה אָעֱרֶה צְאֹנְךָ אֶשְׁמֹר: כָּל־שֶׂה | נָקֹד וְטָלוּא וְכָל־שֶׂה־חוּם בַּכְּשָׂבִים וְטָלוּא וְנָקֹד
לג בָּעִזִּים וְהָיָה שְׂכָרִי: וְעָנְתָה־בִּי צִדְקָתִי בְּיוֹם מָחָר כִּי־תָבוֹא עַל־שְׂכָרִי לְפָנֶיךָ כֹּל אֲשֶׁר־אֵינֶנּוּ נָקֹד וְטָלוּא בָּעִזִּים וְחוּם
לד-לה בַּכְּשָׂבִים גָּנוּב הוּא אִתִּי: וַיֹּאמֶר לָבָן הֵן לוּ יְהִי כִדְבָרֶךָ: וַיָּסַר בַּיּוֹם הַהוּא אֶת־הַתְּיָשִׁים הָעֲקֻדִּים וְהַטְּלֻאִים וְאֵת כָּל־הָעִזִּים הַנְּקֻדּוֹת וְהַטְּלֻאֹת כֹּל אֲשֶׁר־לָבָן בּוֹ וְכָל־חוּם
לו בַּכְּשָׂבִים וַיִּתֵּן בְּיַד־בָּנָיו: וַיָּשֶׂם דֶּרֶךְ שְׁלֹשֶׁת יָמִים בֵּינוֹ וּבֵין יַעֲקֹב וְיַעֲקֹב רֹעֶה אֶת־צֹאן לָבָן הַנּוֹתָרֹת: וַיִּקַּח־לוֹ
לז יַעֲקֹב מַקַּל לִבְנֶה לַח וְלוּז וְעַרְמוֹן וַיְפַצֵּל בָּהֵן פְּצָלוֹת לְבָנוֹת מַחְשֹׂף הַלָּבָן אֲשֶׁר עַל־הַמַּקְלוֹת: וַיַּצֵּג אֶת־
לח הַמַּקְלוֹת אֲשֶׁר פִּצֵּל בָּרֳהָטִים בְּשִׁקֲתוֹת הַמָּיִם אֲשֶׁר תָּבֹאןָ הַצֹּאן לִשְׁתּוֹת לְנֹכַח הַצֹּאן וַיֵּחַמְנָה בְּבֹאָן לִשְׁתּוֹת:
לט וַיֵּחֱמוּ הַצֹּאן אֶל־הַמַּקְלוֹת וַתֵּלַדְןָ הַצֹּאן עֲקֻדִּים נְקֻדִּים

32. וְהָיָה שְׂכָרִי — *That will be my wage.* Rashi explains: "From now on, all goats born spotted and speckled and the brown sheep shall be mine; and as for the ones which already have these colors, separate them from the others and entrust them to your sons, so that you will not claim that the new ones were there from before." This view is also adopted by *Ibn Ezra* and *Radak*. But *Ramban* and other commentators hold that the animals which were then speckled or brown should also have been Jacob's.

The divergent opinions of our classical commentators regarding the details in the following verses revolve in particular around the interpretation of the words הָסֵר (imperative or infinitive-participle), also בָּנָיו (verse 35, sons of Jacob or Laban); the definition of just which animals Jacob had set apart for himself according to their colors; and determining the exact role of the rods. For the text does not clearly indicate whether they were used for both the goats and the sheep.

34. הֵן לוּ יְהִי כִדְבָרֶךָ — *Agreed! If only it will be as you say.* See our commentary to 29:19. In Syria, the sheep are white, the goats black. Hence Jacob's proposal that he keep the sheep which were not white and the goats which were not black was eagerly agreed to by Laban.

35. וַיָּסַר בַּיּוֹם הַהוּא — *So he removed on that very day.* The contract is entirely in Laban's favor. Nevertheless, he begins to trick Jacob by removing all those which had the slightest white mark in order to create as great an obstacle as possible to the growth of the spotted or brown of the flocks. Moreover, he withdrew the he-goats, whereas Jacob's proposal had concerned only the young of the flock. (Brown is considered as a generalized spotting.)

37. וַיְפַצֵּל בָּהֵן פְּצָלוֹת לְבָנוֹת — *He peeled white streaks in them.* Jacob devised three

pasturing and guarding your flocks: ³² *Let me pass through your whole flock today. Remove from there every speckled or spotted lamb, every brownish lamb among the sheep and the spotted or speckled among the goats — that will be my wage.* ³³ *Let my integrity testify for me in the future when it comes before you regarding my wage; any among the goats that is not speckled or spotted, or among the sheep that is not brownish, is stolen, if in my possession."*

³⁴ *And Laban said, "Agreed! If only it will be as you say."*

³⁵ *So he removed on that very day the ringed and spotted he-goats and all the speckled and spotted goats — every one that contained white, as well as all the brownish ones among the sheep — and he left them in charge of his sons.* ³⁶ *And he put a distance of three days between himself and Jacob; and Jacob tended Laban's remaining flock.*

³⁷ *Jacob then took himself fresh rods of poplar and hazel and chestnut. He peeled white streaks in them, laying bare the white of the rods.* ³⁸ *And he set up the rods which he had peeled, in the runnels — in the watering receptacles to which the flocks came to drink — facing the flocks, so they would become stimulated when they came to drink.* ³⁹ *Then the flocks became stimulated by the rods and the flocks gave birth to ringed ones, speckled ones, and*

plans to foil Laban's designs. The procedure he followed, comments *Ramban*, was perfectly legitimate, since Jacob had every right to do as he pleased with the sheep which Laban had given him as his wage. Yet, *Radak* adds, Jacob did not resort to the rods in the first year of the agreement. Only in the second year did he put the rods in front of the sheep, the speckled and spotted sheep born after the agreement, the sheep which now belonged to him. But whatever the case, note the *Tosafists*, Jacob was justified in acting craftily against a man as malicious and wily as Laban, in accordance with the adage (*II Samuel* 22:27), וְעִם עִקֵּשׁ תִּתְפָּל, *with the deceiver be cunning* (cf. our commentary to 27:36).

R' Bachya explains that Jacob resorted to the rods not of his own will but after the vision which he mentions in a later passage. It had been revealed to him that he would be the object of a miracle wrought by God to preserve him from Laban's tricks and that "the he-goats that mounted the flock were ringed, speckled and checkered" (31:10). He then took the rods so that the miracle could be achieved in a natural way, as is generally required. And Jacob attributed the brilliant success of his procedure as much to providential action as to the effect of a natural phenomenon.

39. וַתֵּלַדְןָ הַצֹּאן עֲקֻדִּים נְקֻדִּים וּטְלֻאִים — *The flocks gave birth to ringed ones, speckled ones, and spotted ones.* This verse, continues *R' Bachya*, contains an

מ וּטְלָאִים: וְהַכְּשָׂבִים הִפְרִיד יַעֲקֹב וַיִּתֵּן פְּנֵי הַצֹּאן אֶל־עָקֹד
וְכָל־חוּם בְּצֹאן לָבָן וַיָּשֶׁת לוֹ עֲדָרִים לְבַדּוֹ וְלֹא שָׁתָם
מא עַל־צֹאן לָבָן: וְהָיָה בְּכָל־יַחֵם הַצֹּאן הַמְקֻשָּׁרוֹת וְשָׂם יַעֲקֹב
אֶת־הַמַּקְלוֹת לְעֵינֵי הַצֹּאן בָּרְהָטִים לְיַחְמֵנָּה בַּמַּקְלוֹת:
מב וּבְהַעֲטִיף הַצֹּאן לֹא יָשִׂים וְהָיָה הָעֲטֻפִים לְלָבָן וְהַקְּשֻׁרִים
מג לְיַעֲקֹב: וַיִּפְרֹץ הָאִישׁ מְאֹד מְאֹד וַיְהִי־לוֹ צֹאן רַבּוֹת
לא   א וּשְׁפָחוֹת וַעֲבָדִים וּגְמַלִּים וַחֲמֹרִים: וַיִּשְׁמַע אֶת־דִּבְרֵי
בְנֵי־לָבָן לֵאמֹר לָקַח יַעֲקֹב אֵת כָּל־אֲשֶׁר לְאָבִינוּ וּמֵאֲשֶׁר

important lesson. If the imagination is a determining factor for the nature of the offspring which is to be born, as the example of Jacob's flocks shows, then how much more important will it be in the case of procreating human beings, where the sensibility is greater than that of animals! Accordingly, when husband and wife unite, they should purge their minds of all impure thoughts and every element which is foreign or which concerns third parties. The degree of their moral and spiritual purity will affect the souls of their children.

40. וְהַכְּשָׂבִים הִפְרִיד יַעֲקֹב — *Jacob segregated the lambs.* He put them at the head of the flock so that, just as with the rods, the sight of the lambs could act on the procreating animals. This was Jacob's second plan. The third plan is mentioned in the next verse: Jacob exposed the rods before the strongest ewes (according to *Onkelos* and *Rashi*) in order to be sure of vigorous lambs.

Contrary to *Rashi*, *Ramban* holds that Jacob also included Laban's flocks in this second procedure. The text allows different interpretations. Similarly, opinions vary on the composition of the flocks and on several other details.

As for the *Zohar*, it gives these verses a symbolic meaning. Jacob's ewes represent his children. He had now created his flock just as he had established his own family: fighting with Laban every step of the way and battling tooth and nail with him. But now that his family was formed, he intended to take it away from Laban and to keep his offspring from this greedy, hypocritical, sly individual so that he and his growing children could lead a saintly life, devoted to the love and fear of God. He mapped out his route in the arrangements he made for his flocks: *Jacob segregated the lambs . . . He formed separate droves of his own and did not mingle them with Laban's flocks.* Jacob remains apart, *For Hashem's portion is His people, Jacob is the measure of His inheritance* (Deuteronomy 32:9).

43. וַיִּפְרֹץ הָאִישׁ מְאֹד מְאֹד — *The man became exceedingly prosperous.* Every honest worker is eventually rewarded, without mentioning the promises of the World to Come. Jacob came to Laban's house empty-handed; he left it with flocks amounting to six hundred thousand animals. To be sure, this rapid growth was of a miraculous nature and will only recur in Messianic times (*Midrashim*; עי׳
רמב״ם, הל׳ שכירות י״ג; ה״ז).

spotted ones. [40] Jacob segregated the lambs and he made the flocks
face the ringed ones and all the brownish ones among Laban's
flocks. He formed separate droves of his own and did not mingle
them with Laban's flocks.

[41] Whenever it was mating time for the early-bearing flocks,
Jacob would place the rods in the runnels, in full view of the flock
to stimulate them among the rods. [42] But when the sheep were late
bearing, he would not emplace; thus, the late-bearing ones went to
Laban and the early-bearing ones to Jacob.

[43] The man became exceedingly prosperous and he attained
fecund flocks, maidservants and servants, camels and donkeys.

31 [1] Then he heard the words of Laban's sons, saying, "Jacob has
taken all that belonged to our father, and from that which

The words וַיִּפְרֹץ הָאִישׁ which occur here recall the analogous expression וַיִּגְדַּל
הָאִישׁ, *the man became great*, used in connection with Isaac in 26:13. There the
word הָאִישׁ, *the man*, has a pejorative tone. So too here. It implies a touch of
jealousy and covetousness. For Isaac it was the Philistines and for Jacob it was
Laban — who enviously looked on as "the man became exceedingly prosperous."

וּשְׁפָחוֹת וַעֲבָדִים — *Maidservants and servants.* In speaking of masters possessing
slaves, the Torah expresses itself eleven times in these words, *He had servants
and maidservants.* The only exception to this rule is found here, where the maidservants are referred to before the servants. It will be noted that here the servants
are named right in the middle of the sentence which mentions the smaller
livestock in the beginning and then the camels and asses. The Torah wanted to
mention the maidservants in connection with the smaller livestock for they were
the ones assigned to tend them whereas the servants were to look after the camels
and asses (*Meshech Chochmah;* this also explains the wording of 12:16).

At the end of this chapter *Radak* remarks that the purpose of the Torah's
detailed description of how Jacob acquired his flock is to show us how
Providence watches over the righteous and preserves them from the hands of the
wicked: *The wicked watches the righteous and seeks to slay him . . . God will
not leave him in his hand, nor suffer him to be condemned when he is judged*
(*Psalms 37:32*). But R' Elazar, quoted in the *Zohar*, holds that the Torah is making
a point of teaching us that prayer is far from being the only means by which
man can assure himself of heavenly blessing. Often this blessing will be granted
to the one who does not count on a miracle, but goes ahead and earns it through
his courage and his own hard work. The story of Jacob provides an illustrious
example of this.

31.

1. עָשָׂה אֵת כָּל־הַכָּבֹד הַזֶּה — *He amassed all this wealth.* Literally, כָּבֹד means
honor. In this verse כָּבֹד means wealth, as in *Nahum 2:10* (*Midrash* and *Onkelos*).

ב לְאָבִינוּ עָשָׂה אֵת כָּל־הַכָּבֹד הַזֶּה: וַיַּרְא יַעֲקֹב אֶת־פְּנֵי לָבָן
ג וְהִנֵּה אֵינֶנּוּ עִמּוֹ כִּתְמוֹל שִׁלְשׁוֹם: וַיֹּאמֶר יהוה אֶל־יַעֲקֹב
ד שׁוּב אֶל־אֶרֶץ אֲבוֹתֶיךָ וּלְמוֹלַדְתֶּךָ וְאֶהְיֶה עִמָּךְ: וַיִּשְׁלַח
ה יַעֲקֹב וַיִּקְרָא לְרָחֵל וּלְלֵאָה הַשָּׂדֶה אֶל־צֹאנוֹ: וַיֹּאמֶר לָהֶן
רֹאֶה אָנֹכִי אֶת־פְּנֵי אֲבִיכֶן כִּי־אֵינֶנּוּ אֵלַי כִּתְמֹל שִׁלְשֹׁם
ו וֵאלֹהֵי אָבִי הָיָה עִמָּדִי: וְאַתֵּנָה יְדַעְתֶּן כִּי בְּכָל־כֹּחִי עָבַדְתִּי
ז אֶת־אֲבִיכֶן: וַאֲבִיכֶן הֵתֶל בִּי וְהֶחֱלִף אֶת־מַשְׂכֻּרְתִּי עֲשֶׂרֶת
ח מֹנִים וְלֹא־נְתָנוֹ אֱלֹהִים לְהָרַע עִמָּדִי: אִם־כֹּה יֹאמַר נְקֻדִּים
יִהְיֶה שְׂכָרֶךָ וְיָלְדוּ כָל־הַצֹּאן נְקֻדִּים וְאִם־כֹּה יֹאמַר עֲקֻדִּים
ט יִהְיֶה שְׂכָרֶךָ וְיָלְדוּ כָל־הַצֹּאן עֲקֻדִּים: וַיַּצֵּל אֱלֹהִים אֶת־
י מִקְנֵה אֲבִיכֶם וַיִּתֶּן־לִי: וַיְהִי בְּעֵת יַחֵם הַצֹּאן וָאֶשָּׂא עֵינַי
וָאֵרֶא בַּחֲלוֹם וְהִנֵּה הָעַתֻּדִים הָעֹלִים עַל־הַצֹּאן עֲקֻדִּים

But is it not said in *Avos* (6:3): אֵין כָּבוֹד אֶלָּא תוֹרָה, *Honor is due only for Torah?* Replies the Gaon of Vilna, "Throughout the Torah, the word כָּבוֹד is written in full (with the *vav*), and it signifies the plenitude of honor, i.e., the Torah. But here and in *Nahum* it is written defectively. Hence the word refers to honor solely in the material realm" (*Chofetz Chaim*).

3. וַיֹּאמֶר ה׳ אֶל־יַעֲקֹב — *And HASHEM said to Jacob.* God had promised Jacob prior to his going into Aram: וַהֲשִׁבֹתִיךָ אֶל הָאֲדָמָה הַזֹּאת, *And I will return you to this soil* (28:15). And so, Jacob waited for the Divine command to return to Canaan (*Midrash* on 28:15; cf. *Rashi* on 32:10).

וְאֶהְיֶה עִמָּךְ — *And I will be with you.* There, in Canaan, the other promise too (וְהִנֵּה אָנֹכִי עִמָּךְ, ibid.) will be fulfilled. Jacob had dreaded the possibility that it had been annulled, for God had never revealed Himself to Jacob during his sojourn in Aram. The presence of the *Shechinah* is linked to the Holy Land.

4. וַיִּשְׁלַח יַעֲקֹב — *Jacob sent.* He sent Naphtali the swift messenger (*Targum Yonasan* following *Targum*, 49:21), for he intended to carry out the Divine command without a moment's delay.

הַשָּׂדֶה — *To the field.* R' Akiva said, "I like the Medes for three reasons. One is that they hold their council in the fields" (*Rashi* explains, "because the walls have ears"), and R' Ada added, "That is why Jacob held council with his wives in the fields" (*Berachos* 8b).

5. וֵאלֹהֵי אָבִי הָיָה עִמָּדִי — *But the God of my father was with me.* "Although your father has been very unfair to me, know that I have stolen nothing from him. The God of my father has given all this to me" (*Rashbam*).

6. וְאַתֵּנָה יְדַעְתֶּן — *Now you have known.* The unusual form וְאַתֵּנָה puts emphasis on the personal pronoun: "You yourselves know."

belonged to our father he amassed all this wealth." ² Jacob also noticed Laban's disposition that, behold, it was not toward him as in earlier days. ³ And HASHEM said to Jacob, "Return to the land of your fathers and to your native land, and I will be with you."

⁴ Jacob sent and summoned Rachel and Leah to the field, to his flock, ⁵ and said to them, "I have noticed that your father's disposition is not toward me as in earlier days; but the God of my father was with me. ⁶ Now you have known that it was with all my might that I served your father, ⁷ yet your father mocked me and changed my wage a hundred times; but God did not permit him to harm me. ⁸ If he would stipulate: 'Speckled ones shall be your wages,' then the entire flock bore spotted ones; and if he would stipulate: 'Ringed ones shall be your wages,' then the entire flock bore ringed ones. ⁹ Thus, God took away your father's livestock, and gave them to me. ¹⁰ It once happened at the mating time of the flock that I raised my eyes and saw in a dream — Behold! The he-goats that mounted the flock were ringed,

7. וַאֲבִיכֶן ... וְהֶחֱלִף אֶת־מַשְׂכֻּרְתִּי עֲשֶׂרֶת מֹנִים — Yet your father ... changed my wage a hundred times. Although the Torah mentions only one example of trickery on Laban's part, there must have been many others because later (verse 41), Jacob reproaches him about this, right to his face. It is often the case that the Torah does not give all the details (Ramban).

Rashi explains that the word מֹנִים indicates a minimum of ten times so that "ten מֹנִים" means that Laban changed the conditions one hundred times. But Radak holds that the phrase means exactly ten times. Indeed, Jacob served six years for Laban's flock (verse 41). Now, when the first year passed and Laban saw the prodigious growth of Jacob's flock, he changed his conditions. And he continued to change them every time the animals brought forth young, i.e. twice each year during the five remaining years.

9. אֶת־מִקְנֵה אֲבִיכֶם — Your father's livestock. The word אֲבִיכֶם has a masculine ending whereas it should be feminine, as in verse 7. In this verse it may be that certain shares in the inheritance are being considered. The Tosafists note that the Torah sometimes uses a masculine term when women inherit with the same rights as men (ב״ב קט״ו ד״ה מלמד).

10. הָעַתֻּדִים — The he-goats. Rashi interprets, "Although Laban had separated them so that the ewes would not bear young which resembled them, the angels were bringing them back from the flock entrusted to Laban's sons to the flock kept by Jacob." Ramban, however, considers that this only happened in the vision which Jacob is now recounting to his wives.

יא נְקֻדִּים וּבְרֻדִּים: וַיֹּאמֶר אֵלַי מַלְאַךְ הָאֱלֹהִים בַּחֲלוֹם יַעֲקֹב

יב וָאֹמַר הִנֵּנִי: וַיֹּאמֶר שָׂא־נָא עֵינֶיךָ וּרְאֵה כָּל־הָעַתֻּדִים הָעֹלִים עַל־הַצֹּאן עֲקֻדִּים נְקֻדִּים וּבְרֻדִּים כִּי רָאִיתִי אֵת כָּל־אֲשֶׁר

יג לָבָן עֹשֶׂה לָּךְ: אָנֹכִי הָאֵל בֵּית־אֵל אֲשֶׁר מָשַׁחְתָּ שָּׁם מַצֵּבָה אֲשֶׁר נָדַרְתָּ לִּי שָׁם נֶדֶר עַתָּה קוּם צֵא מִן־הָאָרֶץ הַזֹּאת וְשׁוּב

יד אֶל־אֶרֶץ מוֹלַדְתֶּךָ: וַתַּעַן רָחֵל וְלֵאָה וַתֹּאמַרְנָה לוֹ הַעוֹד לָנוּ

טו חֵלֶק וְנַחֲלָה בְּבֵית אָבִינוּ: הֲלוֹא נָכְרִיּוֹת נֶחְשַׁבְנוּ לוֹ כִּי מְכָרָנוּ

טז וַיֹּאכַל גַּם־אָכוֹל אֶת־כַּסְפֵּנוּ: כִּי כָל־הָעֹשֶׁר אֲשֶׁר הִצִּיל אֱלֹהִים מֵאָבִינוּ לָנוּ הוּא וּלְבָנֵינוּ וְעַתָּה כֹּל אֲשֶׁר אָמַר

יז אֱלֹהִים אֵלֶיךָ עֲשֵׂה: וַיָּקָם יַעֲקֹב וַיִּשָּׂא אֶת־בָּנָיו וְאֶת־נָשָׁיו

יח עַל־הַגְּמַלִּים: וַיִּנְהַג אֶת־כָּל־מִקְנֵהוּ וְאֶת־כָּל־רְכֻשׁוֹ אֲשֶׁר רָכָשׁ מִקְנֵה קִנְיָנוֹ אֲשֶׁר רָכָשׁ בְּפַדַּן אֲרָם לָבוֹא אֶל־יִצְחָק

יט אָבִיו אַרְצָה כְּנָעַן: וְלָבָן הָלַךְ לִגְזֹז אֶת־צֹאנוֹ וַתִּגְנֹב רָחֵל

ששי

---

11. וַיֹּאמֶר אֵלַי מַלְאַךְ הָאֱלֹהִים בַּחֲלוֹם — *And an angel of God said to me in the dream.* In his analysis of the eleven levels of prophecy, *Rambam* stipulates that the appearance of an angel in a dream is something which "applies to most of the prophets," and that it constitutes the sixth level of prophecy (*Guide* 2:45).

13. אָנֹכִי — *I am.* See our commentary to 28:16.

הָאֵל בֵּית־אֵל — *The God of Bethel. Rashi* explains: The article ה in front of the word "God" (which is in the construct state and so should not have an article) is extra, as we sometimes find in the Torah (e.g. *Numbers* 34:2). *Ibn Ezra* and *Radak* interpret the verse to mean that the words, *I am the God of Bethel,* are said by the angel in the name of God. Along the same lines, *Rambam* teaches, "There is no doubt that Jacob vowed to God and not to an angel; but this is the usual practice in the prophets' discourses — I mean that when prophets report the message which the angel has brought them from God, they express themselves as though it were God Himself Who had spoken to them. In passages of this kind, there is a "construct state" which is implied; it is as though it were written, "I am the angel of the Almighty One Who appeared to you in Bethel" (*Guide* 1:27).

However, in the words מַלְאַךְ הָאֱלֹהִים (instead of the usual expression מַלְאַךְ ה'), the Kabbalists see an indication that the revelation did not emanate from the Divinity as an absolute being but from Its terrestrial manifestation (*Shechinah*) embodied in the guardian angel to which Jacob refers at the end of his life: הַמַּלְאָךְ הַגֹּאֵל אֹתִי, *the angel who has redeemed me from all evil* (48:16). Note that while sacrifices must be offered exclusively in the name of Hashem and not in the name of one of His attributes (*Menachos* 110a), when Jacob made his vow (28:17-22) he still invoked only the name אֱלֹהִים, which is an attribute and not the name of His essence. This is explained by the fact

speckled, and checkered. ¹¹ And an angel of God said to me in the dream, 'Jacob!' And I said, 'Here I am.' ¹² And he said, 'Raise your eyes, if you please, and see that all the he-goats mounting the flocks are ringed, speckled, and checkered, for I have seen all that Laban is doing to you. ¹³ I am the God of Bethel where you anointed a pillar and where you made Me a vow. Now — arise, leave this land and return to your native land.' "

¹⁴ Then Rachel and Leah replied and said to him, "Have we then still a share and an inheritance in our father's house? ¹⁵ Are we not considered by him as strangers? For he has sold us and even totally consumed our money! ¹⁶ But, all the wealth that God has taken away from our father belongs to us and to our children; so now, whatever God has said to you, do."

¹⁷ Jacob arose and lifted his children and his wives onto the camels. ¹⁸ He led away all his livestock and all the wealth which he had amassed — his purchased property which he had amassed in Paddan-aram — to go to his father Isaac, to the land of Canaan.

¹⁹ Laban had gone to shear his sheep, and Rachel stole

that the patriarchs did not yet possess a complete knowledge of the Divine essence as contained in the name הַוָיָ. The Torah confirms this in *Exodus* 6:3.

נָדַרְתָּ לִי — *You made Me a vow. Rashi*: "And you must fulfill it, for you said, '[It] shall become a house of God' (28:22); you are to offer sacrifice there." The reason given here for the departure no longer has anything to do with Laban's hostility. So it comes to light that the apparent reasons determining the course of our lives are not always the only ones nor are they always the most profound. Other motives may intervene which, though less apparent, are nevertheless just as decisive.

Why had Jacob delayed in making good his vow and offering sacrifices on the מַצֵּבָה, *pillar*, which he had promised to build (ibid.)? The answer is that from the time of Jacob's sojourn in Aram, the pagans, prompted by his example, also began to build מַצֵּבוֹת in honor of their idols, as we see in verse 52. Now as soon as the מַצֵּבָה became part of a pagan cult, its use was forbidden to all Jews, as *Rashi* notes on *Deuteronomy* 16:22. Accordingly, Jacob waited for the Divine command (*Meshech Chachmah*; cf. *Ramban* on 35:14).

19. וַתִּגְנֹב רָחֵל — *Rachel stole*. With the intention of keeping her father from idolatry (*Rashi*). The next verse also speaks of stealing. This time it is Jacob who outwits Laban (literally: steals Laban's heart). So it was possible to steal in Laban's house; but what Rachel stole was her father's idols and what Jacob stole was Laban's heart. He did this so that he could go where he pleased, which was his most basic right. Can these two acts be considered as really stealing? Apparently not in the opinion of *Onkelos*, who translates "Rachel hid" and "Jacob hid" (ע' נתינה לגר). The same point of view underlies the rule indicated

כ אֶת־הַתְּרָפִים אֲשֶׁר לְאָבִיהָ: וַיִּגְנֹב יַעֲקֹב אֶת־לֵב לָבָן
כא הָאֲרַמִּי עַל־בְּלִי הִגִּיד לוֹ כִּי בֹרֵחַ הוּא: וַיִּבְרַח הוּא
וְכָל־אֲשֶׁר־לוֹ וַיָּקָם וַיַּעֲבֹר אֶת־הַנָּהָר וַיָּשֶׂם אֶת־פָּנָיו הַר
כב־כג הַגִּלְעָד: וַיֻּגַּד לְלָבָן בַּיּוֹם הַשְּׁלִישִׁי כִּי בָרַח יַעֲקֹב: וַיִּקַּח
אֶת־אֶחָיו עִמּוֹ וַיִּרְדֹּף אַחֲרָיו דֶּרֶךְ שִׁבְעַת יָמִים וַיַּדְבֵּק אֹתוֹ
כד בְּהַר הַגִּלְעָד: וַיָּבֹא אֱלֹהִים אֶל־לָבָן הָאֲרַמִּי בַּחֲלֹם הַלָּיְלָה
וַיֹּאמֶר לוֹ הִשָּׁמֶר לְךָ פֶּן־תְּדַבֵּר עִם־יַעֲקֹב מִטּוֹב עַד־רָע:

in the התגין ס׳: the letter ג of the word וַתִּגְנֹב, *she stole*, and also of the word וַיִּגְנֹב, *he stole*, must be adorned with masoretic crowns. This brings out the special significance attached to these words.

הַתְּרָפִים — *Teraphim*. The etymology of the word תְּרָפִים is obscure. It probably refers to idols which served as oracles. The peoples of antiquity attributed different powers to them, such as the ability to remedy a misfortune, to protect the home, or to predict the future. Our classical commentators quote various opinions on the nature of these idols or penates (household gods) and some of them consider that Rachel stole the idols so that they would not reveal to Laban what Jacob's plans were or the direction he would take. She concealed them in the camel's saddle and sat on them, a sign of her supreme disdain; but she refrained from burying them, for such an act might have been seen by one of the slaves, who would tell Laban about it.

20. לָבָן הָאֲרַמִּי — *Laban the Aramean*. This designation also means "Laban the sorcerer." He was אָב הָרַמָּאִים — the greatest sorcerer of his time (*Rabbah* 75). This epithet לָבָן הָאֲרַמִּי is repeated later in verse 24 and seems to want to justify Jacob's trickery here. Jacob was entitled to go to any lengths in order to escape with his family from a perfidious and treacherous man "whose tricks no one could elude" (ibid.). R' Abba said, "Balaam, the great sorcerer, had learned his craft from Laban, his grandfather" (Laban was the father of Beor). Balak, the king of Moab, had brought Balaam from Aram, Laban's land (*Numbers* 23:7). This region formed part of the אֶרֶץ בְּנֵי קֶדֶם, *land of the easterners* (29:1), which was considered in antiquity to be the center of magic and the occult sciences (*Isaiah* 2:6; cf. *Zohar*).

21. וַיִּבְרַח הוּא — *Thus, he fled.* Cf. our commentary on 28:20 and 27:43.

23. וַיִּקַּח אֶת־אֶחָיו עִמּוֹ וַיִּרְדֹּף אַחֲרָיו — *So he took his kinsmen with him and pursued him.* The act of taking his relatives with him in pursuit of Jacob clearly demonstrates Laban's aggressive intentions, confirmed moreover by the remainder of this passage. The phrase in *Deuteronomy* (26:5), אֲרַמִּי אֹבֵד אָבִי, *the Aramean tried to destroy my forefather*, refers to these plans for Jacob's annihilation. The author of the Haggadah of Passover, in commenting on this verse, is even more explicit: "Laban sought to destroy everything (i.e., the whole family)." *Rashi* (*Deuteronomy* ibid.) is entirely of this opinion: "Laban was

the teraphim that belonged to her father. [20] Jacob deceived Laban
the Aramean by not telling him that he was fleeing. [21] Thus, he fled
with all he had. He arose and crossed the river, and he set his
direction toward Mount Gilead.

[22] It was told to Laban on the third day that Jacob had fled. [23] So
he took his kinsmen with him and pursued him a distance of seven
days, catching up with him on Mount Gilead. [24] But God had come
to Laban the Aramean in a dream by night and said to him,
"Beware lest you speak with Jacob either good or bad."

seeking to uproot the House of Israel when he pursued Jacob. Since this was his
intention, God charged him, as it were, with having carried it out since, for the
pagans, God equates [evil] intentions with actions" (cf. *Tosafos* to *Kiddushin*
39b). A similar comment has already been made with respect to Esau, in our
commentary on 27:41.

Laban's cruelty is given as the reason why Jacob, even though he had already
spent 20 years in Syria, could not remain there and begin the 400 year exile
which God had announced to Abraham for his offspring (15:13). "God saw that
the Jews would never be able to bear the cruelties of Syria; He therefore set aside
another land for their exile" (*Pesachim* 87b, according to the version confirmed
by *Ha'amek Davar, Deuteronomy* ibid.). Hence the connection between the two
segments of the phrase quoted above: אֲרַמִּי אֹבֵד אָבִי וַיֵּרֶד מִצְרָיְמָה — *An Aramean*
tried to destroy my forefather, and so he descended to Egypt.

24. וַיָּבֹא אֱלֹהִים אֶל־לָבָן הָאֲרַמִּי בַּחֲלֹם הַלָּיְלָה — *But God had come to Laban the*
Aramean in a dream by night. This is one of the two cases in which the pure
Being became unclean (by coming to a wicked person) on behalf of a righteous
person. The other case was that of Abimelech (20:3) and there the same phrase
is used (*Tanchuma*).

Rambam teaches: "When it is said that God came to someone in a dream of the
night, it is not a reference to prophecy nor is this person a prophet. It means only
that a warning came to this person from God and we are told that this warning
came in a dream . . . One must be careful to distinguish between the expressions,
'in a dream of the night' and 'in the visions of the night.' For of Jacob it is said,
God spoke to Israel in the visions of the night (46:2), whereas it is said of Laban,
God had come . . . in a dream by night. For this reason *Onkelos* translates here,
"A word came from God," and not "God revealed Himself" (*Guide* 2:41).

הִשָּׁמֶר לְךָ פֶּן־תְּדַבֵּר עִם־יַעֲקֹב מִטּוֹב עַד־רָע — *Beware lest you speak with Jacob*
either good or bad. It does not say, "lest you *do* either good or bad to Jacob," but
"lest you *speak* . . . with Jacob." For Laban had come not only with weapons but
also with his sorcerer's art. He wanted to destroy Jacob with his evil spells and his
oracles, with his power to utter a curse. This was the same procedure which his
grandson and disciple Balaam used against the Jews. And in both cases God
intervened to prevent these magical procedures from having any effect (*Zohar*).

כה וַיַּשֵּׂג לָבָן אֶת־יַעֲקֹב וְיַעֲקֹב תָּקַע אֶת־אָהֳלוֹ בָּהָר וְלָבָן תָּקַע
כו אֶת־אֶחָיו בְּהַר הַגִּלְעָד: וַיֹּאמֶר לָבָן לְיַעֲקֹב מֶה עָשִׂיתָ וַתִּגְנֹב
כז אֶת־לְבָבִי וַתְּנַהֵג אֶת־בְּנֹתַי כִּשְׁבֻיוֹת חָרֶב: לָמָּה נַחְבֵּאתָ
לִבְרֹחַ וַתִּגְנֹב אֹתִי וְלֹא־הִגַּדְתָּ לִּי וָאֲשַׁלֵּחֲךָ בְּשִׂמְחָה
כח וּבְשִׁרִים בְּתֹף וּבְכִנּוֹר: וְלֹא נְטַשְׁתַּנִי לְנַשֵּׁק לְבָנַי וְלִבְנֹתָי
כט עַתָּה הִסְכַּלְתָּ עֲשׂוֹ: יֶשׁ־לְאֵל יָדִי לַעֲשׂוֹת עִמָּכֶם רָע וֵאלֹהֵי
אֲבִיכֶם אֶמֶשׁ ׀ אָמַר אֵלַי לֵאמֹר הִשָּׁמֶר לְךָ מִדַּבֵּר עִם־
ל יַעֲקֹב מִטּוֹב עַד־רָע: וְעַתָּה הָלֹךְ הָלַכְתָּ כִּי־נִכְסֹף נִכְסַפְתָּה
לא לְבֵית אָבִיךָ לָמָּה גָנַבְתָּ אֶת־אֱלֹהָי: וַיַּעַן יַעֲקֹב וַיֹּאמֶר
לב לְלָבָן כִּי יָרֵאתִי כִּי אָמַרְתִּי פֶּן־תִּגְזֹל אֶת־בְּנוֹתֶיךָ מֵעִמִּי: עִם
אֲשֶׁר תִּמְצָא אֶת־אֱלֹהֶיךָ לֹא יִחְיֶה נֶגֶד אַחֵינוּ הַכֶּר־לְךָ
מָה עִמָּדִי וְקַח־לָךְ וְלֹא־יָדַע יַעֲקֹב כִּי רָחֵל גְּנָבָתַם:

---

25. וַיַּשֵּׂג לָבָן אֶת־יַעֲקֹב — *Laban overtook Jacob.* Meaning, he wanted to make an attempt on his life. Two circumstances, however, prevented him from carrying out his villainous plan: the warning which he had received from God in his dream at night and the approach of Esau with his four hundred armed men, which will be mentioned later. Laban feared that if he killed Jacob, his brother Esau would in turn, as the avenger of blood, kill him. And so he left him alone. *Then Laban went and returned to his place. Jacob went on his way* (32:1,2) (*Aggadas Bereishis* 54).

29. יֶשׁ־לְאֵל יָדִי — *It is in my power.* The ungodly exalt and glorify themselves in the evil which it is in their power to commit. They renounce it only when forced to do so by the threats of their gods (*Midrash*).

Rashi explains: Laban said, "I have the power to harm you all." Jacob replied, "You say that you have the strength to kill me? Come here, then, with your troops and try to lift this block of stone!" They could not. Then Jacob came forward and *took a stone and raised it up as a monument* (verse 45). He had removed it as one removes the stopper from a bottle (*Tanchuma, Vayishlach*). Jacob possessed extraordinary physical strength; see our commentary on 29:10.

וֵאלֹהֵי . . . לֵאמֹר — *God . . . saying.* לֵאמֹר here means לְדוֹרוֹת, saying also to future generations (to do no harm to the descendants of Jacob) — as it is said (*I Chronicles* 16:22), אַל־תִּגְּעוּ בִּמְשִׁיחָי וּבִנְבִיאַי אַל־תָּרֵעוּ, *Touch not My anointed ones, and do My prophets no harm* (*Midrash Lekach Tov*). The Divine words addressed to Laban thus appear to have unlimited scope, to be applicable at all times, everywhere. And throughout their history, Jacob's descendants are called on to testify before God whether these words are being obeyed or not. They give this evidence in the words of homage to God spoken during the offering of *Bikkurim* (first-fruits): "אֲרַמִּי אֹבֵד אָבִי, וְעָנִיתָ וְאָמַרְתָּ, *you shall testify and say* and the rest of the passage at *Deuteronomy* 26:5-11 (*Zohar*).

²⁵ *Laban overtook Jacob. Jacob had pitched his tent on the mountain, while Laban had stationed his kinsmen on Mount Gilead.* ²⁶ *Laban said to Jacob, "What have you done that you have deceived me and led my daughters away like captives of the sword?* ²⁷ *Why have you fled so stealthily, and cheated me? Nor did you tell me — for I would have sent you off with gladness, with songs, with timbrel, and with lyre!* ²⁸ *And you did not even allow me to kiss my sons and daughters; now you have acted foolishly.* ²⁹ *It is in my power to do you all harm; but the God of your father addressed me last night, saying, 'Beware of speaking with Jacob either good or bad.'* ³⁰ *Now — you have left because you longed greatly for your father's house; but why did you steal my gods?'*

³¹ *Jacob answered and said to Laban, "Because I was afraid, for I thought, perhaps you might steal your daughters from me.* ³² *With whomever you find your gods, he shall not live; in the presence of our kinsmen ascertain for yourself what is with me and take it back." (Now Jacob did not know that Rachel had stolen them.)*

30. . . . וְעַתָּה הָלֹךְ הָלַכְתָּ כִּי־נִכְסֹף נִכְסַפְתָּה — *Now — you have left because you longed greatly . . .* Twice in this sentence we see words repeated (הָלֹךְ הָלַכְתָּ, נִכְסֹף נִכְסַפְתָּה). Given that this sentence was said by an uncouth and uncultured man, R' Yishmael concludes that repetitions in the Torah do not necessarily have any particular significance and that the Torah often speaks in "the language of men" with nothing else being implied (*Talmud Yerushalmi, Shabbos* 19b). But R' Bachya holds that Laban was speaking of the nostalgia which Jacob felt for his father's house, and by repeating נִכְסַפְתָּה, he makes reference also to Jacob's homesickness for the Holy Land, for his homeland. The word נִכְסַפְתָּה means, then, "you are longing for it, i.e. for your land" with the final letter ה (which replaces the direct object in the feminine) referring to אֶרֶץ, *the land*, which is feminine in gender.

לָמָּה גָנַבְתָּ אֶת־אֱלֹהָי — *But why did you steal my gods?* When they heard these words, Laban's grandsons interrupted him: We are ashamed, grandfather, that in your old age you still can say: "my gods!" (*Rabbah* 74).

32. עִם אֲשֶׁר תִּמְצָא אֶת־אֱלֹהֶיךָ לֹא יִחְיֶה — *With whomever you find your gods, he shall not live.* Because of this curse, Rachel died during the journey (*Rashi*). When a righteous man pronounces a curse, Satan grabs hold of it, keeps it until the time of danger is ripe, and then does evil with it, even if the words were spoken by mistake or without realizing what one is saying. Thus, Satan waited until Rachel was in childbirth and then had the curse carried out (*Zohar*). But the same death sentence pronounced just as unwittingly, hastily, and severely on Benjamin by his own brothers, the sons of Jacob, had no consequences, for he had not stolen anything (*Genesis* 44:9).

לג וַיָּבֹא לָבָן בְּאֹהֶל־יַעֲקֹב ׀ וּבְאֹהֶל לֵאָה וּבְאֹהֶל שְׁתֵּי הָאֲמָהֹת
לד וְלֹא מָצָא וַיֵּצֵא מֵאֹהֶל לֵאָה וַיָּבֹא בְּאֹהֶל רָחֵל: וְרָחֵל
לָקְחָה אֶת־הַתְּרָפִים וַתְּשִׂמֵם בְּכַר הַגָּמָל וַתֵּשֶׁב עֲלֵיהֶם
לה וַיְמַשֵּׁשׁ לָבָן אֶת־כָּל־הָאֹהֶל וְלֹא מָצָא: וַתֹּאמֶר אֶל־אָבִיהָ
אַל־יִחַר בְּעֵינֵי אֲדֹנִי כִּי לוֹא אוּכַל לָקוּם מִפָּנֶיךָ כִּי־דֶרֶךְ
לו נָשִׁים לִי וַיְחַפֵּשׂ וְלֹא מָצָא אֶת־הַתְּרָפִים: וַיִּחַר לְיַעֲקֹב
וַיָּרֶב בְּלָבָן וַיַּעַן יַעֲקֹב וַיֹּאמֶר לְלָבָן מַה־פִּשְׁעִי מַה חַטָּאתִי
לז כִּי דָלַקְתָּ אַחֲרָי: כִּי־מִשַּׁשְׁתָּ אֶת־כָּל־כֵּלַי מַה־מָּצָאתָ
מִכֹּל כְּלֵי־בֵיתֶךָ שִׂים כֹּה נֶגֶד אַחַי וְאַחֶיךָ וְיוֹכִיחוּ בֵּין
לח שְׁנֵינוּ: זֶה עֶשְׂרִים שָׁנָה אָנֹכִי עִמָּךְ רְחֵלֶיךָ וְעִזֶּיךָ לֹא שִׁכֵּלוּ
לט וְאֵילֵי צֹאנְךָ לֹא אָכָלְתִּי: טְרֵפָה לֹא־הֵבֵאתִי אֵלֶיךָ אָנֹכִי
מ אֲחַטֶּנָּה מִיָּדִי תְּבַקְשֶׁנָּה גְּנֻבְתִי יוֹם וּגְנֻבְתִי לָיְלָה: הָיִיתִי
מא בַיּוֹם אֲכָלַנִי חֹרֶב וְקֶרַח בַּלָּיְלָה וַתִּדַּד שְׁנָתִי מֵעֵינָי: זֶה־
לִּי עֶשְׂרִים שָׁנָה בְּבֵיתֶךָ עֲבַדְתִּיךָ אַרְבַּע־עֶשְׂרֵה שָׁנָה
בִּשְׁתֵּי בְנֹתֶיךָ וְשֵׁשׁ שָׁנִים בְּצֹאנֶךָ וַתַּחֲלֵף אֶת־מַשְׂכֻּרְתִּי
מב עֲשֶׂרֶת מֹנִים: לוּלֵי אֱלֹהֵי אָבִי אֱלֹהֵי אַבְרָהָם וּפַחַד יִצְחָק

Jacob's spoken word had a direct and irrevocable effect "like that of an angel." When Joseph rejoined his father, why did he not stay with him, instead of keeping his distance and coming only when his father called? It was because Joseph feared questions about the circumstances of his coming to be in Egypt. He would then have been obliged to recount how his brothers had sold him and this might have provoked his father into cursing his brothers. Joseph remembered the effect which such words had had on the fate of his own mother, and he did not want to bring the same fate on his brothers as well (*Daas Zekeinim* from *Baalei Tosafos*, Vayechi *Meshech Chochmah* 1).

33. בְּאֹהֶל־יַעֲקֹב וּבְאֹהֶל לֵאָה — *Into Jacob's tent, and into Leah's tent.* There were three tents according to *Rashi; Ramban* holds that there were five, Jacob having one tent for himself.

35. כִּי לוֹא אוּכַל לָקוּם מִפָּנֶיךָ — *That I cannot rise up before you.* The word לֹא when written with a *vav* can mean both "no" and "him." "For him (Laban) I cannot rise — for anyone else I could" (*Meshech Chochmah*).

כִּי־דֶרֶךְ נָשִׁים לִי — *For the way of women is upon me.* This does not at all prevent a woman from rising up or remaining in a standing position. But in ancient times women were always kept entirely separated during their menses. They stayed in their tents, no one spoke to them; they were shunned completely. That is why Rachel could decline to rise and why Laban did not insist further (*Ramban*). But these arrangements, notes R' Moshe Sofer, are no longer valid in our day and

³³ *Laban came into Jacob's tent, and into Leah's tent, and into the tent of the two maidservants, but he found nothing. When he had left Leah's tent, he came into Rachel's tent.* ³⁴ *Now Rachel had taken the teraphim, put them into the camel's packsaddle and sat on them. Laban rummaged through the whole tent, but found nothing.* ³⁵ *She said to her father, "Let not my lord find it annoying that I cannot rise up before you, for the way of women is upon me." Thus he searched but did not find the teraphim.*

³⁶ *Then Jacob became angered and he took up his grievance with Laban; Jacob spoke up and said to Laban, "What is my transgression? What is my sin that you have hotly pursued me?* ³⁷ *When you rummaged through all my things, what did you find of all your household objects? Set it here before my kinsmen and your kinsmen, and let them decide between the two of us.*

³⁸ *"These twenty years I have been with you, your ewes and she-goats never miscarried, nor did I eat rams of your flock.* ³⁹ *That which was mangled I never brought you — I myself would bear the loss, from me you would exact it, whether it was stolen by day or stolen by night.* ⁴⁰ *This is how I was: By day scorching heat consumed me, and frost by night; my sleep drifted from my eyes.* ⁴¹ *This is my twenty years in your household: I served you fourteen years for your two daughters, and six years for your flocks; and you changed my wage a hundred times.* ⁴² *Had not the God of my father — the God of Abraham and the Dread of Isaac*

age, as physiological conditions now are not the same as they were in those times (שו״ת חת״ם, או״ח סי׳ כ״ג).

36. מַה־פִּשְׁעִי — *What is my transgression?* The anger of the patriarchs is still preferable to the appeasement of their descendants. When Jacob became angry and quarreled with Laban, he only said to him, "What is my transgression, what is my sin?" But when David appeased his generals and forbade them to raise a hand against Saul, he cried out, *As God lives, God will smite him down, or his day will come to die* (I Samuel 26:10; *Midrash Tanchuma*). This example teaches us that the righteous person must be careful with his words and must take care not to stir up hatred, even under those exceptional circumstances when he quarrels with others and allows himself to become angry (*Chofetz Chaim*).

42. וּפַחַד יִצְחָק — *The Dread of Isaac.* The same term is used later in verse 53. While love of God and men characterizes Abraham's form of worship (מִדַּת הַחֶסֶד), Isaac's is characterized by the awe of God (פַּחַד). It was manifest in his absolute obedience to the Divine commands and attained its loftiest expression in the willingness to sacrifice his own person to God (מִדַּת הַדִּין), at the *Akeidah*.

הָיָה לִּי כִּי עַתָּה רֵיקָם שִׁלַּחְתָּנִי אֶת־עָנְיִי וְאֶת־יְגִיעַ כַּפַּי

שביעי   מג רָאָה אֱלֹהִים וַיּוֹכַח אָמֶשׁ: וַיַּעַן לָבָן וַיֹּאמֶר אֶל־יַעֲקֹב הַבָּנוֹת

בְּנֹתַי וְהַבָּנִים בָּנַי וְהַצֹּאן צֹאנִי וְכֹל אֲשֶׁר־אַתָּה רֹאֶה

לִי־הוּא וְלִבְנֹתַי מָה־אֶעֱשֶׂה לָאֵלֶּה הַיּוֹם אוֹ לִבְנֵיהֶן אֲשֶׁר

מד יָלָדוּ: וְעַתָּה לְכָה נִכְרְתָה בְרִית אֲנִי וָאָתָּה וְהָיָה לְעֵד בֵּינִי

מה-מו וּבֵינֶךָ: וַיִּקַּח יַעֲקֹב אָבֶן וַיְרִימֶהָ מַצֵּבָה: וַיֹּאמֶר יַעֲקֹב לְאֶחָיו

לִקְטוּ אֲבָנִים וַיִּקְחוּ אֲבָנִים וַיַּעֲשׂוּ־גָל וַיֹּאכְלוּ שָׁם עַל־הַגָּל:

מז-מח וַיִּקְרָא־לוֹ לָבָן יְגַר שָׂהֲדוּתָא וְיַעֲקֹב קָרָא לוֹ גַּלְעֵד: וַיֹּאמֶר

לָבָן הַגַּל הַזֶּה עֵד בֵּינִי וּבֵינְךָ הַיּוֹם עַל־כֵּן קָרָא־שְׁמוֹ גַּלְעֵד:

מט וְהַמִּצְפָּה אֲשֶׁר אָמַר יִצֶף יְהוָה בֵּינִי וּבֵינֶךָ כִּי נִסָּתֵר אִישׁ

נ מֵרֵעֵהוּ: אִם־תְּעַנֶּה אֶת־בְּנֹתַי וְאִם־תִּקַּח נָשִׁים עַל־בְּנֹתַי

נא אֵין אִישׁ עִמָּנוּ רְאֵה אֱלֹהִים עֵד בֵּינִי וּבֵינֶךָ: וַיֹּאמֶר לָבָן

לְיַעֲקֹב הִנֵּה | הַגַּל הַזֶּה וְהִנֵּה הַמַּצֵּבָה אֲשֶׁר יָרִיתִי בֵּינִי וּבֵינֶךָ:

נב עֵד הַגַּל הַזֶּה וְעֵדָה הַמַּצֵּבָה אִם־אָנִי לֹא־אֶעֱבֹר אֵלֶיךָ אֶת־

אֶת־עָנְיִי וְאֶת־יְגִיעַ כַּפַּי רָאָה אֱלֹהִים — *God saw my wretchedness and the toil of my hands.* Laban had let it be known that for him Jacob had no personal merit but only the merit of his fathers in his favor (*the God of your father addressed me last night,* verse 29). But Jacob replied by stressing the worth of his untiring labor during twenty years of the hardest servitude. ''Hard work is even more precious than the merit of the fathers (זְכוּת אָבוֹת), for although this merit protected Jacob with respect to material possessions (*you would surely have now sent me away empty-handed*), yet it was the labor of his hands which protected the lives of his family (*God ... admonished you last night*) — to save our lives'' (*Rabbah* 74).

45. וַיִּקַּח יַעֲקֹב אָבֶן — *Then Jacob took a stone.* Cf. our commentary on verse 29.

46. לְאֶחָיו — *To his brethren.* According to *Rashi,* ''These were his sons, who were like brothers to him; they were at his side in times of trouble and in battle.'' According to *Ramban,* however, they were Laban's relatives whom Jacob ordered to gather stones out of respect for his father-in-law. But the same term has a different meaning in verse 54 (see our commentary ibid.).

47. וַיִּקְרָא־לוֹ לָבָן יְגַר שָׂהֲדוּתָא — *Laban called it Jegar-sahadutha.* ''The Heap of Witness'' in Laban's language, Syriac. ''Let not the Syriac language,'' R' Yonasan remarks, ''be without value to you, for the Torah uses it — for example in this verse'' (*Yerushalmi, Sotah* 7). According to one Talmudic opinion, it was the language spoken by Adam (*Sanhedrin* 38b) and *R' Yehudah HaLevi* considers it closely related to Hebrew and Arabic (*Kuzari* 2:68; so too *Ibn Ezra* on *Genesis* 30:37).

R' Bachya, however, points out that the word גַּל, *heap,* recurs regularly in Laban's remarks; in contrast Jacob had wanted to erect a מַצֵּבָה, *monument.*

— been with me, you would surely have now sent me away empty handed; God saw my wretchedness and the toil of my hands, so He admonished you last night."

⁴³ Then Laban spoke up and said to Jacob, "The daughters are my daughters, the children are my children and the flock is my flock, and all that you see is mine. Yet to my daughters — what could I do to them this day? Or to their children whom they have borne! ⁴⁴ So now, come, let us make a covenant, I and you, and He shall be a witness between me and you."

⁴⁵ Then Jacob took a stone and raised it up as a monument. ⁴⁶ And Jacob said to his brethren, "Gather stones!" So they took stones and made a mound, and they ate there on the mound. ⁴⁷ Laban called it Jegar-sahadutha, but Jacob called it Galeed.

⁴⁸ And Laban declared, "This mound is a witness between me and you today"; therefore he called its name Galeed. ⁴⁹ And as for the Mizpah — because he said, "May HASHEM keep watch between me and you when we are out of each other's sight. ⁵⁰ If you will ill-treat my daughters or if you will marry wives in addition to my daughters — though no man may be among us — but see! God is a witness between me and you." ⁵¹ And Laban said to Jacob, "Here is this mound, and here is the monument which I have cast between me and you. ⁵² This mound shall be witness and the monument shall be witness that I may not cross over to you past

Now, the repetition of the word גַּל alludes to גַּלְגַּל — the star which Laban worshiped (i.e., the sun) and the "witness" mentioned here (שָׁהֲדוּתָא) is also related to this star, named as a witness to the pact. Quoting the Syriac name in this context is probably intended to draw our attention to what Laban is implying with his words.

50. רְאֵה אֱלֹהִים עֵד בֵּינִי וּבֵינֶךָ — *See! God is a witness between me and you.* The end result of the long discussion between Jacob and Laban was to bring Laban to the recognition of God, whose Name he invokes here. But the good intentions of the wicked are short-lived and Laban immediately (verse 53) returns to his divinity: "Abraham's God and Nahor's gods will judge between us" (*Zohar*). Accordingly, *Rashi* on verse 53 remarks that the first name of God mentioned there in connection with Abraham is of a sacred character whereas the second is not (ibid.).

52. אִם־אָנִי לֹא־אֶעֱבֹר אֵלֶיךָ — *That I may not cross over to you.* Gilead formed a boundary of the land of Israel, as is noted in *Deuteronomy* 34:1.

Laban seems to have wanted to make his covenant with Jacob a second time in order to extend it into the future. Indeed, it was still in force at the time of the wars of David. When David sent Joab, his chief of staff, to fight the Syrians of Tzovah, they said to him, "Are you not a descendant of Jacob? What then do

הַגַּל הַזֶּה וְאִם־אָתָּה לֹא־תַעֲבֹר אֵלַי אֶת־הַגַּל הַזֶּה

נג וְאֶת־הַמַּצֵּבָה הַזֹּאת לְרָעָה: אֱלֹהֵי אַבְרָהָם *וֵאלֹהֵי נָחוֹר
יִשְׁפְּטוּ בֵינֵינוּ *אֱלֹהֵי אֲבִיהֶם וַיִּשָּׁבַע יַעֲקֹב בְּפַחַד אָבִיו יִצְחָק:

נד וַיִּזְבַּח יַעֲקֹב זֶבַח בָּהָר וַיִּקְרָא לְאֶחָיו לֶאֱכָל־לָחֶם וַיֹּאכְלוּ

לב מפטיר א לֶחֶם וַיָּלִינוּ בָּהָר: וַיַּשְׁכֵּם לָבָן בַּבֹּקֶר וַיְנַשֵּׁק לְבָנָיו וְלִבְנוֹתָיו

ב וַיְבָרֶךְ אֶתְהֶם וַיֵּלֶךְ וַיָּשָׁב לָבָן לִמְקֹמוֹ: וְיַעֲקֹב הָלַךְ לְדַרְכּוֹ

ג וַיִּפְגְּעוּ־בוֹ מַלְאֲכֵי אֱלֹהִים: וַיֹּאמֶר יַעֲקֹב כַּאֲשֶׁר רָאָם מַחֲנֵה
אֱלֹהִים זֶה וַיִּקְרָא שֵׁם־הַמָּקוֹם הַהוּא מַחֲנָיִם:

you make of the pact which your ancestor had with Laban the Syrian: *This
mound shall be witness, etc.* Joab did not know what to reply, so he turned to
David, who convened the *Sanhedrin*. The Sages of Israel asserted that the pact
had already been violated twice by the Syrians: first, when they had Balaam
cross the border (*Numbers* 23:7) and then again during the reign of Kushan
Rishathayim, king of Syria (*Judges* 3:10). Then Joab left to do battle, and when
he came back victorious, David sang a hymn to God *when he made war against
Aram-Tzovah,* the Syrians of Tzovah (*Psalms* 60; *Midrash* ibid.).

54. וַיִּזְבַּח יַעֲקֹב זֶבַח בָּהָר. — *Then Jacob slaughtered for a feast on the mountain.*
The word זֶבַח, in the sense of slaughtering a sacrifice, occurs here for the first
time. Jacob has scarcely arrived at the border of the Holy Land, yet he hurries
to offer a sacrifice to God, for he was reluctant to carry on the Divine service
while outside the borders of the land, as *Ramban* points out (26:5).

וַיִּקְרָא לְאֶחָיו לֶאֱכָל־לָחֶם — *And summoned his kinsmen to break bread.* This
refers to his friends who were with Laban (*Rashi*). The way this chapter
concludes might provide us with an explanation for its unusual length and for
the wealth of details regarding Laban's attitude towards Jacob. It makes the
patriarch's magnanimity stand out in bold relief. The righteous man bears no
bitterness against his enemy, despite the implacable hatred, the threat of
extermination, and the outrageous injustices which Laban has so often shown
him. The twenty years of servitude and mental anguish end with a great feast
offered by the victim to his oppressor.

32.

1. וַיֵּלֶךְ וַיָּשָׁב לָבָן לִמְקֹמוֹ — *Then Laban went and returned to his place.* His long
association with a righteous person had no moral influence on Laban. He
returned to his place, that is, to his earlier way of life. As for Jacob, he "went on
his way," making constant, step-by-step progress.

2. וַיִּפְגְּעוּ־בוֹ מַלְאֲכֵי אֱלֹהִים — *And angels of God encountered him.* Laban was
exasperated at having been unable to do Jacob even the slightest harm; when he
got back to Haran he sent a message to Esau through his son Beor and ten
companions. In this note he gave vent to his real sentiments towards his nephew,
despite the tenderness which Laban had shown his sons and daughters as he was

this mound, nor may you cross over to me past this mound and this monument for evil. ⁵³ *May the God of Abraham and the god of Nahor judge between us — the god of their father." And Jacob swore by the Dread of his father Isaac.* ⁵⁴ *Then Jacob slaughtered for a feast on the mountain and summoned his kinsmen to break bread; and they broke bread and spent the night on the mountain.*

32 ¹ **A**nd Laban awoke early in the morning; he kissed his sons and his daughters and blessed them; then Laban went and returned to his place. ² Jacob went on his way, and angels of God encountered him. ³ Jacob said when he saw them, "This is a Godly camp!" So he called the name of that place Mahanaim.

leaving. In this message Laban said to Esau, "Have you heard what your brother Jacob did to me? He came to me empty-handed; I offered him my hospitality, I raised him, I gave him my two daughters and my two bondwomen as wives. Thanks to me he became exceedingly wealthy, he had many children and slaves and amassed a great fortune. And when he saw how great his riches had grown, he stealthily fled from my home while I was away and he took with him all my treasures. He had decided to rejoin his father in Canaan. He carried away my daughters as if they were prisoners of war and he stole my gods from me. I left him in the mountains, in the valley of Yabok, with all of his riches. You can find him there, if you so desire, and you may do with him as you see fit" (*Yashar*).

But Jacob need not have feared either Laban or Esau, for he was escorted on his journey by two camps of guardian angels, one of which accompanied him from Haran to the border. There he was received by the other camp, which escorted him in the Holy Land. Each of these camps was formed of a multitude of angels, and Jacob immediately recognized them as such for no one had seen them approaching and yet, suddenly, "they met him" (*R' Chaim ben Attar*).

The *Zohar* compares the beginning and end of the *sidrah*. At the beginning, it was said, וַיִּפְגַּע בַּמָּקוֹם, *he* [Jacob] *encountered the place*. There, he fell asleep and, in a dream, saw the angels of God on the ladder which rose toward heaven. But at the end of the *sidrah* Jacob, in full consciousness, sees the angels coming to meet him — וַיִּפְגְּעוּ בוֹ. The difference is explained by the fact that at the end of the *sidrah* Jacob returns to the Holy Land as a married man and father of the tribes of Israel. Accordingly, the angels of God come to meet him, וַיִּפְגְּעוּ בוֹ, to welcome and accompany him. But at the outset Jacob was still unmarried; and it was therefore he who was moving toward the holy place (וַיִּפְגַּע בַּמָּקוֹם), with the revelation coming to him only in a dream. When Jacob on his return journey lifts up his eyes and perceives the camp of angels, this vision immediately reminds him of the vision of the "angels of God" in his dream upon arriving at Haran. In his mind he establishes the connection between that heavenly camp then and the earthly camp which is coming to meet him now, and he names this place מַחֲנָיִם, *two camps.*

ד וַיִּשְׁלַח יַעֲקֹב מַלְאָכִים לְפָנָיו אֶל־עֵשָׂו אָחִיו אַרְצָה שֵׂעִיר

ה שְׂדֵה אֱדוֹם: וַיְצַו אֹתָם לֵאמֹר כֹּה תְאמְרוּן לַאדֹנִי לְעֵשָׂו כֹּה

ו אָמַר עַבְדְּךָ יַעֲקֹב עִם־לָבָן גַּרְתִּי וָאֵחַר עַד־עָתָּה: וַיְהִי־לִי

שׁוֹר וַחֲמוֹר צֹאן וְעֶבֶד וְשִׁפְחָה וָאֶשְׁלְחָה לְהַגִּיד לַאדֹנִי

ז לִמְצֹא־חֵן בְּעֵינֶיךָ: וַיָּשֻׁבוּ הַמַּלְאָכִים אֶל־יַעֲקֹב לֵאמֹר בָּאנוּ

4. יַעֲקֹב וַיִּשְׁלַח — *Then Jacob sent.* The aim of this passage is to remind us that the righteous must never rely on their rectitude, but must always do whatever is in their power to assure their well-being. It also serves as an example to future generations of how to conduct themselves in their struggles with the descendants of Esau: Jacob prepared a triple defense of "gifts, prayer and combat." Tradition tells us that R' Yanai used to read these chapters carefully when he was going to the Roman authorities to intercede on behalf of the Jews. He did so in order to be imbued with the same spirit that moved Jacob when he confronted his enemy brother (*Ramban* to 33:15).

מַלְאָכִים — *Angels. Radak* and others hold that the text is speaking literally of messengers sent by Jacob. But *Rashi*, basing himself upon the Midrash (and cf. *Zohar*) explains: "real angels." A third opinion is that of *R' Bachya* (identical, he says, with *Ibn Ezra's*): Given that the word מַלְאָכִים has a double meaning, he holds that Jacob's messengers were preceded by "real angels" from among those who had come out to meet the patriarch, as mentioned in the previous verse.

Rambam teaches that angels are pure intelligences created by God to carry out either occasional or permanent tasks. They can assume corporeal forms depending on which of the ten categories they belong to (cf. *Yesodei HaTorah* 2,7 and *Guide* 1:49; *R' Yehudah HaLevi* in *Kuzari* 4:3 holds similar ideas in this regard, as do *Ibn Gabirol*, quoted by *Abarbanel* on *II Kings* 3, and *R' Bachya* in *Chovos HaLevavos* 1:6). When Jacob wanted to send his men to meet Esau, all were so afraid that they were reluctant to accept the mission, therefore Jacob had his men escorted by ministering angels (*Tanchuma*).

לְפָנָיו — *Ahead of him.* Laban had pursued him and had caught up with him from behind. Scarcely had Jacob been rescued from this peril when he was faced with a new threat, this time ahead of him, from his own brother.

אַרְצָה שֵׂעִיר שְׂדֵה אֱדוֹם — *To the land of Seir, the field of Edom.* Jacob could have returned to his father's house in the south of Canaan via another route, thus avoiding his brother. (*R' Eliyahu Mizrachi* notes here the differences between *Rashi* and *Ramban* in identifying the places.) Consequently the Sages apply the following verse in *Proverbs* to Jacob: *As one who takes a dog by the ears is he who meddles in a dispute which is not his* (26:17). There was no need for Jacob to rekindle the old hatreds and to have to humble himself before Esau.

The *Zohar*, however, gives us its insight into the patriarch's intentions: Jacob felt that the reconciliation he wanted with his brother could only take place

⁴**T**hen Jacob sent angels ahead of him to Esau his brother to the land of Seir, the field of Edom. ⁵ He charged them, saying: "Thus shall you say, 'To my lord, to Esau, so said your servant Jacob: I have sojourned with Laban and have lingered until now. ⁶ I have acquired oxen and donkeys, flocks, servants, and maidservants and I am sending to tell my lord to find favor in your eyes.' "

⁷ The angels returned to Jacob, saying, "We came to

while their father, whom Esau loved dearly, was alive. Now Isaac was already about 157 years old. Jacob decided to attempt a reconciliation without further delay, even before returning to his father's house.

5. וַיְצַו אֹתָם — *He charged them.* "The angels are subordinate to the righteous. When Jacob had to resort to the angels, he took some from their camp, and gave them his orders and sent them to Esau." And they obeyed this righteous man to the letter (*Tanchuma*).

כֹּה תֹאמְרוּן לַאדֹנִי לְעֵשָׂו — *"Thus shall you say, 'to my lord, to Esau."* Right from his opening words, Jacob wanted Esau to understand that he had absolutely no intention of claiming the rights which the paternal blessings had long ago conferred upon him: *Be a lord to your kinsmen, and your mother's sons will prostrate themselves to you* (27:29). Much earlier, Jacob had decided to leave the benefit of this blessing to his descendants and, as it were, to reserve it for the future, as was pointed out in our commentary on 27:40 and 28:4. So it was with complete sincerity that on eight occasions he respectfully called his older brother אֲדֹנִי "my lord" and that he described himself (five times) as Esau's servant. Had Esau understood his brother's true intentions, his reactions certainly would have been different (*Zohar*).

עִם־לָבָן גַּרְתִּי — *I have sojourned with Laban.* Laban had a well-established reputation as אַב הָרַמָּאִים, the master sorcerer of his time. Jacob was intent on informing his brother that despite their twenty years together, Laban's sorcery against him had had no effect; he had left Laban with considerable riches. Jacob felt obliged to win his brother's sympathy with expensive gifts, but at the same time he deemed it essential to impress him with his strength and power.

6. לִמְצֹא־חֵן בְּעֵינֶיךָ — *To find favor in your eyes. Rashi* explains this as "I am coming to you with goodwill and I seek your friendship." Rebecca had sent Jacob a message to let him know of Esau's moves; she had heard about them although she did not know their objective. She warned her son and advised him that were he to encounter Esau, he should speak pleasantly, show himself humble and friendly, and offer him gifts. "You must honor him," she added, "as he is your older brother. Hide nothing from him if he asks you about yourself; perhaps his anger will be appeased and you will save your life and the lives of your family." Jacob decided to follow his mother's good advice (*Yashar*).

אֶל־אָחִ֔יךָ אֶל־עֵשָׂ֑ו וְגַם֙ הֹלֵ֣ךְ לִקְרָֽאתְךָ֔ וְאַרְבַּע־מֵא֥וֹת אִ֖ישׁ
ח עִמּֽוֹ: וַיִּירָ֧א יַעֲקֹ֛ב מְאֹ֖ד וַיֵּ֣צֶר ל֑וֹ וַיַּ֜חַץ אֶת־הָעָ֣ם אֲשֶׁר־אִתּ֗וֹ
ט וְאֶת־הַצֹּ֧אן וְאֶת־הַבָּקָ֛ר וְהַגְּמַלִּ֖ים לִשְׁנֵ֥י מַחֲנֽוֹת: וַיֹּ֕אמֶר אִם־
יָב֥וֹא עֵשָׂ֛ו אֶל־הַמַּחֲנֶ֥ה הָאַחַ֖ת וְהִכָּ֑הוּ וְהָיָ֛ה הַמַּחֲנֶ֥ה הַנִּשְׁאָ֖ר
י לִפְלֵיטָֽה: וַיֹּאמֶר֮ יַעֲקֹב֒ אֱלֹהֵי֙ אָבִ֣י אַבְרָהָ֔ם וֵאלֹהֵ֖י אָבִ֣י יִצְחָ֑ק
יְהֹוָ֞ה הָאֹמֵ֣ר אֵלַ֗י שׁ֧וּב לְאַרְצְךָ֛ וּלְמֽוֹלַדְתְּךָ֖ וְאֵיטִ֥יבָה עִמָּֽךְ:

7. וְגַם הֹלֵךְ לִקְרָאתְךָ — *Moreover, he is heading toward you.* Esau's fear of Jacob
was just as great as Jacob's fear of him. Esau's fear stemmed from his conviction
that Jacob was certainly a grandmaster in sorcery, after twenty years in Laban's
house, and that the magical arts at his disposal could have dire consequences for
him and his family. He took Jacob's opening words, "I have sojourned with
Laban and I have lingered until now" as a warning. The *Zohar* says this is like
a traveler who is told en route that a dangerous bandit is stalking the same road.
He meets a stranger and asks, "Where are you coming from?" He replies, "I am
one of the bandit leader's men." The traveler answers back, "Come no closer; I
am carrying a poisonous snake which kills anyone who comes near." The bandit
returns to tell his leader what he has just heard. The feared bandit then decides
to make the first move and, with his men, goes to meet the traveler and attack
him. But as he approaches, he sees the traveler take fright and bow humbly
before him (for, in fact, he is carrying no serpent). Surprised by this unexpected
mark of respect, he suddenly changes his attitude and, in a show of
magnanimity, leaves the inoffensive traveler unharmed. Such, concludes the
Zohar, was Esau's reaction to Jacob.

8. וַיִּירָא יַעֲקֹב מְאֹד וַיֵּצֶר לוֹ — *Jacob became very frightened, and it distressed him.*
Rashi interprets: "He was fearful of being killed, and distressed because he
might have to kill others." But the Midrash adds, "He was fearful because Esau
could claim the merit of having dwelt in the Holy Land for the twenty years
during which Jacob had been absent; and he was distressed because Esau had the
merit accruing from honoring his parents whereas Jacob himself had been
deprived of doing so all the time he was away." Thus, despite the fact that his
brother was an idolater and a man without morals or scruples, Jacob feared him
just because of his two sole merits, merits which Jacob himself lacked. Faced
with these two advantages of Esau's, Jacob anxiously wondered how much he
could still count on the Divine promises of protection which he had received
earlier. *Happy is the man who always dreads [to do evil]* (Proverbs 28:14).
Concerning the fact that Esau was as frightened of Jacob as Jacob was of him,
cf. our commentary to 27:34.

9. אִם־יָבוֹא עֵשָׂו אֶל־הַמַּחֲנֶה הָאַחַת וְהִכָּהוּ — *If Esau comes to the one camp and
strikes it down. Rashi* points out that מַחֲנֶה, *camp,* can be either masculine or
feminine. The fact that both genders are used here in reference to מַחֲנֶה is
explained by *Maharal.* He points out that the feminine is reserved for instances

*your brother, to Esau; moreover, he is heading toward you,
and four hundred men are with him."*

*⁸ Jacob became very frightened, and it distressed him. So
he divided the people with him, and the cattle, herds, and
camels, into two camps. ⁹ For he said, "If Esau comes to the one
camp and strikes it down, then the remaining camp shall
survive." ¹⁰ Then Jacob said, "God of my father Abraham and
God of my father Isaac; HASHEM Who said to me, 'Return to
your land and to your relatives and I will do good with you' —*

when we are speaking of a minor detail of the object, whereas the masculine is
employed when the object's essence is being referred to. Accordingly, here Jacob
uses the form וְהִכָּהוּ, with the direct complement in the masculine (right after
having used the feminine form). He wants to say that Esau might be able to
smite one of the camps in its very essence, that is, to completely annihilate it.
And as a consequence Jacob is compelled to create a second camp which could
escape.

וְהָיָה הַמַּחֲנֶה הַנִּשְׁאָר לִפְלֵיטָה — *Then the remaining camp shall survive.* That the
second camp will be saved and will escape annihilation is a fact which Jacob
accepts without the slightest doubt. He expresses it in the form of an absolute
certainty. The Sages of the Midrash (as well as *Ramban, R' Bachya* and others)
take this phrase as referring to Jewry's history. "If, in the course of our exile, a
king rises up to drive out or destroy our people, another king will have pity on
us and welcome us." Indeed, throughout history the Jewish people have always
split up into several camps, following Jacob's example, and have attributed their
secret of survival to this dispersion (*Pesachim* 87b).

10. אֱלֹהֵי אָבִי אַבְרָהָם — *God of my father Abraham.* Why does the Divine Name
ה׳ appear here immediately after having been mentioned in the beginning of
this sentence in another form? In his answer *Rashi* points out that above, in 31:3,
God had already appeared to Jacob with the Divine Name ה׳ alone. The *Zohar,*
however, gives another reason. Jacob knew the difference between Abraham's
form of worship and Isaac's. The God of Abraham was essentially God in His
aspect of love (מִדַּת הַחֶסֶד); the God of Isaac was God of justice and law (מִדַּת
הַדִּין), as pointed out in our commentary to 25:27 and 31:42. As for Jacob, he
made his life into the harmonious union of these two principles in the form of
מִדַּת הָרַחֲמִים — the principle of justice tempered with mercy. He attained the
"golden mean," the road which leads to perfection (מִדַּת הַתִּפְאֶרֶת). Indeed, as
Jacob goes about resolving the many conflicts which he had to face in raising
his twelve sons, we see that with absolute integrity he does his utmost to
combine love and justice, pity and uprightness, kindness and fairness. (Joseph
continued his father's example in his attitude toward his long-lost brothers.)
And so, when Jacob implores God to save him from distress, he calls on the
Divine Name ה׳, which refers to the מִדַּת הָרַחֲמִים. But before invoking "his God,"

יא קָטֹנְתִּי מִכֹּל הַחֲסָדִים וּמִכָּל־הָאֱמֶת אֲשֶׁר עָשִׂיתָ אֶת־עַבְדֶּךָ
כִּי בְמַקְלִי עָבַרְתִּי אֶת־הַיַּרְדֵּן הַזֶּה וְעַתָּה הָיִיתִי לִשְׁנֵי
יב מַחֲנוֹת: הַצִּילֵנִי נָא מִיַּד אָחִי מִיַּד עֵשָׂו כִּי־יָרֵא אָנֹכִי אֹתוֹ
יג פֶּן־יָבוֹא וְהִכַּנִי אֵם עַל־בָּנִים: וְאַתָּה אָמַרְתָּ הֵיטֵב אֵיטִיב
עִמָּךְ וְשַׂמְתִּי אֶת־זַרְעֲךָ כְּחוֹל הַיָּם אֲשֶׁר לֹא־יִסָּפֵר מֵרֹב:
שני יד וַיָּלֶן שָׁם בַּלַּיְלָה הַהוּא וַיִּקַּח מִן־הַבָּא בְיָדוֹ מִנְחָה לְעֵשָׂו
טו אָחִיו: עִזִּים מָאתַיִם וּתְיָשִׁים עֶשְׂרִים רְחֵלִים מָאתַיִם
טז וְאֵילִים עֶשְׂרִים: גְּמַלִּים מֵינִיקוֹת וּבְנֵיהֶם שְׁלֹשִׁים פָּרוֹת
יז אַרְבָּעִים וּפָרִים עֲשָׂרָה אֲתֹנֹת עֶשְׂרִים וַעְיָרִם עֲשָׂרָה: וַיִּתֵּן

he invokes the God of his fathers in order to add weight to his prayer. He recalls the various forms of worship by which his ancestors glorified God. Concludes the *Zohar:* "No one understands the art of adding one flourish to another to weave the crown of God as the righteous do in their prayers."

11. קָטֹנְתִּי מִכֹּל הַחֲסָדִים — *I have been diminished by all the kindnesses. Rashi:* "My merit has decreased because of the mercies and faithfulness that You have shown me. And I fear that since the time You made promises to me, I have been so diminished by sin as to be unworthy of deliverance from the hands of Esau." The only Divine words of an unconditional nature are those addressed to the prophets, adds *Maharal*, but this does not include promises to individuals. (So too the *Zohar*.) In his introduction to the Mishnah, *Rambam* discusses the contradiction between the Talmudic assertion (*Shabbos* 55a) that all Divine words are unconditional and R' Yaakov's statement (*Berachos* 4a) that the patriarch was afraid lest the Divine promise made to him be conditional upon his moral conduct. The different views regarding this are summarized by the commentators on these Talmudic passages (cf. for example *Maharsha*, ibid.). See also *Rambam's* commentary in *Yesodei HaTorah* 10:4.

12. כִּי־יָרֵא אָנֹכִי אֹתוֹ — *For I fear him.* God promises His protection to the most perfect of the patriarchs just as to the most perfect of the prophets. Nevertheless, both were seized with fright when they found themselves face to face with their enemies. Moses was afraid of Og, the king of Bashan (*Numbers* 21:34) even though God had assured him of His aid (*Exodus* 3:12). The Sages of the Midrash consider these examples as grounds for the excuses which Jews may make for their lack of confidence in battle, this despite the vehement reproaches of the prophet Isaiah (51:13). "You have forgotten God, your Maker, Who has spread out the heavens and laid the foundations of the earth; and you dread continually, all the day, because of the fury of the oppressor whenever he aims to destroy" (*Rabbah* 76).

13. כְּחוֹל הַיָּם — *Like the sand of the sea.* To Jacob, God had said, *Your offspring shall be as the dust of the earth* (28:14). But here the patriarch is referring to the

¹¹ *I have been diminished by all the kindnesses and by all the truth that You have done Your servant; for with my staff I crossed this Jordan and now I have become two camps.* ¹² *Rescue me, please, from the hand of my brother, from the hand of Esau, for I fear him lest he come and strike me down, mother and children.* ¹³ *And You had said, 'I will surely do good with you and I will make your offspring like the sand of the sea which is too numerous to count.' "*

¹⁴ *He spent the night there, then he took, from that which had come in his hand, a tribute to Esau his brother:* ¹⁵ *Two hundred she-goats and twenty he-goats; two hundred ewes and twenty rams;* ¹⁶ *thirty nursing camels with their colts; forty cows and ten bulls; twenty she-donkeys and ten he-donkeys.* ¹⁷ *He put*

superior blessing addressed to Abraham (22:17), which compares the future generations to the sand upon the seashore, for Jacob's father had handed down Abraham's blessing to him (28:4).

14. וַיָּלֶן שָׁם בַּלַּיְלָה הַהוּא — *He spent the night there.* Jacob spent the whole night searching his mind, trying to discover what transgression he might have committed that had caused the new ordeal to be imposed on him. He felt that he had not fulfilled his vow to offer a tithe of all that God will give him (28:22). And so he separated the tithe and then prepared the present for Esau (*Pirkei D'Rabbi Eliezer* 36; *Midrashim*, cited in *Torah Sheleimah*; cf. our commentary ibid.).

וַיִּקַּח מִן־הַבָּא בְיָדוֹ — *Then he took, from that which had come in his hand.* This phrase implies that he took gifts of mediocre value. *Rashi* interprets: "the separation of the tithe." In the same vein *Baal HaTurim* observes that every word in the next verse which lists the animals ends with a ם, *mem.* This indicates that Jacob sent Esau animals afflicted with a מום, *physical defect*, which rendered them unfit for sacrifices, even sacrifices intended for idols. According to *R' Bachya*, Jacob sent Esau a falcon, Esau's favorite bird of prey, the one Esau liked "to hold in his hand" (the subject of בְיָדוֹ would then be Esau).

16. גְּמַלִּים מֵינִיקוֹת וּבְנֵיהֶם שְׁלֹשִׁים — *Thirty nursing camels with their colts.* Jacob's gifts were not of very great value when one considers his wealth. But the Torah cites them in detail because the numbers involved hint at the future relationships between Jacob's descendants and Esau's (*R' Bachya*). *R' Yitzchak Arama, Baal HaTurim* and others attempt to explain these allusions. *R' Chaim ben Attar* notes that the total number of animals offered to Esau was 580, reckoning 30 nursing camels and 30 colts. This is also the numerical value of the word שָׂעִיר, *goat*, calling to mind the scapegoat sent away each year to Azazel, the embodiment of Esau (himself called שָׂעִיר, 27:11), as *Ramban* explains on *Leviticus* 16:8. Thus, Jacob's gifts foreshadow the future sacrifice of the scapegoat (cf. *Shelah*).

בְּיַד־עֲבָדָיו עֵדֶר עֵדֶר לְבַדּוֹ וַיֹּאמֶר אֶל־עֲבָדָיו עִבְרוּ לְפָנַי
יח וְרֶוַח תָּשִׂימוּ בֵּין עֵדֶר וּבֵין עֵדֶר: וַיְצַו אֶת־הָרִאשׁוֹן לֵאמֹר
כִּי יִפְגָּשְׁךָ עֵשָׂו אָחִי וּשְׁאֵלְךָ לֵאמֹר לְמִי־אַתָּה וְאָנָה תֵלֵךְ
יט וּלְמִי אֵלֶּה לְפָנֶיךָ: וְאָמַרְתָּ לְעַבְדְּךָ לְיַעֲקֹב מִנְחָה הִוא
כ שְׁלוּחָה לַאדֹנִי לְעֵשָׂו וְהִנֵּה גַם־הוּא אַחֲרֵינוּ: וַיְצַו גַּם
אֶת־הַשֵּׁנִי גַּם אֶת־הַשְּׁלִישִׁי גַּם אֶת־כָּל־הַהֹלְכִים אַחֲרֵי
הָעֲדָרִים לֵאמֹר כַּדָּבָר הַזֶּה תְּדַבְּרוּן אֶל־עֵשָׂו בְּמֹצַאֲכֶם אֹתוֹ:
כא וַאֲמַרְתֶּם גַּם הִנֵּה עַבְדְּךָ יַעֲקֹב אַחֲרֵינוּ כִּי־אָמַר
אֲכַפְּרָה פָנָיו בַּמִּנְחָה הַהֹלֶכֶת לְפָנָי וְאַחֲרֵי־כֵן אֶרְאֶה פָנָיו
כב אוּלַי יִשָּׂא פָנָי: וַתַּעֲבֹר הַמִּנְחָה עַל־פָּנָיו וְהוּא לָן בַּלַּיְלָה־
כג הַהוּא בַּמַּחֲנֶה: וַיָּקָם ׀ בַּלַּיְלָה הוּא וַיִּקַּח אֶת־שְׁתֵּי נָשָׁיו
וְאֶת־שְׁתֵּי שִׁפְחֹתָיו וְאֶת־אַחַד עָשָׂר יְלָדָיו וַיַּעֲבֹר אֵת מַעֲבַר

17. וְרֶוַח תָּשִׂימוּ בֵּין עֵדֶר וּבֵין עֵדֶר — *Leave a space between drove and drove.* Jacob implores God, "Master of the Universe! When troubles will rain down upon my descendants, do not send them one after another but put a space between them!" (*Rabbah* 75). The reference is also to the duties and poll taxes which Esau's children will levy on Jacob's children; Jacob prays on their behalf that these taxes will be spaced apart (*Ramban*).

18. וַיְצַו אֶת־הָרִאשׁוֹן לֵאמֹר — *He instructed the first one, saying.* As it frequently is elsewhere, לֵאמֹר is interpreted here to mean לְדוֹרוֹת, *saying to the future generations* (*Midrash Lekach Tov*). This concept implies that Jacob's offspring are to keep to the same kind of language which Jacob used for Esau when they have to defend themselves against aggression and persecution from Esau's descendants. This also concerns the three methods of defense used by Jacob: gifts, prayer, and combat. The wealth of detail in this passage might be explained by its generality and broad applicability. Similarly, later on: "In this manner shall you speak to Esau when you find him" (verse 20).

19. לְעַבְדְּךָ לְיַעֲקֹב — *Your servant Jacob's.* The phrase *your servant Jacob* or *your servant* is repeated five times in total. Accordingly, God reproached Jacob: "You profane that which is sacred!" And the patriarch replied, "I flatter the wicked lest he kill me" (*Pirkei D'Rabbi Eliezer* 37). The Sages of the Talmud consider this reaction legitimate (*Sotah* 41b). Note, however, the different understanding of this episode quoted from the *Zohar* in our commentary on verse 5.

21. כִּי־אָמַר אֲכַפְּרָה פָנָיו — *For he said, "I will appease him."* According to *Ramban*, these words were part of the message transmitted to Esau. But According to *Rashi* and *Ibn Ezra*, they express Jacob's inner thoughts, namely, that gifts were the only way to answer all the questions with which Esau would try to trap him.

in his servants' charge each drove separately and said to his
servants, "Pass on ahead of me and leave a space between drove
and drove." ¹⁸ He instructed the first one, saying, "When my
brother Esau meets you and asks you, saying, 'Whose are you,
where are you going, and whose are these that are before you?' —
¹⁹ You shall say, 'Your servant Jacob's. It is a tribute sent to my
lord, to Esau, and behold he himself is behind us.' "

²⁰ He similarly instructed the second, also the third, as well
as all who followed the droves, saying, "In this manner shall
you speak to Esau when you find him. ²¹ And you shall say,
'Moreover — behold your servant Jacob is behind us.' " (For he
said, "I will appease him with the tribute that precedes me, and
afterwards I will face him; perhaps he will forgive me.") ²² So the
tribute passed on before him while he spent that night in the
camp.

²³ But he got up that night and took his two wives, his two
handmaids, and his eleven sons and crossed the ford of the

---

22. וַתַּעֲבֹר הַמִּנְחָה עַל־פָּנָיו — So the tribute passed on before him. Rashi quotes
the Midrash which imparts to the word פָּנָיו the meaning of anger. Indeed,
"Jacob was angry at having to do all that." The Midrash also states the second
part of the sentence, he spent that night in the camp, as a reference to God Who
stays with the righteous in the night of their distress, as the Psalmist proclaims
I am with him in distress... (91:15), and Who, as it were, shares their affliction
(Meshech Chochmah).

23. וְאֶת־אַחַד עָשָׂר יְלָדָיו — And his eleven sons. Rashi explains, "But where
was Dinah? Jacob had hidden her in a chest so that Esau could not set eyes
upon her. And Jacob was punished for this as Dinah might have had a good
influence on Esau. Accordingly, she later fell into the hands of Shechem."
R' Moshe C. Luzzatto cites this example among others as proof that God is
strict with the righteous, even for the slightest transgression (Mesillas
Yesharim 4). Maharal holds that this transgression is the underlying cause
for the trials described in the next chapter, which Jacob had to suffer on account of his daughter Dinah. Indeed, the Sages of the Midrash work from
the principle that each event occurring in the life of the righteous ultimately
goes back to a moral cause, and it is up to us to seek it out when the Torah does
not explicitly mention it. Using this example Rabbi E. Dessler shows us the
scope, complexity, and subtlety of problems of a moral nature. It is the duty of
the righteous person to weigh the positive and the negative aspects of all of
his proposals, and to choose among the alternatives in order to reach the one
adequate solution — a task which demands an acute sense of moral
responsibility (Michtav Me'Eliyahu I 168).

כד יַבֹּק: וַיִּקָּחֵם וַיַּעֲבִרֵם אֶת־הַנָּחַל וַיַּעֲבֵר אֶת־אֲשֶׁר־
כה לוֹ: וַיִּוָּתֵר יַעֲקֹב לְבַדּוֹ וַיֵּאָבֵק אִישׁ עִמּוֹ עַד עֲלוֹת

24. וַיִּקָּחֵם וַיַּעֲבִרֵם אֶת־הַנָּחַל — *And when he took them and had them cross over the stream.* Why did Jacob make his family cross the stream in the thick of night? It was because he had sensed an ominous feeling in the camp, a sign that evil spirits were stirring. He thought that a move would serve to change this atmosphere, all the more so since the stream would create a boundary between the camp and the "demons of the night." The actions of these demons are neutralized by the element of water (*Zohar*), as is brought out in *Orach Chaim* 4:8 and elsewhere. This remark can also be applied to Jacob's hostile brother. Jacob wanted to place the stream between Esau and his own camp.

25. וַיִּוָּתֵר יַעֲקֹב לְבַדּוֹ — *Jacob was left alone.* The fact that Jacob remained alone on the other side of the river, after he had already led his family across along with all his cattle and possessions, leads R' Elazar to conclude that he had forgotten some small flasks and came back to fetch them. This teaches you that whatever the righteous possess is very dear to them. This is explained by the fact that they take care never to be guilty of even the slightest theft" (*Chullin* 91a). Much later when Joseph invited his father and brothers to leave Canaan to come and join him in Egypt, he advised them, *Do not bother with your utensils* (*Genesis* 45:20), for he knew how meticulous his father was even about the smallest objects (*Baal HaTurim*).

R' Shimon, however, gives this verse a symbolic meaning. The words וַיִּוָּתֵר יַעֲקֹב לְבַדּוֹ echo the words of the prophet, וְנִשְׂגַּב ה' לְבַדּוֹ, *Hashem alone will be exalted* (*Isaiah* 2:11). The comparison is based on the analogy of God reigning over the universe and Jewry residing among the nations, according to the verse in *Deuteronomy* (33:26): אֵין כָּאֵל יְשֻׁרוּן, *there is none like the Almighty, [except] Jeshurun* [Israel] (*Rabbah*). God is unique, that is, alone and exalted in the celestial heights. So too, Israel among the nations of the world remains unique: *This people shall dwell alone and not be reckoned among the nations* (*Numbers* 23:9). Jacob's destiny is to remain alone and to remain exalted.

וַיֵּאָבֵק אִישׁ עִמּוֹ — *And a man wrestled with him.* According to *Rambam*, the struggle and the ensuing dialogue took place only in a prophetic vision, since "it states clearly at the end of the passage that an angel was involved" (*Guide* 2:42; whenever we are told that an angel appears it can only be in a prophetic vision). But *Ramban*, noting that as they fought, Jacob's thigh was strained so that he became lame, cites this as proof that the struggle did in fact take place and was not at all imagined (*Genesis* 18:1). His opinion is shared by *Radak* and *Ibn Ezra*. On the other hand, R' Levi ben Gershon (*Ralbag*, quoted by *Abarbanel*) comes to *Rambam's* defense. He holds that the thigh injury was caused by auto-suggestion, an aftermath of the prophetic vision.

This divergence between the literal and symbolic meanings of the episode is reflected in the many interpretations given to this passage. To be sure, the Torah

Jabbok. [24] *And when he took them and had them cross over the stream, he sent over all his possessions.*

[25] *Jacob was left alone and a man wrestled with him until*

never loses its literal meaning (אֵין מִקְרָא יוֹצֵא מִידֵי פְּשׁוּטוֹ). It remains valid under all circumstances. But in this account the Sages of the Midrash, as well as later scholars and commentators, also see a more general meaning. Some take it as symbolizing the righteous person's inner struggle against the forces of evil. Jacob had sent everything he owned to the other side of the river. Now he stood alone in the vastness, in the profound silence of the night, a mortal human being, defenseless in the anguish of darkness. The Divine messenger struggles with Jacob — he who has already clashed so often with his fellowmen, who has fought and won thanks to his will, his courage, and his intelligence. The prophet Hosea evokes the patriarch's struggle: *He strove with the angel and prevailed; he wept and made supplication unto him ...* (12:5). This prayer for mercy, forgiveness, and protection is fulfilled. Jacob the supplanter becomes Israel the prince of God. The patriarch's mysterious encounter thus becomes a symbolic representation of the fights and struggles taking place on the eve of the approaching ordeal (cf. *R' Bachya* and *Malbim*).

But the struggle in the night has also been taken as a kind of forerunner of the decisive combat which is to occur on the morrow, in broad daylight. It is in the silence of the preceding night that man is judged. It is then that his moral value must assert itself in the struggle against the angel of evil. If he prevails, he will be Israel — who has "striven with the Divine and with man and have overcome." Then, the angel of evil himself will give him his blessing for the imminent trials awaiting him. In the great crises in our lives, our destinies are readied in advance, in the dark night and in the secret recesses of the human conscience. The fratricidal struggle which breaks out the next day has already been decided before the celestial tribune on the preceding night (following the *Shelah*).

Several *Midrashim* identify Jacob's opponent as Esau's "guardian angel" in the celestial spheres. In this interpretation, also reported by *Rashi*, the fight between them symbolizes the historic struggle between Jewry and the nations, and the trials and hurts which Jewry will have to endure until the dawn of our freedom. *When he perceived that he could not overcome him,* means that the enemy cannot separate Jewry from God. *He struck the socket of his hip* is an allusion to the region of circumcision and to the *mitzvah* which the nations will one day forbid Jewry to carry out. *So Jacob's hip-socket was dislocated* alludes to those descendants of Jacob who will forsake Judaism (*Midrash Lekach Tov*).

Thus, Jacob's struggle is a forerunner of those which his descendants will be involved in all through their turbulent history. Jewry will always be the target of underhanded attacks launched by other nations and will be severely hurt by them. Jewry's vitality and even its flesh and blood will be diminished, but our people will never succumb. And in the final outcome Jewry will force the enemy

כו הַשָּׁחַר: וַיַּרְא כִּי לֹא יָכֹל לוֹ וַיִּגַּע בְּכַף־יְרֵכוֹ וַתֵּקַע כַּף־
כז יֶרֶךְ יַעֲקֹב בְּהֵאָבְקוֹ עִמּוֹ: וַיֹּאמֶר שַׁלְּחֵנִי כִּי עָלָה הַשָּׁחַר
כח וַיֹּאמֶר לֹא אֲשַׁלֵּחֲךָ כִּי אִם־בֵּרַכְתָּנִי: וַיֹּאמֶר אֵלָיו מַה־
כט שְּׁמֶךָ וַיֹּאמֶר יַעֲקֹב: וַיֹּאמֶר לֹא יַעֲקֹב יֵאָמֵר עוֹד שִׁמְךָ כִּי

to yield to its great heroism. When the struggle is over, when day breaks on the long hours of "the night of *galus*," the adversary will bless Jewry and will acknowledge their worth. He will pay homage to Jewry's Divine message of the monotheistic ideals. The account of Jacob's struggle with the "angel of Esau" thus harbors the profound confidence of the Jewish people who, despite many tribulations and much suffering, never lose hope of final victory. And so the Torah insisted on keeping the memory of this event alive by prohibiting the consumption of the sinew which was injured in the struggle with the angel.

26. וַיַּרְא כִּי לֹא יָכֹל לוֹ — *When he perceived that he could not overcome him.* Jacob's adversary seeks his weak point. But Jacob is protected on all sides: on his right, the merits of his grandfather Abraham; on his left, those of his father Isaac. He himself is holy, his conduct irreproachable. Now, the adversary knows that Jacob's strength lies in "the voice (study) of the Torah," as it was said (27:22), הַקֹּל קוֹל יַעֲקֹב וְהַיָּדַיִם יְדֵי עֵשָׂו, *The voice is Jacob's voice, but the hands are Esau's hands*, which means that as long as the voice of Jacob is heard in the study of Torah, the hand of Esau will not rule over him. In this case, when he saw that he had not prevailed over the power of the Torah which gave life to Jacob, he wounded him in his thigh. The thighs are the support of the human body. If the antagonist cannot silence the voice of the Torah, he cuts off its "supports" (i.e. those who give material support to Torah students, the תֹּמְכִין דְּאוֹרַיְיתָא). Deprived of such support, the voice of the Torah dies out on its own, leaving Esau able to benefit from the ancestral blessing, *you may cast off his yoke from upon your neck* (27:40). However, even with an injured thigh, Jacob fights on as hard as he can; he does not relent for a moment but perseveres and continues his struggle until morning. For he knows that his adversary has power over him only during the night of *galus*, that with the first rays of daylight the dark shadows and demons of the night will flee. And so it is the adversary who is ultimately conquered when day breaks. In the end it is he who pays homage to Jacob and blesses him there (*Zohar*).

27. וַיֹּאמֶר שַׁלְּחֵנִי כִּי עָלָה הַשָּׁחַר — *Then he said, "Let me go, for dawn has broken."* Jacob's opponent is aware that he has power only at night. He cannot triumph when Jacob fights him with the "light" of the mind and spirit. "Are you a thief afraid of the light of day?" Jacob asked. "No," replied his adversary, whose face Jacob could not make out in the half-light, "I am an angel of God. (אִישׁ designates the lowest category of angels, notes *Rambam* in *Yesodei*

the break of dawn. 26 *When he perceived that he could not overcome him, he struck the socket of his hip; so Jacob's hip-socket was dislocated as he wrestled with him.* 27 *Then he said, "Let me go, for dawn has broken."*

And he said, "I will not let you go unless you bless me."

28 *He said to him, "What is your name?"*

He replied, "Jacob."

29 *He said, "No longer will it be said that your name is Jacob,*

HaTorah 2:7.) But my time has come and now I have to sing the 'song of the day' (*Rashi*) and disappear, for my nocturnal mission is over." Then Jacob realized that his opponent in this tough struggle was none other than the personification of his worst enemy, Esau, his dreaded brother whom he was to meet that very day. And Jacob was aware of his own weak point in facing his brother: his father's blessing which he obtained with guile. Esau still denied the legitimacy of his right to this blessing. And so Jacob said to Esau's guardian angel: "I will not send you away unless you bless me," meaning, "acknowledge my right to my father's blessings which Esau disputes" (*Rashi*). [Note that the Torah has בֵּרַכְתָּנִי, in the past tense, rather than תְבָרְכֵנִי.] The angel answered, "Your name is Jacob, which means *the supplanter* — he who took the place of the other (27:36) or he who takes crooked paths (from עָקֹב, *sinuous*). But now your name will no longer be Jacob. This name will be part of what was past and is no more. Your name will be Israel, for you have fought and won, and this name means that you have obtained the blessings openly and with dignity" (*Rashi*; cf. *Rashi* on 35:10; יִשְׂרָאֵל means *prince* or *noble* (שַׂר) and also יָשָׁר, *one who walks upright with God*). Continued the angel, "God will reveal Himself to you at Beth-El, where He will change your name and bless you. I will be there too and will confirm the blessings. Let me go until He speaks to us there." But Jacob refused (for he was to meet his brother that same day) and the angel, who had only tried for one last reprieve, had to acknowledge the blessings despite himself. This is what is meant by *and he blessed him there* (verse 30). [Taken from *Rashi*, the *Zohar*, and *Chullin* 91b; cf. our commentary to 27:33.]

R' Bachya concludes the above passage by emphasizing its historical importance. After refusing throughout his life to pay homage to the integrity and sincere piety of his brother as a "fighter for God — יִשְׂרָאֵל," the angel of Esau finally gives him his blessing and so acknowledges the words of his father, גַּם בָּרוּךְ יִהְיֶה (ibid.). So, too, in messianic times, the nations which have struggled for so long against Jewry will come to pay homage to Jewry's ideal and historic mission, as the prophet Isaiah proclaims (49:23): *Kings will be your foster fathers and their queens your nursing mother; they will prostrate themselves to you with their face to the earth, and lick the dust of your feet; and you will know that I am God, for they who await Me will not be ashamed.*

אִם־יִשְׂרָאֵל כִּי־שָׂרִיתָ עִם־אֱלֹהִים וְעִם־אֲנָשִׁים וַתּוּכָל:

לֹ וַיִּשְׁאַל יַעֲקֹב וַיֹּאמֶר הַגִּידָה־נָּא שְׁמֶךָ וַיֹּאמֶר לָמָּה זֶּה

שלישי לֹא תִּשְׁאַל לִשְׁמִי וַיְבָרֶךְ אֹתוֹ שָׁם: וַיִּקְרָא יַעֲקֹב שֵׁם הַמָּקוֹם

פְּנִיאֵל כִּי־רָאִיתִי אֱלֹהִים פָּנִים אֶל־פָּנִים וַתִּנָּצֵל נַפְשִׁי:

לֹב וַיִּזְרַח־לוֹ הַשֶּׁמֶשׁ כַּאֲשֶׁר עָבַר אֶת־פְּנוּאֵל וְהוּא צֹלֵעַ

לֹג עַל־יְרֵכוֹ: עַל־כֵּן לֹא־יֹאכְלוּ בְנֵי־יִשְׂרָאֵל אֶת־גִּיד הַנָּשֶׁה

29. יִשְׂרָאֵל — *Israel.* R' Yanai said, "God associated His Name with Israel's. This is like a king who has a small key to open the door of his palace. He says to himself, 'I'll lose the key if I leave it as is, so I'll attach a string in order to find it more easily if it gets lost.' God did the same for Jewry: 'If I leave Jewry alone," He said, 'this people will become lost among the nations. But I shall attach My name to Jewry, so that this people can survive" (*Yerushalmi, Taanis* 2:6).

כִּי־שָׂרִיתָ עִם־אֱלֹהִים וְעִם־אֲנָשִׁים וַתּוּכָל — *For you have striven with the Divine and with man and have overcome.* Onkelos interprets the angel's words: "for you have fought before God with man and have succeeded." Consequently, Israel means "fighter before (or 'for') God," but no indication of the fight with men is to be found in the name יִשְׂרָאֵל, *Israel.* And this is very significant for its mission. Jewry's millennial struggle is within society and its goal is to establish the kingdom of God on earth. But in this struggle Jewry fights only with spiritual weapons. It fights for ideals and principles. Jewry's fight is never directed against human beings.

30. לָמָּה זֶּה תִּשְׁאַל לִשְׁמִי — *Why then do you inquire of my name?* "Knowing my name will be of no use to you, for the power resides solely in God Himself. If you call on me, I will not reply nor will I be able to help you in your distress" (*Ramban*).

31. פְּנִיאֵל — *Peniel* — for I have seen a Divine being face to face. In the following verse this site is called פְּנוּאֵל, which can be explained by the interchangeability of the *vav* and the *yud* (as above, 4:18). The Torah gives this place the name פְּנוּאֵל (cf. *Judges* 8:17). For Jacob, the name of the place has personal meaning and he puts the word פָּנִים in the singular. But for future generations the place-name will signify, פְּנוּ אֵל, *turn to God.*

כִּי־רָאִיתִי אֱלֹהִים פָּנִים אֶל־פָּנִים — *For I have seen the Divine face to face.* How could Jacob, a human being of flesh and blood, grapple with an angel who is, the Torah tells us, nothing but pure spirit?" (e.g., *Psalms* 104:4). In its reply to this question, the *Zohar* states that the angels are capable of adopting a corporeal form when they enter the realm of men, just as, conversely, men adopt the forms of existence of angels when they ascend to their sphere, as we see with Moses (cf. *Exodus* 34:28). *Rambam*, whose theories have already been cited in the commentary on verse 4, says further that the corporeal forms in which angels appear exist only in the mind of the one who sees them —

but Israel, for you have striven with the Divine and with man and have overcome."

³⁰ Then Jacob inquired, and he said, "Divulge, if you please, your name."

And he said, "Why then do you inquire of my name?" And he blessed him there.

³¹ So Jacob called the name of the place Peniel — "For I have seen the Divine face to face, yet my life was spared." ³² The sun rose for him as he passed Penuel and he was limping on his hip. ³³ Therefore the Children of Israel are not to eat the displaced sinew

these forms have no real existence (see also *R' Moshe Chaim Luzzatto,* עקרים, ברוחניים). Accordingly, Jacob stresses here that his encounter with the angel depended only on his sense of vision.

וַתִּנָּצֵל נַפְשִׁי — *Yet my life was spared (saved).* In the historical sense. Had Jewry as a people not heard the Divine voice speak to them "face to face" on Mount Sinai (as it is said, פָּנִים בְּפָנִים דִּבֶּר ה' עִמָּכֶם *God spoke with you face to face on the mount out of the midst of the fire; Deuteronomy* 5:4), they would not have been able to endure the martyrdom of centuries of persecution.

32. וְהוּא צֹלֵעַ עַל־יְרֵכוֹ ... וַיִּזְרַח־לוֹ הַשֶּׁמֶשׁ — *The sun rose for him ... and he was limping on his hip.* The verse alludes to the fact that our suffering appears more difficult to bear when the sun of freedom begins to shine on us. As long as the Jews suffer in exile, they bear their misfortunes, injuries, and ordeals in silence. But when the sun of liberation rises and begins to shine, they feel their past suffering more acutely. Jewry becomes aware of the fact that it "limps on its hip," and is surprised at the extent of its own endurance (*Zohar*).

33. לֹא־יֹאכְלוּ בְנֵי־יִשְׂרָאֵל אֶת־גִּיד הַנָּשֶׁה — *The Children of Israel are not to eat the displaced sinew.* Jewish law insisted on perpetuating the memory of Jacob's struggle by forbidding the consumption of the muscle injured in that struggle. The muscle in question is commonly called the sciatic nerve, which is anatomically inaccurate; but it does give the region of the thigh from which this muscle must be removed. From this stems the obligation to have all meat examined by a specialist, after it is slaughtered, and the practice of not eating the meat from the hindquarters of the animal, for fear that removal of the muscle has not been done in a thorough manner. Indeed, removing the muscle visibly shreds the meat and reduces its commercial value — for this reason butchers prefer not to do it at all.

For the author of the *Sefer HaChinuch*, the aim and object of this law is to reaffirm the faith of the Jewish people and fortify their devotion to God. And indeed, it does make us aware of the fact that Jacob could not be defeated by this adversary, but only wounded in his thigh. This injury has a symbolic value: Jacob's descendants too will be protected by God in struggles against their enemies. They may be wounded and shaken but they will never be

אֲשֶׁר עַל־כַּף הַיָּרֵךְ עַד הַיּוֹם הַזֶּה כִּי נָגַע בְּכַף־יֶרֶךְ יַעֲקֹב בְּגִיד
לג   א   הַנָּשֶׁה: וַיִּשָּׂא יַעֲקֹב עֵינָיו וַיַּרְא וְהִנֵּה עֵשָׂו בָּא וְעִמּוֹ אַרְבַּע
מֵאוֹת אִישׁ וַיַּחַץ אֶת־הַיְלָדִים עַל־לֵאָה וְעַל־רָחֵל וְעַל שְׁתֵּי
ב   הַשְּׁפָחוֹת: וַיָּשֶׂם אֶת־הַשְּׁפָחוֹת וְאֶת־יַלְדֵיהֶן רִאשֹׁנָה וְאֶת־
ג   לֵאָה וִילָדֶיהָ אַחֲרֹנִים וְאֶת־רָחֵל וְאֶת־יוֹסֵף אַחֲרֹנִים: וְהוּא

vanquished. R' S. R. Hirsch points out that Jacob's physical weakness is necessary to open Esau's eyes to the real power which makes Jacob invincible! To be sure, the descendants of Jacob limp through history. But when historical circumstance dictates, they willingly give up this thigh muscle, for Jewry realizes that its historical existence does not depend on the presence or absence of physical might. If Jacob falls, it is not at all because his physical and material power are no match for Esau's but because he has not deserved to keep the Divine protection over him. If Jewry stands firm, without wavering, it does so not because of material or physical power, but because the Almighty bears this people upon "the wings of eagles" through the centuries of history.

With a totally different point of view, the *Zohar* considers that *the Children of Israel are not to eat the displaced sinew on the hip-socket* because this muscle constitutes the physical support for the genital organs which are the source of impure elements. The numerous ramifications of the sciatic nerve surround and fortify these organs. סָבִיב רְשָׁעִים יִתְהַלָּכוּן כְּרֻם זֻלּוּת לִבְנֵי אָדָם, *the wicked walk on every side, when baseness is exalted among the sons of men* (*Psalms* 12:9). And so, eating this muscle has the effect of attracting the forces of impurity toward man. The muscle bears the name הַנָּשֶׁה, derived from the verb נָשָׁה, *to forget*: when man eats it, he consequently forgets himself and forgets his obligation to God. Esau's spirit discovered that Jacob was strong in combat and that his whole body was invulnerable. The only weak point he could find was the region of the genital organs (some see here an allusion to Jacob's sin of having married two sisters). And frequently, in the history of Jacob's descendants, straying (or "forgetfulness") in the domain of morality remained the weak point which enemies were able to attack and severely injure: for example, the debauchery involving the Jews and the daughters of Moab in Shittim, which the Torah recounts in *Numbers* 25. The result was an appalling number of deaths. Another example was that of the foreign wives who turned away the heart of King Solomon after strange gods (*I Kings* 11:4). This eventually led to the division of the Jewish kingdom. Yet another example was "mingling with the daughters of the Canaanite peoples" in Ezra's time — again the cause of numerous misfortunes, as told in the book of *Ezra* (9:7). Thus the prohibition of the sciatic nerve is intended to keep the Jewish people removed from the factor of impurity which is at the root of moral and national degradation.

on the hip-socket to this day, because he struck Jacob's hip-socket on the displaced sinew.

33 ¹ *J*acob raised his eyes and saw — behold, Esau was coming, and with him were four hundred men — so he divided the children among Leah, Rachel, and the two handmaids. ² He put the handmaids and their children first, Leah and her children next, and Rachel and Joseph last. ³ Then he himself

33.

1. וַיִּשָּׂא יַעֲקֹב עֵינָיו וַיַּרְא — *Jacob raised his eyes and saw.* When a righteous person raises his eyes to fix his gaze upon an object, he does so with intentions that are noble and ideal. This was so with Abraham lifting his eyes and perceiving Mount Moriah, the site for the supreme sacrifice (22:4), and then seeing the ram which was to replace Isaac (ibid. verse 13). So too with Isaac, who lifted up his eyes to see his future wife (24:63). And also here with Jacob, that is the case. Lifting up his eyes and finding himself face to face with his mortal enemy, he immediately takes all possible measures to ensure the well-being of his family. But the wicked raise their eyes to admire and covet material riches, as Lot did when he beheld Sodom (13:10), or to fix their gaze on other men's wives, as Esau did in the presence of Jacob's wives (verse 5), or to seduce a stranger, as the wife of Potiphar did to Joseph (39:7), etc. (*Tanchuma Vayeishev*).

וַיַּחַץ אֶת־הַיְלָדִים — *He divided the children.* Why did Jacob change the arrangements he had already made (32:8-9)? The Midrash replies: "This is like a lion who has been enraged by some animals. These animals wonder who could go to appease him. The fox proposes, 'Follow me; I know three hundred parables and with them I can appease him.' The animals accept and go with him. He advances a bit, then stops. 'Why do you stop?' they ask him. 'Because I have forgotten a hundred parables.' But they answer that the remaining two hundred will suffice. Then he stops a second time, declaring that he has forgotten another hundred parables. Nevertheless, at the request of the animals he continues. As he approaches the lion, he cries out, 'Now I have forgotten everything. Each one will have to appease the lion for himself!' So it was with Jacob. He had said, 'I am strong enough to defend you with my prayers or in combat.' But on approaching the lion, he divided his children and said to them, 'Let everyone look after himself!' " (*Rabbah* 78).

2. וְאֶת־רָחֵל וְאֶת־יוֹסֵף אַחֲרֹנִים — *And Rachel and Joseph last.* "But Mordechai did not bow down or prostrate himself before Haman" (*Esther* 3:2). The Jews said to him, "Do you not see that you are exposing us to a risk of death? Why do you transgress the king's command?" He answered, "I am a Jew." But they countered, "And did not Jacob prostrate himself seven times before Esau?" He replied, "Benjamin, the patriarch's youngest son, was not yet born when that

עָבַר לִפְנֵיהֶם וַיִּשְׁתַּ֫חוּ אַ֫רְצָה שֶׁבַע פְּעָמִים עַד־גִּשְׁתּוֹ
ד עַד־אָחִיו: וַיָּ֫רָץ עֵשָׂו לִקְרָאתוֹ וַיְחַבְּקֵהוּ וַיִּפֹּל עַל־צַנָּארָ֫ו
ה וַֽיִּשָּׁקֵ֫הוּ וַיִּבְכּֽוּ: וַיִּשָּׂא אֶת־עֵינָיו וַיַּ֫רְא אֶת־הַנָּשִׁים וְאֶת־
הַיְלָדִים וַיֹּ֫אמֶר מִי־אֵ֫לֶּה לָּ֑ךְ וַיֹּאמַר הַיְלָדִים אֲשֶׁר־חָנַ֫ן
רביעי   ו אֱלֹהִים אֶת־עַבְדֶּֽךָ: וַתִּגַּ֫שְׁןָ הַשְּׁפָחוֹת הֵ֫נָּה וְיַלְדֵיהֶ֫ן
ז וַתִּֽשְׁתַּחֲוֶֽיןָ: וַתִּגַּשׁ גַּם־לֵאָה וִֽילָדֶ֫יהָ וַיִּֽשְׁתַּחֲו֑וּ וְאַחַ֗ר נִגַּשׁ יוֹסֵף

happened. He never bowed down. Now, I am his descendant (Mordechai was
of the tribe of Benjamin; ibid. 2:5) and I will not bow down either" (*Midrash
Esther*). Cf. *Sifre* to *Deuteronomy* 33:12: "The Temple in Jerusalem was erected
in the territory of Benjamin for, of the twelve sons, he alone did not participate
in bowing down before Esau the idolater."

3. וְהוּא עָבַר לִפְנֵיהֶם — *Then he himself went on ahead of them.* The personal
pronoun הוּא is frequently used in the Torah to refer to the *Shechinah*. The
Zohar explains that it was the *Shechinah* which at the critical moment *went on
ahead of them* in order to protect Jacob's family, as God had promised the
patriarch when he left his father's house (28:15). Accordingly, he prostrated
himself before It — not before his pagan brother. See, however, the different
view quoted in our commentary to 29:18.

שֶׁבַע פְּעָמִים עַד־גִּשְׁתּוֹ עַד־אָחִיו — *Seven times until he reached his brother.* The
Jewish calendar is based on the lunar year, whereas the non-Jewish calendar is
based on the solar year. The difference between them in round figures is eleven
days, i.e. 209 days in a cycle of nineteen years. If this difference were not taken
into account, our festivals would gradually come in all seasons. And the festival
of Passover, instead of falling in spring as prescribed by the Torah, would come
to be celebrated in winter. To remedy this we periodically intercalate an entire
month and we add this month seven times every nineteen years. Jacob's
bowing, repeated seven times until he came up to his brother, is symbolic of this
"bowing" of the moon (the star of Jacob) seven times until it catches up with
the cycle of the sun, the star of Esau.

4. וַיִּשָּׁקֵהוּ — *And kissed him.* The word וַיִּשָּׁקֵהוּ is dotted above each letter.
This draws our attention to something implied in the word. Accordingly,
our Sages cast doubt upon the sincerity of Esau's kiss. Some say that these
Masoretic dots are an indication that he did not kiss Jacob with his whole heart.
Faithful are the wounds of a friend, but deceptive are the kisses of an enemy
(*Proverbs* 27:6). It is advisable to be more wary of the hypocritical advances
and seductive ruses of an enemy than of his overt threats or direct attacks.
Jacob was on his guard when Esau welcomed him with such unexpected
cordiality.

But *Rashi* seems to favor the more optimistic interpretation of R' Shimon bar
Yochai: "A permanent rule: It is well known that Esau hates Jacob. But at that

*went on ahead of them and bowed earthward seven times until
he reached his brother.*

*⁴ Esau ran toward him, embraced him, fell upon his neck, and
kissed him; then they wept. ⁵ He raised his eyes and saw the
women and children, and he asked, "Who are these to you?"*

*He answered, "The children whom God has graciously given
your servant."*

*⁶ Then the handmaids came forward — they and their children
— and they bowed down. ⁷ Leah, too, came forward with
her children and they bowed down; and afterwards, Joseph*

moment he was overcome with pity and kissed his brother with genuine
feeling ... He clasped him in his arms, for he was moved when he saw his
brother prostrate himself so many times." "People's hearts," says *Ramban*,
"are in the hands of God; He makes them go where He wishes." Indeed,
God fulfilled Jacob's prayer and made Esau treat him with kindness and
sympathy. True, this sympathy was mixed with fear, for Esau realized the
physical strength of Jacob and his sons as well as their preparedness for
defense and the wealth of their camp. Esau's oldest son Elifaz had also felt
sympathy for his uncle twenty years before and, despite his father's order
to kill Jacob, he had left him unharmed, as *Rashi* notes on 29:11 (*Sefer
HaYashar*). Thus, after having been saved from Laban's hand by the formal
command which God gave him in a dream, Jacob is here saved once more, this
time by the feelings and sentiments which God had aroused in Esau. The
fiercest hatred of the anti-Semites still does not exclude an occasional burst of
sincere sympathy.

5. מִי־אֵלֶּה לָּךְ — *Who are these to you? Rashi* interprets, "Who are these? Are
they yours?" When Esau saw Jacob's large family and his flocks and servants,
he asked him, "Did you not tell me earlier that you wanted only spiritual
wealth and the treasures of the future world? But I see that you, even as I, are
enjoying the riches of this world!" Jacob replied, "God has granted them to me
אֲשֶׁר חָנַן, as an extra gift." Then Esau said to himself, "If these represent only
the interest, how great must be the capital which is reserved for him in the
World to Come" (*Tanna D'Bei Eliyahu Zuta* 19).

6. וַתִּשְׁתַּחֲוֶיןָ — *And they bowed down.* This verb is in the feminine, unlike
the two verbs from the same root which follow in the next verse. It is as
though in this case only the mothers bowed but not the children. In his
lexicon, Shlomoh Parshon (s. נגש) explains: "The actions of the handmaids were
not imitated by their sons because, in their sons' eyes, they were only fulfilling their obligations as servants. But the children felt they did not have to
bow before this wicked person. On the other hand the children of the free
wives, seeing their mothers bowing, could not exempt themselves from doing
likewise."

ח וְרָחֵל וַיִּשְׁתַּחֲווּ: וַיֹּאמֶר מִי לְךָ כָּל־הַמַּחֲנֶה הַזֶּה אֲשֶׁר
ט פָּגָשְׁתִּי וַיֹּאמֶר לִמְצֹא־חֵן בְּעֵינֵי אֲדֹנִי: וַיֹּאמֶר עֵשָׂו יֶשׁ־לִי
י רָב אָחִי יְהִי לְךָ אֲשֶׁר־לָךְ: וַיֹּאמֶר יַעֲקֹב אַל־נָא אִם־נָא
מָצָאתִי חֵן בְּעֵינֶיךָ וְלָקַחְתָּ מִנְחָתִי מִיָּדִי כִּי עַל־כֵּן רָאִיתִי
יא פָנֶיךָ כִּרְאֹת פְּנֵי אֱלֹהִים וַתִּרְצֵנִי: קַח־נָא אֶת־בִּרְכָתִי אֲשֶׁר
הֻבָאת לָךְ כִּי־חַנַּנִי אֱלֹהִים וְכִי יֶשׁ־לִי־כֹל וַיִּפְצַר־בּוֹ וַיִּקָּח:

8. וַיֹּאמֶר לִמְצֹא־חֵן בְּעֵינֵי אֲדֹנִי — *He answered, "To gain favor in my lord's eyes."*
This expression is used by Jacob several times. It provides the answer to Esau's
question regarding the destination or origin of "all this camp" which he met and
was offered by Jacob. All the riches which Jacob possesses and all the presents
which he sends to his adversaries have no other object but "to find favor in their
eyes." In Jewry's millennial struggle against its oppressors, material goods have
provided the means of pacifying their feelings of hatred.

9. יְהִי לְךָ אֲשֶׁר־לָךְ — *Let what you have remain yours.* I.e., that which goes back
to you. Here Esau admits Jacob's right to the blessings (*Rashi*). R' Abba
explained, "When Esau noticed his brother, his anger subsided. It could not have
been otherwise, since 'Esau's angel' had already given his blessing to Jacob the
previous night — וַיְבָרֶךְ אֹתוֹ שָׁם (32:30). Now, everything that happens in this
world has its source in the celestial world. What is decided there is carried out
here. Nothing can prevail in this world unless it has received approval
beforehand in the higher spheres. The worlds form one entity; they are
interdependent" (*Zohar*).

10. כִּי עַל־כֵּן רָאִיתִי פָנֶיךָ — *Inasmuch as I have seen your face.* For me it is as
though I had seen the face of an angel, for I have seen your celestial prince
(*Rashi*). The word אֱלֹהִים thus refers to the angel which Jacob had fought. On
meeting his brother, Jacob remembers this angel. The Sages of the Midrash
interpret the word אֱלֹהִים as an allusion to the principle of supreme justice — מִדַּת
הַדִּין: I stand before you as one stands before the celestial Judge to be judged for
his acts. And even as God commands that none shall appear before Him
empty-handed (וְלֹא יֵרָאוּ פָנַי רֵיקָם; *Exodus* 23:15), but should bring Him offerings
(and this has no connection whatsoever with presents given as bribes), so too is
it is fitting that you accept my gift.

According to this interpretation, the name אֱלֹהִים has a sacred character.
However, *Onkelos* considers it חול (profane) in accord with the indication in
Soferim (IV). He translates it, "I have seen your face as one sees the faces of the
lords."

כִּרְאֹת פְּנֵי אֱלֹהִים — *Which is like seeing the face of a Divine being.* From this
sentence R' Shimon ben Lakish deduces that one is allowed to flatter the wicked
in this world. But he is contradicted by R' Levi, who explains Jacob's words with
a comparison: a guest, invited by his neighbor to a meal, realizes that his host

and Rachel came forward and bowed down.

⁸ *And he asked, "What did you intend by that whole camp that I met?"*

He answered, "To gain favor in my lord's eyes."

⁹ *Esau said, "I have plenty. My brother, let what you have remain yours."*

¹⁰ *But Jacob said, "No, I beg of you! If I have now found favor in your eyes, then accept my tribute from me, inasmuch as I have seen your face, which is like seeing the face of a Divine being, and you were appeased by me.* ¹¹ *Please accept my gift which was brought to you, inasmuch as God has been gracious to me and inasmuch as I have everything." He urged him, and he accepted.*

intends to kill him. He declares, "This meal is just as tasty as the one I had at the king's table." The other concludes from his words that the king knows him; he becomes frightened and does not kill him. This idea of R' Levi's is the one which *Rashi* adopts in his commentary: Why did he tell him he had seen the angel? So Esau would fear him and say, "He has seen angels and has survived. I will be powerless against him" (cf. *Sotah* 41b).

11. וְכִי יֶשׁ־לִי־כֹל — *And inasmuch as I have everything.* Similar expressions בַּכֹּל and מִכֹּל are used with Abraham (24:1) and Isaac (27:33). We mention these three terms in the בִּרְכַּת הַמָּזוֹן, *Grace after Meals,* when we pray for this supreme blessing of the patriarchs: to be satisfied and to be content with whatever we possess.

The Sages of the Talmud tell us that these three terms בַּכֹּל מִכֹּל כֹּל hint at three things: the patriarchs had a foretaste of the future world, they did not have to struggle with the evil instinct, and their bodies were not subject to putrefaction in the grave. *Maharal* explains that the adjective כֹּל, *all,* expresses the wholeness of an object with respect to the number of its parts and its size. It thus includes the notion of perfection in both the moral and the physical senses, as was revealed in the patriarchs. Moreover, it makes us see the object not in its component parts but as a complete whole. (The patriarchs remained "whole"; their bodies did not decompose at all.) *Maharal* notes further that "all" is a collective term which denotes the totality of the integral parts. Now, these parts may have imperfections, whereas only the coherent totality of the individual elements, constituting a whole, an "all," is capable of eliminating them. Accordingly, it is said that the patriarchs, whose blessings included the word כֹּל, were free from the imperfections caused by the יֵצֶר הָרָע (*Bava Basra* 17a). Seen in this light, we can understand the thinking of the Kabbalists who relate the adjective כֹּל to an attribute of holiness attained by a צַדִּיק and they apply it in particular to Joseph (e.g. *Zohar* to *Numbers* 302a; cf. *Ramban* on 24:1).

וַיִּפְצַר־בּוֹ וַיִּקָּח — *He urged him, and he accepted.* "He pretended to refuse but at the same time he held out his hand" (*Midrash*). R' Hoshea said, "An old man explained this to me. In the end of days Esau will return to Jacob all he has taken

יב-יג וַיֹּאמֶר נִסְעָה וְנֵלֵכָה וְאֵלְכָה לְנֶגְדֶּךָ: וַיֹּאמֶר אֵלָיו אֲדֹנִי
יֹדֵעַ כִּי־הַיְלָדִים רַכִּים וְהַצֹּאן וְהַבָּקָר עָלוֹת עָלָי וּדְפָקוּם
יד יוֹם אֶחָד וָמֵתוּ כָּל־הַצֹּאן: יַעֲבָר־נָא אֲדֹנִי לִפְנֵי עַבְדּוֹ וַאֲנִי
אֶתְנָהֲלָה לְאִטִּי לְרֶגֶל הַמְּלָאכָה אֲשֶׁר־לְפָנַי וּלְרֶגֶל הַיְלָדִים
טו עַד אֲשֶׁר־אָבֹא אֶל־אֲדֹנִי שֵׂעִירָה: וַיֹּאמֶר עֵשָׂו אַצִּיגָה־
נָּא עִמְּךָ מִן־הָעָם אֲשֶׁר אִתִּי וַיֹּאמֶר לָמָּה זֶּה אֶמְצָא־חֵן
טז בְּעֵינֵי אֲדֹנִי: וַיָּשָׁב בַּיּוֹם הַהוּא עֵשָׂו לְדַרְכּוֹ שֵׂעִירָה:

from him, as it is said, *The kings of Tarshish and of the isles shall return tribute* (*Psalms* 72:10). Now, if they are to give back those presents which Jacob himself insisted on giving them, how much more so will they return that which they have taken by force!" (*Midrash* ibid.).

12. וְאֵלְכָה לְנֶגְדֶּךָ — *I will proceed alongside you.* Side by side with you (*Rashi*). Referring to this sentence, *Don Isaac Abarbanel* (in his book משמיע ישועה) shows that Christianity, represented by Esau, always developed its doctrine "side by side" with Jacob, that is, taking a path parallel to Jacob's. This positioning is such that Esau could never be able to overpower Jacob. In the light of what has just been said we can understand the reply given by R' Yehoshua ben Chananiah just before his death when his colleagues asked him, "Who will defend us henceforth against the subversive questions of the unbelievers?" He said to them, "Counsel has perished from the children [of Israel]; their wisdom has vanished" (*Jeremiah* 49:7). As soon as good counsel leaves the Jews, the wisdom of the nations of the world is also lost (*Chagigah* 5b).

R' S. Edels (*Maharsha*) points out that although this is true in the spiritual domain it is not so in the domain of temporal power, as we see from the Talmudic passage in *Avodah Zarah* (8b). This passage recounts that, "The Romans engaged in thirty-two battles with the Greeks but could not prevail against them until they made an alliance with the Jews and made an agreement with them ... They succeeded in defeating the Greeks and kept their pact with the Jews for twenty-six years. But then they enslaved them. Upon what verse in the Torah did the Romans base themselves at first (in honoring their word) and upon what did they rely later (in betraying their word)? At first they referred to the words, *Travel on and let us go — I will proceed alongside you.* Later they acted according to the following phrase (verse 14): *Let my lord go ahead of his servant.*" This shows that in the domain of temporal power Jacob allows his brother Esau to surpass him.

13. אֲדֹנִי יֹדֵעַ כִּי־הַיְלָדִים רַכִּים — *My lord knows that the children are tender.* This, however, did not prevent them from slaughtering the inhabitants of Shechem shortly afterwards, as we see in the next chapter. And so our Sages understand this phrase in a figurative sense: The family of Israel is still in its infancy, young and tender. The great leaders, Moses and Aaron, David and Solomon, have not yet made their appearance and in our present state

¹² *And he said, "Travel on and let us go — I will proceed alongside you."*

¹³ *But he said to him, "My lord knows that the children are tender, and the nursing flocks and cattle are upon me; if they will be driven hard for a single day, then all the flocks will die.* ¹⁴ *Let my lord go ahead of his servant; I will make my way at my slow pace according to the gait of the drove before me and the gait of the children, until I come to my lord at Seir."*

¹⁵ *Then Esau said, "Let me assign to you some of the people who are with me."*

And he said, "To what purpose? Let me just have favor in my lord's eyes!"

¹⁶ *So Esau started back that day on his way toward Seir.*

we were no match for Esau. Hence Jacob proposes, "Let my lord go ahead of his servant."

14. וּלְרֶגֶל הַיְלָדִים . . . וַאֲנִי אֶתְנַהֲלָה לְאִטִּי — *I will make my way at my slow pace . . . and the gait of the children.* Let Esau continue on his route toward new conquests. As for Jacob, his only thought is to direct his attention to the progress of his children. Raising them properly is his main preoccupation. Regard for youth, for their upbringing and development, comes before all other considerations. For Jacob what comes first is the moral and spiritual perfection of his children. They should never be "pushed" but instead should "be led along slowly." They are to progress slowly but surely, going constantly forward with unfaltering steps, far from the influence of Esau.

עַד אֲשֶׁר־אָבֹא אֶל־אֲדֹנִי — *Until I come to my lord.* He never did go there, *Rashi* tells us. "He wanted to be far apart from his brother. So when will he come? In the days of the Messiah, as it is written in *Ovadiah* (1:21)." Indeed, this is the last time we see the two brothers together; henceforth they go their separate ways (and will see each other again only at their father's burial; but at this meeting blood will be shed; cf. our commentary on 35:29). They will be together again only in messianic times. Jacob temporarily forgoes the benefit of the paternal blessings; he gives way to his brother who will dominate until Jacob's time comes. This temporary renunciation has already been pointed out, in a quote from the *Zohar* in our commentary to 27:40 and 28:4.

15. אַצִּיגָה־נָּא עִמְּךָ מִן־הָעָם אֲשֶׁר אִתִּי — *Let me assign to you some of the people who are with me.* Jacob declined this offer but Esau insisted. And so it turned out in later history. Converts from the Edomites, descendants of Esau, came to join the ranks of the Jewish people, as was the case with the Prophet Ovadiah (cf. *Rashi* to *Ovadiah* 1:1) among others. Our verse discreetly alludes to this: the numerical value of the words אַצִּיגָה־נָּא עִמְּךָ (290) equals that of the words אֵלּוּ גֵרִים, *these are proselytes* (*Torah Sheleimah*).

16. וַיָּשָׁב בַּיּוֹם הַהוּא עֵשָׂו לְדַרְכּוֹ שֵׂעִירָה — *So Esau started back that day on his way*

יז וְיַעֲקֹב נָסַע סֻכֹּתָה וַיִּבֶן לוֹ בָּיִת וּלְמִקְנֵהוּ עָשָׂה סֻכֹּת עַל־כֵּן
יח קָרָא שֵׁם־הַמָּקוֹם סֻכּוֹת: וַיָּבֹא יַעֲקֹב שָׁלֵם עִיר
שְׁכֶם אֲשֶׁר בְּאֶרֶץ כְּנַעַן בְּבֹאוֹ מִפַּדַּן אֲרָם וַיִּחַן אֶת־פְּנֵי הָעִיר:
יט וַיִּקֶן אֶת־חֶלְקַת הַשָּׂדֶה אֲשֶׁר נָטָה־שָׁם אָהֳלוֹ מִיַּד בְּנֵי־חֲמוֹר
כ אֲבִי שְׁכֶם בְּמֵאָה קְשִׂיטָה: וַיַּצֶּב־שָׁם מִזְבֵּחַ וַיִּקְרָא־לוֹ אֵל

toward Seir. For Esau, the destination, the goal to aim for, is Seir; for Jacob, it is Succoth. These two names reveal the divergence between Christian thought, represented by Esau, and Jewish thought, represented by Jacob. The former sees the highest expression of the religious ideal in the notion of שָׂעִיר (i.e. the שָׂעִיר הַמִּשְׁתַּלֵּחַ, *the scapegoat*). Its direct connection with Esau, called אִישׁ שָׂעִיר, is emphasized by *Ramban* on *Leviticus* 16:8. This idea includes the principle of redemption and absolution, appearing as acts of grace which emanate from Divine love. But Jewish thought goes further; Judaism does not consider the absolution obtained through the scapegoat on יוֹם כִּפּוּר, *the Day of Atonement*, to be a final climax. It continues after Yom Kippur to "journey to Succoth." This festival marks זְמַן שִׂמְחָתֵנוּ, *the time of our rejoicing*. It springs forth from the state of moral purity acquired during the יָמִים נוֹרָאִים, *Days of Awe*, but it has us transcend this to a higher level of Divine service: that of שִׂמְחָה שֶׁל מִצְוָה, the joy of performing religious duties. Although the other religions have been able to imitate the Biblical festivals (with the notable exception of Succos), they still could not conceive of the supreme form of Divine service in an atmosphere of sacred joy as it is exalted in this festival. Thus the two paths separate after the final meeting: Esau returned to Seir. But as for Jacob, he journeyed to Succoth (cf. *Recanati* on *Leviticus* chapter 16).

17. וַיִּבֶן לוֹ בָּיִת — *And built himself a house*. It was a *beis hamidrash*, a house of study, as the *Targum Yonasan* mentions. According to *Rashi*'s calculation, Jacob was to dwell there eighteen months. Whenever Jacob came to a place where he foresaw that he would stay a while, he first had a house of study built (cf. *Rashi* on 46:28).

18. וַיָּבֹא יַעֲקֹב שָׁלֵם — *Jacob arrived intact*. This is the name of a city in the province of Shechem, so interpret *Abarbanel, Rashbam* and others. (It has no connection with the Shalem quoted above in 14:18 as the former name of Jerusalem. The one in the province of Shechem is situated farther to the north.) But the Midrash, quoted by *Rashi*, takes שָׁלֵם as an adjective which means "sound," "whole." Jacob escaped unharmed "from the jaws of lions" (Laban and Esau). He arrived at the border of Canaan physically whole, his dislocation healed; whole financially, despite the gifts he had given his brother; and whole in the Torah, for he had forgotten none of his knowledge during his stay with Laban. The *Zohar* corroborates this concept and notes that peace can come to the soul as a result of dwelling in the *succah*. There man, trusting in the

[17] *But Jacob journeyed to Succoth and built himself a house, and for his livestock he made shelters; he therefore called the name of the place Succoth.* [18] *Jacob arrived intact at the city of Shechem which is in the land of Canaan, upon arriving from Paddan-aram, and he encamped before the city.* [19] *He bought the parcel of land upon which he pitched his tent from the children of Hamor, Shechem's father, for one hundred kesitahs.* [20] *He set up an altar there*

omnipotence of God, finds shelter in His protection. And this is the connection between סֻכּוֹת in the preceding verse and שָׁלֵם (perfection or peace) in our verse. This same connection appears in the expression סֻכַּת שָׁלוֹם which we find in the prayerbook. It refers to the phrase in *Psalms* (76:3): וַיְהִי בְשָׁלֵם סוּכּוֹ, *His succah bestows peace upon him.*

On the other hand, the midrashic interpretation just discussed helps make us more aware of the reasons for Jacob's ordeals as described in the next chapter. The last verses of our chapter are a sort of prelude to the coming chapter. "Because you delayed on the road (before fulfilling your vow) you have been punished through this misfortune which has befallen your daughter" — so explains *Rashi* later on (35:1). Now rich and successful, Jacob is severely criticized for having forgotten to make good the vow which he had uttered in a moment of distress. This is considered the reason for the rape of his daughter and the loss of his wife Rachel (*Tanchuma* 35). He should have gone to Beth-el to build an altar in honor of God as he promised he would do (28:20-22). Now the Torah spells out clearly here, just prior to the tragic story of Dinah, that all the conditions of the vow had been satisfied. The triple protection (physical, material, and spiritual) which Jacob had prayed for (28:20-21) he had indeed received in full measure — Jacob had safely returned to his native land, "whole" physically, materially, and spiritually. But instead of heading to Beth-el to build an altar, he *encamped before the city* of Shechem. What is more, *he bought the parcel of land upon which he pitched his tent . . . for one hundred kesitahs,* that is with current coinage (*Onkelos*), or, for a hundred jewels (*Targum Yerushalmi* based on *Job* 42:11); in any case, for a good price. It was there he erected an altar — but he had vowed to build it at Beth-el where he had received the Divine blessing (*Malbim*).

19. וַיִּקֶן אֶת־חֶלְקַת הַשָּׂדֶה — *He bought the parcel of land.* This is one of the three places the nations cannot vex Jewry about by saying, "You stole it" (for they were acquired in a good and proper manner). These places are the cave of Machpaleh, the site of the Temple in Jerusalem and the tomb of Joseph located in Shechem (*Rabbah* 79). However, the tragic destiny of Jewry was such that these three places have remained in Arab hands throughout the exile. As long as Jewry is in exile, the *Shechinah* which protects us is absent from the Holy Land (cf. our commentary to 23:17).

לד חמישי א אֱלֹהֵי יִשְׂרָאֵל: וַתֵּצֵא דִינָה בַּת־לֵאָה
ב אֲשֶׁר יָלְדָה לְיַעֲקֹב לִרְאוֹת בִּבְנוֹת הָאָרֶץ: וַיַּרְא אֹתָהּ שְׁכֶם
בֶּן־חֲמוֹר הַחִוִּי נְשִׂיא הָאָרֶץ וַיִּקַּח אֹתָהּ וַיִּשְׁכַּב אֹתָהּ וַיְעַנֶּהָ:

20. וַיִּקְרָא־לוֹ אֵל אֱלֹהֵי יִשְׂרָאֵל — *And proclaimed, "God, the God of Israel." Rashi* first gives the textual explanation of the verse: "Jacob gave the altar a name that would commemorate the miracle performed for him: God, the Holy One, Blessed is He, the Master of the Universe — He is God to me, bearing the name Israel." Then *Rashi* quotes the midrashic explanation (as given in *Megillah* 18a). According to this explanation it was God Who gave Jacob the name אֵל ("Who called him אֵל?" — "The God of Israel"). This appellation, R' *Bachya* teaches (33:7) means that a righteous person can attain a degree of holiness so elevated that he can ultimately be identified with a celestial being. R' *Bachya* gives several examples of mortals who attained a moral level such that they were closer to the realm of the angels than of men. This was the case with Jacob when he returned to the land of Canaan.

After quoting the midrashic explanation, *Rashi* concludes: "The words of the Torah are 'like a hammer which shatters rocks' (*Jeremiah* 23:29); they can 'split' into many explanations. As for me, my object is to explain the literal meaning of the text." Surprised here by *Rashi*'s unusual insistence and his stated desire to keep to the literal meaning, R' Tzvi Elimelech of Dinov gives the following explanation in his ס' בני יששכר: Regarding God's proclamation of His thirteen attributes of mercy, ה' ה' אֵל רַחוּם וְחַנּוּן, *Hashem, Hashem God Compassionate and Gracious* (*Exodus* 34:6), R' Yochanan teaches that as He passed before Moses, God exclaimed, "Whenever the Jews sin, let them perform before Me in this order and I will pardon them." Now according to some, this passage (*Rosh Hashanah* 17b) means that to be pardoned the Jews must imitate the Divine attributes in their moral conduct. Others, however, hold that it will suffice just to invoke these attributes by proclaiming them fervently in prayer. But is the first alternative possible? Admittedly, man can imitate God in His attributes of compassion, graciousness, etc. (רַחוּם וְחַנּוּן), but can he imitate Him as אֵל, which is named here as the first of the thirteen attributes? The answer to this will depend on how we interpret our verse. If the midrashic explanation is correct — that it was God Who applied the name אֵל to Jacob — then we see that this attribute can be applied to man. And so to obtain pardon man must really imitate all of the thirteen attributes. But *Rashi* prefers the literal explanation: the name אֵל refers to the altar, not to Jacob, for no man can be called by this Name. From this it follows that the thirteen attributes cannot be achieved by man; hence just invoking them in prayer will suffice to obtain pardon (מאמרי אלול).

34.

1. וַתֵּצֵא דִינָה — *Now Dinah ... went out.* "I said to the joyous ones: Cease your rejoicings." Our Sages cite this verse from *Psalms* (75:5) to introduce the account

and proclaimed, "God, the God of Israel."

34 ¹*Now Dinah — the daughter of Leah, whom she had borne to Jacob — went out to look over the daughters of the land.* ²*Shechem, son of Hamor the Hivvite, the prince of the region, saw her; he took her, lay with her, and violated her.*

which follows (*Tanchuma Shemini*). Joy, they tell us, does not last. And after mentioning the examples of Adam, Abraham, and Isaac, they show how Jacob, who had overcome the terrible trials of the past twenty years and believed that at last he was going to be able to find happiness (as the end of the last chapter seemed to indicate), suddenly faces a setback in his destiny. His household is subjected to a succession of calamities: the rape of his daughter, Rachel's premature death, and Joseph's disappearance. His father Isaac had experienced a very similar fate (cf. our commentary to 27:1). Nevertheless, if we consider the historic mission of Jacob's family we can grasp the meaning of the new trial. This people, which is called on to be a nation of priests and the standard-bearer for God on earth, had to experience a moral outrage upon its own flesh and blood right from its beginnings. It had to undergo this ordeal so that the world could see in its swift and ruthless reaction the sacred character of its ideal of purity. It had to suffer this outrage so that it could harden the steel of the national soul for all time.

בַּת־לֵאָה — *Daughter of Leah.* "And not the daughter of Jacob? But because she 'went out,' she is called the daughter of Leah, for Leah also had the habit of going out, as it says, *And Leah went out to meet him* (30:16). From this we get the proverb: 'Like mother, like daughter'" (*Rashi*). However, this opinion is contradicted by R' Eliezer, who explains that, like her father, Dinah used to stay in her tent, reluctant to leave it. But Shechem aroused her curiosity when he sent dancers and musicians to the door of her tent. These drew her outside. In this appraisal, Dinah's character is more like that of her mother, whom tradition praises for her modesty and reserve, as is noted in the commentary on 29:31 and on 30:16 (*Pirkei D'Rabbi Eliezer* 38). At the same time she was a true daughter of Jacob, as shown by her reserve and modesty in staying in her tent (יֹשֵׁב אֹהָלִים). [The words לִרְאוֹת בִּבְנוֹת הָאָרֶץ, *to look over the daughters of the land*, is given a double meaning in the *Midrash Tanchuma*, as *Rashi* states: לִרְאוֹת וְלֵירָאוֹת, *to see and to be seen*, as the Talmud (*Sanhedrin* 4b) explains in similar cases; cf. שעורי דעת, Vol. 2, no. 3.]

2. וַיַּרְא אֹתָהּ שְׁכֶם בֶּן־חֲמוֹר הַחִוִּי — *Shechem, son of Hamor the Hivvite . . . saw her.* Was he a Hivvite? He was really an Amorite, as we see in *Genesis* 48:22. But חִוְיָא in Aramaic means a serpent (*Onkelos, Genesis* 3:1). Now, *The one who breaks down a fence, a serpent will bite him* (*Ecclesiastes* 10:8), this happened to Dinah. Her parents should have forbidden her to go out (*Rabbah*, ibid.).

ג וַתִּדְבַּק נַפְשׁוֹ בְּדִינָה בַּת־יַעֲקֹב וַיֶּאֱהַב אֶת־הַנַּעֲרָ וַיְדַבֵּר עַל־
ד לֵב הַנַּעֲרָ: וַיֹּאמֶר שְׁכֶם אֶל־חֲמוֹר אָבִיו לֵאמֹר קַח־לִי אֶת־
ה הַיַּלְדָּה הַזֹּאת לְאִשָּׁה: וְיַעֲקֹב שָׁמַע כִּי טִמֵּא אֶת־דִּינָה בִתּוֹ
ו וּבָנָיו הָיוּ אֶת־מִקְנֵהוּ בַּשָּׂדֶה וְהֶחֱרִשׁ יַעֲקֹב עַד־בֹּאָם: וַיֵּצֵא
ז חֲמוֹר אֲבִי־שְׁכֶם אֶל־יַעֲקֹב לְדַבֵּר אִתּוֹ: וּבְנֵי יַעֲקֹב בָּאוּ מִן־
הַשָּׂדֶה כְּשָׁמְעָם וַיִּתְעַצְּבוּ הָאֲנָשִׁים וַיִּחַר לָהֶם מְאֹד כִּי־נְבָלָה
ח עָשָׂה בְיִשְׂרָאֵל לִשְׁכַּב אֶת־בַּת־יַעֲקֹב וְכֵן לֹא יֵעָשֶׂה: וַיְדַבֵּר
חֲמוֹר אִתָּם לֵאמֹר שְׁכֶם בְּנִי חָשְׁקָה נַפְשׁוֹ בְּבִתְּכֶם תְּנוּ נָא
ט אֹתָהּ לוֹ לְאִשָּׁה: וְהִתְחַתְּנוּ אֹתָנוּ בְּנֹתֵיכֶם תִּתְּנוּ־לָנוּ וְאֶת־
י בְּנֹתֵינוּ תִּקְחוּ לָכֶם: וְאִתָּנוּ תֵּשֵׁבוּ וְהָאָרֶץ תִּהְיֶה לִפְנֵיכֶם שְׁבוּ
יא וּסְחָרוּהָ וְהֵאָחֲזוּ בָּהּ: וַיֹּאמֶר שְׁכֶם אֶל־אָבִיהָ וְאֶל־אַחֶיהָ
יב אֶמְצָא־חֵן בְּעֵינֵיכֶם וַאֲשֶׁר תֹּאמְרוּ אֵלַי אֶתֵּן: הַרְבּוּ עָלַי
מְאֹד מֹהַר וּמַתָּן וְאֶתְּנָה כַּאֲשֶׁר תֹּאמְרוּ אֵלָי וּתְנוּ־לִי אֶת־
יג הַנַּעֲרָ לְאִשָּׁה: וַיַּעֲנוּ בְנֵי־יַעֲקֹב אֶת־שְׁכֶם וְאֶת־חֲמוֹר אָבִיו

---

3. וַיֶּאֱהַב אֶת־הַנַּעֲרָ — *He loved the maiden.* R' Shimon ben Lakish says that whenever the word נַעֲרָה is written without the ה (as it is here), it refers to a young girl (*Kesubos* 40b). At the time Dinah was only eight years and one month old, as *R' Bachya* shows.

5. וְהֶחֱרִשׁ יַעֲקֹב עַד־בֹּאָם — *So Jacob kept silent until their arrival.* He immediately realized that recourse to trickery and even to force would be necessary to avenge this outrage against his daughter and his entire family. So he resigned himself to keep silent until his sons returned, for he was counting on their help. What follows in the narrative shows that he entrusted his sons with the task of saving their sister.

7. וְכֵן לֹא יֵעָשֶׂה — *Such a thing may not be done!* to rape virgins. Having learned the lesson of the Flood, even the idolatrous nations had renounced immorality (*Rashi*). *Ramban*, however, counters *Rashi's* argument with the fact that "the morals of the Canaanite peoples were more corrupt than those of all the other nations," which the Torah itself vouches for (cf. *Rashi* on *Leviticus* 18:3). He holds that the words *may not . . .* refer to Jewry. Even though such terrible infamy can take place among the idolatrous nations, it cannot be committed "in Israel." This specification of place in the verse itself seems to support *Ramban's* opinion. Indeed this is the first time that the descendants of Abraham, Isaac, and Jacob are referred to by this name — and it occurs even before the name has been officially proclaimed. They already feel part of the nation which will be a "priestly people" called on to "fight for God." What a lofty conception of duty, virtue, and moral nobility is already connected with this august name! It is particularly significant that the first "struggle for God" with which the name

³ *He became deeply attached to Dinah, daughter of Jacob; he loved the maiden and appealed to the maiden's emotions.* ⁴ *So Shechem spoke to Hamor, his father, saying, "Take me this girl for a wife."*

⁵ *Now Jacob heard that he had defiled his daughter Dinah, while his sons were with his cattle in the field; so Jacob kept silent until their arrival.*

⁶ *Hamor, Shechem's father, went out to Jacob to speak to him.* ⁷ *Jacob's sons arrived from the field, when they heard; the men were distressed, and were fired deeply with indignation, for he had committed an outrage in Israel by lying with a daughter of Jacob — such a thing may not be done!*

⁸ *Hamor spoke with them, saying, "Shechem, my son, longs deeply for your daughter — please give her to him as a wife.* ⁹ *And intermarry with us; give your daughters to us, and take our daughters for yourselves.* ¹⁰ *And among us you shall dwell; the land will be before you — settle and trade in it, and acquire property in it."*

¹¹ *Then Shechem said to her father and brothers, "Let me gain favor in your eyes; and whatever you tell me — I will give.* ¹² *Inflate exceedingly upon me the marriage settlement and gifts and I will give whatever you tell me; only give me the maiden for a wife."*

¹³ *Jacob's sons answered Shechem and his father Hamor*

יִשְׂרָאֵל, *Israel,* is connected is in defense of the sacred ideal of moral purity. The first mission of those who are the "Children of Israel" is to safeguard this ideal.

8. שְׁכֶם בְּנִי חָשְׁקָה נַפְשׁוֹ בְּבִתְּכֶם — *Shechem, my son, longs deeply for your daughter. Rashi* translates the verb חָשַׁק as *desires.* Regarding the commandment, וְאָהַבְתָּ אֵת ה׳, *You shall love Hashem, your God, R' Bachya* wonders why the Torah does not state וְחָשַׁקְתָּ, since this verb appears to express a more intense feeling of love than אָהַב. He suggests that it is because the term חָשַׁק designates an exclusive passionate desire to the point of foregoing the material conditions of life and the necessity of doing *mitzvos,* whereas אָהַב signifies a feeling of love which does not exclude preoccupation with temporal matters. Now the *mitzvos* of the Torah are concerned with these preoccupations. Hence the Torah chooses the word אָהַב to characterize the feeling of love for God (*Deuteronomy* 6:5).

11. וַאֲשֶׁר תֹּאמְרוּ אֵלַי אֶתֵּן — *And whatever you tell me— I will give.* Shechem desired Dinah because she was very beautiful. And yet, although the Torah mentions the beauty of the matriarchs, it does not do so for Dinah. This is because her beauty proved disastrous for her. The Torah only mentions the beauty of those women whose lives can serve as an example (*Ramban*).

13. וַיַּעֲנוּ בְנֵי־יַעֲקֹב אֶת־שְׁכֶם — *Jacob's sons answered Shechem.* They are not criticized for answering in front of their father, as was Laban who spoke up in

יד בְּמִרְמָה וַיְדַבֵּרוּ אֲשֶׁר טִמֵּא אֵת דִּינָה אֲחֹתָם: וַיֹּאמְרוּ
אֲלֵיהֶם לֹא נוּכַל לַעֲשׂוֹת הַדָּבָר הַזֶּה לָתֵת אֶת־אֲחֹתֵנוּ
טו לְאִישׁ אֲשֶׁר־לוֹ עָרְלָה כִּי־חֶרְפָּה הִוא לָנוּ: אַךְ־בְּזֹאת נֵאוֹת
טז לָכֶם אִם תִּהְיוּ כָמֹנוּ לְהִמֹּל לָכֶם כָּל־זָכָר: וְנָתַנּוּ אֶת־בְּנֹתֵינוּ
לָכֶם וְאֶת־בְּנֹתֵיכֶם נִקַּח־לָנוּ וְיָשַׁבְנוּ אִתְּכֶם וְהָיִינוּ לְעַם
יז אֶחָד: וְאִם־לֹא תִשְׁמְעוּ אֵלֵינוּ לְהִמּוֹל וְלָקַחְנוּ אֶת־בִּתֵּנוּ
יח וְהָלָכְנוּ: וַיִּיטְבוּ דִבְרֵיהֶם בְּעֵינֵי חֲמוֹר וּבְעֵינֵי שְׁכֶם בֶּן־
יט חֲמוֹר: וְלֹא־אֵחַר הַנַּעַר לַעֲשׂוֹת הַדָּבָר כִּי חָפֵץ בְּבַת־יַעֲקֹב
כ וְהוּא נִכְבָּד מִכֹּל בֵּית אָבִיו: וַיָּבֹא חֲמוֹר וּשְׁכֶם בְּנוֹ אֶל־שַׁעַר
כא עִירָם וַיְדַבְּרוּ אֶל־אַנְשֵׁי עִירָם לֵאמֹר: הָאֲנָשִׁים הָאֵלֶּה
שְׁלֵמִים הֵם אִתָּנוּ וְיֵשְׁבוּ בָאָרֶץ וְיִסְחֲרוּ אֹתָהּ וְהָאָרֶץ הִנֵּה
רַחֲבַת־יָדַיִם לִפְנֵיהֶם אֶת־בְּנֹתָם נִקַּח־לָנוּ לְנָשִׁים וְאֶת־
כב בְּנֹתֵינוּ נִתֵּן לָהֶם: אַךְ־בְּזֹאת יֵאֹתוּ לָנוּ הָאֲנָשִׁים לָשֶׁבֶת
אִתָּנוּ לִהְיוֹת לְעַם אֶחָד בְּהִמּוֹל לָנוּ כָּל־זָכָר כַּאֲשֶׁר הֵם
כג נִמֹּלִים: מִקְנֵהֶם וְקִנְיָנָם וְכָל־בְּהֶמְתָּם הֲלוֹא לָנוּ הֵם אַךְ
כד נֵאוֹתָה לָהֶם וְיֵשְׁבוּ אִתָּנוּ: וַיִּשְׁמְעוּ אֶל־חֲמוֹר וְאֶל־שְׁכֶם בְּנוֹ
כָּל־יֹצְאֵי שַׁעַר עִירוֹ וַיִּמֹּלוּ כָּל־זָכָר כָּל־יֹצְאֵי שַׁעַר עִירוֹ:

the presence of his father Besuel (see *Rashi* on 24:50). We can therefore conclude
that their reply was given with the patriarch's consent and it saved him from
intervening personally in this humiliating affair. If this is so, asks *Ramban*, how
can we explain Jacob's anger at the way his sons dealt with Shechem (verse 30)?
Jacob's assent concerned punishing the culprit Shechem, even through guile; but
Jacob criticized Simeon and Levi severely for their bloody revenge on all the
townspeople.

בְּמִרְמָה — *Cleverly.* Cf. our commentary to 27:35. According to *R' Chaim ben
Attar,* here the cleverness consisted in presenting their proposition in a way that
aroused no suspicion whatever of any trick. Once again we see Jacob involved
in trickery, this time through his closest kin. From the time he bought the
birthright from his brother Esau, he is successively the perpetrator and victim of
trickery. On this, see our commentary to 27:36.

However, *Rashi* quotes the Midrash which sees the last part of the verse as
the Torah's own reply, that is to say, the reply of the רוּחַ הַקֹּדֶשׁ, *Holy Spirit:*
"You think this is trickery! Not at all! 'Because he had defiled Dinah their sister.'
" Seen in this light, such a reply represents Divine approval; trickery is justified
when it is a matter of a punishment for an immoral act as disgusting as this one
(cf. our commentary to 29:12 and 30:37).

14. כִּי־חֶרְפָּה הִוא לָנוּ — *For that is a disgrace for us. Rashi* explains: "For us it is
a blemish. When one wants to insult another, he says, 'You are uncircumcised,

cleverly and they spoke (because he had defiled their sister Dinah). ¹⁴ *They said to them, "We cannot do this thing, to give our sister to a man who is uncircumcised, for that is a disgrace for us.* ¹⁵ *Only on this condition will we acquiesce to you: If you become like us by letting every male among you become circumcised.* ¹⁶ *Then we will give our daughters to you, and take your daughters to ourselves; we will dwell with you, and become a single people.* ¹⁷ *But if you will not listen to us to be circumcised, we will take our daughter and go."*

¹⁸ *Their proposal seemed good in the view of Hamor, and in the view of Shechem, Hamor's son.* ¹⁹ *The youth did not delay doing the thing, for he wanted Jacob's daughter. Now he was the most respected of all his father's household.*

²⁰ *Hamor — with his son Shechem — came to the gate of their city and spoke to the people of their city, saying,* ²¹ *"These people are peaceable with us; let them settle in the land and trade in it, for see, there is ample room in the land for them! Let us take their daughters for ourselves as wives and give our daughters to them.* ²² *Only on this condition will the people acquiesce with us to dwell with us to become a single people: that all our males become circumcised as they themselves are circumcised.* ²³ *Their livestock, their possessions, and all their animals — will they not be ours? Let us acquiesce to them and they will settle with us."*

²⁴ *All the people who depart through the gate of his city listened to Hamor and his son Shechem, and all the males — all those who depart through the gate of his city — were circumcised.*

or the son of one uncircumcised.' The Hebrew word חֶרְפָּה always indicates something dishonorable." Even though the command of circumcision was then still quite new, it had already acquired such religious and national significance that it served to separate Jews from idolaters. For a Jewish woman to marry an uncircumcised man was something shameful, "a disgrace." The phrase uttered by Jacob's sons sums up in a few telling words the Jewish conception which is still valid to this day: between the pure and the impure no union is possible.

17. וְלָקַחְנוּ אֶת־בִּתֵּנוּ וְהָלָכְנוּ — *We will take our daughter and go.* Here the brothers describe Dinah as their "daughter." In so doing, they want the others to understand that they are determined to avenge their sister's honor as a father avenges the honor of his daughter.

24. כָּל־יֹצְאֵי שַׁעַר עִירוֹ — *All those who depart through the gate of his city.* The fact that all the townspeople were ready to undergo circumcision just so the prince could marry his Dinah seems so extraordinary that it calls for a special explanation. This can be found in the expression: יֹצְאֵי שַׁעַר עִירוֹ used here twice instead of the more usual term בָּאֵי שַׁעַר עִירוֹ (e.g. 23:10 and 18). This expression

כה וַיְהִי בַיּוֹם הַשְּׁלִישִׁי בִּהְיוֹתָם כְּאֲבִים וַיִּקְחוּ שְׁנֵי־בְנֵי־
יַעֲקֹב שִׁמְעוֹן וְלֵוִי אֲחֵי דִינָה אִישׁ חַרְבּוֹ וַיָּבֹאוּ עַל־
כו הָעִיר בֶּטַח וַיַּהַרְגוּ כָּל־זָכָר: וְאֶת־חֲמוֹר וְאֶת־שְׁכֶם
בְּנוֹ הָרְגוּ לְפִי־חָרֶב וַיִּקְחוּ אֶת־דִּינָה מִבֵּית שְׁכֶם וַיֵּצֵאוּ:

apparently means that the inhabitants of Shechem were mainly farmers and peasants whose occupations took them outside the town daily. Hamor and Shechem were therefore probably the lords and proprietors of the land and the townspeople were serfs, used to obeying every demand. Nevertheless, Shechem's request appeared so exorbitant that it became the subject of a proverb among the Jews: "Shechem is in love and the peasant has to get circumcised!" (*Rabbah* 80).

25. בַּיּוֹם הַשְּׁלִישִׁי — *On the third day*. In the Talmud (*Shabbos* 134b) the *Tannaim* refer to this verse to authorize using hot water to wash the wound of the circumcision on the third day, even if it is the Sabbath. "This is because of the risk of physical danger on that day," says *Rambam* (הל׳ שבת פ״ב י״ד וע״ש במ״מ). However, nowadays this danger no longer exists, as the author of the *Shulchan Aruch* points out (*Orach Chaim* 331:9).

שִׁמְעוֹן וְלֵוִי אֲחֵי דִינָה — *Simeon and Levi, Dinah's brothers*. Real brothers. All three were children of the same mother and these brothers felt more responsible for what had happened than the half-brothers. They were 13 years old at the time, the Midrash tells us (*Rabbah* ibid.), and their exploit reveals once again the extraordinary physical strength of Jacob's children (already pointed out in our commentary to 29:10). "Right from their entry into the Promised Land, the members of the family felt that they were in their own country. They no longer concealed their strength, their riches, or their physical beauty. Their strength was seen in the exploit of the two brothers; their riches, in the houses and tents which Jacob constructed (33:17) — even shops were built; their beauty in Dinah, going out to show herself off to the daughters of the land" (*Tanchuma Vayishlach*).

וַיָּבֹאוּ עַל־הָעִיר בֶּטַח — *And they came upon the city confidently*. According to *Onkelos*, it was the city which basked in a feeling of complete security; according to *Rashi*, it was the brothers who had the security, for they knew that the inhabitants were in great pain. Moreover, the Midrash explains that the sons had complete confidence in the power of their father. He was, of course, fundamentally opposed to the savage and ferocious deeds of his sons, but when he understood that they were in mortal danger of a counterattack from neighboring peoples, he armed himself with his sword and bow to fight them. This is what Jacob is referring to when he promises Joseph the town of Shechem which he had conquered "with his sword and with his bow," as *Rashi* brings out on *Genesis* 48:22. See also our commentary to 35:5.

וַיַּהַרְגוּ כָּל־זָכָר — *And killed every male*. *Ramban* remarks that there are many who wonder how righteous men, as Jacob's sons were, could do what they did and shed innocent blood. *Rambam* replies: The descendants of Noah are held

> ²⁵ *And it came to pass on the third day, when they were in*
> *pain, that two of Jacob's sons, Simeon and Levi, Dinah's brothers,*
> *each took his sword and they came upon the city confidently,*
> *and killed every male.* ²⁶ *And Hamor and Shechem his son they*
> *killed at the point of sword. Then they took Dinah from*
> *Shechem's house and left.*

responsible for observing the commandment to set up institutions of justice in
every town so as to guarantee respect for their laws and judge those who
transgress. Now, all descendants of Noah who transgress one of the seven
Noachian laws are liable for the death penalty. This is why the inhabitants of
Shechem were punished with death. Shechem had ravished Jacob's daughter
and the inhabitants did indeed know it, but they did not judge him (הל׳ מלכים
פ״ט י״ד). *Ramban* objects to certain points in this explanation. He holds that
omitting an act of justice does not necessarily entail the death penalty.
Furthermore, he rejects other arguments of *Rambam* concerning the Noachian
laws. (In his *Responsa*, R' Moshe Sofer analyzes the differences of opinion
between these two sages — Volume II, No. 14). He considers that Jacob's sons
had the right to act as they did because the people of Shechem practiced the same
abominations as those which brought the punishment of extermination upon the
peoples of Canaan. The sons were nevertheless severely reprimanded by their
father because they took it upon themselves to exercise judgment without
having been authorized to do so (*Genesis* 49:7).

Other commentators continue the discussion regarding the actions of the two
brothers, but it appears that *Rambam's* opinion is justified, starting from the
principle of collective responsibility for a crime committed in a group and not
brought before the courts. The Torah gives us many examples in which this
principle is applied; the reasons for it we have explained in our commentary to
Chapter 17 and to 18:25.

But, concludes R' *Chaim ben Attar*, neither of these explanations is able to
justify the actions of Jacob's sons in pillaging the town and taking the spoils.

26. וַיִּקְחוּ אֶת־דִּינָה — *They took Dinah.* R' Huna said: A woman who has lived
with an uncircumcised man finds it difficult to separate from him (she loves the
man who deflowered her). When Dinah's brothers came to free her, she said to
them: "Where shall I go to bear my shame?" She refused to go back with them
until Simeon swore that he would marry her. This is what is referred to in 46:10
where Simeon's wife is called a Canaanite woman (*Rashi* ibid.). But the Sages
relate that Dinah remained unmarried and was buried in Canaan by her brother
Simeon (*Rabbah* 80). According to other traditions, Dinah became the wife of
Iyov (ibid.), who was Esau's grandson (*Bava Basra* 15a). In addition, R' Eliezer
says that Dinah, pregnant from Shechem, gave birth in her father's house to a
daughter whom she named Osnath. To protect her from the hostility of his sons,
Jacob sent Osnath to Egypt where she stayed at the house of Potiphar and
became his adopted daughter. Later, Joseph met her there without suspecting her

כז בְּנֵי יַעֲקֹב בָּאוּ עַל־הַחֲלָלִים וַיָּבֹזּוּ הָעִיר אֲשֶׁר טִמְּאוּ
כח אֲחוֹתָם: אֶת־צֹאנָם וְאֶת־בְּקָרָם וְאֶת־חֲמֹרֵיהֶם וְאֵת אֲשֶׁר־
כט בָּעִיר וְאֶת־אֲשֶׁר בַּשָּׂדֶה לָקָחוּ: וְאֶת־כָּל־חֵילָם וְאֶת־
כָּל־טַפָּם וְאֶת־נְשֵׁיהֶם שָׁבוּ וַיָּבֹזּוּ וְאֵת כָּל־אֲשֶׁר בַּבָּיִת:
ל וַיֹּאמֶר יַעֲקֹב אֶל־שִׁמְעוֹן וְאֶל־לֵוִי עֲכַרְתֶּם אֹתִי לְהַבְאִישֵׁנִי
בְּיֹשֵׁב הָאָרֶץ בַּכְּנַעֲנִי וּבַפְּרִזִּי וַאֲנִי מְתֵי מִסְפָּר וְנֶאֶסְפוּ
לא עָלַי וְהִכּוּנִי וְנִשְׁמַדְתִּי אֲנִי וּבֵיתִי: וַיֹּאמְרוּ הַכְזוֹנָה יַעֲשֶׂה
אֶת־אֲחוֹתֵנוּ:

origins. She married him at Pharaoh's command (4:45) and became the mother of Ephraim and Manasseh (*Pirkei D'Rabbi Eliezer* 38).

27. בְּנֵי יַעֲקֹב בָּאוּ עַל־הַחֲלָלִים — *The sons of Jacob came upon the slain.* The *Sefer HaYashar* of R' Joseph ben Gurion states that the victims numbered 645 adults and 276 children. Hamor's father (Chedkam ben Pered) aided by his six brothers, rebelled against the treaty which his son and his grandson Shechem had made with Jacob and his sons. By dire threats, they gained control of the city's inhabitants in order to force them to cancel their decision. Gripped with fear, the people promised to wage war against Jacob's camp the next day. Dinah knew of these plans and sent a messenger to warn her family. Her brothers decided then and there to take advantage of the third day after the circumcision, and they attacked the inhabitants of the city.

30. עֲכַרְתֶּם אֹתִי — *You have discomposed me.* The patriarch's reproaches refer to the dire consequences of his sons' misbehavior, not to the iniquity of their acts of violence. These seem to be beside the point, as least as far as the main culprits were concerned. When the patriarch gathered his children around his deathbed he also condemned their odious action but he did not reprove their real motives.

As for the two sons who were so severely castigated, they had only one reply, "הַכְזוֹנָה וְגוֹ,, should we have let them treat our sister like a harlot?" That was all they said. They realized that this foreign despot would never have allowed himself to commit such an outrage had it not involved a young Jewish girl. This experience made them aware that, right in the family of Jacob, circumstances could arise where they would have to use force to defend their ideal of purity and honor.

They did not try to act with wisdom and reflection; on the contrary, they wanted to make themselves feared, so that no one would ever again dare to commit such an offense against them. And they showed that even if the true might of Israel is הַקֹּל קוֹל יַעֲקֹב, "The voice of prayer and of study of the Torah," still there are exceptional circumstances in the history of the holy people where the use of force can be perfectly legitimate.

Jacob's two sons cried out: "It is not right that it be stated in Jewish houses of prayer and study that the uncircumcised and the idol-worshipers have defiled

²⁷ *The sons of Jacob came upon the slain, and they plundered the city which had defiled their sister.* ²⁸ *Their flocks, their cattle, their donkeys, whatever was in the town and whatever was in the field, they took.* ²⁹ *All their wealth, all their children and wives they took captive and they plundered, as well as everything in the house.*

³⁰ *Jacob said to Simeon and to Levi, "You have discomposed me, making me odious among the inhabitants of the land, among the Canaanite and among the Perizzite; I am few in number and should they band together and attack me, I will be annihilated — I and my household."*

³¹ *And they said, "Should he treat our sister like a harlot?"*

a daughter of Jacob. But it is right for them to hear that the uncircumcised and the idol-worshipers were struck down for having defiled the daughter of Jacob, so that Shechem would not be able to go around boasting that he had abused our sister like a common prostitute and no one had come to her aid" (*Targum Yonasan*).

The reasons which motivated Simeon and Levi thus appear noble and legitimate — it was just the way they acted and their excessive reprisals which were reprimanded. But their way of thinking represents a most indispensable factor for a people which is preparing itself to take on a messianic role within the world community.

When on his deathbed, Jacob cursed their impetuosity and their terrible anger (49:7), he assigned them areas distant from one another in the future territory of Israel. He did this in order to avoid too great a concentration of their physical strength; at the same time this served to ensure the spread of their ideas throughout the various levels of the Jewish people. And the same sword which Simeon and Levi used against strangers to save their sister's honor, we see used again later by Levi, but this time mercilessly against his own brothers in order to keep them from straying and from moral perdition (*Exodus* 32:28), and again by Phineas of the tribe of Levi against the prince of the tribe of Simeon (*Numbers* 25:7-14).

Moses himself praised the tribe of Levi as guardians of the Divine covenant, uniquely faithful to the word of God, who selflessly performed its religious duties without regard to family ties (*Deuteronomy* 33:9). The intransigent zeal and sacred devotion of Simeon and Levi were also rewarded when the blessings were given to Jewry on Mount Gerizim (*Deuteronomy* 27:12). There, the first places were reserved for these two tribes, and this was because of these qualities.

31. הַכְזוֹנָה — *Like a harlot.* They gave him a pertinent reply. For they said, "like a harlot," but not "an actual harlot," which indicates that she had not consented (*Midrash Lekach Tov*). This may also be why there is a Masoretic rule that in this verse the word "sister" is written full (with a *vav* — אֲחוֹתֵנוּ) in contrast to

לה   א וַיֹּאמֶר אֱלֹהִים אֶל־יַעֲקֹב קוּם עֲלֵה בֵית־אֵל וְשֶׁב־שָׁם
וַעֲשֵׂה־שָׁם מִזְבֵּחַ לָאֵל הַנִּרְאֶה אֵלֶיךָ בְּבָרְחֲךָ מִפְּנֵי עֵשָׂו
ב אָחִיךָ: וַיֹּאמֶר יַעֲקֹב אֶל־בֵּיתוֹ וְאֶל כָּל־אֲשֶׁר עִמּוֹ הָסִרוּ אֶת־
אֱלֹהֵי הַנֵּכָר אֲשֶׁר בְּתֹכְכֶם וְהִטַּהֲרוּ וְהַחֲלִיפוּ שִׂמְלֹתֵיכֶם:

the way it is written in verses 13 and 14. As the episode is drawing to a close,
the brothers make a point of saying that Dinah remained "fully" worthy of
being their sister. Could partial reinstatement be what *Rashi* also wants to bring
out when he explains the word אֲחוֹתֵנוּ simply by quoting *Onkelos'* translation:
our sister (without elaborating any further)? *R' Bachya* claims that he does not
understand what *Rashi* wants to tell us here. (According to *Rosh, Onkelos'*
translation shows that the word is in the singular, contrary to what the full form
would have us believe. According to Wolf Heidenheim in הבנת הקרא, *Rashi*
quotes *Onkelos* to re-establish the version with the accusative as authentic, since
there are several versions extant regarding this.)

Getting to the root of the problem, we see that both sides are right. The father,
nearly 100 years old, prudent and moderate, the image of the "old generation,"
argues: "I am only few in number and the enemy will gather themselves
together against me and smite me." But the sons, only thirteen years old, are
uncompromising and ready to fight; they represent the "younger generation."
"Can one treat our sister like a harlot?" they cry out. But what can one do in such
a predicament where one cannot bear to take all that abuse and yet one does not
feel strong enough to offer resistance to it? There is just one way out: קוּם עֲלֵה
בֵית־אֵל, *Arise — go up to Beth-el*, leave here and go elsewhere.

35.

1. וַיֹּאמֶר אֱלֹהִים אֶל־יַעֲקֹב — *God said to Jacob*. The Divine name אֱלֹהִים employed
here and throughout this chapter indicates that the words addressed to Jacob
emanate from God as the Supreme Judge (מִדַּת הַדִּין), Who rewards and Who
punishes. Indeed *Rashi* explains the Divine command, "Arise, go up to Beth-el"
in these words: it is because you have delayed on the way (in fulfilling your vow)
that you have been punished and have suffered this tragedy with your
daughter. This refers to the vow made by Jacob on the dangerous journey to his
uncle Laban (28:19). The importance of this omission on Jacob's part was
discussed in our commentary to 33:18.

The *Midrash Tanchuma* develops this theme in a more general context: on
three occasions, it tells us, the deeds of a man are weighed (that is to say, his case
is examined very carefully to judge if he deserves being saved by a miracle).
These are when a righteous man travels alone (exposing himself to danger),
when he is staying in a house on the verge of collapse, or when he makes a vow
which he forgets to fulfill. Come and see what happened to Jacob: God had
granted him all that he asked for. Now it was up to Jacob to carry out the vow
which he made at a time of suffering but which he had forgotten when times

35 ¹*God said to Jacob, "Arise — go up to Beth-el and dwell there, and make an altar there to God Who appeared to you when you fled from Esau your brother."* ² *So Jacob said to his household and to all who were with him, "Discard the alien gods that are in your midst; cleanse yourselves and change your clothes.*

were good. So God sent him warnings by means of trials — the tense meeting with his brother Esau, the nocturnal struggle with the angel — but Jacob failed to understand. Then Jacob was afflicted with the tragedy with his daughter, and when even then he did not realize what was wrong, God imposed still more unhappiness upon him with the death of Rachel. Then God said: How long will this righteous man be tested without understanding his sin? I will now tell him: "Go to Beth-el, and make an altar there to the Almighty, Who revealed Himself to you when you were running away from your brother Esau." The proverb says, continues the Midrash, "If your sieve becomes clogged, beat upon it." The Torah itself is clear on this point: *When you have made a vow to God, do not delay in carrying it out, otherwise Hashem, your God, will not fail to call you to account and you will have to answer for a sin* (Deuteronomy 23:22).

וְשֶׁב־שָׁם — *And dwell there.* "I do not know for what reason," says *Ramban*. But *R' Bachya, Sforno,* and others interpret this injunction on a spiritual level: "Come back to yourself" (in a figurative sense) after all your past disappointments. Just as Jacob returns to the place which was the starting point for his family life and the creation of the future Jewish nation, he is invited to examine his conscience and to come still closer to God after the many ordeals which he has suffered. This allusion to the return to God, contained in the figurative meaning of the word וְשֶׁב, could be why Jacob ordered the members of his family to prepare themselves, spiritually as well as physically, for a possible Divine revelation at Beth-el. (The term וְשֶׁב also could mean: wait there — for the Divine manifestation.) Indeed, it was at this predestined spot, the future site of the Temple of Jerusalem, that Jacob and his family were to receive the name "Israel," which consecrated their future national and historic mission. Jacob knew Beth-el as "the gate to Heaven," where God had appeared to him for the first time.

2. אֶת־אֱלֹהֵי הַנֵּכָר — *The alien gods.* See *Deuteronomy* 32:16, where *Rashi* explains the term אֱלֹהֵי נֵכָר in the sense of "gods of strangers," whereas *Ramban* and *Ibn Ezra* explain: "gods foreign to the Holy Land."

וְהִטַּהֲרוּ — *Cleanse yourselves. R' Bachya:* Here the Torah teaches us that sin is called an impurity (e.g., *Ezekiel* 20:7), just as forsaking sin is called an act of purification (e.g., *Leviticus* 16:30; *Psalms* 51:4). The Torah considers each sin as a moral blemish, a stain on our soul for as long as it is not completely removed.

וְהַחֲלִיפוּ שִׂמְלֹתֵיכֶם — *And change your clothes.* Note the analogy with the order given by Moses before the Revelation at Sinai: *He sanctified the people and they*

ג וְנָק֨וּמָה וְנַעֲלֶ֖ה בֵּֽית־אֵ֑ל וְאֶֽעֱשֶׂה־שָּׁ֣ם מִזְבֵּ֗חַ לָאֵ֞ל הָעֹנֶ֤ה
ד אֹתִי֙ בְּי֣וֹם צָֽרָתִ֔י וַיְהִי֙ עִמָּדִ֔י בַּדֶּ֖רֶךְ אֲשֶׁ֥ר הָלָֽכְתִּי: וַיִּתְּנ֣וּ
אֶֽל־יַעֲקֹ֗ב אֵ֣ת כָּל־אֱלֹהֵ֤י הַנֵּכָר֙ אֲשֶׁ֣ר בְּיָדָ֔ם וְאֶת־הַנְּזָמִ֖ים
אֲשֶׁ֣ר בְּאָזְנֵיהֶ֑ם וַיִּטְמֹ֤ן אֹתָם֙ יַעֲקֹ֔ב תַּ֖חַת הָאֵלָ֥ה אֲשֶׁ֥ר
ה עִם־שְׁכֶֽם: וַיִּסָּ֑עוּ וַיְהִ֣י ׀ חִתַּ֣ת אֱלֹהִ֗ים עַל־הֶֽעָרִים֙

washed their clothing (*Exodus* 19:14). For the family of Jacob, the ascent to Beth-el, where God had revealed Himself to the patriarch, had the same significance as the assembly at Mount Sinai had for his descendants.

3. לָאֵל הָעֹנֶה אֹתִי — *To God Who answered me.* Of the various attributes of the Supreme Being, the Divine name אֵל is the one which Jacob invokes most frequently. It recurs several times in this chapter and figures both in the name given to the place of revelation (בֵּית אֵל) and in the one given to Jacob as a title of honor: יִשְׂרָאֵל. As the Midrash points out and demonstrates, this name designates God as the Merciful Being, מִדַּת הָרַחֲמִים (*Mechilta, Exodus* 15:2). Cf., for example, the thirteen attributes of Divine goodness: ה' ה' אֵל רַחוּם וְחַנּוּן (ibid. 34:6). Now, not only did Jacob's character tend towards the principle of רַחֲמִים, as was noted in our commentary on 25:27, but his life itself as a whole bore the stamp of מִדַּת הָרַחֲמִים. In contrast to the living conditions of his grandfather Abraham and his father Isaac, Jacob's destiny was under dark clouds and the shadows of night; his life was one long series of painful ordeals while external joys were granted him only for short periods and then only very rarely. But just as the night already looks toward morning, bringing with it the certitude that there exists a God of mercy, Who faithfully watches over those who sleep, so too those who suffer feel that there is a protecting and righteous God, Who never abandons us, even in life's darkest hours. This is why Jacob directs his prayer to God in the evening, at the hour of sunset (cf. our commentary on 28:11). This prayer of *Maariv* is an appeal to the Divine attribute of רַחֲמִים and it begins with the invocation: וְהוּא רַחוּם. The patriarch's repeated appeal to God as אֵל which indicates מִדַּת הָרַחֲמִים (as in אֵל רַחוּם) is based on the same idea.

בְּיוֹם צָרָתִי — *In my time of distress.* God had commanded Jacob to erect an altar to the Almighty, Who had appeared to him when he fled from Esau, but Jacob wants to pay homage to God not only for past kindnesses but also for those of the present. And so he uses the present tense: הָעֹנֶה אֹתִי, to God, *Who answers me* in my time of distress. He experiences Divine salvation as an uninterrupted, continuing reality. Even at the end of his life, he once again uses the present tense to invoke the angel who saves him from all harm (הַמַּלְאָךְ הַגֹּאֵל אֹתִי). For Jacob, Divine Providence is always present, always near to man, always merciful. Accordingly, it is this characteristic faith of Jacob which the Psalmist recommends to all who are in distress: יַעַנְךָ ה' בְּיוֹם צָרָה, *May Hashem answer you on your day of trouble,* יְשַׂגֶּבְךָ שֵׁם אֱלֹהֵי יַעֲקֹב, *May the name of the God of Jacob protect you* (*Psalms* 20:2). *The name of the God of Jacob* refers to

³ *Then come, let us go up to Beth-el; I will make there an altar to God Who answered me in my time of distress, and was with me on the road that I traveled."* ⁴ *So they gave to Jacob all the alien gods that were in their possession, as well as the rings that were in their ears, and Jacob buried them underneath the terebinth near Shechem.* ⁵ *They set out, and there fell a Godly terror on the cities*

the name אֵל, representing the principle of mercy, as was explained above. Divine love is infinite and inexhaustible; it knows neither past nor future but only the eternal present.

4. וְאֶת־הַנְּזָמִים אֲשֶׁר בְּאָזְנֵיהֶם — *The rings that were in their ears.* They handed over to Jacob more than he had asked of them. The rings were not just ornaments but amulets or talismans, as the *Targum Yonasan* points out. The members of Jacob's family understood that the impending appearance before God meant that they would have to rid themselves of all traces of impurity. They would have to devote their entire being to the God of Israel. The external purification was to bring about moral purification. Such, in a general way, is the purpose of the Divine commandments (cf. *Sefer HaChinuch* ס"י כ').

וַיִּטְמֹן אֹתָם יַעֲקֹב תַּחַת הָאֵלָה — *And Jacob buried them underneath the terebinth.* He did not burn them, for he wanted to keep them as a souvenir of their sin of idol-worship (פי' הטור). But an instrument of sin continues to have a harmful effect as long as it is not completely destroyed. As it turned out, many centuries later the Samaritans discovered a statue of a dove high on Mount Gerizim where they built their temple. They took it and worshiped it. This idol was one of those which Jacob had concealed under the terebinth (*Tosafos* to *Chullin* 6a).

עִם־שְׁכֶם — *Near Shechem.* The Torah makes a point of mentioning that Shechem was nearby. The reason for this becomes clearer in the light of what we have just explained: Shechem was indeed "a place predestined for tragedies; it was there that Dinah was raped, there Joseph was sold, and there the kingdom of David was divided, as narrated in *I Kings* 12:1" (*Rashi* on 37:14).

5. וַיִּסָּעוּ — *They set out.* The *Book of Wars of the Sons of Jacob*, also called מִדְרָשׁ וַיִּסָּעוּ after the first word in this verse, describes "the three great wars which the populace near Shechem waged against the family of Jacob. The latter would have been in great peril had it not been for the armed intervention of the patriarch himself, as is mentioned in *Genesis* 48:22" (cf. *Rashi*). The neighboring peoples learned of the exploits of Simeon and Levi at Shechem and felt that if two of Jacob's sons were able to do such a thing, all the sons banding together would be capable of destroying the entire world. And so they united against them. But they were struck with a Divine terror, that is to say, a fear inspired by God (cf. *Pirkei D'Rabbi Eliezer* 38). However, remarks *Ramban*, the Torah limits itself to mentioning that the inhabitants of the neighboring cities broke off their pursuit and that Jacob continued on his way safe and sound, with fully "all the

וֹ אֲשֶׁר סְבִיבֹתֵיהֶם וְלֹא רָדְפוּ אַחֲרֵי בְּנֵי יַעֲקֹב: וַיָּבֹא יַעֲקֹב
לוּזָה אֲשֶׁר בְּאֶרֶץ כְּנַעַן הִוא בֵּית־אֵל הוּא וְכָל־הָעָם
זֹ אֲשֶׁר־עִמּוֹ: וַיִּבֶן שָׁם מִזְבֵּחַ וַיִּקְרָא לַמָּקוֹם אֵל בֵּית־אֵל כִּי
חֹ שָׁם נִגְלוּ אֵלָיו הָאֱלֹהִים בְּבָרְחוֹ מִפְּנֵי אָחִיו: וַתָּמָת דְּבֹרָה
מֵינֶקֶת רִבְקָה וַתִּקָּבֵר מִתַּחַת לְבֵית־אֵל תַּחַת הָאַלּוֹן וַיִּקְרָא
שְׁמוֹ אַלּוֹן בָּכוּת:
טֹ וַיֵּרָא אֱלֹהִים אֶל־יַעֲקֹב עוֹד בְּבֹאוֹ מִפַּדַּן אֲרָם וַיְבָרֶךְ אֹתוֹ:

people who were with him." No more detail is given because a נֵס נִסְתָּר, *a hidden miracle* (attributable to an exceptional physical force), had occurred here and the Torah does not generally note such a fact.

6. וַיָּבֹא יַעֲקֹב לוּזָה — *Thus Jacob came to Luz.* On this name and the name Beth-El, see our commentary to 28:19.

7. וַיִּבֶן שָׁם מִזְבֵּחַ — *And he built an altar there.* When Abraham and Isaac built their altars, as a rule a detail was added in the Torah's description: וַיִּקְרָא בְּשֵׁם ה'. *Ramban* notes that the first two patriarchs loudly proclaimed the name of God to their fellow-citizens before the altars which they erected, whereas Jacob was able to spread the faith in God by his words and by the example of his sons and his great family (12:8). However, the altar which Jacob built here at God's invitation was a concrete act in God's honor and it was meant to express Jacob's profound gratitude for all the kindnesses he had received (*Sforno*).

8. וַתָּמָת דְּבֹרָה מֵינֶקֶת רִבְקָה — *Deborah, the wet-nurse of Rebecca, died. Ramban* rejects *Rashi's* explanation (quoting R' *Moshe HaDarshan*) that Deborah was probably Rebecca's former nurse, mentioned at the time of her marriage (24:59) and that Rebecca had sent this nurse to Jacob to urge him to leave Padan Aram, as she had originally planned with Jacob prior to his departure. It is unlikely that Rebecca would have sent a messenger as old as her nurse. This refers rather to another former nurse who had remained at Laban's and whom, when Jacob left Laban's, he took home with him to help look after his aged mother.

מִתַּחַת לְבֵית־אֵל — *Below Beth-el.* Why is the account of Jacob's sojourn in Beth-el suddenly interrupted by this verse about the death of an aged nurse, whose passing away hardly justifies eternal commemoration and the consecration of an "oak of weeping"? *Ramban* answers that one has to "read between the lines." This can only be explained by the *aggadah* which *Rashi* quotes: by implication it is referring to the death of Rebecca herself which occurred at this time. Jacob wept in mourning for his mother. She had reached the age of 133 (cf. *Tosafos* to *Yevamos* 61b) and had passed away without having seen her beloved son since he had fled on her advice thirty-six years before (on this, see our commentary to 27:45). So that when God appeared to Jacob again (verse 9), it was in order to give him "the blessing for mourners" (*Rashi*).

which were around them, so that they did not pursue Jacob's sons.
⁶ *Thus Jacob came to Luz in the land of Canaan — it is Beth-el — he, and all the people who were with him.* ⁷ *And he built an altar there and called the place El-beth-el, for it was there that God had been revealed to him during his flight from his brother.*
⁸ *Deborah, the wet-nurse of Rebecca, died, and she was buried below Beth-el, below the plateau; and he named it Allon-bachuth.*
⁹ *And God appeared to Jacob again when he came from Paddan-aram, and He blessed him.*

Why does the Torah not let us know clearly the day of Rebecca's death? Why is this death announced only by allusion, in a veiled hint? *Rashi* answers: So that people should not curse her as "the mother who gave birth to Esau." That is why the Torah says nothing about her death. But this argument does not seem satisfactory to *Ramban*. For, on the one hand, the Torah does not mention Leah's death either (there are however special reasons for this, noted in our commentary to 29:31) and, on the other hand, the Torah does not hesitate at all to record the death of Isaac, "buried by Esau and Jacob, his sons" (at the end of this chapter). And so it is quite in order to mention the reason for this as given in the *Midrash Tanchuma* (ד' תצא). When Rebecca died, people said, "Who is there to accompany her coffin? Abraham is dead, Isaac is blind and does not leave his house, Jacob is far away in Padan Aram and the wicked Esau despises her." What did they do? They carried her coffin out at night, and hence the Torah only mentions it indirectly. From this it would seem that Esau was the only member of his family to be present at his mother's burial and this was just what they wanted to avoid publicizing. It is in this perspective that *Rashi's* comment is to be taken.

9. וַיֵּרָא אֱלֹהִים אֶל־יַעֲקֹב עוֹד — *And God appeared to Jacob again*. According to *Rashi*, quoting *Midrash Tanchuma*, the purpose of this appearance was for God to give Jacob "the blessing for mourners" on the loss of his mother. And so the abundant promises which God makes here seem to be ways of comforting and consoling the patriarch. But others explain: "God does not bestow a title of honor on anyone until He has put him to the test. If he triumphs He elevates him to glory." *He who ascends the mountain of Hashem, he who stands in His holy place . . . he shall receive a blessing from Hashem* (Psalms 24:5). Such was the case with Jacob, who gloriously triumphed over a long series of ordeals and received from God the blessing and title of honor: יִשְׂרָאֵל (*Bamidbar Rabbah* 15). Twenty-two years earlier, while he was in a state of depression and material deprivation, Jacob had received promises of Divine protection at this very place. Now he receives proof of God's satisfaction together with the consecration of his offspring into a future nation, whose historic mission is summed up in the name which God had given him: יִשְׂרָאֵל, fighter for the Almighty. And so a new stage begins at the place predestined for the family of Israel.

י וַיֹּאמֶר־לֹו אֱלֹהִים שִׁמְךָ יַעֲקֹב לֹא־יִקָּרֵא שִׁמְךָ עֹוד יַעֲקֹב

יא כִּי אִם־יִשְׂרָאֵל יִהְיֶה שְׁמֶךָ וַיִּקְרָא אֶת־שְׁמֹו יִשְׂרָאֵל: וַיֹּאמֶר

לֹו אֱלֹהִים אֲנִי אֵל שַׁדַּי פְּרֵה וּרְבֵה גֹּוי וּקְהַל גֹּויִם יִהְיֶה מִמֶּךָּ

ששי יב וּמְלָכִים מֵחֲלָצֶיךָ יֵצֵאוּ: וְאֶת־הָאָרֶץ אֲשֶׁר נָתַתִּי לְאַבְרָהָם

וּלְיִצְחָק לְךָ אֶתְּנֶנָּה וּלְזַרְעֲךָ אַחֲרֶיךָ אֶתֵּן אֶת־הָאָרֶץ:

10. לֹא־יִקָּרֵא שִׁמְךָ עֹוד יַעֲקֹב — *Your name shall not always be called Jacob.* On the meaning of the names Jacob and Israel see our commentary on 27:36 and 32:27 and 29. Just as God engraved the seal of His covenant in the flesh of His people, so too He inscribes His name in the name of His people so that the latter will be eternally associated with Him, as it is said: *Israel, my servant, it is by you that I want to be glorified* (Isaiah 49:3; *Tanchuma Kedoshim*).

כִּי אִם־יִשְׂרָאֵל יִהְיֶה שְׁמֶךָ — *But Israel shall be your name.* The Talmud stipulates that the patriarch can be called either Jacob or Israel, but whoever calls Abraham by his original name, Abram, transgresses a positive precept (*Berachos* 13a). The *Zohar* explains the difference by pointing out that Israel is a "qualifier," a characterizing name, whereas the change from Abram to Abraham corresponds to a change in the actual destiny of this person. The change of name "took Abram out of his destiny. He had seen in the stars that he would not have children. Now Abram will not have any children, but Abraham will" (*Rashi* on 15:5). Hence, this change of name is of a fundamental nature. But the name Israel is a title of honor "which means prince (שַׂר) and noble" (*Rashi*). This appellation would thus depend on the level of personal dignity. The Torah brings out the difference when it uses an imperative for Abraham's new name (וְהָיָה שִׁמְךָ אַבְרָהָם, *your name shall be Abraham*), whereas for Jacob it uses the future tense: יִשְׂרָאֵל יִהְיֶה שְׁמֶךָ, *Israel shall be your name.* This means that the name Israel will only be borne exclusively and permanently at some future time when the nation will have become a "kingdom of priests and a holy people." Is not the Name *par excellence* of God Himself the Tetragrammaton (שֵׁם הֲוָיָ), which designates Him as the God of Love? I am הֲוָיָ, such is My name — אֲנִי ה' הוּא שְׁמִי, proclaims God (*Isaiah* 42:8). However, Hashem will similarly only be the one and unique God in messianic times, when the reign of love will extend throughout the universe — בַּיֹּום הַהוּא יִהְיֶה ה' אֶחָד וּשְׁמֹו אֶחָד, *on that day Hashem will be One and His Name will be One* (*Zechariah* 14:9).

11. וַיֹּאמֶר לֹו אֱלֹהִים — *And God said to him.* The constant re-echoing of the Name אֱלֹהִים in this revelation to Jacob is as it were a Divine response directed to the supplication he made at the time of his vow: וְהָיָה ה' לִי לֵאלֹהִים, *And Hashem will be a God to me.* (See our commentary on 28:21 for the meaning of this request.) Here, Jacob is given confirmation that this part of his vow was also fulfilled. However, God will grant His blessing to the patriarch with His name שַׁדַּי, just as Isaac invoked this name when he blessed his son and prayed for the Divine blessings for his offspring (28:3). On that occasion it was shown why the

> ¹⁰ *Then God said to him, "Your name is Jacob. Your name shall not always be called Jacob, but Israel shall be your name." Thus He called his name Israel.* ¹¹ *And God said to him, "I am El Shaddai. Be fruitful and multiply; a nation and a congregation of nations shall descend from you, and kings shall issue from your loins.* ¹² *The land that I gave to Abraham and to Isaac, I will give to you; and to your offspring after you I will give the land."*

name שַׁדַּי regularly appears as being, in the words of the *Baal HaTurim* the One "Who calls forth fruitfulness and procreation" (see our commentary, ibid.).

פְּרֵה וּרְבֵה — *Be fruitful and multiply.* Since eleven of the sons of Jacob were already born, this blessing in a literal sense can refer only to Benjamin, who was not yet born but who was then being carried in the womb (*Rashi*). The subsequent references to nations and kings therefore apply to Benjamin's descendants. But the *Targum Yonasan* relates these blessings more generally to the creation of the Jewish people, which stems from the family of the patriarch: "a holy nation and a community of priests and prophets will be born from you."

גּוֹי וּקְהַל גּוֹיִם — *A nation and a congregation of nations.* The nation which is to descend from Jacob will be in its external relations a single unit (גּוֹי) and internally a united group with different kinds of people and professions (קְהַל גּוֹיִם). Each tribe will constitute a unit by itself. The people issuing from Jacob, called on to transmit the ideal of monotheism to mankind, will not have to be all of the same character. On the contrary, they should have a whole multiplicity of national characteristics; the tribes should possess a range of different aspects, military, mercantile, agricultural, scientific, etc., with the aim of clearly showing to the world that the sanctification of human life by the Divine law does not depend at all on any special profession or any particular national characteristic. The whole of humanity in all its richness and variety is called on to become imbued with the Divine spirit proclaimed by Jewry and to forge all the different individual and national characteristics of mankind into one powerful unit which will build the kingdom of God on earth. The following verse, proclaiming that God will give "the land" to the patriarch's descendants, could then mean (as *Sforno* takes it and as is referred to in *Psalms* 37:29: צַדִּיקִים יִירְשׁוּ אָרֶץ, *the righteous will inherit the earth*) that their heritage will become humanity's heritage and that one day it will reach to the ends of the earth (*R' S.R. Hirsch*). (However, another interpretation is given in our commentary on 48:4.)

12. וְאֶת־הָאָרֶץ אֲשֶׁר נָתַתִּי — *The land that I gave.* The verb "give" is repeated three times in this verse, as if to solemnly confirm, as had been confirmed for his ancestors, Jacob's formal and inviolable rights to possession of the Holy Land. (According to *R' Bachya*, it is only the word אָרֶץ in the second half of the verse that refers to this possession, since the same word at the beginning of the verse refers to blessings of a temporal nature.)

יג־יד וַיַּעַל מֵעָלָיו אֱלֹהִים בַּמָּקוֹם אֲשֶׁר־דִּבֶּר אִתּוֹ: וַיַּצֵּב יַעֲקֹב
מַצֵּבָה בַּמָּקוֹם אֲשֶׁר־דִּבֶּר אִתּוֹ מַצֶּבֶת אָבֶן וַיַּסֵּךְ עָלֶיהָ נֶסֶךְ
טו וַיִּצֹק עָלֶיהָ שָׁמֶן: וַיִּקְרָא יַעֲקֹב אֶת־שֵׁם הַמָּקוֹם אֲשֶׁר דִּבֶּר
טז אִתּוֹ שָׁם אֱלֹהִים בֵּית־אֵל: וַיִּסְעוּ מִבֵּית אֵל וַיְהִי־עוֹד
כִּבְרַת־הָאָרֶץ לָבוֹא אֶפְרָתָה וַתֵּלֶד רָחֵל וַתְּקַשׁ בְּלִדְתָּהּ:
יז וַיְהִי בְהַקְשֹׁתָהּ בְּלִדְתָּהּ וַתֹּאמֶר לָהּ הַמְיַלֶּדֶת אַל־תִּירְאִי
יח כִּי־גַם־זֶה לָךְ בֵּן: וַיְהִי בְּצֵאת נַפְשָׁהּ כִּי מֵתָה וַתִּקְרָא שְׁמוֹ

13. וַיַּעַל מֵעָלָיו אֱלֹהִים — *Then God ascended from upon him.* To this phrase, which is like the one involving Abraham (17:22), the Sages of the Midrash give the following interpretation: הָאָבוֹת הֵן הַמֶּרְכָּבָה, *the patriarchs are the chariot of the Divinity,* that is to say, the upholders and heralds of the Divine Majesty on earth. They are the ones who carry the idea of a living God among mankind. The Torah expresses this concept in these words: *God ascended from over him,* that is, the Divine glory rose in the eyes of people because of Jacob's personality. In *Mesillas Yesharim* (ch. 26), *R' Moshe Chaim Luzzatto* writes, apropos of this: "The difference between purity and holiness is that for those who have attained the level of purity, material (or physical) acts are even for them necessities of nature. They carry them out with this in mind so that such acts lose their inherently gross character and become pure. But they still do not possess the character of sacred acts, since they are looked upon as a necessary evil. However, for the man who is holy, who is constantly in close communion with God, whose soul, filled with love and veneration, is following the Creator in light and truth — this earthly life with all its material necessities is already identical to the eternal life in the presence of God. This man himself becomes as it were a temple, a sanctuary, an altar. The Divine Majesty dwells upon him as it dwelt on the Temple. It is in this sense that the Sages said: 'The patriarchs form the Divine chariot.' "

בַּמָּקוֹם אֲשֶׁר־דִּבֶּר אִתּוֹ — *In the place where He had spoken with him. Rashi:* "I do not know what this wants to teach us." But *Ramban* reminds us here of the words of the prophet *Ezekiel,* בָּרוּךְ כְּבוֹד ה' מִמְּקוֹמוֹ, *the Divine glory is blessed from the* [i.e. every] *place* (3:12). To be sure, the site where God now reveals Himself to Jacob could have been somewhere other than that which he had previously named Beth-el. The Gaon of Vilna teaches that Jacob gave the name Beth-el to three different cities (cf. *Joshua* 16:2). In so doing, he wants to show that the Divine Presence is not at all bound to a particular place. Wherever a man is found worthy of being addressed by the Divine voice, that place can be consecrated as a place of revelation — that place can become a "Beth-el." Not the place but the man is called upon to be the base for the Divine Presence, as was just explained above.

14. וַיַּצֵּב יַעֲקֹב מַצֵּבָה — *Jacob had set up a pillar.* The difference between מַצֵּבָה and מִזְבֵּחַ is pointed out by *Ramban* (on 28:18). A מַצֵּבָה is built of a single stone

¹³ *Then God ascended from upon him in the place where He had spoken with him.*

¹⁴ *Jacob had set up a pillar at the place where God had spoken with him — a pillar of stone — and he poured a libation upon it, and poured oil upon it.* ¹⁵ *Then Jacob called the name of the place where God had spoken with him Beth-el.*

¹⁶ *They journeyed from Beth-el and there was still a stretch of land to go to Ephrath, when Rachel went into labor and had difficulty in her childbirth.* ¹⁷ *And it was when she had difficulty in her labor that the midwife said to her, "Have no fear, for this one, too, is a son for you."* ¹⁸ *And it came to pass, as her soul was departing — for she died — that she called his name*

and is reserved for libations of wine and oil, whereas a מִזְבֵּחַ comprises several stones and is destined for sacrifices. By erecting this monument, by consecrating it and calling it בֵּית־אֵל, Jacob formally carried out the vow which he had made twenty-two years before, when he fled from his brother and departed from his father's house (*Rashi* on 28:2). As for the other part of his vow, concerning the separation of tithes from all that God will give him, this he had already performed previously, as was noted in our commentary to 32:14.

16. וַיִּסְעוּ מִבֵּית אֵל — *They journeyed from Beth-el.* Rachel's death took place in the territory of Canaan and so did her burial, but it was not far from the border, as *Ramban* demonstrates in his controversy with *Rashi* (48:7).

17. אַל־תִּירְאִי — *Have no fear.* Rachel had prayed to God for a second son. Now, in pain from the travail of childbirth, she feared for the life of her child although not caring about her own life (see *Niddah* 44a on the danger for the child in a difficult birth). This is why the midwife comforted her. She assured her that there was no danger for the child and told her not to fear that it would be a girl, the pains of whose birth are usually more difficult than those of a boy's (*R' Chaim ben Attar* and *Sforno*, following *Niddah* 31a).

18. וַיְהִי בְּצֵאת נַפְשָׁה — *And it came to pass, as her soul was departing.* She was still able to give a name to her son, "because a woman in labor is one of the three instances where death can come suddenly even though just before the person had been full of vigor and able to converse" (*Eruvin* 41b).

כִּי מֵתָה — *For she died.* Seder Olam establishes that Rachel died at the age of thirty-six (chapter 2; her sister Leah also died young, at forty-four. However, the Torah passes over her death in silence for the reasons indicated in our commentary on 29:31). Rachel's premature death prompted our Sages to look for its special causes. They stressed two reasons for it, one of which was mentioned by *Rashi* at the time of Jacob's unfortunate utterance condemning to death whoever might be hiding his father-in-law's idols. "It is from this curse that Rachel died on the way," comments *Rashi* (31:32; cf. our commentary there). On

יט בֶּן־אוֹנִי וְאָבִיו קָרָא־לוֹ בִנְיָמִין: וַתָּמָת רָחֵל וַתִּקָּבֵר בְּדֶרֶךְ
כ אֶפְרָתָה הִוא בֵּית לָחֶם: וַיַּצֵּב יַעֲקֹב מַצֵּבָה עַל־קְבֻרָתָהּ
כא הִוא מַצֶּבֶת קְבֻרַת־רָחֵל עַד־הַיּוֹם: וַיִּסַּע יִשְׂרָאֵל וַיֵּט
כב אָהֳלֹה מֵהָלְאָה לְמִגְדַּל־עֵדֶר: וַיְהִי בִּשְׁכֹּן יִשְׂרָאֵל בָּאָרֶץ

the other hand, she was a victim of her husband's negligence concerning the fulfillment of his vow, as was also noted in our commentary on 35:1. The repercussions of such an omission can even affect the spouse (cf. *Shabbos* 32b). However, *Ramban* gives a totally different argument. His starting point is his previously mentioned thesis that the patriarchs observed the Divine laws only on the sacred ground of the Promised Land. *Ramban* holds that marriage to two sisters was legal outside the land but not within it. Accordingly, the death of Rachel (whom Jacob married after marrying her sister) as soon as they entered the Holy Land was an act of Providence (*Ramban* to *Leviticus* 18:25). Moreover, it was for this very reason that Jacob decided to bury Rachel "on the road to Ephrath," and not in the Cave of Machpelah, even though it was not far from where she had died (*Ramban* to *Genesis* 48:7). Leah, the one he married first, was to be buried in the Cave of Machpelah. "He was ashamed in front of his ancestors to bury Rachel there" (ibid.).

וַתִּקְרָא שְׁמוֹ בֶּן־אוֹנִי — *That she called his name Ben Oni.* The life of Rachel, who died en route and was buried along the way, was, despite its brevity, an inspiration, full of passion and struggle, marked by a self-denial and a devotion rarely encountered in the history of man. She gives birth to life once more as she dies. בֶּן אוֹנִי, *the son of my grief,* was what the dying mother called him. But בִּנְיָמִין (בֶּן יְמִין), *son of my right hand,* was his father's name for him; it recalled Rachel, the one who had been his strength and joy, his happiness and light. Benjamin, the fragile child, and Joseph, the son with exceptional intelligence, will take the place which had been Rachel's (*R' S. R. Hirsch*).

וְאָבִיו קָרָא־לוֹ בִנְיָמִין — *But his father called him Benjamin.* Meaning, *Rashi* says, "son of the south." The name was given to him because he alone of all the children was born in Canaan, which is to the south coming from Aram. The word יָמִין is occasionally used to designate the south, as in *Psalms* 89:13. This is why the word is written in full, with the letter *yud* before the final *nun.*

Ramban takes issue with both *Rashi's* logic and his geography. He gives another explanation, involving the double meaning of the word אוֹן. This word can signify grief, suffering, or mourning, as in *Hosea* 9:4 or *Deuteronomy* 26:14, but it can also mean right, strength or success, as in *Genesis* 49:3, *Psalms* 21:9 and 118:16. Now, just after Rachel had given her son a name accentuating the pessimistic significance of the word אוֹן — son of my sorrow — Jacob decided to substitute the optimistic meaning in order to protect the child from any bad omen. The interpretation or the personal meaning which one attaches to the facts and events of existence are among life's imponderables — but it would be wrong

Ben Oni, but his father called him Benjamin. ¹⁹ *Thus Rachel died, and was buried on the road to Ephrath, which is Bethlehem.* ²⁰ *Jacob set up a monument over her grave; it is the monument of Rachel's grave until today.*

²¹ *Israel journeyed on, and he pitched his tent beyond Migdal-eder.* ²² *And it came to pass, while Israel dwelt in that land,*

to neglect them. The Talmud gives us an example of this in the domain of the interpretation of dreams (*Berachos* 57a).

Nevertheless, *Rashi's* view seems just as valid. It is based on the important fact that Benjamin is the only one of Jacob's children to be born in the Holy Land. Abraham had continually headed to the south of the land in search of the place of Divine Inspiration and this site, in the south, was to be the site of the Temple in Jerusalem (*Rashi* on 12:9). The Temple was built on the territory of Benjamin, the one born in the land itself, so that the south appears as his predestined direction. The Divine Majesty "dwells between his shoulders," said Moses of Benjamin (*Deuteronomy* 33:12), and the *Zohar* stresses that the *Shechinah* joined the twelve sons just as Benjamin was born, when the family, as it entered the Holy land, formed a perfect unity. It was the *Shechinah* which filled the void created by Rachel's death. From then on, It faithfully accompanied the family of Israel (*Baal HaTurim* on *Genesis* 46:4) and associated Its name with the names of the twelve tribes in testimony to their dignity (*Rashi* on *Numbers* 26:5). And this earned them the honorable title of שִׁבְטֵי יָ-הּ, *Divine tribes*, which King David gave them (*Psalms* 122:4). [Cf. our commentary on 37:12.]

19. וַתִּקָּבֵר בְּדֶרֶךְ אֶפְרָתָה — *And was buried on the road to Ephrath.* Cf. *Rashi* on 48:7. Jacob said to Joseph before his death, "I know that in your heart you reproach me for having buried her there. But know that it was by God's command that I did it so that she will be able to bring comfort to her children when they pass by on their way to exile in Babylonia under Nebuzaradan. Then Rachel will go out from her tomb and she will cry and pray for Divine mercy on their behalf. As it is said: *A voice is heard in Ramah, etc.* (*Jeremiah* 31:14). And God will answer her, *Your act will have its reward; your children will return to their border* (ibid. 31:15).

20. וַיַּצֵּב יַעֲקֹב מַצֵּבָה עַל־קְבֻרָתָהּ — *Jacob set up a monument over her grave.* As a sequel to the interpretation on the previous verse, the *Zohar* explains: The monument will serve as a landmark for the offspring on their way into exile, showing them Rachel's tomb. And "this monument upon Rachel's grave will remain until the Day," that is to say until the great day of the return to the Holy Land promised to Rachel. The descendants will pass by there again on the way to Ephrath and they will cry with joy and gratitude at Rachel's tomb, and she herself will share their joy and the joy of the *Shechinah*.

21. וַיִּסַּע יִשְׂרָאֵל — *Israel journeyed on.* When the patriarch is called Israel and not Jacob, it is not only a title of honor but also a designation of his moral and spiritual

הַהִוא וַיֵּ֣לֶךְ רְאוּבֵ֗ן וַיִּשְׁכַּב֙ אֶת־בִּלְהָה֙ פִּילֶ֣גֶשׁ אָבִ֔יו
וַיִּשְׁמַ֖ע יִשְׂרָאֵ֑ל
כג וַיִּֽהְי֥וּ בְנֵי־יַעֲקֹ֖ב שְׁנֵ֣ים עָשָׂ֑ר: בְּנֵ֣י לֵאָ֔ה בְּכ֥וֹר יַעֲקֹ֖ב

greatness. Here, after suffering the cruel loss of his young wife coming soon
after that of his mother, Jacob seeks to console himself by heading toward
Jerusalem, the Holy City, the site of Mount Moriah, which was the place of his
father Isaac's *Akeidah*. He spread his tent beyond מִגְדַּל עֵדֶר, the place "where
the king Messiah will reveal himself at the end of days" (*Targum Yonasan*, after
Micah 4:8). The name signifies: *tower of* (the future gathering of) *the* (Jewish)
flock. Jacob again found peace of mind near Mount Moriah and the town of the
future messianic ingathering. He thus surmounted his new trials and became
Israel once again.

From then on, however, he withdrew from earthly cares and consecrated
himself wholly to Divine service (*Radak*). The tent which he had shared with
Rachel (אָהֳלֹה with feminine possessive suffix) he pitched some distance from
the town where the family was encamped. While Rachel was alive Jacob also
lived with Leah and his other wives. But after Rachel's death he separated
himself from them all. This could be what motivated Reuben to remind his
father of his duty to go back and stay with Leah. But the Torah criticizes this
misplaced intervention. It had no effect and Jacob continued to live apart — so
that "the sons of Jacob were (i.e., remained) twelve." This withdrawal could well
be considered the cause for the weakening of the head of the family's authority.
This had dire results. Many errors were committed with dramatic consequences
for the life of a family which had been united in the past, but which now was
witness to growing discord (*R' S. R. Hirsch*).

22. וַיֵּלֶךְ ... וַיִּשְׁכַּב — *Went and lay. Rashi* explains (following the Talmud,
Shabbos 55b): Because he had disturbed the couch of his father, it is considered
as if he had actually lain with her. And why did he do it and defile the couch
of his father (according to the term used by Jacob, *Genesis* 49:4)? Jacob's couch
had been kept constantly in Rachel's tent and not with the other wives. Now
when Rachel died, Jacob removed his couch to Bilhah's tent. Then Reuben came
and took up the cause of his mother, saying: "If my mother's sister was her rival,
must the servant of my mother's sister also be her rival?" That is why "he
disturbed" the couch (either by occupying Bilhah's couch, or by removing that
of his father, or by disturbing the cohabitation of his father with Bilhah —
Midrashim).

R' Shimon ben Elazar adds another argument in defense of Reuben: "Is it
possible," he asks, "that Reuben's descendants would have been called on to
pronounce the curses on Mount Eval and proclaim: *Cursed be he that lies with
his father's wife* (*Deuteronomy* 27:20) — if their ancestor had committed that
very sin?" (*Shabbos* ibid.). Accordingly, he holds that the view that Reuben had
committed a sin is erroneous. But then the question arises, why did the Torah use

that Reuben went and lay with Bilhah, his father's concubine, and Israel heard.

The sons of Jacob were twelve. ²³ *The sons of Leah: Jacob's*

the phrase: "went and lay with"? *Rashi's* reply, that Reuben is held responsible for disturbing his father's couch in the same way "as if he had actually cohabited," seems to contradict the Talmud (*Kiddushin* 40a) which asserts that the intention to commit a sin is not at all equivalent to actually doing the sin. R' Chaim Chizkiya Medini, the author of *S'dei Chemed*, raises this problem and gives detailed arguments for both sides, claiming for *Rashi* that the principle does not apply in the case of incestuous sins (עיי"ש כללים, מערכת מ' כלל כ') (מחשבה רעה דעריות מצרפה למעשה).

But contrary to *Rashi's* opinion (based on the Talmudic source in the name of Rabban Gamliel and R' Elazar Hamodai), two other *Tannaim*, R' Yehoshua and R' Eliezer, take the text literally and consider Reuben guilty of having lain with the wife of his father. This is also the sense of the Aramaic translation of the *Targum Onkelos*, which generally follows these two Sages (עי' נתינה לגר). It has even been suggested that this interpretation of *Onkelos* is why, during the reading of the Torah, this passage of the *Targum* is not to be recited publicly out of respect for Reuben, as the Talmud stipulates in the tractate *Megillah* 25b (ס' העתים). The Sages indeed wanted to protect Reuben's character, for tradition records that he at once realized his sin and that he repented and afflicted himself until the end of his days (*Sifre* to *Deuteronomy* 33). His repentance was accepted and he gained personal merit when he rescued Joseph from the sinister plans of his brothers (cf. *Rashi* on 37:29). According to R' Chanina, Reuben was the only person (besides David) for whom a good deed was accepted as compensation for a sin (*Sifre*, ibid.). His sincere repentance was rewarded by his descendant Hosea's meritorious works on behalf of the duty of *teshuvah*. More than any other prophet, Hosea preached this duty with tireless eloquence (*Genesis Rabbah* 84). Reuben's rehabilitation became complete from the moral point of view when he followed the example of his brother Judah and confessed his sin publicly (*Bava Kamma* 92a; *Tosafos* ד"ה מ'). And so, Moses in his final blessing could erase Jacob's stigmatizing words for his eldest son (49:4) and proclaim: "May Reuben live and not die!" (*Deuteronomy* 33:6). Nevertheless, Reuben's personal rehabilitation did not give him the right to continue in his role as chief of the children of Israel (a right which he had as the firstborn), as *Rashi* notes on the next verse.

וַיִּהְיוּ בְנֵי־יַעֲקֹב שְׁנֵים עָשָׂר — *The sons of Jacob were twelve.* When Israel heard what his son Reuben had done, he was afraid and dreaded that there was amongst his children a bad son, as had been the case with the children of his father and grandfather. But he was told by a heavenly voice that with Reuben's repentance the twelve children were still "Jacob's sons," worthy of their father (*Sifre*, ibid.). The Masoretes marked a pause in the middle of this verse (פִּסְקָה). This indicates that the latter part of the verse is, as it were, the celestial response

כד רְאוּבֵן וְשִׁמְעוֹן וְלֵוִי וְיהוּדָה וְיִשָׂשכָר וּזְבֻלוּן: בְּנֵי רָחֵל יוֹסֵף
כה-כו וּבִנְיָמֵן: וּבְנֵי בִלְהָה שִׁפְחַת רָחֵל דָּן וְנַפְתָּלִי: וּבְנֵי זִלְפָּה
שִׁפְחַת לֵאָה גָּד וְאָשֵׁר אֵלֶּה בְּנֵי יַעֲקֹב אֲשֶׁר יֻלַּד־לוֹ בְּפַדַּן
כז אֲרָם: וַיָּבֹא יַעֲקֹב אֶל־יִצְחָק אָבִיו מַמְרֵא קִרְיַת הָאַרְבַּע הִוא

to Jacob's anguish which was expressed before the pause in the words וַיִּשְׁמַע
יִשְׂרָאֵל, *and Israel heard.*

Here, for the first time, the Torah states the number twelve to enumerate the children of Israel. This number is engraved in the laws of creation. It appears in the twelve signs of the zodiac, in the twelve months of the year, in the twelve hours of the day, and in the twelve hours of the night. Right from its beginnings, the future Jewish nation was established on the same solid and immutable foundation as that which governs the laws of nature (*Genesis Rabbah* 24; cf. our commentary to 46:27).

The Torah enumerates the children of Jacob on sixteen occasions, not always in the same order. This can be explained in the light of *Rashi's* comment: "It wants to teach us that all were equal, all were righteous."

23. בְּכוֹר יַעֲקֹב רְאוּבֵן — *Jacob's firstborn, Reuben.* Right after reporting Reuben's misconduct, the Torah makes a point of telling us that he is Jacob's firstborn. This surely means that Reuben retained his high position as a result of his sincere repentance. He thus acquired his right to personal rehabilitation; however, he could no longer claim that he unreservedly merited the position of leader which his privilege of birth had conferred upon him. "You should be above your brothers in the rights of priesthood and royalty. And why did you lose this and all the advantages that were yours? Because you disturbed your father's bed, you defiled the honor of my couch" (*Rashi* on 49:3). Thus Reuben was deprived of a part of his rights as firstborn, as *Rashi* notes here, but the repercussions would especially be felt by his descendants: the priestly functions ultimately passed (after the sin of the Golden Calf) to the tribe of Levi; the kingship became the prerogative of the tribe of Judah and the "double portion," the legal right of the firstborn, was granted to Joseph (who formed the two tribes of Ephraim and Manasseh) on Jacob's expressed wish (*Genesis* 48:22; cf. *Rashi*). R' Helbo asked R' Shmuel ben Nachmani: "Why did Jacob pick Joseph to receive the double portion?"

"I will answer you with a parable," he replied. "This is like the father of a family who takes an orphan into his home. When the orphan later becomes rich, he says to himself: 'I want to benefit the master of my good fortune.' Now, Jacob and his children were welcomed and fed by Joseph in Egypt like poor orphans and when Jacob was able to do what he wanted with Reuben's double portion, he presented it to Joseph as a sign of gratitude."

"Is that to say," replied R' Helbo, "that if Reuben had not committed a sin Jacob would not have given anything to Joseph? (He could have shown his gratitude without doing so at Reuben's expense.) Your teacher, R' Yochanan,

firstborn, Reuben; Simeon; Levi; Judah; Issachar; and Zebulun.
²⁴ *The sons of Rachel: Joseph and Benjamin.* ²⁵ *The sons of Bilhah,
maidservant of Rachel: Dan and Naphtali.* ²⁶ *And the sons of
Zilpah, maidservant of Leah: Gad and Asher — these are the sons
of Jacob, who were born to him in Paddan Aram.*

²⁷ *Jacob came to Isaac his father, at Mamre, Kiriath-arba; that*

explained it in a different way: The firstborn should have been from Rachel
(whom Jacob had chosen for a wife). However, Leah gave birth first because of
her prayers and supplications. But God restored the firstborn to Rachel as a result
of her modesty (her act of self-denial on Leah's marriage night)" (*Bava Basra*
123a). This argument is also used by the *Zohar* to affirm that Jacob had in no
way transgressed the Biblical prohibition: *He may not designate as firstborn the
son of the preferred one over the son of the disdained one, who is the firstborn*
(*Deuteronomy* 21:16).

For the second time we find Jacob at grips with the problem of the rights of
the firstborn. From the point of view of moral dignity, he proves to be just as
demanding with his own son as he had been with his brother Esau. And we shall
see him once more give the younger son preference over the firstborn with
Joseph's children, Manasseh and Ephraim. We will show on that occasion that
the principle behind the patriarch's actions was to place personal merit before
the privilege of birth (see our commentary to 48:20).

27. וַיָּבֹא יַעֲקֹב אֶל־יִצְחָק אָבִיו — *Jacob came to Isaac his father.* He returned after
being away thirty-six years. Isaac must have been filled with joy at seeing his
son, the heir of the covenant of Abraham, heading such a great family and at
seeing his twelve children "all equal and each one righteous," but alas this joy
was tempered by the recent deaths of Rebecca and Rachel. Jacob dwelt with his
father right up to his death twenty years later. But this stay was once again
deeply saddened by the sale of Joseph in the eighth year. When Isaac died,
twelve years later, they were still under the impression that Joseph was dead.
And so we can see why the words בְּשֵׂיבָה טוֹבָה, *at a good old age,* used in
recording Abraham's death (25:8) are missing in the account of Isaac's death.

Upon departing from his father's house, Jacob had left him in Beer-sheva. It
was there that Abraham had proclaimed the name of God before the altar which
he had built. Isaac had gone there when the famine which had forced him to go
to the land of the Philistines ceased. But now Jacob rejoins his father in Hebron,
where Isaac's parents were buried. Concludes the author of *Sefer Chassidim*
(§306): from this we learn that as a man grows old he should move near the
burial place of his ancestors, if they were righteous, so that he may one day find
eternal rest next to them.

מַמְרֵא — *Mamre. Rashi* adds: That was the name of the plain; Kiriath-arba was
the name of the city. Consequently Jacob and his family settled in the plain on
the outskirts of the city of Hebron, and this once again shows us how he tended

כח חֶבְרֽוֹן אֲשֶׁר־גָּר־שָׁם אַבְרָהָם וְיִצְחָק: וַיֶּהְיוּ יְמֵי יִצְחָק מְאַת
כט שָׁנָה וּשְׁמֹנִים שָׁנָה: וַיִּגְוַע יִצְחָק וַיָּמָת וַיֵּאָסֶף אֶל־עַמָּיו זָקֵן
וּשְׂבַע יָמִים וַיִּקְבְּרוּ אֹתוֹ עֵשָׂו וְיַעֲקֹב בָּנָיו:

לו א-ב וְאֵלֶּה תֹּלְדוֹת עֵשָׂו הוּא אֱדוֹם: עֵשָׂו לָקַח אֶת־נָשָׁיו מִבְּנוֹת
כְּנָעַן אֶת־עָדָה בַּת־אֵילוֹן הַחִתִּי וְאֶת־אָהֳלִיבָמָה בַּת־עֲנָה

to lead a solitary life, apart from the established society. Jacob was aware that he was a גֵּר, a stranger in this land, just as Abraham and Isaac had at times also been a גֵּר in different places (12:10, 21:33, 23:4, 26:3). *Israel dwells in safety (because) alone, that is the desire of Jacob* (Deuteronomy 33:28; according to Netziv). This quality corresponds to a character trait in Jacob already noted in our commentary on 25:27.

28. מְאַת שָׁנָה וּשְׁמֹנִים שָׁנָה — *One hundred and eighty years.* Isaac was able to attain the full cycle of his years; this was not granted to his father Abraham (cf. Rashi on 15:15) nor to his son Jacob, who died at the age of 147.

29. וַיִּגְוַע יִצְחָק וַיָּמָת — *And Isaac expired and died* [painlessly]. See our commentary on 25:8.

וַיִּקְבְּרוּ אֹתוֹ עֵשָׂו וְיַעֲקֹב בָּנָיו — *His sons, Esau and Jacob, buried him.* Jacob let Esau have precedence. He did not wish to take any advantage at all of his legitimate claim to the birthright as indeed he had not done since the first moment they met, for reasons explained in our commentary on 32:5. But the fact that Esau accompanied Jacob does not prompt any favorable comment for Esau although Ishmael was praised when he accompanied Isaac at their father's burial (Rashi on 25:9). On the contrary, R' Levi relates that Isaac had left all his possessions to be divided equally among his two sons and this was why Esau decided to follow his father's coffin. When the time came to divide the inheritance, Esau wanted to choose his share first and to take what was best. But Jacob let him have all the possessions in return for the rights to the land of Canaan and the Cave of Machpelah. After consulting with his next of kin, Esau accepted. He signed a contract duly drawn up, which guaranteed the rights of Jacob in perpetuity (Pirkei D'Rabbi Eliezer 38). A "historical tradition" cited by the Midrash on Psalms 18:41 teaches us that Esau tried to kill Jacob after Isaac's burial. Had he not sworn, "May the days of mourning for my father draw near then I will kill my brother Jacob" (27:41)? But Judah intervened just in time and killed Esau. This tradition contradicts the account given in the Talmud (Sotah 13a) which designates Dan's son Hushim as Esau's executioner and declares that he killed Esau on the day of Jacob's burial, because of Esau's opposition to having this burial in the Cave of Machpelah. The Tosafists try to reconcile these two traditions (Gittin 55b).

36.

1. וְאֵלֶּה תֹּלְדוֹת עֵשָׂו — *And these are the descendants of Esau.* This genealogical listing follows the one for the children of Esau's brother, Jacob. The genealogy is

is Hebron where Abraham and Isaac sojourned. [28] *Isaac's days were one hundred and eighty years.* [29] *And Isaac expired and died, and he was gathered to his people, old and fulfilled of days; his sons, Esau and Jacob, buried him.*

36   [1] *And these are the descendants of Esau, he is Edom.* [2] *Esau had taken his wives from among the Canaanite women: Adah, daughter of Elon the Hittite; and Oholibamah, daughter of Anah,*

interrupted by the report of their father Isaac's death. However, this report was inserted here with a purpose even though "it does not follow the chronological order, for Isaac died much later, in fact twelve years after the sale of Joseph," as *Rashi* demonstrates at length. From this anomaly the *Zohar* concludes that the Torah wanted to associate the name of Isaac solely with the offspring of his son Jacob and not with the descendants of his son Esau, who was judged unworthy. Out of respect for the holy personality of this righteous man, Esau's descendants are mentioned only after his death is recorded.

The break in this genealogical listing takes on still another meaning. Until now, among the children of the patriarchs, there had been a mixture of good and bad elements. To be sure, over the centuries idolatry with its vices and corruption had become too profoundly entrenched in men's souls for a single generation to suffice to uproot this atavism. For this, a long process of selection had become indispensable and, right from Abraham's time, this process of extraction and elimination was operative among his offspring in order to separate the wheat from the chaff. The first generation still witnessed an Ishmael appearing beside an Isaac; the second produced an Esau together with a Jacob. But in the third generation Jacob created מִטָּה שְׁלֵמָה, *a perfect family,"* and his twelve sons were, in *Rashi's* words, "all equal and each one righteous." The work of extraction had now been carried through to such an extent that separation between the pure and the impure had been achieved. From now on, the "pure will give birth to pure, the impure to impure" (*Akeidas Yitzchak*). It is important to maintain this separation in order to protect the pure from the subversive influence of the impure. The Torah considers this requirement important enough to warrant making a noticeable separation in the text. After giving the enumeration of the member's of Jacob's family its due place, the Torah ends the chapter by departing from the chronological order and reporting Isaac's death. After this break, it lists the family of bastard children fathered by Esau.

2. אֶת־עָדָה בַּת־אֵילוֹן — *Adah, daughter of Elon.* She is identical with Basemath (26:34), as *Rashi* explains. Oholibamah, daughter of Anah is identical with Judith (ibid.). Regarding the double names and synonyms to be found in this chapter and in other historical sections of the Torah, remember that even among those of Abraham's family we find quite a few double names, for example: *Abram, Abraham; Sarai, Sarah; Esau, Edom; Jacob, Israel; Benjamin, Ben Oni.*

ג בַּת־צִבְעוֹן הַחִוִּי: וְאֶת־בָּשְׂמַת בַּת־יִשְׁמָעֵאל אֲחוֹת נְבָיוֹת:
ד וַתֵּלֶד עָדָה לְעֵשָׂו אֶת־אֱלִיפָז וּבָשְׂמַת יָלְדָה אֶת־רְעוּאֵל:
ה וְאָהֳלִיבָמָה יָלְדָה אֶת־יְעִישׁ וְאֶת־יַעְלָם וְאֶת־קֹרַח
                                                       יְעוּשׁ ק'
ו אֵלֶּה בְּנֵי עֵשָׂו אֲשֶׁר יֻלְּדוּ־לוֹ בְּאֶרֶץ כְּנָעַן: וַיִּקַּח עֵשָׂו אֶת־
נָשָׁיו וְאֶת־בָּנָיו וְאֶת־בְּנֹתָיו וְאֶת־כָּל־נַפְשׁוֹת בֵּיתוֹ וְאֶת־
מִקְנֵהוּ וְאֶת־כָּל־בְּהֶמְתּוֹ וְאֵת כָּל־קִנְיָנוֹ אֲשֶׁר רָכַשׁ בְּאֶרֶץ
ז כְּנָעַן וַיֵּלֶךְ אֶל־אֶרֶץ מִפְּנֵי יַעֲקֹב אָחִיו: כִּי־הָיָה רְכוּשָׁם
רָב מִשֶּׁבֶת יַחְדָּו וְלֹא יָכְלָה אֶרֶץ מְגוּרֵיהֶם לָשֵׂאת אֹתָם
ח מִפְּנֵי מִקְנֵיהֶם: וַיֵּשֶׁב עֵשָׂו בְּהַר שֵׂעִיר עֵשָׂו הוּא אֱדוֹם:

So the double names of Elon and Anah etc., as derived by textual comparison, are not surprising.

אָהֳלִיבָמָה — *Oholibamah.* Cf. our commentary to 26:34.

בַּת־עֲנָה בַּת־צִבְעוֹן — *Daughter of Anah, daughter of Zibeon. Rashi* explains that Zibeon had cohabited with his daughter-in-law, Anah's wife, so that Oholibamah was born from both of them. "The text teaches us that they were all of incestuous birth." This serves to illustrate our thoughts on the preceding verse. The Midrash is entirely of this opinion, and gives the number of illegitimate children which Esau brought into the world. Regarding this genealogical chapter the Midrash recalls the words of the prophet Jeremiah: *I have made Esau bare, I have uncovered his secrets, he can no longer hide himself* (49:10).

3. בָּשְׂמַת בַּת־יִשְׁמָעֵאל — *Basemath, daughter of Ishmael.* Cf. our commentary to 28:9.

4. וַתֵּלֶד עָדָה לְעֵשָׂו אֶת־אֱלִיפָז — *Adah bore to Esau Eliphaz.* According to *Rashi,* quoting R' Levi (*Rabbah* 82), Eliphaz had cohabited with Oholibamah, his father's wife, and of this adulterous union was born Korah. *Ramban* disputes this and shows that the text allows several other interpretations more favorable to Eliphaz. Indeed, some traditions teach that Eliphaz, Esau's firstborn, was the most deserving of his children. He had "been raised on Isaac's knee and had refused to obey his father's command to kill Jacob," as *Rashi* mentions (on 29:11). He was acknowledged as worthy of Divine Inspiration and the prophet Eliphaz, the friend of Iyov whose words are reported in the book of *Job,* is none other than Eliphaz, son of Esau (*Rashi* on *Job* 4:1). The *Midrash Yalkut* (ibid.) relates the ideological discussion which took place between Iyov and Eliphaz.

6. וַיֵּלֶךְ אֶל־אֶרֶץ מִפְּנֵי יַעֲקֹב אָחִיו — *And went to a land because of his brother Jacob. Rashi* explains the reasons for this departure: "because of the debt (of exile incurred by Abraham) in the Divine decree (*Genesis* 15:13), a debt which was to be paid by the descendants of Jacob. Esau said to himself: 'I will leave here; I have

daughter of Zibeon the Hivvite; ³ and Basemath, daughter of Ishmael, sister of Nebaioth.

⁴ Adah bore to Esau Eliphaz; Basemath bore Reuel; ⁵ and Oholibamah bore Jeush, Jalam, and Korah; these are Esau's sons who were born to him in the land of Canaan.

⁶ Esau took his wives, his sons, his daughters, and all the members of his household — his livestock and all his animals, and all the wealth he had acquired in the land of Canaan — and went to a land because of his brother Jacob. ⁷ For their wealth was too abundant for them to dwell together, and the land of their sojourns could not support them because of their livestock. ⁸ So Esau settled on Mount Seir; Esau, he is Edom.

no share in the gift which made this land his, nor in the payment of the debt.' And also because he was ashamed of having sold the birthright." So it seems that the reason given in the text: for their wealth was too great etc., is only the apparent reason and not the real underlying cause.

Only later does the Torah reveal that Esau dwelt in the mountain land of Seir. First it just tells us that Esau went "to a land," without specifying which land. This leads *Onkelos* to interpret "to another country" whereas *Rashi* has "in order to settle where he could." But for the *Zohar* the mystery with which the Torah surrounds the reasons for Esau's departure and his destination hints at the fact that Esau's destination was actually of little importance to him, and the apparent reasons did not matter. What did matter for him was to get away from Jacob. Esau no longer wanted to share anything with him, whether in the inheritance of the Promised Land or in the spiritual heritage. He wanted to break off from his brother and his only thought was to go "to another land and settle wherever he could." Henceforth the paths of the two brothers separate definitively. Esau goes "to another land" to devote himself to material satisfactions, whereas Jacob, sheltered from bad influences, will become *the people who are God's portion, Jacob, the lot of His inheritance* (Deuteronomy 32:9).

8. וַיֵּשֶׁב עֵשָׂו בְּהַר שֵׂעִיר. — *So Esau settled on Mount Seir.* His wife Oholibamah was originally from this land, a fact which might have influenced Esau in his decision to reside there. But in any case, Mount Seir had been destined "to Esau for an inheritance," as the Torah tells us in *Deuteronomy* 2:5, and *Rashi* (ibid.) gives the following explanation: "[Said God], 'I have given Abraham [the territory of] ten peoples: seven [will be] for you (the Jews) . . . one for Esau, and the [last] two for Lot's children,' as a reward for his having accompanied Abraham to Egypt and for keeping silent when he said of his wife, 'She is my sister,' He treated him as if he were his (Abraham's) son." Esau also deserved a reward for having voluntarily left his home with all his possessions to make way for his brother. And so along with Seir God gave him a hundred provinces stretching from the Orient to the West, as far as Magdiel, which is none other than Rome, as *Rashi* notes at the end of the chapter (*Pirkei D'Rabbi Eliezer* 38).

ט־ וְאֵ֣לֶּה תֹּלְד֧וֹת עֵשָׂ֛ו אֲבִ֥י אֱד֖וֹם בְּהַ֣ר שֵׂעִֽיר: אֵ֖לֶּה שְׁמ֣וֹת
בְּנֵֽי־עֵשָׂ֑ו אֱלִיפַ֗ז בֶּן־עָדָה֙ אֵ֣שֶׁת עֵשָׂ֔ו רְעוּאֵ֕ל בֶּן־בָּשְׂמַ֖ת
יא אֵ֥שֶׁת עֵשָֽׂו: וַיִּֽהְי֖וּ בְּנֵ֣י אֱלִיפָ֑ז תֵּימָ֣ן אוֹמָ֔ר צְפ֥וֹ וְגַעְתָּ֖ם וּקְנַֽז:
יב וְתִמְנַ֣ע ׀ הָיְתָ֣ה פִילֶ֗גֶשׁ לֶֽאֱלִיפַז֙ בֶּן־עֵשָׂ֔ו וַתֵּ֥לֶד לֶאֱלִיפַ֖ז
יג אֶת־עֲמָלֵ֑ק אֵ֕לֶּה בְּנֵ֥י עָדָ֖ה אֵ֥שֶׁת עֵשָֽׂו: וְאֵ֨לֶּה֙ בְּנֵ֣י רְעוּאֵ֔ל
נַ֥חַת וָזֶ֖רַח שַׁמָּ֣ה וּמִזָּ֑ה אֵ֣לֶּה הָי֔וּ בְּנֵ֥י בָשְׂמַ֖ת אֵ֥שֶׁת עֵשָֽׂו:

עֵשָׂו הוּא אֱדוֹם — *Esau, he is Edom.* Esau had acquired the name Edom when he was thirteen, as a result of his affinity for the color of blood and red food (25:30). It became the name of the nation which he founded, a nation coming from the intermixture of his descendants and those of the Horites, relatives through marriage. At first children of Esau were the princes of this nation, but subsequently they dispossessed the Horites inhabiting Seir, "destroyed them and dwelt in their stead" (*Deuteronomy* 2:12).

That Esau is Edom is repeated three times in this chapter. Some take this repetition as the Torah's indication that the important group of nations called Edom and stretching from East to West, was founded by its ancestor Esau, the son of Isaac and grandson of Abraham. Some ideas concerning the existence of God and certain moral principles going back to the patriarch were in this way spread among the peoples of mankind, albeit in softened and "sweetened" form. The purpose of this chapter would then be to sketch a vast historical picture of the cultural evolution within humanity. This seems to be the view of *Ibn Ezra* (*Genesis* 27:40), who consequently holds that the kingdom of Edom which caused Israel's downfall and brought it into exile and which the prophet Obadiah predicted would be wiped out in the end of days, is not at all the same as the Edomite nations listed here.

Other Sages hold, on the contrary, that these nations are really those making up the kingdom of Edom destined ultimately to disappear (*R' Chaim ben Attar; Abarbanel* to *Isaiah* 63). From this perspective, the chapter would be showing us the contrast between the remarkable development of Esau's offspring and the destiny of the descendants of Jacob, who will be living for long centuries in wretched conditions and will go through great hardship before finding peace. Esau and his descendants live according to the "natural law" of the sword. Their prosperity and their greatness stem directly from the easy success achieved by one who does not keep moral law. But, Jacob and his sons work modestly, to build the true city of God, the only one on which the future of the world will depend. Esau and his descendants have disappeared from the world stage despite their rapid rise and their immediate successes. There is a bit of irony in the long list of princes who are sons and grandsons of Esau, a veritable catalogue of kings and lords. For, of all this splendor, what is left? Jacob and his sons humbly founded the nation which would bring spiritual redemption to the world and which to this day has kept a personality quite like that of its ancestors in all its aspects.

⁹ *And these are the descendants of Esau, ancestor of Edom, on Mount Seir.* ¹⁰ *These are the names of Esau's sons: Eliphaz, son of Adah, Esau's wife; Reuel, son of Basemath, Esau's wife.*

¹¹ *The sons of Eliphaz were: Teman; Omar; Zepho; Gatam; and Kenaz.* ¹² *And Timna was a concubine of Eliphaz, son of Esau, and she bore Amalek to Eliphaz; these are the children of Adah, Esau's wife.*

¹³ *And these are the sons of Reuel: Nahath and Zerah; Shammah and Mizzah — these were the children of Basemath, Esau's wife.*

12. וְתִמְנַע הָיְתָה פִילֶגֶשׁ לֶאֱלִיפַז — *And Timna was a concubine of Eliphaz.* Manasseh, the son of King Chizkiyah, took special pleasure in discussing the Torah in a mocking fashion. Did Moses, he asked, have nothing else to do than to write: *Timna was a concubine of Eliphaz,* or *And Lotan's sister was Timna* (*Sanhedrin* 99b). Quoting this, R' *Yosef Albo* (*Ikkarim* 2:25; cf. *Guide* 3:50) remarks that these apparently insignificant phrases are nevertheless not superfluous. Indeed they teach us that Amalek, Timna's descendant, whom the Torah commanded us to wipe out, is to be differentiated from the rest of Edom's descendants — of whom it is said: *You shall not abhor an Edomite for he is your brother* (*Deuteronomy* 23:8).

The Talmud (ibid.) tells us the following about the birth of Amalek, the father of the Amalekites (cf. *Targum Sheni* on *Esther* 3:1): "Timna was a pagan princess, since she is referred to as a sister of prince Lotan (verse 29). She had wanted to become a proselyte. With this in mind, she had turned to Abraham, Isaac and Jacob. But they did not want to accept her. So she became a concubine to Eliphaz, the son of Esau, for she felt that it was better to be a servant in this nation than a princess in another. She gave birth to Amalek who later came to oppress Israel. And for what reason? Because they should not have spurned her."

Once before, Abraham had been reproached for his lack of missionary zeal. It was not overlooked, said R' Yochanan, that although he renounced his personal share of the spoils after the "war of the kings," he also gave up the captives to whom he had a perfectly legitimate right according to the rules of war of that time. In so doing, he missed the opportunity of bringing some pagans to a belief in God (*Nedarim* 32a).

Certainly no Jew fulfilled the duty of converting people to monotheistic belief with such zeal, perseverance, and success as Abraham. But he wanted the conquest of spirits to be based solely on the persuasive force which comes from the truth. And so like the other patriarchs, he refused to accede to Timna's demand, for he knew that she was above all "desirous of joining with the family of Abraham" whose greatness shone forth over the whole of that generation (*Rashi* on verse 20). Abraham refused to keep the prisoners of war and convert them because he felt that such a conversion would be carried out under coercion

יד וְאֵ֣לֶּה הָי֗וּ בְּנֵ֤י אָהֳלִֽיבָמָה֙ בַּת־עֲנָ֔ה בַּת־צִבְע֖וֹן אֵ֥שֶׁת עֵשָֽׂו

טו וַתֵּ֣לֶד לְעֵשָׂ֔ו אֶת־°יְעִ֥ישׁ וְאֶת־יַעְלָ֖ם וְאֶת־קֹֽרַח׃ אֵ֖לֶּה אַלּוּפֵ֣י

בְנֵי־עֵשָׂ֑ו בְּנֵ֤י אֱלִיפַז֙ בְּכ֣וֹר עֵשָׂ֔ו אַלּ֤וּף תֵּימָן֙ אַלּ֣וּף אוֹמָ֔ר

טז אַלּ֥וּף צְפ֖וֹ אַלּ֣וּף קְנַ֑ז אַלּ֤וּף־קֹ֨רַח֙ אַלּ֣וּף גַּעְתָּ֔ם אַלּ֖וּף עֲמָלֵ֑ק

יז אֵ֣לֶּה אַלּוּפֵ֤י אֱלִיפַז֙ בְּאֶ֣רֶץ אֱד֔וֹם אֵ֖לֶּה בְּנֵ֥י עָדָֽה׃ וְאֵ֗לֶּה

בְּנֵ֤י רְעוּאֵל֙ בֶּן־עֵשָׂ֔ו אַלּ֤וּף נַ֨חַת֙ אַלּ֣וּף זֶ֔רַח אַלּ֥וּף שַׁמָּ֖ה

אַלּ֣וּף מִזָּ֑ה אֵ֣לֶּה אַלּוּפֵ֤י רְעוּאֵל֙ בְּאֶ֣רֶץ אֱד֔וֹם אֵ֖לֶּה בְּנֵ֥י

יח בָשְׂמַ֖ת אֵ֥שֶׁת עֵשָֽׂו׃ וְאֵ֗לֶּה בְּנֵ֤י אָהֳלִֽיבָמָה֙ אֵ֣שֶׁת עֵשָׂ֔ו אַלּ֥וּף

יְע֛וּשׁ אַלּ֥וּף יַעְלָ֖ם אַלּ֣וּף קֹ֑רַח אֵ֣לֶּה אַלּוּפֵ֞י אׇהֳלִֽיבָמָ֛ה

יט בַּת־עֲנָ֖ה אֵ֥שֶׁת עֵשָֽׂו׃ אֵ֧לֶּה בְנֵי־עֵשָׂ֛ו וְאֵ֥לֶּה אַלּוּפֵיהֶ֖ם ה֥וּא

כ אֱדֽוֹם׃

כ אֵ֤לֶּה בְנֵֽי־שֵׂעִיר֙ הַחֹרִ֔י

כא יֹשְׁבֵ֣י הָאָ֑רֶץ לוֹטָ֥ן וְשׁוֹבָ֖ל וְצִבְע֥וֹן וַעֲנָֽה׃ וְדִשׁ֥וֹן וְאֵ֖צֶר וְדִישָׁ֑ן

כב אֵ֣לֶּה אַלּוּפֵ֧י הַחֹרִ֛י בְּנֵ֥י שֵׂעִ֖יר בְּאֶ֣רֶץ אֱד֑וֹם׃ וַיִּהְי֥וּ בְנֵֽי־לוֹטָ֖ן

כג חֹרִ֣י וְהֵימָ֑ם וַאֲח֥וֹת לוֹטָ֖ן תִּמְנָֽע׃ וְאֵ֨לֶּה֙ בְּנֵ֣י שׁוֹבָ֔ל עַלְוָ֣ן

כד וּמָנַ֗חַת וְעֵיבָ֛ל שְׁפ֖וֹ וְאוֹנָֽם׃ וְאֵ֥לֶּה בְנֵֽי־צִבְע֖וֹן וְאַיָּ֣ה וַעֲנָ֑ה

ה֣וּא עֲנָ֗ה אֲשֶׁ֨ר מָצָ֤א אֶת־הַיֵּמִם֙ בַּמִּדְבָּ֔ר בִּרְעֹת֥וֹ אֶת־

כה הַחֲמֹרִ֖ים לְצִבְע֥וֹן אָבִֽיו׃ וְאֵ֥לֶּה בְנֵֽי־עֲנָ֖ה דִּשֹׁ֑ן וְאׇהֳלִֽיבָמָ֖ה

כו בַּת־עֲנָֽה׃ וְאֵ֖לֶּה בְּנֵ֣י דִישָׁ֑ן חֶמְדָּ֥ן וְאֶשְׁבָּ֖ן וְיִתְרָ֥ן וּכְרָֽן׃

כז-כח אֵ֖לֶּה בְּנֵי־אֵ֑צֶר בִּלְהָ֥ן וְזַעֲוָ֖ן וַעֲקָ֑ן אֵ֥לֶּה בְנֵֽי־דִישָׁ֖ן ע֥וּץ וַאֲרָֽן׃

and would be incompatible with the very nature of religious faith. However, in both of these cases, Abraham's attitude met with disapproval; he had gone too far in his principles. The truths which he preached had such suggestive power that he could win over even the most independent and refractory minds. And so the patriarchs had to suffer the grave consequences of their refusal. The son of the mother who was rejected became the worst enemy of the Jews.

20. אֵלֶּה בְנֵי־שֵׂעִיר הַחֹרִי — *These are the sons of Seir the Horite.* If the Torah felt obliged to record for us the genealogy of the Horites, it did so in order to come to Timna and to let us know that Abraham's family was held in very high regard since Timna, the sister of prince Lotan, wished to join with it (*Rashi*). *Tanna D'Bei Eliyahu Zuta* notes further: The Torah enters into such detail about the Horites, listing their many descendants and their numerous princes, in order to show us how God rewarded them for having been so gracious to Esau and his people, to the point that Timna became a concubine of his son. This is why the phrase, *And (prince) Lotan's sister was Timna,* is of special significance.

24. הוּא עֲנָה אֲשֶׁר מָצָא אֶת־הַיֵּמִם בַּמִּדְבָּר — *The same Anah who discovered the mules in the desert. Rashi* gives proof that Anah was a bastard. He tended his

¹⁴ *And these were the sons of Oholibamah, daughter of Anah, daughter of Zibeon, Esau's wife: She bore to Esau Jeush, and Jalam, and Korah.*

¹⁵ *These are the chiefs of the children of Esau — the descendants of Esau's firstborn Eliphaz: Chief Teman, Chief Omar, Chief Zepho, Chief Kenaz;* ¹⁶ *Chief Korah, Chief Gatam, Chief Amalek; these are the chiefs of Eliphaz in the land of Edom — these are the descendants of Adah.*

¹⁷ *And these are the descendants of Reuel, Esau's son: Chief Nahath, Chief Zerah, Chief Shammah, Chief Mizzah; these are the chiefs of Reuel in the land of Edom — these are the descendants of Basemath, Esau's wife.*

¹⁸ *And these are the descendants of Ohlibamah, Esau's wife: Chief Jeush, Chief Jalam, Chief Korah — these are the chiefs of Ohlibamah, daughter of Anah, Esau's wife.* ¹⁹ *These are the children of Esau, and these are the chiefs; he is Edom.*

²⁰ *These are the sons of Seir the Horite who were settled in the land: Lotah and Shobal and Zibeon and Anah,* ²¹ *and Dishon and Ezer and Dishan — these are the chiefs of the Horite, the descendants of Seir in the land of Edom.*

²² *The sons of Lotan were: Hori and Hemam; Lotan's sister was Timna.*

²³ *These are the sons of Shobal: Alvan and Manahath and Ebal; Shepho and Onam.*

²⁴ *These are the sons of Zibeon: Aiah and Anah — the same Anah who discovered the mules in the desert while he was pasturing the donkeys for Zibeon, his father.*

²⁵ *These are the children of Anah: Dishon and Oholibamah daughter of Anah.*

²⁶ *These are the sons of Dishan: Hemdan and Eshban and Ithran and Cheran.*

²⁷ *These are the sons of Ezer: Bilhan and Zaavan and Akan.*

²⁸ *These are the sons of Dishan: Uz and Aran.*

father's donkeys in the desert, and he produced the mule by crossing an ass with a foal. "Himself a bastard, he brought abnormal creatures into the world." This act, says *Radak*, was in defiance of the Divine will, which had established the law of the separation of species in creation. The Talmud remarks that creation contains two elements which were formed after God's creation: fire, created by Adam on the evening after the first Sabbath of his life, and the mule, a product of crossing two species, obtained by a deliberate act of Anah the bastard (*Pesachim* 54a).

כט אֵלֶּה אַלּוּפֵי הַחֹרִי אַלּוּף לוֹטָן אַלּוּף שׁוֹבָל אַלּוּף צִבְעוֹן
ל אַלּוּף עֲנָה: אַלּוּף דִּשֹׁן אַלּוּף אֵצֶר אַלּוּף דִּישָׁן אֵלֶּה אַלּוּפֵי
הַחֹרִי לְאַלֻּפֵיהֶם בְּאֶרֶץ שֵׂעִיר:
לא וְאֵלֶּה הַמְּלָכִים אֲשֶׁר מָלְכוּ בְּאֶרֶץ אֱדוֹם לִפְנֵי מְלָךְ־מֶלֶךְ
לב לִבְנֵי יִשְׂרָאֵל: וַיִּמְלֹךְ בֶּאֱדוֹם בֶּלַע בֶּן־בְּעוֹר וְשֵׁם עִירוֹ
לג דִּנְהָבָה: וַיָּמָת בָּלַע וַיִּמְלֹךְ תַּחְתָּיו יוֹבָב בֶּן־זֶרַח מִבָּצְרָה:
לד-לה וַיָּמָת יוֹבָב וַיִּמְלֹךְ תַּחְתָּיו חֻשָׁם מֵאֶרֶץ הַתֵּימָנִי: וַיָּמָת חֻשָׁם
וַיִּמְלֹךְ תַּחְתָּיו הֲדַד בֶּן־בְּדַד הַמַּכֶּה אֶת־מִדְיָן בִּשְׂדֵה מוֹאָב
לו וְשֵׁם עִירוֹ עֲוִית: וַיָּמָת הֲדָד וַיִּמְלֹךְ תַּחְתָּיו שַׂמְלָה
לז מִמַּשְׂרֵקָה: וַיָּמָת שַׂמְלָה וַיִּמְלֹךְ תַּחְתָּיו שָׁאוּל מֵרְחֹבוֹת
לח הַנָּהָר: וַיָּמָת שָׁאוּל וַיִּמְלֹךְ תַּחְתָּיו בַּעַל חָנָן בֶּן־עַכְבּוֹר:
לט וַיָּמָת בַּעַל חָנָן בֶּן־עַכְבּוֹר וַיִּמְלֹךְ תַּחְתָּיו הֲדַר וְשֵׁם
עִירוֹ פָּעוּ וְשֵׁם אִשְׁתּוֹ מְהֵיטַבְאֵל בַּת־מַטְרֵד בַּת מֵי זָהָב:

31. וְאֵלֶּה הַמְּלָכִים — *Now these are the kings.* "The reason for listing the kings who reigned in the lands of Edom is that there is a commandment which says: *Do not put a foreigner over you, who is not your brother* (Deuteronomy 17:15). Now, of all the kings mentioned here, there is not one who originally came from Edom. It seems very likely that the deeds of these kings of Edom were then well known, including how they tyrannized and humiliated Esau's descendants; that is why the Jews are reminded of them. It is as if Jewry were being told: 'Take warning from your brothers, the descendants of Esau, whose kings were so-and-so; for never has a foreigner reigned over a nation without exercising a more or less tyrannical rule" (*Guide* 3:50).

לִפְנֵי מְלָךְ־מֶלֶךְ לִבְנֵי יִשְׂרָאֵל — *Before a king reigned over the Children of Israel.* The eight kings of Edom preceded the eight kings who "will descend from Jacob and will triumph over the power of Esau" (*Rashi*). For the *Zohar*, this chronological order, which is emphasized explicitly by the "parenthetical remark" at the end of the verse, is a general indication that in human societies the reign of the wicked and the vain precedes that of the just and the humble. יַעֲבָר נָא אֲדֹנִי לִפְנֵי עַבְדּוֹ, *Let my lord go ahead of his servant,* Jacob had said to his brother Esau (33:14). From the beginning, he had let Esau come first in temporal matters, as we have noted in several places (e.g., commentary on 27:40 and 28:4). Jacob can wait; he knows that his ambitious brother with his dazzling riches and material power will at first be stronger than his own family with its deep devotion to spiritual yearnings. But he also knows that in the long run the spirit will ultimately dominate and the day will arrive when "the eight kings coming from his descendants will triumph over the eight kings of Edom." From its very origins, the Jewish world has

²⁹ These are the chiefs of the Horite: Chief Lotan, Chief Shobal, Chief Zibeon, Chief Anah, ³⁰ Chief Dishon, Chief Etzer, Chief Dishan — these are the chiefs of the Horite, according to their chiefs, in the land of Seir.

³¹ Now these are the kings who reigned in the land of Edom before a king reigned over the Children of Israel: ³² Bela, son of Beor, reigned in Edom, and the name of his city was Dinhabah. ³³ And Bela died, and Jobab son of Zerah, from Bozrah, reigned after him. ³⁴ And Jobab died and Husham, of the land of the Temanites, reigned after him. ³⁵ And Husham died, and Hadad son of Bedad, who defeated the Midianites in the field of Moab, reigned after him, and the name of his city was Avith. ³⁶ And Hadad died, and Samlah of Masrekah reigned after him. ³⁷ Samlah died, and Saul of Rehoboth nahar reigned after him. ³⁸ And Saul died, and Baal-hanan, son of Achbor, reigned after him. ³⁹ Baal-hanan, son of Achbor, died, and Hadar reigned after him; the name of his city was Pau, and his wife's name was Mehetabel, daughter of Matred, daughter of Me-zahab.

always looked toward the future while the non-Jewish world lays claim to the present.

Authors of Kabbalistic works enlarged upon this thesis. They took this verse in the Torah as a confirmation of the general principle of historical evolution, progressing from the temporal to the spiritual. This manifests itself in the creation of the natural, physical world, for example, by the succession of ever more perfect and more spiritualized worlds emanating from the Creator.

39. וְשֵׁם אִשְׁתּוֹ מְהֵיטַבְאֵל — And his wife's name was Mehetabel. Hadar is the only king whose wife's name is mentioned. By way of explanation, the Baal HaTurim points out that he owed his kingship to her and her rich and illustrious parents. Her father was called Me-zahab, stream of gold. Rashi adds that he was in the habit of saying, מַה זָּהָב, but what is gold? He was so wealthy that gold meant nothing to him. However, Rashi's grandson, R' Shmuel ben Meir (Rashbam), remarks, "I follow the literal meaning and do not attach so much importance to names." But the Zohar declares: "The ways of the Torah are the ways of God; the slightest word within it leaves its mark in the spheres of higher wisdom. See how in the mysteries of higher wisdom R' Yochanan ben Zakkai deduced three hundred rules from the phrase: מְהֵיטַבְאֵל בַּת־מַטְרֵד, Mehetabel, daughter of Matred. But he revealed them only to his companion, R' Elazar. This teaches you that each story and each word of the Torah contains profound mysteries." According to the ס' האמונות of ה"ר שם טוב (7:2) quoted in Torah Sheleimah, R' Yochanan's interpretations also refer to the fact that the Torah does not mention Hadar's

מפטיר מ   וְאֵ֠לֶּה שְׁמ֞וֹת אַלּוּפֵ֤י עֵשָׂו֙ לְמִשְׁפְּחֹתָ֔ם לִמְקֹמֹתָ֖ם בִּשְׁמֹתָ֑ם
מא   אַלּ֥וּף תִּמְנָ֛ע אַלּ֥וּף עַלְוָ֖ה אַלּ֥וּף יְתֵֽת: אַלּ֧וּף אׇהֳלִיבָמָ֛ה אַלּ֥וּף
מב־מג   אֵלָ֖ה אַלּ֥וּף פִּינֹֽן: אַלּ֥וּף קְנַ֛ז אַלּ֥וּף תֵּימָ֖ן אַלּ֥וּף מִבְצָֽר: אַלּ֣וּף
מַגְדִּיאֵ֖ל אַלּ֣וּף עִירָ֑ם אֵ֣לֶּה ׀ אַלּוּפֵ֣י אֱד֗וֹם לְמֹֽשְׁבֹתָם֙ בְּאֶ֣רֶץ
אֲחֻזָּתָ֔ם ה֥וּא עֵשָׂ֖ו אֲבִ֥י אֱדֽוֹם:

death, though it does so for all the other kings (Hadar's death is, however, mentioned in *I Chronicles* 1:51).

40. וְאֵלֶּה שְׁמוֹת אַלּוּפֵי עֵשָׂו — *Now these are the names of the chiefs of Esau.* Cf. our commentary on verse 8.

43. מַגְדִּיאֵל — *Magdiel.* "This is Rome," says *Rashi* (*Maharal* defends this point against *Ramban*, who does not accept it). The city named עִירָם also refers to Rome, as the Midrash explains (*Pirkei D'Rabbi Eliezer* 38), and as we see from *Rashi* on *Numbers* 24:19. And so at the end of the long list of kings and princes, descendants and allies of Esau, we see looming on the horizon that famous and proud city — Rome, the antagonist of Jerusalem. Rome is a direct creation of Esau's successors, and in his commentary on *Genesis* 49:31 *Ramban* amplifies this, quoting the historian Flavius Josephus. Rome, the irreconcilable enemy of

⁴⁰ *Now these are the names of the chiefs of Esau, by their families, by their regions, by their names: the chief of Timna; the chief of Alvah; the chief of Jetheth;* ⁴¹ *the chief of Oholibamah; the chief of Elah; the chief of Pinon;* ⁴² *the chief of Kenaz; the chief of Teman; the chief of Mibzar;* ⁴³ *the chief of Magdiel and the chief of Iram; these are the chiefs of Edom by their settlements, in the land of their possession — he is Esau, father of Edom.*

Jerusalem, was the cause of its downfall, of the destruction of its Temple, and of the fall of the Jewish kingdom. From the time that Esau sold his birthright to Jacob for a bowl of cooked lentils and received the name of Edom (25:30), he remained the constant enemy of his brother. His hatred is being carried on right to the very last of his descendants. The final words of this *sidrah*, הוּא עֵשָׂו אֲבִי אֱדוֹם, *he is Esau, father of Edom,* reveal one of the constants of universal history, namely that Edom's essence which is Rome originates in Esau the rival brother of Jacob (cf. *Megillah* 11a). But the prophet Obadiah has predicted the fate reserved for Edom in future times: *Though you make your nest as high as the eagle and set it among the stars, I will bring you down from there, says God* (verse 4). These words are found in the *haftarah* for this *sidrah;* they provide the response to its closing words.

לז א־ב וַיֵּשֶׁב יַעֲקֹב בְּאֶרֶץ מְגוּרֵי אָבִיו בְּאֶרֶץ כְּנָעַן: אֵלֶּה ו תֹּלְדוֹת
יַעֲקֹב יוֹסֵף בֶּן־שְׁבַע־עֶשְׂרֵה שָׁנָה הָיָה רֹעֶה אֶת־אֶחָיו בַּצֹּאן
וְהוּא נַעַר אֶת־בְּנֵי בִלְהָה וְאֶת־בְּנֵי זִלְפָּה נְשֵׁי אָבִיו וַיָּבֵא יוֹסֵף
ג אֶת־דִּבָּתָם רָעָה אֶל־אֲבִיהֶם: וְיִשְׂרָאֵל אָהַב אֶת־יוֹסֵף מִכָּל־

37.

1. וַיֵּשֶׁב יַעֲקֹב — *Jacob settled*. The account which begins here has excited admiration throughout the generations. It is of incomparable pedagogical value. It deals with the most profound thoughts in a way so simple and direct that they are accessible to every child. And so this episode is of prime importance for the religious and moral education of the child. Its unique character results from the fact that it is dominated by the certainty of the omnipresent Divine Providence, Whose purposes are achieved in the midst of the interplay of human interests. The notions of duty, of sin and expiation; the conflict between our desires and our conscience; and then the ultimate triumph of spiritual and moral values — these are its essential themes. The guiding principle of this episode applies first and foremost to *Genesis* but it is also valid for Biblical history as a whole. It is that the Divine message and the great lesson of duty are taught to man not by means of abstract formulae, but with the help of living examples of human beings who like ourselves feel and give in and sin, and yet even when they do stray they remain aware of the unique path of truth and rise up again. The attitude of Joseph's brothers when they realize the enormity of their crime gives us an example of this.

בְּאֶרֶץ מְגוּרֵי אָבִיו — *In the land of his father's sojournings*. After his many ordeals, Jacob wanted to live in peace in the land where his father had been merely a גֵּר, *stranger*, and a wanderer. He felt he had a right to the peace and quiet of his hopes here in this land, אֶרֶץ כְּנָעַן, the land promised to his descendants. But according to the plans of Providence, the time had not yet come for this. "The righteous seek to live in peace. But the Holy One, Blessed is He, says: The righteous are not content with what is reserved for them in the World to Come, but they still want peace in this world as well!" (*Rashi*). And like Job, Jacob had to admit: *I have neither peace, nor security, nor rest; and now new torments come upon me* (Job 3:26). The truly righteous, said Rav (*Berachos* 64a) have no rest either in this world or in the World to Come. *They go from strength to strength until they appear before God in Zion* (Psalms 84:8).

2. אֵלֶּה תֹּלְדוֹת יַעֲקֹב יוֹסֵף — *These are the chronicles of Jacob: Joseph*. The Midrash explains that the Torah wanted to make the history of Jacob depend on that of Joseph for many reasons (*Rashi*). Indeed the whole history of Jacob's descendants is reflected in Joseph's life. The favorite son of the patriarch, in the prime of his youth, was compelled to flee from the home of his parents and the land of his birth. He was abandoned in a foreign land among a debauched people and they did all they could so that even his name would be forgotten. But

37 ¹Jacob settled in the land of his father's sojournings, in the land of Canaan. ²These are the chronicles of Jacob: Joseph, at the age of seventeen, was a shepherd with his brothers by the flock, but he was a youth with the sons of Bilhah and the sons of Zilpah, his father's wives; and Joseph would bring evil reports about them to their father. ³Now Israel loved Joseph more than all

what happened to him? All the trials and tribulations of his destiny were turned into a springboard for his prodigious ascent. He became a benefactor who gave food to the people. And it ultimately came to pass that his brothers, who had sworn to do away with him, came to kneel before him.

This same destiny will one day come to pass in the life of Jewry. When the time comes for the Messiah, the nations will acknowledge that all the trials and sufferings which have befallen us during our exile were ultimately stages in our ascent. *And you will say on that day: I will thank You, God, that You were angry with me (Isaiah 12:1).* So, just as with Joseph's life, in the final analysis the tribulations and torments willed by Providence are seen to be truly beneficial (*Chofetz Chaim*).

This historical interpretation is certainly not consistent with the view of *Rashbam*, *Rashi's* grandson and fervent advocate of literal interpretations. In his comments on this verse he strongly criticizes those interpretations which lose sight of the textual meaning of the Torah and give preference instead to the meanings hidden in the words and phrases. Along these lines he protests against *Ibn Ezra's* derivation of the word תּוֹלְדוֹת, meaning events, by analogy with the phrase (*Proverbs 27:1*): מַה יֵּלֶד יוֹם, *the events which each day brings forth:* "These are the events which happened to him, the tribulations which he bore." *Rashbam* adds: "I have discussed this (the importance of the literal meaning) with my grandfather *Rashi* and he admitted that, had he had the opportunity, he would have recorded some new explanations according to the literal meaning." According to *Rashbam* the word תּוֹלְדוֹת simply means children or following generations.

וַיָּבֵא יוֹסֵף אֶת־דִּבָּתָם רָעָה — *Joseph would bring evil reports about them. Rashi* explains: "Anything bad that he saw regarding his brothers, the sons of Leah, he used to tell his father." However, *Ramban* holds that Joseph told tales about the sons of Bilhah and Zilpah, and consequently they hated him because of his tales; the sons of Leah hated him because their father showed preference to him.

3. וְיִשְׂרָאֵל אָהַב אֶת־יוֹסֵף מִכָּל־בָּנָיו — *Now Israel loved Joseph more than all his sons.* It is amazing to see that the patriarch, who had suffered so much during his life from the consequences of his own father's preference for his brother Esau, did not take steps to avoid this same situation in his relations with his own children. To explain this preference, the Torah tells us that Joseph was the "son of his old age," which *Rashi* interprets as meaning that Joseph was born during Jacob's later years, or that he had the same facial features as Jacob, or was

ד בָּנָיו כִּי־בֶן־זְקֻנִים הוּא לוֹ וְעָשָׂה לוֹ כְּתֹנֶת פַּסִּים: וַיִּרְאוּ
אֶחָיו כִּי־אֹתוֹ אָהַב אֲבִיהֶם מִכָּל־אֶחָיו וַיִּשְׂנְאוּ אֹתוֹ
ה וְלֹא יָכְלוּ דַּבְּרוֹ לְשָׁלֹם: וַיַּחֲלֹם יוֹסֵף חֲלוֹם וַיַּגֵּד לְאֶחָיו

(according to *Onkelos*) an intelligent child and Jacob had passed on to him all the wisdom he had gained from Shem and Ever. But the *Zohar* gives another reason: Jacob loved Rachel and her son Joseph and he knew that Rachel's children will be instrumental in mankind's final redemption in messianic times. The text discreetly hints at this reason when it designates the patriarch here as Israel. It was indeed as father of the nation given the messianic calling that Jacob cherished Joseph. On this see our commentary to 49:27.

If the patriarch's love might thus seem understandable to us in human terms, it was nevertheless a mistake to show this love openly in front of the other sons. "It was taught in the name of Rav: A man should never single out one of his children among the others. For it was because of a garment weighing two *selaim* which Jacob gave to Joseph and not to his other sons that they became jealous of him. And the matter resulted in the descent of our ancestors into Egypt" (*Shabbos* 10b). Of course, remark the *Tosafists*, the decree of the exile into Egypt goes back to Abraham's time, but the oppression would not have been so severe were it not for this (the unjustified hatred which reigned among the tribes of Israel). And *Rambam* states clearly in his *Mishneh Torah*: "Our Sages have commanded that during his lifetime a man should never make any distinction between his children, no matter how slight, so that there should be no quarrels or jealousy among them as there was between Joseph and his brothers" (הל׳ נחלות, פ״י, ה״ו).

כְּתֹנֶת פַּסִּים — *A fine woolen tunic. Ibn Ezra* and other commentators translate: *a coat of many colors*. According to *Sforno*, a coat of this kind is a sign of high rank and leadership. Frescoes discovered in the Egyptian tombs of the Bene Hassein show that in the patriarchs' times chiefs of Semitic tribes wore multicolored robes; this was the case in the house of King David, as is recorded in *II Samuel* 13:18. We see from this how the father's gesture brought out the hatred and then the jealousy of the brothers. According to an ancient tradition, the cloak was from the bridal gown which Jacob had offered to Rachel and which he later made into a garment for the son of his late wife.

4. וַיִּשְׂנְאוּ אֹתוֹ— *They hated him.* The *Zohar* gives a view which differs from that of the Talmud (quoted in the commentary on the previous verse) according to which Jacob was guilty of showing preference to one of his sons. The *Zohar* recalls that God Himself openly proclaims His affection for Jacob-Israel at the expense of Esau and declares it formally through the prophet Malachi (1:2) and others. So too, the three patriarchs openly show their love for one of their children, not caring about the feelings of hostility which this might stir up among the other children. This is because true love is given completely. When it clings to the ideal of goodness and justice, it excludes everything which stands

*his sons since he was a child of his old age, and he made him
a fine woolen tunic.* ⁴ *His brothers saw that it was he whom their
father loved most of all his brothers so they hated him; and they
could not speak to him peaceably.*
⁵ *Joseph dreamt a dream which he told to his brothers,*

in their way. Knowing how to hate is the corollary of knowing how to love. If
the patriarchs showered their fatherly love on one of their children, it was on the
one in whom they recognized the true guardian of their spiritual heritage. They
gave him this love without reservation and considered it useless to hide it, even
though it might be cause for fierce hatred on the part of the brothers. So too, God
never concealed His love for His "chosen people," although it bore the seeds of
the rancor and the hatred of the nations.

Thus the struggle between the rival brothers of the patriarchal family, as well
as of the vast "family of nations," finds a fertile breeding ground, almost as if
prepared in advance, by the act of a parent in choosing, or exercising his
privilege of bestowing love. No doubt this struggle is deemed necessary for the
attainment of moral perfection and for good to ultimately triumph. Without it,
mankind would lapse into stagnation and indolence. (Cf. also *Tanchuma
Vayigash* 10 for comparison of the destinies of Joseph and Zion. It is interesting
to note that יוֹסֵף and צִיּוֹן have the same numerical value — 156.)

5. וַיַּחֲלֹם יוֹסֵף חֲלוֹם — *Joseph dreamt a dream.* This verse ushers in the series of
dreams which played so great a role in Joseph's life and consequently in the
history of the Jewish people. Because of his dreams, say our Sages of the
Midrash, Joseph fell into great misfortune, but on the other hand he also owed
his prodigious rise to dreams, the dreams of the two imprisoned Egyptian
officers and of Pharaoh. By highlighting dreams in this way, the Torah seems
to want to make us realize the great importance of non-rational factors, such as
dreams, in human existence. A man's whole life can be dominated by this factor
and its influence can have repercussions even on the historical destiny of an
entire nation. From this example we are brought to realize that events and
situations in the social, economic, and political domains are not the only ones to
determine the course of history; there are factors of quite a different nature
which intervene with no less impact on our lives, among them the non-rational
factor of dreams. What is more, in the lifelong historical conflict between Joseph
the dreamer and his brothers the realists, it is ultimately the בַּעַל הַחֲלֹמוֹת, *the
dreamer* who triumphs.

To be sure, Joseph's dreams and those of the Egyptian officers and Pharaoh
contain revelations of future events which can originate only from a
transcendent source. This implication once again raises the old problem of the
relationship between predestination and free will. In the story of Joseph and his
brothers, what share in the responsibility do the actors themselves actually have,
in view of the fact that the sequence of events was determined in advance? *R'
Yitzchak Arama (Akeidas Yitzchak,* chapter 28), *Malbim* (who enters into

ו וַיּוֹסִפוּ עוֹד שְׂנֹא אֹתוֹ: וַיֹּאמֶר אֲלֵיהֶם שִׁמְעוּ־נָא הַחֲלוֹם
ז הַזֶּה אֲשֶׁר חָלָמְתִּי: וְהִנֵּה אֲנַחְנוּ מְאַלְּמִים אֲלֻמִּים בְּתוֹךְ
הַשָּׂדֶה וְהִנֵּה קָמָה אֲלֻמָּתִי וְגַם־נִצָּבָה וְהִנֵּה תְסֻבֶּינָה
ח אֲלֻמֹּתֵיכֶם וַתִּשְׁתַּחֲוֶיןָ לַאֲלֻמָּתִי: וַיֹּאמְרוּ לוֹ אֶחָיו הֲמָלֹךְ
תִּמְלֹךְ עָלֵינוּ אִם־מָשׁוֹל תִּמְשֹׁל בָּנוּ וַיּוֹסִפוּ עוֹד שְׂנֹא אֹתוֹ
ט עַל־חֲלֹמֹתָיו וְעַל־דְּבָרָיו: וַיַּחֲלֹם עוֹד חֲלוֹם אַחֵר וַיְסַפֵּר
אֹתוֹ לְאֶחָיו וַיֹּאמֶר הִנֵּה חָלַמְתִּי חֲלוֹם עוֹד וְהִנֵּה הַשֶּׁמֶשׁ
י וְהַיָּרֵחַ וְאַחַד עָשָׂר כּוֹכָבִים מִשְׁתַּחֲוִים לִי: וַיְסַפֵּר אֶל־אָבִיו
וְאֶל־אֶחָיו וַיִּגְעַר־בּוֹ אָבִיו וַיֹּאמֶר לוֹ מָה הַחֲלוֹם הַזֶּה אֲשֶׁר

controversy with him), and *Rabbi Y.L. Bloch* (שיעורי דעת ח״ב, י״ד) try to answer this question in different ways. R' Yaakov ben Asher declares that Joseph's dreams were just a reflection of what he was thinking during the day and consequently he alone was responsible for them (פי׳ הטור).

But in the final analysis it is to *Rambam* we turn to put this problem in perspective. He stipulates that this eternal problem cannot be resolved in terms of our way of thinking, which is fundamentally different from God's thought. Indeed, the interplay of human deeds and providential acts is such that no living being can discover its mysterious workings (הלכות תשובה, פ״ה, ה׳). In the *Guide to the Perplexed* (2:48), however, *Rambam* seems to be defending the idea that God Himself directed the free will of Jacob's sons so as to have them carry out a great act in the providential plan without their knowing it (cf. ibid., commentary of *Ibn Caspi* and *Efodi*).

6. שִׁמְעוּ־נָא הַחֲלוֹם הַזֶּה אֲשֶׁר חָלָמְתִּי — *Hear, if you please, this dream which I dreamt:* There are three general classes of dreams. The first comprises dreams brought about by "a demon" (*Berachos* 55b); that may mean by impure thoughts or imaginings and by unhealthy influences. The second involves dreams which are simply the natural consequences of our psychophysical constitution. It is to these types of dreams that the prophet Zechariah refers: *The dreams speak vanity* (10:2). The third category includes dreams of prophetic inspiration. The Torah is referring to this category when it says in the name of God: *I make Myself known to him in a vision* (*Numbers* 12:6). This is the way in which *R' Shmuel Edels* (מהרש״א ח״א ברכות נ״ה) and *R' Bachya* (on 41:1) categorize dreams.

Rambam gives an extensive analysis of prophetic dreams and establishes their order of importance (*Guide* 2:36-37). The Talmud, as a matter of fact, takes a dream to be a "minor prophecy." It represents the sixtieth part of prophecy (*Berachos* 57b) and it is described elsewhere as the "abortive fruit of prophecy" (*Bereishis Rabbah* 17 and 44). The inferior character of dreams in relation to direct revelation will affect the ways in which they are interpreted,

and they hated him even more. ⁶He said to them, "Hear, if you please, this dream which I dreamt: ⁷ Behold! — we were binding sheaves in the middle of the field, when, behold! — my sheaf arose and remained standing; then behold! — your sheaves gathered around and bowed down to my sheaf."

⁸ His brothers said to him, "Would you then reign over us? Would you then dominate us?" And they hated him even more — because of his dreams and because of his talk.

⁹ He dreamt another dream, and related it to his brothers. And he said, "Look, I dreamt another dream: Behold! the sun, the moon, and eleven stars were bowing down to me."

¹⁰ And he related it to his father and to his brothers; his father scolded him, and said to him, "What is this dream that you have

as we will see later on. For *R' Shmuel Edels*, Joseph's dreams belong to the third category, prophetic dreams (ibid.).

Is there something to indicate to us the exact nature of a dream? *R' Yehudah HaChassid* tells us that dreams in the first two categories occur during a light sleep, in a semiconscious state (ס׳ חסידים שפי״ב). On the other hand, prophetic dreams come in deep sleep and they are accompanied by a state of very intense exaltation (*Hilchos Yesodei HaTorah* 7:2).

8. הֲמָלֹךְ תִּמְלֹךְ עָלֵינוּ — *Would you then reign over us?* R' Yehudah said: Learn from this that one should not tell a dream to anyone except a good friend. Here, Joseph told his dream to his brothers, who hated him, and they interpreted it in a way that made them most violently opposed to it. And as a result they managed to postpone its realization for twenty-two years. But see in the Talmud (*Megillah* 17a) where this postponement, resulting in Joseph's absence for twenty-two years, is considered a punishment imposed on Jacob, who had stayed away from his own father's house for the same number of years, thus forgoing his duty as a son (cf. *R' Shmuel Edels, Berachos* 55b).

This remark in the *Zohar* is based on the Talmud, which teaches that "dreams follow the mouth," i.e. dreams depend on their interpretation (הַחֲלוֹמוֹת הוֹלְכִים אַחַר הַפֶּה; *Berachos* 55b), as it is said: *Just as he interpreted for us, so did it happen* (41:13). The problem which this statement raises is dealt with by numerous authors: "How is it possible that the effects of a dream can be influenced in one way or another by the interpretation which friends or enemies of the dreamer give to it?"

Certain explanations start from a rationalistic point of view, for example *Ein Yaakov (Berachos* 55b) and *R' Yitzchak Arama (Akeidas Yitzchak* 29). Offering a contradictory view is *R' Shmuel Edels* (חידושי אגדות, *Berachos* ibid.). But *R' Shlomo ben Aderes (Rashba)* points out that the question of dream interpretations goes beyond reason and natural laws (שו״ת ח״א סי׳ ת״ח). Along the same lines the *Tosafists* say that the interpreters of dreams are born under

חֲלַמְתָּ הֲבוֹא נָבוֹא אֲנִי וְאִמְּךָ וְאַחֶיךָ לְהִשְׁתַּחֲוֹת לְךָ אָרְצָה:
שני   יא-יב וַיְקַנְאוּ־בוֹ אֶחָיו וְאָבִיו שָׁמַר אֶת־הַדָּבָר: וַיֵּלְכוּ אֶחָיו לִרְעוֹת
יג אֶת־צֹאן אֲבִיהֶם בִּשְׁכֶם: וַיֹּאמֶר יִשְׂרָאֵל אֶל־יוֹסֵף הֲלוֹא
אַחֶיךָ רֹעִים בִּשְׁכֶם לְכָה וְאֶשְׁלָחֲךָ אֲלֵיהֶם וַיֹּאמֶר לוֹ הִנֵּנִי:
יד וַיֹּאמֶר לוֹ לֶךְ־נָא רְאֵה אֶת־שְׁלוֹם אַחֶיךָ וְאֶת־שְׁלוֹם הַצֹּאן
טו וַהֲשִׁבֵנִי דָּבָר וַיִּשְׁלָחֵהוּ מֵעֵמֶק חֶבְרוֹן וַיָּבֹא שְׁכֶמָה: וַיִּמְצָאֵהוּ
אִישׁ וְהִנֵּה תֹעֶה בַּשָּׂדֶה וַיִּשְׁאָלֵהוּ הָאִישׁ לֵאמֹר מַה־תְּבַקֵּשׁ:

a constellation which favors the faculty of interpretation, the latter having no connection with perspicacity (*Berachos* ibid.). Going further still, the *Zohar* notes that if the interpretation can play a decisive role in the significance of the dream, it is because the dream represents only the sixtieth part of prophecy. Hence it is at the lowest level of Divine revelation and, as such, can produce a mixture of celestial revelations together with products of the imagination. It is upon the latter that the speech of man, whose creative power has been demonstrated, is able to exercise a determining influence. Furthermore, speech serves to concretize and to give form to the abstract thought which constitutes the dream. It is, as it were, the first stage in going from the abstraction of the dream to its materialization in an act. Therefore, in both form and content, it plays a very important role by orienting the dream in a definite direction (עץ יוסף, ברכות, שם).

12. וַיֵּלְכוּ אֶחָיו לִרְעוֹת אֶת־צֹאן אֲבִיהֶם — *Now, his brothers went to pasture their father's flock.* The particle אֶת is dotted. This, says *Rashi*, is the Torah's way of hinting at the fact that the brothers had gone away only in order to "feed themselves." The *Zohar*, on the other hand, says that this particle refers to the *Shechinah* Itself. The brothers, ten in number and pious and righteous men, were accompanied by the Divine Presence. It hovered above them and was with them when Joseph was sold. It stayed with them despite the way they treated Joseph, for they constituted the nucleus of the future Jewish nation (cf. our commentary to 35:18).

13. הֲלוֹא אַחֶיךָ רֹעִים בִּשְׁכֶם — *Your brothers are pasturing in Shechem, are they not?* "A place destined for disaster," declares *Rashi*. Said Jacob, "I fear that the people of Shechem will come and kill your brothers who slew Shechem, his father, and all the population. Therefore go and see how they are" (*Targum Yonasan*).

וַיֹּאמֶר לוֹ הִנֵּנִי — *He said to him: "Here I am."* "Spoken with enthusiasm and zeal. Ready to obey his father's command even though he knew that his brothers hated him" (*Rashi*). As for Jacob, he also knew of their feelings of hostility toward Joseph but he did not think them capable of committing an act of violence, so there was nothing for him to fear (*Zohar*). Moreover, Jacob felt there was no risk involved since Joseph was going on a "sacred mission," as a

dreamt! Are we to come — I and your mother and your brothers — to bow down to you to the ground?" [11] *So his brothers were jealous of him, but his father kept the matter in mind.*

[12] *Now, his brothers went to pasture their father's flock in Shechem.* [13] *And Israel said to Joseph, "Your brothers are pasturing in Shechem, are they not? Come, I will send you to them." He said to him: "Here I am!"* [14] *And he said to him, "Go now, look into the welfare of your brothers and the welfare of the flock, and bring me back word." So he sent him from the depth of Hebron, and he arrived at Shechem.*

[15] *A man discovered him, and behold! — he was blundering in the field; the man asked him, saying, "What do you seek?"*

שָׁלִיחַ מִצְוָה, simply obeying the wish of his father — "those who go to perform a *mitzvah* can come to no harm" (*Pesachim* 8b). "But then how could he have been sold as a slave while on this mission?" asks R' *Chaim ben Attar*. The answer is that harm which ultimately turns out to be of great benefit is not considered harm.

14. וַיִּשְׁלָחֵהוּ מֵעֵמֶק חֶבְרוֹן — *So he sent him from the valley of Hebron.* On this day, notes *Targum Yonasan*, the exile in Egypt began. Indeed, from the day Jacob sent Joseph to meet his brothers the sequence of events leads directly to the exile into Egypt.

The text implies that Jacob accompanied his son as far as Hebron valley. "But Hebron is on a mountain!" remarks *Rashi*. What then does "Hebron valley" signify? The text implies that Jacob went there to follow the profound plan (עָמוֹק, *profound*, being related to עֵמֶק, *valley*) announced to the righteous one who was buried in Hebron (Abraham) and to carry out what was said to him at the time of the "Covenant Between the Parts": *Your offspring shall be aliens in a land not their own* (*Genesis* 15:13).

The story of Joseph and his brothers is thus considered the first step in the realization of what was announced to the first patriarch. This idea recurs frequently and in various forms in the reflections of the Sages of the Midrash as well as of the commentators in their remarks on this chapter. Hence people involved in this episode appear as agents of Providence. God's universal plans for the realization of the messianic goals of history are carried out amidst the comings and goings, the dreams and grudges, the ambitions and vindictiveness of the children of the family of Abraham. And here, the Torah gives us an example of the story of a family in which each person remains totally responsible for his acts although in historical perspective they were acting as שְׁלוּחִים לַמָקוֹם, *agents of Divine Providence* (cf. verse 5, above).

15. וְהִנֵּה תֹעֶה בַּשָׂדֶה — *And behold!* — *he was blundering in the field.* "Blundering" from all points of view, notes the *Zohar*. He was "off the track" in believing that he could trust his brothers. He sought their feelings of

טז וַיֹּאמֶר אֶת־אַחַי אָנֹכִי מְבַקֵּשׁ הַגִּידָה־נָּא לִי אֵיפֹה הֵם

יז רֹעִים: וַיֹּאמֶר הָאִישׁ נָסְעוּ מִזֶּה כִּי שָׁמַעְתִּי אֹמְרִים

נֵלְכָה דֹּתָיְנָה וַיֵּלֶךְ יוֹסֵף אַחַר אֶחָיו וַיִּמְצָאֵם בְּדֹתָן:

יח וַיִּרְאוּ אֹתוֹ מֵרָחֹק וּבְטֶרֶם יִקְרַב אֲלֵיהֶם וַיִּתְנַכְּלוּ אֹתוֹ

יט לַהֲמִיתוֹ: וַיֹּאמְרוּ אִישׁ אֶל־אָחִיו הִנֵּה בַּעַל הַחֲלֹמוֹת

כ הַלָּזֶה בָּא: וְעַתָּה ׀ לְכוּ וְנַהַרְגֵהוּ וְנַשְׁלִכֵהוּ בְּאַחַד הַבֹּרוֹת

וְאָמַרְנוּ חַיָּה רָעָה אֲכָלָתְהוּ וְנִרְאֶה מַה־יִּהְיוּ חֲלֹמֹתָיו:

brotherhood and did not find them. And so the man asked him, "What are you going to look for now?"

מַה־תְּבַקֵּשׁ — *What do you seek?* This verse is written in honor of Joseph. It shows you that he could have had many excuses for giving up the search for his brothers, whom he did not find at Shechem where his father had sent him. But he faced all the dangers and persisted out of respect for his father until he had carried out his mission. The account also teaches us how many means Providence has at Its disposal to achieve Its ends. At the proper moment It sent Gabriel, a ministering angel who, in the guise of a human being, spoke to Joseph and directed him to his brothers. God has many agents to do His work and His plan is carried out in all circumstances (*Ramban*).

17. נֵלְכָה דֹּתָיְנָה — *Let us go to Dothan.* The man said to him: "I have heard from behind the [heavenly] curtain that the exile in Egypt is to begin this very day and that it has been revealed to them (your brothers) prophetically that the Hivites (the inhabitants of Shechem) are preparing to do battle with them." And so they decided to leave for Dothan (*Targum Yonasan*).

But why did an angel have to be sent to put Joseph on the track of his brothers only to have them immediately sell him as a slave? Would it not have been possible to proceed directly to his sale by the Ishmaelites, since this was already foreseen in the plan of Providence, without having to go through an angel?

The Midrash (*Bamidbar Rabbah* 13) replies: Joseph's sale turned out to be the starting point for a great benefit. Joseph became the provider of nations as well as of his own family. Now, the Torah teaches that good should be promoted by good people and that the doers of meritorious deeds should themselves be worthy people: פ׳ ט״ז פיסקא (*Tanna D'Bei Eliyahu Rabba* מְגַלְגְּלִין זְכוּת עַל יְדֵי זַכַּאי ויי״ח). This is why Joseph's brothers had to be the originators of his sale. For they were the most righteous of men at that time, despite the one sin which they committed in their lives.

18. וַיִּתְנַכְּלוּ אֹתוֹ לַהֲמִיתוֹ — *They conspired against him to kill him.* They sought a way to bring about his death by trickery without having to shed his blood themselves. "Let us get dogs after him!" But when he came towards them and they realized they had failed to do this, they said to one another, "Come now, let us kill him" (*Ramban*, following *Rabbah*).

> ¹⁶ And he said, "My brothers do I seek; tell me, please, where they
> are pasturing." ¹⁷ The man said: "They have journeyed on from
> here, for I heard them saying, 'Let us go to Dothan.' " So Joseph
> went after his brothers and found them at Dothan.
>
> ¹⁸ They saw him from afar; and when he had not yet approached
> them they conspired against him to kill him. ¹⁹ And they said to one
> another, "Look! That dreamer is coming! ²⁰ So now, come and let
> us kill him, and throw him into one of the pits; and we will say, 'A
> wild beast devoured him.' Then we shall see what will become of
> his dreams."

19. וַיֹּאמְרוּ אִישׁ אֶל־אָחִיו — *One said to his brother.* "Simeon and Levi, who always collaborated as brothers" (*Rashi* on 49:5).

20. וְנַהַרְגֵהוּ — *And let us kill him.* The brothers felt it perfectly justified to pronounce the death penalty on Joseph. They considered him guilty of slander, talebearing, and giving false witness. *Rashi* (above on verse 2): "He had denounced his brothers, bringing evil report of them to his father, saying: 'They ate flesh torn from a living animal; they humiliated the sons of the bondwomen and called them slaves; they are suspected of immorality.' And Joseph will be correspondingly punished on these three accounts . . ." (cf. *R' Chaim ben Attar,* אוה"ח).

But another opinion suggests that Joseph's brothers considered him a usurper. They looked upon Judah as the brother predestined by his qualities to found the future royal tribe. And they were ready even then to accept him as chief. Now, through his dreams and words, Joseph had shown his intention of taking over as head of the family. Thus he went against the others and seriously threatened the peace and harmony of the family and of the future of Abraham's descendants. This was sufficient to make him deserving of the death penalty (*Torah Sheleimah*).

Sforno points to the grammatical form of the phrase וַיִּתְנַכְּלוּ אֹתוֹ (where the *hispael* verb is not used with a ב as is customary). This means, he says, that they considered him a נוֹכֵל, a man of cunning, who had evil intentions. They thought he was planning to cause their moral or material downfall through some trickery. This inopportune visit happened after the family had met at Shechem to decide what measures to take against the dreaded appearance of a family tyrant. (It is interesting to note that, in the tradition of Jewry, Shechem has remained the symbol of revolt against any threat of dictatorship. When Solomon died and his son Rehoboam made unacceptable demands as heir to the throne, it was again at Shechem that the people assembled and there the schism of the kingdom took place.)

When they passed the death sentence on their brother, the sons of Jacob were convinced that they were acting in legitimate self-defense. They remained convinced of their right and, for many years afterwards, they felt that they

כא וַיִּשְׁמַע רְאוּבֵן וַיַּצִּלֵהוּ מִיָּדָם וַיֹּאמֶר לֹא נַכֶּנּוּ נָפֶשׁ:
כב וַיֹּאמֶר אֲלֵהֶם ׀ רְאוּבֵן אַל־תִּשְׁפְּכוּ־דָם הַשְׁלִיכוּ אֹתוֹ
אֶל־הַבּוֹר הַזֶּה אֲשֶׁר בַּמִּדְבָּר וְיָד אַל־תִּשְׁלְחוּ־בוֹ לְמַעַן
כג הַצִּיל אֹתוֹ מִיָּדָם לַהֲשִׁיבוֹ אֶל־אָבִיו: וַיְהִי כַּאֲשֶׁר־בָּא יוֹסֵף
אֶל־אֶחָיו וַיַּפְשִׁיטוּ אֶת־יוֹסֵף אֶת־כֻּתָּנְתּוֹ אֶת־כְּתֹנֶת הַפַּסִּים
כד אֲשֶׁר עָלָיו: וַיִּקָּחֻהוּ וַיַּשְׁלִכוּ אֹתוֹ הַבֹּרָה וְהַבּוֹר רֵק אֵין
כה בּוֹ מָיִם: וַיֵּשְׁבוּ לֶאֱכָל־לֶחֶם וַיִּשְׂאוּ עֵינֵיהֶם וַיִּרְאוּ וְהִנֵּה
אֹרְחַת יִשְׁמְעֵאלִים בָּאָה מִגִּלְעָד וּגְמַלֵּיהֶם נֹשְׂאִים נְכֹאת
כו וּצְרִי וָלֹט הוֹלְכִים לְהוֹרִיד מִצְרָיְמָה: וַיֹּאמֶר יְהוּדָה
אֶל־אֶחָיו מַה־בֶּצַע כִּי נַהֲרֹג אֶת־אָחִינוּ וְכִסִּינוּ אֶת־דָּמוֹ:

deserved reproach not for the deed itself but only for the manner in which they carried it out and for their lack of pity (42:21).

21. וַיִּשְׁמַע רְאוּבֵן — *Reuben heard.* He said to himself, "I am the firstborn and the biggest of all; the blame will surely fall on me" (*Rashi*). To appreciate Reuben's action, note that as the firstborn he was the one most directly affected by Joseph's ambitions. What is more, it was precisely to Joseph that Reuben was to lose a part of his rights as firstborn, as *Rashi* had noted previously (35:23). Nevertheless, it is "the Holy Spirit Itself which testifies that Reuben said this only with the intention of rescuing Joseph" (*Rashi*). By his whole attitude here, he showed that he possessed true greatness of spirit. He tried to redeem himself from the sin which he had committed against his father and he devoted himself to repentance with his whole heart (cf. our commentary to 35:22).

This affirmation is not at all contradicted by R' Yitzchak's remark which emphasizes a well-known psychological reaction: "The Torah teaches you here the general rule that when one does a *mitzvah* one must carry it out completely. Indeed, had Reuben known that the Torah would write about him: 'Reuben heard and he rescued him from their hand,' he would have carried Joseph on his shoulders and brought him right back to his father (instead of allowing him to be cast into the pit). The same remark applies to certain events in the lives of Aaron and Boaz" (*Vayikra Rabbah* 34).

22. הַשְׁלִיכוּ אֹתוֹ אֶל־הַבּוֹר — *Throw him into this pit.* "It was empty of water but it contained serpents and scorpions," says *Rashi* later, quoting the Midrash. But if this were so, asked the *Zohar*, how could Reuben hope "to rescue him from their hand, to return him to his father" without fearing the fatal bite of the reptiles? Reuben reasoned as follows: Joseph is now in the hands of Simeon and Levi, whose acts of violence are to be feared above all else. They had shown their cruelty and greed in connection with the people of Shechem. They are capable of torturing Joseph to death without leaving any trace of his corpse. It is better, Reuben thought, to throw him into a pit, even one full of snakes and scorpions, than to leave him in the hands of his ruthless brothers who detest him. If he is

²¹*Reuben heard, and he rescued him from their hand; he said,
"We will not strike him mortally!"* ²² *And Reuben said to them:
"Shed no blood! Throw him into this pit in the wilderness, but lay
no hand on him!"* — *intending to rescue him from their hand, to
return him to his father.*

²³ *And so it was, when Joseph came to his brothers they
stripped Joseph of his tunic, the fine woolen tunic that was on
him.* ²⁴ *Then they took him, and cast him into the pit; the pit was
empty, no water was in it.*

²⁵ *They sat to eat food; they raised their eyes and they saw,
behold!* — *a caravan of Ishmaelites was coming from Gilead,
their camels bearing spices, balsam, and lotus* — *on their way to
bring them down to Egypt.* ²⁶ *Judah said to his brothers, "What
gain will there be if we kill our brother and cover up his blood?*

innocent, God will rescue him from the attacks of beasts even if it takes a
miracle. But men, on the other hand, have free will, and Providence only rarely
intervenes when they exercise it. It is in this sense that the twice-repeated phrase:
וַיַּצִּלֵהוּ מִיָּדָם, *and he rescued him from their hand*, is to be understood. Reuben
wanted first and foremost to save Joseph from the hands of Simeon and Levi,
even if it meant exposing him to venomous serpents instead. He was counting
on Divine mercy, just as King David was when he said to the prophet Gad: *Let
us fall then into the hand of God, for He is full of mercy, but let me not fall into
the hand of man* (II Samuel 24:14).

25. וַיֵּשְׁבוּ לֶאֱכָל־לֶחֶם — *They sat to eat food.* This detail proves that they had a
clear conscience and felt that they had committed no crime, as was explained
above (verse 20). But Divine justice must be carried out. Of course it can appear
long-suffering but it never abandons its claim. "You sold your brother," cried
out a voice from Heaven, "and you sit down to a feast?! The time will come
when your children will be sold in the midst of a feast." And many centuries
later this came to pass in Shushan, the capital of Persia, when *the king*
(Ahasueres) *and Haman sat down to drink* (*Esther* 3:15) upon issuing the decree
of extermination of the Jews (*Midrash Psalms* 10).

26. מַה־בֶּצַע — *What gain. Rashi* interprets: "What monetary gain," following
the translation of the *Targum.* But *Ibn Ezra* and others translate the word בֶּצַע
as meaning purpose or profit. This is also how the *Maharsha* explains it in interpreting R' Meir's words (*Sanhedrin* 7a): "Whoever curses Judah for having said
מַה־בֶּצַע is but a blasphemer. To be sure, Judah did not want to stop his brothers
from murdering just because it was not going to bring them any financial gain.
But he wanted to express this idea: what purpose do we have for killing Joseph?
What we really want is to be rid of him. For that we just have to sell him."

כִּי נַהֲרֹג אֶת־אָחִינוּ — *If we kill our brother. Reuben* had already persuaded his
brothers not to kill Joseph but to throw him into a pit where he would die a slow

כז לְכוּ וְנִמְכְּרֶנּוּ לַיִּשְׁמְעֵאלִים וְיָדֵנוּ אַל־תְּהִי־בֹו כִּי־אָחִינוּ
בְשָׂרֵנוּ הוּא וַיִּשְׁמְעוּ אֶחָיו: וַיַּעַבְרוּ אֲנָשִׁים מִדְיָנִים סֹחֲרִים כח
וַיִּמְשְׁכוּ וַיַּעֲלוּ אֶת־יוֹסֵף מִן־הַבּוֹר וַיִּמְכְּרוּ אֶת־יוֹסֵף
לַיִּשְׁמְעֵאלִים בְּעֶשְׂרִים כָּסֶף וַיָּבִיאוּ אֶת־יוֹסֵף מִצְרָיְמָה: וַיָּשָׁב כט
רְאוּבֵן אֶל־הַבּוֹר וְהִנֵּה אֵין־יוֹסֵף בַּבּוֹר וַיִּקְרַע אֶת־בְּגָדָיו:
ל וַיָּשָׁב אֶל־אֶחָיו וַיֹּאמַר הַיֶּלֶד אֵינֶנּוּ וַאֲנִי אָנָה אֲנִי־בָא:

death. Judah now reminds them that such an act is also considered "killing." The
punishment set down for a murderer differs only in degree from the one who
indirectly causes death (*Ramban*).

27. לְכוּ וְנִמְכְּרֶנּוּ לַיִּשְׁמְעֵאלִים — *Come, let us sell him to the Ishmaelites.* Judah
outwitted his brothers with crafty arguments: "Surely, if we kill him, it will
thwart his ambitions and we won't have to become his servants. But things
will be worse. We will still have to submit to the Divine decree of four hundred
years of bondage announced to Abraham. Now, we can rid ourselves of the
two servitudes at the same time by selling Joseph to the Ishmaelites. He will
be their slave and since he will already be in bondage Providence will make
him and his descendants subject to the decree of the four hundred years of
slavery" (*Torah Sheleimah*).

וַיִּשְׁמְעוּ אֶחָיו — *His brothers agreed.* This is the first time that Judah speaks up
and proceeds to impose his will on his brothers. He had the spirit of a leader and
his authority was uncontested, which was not the case with Reuben. But Judah
did not know how to exploit the authority he had over his brothers and he had
to suffer the consequences of this weakness. Indeed, the next chapter deals with
Judah's "going down" from his brothers, that is to say, his downfall. And *Rashi*
explains: This account teaches us that the brothers deposed Judah from his
dignified position when they saw their father's intense grief. They said to him:
"You were the one who said we should sell him. Had you told us to bring him
back to the house, we would have obeyed" (38:1).

28. וַיַּעַבְרוּ אֲנָשִׁים מִדְיָנִים סֹחֲרִים — *Midianite men, traders, passed by.* "This was
a different caravan. From this we see that Joseph was sold several times. His
brothers sold him to the Ishmaelites who sold him to the Midianites and the
Midianites sold him to the Egyptians" (*Rashi*). Several *Midrashim* recount the
many incidents involved in these sales, although how the sales were actually
carried out still remains in question.

These successive transfers from hand to hand are a prefiguration of the future
destiny of the Jewish people whose history is mirrored in Joseph's life (cf. our
commentary on verse 2). *They went from nation to nation, from one kingdom
to another* (*I Chronicles* 16:20). But Joseph went through all these ordeals
without rebelling, without recrimination. And in so doing he serves as an
example to his nation. He utters not a word of complaint. He represents the

27 *Come, let us sell him to the Ishmaelites — but let our hand not be upon him, for he is our brother, our own flesh." His brothers agreed.* 28 *Midianite men, traders, passed by; they drew Joseph up and lifted him out of the pit and sold Joseph to the Ishmaelites for twenty pieces of silver; then they brought Joseph to Egypt.* 29 *Reuben returned to the pit — and behold! — Joseph was not in the pit! So he rent his garments.* 30 *Returning to his brothers he said, "The boy is gone! And I — where can I go?"*

prototype of the "righteous person" of whom it is said, וְצַדִּיק בֶּאֱמוּנָתוֹ יִחְיֶה, *the righteous person lives by his faith in God (Habakkuk 2:4).*

וַיִּמְכְּרוּ אֶת־יוֹסֵף לַיִּשְׁמְעֵאלִים — *And sold Joseph to the Ishmaelites.* The sons of Jacob were never pardoned for the grave sin which they committed (selling Joseph) and for many generations afterwards their descendants had to suffer their share of the punishment. The agony of the "ten martyrs" put to death by Roman tyrants was a late expiation of their sin, as is recounted in several of the *selichos.* The accusation leveled against them was (following from the principle of collective responsibility) based on the crime perpetrated by the sons of Jacob and not brought to justice, despite the Divine command (*Exodus* 21:16): "One who kidnaps a man and sells him, and he was found to have been in his power, shall surely be put to death" (*Midrash Tehillim* 10). *Thus said God,* exclaims the prophet Amos, *because of the threefold, of the fourfold iniquity of Israel, I will not forgive him — because of their selling the righteous one for silver and the weak for a pair of sandals* (2:6) [cf. our commentary on *Genesis* 44:17].

בְּעֶשְׂרִים כָּסֶף — *For twenty pieces of silver.* How can it be that a young man of such noble bearing as Joseph was sold for so little? It is because he had been so terrified by the serpents in the pit that his features had changed and he looked like a different person. Later, however, he regained his composure and his natural appearance, whereupon the merchants added a pair of sandals to their sum of money (as was brought out in the verse just quoted from *Amos*). According to other sources, the brothers divided up the twenty pieces of silver and each bought a pair of sandals, a sign of their supreme disdain for Joseph and his dreams (*Tanchuma*).

29. וַיָּשָׁב רְאוּבֵן — *Reuben returned. Rashi* quotes two explanations from the Midrash: "He was not present at the sale. That day it was his turn to attend upon his father. Another explanation: Dressed in sackcloth at home, he was fasting for having disturbed the couch of his father." According to the second interpretation the word וַיָּשָׁב, which is repeated twice in this context, refers to Reuben's תְּשׁוּבָה, *teshuvah,* "return to God" as shown in his desire to redeem himself by saving Joseph from the hands of his brothers (cf. our commentary to verse 21). Reuben, the Midrash remarks, was the first man to do penance by his own initiative. (To be sure, Adam too had done repentance but he did so only

לא וַיִּקְחוּ אֶת־כְּתֹנֶת יוֹסֵף וַיִּשְׁחֲטוּ שְׂעִיר עִזִּים וַיִּטְבְּלוּ
לב אֶת־הַכֻּתֹּנֶת בַּדָּם: וַיְשַׁלְּחוּ אֶת־כְּתֹנֶת הַפַּסִּים וַיָּבִיאוּ
אֶל־אֲבִיהֶם וַיֹּאמְרוּ זֹאת מָצָאנוּ הַכֶּר־נָא הַכְּתֹנֶת בִּנְךָ הִוא
לג אִם־לֹא: וַיַּכִּירָהּ וַיֹּאמֶר כְּתֹנֶת בְּנִי חַיָּה רָעָה אֲכָלָתְהוּ טָרֹף
לד טֹרַף יוֹסֵף: וַיִּקְרַע יַעֲקֹב שִׂמְלֹתָיו וַיָּשֶׂם שַׂק בְּמָתְנָיו וַיִּתְאַבֵּל
לה עַל־בְּנוֹ יָמִים רַבִּים: וַיָּקֻמוּ כָל־בָּנָיו וְכָל־בְּנֹתָיו לְנַחֲמוֹ

after God had reproached and punished him.) Accordingly, it was his descendant, the prophet Hosea from the tribe of Reuben, who more than any other prophet would call the people of Israel to repent (cf. *Tosafos* to *Bava Kamma* 92a, ד״ה מי).

31. וַיִּשְׁחֲטוּ שְׂעִיר — *Slaughtered a goatling.* The blood of this animal, says *Rashi*, resembles man's blood. This is indeed so, adds the *Zohar*, but there is another reason concealed behind these events. We know that Providence judges the least fault of the righteous with extreme severity (הקב״ה מְדַקְדֵּק עִם הַצַּדִּיקִים כְּחוּט הַשַּׂעֲרָה). This was the case with Jacob. He had received Divine approval for the blessings which his father Isaac had previously given him. But nevertheless he had tricked his father by putting on goatskins and covering his hands with them. Here Jacob suffers the consequences of that act. He too was tricked by the goatskin sent by his sons. And the great shock inflicted on his father (27:33) Jacob was to pay for here by the terror which seized him regarding the fate of his son Joseph. And the question which his sons now ask him: "Is it your son's tunic or not?" reflects the question asked in anguish by his own father, a question provoked by Jacob's deception: "Are you, indeed, my son Esau or not?" (ibid. 21).

33. חַיָּה רָעָה אֲכָלָתְהוּ — *A savage beast devoured him!* And why, asks *Rashi*, did the Holy One, Blessed is He, not reveal the truth to him? It is because they had pronounced a curse and called for the excommunication of anyone who would reveal the truth and they had associated the Holy One, Blessed is He, with it. (Judah had told them that excommunication was valid only when pronounced in the presence of ten people. Now Reuben and Benjamin were absent. So they associated the name of the Holy One, Blessed is He, with their plan, for the *Shechinah* was present among them, as was mentioned in the commentary on verse 12 — *Tanchuma.*) According to *R' Eliyahu Mizrachi*, this association refers to the Divine approval which the brothers were certain they had received. Indeed, they considered themselves messengers of Providence carrying out His plans. But this "association" signifies something more. It includes the presence of the Divine with man whenever it is to assure individual or collective salvation. This procedure should not appear strange to you, writes *R' Bachya*, for Abraham too had asked the Holy One, Blessed is He, to associate His Majesty with the righteous of Sodom in order to make up the ten needed to save the inhabitants. And do not think that our case is different because it involves a

³¹ They took Joseph's tunic, slaughtered a goatling, and dipped the tunic in the blood. ³² They dispatched the fine woolen tunic and they brought it to their father, and said, "We found this; identify, if you please: Is it your son's tunic or not?" ³³ He recognized it and he said, "My son's tunic! A savage beast devoured him! Joseph has surely been torn to bits!" ³⁴ Then Jacob rent his garments and placed sackcloth on his loins; he mourned for his son many days. ³⁵ All his sons and all his daughters arose to comfort him,

calamity, whereas with Sodom it was a matter of saving the city. Not so. The brothers thought that if their father found out the truth, it would bring his eternal curse on them. This would ultimately compromise the future of the Jewish people and consequently the spread of the knowledge of God. It was therefore justifiable to associate the Holy One, Blessed is He, with their oath. However, the prohibition from revealing the truth only concerned revealing it to their father Jacob. It did not apply to Isaac or to Benjamin. According to some sources even Reuben never knew the whole truth. As for Joseph, he probably had been obliged to swear not to enter into any communication with his father without his brother's authorization (Baal HaTurim 42,1). Neither he nor Isaac nor Benjamin ever revealed the secret, and thus the family destiny was able to unfold according to the providential plan.

טָרֹף טֹרַף יוֹסֵף — Joseph has surely been torn to bits! Cf. Rashi on the phrase: מִטֶּרֶף בְּנִי עָלִיתָ, from the prey, my son, you elevated yourself (Genesis 49:9), said by Jacob as he blesses his son Judah for the last time. Referring to the similarity in the words טָרֹף and מִטֶּרֶף, Rashi explains: "You have gone up, i.e., you cleared yourself from that which I had suspected you of when I said, A savage beast has devoured him. Joseph has surely been torn to bits (alluding to Judah, who is described as a wild beast, a young lion, ibid.) when you saved Joseph's life and said, What gain ..."

35. וְכָל-בְּנֹתָיו — And all his daughters. Rashi explains, "R' Yehudah said: A twin sister was born with each of the sons and each married a twin. R' Nechemiah said: 'They were Canaanites. But then why does it say his daughters? They were his daughters-in-law but one readily calls one's son-in-law 'my son' and one's daughter-in-law 'my daughter.' " Ramban, however, points out that R' Nechemiah only speaks of "Canaanite women" to give an opposing opinion to the first, either because he totally denies the existence of the twin sisters or because he holds that union with sisters who have the same mother is forbidden even to the Noachians, as the Talmud stipulates (Sanhedrin 48b). R' Nechemiah employs the term Canaanite as a collective noun designating the Egyptians, the Ammonites, the Moabites, and the descendants of Ishmael and Keturah, but excluding the native women of Canaan. Indeed, it is inconceivable that the children of the patriarchs should marry women who came from the "cursed race" descending from Canaan, which Abraham and Isaac had so often

וַיְמָאֵן לְהִתְנַחֵם וַיֹּאמֶר כִּי־אֵרֵד אֶל־בְּנִי אָבֵל שְׁאֹלָה וַיֵּבְךְּ
לו אֹתוֹ אָבִיו: וְהַמְּדָנִים מָכְרוּ אֹתוֹ אֶל־מִצְרָיִם לְפוֹטִיפַר סְרִיס
פַּרְעֹה שַׂר הַטַּבָּחִים:
לח רביעי א וַיְהִי בָּעֵת הַהִוא וַיֵּרֶד יְהוּדָה מֵאֵת אֶחָיו וַיֵּט עַד־אִישׁ
ב עֲדֻלָּמִי וּשְׁמוֹ חִירָה: וַיַּרְא־שָׁם יְהוּדָה בַּת־אִישׁ כְּנַעֲנִי וּשְׁמוֹ
ג שׁוּעַ וַיִּקָּחֶהָ וַיָּבֹא אֵלֶיהָ: וַתַּהַר וַתֵּלֶד בֵּן וַיִּקְרָא אֶת־שְׁמוֹ

denounced (*Ramban* on 38:2). *Maharal*, though, suggests that the prohibition against marrying Canaanite women only applied to the generations coming soon after Abraham. It no longer applied to the children of Jacob, who already formed the nucleus of the future nation. By that time, the danger coming from marriage with foreign women, if they were ready to serve God, no longer existed. On the contrary, the radiance of Divine truth was growing so intense that it could enlighten pagans and bring them back to God. The *Zohar* draws similar conclusions regarding the "young pagan virgins" when it discusses what Moses said just after the war with the Midianites: *But all the young children among the women who have not known lying with a male, you may keep alive for yourselves* (Numbers 31:18) [cf. our commentary on 26:5 and 29:28].

36. וְהַמְּדָנִים מָכְרוּ אֹתוֹ אֶל־מִצְרָיִם — *Now the Medanites had sold him to Egypt.* The end of the chapter emphasizes that Joseph was sold several times and to several people. And so the brothers completely lost track of him. Joseph could not be found despite their searches. The end of the chapter takes us then right to the heart of the tragedy. The brothers probably shared the vague feeling that Joseph was not gone forever, and this hope gave them the courage to remain unmoved when they faced the poignant suffering of their father. They were convinced that sooner or later the suffering would give way to the joy of finding the lost son. But for the moment, the Patriarchal family found itself plunged into the depths of despair.

38.

1. וַיְהִי בָּעֵת הַהִוא — *It was at that time.* Rashi explains: "Why is this account placed here, interrupting the story of Joseph? It is to teach us that the brothers deposed Judah from his leadership when they saw the grief of their father. They said to Judah, 'It is you who told us to sell him. Had you told us to bring him back home we would have listened to you.'" *Sforno* emphasizes more explicitly Judah's responsibility in the action taken against Joseph. His culpability was great and his wrongdoing in destroying the peace of the family now turned against him. Right in his own household death and jealousy among the brothers broke out. "Measure for measure" — with the loss of his own sons Judah will come to know the cruel suffering he has caused his father.

וַיֵּרֶד יְהוּדָה — *Judah went down.* Coming after the sale of Joseph, Judah's moral downfall (attributable to the causes which have just been mentioned),

but he refused to comfort himself, and said: "For I will go down to the grave mourning for my son." And his father bewailed him. ³⁶ *Now the Medanites had sold him to Egypt, to Potiphar, a courtier of Pharaoh, the Chamberlain of the Butchers.*

¹ *It was at that time that Judah went down from his brothers and turned away towards an Adullamite man whose name was Hirah.* ² *There Judah saw the daughter of a prominent merchant whose name was Shua; he married her and consorted with her.* ³ *She conceived and bore a son and he called his name*

aggravated by his material decline (as emphasized in the *Targum Yonasan*), marks the lowest point in the destiny of the family of Abraham. The future seems tragically jeopardized and the horizon appears bleak. However, the history of our people teaches us with numerous examples that providential help comes just at the moment of deepest despair. For "God creates the cure before the illness' (*Megillah* 13b). And the prophet Isaiah exclaims in his vivid style: *Before she had travailed, she* (the daughter of Zion) *brought children into the world* (66:7). Before beginning the first exile, Providence was preparing the light of the ultimate redeemer. And so, just as the sale of Joseph to Egypt led to the Egyptian exile, the Torah mentions Judah's marriage, the marriage from which will come Peretz, forefather of the kingly line of the house of David, ancestor of the messianic dynasty (*Ruth* 4:18). Once again providential action is seen manifesting itself among and above the comings and goings of men's lives. The Midrash expresses this truth when it strikingly portrays the scene which unfolds in this *sidrah*: "The tribes were involved with the sale of Joseph, Jacob was deep in mourning, and Judah was absorbed in looking for a wife, while God was kindling the spark of the messianic king" (*Rabbah* 85). The greatest purposes of history are born in the secret of silence, unknown to anyone. For "blessing reigns only upon that which is hidden from sight" (*Taanis* 8b).

וַיֵּט עַד־אִישׁ עֲדֻלָּמִי — *And turned away towards an Adullamite man.* Judah headed for the region which his tribe would one day inherit. Adullam was indeed part of Judah's territory, as the book of *Joshua* points out (15:35). There he met a man called Hirah, and "he made friends with him" (*Rashi*). This man liked the family of Judah, as our Sages tell us (*Rabbah* 85), and he was an ancestor of Hiram, the king of Tyre, of whom Scripture relates: *He had always been a friend of David* (I *Kings* 5:15). It was Hiram who provided a large part of the materials for the building of Solomon's Temple (ibid. verse 8) and made a treaty with him. Thus, guided by Providence, Judah showed the way for the destiny of his people, just as the patriarchs had done before him.

2. בַּת־אִישׁ כְּנַעֲנִי — *The daughter of a prominent merchant.* Cf. our commentary to 37:35. R' Shimon ben Lakish holds that the term כְּנַעֲנִי is used here in the sense of "merchant" (as in *Hosea* 12:8) for it is inconceivable that Judah would marry

ד-ה עֵר: וַתַּהַר עוֹד וַתֵּלֶד בֵּן וַתִּקְרָא אֶת־שְׁמוֹ אוֹנָן: וַתֹּסֶף עוֹד
וַתֵּלֶד בֵּן וַתִּקְרָא אֶת־שְׁמוֹ שֵׁלָה וְהָיָה בִכְזִיב בְּלִדְתָּהּ אֹתוֹ:
ו-ז וַיִּקַּח יְהוּדָה אִשָּׁה לְעֵר בְּכוֹרוֹ וּשְׁמָהּ תָּמָר: וַיְהִי עֵר בְּכוֹר
ח יְהוּדָה רַע בְּעֵינֵי יהוה וַיְמִתֵהוּ יהוה: וַיֹּאמֶר יְהוּדָה לְאוֹנָן

a Canaanite woman, going against the warnings of Abraham and Isaac
(*Pesachim* 50b). *Onkelos* and *Rashi* adopt this interpretation. But the question
still arises: Why does the Torah make a point of telling us that Shua was a
merchant and why does it describe him as such with a rarely-used expression
that can be taken in two ways? We can assume that by stressing the Canaanite
origins of Judah's wife right at the beginning of the chapter, the Torah wants
to draw our attention to the same relationship as those previously explained in
our commentary to 19:15. The royal lineage of the house of David, noted the
Midrash on that occasion, descended on its maternal side from the perverse city
of Sodom. It goes back to the daughter of Lot who, through an incestuous union,
gave birth to Moab, the forefather of the nation from which descended Ruth,
David's ancestor. Now, just as the maternal side of the dynasty of the future
messianic king was tainted by sin, so too the paternal side was affected by
Judah's wrongdoing. He married a Canaanite woman and this was the
beginning of his "fall," as the Torah shows; he cohabited with his
daughter-in-law and from this forbidden union came Peretz, the paternal
ancestor of David (*Ruth* 4:18-22).

In order to understand the minds of men of all races, in order to inspire them
with a deep love of God, the future redeemer of mankind will no doubt have to
carry a drop of non-Jewish blood in his veins. And in order to be the supreme
arbiter of justice and altruistic love, he must also have witnessed error and sin
right in the ranks of his own family (פי׳ הרא״ש בהדר זקנים).

וַיִּקָּחֶהָ — *He married her.* She converted and then he married her (*Targum Yonasan*).

5. וְהָיָה בִכְזִיב — *And it was in Chezib. Rashi* explains: "A place-name. And I
think that it is because she stopped having children there that the place was
called כְּזִיב: כזב means *cessation*, *disappointing*, or *deceiving* (following other
examples in Scripture). If not, then what does it come to teach us?" But in his
comments on this, *Maharal* does not consider that the fact that "she stopped
having children there" is sufficient justification for teaching us that the place
was called כְזִיב. And so, it is appropriate to see in this detail a hint that Judah's
wife was physically still capable of having children. And if she ceased bearing,
it was the result of an act of Providence which pursues its historical designs and
carries them out come what may. Mentioning the name of the place where
Judah's wife had her last child therefore serves to remind us that this whole
account fits into the pattern of a vast providential plan.

Historically, the town of Chezib had a role to play in the time of the would-be
messiah, Bar Kochba, in the second century of the common era. He was also

Er. ⁴ *She conceived again and bore a son and she called his name*
Onan. ⁵ *And yet again and she bore a son; and called his name*
Shelah; and it was in Chezib when she bore him.

⁶ *Judah took a wife for Er his firstborn; her name was Tamar.*
⁷ *But Er, Judah's firstborn, was evil in the eyes of* HASHEM,
and HASHEM *caused him to die.* ⁸ *Then Judah said to Onan,*

called Bar Koziba because he came from Chezib. The fact that his father
Hezekiah was descended from the kings of Judea, from the dynasty of David,
and that he was born in Chezib where Judah, the founder of the royal tribe, had
resided (as this passage shows), did much to make his contemporaries look upon
him as the Messiah (*Eichah Rabbah* 2). The city of Chezib belonged to Judah's
territory, as we read in *Joshua* (15:44).

6. לְעֵר בְּכוֹרוֹ — *For Er his firstborn.* He was then seven years old (*Seder Olam*
2). Conclude from this, adds the Midrash, that it is appropriate to marry off one's
children from the time they reach puberty (which took place then at the age
given).

וּשְׁמָהּ תָּמָר — *Whose name was Tamar.* "She was descended from Noah's son
Shem and was as beautiful as a palm" (*Midrash HaGadol*). The word תָּמָר
means *palm.* While the wife of Judah is never named but only called the
daughter of Shua, his daughter-in-law is known only by her name Tamar.
Indeed Tamar was distinguished by her personal worth, whereas the other was
nothing more than her father's daughter. Philo of Alexandria tells us that Tamar
was brought up among idolaters and converted to a belief in One God (as is
confirmed in *Sotah* 10a); the high rank attained by her descendants was due to
her chastity and her virtuous life. Her parents, who were not slaves, had come
from Palestinian Syria (*De Virtutibus* 6).

Some authors compare Tamar's character to Rebecca's. Both were motivated
by a great determination, both did not hesitate to resort to ruse, one in order to
ensure that the paternal blessing would go to the son who she knew was the
most worthy of it, the other to ensure her perpetual attachment to the family of
Abraham. Even after losing both her husbands, Judah's sons, Tamar had but one
desire: to have the joy of founding a branch in the holy family of the patriarchs.
Many generations later her virtue still served as an example. When Boaz married
Ruth, the townspeople blessed him in these words: *May your house be like the*
house of Peretz whom Tamar bore to Judah (*Ruth* 4:12).

7. רַע בְּעֵינֵי ה׳ — *Evil in the eyes of* HASHEM. Just like Onan, he committed the
same corrupt act. For of Onan it is said (in verse 10): *He caused him to die also.*
Just as Er died, so did Onan die. And why did Er do it (the sin of onanism)?
Because he did not want his wife to lose her beauty through pregnancy and
childbirth (*Rashi*). *Radak* adds: "This is why the Torah notes both here and in
verse 10: בְּעֵינֵי ה׳, *in the eyes of* HASHEM. The people, including the father of the
two sons, did not know of this sin; it was seen only by God."

ט בָּא אֶל־אֵשֶׁת אָחִיךָ וְיַבֵּם אֹתָהּ וְהָקֵם זֶרַע לְאָחִיךָ: וַיֵּדַע
אוֹנָן כִּי לֹא לוֹ יִהְיֶה הַזָּרַע וְהָיָה אִם־בָּא אֶל־אֵשֶׁת אָחִיו
י וְשִׁחֵת אַרְצָה לְבִלְתִּי נְתָן־זֶרַע לְאָחִיו: וַיֵּרַע בְּעֵינֵי יהוה
יא אֲשֶׁר עָשָׂה וַיָּמֶת גַּם־אֹתוֹ: וַיֹּאמֶר יְהוּדָה לְתָמָר כַּלָּתוֹ שְׁבִי
אַלְמָנָה בֵית־אָבִיךְ עַד־יִגְדַּל שֵׁלָה בְנִי כִּי אָמַר פֶּן־יָמוּת
יב גַּם־הוּא כְּאֶחָיו וַתֵּלֶךְ תָּמָר וַתֵּשֶׁב בֵּית אָבִיהָ: וַיִּרְבּוּ הַיָּמִים
וַתָּמָת בַּת־שׁוּעַ אֵשֶׁת־יְהוּדָה וַיִּנָּחֶם יְהוּדָה וַיַּעַל עַל־גֹּזֲזֵי
יג צֹאנוֹ הוּא וְחִירָה רֵעֵהוּ הָעֲדֻלָּמִי תִּמְנָתָה: וַיֻּגַּד לְתָמָר
יד לֵאמֹר הִנֵּה חָמִיךְ עֹלֶה תִמְנָתָה לָגֹז צֹאנוֹ: וַתָּסַר בִּגְדֵי
אַלְמְנוּתָהּ מֵעָלֶיהָ וַתְּכַס בַּצָּעִיף וַתִּתְעַלָּף וַתֵּשֶׁב בְּפֶתַח
עֵינַיִם אֲשֶׁר עַל־דֶּרֶךְ תִּמְנָתָה כִּי רָאֲתָה כִּי־גָדַל שֵׁלָה וְהִוא

8. וְיַבֵּם אֹתָהּ — *And enter into levirate marriage with her.* Judah was the first one to perform the duty of levirate marriage (*Rabbah* 85). *Ramban* adds that long before the Torah was given this law was known even among gentiles. The Sages of the world then were aware of the phenomenon of metempsychosis (transmigration of souls) which is possibly at the origin of the law of levirate marriage. This law prescribes that "when brothers dwell together and one of them dies and has no child, the wife of the deceased shall not marry outside the family to one not of his kin; her husband's brother shall come to her ... and it will be that the firstborn that she bears will succeed to the name of his dead brother, so that his name be not blotted out from Israel" (*Deuteronomy* 25:5-6). *Don Isaac Abarbanel* explains that the soul of the one who died before it fulfilled its destiny on earth finds it most perfect reincarnation in the body of his brother (*ibid.*). And so the Torah limits the duty of levirate marriage to the brother of the deceased, whereas beforehand it was carried out by any close relative. This explains Tamar's action and Judah's acknowledgment (verse 26) that his cohabitation with her was legitimate after all, as *Rashi* and *Ramban* point out.

9. וְשִׁחֵת אַרְצָה — *He would let it go to waste on the ground. Rashi* explains, "He had incomplete intercourse with her and ejaculated outside." From the fact that Onan and his brother perished, R' *Yochanan* concludes: "He who commits the sin of onanism is liable to the death penalty" (*Niddah* 13b). Our Sages consider onanism (often wrongly confused with masturbation) to be an exceptionally grave sin and they stigmatize it as an outrage against the Creator, a defiance of the Divine order of nature, an abject and immoral act (*ibid.*). To be sure, the capital punishment mentioned here by the Torah is carried out by heavenly justice, not by a human tribunal. However, the sin was serious enough to warrant this as its punishment even if committed by seven-year-old boys. But R' *Shmuel Edels* remarks that the death penalty would not have been applied

"Consort with your brother's wife and enter into levirate marriage with her, and establish offspring for your brother."

⁹ *But Onan knew that the seed would not be his; so it was, that whenever he would consort with his brother's wife, he would let it go to waste on the ground so as not to provide offspring for his brother.* ¹⁰ *What he did was evil in the eyes of HASHEM, and He caused him to die also.*

¹¹ *Then Judah said to Tamar, his daughter-in-law, "Remain a widow in your father's house until my son Shelah grows up" — for he thought, "Lest he also die like his brothers." — So Tamar went and lived in her father's house.*

¹² *Many days passed and Shua's daughter, the wife of Judah, died; when Judah was consoled, he went up to oversee his sheepshearers — he and his Adullamite friend, Hirah — to Timnah.*

¹³ *And Tamar was told, as follows, "Behold your father-in-law is coming up to Timnah to shear his sheep."* ¹⁴ *So she removed her widow's garb from upon her, covered herself with a veil, and wrapped herself up; she then sat by the crossroads which is on the road toward Timnah, for she saw that Shelah had grown, and she*

to culprits of such a tender age had their father not also been guilty, as we indicated at the beginning of this chapter. The statement in the Decalogue that the iniquity of the fathers is visited upon their children comes into play here and is added to their own crime (*Sotah* 13b).

11. כִּי אָמַר פֶּן־יָמוּת גַּם־הוּא — *For he thought, "Lest he also die."* "This woman leads one to assume that her husbands die one after the other." This argument, which *Rashi* mentions, is rejected by several Sages, since such an assumption does in no way make one exempt from the duty of levirate marriage. In *Ramban's* view, Judah feared that Shelah had the same tendency for this shameful vice as his brothers, but he hoped to have a good influence on him as soon as Shelah reached puberty. He still wanted to wait, but Tamar felt that the time for waiting had come to an end.

14. וַתְּכַס בַּצָּעִיף וַתִּתְעַלָּף — *Covered herself with a veil, and wrapped herself up.* Two women covered their faces with shawls and both had twins. They were Rebecca and Tamar (*Rabbah* 85). On the similar characters of these two women cf. our commentary to verse 6.

וַתֵּשֶׁב בְּפֶתַח עֵינַיִם — *She then sat by the crossroads.* "Our Sages explain: At the gate of Abraham our father, on whom all eyes were fixed (בְּפֶתַח עֵינַיִם), intent on seeing him." This quote from *Rashi* refers, as R' Alexander brings out, to Abraham's tomb. Tamar had gone there to pray that she meet a man of the family of Abraham and be able to give a child to this holy family (*Sotah* 10a).

טו לֹא־נִתְּנָ֥ה ל֖וֹ לְאִשָּֽׁה: וַיִּרְאֶ֣הָ יְהוּדָ֔ה וַֽיַּחְשְׁבֶ֖הָ לְזוֹנָ֑ה כִּ֥י

טז כִסְּתָ֖ה פָּנֶֽיהָ: וַיֵּ֨ט אֵלֶ֜יהָ אֶל־הַדֶּ֗רֶךְ וַיֹּ֨אמֶר֙ הָֽבָה־נָּא֙ אָב֣וֹא

אֵלַ֔יִךְ כִּ֚י לֹ֣א יָדַ֔ע כִּ֥י כַלָּת֖וֹ הִ֑וא וַתֹּ֨אמֶר֙ מַה־תִּתֶּן־לִ֔י כִּ֥י

יז תָב֖וֹא אֵלָֽי: וַיֹּ֕אמֶר אָֽנֹכִ֛י אֲשַׁלַּ֥ח גְּדִֽי־עִזִּ֖ים מִן־הַצֹּ֑אן

יח וַתֹּ֕אמֶר אִם־תִּתֵּ֥ן עֵֽרָב֖וֹן עַ֣ד שָׁלְחֶֽךָ: וַיֹּ֗אמֶר מָ֣ה הָעֵֽרָבוֹן֮

אֲשֶׁ֣ר אֶתֶּן־לָךְ֒ וַתֹּ֗אמֶר חֹתָֽמְךָ֙ וּפְתִילֶ֔ךָ וּמַטְּךָ֖ אֲשֶׁ֣ר בְּיָדֶ֑ךָ

יט וַיִּתֶּן־לָ֛הּ וַיָּבֹ֥א אֵלֶ֖יהָ וַתַּ֣הַר לֽוֹ: וַתָּ֣קָם וַתֵּ֔לֶךְ וַתָּ֥סַר צְעִיפָ֖הּ

כ מֵֽעָלֶ֑יהָ וַתִּלְבַּ֖שׁ בִּגְדֵ֥י אַלְמְנוּתָֽהּ: וַיִּשְׁלַ֨ח יְהוּדָ֜ה אֶת־גְּדִ֣י

הָֽעִזִּ֗ים בְּיַד֙ רֵעֵ֣הוּ הָֽעֲדֻלָּמִ֔י לָקַ֥חַת הָֽעֵרָב֖וֹן מִיַּ֣ד הָֽאִשָּׁ֑ה וְלֹ֖א

כא מְצָאָֽהּ: וַיִּשְׁאַ֞ל אֶת־אַנְשֵׁ֤י מְקֹמָהּ֙ לֵאמֹ֔ר אַיֵּ֧ה הַקְּדֵשָׁ֛ה

הִ֥וא בָֽעֵינַ֖יִם עַל־הַדָּ֑רֶךְ וַיֹּ֣אמְר֔וּ לֹֽא־הָיְתָ֥ה בָזֶ֖ה קְדֵשָֽׁה:

כב וַיָּ֨שָׁב֙ אֶל־יְהוּדָ֔ה וַיֹּ֖אמֶר לֹ֣א מְצָאתִ֑יהָ וְגַ֨ם אַנְשֵׁ֤י הַמָּקוֹם֙

כג אָֽמְר֔וּ לֹֽא־הָיְתָ֥ה בָזֶ֖ה קְדֵשָֽׁה: וַיֹּ֤אמֶר יְהוּדָה֙ תִּֽקַּֽח־לָ֔הּ פֶּ֖ן

נִֽהְיֶ֣ה לָב֑וּז הִנֵּ֤ה שָׁלַ֨חְתִּי֙ הַגְּדִ֣י הַזֶּ֔ה וְאַתָּ֖ה לֹ֥א מְצָאתָֽהּ:

Tamar, says *Rashi* later (39:1), acted for the sake of Heaven (with pure intentions).

15. כִּי כִסְּתָה פָנֶיהָ — *Since she had covered her face.* This detail is mentioned twice, which prompts the Midrash (quoted by *Rashi*) to conclude: "She kept her face covered when she was in her father-in-law's house; she was so virtuous that he could not have any suspicions about her." Later, *Rashi* adds: "Because she lived virtuously in the house of her father-in-law, I have decided that she will give birth to kings. And I have decided that the royal lineage in Israel should come from the tribe of Judah" (verse 26).

This royal lineage goes back to another woman, Ruth the Moabitess. Just like Tamar, her piety and her virtue predestined her to be the ancestor of kings (*Rashi* on *Ruth* 2:5; *Shabbos* 113a). These two women, who became the matriarchs of David, Solomon, and the messianic king, were widows and had no other desire than to ensure that their dead husbands' names and posterity would endure. To this end, one showered her attentions on her father-in-law, in whom she found the soul of her husband, and the other did the same with Boaz, her husband's uncle. Out of love for their dead husbands, motivated by the purest ideal of giving birth to holy and righteous men, they performed the *mitzvah* of levirate marriage. Accordingly, God gave His assistance to these two women and they became pregnant from the first union (*Yevamos* 34b; *Zohar*). And so their union became definitive despite the ephemeral character which Judah had wanted to give it and despite the problem of legitimacy for Boaz regarding Ruth's Moabite origins (*Yevamos* 76b). Consequently, Judah "no longer separated himself" from Tamar, as *Rashi* notes in his second explanation on verse 26.

had not been given to him as a wife.

¹⁵ *When Judah saw her, he thought her to be a harlot since she had covered her face.* ¹⁶ *So he detoured to her by the road and said, "Come, if you please, let me consort with you," for he did not know that she was his daughter-in-law.*

And she said, "What will you give me if you consort with me?" ¹⁷ *He replied, "I will send you a kid of the goats from the flock."*
And she said, "Provided you leave a pledge until you send it." ¹⁸ *And he said, "What pledge shall I give you?"*

She replied, "Your signet, your wrap, and your staff that is in your hand." And he gave them to her, and consorted with her, and she conceived by him.

¹⁹ *Then she arose, left, and removed her veil from upon her, and she put on her widow's garb.*

²⁰ *Judah sent the kid of the goats through his friend the Adullamite to retrieve the pledge from the woman; but he did not find her.* ²¹ *He inquired of the people of her place, "Where is the prostitute, the one at the crossroads by the road?"*

And they said, "There was no prostitute here." ²² *So he returned to Judah and said, "I did not find her; even the local men said, 'There was no prostitute here.'"*

²³ *So Judah said, "Let her keep them, lest we become a laughingstock; I really sent her this kid, but you could not find her."*

16. וַיֵּט אֵלֶיהָ אֶל־הַדֶּרֶךְ — *So he detoured to her by the road.* In his *Guide* (2:6), *Rambam* quotes R' Yochanan's words: Judah was about to pass by — but God sent an angel of lust and said to him: "Where are you going, Judah? From where then will the kings come and from where the redeemers?" (*Rabbah* 85). Our Sages, explains *Rambam*, have clearly stated that all forces (dispositions) which reside in a body are called angels, much more the forces that are active in the universe, and every force has a certain definite action. Here, the natural and psychical forces are also called angels. Be that as it may, R' Yochanan's words emphasize once more that mysterious intertwining of providential action and human action. We have already mentioned its importance at the beginning of this section (עי' אור החיים, מ"ט, ט').

18. חֹתָמְךָ וּפְתִילֶךָ וּמַטְּךָ אֲשֶׁר בְּיָדֶךְ — *Your signet, your wrap, and your staff that is in your hand.* As if inspired by prophecy, she asked for the three objects which became the insignia of her descendants: the signet ring of royalty, the coat of the judge (in the future *Sanhedrin*) and the scepter of the Messiah (*Rabbah* 85).

23. תִּקַּח־לָהּ — *Let her keep them* [or, *let her take for herself* that which she had in hand]. From this verse *Rambam* concludes: "From Judah's action one can learn noble conduct and uprightness in judgment. This is why: before Mosaic

כד וַיְהִי ׀ כְּמִשְׁלְשׁ חֳדָשִׁים וַיֻּגַּד לְיהוּדָה לֵאמֹר זָנְתָה תָּמָר כַּלָּתֶךָ וְגַם הִנֵּה הָרָה לִזְנוּנִים וַיֹּאמֶר יְהוּדָה הוֹצִיאוּהָ וְתִשָּׂרֵף: כה הִוא מוּצֵאת וְהִיא שָׁלְחָה אֶל־חָמִיהָ לֵאמֹר לְאִישׁ אֲשֶׁר־אֵלֶּה לּוֹ אָנֹכִי הָרָה וַתֹּאמֶר הַכֶּר־נָא לְמִי הַחֹתֶמֶת וְהַפְּתִילִים וְהַמַּטֶּה הָאֵלֶּה: כו וַיַּכֵּר יְהוּדָה וַיֹּאמֶר צָדְקָה מִמֶּנִּי

legislation, dealings with a courtesan were as lawful as marriage is since that legislation, that is to say it was permitted and nobody considered it wrong (see *Mishneh Torah, Ishus* 1:4). The hire which was in those days paid to the harlot in accordance with a previous agreement corresponds to the marriage settlement which the husband nowadays pays to his wife when he divorces her. It is a just claim on the part of the wife and the husband is bound to pay it. When Judah then says, *lest we become a laughingstock*, he teaches us that it is shameful for us to speak of things connected with cohabitation, even when it is permitted, and that it is proper to be silent about it, to keep it secret, even if the silence leads to financial loss. This, as you see, is what Judah did when he said: 'It is better for us to lose property and to let her keep what she has than to make this public and bring still more shame upon us.'

This is the lesson of decent conduct which we learn from this incident. As to the uprightness to be learned from it, we see it from Judah's words (spoken to show that he had neither robbed her in any way nor departed in the slightest from his agreement with her): 'I really sent her this kid, etc.' For this kid was probably one of the best of its kind — therefore Judah uses the demonstrative term הַזֶּה, this particular one. Such is the uprightness which he had inherited from Jacob, Isaac and Abraham: that one should neither depart from one's word nor deviate from what one has agreed to; the settlement agreed upon with one's wife is to be treated in the same way as the wages of any hired servant which is due him, and the husband is not to look for a pretext to send her away without paying her the promised sum" (*Guide* 3:49) [וְעַיֵּי מהרש"א ח"א, סוטה י' ע"א].

24. **הוֹצִיאוּהָ וְתִשָּׂרֵף** — *Take her out and let her be burned! Rashi* explains: Ephraim Maksha'a said in the name of R' Meir, "She was the daughter of Shem, who was a priest, a *Kohen* (cf. *Rashi* on 14:18), and so she was condemned to be burned" (cf. *Leviticus* 21:9). But this justification is contested by *Ramban* (and others) from *halachah*. On this point, *Rashi's* opponents hold that Judah condemned his daughter-in-law to death not on legal grounds but by special right, since her loose behavior was an affront to his status as sovereign of the land. According to a "simple explanation," it was probably the custom then, as it was even later in other countries, that when a married woman was unfaithful her punishment was entirely at her husband's discretion; accordingly — although Tamar had been promised to Shelah and, as such, was regarded as his wife — because of Shelah's youth it was his father who sentenced her on his son's behalf.

Another interpretation, given by *Baal HaTurim* in the name of *R' Yehudah HaChassid*, has it that what is involved here is not a sentence to a fiery death,

²⁴ *And it was when about three months had passed, that Judah was told, "Your daughter-in-law has committed harlotry, and moreover, she has conceived by harlotry."*

Judah said, "Take her out and let her be burned!"

²⁵ *As she was taken out, she sent word to her father-in-law, saying, "By the man to whom these belong I am with child." And she said, "Identify, if you please, whose are this seal, this wrap, and this staff."*

²⁶ *Judah recognized; and he said, "She is right; it is from me,*

but a mark made by burning which would brand Tamar as a prostitute (*B. Epstein* in תו״ת sees this point of view as being based on the following fact: the word בָּאֵשׁ which occurs whenever the Torah speaks of death by burning — *Leviticus* 20 and 21:8 — is absent here). The code of Hammurabi (king of Babylon from 1792 to 1750 B.C.E. stipulates that unfaithful wives were to be branded with a mark on their foreheads (§ 126, ed. Berlin, 5683).

25. הוֹא מוּצֵאת וְהִיא שָׁלְחָה אֶל־חָמִיהָ — *As she was taken out, she sent word to her father-in-law.* She did not want to shame him, saying to him: "It is by you that I have conceived." But instead she declared, "By the man to whom these things belong, I am with child." She said to herself: "If he admits it, let him admit it on his own. If not, let them condemn me to be burnt alive for I will not subject him to public disgrace." From this we learn: it is better to let oneself be thrown into a fiery furnace than to shame one's fellowman in public (*Rashi*).

If the Torah makes a special point of telling us that Tamar sent back his pledges only at the last moment, "as she was taken out" to be executed, then there was good reason for it, notes R' Elazar. She had mislaid the pledges and could not find them. This was the work of Satan, who did his utmost to impede the entry of the messianic dynasty into the world, for in it he foresaw his most dangerous enemy. Tamar implored Divine mercy with all her soul and, just as she was being led to the stake, she found the objects as if by a miracle. Thus, historical destinies sometimes hang by a thread and their happy outcome is dependent on a miracle. R' Elazar continues: it is to this slight incident, in reality of very great consequence, that King David refers in his hymn to God (*Psalms* 56:1): לַמְנַצֵּחַ עַל יוֹנַת אֵלֶם רְחֹקִים לְדָוִד מִכְתָּם, *To the victor* [the angel Gabriel who conquered Satan and made the pledges reappear] *regarding the mute dove* [Tamar, who kept silent rather than humiliate Judah] *removed* [whose pledges were mislaid] *on the part of David* [her descendant who pays homage to the victor] *Michtam* [derived from מך ותם, the king, patient and loyal with all] (*Sotah* 10b). The interpretation regarding the mislaid pledges is suggested by the grammatical form of the word מוּצֵאת in our verse. It can be taken as the passive of מָצָא, *to find* — the pledge is found — whereas the usual form would be יוּצֵאת.

26. צָדְקָה מִמֶּנִּי — *She is right; it is from me* [lit. *she is more righteous than I*]. Contrary to the literal meaning, *Rashi* explains: "צָדְקָה, she is right in what she

כִּי־עַל־כֵּן לֹא־נְתַתִּיהָ לְשֵׁלָה בְנִי וְלֹא־יָסַף עוֹד לְדַעְתָּהּ:
כז-כח וַיְהִי בְּעֵת לִדְתָּהּ וְהִנֵּה תְאוֹמִים בְּבִטְנָהּ: וַיְהִי בְלִדְתָּהּ
וַיִּתֶּן־יָד וַתִּקַּח הַמְיַלֶּדֶת וַתִּקְשֹׁר עַל־יָדוֹ שָׁנִי לֵאמֹר
כט זֶה יָצָא רִאשֹׁנָה: וַיְהִי ׀ כְּמֵשִׁיב יָדוֹ וְהִנֵּה יָצָא אָחִיו
ל וַתֹּאמֶר מַה־פָּרַצְתָּ עָלֶיךָ פָּרֶץ וַיִּקְרָא שְׁמוֹ פָּרֶץ: וְאַחַר
יָצָא אָחִיו אֲשֶׁר עַל־יָדוֹ הַשָּׁנִי וַיִּקְרָא שְׁמוֹ זָרַח:

says, מִמֶּנִּי, she is pregnant by me." The literal meaning is subject to the question: how did Judah know that she had become pregnant from him and not from someone else? This is why *Rashi* adopts the interpretation given by R' Elazar: A voice spoke from Heaven and declared, מִמֶּנִּי, *from Me*; it is by My will that this has come about, that she is pregnant from Judah."

It was Shem's tribunal which was sitting when Tamar was to be executed and when she sent the three pledges to her father-in-law. Judah was one of the judges. He then rose to his feet and declared: "With your permission, my brothers, I proclaim here and now that man is dealt with measure for measure, be it for good or bad, but happy is he who recognizes his sin. It is because I dipped Joseph's coat in the blood of a goat and brought it to my father, saying: 'Please identify it. Is it your sons's shirt or not?' that I must now identify before the tribunal to whom the ring, the garment and the staff belong. But it is better to be humiliated and punished in this world than in the next, before my father.So, I acknowledge that Tamar is innocent. She is pregnant from me not because she yielded to any illicit passion but because I did not give her to my son Shelah." When Judah finished speaking, a voice rang out from the heavens and proclaimed: "You are both innocent, for it is by the Divine will that this has come to pass" (*Targum Yerushalmi*).

Judah was rewarded for admitting his sin publicly and removing suspicion from his brothers. From then on he was able to have his share in the World to Come. Judah's eldest brother Reuben followed his example and formally confessed his sin against his father (*Genesis* 35:22), thus clearing the brothers of all suspicion (*Sotah* 7b; cf. *Tosafos* to *Bava Kamma* 92a, ר״ה מי). His name יְהוּדָה then acquired its full significance, resulting from the double meaning of the root הודה, *to thank* (cf. 29:35, אוֹדֶה אֶת ה׳) and *to admit*. God definitively associated His own Name הֲוָיָ with Judah's, thereby showing His affection for the one who had the moral courage to confess his sin publicly (*Sotah* 10b).

27. וְהִנֵּה תְאוֹמִים בְּבִטְנָהּ — *That behold! There were twins in her womb.* That she was predestined to have twins is seen in her name תָּמָר which means date-palm. This plant is in fact a dioecious species of palm tree (*Midrash Bahir* § 138, ed. Leipzig 1923). In the same way, her two sons represent the masculine (sun-Zerah) and feminine (moon-Perez) principles, as explained below.

29. וַיִּקְרָא שְׁמוֹ פָּרֶץ — *And he called his name Perez.* For she cried out: "So, you have made a breach for yourself!" (פִּרְצָה, *a breach*). This action by the newborn

inasmuch as I did not give her to Shelah my son," and he was not intimate with her anymore.

²⁷ And it came to pass at the time she gave birth that behold! There were twins in her womb. ²⁸ And it happened that as she gave birth, one put out a hand; the midwife took a crimson thread and tied it on his hand saying, "This one emerged first!" ²⁹ And it was, as he drew back his hand, that behold! his brother emerged. And she said, "With what strength you asserted yourself!" And he called his name Perez. ³⁰ Afterwards his brother on whose hand was the crimson thread came out; and he called his name Zerah.

is an indication of the royal privilege which will subsequently be held by his descendants. For the king "has the right to open a breach for himself (פּוֹרֵץ גֶּדֶר) without anyone being able to stop him" (*Sanhedrin* 20b).

30. וַיִּקְרָא שְׁמוֹ זָרַח — *And he called his name Zerah.* It means "shining." According to the *Midrash Bahir* (ibid.), quoted by *Ramban*, this refers to the brilliant light of the sun, whereas the name of the younger brother, פֶּרֶץ, is an allusion to the moon which makes its way in the heavens, now visible, now obscured. To be sure, Zerah is the firstborn in the physiological sense, but his younger brother makes his way and is the first son to see the light of the day. This rivalry right from within the mother's womb is especially reminiscent of the rivalry between the two brothers Esau and Jacob, which manifested itself in very similar circumstances. And the deep significance of that earlier rivalry is not unlike that which is to be given to the relationship between Judah's two sons.

The rivalry between Esau and Jacob occurs again and again until the last descendants of Zerah and Perez. The name Perez refers to the moon, which more than any other heavenly body represents Jewry, whereas the sun that shines over the earth is Esau's star (cf. our commentary to 33:3). In its grandeur and its decline, the history of Jewry compares with the waxing and waning of the moon and Perez, the ancestor of the kings of the house of David, incarnates this changing course of the moon in its orbit around the sun. Just as the moon waxes during the first fifteen days of the month, so the Jewish people achieved its rise in the fifteen generations from Abraham to Solomon, while the fifteen generations of kings which followed mark its wane until the destruction of the Temple (cf. *R' Bachya*). The destiny of the house of David is thus outlined in the moon's path. The בִּרְכַּת הַלְבָנָה, *new-moon blessing,* which Jewry pronounces at each new moon, alludes to this with the words דָּוִד מֶלֶךְ יִשְׂרָאֵל חַי וְקַיָם, *David king of Israel still lives.* His hour of glory will come as surely as the moon attains its fullness despite its periodic waning. Certainly this heavenly body must often give way before its twin, the sun, which wins out over it in its resplendent journey over mankind. But has not the prophet Isaiah predicted that the time will come when the moon's light will match that of the sun (30:26)? Until then, just as Esau, who represents the pagan world, lived by the brute force of his hands (הַיָדַיִם יְדֵי עֵשָׂו), so too "the shining star" which Zerah symbolizes raises his hand (וַיִּתֶּן יָד), thereby

לט חמישי א וְיוֹסֵף הוּרַד מִצְרָיְמָה וַיִּקְנֵהוּ פּוֹטִיפַר סְרִיס פַּרְעֹה שַׂר
הַטַּבָּחִים אִישׁ מִצְרִי מִיַּד הַיִּשְׁמְעֵאלִים אֲשֶׁר הוֹרִדֻהוּ
ב שָׁמָּה: וַיְהִי יהוה אֶת־יוֹסֵף וַיְהִי אִישׁ מַצְלִיחַ וַיְהִי
ג בְּבֵית אֲדֹנָיו הַמִּצְרִי: וַיַּרְא אֲדֹנָיו כִּי יהוה אִתּוֹ וְכֹל

showing his domination over his twin brother Perez, the firstborn in the ethical but not in the legal sense. (The moon represents the feminine principle. It is passive and receptive in character for it receives light from the sun, which is identified with the masculine principle, active and impregnating. And on the terrestrial and material plane Jewry, compared with the world of its antagonists, is the weaker.)

39.

1. וְיוֹסֵף הוּרַד מִצְרָיְמָה — *And Joseph had been brought down to Egypt.* The passive form of the verb "to go down" is used here. It suggests that this descent was the work of a higher will. Accordingly, the Midrash begins its treatment of this chapter with a verse from *Psalms:* לְכוּ וּרְאוּ מִפְעֲלוֹת אֱלֹהִים נוֹרָא עֲלִילָה עַל בְּנֵי אָדָם, *Come, let us contemplate the works of God! He is awesome in deed toward mankind* (66:5). God, it then tells us, wanted to carry out His promise to Abraham that his offspring would be in a foreign land. But Jacob (וַיֵּשֶׁב), *settled*, in the land of Canaan and forgot about going down to Egypt. What did God do then? He dealt with Jacob as one deals with a cow being led to the slaughterhouse. If the cow refuses to budge, even when struck, one takes its calf and brings it ahead to the slaughterhouse. Immediately, the cow begins to follow its little one. Hence Joseph was taken from Jacob and "brought down to Egypt." Some years later, his father would follow together with the rest of the family. And so the patriarch came to Egypt, drawn by "human cords, by the ties of (paternal) love" as the prophet Hosea has it (11:4), but he could have been brought there in "chains of iron" or even by coercive measures to have the Divine promise fulfilled.

סְרִיס פַּרְעֹה שַׂר הַטַּבָּחִים — *A courtier of Pharaoh, the Chamberlain of the Butchers.* Some explain the word סְרִיס as king's cook, or executioner. It is also used in the sense of a eunuch. Some traditions have it that Potiphar probably bought Joseph because of his handsomeness, with the intention of engaging in pederasty with him. But he was stricken with impotence and subsequently became mutilated. He was then called פּוֹטִי פֶּרַע, the mutilated one, as in 41:45 (*Sotah* 13b).

מִיַּד הַיִּשְׁמְעֵאלִים — *From the Ishmaelites* [lit. *from the hand of . . .*]. As in *Genesis* 43:9, the expression "to buy from the hand of someone" implies that it is with his guarantee. Thus the Midrash notes here that Potiphar demanded guarantees regarding the origins of this slave. His appearance, his noble bearing, his whole personality, even his light complexion, made Potiphar suspicious, and the Arab sellers had to produce proof that Joseph had been properly acquired as a slave from a merchant caravan.

39   ¹*And Joseph had been brought down to Egypt. Potiphar, a courtier of Pharaoh, the Chamberlain of the Butchers, a prominent Egyptian, purchased him from the Ishmaelites who had brought him down there.* ² *HASHEM was with Joseph, and he came a successful man; and he remained in the house of his Egyptian master.* ³ *His master perceived that HASHEM was with him, and*

As for Joseph, he was urged to answer questions about his origins but he kept completely silent. He did not wish to humiliate his brothers by betraying them, and he kept the promise he had made to them (cf. *Rashi* on 45:27 and our commentary to 37:33). He had inherited the character of his mother who well knew how to keep a secret — as she had proved on her sister Leah's marriage night, even at the cost of her own personal happiness. Joseph's brother Benjamin also possessed this trait; he knew of everything, as is seen from the names he gave to his ten children (*Sotah* 36b), but he kept absolutely quiet (cf. our commentary ibid. and *Genesis Rabbah* 71).

2. וַיְהִי ה' אֶת־יוֹסֵף — *HASHEM was with Joseph.* The word וַיְהִי, *was*, is repeated three times in this verse. This seems to mean that Joseph "was himself" even while a slave in the house of his master. He just as much "was himself" there as he was after receiving the Divine benediction and becoming very successful. In explaining this verse the Sages point out: This is like a father who has ten children living in different countries. The one he visits is the youngest, the one furthest away, and the one who needs him more than the others. However, if God was with Joseph, it could only have been so because Joseph was with God. If man's purpose is identical with God's, circumstances develop in such a way that these purposes can be achieved.

אֲדֹנָיו הַמִּצְרִי — *His Egyptian master.* The epithet "Egyptian" is repeated several times in this chapter, as if to draw our attention to the immense contrast taking place in Joseph's life. From the sublime heights of the holy life he had lived at home, under the guidance of his patriarch father, Joseph had just been "brought down to Egypt," as we are told in the first words of this chapter. Here he will come to know the abysmal depth of an immoral and perverse civilization. One must know Egyptian arrogance, and how scornfully Egypt looked upon a stranger whatever his origins. Especially one must realize the level of morality in the Nile valley, that incredible depravity, that rejection of all moral scruples which makes Potiphar's wife the very prototype of the Egyptian woman, in order to fully appreciate the strength of character and the profound piety of the one whom Jacob later called "the pure among his brothers." What exceptional qualities a person had to have to reach Joseph's position in the house of his Egyptian master!

3. וַיַּרְא אֲדֹנָיו כִּי ה' אִתּוֹ — *His master perceived that HASHEM was with him.* It was due to Joseph that the first rays of the Divine light penetrated into Egypt. The *Shechinah* had "accompanied" Joseph to this land (as we see here from the

ד אֲשֶׁר־הוּא עֹשֶׂה יהוה מַצְלִיחַ בְּיָדְוֹ: וַיִּמְצָא יוֹסֵף חֵן בְּעֵינָיו
ה וַיְשָׁרֶת אֹתוֹ וַיַּפְקִדֵהוּ עַל־בֵּיתוֹ וְכָל־יֶשׁ־לוֹ נָתַן בְּיָדְוֹ: וַיְהִי
מֵאָז הִפְקִיד אֹתוֹ בְּבֵיתוֹ וְעַל כָּל־אֲשֶׁר יֶשׁ־לוֹ וַיְבָרֶךְ יהוה
אֶת־בֵּית הַמִּצְרִי בִּגְלַל יוֹסֵף וַיְהִי בִּרְכַּת יהוה בְּכָל־אֲשֶׁר
ו יֶשׁ־לוֹ בַּבַּיִת וּבַשָּׂדֶה: וַיַּעֲזֹב כָּל־אֲשֶׁר־לוֹ בְּיַד יוֹסֵף וְלֹא־יָדַע
אִתּוֹ מְאוּמָה כִּי אִם־הַלֶּחֶם אֲשֶׁר־הוּא אוֹכֵל וַיְהִי יוֹסֵף
ז יְפֵה־תֹאַר וִיפֵה מַרְאֶה: וַיְהִי אַחַר הַדְּבָרִים הָאֵלֶּה וַתִּשָּׂא
אֵשֶׁת־אֲדֹנָיו אֶת־עֵינֶיהָ אֶל־יוֹסֵף וַתֹּאמֶר שִׁכְבָה עִמִּי:
ח וַיְמָאֵן | וַיֹּאמֶר אֶל־אֵשֶׁת אֲדֹנָיו הֵן אֲדֹנִי לֹא־יָדַע אִתִּי
ט מַה־בַּבָּיִת וְכֹל אֲשֶׁר־יֶשׁ־לוֹ נָתַן בְּיָדִי: אֵינֶנּוּ גָדוֹל בַּבַּיִת הַזֶּה
מִמֶּנִּי וְלֹא־חָשַׂךְ מִמֶּנִּי מְאוּמָה כִּי אִם־אוֹתָךְ בַּאֲשֶׁר אַתְּ־
אִשְׁתּוֹ וְאֵיךְ אֶעֱשֶׂה הָרָעָה הַגְּדֹלָה הַזֹּאת וְחָטָאתִי לֵאלֹהִים:

ששי

use of the preposition אֶת rather than עִם) and It hovered so plainly over him that Potiphar, as it were, "saw It" with his own eyes. It alone can explain the mystery of the superiority of this slave, so radiant with religious piety and moral purity, with a brilliant mind, with physical perfection and personal magnetism. His triumphant success in all that he did could only have been the result of a blessing from a supernatural source.

5. וַיְבָרֶךְ ה׳ אֶת־בֵּית הַמִּצְרִי — *HASHEM blessed the Egyptian's house.* Scripture puts Joseph on equal terms with the Holy Ark, of which it is said: *The ark of God remained in the house of Obed-Edom the Gittite three months, and God blessed Obed-Edom and all his house* (II Samuel 6:11). Later, the Holy Ark and the coffin containing Joseph's bones will travel side by side at the head of the Jewish camp heading through the desert to the Holy Land.

בַּבַּיִת וּבַשָּׂדֶה — *In the house and in the field.* Joseph stayed one year in Potiphar's house; for six months he was appointed over the work in the fields and for the other six months, over the domestic affairs. It was during this period, remarks Philo, that Joseph had the opportunity to acquire the necessary knowledge for becoming a statesman (*De Josepho* 8). However, his stay in prison lasted twelve years (*Midrash*). He had left his father's house at seventeen and he became viceroy of Egypt at thirty.

7. וַיְהִי אַחַר הַדְּבָרִים הָאֵלֶּה — *After these things. Rashi* brings out that whenever the word אַחַר appears (instead of אַחֲרֵי), it indicates that what is about to be described is closely connected with the preceding subject. Here, seeing himself master and knowing that he was handsome in form and features (like his mother, 29:17) Joseph began to indulge himself, eating and drinking and combing his hair. The Midrash also adds that he began to express (mentally) words of gladness (אַחַר הַדְּבָרִים וגו׳) as in 22:1): "When I was in my father's house, my brothers were jealous of me and my father rebuked me. Now that I am here, at last I have some

whatever he did HASHEM *made succeed through him.* ⁴ *Joseph found favor in his eyes, and he attended him; he appointed him over his household, and whatever he had he placed in his custody.*

⁵ *And it happened, that from the time he appointed him in his house and over whatever he had,* HASHEM *blessed the Egyptian's house on Joseph's account, so that* HASHEM'S *blessing was in whatever he owned, in the house and in the field.* ⁶ *He left all that he had in Joseph's custody and with him present he concerned himself with nothing except for the bread he ate. Now Joseph was handsome of form and handsome of appearance.*

⁷ *After these things, his master's wife cast her eyes upon Joseph and she said, "Lie with me."* ⁸ *But he adamantly refused; he said to his master's wife, "Look — with me here, my master concerns himself about nothing in the house, and whatever he has he placed in my custody.* ⁹ *There is no one greater in this house than I, and he has denied me nothing but you, since you are his wife; how then can I perpetrate this great evil and have sinned against God!"*

relief, thank God." Then the Holy One, blessed is He, said to him: "Sated youth, your father is in mourning and you fix your hair! I will incite the 'bear' against you!"

וַתִּשָּׂא אֵשֶׁת־אֲדֹנָיו אֶת־עֵינֶיהָ אֶל־יוֹסֵף — *His master's wife cast her eyes upon Joseph.* Such was the custom of heathens, to ask an astrologer if the time was propitious for buying a slave. The expression "to cast one's eyes" may indeed refer to consulting the stars, as in *Deuteronomy* 4:19. "Thus, through studying the stars she found out that she would have sons with Joseph, but she did not know if this meant herself or her daughter" (*Rabbah* 87; cf. *Rashi* on verse 1). This is why the story of Potiphar's wife immediately follows that of Tamar; both thought they were acting for the sake of Heaven. On this Midrash see our commentary on 41:50.

8. וַיְמָאֵן — *But he adamantly refused.* The "note," the tonic accent for this word, is a שַׁלְשֶׁלֶת and is very rarely used. It indicates that Joseph's refusal of the designs of the temptress was repeated, categorical, and definitive. Potiphar's wife, who is called Zuleika in *Sefer HaYashar*, had certainly told him about the omens she had consulted (see above). But for this pure young man, no argument, no presage or horoscope, could prevail; he kept from sin. Joseph repulsed all her pretexts and passionate supplications with immovable firmness. He saw in this act nothing other than adultery, and adultery was a mortal sin forbidden to the children of Noah and obviously to the children of Abraham (cf. *Rashi* on verse 9).

"Is there among the virtuous a greater hero than a young seventeen-year-old surrounded by libertine women who nevertheless maintains his purity? Accordingly, Joseph was rewarded when, much later, his children received their blessing with the same words — וַיְמָאֵן ... וַיֹּאמֶר (48:19) — as those which had

י וַיְהִי כְּדַבְּרָהּ אֶל־יוֹסֵף יוֹם ׀ יוֹם וְלֹא־שָׁמַע אֵלֶיהָ לִשְׁכַּב
יא אֶצְלָהּ לִהְיוֹת עִמָּהּ: וַיְהִי כְּהַיּוֹם הַזֶּה וַיָּבֹא הַבַּיְתָה
לַעֲשׂוֹת מְלַאכְתּוֹ וְאֵין אִישׁ מֵאַנְשֵׁי הַבַּיִת שָׁם בַּבָּיִת:
יב וַתִּתְפְּשֵׂהוּ בְּבִגְדוֹ לֵאמֹר שִׁכְבָה עִמִּי וַיַּעֲזֹב בִּגְדוֹ בְּיָדָהּ
יג וַיָּנָס וַיֵּצֵא הַחוּצָה: וַיְהִי כִּרְאוֹתָהּ כִּי־עָזַב בִּגְדוֹ בְּיָדָהּ

told how he had resisted this treacherous temptation" (*Zohar*; cf. *Pesachim* 113a-b).

וַיֹּאמֶר — *He said.* He adjured his instincts not to give in, as all righteous do in the time of temptation (*Sifre Deuteronomy* 3:33; cf. our commentary to 14:22). He swore before God never to approach the wife of his master. This is why he said later (verse 9): How then can I do this great wickedness, and sin against God — by breaking my oath (*Tanchuma*).

10. כְּדַבְּרָהּ אֶל־יוֹסֵף יוֹם יוֹם — *Just as she coaxed Joseph day after day.* Two of Rachel's descendants underwent similar tests and enjoyed similar triumphs. Just as the temptress spoke to Joseph day after day, and he did not listen to her at all, so did the servants of Ahasuerus try to persuade Mordechai the Benjaminite (a descendant of Rachel's) by speaking to him day after day. But he did not listen to them (*Esther* 3:4). And both achieved the same glory, both rose to the high position of viceroy (*Midrash*).

לִשְׁכַּב אֶצְלָהּ לִהְיוֹת עִמָּהּ — *To lie beside her, to be with her. Rashi* explains: "*To lie beside her* — even without intercourse (since it does not state לִשְׁכַּב עִמָּהּ) and *to be with her* — in the World to Come (in Hell)." For as soon as a man succumbs to seduction, he is lost in this world and in the next. Sin, said R' Eliezer, attaches itself to the sinner like a dog at the heels of its master (*Sotah* 3b).

11. לַעֲשׂוֹת מְלַאכְתּוֹ — *To do his work. Rashi:* "Rav and Shmuel: one says it really means 'to do his work (checking the account books — *Onkelos*).' The other says: he came also to have relations with her (the phrase וַיָּבֹא הַבַּיְתָה used here calls to mind the term for cohabitation בִּיאָה — *Tosafos* to *Sotah* 36b). But at that moment the image of his father appeared to him and said: Joseph, the names of your brothers will one day be engraved on the precious stones of the *eiphod* (one of the sacred garments of the high priest Aaron; see *Exodus* 28:27) and your name is to be included. Do you want your name to be erased from the rest? Do you want to be called an associate of prostitutes? (cf. *Tosafos* ibid.). This sudden apparition was able to hold Joseph back just as he was about to yield to the temptation. From then on, concludes R' Meir, the patriarch Israel became the true shepherd of his son, as it is said: *Listen, O shepherd of Israel, You Who lead Joseph like a flock (Psalms* 80:2).

No definition can better express the supreme objective of a Jewish upbringing than the midrashic account of Joseph's inner struggle against the temptation of

> ¹⁰ *And so it was — just as she coaxed Joseph day after day, so he would not listen to her to lie beside her, to be with her.* ¹¹ *Then there was an opportune day when he entered the house to do his work — no man of the household staff being there in the house —* ¹² *that she caught hold of him by his garment, saying, "Lie with me!" But he left his garment in her hand, and he fled, and went outside.*
>
> ¹³ *When she saw that he had left his garment in her hand*

Potiphar's wife. The vision of Joseph's venerable father appeared to him just as the will of the young man weakened, just as he was about to sin. She believed she had at last seduced and charmed him. It was then that the sudden vision gave him the strength to control himself, to triumph over his moment of weakness and to conquer his nature, now so high-strung after the long months of heroic resistance. When a child's training and upbringing are such that even if he has long been separated from the family home and even if he is lost in the midst of licentious surroundings in a faraway country, his father's influence still guides him toward moral victory, then this training is the ideal Jewish upbringing.

12. וַיַּעֲזֹב בִּגְדוֹ בְּיָדָהּ — *But he left his garment in her hand.* Although he was the stronger, out of regard for his master's wife he preferred not to snatch his garment from her, but to leave it with her (*Ramban*). In choosing to flee rather than to resist, Joseph teaches us an excellent lesson: in order to overcome a dangerous temptation, the best way is not to fight it but to flee from it (L. Wogue).

וַיָּנׇס וַיֵּצֵא הַחוּצָה — *And he fled and went outside.* Several midrashic sources establish a connection between Joseph's flight from sin and the fleeing of the Red Sea before the Children of Israel as they came out of Egypt, with Joseph's coffin preceding the camp. הַיָּם רָאָה וַיָּנֹס, *the sea saw it and fled* (*Psalms* 114:3). What did it see? It saw the coffin of Joseph, who had fled from sin. Indeed the miracle of the splitting of the Red Sea is due to Joseph's merit (*Rabbah* 87). If creation unreservedly obeys natural law and only consents to a miracle by Divine intervention, it still willingly gives way to the man who is able to control his own nature and it too is ready to control itself. The sea "saw the coffin" of the one who had taken flight and had controlled and held back his virile strength (וַתֵּשֶׁב בְּאֵיתָן קַשְׁתּוֹ; 49:24); and then it did the same, fleeing and returning to its strength (וַיָּשׇׁב הַיָּם ... לְאֵיתָנוֹ; *Exodus* 14:27), thereby miraculously drowning the Egyptians.

13. וַיְהִי כִּרְאוֹתָהּ כִּי־עָזַב בִּגְדוֹ — *When she saw that he had left his garment.* It was this piece of evidence in her hands, proving her own guilt, which led her in the first place to slander Joseph, not merely the simple desire to take revenge on him (*Ramban*).

יד וַיָּנָס הַחוּצָה: וַתִּקְרָא לְאַנְשֵׁי בֵיתָהּ וַתֹּאמֶר לָהֶם לֵאמֹר
רְאוּ הֵבִיא לָנוּ אִישׁ עִבְרִי לְצַחֶק בָּנוּ בָּא אֵלַי לִשְׁכַּב
טו עִמִּי וָאֶקְרָא בְּקוֹל גָּדוֹל: וַיְהִי כְשָׁמְעוֹ כִּי־הֲרִימֹתִי קוֹלִי
טז וָאֶקְרָא וַיַּעֲזֹב בִּגְדוֹ אֶצְלִי וַיָּנָס וַיֵּצֵא הַחוּצָה: וַתַּנַּח בִּגְדוֹ
יז אֶצְלָהּ עַד־בּוֹא אֲדֹנָיו אֶל־בֵּיתוֹ: וַתְּדַבֵּר אֵלָיו כַּדְּבָרִים
הָאֵלֶּה לֵאמֹר בָּא אֵלַי הָעֶבֶד הָעִבְרִי אֲשֶׁר־הֵבֵאתָ לָּנוּ
יח לְצַחֶק בִּי: וַיְהִי כַּהֲרִימִי קוֹלִי וָאֶקְרָא וַיַּעֲזֹב בִּגְדוֹ אֶצְלִי
יט וַיָּנָס הַחוּצָה: וַיְהִי כִשְׁמֹעַ אֲדֹנָיו אֶת־דִּבְרֵי אִשְׁתּוֹ אֲשֶׁר
דִּבְּרָה אֵלָיו לֵאמֹר כַּדְּבָרִים הָאֵלֶּה עָשָׂה לִי עַבְדֶּךָ וַיִּחַר
כ אַפּוֹ: וַיִּקַּח אֲדֹנֵי יוֹסֵף אֹתוֹ וַיִּתְּנֵהוּ אֶל־בֵּית הַסֹּהַר מְקוֹם
אֲשֶׁר־°אסורי הַמֶּלֶךְ אֲסוּרִים וַיְהִי־שָׁם בְּבֵית הַסֹּהַר: °אֲסִירֵי ק'

14. הֵבִיא לָנוּ אִישׁ עִבְרִי — *He brought us a Hebrew man.* After the long series of ordeals which had afflicted the early pioneers of the Jewish nation — persecution, exile, wanderings, the hostility of other peoples, rape, jealousy between brothers, illness, disappointment in the behavior of the children, now a new hardship confronts them: slander. In a sense it is more cruel than the others. For it is based on a revolting injustice which can make a man doubt Divine justice and cause him to lose his moral equilibrium.

By presenting us here with the example of such a calumny, and by exposing in detail the accusation of the slanderer, the Torah seems to want to fill in the picture for coming generations of the destiny awaiting the Jewish people which, as we have seen, mirrors that of the family of Abraham. But Joseph accepts this new setback just as impassively as he had accepted the very recent ordeals of the fierce hatred of his brothers and his sale as a slave. Not one word of justification or rebellion does he utter. Not raising the least protest, he gives in and accepts the infamous punishment of imprisonment for twelve years. However, during this period, his exemplary conduct will permit him to attain the highest of honors. He will appear in all eyes as entirely innocent of the false and shameful accusations. This former slave, thrown into a dungeon, will ultimately rise to glory. Such is the reaction of the just and pious man who, whatever the circumstances, can overcome all hardships. Joseph's attitude will serve as an example to future generations when they face similar situations.

לְצַחֶק בָּנוּ — *To sport with us.* The Midrash describes how Zuleika had stirred up the members of her household and her friends when she began to slander the slave so as to prevent any accusation against her. Thus the use of the term לֵאמֹר in our verse can be explained: She told them "to repeat" (and in what follows, note that the plural is used). The same term recurs frequently in the account of what Potiphar's wife said. It brings out that she stood firmly by her accusations.

and fled outside, [14] *she called out to the men of her household and spoke to them saying, "Look! He brought us a Hebrew man to sport with us! He came to lie with me but I called out with a loud scream.* [15] *And when he heard that I raised my voice and screamed, he left his garment beside me, fled, and went outside!"*

[16] *She kept his garment beside her until his master came home.* [17] *Then she told him a similar account saying, "The Hebrew slave whom you brought to us came to me to sport with me.* [18] *But it happened that when I raised my voice and screamed, he left his garment beside me, and ran outside."*

[19] *And it was, when his master heard his wife's words which she spoke to him, saying, "Your slave did things like these to me," his anger flared up.* [20] *Then Joseph's master took him and placed him in the prison — the place where the king's prisoners were confined — and he remained there in prison.*

בָּא אֵלַי — *He came to . . . me.* Her words contain what is typical of all calumnies: lies, defamation, and the stirring up of anti-Semitic instincts. How often in the history of Joseph's descendants were they to be dealt with in the same odious way — and, like their ancestor, be powerless to oppose it!

19. וַיִּחַר אַפּוֹ — *His anger flared up.* Nevertheless he did not have Joseph executed for attempted adultery as a slave would have deserved. He decided to imprison him at the urging of his wife who still hoped that Joseph would one day consent to her desires. She said to her husband: "It is better to keep him in prison until you can sell him and get back the money which you spent to acquire him" (*Tanchuma*). Another tradition has it that Potiphar did not have him killed because he knew that Joseph was innocent — either because of his great confidence in Joseph; or because he had been told so by his daughter Osnath, who had revealed the whole truth to him; or because Joseph had been proven innocent in a regular trial (*Rabbah* 87, *Yashar*, and *Targum Yonasan*). But he was still obliged to sentence Joseph for the sake of preserving the good name of his wife and children (cf. our commentary to 47:22).

20. וַיִּתְּנֵהוּ אֶל־בֵּית הַסֹּהַר — *And placed him in the prison.* The term בֵּית הַסֹּהַר does not occur anywhere else and, according to *Ibn Ezra*, it seems to be of Egyptian origin. *Radak* relates it to the word סַהַר (*Song of Songs* 7:3), which gives the idea of circuit or curvature such that here it would mean rotunda. According to *Ramban*, it is probably related to the Aramaic word סִיהֲרָא, *moon*, and the Hebrew צֹהַר, *window* (*Genesis* 6:16) and זֹהַר, *radiance, brightness.* The term means, then, a dungeon "constructed underground" and equipped with a skylight allowing the light to shine in from the outside. Accordingly, the unusual use of this term brings out that, although he was cast into a dungeon where he felt shame and despair, Joseph's stay in prison was nevertheless bathed

כא וַיְהִי יהוה אֶת־יוֹסֵף וַיֵּט אֵלָיו חָסֶד וַיִּתֵּן חִנּוֹ בְּעֵינֵי שַׂר
כב בֵּית־הַסֹּהַר: וַיִּתֵּן שַׂר בֵּית־הַסֹּהַר בְּיַד־יוֹסֵף אֵת כָּל־
הָאֲסִירִם אֲשֶׁר בְּבֵית הַסֹּהַר וְאֵת כָּל־אֲשֶׁר עֹשִׂים שָׁם הוּא
כג הָיָה עֹשֶׂה: אֵין ׀ שַׂר בֵּית־הַסֹּהַר רֹאֶה אֶת־כָּל־מְאוּמָה בְּיָדוֹ
בַּאֲשֶׁר יהוה אִתּוֹ וַאֲשֶׁר־הוּא עֹשֶׂה יהוה מַצְלִיחַ:
מ שביעי א וַיְהִי אַחַר הַדְּבָרִים הָאֵלֶּה חָטְאוּ מַשְׁקֵה מֶלֶךְ־מִצְרַיִם
ב וְהָאֹפֶה לַאֲדֹנֵיהֶם לְמֶלֶךְ מִצְרָיִם: וַיִּקְצֹף פַּרְעֹה עַל שְׁנֵי

in light from above because of his unwavering faith and his absolute confidence in God. For Joseph, סֹהַר and זֹהַר, *prison* and *light*, merged into one and the same idea. Note that the text reiterates at the end of the verse that *he remained there in prison*, which was a בֵּית הַסֹּהַר, a "house of light," for, the Torah continues, *Hashem was with Joseph.* For the innocent who suffer imprisonment, the dungeon itself can become a haven of light provided that confidence in God illuminates their souls.

21. וַיְהִי ה' אֶת־יוֹסֵף — *HASHEM was with Joseph.* Joseph's ordeals in prison are a prefiguration of the ordeals Jewry would endure in its exiles. These exiles are comparable to Joseph's stay in the house of detention, which the Torah also calls בּוֹר, *the pit* (41:14). This, notes *R' Bachya*, is why our prayers contain the words יַעֲלֶה וְיָבֹא (may there rise and come), for they rise up from the depths of exile as though they were ascending from the bottom of a pit. And just as the Divine Presence dwells with Joseph in his misfortune, so too does It hover over Jewry in its tribulations in exile. "For," says the prophet Isaiah, *in all their sufferings It suffers with them, and the angel of His presence protects them* (63:9).

If our commentaries are depicting Joseph's misfortunes as trials willed by Providence, or even called by Joseph upon himself as the righteous used to do, it is fitting nevertheless to point out that some of our Sages see them rather as punishments to atone for his faults, particularly the evil reports which he had spread against his brothers (cf. the controversy in *Midrash Rabbah* 87). Right at the beginning of this passage *Rashi* emphasizes this point of view (38:2). To be sure, man is often not able to tell exactly why he meets with adversities. Is it a punishment? Or a hardship which Heaven inflicts upon him? R' Yaakov said that if one keeps his mind free to pursue the study of Torah or, as R' Acha tells us, if he keeps the power of prayer, he will know that his misfortunes are only "trials of love" sent by God to give him the opportunity to raise himself to a higher degree of spiritual greatness (*Berachos* 5a). What counts most of all is the personal reaction in the face of destiny. If man emerges ennobled morally and spiritually from his sufferings, purified in his soul, sanctified in his life, and stronger in his faith in God, these ordeals will have fulfilled their purpose, whatever may have been their cause. And this moral victory will thus have transformed the punishment into a "chastening of love." As for Joseph, the

²¹ HASHEM *was with Joseph, and He endowed him with charisma, and He put his favor in the eyes of the prison warden.* ²² *The prison warden placed all inmates of the prison in Joseph's custody, and everything that was done there, he would accomplish.* ²³ *The prison warden did not scrutinize anything that was in his charge inasmuch as* HASHEM *was with him; and whatever he did* HASHEM *made successful.*

40   ¹ **A**nd *it happened after these things that the cupbearer of the king of Egypt and the baker transgressed against their master, against the king of Egypt.* ² *Pharaoh was enraged at his two*

years which he spent as a slave in Potiphar's house gave him the opportunity to raise himself to the utmost degree of his spiritual strength.

וַיֵּט אֵלָיו חָסֶד — *And He endowed him with charisma.* Or, *piety* (חָסֶד in the sense of piety, as in *Psalms* 37:28). "Each righteous man stands out because of a specific virtue or *mitzvah* which is particularly dear to him. For Abraham, it was circumcision; for Isaac, prayer; for Jacob, truth; for Joseph, deep piety as revealed in his purity of conduct" (*Yalkut Shimoni* to *Numbers* §744). In defending his virtue he even went so far as to risk his master's wife's threat of death (*Tanchuma*). And so, more than anyone else, he deserved the title of "righteous" which was given to him: יוֹסֵף הַצַּדִּיק (*Yoma* 35b). In Kabbalistic literature, where Joseph is counted as one of the seven pillars that are the supports of the *Shechinah* on earth (מֶרְכָּבָה לַשְּׁכִינָה), this quality plays an important part. Joseph's virtue takes away the excuse of the voluptuous. "If such men, on the day of the last judgment, are reproached for abandoning the ways of the Torah and they try to justify themselves by saying: 'We were of handsome appearance and our evil instincts led us astray,' then they will be asked: 'And were you more handsome than Joseph?' " (*Yoma* ibid.).

40.

1. וַיְהִי אַחַר הַדְּבָרִים הָאֵלֶּה — *And it happened, after these things.* This introduction indicates how the episode of the misdeeds and dreams of the two imprisoned officers is tied in with the events which preceded it. There is a direct connection between them. After the guiltless Joseph's imprisonment, Divine Providence in its unfathomable manner paved the way not only for his freedom but also for his brilliant career. This career, which he indirectly owed to his fellow prisoners, will come to constitute an important link in the historical evolution of the Jewish people (cf. *Megillah* 13b). Once again we see here the mysterious interaction between the Divine will, which inexorably carries out its plans, and the human element, which all the while continues to bear its own responsibility (cf. our commentary to 37:5).

חָטְאוּ — *Transgressed.* They were accused of trying to outrage Pharaoh's daughter and of plotting to take Pharaoh's life by poisoning his food and drink

ג סָרִיסָיו עַל שַׂר הַמַּשְׁקִים וְעַל שַׂר הָאוֹפִים: וַיִּתֵּן אֹתָם
בְּמִשְׁמַר בֵּית שַׂר הַטַּבָּחִים אֶל־בֵּית הַסֹּהַר מְקוֹם אֲשֶׁר יוֹסֵף
ד אָסוּר שָׁם: וַיִּפְקֹד שַׂר הַטַּבָּחִים אֶת־יוֹסֵף אִתָּם וַיְשָׁרֶת
ה אֹתָם וַיִּהְיוּ יָמִים בְּמִשְׁמָר: וַיַּחַלְמוּ חֲלוֹם שְׁנֵיהֶם אִישׁ חֲלֹמוֹ
בְּלַיְלָה אֶחָד אִישׁ כְּפִתְרוֹן חֲלֹמוֹ הַמַּשְׁקֶה וְהָאֹפֶה אֲשֶׁר
ו לְמֶלֶךְ מִצְרַיִם אֲשֶׁר אֲסוּרִים בְּבֵית הַסֹּהַר: וַיָּבֹא אֲלֵיהֶם
ז יוֹסֵף בַּבֹּקֶר וַיַּרְא אֹתָם וְהִנָּם זֹעֲפִים: וַיִּשְׁאַל אֶת־סְרִיסֵי
פַרְעֹה אֲשֶׁר אִתּוֹ בְמִשְׁמַר בֵּית אֲדֹנָיו לֵאמֹר מַדּוּעַ פְּנֵיכֶם
ח רָעִים הַיּוֹם: וַיֹּאמְרוּ אֵלָיו חֲלוֹם חָלַמְנוּ וּפֹתֵר אֵין אֹתוֹ
וַיֹּאמֶר אֲלֵהֶם יוֹסֵף הֲלוֹא לֵאלֹהִים פִּתְרֹנִים סַפְּרוּ־נָא לִי:

(*Rabbah* 88 and *Targum Yonasan*). But *Rashi* quotes a Midrash which records
that Pharaoh found a fly in the cup which the butler brought him and a stone
in the bread made by the baker. This negligence cost the baker his life, explains
R' *Bachya*, whereas the butler was forgiven because the fly had fallen into the
cup after he had handed it to the king.

2. שַׂר הַמַּשְׁקִים — *The Chamberlain of the Cupbearers*. Several commentators
hold that the assistants were those who actually did the misdeeds, and the chief
cupbearer and baker were then held responsible for the "sins" of their subordinates. They were high dignitaries and had the privilege of being provided with
someone to look after them during their imprisonment. But according to R' *S.R.
Hirsch* (and others), the butler and baker mentioned in the first verse are the
same as those given here the title of שַׂר, which usually designates a person in
power, a prince or a minister. This designation brings out all the irony and piti-
fulness attendant on this princely dignity. Outwardly, in the eyes of the people,
this person is a שַׂר, a prince; but for the king he is merely a common slave, lower
than a streetsweeper. Indeed, he is entirely dependent on the whims of the king,
since his high dignity consists of nothing other than the distinguished honor of
being able to pour the king his wine or serve him his pastries. So the king has
the same sovereign power over the life and liberty of his "princes" as he does
over his slaves; for him they are merely the butler and the baker. And if anger
takes hold of the master, he gets rid of them and they are sent to prison.

4. וַיִּפְקֹד שַׂר הַטַּבָּחִים אֶת־יוֹסֵף אִתָּם — *The Chamberlain of the Butchers appointed
Joseph to be with them*. *Rashi* interprets: in order that he be with them — and
this for twelve months. (According to other *Midrashim*, their stay in prison
lasted three or even ten years.) So, from Joseph's arrival in Egypt, he was
destined to be constantly in close touch with various high dignitaries of the royal
court so that, from his association with them, he would be prepared for his
future functions as viceroy.

5. בְּלַיְלָה אֶחָד — *On the same night*. It was the night of Rosh Hashanah, and on
the same night exactly two years later, Pharaoh had his dream (*Rosh Hashanah*

*courtiers, the Chamberlain of the Cupbearers and the Chamber-
lain of the Bakers.* ³ *And he placed them in the ward of the house
of the Chamberlain of the Butchers, into the prison, the place where
Joseph was confined.* ⁴ *The Chamberlain of the Butchers appointed
Joseph to be with them, and he attended them and they remained
in the ward for a period of days.*

⁵ *The two of them dreamt a dream, each one had his dream on
the same night, each one according to the interpretation of his
dream — the cupbearer and the baker of the king of Egypt who
were confined in the prison.*

⁶ *Joseph came to them in the morning. He saw them and behold!
they were aggrieved.*

⁷ *And he asked Pharaoh's courtiers who were with him in the
ward of his master's house, saying, "Why do you appear downcast
today?"* ⁸ *And they said to him, "We dreamt a dream, but there
is no interpreter for it." So Joseph said to them, "Do not
interpretations belong to God? Relate it to me, if you please."*

10a). So Joseph immediately understood that the dreams were to have a special
importance, since they had occurred at the time when human destinies are
decided in the heavenly tribunal (cf. *R' S. Edels* on *Berachos* 55a).

אִישׁ כְּפִתְרוֹן חֲלֹמוֹ — *Each one according to the interpretation of his dream.* Each
had a dream corresponding to the explanation of what would happen to him
(*Rashi*). The dreams were very clear by themselves; they referred to their
respective professions, and they hinted directly at what was to happen. The
dreams themselves, as it were, constituted "the interpretation of the dream" and
they seemingly needed only one more detail to do away with the services of an
interpreter altogether. Moreover, the two dreams resembled each other in certain
respects, particularly in the recurrence of the number three. All this contributed
to make them "appear downcast." They guessed that this was a revelation about
their imminent fate. (This is why the Torah tells us that חֲלוֹם שְׁנֵיהֶם, they both
had dreams, as if to say that they shared a single dream which referred to both.)

7. וַיִּשְׁאַל אֶת־סְרִיסֵי פַרְעֹה אֲשֶׁר אִתּוֹ בְמִשְׁמַר בֵּית אֲדֹנָיו — *And he asked Pharaoh's
courtiers who were with him in the ward of his master's house.* Just to have
written וַיִּשְׁאַל אוֹתָם, *he questioned them,* would have sufficed, as *Ramban* points
out. The unusual length of this phrase may be a way of making us grasp
Joseph's inner thoughts. For Joseph, the presence of Pharaoh's two officers in
prison with him had something providential about it. He had a feeling that it
was for him and for his future destiny that Providence had caused these officers
to be held prisoner "with him in the ward of his master's house." And so their
sad and worried appearance made him extremely interested in their plight.

8. הֲלוֹא לֵאלֹהִים פִּתְרֹנִים — *Do not interpretations belong to God?* "It is not the
magician's art which is going to explain your dreams to you," he told the

ט וַיְסַפֵּר שַׂר־הַמַּשְׁקִים אֶת־חֲלֹמוֹ לְיוֹסֵף וַיֹּאמֶר לוֹ בַּחֲלוֹמִי
י וְהִנֵּה־גֶפֶן לְפָנָי: וּבַגֶּפֶן שְׁלֹשָׁה שָׂרִיגִם וְהִוא כְפֹרַ֫חַת עָלְתָה
יא נִצָּהּ הִבְשִׁילוּ אַשְׁכְּלֹתֶיהָ עֲנָבִים: וְכוֹס פַּרְעֹה בְּיָדִי וָאֶקַּח
אֶת־הָעֲנָבִים וָאֶשְׂחַט אֹתָם אֶל־כּוֹס פַּרְעֹה וָאֶתֵּן אֶת־הַכּוֹס
יב עַל־כַּף פַּרְעֹה: וַיֹּאמֶר לוֹ יוֹסֵף זֶה פִּתְרֹנוֹ שְׁלֹשֶׁת הַשָּׂרִגִים
יג שְׁלֹשֶׁת יָמִים הֵם: בְּעוֹד | שְׁלֹשֶׁת יָמִים יִשָּׂא פַרְעֹה
אֶת־רֹאשֶׁךָ וַהֲשִׁיבְךָ עַל־כַּנֶּךָ וְנָתַתָּ כוֹס־פַּרְעֹה בְּיָדוֹ
יד כַּמִּשְׁפָּט הָרִאשׁוֹן אֲשֶׁר הָיִיתָ מַשְׁקֵהוּ: כִּי אִם־זְכַרְתַּנִי אִתְּךָ
כַּאֲשֶׁר יִיטַב לָךְ וְעָשִׂיתָ־נָּא עִמָּדִי חָסֶד וְהִזְכַּרְתַּנִי אֶל־
טו פַּרְעֹה וְהוֹצֵאתַנִי מִן־הַבָּיִת הַזֶּה: כִּי־גֻנֹּב גֻּנַּבְתִּי מֵאֶרֶץ
הָעִבְרִים וְגַם־פֹּה לֹא־עָשִׂיתִי מְאוּמָה כִּי־שָׂמוּ אֹתִי בַּבּוֹר:

officers. He knew that an appeal to the prophetic spirit would be needed to obtain the true explanation. Dreams are six levels below prophetic revelation, so one has to be inspired from the Divine source to understand their significance (*Zohar*; cf. our commentary to 41:16).

9. וְהִנֵּה־גֶפֶן לְפָנָי — *Behold! there was a grapevine in front of me.* As soon as he heard the word vine, Joseph experienced a feeling of exaltation. Is not wine the drink that *gladdens the heart of man* (*Psalms* 104:15) and brings men back to friendship (*Josephus, Antiquities* II:5,2)? Moreover, the vine is the symbol of Israel (e.g. *Hoshea* 10:1). For Joseph, convinced that his meeting with Pharaoh's officers was related to the destiny of the house of Abraham (see above), it was a happy sign to hear the Egyptian praising the splendors of the vine: it had three branches, it was in bud, its blossoms were shooting forth, its clusters were bringing forth ripe grapes — all these were signs which Joseph connected with the future flowering of his people (cf. *Chullin* 92a). It is along these lines that the Midrash (*Rabbah* 88) establishes a connection between the four cups of ''freedom'' on the night of Pesach, and the fourfold mention of כוס in this chapter. Thus the dream was a good omen. And when Joseph heard the chief cupbearer relating the part which concerned him personally: *Pharaoh's cup was in my hand and I took the grapes, etc.* (v. 11) he gave him a favorable interpretation (*Midrash Rabbah* and *Zohar*).

12. שְׁלֹשֶׁת הַשָּׂרִגִים שְׁלֹשֶׁת יָמִים הֵם — *The three tendrils are three days.* And why not three months or three years? Because the dream indicated rapid development. (As soon as the vine budded it produced blossoms, according to *Ramban*, who explains the letter כ"ף of כְּפֹרַחַת in a temporal sense rather than as introducing a comparison, הדמיון כ"ף.) Furthermore, the dream's possible connection with Jewish destiny made Joseph hope for a speedy realization.

14. כִּי אִם־זְכַרְתַּנִי — *If only you would think of me.* ''Please do me a favor and mention me to Pharaoh.'' This is the interpretation given by *Rashi* who takes

⁹ Then the Chamberlain of the Cupbearers recounted his dream to Joseph and said to him, "In my dream — behold! there was a grapevine in front of me! ¹⁰ On the grapevine were three tendrils; and it was as though it budded — its blossoms bloomed and its clusters ripened into grapes. ¹¹ And Pharaoh's cup was in my hand and I took the grapes, pressed them into Pharaoh's cup, and I placed the cup on Pharaoh's palm."

¹² Joseph said to him, "This is its interpretation: The three tendrils are three days. ¹³ In another three days Pharaoh will lift up your head and will restore you to your post, and you will place Pharaoh's cup in his hand as was the former practice when you were his cupbearer. ¹⁴ If only you would think of me with yourself when he benefits you, and you will do me a kindness, if you please, and mention me to Pharaoh, then you would get me out of this building. ¹⁵ For indeed I was kidnaped from the land of the Hebrews, and even here I have done nothing for them to have put me in the pit."

the word נָא as a petition. But *Ramban* explains it in the sense of "then" and takes the sentence to mean: If you remember me (so that I should be) with you . . . and if you then want to do me a favor, tell Pharaoh about me.

וְהוֹצֵאתַנִי מִן־הַבַּיִת הַזֶּה — *Then you would get me out of this building.* Because Joseph put his trust in the chief cupbearer to remember him, he had to remain in prison for two (extra) years. As it is said: *Happy is the man who puts his trust in God, and does not look toward the arrogant.* The latter part of this verse in *Psalms* (40:5) refers to the Egyptians, who were labeled רְהָבִים in *Isaiah* 30:7 (*Rashi*, on verse 23, following *Midrash Rabbah*). Most of our Sages hold that resorting to the intervention of a human being, with the idea that he may serve as an instrument of Divine Providence, is not at all reprehensible in itself as long as this appeal comes from an ordinary individual. But "God is strict to the extreme with those closest to Him" (*Yevamos* 121b). And hence He acted very severely towards Joseph. Throughout his long series of misfortunes, Joseph constantly displayed absolute confidence in God without ever uttering one word of recrimination, complaint, or justification. But here, in his association with an Egyptian functionary, suddenly his faith undergoes a regrettable moment of weakness (*Beis HaLevi* and others; וְעַיֵּי חֲזוֹן אִישׁ עַל אֱמוּנָה וּבִטָּחוֹן, פ"ב).

15. כִּי־גֻנֹּב גֻּנַּבְתִּי מֵאֶרֶץ הָעִבְרִים — *For indeed I was kidnapped from the land of the Hebrews.* According to *Ramban*, this term designates the territory of Hebron, where the patriarchs lived. It was called this because Abraham had come from "the other side" of the river Euphrates (מֵעֵבֶר הַנָּהָר), and this geographical name shows what importance Abraham's offspring had already achieved. But *Ibn Ezra* (*Exodus* 21:2) derives this name from עֵבֶר, *Eber*, the son of Shem, the forefather of the family of Abraham (*Genesis* 10:21).

טז וַיַּרְא שַׂר־הָאֹפִים כִּי טוֹב פָּתָר וַיֹּאמֶר אֶל־יוֹסֵף אַף־אֲנִי
יז בַּחֲלוֹמִי וְהִנֵּה שְׁלֹשָׁה סַלֵּי חֹרִי עַל־רֹאשִׁי: וּבַסַּל הָעֶלְיוֹן
מִכֹּל מַאֲכַל פַּרְעֹה מַעֲשֵׂה אֹפֶה וְהָעוֹף אֹכֵל אֹתָם מִן־הַסַּל
יח מֵעַל רֹאשִׁי: וַיַּעַן יוֹסֵף וַיֹּאמֶר זֶה פִּתְרֹנוֹ שְׁלֹשֶׁת הַסַּלִּים
יט שְׁלֹשֶׁת יָמִים הֵם: בְּעוֹד ׀ שְׁלֹשֶׁת יָמִים יִשָּׂא פַרְעֹה
אֶת־רֹאשְׁךָ מֵעָלֶיךָ וְתָלָה אוֹתְךָ עַל־עֵץ וְאָכַל הָעוֹף
כ אֶת־בְּשָׂרְךָ מֵעָלֶיךָ: וַיְהִי ׀ בַּיּוֹם הַשְּׁלִישִׁי יוֹם הֻלֶּדֶת   מפטיר
אֶת־פַּרְעֹה וַיַּעַשׂ מִשְׁתֶּה לְכָל־עֲבָדָיו וַיִּשָּׂא אֶת־רֹאשׁ ׀ שַׂר
כא הַמַּשְׁקִים וְאֶת־רֹאשׁ שַׂר הָאֹפִים בְּתוֹךְ עֲבָדָיו: וַיָּשֶׁב
אֶת־שַׂר הַמַּשְׁקִים עַל־מַשְׁקֵהוּ וַיִּתֵּן הַכּוֹס עַל־כַּף פַּרְעֹה:
כב-כג וְאֵת שַׂר הָאֹפִים תָּלָה כַּאֲשֶׁר פָּתַר לָהֶם יוֹסֵף: וְלֹא־זָכַר
שַׂר־הַמַּשְׁקִים אֶת־יוֹסֵף וַיִּשְׁכָּחֵהוּ:

God said to Moses (when he wanted to be buried in the Holy Land): "The one who (during his life openly) recognized it (as his country) is buried there, but not the one who did not acknowledge it as such. Joseph acknowledged that he came from the land of the Hebrews and he is buried in Shechem, but you did not declare your country when Jethro's daughters told their father: *An Egyptian man saved us* (*Exodus* 2:19). You will therefore not be buried in the Holy Land" (*Devarim Rabbah* 2). Granted, Moses had never known the land of Israel and had no family there, whereas Joseph's youth was spent in the Holy Land and all his family were still there. But, it would nevertheless have been easier for Moses, welcomed in the house of Jethro after a heroic rescue, to proudly declare: "I am a Jew," than it was for Joseph, an imprisoned slave who was accused of a shameful crime. And yet Joseph was proud of his land and awaited the day when all would know that he was guiltless; when his irreproachable past would be all to the credit and honor of his birthplace, the Holy Land.

16. אַף־אֲנִי — *I, too.* The word אַף, *too*, has another meaning: *anger*. The latter underlies the words of the chief baker (further emphasized by the word חֹרִי, which calls to mind "unleashing anger," as in *Deuteronomy* 29:23: מֶה חֳרִי הָאַף). Consequently *Targum Yerushalmi* interprets: He started to speak in an angry tone. He was indeed angered that this imprisoned slave could wisely interpret dreams which the Egyptian magicians who had been consulted were incapable of explaining (*Ramban*). But anger is not a good counsellor. And so he revealed his dream, but he did so reluctantly. Three (besides the chief baker) started to speak up with the word אַף, that is to say, in a tone of defiant anger, and each was rebuffed with a retort which also began with אַף. These were the serpent in Paradise, Korah and his assembly, and Haman (*Rabbah* 88).

So, concludes the *Zohar*, Joseph trembled when he heard the Egyptian begin his account with the word אַף. And this unfavorable impression was reinforced

¹⁶ *The Chamberlain of the Bakers saw that he had interpreted well, so he said to Joseph, "I, too! In my dream — behold! three wicker baskets were on my head.* ¹⁷ *And in the uppermost basket were all kinds of Pharaoh's food — baker's handiwork — and the birds were eating them from the basket above my head."*

¹⁸ *Joseph responded and said, "This is its interpretation: The three baskets are three days.* ¹⁹ *In three days Pharaoh will lift your head from you and hang you on a tree; birds will eat your flesh from you."*

²⁰ *And it was on the third day, Pharaoh's birthday, that he made a feast for all his servants and he counted the Chamberlain of the Cupbearers and the Chamberlain of the Bakers among his servants.* ²¹ *He restored the Chamberlain of the Cupbearers to his cupbearing and he placed the cup on Pharaoh's palm.* ²² *But the Chamberlain of the Bakers he hung, just as Joseph had interpreted to them.*

²³ *Yet the Chamberlain of the Cupbearers did not remember Joseph, but he forgot him.*

when he heard the chief baker describe his dream: out of the basket upon his head birds were pecking the delicious pastries meant for Pharaoh, and he was powerless to drive them away. Joseph then had the feeling that the anger of Pharaoh, spurned in this way, was inexorably being readied over the head of the chief baker. Moreover, the dream was a bad omen for the destiny of the Jews, a subject which Joseph was continually aware of in his relations with his fellow-prisoners (as was explained above). He considered the vision of the birds darting down upon the food as a symbolic allusion to the enemy nations, birds of prey swooping to attack and smite and scatter Jewry (as in Abraham's vision, 15:11) when the Jews would try to shake off the yoke of the Torah and would no longer uphold the crowns of the Heavenly King placed on their forehead (and represented here by Pharaoh's basket).

18. שְׁלֹשֶׁת הַסַּלִּים שְׁלֹשֶׁת יָמִים הֵם — *The three baskets are three days.* The numerical value of the words שְׁלֹשֶׁת הַסַּלִּים is equal to that of the words שְׁלֹשֶׁת יָמִים הֵם (1175). But what led Joseph to relate the three baskets to three days was the similarity of this dream to the chief cupbearer's (*R' Bachya*).

23. וְלֹא־זָכַר שַׂר־הַמַּשְׁקִים אֶת־יוֹסֵף — *Yet the Chamberlain of the Cupbearers did not remember Joseph.* "That very day (of his liberation)," says *Rashi.* Furthermore, "he forgot him" later on (completely). The forgetfulness of the chief butler in the enjoyment of his own happiness is, alas, only too human. Nothing is more common than ingratitude. Man forgets — but God does not forget His faithful ones. And when the night is darkest, the dawn is already near.

מא   א   וַיְהִי מִקֵּץ שְׁנָתַיִם יָמִים וּפַרְעֹה חֹלֵם וְהִנֵּה עֹמֵד עַל־הַיְאֹר:
ב   וְהִנֵּה מִן־הַיְאֹר עֹלֹת שֶׁבַע פָּרוֹת יְפוֹת מַרְאֶה וּבְרִיאֹת בָּשָׂר
ג   וַתִּרְעֶינָה בָּאָחוּ: וְהִנֵּה שֶׁבַע פָּרוֹת אֲחֵרוֹת עֹלוֹת אַחֲרֵיהֶן
מִן־הַיְאֹר רָעוֹת מַרְאֶה וְדַקּוֹת בָּשָׂר וַתַּעֲמֹדְנָה אֵצֶל הַפָּרוֹת
ד   עַל־שְׂפַת הַיְאֹר: וַתֹּאכַלְנָה הַפָּרוֹת רָעוֹת הַמַּרְאֶה וְדַקֹּת
הַבָּשָׂר אֵת שֶׁבַע הַפָּרוֹת יְפֹת הַמַּרְאֶה וְהַבְּרִיאֹת וַיִּיקַץ
ה   פַּרְעֹה: וַיִּישָׁן וַיַּחֲלֹם שֵׁנִית וְהִנֵּה ׀ שֶׁבַע שִׁבֳּלִים עֹלוֹת בְּקָנֶה
ו   אֶחָד בְּרִיאוֹת וְטֹבוֹת: וְהִנֵּה שֶׁבַע שִׁבֳּלִים דַּקּוֹת וּשְׁדוּפֹת

41.

1. וַיְהִי מִקֵּץ שְׁנָתַיִם יָמִים — *It happened at the end of two years to the day.* קֵץ שָׂם לַחֹשֶׁךְ, *He sets an end to darkness* — with these words from the book of *Job* (28:3) the Midrash begins its comments on our chapter. Everything, it continues, has an end, including the trials inflicted on man. Joseph had to suffer in prison, forgotten by everyone, for twelve seemingly interminable years. His situation must have appeared almost hopeless. Only his belief and faith in God could help him bear such a cruel ordeal. But the turning point of destiny is being readied in the silence of the absolute and it intervenes when the time comes, at the right moment for it in the Divine plan.

The Jewish calendar is set up so that the *sidrah* מִקֵּץ is always read on Chanukah, when the days start to get short and the nights longer. This turning point in the year is accompanied by the Chanukah lights, which symbolically represent the triumph of light over darkness. Thus we see a coincidence, which is not at all fortuitous, with the motif of the history of Joseph: קֵץ שָׂם לַחֹשֶׁךְ, *He sets limits to darkness.* The connection here (and in many other instances) between the cycle of our holidays and the Torah readings on one hand, and the yearly cycle in nature on the other, makes us aware of the profound harmony between the laws governing the destiny of the Jewish people and those establishing the Divine order of creation. Jewry is the second Divine creation (*Psalms* 102:19) and its destiny echoes that of nature: the God of nature is also the God of history.

וּפַרְעֹה חֹלֵם — *Pharaoh was dreaming.* "I will heal you with your (own) wounds," declares the prophet Jeremiah in the name of God (30:17). Dreams were at the root of Joseph's misfortunes; and again dreams bring about his salvation. His life thus unfolds marked by dreams, as was mentioned and explained in our commentary to 37:5.

עֹמֵד עַל־הַיְאֹר — *He was standing over the River.* Literally, on the Nile — not as he later told Joseph: "I was standing on the bank of the Nile." For Pharaoh's dream is a reflection of his secret thoughts filled with arrogance, as the prophet Ezekiel reveals to us: *My Nile is mine and I have made it* (29:3). Hence, in his

41 ¹*It happened at the end of two years to the day: Pharaoh was dreaming that behold! — he was standing over the River,* ² *when behold! out of the River there emerged seven cows, of beautiful appearance and robust flesh, and they were grazing in the marshland.* ³ *Then behold! — seven other cows emerged after them out of the River — of ugly appearance and gaunt flesh; and they stood next to the cows on the bank of the River.* ⁴ *The cows of ugly appearance and gaunt flesh ate the seven cows of beautiful appearance and robust, and Pharaoh awoke.* ⁵ *He fell asleep and dreamt a second time, and behold! seven ears of grain were sprouting on a single stalk — healthy and good.* ⁶ *And behold! seven ears, thin, and scorched*

dream Pharaoh sees himself as a god majestically looking down upon his river. What is more, in this verse the Torah does not use the verb "to dream" in the past tense (Pharaoh dreamed), as one might expect, but in the progressive present tense (Pharaoh was dreaming), expressing a continuity which becomes permanent. His whole life through, Pharaoh had had dreams of grandeur. He believed himself to be a god, the all-powerful creator of Egyptian prosperity, due to "his" river, the Nile. Thus, right from the beginning of his story we see the ultimate cause of his downfall, as the prophet Ezekiel explains (ibid.): *Thus says Hashem, God: I challenge you, Pharaoh, king of Egypt, great crocodile . . . I shall bring a sword upon you and cut off from you man and beast. The land of Egypt will be desolate and waste, and they shall know from it that I am God, because he has said, "My Nile is mine and I have made it."*

It is because of this ultimate decline, foreseen right from the start, that the Torah throughout this passage refrains from adding the title "king of Egypt" to Pharaoh's name. The sole exception is to solemnly announce Joseph's accession to power: "Joseph was thirty years old when he stood before Pharaoh king of Egypt" (verse 46).

3. וַתַּעֲמֹדְנָה אֵצֶל הַפָּרוֹת — *And they stood next to the cows.* Although Pharaoh did not report this to Joseph, he nevertheless took account of it in his interpretation. It meant that the years of famine would immediately follow the years of plenty without a break, and this implied that the reserves were to be built up right from the time of plenty (*Ramban*). The fact that Joseph took this detail into consideration, even though no mention had been made of it, was one of the reasons for Pharaoh's sincere admiration of him.

5. וַיִּישָׁן וַיַּחֲלֹם שֵׁנִית — *He fell asleep and dreamt a second time.* The word שֵׁנִית also signifies "different," in the sense of strange and incredible (מְשֻׁנָּה). The first dream showed animals devouring each other, which is not unrealistic — but how can ears of corn swallow up one another? So it was the second dream, not the first, which troubles Pharaoh's spirit, for it was "incredible" (*Midrash HaGadol*).

ז קָרִים צְמְחוֹת אַחֲרֵיהֶן: וַתִּבְלַעְנָה הַשִּׁבֳּלִים הַדַּקּוֹת אֵת שֶׁבַע הַשִּׁבֳּלִים הַבְּרִיאוֹת וְהַמְּלֵאוֹת וַיִּיקַץ פַּרְעֹה וְהִנֵּה חֲלוֹם:

ח וַיְהִי בַבֹּקֶר וַתִּפָּעֶם רוּחוֹ וַיִּשְׁלַח וַיִּקְרָא אֶת־כָּל־חַרְטֻמֵּי מִצְרַיִם וְאֶת־כָּל־חֲכָמֶיהָ וַיְסַפֵּר פַּרְעֹה לָהֶם אֶת־חֲלֹמוֹ

ט וְאֵין־פּוֹתֵר אוֹתָם לְפַרְעֹה: וַיְדַבֵּר שַׂר הַמַּשְׁקִים אֶת־פַּרְעֹה

י לֵאמֹר אֶת־חֲטָאַי אֲנִי מַזְכִּיר הַיּוֹם: פַּרְעֹה קָצַף עַל־עֲבָדָיו וַיִּתֵּן אֹתִי בְּמִשְׁמַר בֵּית שַׂר הַטַּבָּחִים אֹתִי וְאֵת שַׂר הָאֹפִים:

יא וַנַּחַלְמָה חֲלוֹם בְּלַיְלָה אֶחָד אֲנִי וָהוּא אִישׁ כְּפִתְרֹן

יב חֲלֹמוֹ חָלָמְנוּ: וְשָׁם אִתָּנוּ נַעַר עִבְרִי עֶבֶד לְשַׂר הַטַּבָּחִים וַנְּסַפֶּר־לוֹ וַיִּפְתָּר־לָנוּ אֶת־חֲלֹמֹתֵינוּ אִישׁ כַּחֲלֹמוֹ פָּתָר:

יג וַיְהִי כַּאֲשֶׁר פָּתַר־לָנוּ כֵּן הָיָה אֹתִי הֵשִׁיב עַל־כַּנִּי וְאֹתוֹ תָלָה:

7. וְהִנֵּה חֲלוֹם — *And behold! — it had been a dream.* Rashi explains: The dream was now complete. *Ramban* elaborates: Only one dream was involved. Pharaoh realized on his own that the two dreams referred to the same subject, although his magicians and wise men kept interpreting them as two distinct dreams.

8. וַתִּפָּעֶם רוּחוֹ — *His spirit was agitated.* R' Yochanan said that it was a morning dream (*Rabbah* 89). He taught: "Three kinds of dreams are fulfilled: an early morning dream, a dream which a friend has about one, and a dream which is interpreted in the midst of a dream" (*Berachos* 55b). R' S. Edels explains that the dreams which come just before awakening no longer result from a somatic or psychological deficiency nor from activity of the nervous system, as do dreams occurring at the beginning of sleep. Consequently, early morning dreams belong to the third category (cf. our commentary to 37:6) — those which come from prophetic inspiration. Indeed, the morning hours before waking are known to be a time of great inspiration, even of sudden revelation. The fact that Pharaoh's dreams had taken place at this morning hour, and that there was a "repetition of the dream," convinced the Egyptian king of their very special importance (*R' S. Edels*, ibid.).

וְאֵין־פּוֹתֵר אוֹתָם לְפַרְעֹה — *But none could interpret them for Pharaoh.* The interpretations which they gave, for example, "You will have seven daughters and you will bury seven daughters," referred to Pharaoh as father of a family, whereas he himself felt that the dreams involved him as king of Egypt. Others, contrary to Pharaoh's firm belief, maintained that the two dreams had no connection (*Midrash*). In the end "they explained them, but not for Pharaoh. Their voices were not heard by him (the explanations did not satisfy him) nor did he find any relief" (*Rashi*). The chief butler saw then that Pharaoh was in the grip of an indomitable terror and was in danger of dying of fright. He feared lest Pharaoh die, thinking to himself: I do not know if the new king will keep me in my position. He decided then and there to make mention of Joseph to Pharaoh (*Midrash*).

by the east wind, were growing after them. [7] *Then the seven thin ears swallowed up the seven healthy and full ears; Pharaoh awoke and behold! — it had been a dream.*

[8] *And it was in the morning: His spirit was agitated, so he sent and summoned all the necromancers of Egypt and all its wise men; Pharaoh related his dream to them, but none could interpret them for Pharaoh.*

[9] *Then the Chamberlain of the Cupbearers spoke up before Pharaoh, "My transgressions do I mention today.* [10] *Pharaoh had become incensed at his servants and placed me in the ward of the house of the Chamberlain of the Butchers — me and the Chamberlain of the Bakers.* [11] *We dreamt a dream on the same night, I and he; each of us according to the interpretation of his dream did we dream.* [12] *And there, with us, was a Hebrew youth, a slave of the Chamberlain of the Butchers; we related it to him, and he interpreted our dreams for us; he interpreted for each in accordance with his dream.* [13] *And it was that just as he interpreted for us so did it happen; me he restored to my post and him he hanged."*

12. נַעַר עִבְרִי — *A Hebrew youth.* In Hebrew the term נַעַר, *youth*, often designates a servant of any age. This is the case here with Joseph, even though he was thirty years old. So too with Joshua (*Exodus* 33:11), although he was then over forty (*Guide* 2:32).

עֶבֶד — *A slave.* Although, as we have just explained, the chief butler was interested in helping Pharaoh to find the answer to his dream, he nonetheless wanted to avoid seeing Joseph rise to a high position in the royal court. He feared that Joseph would take revenge and might even have him dismissed for having forgotten about him completely for two years. Hence the chief butler mentions Joseph in a way that will prevent his rise to power: "*A youth* — ignorant, having none of the qualifications needed for an important post; *a Hebrew* — who doesn't even know our language; *a slave* — and it is written in the laws of Egypt that a slave can neither rule nor wear the raiment of a prince" (*Rabbah* ibid.).

13. וַיְהִי כַּאֲשֶׁר פָּתַר־לָנוּ כֵּן הָיָה — *And it was that just as he interpreted for us so did it happen.* From this verse R' Elazar formulates the rule that dreams follow their interpretation, and Rava adds: provided that it is consistent with the dream and is appropriate to its content (*Berachos* 55b and *Rashi* on verse 12). See the explanation in our commentary to 37:8.

To be sure, not only do dreams depend on their interpretation, but more generally, so does human destiny itself. "Everything assumes the reality of the interpretation which one places on it." Might not this apply to the whole of our existence? What is decisive in our lives is not so much the facts and events themselves as the way in which we see them, as optimists or pessimists, idealists

יד וַיִּשְׁלַח פַּרְעֹה וַיִּקְרָא אֶת־יוֹסֵף וַיְרִיצֻהוּ מִן־הַבּוֹר וַיְגַלַּח

שני

טו וַיְחַלֵּף שִׂמְלֹתָיו וַיָּבֹא אֶל־פַּרְעֹה: וַיֹּאמֶר פַּרְעֹה אֶל־יוֹסֵף
חֲלוֹם חָלַמְתִּי וּפֹתֵר אֵין אֹתוֹ וַאֲנִי שָׁמַעְתִּי עָלֶיךָ לֵאמֹר

טז תִּשְׁמַע חֲלוֹם לִפְתֹּר אֹתוֹ: וַיַּעַן יוֹסֵף אֶת־פַּרְעֹה לֵאמֹר

יז בִּלְעָדָי אֱלֹהִים יַעֲנֶה אֶת־שְׁלוֹם פַּרְעֹה: וַיְדַבֵּר פַּרְעֹה

יח אֶל־יוֹסֵף בַּחֲלֹמִי הִנְנִי עֹמֵד עַל־שְׂפַת הַיְאֹר: וְהִנֵּה מִן־
הַיְאֹר עֹלֹת שֶׁבַע פָּרוֹת בְּרִיאוֹת בָּשָׂר וִיפֹת תֹּאַר וַתִּרְעֶינָה

יט בָּאָחוּ: וְהִנֵּה שֶׁבַע־פָּרוֹת אֲחֵרוֹת עֹלוֹת אַחֲרֵיהֶן דַּלּוֹת
וְרָעוֹת תֹּאַר מְאֹד וְרַקּוֹת בָּשָׂר לֹא־רָאִיתִי כָהֵנָּה בְּכָל־אֶרֶץ

כ מִצְרַיִם לָרֹעַ: וַתֹּאכַלְנָה הַפָּרוֹת הָרַקּוֹת וְהָרָעוֹת אֵת

or materialists, believers or atheists. In the final analysis, everything depends on our interpretation. Dreams just provide the classical example where this principle applies in its most direct form.

14. וַיְרִיצֻהוּ מִן־הַבּוֹר — *And they rushed him from the dungeon.* When the time for freedom has come, it happens without delay, at the very moment willed by Providence. So it was with Joseph: *a youth, poor but wise . . . he came forth out of prison in order to rule* (Ecclesiastes 4:14). So it was with the exodus from Egypt, which was made in great haste. And so it will be for the coming of the Messiah: *Suddenly he will enter His temple, the Master whom you have waited for, the messenger of the covenant whom you call with your prayers . . .* (Malachi 3:1; *Sforno*). Every providential act which leads to rescuing someone miraculously from the depths of the abyss comes by surprise, at the moment when one least expects it (*Sanhedrin* 97a), when God sees *His servants with their strength spent, without support and without resources* (Deuteronomy 32:36).

16. בִּלְעָדָי — *That is beyond me. Rashi* explains: The wisdom is not from me, but God will put in my mouth an answer of peace for Pharaoh. Similarly, *R' Bachya* comments: It is God alone Who provides the key to dreams. Joseph had already stressed this to the imprisoned officers when he declared: "But interpretations are God's." And saying this now, he affirms that the explanation could only be the result of Divine inspiration. But, asks *R' Yitzchak Arama* (*Akeidas Yitzchak* 29), how can one reconcile this statement with the idea that "dreams follow the interpretation" which people give to them? *R' Shmuel Edels* replies that the dreams in question came under the category of prophetic dreams (*Berachos* 55b), for which men's interpretations can involve only points of detail.

17. וַיְדַבֵּר פַּרְעֹה אֶל־יוֹסֵף — *Then Pharaoh said to Joseph.* As soon as Pharaoh looked at Joseph, he immediately understood that the young Hebrew was not only a noble and free man but also a sage, perfectly capable of interpreting his dreams (*Philo, De Josepho,* 20).

¹⁴ *So Pharaoh sent and summoned Joseph, and they rushed him from the dungeon. He shaved and changed his clothes, and he came to Pharaoh.* ¹⁵ *And Pharaoh said to Joseph, "I dreamt a dream, but no one can interpret it. Now I heard it said of you that you comprehend a dream to interpret it."*

¹⁶ *Joseph answered Pharaoh, saying, "That is beyond me; it is God Who will respond with Pharaoh's welfare."*

¹⁷ *Then Pharaoh said to Joseph, "In my dream, behold! — I was standing upon the bank of the River.* ¹⁸ *And behold, out of the River there emerged seven cows, of robust flesh and beautiful form, and they were grazing in the marshland.* ¹⁹ *Suddenly, seven other cows emerged after them — scrawny and of very inferior form and of emaciated flesh; I have never seen inferiority like theirs in all the land of Egypt.* ²⁰ *And the emaciated and inferior cows ate up the*

הִנְנִי עֹמֵד עַל־שְׂפַת הַיְאֹר — *I was standing upon the bank of the River.* The detailed repetition of the dreams could mean to show us how Pharaoh tested Joseph by changing some of the details, as was mentioned in our commentary on verses 1 and 3. Some of the other nuances referred to the outward appearance of the cows and the ears on the stalks. But Joseph's interpretation corresponded so exactly to the actual dreams and it was so pertinent that Pharaoh exclaimed: אַחֲרֵי הוֹדִיעַ, "Since [after] God has informed you of all this" (verse 39). Here the term אַחֲרֵי replaces the more usual expression לְפִי. Accordingly, it has been interpreted in the sense of אַחֲרַי, *behind me.* Pharaoh seems to imply to Joseph: "Were you standing behind me when I dreamed?" (*Tanchuma* and *Zohar*).

18. שֶׁבַע פָּרוֹת — *Seven cows.* The number seven plays a major role in Pharaoh's dreams, and as a consequence it determines the number of years of plenty and of famine. R' *Bachya* explains its significance in this way: For the Egyptians, polytheistic, superstitious, and worshiping nature, seven represented the planets. These were supposed to have a determining influence on human destiny and were worshiped by these people. But the years of plenty and of famine, foretold in solemn and spectacular manner in the dreams of the king of Egypt, proved that the seven planets themselves had to obey the will of a superior power, that of the Creator. The number seven, considered as the sacred number of nature, was "demystified" and denounced before the eyes of the heathens as a simple instrument in the hands of Divine Omnipotence. This is why Joseph in several instances calls on the Divine Name אֱלֹהִים which is the attribute of God the Creator (only this name appears in the creation chapter in *Genesis*). The God of heaven and earth alone holds the key to abundance and poverty. He reveals Himself to the peoples of the world as absolute Master of nature. And, at the same time, He demonstrates to us the futility of idols, that resorting to the power of the seven planets cannot have any effect.

כא שֶׁבַע הַפָּרוֹת הָרִאשֹׁנוֹת הַבְּרִיאֹת: וַתָּבֹאנָה אֶל־קִרְבֶּנָה
וְלֹא נוֹדַע כִּי־בָאוּ אֶל־קִרְבֶּנָה וּמַרְאֵיהֶן רַע כַּאֲשֶׁר בַּתְּחִלָּה
כב וָאִיקָץ: וָאֵרֶא בַּחֲלֹמִי וְהִנֵּה | שֶׁבַע שִׁבֳּלִים עֹלֹת בְּקָנֶה
כג אֶחָד מְלֵאֹת וְטֹבוֹת: וְהִנֵּה שֶׁבַע שִׁבֳּלִים צְנֻמוֹת דַּקּוֹת
כד שְׁדֻפוֹת קָדִים צֹמְחוֹת אַחֲרֵיהֶם: וַתִּבְלַעְןָ הַשִּׁבֳּלִים הַדַּקֹּת
אֵת שֶׁבַע הַשִּׁבֳּלִים הַטֹּבוֹת וָאֹמַר אֶל־הַחַרְטֻמִּים וְאֵין
כה מַגִּיד לִי: וַיֹּאמֶר יוֹסֵף אֶל־פַּרְעֹה חֲלוֹם פַּרְעֹה אֶחָד הוּא
כו אֵת אֲשֶׁר הָאֱלֹהִים עֹשֶׂה הִגִּיד לְפַרְעֹה: שֶׁבַע פָּרֹת הַטֹּבֹת
שֶׁבַע שָׁנִים הֵנָּה וְשֶׁבַע הַשִּׁבֳּלִים הַטֹּבֹת שֶׁבַע שָׁנִים הֵנָּה
כז חֲלוֹם אֶחָד הוּא: וְשֶׁבַע הַפָּרוֹת הָרַקּוֹת וְהָרָעֹת הָעֹלֹת
אַחֲרֵיהֶן שֶׁבַע שָׁנִים הֵנָּה וְשֶׁבַע הַשִּׁבֳּלִים הָרֵקוֹת שְׁדֻפוֹת
כח הַקָּדִים יִהְיוּ שֶׁבַע שְׁנֵי רָעָב: הוּא הַדָּבָר אֲשֶׁר דִּבַּרְתִּי
כט אֶל־פַּרְעֹה אֲשֶׁר הָאֱלֹהִים עֹשֶׂה הֶרְאָה אֶת־פַּרְעֹה: הִנֵּה
ל שֶׁבַע שָׁנִים בָּאוֹת שָׂבָע גָּדוֹל בְּכָל־אֶרֶץ מִצְרָיִם: וְקָמוּ שֶׁבַע
שְׁנֵי רָעָב אַחֲרֵיהֶן וְנִשְׁכַּח כָּל־הַשָּׂבָע בְּאֶרֶץ מִצְרָיִם וְכִלָּה
לא הָרָעָב אֶת־הָאָרֶץ: וְלֹא־יִוָּדַע הַשָּׂבָע בָּאָרֶץ מִפְּנֵי הָרָעָב
לב הַהוּא אַחֲרֵי־כֵן כִּי־כָבֵד הוּא מְאֹד: וְעַל הִשָּׁנוֹת הַחֲלוֹם
אֶל־פַּרְעֹה פַּעֲמָיִם כִּי־נָכוֹן הַדָּבָר מֵעִם הָאֱלֹהִים וּמְמַהֵר
לג הָאֱלֹהִים לַעֲשֹׂתוֹ: וְעַתָּה יֵרֶא פַרְעֹה אִישׁ נָבוֹן וְחָכָם

25. אֵת אֲשֶׁר הָאֱלֹהִים עֹשֶׂה הִגִּיד לְפַרְעֹה — *What God is about to do, He has told to Pharaoh.* Joseph then immediately re-emphasizes what he has just said: "It is this matter that I have spoken to Pharaoh: What God is about to do He has shown to Pharaoh" (verse 28). For this insistence on the aspect of Divine revelation in the dreams there were two reasons. On one hand, the dreams had occurred on the night of Rosh Hashanah, as the Talmud tells us (*Rosh Hashanah* 10b). Now, dreams on this night have a particular significance, since the future destiny of the country including its periods of fertility and drought are decided at this time (עי"ש, פ' עין יעקב). On the other hand, these dreams were meant for the king who presided over the destiny of his people and, as R' Yitzchak remarks, the higher the position occupied by a person, the more important is any revelation which he receives. It was therefore of interest to the people as a whole (*Zohar*). *The heart of the king,* said King Solomon, *is in the hand of God like a stream* (*Proverbs* 21:1). So Joseph understood that Pharaoh's dreams were of importance not just to himself and his family but to the whole nation. Addressed to the king of the strongest world power of that era, and on the night of Rosh Hashanah, they could only have been the revelation to Pharaoh of what "God was planning to do."

first seven healthy cows. ²¹ *They came inside them, but it was not apparent that they had come inside them, for their appearance remained as inferior as at first. Then I awoke.* ²² *I then saw in my dream: Behold! — seven ears of grain were sprouting on a single stalk — full and good.* ²³ *And suddenly! — seven ears of grain, withered, thin and scorched by the east wind were growing after them.* ²⁴ *Then the thin ears of grain swallowed up the seven good ears; I said this to the necromancers, but no one could explain it to me."*

²⁵ *Joseph said to Pharaoh, "The dream of Pharaoh is a single one; what God is about to do, He has told to Pharaoh:* ²⁶ *The seven good cows are seven years, and the good ears are seven years; it is a single dream.* ²⁷ *Now, the seven emaciated and bad cows who emerged after them — they are seven years; as are the seven emaciated ears scorched by the east wind. There shall be seven years of famine.* ²⁸ *It is this matter that I have spoken to Pharaoh: What God is about to do He has shown to Pharaoh.*

²⁹ *Behold! — seven years are coming — a great abundance throughout all the land of Egypt.* ³⁰ *Then seven years of famine will arise after them and all the abundance in the land of Egypt will be forgotten; the famine will ravage the land.* ³¹ *And the abundance will be unknown in the land in the face of the subsequent famine — for it will be terribly severe.* ³² *As for the repetition of the dream to Pharaoh — two times — it is because the matter stands ready before God, and God is hastening to accomplish it.*

³³ *Now let Pharaoh seek out a discerning and wise man*

33. וְעַתָּה יֵרֶא פַרְעֹה אִישׁ נָבוֹן וְחָכָם — *Now let Pharaoh seek out a discerning and wise man.* After interpreting the dreams, Joseph takes the initiative of offering Pharaoh advice without being given the authority to do so. No one had solicited these suggestions, but in recommending that the king appoint as chief administrator an understanding and wise man, Joseph was thinking of himself, as *Ramban* indicates. Quite understandably, Joseph must have looked upon the sudden and sensational fashion in which he was brought before Pharaoh as a providential event. He still held a belief in his dreams of adolescence and felt that the long-awaited turning point in his destiny had at last arrived; so he had to take advantage of this unique opportunity. This he did without hesitating and the counsel which he offered to Pharaoh with lightning speed was so pertinent and so favorable to the king that he was tremendously impressed.

נָבוֹן וְחָכָם — *Discerning and wise.* According to *Ramban,* נָבוֹן signifies one who is capable of circumspectly directing the country's economy and חָכָם means gifted with technical knowledge. For *Rashbam,* נָבוֹן is a mind with foresight and חָכָם, an expert. Cf. *Rashi* on *Deuteronomy* 1:13.

לד וְיִשְׁתֵהוּ עַל־אֶרֶץ מִצְרָיִם: יַעֲשֶׂה פַרְעֹה וְיַפְקֵד פְּקִדִים
עַל־הָאָרֶץ וְחִמֵּשׁ אֶת־אֶרֶץ מִצְרַיִם בְּשֶׁבַע שְׁנֵי הַשָּׂבָע:
לה וְיִקְבְּצוּ אֶת־כָּל־אֹכֶל הַשָּׁנִים הַטֹּבֹת הַבָּאֹת הָאֵלֶּה
לו וְיִצְבְּרוּ־בָר תַּחַת יַד־פַּרְעֹה אֹכֶל בֶּעָרִים וְשָׁמָרוּ: וְהָיָה
הָאֹכֶל לְפִקָּדוֹן לָאָרֶץ לְשֶׁבַע שְׁנֵי הָרָעָב אֲשֶׁר תִּהְיֶיןָ בְּאֶרֶץ
לז מִצְרָיִם וְלֹא־תִכָּרֵת הָאָרֶץ בָּרָעָב: וַיִּיטַב הַדָּבָר בְּעֵינֵי פַרְעֹה
לח וּבְעֵינֵי כָּל־עֲבָדָיו: וַיֹּאמֶר פַּרְעֹה אֶל־עֲבָדָיו הֲנִמְצָא כָזֶה
שלישי לט אִישׁ אֲשֶׁר רוּחַ אֱלֹהִים בּוֹ: וַיֹּאמֶר פַּרְעֹה אֶל־יוֹסֵף אַחֲרֵי
הוֹדִיעַ אֱלֹהִים אוֹתְךָ אֶת־כָּל־זֹאת אֵין נָבוֹן וְחָכָם כָּמוֹךָ:

34. וְחִמֵּשׁ אֶת־אֶרֶץ — *And he shall prepare the land.* We are witnessing a veritable lesson in management which Joseph gives to the astonishment of the Egyptian ruler. He advises, according to *Rashbam,* separating a fifth of the annual produce during the seven years of plenty for distribution in the years of famine. Actually, experience proved that, on the average, the yearly consumption in times of plenty surpassed twice that for a normal year, whereas the supply in a year of famine could if necessary be kept at half that for a normal year. Thus, by keeping four-fifths of the produce for current needs, what one would have in reserve would at the very least be enough for coming needs (*R' S. R. Hirsch*).

35. תַּחַת יַד־פַּרְעֹה — *Under Pharaoh's authority.* Joseph's plan puts all the resources of the country at Pharaoh's disposal. At the same time it will reinforce the controls which are indispensable for achieving this veritable wartime economy. Lastly, free trade would temporarily be abolished (Egypt being till then the principal exporting country of grain). Henceforth there would be just one purchaser: the State. As a supplementary measure, one which shows a profound understanding of the way of thinking of the people: the reserves kept as royal property were to remain stored in each town serving as a center of production. The Egyptians would thus see "where the produce went" and could have no suspicions about hidden transactions. It is not surprising that these proposals, showing such evident good political sense, should find an enthusiastic response. Nor is it surprising that it was Joseph, the brilliant author of the plan, who would be appointed to carry it out (ibid.).

38. הֲנִמְצָא כָזֶה אִישׁ אֲשֶׁר רוּחַ אֱלֹהִים בּוֹ — *Could we find another like him — a man in whom is the spirit of God?* "Indeed, Joseph had revealed himself to be both prophet and statesman; he had explained the past and revealed the future and, together with the ailment, he had indicated the remedy" (Wogue). The one whose brothers had nicknamed him "the dreamer," and who possessed the supernatural gift of interpretation, now suddenly reveals himself in an entirely different light — as a politician with an extremely practical turn of mind.

אֲשֶׁר רוּחַ אֱלֹהִים בּוֹ — *In whom is the spirit of God.* The Egyptians did not know the Tetragrammaton, the name of the true God. "I know not הַנֵּי," Pharaoh will

and set him over the land of Egypt. [34] *Let Pharaoh proceed and let him appoint overseers on the land, and he shall prepare the land of Egypt during the seven years of abundance.* [35] *And let them gather all the food of those approaching good years; let them amass fine grain under Pharaoh's authority for food in the cities, and safeguard it.* [36] *The food will be a reserve for the land against the seven years of famine which will befall the land of Egypt, so that the land will not perish in the famine."*

[37] *The matter appeared good in Pharaoh's eyes and in the eyes of all his servants.* [38] *Pharaoh said to his servants, "Could we find another like him — a man in whom is the spirit of God?"*

[39] *Then Pharaoh said to Joseph, "Since God has informed you of all this, there can be no one so discerning and wise as you.*

say to Moses (*Exodus* 5:2). They had only a vague and obscure notion of the existence of a supreme Divinity named אֱלֹהִים, whom Pharaoh mentions on two occasions (*Kuzari* 4:15).

39. אֵין־נָבוֹן וְחָכָם כָּמוֹךָ — *There can be no one so discerning and wise as you.* In order to confer quasi-royal powers upon Joseph, Pharaoh needed to ensure that he had the approval of his servants, for in the eyes of the Egyptians a Hebrew was an impure being, relegated to the status of an outcast. So he said to them: Can we find a man as understanding and wise as this Hebrew? They answered in unanimous acknowledgement of his superiority (*Ramban*). But they pointed out that he was a slave "and it is written in the laws of Egypt that a slave cannot rule." Pharaoh replied: I see in him signs of royalty (*Rashi*) — wisdom, strength, and noble bearing. He is the son of a noble family and he was wrongly sold as a slave (*Rabbi S. Edels*). They replied: If so, he should know the seventy languages (as was the rule for high dignitaries). Pharaoh decided to test him the next day. That night, the angel Gabriel came to teach Joseph these languages but he could not learn them. Then a letter from God's name was added to his name, as it is written (*Psalms* 81:6): עֵדוּת בִּיהוֹסֵף שָׂמוֹ וְגוֹ׳,*He put a sign of testimony on Joseph* (the letter ה of the Divine Name) *when He went out to the land of Egypt. I understood then the language[s which] I had not known.* (The letter of the Divine Name was offered to Joseph in testimony to his chastity throughout all the previous years during which he had reached the level of holiness.) This verse begins and ends with the letter ע, which has a numerical value of 70 (*Rabbi S. Edels*). Thus, Joseph well deserved the miracle which happened to him that night, and when he presented himself before Pharaoh in the morning, he was able to answer him in all the seventy languages. In the end, Joseph addressed Pharaoh in the holy language, in Hebrew, but he did not understand it, and could not master it. So he asked Joseph to swear never to reveal this weakness to anyone, for the king was supposed to know all existing languages. (This oath played an important role at the time of Jacob's burial; cf. *Rashi* on 50:6.) But

מ אַתָּה תִּהְיֶה עַל־בֵּיתִי וְעַל־פִּיךָ יִשַּׁק כָּל־עַמִּי רַק הַכִּסֵּא
מא אֶגְדַּל מִמֶּךָ: וַיֹּאמֶר פַּרְעֹה אֶל־יוֹסֵף רְאֵה נָתַתִּי אֹתְךָ עַל
מב כָּל־אֶרֶץ מִצְרָיִם: וַיָּסַר פַּרְעֹה אֶת־טַבַּעְתּוֹ מֵעַל יָדוֹ וַיִּתֵּן
אֹתָהּ עַל־יַד יוֹסֵף וַיַּלְבֵּשׁ אֹתוֹ בִּגְדֵי־שֵׁשׁ וַיָּשֶׂם רְבִד הַזָּהָב
מג עַל־צַוָּארוֹ: וַיַּרְכֵּב אֹתוֹ בְּמִרְכֶּבֶת הַמִּשְׁנֶה אֲשֶׁר־לוֹ וַיִּקְרְאוּ
לְפָנָיו אַבְרֵךְ וְנָתוֹן אֹתוֹ עַל כָּל־אֶרֶץ מִצְרָיִם: וַיֹּאמֶר פַּרְעֹה
מד אֶל־יוֹסֵף אֲנִי פַרְעֹה וּבִלְעָדֶיךָ לֹא־יָרִים אִישׁ אֶת־יָדוֹ
מה וְאֶת־רַגְלוֹ בְּכָל־אֶרֶץ מִצְרָיִם: וַיִּקְרָא פַרְעֹה שֵׁם־יוֹסֵף
צָפְנַת פַּעְנֵחַ וַיִּתֶּן־לוֹ אֶת־אָסְנַת בַּת־פּוֹטִי פֶרַע כֹּהֵן אֹן
מו לְאִשָּׁה וַיֵּצֵא יוֹסֵף עַל־אֶרֶץ מִצְרָיִם: וְיוֹסֵף בֶּן־שְׁלֹשִׁים שָׁנָה
בְּעָמְדוֹ לִפְנֵי פַּרְעֹה מֶלֶךְ־מִצְרָיִם וַיֵּצֵא יוֹסֵף מִלִּפְנֵי פַרְעֹה
מז וַיַּעֲבֹר בְּכָל־אֶרֶץ מִצְרָיִם: וַתַּעַשׂ הָאָרֶץ בְּשֶׁבַע שְׁנֵי הַשָּׂבָע

Pharaoh was perfectly aware of the supernatural factor which intervened in the extraordinary wisdom and knowledge shown by Joseph. And he exclaimed: "Since God has informed you of all this, there can be no one so discerning and wise as you!" (*Sotah* 36a).

42. וַיִּתֵּן אֹתָהּ עַל־יַד יוֹסֵף — *And put in on Joseph's hand.* R' Shimon ben Gamliel said: Joseph well deserved the honors bestowed upon him because of his virtuous life. The hands, neck, body, and the feet (carried by the chariot) which had refused to sin were now adorned with the glorious signs of royalty (*Rabbah* 90).

45. צָפְנַת פַּעְנֵחַ — *Zaphenath-paneah (revealer of the hidden).* Joseph is granted a new name on his nomination to a state position. This was in accordance with Egyptian custom, and, at times, with Jewish custom (*Numbers* 13:16). The change of name is of importance in the narrative because it will contribute to masking Joseph's identity when his brothers come to Egypt. According to *Onkelos* and *Rashi*, this name means "the explainer of hidden things" (צְפוּנוֹת), an allusion to Joseph's ability to explain dreams. *Ramban* adds that Pharaoh gave the name in a language which was related to Egyptian, just as his daughter Bityah did in naming Moses. According to some other sages, the name is of Egyptian origin, but the meaning of this Egyptian name is not known. The Septuagint and the Coptic version translate: "salvation of the world," or "of the empire."

וַיִּתֶּן־לוֹ אֶת־אָסְנַת בַּת־פּוֹטִי פֶרַע — *And he gave him Asenath daughter of Poti-phera.* Rashi explains: "This is Potiphar. He was called Poti-phera after having become impotent through illness (Poti, the mutilated one) consequent of his sinful lust for Joseph." (Cf. our commentary to 39:1.) *Ramban* tells us that Potiphar was unable to bear this shame, which had become public knowledge, so he resigned his post under Pharaoh and became a priest in the Temple of On. This name designates the town where Osiris (or Frey) the sun-god was worshiped. It is more generally known as Heliopolis, located near Cairo.

⁴⁰ *You shall be in charge of my palace and by your command shall all my people be sustained; only by the throne shall I outrank you."*

⁴¹ *Then Pharaoh said to Joseph, "See! I have placed you in charge of all the land of Egypt." ⁴² And Pharaoh removed his ring from his hand and put it on Joseph's hand. He then had him dressed in garments of fine linen and he placed a gold chain upon his neck. ⁴³ He also had him ride in his second royal chariot and they proclaimed before him: "Avrech!" Thus, he appointed him over all the land of Egypt.*

⁴⁴ *Pharaoh said to Joseph, "I am Pharaoh. And without you no man may lift up his hand or foot in all the land of Egypt."*

⁴⁵ *Pharaoh called Joseph's name Zaphenath-paneah and he gave him Asenath daughter of Poti-phera, Chief of On, for a wife. Thus, Joseph emerged in charge of the land of Egypt. ⁴⁶ Now Joseph was thirty years old when he stood before Pharaoh king of Egypt; Joseph left Pharaoh's presence and he passed through the entire land of Egypt.*

⁴⁷ *The earth produced during the seven years of abundance*

As for Asenath, *Targum Yonasan* tells us that she was the child that Jacob's daughter Dinah bore from Shechem, who had raped her. Several Midrashic sources (and notably *Pirkei D'Rabbi Eliezer* 38) give essentially the following account. When Dinah returned to the family home and gave birth to her daughter, Jacob's sons were not able to bear the presence of this daughter of sin. So Jacob made her an amulet with the inscription: Asenath, daughter of Dinah, daughter of Jacob (אָסְנַת derived from אָסוֹן, daughter of violent tragedy). He attached the amulet to a necklace which she wore around her neck and sent her away. She ultimately came to Egypt, to Potiphar's house, where she was brought up and adopted, for Potiphar had no children, and she was called "daughter of Potiphar." Joseph met her there later without suspecting her origins. But she had such confidence in Joseph that when her adoptive mother began her slanderous accusations against him, she went on her own initiative to convince Potiphar of his innocence (commentary to 39:19). When Joseph became viceroy and rode triumphantly through the town in his royal chariot, "each of the girls climbed heights" (49:22) to see him pass by in his glory, and they threw gifts into his chariot. Asenath, who had nothing else with her, pulled off her necklace and threw it to him. He opened the amulet, read her name and knew then that she was his niece. Thus when Pharaoh wanted Joseph to marry, he chose Asenath. She gave birth to Ephraim and Manasseh, and when the aged patriarch Jacob hesitated to bless them before his death because he had doubts as to their origin, Joseph showed him the amulet (cf. *Rashi* on 48:9). In any case, as a result of his marriage with the daughter of Potiphar, Joseph was clearly vindicated in the eyes

מח לְקָמָצִים: וַיִּקְבֹּץ אֶת־כָּל־אֹכֶל ו שֶׁבַע שָׁנִים אֲשֶׁר הָיוּ בְּאֶרֶץ
מִצְרַיִם וַיִּתֶּן־אֹכֶל בֶּעָרִים אֹכֶל שְׂדֵה־הָעִיר אֲשֶׁר סְבִיבֹתֶיהָ
מט נָתַן בְּתוֹכָהּ: וַיִּצְבֹּר יוֹסֵף בָּר כְּחוֹל הַיָּם הַרְבֵּה מְאֹד עַד
נ כִּי־חָדַל לִסְפֹּר כִּי־אֵין מִסְפָּר: וּלְיוֹסֵף יֻלַּד שְׁנֵי בָנִים בְּטֶרֶם
תָּבוֹא שְׁנַת הָרָעָב אֲשֶׁר יָלְדָה־לּוֹ אָסְנַת בַּת־פּוֹטִי פֶרַע כֹּהֵן

of the Egyptians from the earlier accusations brought against him by the wife of his master.

46. וַיַּעֲבֹר בְּכָל־אֶרֶץ מִצְרָיִם — *And he passed through the entire land of Egypt.* We have already been told this in the previous verse, but here it is mentioned that Joseph went out from before Pharaoh. This additional detail is of particular importance for the *Zohar*, which considers every terrestrial event as only the reflection of metaphysical causes emanating from the higher spheres. There exists, the *Zohar* tells us, a royal chariot on this earth, and a chariot of the Divine Majesty borne by the four archangels in the celestial spheres (*Ezekiel* 1:16). So if honor was lavished on Joseph to the point that he rode through the whole of Egypt in the royal chariot, "emerging from Pharaoh's presence," that is to say, as the herald of the king and surrounded by his radiance of glory, then it is because he had had the merit of being herald for the King of the universe. Joseph had announced His message to mankind and wherever he had lived among pagans he had proclaimed His name and His glory. He was one of the glorious upholders of the chariot of the Divine Majesty (מֶרְכָּבָה לַשְּׁכִינָה), like the four archangels, long before he was carried in triumph on the chariot of the king of Egypt.

48. וַיִּקְבֹּץ אֶת־כָּל־אֹכֶל — *He gathered all food.* The adjective כָּל is not to be taken literally (*Ibn Ezra*) but refers to the fifth part of the produce which Joseph had spoken of previously (*R' Bachya*). This amount remained stored for the subsequent requirements of the famine and, according to *Onkelos'* translation, it included other foods as well as grain. *Ramban*, however, points out the distinction between other foods on the one hand and grain on the other. Joseph had probably gathered all the available food, bought at a low price as a result of overproduction and, rationing it, had resold it for immediate consumption that year in order to prevent any unwise wastage. The surplus, as well as the grain, was held in reserve for the seven years of famine. Joseph was able to manage the fantastic achievement of conserving the foods and grain intact for more than seven years. This was the result of a process noted by the Sages of the Midrash (and cited by *Rashi*): These products can be preserved by storing them in some of the soil in which they are grown (as the second part of verse 48 implies) and this prevents their decay.

49. כְּחוֹל הַיָּם — *Like the sand of the sea.* Right from the beginning of his career, we see Joseph laying the foundations for the prodigious riches of Egypt which more than two centuries later would constitute the "great wealth" taken by the

by the handfuls. ⁴⁸ *He gathered all food of the seven years that came to pass in Egypt, and he placed food in the cities; the food of the field around each city he placed within it.* ⁴⁹ *Joseph amassed grain like the sand of the sea in great abundance until he ceased counting, for there was no number.*

⁵⁰ *Now to Joseph were born two sons — when the year of famine had not yet set in — whom Asenath daughter of Poti-phera, Chief*

Jews when they left this land — in fulfillment of God's words to Abraham (15:14). Thanks to these riches, the Sanctuary with its impressive and sumptuous interior could be constructed in the middle of the desert. Joseph had taken care to divide up the money which poured in from Egypt, as well as from the other countries, into three treasuries of immense value. The Talmud recounts what later happened to them (*Pesachim* 119a). It is thus that Providence prepares long beforehand the works which It wants to carry out.

50. בְּטֶרֶם תָּבוֹא שְׁנַת הָרָעָב — *When the year of famine had not yet set in. Rashi* concludes: From this we learn that one may not cohabit in time of famine. But the *Tosafists* point out that this prohibition applies only to the very pious (*Taanis* 11a). This subject is dealt with by the interpreters of the law in the *Shulchan Aruch, Orach Chaim* §574, 4 (cf. our commentary to 8:16).

אֲשֶׁר יָלְדָה־לּוֹ אָסְנַת — *Whom Asenath . . . bore to him.* The repetition of the name of the mother, as we also find above in 21:9 and in 24:15, usually has a special significance, which the commentators interpret in a light either favorable or unfavorable to her. Thus, *R' S. R. Hirsch* points out that, despite her own upbringing, Asenath raised her children in the spirit of her husband, to the point where they were totally "his" (אֲשֶׁר יָלְדָה לּוֹ). "To be the only Jew in Egypt, to marry a daughter of the house of the priest of On, and yet to bring up children of such virtue that parents to this very day bless their children by wishing them to be like Ephraim and Manasseh, that is indeed so great a merit that the Torah considered it its duty to place special emphasis on it." In contrast, *Radak* attributes certain reprehensible acts which their offspring will commit to the unsavory influence of their mother (*I Kings* 11). Did not Jacob himself feel legitimate apprehensions in this regard (as *Rashi* points out on 48:8)?

The stress which the Torah puts on the name of the mother of Joseph's children can also be explained in another way — by referring to what *Rashi* quotes at the beginning of Chapter 39:1 "Potiphar's wife knew from her horoscope that she would have sons from Joseph, but she was unable to tell if it applied to herself or to her daughter." This is why the Torah emphasizes here the name of the sons' mother, as by so doing it points out an error of astrology. However, concludes *Rashi*, Potiphar's wife had acted with pure intentions, and לְשֵׁם שָׁמַיִם, *for the sake of Heaven,* as did Tamar, whose story comes just before. Tamar also had but one ideal: to help found a family in the house of Israel. But if both of them acted with the same disinterestedness, why has Tamar's memory

נא אוֹן: וַיִּקְרָא יוֹסֵף אֶת־שֵׁם הַבְּכוֹר מְנַשֶּׁה כִּי־נַשַּׁנִי אֱלֹהִים
נב אֶת־כָּל־עֲמָלִי וְאֵת כָּל־בֵּית אָבִי: וְאֵת שֵׁם הַשֵּׁנִי קָרָא
נג אֶפְרָיִם כִּי־הִפְרַנִי אֱלֹהִים בְּאֶרֶץ עָנְיִי: וַתִּכְלֶינָה שֶׁבַע
נד שְׁנֵי הַשָּׂבָע אֲשֶׁר הָיָה בְּאֶרֶץ מִצְרָיִם: וַתְּחִלֶּינָה שֶׁבַע
   שְׁנֵי הָרָעָב לָבוֹא כַּאֲשֶׁר אָמַר יוֹסֵף וַיְהִי רָעָב בְּכָל־
נה הָאֲרָצוֹת וּבְכָל־אֶרֶץ מִצְרַיִם הָיָה לָחֶם: וַתִּרְעַב כָּל־
   אֶרֶץ מִצְרַיִם וַיִּצְעַק הָעָם אֶל־פַּרְעֹה לַלָּחֶם וַיֹּאמֶר
   פַּרְעֹה לְכָל־מִצְרַיִם לְכוּ אֶל־יוֹסֵף אֲשֶׁר־יֹאמַר לָכֶם
נו תַּעֲשׂוּ: וְהָרָעָב הָיָה עַל כָּל־פְּנֵי הָאָרֶץ וַיִּפְתַּח יוֹסֵף אֶת־
   כָּל־אֲשֶׁר בָּהֶם וַיִּשְׁבֹּר לְמִצְרַיִם וַיֶּחֱזַק הָרָעָב בְּאֶרֶץ

רביעי

remained blessed for all eternity, whereas Potiphar's wife has entered into history as a woman of low moral character? The difference lies in their actual behavior. Tamar hears the death sentence pronounced against her, and she accepts it, resigning herself to silence rather than humiliate Judah. But the wife of Potiphar, in marked contrast, chases after Joseph "day in, day out," and when she sees herself defeated, she pushes her treachery to the point of lying and publicly slandering a man she knows is innocent.

51. כִּי־נַשַּׁנִי אֱלֹהִים — *For, "God has made me forget."* Who would not feel indignation at such an attitude? Joseph would then merely be a heartless person and an ungrateful son! And so one should remember that the verb נשה does not only signify to *forget* but also to be a *creditor* (32:33), so that נַשַּׁנִי can just as well mean: "God has turned my misfortunes and my family into my creditors." This is to say that He has transformed my afflictions and the harsh treatment from my family into instruments for my abundant happiness. And thus I feel a debt of gratitude toward my sufferings and my family (*R' S.R. Hirsch*).

52. כִּי־הִפְרַנִי אֱלֹהִים — *For, "God has made me fruitful."* The righteous have a custom of naming their children after events in their lives which recall the memory of miracles they have experienced (*Shemos Rabbah* 1). But Joseph, just like Moses after him, wanted to name his children to bring out memories of his past and his family, and also the fact that, despite his prestigious position in Egypt, he continued to consider that land as the land of "his enslavement." Nothing could be more revealing of his innermost feelings and of his desire to remain attached to his origins and to refuse assimilation in the Egyptian culture than these names he gave to his children. They were constant reminders to him of his duty to be faithful to his family and to the Holy Land.

54. וַיְהִי רָעָב בְּכָל־הָאֲרָצוֹת — *There was famine in all the lands.* The neighboring lands, adds the *Midrash Rabbah*; that is to say, Phoenicia, Arabia, and Canaan. "For if the famine had stricken those lands very distant from Egypt, where there had not been plenty before, the inhabitants would have died of hunger" (*Ramban*).

of On, bore to him. ⁵¹ Joseph called the name of the firstborn
Manasseh for, "God has made me forget all my hardship and all
my father's household." ⁵² And the name of the second son he
called Ephraim for, "God has made me fruitful in the land of my
suffering."

⁵³ The seven years of abundance that came to pass in the land
of Egypt ended. ⁵⁴ And the seven years of famine began
approaching just as Joseph had said. There was famine in all the
lands, but in all the land of Egypt there was bread.

⁵⁵ When all the land of Egypt hungered, the people cried out to
Pharaoh for bread. So Pharaoh said to all of Egypt, "Go to Joseph.
Whatever he tells you, you should do." ⁵⁶ When the famine spread
over all the face of the earth, Joseph opened all the containers and
sold provisions to Egypt; and the famine became severe in the land

55. אֲשֶׁר־יֹאמַר לָכֶם תַּעֲשׂוּ — Whatever he tells you, you should do. Rashi explains:
Joseph told them to have themselves circumcised. When they complained to
Pharaoh, "That is what Joseph said to us!" Pharaoh answered them: "But why
did you not store up provisions of grain? He told you that years of famine were
going to come!" The Egyptians replied: "We stored up a lot, but it rotted." "If
that is so," retorted Pharaoh, "then do exactly what he tells you."

Making the Egyptians undergo circumcision seems at first glance incompre-
hensible. But it is to be connected with the fact that the wheat stored by the
Egyptians rotted whereas that collected by Joseph did not. Some of our Sages,
such as R' Bachya and Maharal, explain that Joseph attributed this difference
to the benefits of the covenant, the בְּרִית, whose sign is circumcision. Indeed, it
has the ability to confer enduring life and possessions on its adherents, as the
history of the Jewish people proves. Accordingly, Joseph held that performing
the sign of the covenant was an antidote against degeneration and a guarantee
of duration and survival. (The usual Aramaic translation for the word בְּרִית is
קְיָם, as in Onkelos to 17:11; it means conservation, permanent existence.) But in
his שלה ס', R' Isaiah Horowitz holds that in the depravity of Egyptian morals
Joseph saw the initial cause of the Divine punishments which were inflicted on
the land of Egypt. The Torah itself confirms this view in Chapter 18 of
Leviticus. Right from his accession to power, Joseph wanted to strike at the roots
of evil and to lead the Egyptians to a more healthy, pure and moral life. He
thought he would be able to achieve this result by first having them undergo
circumcision, whose natural effect is to reduce the power of the sexual instincts.
The Egyptians followed Joseph along this path for as long as he ruled over them,
but they abandoned it very shortly thereafter (Aruch, s.v. מל).

56. וַיִּשְׁבֹּר לְמִצְרָיִם — And sold provisions to Egypt. "When all the land of Egypt
hungered." That, according to Ramban, is the sense of this phrase. Joseph
wanted to open the granaries only after the domestic reserves had been depleted
and he prudently limited the distribution.

נז מִצְרָיִם: וְכָל־הָאָרֶץ בָּאוּ מִצְרַיְמָה לִשְׁבֹּר אֶל־יוֹסֵף כִּי־

מב א חָזַק הָרָעָב בְּכָל־הָאָרֶץ: וַיַּרְא יַעֲקֹב כִּי יֶשׁ־שֶׁבֶר

בְּמִצְרָיִם וַיֹּאמֶר יַעֲקֹב לְבָנָיו לָמָּה תִּתְרָאוּ: וַיֹּאמֶר

ב הִנֵּה שָׁמַעְתִּי כִּי יֶשׁ־שֶׁבֶר בְּמִצְרָיִם רְדוּ־שָׁמָּה וְשִׁבְרוּ־

ג לָנוּ מִשָּׁם וְנִחְיֶה וְלֹא נָמוּת: וַיֵּרְדוּ אֲחֵי־יוֹסֵף עֲשָׂרָה

---

57. בָּאוּ מִצְרַיְמָה לִשְׁבֹּר אֶל־יוֹסֵף — *Came to Egypt to Joseph to buy provisions* (lit. *came into Egypt to buy to Joseph*). "Change the order of the words and explain: All the countries came into Egypt to Joseph in order to buy. If you want to explain it according to the way it is written, the text should have said: in order to buy from Joseph (with the preposition מִן instead of אֶל)." But then why does the Torah choose the less exact form לִשְׁבֹּר אֶל־יוֹסֵף? It is in order to stress the words אֶל־יוֹסֵף, *to Joseph*. Indeed, as this chapter comes to a close, the Torah wants to emphasize that מִקֵּץ, *the end*, of Joseph's misfortunes and his fantastic ascent could only have had as their ultimate objective to make "all the lands" converge "to Joseph" and thus prepare the way for the reunion of the family of Israel. "The reverse order" of this verse, which *Rashi* emphasizes, gives us a glimpse of the providential action on the stage of history which in this case had the purpose of directing events "to Joseph."

42.

1. וַיַּרְא יַעֲקֹב — *Jacob perceived.* Literally. "He saw the merchants buy and bring grain from Egypt" (*Targum Yonasan*). But did his sons not see them as well? Why does the Torah mention only Jacob? *Rashi* cites the midrashic explanation: Jacob saw as a result of Divine Inspiration that there was still *hope* (שֶׁבֶר) for him in Egypt. But it was not a full prophetic vision and he did not know for sure that this hope referred to Joseph himself. R' Yehoshua adds: Here is an old man, confined to his home, who sees what is taking place in Egypt, whereas his ten sons, who come and go freely, see nothing! (*Tanchuma*). [יֶשׁ שֶׁבֶר = בַּר, *the son is there*.)

כִּי יֶשׁ־שֶׁבֶר בְּמִצְרָיִם — *That there were provisions in Egypt.* Apart from its plain meaning of "wheat" or "sale" the word שֶׁבֶר can also be taken to mean *hope* שֵׂבֶר (e.g. *Psalms* 146:5) or *ruin* שֶׁבֶר (e.g. *Isaiah* 51:19). Perhaps it is because of this double meaning that the Torah employs the term here. Indeed, Jacob saw with his prophetic vision that ruin was awaiting his family in Egypt where it would live in exile and be reduced to slavery. But he also understood (שָׁמַע, *to understand*) that hope of survival always remained. Thus ruin and hope intermingle in this one word. The Torah hints at this just as the start of exile begins to loom on the horizon.

לָמָּה תִּתְרָאוּ — *Why do you make yourselves conspicuous? Rashi* derives the word תִּתְרָאוּ from the root רָאָה: Why do you let yourselves *be seen* in the eyes *of Egypt.* ⁵⁷ *All the earth came to Egypt to Joseph to buy provisions, for the famine had become severe in all the earth.*

42   ¹ *Jacob perceived that there were provisions in Egypt; so Jacob said to his sons, "Why do you make yourselves conspicuous?"* ² *And he said, "Behold, I have heard that there are provisions in Egypt; go down there and purchase for us from there, that we may live and not die."* ³ *So Joseph's brothers — ten of them — went down*

of the Ishmaelites and the Edomites as if you were full? For this will cause them to be jealous and could lead to harm. But *Targum Yonasan* derives this word from the root ירא and translates: Why are you *afraid* to go down into Egypt? The venerable father had indeed noticed his sons' apprehension about making this journey. "They were looking one at the other," worried and embarrassed. When Abraham went to Egypt to escape famine, he had gone through severe anguish. As for Isaac, he had been forbidden to go down into Egypt to escape the famine. And regarding themselves, Egypt brought back bad memories of Joseph's sale and deportation to that land. Would they not be going to meet adversity there once again? Furthermore, they had the vague feeling that Egypt would become the land for the exile announced long before to the first patriarch. So Jacob sought to calm their fears by telling them (verse 2): "I have just heard that there is (in spite of everything) hope in Egypt. Go down there (רְדוּ has a numerical value of 210 and alludes to the 210 years that the enslavement was to last instead of the 400 years announced to Abraham; cf. *Rashi*). We shall endure, despite the trials and tribulations of the exile; and we shall not disappear."

2. רְדוּ־שָׁמָּה — *Go down there.* On two successive occasions, here and in 43:2, Jacob insists that his sons go down into Egypt. He, who had hoped so much to live peacefully in Canaan (וַיֵּשֶׁב יַעֲקֹב), now sees himself compelled by the force of circumstances to urge the descent into the land of exile. Thus the Divine will progressively comes to be realized, as was noted in our commentary on 39:1.

3. עֲשָׂרָה — *Ten of them.* According to *Rashi* this detail tells us that all of the ten brothers differed from one another in their feelings of love or hatred as "brothers of Joseph," but they were unanimous in their purpose to "buy grain." *Ramban* holds that the ten were required so that when they all bowed down together the first of Joseph's dreams would come true. But the *Midrash Tanchuma* tells us that Jacob considered a group of ten adult Jews a means of protection — on one hand because recourse to communal prayer requires the presence of a *minyan* and, on the other hand, because of the fact that God, as He had declared to Abraham (18:32), refrains from punishing a group whenever ten righteous men are found gathered (cf. our commentary to verse 6).

ד לִשְׁבֹּר בָּר מִמִּצְרָיִם: וְאֶת־בִּנְיָמִין אֲחִי יוֹסֵף לֹא־שָׁלַח
ה יַעֲקֹב אֶת־אֶחָיו כִּי אָמַר פֶּן־יִקְרָאֶנּוּ אָסוֹן: וַיָּבֹאוּ בְּנֵי
יִשְׂרָאֵל לִשְׁבֹּר בְּתוֹךְ הַבָּאִים כִּי־הָיָה הָרָעָב בְּאֶרֶץ כְּנָעַן:
ו וְיוֹסֵף הוּא הַשַּׁלִּיט עַל־הָאָרֶץ הוּא הַמַּשְׁבִּיר לְכָל־
עַם הָאָרֶץ וַיָּבֹאוּ אֲחֵי יוֹסֵף וַיִּשְׁתַּחֲווּ־לוֹ אַפַּיִם אָרְצָה:
ז וַיַּרְא יוֹסֵף אֶת־אֶחָיו וַיַּכִּרֵם וַיִּתְנַכֵּר אֲלֵיהֶם וַיְדַבֵּר
אִתָּם קָשׁוֹת וַיֹּאמֶר אֲלֵהֶם מֵאַיִן בָּאתֶם וַיֹּאמְרוּ מֵאֶרֶץ
ח כְּנַעַן לִשְׁבָּר־אֹכֶל: וַיַּכֵּר יוֹסֵף אֶת־אֶחָיו וְהֵם לֹא הִכִּרֻהוּ:

4. וְאֶת־בִּנְיָמִין . . . לֹא־שָׁלַח יַעֲקֹב אֶת־אֶחָיו — *But Benjamin . . . Jacob did not send along with his brothers.* This foreshadows the future of the tribe of Benjamin. It did not go into exile with the ten tribes, but remained alongside the tribe of Judah.

פֶּן־יִקְרָאֶנּוּ אָסוֹן — *Lest disaster befall him.* "Could not an accident befall him at home? R' Eliezer ben Yaakov replies: Satan attacks in a time of danger" (*Rashi*). The Midrash continues and informs us that Jacob feared that the journey would bring misfortune to the children of Rachel. Joseph had not returned from his journey and Rachel herself had died on the way. Now what might happen to Benjamin?

5. וַיָּבֹאוּ בְּנֵי יִשְׂרָאֵל — *So the sons of Israel came.* This is the first time that the children of Jacob are called by their historic name: בְּנֵי יִשְׂרָאֵל. (Above, in 34:7, they are called בְּנֵי יַעֲקֹב, this name designates the Jewish people in general.) This time was indeed of crucial importance for the future of the Jewish nation-to-be. And just as the sons of Jacob first come into contact with Egypt, the country of their future exile, their title of honor, בְּנֵי יִשְׂרָאֵל, comes to remind us that their historic vocation is far from sinking into the miseries of exile, but it remains kept in store in its entirety for the future (*R' Bachya* on 45:28).

6. וְיוֹסֵף הוּא הַשַּׁלִּיט עַל־הָאָרֶץ — *Now Joseph — he was the viceroy over the land.* In this position, he of course did not sell grain himself, but he "was the provider" הַמַּשְׁבִּיר. If he nevertheless welcomed the ten brothers personally, it was because they were the first purchasers coming from Canaan and Joseph had ordered that strangers representing the different countries be presented to him. Contrary to this opinion held by *Ramban*, the Sages of the Midrash explain: foreseeing his brothers' journey into Egypt, Joseph had issued three decrees which would enable him to meet them in person: No slave was to enter Egypt to buy grain; no buyer was to load more than one ass; each buyer coming into Egypt was to register his name, the name of his father, and the name of his grandfather. One night, Joseph received a list of strangers and realized that his brothers had arrived, each using a different gate to the city (as their father had instructed them; cf. *Rashi*). He then decreed the closing down of all the granaries except one, thus hoping to trap his brothers. But for three days they

to buy grain from Egypt. ⁴ *But Benjamin, Joseph's brother, Jacob did not send along with his brothers, for he said, "Lest disaster befall him."* ⁵ *So the sons of Israel came to buy provisions among the arrivals, for the famine was in the land of Canaan.*

⁶ *Now Joseph — he was the viceroy over the land, he was the provider to all the people of the land. Joseph's brothers came and they bowed to him, faces to the ground.*

⁷ *Joseph saw his brothers and he recognized them, but he acted like a stranger toward them and spoke with them harshly. He asked them, "From where do you come?" And they said, "From the land of Canaan to buy food."* ⁸ *Joseph recognized his brothers, but they did not recognize him.*

did not appear. He sent his son Manasseh to look for them. Manasseh discovered them wandering about the streets, the parks, and the marketplaces. They were trying to find Joseph and they even went to the most disreputable places, on the supposition that he might have been sold there because of his handsomeness. After spending three days without finding him, they went to buy grain, and when they were to present themselves to Joseph he had already received his son's report about them.

7. וַיְדַבֵּר אִתָּם קָשׁוֹת — *He ... spoke with them harshly.* Three different reasons have been advanced by our principal commentators to explain Joseph's strict attitude of exacting justice on meeting his brothers for the first time in more than twenty years. For *Ramban*, it was the memory of Joseph's dreams which guided his conduct, as is brought out in verse 9: *Joseph recalled the dreams that he had dreamed about them, so he said to them, "You are spies!"* He had never stopped believing in his dreams. His special destiny, his sale as a slave, his astonishing rise to power, were they not all connected with dreams? Now, when his ten brothers came to bow down before him, he understood that none of his dreams had yet been fulfilled, not even the first which involved the bowing down of the "eleven sheaves" before him (37:7). And so he resorted to a stratagem in order to bring the eleventh brother, Benjamin, to Egypt. He knew that it was not in Canaan but only in Egypt, where he was viceroy, that this bowing down could take place. And later, after his first dream was fulfilled, he revealed his identity so as to see the second dream come true — by having his father come to Egypt. But first, using the silver goblet as a means, he tried to keep Benjamin with him, fearing that his brothers would turn hostile toward Benjamin just as they had been toward Joseph himself. It was only after having tested their solidarity and feelings of brotherhood that he consented to let Benjamin go back with them.

Don Isaac Abarbanel, however, objects to this interpretation on certain points. In particular, he holds that the dreams did not imply that the brothers would actually be bowing down, but simply paying homage to Joseph's glory and superiority. According to him, we can explain Joseph's conduct as a desire

ט וַיִּזְכֹּר יוֹסֵף אֵת הַחֲלֹמוֹת אֲשֶׁר חָלַם לָהֶם וַיֹּאמֶר אֲלֵהֶם
י מְרַגְּלִים אַתֶּם לִרְאוֹת אֶת־עֶרְוַת הָאָרֶץ בָּאתֶם: וַיֹּאמְרוּ
יא אֵלָיו לֹא אֲדֹנִי וַעֲבָדֶיךָ בָּאוּ לִשְׁבָּר־אֹכֶל: כֻּלָּנוּ בְּנֵי
אִישׁ־אֶחָד נָחְנוּ כֵּנִים אֲנַחְנוּ לֹא־הָיוּ עֲבָדֶיךָ מְרַגְּלִים:
יב וַיֹּאמֶר אֲלֵהֶם לֹא כִּי־עֶרְוַת הָאָרֶץ בָּאתֶם לִרְאוֹת:
יג וַיֹּאמְרוּ שְׁנֵים עָשָׂר עֲבָדֶיךָ אַחִים אֲנַחְנוּ בְּנֵי אִישׁ־אֶחָד
בְּאֶרֶץ כְּנָעַן וְהִנֵּה הַקָּטֹן אֶת־אָבִינוּ הַיּוֹם וְהָאֶחָד אֵינֶנּוּ:

to punish his brothers. He applied the principle of מִדָּה כְּנֶגֶד מִדָּה, *measure for measure*, to them and, just as they had done to him, he made them suffer mentally rather than physically. From a psychological point of view one can understand Joseph's attitude. In order to become fully and sincerely reconciled with his brothers he had to erase what had happened in the past. But Joseph felt that he could not forgive his brothers as long as they had not received their just punishment. Is it not taught that "suffering wipes away sin"? (*Berachos* 5a). This also seems to be the viewpoint of the *Midrash Tanchuma*, quoted by *Rashi*: Joseph saw (lit. recognized) his brothers; that is to say, he recognized them as true brothers; he wanted to welcome them warmly and to have pity on them. But an angel intervened and reminded him how cruelly they had mistreated him when they wanted to kill him. (This is why the text repeats a second time: he recognized his brothers. This expression is no longer collective as in the previous verse. Once the initial emotion had passed, he could not help remembering the abominable way that each one had treated him.) This Midrash illustrates the conflict which was taking place in Joseph's soul, between the tenderness he felt for his brothers and the bitter memories which obsessed him in spite of himself (or "imposed by an angel"), memories which drove him to call for their punishment.

But *Abarbanel* also admits another interpretation: that Joseph's sole aim was to bring out his brothers' feelings of remorse and so lead them to repent. Although he now has an opportunity for revenge, he reveals his spiritual greatness and shows mankind, for all time, a better way. He puts his brothers to the test. He represses his natural feelings until he is convinced of their reverence for their father, their love for Benjamin, and their heartfelt contrition at having acted criminally towards him. And, at that point, he forgives them without reservation, with all his love.

9. מְרַגְּלִים אַתֶּם — *You are spies.* The connection between the dreams and this accusation is brought out by *Ramban* in his explanation quoted above. The accusation itself was based on Manasseh's report (above, verse 6), bearing witness that the brothers had searched the whole city for three days. Their hunt had taken them even to the streets of prostitutes, which Joseph alludes to when he reproaches them with the words, לִרְאוֹת אֶת עֶרְוַת הָאָרֶץ בָּאתֶם, *you came to see the prostitutes of the land* (according to *Targum Yonasan*).

⁹ Joseph recalled the dreams that he dreamed about them, so he said to them, "You are spies! To see the land's nakedness have you come!"

¹⁰ They answered him, "Not so, my lord! For your servants have come to buy food. ¹¹ All of us, sons of one man are we; we are truthful people; your servants have never been spies."

¹² And he said to them, "No! But the land's nakedness have you come to see."

¹³ And they replied, "We, your servants, are twelve brothers, the sons of one man in the land of Canaan. The youngest is now with our father and one is gone."

11. לֹא־הָיוּ עֲבָדֶיךָ מְרַגְּלִים — Your servants have never been spies. This reply opens the first dialogue between Joseph and Judah, the spokesman for the ten brothers. This dialogue, and the ones which follow, are full of verbal thrusts and parries and they frequently contain underlying meanings. Joseph accusingly says to them as it were, "You are spies who come to discover the weak points of the land, but my descendant Joshua, from the tribe of Ephraim, will not be one of those ten spies trying to find out the weaknesses of the Promised Land." Judah replies: "My descendant Caleb, of the tribe of Judah, will never be a traitor either."

12. לֹא כִּי־עֶרְוַת הָאָרֶץ בָּאתֶם לִרְאוֹת — No! But the land's nakedness have you come to see. Rashi: "For you came into the city through ten gates. Why did you not all enter by the same gate?" By repeating his accusation with such emphasis, Joseph hoped to provoke his brothers into elaborating on their answers and ultimately telling him something about his father. In their reply, the brothers indeed told him that "the youngest is now with our father." Thus Joseph knew that his father was still alive.

Some of our Sages hold that Joseph's repeated accusations were intended to confuse his brothers. Surely they must have known of the extraordinary fact that "a young Hebrew slave" had become viceroy of the country. Joseph might therefore have been afraid that they would recognize him as their brother. But by directing violent accusations against them, he reduced such speculation to naught, and from then on was able to carry out the plan he had concerning his brothers.

13. שְׁנֵים עָשָׂר עֲבָדֶיךָ אַחִים אֲנַחְנוּ — We, your servants, are twelve brothers. And it is inconceivable that a father would risk ten of his children at the same time in espionage. Here, the brothers mentioned the number twelve for the first time. (Hence they use the pronoun אֲנַחְנוּ in its complete form, whereas in verse 11 they had said נַחְנוּ.) However, when they spoke these words they hesitated, for unaware of what had happened to Joseph, they wanted to end by saying הָיִינוּ, we were. This moment of hesitation is marked in the text by a vertical stroke (פְּסִיק) of separation. "But then a spark of prophetic spirit inspired them and they

יד וַיֹּאמֶר אֲלֵהֶם יוֹסֵף הוּא אֲשֶׁר דִּבַּרְתִּי אֲלֵכֶם לֵאמֹר מְרַגְּלִים
טו אַתֶּם: בְּזֹאת תִּבָּחֵנוּ חֵי פַרְעֹה אִם־תֵּצְאוּ מִזֶּה כִּי אִם־
טז בְּבוֹא אֲחִיכֶם הַקָּטֹן הֵנָּה: שִׁלְחוּ מִכֶּם אֶחָד וְיִקַּח אֶת־
אֲחִיכֶם וְאַתֶּם הֵאָסְרוּ וְיִבָּחֲנוּ דִּבְרֵיכֶם הַאֱמֶת אִתְּכֶם
יז וְאִם־לֹא חֵי פַרְעֹה כִּי מְרַגְּלִים אַתֶּם: וַיֶּאֱסֹף אֹתָם
יח אֶל־מִשְׁמָר שְׁלֹשֶׁת יָמִים: וַיֹּאמֶר אֲלֵהֶם יוֹסֵף בַּיּוֹם הַשְּׁלִישִׁי
יט זֹאת עֲשׂוּ וִחְיוּ אֶת־הָאֱלֹהִים אֲנִי יָרֵא: אִם־כֵּנִים אַתֶּם
אֲחִיכֶם אֶחָד יֵאָסֵר בְּבֵית מִשְׁמַרְכֶם וְאַתֶּם לְכוּ הָבִיאוּ שֶׁבֶר
כ רַעֲבוֹן בָּתֵּיכֶם: וְאֶת־אֲחִיכֶם הַקָּטֹן תָּבִיאוּ אֵלַי וְיֵאָמְנוּ
כא דִבְרֵיכֶם וְלֹא תָמוּתוּ וַיַּעֲשׂוּ־כֵן: וַיֹּאמְרוּ אִישׁ אֶל־אָחִיו
אֲבָל אֲשֵׁמִים ׀ אֲנַחְנוּ עַל־אָחִינוּ אֲשֶׁר רָאִינוּ צָרַת נַפְשׁוֹ

ended with the word אֲנַחְנוּ: *we are (still) twelve brothers, the sons of one man*
— thus including Joseph among them" (*Zohar*, referring the explanation which
Rashi had given on verse 11 to this verse).

14. הוּא אֲשֶׁר דִּבַּרְתִּי אֲלֵכֶם — *It is just as I have declared to you* (or, *about you*).
Rashi quotes the Midrash, which shows how Joseph was able to set a trap for
his brothers and turn their arguments against them. But the fact that the word
אֲלֵכֶם, *about you,* is written defectively (without the *yud*) indicates that his
charges were made up, and that he himself was far from believing them.

15. חֵי פַרְעֹה — *By Pharaoh's life. Rashi* explains: When he swore falsely, he
swore by the life of Pharaoh. But *R' Bachya* objects: Joseph never swore falsely:
here too the oath can well accord with the events which followed (they did not
all leave prison, since Simeon remained).

    Rambam notes that when an oath is made on the life of a human being,
the word חֵי is punctuated with the vowel *tzereh,* but when it refers to God,
the vowel is a *patach.* In the first case, it is proper to translate "the life of
Pharaoh" and in the second "the Living God" — for in contrast to human beings
and their lives, God and His life are one and the same (*Hilchos Yesodei
HaTorah,* ch. 2:10).

16. וְאַתֶּם הֵאָסְרוּ — *While you shall remain imprisoned.* The brothers kept silent
regarding this proposal, which meant that they did not accept it. Accordingly,
Joseph put them in prison. They feared that their families would die of
starvation if they had to wait until their return, since one brother alone could not
bring back enough provisions. It was only three days later, when Joseph made
them a new proposal permitting them to go and bring their rations to their
families so that they should not die of hunger, that the Torah notes: וַיַּעֲשׂוּ כֵן, *and
they did so.*

18. בַּיּוֹם הַשְּׁלִישִׁי — *On the third day.* God does not let the righteous suffer
beyond three days (cf. *Hosea* 6:2). The merit of the forefathers protects them: the

¹⁴ *But Joseph said to them, "It is just as I have declared to you: 'You are spies!'* ¹⁵ *By this shall you be tested: By Pharaoh's life you will not leave here unless your youngest brother comes here.* ¹⁶ *Send one of you, and let him fetch your brother while you shall remain imprisoned, so that your words may be tested whether truth is with you; but if not, by Pharaoh's life — surely you are spies!"* ¹⁷ *Then he herded them into a ward for a three-day period.*

¹⁸ *Joseph said to them on the third day, "Do this and live; I fear God:* ¹⁹ *If you are truthful people, let one of your brothers be imprisoned in your place of confinement while you go and bring provisions for the hunger of your households.* ²⁰ *Then bring your youngest brother to me so your words will be verified and you will not die." And they did so.*

²¹ *They then said to one another, "Indeed we are guilty concerning our brother inasmuch as we saw his heartfelt anguish*

merit of Abraham who, on the third day, perceived Mount Moriah where he was going to sacrifice his son (22:4); and the merit of Jewry, who on the third day received the Torah on Mount Sinai (*Exodus* 19:16; *Rabbah* 91).

אֶת־הָאֱלֹהִים אֲנִי יָרֵא — *I fear God.* (The name אֱלֹהִים was known to the Egyptians, as was noted in the commentary on 41:38, so that this profession of faith did not arouse their suspicions.) Some men fear God when they find themselves destitute but reject Him when they become wealthy. Joseph, though, expressed his fear of God both at a time of poverty (39:9) and, as we see here, at the height of his glory (*Midrash Tanchuma*). { When the Divine name is preceded by the definite article, הָאֱלֹהִים it designates God accompanied by His celestial tribunal (*Bereishis Rabbah* 55).} The fear of God which Joseph felt was of the same kind as Abraham's (*Avos D'Rabbi Nosson* 10:13): that is to say, it resulted from love of God, (יִרְאָה מֵאַהֲבָה) (*Sotah* 31b). This form of יִרְאַת ה' is a reverence which differs from a primitive fear of Divine punishment (יִרְאַת הָעוֹנֶשׁ), in that it is based simultaneously on love, worship, and reverence (יִרְאַת הָרוֹמְמוּת). It is, as it were, the epitome of love and its crowning glory.

However, the *Zohar* points out that for Joseph the reference to the fear of God implied first and foremost that he had resolved not to pay back evil with evil. He wanted to follow the maxim which the Torah gives us in these words: *Say not: I will pay back the evil! Have confidence in God; He will help you* (*Proverbs* 20:22).

21. וַיֹּאמְרוּ אִישׁ אֶל־אָחִיו — *They then said to one another.* The same phrase is found in *Genesis* 37:19, when the brothers were plotting to kill Joseph. The words אִישׁ אֶל־אָחִיו referred there to Simeon and Levi, the two brothers who acted in common agreement, and who used the same weapons of violence (49:5). Here too it is these two brothers who come to express their remorse first.

בְּהִתְחַנְנוֹ אֵלֵינוּ וְלֹא שָׁמָעְנוּ עַל־כֵּן בָּאָה אֵלֵינוּ הַצָּרָה

כב הַזֹּאת: וַיַּעַן רְאוּבֵן אֹתָם לֵאמֹר הֲלוֹא אָמַרְתִּי אֲלֵיכֶם ׀

לֵאמֹר אַל־תֶּחֶטְאוּ בַיֶּלֶד וְלֹא שְׁמַעְתֶּם וְגַם־דָּמוֹ הִנֵּה

כג-כד נִדְרָשׁ: וְהֵם לֹא יָדְעוּ כִּי שֹׁמֵעַ יוֹסֵף כִּי הַמֵּלִיץ בֵּינֹתָם: וַיִּסֹּב

מֵעֲלֵיהֶם וַיֵּבְךְּ וַיָּשָׁב אֲלֵהֶם וַיְדַבֵּר אֲלֵהֶם וַיִּקַּח מֵאִתָּם

כה אֶת־שִׁמְעוֹן וַיֶּאֱסֹר אֹתוֹ לְעֵינֵיהֶם: וַיְצַו יוֹסֵף וַיְמַלְאוּ

אֶת־כְּלֵיהֶם בָּר וּלְהָשִׁיב כַּסְפֵּיהֶם אִישׁ אֶל־שַׂקּוֹ וְלָתֵת לָהֶם

כו צֵדָה לַדָּרֶךְ וַיַּעַשׂ לָהֶם כֵּן: וַיִּשְׂאוּ אֶת־שִׁבְרָם עַל־חֲמֹרֵיהֶם

כז וַיֵּלְכוּ מִשָּׁם: וַיִּפְתַּח הָאֶחָד אֶת־שַׂקּוֹ לָתֵת מִסְפּוֹא לַחֲמֹרוֹ

כח בַּמָּלוֹן וַיַּרְא אֶת־כַּסְפּוֹ וְהִנֵּה־הוּא בְּפִי אַמְתַּחְתּוֹ: וַיֹּאמֶר

אֶל־אֶחָיו הוּשַׁב כַּסְפִּי וְגַם הִנֵּה בְאַמְתַּחְתִּי וַיֵּצֵא לִבָּם

וַיֶּחֶרְדוּ אִישׁ אֶל־אָחִיו לֵאמֹר מַה־זֹּאת עָשָׂה אֱלֹהִים לָנוּ:

אֲבָל אֲשֵׁמִים אֲנַחְנוּ — *Indeed we are guilty. Rashi*, following *Onkelos*, translates the term אֲבָל as *truly*. However, the Midrash notes that the word comes from the language of the South and signifies בְּרַם, *alas*. Indeed, it is still used to express the feeling of contrition. And it has passed into our prayers as an introduction to the confession of sins: אֲבָל אֲנַחְנוּ חָטָאנוּ.

The brothers' immediate reaction to the adversity which they had just encountered is authentically Jewish. Far from blaming this high official of the king, the immediate cause of their tribulations, and indulging in self-pity at their sad fate, they look for the real cause of their misfortunes in no one other than themselves. For, אֵין אָנוּ עַזֵּי פָנִים, "We are neither so insolent nor so stubborn that we consider ourselves as righteous people who have never sinned, but alas, we have sinned" (סֵדֶר וִידּוּי). It is always in his own moral or religious conduct that the Jew seeks to find the source of the trials which God inflicts upon him. The Sages of the Midrash stress that, when the brothers looked back into their past, they discovered nothing to blame themselves for except their conduct toward Joseph. This was the only fault which they had committed in their lives (*Bamidbar Rabbah* 13). And even then they did not feel that they had sinned as far as the deed itself was concerned. They regretted only their cruelty: "We saw his anguish when he implored us, but we did not listen" (cf. our commentary to 37:20).

22. וַיַּעַן רְאוּבֵן אֹתָם — *Reuben spoke up to them.* The Torah notes this reply because it brings out the fact that Reuben considered the very condemnation of Joseph bad, not only the way it was carried out and the lack of pity shown, as Simeon and Levi had just asserted. The stinging tone of his response is emphasized in this verse by the repetition of the word לֵאמֹר, saying (*Sforno, ben Attar* and others).

when he pleaded with us and we paid no heed; that is why this anguish has come upon us.''

²² *Reuben spoke up to them, saying, ''Did I not speak to you saying, 'Do not sin against the boy,' but you would not listen! And his blood as well — behold! — is being avenged.''*

²³ *Now they did not know that Joseph understood, for an interpreter was between them.* ²⁴ *He turned away from them and wept; he returned to them and spoke to them; he took Simeon from them and imprisoned him before their eyes.*

²⁵ *Joseph commanded that they fill their vessels with grain, and to return their money, each one's to his sack, and to give them provisions for the journey. And so he did for them.* ²⁶ *Then they loaded their purchase onto their donkeys and departed from there.*

²⁷ *When the one of them opened his sack to give feed to his donkey at the inn, he saw his money, and behold! — it was in the mouth of his sack.* ²⁸ *So he said to his brothers, ''My money has been returned and behold! it, too, is in my sack!'' Their hearts sank, and they turned trembling one to another, saying, ''What is this that God has done to us?''*

24. וַיְדַבֵּר אֲלֵהֶם — *He . . . spoke to them.* In order to get the brothers to designate one of their numbers as hostage. But they refused. So Joseph took Simeon from among them. It follows from this, concludes R' *Bachya*, that it is forbidden for a group of Jews to designate one among them to be handed over when the enemy demands it (עי' ירוש' תרומות, פ"ח ה"י).

וַיֶּאֱסֹר אֹתוֹ לְעֵינֵיהֶם — *And imprisoned him* (or, *had him bound*) *before their eyes.* By his son Manasseh, for the soldiers of the guard were unable to subdue him. Cf. our commentary to 29:10.

27. וַיִּפְתַּח הָאֶחָד — *When the one of them opened.* It was Levi, who separated from Simeon, his constant companion, was now "one" (*Rashi*). According to some, Levi opened his sack because the sight of Simeon being taken away had affected him to such an extent that he had forgotten to bring away his provisions for the journey. Others have it that Levi, the most righteous of the brothers, had intended to give fodder to his donkeys before taking his meal himself, in accordance with the *halachah*. After Levi's discovery, the other brothers also wanted to open their sacks and inspect the contents, but, afraid of being pursued by the Egyptains, they journeyed in haste to reach their homes (Philo, *De Josepho* 21).

28. מַה־זֹּאת עָשָׂה אֱלֹהִים לָנוּ — *What is this that God has done to us? Targum Yerushalmi* adds: when we have done nothing wrong. This interpretation appears to be based on the following episode reported in the Talmud: R' Yochanan passed by the son of R' Shimon ben Lakish, who was sitting and

כט וַיָּבֹאוּ אֶל־יַעֲקֹב אֲבִיהֶם אַרְצָה כְּנָעַן וַיַּגִּידוּ לוֹ אֵת
ל כָּל־הַקֹּרֹת אֹתָם לֵאמֹר: דִּבֶּר הָאִישׁ אֲדֹנֵי הָאָרֶץ אִתָּנוּ
לא קָשׁוֹת וַיִּתֵּן אֹתָנוּ כִּמְרַגְּלִים אֶת־הָאָרֶץ: וַנֹּאמֶר אֵלָיו כֵּנִים
לב אֲנָחְנוּ לֹא הָיִינוּ מְרַגְּלִים: שְׁנֵים־עָשָׂר אֲנַחְנוּ אַחִים בְּנֵי
אָבִינוּ הָאֶחָד אֵינֶנּוּ וְהַקָּטֹן הַיּוֹם אֶת־אָבִינוּ בְּאֶרֶץ כְּנָעַן:
לג וַיֹּאמֶר אֵלֵינוּ הָאִישׁ אֲדֹנֵי הָאָרֶץ בְּזֹאת אֵדַע כִּי כֵנִים
אַתֶּם אֲחִיכֶם הָאֶחָד הַנִּיחוּ אִתִּי וְאֶת־רַעֲבוֹן בָּתֵּיכֶם קְחוּ
לד וָלֵכוּ: וְהָבִיאוּ אֶת־אֲחִיכֶם הַקָּטֹן אֵלַי וְאֵדְעָה כִּי לֹא
מְרַגְּלִים אַתֶּם כִּי כֵנִים אַתֶּם אֶת־אֲחִיכֶם אֶתֵּן לָכֶם
לה וְאֶת־הָאָרֶץ תִּסְחָרוּ: וַיְהִי הֵם מְרִיקִים שַׂקֵּיהֶם וְהִנֵּה־אִישׁ
צְרוֹר־כַּסְפּוֹ בְּשַׂקּוֹ וַיִּרְאוּ אֶת־צְרֹרוֹת כַּסְפֵּיהֶם הֵמָּה
לו וַאֲבִיהֶם וַיִּירָאוּ: וַיֹּאמֶר אֲלֵהֶם יַעֲקֹב אֲבִיהֶם אֹתִי שִׁכַּלְתֶּם
יוֹסֵף אֵינֶנּוּ וְשִׁמְעוֹן אֵינֶנּוּ וְאֶת־בִּנְיָמִן תִּקָּחוּ עָלַי הָיוּ כֻלָּנָה:

---

reciting the verse of *Proverbs* (19:3): *Man by his folly spoils his future, and it is against God that his heart rages!* R' Yochanan exclaimed in astonishment: "Is there then a truth which is expressed in the Hagiographa and yet is mentioned nowhere in the Torah?" The child replied: "But doesn't the Torah tell us regarding Joseph's brothers that their heart failed them and they turned trembling one to another, saying: What has God done to us?' " (*Taanis* 9a).

29. וַיַּגִּידוּ לוֹ אֵת כָּל־הַקֹּרֹת אֹתָם — *And they told him of all that had happened to them.* *Radak* affirms that the changes in wording, the additions, and the omissions in this account are not made with any particular purpose. *Ramban* holds the contrary — the brothers failed to mention that Simeon had been imprisoned and they added that they had the viceroy's authorization to trade freely in Egypt so that their father would consent to send Benjamin.

36. יוֹסֵף אֵינֶנּוּ — *Joseph is gone.* Why did Joseph allow his father to remain unaware of the truth? Why did he not inform his father that he was safe and sound in Egypt? Why did he not send a message during the long years of his sojourn in that land? After all, from Egypt to the city of Hebron was no more than a journey of six days. And wouldn't his love for his father have justified a much longer journey, even one lasting a year? Had Joseph's father received a message, he would surely have redeemed him, whatever the cost might have been. *Ramban* replies to these questions by referring back to the memories of Joseph's dreams of adolescence which he was certain were going to come true. On a previous occasion *Ramban* made use of this peremptory argument, as discussed in our commentary to 42:7. Joseph understood that the dreams could come true only in Egypt and he resolved to wait patiently for the situation to come about, and not to intervene in the unfolding of the providential plan through any personal initiative.

²⁹ *They came to Jacob their father in the land of Canaan and they told him of all that had happened to them, saying:* ³⁰ *"The man, the lord of the land, spoke harshly to us and considered us as if we were spying out the land.* ³¹ *But we said to him, 'We are truthful men: We have never been spies!* ³² *We are twelve brothers, sons of one father. One is gone and the youngest is now with our father in the land of Canaan.'* ³³ *Then the man, the lord of the land, said to us, 'By this I will ascertain whether you are truthful people: One of your brothers, leave with me; and what is needed for the hunger of your households take and go.* ³⁴ *And bring your youngest brother to me so I will know that you are not spies, but truthful people. I will restore your brother to you and you will be free to circulate about the land.' "*

³⁵ *Then, as they were emptying their sacks, behold! — every man's bundle of money was in his sack. When they and their father saw their bundles of money, they were terrified.* ³⁶ *Their father Jacob said to them, "I am the one whom you bereaved! Joseph is gone, Simeon is gone, and now you would take away Benjamin? Upon me has it all fallen!"*

Others assume that Joseph did not want to give his father still more grief by informing him that he was a slave in the house of an Egyptian heathen, or that he was imprisoned because of an accusation of immorality. And later, when he became viceroy, he was afraid that revealing his situation would cause the family to break up. Indeed, his brothers, fearing that Joseph would take revenge, might have decided to flee far and wide, leaving their father to die of sadness. And so Joseph preferred to wait, knowing that sooner or later, because of the famine, his brothers would appear before him, and then he could reveal himself to them and immediately allay their fears (*Tosafists*).

Philo (*De Josepho* 41) considers that the principal reason why Joseph kept silent about this was a desire not to reveal that his brothers had sold him into slavery. He never betrayed this secret; neither his father nor the Egyptians were to know about this infamous act, and rather than shame his own family by revealing himself, he chose to bear all the mental agony that this silence brought him (cf. our commentary to 39:1).

עָלַי הָיוּ כֻלָּנָה — *Upon me has it all fallen!* (i.e. these misfortunes). All these misfortunes (including Rachel's premature death) which befell Jacob made him very pessimistic about Benjamin's journey. "For," said R' Shimon ben Elazar, "when tragic events happen to a family three times, it is a bad sign" (*Chullin* 95b). The word כֻלָּנָה used here expresses the deep anxiety felt by Jacob. It is found only once more in Scripture, in the song of praise to the אֵשֶׁת חַיִל, *woman of valor* (*Proverbs* 31:29). וְאַתְּ עָלִית עַל כֻּלָּנָה, *but you excel them all.* In our verse

לז וַיֹּאמֶר רְאוּבֵן אֶל־אָבִיו לֵאמֹר אֶת־שְׁנֵי בָנַי תָּמִית אִם־
לֹא אֲבִיאֶנּוּ אֵלֶיךָ תְּנָה אֹתוֹ עַל־יָדִי וַאֲנִי אֲשִׁיבֶנּוּ אֵלֶיךָ:
לח וַיֹּאמֶר לֹא־יֵרֵד בְּנִי עִמָּכֶם כִּי־אָחִיו מֵת וְהוּא לְבַדּוֹ נִשְׁאָר
וּקְרָאָהוּ אָסוֹן בַּדֶּרֶךְ אֲשֶׁר תֵּלְכוּ־בָהּ וְהוֹרַדְתֶּם אֶת־
מג א־ב שֵׂיבָתִי בְּיָגוֹן שְׁאוֹלָה: וְהָרָעָב כָּבֵד בָּאָרֶץ: וַיְהִי כַּאֲשֶׁר כִּלּוּ
לֶאֱכֹל אֶת־הַשֶּׁבֶר אֲשֶׁר הֵבִיאוּ מִמִּצְרָיִם וַיֹּאמֶר אֲלֵיהֶם
ג אֲבִיהֶם שֻׁבוּ שִׁבְרוּ־לָנוּ מְעַט־אֹכֶל: וַיֹּאמֶר אֵלָיו יְהוּדָה
לֵאמֹר הָעֵד הֵעִד בָּנוּ הָאִישׁ לֵאמֹר לֹא־תִרְאוּ פָנַי בִּלְתִּי
ד אֲחִיכֶם אִתְּכֶם: אִם־יֶשְׁךָ מְשַׁלֵּחַ אֶת־אָחִינוּ אִתָּנוּ נֵרְדָה
ה וְנִשְׁבְּרָה לְךָ אֹכֶל: וְאִם־אֵינְךָ מְשַׁלֵּחַ לֹא נֵרֵד כִּי־הָאִישׁ
ו אָמַר אֵלֵינוּ לֹא־תִרְאוּ פָנַי בִּלְתִּי אֲחִיכֶם אִתְּכֶם: וַיֹּאמֶר
יִשְׂרָאֵל לָמָה הֲרֵעֹתֶם לִי לְהַגִּיד לָאִישׁ הַעוֹד לָכֶם אָח:

also, the word כֻּלָּנָה implies that the present fear is greater than all the previous harm (*Baal HaTurim*).

38. לֹא־יֵרֵד בְּנִי עִמָּכֶם — *My son shall not go down with you.* *Rashi* explains: Jacob did not accept Reuben's offer, responding: "How stupid my firstborn is! Aren't his sons also my children?" However, *Ibn Ezra* and *Ramban* hold that Reuben's words, "Put my two sons to death," refer rather to a general expression of punishment, similar to that which Judah subsequently uttered: *then I will have sinned to you for all time.* Jacob, though, listened more to his son Judah, for he had more confidence in him than in Reuben, who had previously "tarnished the honor of his couch." Judah, moreover, was clever enough to put off his proposal until there was no food, and the head of the family could not afford to postpone the second journey to Egypt any longer, as *Rashi* notes further on.

וּקְרָאָהוּ אָסוֹן בַּדֶּרֶךְ — *Should disaster befall him on the journey.* Cf. our commentary to 42:4.

וְהוֹרַדְתֶּם אֶת־שֵׂיבָתִי בְּיָגוֹן שְׁאוֹלָה — *Then you will have brought down my hoariness in sorrow to the grave.* This cry of the unfortunate old man reveals the extreme disappointment which engulfed his whole being. For three successive generations a superhuman effort had been made to create the House of Israel, destined to be the nucleus of the new people which would teach mankind to know and to love the One God. Were all these valiant efforts now going to be for naught merely because of a family quarrel? The patriarch certainly did not consider himself guilty. He had wanted the best, but he feared that he would have to witness the worst. And at a hundred and thirty years of age, he no longer felt strong enough to settle this family upheaval. So, with infinite sadness, he invokes the grave which awaits an old man whose life is broken.

³⁷ *Then Reuben told his father, saying, "You may slay my two sons if I fail to bring him back to you. Put him in my care and I will return him to you."*

³⁸ *But he said, "My son shall not go down with you, for his brother is dead and he alone is left. Should disaster befall him on the journey which you shall take, then you will have brought down my hoariness in sorrow to the grave."*

43   ¹ *The famine was severe in the land.* ² *When they had finished eating the provisions which they had brought from Egypt their father said to them, "Go back, buy us some food."* ³ *But Judah told him, saying, "The man sternly warned us saying, 'Do not see my face unless your brother is with you.'* ⁴ *If you are ready to send our brother with us, we will go down and buy you food.* ⁵ *But if you do not send, we will not go down, for the man said to us, 'Do not see my face unless your brother is with you.' "*

⁶ *Then Israel said, "Why did you treat me so ill by telling the man that you had another brother?"*

43.

1. וְהָרָעָב כָּבֵד בָּאָרֶץ — *The famine was severe in the land.* The Torah continues its account by adding many details which at first glance seem to be unimportant. Undoubtedly it wants to vividly depict an example of providential action. On the surface, everything takes place according to the rigorous logic of facts and events and yet you sense at every moment how Providence is exercising Its influence in order to bring about Its historic ends. And this is the very image of earthly existence. Men are only the actors on the stage of history; they are directed and guided according to the universal plan, so that our free will seems to be, in fact, a directed freedom. However, personal responsibility and providential action remain inextricably intertwined in a manner which transcends man's understanding (cf. 37:5).

6. וַיֹּאמֶר יִשְׂרָאֵל — *Then Israel said.* This is the first time that the name Israel reappears since Joseph was sold. It indicates that the patriarch finally regained his self-control and made the decision to send Benjamin away. He realized that it was an absolute necessity since the thirty-seven year-old Benjamin's life was going to be threatened just as much by the famine if he stayed at home (cf. *Rashi* on verse 8). So, knowing that no other solution was humanly possible, Jacob put all his trust in God and recovered his strength as a result of this confident faith. And thus he became once more יִשְׂרָאֵל, the serene man walking with God, and he was no longer יַעֲקֹב, which designates the patriarch in his weakened state, just dragged along in the wake of events (עָקֵב = heel) instead of leading them (*R' S.R. Hirsch*).

ז וַיֹּאמְר֗וּ שָׁא֣וֹל שָֽׁאַל־הָ֠אִישׁ לָ֣נוּ וּלְמֽוֹלַדְתֵּ֘נוּ לֵאמֹ֒ר הַע֨וֹד
אֲבִיכֶ֥ם חַי֙ הֲיֵ֣שׁ לָכֶ֣ם אָ֔ח וַנַּ֨גֶּד־ל֔וֹ עַל־פִּ֖י הַדְּבָרִ֣ים הָאֵ֑לֶּה
הֲיָד֣וֹעַ נֵדַ֔ע כִּ֣י יֹאמַ֔ר הוֹרִ֖ידוּ אֶת־אֲחִיכֶֽם: ח וַיֹּ֨אמֶר יְהוּדָ֜ה
אֶל־יִשְׂרָאֵ֣ל אָבִיו֮ שִׁלְחָ֣ה הַנַּ֣עַר אִתִּי֒ וְנָק֣וּמָה וְנֵלֵ֔כָה
ט וְנִֽחְיֶה֙ וְלֹ֣א נָמ֔וּת גַּם־אֲנַ֥חְנוּ גַם־אַתָּ֖ה גַּם־טַפֵּ֑נוּ אָֽנֹכִי֙
אֶֽעֶרְבֶ֔נּוּ מִיָּדִ֖י תְּבַקְשֶׁ֑נּוּ אִם־לֹ֨א הֲבִיאֹתִ֤יו אֵלֶ֙יךָ֙ וְהִצַּגְתִּ֣יו
לְפָנֶ֔יךָ וְחָטָ֥אתִֽי לְךָ֖ כָּל־הַיָּמִֽים: י כִּ֖י לוּלֵ֣א הִתְמַהְמָ֑הְנוּ
יא כִּֽי־עַתָּ֥ה שַׁ֖בְנוּ זֶ֥ה פַעֲמָֽיִם: וַיֹּ֨אמֶר אֲלֵהֶ֜ם יִשְׂרָאֵ֣ל אֲבִיהֶ֗ם
אִם־כֵּ֣ן ׀ אֵפוֹא֮ זֹ֣את עֲשׂוּ֒ קְח֞וּ מִזִּמְרַ֤ת הָאָ֙רֶץ֙ בִּכְלֵיכֶ֔ם
וְהוֹרִ֥ידוּ לָאִ֖ישׁ מִנְחָ֑ה מְעַ֤ט צֳרִי֙ וּמְעַ֣ט דְּבַ֔שׁ נְכֹ֣את וָלֹ֔ט
יב בָּטְנִ֖ים וּשְׁקֵדִֽים: וְכֶ֥סֶף מִשְׁנֶ֖ה קְח֣וּ בְיֶדְכֶ֑ם וְאֶת־הַכֶּ֜סֶף
הַמּוּשָׁ֨ב בְּפִ֤י אַמְתְּחֹֽתֵיכֶם֙ תָּשִׁ֣יבוּ בְיֶדְכֶ֔ם אוּלַ֖י מִשְׁגֶּ֥ה
יג־יד ה֖וּא: וְאֶת־אֲחִיכֶ֣ם קָ֑חוּ וְק֖וּמוּ שׁ֥וּבוּ אֶל־הָאִֽישׁ: וְאֵ֣ל שַׁדַּ֗י
יִתֵּ֨ן לָכֶ֤ם רַֽחֲמִים֙ לִפְנֵ֣י הָאִ֔ישׁ וְשִׁלַּ֥ח לָכֶ֛ם אֶת־אֲחִיכֶ֥ם
טו אַחֵ֖ר וְאֶת־בִּנְיָמִ֑ין וַֽאֲנִ֕י כַּֽאֲשֶׁ֥ר שָׁכֹ֖לְתִּי שָׁכָֽלְתִּי: וַיִּקְח֣וּ
הָֽאֲנָשִׁים֩ אֶת־הַמִּנְחָ֨ה הַזֹּ֜את וּמִשְׁנֶה־כֶּ֤סֶף לָֽקְחוּ֙ בְיָדָ֔ם
וְאֶת־בִּנְיָמִ֑ן וַיָּקֻ֕מוּ וַיֵּֽרְד֣וּ מִצְרַ֔יִם וַיַּֽעַמְד֖וּ לִפְנֵ֥י יוֹסֵֽף:

---

9. אִם־לֹא הֲבִיאֹתִיו אֵלֶיךָ . . . וְחָטָאתִי לְךָ כָּל־הַיָּמִים — *If I do not bring him back to you . . . then I will have sinned to you for all time. Rashi* interprets: "Even in the World to Come." R' Yehudah said in the name of Rav: "A curse, once pronounced, even conditionally, must be (formally) annulled (in order to avoid its harmful consequences). Here Judah had uttered a curse on himself, and since he did not formally annul it (following the fulfillment of the condition), he paid for it, at least in the World to Come, which he had also included in the curse. Indeed, Judah's remains were not able to find repose in their grave until Moses interceded before God for the peace of his soul" (*Makkos* 11b). Such is the value of the word of a righteous man; it leaves its traces, even though it was bound to a condition which was subsequently fulfilled.

11. אִם־כֵּן אֵפוֹא זֹאת עֲשׂוּ — *If it must be so, then do this.* Judah has overcome his father's opposition. Jacob puts his confidence in the words, the devotion, and the strength of his son Judah. But as Jacob finally acquiesces, he utters the same exclamation of bewilderment (אֵפוֹא) that he had previously caused his father Isaac to voice when Jacob had tricked him into believing that he was Esau. Isaac had been gripped by a very great trembling, and had cried out: מִי־אֵפוֹא הוּא, *Who — where — is the one?* (27:33). Here, Jacob experiences the same terror at the thought of his son Benjamin's departure (*Rabbah* 91). The righteous one is thus punished for the pain, even if justified, which he has caused another.

⁷ And they said, "The man persistently asked about us and our relatives saying, 'Is your father still alive? Have you a brother?' and we responded to him according to these words; could we possibly have known that he would say, 'Bring your brother down'?"

⁸ Then Judah said to Israel his father, 'Send the lad with me, and let us arise and go, so we will live and not die, we as well as you as well as our children. ⁹ I will personally guarantee him; of my own hand you can demand him. If I do not bring him back to you and stand him before you, then I will have sinned to you for all time. ¹⁰ For had we not delayed, by now we could have returned twice."

¹¹ Israel their father said to them, "If it must be so, then do this: Take of the land's glory in your baggage and bring it down to the man as a tribute — a bit of balsam, a bit of honey, wax, lotus, pistachios, and almonds. ¹² And take with you double the money, and the money that was returned in the mouth of your sacks return in your hands; perhaps it was an oversight. ¹³ Take your brother, and arise, return to the man. ¹⁴ And may Almighty God grant you mercy before the man that he may release to you your other brother as well as Benjamin. And as for me, as I have been bereaved, so I am bereaved."

¹⁵ So the men took this tribute and they took double money in their hand, as well as Benjamin. They set out and went down to Egypt and stood before Joseph.

14. וְאֵל שַׁדַּי יִתֵּן לָכֶם רַחֲמִים — And may Almighty God grant you mercy. When Jacob left the house of his parents, his father had invoked this same name of God to give him the Divine blessing: May Almighty God bless you, make you fruitful and make you numerous, and may you be a congregation of peoples (28:3). There, Rashi explains this particular name as follows: "The Almighty God, Who has enough (דַי) blessings for those who are blessed by Him — may He bless you" (ibid.; cf. our commentary). Here, at the critical moment, when Jacob sees a grave threat looming over the future of his family, he looks back to the paternal blessing: "You shall become, with the help of Almighty God, אֵל שַׁדַּי, a congregation of peoples," and he now appeals to אֵל שַׁדַּי for assistance. This same Divine name also appeared in the blessing which God gave the patriarch, promising him great and glorious offspring, and in particular his son Benjamin (Rashi on 35:11). So in the twilight of his life Jacob renders homage to Almighty God Who had blessed him, protected him, and made him prosper.

Rashi adds: "[Jacob said to his sons:] Now you no longer lack anything, except for prayer. And so I'll pray for you." Jacob resorts to his usual weapons to defend his family against their adversaries: gifts and prayer (Rashi on 32:9; his third weapon, going to battle, is not feasible in the present case). As for

טז וַיַּ֣רְא יוֹסֵ֣ף אִתָּם֮ אֶת־בִּנְיָמִין֒ וַיֹּ֗אמֶר לַאֲשֶׁר֙ עַל־בֵּית֔וֹ הָבֵ֥א אֶת־הָאֲנָשִׁ֖ים הַבָּ֑יְתָה וּטְבֹ֤חַ טֶ֙בַח֙ וְהָכֵ֔ן כִּ֥י אִתִּ֛י יֹאכְל֥וּ הָאֲנָשִׁ֖ים בַּֽצׇּהֳרָֽיִם: יז וַיַּ֣עַשׂ הָאִ֔ישׁ כַּאֲשֶׁ֖ר אָמַ֣ר יוֹסֵ֑ף וַיָּבֵ֥א הָאִ֛ישׁ אֶת־הָאֲנָשִׁ֖ים בֵּ֥יתָה יוֹסֵֽף: יח וַיִּֽירְא֣וּ הָֽאֲנָשִׁ֗ים כִּ֣י הֽוּבְאוּ֮ בֵּ֣ית יוֹסֵף֒ וַיֹּֽאמְר֗וּ עַל־דְּבַ֤ר הַכֶּ֙סֶף֙ הַשָּׁ֤ב בְּאַמְתְּחֹתֵ֙ינוּ֙ בַּתְּחִלָּ֔ה אֲנַ֖חְנוּ מֽוּבָאִ֑ים לְהִתְגֹּלֵ֤ל עָלֵ֙ינוּ֙ וּלְהִתְנַפֵּ֣ל עָלֵ֔ינוּ וְלָקַ֧חַת אֹתָ֛נוּ לַעֲבָדִ֖ים וְאֶת־חֲמֹרֵֽינוּ: יט וַֽיִּגְּשׁוּ֙ אֶל־הָאִ֔ישׁ אֲשֶׁ֖ר עַל־בֵּ֣ית יוֹסֵ֑ף וַיְדַבְּר֥וּ אֵלָ֖יו פֶּ֥תַח הַבָּֽיִת: כ וַיֹּאמְר֖וּ בִּ֣י אֲדֹנִ֑י יָרֹ֥ד יָרַ֛דְנוּ בַּתְּחִלָּ֖ה לִשְׁבׇּר־אֹֽכֶל: כא וַֽיְהִ֞י כִּי־בָ֣אנוּ אֶל־הַמָּל֗וֹן וַֽנִּפְתְּחָה֙ אֶת־אַמְתְּחֹתֵ֔ינוּ וְהִנֵּ֤ה כֶֽסֶף־אִישׁ֙ בְּפִ֣י אַמְתַּחְתּ֔וֹ כַּסְפֵּ֖נוּ בְּמִשְׁקָל֑וֹ וַנָּ֥שֶׁב אֹת֖וֹ בְּיָדֵֽנוּ: כב וְכֶ֧סֶף אַחֵ֛ר הוֹרַ֥דְנוּ בְיָדֵ֖נוּ לִשְׁבׇּר־אֹ֑כֶל לֹ֣א יָדַ֔עְנוּ מִי־שָׂ֥ם כַּסְפֵּ֖נוּ בְּאַמְתְּחֹתֵֽינוּ: כג וַיֹּ֩אמֶר֩ שָׁל֨וֹם לָכֶ֜ם אַל־תִּירָ֗אוּ אֱלֹֽהֵיכֶ֞ם וֵֽאלֹהֵ֤י אֲבִיכֶם֙ נָתַ֨ן לָכֶ֤ם מַטְמוֹן֙ בְּאַמְתְּחֹ֣תֵיכֶ֔ם כַּסְפְּכֶ֖ם בָּ֣א אֵלָ֑י וַיּוֹצֵ֥א אֲלֵהֶ֖ם אֶת־שִׁמְעֽוֹן: כד וַיָּבֵ֥א הָאִ֛ישׁ אֶת־הָאֲנָשִׁ֖ים בֵּ֣יתָה יוֹסֵ֑ף וַיִּתֶּן־מַ֙יִם֙ וַיִּרְחֲצ֣וּ רַגְלֵיהֶ֔ם וַיִּתֵּ֥ן מִסְפּ֖וֹא לַחֲמֹֽרֵיהֶֽם: כה וַיָּכִ֙ינוּ֙ אֶת־הַמִּנְחָ֔ה עַד־בּ֥וֹא יוֹסֵ֖ף בַּֽצׇּהֳרָ֑יִם כִּ֣י שָֽׁמְע֔וּ כִּי־שָׁ֖ם יֹ֥אכְלוּ לָֽחֶם: כו וַיָּבֹ֤א יוֹסֵף֙ הַבַּ֔יְתָה וַיָּבִ֧יאּוּ ל֛וֹ אֶת־הַמִּנְחָ֥ה אֲשֶׁר־בְּיָדָ֖ם הַבָּ֑יְתָה וַיִּשְׁתַּֽחֲווּ־ל֖וֹ אָֽרְצָה: כז וַיִּשְׁאַ֤ל לָהֶם֙ לְשָׁל֔וֹם וַיֹּ֗אמֶר הֲשָׁל֛וֹם אֲבִיכֶ֥ם הַזָּקֵ֖ן אֲשֶׁ֣ר אֲמַרְתֶּ֑ם הַעוֹדֶ֖נּוּ חָֽי:

prayer, it should not be left until the time of disaster, but must come before and must rise up to God while everything is still going well. "Isn't your prayer more valuable when it is not (provoked by) distress?" (Job 36:19). So, Jacob prayed for Benjamin to return safe and sound to him, before his son had even left (*Tanchuma*). "The proverb says: Honor your doctor before you require his services" (ibid.).

16. וּטְבֹחַ טֶבַח וְהָכֵן — *Have meat slaughtered, and prepare it.* The verb הָכֵן is the one used to designate the preparations made on the eve of the Sabbath for that holy day. From this we conclude that the brothers came to Joseph's house the second time on Friday, and hence the great occasion when he made himself known (which took place the following day) occurred on the Sabbath day (*Tanchuma*), the day *par excellence* of calm and appeasement.

18. וַיִּירְאוּ הָאֲנָשִׁים — *But the men became frightened.* Even though there was no apparent reason, for they were of awesome strength whereas the "man" who had brought them into the house of Joseph was none other than his son Manasseh, who was then at most nine years old. The sole reason for their fear

¹⁶ Joseph saw Benjamin with them; so he said to the one in charge of his house, "Bring the men into the house. Have meat slaughtered, and prepare it, for with me will these men dine at noon." ¹⁷ The man did as Joseph said, and the man brought the men to Joseph's house. ¹⁸ But the men became frightened when they were brought to Joseph's house, and they said, "Because of the money replaced in our sacks originally are we being brought, so that a charge can be fabricated against us, that it crash down on us, and that we be taken as slaves along with our donkeys."

¹⁹ They approached the man who was in charge of Joseph's house and spoke to him at the entrance of the house. ²⁰ And they said, "If you please, my lord: We had indeed come down originally to buy food. ²¹ But it happened, when we arrived at the inn and opened our sacks, that behold! each one's money was in the mouth of his sack; it was our own money in its full amount, so we have brought it back in our hand. ²² We have also brought other money down in our hand to buy food; we do not know who put our money in our sacks."

²³ He replied, "Peace with you, fear not. Your God and the God of your father has put a hidden treasure in your sacks. Your payment had reached me." And he brought Simeon out to them.

²⁴ Then the man brought the men into Joseph's house. He provided water and they washed their feet, and he gave feed to their donkeys. ²⁵ They prepared the tribute for when Joseph would come at noon, for they had heard that they were to eat a meal there.

²⁶ When Joseph came to the house they brought the tribute that was in their hands to him to the house, and they prostrated themselves to him toward the ground. ²⁷ He inquired after their welfare, and he said, "Is your aged father of whom you spoke at peace? Is he still alive?''

was their troubled conscience, troubled because of the unexpiated sin of selling Joseph. Concludes the *Zohar*: those who do not have a tranquil conscience suffer constantly from fear.

וְלָקַחַת אֹתָנוּ לַעֲבָדִים וְאֶת־חֲמֹרֵינוּ — *And that we be taken as slaves along with our donkeys*. Rambam writes: "Men care as much about their property as they do about themselves; there are some who even put their property above themselves, but most attach equal importance to both: *And that we be taken as slaves along with our donkeys*" (*Guide* 3:40). But R' Bachya affirms that the brothers were concerned about the donkeys because of their vital importance for transportation and for carrying supplies on the desert journeys.

כח וַיֹּאמְרוּ שָׁלוֹם לְעַבְדְּךָ לְאָבִינוּ עוֹדֶנּוּ חָי וַיִּקְּדוּ וַיִּשְׁתַּחֲוּ:
כט וַיִּשָּׂא עֵינָיו וַיַּרְא אֶת־בִּנְיָמִין אָחִיו בֶּן־אִמּוֹ וַיֹּאמֶר הֲזֶה
אֲחִיכֶם הַקָּטֹן אֲשֶׁר אֲמַרְתֶּם אֵלָי וַיֹּאמַר אֱלֹהִים יָחְנְךָ
ל בְּנִי: וַיְמַהֵר יוֹסֵף כִּי־נִכְמְרוּ רַחֲמָיו אֶל־אָחִיו וַיְבַקֵּשׁ לִבְכּוֹת
לא וַיָּבֹא הַחַדְרָה וַיֵּבְךְּ שָׁמָּה: וַיִּרְחַץ פָּנָיו וַיֵּצֵא וַיִּתְאַפַּק
לב וַיֹּאמֶר שִׂימוּ לָחֶם: וַיָּשִׂימוּ לוֹ לְבַדּוֹ וְלָהֶם לְבַדָּם וְלַמִּצְרִים
הָאֹכְלִים אִתּוֹ לְבַדָּם כִּי לֹא יוּכְלוּן הַמִּצְרִים לֶאֱכֹל
לג אֶת־הָעִבְרִים לֶחֶם כִּי־תוֹעֵבָה הִוא לְמִצְרָיִם: וַיֵּשְׁבוּ לְפָנָיו
הַבְּכֹר כִּבְכֹרָתוֹ וְהַצָּעִיר כִּצְעִרָתוֹ וַיִּתְמְהוּ הָאֲנָשִׁים אִישׁ
לד אֶל־רֵעֵהוּ: וַיִּשָּׂא מַשְׂאֹת מֵאֵת פָּנָיו אֲלֵהֶם וַתֵּרֶב מַשְׂאַת
בִּנְיָמִן מִמַּשְׂאֹת כֻּלָּם חָמֵשׁ יָדוֹת וַיִּשְׁתּוּ וַיִּשְׁכְּרוּ עִמּוֹ:

שביעי

28. שָׁלוֹם לְעַבְדְּךָ לְאָבִינוּ — *Your servant our father is at peace.* Rav said: "Why was Joseph called a corpse while he was still alive? (This refers to verse 50:25: *You must bring my bones up out of here.*) It is because he did not intervene to honor his father when his brothers called Jacob 'your servant' in his presence (*Sotah* 13b). R' Yishmael attributes the same reason to the fact that Joseph had ten years taken off his life (he lived only 110 years, instead of 120, the life span for the righteous). Five times he had heard this epithet, "your servant," referring to his father and five more times he listened to it repeated by the interpreter, and he remained silent. And so, he was to bear the consequences of his pride by having his life shortened, consistent with the words of the Decalogue: *Honor your father and your mother, so that your days may be prolonged.* Rashi interprets this: If you honor your father and mother, your days will be prolonged, but if not, your days will be shortened (cf. our commentary on 50:22). In this regard, the author of *Sefer Chassidim* (§1002) notes two divergent opinions. One has it that Jacob was called a servant five times in return for the five times he had accepted to describe himself as a servant of his brother Esau. The other opinion, on the contrary, considers that this repeated act of humility entitled him to be described five times in the books of the Prophets as the servant of God. "For he who is humble will be raised up by God" (*Eruvin* 13b).

29. וַיִּשָּׂא עֵינָיו וַיַּרְא אֶת־בִּנְיָמִין אָחִיו — *Then he lifted up his eyes and saw his brother Benjamin.* But had Joseph not already seen him when he arrived, as we were told in verse 16? Why were his emotions so affected now that he felt the need to cry? It is because he now had a vision of the future which he had not had at first. The text marks this difference by adding the words וַיִּשָּׂא עֵינָיו, *he lifted up his eyes* whereas in verse 16 it had said only וַיַּרְא יוֹסֵף *Joseph saw* Joseph had seen right away that Benjamin was "with them" (אֹתָם). וַיַּרְא יוֹסֵף אִתָּם אֶת־בִּנְיָמִין, *Joseph saw Benjamin with them*). Now, Joseph saw in his vision that Benjamin would always remain at the side of his brother Judah, his great protector. This union was sealed for all time — the two tribes of Judah and

²⁸ They replied, "Your servant our father is at peace; he still lives," and they bowed and prostrated themselves.

²⁹ Then he lifted up his eyes and saw his brother Benjamin, his mother's son, so he said, "Is this your 'little' brother of whom you spoke to me?" And he said, "God be gracious to you, my son."

³⁰ Then Joseph rushed because his compassion for his brother had been stirred and he wanted to weep; so he went into the room and wept there. ³¹ He washed his face and went out, fortified himself and said, "Serve food." ³² They served him separately and them separately and the Egyptians who ate with him separately, for the Egyptians could not bear to eat food with the Hebrews, it being loathsome to Egyptians. ³³ They were seated before him, the firstborn according to his seniority and the youngest according to his youth. The men looked at one another in astonishment.

³⁴ He had portions that had been set before him served to them, and Benjamin's portion was five times as much as the portion of any of them. They drank and became intoxicated with him.

Benjamin formed an indissoluble partnership, but the two tribes issuing from Joseph, Ephraim and Manasseh, were to have no share in this sacred union! When he saw Benjamin was with his brothers instead of with him and his children, Joseph was powerless to hold back his tears (*Zohar*).

33. וַיִּתְמְהוּ הָאֲנָשִׁים אִישׁ אֶל־רֵעֵהוּ — *The men looked at one another in astonishment.* This meal begins to make the brothers suspicious about the viceroy's identity. He eats apart. He assigns the brothers places exactly according to their ages but, above all, the contrast of this warm welcome with the mistrust which he had shown them on their first arrival in Egypt put them on their guard. This meal is particularly significant as a reflection of the way of life which Joseph had maintained in Egypt. Intimately involved with the destiny of the country, having risen to assume the highest duties of the State, Joseph (like Esther in the royal palace of Ahasuerus) had remained faithful to the family traditions. There was no desire for rapid assimilation, no bowing down before the temporal rulers. Joseph had not committed himself to a culture but only to a man, Pharaoh, to whom he owed his freedom. Even in this foreign land, cut off from his kin for many years, he kept the integrity of his ideas and religious practices (*R' S.R. Hirsch*).

34. וַתֵּרֶב מַשְׂאַת בִּנְיָמִן מִמַּשְׂאֹת כֻּלָּם חָמֵשׁ יָדוֹת — *And Benjamin's portion was five times as much as the portion of any of them.* The initial step toward reconciliation was taken when Joseph realized for the first time that a change had occurred in the outlook of his brothers, and that the memory of their misdeed continued to weigh on their conscience. Now, before taking the final, decisive step, as recorded in the next chapter, Joseph puts his brothers to the test. He wants to find out whether his brothers are jealous of Benjamin and prepared

מד

א וַיְצַ֞ו אֶת־אֲשֶׁ֣ר עַל־בֵּיתוֹ֮ לֵאמֹר֒ מַלֵּ֞א אֶת־אַמְתְּחֹ֤ת הָֽאֲנָשִׁים֙ אֹ֔כֶל כַּאֲשֶׁ֥ר יֽוּכְל֖וּן שְׂאֵ֑ת וְשִׂ֛ים כֶּֽסֶף־אִ֖ישׁ בְּפִ֥י אַמְתַּחְתּֽוֹ:
ב וְאֶת־גְּבִיעִ֞י גְּבִ֣יעַ הַכֶּ֗סֶף תָּשִׂים֙ בְּפִי֙ אַמְתַּ֣חַת הַקָּטֹ֔ן וְאֵ֖ת כֶּ֣סֶף שִׁבְר֑וֹ וַיַּ֕עַשׂ כִּדְבַ֥ר יוֹסֵ֖ף אֲשֶׁ֥ר דִּבֵּֽר:
ג הַבֹּ֖קֶר א֑וֹר וְהָֽאֲנָשִׁ֣ים שֻׁלְּח֔וּ הֵ֖מָּה וַֽחֲמֹֽרֵיהֶֽם:
ד הֵ֠ם יָֽצְא֣וּ אֶת־הָעִיר֮ לֹ֣א הִרְחִ֒יקוּ֒ וְיוֹסֵ֤ף אָמַר֙ לַֽאֲשֶׁ֣ר עַל־בֵּית֔וֹ ק֥וּם רְדֹ֖ף אַֽחֲרֵ֣י הָֽאֲנָשִׁ֑ים וְהִשַּׂגְתָּם֙ וְאָֽמַרְתָּ֣ אֲלֵהֶ֔ם לָ֛מָּה שִׁלַּמְתֶּ֥ם רָעָ֖ה תַּ֥חַת טוֹבָֽה:
ה הֲל֣וֹא זֶ֗ה אֲשֶׁ֨ר יִשְׁתֶּ֤ה אֲדֹנִי֙ בּ֔וֹ וְה֕וּא נַחֵ֥שׁ יְנַחֵ֖שׁ בּ֑וֹ הֲרֵֽעֹתֶ֖ם אֲשֶׁ֥ר עֲשִׂיתֶֽם:
ו וַֽיַּשִּׂגֵ֑ם וַיְדַבֵּ֣ר אֲלֵהֶ֔ם אֶת־הַדְּבָרִ֖ים הָאֵֽלֶּה:
ז וַיֹּֽאמְר֣וּ אֵלָ֔יו לָ֚מָּה יְדַבֵּ֣ר אֲדֹנִ֔י כַּדְּבָרִ֖ים הָאֵ֑לֶּה חָלִ֨ילָה֙ לַֽעֲבָדֶ֔יךָ מֵֽעֲשׂ֖וֹת כַּדָּבָ֥ר הַזֶּֽה:
ח הֵ֣ן כֶּ֗סֶף אֲשֶׁ֤ר מָצָ֙אנוּ֙ בְּפִ֣י אַמְתְּחֹתֵ֔ינוּ הֱשִׁיבֹ֥נוּ אֵלֶ֖יךָ מֵאֶ֣רֶץ כְּנָ֑עַן וְאֵ֗יךְ נִגְנֹב֙ מִבֵּ֣ית אֲדֹנֶ֔יךָ כֶּ֖סֶף א֥וֹ זָהָֽב:
ט אֲשֶׁ֨ר יִמָּצֵ֥א אִתּ֛וֹ מֵֽעֲבָדֶ֖יךָ וָמֵ֑ת וְגַם־אֲנַ֕חְנוּ נִֽהְיֶ֥ה לַֽאדֹנִ֖י לַֽעֲבָדִֽים:

to make him pay for this, just as they had made Joseph pay, or whether they had at last overcome their spiteful feelings of jealousy. They did indeed pass this test for *they drank and became intoxicated with him*, without the slightest feeling of resentment. But the time for reconciliation had not yet come! Joseph first wanted to be sure that his brothers were prepared to fight with body and soul to protect a son of Rachel; only then could he proceed to pardon them.

44.

2. וַיַּעַשׂ כִּדְבַר יוֹסֵף אֲשֶׁר דִּבֵּר — *And he followed Joseph's word exactly.* The supervisor was none other than Manasseh, as *Targum Yonasan* points out. His good character shines forth in his attitude toward the ten men who to him were just strangers. When he is to be friendly towards them, he does so at once — hence it states simply: וַיַּעַשׂ הָאִישׁ כַּאֲשֶׁר אָמַר יוֹסֵף, *the man did as Joseph said* (43:17). But when Manasseh is instructed to cause serious difficulties to an innocent person, as he is here, he hesitates and finds it hard to believe that Joseph is serious in giving this order. Joseph has to issue an official command to be sure of being obeyed. This is why it says וַיַּעַשׂ כִּדְבַר יוֹסֵף אֲשֶׁר דִּבֵּר (the word דִּבֵּר signifying harsh words, a command).

3. וְהָאֲנָשִׁים שֻׁלְּחוּ הֵמָּה וַחֲמֹרֵיהֶם — *And the men were sent off, they and their donkeys.* The first letters of the words הֵמָּה וַחֲמֹרֵיהֶם and of the next two words הֵם יָצְאוּ form the Divine name הֲוָיָ' but in reverse order. This, writes R' *Bachya*, indicates that Divine justice (the reverse of מִדַּת הָרַחֲמִים expressed by the name הֲוָיָ') loomed over the brothers on their way back to Canaan. This was because of their earlier sin against Joseph which they had not yet atoned for. But they were protected thanks to the merit which their ancestor, the patriarch Abraham,

44 ¹Then he instructed the one in charge of his house, saying, "Fill the men's sacks with as much food as they can carry and put each man's money in the mouth of his sack. ² And my goblet — the silver goblet — place in the mouth of the youngest one's sack along with the money of his purchase." And he followed Joseph's word exactly.

³ The day dawned and the men were sent off, they and their donkeys. ⁴ They had left the city, had not gone far, when Joseph said to the one in charge of his house, "Get up, chase after the men; when you overtake them, you are to say to them, 'Why do you repay evil for good? ⁵ Is it not the one from which my master drinks, and with which he regularly divines? You have done evil in how you acted!' "

⁶ He overtook them and spoke those words to them. ⁷ And they said to him, "Why does my lord say such things? It would be sacrilegious for your servants to do such a thing! ⁸ Here, look: The money that we found in the mouth of our sacks we brought back to you from the land of Canaan. How then could we have stolen from your master's house any silver or gold? ⁹ Anyone among your servants with whom it is found shall die, and we also will become slaves to my lord."

had earned through his deep love of God. This love for God also manifested itself "early in the morning,"(הַבֹּקֶר אוֹר, *the day dawned*),when Abraham made his way "with his donkey" to Mount Moriah to sacrifice Isaac — וַיַּשְׁכֵּם אַבְרָהָם בַּבֹּקֶר וַיַּחֲבֹשׁ אֶת־חֲמֹרוֹ, *So Abraham woke up early in the morning and he saddled his donkey* (22:3).

4. וְהִשַּׂגְתָּם — *When you overtake them.* The word וְהִשַּׂגְתָּם is interpreted to mean הֱוֵי שׁוֹגֵג אוֹתָם, confuse them, lead them into error. "Speak to them in turn harshly and gently" (*Tanchuma*). Joseph's advice reflects his own tactics toward his brothers and it reminds us of the methods of oriental diplomacy. Its purpose was to jar their peace of mind and to awaken their conscience.

9. אֲשֶׁר יִמָּצֵא אִתּוֹ מֵעֲבָדֶיךָ וָמֵת — *Anyone among your servants with whom it is found shall die.* In this, the final test which he inflicted on his brothers, Joseph wanted to find out the fate they had in store for Rachel's second son. Would they be so pleased at the opportunity of finally bringing their purchases back to their father that they would abandon Benjamin and invent a new story about a wild beast, or this time would they make their decision out of a sense of responsibility and family solidarity? It is not without reason that Joseph chose the goblet; for the Egyptians it was an object of religious worship. The brothers must have known this fact. They could react in one of two ways: either they were already sullied with the pagan Egyptian spirit and would try to keep this

י וַיֹּאמֶר גַּם־עַתָּה כְדִבְרֵיכֶם כֶּן־הוּא אֲשֶׁר יִמָּצֵא אִתּוֹ
יא יִהְיֶה־לִּי עָבֶד וְאַתֶּם תִּהְיוּ נְקִיִּם: וַיְמַהֲרוּ וַיּוֹרִדוּ אִישׁ
יב אֶת־אַמְתַּחְתּוֹ אָרְצָה וַיִּפְתְּחוּ אִישׁ אַמְתַּחְתּוֹ: וַיְחַפֵּשׂ
בַּגָּדוֹל הֵחֵל וּבַקָּטֹן כִּלָּה וַיִּמָּצֵא הַגָּבִיעַ בְּאַמְתַּחַת בִּנְיָמִן:
יג וַיִּקְרְעוּ שִׂמְלֹתָם וַיַּעֲמֹס אִישׁ עַל־חֲמֹרוֹ וַיָּשֻׁבוּ הָעִירָה:
יד וַיָּבֹא יְהוּדָה וְאֶחָיו בֵּיתָה יוֹסֵף וְהוּא עוֹדֶנּוּ שָׁם וַיִּפְּלוּ לְפָנָיו   מפטיר
טו אָרְצָה: וַיֹּאמֶר לָהֶם יוֹסֵף מָה־הַמַּעֲשֶׂה הַזֶּה אֲשֶׁר עֲשִׂיתֶם
טז הֲלוֹא יְדַעְתֶּם כִּי־נַחֵשׁ יְנַחֵשׁ אִישׁ אֲשֶׁר כָּמֹנִי: וַיֹּאמֶר
יְהוּדָה מַה־נֹּאמַר לַאדֹנִי מַה־נְּדַבֵּר וּמַה־נִּצְטַדָּק הָאֱלֹהִים
מָצָא אֶת־עֲוֺן עֲבָדֶיךָ הִנֶּנּוּ עֲבָדִים לַאדֹנִי גַּם־אֲנַחְנוּ גַּם
יז אֲשֶׁר־נִמְצָא הַגָּבִיעַ בְּיָדוֹ: וַיֹּאמֶר חָלִילָה לִּי מֵעֲשׂוֹת זֹאת

goblet safe and thus have for themselves a powerful instrument of sorcery, or else they would see this goblet merely as a metal object of some commercial value, and their honesty alone would be put to the test. In any case, the brothers would have one last chance of proving that the past with its lies and treachery had definitely given way to new times where only the honor of the family, the well-being of its members, and the service of the ideal of its ancestors would determine the actions of the sons of Jacob (R' S.R. Hirsch).

12. וַיִּמָּצֵא הַגָּבִיעַ בְּאַמְתַּחַת בִּנְיָמִן — *And the goblet was found in Benjamin's sack.* The Midrash shows us here how quickly suspicion is awakened in the hearts of men, and at the slightest pretext: "When the cup was found in Benjamin's sack, his brothers struck him on the shoulders and said to him: 'Thief, son of a thieving mother! You have shamed us, just as your mother shamed our father when she stole Laban's *teraphim'* (*Genesis* 31:19). Benjamin solemnly swore that he was innocent and the brothers believed him, for he did not make a habit of swearing (*Tanchuma* and *Midrash Aggada*). Moreover, R' Yose adds: Those who are suspected wrongly always have the right to compensation. For the blows which Benjamin took on his shoulders because of these false suspicions, his descendants received compensation. They had the privilege of being able to welcome the *Shechinah* "between their shoulders" (*Deuteronomy* 33:12). The Temple was built on Benjamin's territory in Jerusalem.

13. וַיִּקְרְעוּ שִׂמְלֹתָם — *They rent their garments.* Everything is repaid. Twenty-two years after having made their father go into mourning because of a falsehood, to the point where "he rent his garments" (37:34), the sons, now falsely accused of a crime, also had to go through the same anguish and here, in deep despair, they too tear their clothes.

14. וַיִּפְּלוּ לְפָנָיו אָרְצָה — *They fell to the ground before him.* For the third time since their last visit, the brothers, including Benjamin, bow down before Joseph. When Joseph sees the dreams of his youth coming true in such striking fashion,

¹⁰ He replied, "What you say now is also correct. The one with whom it is found shall be my slave, but the rest of you shall be exonerated."

¹¹ Hurriedly, each one lowered his sack to the ground, and each one opened his sack. ¹² He searched; he began with the oldest and ended with the youngest; and the goblet was found in Benjamin's sack. ¹³ They rent their garments. Each one reloaded his donkey and they returned to the city.

¹⁴ When Judah arrived with his brothers to Joseph's house, he was still there. They fell to the ground before him. ¹⁵ Joseph said to them, "What is this deed that you have done? Do you not realize that a man like me practices divination!"

¹⁶ So Judah said, "What can we say to my lord? How can we speak? And how can we justify ourselves? God has uncovered the sin of your servants. Here we are: We are ready to be slaves to my lord — both we and the one in whose hand the goblet was found."

¹⁷ But he replied, "It would be sacrilegious for me to do this.

he realizes that there is no longer any purpose in putting off the time for their reconciliation.

16. הָאֱלֹהִים מָצָא אֶת־עֲוֹן עֲבָדֶיךָ — God has uncovered the sin of your servants. Rashi explains: "We know that we have not done anything wrong. But what has happened to us has come from the Holy One, Blessed is He. The creditor has found occasion to collect his debt." Thus these words imply admission of the earlier sin committed against Joseph. Judah considers their new ordeal a Divine punishment. So he at first renounces all the formal commitments to his father regarding Benjamin and he goes so far as to declare: "Here we are: We are ready to be slaves to my lord — both we and the one in whose hand the goblet was found." Only when Joseph shows that he has his mind set solely on Benjamin does his brother, his "guarantor," come forward to defend him with all his might.

17. וְאַתֶּם עֲלוּ לְשָׁלוֹם אֶל־אֲבִיכֶם — And as for you — go up in peace to your father. With these words the sidrah comes to an end on an optimistic note. According to R' Bachya, this happy outlook, after all the tragic events that had happened, is to be seen in connection with the historical allusion in the tenfold repetition of the word אֲנָשִׁים (the men) in the last two chapters, 43 and 44. If the Torah employs this term to describe Jacob's ten sons rather than the more usual אֲחֵי יוֹסֵף or בְּנֵי יַעֲקֹב, it is because the Torah is hinting to us that they are somehow connected with the "ten martyrs." About the second century of the common era, ten sages from among the most important leaders of the Jewish nation were tortured and put to death on the orders of Roman emperors who

הָאִישׁ אֲשֶׁר נִמְצָא הַגָּבִיעַ בְּיָדוֹ הוּא יִהְיֶה־לִּי עָבֶד וְאַתֶּם
עֲלוּ לְשָׁלוֹם אֶל־אֲבִיכֶם:

claimed that they wanted to make the Jews atone for the sin which their ancestors had committed against Joseph, in conformity with Divine law (*Exodus* 21:16; *Midrash Rabbah* on *Lamentations* 2). With its discreet allusion here to the "ten martyrs," the Torah is telling us that the crime of the brothers was never brought to justice in a court of law, and as a result it had never been atoned for. Consequently, God could not pardon it and it continued to weigh

The man in whose possession the goblet was found, only he shall
be my slave, and as for you — go up in peace to your father."

heavily as a permanent threat over the destinies of the people. This situation
lasted for many centuries and it was only when the ten leaders of Jewry
underwent death in order to atone for this sin (ibid.) that it was finally expiated.
Then, thanks to their sacrifice, the brothers could "go up in peace to their
Heavenly Father (cf. our commentary on 27:28; cf. *Midrash Mishlei* 1 for
another view).

יח וַיִּגַּ֨שׁ אֵלָ֜יו יְהוּדָ֗ה וַיֹּאמֶר֮ בִּ֣י אֲדֹנִי֒ יְדַבֶּר־נָ֨א עַבְדְּךָ֤ דָבָר֙ בְּאָזְנֵ֣י אֲדֹנִ֔י וְאַל־יִ֥חַר אַפְּךָ֖ בְּעַבְדֶּ֑ךָ כִּ֥י כָמ֖וֹךָ כְּפַרְעֹֽה: יט אֲדֹנִ֣י שָׁאַ֔ל אֶת־עֲבָדָ֖יו לֵאמֹ֑ר הֲיֵשׁ־לָכֶ֥ם אָ֖ב אוֹ־אָֽח: כ וַנֹּ֙אמֶר֙ אֶל־אֲדֹנִ֔י יֶשׁ־לָ֙נוּ֙ אָ֣ב זָקֵ֔ן וְיֶ֥לֶד זְקֻנִ֖ים קָטָ֑ן וְאָחִ֣יו מֵ֔ת

18. וַיִּגַּשׁ אֵלָיו יְהוּדָה וַיֹּאמֶר — *Then Judah approached him and said.* The word הַגָּשָׁה, which expresses the action of approaching someone, is used in three different senses. It can mean to come forward for presenting a case for judgment (*Deuteronomy* 25:1); to appease an adversary (*Joshua* 14:6); or else to engage in battle (*II Samuel* 10:13). As he came forward, Judah resolved to achieve his goal using these three means — pleas and arguments for Benjamin, words of appeasement — *let not your anger flare up at your servant* — *for you are like Pharaoh* and battle — *If you anger me, I will kill you and your master* (*Rashi*).

R' *Bachya* stresses, however, that Judah first resorted to appeasement as his long speech bears out. He thus acted in conformity with the recommendation in *Proverbs: A reply full of gentleness turns away anger; a wounding word stirs up rage* (15:1). This view is brought out also in the *Midrash Tanchuma:* to Judah's rhetorical prowess it applies the verse from *Proverbs: Like deep water is the counsel in the heart of man: but the wise man knows how to draw it out* (20:5). This, explains the Midrash, is to be compared to a well so deep that no one can draw water from it. Then along comes a man who ties ropes together and joins pails together until the water at the bottom of the well can be drawn up. So the secret thought which dwelt deep in Joseph's heart appeared impenetrable to the ten brothers. But thanks to his keen psychological insight, Judah knew "how to go down into the depths of Joseph's thinking." He was able to touch Joseph's heartstrings when he described so poignantly the terrible suffering which his father would endure were Benjamin not to return. And so he succeeded in overcoming Joseph's cold reserve. As intelligent as Joseph was, concludes our Sages, Judah nevertheless gained the upper hand.

יְדַבֶּר־נָא עַבְדְּךָ דָבָר — *May your servant speak a word. Ramban* notes that he does not know why Judah spoke at such length to recount what had previously taken place between them. Nor does *Rashi's* answer seem to satisfy him. It makes mention of Judah's criticism of Joseph: You act like Pharaoh, you promise something and do not keep your word. You had told us that you wanted "to set an eye upon Benjamin." Is this what you call "setting eyes upon" someone? Judah's lengthy speech was then just the development of this criticism. *Ramban* holds, on the other hand, that Judah was only endeavoring to stir up pity for Benjamin by playing on Joseph's "fear of God" as revealed by his words (42:18) and deeds (43:23). And so he pointed out that Benjamin's coming to Egypt was only due to Joseph's exaggerated demand and it had taken place against the will of their broken-hearted father. Was it right to seize Benjamin and keep him as a slave just because of a trick? "You have tried to pick a quarrel with us. Why did you ask us all these questions (which you did

¹⁸Then Judah approached him and said, "If you please, my
lord, may your servant speak a word in my lord's ears and
let not your anger flare up at your servant — for you are like
Pharaoh. ¹⁹ My lord has asked his servants, saying, 'Have you
a father or brother?' ²⁰ And we said to my lord, 'We have an old
father and a young child of [his] old age; his brother is dead,

not ask any of the other buyers)? Were we asking for your daughter, or did you
want our sister?" (Rashi). "Then spare our aged father," says Judah, "and
enslave me instead of Benjamin, and you will have acted fairly." Thus, pursuing
his previously mentioned aim, Judah goes with consummate skill from
sentimental arguments to scarcely concealed reproach, from appeals to Joseph's
sense of justice and his piety right to veiled threats which thunder in the furious
tone of his voice (Midrash).

וְאַל־יִחַר אַפְּךָ — And let not your anger flare up. Rashi: From this you can
conclude that he spoke to him harshly. To the verbal duel being fought here
between the lion (referring to Judah, cf. 49:9) and the ox (Joseph, Deuteronomy
33:17), the Zohar applies the verse of Psalms (48:5): כִּי הִנֵּה הַמְּלָכִים נוֹעֲדוּ עָבְרוּ
יַחְדָּו, For behold the kings assembled, they came together. It interprets it thus:
Here are the kings meeting face to face (Judah and Joseph were the two
principal leaders among the brothers): they are both enraged; הֵמָּה רָאוּ וגו' —
they (the others) see them and are struck with perplexity, dread seizes them . . .
anguish takes hold of them. They tremble with fear, continues the Zohar, that
they will have to kill or be killed. But the confrontation of the two giants turned
out for the best. For the establishment of harmony within the family and in
society is conditioned by the union of temporal power (represented by Judah,
the father of the royal tribe) and spiritual power (represented by יוֹסֵף הַצַּדִּיק, the
righteous Joseph). Indeed, no source of blessing is more beneficial to man than
that which emanates from the alliance of royalty and the fear of God.
Accordingly, the introductory verse of this section, וַיִּגַּשׁ אֵלָיו יְהוּדָה, announcing
that Judah comes forward to confront Joseph, marks an auspicious turning
point in the evolution of history.

R' Yonasan adds: The angels themselves descended from heaven to be
present at the furious combat between "the lion and the ox." In most battles,
they said, the ox stands in fear of the lion, but this battle will not cease until the
Messiah comes, as the prophet Isaiah declares concerning the coming of the
Redeemer: Then will end the rivalry of Ephraim (representative of the
descendants of Joseph), and the hatred of Judah will disappear; Ephraim will
no longer be jealous of Judah, and Judah will no longer be hostile to Ephraim
(11:13 — Tanchuma). Seen in historical perspective, the reconciliation of the
two brothers taking place here did not survive the test of time. When the Jewish
kingdom was divided into two opposing groups after King Solomon's death,
one was called Judah, the other Ephraim. As for Benjamin, he remained ever
loyal to Judah, his great protector, and never rallied to the side of Joseph's

כא וַיִּוָּתֵר הָוּא לְבַדָּוֹ לְאִמֹּו וְאָבִיו אֲהֵבְוֹ: וַתֹּאמֶר אֶל־עֲבָדֶיךָ

כב הוֹרִדֻהוּ אֵלָי וְאָשִׂימָה עֵינִי עָלָיו: וַנֹּאמֶר אֶל־אֲדֹנִי לֹא־יוּכַל

כג הַנַּעַר לַעֲזֹב אֶת־אָבִיו וְעָזַב אֶת־אָבִיו וָמֵת: וַתֹּאמֶר אֶל־

עֲבָדֶיךָ אִם־לֹא יֵרֵד אֲחִיכֶם הַקָּטֹן אִתְּכֶם לֹא תֹסִפוּן

כד לִרְאוֹת פָּנָי: וַיְהִי כִּי עָלִינוּ אֶל־עַבְדְּךָ אָבִי וַנַּגֶּד־לֹו אֵת דִּבְרֵי

כה-כו אֲדֹנִי: וַיֹּאמֶר אָבִינוּ שֻׁבוּ שִׁבְרוּ־לָנוּ מְעַט־אֹכֶל: וַנֹּאמֶר

לֹא נוּכַל לָרֶדֶת אִם־יֵשׁ אָחִינוּ הַקָּטֹן אִתָּנוּ וְיָרַדְנוּ כִּי־לֹא

נוּכַל לִרְאוֹת פְּנֵי הָאִישׁ וְאָחִינוּ הַקָּטֹן אֵינֶנּוּ אִתָּנוּ:

כז וַיֹּאמֶר עַבְדְּךָ אָבִי אֵלֵינוּ אַתֶּם יְדַעְתֶּם כִּי שְׁנַיִם יָלְדָה־

כח לִּי אִשְׁתִּי: וַיֵּצֵא הָאֶחָד מֵאִתִּי וָאֹמַר אַךְ טָרֹף טֹרָף וְלֹא

כט רְאִיתִיו עַד־הֵנָּה: וּלְקַחְתֶּם גַּם־אֶת־זֶה מֵעִם פָּנַי וְקָרָהוּ

ל אָסֹון וְהוֹרַדְתֶּם אֶת־שֵׂיבָתִי בְּרָעָה שְׁאֹלָה: וְעַתָּה כְּבֹאִי

אֶל־עַבְדְּךָ אָבִי וְהַנַּעַר אֵינֶנּוּ אִתָּנוּ וְנַפְשׁוֹ קְשׁוּרָה בְנַפְשׁוֹ:

לא וְהָיָה כִּרְאוֹתוֹ כִּי־אֵין הַנַּעַר וָמֵת וְהוֹרִידוּ עֲבָדֶיךָ אֶת־

שני

לב שֵׂיבַת עַבְדְּךָ אָבִינוּ בְּיָגוֹן שְׁאֹלָה: כִּי עַבְדְּךָ עָרַב אֶת־

הַנַּעַר מֵעִם אָבִי לֵאמֹר אִם־לֹא אֲבִיאֶנּוּ אֵלֶיךָ וְחָטָאתִי

לג לְאָבִי כָּל־הַיָּמִים: וְעַתָּה יֵשֶׁב־נָא עַבְדְּךָ תַּחַת הַנַּעַר עֶבֶד

לד לַאדֹנִי וְהַנַּעַר יַעַל עִם־אֶחָיו: כִּי־אֵיךְ אֶעֱלֶה אֶל־אָבִי

וְהַנַּעַר אֵינֶנּוּ אִתִּי פֶּן אֶרְאֶה בָרָע אֲשֶׁר יִמְצָא אֶת־אָבִי:

children, Ephraim and Manasseh, just as Joseph had painfully foreseen (cf. our
commentary on 43:29).

21. וְאָשִׂימָה עֵינִי עָלָיו — *And I will set my eye on him. Rambam* notes that Joseph
never actually said this. And thus some commentators hold that these words are
to be attributed to the speaker, that is to say, to Judah, who wanted to express
his desire to examine the case of his brother more closely (*Chizkuni*). "What
right have you to condemn Benjamin?" he asked Joseph. "Is it by Egyptian law?
It permits you only to confiscate our property, as the law stipulates in the case
of theft. Is it by the law that we uphold? That states explicitly: *If a thief is found
breaking in . . . he shall make restitution; and if he cannot* (through lack of
money) *then he shall be sold for his theft* (Exodus 22:2). But," continued Judah,
"our brother has money; therefore you do not have the right to hold him as a
slave" (*Tanchuma*).

32. כִּי עַבְדְּךָ עָרַב אֶת־הַנַּעַר — *For your servant took responsibility for the youth.*
Rashi explains: "And if you ask me why I enter the fray more than my other
brothers, it is because they are not involved. But I myself am running the risk
of banishment from both this world and the next." Several midrashic sources

he alone is left from his mother, and his father loves him.' ²¹ Then
you said to your servants, 'Bring him down to me, and I will set my
eye on him.' ²² We said to my lord, 'The youth cannot leave his
father, for should he leave his father he will die.' ²³ But you said to
your servants, 'If your youngest brother does not come down with
you, you will not see my face again!'

²⁴ *"And it was, when we went up to your servant my father, we*
told him my lord's words; ²⁵ and our father said, 'Go back, buy us
some food.' ²⁶ We said, 'We cannot go down; only if our youngest
brother is with us, then we will go down, for we cannot see the
man's face if our youngest brother is not with us.' ²⁷ Then your
servant my father said to us, 'You know that my wife bore me two
[sons]. ²⁸ One has left me and I presumed: Alas, he has surely been
torn to pieces, for I have not seen him since! ²⁹ So should you take
this one, too, from my presence, and disaster befall him, then you
will have brought down my hoariness in evil to the grave.'

³⁰ *"And now, if I come to your servant my father and the youth*
is not with us — since his soul is so bound up with his soul — ³¹ it
will happen that when he sees the youth is missing he will die, and
your servants will have brought down the hoariness of your
servant our father in sorrow to the grave. ³² For your servant took
responsibility for the youth from my father saying, 'If I do not
bring him back to you then I will be sinning to my father for all
time.' ³³ Now, therefore, please let your servant remain instead of
the youth as a servant to my lord, and let the youth go up with his
brothers. ³⁴ For how can I go up to my father if the youth is not with
me, lest I see the evil that will befall my father!''

give the successive stages of the epic and extremely violent dialogue between
Judah and Joseph. When Joseph heard Judah's reply regarding his responsibility
for Benjamin, he answered back in stinging tones: "And why didn't you take
responsibility for your other brother whom you sold for twenty pieces of silver?
Then you weren't concerned at all with your father's anguish upon hearing that
a wild beast had devoured him. However, that brother had not done anything
wrong, whereas Benjamin stole! Go and tell your father: The rope has followed
the bucket." These words exasperated Judah and his brothers to the point that
they became furious and were prepared to attack the officers and the soldiers of
the guard, for they were endowed with extraordinary strength. But Judah
controlled his anger and said to Joseph: "What will we tell our father when he
sees that our young brother is not with us? He will die of sorrow." Joseph
repeated: "Tell him that the rope has followed the bucket." Judah: "You are a
king. Why do you speak like this, why do you advise us to lie?" Joseph: "Is it

א וְלֹא־יָכֹל יוֹסֵף לְהִתְאַפֵּק לְכֹל הַנִּצָּבִים עָלָיו וַיִּקְרָא
הוֹצִיאוּ כָל־אִישׁ מֵעָלָי וְלֹא־עָמַד אִישׁ אִתּוֹ בְּהִתְוַדַּע
ב יוֹסֵף אֶל־אֶחָיו: וַיִּתֵּן אֶת־קֹלוֹ בִּבְכִי וַיִּשְׁמְעוּ מִצְרַיִם
ג וַיִּשְׁמַע בֵּית פַּרְעֹה: וַיֹּאמֶר יוֹסֵף אֶל־אֶחָיו אֲנִי יוֹסֵף הַעוֹד
אָבִי חָי וְלֹא־יָכְלוּ אֶחָיו לַעֲנוֹת אֹתוֹ כִּי נִבְהֲלוּ מִפָּנָיו:

a bigger lie than the one you told your father when you said that a wild beast had devoured your brother?" Judah: "I can feel the fire of Shechem burning within me! I am going to do to your land as we did to Shechem!" Joseph: "Yes, the same fire that burned when you wanted to slay your daughter-in-law Tamar, a fire which was never kindled!" Judah: "My brothers and I are capable of turning the whole of Egypt into a blood bath!" Joseph: "Yes, that is indeed your trade. Did you not dip the tunic of your brother in a bath of blood?" At these words, Judah and his brothers could no longer control their anger, and Joseph sensed that a full battle was about to rage, something he of course wanted to avoid.

But he at last had the absolute and irrefutable proof he had been seeking of their devotion to their brother. And, on the other hand, his brothers had had their share of the expiatory humiliation which they had deserved. He therefore felt that the time for reconciliation had at last arrived.

45.

1. וְלֹא־יָכֹל יוֹסֵף לְהִתְאַפֵּק — *Now Joseph could not restrain himself. Rashi* explains: "Joseph could not bear having the Egyptians there, witnessing how humiliated his brothers would be when he made himself known to them." But other commentators hold that Joseph could not wait any longer for he was gripped with emotion at the thought of his aged father's misery, which Judah had so poignantly described on several occasions (*Ibn Ezra*). *Ramban* attributes the fact that Joseph could not "stand firm" (*Onkelos'* translation) any longer "in the presence of all who were in attendance on him" to the supplications of the bystanders that he show mercy to Benjamin after Judah's brilliant pleadings.

הוֹצִיאוּ כָל־אִישׁ מֵעָלָי — *Remove everyone from before me.* "In so doing Joseph risked great danger, for if the brothers (put to shame by his decision) had attacked him, there was no one to come to his rescue. But well aware of this danger, Joseph said to himself: It is better that I die than humiliate my brothers in front of the Egyptians!" This is the opinion of R' Chama ben Chanina. But it is opposed by the son of R' Nachman: "Joseph had no reason to be afraid. He was aware of the piety of his brothers and knew that they were not murderers" (*Rabbah* 93). Furthermore, from the latest events Joseph had seen the great solidarity which united the family, and he now had the sincerest feelings of fraternal love for his eleven brothers. And he could count on the same feelings in return, according to the teaching expressed in these words by King Solomon

45　　¹*Now Joseph could not restrain himself in the presence of all who stood before him, so he called out, "Remove everyone from before me!" Thus no one remained with him when Joseph made himself known to his brothers.*

²*He cried in a loud voice. Egypt heard, and Pharaoh's household heard.*

³*And Joseph said to his brothers, "I am Joseph. Is my father still alive?" But his brothers could not answer him because they were left disconcerted before him.*

(*Proverbs* 27:19): *As in water a face [reflects] a face, so with one man's heart to another* (cf. *Rashi* on verse 12).

2. וַיִּתֵּן אֶת־קֹלוֹ בִּבְכִי — *He cried in a loud voice.* They were tears of happiness prompted by the great joy of finally seeing the long years of terrible trials and moral suffering come to an end. When Joseph once again found his brothers and his family, under circumstances so glorious for him, he saw his most cherished wish come true beyond all his expectations. Alas, notes the Midrash, when Jewry will at the end of time again find God in its land, this rediscovery will be of the same nature: with tears of joy will be mingled the memory of indescribable suffering endured through the seemingly endless years of exile. Such is the destiny of Jewry, as *Jeremiah* predicts, *They will return in tears, I shall bring them back with sighing* (31:8).

3. אֲנִי יוֹסֵף — *I am Joseph.* "Woe to us on the day of judgment, woe to us on the day of rebuke! If the brothers were so dismayed that they were unable to answer Joseph's rebuke, and he was after all only their younger brother, what will it be like on the day of the final judgment when the Holy One, Blessed is He, will demand an account from every human being?" This passage is mentioned (with some variation) in the Talmud (*Chagigah* 4b), in the *Midrash Rabbah*, and in *Tanchuma*, quoting different Sages. It brings the following to mind:

The brothers had always considered themselves absolutely right in their treatment of Joseph. They had a whole series of legal motives, as we have shown in our commentary on 37:20, and little by little they had become convinced of their complete innocence. But, when the hour of truth came, twenty-two years later, they needed only to hear Joseph utter two words — אֲנִי יוֹסֵף — and they were petrified, speechless. This simple two-word rebuke abruptly tore away the veil of falsehood and the brothers suddenly realized the shallowness of all their excuses and all their pretexts — the whole beautiful "system of defense" which they had built up over the years suddenly crumbled. All the good reasons which we use to exonerate ourselves cannot withstand the blinding light of truth. "What will it be like then on the day of supreme judgment, when God will ask us to account for our deeds!"

הַעוֹד אָבִי חָי — *Is my father still alive?* "Can it really be that our father, so old and having gone through so much, is still alive?" This seems to be the sense of

ד וַיֹּ֨אמֶר יוֹסֵ֤ף אֶל־אֶחָיו֙ גְּשׁוּ־נָ֣א אֵלַ֔י וַיִּגָּ֑שׁוּ וַיֹּ֕אמֶר אֲנִי֙ יוֹסֵ֣ף
ה אֲחִיכֶ֔ם אֲשֶׁר־מְכַרְתֶּ֥ם אֹתִ֖י מִצְרָֽיְמָה: וְעַתָּ֣ה ׀ אַל־תֵּעָ֣צְב֗וּ
וְאַל־יִ֙חַר֙ בְּעֵ֣ינֵיכֶ֔ם כִּֽי־מְכַרְתֶּ֥ם אֹתִ֖י הֵ֑נָּה כִּ֣י לְמִֽחְיָ֔ה שְׁלָחַ֥נִי
ו אֱלֹהִ֖ים לִפְנֵיכֶֽם: כִּי־זֶ֛ה שְׁנָתַ֥יִם הָרָעָ֖ב בְּקֶ֣רֶב הָאָ֑רֶץ וְעוֹד֙
ז חָמֵ֣שׁ שָׁנִ֔ים אֲשֶׁ֥ר אֵין־חָרִ֖ישׁ וְקָצִֽיר: וַיִּשְׁלָחֵ֤נִי אֱלֹהִים֙
לִפְנֵיכֶ֔ם לָשׂ֥וּם לָכֶ֛ם שְׁאֵרִ֖ית בָּאָ֑רֶץ וּלְהַחֲי֣וֹת לָכֶ֔ם לִפְלֵיטָ֖ה
שלישי ח גְּדֹלָֽה: וְעַתָּ֗ה לֹֽא־אַתֶּ֞ם שְׁלַחְתֶּ֤ם אֹתִי֙ הֵ֔נָּה כִּ֖י הָאֱלֹהִ֑ים
וַיְשִׂימֵ֨נִי לְאָ֜ב לְפַרְעֹ֗ה וּלְאָדוֹן֙ לְכָל־בֵּית֔וֹ וּמֹשֵׁ֖ל בְּכָל־אֶ֥רֶץ
ט מִצְרָֽיִם: מַהֲרוּ֮ וַעֲל֣וּ אֶל־אָבִי֒ וַאֲמַרְתֶּ֣ם אֵלָ֗יו כֹּ֤ה אָמַר֙ בִּנְךָ֣
יוֹסֵ֔ף שָׂמַ֧נִי אֱלֹהִ֛ים לְאָד֖וֹן לְכָל־מִצְרָ֑יִם רְדָ֥ה אֵלַ֖י אַֽל־תַּעֲמֹֽד:

this question. The thought of his venerable father is uppermost in Joseph's mind, and his question is rather an expression of astonishment; therefore he did not wait for an answer.

4. גְּשׁוּ־נָ֣א אֵלַ֔י — *Come close to me, if you please. Rashi* explains: "He saw that they were withdrawing. He said to himself: 'Now my brothers are filled with shame.' He spoke to them gently, appealing to them, and he showed them that he was circumcised" (*Bereishis Rabbah* 93:8) *Rashi* later explains that Joseph resorted to the fact that he spoke Hebrew and was circumcised as double proof that he really was their brother.

But the *Zohar* interprets this remark in a figurative sense. When Joseph saw his brothers utterly dumbfounded by the royal rank to which the former slave had been elevated, he explained to them that he attributed his ascent to having constantly respected the covenant of Abraham. Now, the sign of this covenant is circumcision, an indelible sign of sexual purity. It represents the seal of the Divine applied to the most private areas on a man's body and it also makes us aware of the fact that moral purity is to constitute the eternal hallmark of the sons of the covenant. It was just when Joseph categorically refused to yield to debauchery with his master's wife that his destiny took the decisive turn which ultimately led to royalty. Respect for the sacred covenant, concludes the *Zohar*, leads man to rulership, as we also see from other Biblical examples, in particular that of Boaz.

5. כִּ֣י לְמִֽחְיָ֔ה שְׁלָחַ֥נִי אֱלֹהִ֖ים לִפְנֵיכֶֽם — *For it was to be a provider that God sent me ahead of you.* In order to persuade his brothers that he no longer judged them harshly for their past fault, Joseph explains to them with great insistence (verses 7 and 8) that he considers the chain of events and his own extraordinary destiny as part of a plan prearranged by God. The purpose of this plan was to save the tribe of Jacob from a famine which would have destroyed it. Rarely indeed does a historical account make so apparently clear the ways of Divine Providence, which King Solomon describes in these terms (*Proverbs* 26:10). *The Master* (of

⁴ Then Joseph said to his brothers, "Come close to me, if you please," and they came close. And he said, "I am Joseph your brother — it is me, whom you sold into Egypt. ⁵ And now, be not distressed, nor reproach yourselves for having sold me here, for it was to be a provider that God sent me ahead of you. ⁶ For this has been two of the hunger years in the midst of the land, and there are yet five years in which there shall be neither plowing nor harvest. ⁷ Thus God has sent me ahead of you to insure your survival in the land and to sustain you for a momentous deliverance. ⁸ And now: It was not you who sent me here, but God; He has made me father to Pharaoh, master of his entire household, and ruler throughout the entire land of Egypt. ⁹ Hurry — go up to my father and say to him, 'So said your son Joseph: "God has made me master of all Egypt. Come down to me; do not delay.

the Universe) *Who creates everything* (from the minute seed) *has at His service the fool as well as the criminal.* Folly and sin serve the Creator, without knowing it and in spite of themselves. In this episode the connections appear clear, in other incidents less so; but from this one we can learn the ways of God. The promise made to Abraham at the בְּרִית בֵּין הַבְּתָרִים (Chapter 15) came true because of, as our Sages expressed it, "two ounces of silk" with which Jacob had embroidered Joseph's cloak, which caused his brothers' jealousy. To conserve its integrity, this family of Jacob had to be formed into a nation in the midst of hostile surroundings, both from a national and a cultural point of view. No country complied better with these conditions than Egypt, which thus became the crucible, the "iron furnace" (*Deuteronomy* 4:20) wherein the Jewish people was forged (*R' S.R. Hirsch*).

From his own past Joseph gained a steadfast confidence in the One Who directs human destiny. It was on justifiable grounds that he later uttered the words which were to guide the oppressed people: "God will surely remember you and bring you up out of this land to the land of the forefathers." He was able in all good conscience to announce to his descendants that there would be a future redemption, because he himself had been the object of the great workings of God's invisible hand.

7. וַיִּשְׁלָחֵנִי אֱלֹהִים לִפְנֵיכֶם — *Thus God has sent me ahead of you.* In his *Guide for the Perplexed* (2:48), *Rambam* develops the theory that in the Bible all subsequent or secondary causes are directly attributed to God as the first cause. For example, one says that God made, or ordained, or said, or sent something, even though it is a question only of the effect of some well-known cause. So too with the meaning of this verse, which *Rambam* cites as one of the examples of a cause due to "chance." According to commentators on *Rambam* (*Abarbanel, Ibn Caspi* and *Efodi*), the author apparently wants to convey that, having attributed to God the accidental result of the act which came from the free will

י וְיָשַׁבְתָּ בְאֶרֶץ־גֹּשֶׁן וְהָיִיתָ קָרוֹב אֵלַי אַתָּה וּבָנֶיךָ וּבְנֵי בָנֶיךָ
יא וְצֹאנְךָ וּבְקָרְךָ וְכָל־אֲשֶׁר־לָךְ: וְכִלְכַּלְתִּי אֹתְךָ שָׁם כִּי־עוֹד
חָמֵשׁ שָׁנִים רָעָב פֶּן־תִּוָּרֵשׁ אַתָּה וּבֵיתְךָ וְכָל־אֲשֶׁר־לָךְ:
יב וְהִנֵּה עֵינֵיכֶם רֹאוֹת וְעֵינֵי אָחִי בִנְיָמִין כִּי־פִי הַמְדַבֵּר
יג אֲלֵיכֶם: וְהִגַּדְתֶּם לְאָבִי אֶת־כָּל־כְּבוֹדִי בְּמִצְרַיִם וְאֵת
יד כָּל־אֲשֶׁר רְאִיתֶם וּמִהַרְתֶּם וְהוֹרַדְתֶּם אֶת־אָבִי הֵנָּה: וַיִּפֹּל
עַל־צַוְּארֵי בִנְיָמִן־אָחִיו וַיֵּבְךְּ וּבִנְיָמִן בָּכָה עַל־צַוָּארָיו:
טו וַיְנַשֵּׁק לְכָל־אֶחָיו וַיֵּבְךְּ עֲלֵהֶם וְאַחֲרֵי כֵן דִּבְּרוּ אֶחָיו אִתּוֹ:

of his brothers, Joseph wishes to explain to them right away (verse 8) that a result of such great importance could not just be purely accidental. It must necessarily have been God Himself Who directed the free will of the sons of Jacob so that, without knowing it, they were made to act out a great deed in accord with the plan of His Divine Providence.

10. וְיָשַׁבְתָּ בְאֶרֶץ־גֹּשֶׁן — *You will reside in the land of Goshen.* Joseph knew that his father would not consent to reside in the Egyptian capital, a center of pagan idolatry (*Ramban*). Without hesitation he was able to assign him this province, situated in lower Egypt, for he knew that his choice would be ratified by Pharaoh. This was so since one of Pharaoh's predecessors had given it to Sarah as a gift in perpetuity after he had abducted her and then restored her to Abraham (*Pirkei D'Rabbi Eliezer* 26). Hence this region was rightfully returned to Sarah's descendants and Pharaoh, eager to keep Joseph in his service, and fearing his possible return with his family to Canaan, hastened to reconfirm their rights over this district (*Yalkut Reuveni*, end of 47). It indeed remained under Semitic influence, as is apparent from the names of the cities where the Jews stopped on their way to the Red Sea: Succoth, Etham, Pi Hahiroth, Migdol, Baal Zefon (all are of Semitic origin). But the identification of Goshen with the territory given to the tribe of Judah, as *Radak* holds in *Joshua* 11:16, is contested by R' David Luria in his commentary to *Pirkei D'Rabbi Eliezer* ibid. (cf. our commentary on 46:28).

12. וְהִנֵּה עֵינֵיכֶם רֹאוֹת — *Behold! Your eyes see.* For *Rashi*, the circumcision which the brothers could see with their own eyes and the Holy Tongue coming from Joseph's lips constituted the two proofs "that he was their brother." The second argument is hardly convincing, *Ramban* holds, since many Egyptians, and particularly the leading dignitaries, knew this language. But the fact which was to convince Jacob was that the viceroy, whom the brothers had seen with their own eyes in the midst of his glory and power, had himself ordered Jacob to be brought to him and fed along with the rest of his family to spare them from distress. As for the proof that Joseph spoke לְשׁוֹן הַקֹּדֶשׁ, the *Holy Tongue,* it is meant, says *R' Chaim ben Attar* among others, in the sense that the brothers had not recognized Joseph's voice when he spoke Egyptian, but they recognized it when he spoke his mother tongue.

¹⁰ You will reside in the land of Goshen and you will be near to me — you, your sons, your grandchildren, your flock and your cattle, and all that is yours. ¹¹ And I will provide for you there — for there will be five more years of famine — so you do not become destitute, you, your household, and all that is yours.' '

¹² "Behold! Your eyes see as do the eyes of my brother Benjamin that it is my mouth that is speaking to you. ¹³ Therefore, tell my father of all my glory in Egypt and all that you saw; but you must hurry, and bring my father down here."

¹⁴ Then he fell upon his brother Benjamin's neck and wept; and Benjamin wept upon his neck. ¹⁵ He then kissed all his brothers and wept upon them; afterwards his brothers conversed with him.

14. וַיִּפֹּל עַל־צַוְּארֵי בִנְיָמִן־אָחִיו — *Then he fell upon his brother Benjamin's neck.* The word צַוְּארֵי, says *Rashi*, is written in the plural: Joseph cried over the "two necks," symbolizing the two Temples which would be located in Benjamin's territory and would suffer destruction. As for Benjamin, he cried on Joseph's neck, for the Tabernacle of Shiloh which was destined to be in Joseph's territory and would likewise be destroyed. The *Zohar* adds that Joseph cried afterwards "over his brothers" (verse 15), whose descendants would be sent into exile and scattered among the nations. But they did not cry, for they were not inspired by the prophetic spirit as Joseph was. (On the connection between the neck and the Temple, as alluded to in the *Song of Songs* (4:4) see *R' S. Edels* in חִידּוּשֵׁי אַגָּדוֹת to *Berachos* 30a, ד״ה כמגדל).

Joseph had cried previously when he revealed himself to his brothers, but his tears then were tears of joy. Now, at the end of his heartfelt words, his tears are brought on by sadness and suffering. He had in effect just formally invited his father to go down into Egypt with all his family. This meant the beginning of a national existence in exile. It was impossible for Joseph not to be fully conscious of this, and even though he acted as he did and as he had to, he still clearly foresaw that this Egyptian exile would not be the last in the history of his people. As he embraced his brothers, he had the vision that Providence had many other trials and hardships in store for them. The rejoicings of the Jewish people are such that even while thanking God for His infinite mercy (הוֹדוּ לַה׳ כִּי טוֹב), they tremble at the thought of what the future holds in store — and thereupon beseech God's help, אָנָּה ה׳ הוֹשִׁיעָה נָא.

15. וְאַחֲרֵי כֵן דִּבְּרוּ אֶחָיו אִתּוֹ — *Afterwards his brothers conversed with him.* *Rashi*: "When they saw that he cried and that his heart was sincerely with them, his brother spoke to him. For at first they were filled with shame before him." The *Midrash HaGadol* gives other details: "When Joseph saw the shame of his brothers he tried to calm them, saying: 'It is not you who have sent me here but God.' However, this argument did not succeed in ridding them of their feeling of shame. So he continued: 'You surely understand that I have no hatred in my heart for Benjamin since he was not there when I was sold; in the same way, in

טז וְהַקֹּל נִשְׁמַע בֵּית פַּרְעֹה לֵאמֹר בָּאוּ אֲחֵי יוֹסֵף וַיִּיטַב בְּעֵינֵי
יז פַרְעֹה וּבְעֵינֵי עֲבָדָיו: וַיֹּאמֶר פַּרְעֹה אֶל-יוֹסֵף אֱמֹר אֶל-
אַחֶיךָ זֹאת עֲשׂוּ טַעֲנוּ אֶת-בְּעִירְכֶם וּלְכוּ-בֹאוּ אַרְצָה כְּנָעַן:
יח וּקְחוּ אֶת-אֲבִיכֶם וְאֶת-בָּתֵּיכֶם וּבֹאוּ אֵלָי וְאֶתְּנָה לָכֶם
רביעי יט אֶת-טוּב אֶרֶץ מִצְרַיִם וְאִכְלוּ אֶת-חֵלֶב הָאָרֶץ: וְאַתָּה
צֻוֵּיתָה זֹאת עֲשׂוּ קְחוּ-לָכֶם מֵאֶרֶץ מִצְרַיִם עֲגָלוֹת לְטַפְּכֶם
כ וְלִנְשֵׁיכֶם וּנְשָׂאתֶם אֶת-אֲבִיכֶם וּבָאתֶם: וְעֵינְכֶם אַל-תָּחֹס
כא עַל-כְּלֵיכֶם כִּי-טוּב כָּל-אֶרֶץ מִצְרַיִם לָכֶם הוּא: וַיַּעֲשׂוּ-
כֵן בְּנֵי יִשְׂרָאֵל וַיִּתֵּן לָהֶם יוֹסֵף עֲגָלוֹת עַל-פִּי פַרְעֹה
כב וַיִּתֵּן לָהֶם צֵדָה לַדָּרֶךְ: לְכֻלָּם נָתַן לָאִישׁ חֲלִפוֹת שְׂמָלֹת
וּלְבִנְיָמִן נָתַן שְׁלֹשׁ מֵאוֹת כֶּסֶף וְחָמֵשׁ חֲלִפֹת שְׂמָלֹת:

my heart there is no hatred for you.' But this new argument did not convince them either. Then Joseph said to them: 'How could you, my brothers, think that it would be in my power to do you harm? If ten flames were not able to extinguish just one flame, how can one flame extinguish ten?' This argument convinced them and after these words and tearful embraces they were finally able to speak freely with him" (cf. *Rashi* to 50:21). To be sure, the brothers, who the Torah had previously told us could not speak peaceably to Joseph at the time of his dreams, were incapable of any hypocrisy. Their character did not permit them to say anything which was in contradiction with their feelings (*Rashi* on 37:4).

16. בָּאוּ אֲחֵי יוֹסֵף — *Joseph's brothers have come.* Pharaoh and his ministers rejoiced at this because it had been humiliating for them to have at the head of their government a foreign slave who had been in prison. Now they had proof that Joseph came from a very honorable family, and that he had been abducted from the land of the Hebrews just as he had constantly claimed (45:15; *Ramban*).

18. וְאֶתְּנָה לָכֶם אֶת-טוּב אֶרֶץ מִצְרַיִם — *I will give you the best of the land of Egypt.* *Rashi* explains: "The land of Goshen. He was prophesying without knowing what he was prophesying. For they would make the land like depths where there are no fish." This explanation refers to the interpretation of *Exodus* 12:36, as given by R' Shimon ben Lakish in the Talmud (*Berachos* 9b). It points out that the Jews ultimately consumed "the substance of the land" (lit. חֵלֶב, *the fat*, which always designates the best part) in a double sense. They emptied the country of its riches and made it like "depths (in the sea) where there are no fish" for they took with them the gold and silver vessels of the Egyptians, as well as the treasuries of money which had been brought to Egypt to purchase corn during the famine. Joseph had collected and hidden them in secret caches which the Jews discovered as they left Egypt (*Pesachim* 119a). But they also emptied the land in a figurative sense, for they took with them all the valuable elements

¹⁶ *The news was heard in Pharaoh's palace saying, "Joseph's brothers have come!" And it was pleasing in the eyes of Pharaoh and in the eyes of his servants.* ¹⁷ *Pharaoh said to Joseph, "Say to your brothers, 'Do this: Load up your animals and go directly to the land of Canaan.* ¹⁸ *Bring your father and your households and come to me. I will give you the best of the land of Egypt and you will eat the fat of the land.'* ¹⁹ *And you are commanded [to say], 'Do this: Take for yourselves from the land of Egypt wagons for your small children and for your wives; transport your father and come.* ²⁰ *And let your eyes not take pity on your belongings, for the best of all the land of Egypt — it is yours.'"*

²¹ *The sons of Israel did so, and Joseph gave them wagons by Pharaoh's word, and he gave them provisions for the journey.* ²² *To each of them he gave changes of clothing; but to Benjamin he gave three hundred pieces of silver and five changes of clothing.*

of the Egyptian population — those who believed in God and who joined the Jewish people as proselytes. Thus they liberated all "the sacred sparks which were smoldering under the embers." (Cf. our commentary on 46:3 and *Exodus* 11:2.)

19. וְאַתָּה צֻוֵּיתָה זֹאת עֲשׂוּ — *And you are commanded [to say], 'Do this.'* "Tell them that it is with my authority" (*Rashi*). Exporting grain in vehicles had been forbidden since the famine, and permission to export by this means required Pharaoh's formal authorization (*Rashbam*). Hence the wagons sent by Joseph at Pharaoh's command were seen by Jacob as concrete proof of Pharaoh's benevolence and Joseph's power. The wagons would serve both for transporting the grain and for helping to resettle the patriarchal family, and it was when Jacob saw them that *Jacob's spirit* (Divine Inspiration) *revived* (verse 27). However, the initiative of sending the wagons came not from Pharaoh but from Joseph, as is apparent from verse 27. The reasons which prompted him to do this will be explained later. The fact that the word צֻוֵּיתָה in this verse ends with a ה (contrary to normal practice) is taken by the *Zohar* as an indication that the phrase could be interpreted: "What you have ordered, they should do."

20. וְעֵינְכֶם אַל־תָּחֹס עַל־כְּלֵיכֶם — *And let your eyes not take pity on your belongings.* Do not be concerned about them. Cf. our commentary on 32:25.

22. וּלְבִנְיָמִן נָתַן . . . וְחָמֵשׁ חֲלִפֹת שְׂמָלֹת — *But to Benjamin he gave . . . five changes of clothing.* How can it be, ask the Sages of the Talmud, that Joseph repeated the same tragic error which his father had made? He seems to favor one of his brothers and gives him five changes of clothes, thereby provoking the jealousy of the other brothers. The five garments, it is answered, were only an allusion from Joseph to Benjamin regarding his descendant Mordechai who would one day go out of the royal palace attired in five kingly garments (*Esther* 8:15;

כג וּלְאָבִ֞יו שָׁלַ֤ח כְּזֹאת֙ עֲשָׂרָ֣ה חֲמֹרִ֔ים נֹשְׂאִ֖ים מִטּ֣וּב מִצְרָ֑יִם
כד וְעֶ֣שֶׂר אֲתֹנֹ֡ת נֹֽשְׂאֹת֩ בָּ֨ר וָלֶ֧חֶם וּמָז֛וֹן לְאָבִ֖יו לַדָּֽרֶךְ: וַיְשַׁלַּ֤ח
כה אֶת־אֶחָיו֙ וַיֵּלֵ֔כוּ וַיֹּ֣אמֶר אֲלֵהֶ֔ם אַֽל־תִּרְגְּז֖וּ בַּדָּֽרֶךְ: וַֽיַּעֲל֖וּ
כו מִמִּצְרָ֑יִם וַיָּבֹ֙אוּ֙ אֶ֣רֶץ כְּנַ֔עַן אֶֽל־יַעֲקֹ֖ב אֲבִיהֶֽם: וַיַּגִּ֨דוּ ל֜וֹ לֵאמֹ֗ר
ע֚וֹד יוֹסֵ֣ף חַ֔י וְכִֽי־ה֥וּא מֹשֵׁ֖ל בְּכָל־אֶ֣רֶץ מִצְרָ֑יִם וַיָּ֣פָג לִבּ֔וֹ
כז כִּ֥י לֹֽא־הֶאֱמִ֖ין לָהֶֽם: וַיְדַבְּר֣וּ אֵלָ֗יו אֵ֣ת כָּל־דִּבְרֵ֤י יוֹסֵף֙ אֲשֶׁ֣ר

Megillah 16b). In reality, adds *R' Shmuel Edels*, the question is hardly valid, since Joseph had a perfect right to feel a special affection for Benjamin, his only brother from his mother. So these presents would not have caused any jealousy. As for the choice of the number five, some *Midrashim* explain it in the way *Rashi* quoted on 43:34: "Benjamin's own portion, like that of the others, and in addition the portions offered by Joseph, Osnath, Manasseh and Ephraim" (מדר׳ חפץ). The *Midrash Sechel Tov* notes that five was Joseph's favorite number: *Let the country be divided into five parts* (41:34); *You will give a fifth to Pharaoh* (47:24). *R' Bachya* (on 46:4) explains at length Joseph's preference for the number five and relates it to the letter ה (with a numerical value of five), the sign of the Divine name (cf. our commentary to 41:39).

24. אַל־תִּרְגְּזוּ בַּדָּרֶךְ — *Do not become agitated on the way.* According to *Rashi* the literal meaning is that, "as they were filled with shame, Joseph feared lest on the way back they would quarrel about having sold him and be led to say to one another: 'It is because of you that he was sold: you spoke evil about him and made us despise him.' " But this explanation would require the expression אַל־תְּרִיבוּ, *do not quarrel.* Accordingly, *Rashi* cites as well the midrashic interpretation given by *R' Elazar* (*Taanis* 10b). It teaches that Joseph advised his brothers not to become involved in any *halachic* discussions (which can lead to heated arguments, that is to say, becoming excited, *Maharsha*) so as not to lose their way. True, remarks the Talmud, it is recommended that students of the Torah exchange words of the Law when they travel together, but this refers only to conversation, not to thorough study. However, the expression אַל־תִּרְגְּזוּ can also be interpreted in the sense of: "Do not hurry" (ibid.), which justifies the "other explanation" mentioned by *Rashi*: "Do not take large strides, and enter the town with the sun." This special recommendation seems all the more pertinent since previously Joseph had urged his brothers to hurry when they were going back to bring their father.

25. וַיַּעֲלוּ מִמִּצְרָיִם — *They went up from Egypt.* "The holy Land stands higher than all the other lands" (*Rashi* on verse 9, following *Kiddushin* 69a). This is to be taken in a figurative sense, explains *Maharal* (באר הגולה, ו). It refers to the statement that the Holy Land is situated at the center of the world (*Kiddushin* ibid.). Each point on the circumference of a spherical body is more elevated than all the other points situated on its various sectors. But here it is not a question of the geographical center. It is a matter of the ideal center which constitutes the

²³ *And to his father he sent the following: ten he-donkeys laden with the best of Egypt and ten she-donkeys laden with grain, bread, and food for his father for the journey.* ²⁴ *And he sent off his brothers, and they went. He said to them, "Do not become agitated on the way."*

²⁵ *They went up from Egypt and came to the land of Canaan to Jacob their father.* ²⁶ *And they told him, saying, "Joseph is still alive," also that he is ruler over all the land of Egypt; but his heart rejected it, for he could not believe them.* ²⁷ *However, when they related to him all the words that Joseph*

point of connection between opposite extremes such as the spiritual and the material. The Holy Land is the land destined to achieve this harmonious union and to make it shine forth on the world. In this moral sense it represents the central region of the planet, and its highest point.

26. וַיַּגִּדוּ לוֹ — *And they told him.* The word וַיַּגִּדוּ is written defectively (without the letter *yud*); this indicates that they did not tell him themselves but they had the wonderful news announced by someone else: לֵאמֹר, *saying.* They were afraid that suddenly announcing so extraordinary a surprise would affect the health of the old man. "Now, as they were nearing their destination, they saw Serah, the daughter of Asher. Full of wit and charm, she played the harp to perfection. They summoned her and asked her to go and play for their father Jacob and to sing the words that they would tell her. So she went and sat before Jacob and sang the following words to a beautiful melody accompanied by the rhythms of her harp: עוֹד יוֹסֵף חַי, 'Joseph, my uncle, is still alive. He rules the whole of Egypt, for he did not die.' As she repeated this refrain over and over again, Jacob began to listen to it and became deeply moved. He felt an intense joy and little by little his spirits began to revive. Since being separated from Joseph he had lived in sadness and prophetic inspiration had departed from him. But with Serah's touching words, his heart overflowed with immense happiness and he asked her to sing her song again. 'For your reward,' he told her, 'I pray that death never have dominion over you, for you have restored me to life.' And this wish came true. Serah never knew death; she entered alive into Paradise. While he was speaking with her, the brothers entered the room. They stood before him in their splendor and exclaimed: 'There is wonderful news! Our brother Joseph is still alive, he is governor over the land of Egypt, and he sends you a message of joy!' But the surprise was so unexpected that Jacob still could not believe it" (*Sefer HaYashar*).

וַיָּפָג לִבּוֹ כִּי לֹא־הֶאֱמִין לָהֶם — *But his heart rejected it, for he could not believe them.* According to *Ramban* and *Ibn Ezra*, וַיָּפָג לִבּוֹ means: his heart stopped (beating). However, *R' Yitzchak Arama* and *Abarbanel* support *Rashi's* explanation.

27. וַיְדַבְּרוּ אֵלָיו אֵת כָּל־דִּבְרֵי יוֹסֵף אֲשֶׁר דִּבֶּר אֲלֵהֶם — *However, when they related to him all the words that Joseph had spoken to them.* The message from Joseph

דִּבֶּר אֲלֵהֶם וַיַּרְא אֶת־הָעֲגָלוֹת אֲשֶׁר־שָׁלַח יוֹסֵף לָשֵׂאת אֹתוֹ
כח וַתְּחִי רוּחַ יַעֲקֹב אֲבִיהֶם: וַיֹּאמֶר יִשְׂרָאֵל רַב עוֹד־יוֹסֵף בְּנִי
א חָי אֵלְכָה וְאֶרְאֶנּוּ בְּטֶרֶם אָמוּת: וַיִּסַּע יִשְׂרָאֵל וְכָל־אֲשֶׁר־
לוֹ וַיָּבֹא בְּאֵרָה שָּׁבַע וַיִּזְבַּח זְבָחִים לֵאלֹהֵי אָבִיו יִצְחָק:

(margin: חמישי / מו)

which the brothers were to bring to their father made no reference to his sale as
a slave (verses 9-13). Accordingly, *Ramban* holds that all his life Jacob remained
unaware of the fact that this sale was the work of his sons. He thought that
Joseph had lost his way in the countryside and had been sold by strangers. But
his sons kept their crime secret, afraid that if it was revealed Jacob would have
grounds to curse them and the whole family would split up. As for Joseph, he
also kept silent to spare his brothers shame and the anger of their father.
Ramban finds support for his view in certain passages in the text. But *Rashi*,
quoting the Talmud and the Midrash, seems to hold that Jacob was aware of the
whole truth. (Cf. 49:9 and 50:16; he never asked Joseph to forgive the sin of his
brothers, believing Joseph incapable of bearing a grudge toward them for so
long, but he was aware of the sin involved in Joseph's sale.)

וַיַּרְא אֶת־הָעֲגָלוֹת אֲשֶׁר־שָׁלַח יוֹסֵף — *And he saw the wagons that Joseph had sent.*
By emphasizing that the wagons had been sent by Joseph, not by Pharaoh, the
Torah wants to point out that they constituted "a sign" from Joseph to his
father. This sign involved the Biblical passage about the עֶגְלָה, *heifer* (a
heteronym of עֲגָלָה, *wagon*) which he was in the process of studying with his
father when they were separated. The midrashic account referring to this verse
exists in several variations. It is quoted as follows by the *Zohar*, in the name of
R' Elazar: The heifer is offered in atonement for a murder when the murderer
is not known. This sacrifice is to be brought by the elders of the city nearest to
the body; they declare that their hands did not shed this blood, and they were
not guilty of letting the victim leave their town unaccompanied and without
provisions (*Deuteronomy* 21:1-9). Now, Jacob had sent his son to meet his
brothers who, he knew, hated him: yet he had let him depart alone and without
food. So he felt personally guilty for the disappearance of his son, and he had
cried out: *I will go down to the grave (guilty toward) mourning for my son*
(37:35). When Joseph sensed his father's deep remorse, he sent him the wagons
as an allusion to the sacrifice of the heifer, as though to calm him and let him
know that he too could openly declare: "Our hands have not shed this blood
neither have our eyes seen it spilled." Jacob then understood that in Joseph's eyes
he was perfectly innocent, "and his spirit revived."

וַתְּחִי רוּחַ יַעֲקֹב — *Then the spirit of . . . Jacob was revived.* "The Divine Presence
which had withdrawn from him came again to hover over him" (*Rashi*). In his
Guide to the Perplexed (2:36), *Rambam* notes that some Biblical personages
gifted with prophetic spirit were temporarily deprived of prophecy as a result
of an external event. For prophecy depends on the faculty of imagination which,

*had spoken to them, and he saw the wagons that Joseph had sent
to transport him, then the spirit of their father Jacob was revived.*
*²⁸ And Israel said, "How great! My son Joseph still lives! I shall
go and see him before I die."*

46 *¹So Israel set out with all that he had and he came to Beer-sheba
where he slaughtered sacrifices to the God of his father Isaac.*

like every faculty of a corporeal nature, sometimes becomes blunted, weakens,
and deteriorates, and sometimes becomes strengthened. "This is why you find
that in times of sadness or anger and other similar feelings, prophets cease to
prophesy. You know that the Sages say prophecy comes neither during sadness
nor gloom (*Shabbos* 30b). Accordingly, our patriarch Jacob did not receive any
revelation while he was in mourning, for his imaginative faculty was occupied
with the loss of Joseph. Similarly, Moses ceased having any revelation from
the time of the evil report of the spies until the entire generation of the
desert had perished (*Taanis* 30b) because he was overwhelmed by the enormity
of their sin."

28. וַיֹּאמֶר יִשְׂרָאֵל — *And Israel said.* As soon as the Divine Presence returned to
rest upon him, Jacob reappeared in his name Israel, his title of nobility, grandeur,
and power. Cf. our commentary on 42:5.

רַב — *How great.* "Much joy and satisfaction still await me for my son Joseph
is alive." So *Rashi*, interprets the word עוֹד, *much*, but *Rashbam* explains: "It is
enough! What care I for all his glory? He is alive — that is all I want." *Targum
Yonasan* translates Jacob's thought in this way: "Many are the blessings which
God has bestowed upon me. He saved me from the hands of Esau, from Laban,
and from the Canaanites who were persecuting me. I have had many joys and
I hope to experience still others. But I had given up hope of ever setting eyes on
Joseph again. Now I want to go and see him before I die."

46.

1. יִשְׂרָאֵל . . . וַיָּבֹא בְּאֵרָה שָּׁבַע — *Israel . . . and he came to Beer-sheba.* Filled with
a joy unlike any other he had known, Israel takes all his family and goes to meet
Joseph, his beloved son. He journeys southward and stops near the border, at
Beer-sheba, the town made famous by the story of his ancestors. Previously,
when Jacob had left his father's house to go to his uncle Laban's at Padan Aram,
he had first stopped off at Beer-sheba. For he thought: "My father and mother
have told me to go to Aram, beyond the Promised Land. First I will go to
Beer-sheba where my father heard God refuse him permission to leave the Holy
Land, so that I can learn whether God now approves of my departure." And so,
Jacob went to Beer-sheba to meditate before heading for a foreign land to settle
with his family and begin a new life (cf. our commentary on 28:10). Here again
we see Jacob head for this town before continuing his journey. Once more he
goes there to seek Divine Inspiration and to learn whether God, Who had

ב וַיֹּאמֶר אֱלֹהִים ׀ לְיִשְׂרָאֵל ׀ בְּמַרְאֹת הַלַּיְלָה וַיֹּאמֶר יַעֲקֹב ׀

forbidden his father to emigrate from the Holy Land, approves of his departure. The desire to receive the Divine blessing before undertaking the descent into Egypt is all the more understandable since Jacob and his sons still felt very apprehensive at the prospect of having to leave the Promised Land, the land of their birth, and go to another country where new hardships might await them. This feeling of anxiety had already caused the brothers to hesitate when they first went down to Egypt, as was mentioned in our commentary on 42:1.

But Jacob had yet another entirely different reason for going first to Beer-sheba. "He went to cut the trees which Abraham had planted there" (as reported in *Genesis* 21:33 — *Rabbah* 94). He had these trees brought down to Egypt, as *Rashi* mentions regarding the construction of the Tabernacle: "From where did the Jews have acacia-wood in the desert? With his prophetic spirit, the patriarch Jacob had foreseen that the Jews would one day have to build the Tabernacle in the desert. So he had trees brought to Egypt. He had them replanted there and ordered his children to bring them along when they went out of Egypt" (*Exodus* 25:5). Even before entering the country that was to be the future land of exile for his descendants, Jacob (just like his grandfather Abraham before him) prepared for the building of the Sanctuary, which would later constitute the moral bulwark of the people against assimilation and decadence. It would be the central point from which the ideal of holiness would shine forth. And at the same time it would ensure that the people would be protected and that the Divine Presence would dwell in their midst.

וַיִּזְבַּח זְבָחִים — *Where he slaughtered sacrifices.* The word זְבָחִים refers to sacrifices of שְׁלָמִים [*shelamim*], *remuneratory offerings*, as is apparent from *Exodus* 24:5. This translation follows the *Rashbam* who defines the sacrifices in the category of שְׁלָמִים as "payment (from שִׁלֵּם, *to pay*) of moral debts of gratitude (תּוֹדָה) or of voluntary commitments (נֶדֶר וּנְדָבָה)." Up to that time the sacrifices offered by Noah, Abraham and Isaac were עוֹלָה, *burnt-offerings*, the only type of sacrifice known to the Noachians (*Zevachim* 116a). But now, as thankfulness fills Jacob's heart and he prepares to go to his long-lost son, he offers, for the first time, the sacrifice of שְׁלָמִים, meant as an expression of gratitude for the kindnesses of Providence (*Leviticus* 7:12).

Rashi, though quotes the midrashic interpretation (ת"כ, ט"ז, א) to the effect that sacrifices of שְׁלָמִים establish peace in the world (שָׁלוֹם). Developing this explanation, *Ramban* (and also *Recanati* and R' *Bachya*) holds the following: Afraid that his descent into Egypt would have grave consequences for all his descendants (as was shown above), Jacob wanted to pave the way for peace and conciliation as he set out on this new road into the future. So he offered his sacrifice of peace to the God of his father Isaac (rather than of Abraham) for it was his father whom God had warned not to go down into Eygpt. Recalling this solemn warning but compelled by circumstances to go to settle there, Jacob

² *God spoke to Israel in night visions and He said, "Jacob,*

offers his sacrifice at the very threshold of the land of Egypt and he prays for a "twofold peace," שְׁלָמִים: the peace he would like to witness within his family, and the external peace with his potential enemies.

R' S. R. Hirsch makes reference to another characteristic of the שְׁלָמִים sacrifices. In contrast to burnt-offerings, they are consumed for the most part by those who offered them. They are called שְׁלָמִים because "they bring peace to the altar, the priests, and the owners — to all who participate" (*Rashi* on *Leviticus* 3:1). To be sure, the descendants of Noah also had some idea of עוֹלָה, of the burnt-offering which symbolizes giving oneself up completelyto God in a mystical union. But the idea of שְׁלָמִים which reunites all the family around the table to partake in a meal sanctified by God, in an atmosphere of serene joy and profound gratitude — this idea of the sanctification of the family home in everyday life remains something specifically Jewish. The reason, then, that Jacob offered sacrifices of this kind lay in the fact that now, for the first time, he felt happy and joyful in his family circle. He offered them in the name of the God of his father Isaac, for he was fully aware that he owed his happiness not to his own merits but to זְכוּת אָבוֹת, the merits of his ancestors. (On the use of the Divine name אֱלֹהִים in this verse, cf. our commentary on 31:13.)

לֵאלֹהֵי אָבִיו יִצְחָק — *To the God of his father Isaac. Rashi:* "A man owes more honor to his father than to his grandfather. That is why he refers to Isaac and not to Abraham." But for *Ramban* this is not convincing and he gives the reason quoted above, which, in turn, is questioned by *Abarbanel*. But R' Yehoshua ben Levi offers another reason which seems to go back to the one cited by *Rashi* (it too being quoted from the Midrash): "When one meets a teacher and his disciple on the way, one first greets the disciple (who walks before to herald his teacher)." Thus Jacob greeted his father, Abraham's disciple, first (*Rabbah* 94).

2. בְּמַרְאֹת הַלַּיְלָה — *In night visions.* In *Rambam's* analysis of the eleven levels of prophecy (*Guide* 2:45), the prophetic dream in which it seems to someone that God speaks to him constitutes the seventh degree. Moreover, *Rambam* affirms that all prophecy, all revelation (excluding that of Moses) comes only in a dream or a vision, and only through the intermediary of an angel. Hence the word אֱלֹהִים employed here metaphorically designates the angels (just as it sometimes indicates judges or rulers). Cf. *Guide*, ibid. 41 and 6, and our commentary on 31:11.

Here, however, the Torah is speaking of visions of the night, rather than just of dreams, as is so often the case. And hence, notes *Ramban*, it brings out the importance of the night period, the time of דִּין רָפֶה, of clemency in judgment. On a temporal plane, Jacob's entire life corresponds to the period of night, as we have seen in our commentary on 28:11. His life, which was nothing but a long series of painful ordeals, is covered by the shadows of night. But even as the night already looks toward the morning, bringing with it the certainty that there exists a God of mercy Who faithfully watches over those who sleep, so too

ג יַעֲקֹב וַיֹּאמֶר הִנֵּנִי: וַיֹּאמֶר אָנֹכִי הָאֵל אֱלֹהֵי אָבִיךָ אַל־תִּירָא
ד מֵרְדָה מִצְרַיְמָה כִּי־לְגוֹי גָּדוֹל אֲשִׂימְךָ שָׁם: אָנֹכִי אֵרֵד עִמְּךָ
מִצְרַיְמָה וְאָנֹכִי אַעַלְךָ גַם־עָלֹה וְיוֹסֵף יָשִׁית יָדוֹ עַל־עֵינֶיךָ:

there filtered into Jacob's life a ray of hope leading from darkness to light. In the same way also, God reveals Himself to Jacob in the visions of the night, precisely when the "night of the exile" is about to commence. He solemnly announces then that the night now beginning will be followed by the dawn of freedom. For if God goes down with him into Egypt, He will also go up out of Egypt with him. (The night appears as the time when judgment is tempered with mercy, which is why at the beginning of the evening prayer we appeal to the attribute of mercy — וְהוּא רַחוּם.) And just as Abraham's destiny was bound up with the morning, and Isaac's with dusk (commentary on 24:11), so is Jacob's destiny linked to the night hours — the vision of the celestial ladder on the night of his departure for Haran; the night he was misled by Leah; the night he fought the angel of Esau; the night God commanded him to go down to Egypt.

יַעֲקֹב יַעֲקֹב — *Jacob, Jacob.* A forceful appeal, full of warmth and yet stern at the same time, which presaged new tasks to carry out. These tasks might not involve playing a glorious role since the patriarch is called by his name Jacob and not Israel, the title of nobility which God Himself had given him. But Jacob replies without hesitation: Here I am, ready to accept whatever task God will ask of me (cf. our commentary to 22:11.) When God called to Abraham, Jacob, and Samuel, repeating their names, the names are separated by a vertical line called a פְּסִיק. This, notes the *Zohar,* teaches that during their lives these people underwent a spiritual change and their degree of perfection increased greatly as they grew older. Only with Moses does this disjunctive vertical stroke not appear when God twice called out his name — as he stood before the burning bush (*Exodus* 3:4). Moses was already perfect from the time he came into the world (ibid. 2:2).

3. אָנֹכִי הָאֵל אֱלֹהֵי אָבִיךָ — *I am the God — God of your father.* Cf. our commentary to אָנֹכִי 28:16.

אַל־תִּירָא — *Have no fear.* These encouraging words were spoken on different occasions to each of the three patriarchs: to Abraham after the war with the four kings (15:1); to Isaac during the quarrels with the Philistines and the shortage of water (26:24), and to Jacob on his departure for the land of exile. These three promises of Divine protection, referring to different ordeals in life, make us conscious of the fact that Providence manifests Itself at all time and in all circumstances. They lead us to a trust in God which banishes fear and despair.

מֵרְדָה מִצְרַיְמָה — *Of descending to Egypt.* "Why are you afraid?" God asked him. He replied: "I fear that my family will succumb there, that the Divine Presence will no longer dwell among us, that I will not be buried with my ancestors, and that I will not see the redemption of my children." God reassured him on each of these accounts: "I shall make you into a great nation there; I shall go down

Jacob."

And he said, "Here I am."

³ And He said, "I am the God — God of your father. Have no fear of descending to Egypt, for I shall establish you as a great nation there. ⁴ I shall descend with you to Egypt, and I shall also surely bring you up; and Joseph shall place his hand on your eyes."

with you to Egypt and I shall also bring you up from there, and Joseph will place his hand over your eyes" (*Zohar*).

כִּי־לְגוֹי גָּדוֹל אֲשִׂימְךָ שָׁם — *I shall establish you as a great nation there.* Referring to the teaching of R' Shimon bar Yochai, *R' Chaim ben Attar* develops here (and elsewhere) his conception of the exile. Undoubtedly Jacob thought of returning to the Holy Land as soon as the famine was over. But God gave him to understand that according to the providential plan "a great nation" issuing from his children would be founded, not in the Holy Land, but right there in the land of exile. The mission of the chosen people is to reunite the sparks of light which lie smoldering under the ashes of a fallen humanity and, with this sparkling convergence of light, to re-establish the Divine radiance which had inundated the world with holiness at the beginning of the creation. Ever since the first sin, when the ideal of good which sovereignly dominated the forces of evil faded, confusion between "good and evil" set in, producing within society an inextricable jumble of moral ideas. Jewry's mission as it wanders among the nations of the world is to reassemble all the elements of good which have scattered throughout humanity since the fall resulting from the first sin. It is Jewry's task to free them from the thick shell (קְלִיפָּה) covering them and then to recast and reconstitute them into "a great nation." Now, the positive elements are always proportional to the number of negative elements, and hence it follows that the more a particular zone contains factors of טוּמְאָה, *impurity*, the more it includes, in return factors of קְדוּשָׁה, *holiness.* Accordingly, in early history the land of Egypt offered the greatest possibility for the people of God to raise themselves to the level of holiness. It was there that the spirit of impurity from debauchery, perversion and immorality had occupied all the "49 gates of impurity." And hence it was there in the "iron furnace" of discipline, self-denial and austerity that Jewry — inspired by faith in God and by His moral laws, and purified by the moral and physical suffering of slavery — could progressively conquer the 49 gates of holiness. Only in Egypt could Jewry really become "a great nation." As our verse states, *for I shall establish you as a great nation there.* Moses himself testified to this when he exclaimed about Jewry, כִּי מִי גוֹי גָּדוֹל, *For which is a great nation, etc.* (*Deuteronomy* 4:7). Such were the considerations concerning the providential plan which God indicated to Jacob, who had hoped to go down to Egypt only for a short while, לָגוּר שָׁם, as he himself would tell Pharaoh (47:4).

4. אָנֹכִי אֵרֵד עִמְּךָ מִצְרַיְמָה — *I shall descend with you to Egypt. Rambam* (*Guide,* 1:27) comments on this verse as follows: "*Onkelos* the proselyte, who knew the

ה וַיָּקָם יַעֲקֹב מִבְּאֵר שָׁבַע וַיִּשְׂאוּ בְנֵי־יִשְׂרָאֵל אֶת־יַעֲקֹב
אֲבִיהֶם וְאֶת־טַפָּם וְאֶת־נְשֵׁיהֶם בָּעֲגָלוֹת אֲשֶׁר־שָׁלַח
ו פַּרְעֹה לָשֵׂאת אֹתוֹ: וַיִּקְחוּ אֶת־מִקְנֵיהֶם וְאֶת־רְכוּשָׁם אֲשֶׁר
רָכְשׁוּ בְּאֶרֶץ כְּנַעַן וַיָּבֹאוּ מִצְרָיְמָה יַעֲקֹב וְכָל־זַרְעוֹ אִתּוֹ:
ז בָּנָיו וּבְנֵי בָנָיו אִתּוֹ בְּנֹתָיו וּבְנוֹת בָּנָיו וְכָל־זַרְעוֹ הֵבִיא
ח אִתּוֹ מִצְרָיְמָה: וְאֵלֶּה שְׁמוֹת בְּנֵי־
יִשְׂרָאֵל הַבָּאִים מִצְרַיְמָה יַעֲקֹב וּבָנָיו בְּכֹר יַעֲקֹב רְאוּבֵן:

Hebrew and Syriac languages perfectly, made every effort to avoid anthropo-
morphisms (attributions of human form to God). Whenever the Torah (speaking
of God) employs a term which might imply corporealization, *Onkelos* interprets
it according to its literal sense. Every time he finds such a term indicating one
of the different forms of movement, he takes the movement in the sense of
manifestation or appearance, etc. . . . However, to the words אָנֹכִי אֵרֵד עִמְּךָ מִצְרָיְמָה
he gives a literal translation: אֲנָא אֵחוֹת עִמָּךְ לְמִצְרָיִם, *I shall descend with you to
Egypt* (also our translation of the text) this is very noteworthy and proves the
exceptional talent of this master and the excellence of his manner of interpretation. For through this translation he lets us glimpse one of the main points
of prophecy. At the beginning of this episode, it is said that God spoke to Israel
in night visions, etc. Now, it is clear from the beginning of the discourse that this
took place in visions of the night, and hence *Onkelos* sees no harm in giving a
literal rendering of what had been said in these night visions. And he is right in
doing so, for he is relating something which had been said rather than an actual
happening, as for example when God came down upon Sinai (*Exodus* 19:20)."
    After quoting these views of *Rambam* on *Onkelos'* ideas, *Ramban* goes on to
give a detailed analysis of his principles of translation and he reaches a somewhat
different conclusion. He holds that *Onkelos'* main idea is not to avoid
anthropomorphism but is rather based on Kabbalistic grounds. In particular he
suggests that when *Onkelos* translated the phrase, "I shall go down with you
to Egypt" in a literal sense, he wanted to refer to the Talmudic statement that
the *Shechinah* (Divine Presence) accompanies Jewry in its wanderings among
the nations (*Shabbos* 89b and *Megillah* 29a). This idea emphasizing the Divine
solicitude for Jewry as it wanders miserably among the nations seems of such
supreme importance to him that he refuses to paraphrase the verse. A similar
opinion is expressed by such commentators as *R' Yitzchak Arama, R' Bachya*
and *R' Chaim ben Attar*. The latter adds (and proves with numerous examples)
that the Divine Presence hovering near people who are suffering can vary in its
degree of attachment depending on their numbers and quality, and also on the
time and place.

וְיוֹסֵף יָשִׁית יָדוֹ עַל־עֵינֶיךָ — *And Joseph shall place his hand on your eyes.* The
patriarch is informed that he will remain in Egypt until the day of his death
(*Rabbah*).

⁵ So Jacob arose from Beer-sheba; the sons of Israel transported Jacob their father, as well as their young children and wives, in the wagons which Pharaoh had sent to transport him. ⁶ They took their livestock and their wealth which they had amassed in the land of Canaan and they came to Egypt — Jacob and all his offspring with him. ⁷ His sons and grandsons with him, his daughters and granddaughters and all his offspring he brought with him to Egypt.

⁸ Now these are the names of the children of Israel who were coming to Egypt — Jacob and his children: Jacob's firstborn, Reuben.

5. וַיָּקָם יַעֲקֹב מִבְּאֵר שָׁבַע — So Jacob arose from Beer-sheba. He had gone there to consult the Divine will about his proposed journey. Now, having obtained approval in the night visions he leaves for good with his whole family. What God had said to him in this revelation was really nothing more than indirect encouragement: Do not be afraid to go down to Egypt. This was not an order but, as it came from God, Jacob took this indirect message as a formal command. This is what the Passover Haggadah is referring to when it says: אָנוּס עַל פִּי הַדִּבּוּר, Jacob went down to Egypt constrained by the Divine command (Abarbanel). Maharal explains: If the characteristic of "constraint" is stressed here, as in other similar circumstances, it is because it is impossible to imagine that the exile and the liberation of the Jewish people were the result of chance happenings. They constitute an essential link in the realization of the messianic purposes of history. Accordingly, their occurrence is "constrained and forced" (גבורות ה', נ״ד).

8. וְאֵלֶּה שְׁמוֹת בְּנֵי-יִשְׂרָאֵל — Now these are the names of the children of Israel. From this list we see that all the children of Jacob kept their Jewish names, since only these names are used whenever the children are mentioned in the Torah. By recording these names as the family of Jacob departs from Canaan, and again as they arrive in Egypt, the Torah brings out the importance of keeping names of Jewish origin when facing the danger of assimilation, a danger which threatens those who "came into the land of exile." By keeping their original names, the children of Jacob created for themselves an important moral and spiritual protection which continued to serve them as a means of self-defense until the day of their deliverance. This was one of their principal merits: שֶׁלֹּא שִׁינּוּ אֶת שְׁמָם, they did not change their names, and in this way they kept their Jewish identity (Vayikra Rabbah 32). Apart from this consideration, one can see why this present enumeration is of general interest. Here for the first time we see all the members of a family living in perfect harmony, united in the service of the same sacred ideal, and ready to defend it with complete devotion. Like the branches of a tree which are all nourished from one root, the seventy members of the family draw their strength from the same source, rooted deeply in the faith of the patriarchs. This family formed the nucleus of the future people of God.

ט וּבְנֵי רְאוּבֵן חֲנוֹךְ וּפַלּוּא וְחֶצְרֹן וְכַרְמִי: וּבְנֵי שִׁמְעוֹן יְמוּאֵל

יא וְיָמִין וְאֹהַד וְיָכִין וְצֹחַר וְשָׁאוּל בֶּן־הַכְּנַעֲנִית: וּבְנֵי לֵוִי גֵּרְשׁוֹן

יב קְהָת וּמְרָרִי: וּבְנֵי יְהוּדָה עֵר וְאוֹנָן וְשֵׁלָה וָפֶרֶץ וָזָרַח וַיָּמָת

יג עֵר וְאוֹנָן בְּאֶרֶץ כְּנַעַן וַיִּהְיוּ בְנֵי־פֶרֶץ חֶצְרֹן וְחָמוּל: וּבְנֵי

יד יִשָּׂשכָר תּוֹלָע וּפֻוָּה וְיוֹב וְשִׁמְרֹן: וּבְנֵי זְבֻלוּן סֶרֶד וְאֵלוֹן

טו וְיַחְלְאֵל: אֵלֶּה ׀ בְּנֵי לֵאָה אֲשֶׁר יָלְדָה לְיַעֲקֹב בְּפַדַּן אֲרָם

טז וְאֵת דִּינָה בִתּוֹ כָּל־נֶפֶשׁ בָּנָיו וּבְנוֹתָיו שְׁלֹשִׁים וְשָׁלֹשׁ: וּבְנֵי

יז גָד צִפְיוֹן וְחַגִּי שׁוּנִי וְאֶצְבֹּן עֵרִי וַאֲרוֹדִי וְאַרְאֵלִי: וּבְנֵי אָשֵׁר

יח יִמְנָה וְיִשְׁוָה וְיִשְׁוִי וּבְרִיעָה וְשֶׂרַח אֲחֹתָם וּבְנֵי בְרִיעָה

חֶבֶר וּמַלְכִּיאֵל: אֵלֶּה בְּנֵי זִלְפָּה אֲשֶׁר־נָתַן לָבָן לְלֵאָה בִתּוֹ

So the Torah makes a point of recording for posterity the names of its members. At the same time, by presenting this picture of a family of ancient patriarchal stock, sincerely pious and held in the highest esteem by Egyptian royalty, it shows us that the origins of this people were not from an anonymous tribe of nomads, nor from a clique of revolutionaries, nor from a brotherhood of exalted prophets.

הַבָּאִים מִצְרַיְמָה — *Who were coming to Egypt. Rashi* explains the use of the present tense in this verse as referring to the time when they were just arriving in Egypt, "and it is not surprising that it does not say: "who had arrived in Egypt." However, the same form with the present tense is also employed in the first verse of *Exodus:* "And these are the names of the children of Israel who come (הַבָּאִים) into Egypt." This indicates a more general intention which the Rebbe of Belz explained as follows: the Jews must always look upon themselves as if they have arrived on this very day in the land of their exile, "with Jacob," that is to say, drawing inspiration daily from the spirit of the patriarch. No matter how many years they have already spent among the nations, they should always consider themselves not as native inhabitants rooted in the culture of the land but as new arrivals who remain attached to their country of origin and to their national culture (cf. our commentary to *Exodus* 1:1).

10. וְשָׁאוּל בֶּן־הַכְּנַעֲנִית — *And Shaul, son of the Canaanite woman. Rashi* explains: "the son of Dinah who had cohabited with the Canaanite. When her brothers had killed Shechem, Dinah consented to depart only after Simeon had promised to marry her" (cf. our commentary on 34:26). But the *Targum Yonasan* notes: Shaul is Zimri, who at Shittim behaved like the Canaanites. This refers to the act of debauchery (a common practice among the Canaanites) committed at Shittim by Zimri, the son of Salu (Shaul?) who was the prince of a family in Simeon's tribe, as recorded in *Numbers* 25:14 (cf. *Sanhedrin* 82b). There was, to be sure, an interval of several centuries from Dinah's time to the time of Zimri's act, so that calling the latter the "son of the Canaanite woman" seems somewhat striking.

⁹ *Reuben's sons: Hanoch, Pallu, Hezron, and Carmi.*
¹⁰ *Simeon's sons: Jemuel, Jamin, Ohad, Jachin, Zohar, and Shaul, son of the Canaanite woman.*
¹¹ *Levi's sons: Gershon, Kohath, and Merari.*
¹² *Judah's sons: Er, Onan, Shelah, Perez, and Zerah; but Er and Onan had died in the land of Canaan — and Perez's sons were Hezron and Hamul.*
¹³ *Issachar's sons: Tola, Puvah, Iov, and Shimron.*
¹⁴ *Zebulun's sons: Sered, Elon, and Jahleel.* ¹⁵ *These are the sons of Leah whom she bore to Jacob in Paddan-aram, in addition to Dinah his daughter. All the people — his sons and daughters — numbered thirty-three.*
¹⁶ *Gad's sons: Ziphion, Haggi, Shuni, Ezbon, Eri, Arodi, and Areli.*
¹⁷ *Asher's sons: Imnah, Ishvah, Ishvi, Beriah, and their sister Serah; and Beriah's sons, Heber and Malchiel.* ¹⁸ *These are the sons of Zilpah whom Laban had given to Leah his daughter.*

Hence, it is probable that the Midrash wants to explain the immoral behavior of Zimri, completely immersed in Canaanite depravity, by the fact that the soul of his ancestor Dinah had been soiled by cohabitation with Shechem the Canaanite (cf. *R' Zvi H. Chajes, Student's Guide through the Talmud*, Chapter 20).

12. וַיָּמָת עֵר וְאוֹנָן — *But Er and Onan had died.* Why does the Torah mention this fact here when it is already known from before? It is to bring out that the souls of these two sons were reincarnated in חֶצְרֹן וְחָמוּל after Judah had performed the levirate duty toward their widow Tamar, as was noted in the commentary on 38:8 (*R' Chaim ben Attar*).

13. וּבְנֵי יִשָּׂשכָר — *Issachar's sons.* יוֹב, *Iov*, is given the name יָשׁוּב in *Numbers* 26:24. Cf. our explanation in our commentary to 30:18.

15. כָּל־נֶפֶשׁ ... שְׁלֹשִׁים וְשָׁלֹש — *All the people ... numbered thirty-three. Rashi:* "If you count them carefully, you will find only thirty-two. Jochebed was born between the walls just as they were entering the city, as it is said: *Jochebed ... who was born to Levi in Egypt* (*Numbers* 26:59). The birth was in Egypt — not the conception." But *Radak* and *Ibn Ezra* hold that Jacob himself is included in the thirty-three, as verse 8 seems to show. *Ibn Ezra* takes issue with *Rashi* and points out that his opinion would make Jochebed 130 years old when she gave birth to Moses, a miracle that the Torah would not have passed by without mentioning. *Ramban* refutes this argument for the reasons indicated in our commentary to 17:18 and to *Exodus* 2:2.

18. אֵלֶּה בְּנֵי זִלְפָּה — *These are the sons of Zilpah.* Although the Torah generally lists Leah's children first and then Rachel's and finally the servants', here it follows a different order, going according to numerical importance. Hence Zilpah's children are named before Rachel's.

יט וַתֵּ֤לֶד אֶת־אֵ֙לֶּה֙ לְיַעֲקֹ֔ב שֵׁ֥שׁ עֶשְׂרֵ֖ה נָֽפֶשׁ: בְּנֵ֤י רָחֵל֙ אֵ֣שֶׁת
כ יַעֲקֹ֔ב יוֹסֵ֖ף וּבִנְיָמִֽן: וַיִּוָּלֵ֣ד לְיוֹסֵף֮ בְּאֶ֣רֶץ מִצְרַ֒יִם֒ אֲשֶׁ֨ר
יָֽלְדָה־לּ֜וֹ אָֽסְנַ֗ת בַּת־פּ֤וֹטִי פֶ֙רַע֙ כֹּהֵ֣ן אֹ֔ן אֶת־מְנַשֶּׁ֖ה וְאֶת־
כא אֶפְרָֽיִם: וּבְנֵ֣י בִנְיָמִ֗ן בֶּ֤לַע וָבֶ֙כֶר֙ וְאַשְׁבֵּ֔ל גֵּרָ֥א וְנַעֲמָ֖ן אֵחִ֥י
כב וָרֹֽאשׁ מֻפִּ֥ים וְחֻפִּ֖ים וָאָֽרְדְּ: אֵ֚לֶּה בְּנֵ֣י רָחֵ֔ל אֲשֶׁ֥ר יֻלַּ֖ד לְיַעֲקֹ֑ב
כג־כד כָּל־נֶ֖פֶשׁ אַרְבָּעָ֥ה עָשָֽׂר: וּבְנֵי־דָ֖ן חֻשִֽׁים: וּבְנֵ֣י נַפְתָּלִ֔י יַחְצְאֵ֥ל
כה וְגוּנִ֖י וְיֵ֥צֶר וְשִׁלֵּֽם: אֵ֚לֶּה בְּנֵ֣י בִלְהָ֔ה אֲשֶׁר־נָתַ֥ן לָבָ֖ן לְרָחֵ֣ל
כו בִּתּ֑וֹ וַתֵּ֧לֶד אֶת־אֵ֛לֶּה לְיַעֲקֹ֖ב כָּל־נֶ֥פֶשׁ שִׁבְעָֽה: כָּל־הַ֠נֶּפֶשׁ
הַבָּאָ֨ה לְיַעֲקֹ֤ב מִצְרַ֙יְמָה֙ יֹצְאֵ֣י יְרֵכ֔וֹ מִלְּבַ֖ד נְשֵׁ֣י בְנֵֽי־יַעֲקֹ֑ב
כז כָּל־נֶ֖פֶשׁ שִׁשִּׁ֥ים וָשֵֽׁשׁ: וּבְנֵ֥י יוֹסֵ֛ף אֲשֶׁר־יֻלַּד־ל֥וֹ בְמִצְרַ֖יִם
נֶ֣פֶשׁ שְׁנָ֑יִם כָּל־הַנֶּ֧פֶשׁ לְבֵֽית־יַעֲקֹ֛ב הַבָּ֥אָה מִצְרַ֖יְמָה שִׁבְעִֽים:

20. אָסְנַת בַּת־פּוֹטִי פֶרַע — *Asenath daughter of Poti-phera*. Cf. our commentary on 41:45.

21. וּבְנֵי בִנְיָמִן — *Benjamin's sons*. You find certain variations in the names here compared with the lists of Jacob's descendants in *Numbers* 26 and in *I Chronicles* 4:24. *Radak* notes here that such variations in proper names and place names were common in those times and they are of no special significance (ibid.). The very names of Benjamin's sons are all veiled references to Joseph and his disappearance, as we are told by the Midrash (in several places) and the Talmud (*Sotah* 36b). [From this we learn that Benjamin must have been aware of the sale of his brother, as was pointed out in the commentary on 39:1.]

מֻפִּים — *Muppim*. Muppim is the only one of the ten children of Benjamin whose name is not explained in the Talmudic passage mentioned above. But *Rashi*, quoting the *Midrash Tanchuma*, interprets: "His mouth was like his father's (מופים, *two mouths*), filled with the words of wisdom (which Jacob had learned at the school) of Shem and Eber." (See also *Rashi* on *Numbers* 26:39.)

23. וּבְנֵי־דָן חֻשִׁים — *Dan's sons: Hushim*. The fact that the word *sons* is in the plural while Dan had only one son is explained in various ways. Some hold that it is not unusual on the part of a father to say "children" when speaking of his only child; others suggest that the word חֻשִׁים means productive (or prolific) and implies that the children of Dan were "innumerable" (*Targum Yonasan*). The school of Hezekiah, quoted in the Talmud (*Bava Basra* 143b) translates the word חֻשִׁים as bush, undergrowth, and recalls that in the following generations the tribe of Dan became one of the largest of the twelve tribes. It branched out rapidly and in large numbers from the only son of the ancestor of the tribe, just as the undergrowth develops from a single root.

Knowing of this later proliferation gives us a better grasp of the Midrash (*Rabbah* 94) which teaches: "In the *sefer Torah* of R' Meir it is written (in the singular) — וּבֶן דָן חֻשִׁים." Of our Sages, R' Meir is the one who demands taking

These she bore to Jacob — sixteen people.

¹⁹ *The sons of Rachel, Jacob's wife: Joseph and Benjamin.*

²⁰ *To Joseph were born in the land of Egypt — whom Asenath daughter of Poti-phera Chief of On bore to him — Manasseh and Ephraim.*

²¹ *Benjamin's sons: Bela, Becher, Ashbel, Gera, Naaman, Ehi, Rosh, Muppim, Huppim, and Ard.* ²² *These are the sons of Rachel who were born to Jacob — fourteen persons in all.*

²³ *Dan's sons: Hushim.*

²⁴ *Naphtali's sons: Jahzeel, Guni, Jezer, and Shillem.* ²⁵ *These are the sons of Bilhah whom Laban had given to Rachel his daughter. She bore these to Jacob — seven people in all.*

²⁶ *All the persons coming with Jacob to Egypt — his own descendants, aside from the wives of Jacob's sons — sixty-six persons in all.*

²⁷ *And Joseph's sons who were born to him in Egypt numbered two persons. All the people of Jacob's household who came to Egypt — seventy.*

into consideration the minority as well as the majority (*Chullin* 11b). Accordingly, he makes a point of stressing in his *sefer Torah*, that is to say, in his teaching, the example of the value of the minority as given by the history of the tribe of Dan. Although its ancestor had only one son, it ultimately became the second most numerous tribe (*Numbers*, Chapters 1 and 26).

26. מִלְּבַד נְשֵׁי בְנֵי-יַעֲקֹב — *Aside from the wives of Jacob's sons. Rashi* comments: "As for the opinion that a twin sister was born with each head of the future tribes, we are obliged to say that they died before the descent into Egypt, since they are not counted here." However, *Ramban* recalls the words of R' Yehudah (quoted by *Rashi* on 37:35) who held that each of the sons had married his twin sister (which he does not consider forbidden to the Noachians; cf. our commentary ibid.). The twin sisters would therefore be identical to the wives of Jacob's sons. These the Torah does not count, even though they were among those "that came out of his loins" because "the enumeration was intended to highlight the extraordinarily rapid increase which took place in Egypt, starting from only seventy souls — and in this regard man and wife together form just 'one flesh.' " (Regarding the interpretations of this verse, see the controversy between *Ramban* and R' S. Edels on *Bava Basra* 123b.) Serah, the daughter of Asher, and Dinah, the daughter of Leah, are the only women mentioned here; they were unmarried at the time of the census.)

27. שִׁבְעִים — *Seventy.* Many replies have been given to the problem which our Sages of the Talmud raise: "The complete total is seventy but counting one by one you find only sixty-nine" (*Bava Basra* 123b). In verse 15 we mentioned the views of those who would complete the total number by adding Jochebed, the

כח וְאֶת־יְהוּדָ֞ה שָׁלַ֤ח לְפָנָיו֙ אֶל־יוֹסֵ֔ף לְהוֹרֹ֥ת לְפָנָ֖יו גֹּ֑שְׁנָה וַיָּבֹ֖אוּ
כט אַ֣רְצָה גֹּֽשֶׁן: וַיֶּאְסֹ֤ר יוֹסֵף֙ מֶרְכַּבְתּ֔וֹ וַיַּ֛עַל לִקְרַֽאת־יִשְׂרָאֵ֥ל

שׁשׁי

daughter of Levi who was born just as they were entering Egypt, or by including the patriarch himself. Others propose to make up the number by counting Dinah's daughter, Asenath, or her twin sister, etc. *Rabbeinu Asher*, at the end of *Pesachim* (40), holds that it is a custom for Scripture to round off the number when just one unit is missing. R' Eliezer replies that God Himself joined the sixty-nine members of the family, as it is said: "I shall go down with you to Egypt" (*Pirkei D'Rabbi Eliezer* 39).

The Divine Presence (*Shechinah*) shown to us here as accompanying Israel in its wanderings among the nations (see commentary on verse 4) dwells with men in order to protect them in times of trial, as was also the case with the inhabitants of Sodom. "God wanted to associate Himself with the nine righteous people of the town to complete the required number of ten" (*Rashi* on 18:28). So too, in similar conditions, He associated Himself with the sons of Jacob when Joseph was sold, as was mentioned in the commentary on 37:33. And hence it is to God Who manifested all His solicitude for Jacob that the Psalmist turns when he proclaims: *May HASHEM answer you in the day of distress, may the name of the God of Jacob protect you* (*Psalms* 20:2).

It is significant that the Torah mentions the number seventy here and repeats it in *Exodus* 1:5 and in *Deuteronomy* 10:22, even though the make-up of this total is uncertain and is explained in several ways. It brings to mind the analogous case of 613 for the total number of the *mitzvos* as given by the Midrash on *Deuteronomy* 33:4: the composition of this number also is the object of numerous controversies. In these examples, the number appears to have been established *a priori* — axiomatically. R' Bachya deals with this question and goes back to the ancient sources of the *Sefer HaBahir*. He bases himself on the verse of *Exodus*: *They arrived to Elim, where there were twelve springs of water and seventy date-palms and they encamped there by the water* (15:27). The twelve springs mentioned in this verse are destined to nourish the seventy palm trees. Now, the same relationship exists on the spiritual plane between the twelve Jewish tribes and the seventy nations of the world (cf. *Rashi* on *Numbers* 29:35). This is mirrored in the seventy members of the patriarchal family, the nucleus of the Jewish people. The number seventy thus acquires its full significance, as *Rashi* explains on *Deuteronomy* 32:8.

But these numbers are by no means arbitrary. They have their origin in the natural structure of the universe as it was created and they are found at the foundation of the dimensions of time and space. The number twelve appears in the twelve signs of the zodiac, to which correspond the twelve months of the year, as well as in the twelve divisions of the solar day. And this number also determines the categories of space, since each of the four cardinal points of the compass is subdivided into three main sectors. The division of time into twelve

²⁸ *He sent Judah ahead of him to Joseph, to prepare ahead of him in Goshen; and they arrived in the region of Goshen.*
²⁹ *Joseph harnessed his chariot and went up to meet Israel his*

months of the year and twelve hours of the day also derives from the threefold multiplication of the four basic elements which are the four seasons or the four successive divisions of the day (dawn, morning, noon, dusk) from morning to evening.

This four-sided system which rules in all spheres of the universe was revealed to the prophet Ezekiel in his vision of the Divine chariot. In this vision, the chariot was upheld by four archangels — he describes them in his first prophecy. From this center of gravity of cosmogonic elements emanate the rays which carry the vital forces throughout the world (cf. *Rambam, Guide* 3:4). And just as the principles and laws of the upper world materialize on earth with repercussions throughout the different spheres of existence, so too is the system of the celestial chariot reflected here below in reduced forms. Its manifestation within the framework of human society is found in the camp of the children of Israel, at whose center stands the Holy Ark. It was patterned after the celestial chariot over which hovered the Divine Majesty. The camp was organized in the form of a quadrilateral; at each of its sides were grouped three tribes, making a total of twelve. And from this camp emanated the rays of spiritual force, heading toward the seventy nations of the world, bringing them their source of inspiration. Thus, in the relationship between the twelve sons and the seventy descendants of Jacob, we see the macrocosm depicted in microcosm. Just as Israel goes down into Egypt and so begins the long journey across the centuries and the nations, this tableau reminds them of their eternal calling in history (cf. *R' Yitzchak Arama, Akeidas Yitzchak,* 31).

28. וְאֶת־יְהוּדָה שָׁלַח לְפָנָיו — *He sent Judah ahead of him.* Judah was not only considered the leader among his brothers, but it was he who had begun the *mitzvah* of reuniting the family by pleading with Joseph for Benjamin's sake. Accordingly, the merit of completing the *mitzvah* rightfully belonged to Judah. On the other hand, Judah was responsible for Joseph's coming to Egypt in the first place, for he was the one who had suggested his sale to the Ishmaelites. Therefore it was now up to him to prepare the restoration of the family unit. Later, the tribe of Judah and its chief played a prominent role at the time of the Exodus from Egypt and this tribe was then completely rehabilitated (*Psalms* 114:2): הָיְתָה יְהוּדָה לְקָדְשׁוֹ *Judah became His sanctuary* (*Midrashim*).

לְהוֹרֹת לְפָנָיו — *To prepare ahead of him. Rashi* explains, "As the *Targum* translates: In order to prepare a place for him," but then *Rashi* adds: "and to show how to settle there." Undoubtedly, Jacob at first had no intention of establishing himself in Goshen permanently, as has already been emphasized previously. And yet, the Torah tells us at the end of the *sidrah* that the family "took possession" of this Egyptian province, over which they had inherited

אָבִיו גּֽשְׁנָה וַיֵּרָא אֵלָיו וַיִּפֹּל עַל־צַוָּארָיו וַיֵּבְךְּ עַל־צַוָּארָיו
ל עוֹד: וַיֹּאמֶר יִשְׂרָאֵל אֶל־יוֹסֵף אָמוּתָה הַפָּעַם אַחֲרֵי
לא רְאוֹתִי אֶת־פָּנֶיךְ כִּי עוֹדְךָ חָי: וַיֹּאמֶר יוֹסֵף אֶל־אֶחָיו
וְאֶל־בֵּית אָבִיו אֶעֱלֶה וְאַגִּידָה לְפַרְעֹה וְאֹמְרָה אֵלָיו אַחַי

some rights from Sarah (see commentary on 45:10). The *Zohar* remarks that they took possession of it in perpetuity, for the province belonged to them legally. If one accepts the view quoted by *Radak* (*Joshua* 11:16) that this province was incorporated into the territory of the ancestors, then we can see why Jacob, although he felt so unhappy at being obliged to leave the Holy Land, had consented to "settle there." This is what *Rashi* perhaps wants to bring to light when he adds his words to the *Targum's* translation.

Rashi also mentions the interpretation of the verb לְהוֹרֹת in the sense of "to teach": he sent Judah to prepare a house of study for him, a place for learning. Every time he moved to a new land, Jacob's first concern was to strengthen himself morally ("for himself" as is indicated by the word לְפָנָיו, which is repeated twice in this verse) by drawing inspiration from sacred studies, just as we witnessed when he left for Haran (cf. our commentary to 28:10). To Jews of every era who find themselves immigrants in a new country, Jacob gives the example of fulfilling the most noble of their duties: to ensure for themselves and their children the continuance of the sacred teachings.

גּֽשְׁנָה — *In Goshen*. The word גּֽשְׁנָה has the same numerical value (358) as the word מָשִׁיחַ, *Messiah*. The redeemer is called on to deliver Jewry from the yoke of the four nations which enslaved it — the Egyptians, the Babylonians, the Greeks, and the Romans. The Messiah, the son of David, from the tribe of Judah, will be preceded by מָשִׁיחַ בֶּן יוֹסֵף, the Messiah descending from Joseph. On reaching Egypt, Jacob ardently hopes to see this Messianic union of his two children, Judah and Joseph, come about one day. He sends Judah to meet Joseph so that these two (who represent the ten lost tribes and the two who remained faithful) might together pave the way for the coming of the Messiah מָשִׁיחַ=גּֽשְׁנָה. (The second part of the verse refers then to Joseph; he shows the path of the Messiah "before" Judah.)

The author of this explanation, *R' Zvi E. Shapiro*, continues in his *Sefer B'nai Yissachar*: The four letters of the word גּֽשְׁנָה — ג-ש-נ-ה — are the same as those inscribed on the four sides of the Chanukah top (the *dreidel*). Moreover, Chanukah is celebrated about the time that the *sidrah Vayigash* is read in the synagogue. The letters are the initials of four words designating certain forces in man and it was the corruption of these forces which brought about the sufferings of the exile in the above-mentioned four nations, with the intention of removing this corruption. The forces are those of the physical (גּוּף), intellectual (שֵׂכֶל), and emotional (נֶפֶשׁ) elements of the soul plus the general force which comprises the totality (הַכֹּל) of human aptitudes: גּוּף, שֵׂכֶל, נֶפֶשׁ, הַכֹּל. The first letters of these words form the word גּֽשְׁנָה. On the festival of Chanukah,

father in Goshen. He appeared before him, fell on his neck, and he wept on his neck excessively. ³⁰ *Then Israel said to Joseph, "Now I can die, after my having seen your face, because you are still alive."*

³¹ *And Joseph said to his brothers and to his father's household, "I will go up and tell Pharaoh, and I will say to him, 'My brothers*

when the flame of messianic hope again begins to brighten the nights of our exile, the *dreidel* becomes the symbol of the four kingdoms which enslaved us because of our fourfold decline, but at the same time it reminds us that all of human existence and all of human history rotate about the messianic axis and that everything ultimately comes to "גִּשְׁנָה," that is, to messianic redemption (שם, חֹדֶשׁ בְּסָלַו).

29. וַיֵּרָא אֵלָיו — *He appeared before him.* According to *Rashi*, this was Joseph, who presented himself to Jacob and fell on his neck and wept. But *Ramban* takes the subject of the sentence to be Jacob. He fell on the neck of his long-lost son and wept with joy and emotion. We know full well, he continues, who would be first to shed tears, the old father who finds his son alive after having believed him dead for twenty-two years, or the son, still young and at the height of his glory.

However, *Rashi* continues his explanation, adding: Joseph wept and kept on weeping. But Jacob did not fall on his neck nor did he kiss him. Our Sages tell us that (at that moment) he was reciting *Shema. Maharal* explains this *aggadic* statement as follows: When the opportunity arises for the righteous to express the sentiments of love they feel, they do not want to keep these feelings of joy just for their own personal happiness, but they want to pay tribute to God for them. Such was the case with Jacob. Just when he had the immense joy of finding the son whom he had believed lost, just as he sensed the flame of paternal love blaze up in his heart, he controlled his feelings and recited *Shema*, offering all his love to God. At this, the happiest hour of his life, he wanted to have but one thought: וְאָהַבְתָּ אֵת ה' אֱלֹהֶיךָ, *you shall love Hashem, your God.*

30. אָמוּתָה הַפָּעַם אַחֲרֵי רְאוֹתִי אֶת־פָּנֶיךָ כִּי עוֹדְךָ חָי — *Now I can die, after my having seen your face, because you are still alive.* Knowing that Joseph was still alive brought joy to Jacob, but his happiness remained incomplete as long as he had not assured himself of one fact: that Joseph had maintained a high standard of piety while a slave and then as viceroy of Egypt. How can one rejoice at rediscovering a son if he has abandoned his faith and his fear of God? But Jacob possessed the ability of the righteous to recognize the spiritual state of an individual by looking at his features. So it was sufficient for him "to see Joseph's face" in order to assure himself that he had remained pure and pious. "Now," he exclaimed, "I can die in peace, since I have seen your face (and know) that you are yet alive," that is to say, you have still remained righteous, for only the righteous are truly alive (*Berachos* 18a; *R' Chaim ben Attar*).

לב וּבֵית־אָבִ֛י אֲשֶׁ֥ר בְּאֶֽרֶץ־כְּנַ֖עַן בָּ֣אוּ אֵלָ֑י וְהָאֲנָשִׁים֙ רֹ֣עֵי צֹ֔אן
כִּֽי־אַנְשֵׁ֥י מִקְנֶ֖ה הָי֑וּ וְצֹאנָ֧ם וּבְקָרָ֛ם וְכָל־אֲשֶׁ֥ר לָהֶ֖ם הֵבִֽיאוּ:

לג-לד וְהָיָ֕ה כִּֽי־יִקְרָ֥א לָכֶ֖ם פַּרְעֹ֑ה וְאָמַ֖ר מַה־מַּֽעֲשֵׂיכֶֽם: וַֽאֲמַרְתֶּ֗ם
אַנְשֵׁ֨י מִקְנֶ֜ה הָי֤וּ עֲבָדֶ֨יךָ֙ מִנְּעוּרֵ֣ינוּ וְעַד־עַ֔תָּה גַּם־אֲנַ֖חְנוּ
גַּם־אֲבֹתֵ֑ינוּ בַּֽעֲב֗וּר תֵּֽשְׁבוּ֙ בְּאֶ֣רֶץ גֹּ֔שֶׁן כִּֽי־תֽוֹעֲבַ֥ת מִצְרַ֖יִם

מז א כָּל־רֹ֥עֵה צֹֽאן: וַיָּבֹ֣א יוֹסֵף֮ וַיַּגֵּ֣ד לְפַרְעֹה֒ וַיֹּ֗אמֶר אָבִ֨י וְאַחַ֜י
וְצֹאנָ֤ם וּבְקָרָם֙ וְכָל־אֲשֶׁ֣ר לָהֶ֔ם בָּ֖אוּ מֵאֶ֣רֶץ כְּנָ֑עַן וְהִנָּ֖ם
ב בְּאֶ֥רֶץ גֹּֽשֶׁן: וּמִקְצֵ֣ה אֶחָ֔יו לָקַ֖ח חֲמִשָּׁ֣ה אֲנָשִׁ֑ים וַיַּצִּגֵ֖ם
ג לִפְנֵ֥י פַרְעֹֽה: וַיֹּ֧אמֶר פַּרְעֹ֛ה אֶל־אֶחָ֖יו מַה־מַּֽעֲשֵׂיכֶ֑ם וַיֹּֽאמְר֣וּ
ד אֶל־פַּרְעֹ֗ה רֹעֵ֥ה צֹאן֙ עֲבָדֶ֔יךָ גַּם־אֲנַ֖חְנוּ גַּם־אֲבוֹתֵֽינוּ:
וַיֹּֽאמְר֣וּ אֶל־פַּרְעֹ֗ה לָג֣וּר בָּאָרֶץ֮ בָּאנוּ֒ כִּי־אֵ֣ין מִרְעֶ֗ה לַצֹּאן֙
אֲשֶׁ֣ר לַֽעֲבָדֶ֔יךָ כִּֽי־כָבֵ֥ד הָֽרָעָ֖ב בְּאֶ֣רֶץ כְּנָ֑עַן וְעַתָּ֛ה יֵֽשְׁבוּ־
ה נָ֥א עֲבָדֶ֖יךָ בְּאֶ֥רֶץ גֹּֽשֶׁן: וַיֹּ֣אמֶר פַּרְעֹ֔ה אֶל־יוֹסֵ֖ף לֵאמֹ֑ר אָבִ֥יךָ
ו וְאַחֶ֖יךָ בָּ֥אוּ אֵלֶֽיךָ: אֶ֤רֶץ מִצְרַ֨יִם֙ לְפָנֶ֣יךָ הִ֔וא בְּמֵיטַ֣ב הָאָ֔רֶץ
הוֹשֵׁ֥ב אֶת־אָבִ֖יךָ וְאֶת־אַחֶ֑יךָ יֵֽשְׁבוּ֙ בְּאֶ֣רֶץ גֹּ֔שֶׁן וְאִם־יָדַ֗עְתָּ
וְיֶשׁ־בָּם֙ אַנְשֵׁי־חַ֔יִל וְשַׂמְתָּ֛ם שָׂרֵ֥י מִקְנֶ֖ה עַל־אֲשֶׁר־לִֽי:

32. וְהָאֲנָשִׁים רֹעֵי צֹאן — *The men are shepherds.* According to *R' Bachya ibn Pakuda*, two reasons prompted Jacob's children and the most illustrious of Biblical characters to choose to be shepherds. On one hand this profession is healthy and profitable. On the other hand, it keeps to a minimum the association with idolaters who consider that *shepherds are abhorrent* (v. 34) since "they look upon sheep as an object of worship" (*Rashi* ibid.). Thus shepherds lead their lives for themselves, living close to pasture-land and far from large settlements. This has two advantages: the shepherd is better able to safeguard his spiritual and religious heritage, and it is easier to avoid the many vices which are brought out by the sophisticated social life of big cities — gossip, slander, depravity, thievery, hypocrisy, and falsehood. Being a shepherd allows one to be alone, far from men and their evil ways, and for this the righteous and the prophets have always searched. It answers their wish to devote themselves to meditation and to an austere and holy way of life which would elevate them until they reached the Source of Divine Inspiration (cf. our commentary to 4:2).

34. בַּֽעֲבוּר תֵּֽשְׁבוּ בְּאֶרֶץ גֹּשֶׁן — *So that you may be able to settle in the region of Goshen.* Even though his brothers had only just entered Egypt, Joseph already feels obligated to advise them to be prudent and cautious in order to ensure that they have a peaceful life, consistent with their family ideal. Knowing how difficult it would be for this insignificant national minority to safeguard its cultural autonomy amid the Egyptian people, he tells them to behave so as to appear in the eyes of Pharaoh very unexceptional from every point of view

and my father's household who were in the land of Canaan have come to me. ³² *The men are shepherds, for they have been cattlemen; their flocks and cattle — and everything they own — they have brought.'* ³³ *And it shall be, when Pharaoh summons you, and says, 'What is your occupation?'* ³⁴ *Then you are to say, 'Your servants have been cattlemen from our youth till now, both we and our forefathers,' so that you may be able to settle in the region of Goshen, since all shepherds are abhorrent to Egyptians.''*

47 ¹ *Then Joseph came and told Pharaoh, and he said, "My father and my brothers, their flocks, their cattle, and everything they own, have arrived from the land of Canaan and they are now in the region of Goshen." ² From the least of his brothers he took five men and presented them to Pharaoh. ³ Pharaoh said to his brothers, "What is your occupation?" They answered Pharaoh, "Your servants are shepherds — we as well as our forefathers." ⁴ And they said to Pharaoh, "We have come to sojourn in the land, since there is no grazing for your servants' flocks, for the famine is severe in the land of Canaan; now, if you please, allow your servants to dwell in the region of Goshen."*

⁵ *And Pharaoh said to Joseph saying, "Your father and your brothers have come to you. ⁶ The land of Egypt is before you — in the best part of the land settle your father and your brothers; let them settle in the region of Goshen, and if you know that there are capable men among them, appoint them as chamberlains over the livestock that belongs to me."*

(verse 2). They will have to shun any situation which will make them conspicuous, and they are to use diplomacy and cunning in order to be given land far from the capital, in the region of Goshen. All the outstanding honors which were bestowed on Jacob and his household when they arrived in Egypt did not make them forget the danger of assimilation and the urgent necessity of taking all the appropriate measures for resisting it. Thus we see the precarious situation of the Jews among the nations. The Torah gives us a typical example of it right from the first descent into a land of exile, even though this seemed at first to augur well for the Jews.

47.

1. וַיָּבֹא יוֹסֵף וַיַּגֵּד לְפַרְעֹה — *Then Joseph came and told Pharaoh.* By continuing to portray the attitude of the family of Israel on its arrival in Egypt in such detail, the Torah intends to give us an example of foresight and the precautionary measures to be taken when similar circumstances recur in its history. All these arrangements stem from the objectives which we have just indicated. Perhaps

ז וַיָּבֵא יוֹסֵף אֶת־יַעֲקֹב אָבִיו וַיַּעֲמִדֵהוּ לִפְנֵי פַרְעֹה וַיְבָרֶךְ
ח יַעֲקֹב אֶת־פַּרְעֹה: וַיֹּאמֶר פַּרְעֹה אֶל־יַעֲקֹב כַּמָּה יְמֵי שְׁנֵי
ט חַיֶּיךָ: וַיֹּאמֶר יַעֲקֹב אֶל־פַּרְעֹה יְמֵי שְׁנֵי מְגוּרַי שְׁלֹשִׁים
וּמְאַת שָׁנָה מְעַט וְרָעִים הָיוּ יְמֵי שְׁנֵי חַיַּי וְלֹא הִשִּׂיגוּ
י אֶת־יְמֵי שְׁנֵי חַיֵּי אֲבֹתַי בִּימֵי מְגוּרֵיהֶם: וַיְבָרֶךְ יַעֲקֹב אֶת־
שביעי יא פַּרְעֹה וַיֵּצֵא מִלִּפְנֵי פַרְעֹה: וַיּוֹשֵׁב יוֹסֵף אֶת־אָבִיו וְאֶת־אֶחָיו
וַיִּתֵּן לָהֶם אֲחֻזָּה בְּאֶרֶץ מִצְרַיִם בְּמֵיטַב הָאָרֶץ בְּאֶרֶץ
יב רַעְמְסֵס כַּאֲשֶׁר צִוָּה פַרְעֹה: וַיְכַלְכֵּל יוֹסֵף אֶת־אָבִיו וְאֶת־
יג אֶחָיו וְאֵת כָּל־בֵּית אָבִיו לֶחֶם לְפִי הַטָּף: וְלֶחֶם אֵין בְּכָל־
הָאָרֶץ כִּי־כָבֵד הָרָעָב מְאֹד וַתֵּלַהּ אֶרֶץ מִצְרַיִם וְאֶרֶץ כְּנַעַן

the Torah also wants to put us on our guard against the capriciousness of the rulers and peoples who receive us in their lands. To be sure, out of gratitude to Joseph, the Egyptian people at first welcomed his father and brothers with princely honors and the greatest magnanimity, but they quickly changed their mood. And then their generosity was transformed into barbarity and cruel tyranny.

9. יְמֵי שְׁנֵי מְגוּרַי — *The days of the years of my sojourns.* "The years I dwelt as a stranger, all my days I have been a stranger on earth" (*Rashi*). Cf. our commentary to 26:3. The disillusioned reply of the old patriarch might seem astonishing from someone who had always been suffused with confidence in God. *Ramban* explains that Jacob appeared older than he really was, and he wanted simply to explain this premature aging. Other commentators hold that this answer followed the general trend in the conduct of Jacob and his sons: they tried to lessen themselves in the eyes of Pharaoh and the Egyptians and to appear as just an ordinary family so that they could withdraw and live in a far-off province. Even to God, Jacob said: My merit has been depleted by all the favors and all the fulfillment of promises You have granted Your slave (*Genesis* 32:11); and to Pharaoh: The years of my life were few and bad (*Daas Zekeinim*).

However, several *midrashic* sources record another view: Divine justice held Jacob to account for the ingratitude shown in his reply. "You lament your unhappy life," God reproached him, "even after I saved you from the hands of Esau and Laban and then brought back your daughter Dinah and your son Joseph! So your years will not number those of your forefathers, just as you yourself have said prematurely. Isaac lived one hundred eighty years; thirty-three years will be taken off your life (Jacob died at one hundred forty-seven years). This corresponds to the thirty-three words in these two verses (8 and 9)." One can understand this Midrash from the Talmudic statement that God is not lenient with the righteous, punishing even their slightest mistakes (*Taanis* 11a). For even the legal responsibility of a person increases with the level of his moral stature. That is why the above opinion is

⁷ Then Joseph brought Jacob, his father, and presented him to Pharaoh, and Jacob blessed Pharaoh. ⁸ Pharaoh said to Jacob, "How many are the days of the years of your life?"

⁹ Jacob answered Pharaoh, "The days of the years of my sojourns have been a hundred and thirty years. Few and bad have been the days of the years of my life, and they have not reached the life spans of my forefathers in the days of their sojourns." ¹⁰ Then Jacob blessed Pharaoh, and left Pharaoh's presence.

¹¹ So Joseph settled his father and his brothers and he gave them a possession in the land of Egypt in the best part of the land, in the region of Rameses, as Pharaoh had commanded. ¹² Joseph sustained his father and his brothers and all of his father's household with food according to the children.

¹³ There was no bread in all the earth for the famine was very severe; the land of Egypt and the land of Canaan became weary

not in contradiction with the other reason for Jacob's life being shortened (the reason given by the *Baal HaTurim* in this same chapter, verse 28): previously Jacob had unwittingly pronounced a curse on the one of his family with whom Laban's gods would be found. He had exclaimed, "לֹא יִחְיֶה, *he shall not live*" (31:32). This unjustified curse struck his wife Rachel who died prematurely. But now it fell back on him and he died thirty-three years before his natural life span, corresponding to the numerical value of the word יִחְיֶה.

10. וַיְבָרֶךְ יַעֲקֹב — *Then Jacob blessed.* "What was this blessing? That the waters of the Nile should rise to his feet, for Egypt does not receive rainwater; the Nile irrigates it when it overflows. Now, from the time that Pharaoh received the blessing from Jacob, he used to go down to the Nile and the river would rise and water the land" (*Rashi*). This blessing of a righteous man came to fruition: the famine stopped with the arrival of Jacob, that is to say five years before the specified time, as *Rashi* points out in his commentary to verse 19.

11. בְּאֶרֶץ רַעְמְסֵס — *In the region of Rameses.* This town received its name in the reign of Rameses II. He is generally held to be the Pharaoh who oppressed the Jews. According to the *Targum Yonasan*, this name designates the land of beautiful fabrics.

12. לֶחֶם לְפִי הַטָּף — *With food according to the children. Rashi* explains, "according to what was necessary for all family members." *Sforno* adds: Although Joseph could have increased their ration, he gave them only the basic amount.

13. וַתֵּלַהּ אֶרֶץ מִצְרַיִם. . .מִפְּנֵי הָרָעָב — *The land of Egypt . . . became weary from hunger. Menachem ben Saruk* connects this word וַתֵּלַהּ with מִתְלַהְלֵהַּ in *Proverbs* 26:18 and translates it to mean: to be stricken with insanity. Historical descriptions of similar famines in Egypt give an idea of the frightening deprivation from which Joseph spared the country. "The consumption of

יד מִפְּנֵי הָרָעָב: וַיְלַקֵּט יוֹסֵף אֶת־כָּל־הַכֶּסֶף הַנִּמְצָא בְאֶרֶץ־
מִצְרַיִם וּבְאֶרֶץ כְּנַעַן בַּשֶּׁבֶר אֲשֶׁר־הֵם שֹׁבְרִים וַיָּבֵא יוֹסֵף
טו אֶת־הַכֶּסֶף בֵּיתָה פַרְעֹה: וַיִּתֹּם הַכֶּסֶף מֵאֶרֶץ מִצְרַיִם וּמֵאֶרֶץ
כְּנַעַן וַיָּבֹאוּ כָל־מִצְרַיִם אֶל־יוֹסֵף לֵאמֹר הָבָה־לָּנוּ לֶחֶם
טז וְלָמָּה נָמוּת נֶגְדֶּךָ כִּי אָפֵס כָּסֶף: וַיֹּאמֶר יוֹסֵף הָבוּ מִקְנֵיכֶם
יז וְאֶתְּנָה לָכֶם בְּמִקְנֵיכֶם אִם־אָפֵס כָּסֶף: וַיָּבִיאוּ אֶת־מִקְנֵיהֶם
אֶל־יוֹסֵף וַיִּתֵּן לָהֶם יוֹסֵף לֶחֶם בַּסּוּסִים וּבְמִקְנֵה הַצֹּאן
וּבְמִקְנֵה הַבָּקָר וּבַחֲמֹרִים וַיְנַהֲלֵם בַּלֶּחֶם בְּכָל־מִקְנֵהֶם
יח בַּשָּׁנָה הַהִוא: וַתִּתֹּם הַשָּׁנָה הַהִוא וַיָּבֹאוּ אֵלָיו בַּשָּׁנָה הַשֵּׁנִית
וַיֹּאמְרוּ לוֹ לֹא־נְכַחֵד מֵאֲדֹנִי כִּי אִם־תַּם הַכֶּסֶף וּמִקְנֵה
הַבְּהֵמָה אֶל־אֲדֹנִי לֹא נִשְׁאַר לִפְנֵי אֲדֹנִי בִּלְתִּי אִם־גְּוִיָּתֵנוּ
יט וְאַדְמָתֵנוּ: לָמָּה נָמוּת לְעֵינֶיךָ גַּם־אֲנַחְנוּ גַּם־אַדְמָתֵנוּ קְנֵה־
אֹתָנוּ וְאֶת־אַדְמָתֵנוּ בַּלָּחֶם וְנִהְיֶה אֲנַחְנוּ וְאַדְמָתֵנוּ עֲבָדִים
לְפַרְעֹה וְתֶן־זֶרַע וְנִחְיֶה וְלֹא נָמוּת וְהָאֲדָמָה לֹא תֵשָׁם:

human flesh became so commonplace that it no longer astonished anyone," wrote a witness to one of these famines in the Middle East. "The route from Syria to Egypt resembled one vast field strewn with corpses."

וְאֶרֶץ כְּנַעַן — *And the land of Canaan.* Anyone other than Joseph would have been tempted to weaken the people of Canaan, whose land was subsequently to be conquered by his descendants, as everyone in the family of Abraham well knew. But Joseph was concerned only with carrying out his humanitarian duty: to nourish the unfortunate ones who appealed to him for help. Pharaoh, though, wanted to keep the grain in his silos, as historical tradition tells us. Of these two rulers of Egypt the verse in *Proverbs* says (11:26): "He who withholds grain, the people will curse him" — this was the lot of Pharaoh — "but blessing will be upon the head of him that sells it" — this was Joseph (*Rabbah* 91).

14. וַיְלַקֵּט יוֹסֵף אֶת־כָּל־הַכֶּסֶף — *Joseph gathered all the money.* Cf. our commentary to 41:49.

18. וַתִּתֹּם הַשָּׁנָה הַהִוא — *And when that year ended.* According to the opinion which *Rashi* expressed in verse 10, this refers to the end of the first year and then to the second year, counting from the beginning of the famine, since it had ceased as soon as Jacob had arrived. *Ramban* takes issue with this view as inconsistent with the interpretation which Joseph had given to Pharaoh's dreams; he therefore casts doubt on it. Moreover, is it not written that Joseph sustained his father and brothers and gave them the food rations even after the arrival of the patriarch? Accordingly, *Ramban* holds that verses 17 and 18 refer

from hunger. ¹⁴ *Joseph gathered all the money that was to be found in the land of Egypt and in the land of Canaan through the provisions that they were purchasing, and Joseph brought the money into Pharaoh's palace.* ¹⁵ *And when the money was exhausted from the land of Egypt and from the land of Canaan, all the Egyptians came to Joseph, saying, "Give us bread; why should we die in your presence? — for the money is gone!"*

¹⁶ *And Joseph said, "Bring your livestock and I will provide for you in return for your livestock if the money is gone."* ¹⁷ *So they brought their livestock to Joseph, and Joseph gave them bread in return for the horses, for the flocks of sheep, for the herds of cattle, and for the donkeys; thus he provided them with bread for all their livestock during that year.*

¹⁸ *And when that year ended, they came to him in the next year and said to him, "We will not withhold from my lord that with the money and flocks of cattle having been exhausted to my lord, nothing is left before my lord but our bodies and our land.* ¹⁹ *Why should we die before your eyes, both we and our land? Acquire us and our land for bread; and we — with our land — will become serfs to Pharaoh; and provide seed so that we may live and not die, and the land will not become desolate."*

to the sixth and seventh years of the famine. He also cites the controversy between R' Shimon and his son, R' Elazar. The former disagreed with R' Yose's statement that the last five years of the famine came after the death of the patriarch. It is no honor for the righteous, he objected, that their words come true in their lifetime and then are null and void after their death. On the contrary, replied his son, the honor lies in the fact that the blessing continues for as long as the righteous are among the living and that it disappears when they die. In any case, Joseph's prophecy did come to pass in its entirety, according to this latter tradition (*Sifre* to *Deuteronomy* 38), although not in consecutive years.

19. וְתֶן־זֶרַע — *And provide seed.* Even admitting with *Rashi* that this dialogue between Joseph and the Egyptians took place at the end of the second year, shortly after Jacob's arrival, we see how greatly the Egyptians feared that they would see their country transformed into an arid desert, were the land to lie fallow for five years. Far from having the effect of resting and strengthening the arable land, a seven-year pause causes a very noticeable weakening of its productive capacity. Not yet aware of the beneficial effect of the blessing which Jacob had given to Pharaoh, the Egyptians were apprehensive that their "land would become desolate." The prophet Ezekiel paints a very bleak picture of what such desolation means for Egypt (29:8-12).

כ וַיִּ֣קֶן יוֹסֵ֣ף אֶת־כָּל־אַדְמַ֣ת מִצְרַ֘יִם֮ לְפַרְעֹה֒ כִּי־מָכְר֤וּ מִצְרַ֙יִם֙
אִ֣ישׁ שָׂדֵ֔הוּ כִּֽי־חָזַ֥ק עֲלֵהֶ֖ם הָרָעָ֑ב וַתְּהִ֥י הָאָ֖רֶץ לְפַרְעֹֽה:
כא וְאֶ֨ת־הָעָ֔ם הֶעֱבִ֥יר אֹת֖וֹ לֶֽעָרִ֑ים מִקְצֵ֥ה גְבֽוּל־מִצְרַ֖יִם וְעַד־
קָצֵֽהוּ: כב רַ֛ק אַדְמַ֥ת הַכֹּֽהֲנִ֖ים לֹ֣א קָנָ֑ה כִּי֩ חֹ֨ק לַכֹּֽהֲנִ֜ים מֵאֵ֣ת
פַּרְעֹ֗ה וְאָֽכְל֤וּ אֶת־חֻקָּם֙ אֲשֶׁ֨ר נָתַ֤ן לָהֶם֙ פַּרְעֹ֔ה עַל־כֵּ֕ן לֹ֥א
מָֽכְר֖וּ אֶת־אַדְמָתָֽם: כג וַיֹּ֤אמֶר יוֹסֵף֙ אֶל־הָעָ֔ם הֵן֩ קָנִ֨יתִי אֶתְכֶ֥ם
הַיּ֛וֹם וְאֶת־אַדְמַתְכֶ֖ם לְפַרְעֹ֑ה הֵֽא־לָכֶ֣ם זֶ֔רַע וּזְרַעְתֶּ֖ם אֶת־
הָֽאֲדָמָֽה: כד וְהָיָה֙ בַּתְּבוּאֹ֔ת וּנְתַתֶּ֥ם חֲמִישִׁ֖ית לְפַרְעֹ֑ה וְאַרְבַּ֣ע
הַיָּדֹ֡ת יִֽהְיֶ֣ה לָכֶם֩ לְזֶ֨רַע הַשָּׂדֶ֧ה וּֽלְאָכְלְכֶ֛ם וְלַֽאֲשֶׁ֥ר בְּבָֽתֵּיכֶ֖ם

20. וַיִּ֣קֶן יוֹסֵ֣ף אֶת־כָּל־אַדְמַ֣ת מִצְרַ֘יִם — *Thus Joseph acquired all the land of Egypt.*
But not the people themselves, as the Egyptians had proposed. They had asked
for the nationalization of their lands and for the sale of themselves to Pharaoh
as slaves. But Joseph carefully avoids (in verse 23) using the term slavery or
servitude. Henceforth, a rent of one-fifth of the produce was to be given
annually to the collectors. This excludes a usual system of metayage (payment
of rent in kind) where the tariff is fixed at four-fifths — which effectively
reduces the beneficiary to the status of a slave (historians report numerous
examples of very high rates of metayage throughout the Middle Ages). Egypt
was to have a system whereby a free peasantry could live as they wished on
their land, and have the majority of their produce at their own disposal. The
only hindrance would be the impossibility of selling or transferring their land
without the prior consent of the actual proprietor — the Crown. Thus the birth
of feudalism was prevented and Pharaoh remained the uncontested master of
his provinces (*R' S.R. Hirsch*).

21. וְאֶ֨ת־הָעָ֔ם הֶעֱבִ֥יר אֹת֖וֹ לֶֽעָרִ֑ים — *As for the nation, he resettled it by cities.*
According to *Rashi*, the intent was to make it clear to the owners that the land
no longer belonged to them. He transplanted the people in order to make their
dispossession all the clearer. However, he respected social and communal
affinities and organized the transfer so that it would not be made through
isolated individuals, which would have been greatly resented, but "by cities,"
that is to say, by collective entities. The grammatical form of the term לֶֽעָרִים
indeed signifies "by cities" (to express the idea of a transfer *in* cities would have
required אֶל הֶעָרִים; *Luzzatto*). But why, asks R' Shimon ben Lakish, did the
Torah need to record this detail? There are in this regard "a number of verses
which to all appearances ought to be burnt, but are really essential elements in
the Torah." Here, the Torah's intention is to pay tribute to Joseph who
endeavored to spare his brothers (by this means of the transfer of population)
from the shame of being treated as the only exiles (*Chullin 60b*).

22. רַ֛ק אַדְמַ֥ת הַכֹּֽהֲנִ֖ים לֹ֣א קָנָ֑ה — *Only the land of the priests he did not buy.*
There is a striking contrast between Jewish legislation, which does not

²⁰ *Thus Joseph acquired all the land of Egypt for Pharaoh, for every Egyptian sold his field because the famine had overwhelmed them; and the land became Pharaoh's.* ²¹ *As for the nation, he resettled it by cities, from one end of Egypt's borders to the other.* ²² *Only the land of the priests he did not buy, since the priests had a stipend from Pharaoh, and they lived off their stipend that Pharaoh had given them; therefore they did not sell their land.*

²³ *Joseph said to the people, "Look — I have acquired you this day with your land for Pharaoh; here is seed for you — sow the land.* ²⁴ *At the ingathering of the harvests you will give a fifth to Pharaoh; the [other] four parts shall be yours — as seed for the field, and food for yourselves and for those in your household,*

recognize any territorial possession by the *Kohanim,* who were to dedicate themselves exclusively to their double vocation of priests and teachers, and the Egyptian system where, under pressure from the dominant class of the clergy, the lands belonging to the priests remained out of the control of the state. Here we see the beginning of the system of the "grand fiefs" held by the ecclesiastical power which gradually led to tyranny in feudal society.

But why, it is asked, did Joseph, who governed with such wisdom and foresight, not oppose this pressure from the clergy? It was because he remained grateful to Potiphera, the priest of On (Heliopolis) whose daughter he had married, and to the Egyptian priests who had spoken up in his defense against the accusations of his master's wife. They had saved him from being condemned to death, as *Targum Yonasan* tells us in 39:20 (פי' הטור). Accordingly, Joseph did not want to upset them.

23. הֵא־לָכֶם זֶרַע — *Here is seed for you.* The word הֵא, meaning "here," is not found anywhere else in the Pentateuch. Its use in our verse instead of הִנֵּה has a special significance which is brought out by R' *Bachya* on *Genesis* 2:4 and 46:4. The spelling of the interjection הֵא is the same as that of the letter ה. Now, it is "with the letter ה that God created the terrestrial world," as *Rashi* explains on *Genesis* 2:4. However, Divine Omnipotence which creates the laws of nature also has the power to modify them. The example of Abraham demonstrates this. The patriarch could not procreate according to natural laws. But by adding the letter ה to his name God gave him the power to procreate (*Rashi* on 15:5). So too, although on a different plane, with the Egyptian famine. Natural conditions had made the earth barren during the time of the drought. But a new source of blessing spread over the land when the patriarch came. Accordingly, the rich crop which now suddenly begins to spread throughout starving Egypt is placed under the sign of the letter ה, coming from the Divine name שֵׁם הֲוָיָ״, the source of productive power and fertility (cf. *Zohar* to *Leviticus* 216b).

מפטיר   כה וְלֶאֱכֹל לְטַפְּכֶם: וַיֹּאמְרוּ הֶחֱיִתָנוּ נִמְצָא־חֵן בְּעֵינֵי אֲדֹנִי

כו וְהָיִינוּ עֲבָדִים לְפַרְעֹה: וַיָּשֶׂם אֹתָהּ יוֹסֵף לְחֹק עַד־הַיּוֹם הַזֶּה

עַל־אַדְמַת מִצְרַיִם לְפַרְעֹה לַחֹמֶשׁ רַק אַדְמַת הַכֹּהֲנִים

כז לְבַדָּם לֹא הָיְתָה לְפַרְעֹה: וַיֵּשֶׁב יִשְׂרָאֵל בְּאֶרֶץ מִצְרַיִם

בְּאֶרֶץ גֹּשֶׁן וַיֵּאָחֲזוּ בָהּ וַיִּפְרוּ וַיִּרְבּוּ מְאֹד:

---

25. הֶחֱיִתָנוּ — *You have saved our lives.* The verbal form employed here is הֶחֱיִתָנוּ rather than חִיִּיתָנוּ, and from this the Midrash concludes that the Egyptians were grateful to Joseph for the "double life" he had given them — the material life on earth and the future life in the hereafter. He had led them toward a more wholesome moral life by imposing the law of circumcision upon them, as was explained in our commentary on 41:55.

וְהָיִינוּ עֲבָדִים לְפַרְעֹה — *And we will be serfs to Pharaoh.* If the measures taken in Egypt clearly demonstrate Joseph's high degree of political wisdom, one nevertheless wonders why the Torah considers them of such great importance from an educational or doctrinal point of view that it describes them in detail. It appears that they contain a value judgment of importance. The Torah is revealing the historical events which turned Egypt into the "house of bondage בֵּית עֲבָדִים." It was the Egyptians themselves who expressed willingness to give up their lands. It was they who came to plead with Joseph, "May we find favor in your eyes,sir, and be slaves to Pharaoh." This slave mentality was behind the actions of the Egyptian people, and the Jews lived in contact with it for centuries. In Egypt they went through all the mental and physical tortures of persecution and the worst humiliation which scorn for human dignity and individual freedom could cause. These ordeals made them fit and ready to understand and to cherish the Law which they received when they were freed from the house of bondage, the Law which exalted the virtues of freedom and human dignity. They realized that man is not to be a slave to anyone save God — He alone is to be master of all creatures and dispenser of all the lands. "From the most developed tyranny of the ancient world emerged a people ready to

and to feed your young ones."

²⁵ *And they said, "You have saved our lives; may we find favor in your eyes, my lord, and we will be serfs to Pharaoh."*

²⁶ *So Joseph imposed it as a statute till this day regarding the land of Egypt: It was Pharaoh's for the fifth; only the priests' land alone did not become Pharaoh's.*

²⁷ *Thus Israel settled in the land of Egypt in the region of Goshen; they acquired property in it and they were fruitful and multiplied greatly.*

accept the system which placed the principle of freedom of the human personality above all else" (*Henry George*).

26. רַק אַדְמַת הַכֹּהֲנִים לְבַדָּם לֹא הָיְתָה לְפַרְעֹה — *Only the priests' land alone did not become Pharaoh's.* In principle, the *sidrah* of וַיִּגַּשׁ should have ended here, for the next verse really belongs with the episode which follows. But the communities, not wanting to end the section with the lengthy account (verses 20 to 26) of Pharaoh's rights to the land, added verse 27 to it (*Rashbam*).

27. וַיֵּאָחֲזוּ בָהּ — *They acquired property in it.* Cf. our commentary to 45:10. "Israel" dwelt in the land of Egypt, but the members of the family (a sylleptic plural) "were possessed" by it (וַיֵּאָחֲזוּ, the *nif'al* form of אחז, *to take possession*). They allowed themselves to be gripped by the land of Egypt. This term also alludes to the start of the transgression which the prophet Ezekiel (Chapter 20) later mentioned in his fiery speeches. The pleasant feeling of being able to dwell in this beautiful province gradually led to the danger of forsaking the ancient traditions and abandoning the great calling of the Abrahamic family (*R' S.R. Hirsch*).

וַיִּפְרוּ וַיִּרְבּוּ מְאֹד — *They were fruitful and multiplied greatly.* For (at first) they had no cares and lived in the midst of plenty (*Zohar*). The exceptional growth in population was merely a natural phenomenon, a result of enjoying excellent living conditions. But later, during the period of slavery and oppression, that extraordinary increase in numbers noted by the Torah at the beginning of *Exodus* can only be explained as the result of providential intervention, supernatural in character (*Ramban* on *Numbers* 3:14).

כח וַיְחִי יַעֲקֹב בְּאֶרֶץ מִצְרַיִם שְׁבַע עֶשְׂרֵה שָׁנֶה וַיְהִי יְמֵי־

28. וַיְחִי יַעֲקֹב — *Jacob lived.* The *sidrah* which tells of the death of Jacob is entitled: *Jacob lived.* Similarly, the one recounting the death of Sarah is called חַיֵּי שָׂרָה, *the life of Sarah.* The righteous continue to live on after death, the Sages tell us (*Berachos* 18b), because of the example which they have given and the spiritual heritage which they have bequeathed to posterity. So "our father Jacob did not die," as *Rashi* notes on 49:33.

This last *sidrah* in *Genesis* illuminates the end of Jacob's life with the soft light of dusk. His existence had been rocked by furious tempests and had quite often been shaken to its very foundations. Now the old patriarch lies on his deathbed and gives his supreme blessing to his children. He is at peace with God; he is no longer afraid of death. "I want to sleep with my fathers," he says. We hear him pray with his last words: "I hope for Your salvation, Hashem." For he knows that he will never be able to attain his goal without help from God. How many struggles — Esau, Laban, Dinah, Joseph — how much suffering and sorrow each of these tragedies brought him! Yet he dies while giving blessings. Although he had begun as "a quiet man, dwelling in tents," he had never turned away from the things of this world. Jacob possessed a very rare art: as each one of the trials came upon him, he could see the good which it brought for the future. Thus, he erred and he stumbled but he always raised himself once again to his level of moral perfection. For his greatness of spirit had been forged on the anvil of suffering. In the land of Egypt, the *Zohar* tells us, Jacob lived the best years of his life. There he lived in tranquility, free of cares, with family harmony and the honors which the Egyptians bestowed upon him thanks to the prestige of his son Joseph. And there too he had the joy of seeing that his family "were fruitful and multiplied greatly," as was mentioned in the previous verse. The *Zohar* explains that this direct connection with "real life," which Jacob at last had the privilege of experiencing in Egypt, is why the two *sidros* of *Vayigash* and *Vayechi* are linked without any indentation in the text.

Rashi provides two other reasons for this continuity: "As soon as Jacob died, the eyes and the hearts of Jewry were 'closed' (closed like the new *sidrah* which is linked to the previous one without any new opening) by the sufferings of the bondage which now came upon them." (This could only refer to spiritual bondage, since *Rashi* notes on *Exodus* 6:16 that the slavery did not commence as long as one of Jacob's sons remained alive.) Another explanation: "Jacob wanted to reveal the End of Days to his children but it was 'closed' to him" (on this see our commentary to 49:1).

R' S. R. Hirsch, however, puts forward an entirely different view. One might think that the seventeen years of peaceful life in Egypt were to be considered as the main phase of Jacob's existence and that as such they deserved to be recounted in a separate chapter, distinct from the others. But, quite the contrary, the Torah makes it follow right on the heels of the account of years filled with

²⁸ *Jacob lived in the land of Egypt seventeen years; and the days*

suffering and torment — without bringing it into any special prominence. It was precisely during those years that Jacob became Israel and prepared his family for their future messianic calling. From the national point of view, the years of hardship were the ones of greatest importance, whereas the years of happiness appear as the height of Jacob's existence only from the perspective of the individual. And so they are presented simply as the natural consequence of the life which preceded them.

שְׁבַע עֶשְׂרֵה שָׁנָה — *Seventeen years*. Joseph was the image of his mother. Whenever Jacob looked at him, he seemed to be seeing his beloved wife Rachel who had been taken prematurely from him. As a result he felt intense joy at having Joseph near him. But when Joseph reached the age of seventeen, he too was taken away from him (37:2), and from that time, a day did not pass without Jacob crying over his lost happiness. And so God compensated him for all his sufferings and, as his life drew to a close, Jacob was granted seventeen more years at the side of his son Joseph (*Zohar*).

It might indeed seem astonishing that the best years of the patriarch's life were those he spent in a land of exile after he had left the Promised Land. We can understand more clearly *Rashi's* opening remarks on the *sidrah*, already quoted above: despite the carefree and happy existence in Egypt, despite the blessing of "multiplying greatly," the "eyes and hearts of the Jews were closed," that is to say, they retired within themselves because of "the spiritual bondage" which had threatened them right from their arrival in Egypt. The patriarch's visionary powers, too, began to diminish until he could not reveal the future to his children. If a life of comfort and material wealth is the lot of the nations of the world, prophetic inspiration and the light of truth are the prerogatives of the Holy Land.

The *sidrah Vayeitzei* offers us a similar example. It contains no indentation or break in the text and thus it appears as a "closed" *sidrah*. It deals with the first emigration from the Promised Land by the patriarch, with a view to founding his family. His children enter the world and grow up in a foreign land, but when it comes to raising and educating them, Jacob "closes his eyes and his heart" to his pagan surroundings. His eyes and his thoughts are turned solely to the land of his ancestors.

וַיְהִי יְמֵי־יַעֲקֹב שְׁנֵי חַיָּיו — *And the days of Jacob — the years of his life*. Consistent with his previously expressed view (43:14), *Ramban* explains at the beginning of this chapter that Jacob's descent into Egyptian exile is a forerunner of the descent of his offspring into exile in Edom or the Roman empire, the exile we find ourselves in now. The analogy extends to a series of circumstances. In both cases it was the "causeless hatred between brothers" which brought about the exile. Like Jacob, who thought he would be going to a friendly king, so Agrippa, the last king of Jewish Palestine, went to the Roman court, to Caius Caligula, his intimate friend. As for the inhabitants of

כט יַעֲקֹב֙ שְׁנֵ֣י חַיָּ֔יו שֶׁ֤בַע שָׁנִים֙ וְאַרְבָּעִ֣ים וּמְאַ֣ת שָׁנָ֑ה: וַיִּקְרְב֣וּ
יְמֵֽי־יִשְׂרָאֵל֮ לָמוּת֒ וַיִּקְרָ֣א ׀ לִבְנֹ֣ו לְיוֹסֵ֗ף וַיֹּ֤אמֶר לוֹ֙ אִם־
נָ֨א מָצָ֤אתִי חֵן֙ בְּעֵינֶ֔יךָ שִֽׂים־נָ֥א יָדְךָ֖ תַּ֣חַת יְרֵכִ֑י וְעָשִׂ֤יתָ

besieged Jerusalem, they were made captives because of famine, just as the
family of Jacob had been compelled to emigrate because of a famine. In both
cases the exile lasted longer than anyone foresaw and "the end remained
hidden." Nevertheless the day is coming when *they shall bring all your brethren
out of all the nations . . . upon horses and in chariots . . . to My holy mountain,
Jerusalem (Isaiah 66:20),* even as the Egyptians ultimately accompanied Jacob's
remains with great honors to the Holy Land.

שֶׁבַע שָׁנִים וְאַרְבָּעִים וּמְאַת שָׁנָה — *Were one hundred and forty-seven years* (lit.
seven years and forty and one hundred years). The Torah, informs us of Jacob's
age with the small number preceding the larger, contrary to the general rule.
This is in order to have the number forty-seven closer to the words שְׁנֵי חַיָּיו, the
years when Jacob "really lived." That was the time when he felt happy because
Rachel or Joseph was with him. These years did in fact number forty-seven, as
R' Chaim ben Attar points out.

29. וַיִּקְרְבוּ יְמֵי־יִשְׂרָאֵל לָמוּת — *The time approached for Israel to die.* When the
Torah says of someone that he drew near to death, it means that he did not live
as long as his fathers (*Rashi*). This term suggests that death draws near with
giant strides, that is to say, prematurely. See our commentary on 47:9 on why
Jacob did not attain the age of his fathers.

יְמֵי־יִשְׂרָאֵל — *The time . . . for Israel.* In the previous verse, which speaks of the
life of the patriarch, he is called Jacob, whereas here, when his death is
mentioned, he is called Israel. The contrary would seem to be more consistent
with the usual usage — the Torah generally calls the patriarch "Jacob" when he
appears in a state of weakness and "Israel" in the opposite context. Accordingly,
R' Yose explains that, as Jacob's life drew to a close, all his days appeared
encircled with an aura of glory, which the name of Israel designates. It is with
his highest title of nobility that the holy man will appear before the Celestial
Judge at the hour of his death (*Zohar*).

יְמֵי . . . לָמוּת — *Time . . . to die.* How did he know that he was going to die? At
that time he was thirty-three years younger than his father had been when he
died, and did we not learn that when a man approaches the age at which his
parents died, he should be concerned for five years before and five years after
(*Rashi* on 27:2)? But, says *Ramban*, he felt his powers declining and weakness
overcoming him, without being really ill. *R' Chaim ben Attar* replies that the
onset of physical weakness is far from proving that death is approaching. But
the righteous know of certain symptoms which they perceive thirty days before
the end, when death is decreed in the celestial spheres. From that moment the
image of God which is reflected in the human face becomes obscured.

of Jacob — the years of his life — were one hundred and forty-seven years. ²⁹ The time approached for Israel to die, so he called for his son, for Joseph, and said to him, "Please — if I have found favor in your eyes, please place your hand under my thigh and do

אִם־נָא מָצָאתִי חֵן בְּעֵינֶיךָ — *Please — if I have found favor in your eyes.* The old man begs his son and implores his kindness — נָא appears three times in this one verse. This is proof of the exceptional importance that he attaches to the prayer he is about to utter.

Under no circumstances and on no account did Jacob want to be buried in Egypt, not even temporarily. He had several reasons for this. First of all he wanted the Egyptians to see that the members of the family of Israel still did not consider themselves naturalized Egyptians. Their hearts still belonged to their ancient homeland. He wanted, in addition, to set in the hearts and minds of his children and of his children's children for all time the conviction that their true inheritance was none other than the Promised Land. To do so, no means would be more effective than having his tomb there. He knew that it would establish sentimental ties indestructibly linking the country where the ancestors lay buried with the families of their descendants, wherever they dwelt. They would often feel the desire to come and prostrate themselves upon the tomb of their ancestors, and would never give up to their enemies the land where the three patriarchs Abraham, Isaac, and Jacob lay buried. The plan of action decided on by Jacob was all the more urgent now that his children had begun to "let themselves be possessed by the land of Goshen," as was pointed out previously (cf. our commentary to verse 27). Life in Egypt threatened to have a profound influence on them. Soon they might substitute the Nile for the Jordan and their sojourn in Egypt would no longer seem to them an exile.

Rashi, however, brings arguments of quite a different sort. It was repugnant to Jacob to be buried in Egypt "where the earth would become vermin" (at the time of the third plague). This reason gives us insight into the patriarch's concern that his mortal remains be protected against destruction even in the grave (by insects, etc.). He was intent on making known his view that the body represents the envelope of the soul which issues from celestial spheres and hence, even after death, it deserves to be treated with the greatest respect. Jacob's children were aware of this lesson and gave their father's remains the most attentive care and the greatest respect (cf. our commentary to 50:2). This attitude regarding the treatment of the departed is basic in Jewish tradition.

Another of the patriarch's reasons is given by *Rashi*: "I do not want the Egyptians to idolize me." But most of all Jacob wished to be buried in the Holy Land, knowing that its earth brings peace and eternal rest to the dead. Regarding this, *Rashi* quotes the Talmud where this truth is expressed as follows (*Kesuvos* 111b): the dead outside the Holy Land will be resurrected only through the sufferings of underground migrations (in order to reach the Holy Land). Without claiming to interpret the sense of this image, we can nevertheless hold

ל עֲמָדִי חֶסֶד וֶאֱמֶת אַל־נָא תִקְבְּרֵנִי בְּמִצְרָיִם: וְשָׁכַבְתִּי
עִם־אֲבֹתַי וּנְשָׂאתַנִי מִמִּצְרַיִם וּקְבַרְתַּנִי בִּקְבֻרָתָם וַיֹּאמַר
לא אָנֹכִי אֶעֱשֶׂה כִדְבָרֶךָ: וַיֹּאמֶר הִשָּׁבְעָה לִי וַיִּשָּׁבַע לוֹ וַיִּשְׁתַּחוּ
יִשְׂרָאֵל עַל־רֹאשׁ הַמִּטָּה:

מח א וַיְהִי אַחֲרֵי הַדְּבָרִים הָאֵלֶּה וַיֹּאמֶר לְיוֹסֵף הִנֵּה אָבִיךָ
חֹלֶה וַיִּקַּח אֶת־שְׁנֵי בָנָיו עִמּוֹ אֶת־מְנַשֶּׁה וְאֶת־אֶפְרָיִם:

that the human body naturally aspires to rejoin its land of origin and that it suffers when far away from it. "And the dust returns to the earth where it was and the spirit returns to God Who gave it" (*Ecclesiastes* 12:7). This natural tendency to return to one's origins is common to all the elements of creation. Now, when God created man "from the dust of the earth," He "took it from the place where the altar of the Temple of Jerusalem would ultimately stand, as a widely held tradition teaches us" (הלכ׳ בית הבחירה, פ״ב). This spot is the "navel of the world," and the point of origin for creation. Accordingly, one can see that in Jerusalem and its environs the physical remains of man find the highest degree of peace and repose.

Concludes the *Zohar*, it is important to know all these reasons, for without them it would have been more in keeping with the patriarch's feelings to leave his tomb near his children and descendants. For them it would have been a place of comfort and protection amid the sufferings and calamities which Egyptian exile would inflict upon them.

שִׂים־נָא יָדְךָ תַּחַת יְרֵכִי — *Please place your hand under my thigh.* An allusion to the circumcised organ. At the time of the patriarchs, this *mitzvah* represented their sole sacred object; it was upon this that they swore until the day of the giving of the Torah (*Pirkei D'Rabbi Eliezer* 39). However, the feeling of natural modesty held the son back from doing this "under the thigh" of his father, and he just promised him: "I personally will do as you have said" (*Targum Yonasan*). In an analogous case, Abraham's servant Eliezer did put his hand under the thigh of his master, as the Torah tells us (24:9) — but Eliezer did not have the sentiments which a son has for his father.

וְעָשִׂיתָ עִמָּדִי חֶסֶד וֶאֱמֶת — *And do kindness and truth with me.* "Truth" — tell Pharaoh the whole truth, and do not hide the real reasons which prompted the last wishes of the dead father. "Kindness" — for this will be the final proof of filial devotion which will repay Jacob for all the disappointments, all the desertions, his sons had caused. Truth and loving-kindness — Jacob's testament will thus be the motto for the future conduct of his sons and it will serve them as a guide throughout the years of oppression (*R' S.R. Hirsch*).

30. וְשָׁכַבְתִּי עִם־אֲבֹתַי — *For I will lie down with my fathers.* It has already been noted (in our commentary to 25:8) that this expression does not refer to the earthly grave but to the repose of the soul. Now, these words precede the part of the verse where Jacob orders that his body be brought out and buried in the

kindness and truth with me — please do not bury me in Egypt.
³⁰ *For I will lie down with my fathers and you shall transport me out of Egypt and bury me in their tomb."*
   He said, "I personally will do as you have said."
   ³¹ *He replied, "Swear to me," and he swore to him; then Israel prostrated himself towards the head of the bed.*

48   ¹ *And it came to pass after these things that someone said to Joseph, "Behold! — your father is ill." So he took his two sons, Manasseh and Ephraim, with him.*

burial place of his fathers. The *Midrash Aggadah* concludes: the repose of the soul precedes that of the body. The soul goes "to rejoin the fathers," regardless of where their remains are buried.

31. הִשָּׁבְעָה לִי — *Swear to me.* Not that Jacob suspected that his son would not keep his word when the time came, but he made him swear knowing that this favor he demanded constituted an insult to the land which had given him hospitality. So he wanted to make it binding with a solemn oath to which Joseph could make reference if, on the death of his father, he was faced with a refusal from Pharaoh. The foresight of the patriarch turned out to be justified. Pharaoh acceded to Joseph's request solely because of the oath he had made to his father (*Ramban*). *Rashi* mentions: "Were it not for this oath, I would not have given you my permission." Pharaoh told him to have his oath annulled. But Joseph answered him back: "if I have this oath annulled I will also have the one I made to you annulled — not to reveal that in addition to the seventy languages I know the Holy Tongue, but you do not know it" (*Sotah* 36b; commentary to 50:6).

וַיִּשְׁתַּחוּ יִשְׂרָאֵל עַל־רֹאשׁ הַמִּטָּה — *Then Israel prostrated himself towards the head of the bed.* According to the Talmudic interpretation (*Megillah* 16b), this refers to Joseph. The old patriarch gave honor to Joseph who was now "at the head" of his descendants. In this regard, *Rashi* quotes the saying: "When it is the fox's time, bow down even before him." Of all the sons, only Joseph had the power to make his last wish come true. Thus came about, in any event, that part of Joseph's thirty-nine-year-old dream in which he had seen the sun (i.e. his father) bow down before him. This gesture represents a supreme tribute to Joseph in his position as viceroy of Egypt, after he had sworn to do a favor for Jacob which risked putting himself in disgrace before Pharaoh. But the bowing can also be taken as a mark of gratitude to the Divine Presence which, as *Rashi* notes, hovers above the head of a sick person. A third interpretation is given by the *Midrash Rabbah*; it is quoted in our commentary to 29:30.

48.

1. וַיְהִי אַחֲרֵי הַדְּבָרִים הָאֵלֶּה — *And it came to pass after these things.* This expression does not only refer to the preceding "things," but it usually implies certain reflections which those involved had in their minds. Here it refers to

ב וַיַּגֵּד לְיַעֲקֹב וַיֹּאמֶר הִנֵּה בִּנְךָ יוֹסֵף בָּא אֵלֶיךָ וַיִּתְחַזֵּק
ג יִשְׂרָאֵל וַיֵּשֶׁב עַל-הַמִּטָּה: וַיֹּאמֶר יַעֲקֹב אֶל-יוֹסֵף אֵל
ד שַׁדַּי נִרְאָה-אֵלַי בְּלוּז בְּאֶרֶץ כְּנָעַן וַיְבָרֶךְ אֹתִי: וַיֹּאמֶר אֵלַי
הִנְנִי מַפְרְךָ וְהִרְבִּיתִךָ וּנְתַתִּיךָ לִקְהַל עַמִּים וְנָתַתִּי אֶת-
ה הָאָרֶץ הַזֹּאת לְזַרְעֲךָ אַחֲרֶיךָ אֲחֻזַּת עוֹלָם: וְעַתָּה שְׁנֵי-
בָנֶיךָ הַנּוֹלָדִים לְךָ בְּאֶרֶץ מִצְרַיִם עַד-בֹּאִי אֵלֶיךָ מִצְרַיְמָה

thoughts which had disturbed the patriarch since his coming down to Egypt. —
Was he going to die and be buried in Egypt, and would his children then settle
down in this land, and lose themselves in the Egyptian population? These grave
sources of anxiety had just been dispelled by Joseph's oath, and the patriarch
realized that the promise he had received from God would be carried out to the
letter: *And I shall also surely bring you up; and Joseph shall place his hand on
your eyes* (46:4). It was after these reassuring thoughts that an illness made Jacob
aware that his time was drawing near (*Midrash HaGadol*).

וַיֹּאמֶר לְיוֹסֵף — *Someone said to Joseph. Rashi* explains: "One of the messengers.
Some say that it was Ephraim, who studied with Jacob; when Jacob had become
sick in Goshen, he went back to Egypt to tell his father." We see from this, add
the *Tosafists*, that Joseph was not usually with his father. Indeed, he feared
Jacob's questions regarding the circumstances of his sale to Egypt — these might
lead him to denounce the unspeakable behavior of his brothers. Above all he
wanted to avoid having his father pronounce a curse on them, for it would have
meant the ruin of the entire family. Had he not lost his own mother so prematurely because of a few words which his father had unwittingly uttered (31:32)?

הִנֵּה אָבִיךָ חֹלֶה — *Behold! — your father is ill.* "There were seven wondrous
events in the world since the creation of heaven and earth. The fourth was the
natural phenomenon of sickness. From the time of creation, a man had never
been afflicted with illness before his death (cf. *Tosafos* to *Bava Basra* 16b).
Whether on the road or in the marketplace, he simply sneezed and expired. But
Jacob besought God saying: 'Master of the Universe, do not take back my soul
before I have had time to make my last wishes known to my children and to
repent.' God heard his prayer and made him fall sick some days before his death.
The nations were astonished to learn of this new phenomenon. From that time,
we make a habit of wishing someone good health when we hear him sneeze so
that this sudden and convulsive movement not have mortal consequences"
(*Pirkei D'Rabbi Eliezer* 52; *Magen Avraham* §230, 7).

וַיִּקַּח אֶת-שְׁנֵי בָנָיו — *So he took his two sons.* Aware that his grandfather Isaac had
reserved the blessing for his children until he felt the approach of death, Joseph
now took his two sons to have them benefit at the same time as himself from
his father's ultimate blessing. (Final rebukes are also kept for the days which
precede death, for the four reasons which *Rashi* gives in his commentary to

² *Jacob was told, "Behold! — your son Joseph has come to you."*
So Israel exerted himself and sat up on the bed.

³ *Jacob said to Joseph, "El Shaddai had appeared to me in Luz*
in the land of Canaan and He blessed me. ⁴ *He said to me, 'Behold*
— I will make you fruitful and numerous; I will make you a
congregation of nations, and I will give this land to your offspring
after you as an eternal possession.' ⁵ *And now, your two sons who*
were born to you in Egypt before my coming to you in Egypt shall

Deuteronomy 1:3.) Joseph was intent on making sure that his own posterity
would continue the great family tradition. This motivated him to bring his
children to his father, so that before he died they might receive his blessing,
which also included the blessing of his forefathers, Abraham and Isaac. This
scene, wherein we see Joseph experiencing the joy of being able to present his
children to his father and of having them blessed by him, represents the
crowning glory of Jacob's life. It offers to every Jewish father the ideal picture
of the perfect harmony which embraces past and future generations with the
same aspirations. As for Joseph, the paternal blessing upon his children must
have given him immense satisfaction, after his heroic struggles in Egypt to
safeguard the ancestral faith within his home.

2. וַיִּתְחַזֵּק יִשְׂרָאֵל — *So Israel exerted himself.* He prepared himself to receive
prophetic inspiration in order to give his paternal blessing. Since his arrival in
the land of exile, inspiration only came to him in darkness, intermittently, like
a flash of lightning in the night. But as death approached it became more
luminous, like a candle flame which has a sudden brilliance before it goes out
(*Ha'amek Davar*).

3. אֵל שַׁדַּי נִרְאָה־אֵלַי בְּלוּז — *El Shaddai had appeared to me in Luz.* The
introductory word וְעַתָּה, *and now,* at the beginning of verse 5 makes it clear that
the privilege of the birthright accorded to Joseph by the investiture of his two
sons as distinct tribes is to find its justification in the explanation of the verses
which precede it.

4. וּנְתַתִּיךָ לִקְהַל עַמִּים — *I will make you a congregation of nations.* "God
announced to me that He will make me the ancestor of a community of nations.
Although He had told me: *A nation and a congregation of nations* (35:11), the
nation refers to Benjamin (the other sons were born before this announcement).
And the *congregation of nations* means two nations beside Benjamin. Now,
since that time, I have not had any sons. From this He taught me that one of my
tribes is to be split into two. And now, this privilege I give to you" (*Rashi*).

Jacob's reasons for granting this privilege to Joseph have been explained in
our commentary to 35:23. But, in a more general way, it appears that Jacob
constantly sought to put personal merit ahead of the privilege of birth (see our
commentary to verses 14 and 20 of this chapter).

ו לִי־הֶם אֶפְרַ֫יִם וּמְנַשֶּׁ֗ה כִּרְאוּבֵ֥ן וְשִׁמְע֖וֹן יִֽהְיוּ־לִ֑י: וּמוֹלַדְתְּךָ֞
אֲשֶׁר־הוֹלַ֣דְתָּ אַחֲרֵיהֶ֖ם לְךָ֣ יִֽהְי֑וּ עַ֣ל שֵׁ֧ם אֲחֵיהֶ֛ם יִקָּרְא֖וּ
ז בְּנַחֲלָתָֽם: וַאֲנִ֣י ׀ בְּבֹאִ֣י מִפַּדָּ֗ן מֵ֩תָה֩ עָלַ֨י רָחֵ֜ל בְּאֶ֤רֶץ
כְּנַ֨עַן֙ בַּדֶּ֔רֶךְ בְּע֥וֹד כִּבְרַת־אֶ֖רֶץ לָבֹ֣א אֶפְרָ֑תָה וָאֶקְבְּרֶ֤הָ
ח שָּׁם֙ בְּדֶ֣רֶךְ אֶפְרָ֔ת הִ֖וא בֵּ֣ית לָֽחֶם: וַיַּ֥רְא יִשְׂרָאֵ֖ל אֶת־
ט בְּנֵ֣י יוֹסֵ֑ף וַיֹּ֖אמֶר מִי־אֵֽלֶּה: וַיֹּ֤אמֶר יוֹסֵף֙ אֶל־אָבִ֔יו בָּנַ֣י הֵ֔ם
אֲשֶׁר־נָֽתַן־לִ֥י אֱלֹהִ֖ים בָּזֶ֑ה וַיֹּאמַ֕ר קָֽחֶם־נָ֥א אֵלַ֖י וַאֲבָרְכֵֽם:

Finally, it should not be forgotten that Levi, third son of Jacob, had long been destined by his father to be in charge of the Divine service, for the reasons indicated in our commentary on 28:22. As a consequence, the tribe issuing from him would not have a portion of territory in the Promised Land (*Deuteronomy* 14:27); this meant that the number of tribes receiving a share of the land would not total twelve (the number foreseen from the beginning; cf. our commentary to 35:22). Accordingly, Jacob wanted to reattain this number by substituting Manasseh and Ephraim for Levi and also for Joseph himself, since Joseph too was not to be counted as one of the twelve tribes, as *Rashi* explains on 50:13.

5. אֶפְרַיִם וּמְנַשֶּׁה — *Ephraim and Manasseh.* The numerical value of these two names equals רְאוּבֵן וְשִׁמְעוֹן (*Baal HaTurim*). The two sons of Joseph had the same rights as the sons of Jacob, and in their travels through the desert these two tribes had their own banners.

6. וּמוֹלַדְתְּךָ אֲשֶׁר־הוֹלַדְתָּ אַחֲרֵיהֶם — *But progeny born to you after them.* They will not form new tribes but will be taken in and allotted places in the tribes of Ephraim and Manasseh, without being given a special name. Indeed, *Rashi* holds that the land was divided up "according to the number of heads," that is to say that everyone received an equal share, but only the firstborn, who received a double portion, bore the names of the tribes. The title in question would therefore be purely honorific. But this is not *Ramban's* opinion. He holds that the country was divided into twelve equal parts and Joseph received two of these portions because of the right of the firstborn which had just been granted to him. His other children, though, only received a single share, in conformity with the rule of dividing the land according to the number of people (*Numbers* 26:54), which refers to families but not to the twelve tribes. Furthermore, contrary to *Rashi*, *Ramban* (and *Ibn Ezra*) maintains that Joseph did have other children besides Ephraim and Manasseh!

7. וַאֲנִי בְּבֹאִי מִפַּדָּן — *But as for me — when I came from Paddan.* This phrase, which seemingly has no connection with Jacob's previous words, *Rashi* explains as follows: Although I demand from you the task of carrying my body up for burial in the land of Canaan in the Cave of Machpelah, I myself did not do so for your mother, even though she died near Bethlehem . . . and I know that in your heart you reproach me for it. But know that it was at God's command that I buried her at that place so that she will be a comfort to her children when

> be mine; Ephraim and Manasseh shall be mine like Reuben and
> Simeon. [6] But progeny born to you after them shall be yours; they
> will be included under the name of their brothers with regard
> to their inheritance. [7] But as for me — when I came from Paddan,
> Rachel died on me in the land of Canaan on the road, while there
> was still a stretch of land to go to Ephrath; and I buried her there
> on the road to Ephrath, which is Bethlehem."
>
> [8] Then Israel saw Joseph's sons and he said, "Who are these?"
> [9] And Joseph said to his father, "They are my sons whom God
> has given me here."
>
> He said, "Bring them to me, if you please, and I will bless
> them."

Nebuzaradan drives them into exile and they pass there. Then Rachel will come out of her tomb, she will cry and pray for God's mercy for them, as is stated in the book of Jeremiah (31:14). [The word בַּדֶּרֶךְ, on the road, alludes to the future route of the exiles.]

For Ramban, however, Jacob's justification for not burying Rachel in the family tomb of Machpelah is entirely different and he derives it from the text which puts the greatest emphasis on the fact that she died suddenly "on the road." Jacob was struggling hard to take care of the needs of his large family and extensive herds. While he was on the road, he lacked the appropriate means for transferring the mortal remains of his wife with the honor due her. Hence he gave up this project. But, continues Ramban, these arguments put forward by the patriarch were only outward reasons serving as excuses. The real reasons are on an entirely different level. They were mentioned in our commentary on 35:18, and they, along with the explanation previously quoted from Rashi, teach us that Rachel's burial "along the way" had profound significance. Accordingly, Jacob could not accede to Joseph's wish (Pesikta Rabbasi) that the remains of his mother be brought to the Cave of Machpelah.

8. מִי־אֵלֶּה — Who are these? R' Shmuel ben Nachman remarks that the prophetic spirit left Jacob on two occasions: when he wanted to bless his two grandsons, and later when he wanted to reveal the ultimate end of exile to his children (Tanchuma). Similar obstacles, although of another type, had already been encountered when his father and his grandfather wanted to bless their children. Praying that a man be granted prosperity, power, and wisdom as well as Divine protection presupposes a very high degree of moral dignity on the part of the beneficiary and his descendants. Now, when Jacob felt inspiration leaving him, he understood that the offspring of his grandchildren were not to be worthy of his blessing (whereas he had full confidence in Ephraim and Manasseh, whom he had known well for seventeen years). He saw (not with his eyes — since it will be mentioned shortly in the Torah that the eyes of Israel were dim with age and he could no longer see — but with an inner vision) that "from Ephraim would one day come Jeroboam and Ahab, and from Manasseh,

שני

י וְעֵינֵי יִשְׂרָאֵל כָּבְדוּ מִזֹּקֶן לֹא יוּכַל לִרְאוֹת וַיַּגֵּשׁ אֹתָם

יא אֵלָיו וַיִּשַּׁק לָהֶם וַיְחַבֵּק לָהֶם: וַיֹּאמֶר יִשְׂרָאֵל אֶל־יוֹסֵף רְאֹה

פָנֶיךָ לֹא פִלָּלְתִּי וְהִנֵּה הֶרְאָה אֹתִי אֱלֹהִים גַּם אֶת־זַרְעֶךָ:

יב-יג וַיּוֹצֵא יוֹסֵף אֹתָם מֵעִם בִּרְכָּיו וַיִּשְׁתַּחוּ לְאַפָּיו אָרְצָה: וַיִּקַּח

יוֹסֵף אֶת־שְׁנֵיהֶם אֶת־אֶפְרַיִם בִּימִינוֹ מִשְּׂמֹאל יִשְׂרָאֵל

יד וְאֶת־מְנַשֶּׁה בִשְׂמֹאלוֹ מִימִין יִשְׂרָאֵל וַיַּגֵּשׁ אֵלָיו: וַיִּשְׁלַח

יִשְׂרָאֵל אֶת־יְמִינוֹ וַיָּשֶׁת עַל־רֹאשׁ אֶפְרַיִם וְהוּא הַצָּעִיר

וְאֶת־שְׂמֹאלוֹ עַל־רֹאשׁ מְנַשֶּׁה שִׂכֵּל אֶת־יָדָיו כִּי מְנַשֶּׁה

Jehu and his sons" (*Rashi*). Indeed, in later history the tribes of Ephraim and Manasseh were at the origin of the defection which ultimately led to a national catastrophe for Jewry. So much was this so that among the prophets, Ephraim, representing the tribes in the North, became the symbol of infidelity and treason (e.g. *Hosea*, chapters 4-7; see, however, the commentary on verse 19). Israel said then: *"Who are these? From where did these come?"* — that is to say, his two grandsons (ibid.). His first thought was that their birth might have been tainted and blemished. Was not their mother Asenath, whom Pharaoh had given to Joseph for a wife, of pagan birth? Then Joseph showed his father "his contract of betrothal and his marriage contract" (ibid.). He presented him with the proofs that his wife descended from Abraham (see our commentary on 41:45). He then prayed for Divine mercy, and the Holy Spirit came to hover again over Jacob, who was then able to bestow his blessing upon his grandchildren. And Joseph thought: "Despite the hesitation on Abraham's part, had not God Himself given His blessing to Isaac even though it implicitly included Esau as well? (cf. our commentary to 25:11). Why then should Jacob refuse to bless his sons because of some impious descendants?"

10. וְעֵינֵי יִשְׂרָאֵל כָּבְדוּ מִזֹּקֶן — *Now Israel's eyes were heavy with age.* The *Kohanim* close their eyes while giving the priestly blessing. The Torah tells us that Jacob and his father Isaac (27:1) had their eyes closed when the *Shechinah* descended over them and inspired them as they bestowed their blessings (*Sefer Chassidim*, ed. Freimann, No. 1588). When a man is under the sway of the higher spirit, emanating from sacred spheres, he must eliminate all extraneous impressions from his sight and direct all his thoughts to the spirit which inspires him and which gives him the power to bless.

וַיִּשַּׁק לָהֶם וַיְחַבֵּק לָהֶם — *And he kissed them and hugged them.* With his beloved children he wanted to feel profound joy so that the *Shechinah* could come to dwell over him. For It resides not amid sadness and despair, but where there is serene joy (*Midrash Aggadah*). However, when he saw that the *Shechinah* delayed in giving him inspiration, he began to speak about other matters (as the next verse tells us) until Joseph bowed to the ground before him and prayed to God for the paternal benediction for his children.

¹⁰ *Now Israel's eyes were heavy with age, he could not see; so he brought them near him and he kissed them and hugged them.* ¹¹ *Israel said to Joseph, "I dared not accept the thought that I would see your face, and here God has shown me even your offspring!"* ¹² *Joseph then removed them from his knees and he prostrated himself with his face toward the ground.* ¹³ *Joseph took the two of them — Ephraim with his right [hand], to Israel's left, and Manasseh with his left, to Israel's right — and he drew close to him.* ¹⁴ *But Israel extended his right hand and laid it on Ephraim's head though he was the younger and his left hand on Manasseh's head. He maneuvered his hands, for Manasseh was*

11. לֹא פִלָּלְתִּי — *I dared not accept the thought.* According to *Rashi*, פִלָּלְתִּי has the sense of thinking. But *Onkelos* translates, "I had not hoped," and *Rashbam*, "I did not deem myself (sufficiently worthy)." The *Midrashim* interpret: I did not even pray to see you again (for I thought you were dead).

12. וַיּוֹצֵא יוֹסֵף אֹתָם מֵעִם בִּרְכָּיו — *Joseph then removed them from his knees.* In a figurative sense: He took them off his lap and said to them: "Look no longer for the princely honors which you have enjoyed so far — they are only temporary. Instead, pray that the Divine Spirit should come to inspire your grandfather to bestow his blessing upon you" (*Midrash HaGadol*). Here we find the underlying reason why Joseph brought his children with him and why he insisted so much that they be blessed by his father. Indeed, throughout *Genesis*, the patriarchal benediction signifies the investiture of the messianic vocation of the Jewish people.

14. וַיָּשֶׁת עַל־רֹאשׁ אֶפְרַיִם — *And laid it on Ephraim's head.* Not only is the hand the organ *par excellence* for carrying out what the human brain dictates, but it is also through the hands that the Holy Spirit is transmitted at the time of ordination (*Numbers* 27:18), of consecration (*Leviticus* 1:4), and of blessing (ibid. 9:22). These direct links between the Spirit and the hands enable us to understand *Onkelos'* translation of the words שִׂכֵּל אֶת־יָדָיו: אַחְכִּימִנּוּן לִידוֹהִי, *he placed his hands intelligently*, שִׂכֵּל being derived from שֵׂכֶל, *intelligence*, and not from סֶכֶל, *folly*, as R' *Yitzchak Arama* had emphasized in *Akeidas Yitzchak*.

שִׂכֵּל אֶת־יָדָיו — *He maneuvered his hands.* R' Chananel, quoted by R' *Bachya*, interprets this to mean that he crossed his hands. Instead of making his two grandsons change places, as the latter states, Jacob preferred to cross his hands over their heads so as "not to humiliate Manasseh, who was the firstborn" (*Maharshal*). Accordingly, the words כִּי מְנַשֶּׁה הַבְּכוֹר are taken to mean "for Manasseh was the firstborn" and not "although he was the firstborn," as *Rashi* proposes. Jacob's concern not to humiliate Joseph's firstborn appears even more comprehensible since on several occasions he had shown a marked preference for the younger son and this had already provoked very serious crises in the

טו הַבְּכֹר: וַיְבָ֣רֶךְ אֶת־יוֹסֵף֮ וַיֹּאמַר֒ הָאֱלֹהִ֡ים אֲשֶׁר֩ הִתְהַלְּכ֨וּ
אֲבֹתַ֤י לְפָנָיו֙ אַבְרָהָ֣ם וְיִצְחָ֔ק הָאֱלֹהִים֙ הָרֹעֶ֣ה אֹתִ֔י
טז מֵעוֹדִ֖י עַד־הַיּ֥וֹם הַזֶּֽה: הַמַּלְאָךְ֩ הַגֹּאֵ֨ל אֹתִ֜י מִכָּל־רָ֗ע
יְבָרֵךְ֮ אֶת־הַנְּעָרִים֒ וְיִקָּרֵ֤א בָהֶם֙ שְׁמִ֔י וְשֵׁ֥ם אֲבֹתַ֖י אַבְרָהָ֥ם

family. To be sure, Jacob showed preferences openly, doing so for the reasons indicated in our commentary to 37:4, but a certain circumspection in their expression was nevertheless needed in the interests of keeping peace in the family.

As for Jacob's reasons for preferring the younger grandson, he himself states them: Manasseh "will also become a people and he will also grow great; yet his younger brother will surpass him and his descendants will be the talk of the nations." The patriarch thus attributes the pre-eminence of the younger brother to his future destiny and not to the effect of his blessing, but one may assume that this distinction stems from moral causes. Now, for seventeen years Ephraim devoted himself to sacred studies with his grandfather whereas Manasseh, the supervisor in Joseph's palace (*Rashi* on 42:23 and 48:1), was inclined toward temporal matters. In these differences of character Jacob could see confirmation of what he had already experienced several times: the moral and spiritual calling was better safeguarded by the younger brother than by the elder. And so he acted accordingly, with his thoughts on the very somber future of the two tribes of Ephraim and Manasseh which he had just glimpsed in his prophetic vision. Jacob's benediction, then, was aimed at assuring his grandsons of זְכוּת אָבוֹת, *the merit of the fathers,* and Divine protection.

15. וַיְבָרֶךְ אֶת־יוֹסֵף וַיֹּאמַר — *He blessed Joseph and he said.* He blessed Joseph by blessing his children; for is not the greatest blessing for a father that which is bestowed on his children? (*Ramban*). However, R' Chaim ben Attar interprets the verse thus: He blessed Joseph, then, he said [to his sons, etc.].

הָאֱלֹהִים אֲשֶׁר הִתְהַלְּכוּ אֲבֹתַי לְפָנָיו — *O God before Whom my forefathers ... walked.* The first part of this phrase invokes the merit of the fathers, the last resort in grave circumstances, as we see from Moses' prayer (*Exodus* 32:13) and Solomon's (*Psalms* 132:10; cf. *Shemos Rabbah* 8). But the words can be interpreted in two ways, as is recorded in the *Midrash Rabbah.* "Walking before God" could mean as a herald who precedes the King to proclaim his coming, or as a shepherd who is preceded by his flock in order that he may be better able to watch over them. The first interpretation emphasizes the glory which the ancestors brought to God, whereas the second brings out the honor which they received from God. In any case, Jacob seems to be thinking of the second meaning because, as he speaks modestly of himself, he says: "God Who shepherds me" (on the use of the present in the phrases הָרֹעֶה אֹתִי and הַגֹּאֵל אֹתִי, see our commentary on 35:3).

16. הַמַּלְאָךְ הַגֹּאֵל אֹתִי — *May the angel who redeems me.* Jacob's blessing refers to two things, daily subsistence (פַּרְנָסָה) and deliverance from all danger (גְּאֻלָּה).

the firstborn. ¹⁵ *He blessed Joseph and he said, "O God before Whom my forefathers Abraham and Isaac walked — God Who shepherds me from my inception until this day:* ¹⁶ *May the angel who redeems me from all evil bless the lads, and may my name be declared upon them, and the names of my forefathers Abraham*

According to the Midrash, the first comes from the words: "God Who shepherds me *from my inception until this day,*" an image which evokes Providence leading man to his "pasture." In Jacob's eyes, continues R' Eliezer in *Yalkut Shimoni,* both benefits depend on a daily miracle, and when Jacob gives his blessing to his grandchildren he prays that this solicitude from Providence be upon them.

However, Jacob makes a distinction between these two benefits. He attributes daily subsistence to a Divine act, הָאֱלֹהִים וגו׳, and deliverance from danger to the action of the appointed angel (הַמַּלְאָךְ). Philosophers and commentators attempt to explain the differences between the one and the other. It appears that the subsistence accorded daily to all creatures, from the largest to the most minute, is something supernatural, for which the Creator alone holds the keys in His hands (*Taanis* 2a). This means that this phenomenon does not follow from natural laws but is subordinate to an act of Providence. How many times through the long years of hardship, misery and then prosperity had Jacob felt the wonder of Divine mercy which never abandons those who have faith in it? As his life comes to a close, he eagerly wishes that this blessing carry on and continue to benefit his beloved grandchildren.

Together with this Jacob is thinking about the permanent protection which he had enjoyed while surrounded by threats of death, blackmail, ignoble tricks, enemy aggression — in short by the countless hardships which had plagued him since his youth. He attributes this "redemption from all evil" to the "guardian angel," this מַלְאָךְ which one meets so often in life. It is accepted that, at the time of creating man, God appoints a guardian angel to protect him from the harm which elements of the physical world hold in store, as well as from the dangers, no less serious, which lie in wait for him in his social life. Such angels are referred to in the Poem About Evil Forces, שִׁיר שֶׁל פְּגָעִים (*Shevuos* 15b thus calls Psalm 91): *No evil will befall you,...For He will appoint His angels over you to protect you in all your ways* (vs. 10-11). This protective function derives then from a factor of creation — it does not have the character of natural law or of an act of Divine mercy that is granted indiscriminately. Accordingly, one must constantly pray for it, and this conviction led Jacob to express the wish: *May the angel who redeems me from all evil bless the lads.*

יְבָרֵךְ אֶת־הַנְּעָרִים — *Bless the lads.* In his book *Emunah Ramah* the philosopher R' Avraham ben David Halevi explains why the singular יְבָרֵךְ is used here, even though the reference in this verse includes also the Divinity mentioned in the preceding verse. Since the angel is only the representative of God and His instrument, there is in reality only one agent (pp. 83-84).

שלישי יז וְיִצְחָק וְיִדְגּוּ לָרֹב בְּקֶרֶב הָאָרֶץ: וַיַּרְא יוֹסֵף כִּי־יָשִׁית
אָבִיו יַד־יְמִינוֹ עַל־רֹאשׁ אֶפְרַיִם וַיֵּרַע בְּעֵינָיו וַיִּתְמֹךְ
יַד־אָבִיו לְהָסִיר אֹתָהּ מֵעַל רֹאשׁ־אֶפְרַיִם עַל־רֹאשׁ מְנַשֶּׁה:

וְיִקָּרֵא בָהֶם שְׁמִי — *And may my name be declared upon them.* May they be
worthy of having my name and those of my fathers, Abraham and Isaac, linked
with theirs (*Sforno*). The importance that the patriarch attaches here to family
honor (which is at the basis of the Jewish concept of יחוס) is also borne out
contrariwise when Jacob purposely separates himself from his sons Simeon and
Levi for tarnishing his name: *With their congregation, do not join, my honor*
(49:6).

The text permits another interpretation: "Let my name be invoked by them."
The patriarch blesses his children by wishing that his own name and that of his
ancestors be known, revered, and celebrated because of their works and their
merits. That the name of the father be exalted as a result of the exemplary
conduct of his children and grandchildren — this is the most wonderful blessing
which he can bestow.

וְיִדְגּוּ לָרֹב — *And may they proliferate abundantly.* *Rashi* explains that fish are
fruitful and multiply without the evil eye having power over them. The term
דָּגָה refers to the act of procreation (as *Rashi* notes in *Yoma* 75a). This
benediction was to come to fruition when they will arrive in the land of Canaan
after their journey in the desert. But, given that when they left Egypt these two
tribes were no more numerous than the others, it follows that the share of the
Promised Land set aside for them according to their numbers at the time of the
Exodus eventually no longer sufficed. And so Joseph's descendants complained
to Joshua, saying: "Why have you given us only one portion and one district
when we are a great people, as God has blessed us?" Joshua replied to them: "*If
you are so numerous, go up to the forest . . . the hill country will be yours, etc.*"
(*Joshua* 17:14-15). He gave them this advice, add the Sages of the Talmud,
because he wanted to shield them from the evil eye by concealing them in
wooded areas. He was afraid that the evil eye would be attracted to them because
of their exceptional growth in numbers. But they did not accept this offer (ibid.
verse 16), pointing out that: "We are the descendants of Joseph and the evil eye
has no power over us because of the blessing of our ancestor" (*Bava Basra* 118b).

This part of the benediction was considered so basic that the fish served as the
emblem on the banner of the tribe of Ephraim (cf. *Torah Sheleimah* by M.M.
Kasher). Some pagan peoples worshiped it as an idol of fertility. Even to this day
the emblem of the fish frequently serves as a talisman against the effect of the
evil eye which stems from the occult power of the jealousy, hatred and envy of
others.

If Joseph and his offspring were found worthy of being protected from the
effect of the evil eye, it was because of the great merit he had acquired by closing
his eyes to the temptress, the wife of his master, when staying at his house. בֵּן

and Isaac, and may they proliferate abundantly like fish within the land."

¹⁷ Joseph saw that his father was placing his right hand on Ephraim's head and it displeased him; so he supported his father's hand to remove it from upon Ephraim's head to Manasseh's head.

פּוֹרָת עֲלֵי עָיִן, he was the wonderful son "because of the eye" and so he received the paternal blessing which raised him "above the evil eye" (49:22), as R' Abbahu points out (*Zevachim* 118b). Joseph deserved the title of צַדִּיק because of the sanctification of his vision (קְדוּשַׁת הָעַיִן) which he had been able to achieve (*Sfas Emes*).

However, Jacob may have had very different reasons for evoking the life of fish. We have already seen several times how Jacob tended to lead a solitary life, keeping his distance from the native population and only looking for the best means of raising and instructing his children in a homogeneous milieu, sheltered from foreign influences (cf. our commentary to 35:27). Accordingly, in blessing his children he sees before him the image of the aquatic world. Fish live their own lives, in an element apart, in calm, and in depths unseen. And men, inhabitants of another element, hardly suspect this joyous, carefree, happy existence of theirs which continues from generation to generation. This is how the patriarch wanted to see his descendants live, but בְּקֶרֶב הָאָרֶץ, in the midst of the earth, flourishing in security and happiness, in the element which is their very own, in a place where the surrounding world can neither follow them nor appreciate the profound significance of their lives. They will then be, as *Onkelos* interprets, "in the midst of humanity, on earth, like the fish in the sea."

17. וַיַּרְא יוֹסֵף — *Joseph saw.* Some commentators hold that Joseph's gesture took place prior to the blessings reported above since the phrase, "his father had placed his right hand, etc." is not in the past tense (שָׁת) but in the future: יָשִׁית. Joseph saw that his father was going to put his right hand down . . . and that displeased him. There had already been several dramatic crises within his family as a result of preference being openly shown to the younger son, and, well aware of these, Joseph believed he was justified in doing everything possible to avoid any repetition among his own children. But his father held a different opinion, as is apparent from his reply. Hence we see here the outbreak of a brief but vehement conflict between father and son, and with it the peremptory action of the latter.

יַד־יְמִינוֹ — *His right hand.* Regarding the importance attributed to the right hand, see *Rashi* on *Exodus* 15:6 and commentaries (cf. our commentary to verse 14).

וַיִּתְמֹךְ יַד־אָבִיו לְהָסִיר אֹתָהּ — *So he supported his father's hand to remove it.* To this audacious gesture, the father replied: "You want to remove this hand which fought the Angel of God and vanquished him?" R' Yochanan asked: "Jacob's arms were like the two columns in the palaces at Tiberias." These remarks

יח וַיֹּאמֶר יוֹסֵף אֶל־אָבִיו לֹא־כֵן אָבִי כִּי־זֶה הַבְּכֹר שִׂים יְמִינְךָ
יט עַל־רֹאשׁוֹ: וַיְמָאֵן אָבִיו וַיֹּאמֶר יָדַעְתִּי בְנִי יָדַעְתִּי גַּם־
הוּא יִהְיֶה־לְעָם וְגַם־הוּא יִגְדָּל וְאוּלָם אָחִיו הַקָּטֹן יִגְדַּל
כ מִמֶּנּוּ וְזַרְעוֹ יִהְיֶה מְלֹא־הַגּוֹיִם: וַיְבָרֲכֵם בַּיּוֹם הַהוּא לֵאמוֹר

emphasize the patriarch's determined wish to bestow the benediction in the manner he intended.

19. וַיְמָאֵן אָבִיו וַיֹּאמֶר — *But his father refused, saying.* Cf. our commentary to 39:8.

יָדַעְתִּי בְנִי יָדַעְתִּי — *I know, my son, I know.* Rashi explains: "I know who is the firstborn." And the second affirmation of יָדַעְתִּי, the Midrash interprets: "I know also of the incident of Reuben and Bilhah, and of Judah and Tamar." The implications of this allusion, continues the *Zohar*, let Joseph see the reasons for Jacob's lack of esteem for the right of primogeniture. Jacob knew that the firstborn of his sons, as well as the first among them in authority, had been guilty of moral misdeeds, whereas the second youngest, Joseph, had conducted himself as his true son (בְּנִי) even though separated from his father for many years. Indeed it was the awareness of being the son of his saintly father that at the critical moment had kept Joseph from yielding to the temptation to sin with Potiphar's wife (cf. our commentary to 39:11).

וְאוּלָם אָחִיו הַקָּטֹן יִגְדַּל מִמֶּנּוּ — *Yet his younger brother shall become greater than he.* For from him will descend Joshua, who will give Jewry the Holy Land as an inheritance and teach them Torah (*Rashi*). We have already noted that the study of the Torah was the prerogative of Ephraim (see our commentary on verse 14) and that the patriarch gave him pre-eminence because of this spiritual calling. But the tribe of Ephraim also stood out because of its profound ties to the Holy Land. It was Joshua who had the great merit, known the world over, of conquering the Holy Land, but long before him the tribe of Ephraim had shown its deep attachment to the land of the ancestors when it threw off the yoke of Egyptian slavery and departed en masse to settle there (*Sanhedrin* 92b). This premature venture toward freedom came to an end with the defeat of the valiant warriors of Ephraim. But their remains, strewn over the valley of the land of the Philistines, were restored to life in the time of the prophet Ezekiel who proclaimed: "Thus says God: Behold I shall open your graves and cause you to come up out of your graves, My people, and I shall bring you back into the land of Israel ... (37:12). If the tribe of Ephraim did make the error of breaking the chains of exile before the time fixed by Providence, they did so with pure intentions. They aspired to free themselves from a life in exile, motivated by a yearning for the Holy Land, in order to be better able to serve God there. And so we see this tribe given credit by the prophet in his words of consolation to the children of Rachel: *I have indeed heard (said God) Ephraim bemoaning himself: "You have chastised me and I was chastised as an untamed calf; cause me to return and I will return; for You alone, God, will be my God ...I have repented, I am aware of my faults, I have beat my breast. I am ashamed and confounded*

¹⁸ *And Joseph said to his father, "Not so, Father, for this is the firstborn; place your right hand on his head."*

¹⁹ *But his father refused, saying, "I know, my son, I know; he too will become a people, and he too will become great; yet his younger brother shall become greater than he, and his off-spring['s fame] will fill the nations." ²⁰ So he blessed them that day, saying,*

because I bear the disgrace of my youth." Is not Ephraim then a son dear to Me? Or a child that I cherish? For whenever I speak of him, I do earnestly remember him again. Therefore are my inward parts moved for him; I shall surely have mercy upon him, says God (Jeremiah 31:17-19). These were also the sentiments of the patriarch when he foresaw the future of his children. For him also, Ephraim was "the dear son, the child that I cherish" (*Zohar*).

וְזַרְעוֹ יִהְיֶה מְלֹא־הַגּוֹיִם — *And his offspring['s fame] will fill the nations.* The name Ephraim, particularly among the prophets, is a collective name for the northern kingdom, made up of the ten tribes who "were lost" when they subsequently were scattered among the nations. *Ephraim is mixed with the nations (Hosea 7:8).* Was it it this world-wide dispersion which the patriarch had in mind when he uttered that prophetic phrase *his offspring['s fame] will fill the nations?* Some of our commentators think so. True, the punishment of dispersion was due to the unfaithfulness and sinfulness of Ephraim's descendants (*Hosea*, ibid.), yet upon their ancestor Jacob does confer his blessing, for "they will return to God" and will have their share in the World to Come (*Sanhedrin* 110b). And R' Eliezer adds: "Even the darkness in which the ten tribes were lost will one day become as radiant as the day" (according to the version of *Avos D'Rabbi Nosson* 36). And in retrospect do we not see that these children of Abraham, Isaac and Jacob, scattered among the nations, did indeed "enlighten" them? They did so by bringing them the fundamental ideals of the knowledge and love of the God of their forefathers, ideas which they had never forsaken. Hence they too have a messianic vocation and their Messiah, מָשִׁיחַ בֶּן יוֹסֵף (*Sukkah* 52a), also called מָשִׁיחַ בֶּן אֶפְרַיִם (*Targum Yonasan* on *Exodus* 40:11), will be a redeemer of humanity as the precursor of מָשִׁיחַ בֶּן דָוִד, the Messiah son of David. It is therefore not surprising to find that the prophet Jeremiah speaks with tender affection for the kingdom of Ephraim (just as he did in his words previously quoted): *Go, says God, and proclaim these words to [the kingdom of] the North, and say: Return, you backsliding Israel. I will no longer cause My anger to fall upon you; for I am full of kindness, says God, I will not bear a grudge forever . . . Return, backsliding children, for I want to make a union with you. I will take you one of a city and two of a family, and I will bring you to Zion (3:12,14).* Seen in this light, the patriarch's words, "his descendants will be the talk of all the nations," assume the significance of a blessing.

20. וַיְבָרְכֵם בַּיּוֹם הַהוּא — *So he blessed them that day.* The text does not say בַּיּוֹם הַזֶּה, *on this day,* but בַּיּוֹם הַהוּא, *on that particular day,* when, according to *Rashi,* one will want to bless his children. The *Targum Yonasan* is more explicit: "on

בְּךָ֡ יְבָרֵ֣ךְ יִשְׂרָאֵל֩ לֵאמֹ֨ר יְשִֽׂמְךָ֤ אֱלֹהִים֙ כְּאֶפְרַ֣יִם וְכִמְנַשֶּׁ֔ה
כא וַיָּ֥שֶׂם אֶת־אֶפְרַ֖יִם לִפְנֵ֥י מְנַשֶּֽׁה: וַיֹּ֤אמֶר יִשְׂרָאֵל֙ אֶל־יוֹסֵ֔ף
הִנֵּ֥ה אָנֹכִ֖י מֵ֑ת וְהָיָ֤ה אֱלֹהִים֙ עִמָּכֶ֔ם וְהֵשִׁ֣יב אֶתְכֶ֔ם אֶל־אֶ֖רֶץ

the day a newborn child is circumcised." Oriental communities have adopted the custom of pronouncing the blessing recorded here on such occasions. (The first לֵאמֹר in this verse is written out in full and refers, as is often the case, to לְדוֹרוֹת, to repeat it in coming generations, that is to say, to have it "fully" affirmed.)

בְּךָ יְבָרֵךְ יִשְׂרָאֵל — *By you shall Israel bless.* Even now it is still customary on the eve of the Sabbath for every pious Jewish father to place his hand over the head of his son and to bless him with the words: "May God make you like Ephraim and like Manasseh." In his two grandsons Jacob saw the triumph of an ideal for which he had struggled his whole life. Joseph's two sons were born in a foreign land, and were brought up in an environment diametrically opposed to the ancestral principles, whereas Jacob's other sons had been favored by being raised right in the family home which they had never left for any length of time. Despite the temptations and daily attractions of the society around them, Joseph's sons had remained loyal to the faith of their forefathers. They had never thought of exchanging their Judaism for high social standing or the brilliant political careers which the Egyptian state offered them. On the contrary, they had abandoned their positions in the Egyptian aristocracy in order to go openly and willingly to join their "foreign" relatives, who were viewed as contemptible immigrant shepherds. In so doing, they set the example of an upbringing based entirely on an ideal of life and given strong direction by a father conscious of his duty. And Jacob expresses the hope that every Jewish father would pray for his own children to show the same devotion to their father and to the God of their father as had Ephraim and Manasseh, his own offspring, who throughout the ages remain the striking example of this. By thus ignoring his dark visions of the future, the patriarch responds fully to Joseph's entreaty (see our commentary to verse 8).

וַיָּשֶׂם אֶת־אֶפְרַיִם לִפְנֵי מְנַשֶּׁה — *And he put Ephraim before Manasseh.* Once again the Torah stresses that the patriarch gave precedence to the younger son over the firstborn. This is the third time in the life of Jacob that such a situation occurs. While still young, he had denied his brother the birthright; then, as a father, he deprived his firstborn Reuben of this right and conferred it on Joseph. Now, as patriarch and grandfather, he puts Ephraim before Manasseh. It is obvious that Jacob has a specific purpose in mind: he places personal merit above the privilege of birth.

R' Yitzchak Arama deals with this subject in his book *Akeidas Yitzchak* (23). He describes the Biblical conception and quotes the following parable to illustrate this point: In one of the great kingdoms of antiquity it was the custom to elect

"By you shall Israel bless saying, 'May God make you like Ephraim and like Manasseh' " — and he put Ephraim before Manasseh.

²¹ *Then Israel said to Joseph, "Behold! — I am about to die; God will be with you and will bring you back to the land of your*

the wisest, worthiest, and most valiant of the citizens as king. The royal prince did not inherit the crown. Now, it happened that one of the kings who came to the throne had acquired extraordinary popularity because of his goodness, his wisdom, his conquests, and his beneficial reforms. The people loved him deeply and, in recognition of his merits, they promised to establish his dynasty over the kingdom and henceforth to have the royalty become a hereditary right of the firstborn son. For several generations the people kept their word, but it happened that a descendant of the illustrious founder of the dynasty had a firstborn son who was an incapable person; he was simple-minded and delinquent. It also happened that the latter's younger brother was virtuous, intelligent, and courageous. After the king died, the subjects decided to organize a great feast in honor of the heir to the crown. When the heir to the throne had drunk and had filled himself with all manner of delicacies, the sages of the kingdom came to speak to him about the heavy responsibilities and personal sacrifices which the position of royalty entailed. They strongly urged him to give up the throne in favor of his younger brother so that he could completely devote himself to all the pleasures which life offered him. The prince accepted. Thereupon the council of the kingdom met, proclaimed the younger son king, and decided that the law of the hereditary right to the throne, previously accorded to the firstborn as a tribute to the valiant founder of the dynasty, should be abolished.

This parable affords a comparison with the evolution of the birthright in the Torah. No privilege of birth had been envisaged at the beginning of the history of humanity. The examples of Seth son of Adam and Shem son of Noah show us the important role which the younger son then played. But when Abraham, the beloved of God, appeared on the scene of history, God made him "the father of a multitude of nations" (17:4) and He established His eternal covenant with him and his descendants. It was the firstborn who was to be the repository of the Divine message. But in the third generation, the firstborn, who was Esau, proved to be unworthy of this inheritance. His younger brother Jacob made him a feast during which he bought his rights as firstborn. From then on, Jacob understood that this privilege was to be abolished, and that it was important to revert to the original right by which pre-eminence was given to the most worthy and wisest of the brothers. The Torah also confirms for us that the privilege of the firstborn among Jewry was in effect only for a very short time. They had been appointed to serve in worship and minister in the Divine service when the Egyptian firstborn died in the tenth plague (*Exodus* 13:15). But they did not prove worthy of this honor, for soon afterwards they participated in the sin of

כב אֲבֹתֵיכֶם: וַאֲנִי נָתַתִּי לְךָ שְׁכֶם אַחַד עַל־אַחֶיךָ אֲשֶׁר לָקַחְתִּי
מִיַּד הָאֱמֹרִי בְּחַרְבִּי וּבְקַשְׁתִּי:
מט רביעי א וַיִּקְרָא יַעֲקֹב אֶל־בָּנָיו וַיֹּאמֶר הֵאָסְפוּ וְאַגִּידָה לָכֶם אֵת אֲשֶׁר־
ב יִקְרָא אֶתְכֶם בְּאַחֲרִית הַיָּמִים: הִקָּבְצוּ וְשִׁמְעוּ בְּנֵי יַעֲקֹב

the Golden Calf. From that time on, the Levites replaced the firstborn (*Numbers* 3:45). As far as legislation is concerned, the institution of פִּדְיוֹן בְּכוֹר seems to confirm that the Torah does not consider the birthright as an absolute, irrevocable privilege. The redemption of the firstborn (which in effect cancels the privilege) is expressly adumbrated by the Torah.

21. וַיֹּאמֶר יִשְׂרָאֵל אֶל־יוֹסֵף הִנֵּה אָנֹכִי מֵת — *Then Israel said to Joseph, "Behold! — I am about to die."* These words were said as death neared, and this gave them a prophetic meaning. To Joseph they brought the absolute certainty that God would remain among the Jews in the land of their exile and that He would deliver them and bring them back to the land of their ancestors. And so, these words became an unending source of confidence in God, enduring for Jewry throughout the centuries of exile and hardship. Joseph repeats them almost word for word to all his brothers before his death (50:24), adding certain allusions to the signs which will announce the redemption (סִימָנֵי גְאוּלָה) which he heard from the mouth of his father. And, before his death, Moses too refers to this solemn promise of deliverance for the Jewish people which the patriarch had uttered on his deathbed, as *Rashi* points out (*Deuteronomy* 33:28).

22. וַאֲנִי נָתַתִּי לְךָ — *And as for me, I have given you. Rashi* explains the literal meaning of this verse. The *Midrash Rabbah*, however, gives the following interpretation: Joseph received two gifts from his father (as a sign of affection and also as compensation for the injustices which he had suffered for so long within the family — *Ramban*). The first was the city of Shechem in the territory of Canaan (where he was later buried). The city of Shechem had been conquered by Jacob with his "sword" and his "bow" when the Emorite kings made war on the family of the patriarch in retaliation for the destructive attack by two of his sons (cf. our commentary to 35:5). He had chosen this city because Joseph's chastity when he stayed in Potiphar's house had wiped away the shame of the degradation which had taken place in Shechem, where Dinah had suffered outrage at the hands of a stranger. The reputation for perfect morality, blemished for the first time at Shechem, had thus been re-established due to Joseph's exemplary conduct. Furthermore, Shechem was the city where Joseph had previously gone to look for his brothers; it was there that the episode of his deportation to Egypt began to unfold (37:13). Now, Jacob asserted his legal rights over Shechem and transferred them to Joseph. Indeed, Shechem, the lord of the city, had offered it to Dinah as a gift, and, given that Dinah's daughter Asenath had married Joseph (cf. our commentary to 41:45), he then had full rights to this city (See *Tzror Hamor*).

fathers. [22] *And as for me, I have given you Shechem — one portion more than your brothers, which I took from the hand of the Emorite with my sword and with my bow."*

49 [1] *Then Jacob called for his sons and said, "Assemble yourselves and I will tell you what will befall you in the End of Days.* [2] *Gather yourselves and listen, O sons of Jacob,*

The second gift was the precious "garment of Adam" in which Rebecca had clothed her son Jacob to receive the paternal blessing. These "garments of skin" had then played a decisive role and had thereafter remained in Jacob's hands. He had taken them from his brother Esau, who had proved unworthy, for he had behaved like an Emorite. But the only weapons which Jacob used to take them away were "wisdom and prayer" (*Rashi*). These כָּתְנוֹת עוֹר, coming from Paradise and fashioned by God, had passed through various hands, as was noted in our commentary on 27:27. And they were used in the investiture of those firstborn who were the first servants of God in their generations (*Bamidbar Rabbah* 4). Hence Jacob bequeathed them to Joseph when he gave him the extra portion (שְׁכֶם אֶחָד) deriving from the right of the firstborn. One may assume that there is a connection between these garments and the "fine cloak" which had been given to Joseph more than forty years earlier. It too is designated as כְּתֹנֶת (37:3), and ancient *midrashic* sources identify it as one of the garments coming from Paradise. The cloak had been brought back bloodstained to Jacob, and it had then almost torn apart the family of the patriarch. Now, on the eve of his death, Jacob gives it again to his dearly beloved son, thus confirming that Joseph had always been his choice. The course of Joseph's eventual existence proved him to be right.

שְׁכֶם אַחַד עַל־אַחֶיךָ — *Shechem — one portion more than your brothers. Rashi* adds: "Because you will have taken the trouble to arrange for my burial, I in turn give you an inheritance where you will be buried. And what is it? It is Shechem" (cf. our commentary to 23:17).

49.

1. וַיִּקְרָא יַעֲקֹב אֶל־בָּנָיו — *Then Jacob called for his sons.* Jacob began his blessing where Isaac had left off. (The word וַיִּקְרָא here continues with the same term Isaac had used in 28:1.) And Moses began where Jacob ended his benediction (וְזֹאת הַבְּרָכָה, *Deuteronomy* 33:1, recalls Jacob's final words, וְזֹאת אֲשֶׁר דִּבֶּר, verse 28). And lastly, David began his hymns where Moses had left off his blessings (אַשְׁרֵי הָאִישׁ, *Psalms* 1:1, echoes the last wish of Moses in the Torah, אַשְׁרֶיךָ יִשְׂרָאֵל, *Deuteronomy* 33:29). Thus, each of the three successive phases of Jewish history is accompanied by the ancestral benediction which gave inspiration to the future leaders of the generations. Jacob gave his blessings for the definitive constitution of the Jewish people, and he based them on the benediction which he had received from his father. Moses blesses his people at the threshold of the Promised Land to take possession of it, and he was inspired by the solemn

benediction of the patriarch. As for David, his book of *Psalms* represents the blessing which he bestowed upon Jewry — he bequeathed to Jewry a universal means of expression for the propagation of the faith in one God and for the realization of its messianic task. Seen in this light, David's blessing is nothing but the continuation of the previous benedictions.

Blessings occupy a prominent place throughout the Torah and particularly in the book of *Genesis*. From the time that the power to bless was first conferred on Abraham so that "he could bless whom he wanted" (*Rashi* on 12:2), the factor of blessing played a role of ever-increasing importance. The benediction accorded by the righteous is considered as proceeding from a metaphysical force which confers upon it an actual, concrete efficacy. To bless is a privilege conferred by God.

Blessing is a dimension *sui generis* (altogether unique) in the framework of human existence. There are, to be sure, certain imponderables in the social and economic spheres, for the law of cause and effect which orders our existence contains gaps which introduce an element of uncertainty into all of man's endeavors. Nothing is sure, nothing can be foreseen. And so man readily speaks of the abstract factor called "chance" which plays a prominent role in our daily lives. Some English economists have demonstrated the great importance of this "something," this factor which can take the form of a gift, a talent, or a personal ability.

The doctrine of Judaism conceives of this metaphysical element in a more direct and more personal way. Where man sees only the effect of blind chance, Judaism recognizes the action of providential intervention. It manifests itself as an immaterial factor, independent of human will, coming from a supernatural sphere. It is interwoven in the fabric of our economic, social, scientific, or cultural activities, bringing its determining influence to bear. This factor is the heavenly blessing which brings the element of success, achievement, and prosperity to man's efforts; it develops and brings his enterprises to fruition. It can neither be foreseen nor calculated, neither counted nor measured. The wish of "good luck" which people give one another at each new undertaking, and which reveals their belief in a metaphysical factor operating in economic life, is nothing other than the secular translation of God's blessing. It thus constitutes a constructive and creative element in all of our existence. *God's blessing makes rich* (*Proverbs* 10:22).

Just as the Jews embark on the historic task of constituting an independent nation, the patriarch, before he dies, wishes to confer upon them the Divine blessing for success in this undertaking of universal importance.

הֵאָסְפוּ — *Assemble yourselves.* In the next verse Jacob repeats: "Gather yourselves and listen, O sons of Jacob." For Jacob the union of his sons, the lasting solidarity of the families of Jewry, constitutes the primary condition for realization of the benediction. The past had taught him the harm resulting from disunity, hatred, and jealousy. As Jacob thought of the future, when he would no longer be able to serve as the rallying point for the family, what could have seemed more pressing for constituting the future nation than an unshakable family solidarity? Let Jewry form a permanent band to resist all attacks so that the enemy's blows come up against a unified will, an unflinching spirit of brotherhood which nothing can destroy. First, this union, and then, "listen to Israel your father." Draw each moment on the spiritual heritage of the patriarchs; persevere as long as the task remains; always take inspiration from the prophetic words of the "three fathers" — this was the supreme wish of the dying patriarch.

וְאַגִּידָה לָכֶם — *And I will tell you.* Jacob intended to reveal the End of Days to them, but the *Shechinah* departed from him and he spoke of other matters (*Rashi*). This remark results from the fact that Jacob's subsequent words have no connection with his announced intention of revealing "what will happen at the messianic end of time" (which *Ramban* tells us is the unanimous interpretation of the term בְּאַחֲרִית הַיָּמִים).

In this connection the Talmud cites the following statement in the name of R' Shimon ben Lakish: "Jacob saw that Divine Inspiration was departing from him when he wanted to reveal the End of Days to his children, and he said, 'Perhaps there is among my offspring an unworthy son, as with Abraham who had Ishmael for a son, and my father Isaac who had Esau.' His sons answered him: 'Hear, Israel, HASHEM is our God, HASHEM is one! Just as He is unique in your heart, so is He in ours. (We have no doubts in our heart regarding God).' At that moment, Jacob cried out: 'Blessed be His Name of glorious kingship for ever and ever! בָּרוּךְ שֵׁם כְּבוֹד מַלְכוּתוֹ לְעוֹלָם וָעֶד' " (*Pesachim* 56a).

Jacob's idea to reveal the End of Days to his children was most likely prompted by a desire to comfort them and raise their spirits at a time when they were faced with the bleak perspective of a life of slavery in a land of exile — a situation which was to last for several centuries according to the well-known Divine announcement made to Abraham. For Jewry, the messianic end of time represents eternal hope, unshakable confidence, and the certainty that good will ultimately triumph over evil. It was this faith in the End of Days, reinforced by the circumstances which will surround it, that Jacob wanted to communicate to his sons.

But the *Shechinah* withdrew from him, and he was unable to reveal what he wanted. Regarding the בְּרִית בֵּין הַבְּתָרִים, *Covenant Between the Parts*, made with Abraham, we have pointed out that the end of suffering in exile remains shrouded in mystery (see our commentary to 15:13). In addition to the motives mentioned there, the dialogue between Jacob and his sons, quoted above, brings out another reason for this: the Jews have no need of knowing the duration of their sufferings as long as they are supported by their שְׁמַע יִשְׂרָאֵל! Their proclamation of absolute faith in their historic mission, in the words of the שְׁמַע יִשְׂרָאֵל, containing the manifesto of monotheism, ought to suffice to give them courage, enthusiasm, and perseverance until the end of time. It is to fill their soul to such a point that the will to achieve the messianic goal for which they live puts any anticipation of an early redemption in the background. The ardor of

ג וְשִׁמְעוּ אֶל־יִשְׂרָאֵל אֲבִיכֶם: רְאוּבֵן בְּכֹרִי אַתָּה כֹּחִי
ד וְרֵאשִׁית אוֹנִי יֶתֶר שְׂאֵת וְיֶתֶר עָז: פַּחַז כַּמַּיִם אַל־תּוֹתַר כִּי

faith ought to be a more powerful reason for loyalty to God than hope of salvation. For the one who has faith, what does it matter to know when his trials will come to an end?

Accordingly, when the patriarch heard the profession of faith of the future people being unanimously proclaimed by his children, he cried out: "בָּרוּךְ שֵׁם כְּבוֹד וגו׳, *May God be blessed for ever!* And later, the Sages included this phrase in the prayer of *Shema*, but they ordained that it be recited in a low voice, since it is not part of the Torah text (*Pesachim* ibid.). In this context, then, the words שְׁמַע יִשְׂרָאֵל, which were pronounced for the first time at the bedside of a dying man, signify: "Hear, Israel (our father)," and this tradition in the Talmud is based on the fact that the words וְשִׁמְעוּ אֶל־יִשְׂרָאֵל אֲבִיכֶם in the following verse echo these words.

2. הִקָּבְצוּ — *Gather yourselves.* From the beginning of humanity, in each generation there had been only one individual who was the chosen of God, only one upon whom the Holy Spirit rested. But here for the first time an entire group was found worthy of this distinction. They formed the nucleus of the future chosen people (*Kuzari* 1:95).

וְשִׁמְעוּ בְּנֵי יַעֲקֹב — *And listen, O sons of Jacob.* The solemn convocation was intended to give the paternal blessing to each of them. But *Ibn Ezra* holds that this opinion, expressed by R' *Saadyah Gaon*, is mistaken. The patriarch wanted to inform them of his prophecies for the future. *Abarbanel* holds that the words of Jacob are to be taken on four levels simultaneously: as blessing (and prayer), as reprimand, as prophecy, and as giving the particulars of their future inheritance in the Promised Land.

וְשִׁמְעוּ אֶל־יִשְׂרָאֵל אֲבִיכֶם — *And listen to Israel your father.* Jacob speaks his last words in poetic form. Hence they are expressed using "parallelism" or the rhythmical thought which is characteristic of all Hebrew poetry. This verse represents the introduction to the principal theme of the chapter, and Jacob demands from his children the most serious attention for the message which he is about to bring them, a message which will direct their destiny.

3. רְאוּבֵן בְּכֹרִי אַתָּה — *Reuben, you are my firstborn.* Don Isaac Abarbanel describes the leading idea which is central to Jacob's blessings in these terms: "Before he died, the patriarch wanted to determine to which of his sons royalty should belong. Thanks to his prophetic spirit he knew that his offspring would be very numerous. Hence it was essential to designate the future leader who would impose discipline and would serve as a guide for the brothers. He wanted to make this central figure known in his lifetime in order to avoid quarrels among the tribes. It was above all the search for this leader and then naming him that occupied Jacob's last thoughts. One after the other he went over his sons in his mind, examining each one according to his merits and faults. And the

and listen to Israel your father.
³ *"Reuben, you are my firstborn, my strength and my initial vigor, foremost in rank and foremost in power.* ⁴ *Water-like impetuosity — you cannot be foremost, because*

blessing which he will bestow on each will often take the form of a warning, a lesson to be remembered, a recommendation, rather than a simple word of fatherly kindness."

Already the eldest of his sons had to be eliminated from the role of leadership, although it should have been his as firstborn. The unforgotten sin when he "profaned his father's couch" (35:22) had revealed his nature — "water-like impetuosity" (*Rashi:* the instability, the impetuosity, the haste with which you rushed to vent your anger — like the water which rushes in its flow). To be sure, Reuben had repented. But although this helped to rehabilitate him on the personal level, he was nevertheless disqualified as leader of his brothers. For the tempestuous foundations of his character were not at all changed by his repentance.

Does this mean that he did not merit his father's blessing? Such does not seem to be the case if one considers his father's words, which can be taken favorably as well as unfavorably. In the *midrashic* analysis of the text (*Rabbah* 98) we find the same controversy between R' Yehoshua and R' Eliezer on the one hand, and R' Elazar Hamoda'i on the other, as that mentioned in our commentary to 35:22, concerning Reuben's sin. The first *Tannaim* are more severe in their judgment than R' Elazar Hamoda'i, who gives Jacob's words a favorable, benevolent meaning with regard to his firstborn. Faced with this divergence of opinion arising from the ambiguity of the patriarch's words, the Sages conclude by having him say the following: "I do not push you away, I do not draw you closer, I leave it in doubt until Moses comes; he will deal with you as he sees fit." Did Jacob want to put off the final decision and make it dependent on the future behavior of his son? This is indeed what comes out of the parable quoted in this connection by the *Zohar:* "The father of a family saw the king coming toward him just as he was dying. He said: 'Let my fortune remain in the hands of the king, in trust for my son, to be given to him when the king deems him worthy.' This is how Jacob acted toward Reuben. He bestowed upon him his blessing, but he kept it in reserve until Reuben would show himself worthy of it."

Over two centuries later, Reuben obtained his posthumous rehabilitation from the moral point of view, if not from the point of view of his birthright. Moses declared him worthy of benefiting from the paternal blessing held in reserve and, wiping away the words of stigma which Jacob had pronounced on his firstborn son, Moses exclaimed: "Let Reuben live and be immortal!" May he live, adds *Sifre* (*Deuteronomy* 33:6), for the merit of saving Joseph from the hands of his brothers, and may the affair of Bilhah no longer be mentioned (cf. our commentary ibid. on the principle of the compensation). Moses, himself seemingly easily angered, undoubtedly had a greater understanding of

עָלִיתָ מִשְׁכְּבֵי אָבִיךָ אָז חִלַּלְתָּ יְצוּעִי עָלָה:
ה־ו שִׁמְעוֹן וְלֵוִי אַחִים כְּלֵי חָמָס מְכֵרֹתֵיהֶם: בְּסֹדָם אַל־תָּבֹא
נַפְשִׁי בִּקְהָלָם אַל־תֵּחַד כְּבֹדִי כִּי בְאַפָּם הָרְגוּ אִישׁ וּבִרְצֹנָם
ז עִקְּרוּ־שׁוֹר: אָרוּר אַפָּם כִּי עָז וְעֶבְרָתָם כִּי קָשָׁתָה אֲחַלְּקֵם
בְּיַעֲקֹב וַאֲפִיצֵם בְּיִשְׂרָאֵל:

Reuben's impetuous character. But above all it was the tribes who intervened in his favor. To Moses they said: "We ask but one thing — reconciliation with our eldest brother." This is seen from the two phrases coming one after the other: יַחַד שִׁבְטֵי יִשְׂרָאֵל, יְחִי רְאוּבֵן וְגו', all the tribes of Jewry together: Let Reuben live (Sifre ibid.).

4. פַּחַז כַּמַּיִם — Water-like impetuosity. According to the favorable interpretation it means: "You deserve superiority in dignity and power (verse 3) for you rush like the torrent (to lead the way in the conquest of Canaan; Numbers 32:17) and hence you will not lose one man (in battle). It is because you 'entered your father's bedroom' (an allusion to the Promised Land, according to 28:13, הָאָרֶץ אֲשֶׁר אַתָּה שֹׁכֵב עָלֶיהָ) that you smite (the enemy — חִלַּלְתָּ being derived from חוֹלֵל to strike) in order (to allow me) to go up to my couch" (Hadar Zekeinim; other favorable interpretations are given in the Midrash Rabbah).

5. שִׁמְעוֹן וְלֵוִי אַחִים — Simeon and Levi are comrades. The honors reserved for the firstborn should have gone then to the next-oldest sons. But neither the second son nor the third was worthy. In the episode involving Dinah at Shechem (Chapter 34), both had shown an attitude of fraternal responsibility for which their father could have had nothing but praise, had this feeling not degenerated into an act of brutal violence, unworthy of Jacob's heirs. To avenge the honor of an outraged sister gives evidence of a very strong sense of purity. But a long way from this honorable sentiment was the massacre perpetrated by the brothers. There is danger in their violence; their savage fury can have very grave consequences. Neither brother could be invested with the authority of a leader.

With regard to Simeon and Levi, Jacob finds himself in a dilemma similar to that involving Reuben. Should he, because of the savagery of their acts, refuse to give his blessing to two children whose descendants were going to be part of the nation of God? His upright character caused him to hesitate and, then, once again he decided to grant his benediction, but to have it given by the future prophet who would be closer to God than himself. When the time came, when that prophet, who was none other than Moses, was to bless the Jewish tribes, a change had taken place. There was now a gulf between the two previously inseparable brothers (Zohar). Levi was like "a man who had borrowed a sum of money from the king, then repaid it, and could even advance him some money in return. But Simeon resembled a man who had borrowed money from the king and then, far from repaying, had again become indebted to him." Levi had previously become guilty toward God because of the massacre at Shechem. But

*you mounted your father's bed; then you desecrated Him Who
ascended my couch.*

⁵ *"Simeon and Levi are comrades, their weaponry is a stolen
craft.* ⁶ *Into their conspiracy, may my soul not enter! With their
congregation, do not join, O my honor! For in their rage they
murdered people and at their whim they maimed an ox.*
⁷ *Accursed is their rage for it is intense, and their wrath for it is
harsh; I will separate them within Jacob, and I will disperse them
in Israel.*

he had "repaid his debt" in the desert at the time of the Golden Calf, for, of all
the tribes, only Levi had answered Moses' call: "Whoever is on God's side, let
him come to me!" What is more, it was a member of the tribe of Levi, Phinehas,
who gloriously defended the Divine cause at Shittim, and he did so on his own
initiative. And as a result of this, he "had turned the wrath of God away from
the Children of Israel" (*Numbers* 25:11). As for Simeon, he had not only
remained indebted to God for his crimes at Shechem, but he had again become
guilty at Shittim. There Zimri, who headed a house within the tribe of Simeon,
had publicly engaged in debauchery with a Midianite woman (ibid.). When this
happened, even though their ancestors had been inseparable brothers, the two
tribes met face to face in fierce opposition. The act of חִלּוּל הַשֵׁם perpetrated by
the Simeonites was avenged, once again, by unconditional devotion to the
Divine cause on the part of a Levite. Accordingly, Moses bestowed his blessing
on Levi but not on Simeon. Instead he included Simeon's blessing, without
explicitly naming him, in the blessing he gave to Judah (*Sifre to Deuteronomy*
33:8; cf. *Ramban*, ibid.). For "the Simeonites had their inheritance in the midst
of the inheritance of the children of Judah" (*Joshua* 19:1).

6. וּבִרְצֹנָם עִקְּרוּ־שׁוֹר — *And at their whim they maimed an ox.* Rashi explains:
"They had wanted to strike Joseph, who is likened to an ox (*Deuteronomy*
33:17)." But this explanation assumes that Jacob knew of Joseph's sale and of the
part that Simeon and Levi had played in it, which is far from certain.
Accordingly, most of the other commentators hold that the word שׁוֹר refers
either to cattle or to the wall of Shechem, which the brothers had destroyed.

7. אָרוּר אַפָּם — *Accursed is their rage.* "Even at the moment of condemnation,"
says *Rashi*, "it is not them but their anger which Jacob curses." It has already
been pointed out in our commentary to 34:30 that the patriarch's reproaches are
directed not toward the actual motivation of his sons, but toward their heinous
methods. It follows that under no circumstances did Jacob want to tolerate the
false principle that the end justifies the means.

Rashi continues by quoting Balaam's exclamation: *How shall I curse whom
God has not cursed?* See our commentary to 34:13: God had not condemned the
decision of the brothers in itself, "since someone had outraged their sister
Dinah." All that was cursed was their excessive rage and violence and, coming

ח יְהוּדָה אַתָּה יוֹדוּךָ אַחֶיךָ יָדְךָ בְּעֹרֶף אֹיְבֶיךָ יִשְׁתַּחֲווּ
ט לְךָ בְּנֵי אָבִיךָ: גּוּר אַרְיֵה יְהוּדָה מִטֶּרֶף בְּנִי עָלִיתָ
י כָּרַע רָבַץ כְּאַרְיֵה וּכְלָבִיא מִי יְקִימֶנּוּ: לֹא־יָסוּר שֵׁבֶט

at the time of the consecration of the future Jewish nation, this verdict is of paramount importance. Contrary to the view of the majority of nations, it proclaims that moral principles are valid not just in one's private life but also, and every bit as much, in the collective life of nations and societies. The use of brute force is formally condemned, even in a case such as this where common interests or ethical ideals are at stake. This is the teaching which Jacob bequeaths to his descendants, a teaching which will never lose its value for all eternity.

אֲחַלְּקֵם בְּיַעֲקֹב — *I will separate them within Jacob.* Levi will not form any concentrated nucleus within the future Jewish state. Because of their priestly function, the Levites will be domiciled in levitical towns spread over the whole territory. Simeon's portion in the future Land of Israel will form an enclave within Judah's (*Joshua* ibid.). Neutralized in this way, the threat which the violent deeds and lack of sociability that these two brothers presented will be reduced to a minimum. On the other hand, their dispersion among all the tribes of Israel was to have a highly salutary effect on the entire nation. For to their brothers, particularly in times of persecution and defeat, they brought their natural gifts of courage and strength as well as their religious intensity and their noble sentiment of pride in their Jewishness. Moreover, the spiritual activities of these two tribes became exemplary. On the one hand, "the poor, the scribes of the Torah and the teachers of the young children will only be found in the tribe of Simeon" (*Rashi*), and on the other, "the Levites teach the Divine Laws to Jacob and the Torah to Israel" (*Deuteronomy* 33:10). Their physical power will be redirected and will find a happier and more productive outlet when transformed into spiritual strength. Then the generosity and vigor of the two brothers will come to serve the common good. The initial harm thus transformed itself into a source of benefit and blessing in the service of God.

8. יְהוּדָה אַתָּה יוֹדוּךָ אַחֶיךָ — *Judah — you, your brothers shall acknowledge* [your royalty]. After eliminating the three older brothers as future leaders, in his fourth son Jacob recognized the virtues necessary for this honor. The reasons which prompted this choice are four in number, according to *Abarbanel.* First of all, Judah's brothers respected his natural authority without feeling the slightest jealousy towards him. Next, he had emerged victorious from all his undertakings and had succeeded in finally establishing a harmonious peace among the brothers. He was not impetuous like Reuben, nor did he have violent tendencies like Simeon and Levi. Instead he possessed that majestic calm which comes from confidence in one's own powers. And by using the metaphor of a lion cub for Judah, his father heightened the impression of majesty and power which was manifest in his personality.

יִשְׁתַּחֲווּ לְךָ בְּנֵי אָבִיךָ — *Your father's sons will prostrate themselves to you.* As

⁸ "*Judah — you, your brothers shall acknowledge; your hand will be at your enemies' nape; your father's sons will prostrate themselves to you.* ⁹ *A lion cub is Judah; from the prey, my son, you elevated yourself. He crouches, lies down like a lion, and like an awesome lion, who dares rouse him?* ¹⁰ *The scepter shall not depart*

they were sons of several wives, Jacob did not say "your mother's sons," as Isaac said (27:29). The *Zohar* adds: "All the tribes, even those which broke away and formed the Kingdom of the North, recognized the authority of the kingdom established in Jerusalem, and they bowed down before the kings of Judah when they went to Jerusalem, just as the authority of the Exilarchs, descendants of the kings of Judah was recognized by the entire Jewish people."

9. גּוּר אַרְיֵה יְהוּדָה — *A lion cub is Judah.* In you, Judah, are combined the courage of youth and the reflection of maturity. (First a cub, says *Rashi*, then a lion.) You take no pleasure in war or pillage, you are neither a hyena nor a wolf — you are a lion, and you disdain the carnage of beasts of prey.

מִטֶּרֶף בְּנִי עָלִיתָ — *From the prey, my son, you elevated yourself.* Cf. our commentary to 37:33, where these words are linked to the sale of Joseph, in *Rashi's* interpretation. But the majority of commentators attribute a different meaning to this phrase. Far from giving free reign to brutality in the wake of his fighting, Judah "goes back up" to his moral level once he has caught and brought back his trophy.

10. לֹא־יָסוּר שֵׁבֶט מִיהוּדָה — *The scepter shall not depart from Judah. Rashi* explains: "From David onwards. This is an allusion to the Exilarchs in Babylon who will rule over the people with their scepters, for they were appointed by the king. וּמְחֹקֵק מִבֵּין רַגְלָיו — *Nor a scholar from among his descendants.* I.e. the disciples of the Torah. These are the princes, *nesi'im* (of the *Sanhedrin*) of the Holy Land. עַד כִּי־יָבֹא שִׁילֹה — *Until Shiloh arrives.* This is the king Messiah *to whom* (שֶׁ־לוֹ) belongs sovereignty."

Here *Rashi* follows *Onkelos*' translation (עַד דְּיֵיתֵי מְשִׁיחָא דְּדִילֵהּ הִיא מַלְכוּתָא). Regarding this R' Yosef Albo remarks (in his book *Ikarim*): "The messianic faith is based on tradition, for *Onkelos* the proselyte, a disciple of Shemaya and Avtalyon who lived at the time of the Second Temple, refers these words to the Messiah. This tradition has been carried on right to the present and it cannot be rejected. For if we wanted to reject it, we could reject the whole religious faith and explain the verses in another manner. All is therefore based on tradition" (4:42).

In contrast to *Rambam*, who includes messianic faith among the thirteen principles of faith in Jewish doctrine, R' Yosef Albo holds that it is anchored in tradition, as is borne out by numerous passages in the Prophets relating to the Messiah, but does not however constitute a special article of faith. For this messianic faith derives from the principle of retribution for good and evil. It proceeds from belief in the ultimate victory of good.

מִיהוּדָה וּמְחֹקֵק מִבֵּין רַגְלָיו עַד כִּי־יָבֹא שִׁילֹה וְלוֹ יִקְּהַת עַמִּים:

In any case, the primary Biblical source for the belief that the Messiah will come in the distant future is contained in this verse. It is often quoted in support of our faith in the coming of the Redeemer, and in the Middle Ages the wisest dignitaries of Jewish communities always made reference to it when they had to engage in the many debates with the ecclesiastics of the other religions. A vast exegetic and apologetic literature has developed around this Biblical passage which can be interpreted in many ways. But its fundamental meaning nevertheless remains unalterable.

What might, however, seem in doubt is the scope and importance which the patriarch himself wanted to give to his words. Was it a foretelling of future developments, or an order which instituted the tribe of Judah exclusively, and not any of the other tribes, as "the royal tribe"? This latter view is held by *Rambam* (*Hilchos Melachim* 1:9) and *Ramban*, who consider sovereignty from any tribe other than Judah an illicit act of usurpation. Accordingly, kingship under such circumstances was generally only of limited duration. This was the case with the dynasty of the Hasmoneans, who were descended from the tribe of Levi; their reign crumbled in dishonor after a few generations (this dynasty was also guilty of filling both priestly and royal functions, contrary to the law stated in *Numbers* 18:7).

But R' Nissim Gerondi objects that if the patriarch's words are equivalent to a command, one would have to admit that all the kings of the kingdom of Israel were usurpers, and that, on the other hand, the patriarch's command was never fully carried out except in the times of David and Solomon, who reigned over all twelve tribes. And so he concludes that these words are either words of prophecy or of benediction, referring to a time of national sovereignty (thus excluding the Hasmonean kings) and which takes into account only the historical period "from David onwards" (cf. *Rashi*), that is to say, starting from the reign of the tribe of Judah (which leaves out the reign of Saul). From that time on, the scepter will never be completely away from Judah (דרוש ז). The *Tosafists* also hold that this verse is intended as a blessing (*Yoma* 26a); however, its effect was only partially achieved because of the unworthiness of certain descendants of the Davidic line (*II Samuel* 7).

וּמְחֹקֵק מִבֵּין רַגְלָיו — *Nor a scholar from among his descendants*. A blessing which came about in the time of Hillel's descendants, who were from the tribe of Judah. They were the princes (*nesi'im* of the *Sanhedrin*) in the Holy Land (*Sanhedrin* 5a). Their successors, the Exilarchs in Babylon, were given civil authority by the Babylonian kings; they are alluded to by the first phrase of this verse. Thanks to their descent from the Davidic dynasty, they enjoyed immense prestige both at home and abroad. According to *Seder Olam*, the last representative was the Exilarch Bustenai who lived in Persia in the first half of the seventh century under Arab domination. Several legends have arisen

from Judah nor a scholar from among his descendants until Shiloh arrives and his will be an assemblage of nations.

regarding this historical personage, of whom the Gaon Rav Sherira tells us he is a descendant (53, אגרת רש״ג).

עַד כִּי־יָבֹא שִׁילֹה — *Until Shiloh arrives.* "This is the king Messiah, to whom sovereignty belongs" (*Rashi*). Until his coming, Judah will hold the royal scepter in the midst of his nation, but the Messiah, son of David, will be king over all the gathered nations וְלוֹ יִקְּהַת עַמִּים, his will be an assemblage of nations."

In his *Encyclopedia of Biblical Interpretation*, M.M. Kasher quotes eleven different interpretations of the word שִׁילֹה. But Jewish tradition has retained only that of *Rashi* and *Onkelos*, who give it the meaning of Messiah, for the reasons mentioned by *Rashi*. Some Christian theologians state, without any solid foundation, that Shiloh is a name designating the founder of Christianity. "Until the coming of Shiloh" has in this sense become a favorite text for Christian missionaries who use it to try to convert Jews who know little or nothing of the Holy Scripture. It is however worthy of note that this translation dates only from the year 1534; in that year it appears for the first time in the German Bible of Sebastian Münster. It is now rejected by all who have gone into the subject in depth. In his responsa (Vol. IV, No. 187), R' Shlomo ben Adereth (who lived in the thirteenth century) gives a detailed report of the public debate which he had with the learned preacher Martini, who took this verse as demonstrating that the Messiah has already come. The same arguments are found in the book וִיכּוּחַ הָרַמְבַּ״ן (Constantinople, 1710), It records the debate which took place in Barcelona in 1263 between *Ramban* and the Dominican Fra Paola, a converted Jew from Montpelier, in the presence of King James of Aragon. In this report *Ramban* also quotes his reply to the king: the Messiah will come, that is certain, and he will be a man born of a father and mother from the dynasty of David, as it is said: עַד כִּי־יָבֹא שִׁילֹה, until the coming of his son, the term שִׁילֹה being derived from שִׁלְיָה meaning his little child, as in *Deuteronomy* 28:57. Thus, he will come into the world normally, like all men. (A detailed refutation of the christological arguments concerning this verse are given in ס׳ חזוק אמונה, Breslau, 1873, part 1, chapter 14; cf. *Rambam*, סוף הלכות מלכים (מהדורת רומא, או מהדורת מוסד הרב קוק).

וְלוֹ יִקְּהַת עַמִּים — *And his will be an assemblage of nations.* This means the assembly of peoples around the Messiah, also mentioned by the prophet Isaiah (11:10), as *Rashi* explains. But *Ibn Ezra* and *Radak* translate: he will have the obedience of the peoples (as in *Proverbs* 30:17). According to these two views, Judah here personifies the Jewish nation, the Jews. The patriarch intends to say that they will exert moral supremacy over the gathered nations and their principles will be imposed successively on all the nations, until the final revolution ultimately led by the Messiah. He will be the prince of peace in the sense that the definitive character of his mission will be peace and universal

יא אֹסְרִי לַגֶּפֶן עִירֹה וְלַשֹּׂרֵקָה בְּנִי אֲתֹנוֹ כִּבֵּס בַּיַּיִן לְבֻשׁוֹ
יב וּבְדַם־עֲנָבִים סוּתֹה: חַכְלִילִי עֵינַיִם מִיָּיִן וּלְבֶן־שִׁנַּיִם
מֵחָלָב:
יג זְבוּלֻן לְחוֹף יַמִּים יִשְׁכֹּן וְהוּא לְחוֹף אֳנִיֹּת וְיַרְכָתוֹ עַל־צִידֹן:

harmony (שׁילה derived from שׁלה, the root of שָׁלְוָה and שָׁלוֹם, *happiness* and *peace*, following *Sforno's* etymology). Then the scepter of Judah will no longer reign only over his own nation but over the "assemblage of nations."

11. אֹסְרִי לַגֶּפֶן עִירֹה — *He will tie his donkey to the vine.* "Thus Jacob visualizes the Messiah. But how does he see him? He sees the conqueror of humanity not on a steed, but with a young donkey. The donkey is the beast of burden which always represents peaceful well-being, peaceful national greatness, whereas the steed represents military might. Similarly, of all the unclean animals it is the donkey which is chosen through פֶּטֶר חֲמוֹר to represent the consecration of all movable possessions. It is this animal that carries man and his goods at a leisurely pace. Accordingly, the Jewish conception of royal power is not represented by the number of horses, and it is forbidden for the king לְהַרְבּוֹת סוּס. The future redeemer of Jewry and humanity appears then here in connection with the donkey, and this image supports the twofold vision of peace and material well-being. For to tie up his animal and especially the עִיר, the frisky donkey's colt, to the vine, is a sign of a very greatly increased development of nature (the vine being as vigorous as our trees) and of an extraordinary abundance. The image of the Messiah "riding on a donkey" is also how the coming of the Redeemer appeared to the prophet Zechariah in his messianic vision: "Rejoice greatly O daughter of Zion, shout with joy O daughter of Jerusalem! Look how your king comes to you, righteous and victorious, humbly riding upon an ass, upon the colt of an ass" (9:9) (*R' S.R. Hirsch*).

וְלַשֹּׂרֵקָה בְּנִי אֲתֹנוֹ — *To the vine branch his donkey's foal.* The name of God is twice alluded to in this verse. The letter י as a suffix to the verb אָסַר and the letter ה, written in place of a *vav* as modifier of the word עִיר, form the Divine name י־ה. And this name is constituted once more by the letter י, the suffix on the word בֶּן, with the letter ה, suffix of שׂרֵק (the usual form, as in *Jeremiah* 2:21). This double allusion is to emphasize that the mission of the true Messiah will only be accomplished "when God will be recognized as King over all the earth" (*Zohar*).

12. חַכְלִילִי עֵינַיִם מִיָּיִן — *Red eyed from wine.* As *Rashi* emphasizes, these last two verses describe in hyperbolic form the abundance of good things which the earth will yield at the end of time. Jacob sees the messianic era — whose time he was not able to reveal, as was his original intention — from the point of view of a paradisical rejuvenation involving the whole of nature. The blessings of heaven, the understanding among men, will create a temporal happiness wherein man's greatness will no longer manifest itself by the enslavement or destruction of peoples. The garments of the world's great men will not be stained

¹¹ *He will tie his donkey to the vine; to the vine branch his donkey's foal; he will launder his garments in wine and his robe in the blood of grapes.* ¹² *Red eyed from wine, and white toothed from milk.*

¹³ *"Zebulun shall settle by seashores. He shall be at the ship's harbor, and his last border will reach Zidon.*

with the blood of other human beings; the generation of the Messiah will be brilliant, glowing with vitality (with eyes sparkling) and physical vigor (teeth whiter than milk).

The messianic idea of Judaism is inseparable from the notion of material well-being, when *every man will sit under his vine and under his fig-tree* (*Micah* 4:4). In contrast to other religions, Judaism has never despised the material domain as being beneath its teachings. It aspires to assure individual and collective happiness on earth, which is in answer to the legitimate wish of every human being, and to elevate man to a level of material well-being and culture which, far from being an obstacle to virtue, actually facilitates its practice, provided one makes use of it wisely. One only has to read the many promises in the Torah relating to earthly goods in order to realize that Judaism has never deserved the reproach of being "an opiate for the masses." In its legislation, it covers a vast social and economic system, giving material goods their proper emphasis and striving to ennoble all human aspirations through an atmosphere of purity and holiness within a peaceful and happy humanity.

After finding in Judah those qualities for the leader of the future house of Jewry which he sought, the patriarch turns to his other children. He bestows upon them his blessing, assigning to each, according to his particular aptitudes, his role in the harmony of the twelve tribes.

13. זְבוּלֻן לְחוֹף יַמִּים יִשְׁכֹּן — *Zebulun shall settle by seashores.* When Moses gives his final benediction, Zebulun is mentioned before Issachar, as he is here, although the latter was the elder. There *Rashi* explains: "Zebulun and Issachar had become partners. Zebulun will dwell at the shore of the sea, going out with his ships to trade and grow prosperous and look after the needs of Issachar who will settle down to study the Torah — hence Zebulun is mentioned before Issachar, for Issachar's Torah exists only because of Zebulun" (*Deuteronomy* 33:18).

This priority, however, only involves one situation: when the subsistence of the elder who devotes himself to the study of Torah depends on his younger brother. But if this is not the case, it is the representative of the Torah who should be honored before any other, even a great dignitary, as we see from the example of Ephraim, upholder of the Torah, and Manasseh, representing temporal power (*Ha'amek Davar*, 48:20).

וְיַרְכָתוֹ עַל־צִידֹן — *And his last border will reach Zidon.* In his blessing for the two brothers, Moses adds this detail: "They shall call peoples unto the

יד־טו יִשָּׂשכָר חֲמֹר גָּרֶם רֹבֵץ בֵּין הַמִּשְׁפְּתָיִם: וַיַּרְא מְנֻחָה כִּי טוֹב
וְאֶת־הָאָרֶץ כִּי נָעֵמָה וַיֵּט שִׁכְמוֹ לִסְבֹּל וַיְהִי לְמַס־
טז עֹבֵד: דָּן יָדִין עַמּוֹ כְּאַחַד שִׁבְטֵי יִשְׂרָאֵל:

mountain," (*Deuteronomy* 33:19) which *Rashi* (ibid.) explains in these terms:
"Attracted by trade with Zebulun, foreign merchants will come into his
territory, while he remains at the border. Then they will say: 'Since we have
already taken the trouble to come this far, let us continue to Jerusalem and see
what divinity is worshiped by this nation and what He has done'; and they will
see all Jewry worshiping one God and following the same dietary laws, for
among the other nations the god of one of them is not like that of the other.
Then they will say: 'There is no other people as pure as this,' and they will
become converts there, as it is said (ibid.): 'There they shall offer sacrifices of
righteousness' (שָׁם יִזְבְּחוּ זִבְחֵי צֶדֶק)." [In another version, attributed by the
Midrash Rabbah (chapter 99) to R' Acha, the conversion of the peoples drawn
to the Holy Land by trade with Zebulun is due to their admiration for the tribe
of Issachar which enjoys material ease even though it devotes itself to sacred
studies. In this way, Issachar brings "material for the proselytes" (= חֲמֹר גָּרֶם
חוֹמֶר לַגֵּרִים).]

14. יִשָּׂשכָר חֲמֹר גָּרֶם — *Issachar is a strong-boned donkey.* Cf. our commentary
on 30:16.

רֹבֵץ בֵּין הַמִּשְׁפְּתָיִם — *He rests between the boundaries.* The *Targumim* translate
"between the borders," which from a geographical point of view permits
various interpretations, quoted by M.M. Kasher in the *Encyclopedia of Biblical
Interpretation.* But also quoted there is the statement of the *Yalkut of the
Yemenites* which explains the phrase in a figurative sense: "between the
borders," that is to say, between the mystery of creation and the mystery of
theosophy. This Midrash seems to be alluding to the essential contribution
which the tribe of Issachar made to Jewry's religious life — the establishment of
the calendar by calculating the months and leap years, as it is said in *Chronicles:
And of the sons of Issachar, instructed in discerning the dates* (I *Chronicles*
12:33). These calculations depend on the distinction between the two spheres of
creation, the natural order, where the solar year rules, and the sphere of religious
observance, based on the lunar system. It is on the border between these two
zones that the Jewish calendar is situated. [בֵּין הַמִּשְׁפְּתָיִם, *between the boundaries,*
echoes the phrase יוֹדְעֵי בִינָה (I *Chronicles* ibid.), knowing how to discern
between the spheres in order to calculate the dates.]

15. מְנֻחָה כִּי טוֹב — *Tranquility that it was good. Rashi* explains: "He saw that his
portion was a land that was blessed, goodly and fruitful, but (nevertheless)
lowered his shoulder to bear the yoke of Torah and he became a servant under
taskwork (of Jewry), accepting the task of settling the rulings of the Torah for
them and answering their questions."

¹⁴ *"Issachar is a strong-boned donkey; he rests between the boundaries. ¹⁵ He saw tranquility that it was good, and the land that it was pleasant, yet he bent his shoulder to bear and he became an indentured laborer.*

¹⁶ *"Dan will avenge his people, the tribes of Israel will be united*

Malbim and *R' S.R. Hirsch*, however, take the word הָאָרֶץ literally and translate: he saw that work on the land was pleasant. If Judah forms the royal tribe and Zebulun the tribe of commerce, then Issachar's tribe represents agriculture and, as a result, constitutes the nucleus of the Jewish people. A man of the Jewish people does not work for the love of work and earnings; he works in order to assure himself of מְנֻחָה, leisure time. He leaves power and riches to the others. For him the leisure obtained by personal effort is the greatest benefit which labor can provide. Accordingly, this tribe became the one which cultivated the spiritual treasures of the nation. Deep knowledge of the Torah is not acquired in incessant work devoted to business affairs, but in the hours of leisure which are the real "benefit" of work (מְנֻחָה כִּי טוֹב). And in agriculture, Issachar sees the best means of reaching the ideal state where man "makes Torah his main purpose, and his work the accessory means." Issachar formed the most intellectual tribe of the Jewish nation and this was so because it had agreed to pay "the tax of agricultural work, וַיְהִי לְמַס עֹבֵד."

16. דָּן יָדִין עַמּוֹ — *Dan will avenge* [lit. *judge*] *his people.* To Jacob in his prophetic vision is revealed the grandeur and decadence of the future tribe of Dan. This tribe was to have been the counterpart of the tribe of Judah; for Dan formed the rear guard of the Jewish camp in its forty years of wandering in the desert (*Numbers* 10:25), whereas the tribe of Judah formed the advance guard (ibid. 14). However, while Judah, with the courage of a lion, always attacked the enemy head on, Dan fought a war of surprise and ambush. Like the serpent, "more cunning than any beast," it "bites the horse's heels so its rider falls backwards." These words of Jacob are often applied to Samson, the judge and avenger (in the double meaning of יָדִין) of his people. He descended from the tribe of Dan and was most perfectly representative of it. His tactics in battle against the Philistines corresponded to Jacob's description, as *Ramban* and *Rashi* observe. But although Samson valiantly defended his people and brought his tribe glory, he ultimately fell into dishonor and shame. "He alone of the Jewish judges was to fall into the hands of the enemy" (*Ramban*).

18. לִישׁוּעָתְךָ קִוִּיתִי ה׳ — *For Your salvation do I long, O HASHEM!* This supplication, the closing words addressed to Dan, seems quite understandable when one considers this tribe's future destiny. From the viewpoint of its geographical position in the Holy Land, the tribe of Dan was the most exposed of all the tribes. But it was also the most vulnerable on the moral plane. It is clearly designated as forming "the black mark" in the Jewish camp and needs to be surrounded by the two worthy tribes of Asher and Naphtali (*Bamidbar*

יז יְהִי־דָן נָחָשׁ עֲלֵי־דֶרֶךְ שְׁפִיפֹן עֲלֵי־אֹרַח הַנֹּשֵׁךְ עִקְּבֵי־סוּס

חמישי יח-יט וַיִּפֹּל רֹכְבוֹ אָחוֹר: לִישׁוּעָתְךָ קִוִּיתִי יהוה: ✳ גָּד גְּדוּד

כ יְגוּדֶנּוּ וְהוּא יָגֻד עָקֵב: מֵאָשֵׁר שְׁמֵנָה לַחְמוֹ וְהוּא

כא יִתֵּן מַעֲדַנֵּי־מֶלֶךְ: נַפְתָּלִי אַיָּלָה שְׁלֻחָה הַנֹּתֵן

כב אִמְרֵי־שָׁפֶר: בֵּן פֹּרָת יוֹסֵף בֵּן פֹּרָת עֲלֵי־עָיִן

Rabbah 2). Indeed it appears as being "the tribe of idolaters." In Dan was found Micah's idol (*Judges* 18), the one the tribe had taken with it when it left Egypt (*Sanhedrin* 103b). Moreover, only the children of Dan went to worship the golden calves set up by King Yeroboam at Dan (*I Kings* 12:28-30). Centuries before, this infidelity had stopped the drive of the patriarch Abraham in his war against the kings (cf. commentary on 14:14). When he glimpsed this dark future, Jacob feared that the entire tribe would undergo the same tragic fate as its most famous representative, Samson, whose downfall was partly due to intermarriage. And so he prayed for God's help for this tribe.

19. גָּד גְּדוּד יְגוּדֶנּוּ — *Gad will recruit a regiment.* With this concise phrase the patriarch pays tribute to the overpowering strength of the tribe of Gad. It guarded the frontier and, on numerous occasions, repulsed attacks by the Amorites, Moabites, and Arameans (*Ramban*). Moses compares it to a lion whose strength, speed, and courage overcome any attempt to trespass its borders (*Deuteronomy* 33:20). Our Sages connect Jacob's prophetic words with different events in the history of the tribe, but *Ibn Ezra* remarks: "We now no longer know all the tribulations which our ancestors went through."

20. מֵאָשֵׁר שְׁמֵנָה לַחְמוֹ ... מַעֲדַנֵּי־מֶלֶךְ — *From Asher — his bread will have richness ... kingly delicacies.* In our commentary on 30:13, when the two children "of happiness," Gad and Asher, came into the world, it was pointed out under what circumstances Asher was able to redeem the wrongdoing of his brother Gad. By having the two blessings for the brothers come one right after the other and by adding to Asher's name the prefix מ ("from Asher"), the Torah is alluding to the merit of the latter. Gad's blessing comes to him "from Asher."

Apart from the literal meaning of the blessings (which *Rashi* notes), placing Asher in the foremost position among the tribes producing agricultural goods, the Sages of the Midrash hold that this tribe was blessed "by the beauty of its women, who will be sought after in marriage by kings and high priests." Even at Asher's birth his mother had foretold(30:13): בְּאָשְׁרִי, (he will be) for my salvation, for the daughters (of his descendants) will make me happy. The word מַעֲדַנֵּי, *delicacies*, refers to the jeweled ornaments destined for the princesses, as is mentioned in *II Samuel* 1:24. Accordingly, jewels appear on the banner of Asher (*Bamidbar Rabbah* 2.)

21. אַיָּלָה שְׁלֻחָה — *A hind (doe) let loose.* The tribes of Israel are compared to animals (*Sotah* 11b). Judah is compared to a young lion, Issachar to a strong-boned donkey, Dan to a serpent, Naphtali to a hind, Benjamin to a wolf.

as one. [17] *Dan will be a serpent on the highway, a viper by the path, that bites a horse's heels so its rider falls backward.* [18] *For Your salvation do I long, O HASHEM!*

[19] *"Gad will recruit a regiment and it will retreat on its heel.*

[20] *"From Asher — his bread will have richness, and he will provide kingly delicacies.*

[21] *"Naphtali is a hind let loose who delivers beautiful sayings.*

[22] *"A charming son is Joseph, a charming son to the eye; each*

According to *R' S. Edels*, this Talmudic statement stresses that the characteristic traits which distinguish each of the great Jewish families are to be maintained as basic powers which remain unaffected by the blemishes of society and civilization — just as is the case with the corresponding characteristics embodied in these representatives of the animal kingdom.

"The rulers of the lands used to send does to each other. The does, coming into the world in a Nordic land, were raised in the court of a king in a Mediterranean land; then a message was attached to their horns and they ran rapidly back to their birthplace, thus becoming messengers of 'אִמְרֵי שָׁפֶר, *words of praise.*' We read in *Talmud Yerushalmi* that the Roman emperor Diocletian imposed such heavy taxes on the inhabitants of Panage that they resolved to leave their town. One of the emperor's counselors then said to him: 'If they leave, they will return, for such is the nature of creatures. Let us see by sending does from our land to a distant country. They will eventually return.' And so they did send does to Africa where they were tied up to keep them from fleeing. When they were freed thirteen years later, they immediately returned to the land of their birth" (*Ramban*).

Naphtali was the prototype of the satisfied man, *satisfied with Divine favor, and full with the blessing of HASHEM* (*Deuteronomy* 33:23). In addition he had the gift of eloquence and "when he began to speak at gatherings, his words flowed like honey" (*Targumim:* נַפְתָּלִי formed from נוֹפֶת לוֹ, the honey which flows from him, as in *Proverbs* 24:13.) Thus, as a result of his natural ability and his eloquence, he was predestined to be the bearer of good news. He himself had had the occasion to fulfill this role in his lifetime. (Some sources have it that it was Naphtali who first announced to Jacob that Joseph was still alive — *Targumim*.) Later his descendants proved themselves to be born diplomats thanks to their charm, their cleverness and their dexterity (*Tanchuma*). Naphtali became the messenger who did not fail in his mission; he will be capable of carrying out the most arduous undertaking, for his penetrating and inspired spirit and his disarming grace were to make this brother the best "bearer of news," in the highest sense of the term.

22. בֵּן פֹּרָת יוֹסֵף — *A charming son is Joseph.* To *Rashi*, בֵּן פֹּרָת signifies a magnificent son; to *Ibn Ezra*, a fertile branch; to *Onkelos*, a fruitful son. The grammarians cited by *Ramban* interpret: Son! Branched out is Joseph, Son! with branches right from the source. (The word בֵּן, punctuated with a צֵירָה and not

כג בָּנוֹת צָעֲדָה עֲלֵי־שׁוּר: וַיְמָרֲרֻהוּ וָרֹבּוּ וַיִּשְׂטְמֻהוּ בַּעֲלֵי חִצִּים:
כד וַתֵּשֶׁב בְּאֵיתָן קַשְׁתּוֹ וַיָּפֹזּוּ זְרֹעֵי יָדָיו מִידֵי אֲבִיר יַעֲקֹב מִשָּׁם
כה רֹעֶה אֶבֶן יִשְׂרָאֵל: מֵאֵל אָבִיךָ וְיַעְזְרֶךָּ וְאֵת שַׁדַּי וִיבָרֲכֶךָּ

a סֶגוֹל, is in the absolute state. The repetition in this phrase refers to the two branches issuing from Joseph: Ephraim and Manasseh.)

The blessing addressed to Joseph is imbued with terms of the warmest affection. It is for Joseph, the one twice called simply "Son!" that the father keeps his most complimentary and tender words. This son, after going through so much, receives his reward, which is nothing but favorable.

To be sure, Judah was recognized as the uncontested leader of Israel's children. "You your brothers shall acknowledge," his father had said to him. He had natural authority and enjoyed undisputed popularity, while Joseph, whose spiritual and physical gifts were without doubt even more outstanding than Judah's had always provoked the jealousy and then the hatred of his brothers. "They embittered him and became antagonists the arrow-[tongued] men hated him." As a consequence, he could not aspire to the position of leader.

And yet, in grandeur of soul and in moral worth, Joseph was superior to Judah. It was he, not Judah, who earned the title of צַדִּיק, *righteous one*, with which Jewish tradition has honored him (*Yoma* 35b). His father calls him here "the crown among his brothers," the one who wears, unseen by others, the diadem of moral perfection. This exceptional tribute from the dying patriarch is due to the strength of character and nobleness of heart which Joseph had demonstrated on two decisive occasions in his life. Jacob discreetly recalls them through the euphemistic words he now addresses to Joseph.

Joseph's first moral victory over himself concerned the chastity which he had maintained in Egypt, despite the daily temptations from all sides. "Each day," exclaims R' Yochanan, "God Himself praises the virtue of the bachelor who lives in a large town without yielding to sin" (*Pesachim* 113a). Now, Egypt was the land where moral perversion and sexual license were practiced in their most ignoble form, as the Torah itself attests (*Leviticus* 18:3). But Joseph remained supremely unaffected by the debauchery of his surroundings. He was able to resist the constant temptations from the wife of his master. He had defended his virtue even at the risk of death (with which she threatened him) whereas Judah in a moment of weakness had yielded to an act of debauchery. Joseph had never faltered in this way, though he had possessed such extraordinary handsomeness that "girls climbed heights to gaze" in order to behold him as he passed. He had been capable of controlling his instincts by "restraining his virile strength" (cf. our commentary to 39:12, following *Sotah* 36b). This spiritual strength he displayed was due to the distant effect of the "mighty Jacob" (מִידֵי אֲבִיר יַעֲקֹב; ibid.). Thus it was from far (מִשָּׁם) that the patriarch, the rock of Israel, guided his son like a shepherd (רֹעֶה אֶבֶן יִשְׂרָאֵל). The Psalmist, too, sings of this astonishingly strong paternal influence on the son even after a separation of

*of the girls climbed heights to gaze. ²³ They embittered him and
became antagonists; the arrow-tongued men hated him. ²⁴ But his
bow was firmly emplaced and his arms were gilded, from the
hands of the Mighty Power of Jacob — from there, he shepherded
the stone of Israel. ²⁵ [That was] from the God of your father and
He will help you, and with Shaddai — and He will bless you [with]*

many years in a distant land: "O Shepherd, Israel, listen, you who lead Joseph
like a flock" (נֹהֵג כַּצֹּאן יוֹסֵף; 80:2).

The self-mastery and self-control which Joseph demonstrated in his struggle
against the attractions of the senses reaffirmed itself once more in the domain
of moral virtues. Jacob alludes to it when he juxtaposes the two great reasons for
his son's merit. His brothers had harrassed him and "the archers shot at him with
their arrows," and yet he did not exploit a ready opportunity to take revenge on
the guilty. A viceroy of Egypt with almost unlimited powers, Joseph was still
able to forgive. He proved capable of generosity and of renouncing an
opportunity to show hatred, however justified it might be. Far from turning his
bow against his brothers when he was well able to do so, "his bow remained at
rest (וַתֵּשֶׁב בְּאֵיתָן קַשְׁתּוֹ), even though the arms of his hands already bore the
golden ornaments (of royalty) (וַיָּפֹזּוּ זְרֹעֵי יָדָיו)." Joseph owed this miraculous
turning point in his life to the same Divine Providence which had guided the
life of Jacob. He too recognized in God the "All-powerful Force, אָבִיר" (as in
Isaiah 1:24), Who had raised him from the depths of human misery. In all the
phases of his existence, Joseph experienced God as the Shepherd Who led him
as He had led his father Jacob and Who had bestowed all His solicitude upon
the "stone of Israel" (אֶבֶן יִשְׂרָאֵל). This stone was none other than the one which,
in the midst of desolation, Jacob had previously consecrated to become Beth-El,
the cornerstone of the family belonging to God (וְהָאֶבֶן הַזֹּאת וכו'; 28:22). On it
Jacob had rested his weary head when he left the paternal home to flee from his
brother's threats on his life, and since then he had never ceased to look upon it
as the symbol not only of his deepest misery, but also of the marvelous Divine
blessing which he had received in the dream. The blessing had been completely
fulfilled and now, in the evening of his life, with a heart full of thanksgiving,
Jacob directed his thoughts towards this "stone of Israel" (*R' Hirsch*).

As for Joseph, in him the patriarch recognized the one son who had
understood more deeply than the others the meaning of the moral mission of
mankind. He is the true heir, the "crown of his brothers." His nobility of heart
and exceptional natural gifts combine to form the truly "righteous one." He
merits the title of honor, צַדִּיק, because at moments of great temptation he had
been master of himself and remained absolutely faithful to his beliefs and to the
God of his father. And so it is to the God of his father (מֵאֵל אָבִיךָ) that Jacob
prays, asking that He continue to watch over his son Joseph.

25. וְאֵת שַׁדַּי — *And with Shaddai. Rashi* interprets: "And with God was your
heart when you did not listen to the words of your master's wife, and it is He

בִּרְכֹת שָׁמַ֫יִם֙ מֵעָ֔ל בִּרְכֹ֥ת תְּה֖וֹם רֹבֶ֣צֶת תָּ֑חַת בִּרְכֹ֥ת שָׁדַ֖יִם

כו וָרָ֑חַם: בִּרְכֹ֣ת אָבִ֗יךָ גָּֽבְרוּ֙ עַל־בִּרְכֹ֣ת הוֹרַ֔י עַד־תַּאֲוַ֖ת גִּבְעֹ֣ת

עוֹלָ֑ם תִּֽהְיֶ֙יןָ֙ לְרֹ֣אשׁ יוֹסֵ֔ף וּלְקָדְקֹ֖ד נְזִ֥יר אֶחָֽיו:

ששי   כז   בִּנְיָמִין֙ זְאֵ֣ב יִטְרָ֔ף בַּבֹּ֖קֶר יֹ֣אכַל עַ֑ד וְלָעֶ֖רֶב יְחַלֵּ֥ק שָׁלָֽל:

Who will bless you." The word אֶת is taken as a preposition meaning "with." But the Zohar considers it as having to take the place of the Divine name אֵל. The Torah chooses instead the word אֶת, beginning with א and ending with ת, to illustrate the idea of the totality of the elements (whereas the name אֵל, terminating with a ל, comes to an end at the halfway mark of the alphabet). Now, it is precisely this idea of the universality of the Divine blessings which the patriarch emphasizes in what he is about to say.

Jacob had indeed been granted blessings far surpassing those of his progenitors, as we have pointed out in our commentary on 28:14. His father had blessed him with "the blessings from heaven above and from the depths that lie below" בִּרְכֹת שָׁמַיִם מֵעַל וְגוֹ', through the words מִטַל הַשָׁמַיִם וּמִשְׁמַנֵּי הָאָרֶץ; (27:28). God had bestowed upon him blessings "without limit": "Your descendants will be like the dust of the earth, and you will expand westward, eastward, northward, and southward; and all the families of the earth will be blessed through you and through your descendants" (28:14). This blessing, surpassing those of his progenitors (גָּבְרוּ עַל בִּרְכֹת הוֹרַי), indeed extended to the far reaches of the world (עַד תַּאֲוַת גִּבְעֹת עוֹלָם). However, Jacob had never profited from his rich blessings; he wanted them to be kept in reserve for the future (cf. our commentary, ibid. 4). And now the time had come to bequeath them to the son who appeared the most worthy. This son was Joseph, the צַדִּיק, for it is always necessary that "the instrument of good be good itself (מְגַלְגְּלִין זְכוּת עַ"י זַכַּאי; Shabbos 32a). Accordingly, it is fitting that "the blessings be upon the head of the righteous" (Proverbs 10:6).

בִּרְכֹת שָׁדַיִם וָרָחַם — *Blessings of the bosom and womb.* According to the *Midrash Rabbah*, this refers to Rachel, the never-to-be-forgotten wife, the mother of Joseph. Before his death, Jacob wanted to recall her memory in order to remind his son of how many blessings he owed to his mother whose breasts had nourished him and whose womb had given birth to him. But for *Rashi* and *Onkelos*, this phrase depicts the fruitfulness of Joseph's descendants. The patriarch's blessing was, however, not able to last. As time went on Joseph's offspring became unworthy, forfeiting this blessing and causing Hosea, the first prophet after the destruction of the Temple, to exclaim: *Give them, HASHEM, whatsoever You will give; give them a barren womb and dried-up breasts* (9:14).

26. נְזִיר אֶחָיו — *The exile from his brothers.* Joseph deserved the title of *nazir* by his abstinence from all impure contact while he was in Egypt, as was mentioned previously. This virtue earned him the "crown" among his brothers, which the term נְזִיר also designates.

blessings of heaven from above, blessings of the deep crouching below, blessings of the bosom and womb. [26] *The blessings of your father surpassed the blessings of my parents to the endless bounds of the world's hills. Let them be upon Joseph's head and upon the head of the exile from his brothers.*

[27] *"Benjamin is a predatory wolf; in the morning he will devour prey and in the evening he will distribute spoils."*

Joseph thus appears as the brother who, beside Judah, occupies a pre-eminent position in the family of Israel. This family is crystalized around two poles, one representing the authority of the leader (מַלְכוּת), the other, the basis of righteousness and integrity (צַדִּיק). The origins of this polarity show up in Jacob's blessings and through Biblical history from beginning to end. But while the tribe of Judah remains faithful to its messianic calling as history unfolds, Joseph's descendants strayed from their path. And as a consequence, the brotherly unity between the royal tribe and the tribe of faithful piety, the *entente* which was sought from the start, did not stand the test of time. The schism which developed between the kingdoms of Judah and Joseph-Ephraim illustrates this tragic opposition. However, an end to this antagonism is announced in the name of God — we find it in the prophet Ezekiel's messianic vision: *I shall take the staff of Joseph ... and the staff of Judah, and I shall make of them one staff and they will be one in my hand ... Only one king will be king to both of them ... neither will they be divided into two kingdoms any more at all* (37:19-22).

27. בִּנְיָמִין זְאֵב יִטְרָף — *Benjamin is a predatory wolf.* In his interpretation of these words to Benjamin, *Rashi* remains consistent with his view that all of Jacob's blessings have the sense of prophecies regarding the future destinies of each tribe. Seen in this perspective, the solemn convocation of the patriarch was intended to assign to each son in turn his historic vocation, which would characterize his tribe until the end of time.

But the *Zohar* and the *Targumim* take this phrase concerning Benjamin and refer it to the sacrificial service which will take place in the Temple at Jerusalem, in Benjamin's territory (*Zevachim* 44b). For Jacob, the glorious future of his youngest son is connected with this exceptional privilege (the reasons for it have been given in our commentary to 33:2 and 35:18). The verse, then, has the following meaning: Benjamin is a "wolf" that devours! The altar where the holy animals are consumed is also called אֲרִיאֵל, the *lion of God*, because the celestial fire appears crouching like a lion (*Rashi* on *Isaiah* 29:1). "In the morning he will devour" the spoils of the daily sacrifice which is offered then (עוֹלַת הַבּוֹקֶר). The morning offering is a sign of love on the part of man; right from the beginning of the day he wants to raise himself up to God. The word עַד used here echoes the phrase וְשַׁבְתָּ עַד ה׳ אֱלֹהֶיךָ, *you will return to HASHEM, your God* (*Deuteronomy* 30:2). And at night he "will distribute spoils," referring to the rich blessings which, thanks to the altar, are

כח כָּל־אֵ֣לֶּה שִׁבְטֵ֧י יִשְׂרָאֵ֛ל שְׁנֵ֥ים עָשָׂ֖ר וְ֠זֹאת אֲשֶׁר־דִּבֶּ֨ר לָהֶ֤ם

כט אֲבִיהֶם֙ וַיְבָ֣רֶךְ אוֹתָ֔ם אִ֛ישׁ אֲשֶׁ֥ר כְּבִרְכָת֖וֹ בֵּרַ֣ךְ אֹתָֽם: וַיְצַ֣ו

אוֹתָ֗ם וַיֹּ֤אמֶר אֲלֵהֶם֙ אֲנִי֙ נֶאֱסָ֣ף אֶל־עַמִּ֔י קִבְר֥וּ אֹתִ֖י אֶל־

ל אֲבֹתָ֑י אֶל־הַ֨מְּעָרָ֔ה אֲשֶׁ֥ר בִּשְׂדֵ֖ה עֶפְר֣וֹן הַֽחִתִּֽי: בַּמְּעָרָ֞ה אֲשֶׁ֣ר

bestowed every evening in consequence of the holy service performed there every morning.

וְלָעֶרֶב יְחַלֵּק שָׁלָל — *And in the evening he will distribute spoils.* According to *R' S.R. Hirsch,* after having accompanied his sons in his prophetic vision through the torments of history the patriarch foresees that it will be the smallest and the youngest among them who will ultimately at the End of Days repulse the "ravenous wolf," the eternal Amalek, and drive him far from the flock of Israel (זְאֵב יִטְרָף is then translated: *he will tear the wolf,* since it is not written זְאֵב טוֹרֵף). In the era of justice and love, not the strongest or the best-armed but the weakest of the brothers will triumph over the ferocious beast. In the morning of Jewry's history, Shaul, the Benjaminite, will inflict a temporary defeat on the Amalekites. And in the twilight of time, Benjamin will destroy them completely and will divide their spoils. *The youngest of the flock will repulse them* (Jeremiah 49:20).

Comparing Jacob's blessings with those of Moses at the end of the Torah, *Don Isaac Abarbanel* upholds the view that Moses' words are in anticipation of the future establishment of the tribes in the Promised Land, whereas Jacob was inspired with the character and vocation of each of his sons. This would explain the difference regarding Benjamin. Jacob characterizes him as a killing wolf whereas Moses calls him: *The beloved of God ... who gives Him his shelter forever, and He dwells between his shoulders* (a reference to the Temple amid the hills surrounding Jerusalem).

28. כָּל־אֵלֶּה שִׁבְטֵי יִשְׂרָאֵל שְׁנֵים עָשָׂר — *All these are the tribes of Israel-twelve.* All equal in righteousness, all צַדִּיקִים (*Targum Yonasan*) despite their faults which have just been criticized. The twelve sons are worthy of their father, they are all included in שִׁבְטֵי יִשְׂרָאֵל, *the tribes of Israel,* a title of honor appearing here for the first time. When the tree-root is good, says *Abarbanel,* all the boughs, branches, and trunks are good. Thus the work of selecting the good from the bad which had started with the descendants of the first patriarch in order to create the holy nation (cf. our commentary to 16:15) comes to completion in the offspring of the third patriarch — *His couch is perfect* (Rashi on 47:31).

שְׁנֵים עָשָׂר — *Twelve.* See our commentary to 46:27. The Torah makes a point of reaffirming the number twelve, already established in 35:22, despite the fact that the tribe of Joseph had since been split into two. This tribe is counted as one entity whenever Levi is counted among the sons; this excludes the cases where the tribes encamp or settle in Canaan.

וַיְבָרֶךְ אוֹתָם — *And he blessed them. Rashi:* But the text should have said: "Each according to his blessing he blessed *him.*" Why does the text say, "he blessed

²⁸ *All these are the tribes of Israel — twelve — and this is what their father spoke to them and he blessed them; he blessed each according to his appropriate blessing.*

²⁹ *Then he instructed them; and he said to them, "I shall be gathered to my people; bury me with my fathers in the cave that is in the field of Ephron the Hittite. ³⁰ In the cave that is in the*

them?" It is because the collective blessing (אוֹתָם) benefited every single one, and every single blessing benefited all the brothers.

אִישׁ אֲשֶׁר כְּבִרְכָתוֹ — *Each according to his appropriate blessing.* The blessing is not uniform. It varies according to the character of each child, for the Jewish nation is founded on the principle of unity in plurality, as has been explained in our commentary to 35:11. Each of the twelve tribes is called upon to perform its particular function, resulting from its special character and its regional location in the land. Thus there is set up a veritable "division of labor" which determines the economic and cultural life of the nation. Reuben, Gad and Manasseh, occupying Transjordan, specialized in raising cattle and grazing them (*Numbers* 32). From Simeon came the nation's scribes and teachers (*Rashi* on verse 7) and from Issachar its sages (*Judges* 5:14). Levi provided the clergy, and Judah the royal dynasty. Ephraim and Benjamin provided the best soldiers (*Psalms* 80:3), while Zebulun devoted himself to foreign trade and maritime commerce. Asher excelled in agriculture, as did Naphtali, who, in addition, produced orators. Lastly, the tribe of Dan distinguished itself (*Pesachim* 4a) by its great competence in judicial matters.

The characteristics noted by the patriarch marked the Jewish tribes for all time. While remaining loyal to their common faith, the Jews developed characteristics for each tribe, recognized as completely legitimate. It is these characteristics which are at the origin of the various customs in prayer ritual prevalent among the different sectors of the Jewish nation. There are "twelve heavenly gates, one for each of the twelve tribes. Each tribe possesses its form of prayer, which ascends to God by one of these gates. So it is proper not to change the מִנְהָגִים, the established customs" (מגן אברהם, סי׳ ס״ח).

29. וַיְצַו אוֹתָם — *Then he instructed them.* According to *Ramban*, the basis for this command, which Jacob addressed to his children after Joseph had already promised to bury him in the Holy Land, lies in the patriarch's apprehension that Pharaoh, afraid that Joseph would leave Egypt never to return, would refuse his request. So, Jacob gave this most categorical command to the whole family together, adding a last wish regarding the transfer of his remains, "which no uncircumcised person should touch" (*Midrash* and *Rashi* on 50:13). The detailed account of the patriarch's arrangements shortly before his death is given both at the beginning and at the end of the *sidrah* and it emphasizes the exceptional importance attached to the Holy Land and its soil. The reasons for this have been

בִּשְׂדֵ֤ה הַמַּכְפֵּלָה֙ אֲשֶׁ֣ר עַל־פְּנֵ֣י מַמְרֵ֔א בְּאֶ֖רֶץ כְּנָ֑עַן אֲשֶׁר֩
קָנָ֨ה אַבְרָהָ֜ם אֶת־הַשָּׂדֶ֗ה מֵאֵ֛ת עֶפְרֹ֥ן הַחִתִּ֖י לַאֲחֻזַּת־
לא קָ֑בֶר: שָׁ֣מָּה קָֽבְר֞וּ אֶת־אַבְרָהָ֗ם וְאֵת֙ שָׂרָ֣ה אִשְׁתּ֔וֹ
שָׁ֚מָּה קָֽבְר֣וּ אֶת־יִצְחָ֔ק וְאֵ֖ת רִבְקָ֣ה אִשְׁתּ֑וֹ וְשָׁ֥מָּה קָבַ֖רְתִּי
לב אֶת־לֵאָֽה: מִקְנֵ֧ה הַשָּׂדֶ֛ה וְהַמְּעָרָ֥ה אֲשֶׁר־בּ֖וֹ מֵאֵ֥ת בְּנֵי־
לג חֵֽת: וַיְכַ֤ל יַעֲקֹב֙ לְצַוֺּ֣ת אֶת־בָּנָ֔יו וַיֶּאֱסֹ֥ף רַגְלָ֖יו אֶל־
א הַמִּטָּ֑ה וַיִּגְוַ֖ע וַיֵּאָ֥סֶף אֶל־עַמָּֽיו: וַיִּפֹּ֥ל יוֹסֵ֖ף עַל־פְּנֵ֣י
ב אָבִ֑יו וַיֵּ֥בְךְּ עָלָ֖יו וַיִּשַּׁק־לֽוֹ: וַיְצַ֨ו יוֹסֵ֤ף אֶת־עֲבָדָיו֙ אֶת־
הָרֹ֣פְאִ֔ים לַחֲנֹ֖ט אֶת־אָבִ֑יו וַיַּחַנְט֥וּ הָרֹפְאִ֖ים אֶת־יִשְׂרָאֵֽל:

נ

stated in our commentary to 47:29. On this note and on the long description of
the burial in the cave of the patriarchs, *Genesis* comes to an end.

30. בַּמְּעָרָה אֲשֶׁר בִּשְׂדֵה הַמַּכְפֵּלָה — *In the cave that is in the field of Machpelah.*
Cf. our commentary to 23:17.

31. שָׁ֣מָּה קָֽבְרוּ אֶת־יִצְחָק וְאֵת רִבְקָה אִשְׁתּוֹ — *There they buried Isaac and Rebecca
his wife.* Although it is forbidden to call one's father by his first name even after
his death, it is nevertheless permitted when to the first name one adds the term
אַבָּא, *my father* (הגר״א, יו״ד, רמ״ב ס״ק ל״ו). Now here, Jacob had prefaced the first
names with the term אֲבֹתַי, *my fathers.* According to *Ritva,* the names of the
patriarchs were specific names given by God, and this allowed the sons to
mention them. The same remark applies to 50:24.

33. וַיְכַל יַעֲקֹב לְצַוֺּת אֶת־בָּנָיו — *When Jacob finished instructing his sons.* Until his
last breath the righteous one remains master over death. Death waits as it were
until he finishes expressing his final wishes to his sons. Jacob is one of the six
righteous people over whom the Angel of Death had no authority — they died
from the kiss of God (*Bava Basra* 16a) — nor are their remains consumed by the
worms (ibid.).

But *Rashi* quotes the Talmud (*Taanis* 5b) which points out that the word וַיָּמָת
is not mentioned concerning Jacob. And our Sages say: "Jacob our father did not
die." This remark, which of course cannot be taken in a literal sense, as the
commentators tell us, has a more general meaning which was developed in our
commentary at the beginning of the *sidrah* (to 47:28).

Why is this distinction attributed to Jacob and not to the other patriarchs? *R'
Bachya* reminds us that in his lifetime Jacob achieved the harmonious union of
those virtues which each of his ancestors only possessed singly: Abraham's
infinite love of God and man, and the spirit of obedience and unconditional
discipline characterized Isaac. While Abraham incarnated the principle of חֶסֶד
(*love*) and Isaac that of דִּין (*law* and *legality*), Jacob took the royal path, the
happy medium (תִּפְאֶרֶת = רַחֲמִים), of love tempering justice (cf. our commentary
to 25:27). This way is the way of harmony and truth (תִּתֵּן אֱמֶת לְיַעֲקֹב). And while
throughout the course of history, love and justice experience periods of eclipse

*field of Machpelah, which faces Mamre, in the land of Canaan,
which Abraham bought with the field from Ephron the Hittite
as a burial estate.* [31] *There they buried Abraham and Sarah his
wife; there they buried Isaac and Rebecca his wife; and there
I buried Leah.* [32] *Purchase of the field and the cave within it was
from the sons of Heth."*

[33] *When Jacob finished instructing his sons, he drew his feet
onto the bed; he expired and was gathered to his people.*

50   [1] *Then Joseph fell upon his father's face; he wept over him and
kissed him.* [2] *Joseph ordered his servants, the physicians, to
embalm his father; so the physicians embalmed Israel.*

and defeat, and carry in them the seeds of their opposition, the way of
harmonious union (רַחֲמִים בַּדִּין) asserts itself at all times and in all places. It is
everlasting and does not fade or decay. This principle of Jacob overcomes death.

וַיֵּאָסֶף אֶל־עַמָּיו — *And was gathered to his people.* Cf. our commentary to 25:8.

50.

1. וַיִּשַּׁק־לוֹ — *And kissed him.* R' *Chaim ben Attar* remarks: "It is not proper to
cover a corpse with kisses, because its impurity is passed on to the one who
embraces it. Jacob, however, was an exception for, in the higher sense, he
continued to live. Death did not change him." In the fourth paragraph of his will,
R' *Yehudah HaChassid* declares that to kiss one's dead child is a bad omen, and
A.Z. *Eisenstadt* comments that this refers only to a son or daughter, but not to
parents, as we see from Joseph's example (פ"ת יו"ד, סי' שצ"ד).

2. וַיְצַו יוֹסֵף ... לַחֲנֹט אֶת־אָבִיו — *Joseph ordered ... to embalm his father.* R'
Yehudah HaChassid differs with the Sages over the appropriateness of this
order given by Joseph. He considers it out of place and puts these words in the
mouth of God: "Would I not have been able to protect the righteous Myself? Will
I not say of him: *The worms will not touch Jacob, the remains of Israel! It is I
Who help you, says HASHEM (Isaiah 41:14).* And so Joseph had to bear the
consequences of this error. But the Sages defend Joseph's decision, affirming that
he was in effect following his father's orders, as we see from verse 12: *His sons
did for him exactly as he had instructed them.*

These two opinions correspond to the two opposing points of view concerning
the appropriateness of embalming. Some see it not only as an affront to the
human body which, even after death, retains its character of inviolability, but
also as a means of delaying or preventing putrefaction. Now, the latter is one of
the conditions of atonement, as is taught in *Sanhedrin 47b* (R' *Yechezkel Landau*
and R' *Moshe Sofer, Responsa*). Considering the matter in a more general way,
R' *S.R. Hirsch* points out that embalming marks one of the most characteristic
differences between the Jewish outlook and that of pagans. The Egyptians
embalmed the body in order to preserve its personal individuality.

ג וַיִּמְלְאוּ־לוֹ אַרְבָּעִים יוֹם כִּי כֵּן יִמְלְאוּ יְמֵי הַחֲנֻטִים
ד וַיִּבְכּוּ אֹתוֹ מִצְרַיִם שִׁבְעִים יוֹם: וַיַּעַבְרוּ יְמֵי בְכִיתוֹ
וַיְדַבֵּר יוֹסֵף אֶל־בֵּית פַּרְעֹה לֵאמֹר אִם־נָא מָצָאתִי חֵן
ה בְּעֵינֵיכֶם דַּבְּרוּ־נָא בְּאָזְנֵי פַרְעֹה לֵאמֹר: אָבִי הִשְׁבִּיעַנִי

The soul, they held, does not retain its individuality; it goes through numerous transmigrations, and goes from body to body even by way of animal bodies, continually undergoing changes. Jews, on the other hand, are taught that the soul is everlasting while the body decomposes "in the soil of the earth." They consider that the immediate return of the dead body to the earth is a *mitzvah;* the body is absorbed in the earth and can undergo all the transformations of terrestrial substances. The Egyptians believed in metempsychosis (transmigration of souls), and they tried to protect the body from all change, while the Jews believe in the eternal and personal existence of the soul, and they allow the body to suffer the fate of all physical matter. No doubt it is this negation of the belief in the immortal individuality of the soul which led the Egyptians to embalm their dead — and to erect those colossal edifices, the pyramids, intended as a final resting place for them. They wanted at least to retain the body, since the soul was supposedly in perpetual migration. If Joseph took into account this Egyptian custom, diametrically opposed to the Jewish conception, it could only have been for one reason: to avoid being accused of a lack of filial piety.

The *Zohar,* however, maintains a fundamentally different point of view. Do not think, it says, that Joseph ordered the embalming to preserve his father's body for the long journey to Canaan. In embalming him, he was following his father's wish. Having reached the highest degree of holiness, Jacob's body was free of all impurity. Jacob resembled Adam, physically and spiritually, and his life complemented Adam's (as was explained in our commentary on 27:28). Accordingly, his body was to rest in the Cave of Machpelah beside Adam's body, which, as it had been created by the hand of God, remained for all time in its original condition. Therefore it was "fitting and proper" that the body of Jacob should also remain intact. And it is in this sense that the *Zohar* understands the phrase יַעֲקֹב אָבִינוּ לֹא מֵת. (The body of a holy man who dies by the Divine kiss is not affected by impurity — *Ramban* on *Numbers* 19:2. See also *Tosafos* to *Kesubos* 103b.)

וַיַּחַנְטוּ הָרֹפְאִים אֶת־יִשְׂרָאֵל — *So the physicians embalmed Israel.* The patriarch had given orders to keep all Egyptians, and even his grandchildren who had married Canaanites, away from his coffin (*Rashi* on verse 13) so as "not to chase away the *Shechinah*" (*Midrash*). How then could Joseph hand over the body of his father to the pagan physicians? *R' Yehudah HaChassid* attempts to answer this question by showing that the doctors acted only through intermediaries (servants who had adopted the faith of Joseph) or through the sons themselves (*Sefer Chassidim* §1563).

³ *His forty-day term was completed, for such is the term of the embalmed; and Egypt bewailed him for seventy days.* ⁴ *When his bewailing period passed, Joseph spoke to Pharaoh's household, saying, "If you please — if I have found favor in your eyes, speak now in the ears of Pharaoh, saying:* ⁵ *My father had adjured me,*

3. וַיִּמְלְאוּ־לוֹ אַרְבָּעִים יוֹם — *His forty-day term was completed.* Don Isaac Abarbanel holds that the body was artificially preserved by means of balsamic substances once the brain, intestines, and thoracic organs had been removed. But referring to a passage in the *Zohar, R' Moshe Sofer* maintains that the embalming of Jacob might have taken place exceptionally without removal of these organs (*Responsa, Yoreh De'ah* 336).

4. וַיַּעַבְרוּ יְמֵי בְכִיתוֹ — *When his bewailing period passed.* On the death of Moses, the Torah remarks, וַיִּתְּמוּ יְמֵי בְּכִי, *the days of bewailing were ended* (*Deuteronomy* 34:8). This difference in wording is explained by the fact that Moses died on the threshold of the Promised Land. The Jews were living with the joyful prospect of soon gaining the status of a free people, dwelling in their own land. And so, the mourning for Moses ended with the completion of the usual period of thirty days. Jacob's passing, though, was felt as a national calamity. The last representative of the glorious epoch of the patriarchs had passed away. His descendants felt deprived of their great protector, and they were perfectly aware that their position in the land of the Egyptians would become more precarious. This is why "his bewailing period passed" without however being ended, as was stated in Moses' case.

וַיְדַבֵּר יוֹסֵף אֶל־בֵּית פַּרְעֹה — *Joseph spoke to Pharaoh's household.* Joseph could not present himself before Pharaoh in garments of mourning nor did he want to interrupt the period of lamentation — but these do not seem to have been the only reasons which prompted him to turn to the people of Pharaoh's court. The Midrash mentions his fear that the courtiers might oppose his request to Pharaoh. So he acted according to the proverb: "Win the accuser over to your cause if you want him not to act against you." He was obliged to speak first with the lady-in-waiting to the queen; she influenced her mistress, who in her turn persuaded Pharaoh on Joseph's behalf (*Rabbah* 100).

But, remarks *R' Shmuel Edels*, what Joseph feared most of all was that Pharaoh himself would refuse to let the coffin leave Egypt. Joseph was well aware that the Egyptian king and his subjects had looked upon Jacob as a saint who "right from his arrival in Egypt had brought them blessing, since from that time the famine had ended and the Nile had begun to rise again" (*Rashi*). Consequently, Pharaoh insisted on ensuring that his country would have the beneficial presence of the coffin (*Sotah* 36a). And finally, after all the steps which Joseph had taken, Pharaoh only agreed to this request because he feared that Joseph might reveal a secret, one which could cost his throne, as *Rashi* explains on verse 6. "Were it not for the oath which you made to your father,

לֵאמֹר הִנֵּה אָנֹכִי מֵת בְּקִבְרִי אֲשֶׁר כָּרִיתִי לִי בְּאֶרֶץ כְּנַעַן
שָׁמָּה תִּקְבְּרֵנִי וְעַתָּה אֶעֱלֶה־נָּא וְאֶקְבְּרָה אֶת־אָבִי וְאָשׁוּבָה:
ו־ז וַיֹּאמֶר פַּרְעֹה עֲלֵה וּקְבֹר אֶת־אָבִיךָ כַּאֲשֶׁר הִשְׁבִּיעֶךָ: וַיַּעַל
יוֹסֵף לִקְבֹּר אֶת־אָבִיו וַיַּעֲלוּ אִתּוֹ כָּל־עַבְדֵי פַרְעֹה זִקְנֵי בֵיתוֹ
ח וְכֹל זִקְנֵי אֶרֶץ־מִצְרָיִם: וְכֹל בֵּית יוֹסֵף וְאֶחָיו וּבֵית אָבִיו
ט רַק טַפָּם וְצֹאנָם וּבְקָרָם עָזְבוּ בְּאֶרֶץ גֹּשֶׁן: וַיַּעַל עִמּוֹ גַּם־רֶכֶב
י גַּם־פָּרָשִׁים וַיְהִי הַמַּחֲנֶה כָּבֵד מְאֹד: וַיָּבֹאוּ עַד־גֹּרֶן הָאָטָד
אֲשֶׁר בְּעֵבֶר הַיַּרְדֵּן וַיִּסְפְּדוּ־שָׁם מִסְפֵּד גָּדוֹל וְכָבֵד מְאֹד

I would not permit you to do it." For when Pharaoh told him, "Break your oath,"
Joseph replied: "In that case I will also break the oath I made to you — not to
reveal that in addition to the seventy languages, I know the Holy Language
whereas you do not" (and so according to the prevailing laws you do not have
the right to occupy the throne; cf. our commentary on 41:39).

5. בְּקִבְרִי אֲשֶׁר כָּרִיתִי לִי — *In my grave, which I have hewn for myself. Rashi*
quotes the *midrashic* explanation which interprets the word כָּרִיתִי in the sense
of "I have bought." Perhaps Joseph thought that wanting to be buried in a
duly-acquired cave would make more of an impression on Pharaoh than the
desire to be buried with his ancestors, the reason which Jacob himself gave.

7. וַיַּעַל יוֹסֵף לִקְבֹּר אֶת־אָבִיו — *So Joseph went up to bury his father.* He wanted
to perform this *mitzvah* personally, in spite of his royal position. "Measure for
measure," declares the *Mishnah*. The greatest of mortals, Moses, subsequently
looked after Joseph's burial (*Exodus* 13:19; *Sotah* 9b).

9. גַּם־רֶכֶב גַּם־פָּרָשִׁים — *Both chariots and horsemen.* "The cortege was going in
honor of the deceased, but the chariots and the infantry were there in case of
war" (*Midrash*). Joseph foresaw that a battle would be waged with Esau and his
troops. He suspected that Esau would want to contest Jacob's right to the last
remaining place in the Cave of Machpelah. And this deed indeed come about.
In his *Antiquities*, Flavius Josephus recounts the battles fought by the two
camps before the ancestral cave. Esau's grandson, Tz'fo son of Eliphaz, taken
prisoner during an attack against the children of Israel, was brought to Egypt,
where he remained a captive. After Joseph's death, he escaped and fled to Italy,
where he became the first king of Rome. There he built its first palace (*Ramban*;
cf. our commentary to 25:23).

10. גֹּרֶן הָאָטָד — *Goren HaAtad* [lit. *field of thorns*]. The name אָטָד can only
be symbolic, since it is found nowhere else in Scripture, said R' Shmuel
ben Nachman (*Yerushalmi, Sotah* 1:10). Accordingly *Rashi*, citing the
Talmud (*Sotah* 13a) explains: "It was given this name because of the event
which took place there. All the kings of Canaan and the princes of Ishmael
came there to wage war. But when they saw Joseph's crown hanging upon
Jacob's coffin, they desisted and hung their crowns on it also, surrounding it

saying, 'Behold, I am about to die; in my grave, which I have hewn for myself in the land of Canaan — there you are to bury me.' Now, I will go up if you please, and bury my father; then I will return."

⁶ And Pharaoh said, "Go up and bury your father as he adjured you."

⁷ So Joseph went up to bury his father, and with him went up all of Pharaoh's servants, the elders of his household, and all the elders of the land of Egypt, ⁸ and all of Jacob's household — his brothers, and his father's household; only their young children, their flocks, and their cattle did they leave in the region of Goshen. ⁹ And he brought up with him both chariots and horsemen; and the camp was very imposing. ¹⁰ They came to Goren HaAtad, which is across the Jordan, and there they held a very great and imposing eulogy;

with crowns just like a field which is encircled with a protective hedge of thorns." The crowns around the patriarch's coffin numbered thirty-six: twelve from the princes of Ishmael, twenty-three from the princes of Esau, and Joseph's crown (Rashi, ibid.). The crowns which the kings of the nations now and then offer to the Jews in a burst of magnanimity are, alas, covered with thorns.

The Zohar, however, gives a different interpretation. Its starting point is the Torah's remark emphasizing that there was very great mourning in a place called אָטָד and that this mourning was אֵבֶל מִצְרַיִם, a mourning for Egypt, not for the children of Israel. The wise men of Egypt had joyfully welcomed the news of Jacob's death, for the presence alone of this holy man had protected his descendants from every attempt by the Egyptian people to dominate them. But when they came to אָטָד, a name which signifies "thorns," the Egyptian diviners read in the stars that the future of their own people would be full of brambles and thorns, and that their rule would not outlast the rise of the Jewish nation. אָטָד has a numerical value of fourteen, equal to the word יָד, hand, and it hints at the great hand (הַיָּד הַגְּדֹלָה) which HASHEM stretched out against the Egyptians (Exodus 14:31), to swallow them up in the waters of the Red Sea. The astrologers saw a hand directed against the Egyptians — from its fingers grew thorns ready to prick them mercilessly. And so here they were plunged into deep mourning and this place was given the name of "mourning for Egypt."

אֲשֶׁר בְּעֵבֶר הַיַּרְדֵּן — Which is across the Jordan. בְּעֵבֶר sometimes means "across" and sometimes "on the side." This latter meaning is held by Chizkuni: The text is referring to the land of Canaan. Indeed, it was the inhabitants of Transjordan who saw the great mourning at Atad in Canaan. Relative to them, Atad was located on the other side of the Jordan (similarly, Rashbam on Deuteronomy 1:1, and others).

יא וַיַּעַשׂ לְאָבִיו אֵבֶל שִׁבְעַת יָמִים: וַיַּרְא יוֹשֵׁב הָאָרֶץ הַכְּנַעֲנִי
אֶת־הָאֵבֶל בְּגֹרֶן הָאָטָד וַיֹּאמְרוּ אֵבֶל־כָּבֵד זֶה לְמִצְרָיִם
יב עַל־כֵּן קָרָא שְׁמָהּ אָבֵל מִצְרַיִם אֲשֶׁר בְּעֵבֶר הַיַּרְדֵּן: וַיַּעֲשׂוּ
יג בָנָיו לוֹ כֵּן כַּאֲשֶׁר צִוָּם: וַיִּשְׂאוּ אֹתוֹ בָנָיו אַרְצָה כְּנַעַן
וַיִּקְבְּרוּ אֹתוֹ בִּמְעָרַת שְׂדֵה הַמַּכְפֵּלָה אֲשֶׁר קָנָה אַבְרָהָם
אֶת־הַשָּׂדֶה לַאֲחֻזַּת־קֶבֶר מֵאֵת עֶפְרֹן הַחִתִּי עַל־פְּנֵי מַמְרֵא:

וַיַּעַשׂ לְאָבִיו אֵבֶל שִׁבְעַת יָמִים — *And he ordained a seven-day mourning period for his father.* This was after Jacob's burial, *Ibn Ezra* tells us. But the *Tosafists* hold that, in the period before the Torah was given, the seven days of mourning took place before burial (*Moed Katan* 20a), as it seems to appear from the text. Whichever is the case, we see that the custom of having a period of mourning lasting seven days goes back to the time of the patriarchs. In this regard, *Rambam* stipulates: "According to the Torah, the mourning period is for just one day, the day of death and burial. But the seven days are not a Mosaic law, although the Torah does contain the words: *he ordained a seven-day' mourning period for his father.* For when the Torah was given, the law was established anew (and the duration of mourning was set at one day only). The basis for the custom of the seven days of mourning, just as for the the seven days of festivity after a marriage (הלכ' אבל פ"א, א) was established for Jewry by Moses, our teacher" (cf. our commentary to 7:4).

11. עַל־כֵּן קָרָא שְׁמָהּ אָבֵל מִצְרָיִם — *Therefore, it was named Avel Mizraim.* The local population was so impressed by the extent of national mourning of the great Egyptian state that their ruler decided upon this place-name to immortalize the love and respect for a Jewish ancestor in the midst of a foreign nation.

12. וַיַּעֲשׂוּ בָנָיו לוֹ כֵּן כַּאֲשֶׁר צִוָּם — *His sons did for him exactly as he had instructed them.* כֵּן also has the meaning of "with sincerity," as in *Proverbs* 11:19. His sons acted with sincerity, that is to say, without trying to discover the reasons which had prompted their father to arrange them in the order mentioned later on. They acted with sincerity, simply because "he had instructed them."

13. וַיִּשְׂאוּ אֹתוֹ בָנָיו — *His sons carried him. Rashi* explains: "And not the sons of his sons. For that is what Jacob had ordered: Let not an Egyptian carry my coffin, nor any of your sons, for they are the children of Canaanite women, but you yourselves carry it. Jacob assigned each one his place, three on each of the four sides, in the same order that they would later occupy as they journeyed with the banners of the tribes. Levi was not to carry the coffin, for he was destined to bear the Holy Ark. Joseph too was excluded for he was king. Their places were taken by Manasseh and Ephraim. This is the meaning of the words: *Each man by his banner, according to the insignias* (*Numbers* 2:2). That is to say, according to the signs their father had given them for carrying his coffin."

This order of procession, fixed by the patriarch and reflected in the arrangement of Israel's camp in the desert, was as follows: In the forefront, to

and he ordained a seven-day mourning period for his father.
*¹¹ When the Canaanite inhabitants of the land saw the mourning
in Goren HaAtad, they said, "This is a grievous mourning for
Egypt." Therefore, it was named Avel Mizraim, which is across
the Jordan.*
*¹² His sons did for him exactly as he had instructed them. ¹³ His
sons carried him to the land of Canaan and they buried him in
the cave of the Machpelah field, the field that Abraham had
bought as a burial estate from Ephron the Hittite, facing Mamre.*

the east, were the tribes of Judah, Issachar and Zebulun. They represented the
political and spiritual direction of the nation. To the south were the tribes of
Simeon and Gad under the leadership of Reuben, the prototype of the *baal
teshuvah*. In this sense, this side represented moral government. Located
opposite on the north side were the three tribes of Dan, Asher, and Naphtali,
possessors of material wealth. And in the west, the tribes of Ephraim, Manasseh
and Benjamin, who had the responsibility for national defense (*Psalms* 80:3).

This social and national arrangement is a reflection on a reduced scale of the
pre-established harmonious order of elementary forces in the universal spheres.
The prophet Ezekiel unveils a little of this concept when he reveals the order of
the four forces surrounding the celestial chariot where the Divine Majesty is
enthroned (1:10). The first of these four חַיּוֹת or universal forces, situated in the
east, had a human face. It represented the supremacy of the spirit, the
prerogative of man. Its position in the east is in the direction of the Orient, the
cradle of humanity, where the man formed by God was placed (*Genesis* 2:8).
The second force, set in the south, had "the face of a lion." The king of beasts
symbolizes the element of strength. Now, the acme of strength is not physical,
but moral. *He who rules his passions is better than the conqueror* (*Proverbs*
16:32). Hence, faithfulness to God requires *the strength, the courage of the lion*
(*Avos* 5:23). The third force, placed at the north of the Divine chariot, had the
face of an ox; it represents the physical and material aspects of the structure of
the universe. Lastly, the fourth חַיָּה had the face of an eagle, the symbol of
majesty and victory. It guarantees that the existing forces will endure. From the
west she "stirs up her nest, hovers over her young, spreads out her wings, takes
them, bears them on her pinions" (*Deuteronomy* 32:11).

Corresponding to this pre-established arrangement of the "chariot" of
universal life is the functional arrangement of Israel's camp. The twelve tribes
which revolve around the four elements are organized in conformity with the
eternal laws which govern the cosmos. The image of the macrocosm is
rediscovered in the microcosm of Israel. And when King Solomon built the
Temple in Jerusalem, he wanted to materialize this ideal principle of the
harmony of the upper and lower spheres. He made the "sea," the great laver, and
supported it by twelve oxen, "three looking toward the north, and three looking

יד וַיָּשָׁב יוֹסֵף מִצְרַיְמָה הוּא וְאֶחָיו וְכָל־הָעֹלִים אִתּוֹ לִקְבֹּר
טו אֶת־אָבִיו אַחֲרֵי קָבְרוֹ אֶת־אָבִיו: וַיִּרְאוּ אֲחֵי־יוֹסֵף כִּי־מֵת
אֲבִיהֶם וַיֹּאמְרוּ לוּ יִשְׂטְמֵנוּ יוֹסֵף וְהָשֵׁב יָשִׁיב לָנוּ אֵת כָּל־
טז הָרָעָה אֲשֶׁר גָּמַלְנוּ אֹתוֹ: וַיְצַוּוּ אֶל־יוֹסֵף לֵאמֹר אָבִיךָ צִוָּה

toward the west, and three looking toward the south, and three looking toward the east. And the sea rested above upon them" — and the *Shechinah* hovered above it, even as, at the beginning of the Creation, "a breath from God was hovering over the water" (*I Kings* 7:25, according to the *Zohar*). These were the prophetic visions which inspired the final arrangements made by Jacob.

וַיִּקְבְּרוּ אֹתוֹ בִּמְעָרַת — *And they buried him in the cave.* "When they came to the cave, Esau drew near and barred the way, saying that the last of the eight places in the cave belonged to him. They replied that he had sold not only his birthright but also his own portion of the inheritance of his fathers in the Cave of Machpelah (*Rashi* on verse 5). He said to them: 'Show me the contract of the sale' (assuming that they did not have it with them). So they sent Naphtali, who was as fleet as a doe, to go and find the contract in Egypt. Now, among them was Hushim, the son of Dan. He was hard of hearing and asked what was happening. They told him that Esau was holding up the burial until Naphtali returned. He replied: 'And is my grandfather to lie there dishonored until Naphtali returns from Egypt?' Thereupon he took a club and struck Esau on the head, killing him and causing his eyes to fall at Jacob's feet. On that day Rebecca's prophecy was fulfilled, as it is written: *Why should I be bereaved of both of you on the same day?*" (27:45; *Sotah* 13a).

14. וְכָל־הָעֹלִים אִתּוֹ — *And all who had gone up with him.* Despite the battles which Esau's sons had waged against them to avenge their father's death, "after he (Joseph) had buried his father," not one person was missing on the return journey to Egypt. These raids by the armies of Esau provoked a series of wars not only between enemies but also between former allies, and the wars successively spread to numerous countries in Asia Minor and Africa and even to Italy, where a grandson of Esau, Tz'fo ben Eliphaz, succeeded in establishing the first monarchy. The description of this historical period is given by Yosef HaKohen ben Gurion, the presumed author of the chronicles called the *Seder HaYashar* and *Yosifon*.

15. לוּ יִשְׂטְמֵנוּ יוֹסֵף — *Perhaps Joseph will nurse hatred against us.* A noteworthy example of the voice of a bad conscience which cannot be calmed. Completely fantastic interpretations are placed on certain of Joseph's acts in such a way that his brothers see phantoms everywhere. Thus, while his father was still alive, Joseph used to welcome his brothers at his table and dine with them out of respect for Jacob. Right after Jacob's death he no longer received them in this way. However, adds R' Tanchuma, his intentions were pure, they were not at all prompted by feelings of resentment. It was just that Joseph's father had made him take the place of honor at the table (which in reality should have gone to

> ¹⁴ *Joseph returned to Egypt — he and his brothers, and all who had gone up with him to bury his father — after he buried his father.*
> ¹⁵ *Joseph's brothers perceived that their father was dead, and they said, "Perhaps Joseph will nurse hatred against us and then he will surely repay us all the evil that we did him." ¹⁶ So they instructed that Joseph be told, "Your father gave orders before*

Reuben the firstborn or the leader, Judah), and now Joseph was embarrassed to occupy that place. Another example: when they came back from the burial, Joseph detoured to stop at the pit where he had been cast before being sold to the Ishmaelites. The brothers took this as a sign that old grudges were reviving whereas in reality Joseph's only intention was to pay tribute to God, Who "had made a miracle at this place" for him (*Tanchuma*).

Rashi explains at length that here the conjunction לוּ has the meaning of *perhaps* — the one place in all of Scripture where this is so. Why is this term used here instead of אוּלַי? R' *Chaim ben Attar* replies that the principle meaning of לוּ — *if only*, or, *provided that* — is implied in the words of the brothers. Deep in their hearts they thought: If only Joseph would detest us and pay us back for all the harm which we have caused him! Then there would no longer be any trace of our sin and we would have no fear of seeing it fall back on our children and our descendants. The sin did not go unpunished; Divine justice was only carried out centuries later at the time of the ten martyrs (cf. our commentary to 44:17).

16. אָבִיךָ צִוָּה — *Your father gave orders. Rashi:* "In the interests of peace, they altered the words somewhat. Jacob had never given such a command, for he did not suspect that Joseph would harbor resentment towards his brothers." The Talmudic statement which *Rashi* is quoting from here concludes from this verse that it is permitted to tell a "white lie" for the sake of peace (*Yevamos* 65b). But a restriction to this is brought down in *Sefer Chassidim* (§426): "If a Jew or a non-Jew comes to you for a loan and you do not want to give the money to him for fear that he will not repay it, you do not have the right to lie and say that you do not have the means, for permission to tell a 'white lie' in the interest of peace applies only to cases which have already happened, but not to events that are in the future." This is also the decision set down in *Magen Avraham* §156:2.

But were the words which the brothers spoke in the name of their father really a lie? Far from it, replies R' *Shmuel Edels* (on *Yevamos* ibid.). They had heard their father bless Joseph in these terms: *They embittered him and became antagonists . . . [But this came about] from the hands of the Mighty Power of Jacob*, etc. With these words, the patriarch had considerably lessened the responsibility of the brothers. Might not this formal reference to providential action directing Joseph's destiny have been interpreted as an indirect invitation to Joseph to show magnanimity toward his brothers? His reply proves that he himself had drawn the same conclusion from his father's words. Hence, the brothers were not guilty of a "white lie," but rather of a change of wording, as

יז לְפָנֵי מוֹתוֹ לֵאמֹר: כֹּה־תֹאמְרוּ לְיוֹסֵף אָנָּא שָׂא נָא פֶּשַׁע
אַחֶיךָ וְחַטָּאתָם כִּי־רָעָה גְמָלוּךָ וְעַתָּה שָׂא נָא לְפֶשַׁע
יח עַבְדֵי אֱלֹהֵי אָבִיךָ וַיֵּבְךְּ יוֹסֵף בְּדַבְּרָם אֵלָיו: וַיֵּלְכוּ גַּם־
יט אֶחָיו וַיִּפְּלוּ לְפָנָיו וַיֹּאמְרוּ הִנֶּנּוּ לְךָ לַעֲבָדִים: וַיֹּאמֶר אֲלֵהֶם
כ יוֹסֵף אַל־תִּירָאוּ כִּי הֲתַחַת אֱלֹהִים אָנִי: וְאַתֶּם חֲשַׁבְתֶּם עָלַי
רָעָה אֱלֹהִים חֲשָׁבָהּ לְטֹבָה לְמַעַן עֲשֹׂה כַּיּוֹם הַזֶּה לְהַחֲיֹת
כא עַם־רָב: וְעַתָּה אַל־תִּירָאוּ אָנֹכִי אֲכַלְכֵּל אֶתְכֶם וְאֶת־   שביעי
כב טַפְּכֶם וַיְנַחֵם אוֹתָם וַיְדַבֵּר עַל־לִבָּם: וַיֵּשֶׁב יוֹסֵף בְּמִצְרַיִם
כג הוּא וּבֵית אָבִיו וַיְחִי יוֹסֵף מֵאָה וָעֶשֶׂר שָׁנִים: וַיַּרְא יוֹסֵף   מפטיר

they alluded to Jacob's words מֵאֵל אָבִיךָ in saying to Joseph, "please forgive the guilt of the servants *of your father's God.*"

17. וַיֵּבְךְּ יוֹסֵף בְּדַבְּרָם אֵלָיו — *And Joseph wept when they spoke to him.* He had never wept during the long, hard years of his trials and humiliations. But he was easily brought to tears when his emotions were stirred, as by the sight of his brothers after the long separation or by the memory of his father, as here. Even though he was a great statesman and an eminent economist, Joseph was at the same time a great dreamer and very emotional.

19. כִּי הֲתַחַת אֱלֹהִים אָנִי — *For am I instead of God?* Cf. our commentary to 30:2. According to *Onkelos:* For I am subordinate to God.

20. וְאַתֶּם חֲשַׁבְתֶּם עָלַי רָעָה — *Although you intended me harm.* "It is true that you had evil intentions towards me, but in the plan of the Holy One, Blessed is He, it was for the best. How then can I do you harm?" (*Rashi*).

Had Joseph forgiven his brothers or not? By attributing to Providence the fact that their evil intentions turned out favorably, does this mean that they were absolved? Nothing is less certain, and opinions are divided on this matter, especially since the Torah nowhere makes any mention of a formal pardon.

Some consider that since the brothers' bad deeds did ultimately result in good, their guilt was wiped out as far as Joseph was concerned, but not with respect to God (*Sefer Chassidim*, ed. M. N., p. 437). Others, though, are of the opinion that if God did not hold them accountable for their sin because it had turned out to be the instrument of a great good, nevertheless the brothers were not acquitted before human justice. The punishment was postponed but it was ultimately meted out at the time of the ten martyrs, who, according to kabbalistic sources carried the transmigrated souls of the brothers (*R' Bachya*). Another opinion, the basis for which is however contested: the fact that the brothers had been chosen by Providence as the instrument of good proves that they were guilty neither before God nor before men. Moreover, they had acted unknowingly, and their conduct had been based on an error of judgment (ר״י בכור שור ואוה״ח). Lastly, the *Zohar* holds that the brothers had repented several times and this

his death, saying: [17] *'Thus shall you say to Joseph: "O please,
kindly forgive the spiteful deed of your brothers and their sin
for they have done you evil" '; so now, please forgive the spiteful
deed of the servants of your father's God." And Joseph wept
when they spoke to him.*

[18] *His brothers themselves also went and flung themselves
before him and said, "We are ready to be your slaves."*

[19] *But Joseph said to them, "Fear not, for am I instead of God?*
[20] *Although you intended me harm, God intended it for good: in
order to accomplish — it is as clear as this day — that a vast
people be kept alive.* [21] *So now, fear not — I will sustain you and
your young ones." Thus he comforted them and spoke to their
heart.*

[22] *Joseph dwelt in Egypt — he and his father's household —
and Joseph lived one hundred and ten years.* [23] *Joseph saw*

entitled them to be pardoned for their transgression. Accordingly, Joseph had
forgiven them. What is more, he felt obliged to console them and to appease the
guilt feelings they had since death had taken away their father who had been
the veritable "guardian angel" of the family. They felt they had to look upon
the exile and its trials, which they now foresaw in all its merciless hardships, as
a Divine punishment for their transgressions. "Fear nothing," Joseph repeatedly
told them, "I will sustain you," meaning, "I will continue to protect you from
the harm of life in exile."

In the light of these various opinions, it appears that some doubt still persists
regarding the moral rehabilitation of Joseph's brothers. Would this not be
confirmation of what R' Meir taught, that the principles which determine mercy
and forgiveness have not been revealed to any mortal, not even to the greatest
of the prophets, Moses (*Berachos* 7a). The path of good and virtue remains
independent of the prospects of mercy and pardon.

22. וַיֵּשֶׁב יוֹסֵף בְּמִצְרַיִם — *Joseph dwelt in Egypt.* וַיֵּשֶׁב frequently implies: he
settled. Joseph settled down in exile, remembering the Divine words addressed
to his father: *Have no fear of descending to Egypt, for I shall establish you as
a great nation there* (46:3). Neither he nor the house of his father tried to look
for ways of leaving the land of Egypt. They resolved to trust in God's words and
to wait for the end (ibid.) which He had promised. Joseph knew that this end
could not be too far off, since the "fourth generation" was approaching, the
generation which God had announced would return to Canaan (15:16). He was
satisfied just to reveal the signs of the future redemption to his brothers. It was
his last act before his death (verse 24).

וַיְחִי יוֹסֵף מֵאָה וָעֶשֶׂר שָׁנִים — *And Joseph lived one hundred and ten years.* "Public
responsibility shortens the life of man. Here was Joseph who, save for Benjamin,
was the youngest of the brothers, and yet he died before the others" (*Midrash*

לְאֶפְרָיִם בְּנֵי שִׁלֵּשִׁים גַּם בְּנֵי מָכִיר בֶּן־מְנַשֶּׁה יֻלְּדוּ עַל־בִּרְכֵּי
כד יוֹסֵף: וַיֹּאמֶר יוֹסֵף אֶל־אֶחָיו אָנֹכִי מֵת וֵאלֹהִים פָּקֹד יִפְקֹד
אֶתְכֶם וְהֶעֱלָה אֶתְכֶם מִן־הָאָרֶץ הַזֹּאת אֶל־הָאָרֶץ אֲשֶׁר
כה נִשְׁבַּע לְאַבְרָהָם לְיִצְחָק וּלְיַעֲקֹב: וַיַּשְׁבַּע יוֹסֵף אֶת־בְּנֵי
יִשְׂרָאֵל לֵאמֹר פָּקֹד יִפְקֹד אֱלֹהִים אֶתְכֶם וְהַעֲלִתֶם אֶת־

Lekach Tov). It was also while carrying out his high functions that he erred by
failing to show respect for his father (cf. our commentary to 43:28) and he had
to atone for this by having his life shortened. (Cf. *Rashi* on *Exodus* 20:12: *Honor
your father and your mother so that your days may be prolonged.* If you honor
them, your days will be prolonged. If not, they will be shortened.)

23. וַיַּרְא יוֹסֵף לְאֶפְרַיִם בְּנֵי שִׁלֵּשִׁים — *Joseph saw three generations through
Ephraim.* According to *Ibn Ezra,* this refers to the children born to the third
generation (בְּנֵי being in the construct state). It follows from this verse that despite
what had just been said, Joseph was granted the joy of being a grandfather in
greater measure than all his brothers. Thus at the end of his life, the Torah gives
us an illustration of the *midrashic* statement: "For the righteous, as opposed to
the wicked, life begins with hardships but ends in happiness" (*Bereshis Rabbah*
66). None of the brothers had experienced a life so full of hardships.

בְּנֵי מָכִיר — *The sons of Machir.* He had a son named Gilad, the ancestor of
Zelophehad whose five daughters are known for their extraordinary attachment
to the inheritance of the Promised Land (*I Chronicles* 7:15). By this reference,
made just as Joseph urges his brothers to bury him in the Holy Land, the Torah
draws our attention to the influence which the faith of an ancestor can have even
on distant generations of his descendants (*R' Bachya*).

עַל־בִּרְכֵּי יוֹסֵף — *On Joseph's knees.* An allusion to the circumcision of his
grandchildren, which was carried out by Joseph himself (*Targum Yonasan*).

24. וַיֹּאמֶר יוֹסֵף אֶל־אֶחָיו אָנֹכִי מֵת — *Joseph said to his brothers, "I am about to die."*
Cf. our commentary to 48:21.

וֵאלֹהִים פָּקֹד יִפְקֹד אֶתְכֶם — *But God will surely remember you.* The term פָּקַד, like
זָכַר, usually announces the appearance of הַשְׁגָּחָה, *Divine Providence.* God
remembers the merits of men in their distress, or the merit of their fathers, as was
the case for Noah in the Flood, for Sarah remaining barren, and for the Children
of Israel when reduced to slavery, and He decided to come to their aid. Cf. our
commentary to 8:1.

At the burning bush, when Moses was given the mission to go and deliver the
Jews from bondage, God promised him: "They will listen to you." *Rashi*
explains: "As soon as you address them with these words: פָּקֹד פָּקַדְתִּי אֶתְכֶם, *I
have doubly remembered you* (*Exodus* 3:16), they will listen to your voice. For
this sign had been passed on to them from the time of Jacob and Joseph. [They
know] that these are the words which will announce the redemption. Jacob and

*three generations through Ephraim; even the sons of Machir son
of Manasseh were raised on Joseph's knees.*

²⁴ *Joseph said to his brothers, "I am about to die, but God will
surely remember you and bring you up out of this land to the land
that He swore to Abraham, to Isaac, and to Jacob."*

²⁵ *Then Joseph adjured the children of Israel saying, "When God
will indeed remember you, then you must bring my bones up*

Joseph had said to them: פָּקֹד יִפְקֹד אֱלֹהִים אֶתְכֶם (ibid. verse 25 — Joseph repeats
this phrase twice; the first time he quotes what his father had said, the second
time he makes a formal announcement of them; *R' Eliyahu Mizrachi*). This sign
of the authentic "language of redemption" had been revealed to Abraham and
then transmitted successively to Isaac, Jacob, and Joseph. The latter entrusted
these declamatory terms to his brothers, and they ultimately came down to
Serah, the daughter of Asher, sole survivor of Jacob's grandchildren in the time
of Moses. When Moses came to the Jewish elders, they asked Asher's daughter
if his words corresponded to the secret tradition which she had received, and
when she confirmed that they did, the elders believed in his words (*Pirkei
D'Rabbi Eliezer* 48).

אֶל־הָאָרֶץ אֲשֶׁר נִשְׁבַּע לְאַבְרָהָם לְיִצְחָק וּלְיַעֲקֹב — *To the land that He swore to
Abraham, to Isaac and to Jacob.* Trust not in any prophet who will claim to
redeem you and lead you to a country other than the Promised Land. (On the
use of the father's first name by the son, see our commentary on 49:31.)

25. וַיַּשְׁבַּע יוֹסֵף אֶת־בְּנֵי יִשְׂרָאֵל — *Then Joseph adjured the children of Israel.* In
the preceding verse, Joseph was speaking to his brothers; here he speaks to all
the descendants of Israel and the text adds the term לֵאמֹר which signifies "in
order to retell it." This is why the *Targum Yonasan* interprets this oath as being
addressed to the future generations. It is Joseph's offspring who, more than two
centuries later, will have the mission of carrying his bones to the Holy Land.
"And why did he not make his sons swear to carry his remains to the land of
Canaan immediately, just as Jacob had made him swear? Joseph said to himself:
'I am master in Egypt and I have the power to have this done. But the Egyptians
will not allow my sons to do it.' So he made them swear to carry his remains with
them when they finally leave Egypt' (*Rashi* on *Exodus* 13:19). But the *Targum*
also points out that an oath usually includes a warning. This only appears
indirectly in our verse, but it has a precise meaning: when you are enslaved in
Egypt, do not venture to go back to the land of Israel before the coming of the
redeemer who will announce to you, פָּקֹד יִפְקֹד וגו'.

פָּקֹד יִפְקֹד אֱלֹהִים אֶתְכֶם — *When God will indeed remember you.* A twofold
remembering: פָּקֹד יִפְקֹד, one referring to Moses, the other to the Messiah. Thus
Joseph's last message was one of confidence in God, amid all the distress which
the future might hold for His people. God will surely remember, and He will
send His redeemer, to save them not only from Egyptian tyranny but also from

כו עַצְמֹתַי מִזֶּה: וַיָּמָת יוֹסֵף בֶּן־מֵאָה וָעֶשֶׂר שָׁנִים וַיַּחַנְטוּ אֹתוֹ
וַיִּישֶׂם בָּאָרוֹן בְּמִצְרָיִם:

all the other suffering, until the final coming of the messianic king. So often in his life Joseph had experienced miraculous reversals, and he was better qualified than any of his brothers to sum up every experience with an expression of confidence in God. But he did not forget either that it was his presence in Egypt which had brought about, albeit involuntarily, the descent of the whole family into exile. Accordingly, before he died, he made a point of revealing to them the certainty of the national redemption. Just before the page is turned and a new book takes us to the depths of sufferings in Egypt, the promise of the messianic salvation, solemnly proclaimed here at the end of *Genesis*, reminds us of Jewry's eternal belief: God sends the cure before the ailment רְפוּאָה קוֹדֶם הַמַּכָּה (*Megillah* 13b).

וְהַעֲלִתֶם אֶת־עַצְמֹתַי מִזֶּה — *Then you must bring my bones up out of here.* Knowing by tradition that the Cave of Machpelah was reserved only for the patriarchs (and the first couple), Joseph did not mention the place of his burial. He was content to tell them: Bury me where you will (*Ramban* on 49:31). His sole desire was to be laid to rest in the Holy Land. His coffin was finally buried at Shechem (*Joshua* 24:32) — the tribes brought his remains to the very place where he had been sold as a slave many years before. In so doing, they wanted to make amends, at least in part, for the transgression of their ancestors. They would bury him with all the honors owing to a dead prince and a holy man at the very place which had seen the hatred and treachery.

"When the bodies of the righteous who have never known sin are buried in the Holy Land, they do not affect the purity of the land. But the unclean bodies of the impious are a defilement for it. As for those who left the land, became sullied with the impurity of the nations, and then returned in order to be buried there, of them the prophet has said: *You come, you make My land unclean and My heritage you make an abomination* (*Jeremiah* 2:7). As for Joseph, although he had settled outside the Holy Land, he had kept his body in perfect purity. In spite of this, he did not want the flesh of his body to be buried in the Holy Land. In contrast to his father, he was content to ask only that his bones be buried there. Happy are those who live and die in righteousness in the Holy land and whose body and soul remain forever preserved" (*Zohar*).

From these ideas (and similar views quoted in *Kesubos* 3a), *Rambam* states: Whoever is buried in the Holy Land is granted absolution there (following *Deuteronomy* 32:43: וְכִפֶּר אַדְמָתוֹ עַמּוֹ). However, someone who is received there after his death cannot be compared to one who lived his life there. Nevertheless the Sages arranged for their bodies to be taken to the Holy Land, following the examples of Joseph and Jacob (*Hilchos Melachim* 5:11).

מִזֶּה — *Out of here.* When this oath of Joseph's is reported in *Exodus* (13:19), the word אֶתְכֶם, *with you*, is added, which gives rise to the following interpretation

out of here."

²⁶ *Joseph died at the age of one hundred and ten years; they embalmed him and he was placed in a coffin in Egypt.*

from *Rashi:* From this we adduce that they carried with them also the remains of all the sons of Jacob, since it is said: "with you" (at the same time as yours).

26. וַיָּמָת יוֹסֵף בֶּן־מֵאָה וָעֶשֶׂר שָׁנִים — *Joseph died at the age of one hundred and ten years.* The repetition of this point is of importance from a chronological point of view. The Torah frequently provides details of this kind enabling us to put the Biblical events in historical perspective. Joseph survived his father by fifty-four years. As viceroy, he had presided over the destiny of Egypt for eighty consecutive years, which is an exceptional phenomenon (he had been thirty years old when he appeared before Pharaoh, 41:46). Seventy-one years had passed since Jacob arrived in Egypt, and during this time the children of Jacob had led a peaceful existence which was to continue for another twenty-three years until the death of Levi. The 116 years of slavery and servitude began only after this happy period, which lasted for ninety-four years (*Rashi* on *Exodus* 6:16). The period of slavery and oppression which was to have lasted 400 years (15:13) was shortened by God to 210 years. Out of love for Jewry God rushed to its aid in order to rescue it well before the prescribed end of its ordeals. This premature redemption which knew no obstacles and stages is celebrated in allegorical form in the *Song of Songs: Hark! My beloved! Behold he comes, leaping upon the mountains, skipping over the hills* (2:8; cf. *Rashi* ibid.).

וַיַּחַנְטוּ אֹתוֹ — *They embalmed him.* Did the embalming take place on the initiative of the brothers, who wanted to honor Joseph as he himself had honored their father, or was it carried out by the doctors in order to give royal honors to his mortal remains in accordance with Egyptian custom? R' Yehudah holds one opinion and R' Pinchas the other (*Rabbah* 100). Whatever the case, Joseph's embalming did not have the same significance as his father's, for the reasons developed in our commentary to verse 2 of this chapter.

וַיִּישֶׂם בָּאָרוֹן — *And he was placed in a coffin.* The name אָרוֹן is also given to the holy ark which contains the twin tablets of the Torah. It is called אֲרוֹן הַבְּרִית, *the ark of the covenant* (*Joshua* 3:6). By repeating the letter *yud* in the word וַיִּישֶׂם, the Torah is hinting at the second אָרוֹן, the holy ark where Joseph had, figuratively speaking, the supreme honor of being welcomed. He had indeed earned the title of יוֹסֵף הַצַּדִּיק, Joseph the righteous, owing to his great virtue, the virtue of chastity. The holiness which he had acquired made his whole personality an אֲרוֹן הַבְּרִית, an *ark of the covenant*, which bore witness on earth to the majesty of God. Joseph was laid to rest in Egypt in an אָרוֹן which is none other than the reflection of the holy ark where his soul rests in the holy spheres (*Zohar*).

בְּמִצְרָיִם — *In Egypt.* Nowhere does the Torah speak of the burial of the coffin, and from this the Sages deduce that it was lowered into the depths of the Nile

so that "its waters would be blessed by Joseph's coffin." But R' Nosson teaches
that the coffin was buried in "the labyrinth of the kings." In either case, Moses
had to pray for a miracle in order to find its exact location (*Sotah* 13a). Whatever
the reasons why Joseph had not demanded the immediate transfer of his coffin
to Canaan, as his father had done, the fact remains that his spirit dwelt with his
children during the difficult hardships which awaited them "in Egypt." On this
note of moral comfort *Genesis* comes to an end.

The end of the patriarchal epoch is not a conclusion. On the contrary, it is a
beginning of realization, a hope: the nucleus of the future "nation of priests" is
created and firmly established. The period of great trials is about to begin, and
this nation will emerge from it with its spiritual strength formed to endure for
all time.